The Handbook of International Crisis and Risk Communication Research

Handbooks in Communication and Media

This series aims to provide theoretically ambitious yet accessible volumes devoted to the major fields and subfields within communication and media studies. Each volume sets out to ground and orientate the student through a broad range of specially commissioned chapters, while also providing the more experienced scholar and teacher with a convenient and comprehensive overview of the latest trends and critical directions.

The Handbook of Organizational Rhetoric and Communication, *edited by Øyvind Ihlen and Robert L. Heath*
The Handbook of Communication Engagement, *edited by* Kim A. Johnston and Maureen Taylor
The Handbook of Financial Communication and Investor Relations, *edited by* Alexander V. Laskin
The Handbook of Children, Media, and Development, *edited by Sandra L. Calvert and Barbara J. Wilson*
The Handbook of Internet Studies, *edited by Mia Consalvo and Charles Ess*
The Handbook of Rhetoric and Public Address, *edited by Shawn J. Parry-Giles and J. Michael Hogan*
The Handbook of Global Communication and Media Ethics, *edited by Robert S. Fortner and P. Mark Fackler*
The Handbook of Communication and Corporate Social Responsibility, *edited by Øyvind Ihlen, Jennifer Bartlett, and Steve May*
The Handbook of Gender, Sex, and Media, *edited by Karen Ross*
The Handbook of Global Health Communication, *edited by Rafael Obregon and Silvio Waisbord*
The Handbook of Global Media Research, *edited by Ingrid Volkmer*
The Handbook of Global Online Journalism, *edited by Eugenia Siapera and Andreas Veglis*
The Handbook of Communication and Corporate Reputation, *edited by Craig E. Carroll*
The Handbook of Media and Mass Communication Theory, *edited by Robert S. Fortner and P. Mark Fackler*
The Handbook of International Advertising Research, *edited by Hong Cheng*
The Handbook of Psychology of Communication Technology, *edited by S. Shyam Sundar*
The Handbook of Magazine Studies, *edited by Miglena Sternadori and Tim Holmes*
The Handbook of European Communication History, *edited by Klaus Arnold, Paschal Preston, and Susanne Kinnebrock*
The Handbook of Public Sector Communication, *edited by Vilma Luoma-aho and María José Canel*
The Handbook of Applied Communication Research, *2 Volume Set, edited by H. Dan O'Hair and Mary John O'Hair*
The Handbook of Listening, *edited by Debra L. Worthington and Graham D. Bodie*
The Handbook of Communication Rights, Law, and Ethics, *edited by Loreto Corredoira, Ignacio Bel Mallen, and Rodrigo Cetina Preusel*
The Handbook of Strategic Communication, *edited by Carl H. Botan*
The Handbook of Peer Production, *edited by Mathieu O'Neil, Christian Pentzold, and Sophie Toupin*
The Handbook of Crisis Communication, second edition, *edited by W. Timothy Coombs and Sherry J. Holladay*
The Handbook of Critical Intercultural Communication, second edition, *edited by Thomas K. Nakayama and Rona Tamiko Halualani*

The Handbook of International Crisis and Risk Communication Research

Second Edition

Edited By

Andreas Schwarz

Matthew W. Seeger

Sora Kim

WILEY Blackwell

Published by John Wiley & Sons, Inc., Hoboken, New Jersey.

Published simultaneously in Canada.

Library of Congress Cataloging-in-Publication Data

Names: Schwarz, Andreas, 1979- editor. | Seeger, Matthew W. (Matthew Wayne), 1957- editor. | Kim, Sora, editor.
Title: The handbook of international crisis and risk communication research / edited by Andreas Schwarz, Matthew W. Seeger, Sora Kim.
Description: Second edition. | Hoboken, New Jersey : Wiley-Blackwell, [2025] | Series: Handbooks in communication and media | Includes bibliographical references and index.
Identifiers: LCCN 2025000605 (print) | LCCN 2025000606 (ebook) | ISBN 9781394180806 (cloth) | ISBN 9781394180820 (adobe pdf) | ISBN 9781394180837 (epub)
Subjects: LCSH: Crisis management–Handbooks, manuals, etc. | Risk communication–Handbooks, manuals, etc. | Communication, International–Handbooks, manuals, etc.
Classification: LCC HD49 .H354 2025 (print) | LCC HD49 (ebook) | DDC 658.4/056–dc23/eng/20250321
LC record available at https://lccn.loc.gov/2025000605
LC ebook record available at https://lccn.loc.gov/2025000606

Cover Design: Wiley
Cover Image: © imagedepotpro/Getty Images

Set in size of 10/12pt ITC Galliard Std by Straive, Pondicherry, India

Contents

List of Contributors

Tariku Abas
Loyola Marymount University, Marymount Institute-TSEHAI Publishers, Los Angeles, CA, USA

Wole Adamolekun
Department of Mass Communication, Elizade University, Ilara-Mokin, Nigeria

Ilhem Allagui
Journalism and Strategic Communication Program, Northwestern University, Doha, Qatar

Jesús Arroyave
Departamento de Comunicación Social, Universidad del Norte, Barranquilla, Colombia

Alina Bârgăoanu
National University of Political Studies and Public Administration (SNSPA), European Digital Media Observatory (EDMO), Bucharest, Romania

Cynthia Baur
Department of Behavioral and Community Health, Horowitz Center for Health Literacy, School of Public Health, University of Maryland, College Park, MD, USA

Zenebe Beyene
University of Mississippi, Media & Communication, Oxford, MS, USA

Monica Bîră
National University of Political Studies and Public Administration (SNSPA), Bucharest, Romania

Frederic Bouder
Faculty of Science and Technology, Department of Safety, Economic and Planning, University of Stavanger, Stavange, Norway

Corina Buzoianu
National Univeristy of Political Studies and Public Administration (SNSPA), Bucharest, Romania

An-Sofie Claeys
Department of Translation, Interpreting and Communication, Ghent University, Gent, Belgium

Ester Cohen-Rinski
School of Communication, Bar Ilan University, Ramat Gan, Israel

Ruth DeFoster
Hubbard School of Journalism and Mass Communication, University of Minnesota, Minneapolis, MN, USA

Ganga S. Dhanesh
Department of Communication, University of Maryland, College Park, MD, USA

Audra Diers-Lawson
Institute for Communication, Kristiania University of Applied Sciences, Oslo, Norway

Iuliia Dolmatova
Gaylord College of Journalism and Mass Communication, University of Oklahoma, Norman, OK, USA

Ben Duncan
Self-employed crisis and risk communication consultant, Consultant to WHO Health Emergencies Programme, Brussels, Belgium

Ana María Erazo-Coronado
Dirección Especialización Endodoncia, Universidad Metropolitana, Barranquilla, Colombia

Pauline Gidget Estella
Department of Media Studies, Institute of Media and Communication Science, Technische Universität Ilmenau, Ilmenau, Germany

Finn Frandsen
Department of Management, Aarhus School of Business and Social Sciences, Aarhus University, Denmark

Ryan P. Fuller
Department of Management & Organizations, College of Business, California State University-Sacramento, Sacramento, CA, USA

Christopher Galloway
Massey Business School, Massey University, Auckland, New Zealand

Rozália Del Gáudio Soares
Inspiria 3 Consulting, São Paulo, SP, Brazil

Amiso M. George
Department of Strategic Communication, Bob Schieffer College of Communication, Texas Christian University, Fort Worth, TX, USA

Eytan Gilboa
School of Communication, Bar Ilan University, Ramat Gan, Israel

Rob Grace
University of Cincinnati, School of Information Technology, Cincinnati, OH, USA

Michel M. Haigh
School of Journalism and Mass Communication, Texas State University, San Marcos, TX, USA

Robert L. Heath
Valenti School of Communication, University of Houston, Houston, TX, USA

Øyvind Ihlen
Department of Media and Communication, Faculty of Humanities, University of Oslo, Oslo, Norway

Yingru Ji
College of Media and International Culture, Zhejiang University, Hangzhou, China

Yan Jin
Grady College of Journalism and Mass Communication, University of Georgia, Athens, GA, USA
Amsterdam School of Communication Research (ASCoR), University of Amsterdam, Amsterdam, The Netherlands

Winni Johansen
Department of Management, Aarhus School of Business and Social Sciences, Aarhus University, Denmark

Bengt Johansson
Department of Journalism, Media, and Communication, University of Gothenburg, Gothenburg, Sweden

Soo-Yeon Kim
College of Media, Arts, and Science, Sogang University in Seoul, Seoul, Korea

Sora Kim
School of Journalism and Communication, Chinese University of Hong Kong, Shatin, Hong Kong

Marjorie Kyomuhendo
Department of Journalism and Communication, Makerere University, Kampala, Uganda

Kenneth A. Lachlan
University of Connecticut, Storrs, CT, USA

Elin Strand Larsen
Department of Computer Science and Communication, Faculty of Computer Science, Engineering and Economics, Østfold University College, Halden, Norway

Jason Shi-yang Lim
Lee Kong Chian School of Business, Singapore Management University, Singapore, Singapore

Brooke Fisher Liu
Department of Communication, University of Maryland, College Park, MD, USA

Martin Löffelholz
Institut für Medien und Kommunikationswissenschaft, Technische Universität Ilmenau, Ilmenau, Germany

Marta N. Lukacovic
Department of Communication and Mass Media, Angelo State University, San Angelo, TX, USA

Clila Magen
School of Communication, Bar Ilan University, Ramat Gan, Israel

Toni G.L.A. van der Meer
Grady College of Journalism and Mass Communication, University of Georgia, Athens, GA, USA
Amsterdam School of Communication Research (ASCoR), University of Amsterdam, Amsterdam, The Netherlands

Aisha Sembatya Nakiwala
Department of Journalism and Communication, Makerere University, Kampala, Uganda

Angella Napakol
School of Journalism, Media and Communication, Uganda Christian University, Mukono, Uganda

Jerena Ng
Lee Kong Chian School of Business, Singapore Management University, Singapore, Singapore

Michael J. Palenchar
Tombras School of ADPR, University of Tennessee, Knoxville, TN, USA

Augustine Pang
Lee Kong Chian School of Business, Singapore Management University, Singapore, Singapore

Damián Fernández Pedemonte
Universidad Austral, Graduate School of Communication, Buenos Aires, Argentina

Andrew S. Pyle
Department of Communication, Clemson University, Clemson, SC, USA

Constanze Rossmann
Department of Media and Communication, University of Munich, Munich, Germany

Liane Rothenberger
School of Journalism, Catholic University of Eichstätt-Ingolstadt, Eichstätt, Germany

Aino Ruggiero
Humanitarian Logistics and Supply Chain Research Institute, Department of Marketing, Hanken School of Economics, Helsinki, Finland

Mihoko Sakurai
Graduate School of International Management, International University of Japan, Niigata, Japan

Sergei A. Samoilenko
Department of Communication, George Mason University, Washington, Fairfax, VA, USA

Aynur Sarısakaloğlu
Department of Media Studies, Institute of Media and Communication Science, Technische Universität Ilmenau, Ilmenau, Germany

Kathrin Schleicher
Institute of Media and Communication Science, Technische Universität Ilmenau, Ilmenau, Germany

Andreas Schwarz
Institute of Media and Communication Science, Technische Universität Ilmenau, Ilmenau, Germany

Matthew W. Seeger
Center for Emerging and Infectious Diseases, Wayne State University, Detroit, MI, USA

Deanna D. Sellnow
Department of Communication, Clemson University, Clemson, SC, USA

Timothy L. Sellnow
Department of Communication, Clemson University, Clemson, SC, USA

Greg Simons
Department of Journalism, Media & Communication, Daffodil International University in Dhaka, Bangladesh

Paulo Henrique Soares
Brazilian Mining Institute, Belo Horizonte, MG, Brazil

Rodrigo Soares
University of Vermont, Department of Agriculture, Landscape & Environment, Burlington, VT, USA

Patric R. Spence
University of Central Florida, Orlando, FL, USA

Krishnamurthy Sriramesh
Advertising, Public Relations, and Design, University of Colorado, Boulder, CO, USA

Minttu Tikka
Faculty of Social Sciences, University of Helsinki, Helsinki, Finland

W. Timothy Coombs
Centre for Crisis and Risk Communications, Calgary, Canada

Katerina Tsetsura
Gaylord College of Journalism and Mass Communication, University of Oklahoma, Norman, OK, USA

Robert R. Ulmer
Greenspun College of Urban Affairs, University of Nevada Las Vegas, Las Vegas, NV, USA

Shari R. Veil
College of Journalism and Mass Communications, University of Nebraska-Lincoln, Lincoln, NE, USA

Melanie Verhovnik-Heinze
Faculty of Business, Ansbach University of Applied Science, Ansbach, Germany

Orla Vigsø
Department of Journalism, Media, and Communication, University of Gothenburg, Gothenburg, Sweden

Daniel Vogler
Research Center for the Public Sphere and Society (fög), University of Zurich, Zurich, Switzerland

Chang Wan
College of Media and International Culture, Zhejiang University, Hangzhou, China

Carla White
Tombras School of ADPR, University of Tennessee, Knoxville, TN, USA

Annemarie Wiedicke
Institute for Media Research, Chemnitz University of Technology, Chemnitz, Germany

Yi Xu
Institut für Kommunikationswissenschaft, Friedrich Schiller University Jena, Jena, Germany

Theodore E. Zorn
Massey Business School, Massey University, Auckland, New Zealand

Preface and Acknowledgments

The second edition of the *International Handbook of Crisis and Risk Communication Research*, like the first edition, was based on the aspirational goal of continuing to expand, integrate, and internationalize the field. In this edition, we have included 50 chapters describing programs of research from around the globe, addressing diverse audiences, cultures, and risk/crisis types from a variety of methodological and disciplinary perspectives. A project of this scope and complexity simply could not be accomplished without the active support of others.

First and foremost, we wish to acknowledge and thank our two research assistants, Dr. Najma Akhther and Muhammad Zakaria. Their attention to detail, organizational skills, technical expertise, and tireless commitment were essential to the success of this project. Without their involvement, this project would have languished at many points. We hope that the experiences gained through this project will significantly contribute to the continued development of your own careers in risk and crisis communication research. Thank you.

Second, we wish to express our thanks and deep appreciation to all chapter authors. Many of you have taken on the responsibility of summarizing research from regions that have only recently begun developing systematic programs of inquiry. Other authors have taken fresh approaches to well-developed bodies of research. In many cases, we requested that authors fit their analyses into the framework of this handbook.

Each of us also like to express our thanks and appreciation to our fellow co-editors. We represent three continents and three diverse approaches to the field. This diversity was essential to the success of this project and to the growth and development of the field. Despite the challenges of working across time zones in Hong Kong, Germany, and the United States, we have learned a great deal from one another and developed and strengthened our friendships.

Finally, we thank the staff and editors at Wiley, especially Nicole Allen. Thank you for sharing the vision of internationalizing this field through a handbook of this scope and for your patience.

Our world is becoming more hazardous, as vividly demonstrated by the COVID-19 pandemic. Climate change has a profound impact, creating a diverse set of crises and disasters. It is our hope that this handbook helps students, scholars, and practitioners communicate about these hazards in ways that limit the frequency, scope, and harm of these events.

Part I

History, Status Quo, and Trends in Global Crisis and Risk Communication Research

1

Global Threats and the Significance of International Risk and Crisis Communication Research: Advancing Integration, Diversity, and Complexity

Andreas Schwarz
Institute of Media and Communication Science,
Technische Universität Ilmenau, Ilmenau, Germany

Since the first edition of this handbook was published in 2016, global threats have continued to emerge and, depending on the type of hazard, have become more severe. Although experts caution against bias in disaster reporting (Ritchie & Rosado, 2024), there appears to have been a recent increase in global damage and fatalities caused by small- and medium-sized disasters. In particular, floods, earthquakes, storms, and wildfires have taken a severe toll on the world's population and were often attributed to climate change (Centre for Research on the Epidemiology of Disasters (CRED), 2024). In 2023, the CRED reported 86,473 fatalities, 93 million people affected, and economic losses of US$203 billion due to disasters. While progress has been made in reducing global hunger over time, levels of undernourishment have increased since 2017. For 2023, 735 million people were estimated to be undernourished, with South Asia and Sub-Saharan Africa being the most affected regions. According to the World Hunger Index 2023 (Grebmer et al., 2023):

> "This stagnation relative to 2015 largely reflects the combined effects of several crises. These include the COVID-19 pandemic, the Russia-Ukraine war, economic stagnation, the impacts of climate change, and the intractable conflicts facing many countries of the world. Their compounding effects have led to a cost-of-living crisis and exhausted the coping capacity of many countries, especially those where hunger was already high before the crises [...] (p. 7)."

Armed conflicts, terrorism, and gun violence remain severe threats within countries and globally. In 2020, the US National Consortium for the Study of Terrorism and Responses to Terrorism reported a total of 10,126 terrorist attacks worldwide, resulting in more than 29,000 deaths, with Africa, the Middle East, and South Asia being the most affected regions, where perpetrators such as ISIS, Al-Shabaab, Boko Haram, Hamas, or the Communist Party of the Philippines are operating, with many of them being active transnationally and/or sponsored by foreign states (Global Terrorism Trends and Analysis Center, 2023). Their main tactics include shootings, improvised explosives, bombings, and kidnapping. Although the number of armed conflicts and wars, as well as the number of battle fatalities, has been

The Handbook of International Crisis and Risk Communication Research, Second Edition.
Edited by Andreas Schwarz, Matthew W. Seeger, and Sora Kim.

decreasing since World War II, the Department of Peace and Conflict Research at Uppsala University (2024) reported a growing number of state-based violence after 2012. With Russia's invasion of Ukraine in 2022, war has returned to Europe, claiming more than 160,000 lives between 2022 and 2023 and leading to a re-militarization of the continent.

One of the most devastating transnational crises since the first edition of this handbook was published was undoubtedly the COVID-19 pandemic. By July 2024, the World Health Organization (WHO) reported more than seven million deaths worldwide, with Europe, the United States, Brazil, India, and Russia among the hardest hit at the country level (World Health Organization, 2024). Failures in crisis response and unethical, incomplete, and misleading risk communication by governments and/or individual political leaders, as in the United States, Brazil, Russia, and the United Kingdom, as well as the spread of misinformation through social media, had tragic consequences for citizens. COVID-19 also demonstrated the essential role of crisis and risk communication in global emergencies. Economic crises and inflation, which in part resulted from the COVID-19 pandemic and/or Russia's attack on Ukraine, but also several crises involving large corporations such as Boeing or Volkswagen have shaped the world and the news agenda since 2016. With the rise of extremist right-wing parties in many Western countries, often supported by foreign states (e.g., Russia's interference in elections, Brexit, etc.) and the possibilities of new technologies such as artificial intelligence (AI) (e.g., covert influence operations by Russia, China, and Iran using AI as reported by OpenAI (2024)), misinformation and disinformation tactics have increasingly destabilized democracy and political and social cohesion. Most of these right-wing groups, for instance in the United States, Latin America, and Europe, promote climate change denial, seek to defund environmental protection programs, spread disinformation about public health threats and vaccinations, reinforce racism, and oppose support for most minority groups or diversity in general. The political gains of these groups have aggravated the causes and impact of crises in many regions of the world.

Hence, the trends we outlined in the handbook's first edition, that risks and crises are becoming more international in terms of physical causes and consequences as well as symbolic effects through global (digital) communication, are still on the agenda of international risk and crisis communication research. Indeed, with the manifestations of anthropogenic climate change, global diseases, growing political instability, and the second-order effects of these developments (e.g., migration, crime, famine, etc.), the need for multidisciplinary cross-national comparative research on the role of risk and crisis communication has increased. A more recent development in this context is the rise of AI and more awareness of the impact of algorithms on global communication with positive and negative outcomes (Park & Park, 2024; Schwarz & Unselt, 2024). The use of machine learning and automation has also changed the research landscape and possibilities in the social sciences in terms of methodology, including risk and crisis communication research (see Chapter 46, Vogler).

To understand recent developments in risk and crisis communication research before and after the first edition of this handbook was published, we first report the results of a Scopus-based literature analysis of the last 15 years. We will then discuss the current trends and needs for studying risk and crisis communication internationally and how these trends relate to the goals and structure of the second edition.

The State of International Crisis and Risk Communication Research

Scholars have pointed to several limitations of the field, including a lack of integrating risk communication and crisis communication conceptually as well as empirically. In addition, the literature published in English is still largely dominated by authors with US and European affiliations (Diers-Lawson et al., 2024). To verify these observations, we conducted a

Scopus-based literature analysis of publications in the last 15 years (2009–2024). Being aware of several limitations, we searched the database for all journal articles, books, and book chapters in English, which included the terms "risk communication" or "crisis communication" in titles *or* abstracts *and* as one of their author keywords.[1] Although much of the research addresses risk or crisis empirically, authors often fail to relate it in a meaningful way to risk communication and/or crisis communication as somewhat important and explicit concepts or to the related body of literature, as found in studies of media coverage of COVID-19 (Schwarz et al., 2023). Using one of these terms in titles/abstracts *and* author keywords was therefore regarded as a useful indicator for a first quantitative review of the field. Within the search results, we split the sample in two parts by using Scopus' exact keyword function to compare publications on "risk communication" with publications on "crisis communication."

Altogether, we found 2,540 publications on crisis and risk communication between 2009 and early August 2024. The share of research indexed as "risk communication" was almost twice as high (n = 1,416) as the share of texts on "crisis communication" (n = 748). Over time, the research output steadily increased, especially after 2015, but even more significantly after 2019. However, a significant share of that growth between 2020 and 2023 may be attributed to a temporary impact of the COVID-19 pandemic, which led to a considerable number of publications related to risk and crisis communication (Figure 1.1).

Most publications either appeared in journals related to public relations, strategic communication, and management or in journals on risk and disaster research (Figure 1.2). Very few studies were published in more general mainstream communication journals such as *Communication Research* or *Communication Studies.* Altogether, the most relevant journals included *Public Relations Review* (6%), the *Journal of Risk Research* (4%), *Risk Analysis* (3%), the *International Journal of Disaster Risk Reduction* (3%), the *International Journal of Environmental Research and Public Health* (2%), and the *Journal of Contingencies and Crisis*

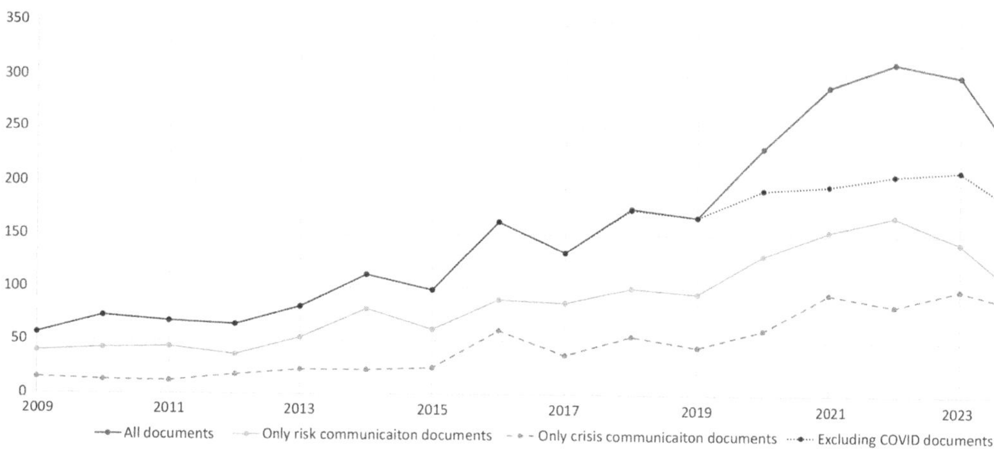

Figure 1.1 Number of publications in risk and crisis communication journals and books from 2009 to 08/2024. *Source*: Adapted from Scopus.

[1] Search string used on Scopus: (TITLE-ABS ("crisis communication") OR TITLE-ABS ("risk communication") AND (AUTHKEY ("crisis communication") OR AUTHKEY ("risk communication"))) AND PUBYEAR > 2008 AND PUBYEAR < 2025 AND (LIMIT-TO (SRCTYPE, "b") OR LIMIT-TO (SRCTYPE, "j") OR LIMIT-TO (SRCTYPE, "k")) AND (LIMIT-TO (DOCTYPE, "ch") OR LIMIT-TO (DOCTYPE, "ar")) AND (LIMIT-TO (LANGUAGE, "English"))

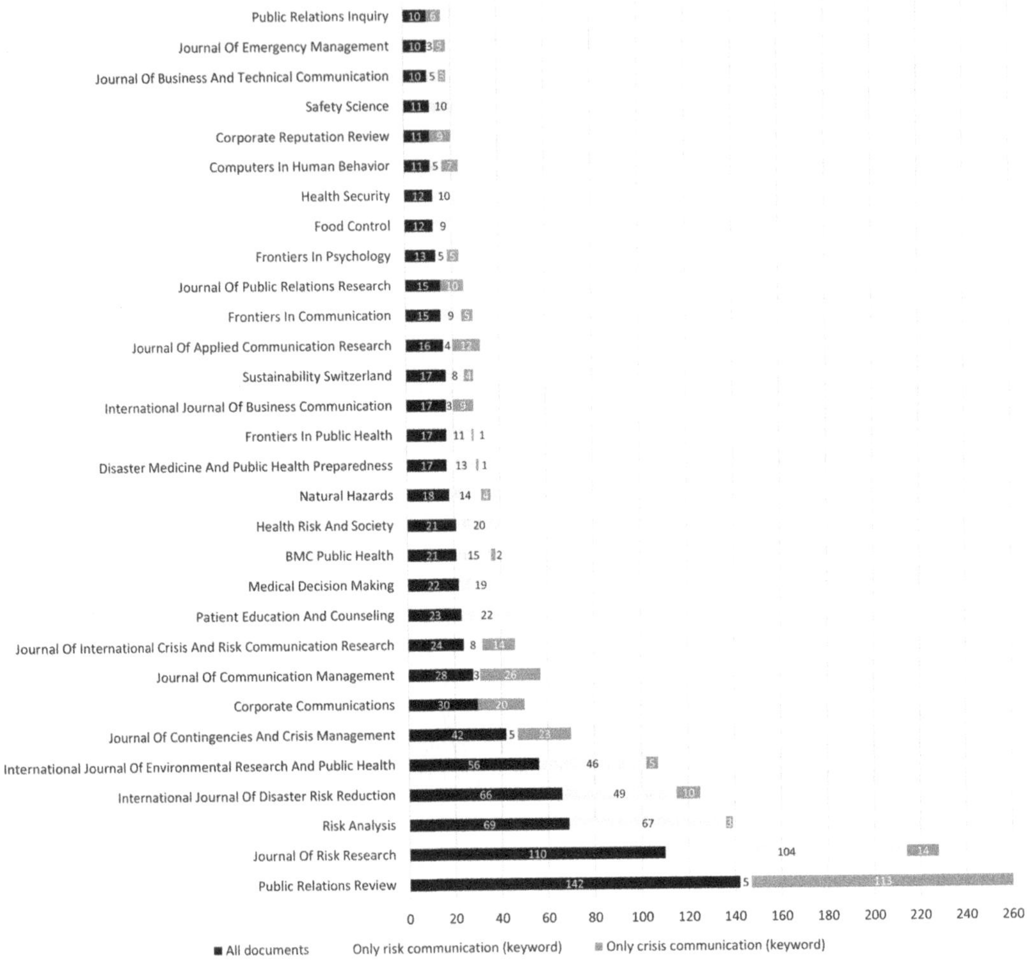

Figure 1.2 Number of publications in risk and crisis communication by journal and topic from 2009 to 08/2024 (sub-samples may overlap in a few cases). *Source*: Adapted from Scopus.

Management (2%). The comparison of risk communication and crisis communication suggests a disciplinary and/or conceptual divide between publication outlets since very few journals overlap in this regard. Most journals are either primarily dedicated to risk communication or to crisis communication. In crisis communication, journals with a PR or management focus dominate (e.g., *Public Relations Review, Journal of Communication Management, Corporate Communications*), while in risk communication, journals with a general focus on risk, environmental, and public health research stand out (e.g., *Risk Analysis, International Journal of Environmental Research* and *Public Health*). Journals with some but limited overlap were the *Journal of Risk Research, the International Journal of Disaster Risk Reduction*, or the *Journal of International Crisis and Risk Communication Research*. Based on Scopus' categorization of subject areas, risk communication research seems to be more multidisciplinary since most publications are scattered across medicine, the social sciences, environmental sciences, and engineering. Crisis communication research was mainly found in the social sciences and business/management research (Figure 1.3).

We also analyzed people and institutions producing risk and crisis communication research in the last 15 years. Among the most productive according to this database search were Yan Jin

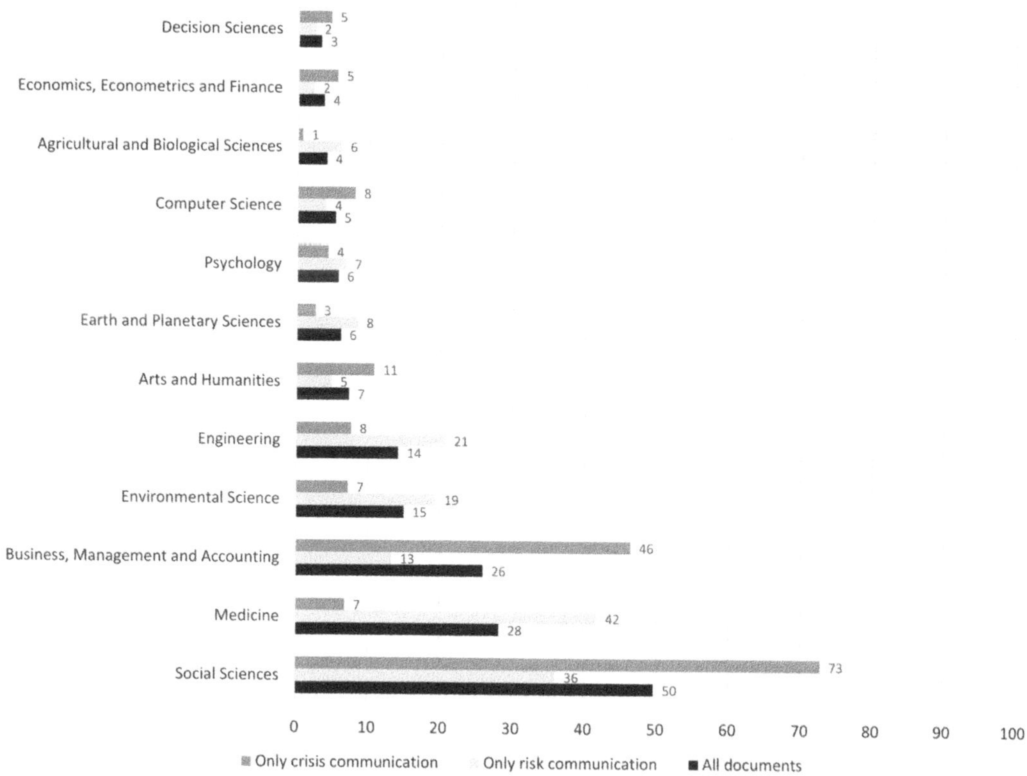

Figure 1.3 Number of publications in risk and crisis communication (in % of total sample or risk/crisis sub-sample) by subject area and topic from 2009 to 08/2024. *Source*: Adapted from Scopus.

(University of Georgia), An-Sofie Claeys (Ghent University), W. Timothy Coombs (Texas A&M University), Patrick R. Spence (University of Central Florida), and Timothy L. Sellnow (Clemson University). With the exception of Claeys (Belgium), these authors were affiliated to US-based institutions (Figure 1.4). Besides the United States, further prolific authors were based at European and Asian universities. Almost half of the authors in the top 40 have contributed to this handbook. A similar result was found for the publication output by institution, with the most relevant being based in the United States (U of Georgia, U of Central Florida, U of Maryland, and U of Kentucky) (Figure 1.5). The most important non-US institutions were King's College London (United Kingdom), Aarhus University (Denmark), Ghent University (Belgium), two universities in Amsterdam, Kyoto University (Japan), ETH Zürich (Switzerland), Max Planck Institute (Germany), and the University of Ottawa (Canada). The breakdown by country shows the overwhelming dominance of US institutions (38%), followed by the United Kingdom (10%), Germany (7%), China (7%), Canada (5%), and Australia (5%) (Figure 1.6). In the long tail, we mainly found further European, Asian (e.g., Japan, South Korea, India, Malaysia), and a few African institutions (South Africa, Nigeria). Latin American countries were only scarcely represented. The funding sources of risk and crisis communication research that were listed most frequently were the European Commission and its different framework programs (n = 63), followed by the US National Science Foundation (n = 56), the National Natural Science Foundation of China (n = 53), the US National Institutes of Health (n = 40), and the Japan Society for the Promotion of Science (n = 37).

To get an impression of how much of that research was designed to study more than one country or to study transnational causes, processes, or outcomes of risk and crisis

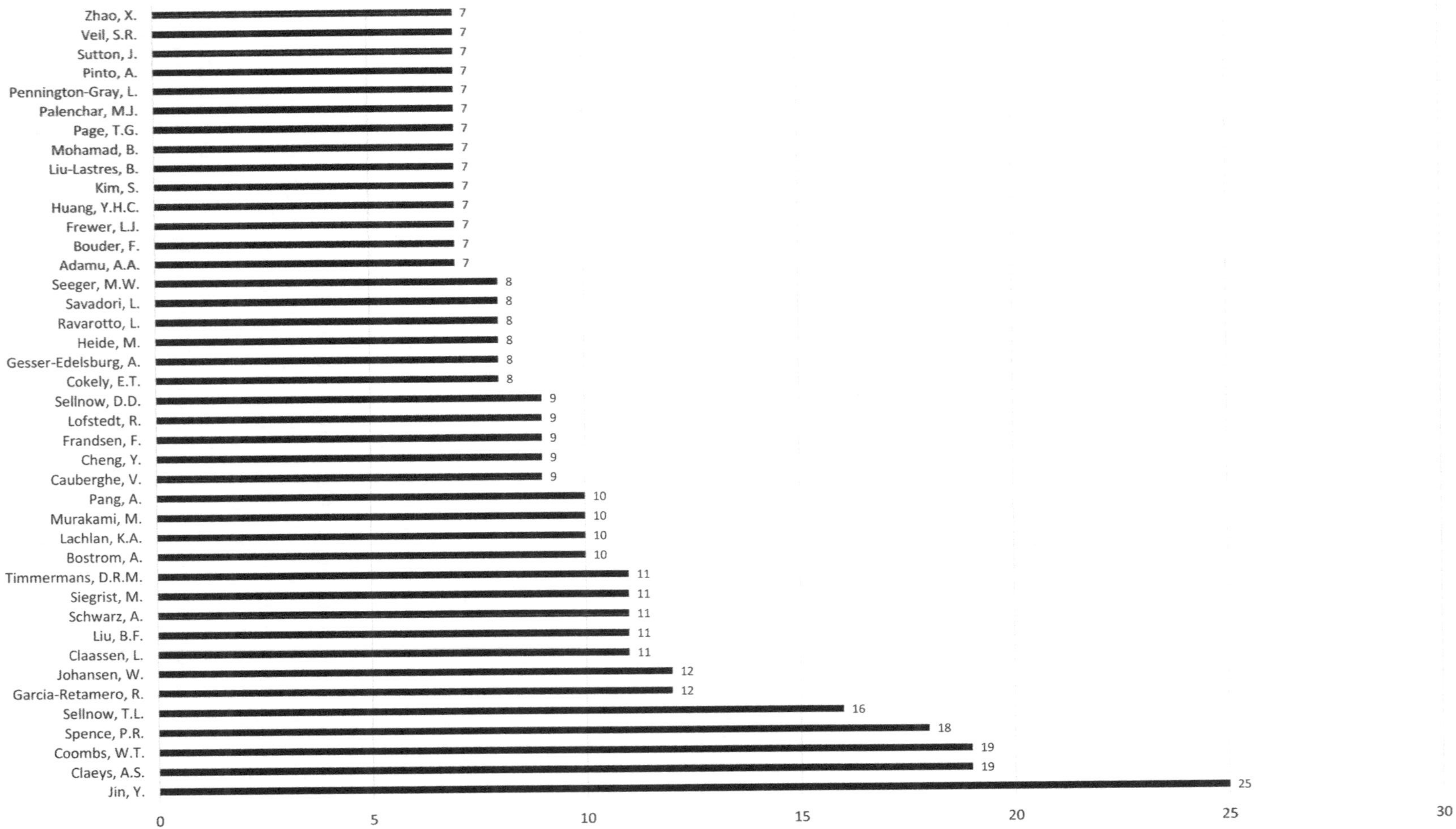

Figure 1.4 Number of publications in risk and crisis communication by author from 2009 to 08/2024. *Source*: Adapted from Scopus.

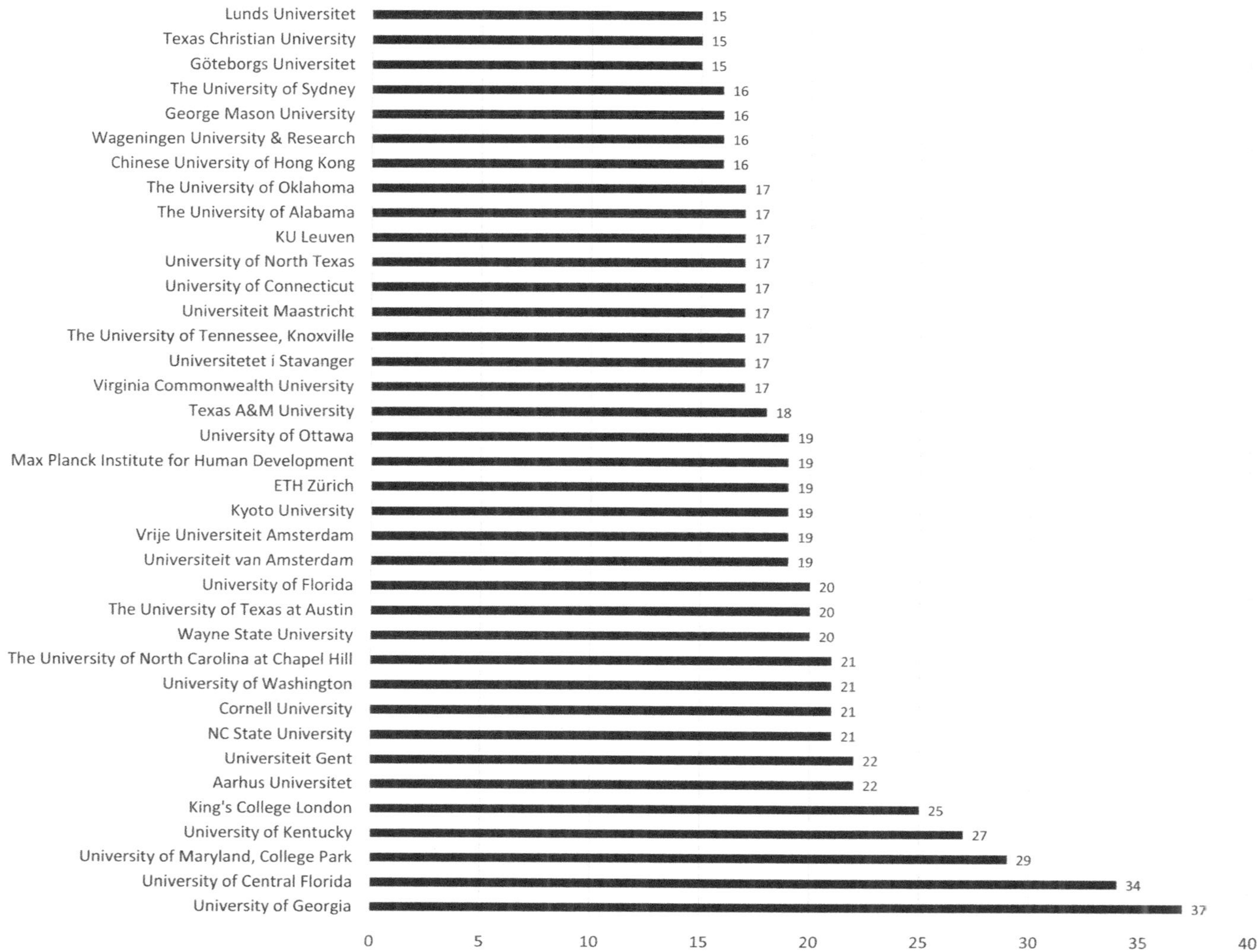

Figure 1.5 Number of publications in risk and crisis communication by affiliation from 2009 to 08/2024. *Source*: Adapted from Scopus.

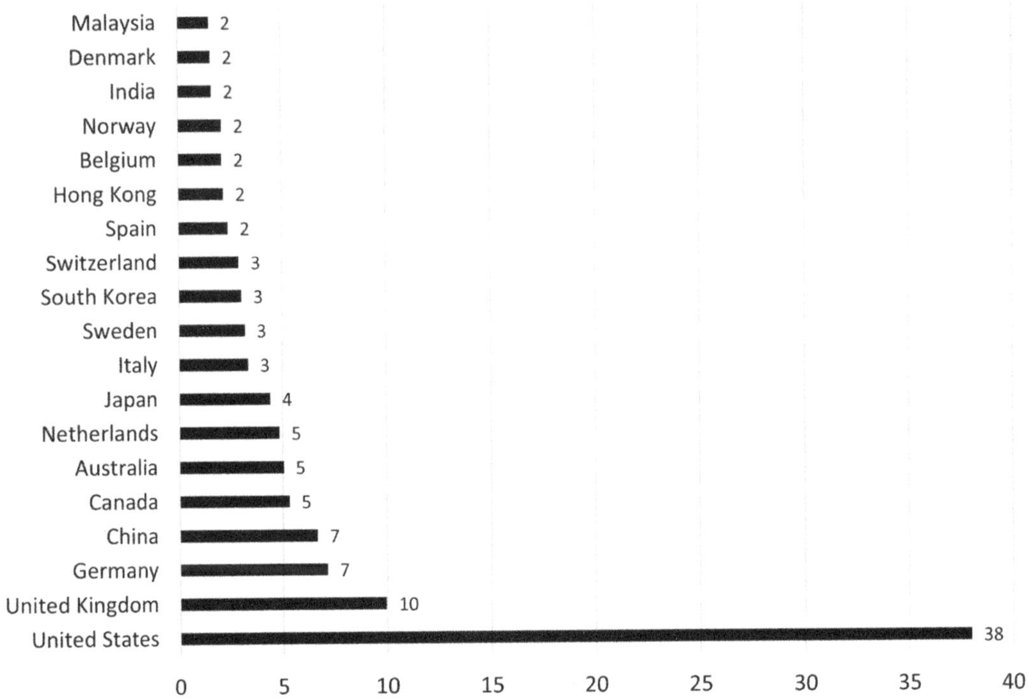

Figure 1.6 Number of publications in risk and crisis communication by country (in %) from 2009 to 08/2024 (N = 2,540). *Source*: Adapted from Scopus.

communication, we further searched the results for publications using the keywords *cross-cultural, cross-national, comparative,* or *transnational* in titles or abstracts. Only 82 publications were found (3%), a considerable number of which were indexed as comparative without collecting data across countries. Almost a third of them (n = 26) were published in 2022 and 2023. Based on titles and abstracts, most of that recent research dealt with different aspects of the COVID-19 pandemic, including studies of public health communication (Cristea et al., 2022), political communication (Nicasio Varea et al., 2023), news media framing (Sørensen & Evensen, 2023), corporate communication (Parmelee & Greer, 2023), or internal instructional risk communication (Schwarz et al., 2024). Altogether, cross-national research was almost evenly distributed across risk communication (n = 40) and crisis communication (n = 34), as well as a broad range of publication outlets. The most relevant in that regard were *Public Relations Review* (6), the *Handbook of International Crisis Communication Research* (1st ed.) (4), *Risk Analysis* (4), *Corporate Communications* (3), and the *Journal of Risk Research* (3).

Despite database limitations and the occasional lack of appropriate indexing by journals or authors, this analysis of 15 years points to the following observations of risk and crisis communication as a field:

1. The international research output is still dominated by US institutions and authors, followed by European and Asian researchers. However, many authors from these institutions may actually come from different countries, as academic systems have become more international in the United States and Europe. The representation of the Global South in English publication outlets remains scarce, the regions of Africa and Latin America in particular.

2. The field is multidisciplinary, especially in risk communication research, while crisis communication research tends to have a PR or management focus. The disciplinary divide between risk communication and crisis communication persists and the two fields lack integration. Most journals stress either one or the other with little overlap.
3. Cross-national or cross-cultural research seems to remain rare in terms of publication output. Specific events such as the COVID-19 pandemic have the potential to trigger more efforts in that regard, which may be related to the global character of such crises, high levels of societal and political attention, as well as more funding opportunities (Liu et al., 2024).

Goals and Structure of the Handbook

Recent edited volumes on risk and crisis communication have contributed important overviews of the body of knowledge in the field (Coombs & Holladay, 2023; Diers-Lawson et al., 2024; Liu & Mehta, 2024; Sellnow & Sellnow, 2024). However, they either focus on a range of specific crisis types or lack a more global as well as interdisciplinary representation of scholarship. With the second edition of this handbook, we tried to take these limitations into account. In addition, we addressed some of the gaps that resulted from the literature review presented in this chapter.

A major concern is the still-lacking integration of crisis and risk communication scholarship. Although improvement is visible based on handbook and journal publications, the divide keeps being an institutional and disciplinary reality. There is, for example, little overlap in membership and collaboration between the specialty group for risk communication at the Society of Risk Analysis (focus on risk) and the Risk and Crisis Communication Section at the European Communication Research and Education Association (ECREA) (somewhat focused on crisis). Although the first edition of this handbook already included chapters addressing both risk and crisis communication, the predominant focus was on crisis communication. Therefore, in the second edition, we asked our contributors to cover both fields more explicitly in their reviews of the literature and/or to address matters of conceptual and empirical integration in all sections of the handbook.

In the first section of this volume, we excluded the disciplinary foundations of the field (e.g., political science, psychology, anthropology) that were part of the first edition since they have not fundamentally changed. Instead, the editors give a condensed overview on risk and crisis communication research to deduce the field's significance and major gaps (Chapter 1, Schwarz), describe the historical development and structure of the field (Chapter 2, Seeger), and analyze the role of culture in international crisis and risk communication research (Chapter 3, Kim).

The sections two, three, and four follow a similar structure as in the first edition using a two-dimensional matrix of risk/crisis context (war, terrorism/shootings, disaster, public health threats/pandemics, organizational crises, political crises) and communication perspective (strategic/institutional risk and crisis communication, social/news media constructions of risks and crises, stakeholder/audience perspective of risk and crisis perception and communication). In the resulting 18 chapters, authors elaborate different perspectives according to their respective expertise. By largely maintaining this matrix, we were able to avoid one-sided emphases on specific objects of study (e.g., corporate crises and public relations), as we found them in many of the publication outlets in our previous analysis. We also incorporate different sub-disciplines to offer a comparative perspective of the multidisciplinary and in part fragmented field (e.g., strategic communication, political communication, scandal research, instructional communication, journalism, media effects, risk perception, etc.).

Three major changes were made in sections two to four. First, since the COVID-19 pandemic had significant global impact on societies as well as the publication output, we dedicated additional chapters to the risk/crisis context of pandemics and public health crises (e.g., Chapter 7, Löffelholz & Xu; Chapter 13, Liu & Baur; Chapter 19, Wiedicke & Rossmann). Second, the role of misinformation and disinformation was given more room because of its increasing relevance in the context of public health crises, political crises, as well as armed conflicts (e.g., Chapter 6, Palenchar & Heath). In addition, the chapters on terrorism include more references to shootings (e.g., Chapter 11, Rothenberger & Verhovnik-Heinze) since the number of active shooter incidents (Gramlich, 2023) and mass shootings (Statista, 2024) has increased significantly after 2016, especially in the United States. Third, section three was no longer only focused on the role of traditional news media (journalism). The authors were asked to incorporate both the role of social media/algorithms and news media in their reviews of the literature (e.g., Chapter 14, Jin & van der Meer).

Scholars have repeatedly criticized the lack of diversity in approaches, countries represented in research affiliations, and/or empirical data, as it was also confirmed by our literature analysis. While the first edition already included a broad range of international authors and overviews on several regions, in this edition we increased global representation, for example by including more regional overviews on the Global South in section five. This includes chapters on East Africa (Chapter 22, Napakol et al.), Ethiopia (Chapter 23, Abas & Beyene), Nigeria (Chapter 24, George & Adamolekum), Latin America (Chapter 38, Arroyave & Erazo-Coronado), Brazil (Chapter 39, Soares et al.), and Argentina (Chapter 40, Fernández Pedemonte). We included additional overviews on Eastern European countries (Chapter 35, Buzoianu et al.; Chapter 36, Tsetsura et al.) and the Middle East (Chapter 31, Allagui). We also added Japan for the East Asian region (Chapter 29, Sakurai). The chapters in section five give international scholars, students, and practitioners insights into different national and cultural contexts of risk and crisis communication. They also facilitate an understanding of national research priorities and access to publications, which otherwise would not have been noticed because of language barriers. In many countries, scholars publish extensively on risk and crisis communication in books and book chapters in their respective language and are not necessarily represented in English peer-reviewed journals (Klingelhöfer, 2023). Hence, this handbook aims to raise awareness of these diverse contexts in order to facilitate cross-national collaboration among researchers and practitioners. Managing such global and/or multicultural teams has been identified as both a major challenge and opportunity for attracting and conducting funded research in global risk and crisis communication research (Liu et al., 2024).

Finally, section six includes several chapters that address current theoretical, methodological, technological, and practice-related trends in the field. In Chapter 42, for example, Soares and Sellnow present the results of a literature analysis of publications in two major journals of the field to assess the extent to which recent research has addressed international dimensions of crises and disasters. To do so, the authors discuss their findings in the context of mega-crises and wicked problems, as these concepts have gained importance with the increasingly severe manifestations of climate change, the occurrence of major pandemics, and the general overlap of multiple crises. In Chapter 44, Frederic Bouder reviews contributions from risk science and risk analysis to best practices in risk and crisis communication. Further conceptual innovations in the field can be linked to instructional communication theory and its increasing application in risk and crisis communication, as Deanna Sellnow points out (Chapter 43). Methodological trends and challenges were discussed in Chapters 45–47. Daniel Vogler (Chapter 46), for instance, discusses the opportunities and limitations of computational communication science for analyzing international risk and crisis communication with regards to the complexity of multilingual analysis or the adaptation of models to less widely spoken languages. Audra Diers-Lawson (Chapter 45) addresses epistemological challenges and limitations in diversity as well as alignment of theory and research designs in studying risk and crises cross-culturally based on an extensive systematic literature review. We also included a chapter on recent developments in technologies, which are applied in risk and crisis communication processes involving public safety authorities and citizens (Chapter 48, Grace). The author analyzes developments and the potential of public warning systems, social media, monitoring systems, and common operational pictures, including the risks and benefits of artificial intelligence. Chapter 49 (Duncan & Diers-Lawson) elaborates on the structures, conditions, and challenges of international health emergency response from the perspective of practitioners and global organizations such as the WHO. In the final section (Chapter 50), the editors sum up the main insights from this handbook for cross-cultural and cross-national risk and crisis communication and draw conclusions for future research and practices.

In conclusion, the second edition of this handbook offers a substantial update of global research and addresses prevalent gaps in the literature to:

1. advance the integration of risk communication and crisis communication as fields with, in part, separate conceptual foundations, empirical foci, and institutional structures,
2. support the increase in diversity of global voices and international collaboration contributing to risk and crisis communication research and practice,
3. and to facilitate the conceptual integration and methodologically innovative exploration across risk and crisis contexts, including transnational and protracted crises, to overcome the still prevalent fragmentation of the field within and across academic disciplines.

References

Centre for Research on the Epidemiology of Disasters (CRED) (2024). *2023 disasters in numbers.* https://files.emdat.be/reports/2023_EMDAT_report.pdf

Coombs, W. T., & Holladay, S. J. (Eds.). (2023). *The Handbook of Crisis Communication* (2nd ed.). Wiley Blackwell.

Cristea, F., Weishaar, H., Geurts, B., Delamou, A., Tan, M. M. J., Legido-Quigley, H., Aminu, K., Mari-Sáez, A., Rocha, C., Camara, B., Barry, L., Thea, P., Boucsein, J., Bahr, T., Al-Awlaqi, S., Pozo-Martin, F., Boklage, E., Jegede, A. S., & Bcheraoui, C. E. (2022). A comparative analysis of experienced uncertainties in relation to risk communication during COVID19: A four-country study. *Globalization and Health, 18*(1), Article 66. https://doi.org/10.1186/s12992-022-00857-x

Department of Peace and Conflict Research (2024). *UCDP Uppsala Conflict Data Program.* Uppsala Universitet. Retrieved August 16 from https://ucdp.uu.se/

Diers-Lawson, A., Schwarz, A., Meissner, F., & Ravazzani, S. (2024). *Risk and Crisis Communication in Europe: Towards Integrating Theory and Practice in Unstable and Turbulent Times.* Routledge. https://doi.org/10.4324/9781003375296

Global Terrorism Trends and Analysis Center (2023). *Annex of statistical information 2022: Country reports on terrorism 2022.* https://www.state.gov/wp-content/uploads/2023/11/2022_Statistical_Annex_Final__508_Compliant.pdf

Gramlich, J. (2023). *What the data says about gun deaths in the U.S.* Retrieved August 16 from https://www.pewresearch.org/short-reads/2023/04/26/what-the-data-says-about-gun-deaths-in-the-u-s/

Grebmer, K. v., Geza, W., Ndlovu, M., Bernstein, J., Wiemers, M., Reiner, L., Bachmeier, M., Hanano, A., Chéilleachair, R. N., Foley, C., Sheehan, T., Gitter, S., Larocque, G., & Fritschel, H. (2023). *2023 Global Hunger Index: The Power of Youth in Shaping Food Systems.* Welthungerhilfe (WHH). https://concernusa.org/public/uploads/2023-global-hunger-index_en.pdf

Klingelhöfer, J. (2023). *The Power of Crisis Communication: A Qualitative Study of the Establishment of a Scientific Field.* Springer VS.

Liu, B. F., Jin, Y., Zhao, W. Q., Schwarz, A., Truban, O., & Seeger, M. (2024). Building the new architecture of crisis management: Global experts' insights on best and worst practices for securing external funding. *Journal of Contingencies & Crisis Management, 32*(1), 12, Article e12539. https://doi.org/10.1111/1468-5973.12539

Liu, B. F., & Mehta, A. M. (Eds.). (2024). *Routledge Handbook of Risk, Crisis, and Disaster Communication.* Routledge.

Nicasio Varea, B., Pérez-Gabaldón, M., & Chavez, M. (2023). Communication strategies in divergence: Between rigor and manipulation. A comparative analysis of the political communication of the United States and Spain during the initial stage of the COVID-19 crisis. *Revista Latina de Comunicación Social, 2023*(81), 275–296. https://doi.org/10.4185/RLCS-2023-1899

OpenAI (2024). *Disrupting deceptive uses of AI by covert influence operations.* Retrieved August 15 from https://openai.com/index/disrupting-deceptive-uses-of-AI-by-covert-influence-operations/

Park, H. W., & Park, S. (2024). The filter bubble generated by artificial intelligence algorithms and the network dynamics of collective polarization on YouTube: The case of South Korea. *Asian Journal of Communication, 34*(2), 195–212. https://doi.org/10.1080/01292986.2024.2315584

Parmelee, S. D., & Greer, C. F. (2023). Corporate responses to the COVID-19 pandemic by Fortune 500 companies. *Public Relations Review, 49*(1), Article 102285. https://doi.org/10.1016/j.pubrev.2022.102285

Ritchie, H., & Rosado, P. (2024). *Is the number of natural disasters increasing?* https://ourworldindata.org/disaster-database-limitations

Schwarz, A., Alpers, F., Wagner-Olfermann, E., & Diers-Lawson, A. (2023). The Global Study of COVID News: Scope, findings, and implications of quantitative content analyses of the COVID-19 news coverage in the first two years of the pandemic. *Health Communication, 39*(8), 1568–1581. https://doi.org/10.1080/10410236.2023.2226932

Schwarz, A., Sellnow, D. D., Sellnow, T. D., & Taylor, L. E. (2024). Instructional risk and crisis communication at higher education institutions during COVID-19: Insights from practitioners in the global south and north. *Journal of International Crisis and Risk Communication Research, 7*(1), 1–47. https://doi.org/10.56801/jicrcr.V7.i1.1

Schwarz, A., & Unselt, J. J. (2024). Rage against the machine? Framing societal threat and efficacy in YouTube videos about artificial intelligence. *Risk Analysis, 44*(10), 2377–2395. https://doi.org/10.1111/risa.14299

Sellnow, T. L., & Sellnow, D. D. (Eds.). (2024). *Communicating Risk and Safety.* De Gruyter Mouton.

Sørensen, M., & Evensen, D. (2023). Framing the Covid-19 pandemic: A comparative analysis of Swedish and Danish crisis communication. *Journal of Contingencies & Crisis Management, 31*(4), 960–967. https://doi.org/10.1111/1468-5973.12486

Statista (2024). *Number of mass shootings in the United States between 1982 and June 2024.* Retrieved August 16 from https://www.statista.com/statistics/811487/number-of-mass-shootings-in-the-us/

World Health Organization (2024). *Number of COVID-19 deaths reported to WHO.* Retrieved August 15 from https://data.who.int/dashboards/covid19/deaths

Author's Bio

Andreas Schwarz (PhD, TU Ilmenau, 2009) is a senior researcher in risk and crisis communication at Technische Universität Ilmenau in Germany where he serves as co-director of the International Research Group on Crisis Communication. He was the founding chair of the Crisis Communication Section of the European Communication Research and Education Association (ECREA), 2011–2018. His research interests include cross-cultural risk and crisis communication, crisis response of nongovernmental and higher education organizations, and the science and risk communication of emerging technologies such as artificial intelligence. Schwarz received research grants to study risk communication of COVID-19, crisis communication of child protective services and nonprofit organizations, and perceptions of artificial intelligence or automated mobility. His research has been published in journals like *Health Communication, International Journal of Strategic Communication, Public Relations Review, Journal of Public Relations Research, Risk Analysis,* Journal of Risk Research, and *Science Communication.* He has conducted trainings and consulted on risk and crisis communication for several government agencies, nonprofit organizations, and corporations.

2

History of Crisis and Risk Communication

The Development of a Global Community of Multi-Disciplinary Research, Theory and Practice

Matthew W. Seeger
Department of Communication and Center for Emerging and Infectious Diseases, Wayne State University, Detroit, MI, USA

Introduction

The 2016 *International Handbook of Crisis Communication Research* includes several discussions of the history and development of the crisis communication field. In addition, many other authors have discussed the development of the field (See Frandsen & Johansen, 2020; Lachlan et al., 2019; Palenchar, 2020). The development of risk communication as a field has been examined by several authors, including Fischhoff (1995), Plough and Krimsky (2013), and Balog-Way et al. (2020). Several efforts have also sought to identify connections between the risk and crisis communication fields.

In this chapter, the history(s) of these field(s) are examined to trace the trajectory of crisis and risk communication theory and research. Dominate theories of crisis communication and risk communication are identified. The various ways crisis and risk communication have been linked are also described. Conclusions are offered about the future of the field going forward.

Crisis Communication

Systems for communicating crisis warnings appear to arise as an evolutionary adaptation to recurring risks. In fact, animal alarm signals have been documented among a variety of species, including birds, mammals, and insects. Several bird species signal the presence of predators with specific vocalizations or alarm signals. Some mammal species, including Meerkats, have designated lookouts watching for danger. Herd animals may depend on other species to signal risks. Many primates use specific alarms, as well as clear vocalizations. Bees use chemical pheromones to signal danger to other members of the hive (Gill & Bierema, 2013; Smith, 1986; Verheggen et al., 2010).

Similar systems of warnings and alerts for humans have likely existed as long as organized groups of humans faced hazards and sought to avoid them. Specialized signal fires, horns, or other wind instruments, and later alarm bells were used to warn communities of impending dangers and the need to take mitigating actions (Telegraphia, 2023). "Ringing the

The Handbook of International Crisis and Risk Communication Research, Second Edition.
Edited by Andreas Schwarz, Matthew W. Seeger, and Sora Kim.

warning bell" has become a term to denote an effort to call attention to some impending or emerging danger.

As technology developed, the alarm bell was replaced by sirens and broadcasting systems, such as the US CONELRAD (*Control of Electromagnetic Radiation*) system introduced in 1951 in response to fears of a nuclear attack, the Emergency Broadcast System introduced in 1963, and the Emergency Alert System, introduced in 1997. More recently, Wireless Emergency Alerts (WEAS) have been developed using text-based warning systems (Bean et al., 2016).

Alerts and warnings as forms of risk and crisis communication have been examined from a variety of perspectives. This includes differentiating alerts, as signals that something may be happening, from warnings, messages with more specific information, and recommended protective actions (Mileti & Sorensen, 1990). These systems of warnings are used for a wide range of hazards, including tsunamis, earthquakes, hurricanes, tornadoes, floods, toxic spills, fires, mudslides, volcanic activity, and earthquakes within a range of local, national, and international contexts (Villagrán et al., 2013). Much of this work focused on improving the effectiveness of warnings by enhancing dissemination, understanding, and compliance. This work has led to frameworks such as Mileti's Hear-Confirm-Understand-Decide-Response model (Mileti & Fitzpatrick, 1992; Mileti & Peek, 2000) and the Protection Action Defense Model (Lindell & Perry, 2004, 2012).

The systematic investigation of disasters from a social science perspective began in the 1950s, primarily within the field of sociology. These studies focused on a variety of behavioral phenomena, including the impact of disasters on social structures, organization and disorganization, evacuation behaviors, emergency services, response training, the features of specific disaster types such as tornadoes, floods, and bombings, and investigations of alerts and warnings (See Rayner, 1957). Efforts were also directed to understanding fundamental questions of disaster behavior, including effective warnings, behavior during various disaster stages, flocking to disaster zones, coordination and control of rescue and relief activities, victim trauma, and the sources of possible conflicts (Fritz & Williams, 1957).

The development of risk and crisis communication research in the U.S. was also guided by the work of two academic centers: the Disaster Research Center at Ohio State University, led by the sociologist Enrico Quarantelli, and the Natural Hazards Center, founded in 1975 at the University of Colorado, led by geography professor Gilbert White. White was especially interested in multi-disciplinary approaches to natural hazards and strategies for mitigating harm. Quarantelli and colleagues examined a wide range of behavioral factors in human responses to hazards. This included communicative behaviors such as the use of media.

Several authors have noted that crisis communication research was heavily influenced by crisis events that demonstrated the central role of communication in crisis management and the need for research (Frandsen & Johansen, 2016, Lachlan et al., 2019). A major train derailment accident in 1906 in New Jersey in the US promoted the first use of a formal press release by Ivy Lee, who would go on to help found the public relations profession. Research on the Tylenol poisoning in 1982 and Johnson and Johnson's response (Benson, 1988), the Three Mile Island disaster (Dionisopoulos & Crable, 1988), the Challenger Space Shuttle explosion (Seeger, 1986), and the Exxon Valdez Oil Spill (Williams & Treadaway, 1992) added to a growing body of crisis event scholarship.

Outside of the US, international crises generating the attention of investigators included the 1984 Bhopal/Union Carbide disaster (Shrivastava, 1987; Weick, 2010), the 1986 Chernobyl disaster (Dombrowsky, 1987; Teichert, 1987), and infectious disease outbreaks, including the AIDS pandemic of the early 1980s and the outbreak of Avian Influenza in Hong Kong in 1997 (Seeger et al., 2020). The scale of these events called research attention to global disasters. The Bhopal / Union Carbide disaster influenced the expansion of sensemaking and enactment in crisis communication (Weick, 2010). The Avian Influenza threat helped motivate the U.S. Centers for Disease Control and Prevention to integrate crisis communication into their health communication programs (Reynolds & Seeger, 2005).

Other disasters prompting research interest included the 9/11 Terrorist Attacks (Ulmer et al., 2007), war (See Schwarz, Chapter 32) Hurricane Katrina (Garnett & Kouzmin, 2007), the Great Hanshin/Kobe Earthquake in Japan (Heath, 1995, Acar & Muraki, 2011), and the Fukushima-Daiichi disaster (Utz et al., 2013). The COVID-19 pandemic once again generated widespread interest in crisis communication research related to health and also pointed out the global reach of some disasters (Croucher & Diers-Lawson, 2023; Malecki et al., 2021).

Event-driven crisis communication research is primarily grounded in a case study epistemology, but events also drive extramural funding (See Liu et al., 2024). Because the focus is on a specific event in a specific location with limited impacts, the results of these studies may have limited generalizability and support middle-range explanations rather than grand theory (Seeger, 2022). Nonetheless, they have significantly advanced the field, provided a broad understanding of the kinds of crisis events that occur and their impact, and facilitated the development of theory.

In addition to examination of events using primarily case study approaches, investigations have turned to other methods, including experiments, interviews with practitioners, and surveys of audiences, to examine how communication may function in crisis contexts (Cameron, 1994; Coombs & Holladay, 1996; Jin et al., 2014; Lyon & Cameron, 2004; Westerman et al., 2014). These and other studies drove a number of research programs into such issues as reputational defense and image repair, the role of emotions in crisis communication, channel and message features, and the use of social media, among others.

Multidisciplinary Approaches

Crisis communication research is dispersed among a variety of fields, creating both challenges and opportunities. Anthropology, sociology, political science, business, and various traditions in communication, have contributed to the literature. Anthropologists Mary Douglas' (1970; Douglas & Wildavsky, 1983) work on culture and risk, Kai Erickson's (1976) investigation of the sociology of the Buffalo Creek disaster, Barry Turner's (1976) thesis on the development of disasters, and Birkland's (1997) development of the theory of crisis-focusing events in political science have all contributed to a rich and diverse literature on crises and disasters. Business and organizational studies contributed important conceptual frameworks to the study of crisis. Hermann's (1963) description of the features of a crisis, Fink's (1971) developmental model, and Smart and Vertinsky's (1977) analysis of crisis decision-making helped establish crisis management as an important subdiscipline within organizational studies.

Within the field of communication, crisis studies have followed two somewhat distinct paths. First, public relations has been interested in questions of the reputational impact of crises and strategies for image restoration and repair. Early work in this area broadly followed the genre of apologia as a form of rhetorical defense (Ware & Linkugel, 1973). William Benoit's (1997) work on image repair became very influential as a framework for describing and informing strategic responses to accusations of wrongdoing. A second framework for understanding accusations of wrongdoing was developed by Timothy Coombs and colleagues (1990; Coombs & Holladay, 1996) and is broadly grounded in concepts of attribution theory. This situational crisis communication theory seeks to account for a range of contextual factors in understanding organizational responses to accusations of wrongdoing and has become what is arguably the most influential approach to crisis communication scholarship.

A second body of crisis communication work is more fully grounded in an organizational communication perspective. This body of work has focused on the impact of disruptive events on organizations, including businesses and corporations, and the methods of management, including planning and management (Mitroff et al., 1987, Fink, 1986), risk and threat recognition (Mitroff, 1988), and crisis stages (Fink et al., 1971). Ian Mitroff's work on organizations and crisis management phases (1988) and the theory of crisis-prone and crisis-proof organizations helped to position crisis management as an essential issue in organizational studies (Pearson & Mitroff, 2019). Similarly, Karl Weick's extension of his sensemaking and enactment framework to crises (1988, 1995) and the subsequent development of the high-reliability framework provided important theoretical frameworks that positioned communication as central to organizational crises.

In addition to image repair and Situational Crisis Communication Theory, other theoretical frameworks for crisis communication have developed. These include the Rhetorical Arena Model (Frandsen & Johansen), Social-mediated crisis communication (SMCC) (Austin et al., 2012), Resilience (Buzzanell, 2010), and Renewal (Seeger & Ulmer, 2002; Seeger et al., 2024). The rhetorical area theory (RAT) suggests that a communicative space opens following a crisis and that a variety of stakeholder voices will be represented in post-crisis communication. The representation of the multiple voices in the post-crisis context reflects the inherent complexity and the dynamics of conflict and agreement among groups. SMCC describes the information flows between organizations and three groups of crisis stakeholders:"(1) influential social media creators; (2) social media followers: and (3) social media inactives." (Austin et al., 2012, p. 192). Social media distributes information to these stakeholders both directly and indirectly.

Risk Communication

Risk communication was undoubtedly widely practiced before it became a topic of research and formal policy (Palenchar & Heath, 2007). In the 1980s, risk communication emerged as an "organizing theme for a set of diverse but conceptually related problems concerning the political management of public risk perceptions and individual behavioral responses to risks" (Plough & Krimsky, 1987, p. 4). The expansion of risk communication research, policy, and practice can be attributed at least in part to the adoption of programs by government agencies, first with the US Environmental Protection Administration and later with the Centers for Disease Control and Prevention and the World Health Organization. Palenchar and Heath (2007) attributed the growth of risk communication to US legislation addressing large-scale chemical contamination and community right-to-know legislation in the mid-1980s. Since its emergence, research and practice have expanded into a multi-disciplinary area of research and practice. Risk communication is broadly understood "as an iterative exchange of information among individuals, groups, and institutions related to the assessment, characterization, and management of risk" (McComas, 2006, p. 76; National Research Council, 1989). It may take a variety of forms and diverse channels and social, professional, and organizational contexts (Covello et al., 1986).

In addition, anthropologist Mary Douglas theoretical framing of social structures and processes as essentially serving the cooperative management of risk elevated and expanded the field (Douglas & Wildavsky, 1983). The management of risk, including through communication, was positioned as central to all components of society. This view also contributed to the arguments that risk is socially constructed as a composite of social and individual values, specific contexts, and expectations and assumptions about future events (Bostrom, 2003, p. 554).

Leiss (1996) identified three phases of risk communication research, with Phase 1 running from 1975 to 1984 and focusing on quantitative risk assessments and comparative analysis for regulatory actions. Risk as a quantity Phase 2 (1985–1994) focused on effective communication to close the understanding deficit so that audiences had an accurate understanding of risks. Phase 3 recognizes the social dimensions and diverse experiences, including personal, community, and cultural, with risks and addresses consensus building, meaningful interaction between stakeholders, and acceptance of government regulations. The understanding of the information deficit view is based on the assumption that audiences have insufficient information about risks and that by providing additional information from credible, often expert sources, they will have the correct understanding and associated behaviors (Balog-Way et al. 2020).

Baruch Fischhoff (1995), one of the most influential investigators in risk perception and communication, identified several stages in the development of risk communication based on themes of practitioner understanding of effectiveness. These include:

> All we have to do is get the numbers right
> All we have to do is tell them the numbers
> All we have to do is explain what we mean by the numbers
> All we have to do is show them that they've accepted similar risks in the past
> All we have to do is show them that it's a good deal for them
> All we have to do is treat them nice
> All we have to do is make them partners
> All of the above (Fischhoff, 1995, p. 138).

The first three stages focus on closing the audience's informational deficits so as to create a correct or accurate understanding of risk. The emphasis is on empirical assessment of risk and reliance on expert knowledge. The second two stages focus on how audiences might make sense of risk and the importance of community-based risk knowledge. Finally, the last two stages acknowledge the value of active and authentic audience engagement in the mutual exchange of information, opinions, and values about risk. Fischhoff also acknowledges that risk communication is a challenging and dynamic process that takes time, facts, and careful planning.

McComas (2006) conducted a review of risk communication research beginning in 1996 and identified studies focusing on the role of social trust, the social amplification of risk, and affect heuristics, as well as, risk in mass media and the use of risk comparisons, narratives, and visual portrayals of risk. Trust in society, institutions, and specific sources of information continues to be an essential aspect of risk communication research. Affect heuristics, of what people feel, as well as, believe about a risk, was positioned as a way to broaden understandings of risk perceptions (Kasperson et al., 2022). The social amplification of risk continues to be a useful framework for understanding public responses to health risks and may have particular utility for understanding the role of legacy and social media in the formation of risk perceptions. Taken together, these trends suggest that research in risk communication continues to expand the focus on social processes for understanding the formation of risk perceptions and ways to use communication processes and strategies to effectively engage with audiences. This includes moving beyond simple information deficit and persuasion models to "a broader understanding of the psychological, cultural, and social influences on risk communication" (Leiss, 1996; McComas, 2006, p. 85).

In an effort to summarize and characterize the dynamic, evolving, and growing field of risk communication, Balog-Way et al. (2020) conducted a systematic review of thirty years of literature. This included examining various arguments about the role and function of risk communication. *Instrumental* arguments in the literature, for example, centered on effective multiway risk communication as a form of strategic communication for individuals, groups, or organizations to achieve goals. *Substantive* arguments in the risk communication literature focus on its capacity to generate new insights and knowledge. In addition, Balog-Way et al. (2020) describe three major foci of research: messengers, messages, and audiences. *Messengers* refer to individual, group, and organizational sources, and research has explored questions about trust and transparency. *Message attributes* refer to research focusing such as message frames, affect components, and messages that address uncertainty. *Audiences* concern the recipients who are engaged in risk communication, and research has explored issues such as the impact of audience attributes, risk perception, and cultural values.

Balog-Way et al. (2020) conclude by observing that risk communication, like crisis communication, is driven by contemporary events, that risk communication is complex and requires a multifaceted approach, that many risk communication concepts are also multidimensional and require more nuanced discussions, and that effective risk communication requires an ongoing process of engagement. Or, as they have noted, risk communication has moved from an information deficit model to a stakeholder dialogue model.

The robustness of risk communication research belies its relatively short history as a focused area of multidisciplinary study. The plethora of work does suggest that risk communication is seen as an essential area of research to inform practice in a variety of fields, including health and medicine, natural hazards, such as hurricanes, fires, and floods, and human-caused hazards such as chemical spills, contamination events, and radiological hazards.

Theoretical and Interdisciplinary Perspectives

As with crisis communication research, risk communication research is dispersed among a variety of fields, including psychology, communication, engineering, sociology, geography, anthropology, political science, and the various decision sciences, among others (Balog-Way et al., 2020; Plough & Krimsky, 2013). Communication and psychology are probably the two dominant research traditions, followed closely by sociology and anthropology. Psychology has a primary interest in risk perception and associated cognitive processes. Communication has also focused on risk perception and the ways messages may change perceptions, and the interaction between various risk stakeholders. Anthropology might broadly be described as focusing on culture and risk, while sociology is concerned with the impact of social processes and structures on risk and risk perception. Engineering, business, medicine, and political science have more practical and applied interests in risk communication. In practice, there is a great deal of overlap between these fields to the degree that risk communication is generally recognized as a multidisciplinary field.

There are, however, theoretical frameworks that are associated with specific fields. One of the most prominent, the mental models approach developed by Baruch Fischhoff and colleagues, grew out of psychology. Mental models are mental representations or images about the world and how it should work that allow for inferences that influence both beliefs and behaviors (Bostrom, 2017; Downs et al., 2020). Existing mental models may impede or facilitate the integration of new information about risks. Risk communication, therefore, must begin with an audience focus and an effort to understand existing mental models. Thus, risk communication requires dialogue to know what audiences think and believe (Morgan & Fischhoff, 2023).

Morgan & Fischhoff (2023) suggest that risk communication should seek to close the gap between subject matter experts' mental models and the mental models of the target audience. Risk communication, then, follows a process of identifying the relevant scientific domain, conducting audience analysis using methods such as open-ended interviews, comparing the mental models of the audience and those from experts, and developing messages that reduce the gaps, address misperceptions, and reinforce models.

A second framework for risk communication from psychology is the theory of planned behavior. According to Icek Ajzen (1991, 2020; Bosnjak et al., 2020), behaviors are influenced by intentions, which are determined by three attitudinal factors: the individual's attitude toward the behavior, perceived subjective norms, group or community, concerning the behavior, and perceived behavioral control or a belief that behavior will be facilitated or inhibited by some factors (Ajzen, 2020). A favorable attitude and perceived supportive subjective norms are motivations to engage in the behavior. The intention to engage in the behavior only occurs when there is a perception of power to perform a behavior and the perception of ease or difficulty in performing the behavior (Ajzen, 2020). While developed as a general theory of behavior, it has been very widely applied in areas such as health communication and risk communication. It has also been demonstrated to have strong predictive power and is used widely in message design.

A third dominant theory of risk communication comes from the communication field and addresses the utility and functioning of fear appeals. The Extended Parallel Processing Model (EPPM) was developed by Kim Witte and colleagues to explain the impact of fear appeals. Witte (1992, 1994) posited that fear appeals in risk messages led to one of three responses by audiences: non-responses, danger control responses, and fear control responses. Danger control responses may include taking recommended protective actions, while fear control may involve rejecting or ignoring the threat. The specific response was determined by the interaction between the audience's perceptions of the threat and perceptions of their ability to respond effectively to the threat. This perceived response capacity is usually framed as efficacy to avert the threat. EPPM suggests that fear appeals that undermine perceived efficacy may backfire and reduce desired behaviors. Message components typically address self-efficacy, response efficacy, threat susceptibility, and severity. These impact perceptions of efficacy and threat. These perceptions, then, lead to protection motivation, or defense motivation, with the former leading to danger control mechanisms, while the latter leads to message rejection and fear control (Maloney et al., 2011; Witte, 2019).

Finally, the Crisis and Emergency Risk Communication Model (CERC) seeks to match message type to the conditions of threat as specified by the developmental stages or phases (Reynolds & Seeger, 2005). These include pre-crisis, initial events, maintenance, resolution, and evaluation. Thus, CERC is a kind of contingency model of crisis communication. CERC was developed by the US Centers for Disease Control and Prevention in response to events surrounding the 9/11 terrorist attacks on the World Trade Center and the subsequent distribution of letters contaminated with anthrax spores. The CDC developed the CERC in recognition that their existing models were not sufficient.

CERC argues that risk communication is primary at some stage, including pre-crisis as part of preparedness and warning goals. Risk communication also has an important function in the initial event stage but becomes less salient in the maintenance and resolution stages. Risk messages may again be important in the evaluation stage as efforts are made to communicate lessons learned and a new understanding of risks.

The Relationship Between Crisis and Risk Communication

As the previous discussions have suggested, crisis and risk communication are linked concepts and domains of research and practice. They share somewhat distinct origin histories and disciplinary roots. Crisis communication grew primarily from work in public relations, image management, repair theories, and work in disaster sociology focusing on warnings and alerts (Reynolds & Seeger, 2005; Sellnow & Seeger, 2021). Public relations has developed communication models and frameworks to inform practice and limit the damage to organizations, communities, and stakeholders (Seeger et al., 1998). Warning messages function to inform a specific target audience of some impending, likely, or probable threat (Sellnow & Seeger, 2021). Risk communication is more firmly rooted in traditions from psychology and social psychology and seeks "to enable people at risk to make informed decisions to mitigate the effects of a threat (hazard) – such as a disease outbreak – and take protective and preventive measures" (WHO, 2024, n.p.). Risk communication is associated with the identification of risks to the public efforts to persuade the public to adopt safer, more healthy, less risky behaviors (Freimuth et al., 2000). Including hazards such as tobacco use, safe sex, drunk driving, binge drinking, vaccines, drug abuse, infectious diseases, exercise, and various kinds of disease and health screenings, as well as the dissemination of information about environmental hazards, chemicals and toxic contaminants, pathogens, UV radiation, and related environmental hazards (Powell & Leiss, 1997).

The relationship between risk communication and crisis communication may be described in three ways. First, risk and crisis may be entirely distinct forms of communication, with no overlap in function, audience, channels, messages, or goals. In this view, risk and crisis occur within distinct communication contexts and use distinct communication strategies. Although given what have been somewhat distinct developments of disciplines and histories, it may appear that risk and crisis are entirely distinct; as the previous review indicates, there are many points of connection. In fact, some suggest that crisis communication is just a more limited form of risk communication (Lundgren & McMakin, 2018).

This suggests second-way risk communication is related. The CERC development model described earlier, for example, suggests that risk communication and crisis communication are overlapping, time- and context-specific processes that are more or less prominent at various stages in a risk-crisis life cycle. There are some communication contexts where risk communication is more appropriate and others where communication is better matched to the context. Crisis and risk communication, therefore, may also essentially be the same processes only practiced in different contexts by different communicators.

A third view is that risk and crisis communication are essentially the same forms of communication manifest in different ways, at different times, with different audiences. Although the form, participants, context, and channels may vary, risk and crisis communication share the underlying goal of using the exchange of informative and persuasive messages between risk, threat, and response stakeholders to prepare for, mitigate, limit, and recover from harmful events and circumstances.

Future Developments

The emerging and merging field(s) of risk and crisis communication have grown rapidly in response to new threats, new stakeholder expectations, and new methods of communication (Palenchar & Heath, 2007). COVID-19 as a global pandemic highlighted the importance of communication processes. Many of these threats defy traditional boundaries, while new forms of communication mean that more stakeholders are involved in sharing opinions and information about risks more quickly and more widely. Public expectations for timely and effective communication have also grown, and the communication capacity of agencies is often unable to meet these expectations.

At the same time, the size and scope of several risk factors are now more evident, creating public perceptions of existential threats. In some cases, these threats motivate actions, and in other cases, they result in a fatalistic view. According to a 2023 Pew survey, overall, a majority of U.S. adults (54%) describe climate change as a major threat (Tyson et al., 2023). Moreover, about 14% of the couples who indicate they will not have children indicate that their decision is based on climate change and environmental factors or the general state of the world (Pew, Nov. 9, 2021).

In addition, risk and crisis communication research is increasingly global, driven in part by a recognition that disasters, infectious disease outbreaks, terrorism, war, and climate change do not expect regional or national boundaries. COVID-19 was probably the most vivid example of a disaster with global reach. This suggests the need for more international research addressing questions about how diverse regions, nations, and cultures address risk and crisis and how different systems manage preparation, response, and recovery. Despite many efforts to globalize the field, including those represented in this Handbook, crisis and risk communication remains a largely United States and Western Europe-centric field. Some important centers for research, however, have emerged in Asia, including in Hong Kong, Singapore, and Australia. Additional efforts are needed to build an international research community to address global risks. In particular, these efforts need to engage the Middle East, African continent, and Central and South America. At the same time, global response agencies need to be strengthened. This includes institutions such as the World Health Organization and UN Office for Disaster Risk Reduction (UNDRR). Frameworks such as the UN 2015 Sendai Framework for Disaster Risk Reduction 2015 – 2030 can be useful tools in guiding efforts to build global capacity (Mizutori, 2020).

Finally, global events such as COVID-19 point to an emerging form of crisis, the mega-crisis, that defies traditional boundaries, limits, and has extended non-linear, often long-term consequences, creates second- and third-level impacts, very high levels of uncertainty, and often intersects with other risk factors. They also have the potential of creating high levels of harm (Helsloot et al., 2012). These events will require substantial multi-national efforts and cooperation and social, political, and economic change (Sellnow & Seeger, 2021, p. 6). They also will require fundamentally new models that emphasize not just system resilience and stability as a strategy but change and renewal in response to a new understanding of risks (Seeger et al., 2024).

Conclusion

It is easy for those of us who study and practice crisis and risk communication to be overwhelmed by the devastation of these events, the scope of the harm, and the tendency of organizations, communities, and societies to ignore warnings and fail to learn post-crisis lessons. Too often, the same or similar disasters are repeated. Those of us who study and practice crisis and risk communication, however, are part of the solution to both a risky world facing known and unknown hazards, emerging risks, and mega crises and the struggles of organizations, communities, nations, and the world to prepare for, manage, and respond to these threats.

References

Acar, A., & Muraki, Y. (2011). Twitter for crisis communication: Lessons learned from Japan's tsunami disaster. *International Journal of Web Based Communities*, *7*(3), 392–402.

Ajzen, I. (1991). The theory of planned behavior. *Organizational Behavior and Human Decision Processes*, *50*(2), 179–211.

Ajzen, I. (2020). The theory of planned behavior: Frequently asked questions. *Human Behavior and Emerging Technologies*, *2*(4), 314–324.

Austin, L., Fisher Liu, B., & Jin, Y. (2012). How audiences seek out crisis information: Exploring the social-mediated crisis communication model. *Journal of Applied Communication Research*, *40*(2), 188–207.

Bean, H., Liu, B. F., Madden, S., Sutton, J., Wood, M. M., & Mileti, D. S. (2016). Disaster warnings in your pocket: How audiences interpret mobile alerts for an unfamiliar hazard. *Journal of Contingencies & Crisis Management*, *24*(3), 136–147.

Balog-Way, D., McComas, K., & Besley, J. (2020). The evolving field of risk communication. *Risk Analysis*, *40*(S1), 2240–2262.

Benoit, W. L. (1997). Image repair discourse and crisis communication. *Public Relations Review*, *23*(2), 177–186.

Benson, J. A. (1988). Crisis revisited: An analysis of strategies used by Tylenol in the second tampering episode. *Communication Studies*, *39*(1), 49–66.

Birkland, T. A. (1997). *After Disaster: Agenda Setting, Public Policy, and Focusing Events.* Georgetown University Press.
Bosnjak, M., Ajzen, I., & Schmidt, P. (2020). The theory of planned behavior: Selected recent advances and applications. *Europe's Journal of Psychology, 16*(3), 352.
Bostrom, A. (2017). Mental models of risk. In *Oxford Research Encyclopedia of Communication* (pp. 82–92). Oxford University Press.
Bostrom, A. (2003). Future risk communication. *Futures, 35*(6), 553–573.
Buzzanell, P. M. (2010). Resilience: Talking, resisting, and imagining new normalcies into being. *Journal of Communication, 60*(1), 1–14.
Cameron, G. (1994). Does publicity outperform advertising? An experimental test of third party endorsement. *Journal of Public Relations Research, 6*, 185–207.
Coombs, W. T. (1990). *Ongoing Crisis Communication: Planning, Managing, and Responding.* Sage.
Coombs, W. T., & Holladay, S. J. (1996). Communication and attributions in a crisis: An experimental study in crisis communication. *Journal of Public Relations Research, 8*(4), 279–295.
Covello, V., von Winterfeldt, D., & Slovic, P. (1986). Risk communication: A review of the literature. *Risk Abstracts, 3*, 171–182.
Croucher, S. M., & Diers-Lawson, A. (Eds.). (2023). *Pandemic Communication.* Taylor & Francis.
Dionisopoulos, G. N., & Crable, R. E. (1988). Definitional hegemony as a public relations strategy: The rhetoric of the nuclear power industry after Three Mile Island. *Communication Studies, 39*(2), 134–145.
Dombrowsky, W. R. (1987). *Das Tschernobyl-Syndrom: Katastrophen als verhaltensändernde Ereignisse [The Chernobyl Syndrome: Disasters as Events that Change Behavior].* Opladen: Westdeutscher Verlag.
Douglas, M. (1970). *Natural Symbols*, London: Barrie & Rockliff.
Douglas, M., & Wildavsky, A. (1983). *Risk and Culture: An Essay on the Selection of Technological and Environmental Dangers.* Univ of California Press.
Downs, J. S., de Bruin, W. B., Fischhoff, B., Hesse, B., & Maibach, E. (2020). How people think about cancer: A mental models approach. In *Handbook of Risk and Crisis Communication* (pp. 507–524). Routledge.
Erikson, K. (1976). *Everything in Its Path.* Simon and Schuster.
Fink, S. L., Beak, J., & Taddeo, K. (1971). Organizational crisis and change. *The Journal of Applied Behavioral Science, 7*(1), 15–37.
Fink, S. (1986). *Crisis Management: Planning for the Inevitable.* American Management Association.
Fischhoff, B. (1995). Risk perception and communication unplugged: Twenty years of process 1. *Risk Analysis, 15*(2), 137–145.
Frandsen, F., & Johansen, W. (2016). *Organizational Crisis Communication: A Multivocal Approach.* Sage.
Frandsen, F., & Johansen, W. (2020). Reframing the field: Public crisis management, political crisis management, and corporate crisis management. *Crisis Communication*, 59–102.
Freimuth, V., Linnan, H. W., & Potter, P. (2000). Communicating the threat of emerging infections to the public. *Emerging Infectious Diseases, 6*(4), 337.
Fritz, C. E., & Williams, H. B. (1957). The human being in disasters: A research perspective. *The Annals of the American Academy of Political and Social Science, 309*(1), 42–51.
Garnett, J. L., & Kouzmin, A. (2007). Communicating throughout Katrina: Competing and complementary conceptual lenses on crisis communication. *Public Administration Review, 67*, 171–188.
Gill, S. A., & Bierema, A. M. K. (2013). On the meaning of alarm calls: A review of functional reference in avian alarm calling. *Ethology, 119*(6), 449–461.
Heath, R. (1995). The Kobe earthquake: Some realities of strategic management of crises and disasters. *Disaster Prevention and Management: An International Journal, 4*(5), 11–24.
Helsloot, I., Boin, A., Jacobs, B., & Comfort, L. K. (2012). *Mega-Crises: Understanding the Prospects, Nature, Characteristics, and the Effects of Cataclysmic Events.* Charles C Thomas Publisher.
Hermann, C. F. (1963). Some consequences of crisis which limit the viability of organizations. *Administrative Science Quarterly, 8*, 61–82.
Jin, Y., Liu, B. F., & Austin, L. L. (2014). Examining the role of social media in effective crisis management: The effects of crisis origin, information form, and source on publics' crisis responses. *Communication Research, 41*(1), 74–94.

Lindell, M. K., & Perry, R. W. (2004). *Communicating Environmental Risk in Multiethnic Communities.* Thousand Oaks, CA: Sage.

Lindell, M. K., & Perry, R. W. (2012). The protective action decision model: Theoretical modifications and additional evidence. *Risk Analysis: An International Journal, 32*(4), 616–632.

Liu, B. F., Jin, Y., Zhao, W., Schwarz, A., Truban, O., & Seeger, M. (2024). Building the new a rchitecture of crisis management: Global experts' insights on best and worst practices for securing external funding. *Journal of Contingencies & Crisis Management, 32*(1), e12539.

Lundgren, R. E., & McMakin, A. H. (2018). *Risk Communication: A Handbook for Communicating Environmental, Safety, and Health Risks.* John Wiley & Sons.

Lyon, L., & Cameron, G. T. (2004). A relational approach examining the interplay of prior reputation and immediate response to a crisis. *Journal of Public Relations Research, 16*(3), 213–241.

Kasperson, R. E., Webler, T., Ram, B., & Sutton, J. (2022). The social amplification of risk framework: New perspectives. *Risk Analysis, 42*(7), 1367–1380.

Lachlan, K. A., Spence, P. R., Seeger, M., Gilbert, C., & Lin, X. (2019). Crisis communication in context: History and publication trends. *Journal of the Association for Communication Administration, 38*(2), 2.

Leiss, W. (1996). Three phases in the evolution of risk communication practice. *The Annals of the American Academy of Political and Social Science, 545*(1), 85–94.

Malecki, K. M., Keating, J. A., & Safdar, N. (2021). Crisis communication and public perception of COVID-19 risk in the era of social media. *Clinical Infectious Diseases, 72*(4), 697–702.

Maloney, E. K., Lapinski, M. K., & Witte, K. (2011). Fear appeals and persuasion: A review and update of the extended parallel process model. *Social and Personality Psychology Compass, 5*(4), 206–219.

McComas, K. A. (2006). Defining moments in risk communication research: 1996–2005. *Journal of Health Communication, 11*(1), 75–91.

Mileti, D. S., & Fitzpatrick, C. (1992). The causal sequence of risk communication in the Parkfield earthquake prediction experiment. *Risk Analysis, 12*(3), 393–400.

Mileti, D. S., & Peek, L. (2000). The social psychology of public response to warnings of a nuclear power plant accident. *Journal of Hazardous Materials, 75*(2–3), 181–194.

Mileti, D. S., & Sorensen, J. H. (1990). Communication of emergency public warnings. *Landslides, 1*(6), 52–70.

Mitroff, I. I. (1988). Crisis management: Cutting through the confusion. *MIT Sloan Management Review, 29*(2), 15.

Mitroff, I. I., Shrivastava, P., & Udwadia, F. E. (1987). Effective crisis management. *Academy of Management Perspectives, 1*(4), 283–292.

Mizutori, M. (2020). Reflections on the Sendai Framework for disaster risk reduction: Five years since its adoption. *International Journal of Disaster Risk Science, 11*(2), 147–151.

Morgan, K., & Fischhoff, B. A. R. U. C. H. (2023). Mental models for scientists communicating with the public. *Issues in Science and Technology, 39*, 58–61.

National Research Council (1989). Recommendations for improving risk communication. In *Improving Risk Communication.* National Academies Press (US).

Palenchar, M. J., & Heath, R. L. (2007). Strategic risk communication: Adding value to society. *Public Relations Review, 33*(2), 120–129.

Palenchar, M. J. (2020). Historical trends of risk and crisis communication. In *Handbook of Risk and Crisis Communication* (pp. 31–52). Routledge.

Pearson, C. M., & Mitroff, I. I. (2019). From crisis prone to crisis prepared: A framework for crisis management. In *Risk Management* (pp. 185–196). Routledge.

Pew (November 9, 2021). https://www.pewresearch.org/short-reads/2021/11/19/growing-share-of-childless-adults-in-u-s-dont-expect-to-ever-have-children

Powell, D. A., & Leiss, W. (1997). *Mad Cows and Mother's Milk: The Perils of Poor Risk Communication.* McGill-Queen's Press-MQUP.

Plough, A., & Krimsky, S. (1987). The emergence of risk communication studies and social and political context. *Science, Technology and Human Values, 12*(3/4), 4–10.

Plough, A., & Krimsky, S. (2013). The emergence of risk communication studies: Social and political context. In *Readings in Risk* (pp. 223–231). RFF Press.

Rayner, J. (1957). Studies of disasters and other extreme situations– An annotated selected bibliography. *Human Organization, 16*(2), 30–40.Special Issue: Human Adaptation to Disaster

Reynolds, B., & Seeger, M. W. (2005). Crisis and emergency risk communication as an integrative model. *Journal of Health Communication, 10*(1), 43–55.

Smart, C., & Vertinsky, I. (1977). Designs for crisis decision units. *Administrative Science Quarterly, 22*, 640–657.

Smith, R. J. F. (1986). Evolution of alarm signals: Role of benefits of retaining group members or territorial neighbors. *The American Naturalist, 128*(4), 604–610.

Seeger, H. S. (2022). A meta-theoretical orientation to crisis communication. In T. Coombs, & S. Holliday, Eds., *The Handbook of Crisis Communication* (pp. 67–79). Wiley-Blackwell.

Seeger, M. W. (1986). The challenger tragedy and search for legitimacy. *Central States Speech Journal, 37*(3), 147–157.

Seeger, M. W., Nowling, W., & Seeger, H. S. (2024). Keystone theories of postcrisis discourse: Communication theory of resilience and discourse of renewal. *Journal of Contingencies & Crisis Management, 32*(1), e12533.

Seeger, M. W., Sellnow, T. L., & Ulmer, R. R. (1998). Communication, organization, and crisis. *Annals of the International Communication Association, 21*(1), 231–276.

Seeger, M. W., Reynolds, B., & Sellnow, T. L. (2020). Crisis and emergency risk communication in health contexts: Applying the CDC model to pandemic influenza. In *Handbook of risk and crisis communication* (pp. 493–506). Routledge.

Sellnow, T. L., & Seeger, M. W. (2021). *Theorizing Crisis Communication*. John Wiley & Sons.

Seeger, M., & Ulmer, R. (2002). A post-crisis discourse of renewal: The cases of Malden Mills and Cole Hardwoods. *Journal of Applied Communication Research, 30*(2), 126–142.

Shrivastava, P. (1987). *Bhopal: Anatomy of a Crisis* (p. 1853961922). Sage.

Teichert, W. (1987). Tschernobyl in den Medien: Ergebnisse und Hypothesen zur Tschernobyl-Berichterstattung [Chernobyl in the media: Results and hypotheses on the Chernobyl coverage]. *Rundfunk und Fernsehen, 35*(2), 185–204.

Telegraphia (2023). *History of early warning and emergency notification systems*. https://www.electronic-sirens.com/history-early-warning-emergency-notification-systems/

Turner, B. A. (1976). The organizational and interorganizational development of disasters. *Administrative Science Quarterly, 21*, 378–397.

Tyson, A., Funk, C., & Kennedy, B. (2023). *What the Data Says About Americans' Views of Climate Change*. Pew Research Center. https://www.pewresearch.org/short-reads/2023/08/09/what-the-data-says-about-americans-views-of-climate-change/

Ulmer, R. R., Seeger, M. W., & Sellnow, T. L. (2007). Post-crisis communication and renewal: Expanding the parameters of post-crisis discourse. *Public Relations Review, 33*(2), 130–134.

Utz, S., Schultz, F., & Glocka, S. (2013). Crisis communication online: How medium, crisis type and emotions affected public reactions in the Fukushima Daiichi nuclear disaster. *Public Relations Review, 39*(1), 40–46.

Verheggen, F. J., Haubruge, E., & Mescher, M. C. (2010). Alarm pheromones – Chemical signaling in response to danger. *Vitamins and Hormones, 83*, 215–239.

Villagrán de León, J. C., Pruessner, I., & Breedlove, H. (2013). *Alert and warning frameworks in the context of early warning systems*. http://collections.unu.edu/eserv/UNU:1866/pdf11123.pdf

Ware, B. L., & Linkugel, W. A. (1973). They spoke in defense of themselves: On the generic criticism of apologia. *The Quarterly Journal of Speech, 59*(3), 273–283.

Weick, K. E. (1988). Enacted sensemaking in crisis situations [1]. *Journal of Management Studies, 25*(4), 305–317.

Weick, K. E. (1995). *Sensemaking in Organizations* (Vol. 3, pp. 1–231). Thousand Oaks, CA: Sage Publications.

Weick, K. E. (2010). Reflections on enacted sensemaking in the Bhopal disaster. *Journal of Management Studies, 47*(3), 537–550.

Westerman, D., Spence, P. R., & Van Der Heide, B. (2014). Social media as information source: Recency of updates and credibility of information. *Journal of Computer-Mediated Communication, 19*(2), 171–183.

Williams, D. E., & Treadaway, G. (1992). Exxon and the Valdez accident: A failure in crisis communication. *Communication Studies, 43*(1), 56–64.

Witte, K. (1992). Putting the fear back into fear appeals: The extended parallel process model. *Communications Monographs, 59*(4), 329–349.

Witte, K. (1994). Fear control and danger control: A test of the extended parallel process model (EPPM). *Communications Monographs*, *61*(2), 113–134.
Witte, K. (2019). The role of threat and efficacy in AIDS prevention. In Progress in Preventing AIDS? (pp. 87–112). Routledge.
World Health Organization (2024). *Risk communication and community engagement*. https://www.who.int/emergencies/risk-communications#:~:text=The%20purpose%20of%20risk%20communication,in%20emergency%20preparedness%20and%20response

Author's Bio

Matthew W. Seeger (PhD, 1982, Indiana University) is a Distinguished University Professor and Co-Director of the Center for Emerging and Infectious Diseases at Wayne State University. Seeger's research concerns crisis and risk communication, health promotion, crisis and ethics, failure of complex systems, and post-crisis renewal.

His work has appeared in more than 200 peer-reviewed articles and book chapters including the *Handbook of Crisis and Risk Communication*, *International Encyclopedia of Communication*, *Journal of Health Communication Research*, *Health Promotion Practice*, *Communication Monographs*, *International Journal of Crisis and Contingency Management*, *Communication Yearbook*, *Handbook of Public Relations*, *Handbook of Applied Communication Research*, *Communication Monographs*, *Public Relations Review*, *Communication Studies*, *Southern Communication Journal*, *Journal of Business Ethics*, *Journal of Business Communication*, *Management Communication Quarterly*, *Journal of Applied Communication Research*, and *Journal of Organizational Change Management*, among several others.

Seeger is the author or co-author of eight books on crisis and risk communication, including *Communication and Organizational Crisis* (2003), *Crisis Communication and the Public Health* (2008), *Effective Crisis Communication* (2007), *Effective Risk Communication* (2009), *Theorizing Crisis Communication* (2014), *Crisis and Emergency Risk Communication* (Second Edition, 2015), *Narratives of Crisis: Stories of Ruin and Renewal* (2016), and the *International Handbook of Crisis Communication* (2016). He is currently completing *Best Practices in Crisis and Emergency Risk Communication*. He is the founding co-editor of *Crisis and Risk Communication*. He has advised over 40 doctoral dissertations.

3

Beyond Borders and Bridging Worlds

Unveiling Cultural Dynamics in International Risk and Crisis Communication

Sora Kim

School of Journalism and Communication, Corporate Communication Program MSSc, The Chinese University of Hong Kong, Shatin, New Territories, Hong Kong

Why Culture Matters in Risk and Crisis Communication?

Crises and risks today transcend national and cultural boundaries both physically and symbolically, in terms of their causes, consequences, and public discourse (Schwarz et al., 2016). Take such ongoing global challenges as climate change and pandemics. These are transboundary threats that impact and instigate crises in diverse cultural societies worldwide. Moreover, the advancement of technology has shrunk the world, creating an interconnected global community. The Internet accelerates public discourse regarding crises and risks, rendering local threats visible to people worldwide and heightening the potential of such threats to evolve into global ones.

It is crucial to consider the relevance, significance, and role of culture in the dynamics of crisis and risk communication. The notion of crisis is a deeply culture-sensitive social construct. Indeed, crises often emerge when someone or some organization violates established social norms, values, beliefs, and expectations (Schwarz et al., 2016). Culture plays a pivotal role in shaping both individual and collective worldviews, norms, expectations, and behaviors, thereby serving as a fundamental reference point for identifying and understanding what constitutes a crisis within a society (Alegria et al., 2010; Schwartz, 2006; Suh et al., 1998). Moreover, from an institutional standpoint, culture shapes the preparedness and response strategies of involved entities such as governments, corporations, and non-profit organizations, influencing their approaches to global risks and crises (Beekun et al., 2003; Dhanesh & Sriramesh, 2018; Haruta & Hallahan, 2003; Kim & Lee, 2021). Similarly, culture molds individuals' perceptions, attitudes, and behaviors toward crises, risks, response strategies, and policies (Huang et al., 2016; Ji & Kim, 2019; Kim et al., 2021; Renn & Rohrmann, 2000; Xu, 2018). Consequently, communication scholars have increasingly recognized the international and intercultural dimensions of crises and risks, emphasizing the pivotal role and significance of culture in both global and local threats (Claeys & Schwarz, 2016; Haruta & Hallahan, 2003; Schwarz et al., 2016).

The Handbook of International Crisis and Risk Communication Research, Second Edition.
Edited by Andreas Schwarz, Matthew W. Seeger, and Sora Kim.

Culture: Definition and Its Levels

To grasp the pivotal role of culture in international crisis and risk communication, one must clearly define it within this context. Culture encompasses a wide array of meanings across various disciplines, encompassing national beliefs, values, shared assumptions, and daily life patterns (Schein, 1991). Essentially, culture embodies collectively shared values, norms, and customs that distinguish one group of people from another (Hofstede, 1980; Schein, 1991).

Culture operates on multiple layers, many scholars assert, due to its inherent differentiation among diverse groups. Erez and Gati (2004) proposed a hierarchical structure consisting of four layers of culture, with global culture occupying the highest tier, followed by national, organizational, and group cultures. Similarly, Wilhelms et al. (2009) proposed a five-level classification of culture – micro, meso, macro, meta, and global cultures. Each level represents the scale of the environment in which cultural dynamics operate. Microculture emerges within small groups and, in this chapter, pertains to organizational culture. Mesoculture denotes shared values, norms, and behavioral patterns among mid-sized groups, positioned between micro and macro cultural layers. Examples of mesoculture include professional and industry cultures, typically larger than microcultures (e.g., organizational culture) but smaller than macrocultures (national culture).

Macroculture refers to collectively shared values within a specific geographic region, with the national framework serving as its upper limit, such as national culture. Meta culture comprises more than two national cultures or multinational geographical regions (e.g., EU, Global South, Middle East, etc.). Global culture represents the broadest layer, comprising shared values on a worldwide scale. Given that investigations at the global culture level are not directly relevant to understanding cultural dynamics in crisis and risk communication, I focus my discussion on the role of culture within the meta, macro, meso, and micro levels, with a primary emphasis on macroculture, namely national culture.

Cultural Investigation Matrix in International Crisis and Risk Communication

Cultural investigations can take two primary approaches – cultural comparisons across different levels of cultures and individual investigations focusing on specific cultural contexts. The former involves examining cultural differences at various levels, including meta, national, industrial, and organizational levels. On the other hand, individual investigations delve into the cultural dynamics of a single nation, industry, or organization, particularly in the context of crisis and risk communication and corresponding public responses. Individual cultural investigations, especially those concerning under-researched nations in regions like Africa and Latin America, advance our knowledge of local culture. In contrast, cultural comparisons across multiple levels shed light on the role of different cultures. Hence, this chapter places greater emphasis on cultural comparisons rather than individual investigations of single cultures.

For easier reference and comparison, I propose classifying cultural investigations according to three factors: (1) Level of culture, (2) Scope of crisis/risk, and (3) Focus of crisis/risk analysis. First, concerning levels of culture, I use the scale of the environment to propose the following four levels: (1) meta (e.g., Eastern vs. Western), (2) macro (nation), (3) meso (industry), and (4) micro (organization) level cultures. Individual-level cultures are excluded here because culture denotes shared values, norms, and behavioral patterns held by a group of people not by an individual. Thus, individuals, as cultural self-presentations, are considered the foundations of all these varying layers of culture (Erez & Gati, 2004; Wilhelms et al., 2009).

Second, the scope of crisis/risk pertains to the geographical, jurisdictional, or organizational level in which the crisis/risk unfolds and its potential impact. The scope encompasses three levels – (1) global, (2) national, and (3) organizational. Global-level crises/risks refer to events that impact global systems and countries around the world and can entail various social, political, economic, and other issues. Examples include the COVID-19 pandemic, climate change, and refugee issues. National crisis/risk refers to situations wherein a nation faces threats that affect its national systems and numerous organizations within the country. Examples encompass a nation's economic crises or natural disasters such as floods or earthquakes. Organizational-level crisis/risk involves crises or risks specific to a particular organization or entity, influencing its operations, performance, reputation, or stakeholders. Examples include product recalls or organizational misconduct.

Third, given that culture influences both (a) institutional and (b) individual responses to crises and risks, it is essential, in a cultural investigation, to explore both institution-centric and public-centric perspectives. Institution-centric perspectives encompass government- and organization-level perceptions and responses to crises and risks, reflecting institutional responses. Public-centric perspectives, conversely, are represented by examining individual-level perceptions and responses.

In the current landscape of international crisis and risk communication research, the majority of culture-focused studies concentrate on the macroculture level, national culture in particular. While some studies delve into metacultural investigations, such as comparisons between EU and non-EU cultures or Eastern and Western cultures, they remain relatively limited in scope (Schwarz et al., 2024; Zhou & Shin, 2017). Metacultural comparisons often rely on macro (national) cultural level analyses by selecting representative countries from meta-level regions (e.g., Eastern vs. Western) and speculating on metacultural differences (e.g., Zhou & Shin, 2017).

Furthermore, the literature has devoted even less attention to the role of organizational (micro) culture or industry (meso) culture than to macroculture and metaculture. Thus, while calling for more research to focus on the impact of micro- (organizational) or meso- (industry) level cultures, this chapter mainly discusses macro (national) level culture, with some exploration of metaculture.

The Status of Research on Culture in Crisis and Risk Communication

In the last two decades, more scholars have taken a non-Western perspective and explored cultural differences in crisis and risk communication from various aspects (Barkley, 2020; Cornia et al., 2016; Diers-Lawson, 2017; George & Kwansah-Aidoo, 2017; Manzie, 2018). Specifically, the cultural contexts of risk and crisis communication research have become more diversified with increasing numbers of studies focusing on Europe and Asian countries (Barkley, 2020; Cornia et al., 2016; Zhu et al., 2017). Despite this increased diversity, crisis communication research remains America-focused or Western-focused, not yet fully representing the global reality of crisis communication (Diers-Lawson, 2017). While there has been an increase in studies exploring Asian countries, these efforts predominantly focus on East Asian nations such as China and South Korea. Remaining notably scarce is research in regions such as Africa, Latin America, and other Asian countries outside of East Asia, significantly limiting our comprehension of crisis and risk communication in these areas.

Another observation concerns the differing focuses between crisis communication and risk communication. Early research in crisis communication primarily concentrated on institutional perspectives, analyzing how institutions managed crises through case studies or content analysis approaches (Benoit, 1997; Wertz & Kim, 2010). In recent years, however, a more balanced approach has emerged in crisis communication research, with greater attention paid to public perspectives. This includes investigating public perceptions, attitudes, and behaviors toward crises (Cornia et al., 2016; Shim et al., 2021).

In risk communication, on the other hand, trends have consistently leaned towards a more public-centric approach. A good deal of research has focused on understanding public perceptions of risks and their behavioral responses. This distinction between the two disciplines may be linked to their varying natures. Crises are tangible and visible threat events that have already occurred; risks represent perceived threats yet to occur. For crises, then, organizations often employ easily observable management and response strategies. For risk communication, their approaches are less obvious. This discrepancy likely contributes to a greater emphasis on institutional management approaches in crisis communication research compared to risk communication research. In a similar vein, the proliferation of crisis-response strategy taxonomies, such as image restoration (Benoit, 1997) and situational crisis communication theory (SCCT, Coombs, 2007), may have bolstered the prevalence of institutional perspectives in crisis communication research relative to risk communication research.

In the subsequent section, I examine cultural insights derived from previous research in crisis and risk communication, with a focus on two primary perspectives: institution-centric and public-centric perspectives.

Role of Culture from Institutional Perspectives

The bulk of current international crisis communication research has focused on exploring national-level (macro) cultural disparities, particularly in how governments or organizations respond to global, national, and organizational-level crises and risks. First, at the global level, such as in the case of crises like COVID-19 and climate change, there has been a significant emphasis on investigating how cultural differences influence the crisis communication strategies and management of local authorities. For instance, amidst the recent COVID-19 pandemic, prior studies have aimed to elucidate how cultural variations impact crisis management and communication with the public (Ansah, 2022; Petridou & Zahariadis, 2021; Ruiu, 2020; Zeemering, 2021). Many studies have scrutinized macro-cultural differences in how different governments contended with the pandemic (Lee et al., 2020; Petridou & Zahariadis, 2021), and how various institutions such as the media reported on it (Ng & Tan, 2021). These cross-cultural disparities have been observed to influence sense-making, decision-making, sense-giving, and meaning-making throughout the different stages of crisis management (Bajaj et al., 2021).

Expanding beyond the context of COVID-19, refugee issues have also garnered attention. Many studies related to refugee issues tend to concentrate on variations in media coverage, exploring how macro-cultural differences influence the portrayal of the refugee issue in different countries' media (De Cock et al., 2018; Jiang et al., 2021). For example, Jiang et al. (2021) observed cultural disparities in media coverage of the refugee issue, noting that Belgian and Swedish newspapers placed more emphasis on welcoming refugees than their Chinese counterparts. Conversely, Chinese newspapers tended to discuss the Islamic religion more in their refugee reports than Belgian and Swedish newspapers did. These differences were attributed to varying political interests and relationships that each country holds concerning the refugee issue.

Second, compared to culture-related studies focusing on global-level crises and risks, little research exists at the level of national crises and risks. This discrepancy arises from the challenge of directly comparing cultures in response to national-level crises, which often occur at different times in each country. As a result, much of the existing culture research in this category has opted to study similar types of national-level crises or risks, such as natural disasters (e.g., floods or earthquakes), examining how different countries respond to or implement policies in the face of similar types of national-level crises or risks (Marincioni, 2001; Paul et al., 2016).

Third, concerning organizational-level crises and risks, the majority of previous research has delved into cultural influences regarding how organizations adopt varying crisis response strategies for specific crisis types (e.g., product recalls, airline crashes; Haruta & Hallahan, 2003), or the cultural differences in media coverage of similar crisis types (e.g., food crises; Wertz & Kim, 2010). In a classic and seminal cultural investigation, Haruta and Hallahan (2003) analyzed how Delta Airlines and Japan Airlines dealt with airplane crash crises differently, applying Hofstede's (1980) cultural dimensions. They found that power distance differences between the two countries (low in the US, high in Japan) explained disparities in CEO involvement in corporate responses (i.e., no CEO involvement in the US vs. a strong presence of the CEO in Japan). Additionally, uncertainty avoidance differences (low in the US vs. high in Japan) were used to elucidate why Japan Airlines issued an immediate apology to its public, whereas Delta did not.

For cultural comparisons of institutional responses at the organizational crisis level, researchers may opt to investigate specific crises involving multinational corporations instead of examining similar types of organizational crises. As an illustration of macro-cultural comparison studies, Taylor (2000) scrutinized a crisis faced by a multinational company, namely Coca-Cola, by employing Hofstede's (1980) cultural dimensions. She explored how governments in various European countries handled this crisis differently. Taylor argued that the immediate ban on Coke products implemented in Western European countries such as Belgium, Spain, and France could be attributed to a relatively higher tendency toward uncertainty avoidance in those nations. In contrast, in Northwestern European countries such as Denmark, Norway, and Sweden, where uncertainty avoidance tendencies are lower, no ban on Coke products was implemented.

Another significant line of research in this category explores how, during crises, multinational companies navigate cultural differences between their organizational culture and the host country's culture (Dhanesh & Sriramesh, 2018; Lehmberg & Hicks, 2018; Manzie, 2018; Zhu et al., 2017). This research stream delves into the influences of both micro-level culture (i.e., organizational culture) and macro-level culture (national), often focusing on individual investigations of organizational-level crises involving multinational companies in a single country, rather than macro-cultural comparisons.

Many of these studies have highlighted a lack of emphasis on local national culture when multinational companies attempt to manage local crises, advocating for a "glocalization" approach (i.e., considering both local and global factors) to international crisis and risk communication (Lehmberg & Hicks, 2018). For instance, Dhanesh and Sriramesh (2018) pointed out that Nestlé India's crisis management strategies during the Maggi Noodles crisis in 2015 were primarily guided by its corporate culture rather than India's local culture. They argued that the crisis was exacerbated by the corporate failure to adapt to local cultural nuances, such as the inability to quickly respond to shifting local needs.

Similarly, Manzie (2018) observed during the 2014 Royal Dutch Shell oil crisis in Nigeria that the adoption of renewal strategies by the multinational company did not align well with Nigerian cultural norms, although these strategies were generally effective for managing preventable crises elsewhere. Manzie suggested that accommodating public demands within Nigerian culture was crucial and recommended a significant reorientation of renewal strategies to align with local historical and cultural norms in Nigeria.

Furthermore, cultural disparities in the utilization and adoption of crisis response strategies are extensively documented. American companies, for instance, are often reluctant to issue apologies due to potential legal repercussions (Myers, 2016). Conversely, in Asian countries such as China, Japan, and Korea, the adoption of apology strategies typically occurs without significant concern for corresponding legal ramifications (Barkley, 2020; Ha, 2016; Zhu et al., 2017). Korean companies tend to frequently resort to apologies, considering it a one-size-fits-all strategy irrespective of the type of crisis, largely influenced by the prevailing anti-*chaebol* sentiment in Korea (Ha, 2016). Additionally, cultural variances are discerned even among closely related Chinese societies, such as China and Taiwan. In instances like the melamine-tainted milk powder crisis, mainland Chinese companies often opted initially to go with defensive strategies, but eventually transitioned to more accommodative approaches. In contrast, Taiwanese companies tended to exhibit a reverse pattern (Lyu, 2012).

Role of Culture from Public-centric Perspectives

In crisis and risk communication research, there has in recent years been a growing emphasis on public-centric perspectives. In particular, researchers have tended to focus on individuals' cognitive, affective, and behavioral responses. At the global level of crises and risks, considerable attention has been directed towards individuals' psychological perspectives, exploring how national culture influences their perceptions of such crises as COVID-19 (Dryhurst et al., 2020; Zeng et al., 2022; Zhang, 2021). In addition, some researchers have delved into how national culture shapes individuals' inclination to seek information and adopt preventive measures (Kim et al., 2022; Wang et al., 2022).

Using ten countries across Europe, Asia, and America, Dryhurst et al. (2020) studied variations in publics' risk perceptions of COVID-19. The researchers identified cultural differences in individualistic worldviews and recorded the extent of social amplification through interpersonal networks. Such amplification, in turn, gave rise to diverse risk perceptions and various levels of adopting preventive measures. Similarly, Zhang (2021) observed that fear appeals employed during the COVID-19 pandemic were culturally sensitive; Chinese individuals generally exhibited higher perceived severity, susceptibility, and self-efficacy towards fear appeals than their American counterparts.

Studies beyond the scope of COVID-19 have delved into global-level risks such as climate change and environmental issues, offering insights from public-centric perspectives (Cordano et al., 2010; Onwezen et al., 2014; Schultz, 2002). Culture significantly influences individuals' opinions, risk perceptions, attitudes, and behaviors concerning climate change and environmental matters, for indeed these issues are culturally and socially constructed (Renn & Rohrmann, 2000). Cordano et al. (2010) discovered, for example, distinct differences between Chilean business students and their American counterparts in their understanding of environmental issues, sense of obligation to protect the environment, and inclination towards pro-environmental behaviors. These variations can be attributed to differing levels of peer and societal pressures stemming from in-group and out-group dynamics within the two countries.

In examining national-level crises and risks from public-centric perspectives, previous studies have scrutinized macro-cultural disparities in people's perceptions of risk or attribution of responsibility during nation-wide natural disasters (Cornia et al., 2016; Kalayjian et al., 2002). By analyzing, for instance, how individuals across seven European countries perceived disasters, Cornia et al. (2016) delineated three distinct risk cultures – individual-oriented, state-oriented, and fatalistic.

Individual-oriented risk culture pertains to societies, exemplified by the Netherlands, in which individuals are perceived as primarily responsible for managing disasters. State-oriented risk culture pertains to societies, exemplified by Sweden, Austria, and Germany, in which the government is perceived as primarily responsible for intervening to mitigate disasters. Fatalistic risk culture pertains to societies, exemplified by Italy and Hungary, in which the populace feels powerless and vulnerable in the face of disasters. Italy and Hungary in fact also possess elements of state-oriented risk culture. In the context of epidemics such as Ebola and Cholera, Thompson (2020) underscored the profound impact of societal experiences on risk perceptions in Ghana, shaped by the nation's historical, religious, and sociocultural processing of related risk signals. These varying societal experiences elucidate the divergence in risk judgments concerning these diseases in Ghana compared to other nations.

Finally, in examining the public-centric perspective toward organization-level crises and risks, previous research has delved into cultural variations in individuals' cognitive, affective, and behavioral responses to such crises. Shim et al. (2021) explored how individuals' moral foundations – specifically individualizing and binding morals – shaped their perceptions and reactions to corporate crises across different cultures, including Singapore, South Korea, and the US. The authors' findings revealed that across national cultures the extent of public anger and intentions to boycott organizations caught in crisis varied significantly. These differences were attributed to divergent emphases on distinct aspects of morality. Singaporeans and South Koreans were less forgiving towards companies causing harm to the local community or group, reflecting a stronger emphasis on binding moral principles. In contrast, Americans were more inclined to penalize companies for infringing upon the rights of individual consumers or employees, indicating a greater emphasis on individualizing moral values.

Researchers have extensively documented cultural variations in public perceptions of and reactions to crisis response strategies (Barkley, 2020; Huang & Bedford, 2009). One example of such variation is the interpretation and acceptance of an apology. In collectivistic cultures, such as those found in Asian countries, an apology does not necessarily imply an admission of fault or mistake. Individuals in these cultures perceive an apology as an acknowledgment by the organization in crisis of the difficulties or burdens experienced by the victims or those affected, and a demonstration of concern for their well-being (Barkley, 2020; Zhu et al., 2017).

Furthermore, cultural differences also influence the public's response to and acceptance of defensive crisis strategies. Individuals in the Middle East tend to be more receptive to defensive crisis response strategies than their Western counterparts, possibly due to the shame-avoidance tendency prevalent in Arab culture (Gribas et al., 2021).

Some scholars have emphasized the importance of considering local cultural concepts when tailoring crisis and risk communication strategies so that such strategies better resonate with locals. To underscore the significance of face-saving, face-giving, and social relationships among Chinese populations, for instance, Huang and Bedford (2009) introduced and elucidated the Chinese notions of *guanxi* ("relationship") and *mianzi* ("face"). Similarly, to shed light on how Koreans perceive social risks, including environmental and economic, Yang (2015) explicated the Korean notions of *jeong* (deep attachment), *uri* ("our" or "we"), and *chemyon* ("face"). In terms of public behavioral reactions to organizational crises, previous studies have highlighted distinct tendencies across national cultures. Kim et al. (2021) observed that, during online firestorms, Chinese users tend to attribute blame to social institutions or external factors and engage in collective actions against organizations. American users are more inclined to target individuals or representatives of the organizations. These differences in attributional tendencies are consistent with findings from cultural psychology research, indicating that Westerners typically lean towards internal and dispositional attributions, while Easterners tend to make situational attributions, emphasizing external, environmental, and situational factors (Choi et al., 1999).

Theoretical and Methodological Framework of Culture Research in Risk and Crisis Communication

To discern trends in theoretical and methodological frameworks within culture-focused research in risk and crisis communication, a quick quantitative content analysis was conducted on 130 articles published between 1991 and 2023. These articles were obtained from keyword searches of "culture," "crisis," and "risk communication" in academic journal databases such as Business Source Premier and Communication Source. Up until 2000, there was minimal growth in culture-focused research in crisis and risk communication. Since 2010, however, the growth has been exponential, with more than two-thirds of the articles published between 2010 and 2023. Regarding the adoption trends in theoretical frameworks in crisis and risk communication, the analysis reveals a lack of theory-driven research. Only one-third of culture-focused research has employed specific theories to explain cultural aspects of crisis and risk communication. Among these specific theory-adopted studies, three dominant theoretical frameworks emerge – (1) crisis and risk management theories, such as image restoration (Benoit, 1997), SCCT (Coombs, 2007), and attribution theory; (2) Hofstede's (1980) cultural dimension theory; and (3) rhetoric- or message-focused theories, such as rhetoric area theory and framing theory.

In the past decade, there has been a notable uptick in the adoption of crisis and risk management theories. Significant attention has been given to prominent theories within this category, including image restoration, SCCT, and attribution theory (Barkley, 2020; Lyu, 2012; Wertz & Kim, 2010; Zhou & Shin, 2017). Studies employing these theories primarily explore the efficacy of theory-proposed response strategies across diverse cultural contexts. The second group of studies adopts a comparative and cross-cultural perspective, often leveraging Hofstede's (1980) cultural dimensions theory to examine cultural disparities in both crisis and risk communication (Haruta & Hallahan, 2003; Taylor, 2000; Xu, 2018; Yang, 2015). For example, researchers may designate certain nations as representatives of distinct cultural dimensions and conduct comparative analyses of risk and communication strategies across them (Barkley, 2020; Zhu et al., 2017). Other scholars seek to explore how specific cultural dimensions may shape individuals' perceptions and behaviors in risk and crisis communication, both within and beyond national boundaries (Xu, 2018; Yang, 2015). Xu (2018), for instance, proposed that, compared to individualists, collectivists may experience heightened emotions and risk perceptions due to stronger influences from collectivistic groups.

The third theoretical framework category adopts a rhetoric- and message-focused perspective, employing theories such as rhetorical arena theory, and framing theory in order to elucidate the interplay between culturally rooted messages and crisis/risk communication dynamics (Manzie, 2018; Rodin et al., 2018). While it is acknowledged that a single theory can provide only partial insights into the intricate phenomenon of cultural variations in crisis and risk communication, the current analysis underscores the importance of prioritizing theory-driven research in culture-focused studies. To delve deeper into cultural variations within this field, a significant need exists for the adoption of more specific theories.

Regarding the adoption trends of methodological frameworks, the most prevalent methodology is the case study approach, making up approximately one out of five studies. The majority of studies (42%) have embraced qualitative research methods, including the case study method, historical or conceptual analysis. Slightly less commonly seen are quantitative research methods such as surveys and experiments. They make up approximately one-third of the research. Since 2018, there has been a gradual increase in studies utilizing experiments or computational methods, though these remain relatively limited. The analysis strongly suggests a pressing need for a broader adoption of quantitative research methods.

Challenges and Future Directions in Cultural Investigations

A review of the existing culture-focused research in crisis and risk communication reveals several challenges. First, the predominant emphasis is on macro-level cultural investigations. This fact implies a neglect of meso-level (e.g., industry) or micro-level (e.g., organization) cultural inquiries across various scopes of crises and risks, spanning global, national, and organizational levels. This dearth of attention towards micro or meso-level cultural investigations can be partly ascribed to researcher' limited access to specific organizations or industries for data collection, stemming from privacy and confidentiality concerns. However, this obstacle can be surmounted by adopting cross-sectional approaches in data collection. In such approaches, the study's focus need not be a specific organization's cultural aspects. Instead, researchers can solicit insights from diverse employees by adopting a cross-sectional approach regarding their respective organizations' cultural dynamics and crisis/risk communication practices. This involves specifying a study's sample as employees from various organizations and industries. Thus, to meet the need to expand the current scope to micro- and meso-level cultural investigations, I call for future research to target specific groups of individuals, such as employees, rather than targeting the general public.

Second, the central inquiry within culture-focused research in risk and crisis communication revolves around establishing comprehensive theoretical frameworks to guide practices and facilitate theory development (Schwarz et al., 2016). Our analysis of theoretical frameworks affirms the continued absence of theory-driven research in the current literature, emphasizing the ongoing relevance and necessity of this central inquiry. One finding is particularly concerning, that only one-third of culture-focused research integrates a specific theory. The field urgently needs more theory-driven research.

This observation is also tied to another critical issue – the dearth of empirical testing regarding the reasons behind cultural differences in culture-focused research. Many studies aim solely to showcase the existence of cultural variations without delving into their underlying causes or predictive factors. Rather than rigorously testing cultural elements, they often rely on post hoc explanations for these differences. For instance, when applying a widely adopted culture-focused theory – Hofstede's (1980) cultural dimensions theory – to analyze cultural variations in crisis communication, dimensions like individualism versus collectivism or high versus low uncertainty avoidance are rarely measured at the individual level to ascertain if individuals' diverse inclinations on these dimensions predict cultural differences in attributional or behavioral responses during crises across different nations. Instead, how culture differs on a large scale in these cultural dimensions is often provided as a potential explanation. Hofstede's theory is a macro-level theory; it examines broad cultural patterns and tendencies across entire nations rather than individual or small-group dynamics. Nevertheless, researchers should not automatically assume that there are national differences in these dimensions, as the theory proposes. Macro-level (national) cultural differences stem from the collective aggregation of individual differences. Thus, without measuring individual patterns and tendencies, we cannot presume the existence of broad cultural patterns and tendencies across entire nations. This is especially true in our rapidly changing world, where elucidating cultural disparities in crisis or risk-related perceptions or behaviors is increasingly complex. Therefore, I advocate for increased research efforts to incorporate specific theories in examining cultural aspects. When employing such theories, researchers should rigorously test cultural elements that can help explain the underlying reasons or antecedents of cultural differences.

Third, given the nuances and diversity of cultures, it is imperative to elevate more local, culture-based concepts and non-Western theories in the realm of crisis and risk communication. While Western-based theories continue to dominate current culture-focused research in crisis and risk communication, previous studies have underscored the limitations and cultural insensitivity inherent in these frameworks when applied to diverse cultural norms and values (Barkley, 2020; Guerber et al., 2020). Our comprehension of local cultures in crisis and risk communication has been enriched by non-Western concepts such as *guanxi* (relationships in Chinese; Huang & Bedford, 2009), *jeong* (deep attachment in Korean; Yang, 2015), and the shame avoidance tendency in Arab culture (Gribas et al., 2021). However, our understanding of the role of culture in crisis and risk communication remains largely confined to a handful of countries, including the US, European nations, and East Asian countries. Countries in Africa, the Middle East, Latin America, and Southeast Asia remain largely unexplored. This research gap partly arises from a scarcity of international scholars with expertise in these regions. Additionally, scholars with such expertise often face challenges in disseminating their findings to a global audience due to language barriers. To address this challenge, greater international collaboration among scholars from diverse cultural backgrounds is strongly encouraged.

Lastly, there is a critical imperative for a wider embrace of quantitative research methods in culture-focused research, expanding the heavy reliance on case study approaches. While it is understandable that many studies in risk and crisis communication, still in its nascent stage, have favored case study or conceptual analysis approaches to delineate various cultural practices, there exists a need for methodological diversification. To elucidate the underlying mechanisms of cultural differences and enhance research generalizability, future studies should broaden their methodological spectrum to incorporate more quantitative approaches, such as experiments, surveys, and computational research methods. For instance, research adopting experimental designs can help us rule out the potential impact of confounding factors and clarify any causal relationships between cultural elements and crisis or risk communication. Similarly, research employing computation methodologies has the potential to enrich our understanding of culture by providing a more nuanced and non-intrusive portrayal of how diverse cultures navigate and respond to risks and crises.

References

Alegria, M., Atkins, M., Farmer, E., Slaton, E., & Stelk, W. (2010). One size does not fit all: Taking diversity, culture and context seriously. *Administration and Policy in Mental Health and Mental Health Services Research*, *37*, 48–60. https://doi.org/10.1007/s10488-010-0283-2

Ansah, P. (2022). COVID-19 dialogue on Facebook: Crisis Communication relationship between Ghanaian Authorities and Citizens. *Journal of International Crisis and Risk Communication Research*, *5*(1), 57–86. https://doi.org/10.30658/jicrcr.5.1.3

Bajaj, G., Khandelwal, S., & Budhwar, P. (2021). COVID-19 pandemic and the impact of cross-cultural differences on crisis management: A conceptual model of transcultural crisis management. *International Journal of Cross Cultural Management*, *21*(3), 569–601. https://doi.org/10.1177/14705958211060189

Barkley, K. (2020). Does one size fit all? The applicability of situational crisis communication theory in the Japanese context. *Public Relations Review*, *46*(3), 101911. https://doi.org/10.1016/j.pubrev.2020.101911

Beekun, R. I., Stedham, Y., & Yamamura, J. H. (2003). Business ethics in Brazil and the U.S.: A comparative investigation. *Journal of Business Ethics*, *42*(3), 267–279. https://doi.org/10.1023/A:1022200702149

Benoit, W. L. (1997). Image repair discourse and crisis communication. *Public Relations Review*, *23*(2), 177–186. https://doi.org/10.1016/S0363-8111(97)90023-0

Choi, I., Nisbett, R. E., & Norenzayan, A. (1999). Causal attribution across cultures: Variation and universality. *Psychological Bulletin*, *125*, 47–63. https://doi.org/10.1037/0033-2909.125.1.47

Claeys, A.-S., & Schwarz, A. (2016). Domestic and international audiences of organizational crisis communication. In A. Schwarz, M. W. Seeger, & C. Auer, Eds., *The Handbook of International Crisis Communication Research* (pp. 224–235). John Wiley & Sons, Ltd.

Coombs, T. W. (2007). *Ongoing Crisis Communication: Planning, Managing, and Responding* (2nd ed.). Sage.

Cordano, M., Welcomer, S., Scherer, R., Pradenas, L., & Parada, V. (2010). Understanding cultural differences in the antecedents of pro-environmental behavior: A comparative analysis of business students in the United States and Chile. *The Journal of Environmental Education*, *41*(4), 224–238. https://doi.org/10.1080/00958960903439997

Cornia, A., Dressel, K., & Pfeil, P. (2016). Risk cultures and dominant approaches towards disasters in seven European countries. *Journal of Risk Research*, *19*(3), 288–304. https://doi.org/10.1080/13669877.2014.961520

De Cock, R., Mertens, S., Sundin, E., Lams, L., Mistiaen, V., Joris, W., & d'Haenens, L. (2018). Refugees in the news: Comparing Belgian and Swedish newspaper coverage of the European refugee situation during summer 2015. *Communications*, *43*(3), 301–323. https://doi.org/10.1515/commun-2018-0012

Dhanesh, G. S., & Sriramesh, K. (2018). Culture and crisis communication: Nestle India's maggi noodles case. *Journal of International Management, 24*(3), 204–214. https://doi.org/10.1016/j.intman.2017.12.004

Diers-Lawson, A. (2017). A state of emergency in crisis communication an intercultural crisis communication research agenda. *Journal of Intercultural Communication Research, 46*(1), 1–54. https://doi.org/10.1080/17475759.2016.1262891

Dryhurst, S., Schneider, C. R., Kerr, J., Freeman, A. L. J., Recchia, G., van der Bles, A. M., Spiegelhalter, D., & van der Linden, S. (2020). Risk perceptions of COVID-19 around the world. *Journal of Risk Research, 23*(7–8), 994–1006. https://doi.org/10.1080/13669877.2020.1758193

Erez, M., & Gati, E. (2004). A dynamic, multi-level model of culture: From the micro level of the individual to the macro level of a global culture. *Applied Psychology. An International Review, 53*(4), 583–598. https://doi.org/10.1111/j.1464-0597.2004.00190.x

George, A. M., & Kwansah-Aidoo, K. (Eds.). (2017). *Culture and Crisis Communication: Transboundary Cases from Nonwestern Perspectives.* John Wiley & Sons.

Gribas, J., DiSanza, J. R., Hartman, K. L., Carr, D. J., & Legge, N. J. (2021). Exploring the effectiveness of image repair tactics: Comparison of U.S. and Middle Eastern audiences. *Communication Research Reports, 38*(3), 150–160. https://doi.org/10.1080/08824096.2021.1909550

Guerber, A. J., Anand, V., Ellstrand, A. E., Waller, M. A., & Reychav, I. (2020). Extending the situational crisis communication theory: The impact of linguistic style and culture. *Corporate Reputation Review, 23*(2), 106–127. https://doi.org/10.1057/s41299-019-00081-1

Ha, J.-H. (2016). 기업 위기와 사과 전략 활용에 관한 분석연구 위기 유형과 사과 시점을 중심으로 [A content analysis of the relations between crisis types and apology response strategies]. *광고연구, 109*, 76–100.

Haruta, A., & Hallahan, K. (2003). Cultural issues in airline crisis communications: A Japan-US comparative study. *Asian Journal of Communication, 13*(2), 122–150. https://doi.org/10.1080/01292980309364841

Hofstede, G. (1980). *Culture's Consequences: International Differences in Work-Related Values.* Sage.

Huang, Y.-H. C., Wu, F., Cheng, Y., & Lyu, J. C. (2016). Crisis communication research in the Chinese mainland. In A. Schwarz, M. W. Seeger, & C. Auer, Eds., *The Handbook of International Crisis Communication Research* (pp. 269–282). John Wiley & Sons, Ltd.

Huang, Y.-H. C., & Bedford, O. (2009). The role of cross-cultural factors in integrative conflict resolution and crisis communication: The Hainan incident. *American Behavioral Scientist, 53*(4), 565–578. https://doi.org/10.1177/0002764209347631

Ji, Y., & Kim, S. (2019). Communication-mediated psychological mechanisms of Chinese publics' post-crisis corporate associations and government associations. *Journal of Contingencies & Crisis Management, 27*(2), 182–194. https://doi.org/10.1111/1468-5973.12255

Jiang, S., d'Haenens, L., & Zhang, L. (2021). Differences in journalism culture or is there more to it? Comparing news on the European refugee issue in Western Europe and China. *International Communication Gazette, 83*(5), 451–473. https://doi.org/10.1177/17480485211029021

Kalayjian, A., Kanazi, R. L., Aberson, C. L., & Feygin, L. (2002). A cross-cultural study of the psychosocial and spiritual impact of natural disaster. *International Journal of Group Tensions, 31*, 175–186. https://doi.org/10.1023/A:1015260717000

Kim, N., & Lee, S. (2021). Cybersecurity breach and crisis response: An analysis of organizations' official statements in the United States and South Korea. *International Journal of Business Communication, 58*(4), 560–581. https://doi.org/10.1177/2329488418777037

Kim, S., Sheng, X., & Ketron, S. C. (2022). The roles of legacy versus social media information seeking in American and Chinese consumers' hoarding during COVID-19. *Journal of International Marketing, 30*(2), 38–55. https://doi.org/10.1177/1069031X221089347

Kim, S., Sung, K. H., Ji, Y., Xing, C., & Qu, J. G. (2021). Online firestorms in social media: Comparative research between China Weibo and USA Twitter. *Public Relations Review, 47*(1), 102010. https://doi.org/10.1016/j.pubrev.2021.102010

Lee, S., Yeo, J., & Na, C. (2020). Learning before and during the COVID-19 outbreak: A comparative analysis of crisis learning in South Korea and the US. *International Review of Public Administration, 25*(4), 243–260. https://doi.org/10.1080/12294659.2020.1852715

Lehmberg, D., & Hicks, J. (2018). A 'glocalization' approach to the internationalizing of crisis communication. *Business Horizons, 61*(3), 357–366. https://doi.org/10.1016/j.bushor.2018.01.002

Lyu, J. C. (2012). A comparative study of crisis communication strategies between Mainland China and Taiwan: The melamine-tainted milk powder crisis in the Chinese context. *Public Relations Review*, *38*(5), 779–791. https://doi.org/10.1016/j.pubrev.2012.07.003

Manzie, V. (2018). Applying the rhetoric of renewal model in a contemporary African context: Lessons learned from the royal Dutch shell oil crisis in Nigeria. *Journal of International Crisis and Risk Communication Research*, *1*(2), 201–224. https://doi.org/10.30658/jicrcr.1.2.2

Marincioni, F. (2001). A cross-cultural analysis of natural disaster response: The Northwest Italy floods of 1994 compared to the U.S. Midwest floods of 1993. *International Journal of Mass Emergencies and Disasters*, *19*(2), 209–235. https://doi.org/10.1177/028072700101900204

Myers, C. (2016). Apology, sympathy, and empathy: The legal ramifications of admitting fault in US public relations practice. *Public Relations Review*, *42*(1), 176–183. https://doi.org/10.1016/j.pubrev.2015.10.004

Ng, R., & Tan, Y. W. (2021). Diversity of covid-19 news media coverage across 17 countries: The influence of cultural values, government stringency and pandemic severity. *International Journal of Environmental Research and Public Health*, *18*(22), 11768. https://doi.org/10.3390/ijerph182211768

Onwezen, M. C., Bartels, J., & Antonides, G. (2014). Environmentally friendly consumer choices: Cultural differences in the self-regulatory function of anticipated pride and guilt. *Journal of Environmental Psychology*, *40*, 239–248. https://doi.org/10.1016/j.jenvp.2014.07.003

Paul, R., Bouder, F., & Wesseling, M. (2016). Risk-based governance against national obstacles? Comparative dynamics of Europeanization in Dutch, French, and German flooding policies. *Journal of Risk Research*, *19*(8), 1043–1062. https://doi.org/10.1080/13669877.2015.1074936

Petridou, E., & Zahariadis, N. (2021). Staying at home or going out? Leadership response to the COVID-19 crisis in Greece and Sweden. *Journal of Contingencies & Crisis Management*, *29*(3), 293–302. https://doi.org/10.1111/1468-5973.12344

Renn, O., & Rohrmann, B. (2000). *Cross-Cultural Risk Perception: A Survey of Empirical Studies*. Springer Science & Business Media.

Rodin, P., Ghersetti, M., & Odén, T. (2018). Disentangling rhetorical subarenas of public health crisis communication: A study of the 2014–2015 Ebola outbreak in the news media and social media in Sweden. *Journal of Contingencies & Crisis Management*, *1468–5973*, 12254. https://doi.org/10.1111/1468-5973.12254

Ruiu, M. L. (2020). Mismanagement of Covid-19: Lessons learned from Italy. *Journal of Risk Research*, *23*(7–8), 1007–1020. https://doi.org/10.1080/13669877.2020.1758755

Schein, E. H. (1991). What is culture? In P. J. Frost, L. F. Moore, M. R. Louis, C. C. Lundberg, & J. Martin, Eds., *Reframing Organizational Culture* (pp. 243–253). Sage.

Schultz, P. W. (2002). Environmental attitudes and behaviors across cultures. *Online Readings in Psychology and Culture*, *8*(1), 2307–0919. https://doi.org/10.9707/2307-0919.1070

Schwartz, S. H. (2006). A theory of cultural value orientations: Explication and applications. *Comparative Sociology*, *5*(2–3), 137–182. https://doi.org/10.1163/156913306778667357

Schwarz, A., Seeger, M. W., & Auer, C. (2016). Significance and structure of international risk and crisis communication research: Toward an integrative approach. In A. Schwarz, M. W. Seeger, & C. Auer, Eds., *The Handbook of International Crisis Communication Research* (pp. 1–10). John Wiley & Sons, Ltd.

Schwarz, A., Sellnow, D. D., Sellnow, T. D., & Taylor, L. E. (2024). Instructional risk and crisis communication at higher education institutions during COVID-19: Insights from practitioners in the global south and north. *Journal of International Crisis and Risk Communication Research*, *7*(1), 1–47. https://doi.org/10.56801/jicrcr.V7.i1.1

Shim, K., Cho, H., Kim, S., & Yeo, S. L. (2021). Impact of moral ethics on consumers' boycott intentions: A cross-cultural study of crisis perceptions and responses in the United States, South Korea, and Singapore. *Communication Research*, *48*(3), 401–425. https://doi.org/10.1177/0093650218793565

Suh, E., Diener, E., Oishi, S., & Triandis, H. C. (1998). The shifting basis of life satisfaction judgments across cultures: Emotions versus norms. *Journal of Personality and Social Psychology*, *74*(2), 482. https://doi.org/10.1037/0022-3514.74.2.482

Taylor, M. (2000). Cultural variance as a challenge to global public relations: A case study of the Coca-Cola scare in Europe. *Public Relations Review*, *26*(3), 277–293. https://doi.org/10.1016/S0363-8111(00)00048-5

Thompson, E. E. (2020). Risk communication in a double public health crisis: The case of Ebola and cholera in Ghana. *Journal of Risk Research*, *23*(7–8), 962–977. https://doi.org/10.1080/13669877.2020.1819386

Wang, H., Xiong, L., Wang, C., & Chen, N. (2022). Understanding Chinese mobile social media users' communication behaviors during public health emergencies. *Journal of Risk Research*, *25*(7), 874–891. https://doi.org/10.1080/13669877.2022.2049621

Wertz, E. K., & Kim, S. (2010). Cultural issues in crisis communication: A comparative study of messages chosen by South Korean and US print media. *Journal of Communication Management*, *14*(1), 81–94. https://doi.org/10.1108/13632541011017825

Wilhelms, R. W., Shaki, M. K., & Hsiao, C. (2009). How we communicate about cultures: A review of systems for classifying cultures, and a proposed model for standardization. *Competitiveness Review: An International Business Journal*, *19*(2), 96–105. https://doi.org/10.1108/10595420910942261

Xu, S. (2018). When individual cultural orientation and mediated portrayal of risk intersect: Effects of individualism-collectivism and media framing on risk perception and attribution of responsibility. *Journal of Contingencies & Crisis Management*, *26*(4), 499–509. https://doi.org/10.1111/1468-5973.12219

Yang, J. (2015). The influence of culture on Koreans' risk perception. *Journal of Risk Research*, *18*(1), 69–92. https://doi.org/10.1080/13669877.2013.879490

Zeemering, E. S. (2021). Functional fragmentation in city hall and Twitter communication during the COVID-19 pandemic: Evidence from Atlanta, San Francisco, and Washington, DC. *Government Information Quarterly*, *38*(1), 101539. https://doi.org/10.1016/j.giq.2020.101539

Zeng, J., Yuan, M., & Huang, G. (2022). Individual characteristics or cultures? Public risk perception in the coronavirus pandemic. *Journal of Risk Research*, *25*(11–12), 1413–1443. https://doi.org/10.1080/13669877.2022.2142951

Zhang, X. A. (2021). Understanding the cultural orientations of fear appeal variables: A cross-cultural comparison of pandemic risk perceptions, efficacy perceptions, and behaviors. *Journal of Risk Research*, *24*(3–4), 432–448. https://doi.org/10.1080/13669877.2021.1887326

Zhou, L., & Shin, J.-H. (2017). Does stealing thunder always work? A content analysis of crisis communication practice under different cultural settings. *Public Relations Review*, *43*(5), 1036–1047. https://doi.org/10.1016/j.pubrev.2017.08.004

Zhu, L., Anagondahalli, D., & Zhang, A. (2017). Social media and culture in crisis communication: McDonald's and KFC crises management in China. *Public Relations Review*, *43*(3), 487–492. https://doi.org/10.1016/j.pubrev.2017.03.006

Author's Bio

Sora Kim is a professor in the School of Journalism and Communication and the director of the Corporate Communication MSc program at the Chinese University of Hong Kong. Her research focuses on crisis and corporate social responsibility (CSR) communication. She has published more than 130 publications including refereed international journal articles, conference papers, book chapters, and other publications. Her work has been published in top international journals across communication, business, management, and ethics. She has presented at leading international conferences, received six prestigious top research awards, and secured significant research funding from organizations such as the General Research Fund (GRF)/Research Grants Council (RGC), Toyota Foundation Research Grants, and the Arthur W. Page Center. Sora Kim has been recognized on the Top 2% Scientists list by Stanford University in the subfield of communication and media studies for five consecutive years, from 2020 to 2024.

Part II

Strategic and Institutional Communicators in International Crises and Risks

4

Military, Government, and Media Management in Wartime

Kathrin Schleicher
Institute of Media and Communication Science,
Technische Universität Ilmenau, Ilmenau, Germany

Introduction

"War is among the most horrific of activities pursued by mankind" (Hudson & Stanier, 1998, p. xi). Wars affect almost every area of social life: They lead to harm and uncertainty among the civilian population and affect policy options for many years afterward (Aday et al., 2012). But as Robinson (2012, p. 352) claims, "there needs to be greater precision in terms of what we mean and understand by war".

In crisis communication studies there is an apparent lack of agreement on whether war represents a crisis or not. For example, Sellnow and Seeger (2013, p. 5) have argued that war is "the outcome of some extended conflict and as such is not surprising in the same way as most crisis", and therefore should not be classified as crisis. Others have suggested that war is a specific form of crisis (e.g. Brecher & Wilkenfeld, 1997; James, 1988) – for example as a "humanitarian crisis in disguise" (Jain et al., 2022).

According to Brecher and Wilkenfeld (1997), typically international crises occur in a non-war setting and some of them do escalate to war.

This chapter, however, follows the suggestion that war is not a type of crisis but one of a variety of possible approaches to resolving a crisis. Therefore, war is seen as one political instrument (e.g. von Clausewitz, 2006) among others such as diplomatic or economic embargoes, and yet can be considered as continuing crises as well.

On a phenomenon level, there is no consistent definition of war: It is seen as a distinct and intense form of violent conflict, but with no agreed differentiation between the two (Jungblut, 2023). In a broad sense, conflict can be defined as a "severe disagreement between at least two sides, where their demands cannot be met by the same resources at the same time" (Wallensteen 2007, p. 14). Conflicts can range from latent – with minimal efforts to address the underlying issue – to manifest: with a wide range of actions, from demonstrations and riots to, at the extreme end, full-blown war (Meyer et al., 2018). Hence, conflicts vary in terms of actors (states, non-state actors, or both), the disputed issue (e.g. ideology, autonomy, resources), conflict type (interstate, intrastate, substate, transstate), and the level of violence (Heidelberg Institute for International Conflict Research, 2022; Jungblut, 2023).

The Handbook of International Crisis and Risk Communication Research, Second Edition.
Edited by Andreas Schwarz, Matthew W. Seeger, and Sora Kim.

Following Howard (2000, p. 1), in this chapter war is defined as "armed conflict between organized political groups". James (1988, p. 6) mentions two general criteria to distinguish wars: First, the participants must be nation-states and second, the conflict must have led to one thousand or more combat-related casualties. But nowadays, the first criterion is no longer applicable, because of the appearance of the so-called *new wars*. New wars are characterized to a high extent by asymmetric warfare. Asymmetric warfare means that: (1) armed non-state actors are fighting, (2) free from the geographical constraints of nation-states, and (3) without a clear distinction between combatants and civilians (Theiler, 2009, p. 26). Typically, they are domestic wars, being waged to gain or stabilize the political and economic power of clans, religious or ideological groups, etc., with no clear lines of conflict.

With the rise of the new media environment – global media, internet, and mobile communication devices – the new paradigm of war is also characterized by an increasing mediatization of war (e.g. Boichak & Hoskins, 2022; Hjarvard et al., 2015).

Mediatization means that "the planning, waging and consequences of warfare do not reside outside of the media" (Hoskins & O'Loughlin, 2010, p. 5). War and conflict "are dependent upon media and, consequently, have been transformed to increasingly follow media logics" (Hoskins & O'Loughlin, 2015, p. 1323). As a result, the media not only offer the setting, in which war is performed but also have an impact on how it is performed (Maltby, 2012, p. 109). Media and communication technologies have deeply influenced the ways in which the wars were fought (Boichak & Hoskins, 2022, p. 2) and have become an "integrated component of the overall military strategy" (Hjarvard et al. 2015, p. 17). For example, since the 2003 Iraq War, the internet and digital communication have given a voice to new actors, including ordinary people, and provides policymakers and militaries with unexpected feedback to manage (Hoskins & O'Loughlin, 2010). But policymakers and militaries are also benefiting from the new media, – for instance, a "recent example of the elite reclaiming of the new media ecology is the Russian Troll Army" (Hoskins & Loughlin, 2015, p. 1328).

Against this background, this chapter focuses on the main actors in the context of war and examines communication studies with regard to the following questions: What impact do traditional communicators of war – military and government – have on news media coverage in war settings? How do they strategically communicate to attain their goals – for example, which types of media control do they typically use? Is news media independent of or dependent upon military and governmental influence? And, which new actors are important communicators in the mediated reporting of war, and how do digitization and new communication technologies impact strategic communication in warfare?

Military Media Management

In communication science, most studies of war communication only focus on the media's side, mostly on journalistic war reporting or on the content and patterns of war coverage (cf. Löffelholz, 2004; Schleicher, 2023). Due to the difficult access to the military as a research object, military communication strategies and tactics are either analyzed by drawing conclusions from media coverage, e.g. with which strategic frames the military appears (e.g. Jungblut, 2020b), or only partially examined.

Scholarly research in military media management mostly refers to official military communication (e.g. Taradai, 2019) or military practices of information control and treatment of journalists (e.g., the pool system), and is – apart from a few exceptions (e.g. Rid, 2007) – usually limited to a single conflict (e.g. Wolfgram, 2008). A well-researched example of the impact of media treatment on defense issues is the 1955–1975 Vietnam War. In the perception of the US military, independent news coverage during the Vietnam War was the reason for losing it, because it seemed to contradict the official war narrative and undermine public support. Hence, the Vietnam War was not lost on the Southeast Asian battlefield, but on the North American media stage. This, however, quite soon proved to be a gross simplification. But still, academics debate which role media coverage plays in the decision-making process of the government. However, the media was blamed for the loss of the Vietnam War by members of the military and led according to Rid (2007, p. 177) to "a culturally deep-rooted anti-media bias in the US armed forces."

As a reaction to Vietnam, restrictive public affairs – marked by high information control through censorship and limited media access to the battlefield – dominated until the mid-1990s (Maltby, 2012). Starting with the 1990–1991 Persian Gulf War, commentators stressed that the military has focused on "integration instead of repression" (Rid, 2007, p. 178) and open information policies. According to some scholars (Maltby, 2012; Thrall, 2000), the apparent greater transparency was, however, only an indication of how militaries have become more manipulative in their media management strategies:

"Military media management is now founded on minimizing access to the battle space (and hence information) while maximizing control through other means" (Maltby, 2012, p. 2).

In this context, one employed maneuver is the embedding of journalists with military troops. First tested in 1992–1995 Bosnian War (Rid, 2007), embedding was implemented in the 2003 Iraq War. However, only a few scholars are engaged in empirical studies about the effects of media on military practices. Like Rid (2007), they mostly are limited to the US armed forces (exceptions include e.g. studies on the Australian military [Forster & Pallant, 2013], and the British military [Maltby, 2012]).

Government–Media Relationships in Wartime – Theoretical Models

The relevance of strategic communication for warfare has increased in recent decades: On the one hand, there is a noticeable growth in asymmetric conflicts where the parties perceived as weaker strategically employ communication tactics to demoralize their adversaries or garner support from other nations; on the other hand, with the rising of social media and the digitalization of strategic communication, the focus has increasingly shifted to direct contact between strategic communicators and recipients (Wolfsfeld, 2018). For example, mobile phone cameras offer the possibility of directly documenting the events of war and sharing atrocities committed by the enemy online with the global public (Wolfsfeld, 2018). Politicians rely on the media as a source of information and can capitalize on the momentum generated by media coverage, but the elites also need access to the media to promote themselves and their issues (Van Aelst & Walgrave, 2016). Conflicting nations actively seek to shape events in their favor through strategic information presentation and narrative control. This involves employing traditional tools such as public relations, propaganda, censorship, and exerting influence over correspondents on the ground, along with controlling access to conflict zones (Wolff, 2018).

In the field of communication research, scholars delve into the history of propaganda, media censorship and control, and the strategies, content, and agents of persuasive communication (e.g. Wilke, 2007). Various conflicts, including the Second Gulf War in 1991 (e.g. Taylor, 1992), the Kosovo conflict (e.g. Nacos et al., 2000), the Iraq War (e.g. Kutz, 2006), the Afghanistan War (e.g. Taylor, 2003), the "War on Terrorism" (e.g. Brown, 2003), and more recent escalations such as the conflicts between Israel and Palestine (e.g. Wolfsfeld, 2018) and Ukraine and Russia (e.g. Alyukov, 2022; Taradai, 2019), have garnered significant scholarly attention.

Communication scholars have noted the growing sophistication of government news media management techniques (Robinson, 2012). Findings from communication science (e.g. Aday et al., 2012; Hjarvard et al., 2015) show that governments maintain their dominance as a news source through various strategies. These include public diplomacy, political public relations, propaganda and disinformation (such as Russian President Putin's troll army), strategic framing (such as the prominent 'war on terror') and military practices, especially information control through methods such as pooling, embedding and censorship.

Strategic communication aims to influence public opinion both domestically and internationally (Van Aelst and Walgrave, 2016). This has the potential to influence the foreign policy of other nations (Sheafer et al., 2014), including gaining public support for political decisions and measures (Aday et al., 2012).

Closely linked to the issue of governmental effort in dominating news media coverage as the main source is the question, of whether news media is dependent upon governmental impact – and therefore only serves as an instrument of government and military in wartime settings – or plays a leading role as an independent actor, influencing the behavior of governments. As Robinson (2004) claims:

> "[An] important question raised for those who have attempted to assess the relative balance of power between the US media and the state during wartime is whether we have witnessed an empowered wartime media or, conversely, continued domination of the news agenda by official viewpoints (p. 96)."

In communication studies, scholars have argued about this question and offered a variety of competing views. They have articulated theoretical positions concerning the interplay between news media and political power, and the role of media in strategic political communication. According to Brüggemann and Weßler (2009), these perspectives or models can be broadly classified into three categories:

- *The independent model*: This perspective tends to frame news media as an independent actor. In this concept, the news media wartime coverage is able to set out the security political agenda, and affect or even shape security political and military decisions (e.g., the CNN effect).
- *The dependent model*: This view emphasizes news media in wartime as governmental mouthpieces on security, political and military issues. Elite-driven approaches highlight the dominance of official sources; news media tend to matter only as a governmental instrument in forming public opinion (e.g., elite-driven theories: indexing hypothesis, propaganda model).
- *The interaction models*: These assume a complex dependency relationship between media and government: under certain conditions, news media dominates the government whereas, in other conditions, it is the military that impacts journalism (e.g., the *political context* model, the *cascading activation* model).

Independent Model (CNN Effect)

In recent decades, technological developments, including digitization, cable and satellite technology, or cellular telephony have revolutionized the speed of communication and changed the way western audiences experience war (e.g. Jungblut, 2020a). This development is accompanied by a general mediatization of society (e.g. Hjarvard et al., 2015). As a result, social actors assign media an increasing importance. In order to be present in media coverage, politicians must therefore adapt to the media logic. Some scholars stress that the balance of power between the security political sector and the military on one side and journalism on the other side shifts in favor of journalism. News coverage of war is said to have strong effects on the security political processes by shaping perceptions and public opinion, and thus influencing the political decision-making.

A prominent approach that deals with these effects of journalism on strategic communication is the so-called CNN effect. It describes the process by which the coverage of an event by

Cable News Network (CNN) causes a government to act and presupposes that the portrayal of conflicts in the media has the potential to force a government to change its policies (Gilboa, 2005). In academic research, CNN therefore is representative for global round-the-clock news with a significant impact on foreign policymaking, specifically on governmental decisions to deployment or withdrawal of U.S. troops. As Robinson (2012, p. 347) argues, "news media were an active force in causing policymakers to engage in humanitarian warfare."

Since the 1990–1991 Persian Gulf War, the CNN effect has been the subject of considerable academic analysis, but the empirical verification of the CNN effect was very limited. There are some crucial conditions that must be in place for the CNN effect to influence foreign-policy decision-making. Robinson (2012, p. 348), for example, argues that "initial claims regarding the CNN effect [...], were almost undoubtedly inaccurate and exaggerated." Furthermore, Robinson (2012, p. 348) concludes, "[a]t best, news media was one factor among many". Gilboa et al. (2016) also argue that the concept of the CNN effect is outdated and needs to be updated to understand the complex relationships between media and conflict.

Dependent Models (Indexing Hypothesis and Propaganda Model)

As shown, academics controversially debate the role media coverage plays in the governmental decision-making process. Above all, US political communication scholars tend to emphasize the strong influence of strategic communication on media coverage (e.g. Bennett, 1990). Because of the very limited access to objective information, the media was not seen as an independent actor but as an elite-dominated instrument to form public opinion.

With respect to the instrumentalization of news media by the government, the indexing hypothesis (Bennett, 1990) is a prominent approach. Bennett states that the media coverage of violent conflicts in the US is only an index of the opinions of the political elites. Therefore, it always focused on the opinion spectrum of the system. In the case of a parliamentary consensus, the journalists expressed only marginal criticism of the political system. In contrast, the impact of news media is more likely to occur if the political line itself is uncertain.

The indexing hypothesis has been widely confirmed, at least for the US (Bennett et al., 2006), and the far-reaching assertion that the governments even control the public debate.

Another theoretical framework that has sought to describe the dependence of news media upon official sources – and therefore critically stresses the government's influence on media coverage – is the propaganda model. Developed by US political communication researchers Herman and Chomsky (1988), the model identifies structural factors that limit the ability of the media to enforce an independent reporting of state interests. Although implicit, it refers to the inability of the media to set the news agenda. "Treetops propaganda," spread from prestigious agenda-setting print media in the US, is identified as an important factor in forming public opinion (Boyd-Barrett, 2004).

However, journalism research contests these models by presenting empirical evidence that highlights how journalist disparities, such as political views and gender, impact the selection and dissemination of news (Jungblut, 2020a). For example, a study shows that the journalistic framing of conflict events is context-dependent and far more independent of the strategic communication of political elites than the indexing hypothesis suggests (Jungblut, 2020b). Dependent models underscore the active involvement of journalists in the news production process (e.g. Hoxha & Hanitzsch, 2018; Tenenboim-Weinblatt & Baden, 2021).

Interaction Models (Political Contest Model and Cascading Activation Model)

As the contradictory findings show, research indicates that media effects range from strong to weak with explanations given for both ends of the continuum. In this respect, the thesis here is that a complex dependency relationship with reciprocal influences between media and government should be assumed. Under certain conditions media dominated the government; among other conditions, it is for the military to impact journalism: "Rather than continuing to debate the extremes of [media] autonomy or dependence, it makes more sense to explore the uneasy and often disjointed combinations of the two" (Bennett & Livingston, 2003, pp. 360–361).

This is one reason recent research has focused on analyzing the circumstances in which media plays a more or less influential role. Therefore, Robinson (2011) summarizes important variables, which explain the variability of media influence on security political decisions:

- *Elite dissensus/consensus*: Wolfsfeld's (1997) political contest model, Entman's (2004) cascading activation model, and Robinson's (2002) policy – media interaction model identify elite dissensus as an important condition for media independence.
- *Policy type*: With reference to the communication studies of Livingston (1997), Robinson (2011, p. 7) noticed that "not all policy areas appear amenable to signification media influence while others are likely to invite signification amounts of influence." Policies with high economic and political costs seem not to be strongly determined by media coverage, but foreign policy decisions over policies with lower costs, for example supplying humanitarian aid, might be significantly influenced by media pressure (Robinson, 2011).
- *Policy stage*: Robinson (2011, p. 7) stresses the idea that the influence of news media possibly is high at some points of the policy stage, "for example at the early agenda setting stage, and less at later stages, such as the policy implementation stage, is a cogent one and worth exploring." But to explain the contradictory findings more deeply, this variable needs further research.

According to Brüggemann and Weßler (2009), in addition to the influences within the political system already described, this also includes influences within the media system (e.g. journalism culture), cultural influencing factors (e.g. practices of interaction between journalists and political actors) and situational factors (e.g. control over the conflict situation). Although there are numerous case studies that have identified potential influencing factors on the relationship between politics and media, there is still a lack of comprehensive comparative studies that determine the influence of these factors across different contexts and conflicts (Jungblut, 2020a). A first attempt is made by Meyer et al. (2018): Based on an empirical analysis of six conflicts, media influence in the emergence, escalation, pacification, or prevention of violence hinges on how they process conflict actors' strategic communication as news. The authors attribute variations in media roles to contextual factors such as culturally embedded conflict perceptions, public trust in the media, media configuration, diversity, freedom, the constellation of conflict actors, including regional and international powers, and the course and intensity of the conflict. Meyer and Baden (2018, pp. 44–45) suggest that theoretical considerations on the media's role in conflicts should integrate insights into determining factors for specific media roles and the case-specific characteristics of the conflict.

As a good example of the variability of media influence, Robinson (2001) identifies different roles of the media during the 1955–1975 Vietnam War that explain the contradictory findings. According to Robinson (2001, p. 536), until 1968 the "news media coverage of the war in Vietnam [...] was largely supportive of the war." But from 1968 "elite dissensus started to be reflected in media coverage" (Robinson 2001, p. 537) and media coverage was adopting the perspective of those opposed to official policy. As time went by, the media became more and more critical:

> "In doing so, media coverage ... became an active participant in elite debate by adopting the side of those opposed to the war and, in the presence of executive policy uncertainty, influencing key policy-makers to move to withdrawal" (Robinson, 2001, p. 538).

In this respect, assumptions that the Vietnam explanation is nothing more than a myth of the power of the media in times of war are too narrowly considered, because the criticism of the Vietnam War was only reproduced by journalists, according to the assumptions of the indexing theory explained previously. The analysis of the relationship between the U.S. government and the media during the Vietnam War supports explanations that assume political-media interdependence – an interaction between politics and the media, in which neither party can control the other totally. To conclude with Aday et al. (2012, p. 333), "[a] careful reading of the literature suggests that context determines if and when the media influence foreign policymaking generally and particularly in times of war and conflict."

Digitization and Emerging Voices in War Communication

In the late twentieth century, the prevailing assumptions of war representations were linked to a media model characterized by a simple "broadcast ecology" (Boichak & Hoskins, 2022) that allowed the government and military to control the flow of information around operations (Merrin, 2018). Now, however, according to Boichak and Hoskins (2022), the link between top-down media control and military authority has dissolved. Contemporary discussions introduce concepts such as participatory war (Merrin, 2018), or radical war (Ford & Hoskins, 2022), reflecting a more decentralized relationship between media and military dynamics (Boichak & Hoskins, 2022).

In recent years, the use of social media for government communication has increased significantly. Politicians use it to connect directly with their audiences, making it a key battleground (Criado et al., 2013). While social media allows governments and politicians to communicate their political agenda directly to audiences (Yang et al., 2016), it is also transforming into a platform for the population (Warnick & Heineman, 2012). The key question in relation to digital media and government communication is therefore whether the power of government is diminished through political engagement (Nisch, 2023).

A growing number of studies deal with the use of social media in governments' strategic communication during times of war, for example, an analysis of the media's role as perceived by Israeli and Palestinian leaders (Wolfsfeld, 2018), a study by German Chancellor Scholz's Twitter communication during the Russian invasion of Ukraine (Nisch, 2023), an analysis of Canadian Prime Minister Justin Trudeau's tweets on the Russia–Ukraine War (Jaber, 2022) or the Russian propaganda campaign (Geissler & Feuerriegel, 2023) and the phenomenon of "participatory propaganda" – emerging propaganda strategies on social networks in Ukraine and Russia, offering insights into the "rewiring" of traditional propaganda for the digital age (Asmolov, 2022).

Also, the military is taking advantage of online platforms and social network sites. According to Massa and Anzera (2023), armies are currently using digital media as promotion, involving the "normalization" of militarism, and as conflict management, entailing the handling of conflicts (Massa & Anzera, 2023) and as visual meaning-making (Shim & Stengel, 2017).

Besides military and governmental communicators, scholars cannot ignore the new actors, which have emerged in wartime communication arenas. The entire battlefield is changing as smartphones, messaging apps and social media platforms in particular form a global and participatory arena (Merrin & Hoskins, 2020). In this space, the traditional distinctions between combatants, civilians and information warriors are blurring (Merrin & Hoskins, 2020):

> "Rather, the pervasive use of everyday internet-connected devices, such as smartphones, social media apps, and platforms, in targeting, hacking, cyberattacks, propaganda, and disinformation, blurs the distinction between who is civilian and who is combatant" (Boichak & Hoskins, 2022, pp. 1–2).

Changing circumstances such as the new warfare and technological developments allow these new voices to be expressed (see a more detailed discussion in Kampf and Liebes, 2013, p. 6). With the emergence of the internet as a new medium for alternative coverage, anti-war and pro-war blogs allowed citizens, independent journalists, and alternative agencies in the 2003 Iraq War to report directly from Iraq (Allan, 2004).

New forms of witnesses have also emerged in war coverage (Hoskins & O'Loughlin, 2010). For example, since the 2003 Iraq War, ordinary soldiers have been speaking publicly about military life and policy. Hoskins and O'Loughlin (2010, p. 77) describe the importance of soldiers' blogs, which change the relationship between media and military: "A journalist can potentially find a story directly from a soldier rather than indirectly through an authorized military press officer."

To take one example, Bennett (2013) analyzes the evolution of a war and terror "blogosphere" between 2001 and 2011. He contributes to the broader debate by explaining the changing nature of such a war and terror blogosphere. Bennett (2013, p. 39) identifies several categories of blogs and bloggers that might be of particular interest to journalists covering defense and security political questions: eyewitness accounts; independent journalists, NGOs and activists; diasporic blogs or "bridgebloggers"; experts, analysts and specialists; front line soldiers' blogs and military blogging; official military blogs; and microblogging insurgents.

In the advent of the digital age, the major question has arisen as to whether the role of the media has significantly changed in conflicts (Ciuriak, 2022). Despite the proliferation of social media, traditional news organizations continue to play a crucial role in amplifying the voices of various actors in armed conflicts (Zahoor & Sadiq, 2021). Bloggers and activists, often acting as citizen journalists in conflict zones, rely on coverage by traditional news outlets (Bennett, 2013).

Besides bloggers and activists, NGOs – a highly diverse array of organizations with varying goals and resources – were also relevant new communicators. Bennett (2013, p. 42) argues that collaborations between NGOs and traditional media journalists are mutually beneficial, because "the NGO gains more publicity while the journalists gain access to local sources, knowledge and expertise." NGO as eye-witnesses often seek to raise funds or awareness of the conflict (Hoskins & O'Loughlin, 2010) – as Hoskins and O'Loughlin (2010, p. 79) argue, "[m]edia become weaponized, not as a weapon of terror but as a weapon of care." The research landscape on the impact of NGOs on war reporting lacks consensus. On the one hand, they are recognized as having an increasing influence (Fröhlich & Jungblut, 2018). On the other hand, studies point to a rather low overall influence of NGOs in conflict reporting. These emphasize that NGOs are rarely quoted in the media, with the majority of quotes being attributed to large transnational NGOs (Jungblut, 2020b).

Thus, scholars have also focused on terrorism and its relationship to news media. Liebes and Kampf (2004, p. 78) for example argue that, "September 11 changed the image of terror and the journalistic approach to terror." Furthermore, Liebes and Kampf (2004, p. 78) stress that there has been a gradual shift whereby terrorists achieve "a status in which they speak for themselves, are listened to, explain their motives, and, to some extent, set the news agenda." According to Liebes and Kampf (2004, p. 81) western news channels now have more flexibility in giving voice to terrorists due to satellite channels, broadcasting from Arab states and are perceived to be somehow "democratic." Some scholars compare Al-Jazeera with CNN – and in the role of an "Arab CNN." Al-Jazeera also reached western audiences to offer alternative views.

Conclusion and Implications for Communicator Research

In summary, this chapter shows that in the area of security policy, research results indicate media effects ranging from strong to weak effects. The so-called CNN effect, for instance, describes the process by which the coverage of an event by CNN causes a federal government to act. Empirical studies however also show clear indications for weak media effects. The much-debated approach in this context is the so-called indexing hypothesis that Lance Bennett (1990) has established. In his view, the range of opinion in media coverage is just an index of the opinions of the political elite. Because of these contradictory findings, further research about the relationship between the military and the media, which both shape public image of wars, needs to be conducted. But in communication studies, the research focus is still on the media's side, for example on journalistic war reporting, the content of war coverage, or the role of the media at large. Maybe because of the difficult access to the military as the research object their communication strategies and tactics still were only partially examined (e.g. Maltby, 2012).

Due to the primacy of politics over the military system, the governmental influence on the military should be considered, too, because – as Ethiel (2002, p. 13) points out – it is more "a complex, conflictive, and peculiarly intimate triangular relationship" between government, military, and the media. Hence, in the future, more research is necessary to explore the complex relationship between the military and government.

Digital media are an integral part of warfare (Jungblut et al., 2023). The influence of a single viral picture or video from a conflict zone holds the potential to (re)shape public opinion and influence governmental stances and policies (Zahoor & Sadiq, 2021). In this context, strategic communication of conflict parties attempts to control the narrative and influence public opinion through targeted disinformation campaigns and participatory propaganda. The role of social media in strategic communication requires further investigation, particularly through cross-conflict studies.

References

Aday, S., Entman, R. M., & Livingston, S. (2012). Media, power and US foreign policy. In H. A. Semetko, & M. Scammell, Eds., *The SAGE Handbook of Political Communication* (pp. 327–341). London: SAGE Publications.

Allan, S. (2004). The culture of distance. Online reporting of the Iraq war. In S. Allan, & B. Zelizer, Eds., *Reporting War. Journalism in Wartimes* (pp. 347–356). London and New York: Routledge.

Alyukov, M. (2022). Propaganda, authoritarianism and Russia's invasion of Ukraine. *Nature Human Behavior, 6*, 763–765. https://doi.org/10.1038/s41562-022-01375-x

Asmolov, G. (2022). The transformation of participatory warfare: The role of narratives in connective mobilization in the Russia–Ukraine war. *Digital War, 3*, 25–37. https://doi.org/10.1057/s42984-022-00054-5

Bennett, D. (2013). Exploring the impact of an evolving war and terror blogosphere on traditional media coverage of conflict. *Media, War & Conflict, 6*(1), 37–53. https://doi.org/10.1177/1750635212469907

Bennett, W. L. (1990). Toward a theory of press-state relations in the United States. *Journal of Communication, 40*(2), 103–125.

Bennett, W. L., & Livingston, S. (2003). A semi-independent press: Government control and journalistic autonomy in the political construction of news. *Political Communication, 20*, 359–362.

Bennett, W. L., Lawrence, R. G., & Livingston, S. (2006). None dare call it torture: Indexing and the limits of press independence in the Abu Ghraib scandal. *Journal of Communication, 56*(3), 467–485. https://doi.org/10.1111/j.1460-2466.2006.00296.x

Boichak, O., & Hoskins, A. (2022). My war: Participation in warfare. *Digital War, 3*, 1–8. https://doi.org/10.1057/s42984-022-00060-7

Boyd-Barrett, O. (2004). Understanding the second casualty. In S. Allan, & B. Zelizer, Eds., *Reporting War. Journalism in Wartimes* (pp. 25–42). London and New York: Routledge.

Brecher, M., & Wilkenfeld, J. (1997). *A Study of Crisis*. Ann Arbor: University of Michigan Press.

Brüggemann, M., & Weßler, H. (2009). Medien im Krieg. Das Verhältnis von Medien und Politik im Zeitalter transnationaler Konfliktkommunikation. In F. Marcinkowski, & B. Pfetsch, Eds., *Politik in der Mediendemokratie* (pp. 635–657). Wiesbaden: Springer VS.

Ciuriak, D. (2022). *The role of social media in Russia's war on Ukraine*. Retrieved from http://dx.doi.org/10.2139/ssrn.4078863

Criado, J. I., Sandoval-Almazán, R., & Gil-Garcia, J. (2013). Government innovation through social media. *Government Information Quarterly*, *30*, 319–326.

Entman, R. M. (2004). *Projections of Power: Framing News, Public Opinion and US Foreign Policy*. Chicago: University of Chicago Press.

Ethiel, N. (Ed.). (2002). *The Military, the Media, and the Administration: An Irregular Triangle*. Chicago: McCormick Tribune Foundation.

Ford, M., & Hoskins, A. (2022). *Radical War: Data, Attention and Control in the Twenty-First Century*. Oxford University Press.

Foster, K., & Pallant, J. (2013). Familiarity breeds contempt? What the Australian Defence Force thinks of its coverage in the Australian media, and why. *Media International Australia*, *148*, 22–38.

Fröhlich, R., & Jungblut, M. (2018). Between factoids and facts: The application of 'evidence' in NGO strategic communication on war and armed conflict. *Media, War & Conflict*, *11*(1), 85–106. https://doi.org/10.1177/1750635217727308

Geissler, D., & Feuerriegel, S. (2023). *Analyzing the strategy of propaganda using inverse reinforcement learning: Evidence from the 2022 Russian invasion of Ukraine*. Retrieved from https://arxiv.org/pdf/2211.04154.pdf

Gilboa, E., Gabrielsen Jumbert, M., Miklian, J., & Robinson, P. (2016). Moving media and conflict studies beyond the CNN effect. *Review of International Studies*, *42*(4), 654–672. https://doi.org/10.1017/S026021051600005X

Heidelberg Institute for International Conflict Research (2022). *Methodik*. Retrieved from https://hiik.de/hiik/methodik/

Herman, E., & Chomsky, N. (1988). *Manufacturing Content: The Political Economy of the Mass Media*. New York: Pantheon.

Hjarvard, S., Mortensen, M., & Eskjær, M. (2015). Three dynamics of mediatized conflicts. In M. Eskjær, S. Hjarvard, & M. Mortensen, Eds., *The Dynamics of Mediatized Conflicts* (pp. 1–27). New York: Peter Lang.

Hoskins, A., & O'Loughlin, B. (2015). Arrested war: The third phase of mediatization. *Information, Communication & Society*, *18*, 1320–1338. https://doi.org/10.1080/1369118X.2015.1068350

Hoskins, A., & O'Loughlin, B. (2010). *War and Media. The Emergence of Diffused War*. Cambridge, UK: Polity Press.

Howard, M. (2000). *The Invention of Peace: Reflections on War and International Order*. London: Profile.

Hoxha, A., & Hanitzsch, T. (2018). How conflict news comes into being: Reconstructing 'reality' through telling stories. *Media, War & Conflict*, *11*(1), 46–64. https://doi.org/10.1177/1750635217727313

Hudson, M., & Stanier, J. (1998). *War and the Media: A Random Searchlight*. New York: New York University Press.

Jaber, F. (2022). Social media framing of the 2022 'War in Ukraine': A content analysis study of the Canadian prime minister's tweets. *Journal of Applied Journalism & Media Studies*. https://doi.org/10.1386/ajms_00099_1

Jain, N., Prasad, S., Bordeniuc, A., Tanasov, A., Shirinskaya, A. V., Béla, B., Cheuk, C. P., Banica, D. C. N., Panag, D. S., Świątek, D., Savchenko, E., Platos, E., Lolita, J., Betka, M. M., Phiri, M., Patel, S., Czárth, Z. C., Krygowska, A. M., Jain, S., & Reinis, A. (2022). European countries step-up humanitarian and medical assistance to Ukraine as the conflict continues. *Journal of Primary Care & Community Health*. https://doi.org/10.1177/21501319221095358

James, P. (1988). *Crisis and War*. Montreal: McGill-Queen's University Press.

Jungblut, M. (2020a). Kriegs- und Konfliktberichterstattung im digitalen Zeitalter. In I. Borucki, K. Kleinen-von Königslöw, S. Marschall, & T. Zerback, Eds., *Handbuch Politische Kommunikation* (pp. 313–326). Wiesbaden: Springer VS. https://doi.org/10.1007/978-3-658-26242-6_23-1

Jungblut, M. (2020b). *Strategic Communication and Its Role in Conflict News. A Computational Analysis of the International News Coverage on Four Conflicts*. Wiesbaden: Springer Fachmedien.

Jungblut, M. (2023). Content analysis in the research field of war coverage. In F. Oehmer-Pedrazzi, S. H. Kessler, E. Humprecht, K. Sommer, & L. Castro, Eds., *Standardisierte Inhaltsanalyse in der*

Kommunikationswissenschaft – Standardized Content Analysis in Communication Research. Springer VS: Wiesbaden. https://doi.org/10.1007/978-3-658-36179-2_11

Jungblut, M., Kümpel, A. S., Peter, C., & Wulf, T. (2023). Editorial: The Russian invasion of Ukraine in modern information environments: Content, consumers, and consequences of digital conflict communication. *Frontiers in Political Science, 5.* https://doi.org/10.3389/fpos.2023.1227005

Kampf, Z., & Liebes, T. (2013). *Transforming Media Coverage of Violent Conflicts: The New Face of War.* Basingstoke: Palgrave McMillan.

Liebes, T., & Kampf, Z. (2004). The PR of terror. In S. Allan, & B. Zelizer, Eds., *Reporting War: Journalism in Wartime* (pp. 77–95). London and New York: Routledge.

Livingston, S. (1997). *Clarifying the CNN effect: An examination of media effects according to type of military intervention.* Research paper R-18. Cambridge, MA: The Joan Shorenstein Center on the Press, Politics and Public Policy at Harvard University.

Löffelholz, M. (2004). Krisen- und Kriegskommunikation als Forschungsfeld. Trends, Themen und Theorien eines hoch relevanten, aber gering systematisierten Teilgebietes der Kommunikationswissenschaft. In M. Löffelholz, Ed., *Krieg als Medienereignis. Krisenkommunikation im 21. Jahrhundert* (pp. 13–55). Wiesbaden: VS Verlag für Sozialwissenschaften.

Maltby, S. (2012). *Military Media Management. Negotiating the "Front" Line in Mediatized War.* London and New York: Routledge.

Massa, A., & Anzera, G. (2023). The platformization of military communication: The digital strategy of the Israel Defense Forces on Twitter. *Media, War & Conflict, 16*(3), 364–382. https://doi.org/10.1177/17506352221101257

Merrin, W., & Hoskins, A. (2020). Tweet fast and kill things: Digital war. *Digital War, 1*, 184–193. https://doi.org/10.1057/s42984-020-00002-1

Merrin, W. (2018). *Digital War: A Critical Introduction.* London: Routledge.

Meyer, C. O., & Baden, C. (2018). Dissecting media roles in conflict. A transactionist process model of conflict news production, dissemination and influence. In R. Fröhlich, Ed., *Media in War and Armed Conflict. The Dynamics of Conflict News Production and Dissemination* (pp. 23–48). London: Routledge.

Meyer, C. O., Baden, C., & Frère, M.-S. (2018). Navigating the complexities of media roles in conflict: The INFOCORE approach. *Media, War & Conflict, 11*(1), 3–21. https://doi.org/10.1177/1750635217719754

Nisch, S. (2023). Frames and sentiments of the Twitter communication by German Chancellor Scholz during the Russian invasion of Ukraine. *Politics in Central. Europe, 19*(3). https://doi.org/10.2478/pce-2023-0028

Rid, T. (2007). *War and Media Operations. The US Military and the Press from Vietnam to Iraq.* London: Routledge.

Robinson, P. (2001). Theorizing the influence of media on world politics. Models of media influence on foreign policy. *European Journal of Communication, 16*(4), 523–544.

Robinson, P. (2002). *The CNN Effect: The Myth Of News, Foreign Policy and Intervention.* London: Routledge.

Robinson, P. (2004). Researching US media-state relations and twenty-first century wars. In S. Allan, & B. Zelizer, Eds., *Reporting War. Journalism in Wartime* (pp. 96–112). London and New York: Routledge.

Robinson, P. (2011). The CNN effect reconsidered: Mapping a research agenda for the future. *Media, War & Conflict, 4*(1), 3–11. https://doi.org/10.1177/1750635210397434

Robinson, P. (2012). News media and war. In H. A. Semetko, & M. Scammell, Eds., *The SAGE Handbook of Political Communication* (pp. 342–355). London: SAGE Publications.

Schleicher, K. (2023, in print). Journalismus und Militär. In M. Löffelholz, & L. Rothenberger, Eds., *Handbuch Journalismustheorien* (2nd ed.). Wiesbaden: Springer VS.

Sellnow, T. L., & Seeger, M. W. (2013). *Theorizing Crisis Communication.* Hoboken, NJ: Wiley-Blackwell.

Sheafer, T., Shenhav, S. R., Takens, J., & Van Atteveldt, W. (2014). Relative political and value proximity in mediated public diplomacy: The effect of state-level homophily on international frame building. *Political Communication, 31*(1), 149–167.

Shim, D., & Stengel, F. A. (2017). Social media, gender and the mediatisation of war: Exploring the German armed forces' visual representation of the Afghanistan opera-tion on facebook. *Global Discourse, 7*, 330–347.

Taradai, D. (2019). Who is Ukraine's enemy: Narratives in the military communication regarding the war in Donbas. *Russian Journal of Communication, 11*, 141–156.

Tenenboim-Weinblatt, K., & Baden, C. (2021). Gendered communication styles in the news: An algorithmic comparative study of conflict coverage. *Communication Research, 48*(2), 233–256. https://doi.org/10.1177/0093650218815383

Theiler, O. (2009). Die Eigendarstellung staatlicher Sicherheitsakteure in den Medien. Das Beispiel der Bundeswehr. In T. Jäger, & H. Viehrig, Eds., *Sicherheit und Medien* (pp. 25–34). Wiesbaden: VS Verlag für Sozialwissenschaften.

Thrall, A. T. (2000). *War in the Media Age*. Cresskill, NJ: Hampton Press.

Van Aelst, P., & Walgrave, S. (2016). Information and arena: The dual function of the news media for political elites. *Journal of Communication, 66*(3), 496–518.

von Clausewitz, K. (2006). *On war*. Retrieved from http://www.gutenberg.org /files/1946/1946-h/1946-h.htm

Wallensteen, P. (2007). *Understanding Conflict Resolution*. London: Sage.

Warnick, B., & Heineman, D. S. (2012). *Rhetoric online: The Politics of New Media* (2nd ed.). New York, NY: Peter Lang.

Wolff, M. A. (2018). *Kriegsberichterstattung und Konfliktsensitivität. Qualitätsjournalismus zwischen Anspruch und Wirklichkeit*. Wiesbaden: Springer Vieweg.

Wolfgram, M. A. (2008). Democracy and propaganda: NATO's war in Kosovo. *European Journal of Communication, 23*(2), 153–171.

Wolfsfeld, G. (1997). *The Media and Political Conflict. News from the Middle East*. Cambridge: Cambridge University Press.

Wolfsfeld, G. (2018). The role of the media in violent conflicts in the digital age: Israeli and Palestinian leaders' perceptions. *Media, War & Conflict, 11*(1), 107–124.

Yang, X., Chen, B. C., Maity, M., & Ferrara, E. (2016). Social politics: Agenda setting and political communication on social media. In E. Spiro, & Y. Y. Ahn, Eds., *Social Informatics. SocInfo 2016* (Lecture Notes in Computer Science(), Vol. 10046). Cham: Springer. https://doi.org/10.1007/978-3-319-47880-7_20

Zahoor, M., & Sadiq, N. (2021). Media and armed conflicts: An overview. *NUST Journal of International Peace & Stability*. https://doi.org/110.37540/NJIPS.V4I1.80

Author Bio

Kathrin Schleicher is a research assistant at the Institute for Media and Communication Studies at the Technical University of Ilmenau. She is a member of the International Research Group on Crisis Communication (IRGoCC). Her research interests include crisis communication, strategic communication and organisational communication. She is currently working on a research project led by Martin Löffelholz that analyses state risk and crisis communication in Germany in the context of the Covid-19 pandemic.

5

Crisis Communication in the Context of Terrorism

Process Approach to Complex Crises

Aino Ruggiero[1] and Minttu Tikka[2]

[1] Humanitarian Logistics and Supply Chain Research Institute, Department of Marketing, Hanken School of Economics, Helsinki, Finland

[2] Faculty of Social Sciences, University of Helsinki, Helsinki, Finland

In the wake of the 9/11 terrorist attacks, which shocked the Western world at the turn of the millennium, crisis communication in the context of terrorism gained importance as a field of research. Broadly defined, crisis communication consists of an ongoing process of creating, amid crises, shared meanings among and between different individuals, groups, communities, and organizations in order to prepare for and respond to risks and crises in ways that minimize harm and enhance resilience (Sellnow & Seeger, 2013, p. 13). Terrorism is a risk that can turn into a crisis in the event of a terrorist attack. Hence, in an integrated view, risk and crisis communication form a continuum with pre-crisis, crisis, and post-crisis phases (cf. Reynolds & Seeger, 2005; Veil et al., 2008).

Terrorism is a contested term. It is generally used to refer to a complex phenomenon intended to create chaos and fear. Terrorism takes the form of a violent attack carried out with, for example, explosive devices, firearms, or bladed weapons. Violence is targeted against civilians and innocent people who become victims indiscriminately (Walzer, 1977), due to ideological reasons (Fletcher, 2006; Meisels, 2009), or for a combination of both reasons. Compared to many other types of crises and disasters, terrorism has a special connection with mediated communication: The purpose of terrorist attacks is to convey a message, making terrorism an inherently communicative act. More than instilling fear in the actual targets of terrorism, contemporary acts of terrorism are often planned to maximize the attention they receive through digital media platforms, thereby reaching a broader audience among the population (Nacos, 2016). Consequently, to generate society-wide terror, such attacks are designed "for the media" as much as [they are] "for the chaos" (Cui & Rothenbuhler, 2018, p. 157). An illustrative case is the 2019 attack in Christchurch, New Zealand, in which the right-wing perpetrator live-streamed the massacre on Facebook. This is to say, terror attacks are grounded in symbolic violence that aims at psychological effects and social disruption through vast, real-time media attention (Falkheimer, 2014; Sumiala et al., 2018).

Terrorism as a concept indicates substantive political and moral disapproval. In essence, it is a social construct shaped by its public use in diverse socio-political contexts, making it difficult

The Handbook of International Crisis and Risk Communication Research, Second Edition.
Edited by Andreas Schwarz, Matthew W. Seeger, and Sora Kim.

to pinpoint an unequivocal meaning of terrorism. Consequently, not all acts of violence are considered terrorism; often, it is the intention behind an act that determines whether an attack is perceived as terroristic or not. The key tensions regarding the public use of this concept intertwine around the motives behind a given attack and the collective identities of its targets. For an act to be considered terrorist, it should be politically or religiously motivated. However, intentions can be difficult to unmask, leading to challenges in deducing if an attack is politically motivated or, for example, a result of mental health problems. Moreover, the identity of a perpetrator and the political conceptions of "enemies" and "friends" play an important role in who is regarded as a terrorist and who is not (Betus et al., 2021; Norris, 2020). Scholars have noted that in Western discourse, the term terrorist is quickly activated in case of violent attacks committed by "others," i.e., persons with different cultural and religious backgrounds often associating with Islamic actors (Abbas, 2021). In contrast, far-right attacks are often associated with mental illnesses or street gangs instead of framing them as terrorism (Gardell, 2018). Consequently, the threat of violent right-wing extremism remains underestimated by authorities (Hartleb, 2020), and attacks inspired by far-right ideology are underreported in official statistics (Bjørgo & Ravndal, 2019).

Labeling something as terrorism carries strong political and moral implications (Baele et al., 2019), yet there is no widely accepted international legal definition of the term. Different states have varying definitions of terrorism, and institutions – even within the same country – sometimes devise their own definitions, correlating and justifying their role in combating terrorism (Haghani et al., 2022). These conceptual challenges are reflected in the databases that keep records on terrorist events, raising the question of which events are actually reported as terrorism (Freilich et al., 2015). Nevertheless, the databases indicate the recent development of this phenomenon. According to the Global Terrorism Database (GTD), the overall number of reported terrorist incidents decreased from 2015 to 2020, from around 1500 to 650 (GDT, 2023). Most attacks during this period occurred in the Middle East and North Africa (35.10%), in South Asia (31.76%), and in Sub-Saharan Africa (18.11%); 4% of the attacks took place in Europe. These figures reflect the longer-term regional trend in the number of attacks. Still, the field of terrorism studies has a notable Eurocentric focus, with its knowledge produced mostly within a Western academic system. This bias in focus has led to the emergence of critical terrorism studies (CTS), which aim to address and acknowledge the colonial roots of terrorism studies, state-centrism, and pro-Western bias and the inordinate focus on so-called Islamic terrorism, diversifying the discussion to listen to participating voices beyond those in the West (Achieng et al., 2023).

Instances of terrorism can be categorized in many ways based on their type of attack or ideology. According to the recent European Union Terrorism Situation and Trend Report (TE-SAT, 2023), jihadist acts of violence are perceived as the most salient terrorist threat to the EU, while the threat from far-right terrorist actors is considered notable, and left-wing violent extremists also pose a hazard to public safety (TE-SAT, 2023). In the aftermath of the 9/11 attacks and the following anthrax crisis in the US, which had illustrated how terrorists were inventing new ways to terrorize and how any human invention could potentially be used as a device to conduct a terror attack, the concern for the use of CBRN (chemical, biological, radiological, or nuclear) materials for terrorist purposes was intensified (Beck, 2002; Slovic, 2002). The likelihood of such attacks is uncertain and difficult to quantify (Mäkelä, 2007; Slovic, 2002); however, they constitute worst-case scenarios with potentially devastating material and immaterial consequences that cannot be excluded from crisis preparedness and exemplify the extreme level of complexity that a terrorist attack could potentially produce (Ruggiero, 2017).

Similarly, as with all events that suddenly disrupt the security and safety of societies, terrorism-related risks and crises require fast and coordinated responses, communication, and management from all institutional actors involved with them. A shared understanding is important to prevent or manage terrorism-related events in a coordinated manner. In this regard, the European Union is one of the few international actors that has succeeded in achieving consensus on terrorism (Malkki, 2020). In the EU, the concept is applied as a judicial term that offers a basis for authorities' international and national collaboration. Specifically, EU Directive 2017/541 on combating terrorism establishes a legal framework common to all member states and, notably, a uniform definition of terrorism. At the core of this definition are the purpose and motivation behind the terroristic act of violence. In the directive, the terrorist's aim is defined as intimidating a population, unduly coercing a government or an international organization to perform or prevent from performing any act, or seriously destabilizing or destroying the fundamental political, economic, constitutional, or social structures of a country or international organization (EU Directive, 2017/541). The EU Directive obligated member states to enact legislation in their own countries according to this law. In the fight against and prevention of terrorist crimes, the authorities are given more extensive means than usual. From the viewpoint of government organizations, this directive serves as the basis for jurisdiction and, consequently, creates a framework for their crisis management and communication strategies in the context of terror attacks.

Multi-Actor Response Network

Terror attacks are complex and highly unexpected events that affect all levels of society. They require a coordinated response from all involved institutional actors who could address the situational complexity that emerges from the event and its consequences (Curtis, 2018). Among the ways to manage such crises, the relational approach to crisis management draws on complexity-based thinking (Gilpin & Murphy, 2010) and acknowledges how the ambiguity of the situation necessitates a processual orientation for managing crises through communication. Unlike traditional centralized management approaches, the relational approach to crisis management stresses the need for multi-agency collaboration, coordination, and networked communication in crises (Falkheimer & Heide, 2010; Frandsen & Johansen, 2017); in complex crises, multi-organizational networks that cross organizational and jurisdictional boundaries constitute the crisis response entity (Adkins, 2010; Boin et al., 2005; Palttala & Vos, 2012). Terrorist attacks involve a high level of uncertainty, threat, and urgency – the epitome of a crisis (Boin & 't Hart, 2007) – each affecting, for example, the number of assaults, perpetrators, and victims. As one illustrative instance, in November 2015 in Paris, a suicide bombing near the Stade de France was the first incident in a series of coordinated attacks on streets, café terraces, restaurants, and a theatre that were executed with explosives and assault rifles. The multiple simultaneous attacks, combined with the presence of active gunmen, hostage-taking, and an unforeseen number of casualties, created an intensely complex crisis for institutional actors to manage (Kouri & Tziaferi, 2016). Notably, if such an attack were combined with the use of an unknown agent, such as a biological weapon, a dimension of further complexity would be added.

A terrorist crisis like the one in Paris involves a multiplicity of public and private institutional actors on all levels – local, regional, national, and international. These actors are expected to mitigate terrorism-related risks and crises according to their areas of jurisdiction and expertise. Their responses can be categorized in three ways.

First, terrorist attacks always occur in specific geographical locations involving local public authorities and official bodies, with examples including fast-response organizations, such as police and other emergency response organizations (e.g., fire departments and health services) that operate on tactical, operational, and strategic levels (Bye et al., 2019). As terrorist attacks are criminal offenses, police organizations hold a prominent role in their prevention, management, investigation, and communication, according to jurisdiction, but they also require involvement from several other agencies. Specifically, municipal actors, local religious communities (e.g., churches, mosques, and synagogues), and NGO divisions (e.g., local Red Cross divisions) are often involved in organizing media centers for journalists and evacuation centers for the affected civilians or coordinating public traffic and other public premises in the event of a city lockdown.

Secondly are political responses, which can vary in what level they occur. In certain countries, such as France, a military response would occur at a national level (Kouri & Tziaferi, 2016), often involving public announcements from the head of state and interministerial coordination of the situation. Psycho-social support for the victims is also coordinated on a national level by, for example, the country's Red Cross.

Third, terrorism is a cross-border phenomenon, and institutional responses often involve an international level of engagement, connecting a local area to the international debate on terrorism and the threats involved (Falkheimer, 2014). Post-attack, the political leaders of other countries often express their condolences, condemn the attack, and declare their support for the target country. International agencies and bodies, such as the EU, UN, NATO, and NGOs like the International Committee of Red Cross (ICRC), express solidarity and provide psychosocial support for civilians to cope with uncertainty and stress. Notably, in response to research and public pressure, reputational incentives, and the threat of legislation, social media corporations have recently entered as novel institutional actors in the international crisis response. Indeed, research has established that terrorist actors utilize new technologies and exploit social media services (TE-SAT, 2023; Tikka et al., 2020). Accordingly, these findings and public pressure have forced social media giants like Meta (Facebook and Instagram), Alphabet (Google and YouTube), and X (Twitter) to become more proactively engaged in counterterrorism efforts (Borelli, 2023). Defying a neat categorization into local, regional, national, or international, news media in the age of digital platforms – and affected citizens and the interested public – all operate across these levels, creating communicative conditions for terrorism and its public framing and responses.

The multi-actor crisis response network involves pre-existing institutions that often merge into a new entity (Hu et al., 2022; Scott & Nowell, 2020). A situation entailing high uncertainty, such as a terrorist attack, creates challenging conditions for the emerging crisis management network, especially regarding distributed sensemaking, inter-organizational coordination, and communication (Tikka et al., 2023). A crisis caused by a terrorist attack represents a cosmology episode, a situation where "both the sense of what is occurring and the means to rebuild that sense collapse together" (Weick, 1993, p. 633), and this episode activates an intense need for sensemaking and to understand the causes and consequences of the crisis. Making sense of the evolving situation is vital for all crisis response activities, yet in multi-actor crisis response networks, the partial pieces of information held by different actors are not easily synchronized into a coherent situational awareness (Wolbers, 2022). In addition, the dynamic changes in the situation may affect the roles between the actors, which may, for example, require new institutional actors to become involved or assume new roles. However, at times, some institutional actors may stall, fail to recognize their role and responsibility in the situation or be restricted in their participation, further complicating the response (Curtis, 2018). As another notable feature of this crisis management network, the complexity increases along with the number of actors involved (Christensen et al., 2015). Managing complexity thus necessitates effective risk and crisis communication, which facilitates both the sensemaking, coordination, and collaboration between organizations of the emerging crisis management network and the engagement of the citizens and other stakeholders.

The Process Approach, from Preparedness to Recovery

Crisis communication is an ongoing process of co-creating meanings and actions among and between the different actors in the response network formed around terrorist threats and crises, with this process taking the form of networked crisis communication and management (Palttala & Vos, 2012; Ruggiero, 2017; Sellnow & Seeger, 2013). In a co-creational view of communication, relationships are at the heart of interaction and cooperation (Botan & Taylor, 2004). Communication is, therefore, constitutive in crisis management, enabling many sub-processes (Jahn & Johansson, 2018). For example, warnings and emergency messages can be delivered through crisis communication. Risk communication, on the other hand, focuses on pre-event readiness, aiming to inform, prepare, and advise in building preparedness. A process view of crisis communication consists of an integrated approach to risk and crisis communication.

According to the process approach, also called the developmental or phased approach (e.g., Coombs, 2015), risk and crisis communication approaches, strategies, and activities are divided into different developmental stages of crises. Among the models for these stages, the three-stage one – splitting crises and related communication activities into pre-crisis, crisis, and post-crisis phases – is the most popular and commonly used (Sellnow & Seeger, 2013). Another well-known model is the Crisis and Emergency Risk Communication Model (CERC), with five phases: (1) pre-crisis, (2) initial event, (3) maintenance, (4) resolution, and (5) evaluation (Reynolds & Seeger, 2005). The CERC model has also been applied to the terrorism context as a framework that specifies and describes crisis communication tasks per terrorist crisis phase and stakeholder group (see Ruggiero et al., 2015).

Preparedness

The pre-crisis phase encompasses building preparedness and creating crisis communication plans in the crisis management network. In this regard, an all-hazards approach has been suggested as a method to create preparedness for terrorism that constitutes a low-probability, potentially high-impact risk based on the kind of device used to execute the attack (Ruggiero & Vos, 2015). The pre-crisis phase includes preparations for collaboration and coordination in the crisis management network, during which procedures for information exchange and distributed sensemaking in the network are established. Overall, crisis management preparedness intersects with counterterrorism activities in monitoring the development of terrorism and threat assessment, including the radicalization of potential terrorist threats. In the sphere of strategic communication, this threat monitoring would include detecting and countering terrorist propaganda – including disinformation – and the spread of messages spurring hatred and violence over the internet and social media (e.g., Finnish Ministry of Interior, 2022; Ruggiero & Vos, 2014; TE-SAT, 2023).

A community approach to crisis communication, which entails partnering with the public and including them in pre-event planning, is also valid for communicating about terrorism (Blanchard et al., 2005). It has also been indicated as a means to build and cultivate trust: what terrorism puts to the test and aims to shatter (Rogers et al., 2007). In this approach, identifying risk groups and vulnerabilities according to a terrorist scenario and developing communication strategies are part of the preparedness phase (Stevens et al., 2009; Wray et al., 2008). Recent research supports the use of pre-event communication about terrorism and cites its benefits: enhancing perceptions of response organizations' preparedness to respond, increasing trust in official instructions during an incident, and positively influencing behavioral actions that could save lives while discouraging nonprotective behaviors (Pearce et al., 2019). Traditionally, however, the trend among governments has been to avoid communicating about the risk of terrorism to avoid creating unnecessary anxiety among the publics of various countries.

During the preparedness phase, the tasks of crisis communicators are mapping risk perceptions and understanding the publics' information needs regarding terrorism. For example, in the Western cultural context, messages with exemplars aimed at behavioral intentions have been found useful in targeting women, who are more proactive or reactive and susceptible to them compared to men (Spence et al., 2017). By increasing knowledge and understanding of terrorism and making it less formidable, risk communication aims to augment resilience among the publics (Sheppard, 2011). Especially in the case of terrorism that involves the use of CBRN materials, the unknown content employed in the attack should be explained in understandable language. For example, relevant information for message construction and planning in cases of bioterrorism includes signs and symptoms of infection and related health advice. Communication expertise must, therefore, be coupled with a multidisciplinary task-force that includes subject-matter specialists and risk analysts (Fischhoff, 2011). Overall, terrorism risks should be communicated in an actionable way, providing concrete advice for preparedness actions one may take (Wood et al., 2012). This resonates with the IDEA framework, in which message construction for instructional risk and crisis communication is guided by four aims: internalization, distribution, explanation, and action (Sellnow et al., 2017).

Planning and preparing for various psychological factors and reactions is integral to terrorism crisis communication preparedness (DiGiovanni, 2003). Overall, the roles of affect and emotion in risk communication are imperative to acknowledge, as risk is more likely to manifest in people as a feeling or an emotional response rather than as an analytical outcome (Spence et al., 2017). As terrorist events are always publicized by and involve the media, working with media organizations in the pre-event phase is essential. Pre-crisis training and exercises are important but are presently outdated or lacking in their content, especially regarding the worst-case scenarios that involve the use of CBRN materials (Ruggiero & Vos, 2015). Pre-crisis training and exercises involving cooperation with journalists could include topics such as tensions between journalistic reporting and official communication when a criminal investigation is ongoing, the protection of victim privacy, and the upholding of ethical principles (e.g., how to avoid fostering generalizations and stigma when describing perpetrators). Recent research shows that crisis exercises are beneficial in terms of improved agility, understanding of response roles, and coordination among participants and can thus improve the capacity for distributed sensemaking (Skryabina et al., 2020).

Response

In the acute crisis phase, crisis communication in response to a terrorist attack aims to help people take appropriate self-protective measures, limit adverse social and psychological effects, and reduce morbidity and mortality (Becker, 2004). In this regard, maintaining trust and encouraging the publics to keep fears in perspective are important goals for communication (Gray & Ropeik, 2002). While the direct effects of terrorism are often limited and the domain of operational crisis management, the indirect effects are often wide and depend on the success or failure of communication around the event (Fischhoff, 2011). Hence, whether terrorists succeed in their primary objective – in spreading fear, anxiety, distrust, and uncertainty – is an outcome of crisis communication. Although terrorism may provoke intense emotional reactions and responses among the publics, outright panic is rare (Sheppard et al., 2006); indeed, people's coping capacities should not be underestimated. Post-attack, the provision of non-specific reassurance can be a source of suspicion (Rubin et al., 2011). Messages should thus contain simple, practical advice and steps along with basic information (Wray et al., 2008). Language should be straightforward, easy to follow, accompanied by pictures, and available for multiple language groups (Becker, 2004). If CBRN materials are used, health literacy and the simplification of complex materials and the attack or device type must also be accounted for in the message creation (Clements-Nolle et al., 2005; Wray et al., 2004).

As terrorist crises evoke security concerns, responses to them are often scaled up to the highest level, which involves governmental actors and heads of state. Aside from supporting overall crisis management, for example, issuing warnings or facilitating cooperation and coordination, communication serves as a vehicle of leadership (Ruggiero, 2017). For example, in the case of the Christchurch attacks in 2019, New Zealand Prime Minister Jacinda Ardern explicitly refused to name the perpetrator and focused instead on the victims and narratives of solidarity and togetherness, employing symbolic communication and rituals of belonging (Valaskivi et al., 2022). Through a restorative rhetorical approach, leaders can facilitate the process of recovery, aiming to maintain or restore faith in a society's core values and beliefs, strengthen the publics' sense of security, and establish a vision for the future (Griffin-Padgett & Allison, 2010). This healing process is initiated during the response phase and continues into the post-crisis period. The media's coverage of the event plays a crucial role in determining the kind of publicity the terrorists receive; in the absence of direct experience with terrorism, people rely on indirect experience, including reports by news media, to form their opinions (Aldoory et al., 2010). Therefore, during the crisis phase, it is important to work with the media on how to implement the ethical principles of communication, including how to protect victims and their privacy and avoid stereotypes when describing the perpetrators. In addition, the use of social media in emergency responses (e.g., Simon et al., 2014) has increased the number of communicators, voices, and topics of discussion in various arenas (Frandsen & Johansen, 2017; Vos et al., 2014). Aside from democratizing and decentralizing the crisis communication process from one to many, social media has also brought along various challenges, often adding conflicting, confusing, and misleading information. In the case of the Westgate Mall terrorist attack in Kenya in 2013, Twitter was the main communication channel between the government, emergency responders, and the public and facilitated the emergency management of the event (Simon et al., 2014). However, the unregulated real-time sharing of information pertinent to a threat or attack may aid terrorists in creating their situational picture, as noted in a study on the 2008 Mumbai terrorist attack (Oh et al., 2011).

In addition, companies are often affected by terrorist attacks, thereby becoming part of the crisis response. For example, the venue that the perpetrators use may be owned by a company, as in the aftermath of the 9/11 attacks, when airline companies suffered immense losses. According to a recent study by Domschat et al. (2023), the selection of appropriate communication strategies after a terrorist attack that involved the loss of lives can protect companies from brand image loss or brand burn. Apologizing and providing compensation, irrespective of the attribution of guilt, were the preferred strategies by the publics, as shown by increases in the brand image. Issues of reputation and lost trust also threaten public organizations if they fail to address the needs of terrorist attack victims. However, a study of the government's crisis response following the Brussels terrorist attacks in March 2016 – a response that applied a communication strategy that sought to address and alleviate the anxiety and stress levels of the entire population exposed to the attack – demonstrated how these organizations' priority is to address the concerns of the directly and indirectly affected public (Marynissen & Lauder, 2019). The study also favored the use of a contingent approach to crisis communication over pre-defined communication strategies. In a similar vein, a study on crisis communication strategy-making – based on a tabletop exercise that involves a scenario of an anthrax attack – concluded that deciding on communication actions during a terrorist crisis is an ongoing, adaptive process (Ruggiero, 2016). This process occurs through continuous monitoring of the situation in concert with interpreting situational inputs for communication strategy choices, and balancing contingent approaches with the tools and resources defined in the preparedness plans.

Recovery

In the post-crisis phase, crisis communication aims to facilitate recovery of the directly and indirectly affected public. Once acute operational needs have been met, the primary focus is shifted to the intangible effects of the terrorist attack. This process of recovery entails the evaluation of lessons learned from the crisis management network and among the affected community. Here, a key question is how crisis communication can support resilient recovery in the form of a bouncing-forward capability – that is, growing stronger instead of merely bouncing back. Tools for reflection and learning after a crisis can facilitate this process, with examples like the crisis communication scorecard for crises caused by terrorism (Ruggiero et al., 2015). The more inclusive the process and the more it involves open public discourse while addressing the needs of the entire community of directly and indirectly affected stakeholders, the more holistic the recovery will likely be. One strategy developed to meet these goals is based on a discourse that emphasizes renewal and growth through stakeholder commitment and re-establishing core values relevant to the affected community (Ulmer & Sellnow, 2002). Likewise, the role of NGOs and local municipalities in offering psycho-social support and care is significant (Stene et al., 2022).

Key to understanding stakeholder needs and developing appropriate communication strategies to meet these needs post-attack is the continuous monitoring of risk perceptions, information needs, emotions, and evolutions of the debate in issue arenas (Vos et al., 2014). The type of attack and device used defines the nature of the crisis and its duration, including its recovery phase. An attack conducted with CBRN materials could, for example, have long-lasting effects, with an extended recovery phase wherein victims would require information about when it is safe to return to contaminated areas (Sheppard, 2011). Accordingly, a comprehensive strategy covering emergency response while extending to long-term health care, risk communication, research, and economic assistance may be needed for such crises (Hyams et al., 2002). Continued attention to ethical principles, including victim privacy and the avoidance of stereotypes when communicating the results of criminal investigations about perpetrators and their backgrounds, is vital to avoid fueling social discourses that promote otherness, hate speech, or discrimination.

Important questions for the leadership to address in public communication are those involving responsibility. For example, although there is typically no single entity that can be held accountable beyond the terrorists themselves in a terrorist crisis, several factors must be addressed, including the potential systemic failures that enabled the attack, the success or failure of the emergency response, and countermeasures to prevent similar risks from manifesting themselves in the future. Although most people tend to be willing to forget a crisis and move forward as soon as the acute phase is over, continuous support and empathy via post-crisis communication to all affected parties is needed to ensure psychological recovery and avoid anyone being left behind during recovery. This process requires channels for dialogue and participation for people to express their concerns and needs, participate in recovery efforts, and gain control over their own lives and the future of their community (e.g., Ruggiero et al., 2015).

Concluding Remarks

Government officials, journalists, and crisis experts alike are prone to thinking that people will likely panic in response to terrorist attacks (Pearce et al., 2019; Ruggiero & Vos, 2015; Sheppard et al., 2006). However, research shows that although people may act differently from what is considered rational from an expert point of view, most of the time, people act to the best of their knowledge during terrorist crises. Thus, in actual terrorist crises, although fear, anxiety, and stress levels are expected to be high, panic is rare (Sheppard et al., 2006). The difference between the former emotions and panic is important, as "panic implies the adoption of selfish, irrational behaviour," while the others do not (Pearce et al., 2019, p. 1676). The misleading belief of a panic-prone public may, therefore, be counterproductive, potentially directing emergency planning efforts in ways that continue to neglect citizen involvement and participation. It is even more contradictory in light of the evidence that most mistakes during crisis responses arise from problems and difficulties in management, such as poor coordination, obstacles in the information exchange, or clashing organizational cultures and silo-thinking (Quarantelli, 1988).

Involving the publics in risk and crisis communication about terrorism can be considered an ethical approach – indeed, it is grounded in the ethical principles of empowerment, participation, pluralism, collectivism, and civic responsibility (Deetz, 1992; Ruggiero, 2017; Seeger et al., 2009; Veil et al., 2008). By contrast, abstaining from risk communication and public education campaigns concerned with creating an unnecessary state of alarm among the publics may contribute to a lack of societal preparedness. Finally, propagating a lack of information and actionable advice for how to protect oneself and others in terrorist scenarios would mean that terrorism risks continue to be unknown, uncontrollable, and thus feared – at the cost of societal resilience.

Despite the growing research interest in crisis communication in the context of terrorism in the period after the 9/11 terrorist attacks (see Ruggiero & Vos, 2013), Hargie and Irving's (2016) conclusion in the previous edition of this book remains valid today: theory is still under-developed, and crisis communication theory specific to terrorism requires advancement (see also Falkheimer, 2014; Ruggiero, 2017; Schmid, 2011; Sparks et al., 2005). As terrorism is a complex crisis type, a multidisciplinary theory basis combining insights from terrorism studies, media research, psychology, and behavioral sciences would be beneficial. Furthermore, terrorism is an international threat that thrives on globalization and open communications, so the international dimension of crisis communication should be considered, and more insights and research are needed on cultural issues and intercultural communication. Although there are some examples of research that have focused on non-Western contexts (e.g., Musoma, 2021; Oh et al., 2011; Simon et al., 2014), more research is needed in different countries and cultural contexts in line with the CTS approach to tackle the Western bias that characterizes the field (Achieng et al., 2023). Indeed, as shown by the Global Terrorism Database, most terrorist attacks occur in non-western countries (GDT, 2023). As terrorism is a concept charged with value-related issues and intertwined in the discourse about politics, power, and international relations, ethical issues are also key to crisis communication in the context of terrorism, and this topic warrants further research.

The overall number of reported terrorist incidents has decreased worldwide in recent years (GDT, 2023). Similarly, the public concern for the topic in the EU has declined in favor of other current issues, such as international security and climate change. This is a notable change compared to 2017 when terrorism shared the leading spot with immigration as a top perceived risk for the EU (European Union, 2023). However, researchers can benefit from studying the topic further. In an era of hybrid threats with unpredictable state and non-state actors, and ideological identifications and affiliations rising, crisis communication research in the context of terrorism may offer insights for the broader crisis communication research too. Crisis communication in complex crises, which terrorism is an example of, needs to account for multiple layers of complexities, including emerging multi-actor response networks, the dynamic evolving situation, inter-acting unpredictable events, high levels of uncertainty, multiple risks, and unpredictable response along with heightened fear levels among publics. What that means across various dimensions merits further research. One such area of inquiry spans crisis communicators' skills and competencies, such as the ability to improvise and implement flexible decision-making or processes of communication strategy-making and distributed sense-making in the response network. In practice, preparedness for the most complex scenarios can also enhance preparedness and resilience for the less severe events.

Acknowledgments

This paper has been supported by funding from the European Union's Horizon 2020 research and innovation program under grant agreement number 101021746, as well as funding from the Research Council of Finland's special funding for research into crisis preparedness and security of supply 2020 under funding decision number 339931.

References

Abbas, T. (2021). Reflection: The "war on terror", Islamophobia and radicalisation twenty years on. *Critical Studies on Terrorism, 14*(4), 402–404. http://doi.org/10.1080/17539153.2021.1980182

Achieng, S., Oando, S., & Jackson, R. (2023). Critical terrorism studies. In L. A. Frumkin, J. F. Morrison, & A. Silke, Eds., *A Research Agenda for Terrorism Studies* (pp. 63–77). Elgar.

Adkins, G. L. (2010). Organizational networks in disaster response: An examination of the US government network's efforts in Hurricane Katrina. In W. T. Coombs, & S. J. Holladay, Eds., *Handbook of Crisis Communication* (pp. 93–114). Wiley-Blackwell. https://doi.org/10.1002/9781444314885.ch4

Aldoory, L., Kim, J.-N., & Tindall, N. (2010). The influence of perceived shared risk in crisis communication: Elaborating the situational theory of publics. *Public Relations Review, 36*(2), 134–140. https://doi.org/10.1016/j.pubrev.2009.12.002

Baele, S. J., Sterck, O. C., Slingeneyer, T., & Lits, G. P. (2019). What does the "terrorist" label really do? Measuring and explaining the effects of the "terrorist" and "Islamist" categories. *Studies in Conflict & Terrorism, 42*(5), 520–540. https://doi.org/10.1080/1057610X.2017.1393902

Beck, U. (2002). The terrorist threat: World risk society revisited. *Theory, Culture and Society, 19*(4), 39–55. https://doi.org/10.1177/0263276402019004003

Becker, S. M. (2004). Emergency communication and information issues in terrorist events involving radioactive materials. *Biosecurity and Bioterrorism: Biodefense Strategy, Practice and Science, 2*(3), 195–207. https://doi.org/10.1089/bsp.2004.2.195

Betus, A. E., Kearns, E. M., & Lemieux, A. F. (2021). How perpetrator identity (sometimes) influences media framing attacks as "terrorism" or "mental illness". *Communication Research, 48*(8), 1133–1156. https://doi.org/10.1177/009365022097114

Bjørgo, T., & Ravndal, J. A. (2019). *Extreme-right violence and terrorism: Concepts, patterns, and responses.* ICCT Policy Brief. Retrieved December 12, 2023 from https://www.icct.nl/publication/extreme-right-violence-and-terrorism-concepts-patterns-and-responses

Blanchard, J. C., Haywood, Y., Stein, B. D., & Tanielian, T. L. (2005). In their own words: Lessons learned from those exposed to anthrax. *American Journal of Public Health, 95*(3), 489–495.

Boin, A., & t' Hart, P. (2007). The crisis approach. In H. Rodríguez, E. L. Quarantelli, & R. R. Dynes, Eds., *Handbook of Disaster Research. Handbooks of Sociology and Social Research* (pp. 42–54). New York: Springer.

Boin, A., t' Hart, P., Stern, E., & Sundelius, B. (2005). *The Politics of Crisis Management, Public Leadership Under Pressure.* Cambridge University Press.

Borelli, M. (2023). Social media corporations as actors of counter-terrorism. *New Media & Society, 25*(11), 2877–2897. https://doi.org/10.1177/14614448211035121

Botan, C. H., & Taylor, M. (2004). Public relations: State of the field. *Journal of Communication, 54*(4), 645–661. https://doi.org/10.1111/j.1460-2466.2004.tb02649.x

Bye, R. J., Almklov, P., Antonsen, S., Nyheim, O. M., Aalberg, A. L., & Johnsen, S. O. (2019). The institutional context of crisis. A study of the police response during the 22 July terror attacks in Norway. *Safety Science, 111*, 67–79. https://doi.org/10.1016/j.ssci.2018.09.011

Christensen, T., Lægreid, P., & Rykkja, L. H. (2015). The challenges of coordination in national security management – The case of the terrorist attack in Norway. *International Review of Administrative Sciences, 81*(2), 352–372. https://doi.org/10.1177/0020852314564307

Clements-Nolle, K., Ballard-Reisch, D. S., Todd, R. L., & Jenkins, T. (2005). Nevada's Academic-Practice Collaboration: Public health preparedness possibilities outside an academic center. *Public Health Reports, 120*(1), 100–108. https://doi.org/10.1177/00333549051200S1

Coombs, W. T. (2015). *Ongoing Crisis Communication: Planning, Managing, and Responding* (4th ed.). SAGE.

Cui, X., & Rothenbuhler, E. (2018). Communicating terror. Mediatization and ritualization. *Television and New Media, 19*(2), 155–162. https://doi.org/10.1177/1527476417715685

Curtis, C. A. (2018). Organizational networks in times of crisis: Lessons from Katrina. *Journal of Contingencies & Crisis Management, 26*(2), 202–211. https://doi.org/10.1111/1468-5973.12138

Deetz, S. (1992). *Democracy in an Age of Corporate Colonization: Developments in Communication and the Politics of Everyday Life.* State University of New York Press.

DiGiovanni, C. J. (2003). The spectrum of human reactions to terrorist attacks with weapons of mass destruction: Early management considerations. *Prehospital and Disaster Medicine, 18*(3), 253–257. https://doi.org/10.1017/S1049023X00001138

Domschat, L., Stephens, M., & Saeed, H. (2023). Communication to protect brand image during a terrorism crisis: Application of situational crisis communication theory. *Journal of Contingencies and Crisis Management, 31*(4), 913–927. https://doi.org/10.1111/1468-5973.12489

EU Directive 2017/541. (2017). *Directive (EU) 2017/541 of the European Parliament and of the Council of 15 March 2017 on combating terrorism and replacing Council Framework Decision 2002/475/JHA and amending Council Decision 2005/671/JHA.* Retrieved December 12, 2023 from https://eur-lex.europa.eu/legal-content/EN/TXT/?uri=celex%3A32017L0541

European Union. (2023). *Eurobarometer. All surveys.* Retrieved December 12, 2023 from https://europa.eu/eurobarometer/surveys/browse/all/series/4961

Falkheimer, J. (2014). Crisis communication and terrorism: The Norway attacks on 22 July 2011. *Corporate Communications: An International Journal, 19*(1), 52–63. https://doi.org/10.1108/CCIJ-08-2012-0053

Falkheimer, J., & Heide, M. (2010). Crisis communicators in change: From plans to improvisations. In W. T. Coombs, & S. J. Holladay, Eds., *Handbook of Crisis Communication* (pp. 511–526). Wiley. https://doi.org/10.1002/9781444314885.ch25

Finnish Ministry of Interior. (2022). *National counter-terrorism strategy 2022–2025.* Publications of the Ministry of the Interior (2022:38), Ministry of the Interior. Retrieved November 27, 2023 from https://urn.fi/URN:ISBN:978-952-324-578-5

Fischhoff, B. (2011). Communicating about the risks of terrorism (or anything else). *American Psychologist, 66*(6), 520–531. https://doi.org/10.1037/a0024570

Fletcher, G. (2006). The indefinable concept of terrorism. *Journal of International Criminal Justice, 4*(5), 1–14. https://doi.org/10.1093/jicj/mql060

Frandsen, F., & Johansen, W. (2017). *Organisational Crisis Communication.* SAGE. https://doi.org/10.1515/commun-2018-2010

Freilich, J. D., Chermak, S. M., & Gruenewald, J. (2015). The future of terrorism research: A review essay. *International Journal of Comparative and Applied Criminal Justice, 39*(4), 353–369. https://doi.org/10.1080/01924036.2014.922321

Gardell, M. (2018). Urban terror: The case of lone wolf Peter Mangs. *Terrorism and Political Violence, 30*(5), 793–811. https://doi.org/10.1080/09546553.2018.1444796

GDT. (2023). *Global terrorism database.* Retrieved December 12, 2023 from https://www.start.umd.edu/gtd/

Gilpin, D. R., & Murphy, P. (2010). Complexity and crises: A new paradigm. In W. T. Coombs, & S. J. Holladay, Eds., *The Handbook of Crisis Communication* (pp. 683–690). Wiley-Blackwell. https://doi.org/10.1002/9781444314885.ch34

Gray, G. M., & Ropeik, D. P. (2002). Dealing with the dangers of fear: The role of risk communication. *Health Affairs, 21*(6), 106–116. https://doi.org/10.1377/hlthaff.21.6.106

Griffin-Padgett, D. R., & Allison, D. (2010). Making a case for restorative rhetoric: Mayor Rudolph Giuliani & Mayor Ray Nagin's response to disaster. *Communication Monographs, 77*(3), 376–392. DOI: 10.1080/03637751.2010.502536.

Haghani, M., Kuligowski, E., Rajabifard, A., & Lentini, P. (2022). Fifty years of scholarly research on terrorism: Intellectual progression, structural composition, trends and knowledge gaps of the field. *International Journal of Disaster Risk Reduction, 68.* https://doi.org/10.1016/j.ijdrr.2021.102714

Hargie, O., & Irving, P. (2016). Crisis communication and terrorist attacks. In A. Schwarz, C. Auer, & M. W. Seeger, Eds., *Handbook of International Crisis Communication Research* (pp. 85–95). Wiley. https://doi.org/10.1002/9781118516812.ch9

Hartleb, F. (2020). *Lone Wolves. The New Terrorism of Right-Wing Single Actors*. Springer. https://doi.org/10.1007/978-3-030-36153-2_1

Hu, Q., Yeo, J., & Kapucu, N. (2022). A systematic review of empirical emergency management network research: Formation and development, properties, and performance. *The American Review of Public Administration, 52*(4), 280–297. https://doi.org/10.1177/02750740221077348

Hyams, K. C., Murphy, F. M., & Wessely, S. (2002). Responding to chemical, biological, or nuclear terrorism: The indirect and long-term health effects may present the greatest challenge. *Journal of Health Politics, Policy and Law, 27*(2), 273–291. https://doi.org/10.1215/03616878-27-2-273

Jahn, J. L. S., & Johansson, C. (2018). The communicative constitution of adaptive capacity during Sweden's Västmanland wildfire. *Corporate Communications: An International Journal, 23*(2), 162–179. https://doi.org/10.1108/CCIJ-04-2017-0031

Kouri, G. D., & Tziaferi, S. G. (2016). Case study: Paris terrorist attack November 2015, crisis management and the role of media. *International Journal of Occupational Health and Public Health Nursing, 3*(2), 31–43.

Mäkelä, J. (2007). *CBRNE-terrorismi: Turhaa pelottelua vai varteenotettava riski?* National Defence University, Department of Strategic and Defence Studies, series 4(21). Edita Prima. https://urn.fi/URN:NBN:fi-fe201201241140

Malkki, L. (2020). *Mitä tiedämme terrorismista*. Otava.

Marynissen, H., & Lauder, M. (2019). Stakeholder-focused communication strategy during crisis: a case study based on the brussels terror attacks. *International Journal of Business Communication. 57*(2), 176–193. https://doi.org/10.1177/2329488419882736

Meisels, T. (2009). Defining terrorism – A typology. *Critical Review of International Social and Political Philosophy, 12*(3), 331–351. https://doi.org/10.1080/13698230903127853

Musoma, A. L. (2021). Multi agency response to international terrorism in Kenya: A comparison of Dusit D2 and Westgate terror attack. *African Journal of Empirical Research, 2*(1), 68–84. https://doi.org/10.51867/ajer.v2i2.23

Nacos, B. (2016). *Terrorism and Counterterrorism* (4th ed.). Routledge.

Norris, J. J. (2020). When (and where) can right-wing terrorists be charged with terrorism? *Critical Studies on Terrorism, 13*(4), 519–544. https://doi.org/10.1080/17539153.2020.1810991

Oh, O., Agrawal, M., & Rao, H. R. (2011). Information control and terrorism: Tracking the Mumbai terrorist attack through twitter. *Information Systems Frontiers, 13*, 33–43. https://doi.org/10.1007/s10796-010-9275-8

Palttala, P., & Vos, M. (2012). Quality indicators for crisis communication to support emergency management by public authorities. *Journal of Contingencies & Crisis Management, 20*(1), 39–51. https://doi.org/10.1111/j.1468-5973.2011.00654.x

Pearce, J. M., Lindekilde, L., Parker, D., & Rogers, M. B. (2019). Communicating with the public about marauding terrorist firearms attacks: Results from a survey experiment on factors influencing intention to "run, hide, tell" in the United Kingdom and denmark. *Risk Analysis, 39*(8), 1675–1694. https://doi.org/10.1111/risa.13301

Quarantelli, E. L. (1988). Disaster crisis management: A summary of research findings. *Journal of Management Studies, 25*(4), 373–385. https://doi.org/10.1111/j.1467-6486.1988.tb00043.x

Reynolds, B., & Seeger, M. W. (2005). Crisis and emergency risk communication as an integrative model. *Journal of Health Communication, 10*(1), 43–55. https://doi.org/10.1080/10810730590904571

Rogers, M. B., Amlôt, R., Rubin, G. J., Wessely, S., & Krieger, K. (2007). Mediating the social and psychological impacts of terrorist attacks: The role of risk perception and risk communication. *International Review of Psychiatry, 19*(3), 279–288. https://doi.org/10.1080/09540260701349373

Rubin, G. J., Amlôt, R., & Page, L. (2011). The London polonium incident: Lessons in risk communications. *Health Physics, 101*(5), 545–550. https://doi.org/10.1097/HP.0b013e3182259a61

Ruggiero, A. (2016). Making communication strategy choices in a fast-evolving crisis situation – Results from a table-top discussion on an anthrax scenario. *Social Sciences, 5*(2), 19. https://doi.org/10.3390/socsci5020019

Ruggiero, A. (2017). *Crisis communication and terrorism. Mapping challenges and co-creating solutions* (Jyväskylä Studies in Humanities 324) [Doctoral dissertation, University of Jyväskylä]. http://urn.fi/URN:ISBN:978-951-39-7172-4

Ruggiero, A., & Vos, M. (2013). Terrorism communication: Characteristics and emerging perspectives in the scientific literature 2002–2011. *Journal of Contingencies & Crisis Management*, *21*(3), 153–166. https://doi.org/10.1111/1468-5973.12022

Ruggiero, A., & Vos, M. (2014). Social media monitoring for crisis communication: Process, methods and trends in the scientific literature. *Online Journal of Communication and Media Technologies*, *4*(1), 105–130. https://doi.org/10.29333/ojcmt/2457

Ruggiero, A., & Vos, M. (2015). Communication challenges in CBRN terrorism crises: Expert perceptions. *Journal of Contingencies & Crisis Management*, *23*(3), 138–148. https://doi.org/10.1111/1468-5973.12065

Ruggiero, A., Vos, M., & Palttala, P. (2015). The CBRN communication scorecard. In S. Schmidt, & M. Vos, Eds., *Behavior and Communication in CBRN Crises – Findings and Recommendations in Case of Chemical, Biological, Radiological, and Nuclear Attacks on Society* (pp. 106–139). Pabst Science.

Schmid, A. P. (2011). 50 un- and under-researched topics in the field of (counter-) terrorism studies. *Perspectives on Terrorism*, *5*(1), 76–78. https://www.jstor.org/stable/26298505

Scott, R., & Nowell, B. (2020). Networks and Crisis Management. *Oxford Research Encyclopedias*. https://doi.org/10.1093/acrefore/9780190228637.013.1650

Seeger, M. W., Sellnow, T. L., Ulmer, R. R., & Novak, J. M. (2009). Applied communication ethics: A summary and critique of research literature. In L. R. Frey, & K. N. Cissna, Eds., *Routledge Handbook of Applied Communication Research* (pp. 280–306). Routledge.

Sellnow, T. L., & Seeger, M. W. (2013). *Theorizing Crisis Communication. Foundations of Communication Theory*. Wiley-Blackwell.

Sellnow, D. D., Lane, D. R., Sellnow, T. R., & Littlefield, R. S. (2017). The IDEA model as a best practice for effective instructional risk and crisis communication. *Communication Studies*, *68*(5), 552–567. https://doi.org/10.1080/10510974.2017.1375535

Sheppard, B. (2011). Mitigating terror and avoidance behavior through the risk perception matrix to augment resilience. *Journal of Homeland Security and Emergency Management*, *8*(1), 26. https://doi.org/10.2202/1547-7355.1840

Sheppard, B., Rubin, G. J., Wardman, J. K., & Wessely, S. (2006). Viewpoint: Terrorism and dispelling the myth of a panic prone public. *Journal of Public Health Policy*, *27*(3), 219–245. https://doi.org/10.1057/palgrave.jphp.3200083

Simon, T., Goldberg, A., Aharonson-Daniel, L., Leykin, D., & Adini, B. (2014). Twitter in the cross fire – The use of social media in the Westgate Mall terror attack in Kenya. *PLoS One*, *9*(8), e104136. https://doi.org/10.1371/journal.pone.0104136

Skryabina, E. A., Betts, N., Reedy, G., Riley, P., & Amlôt, R. (2020). The role of emergency preparedness exercises in the response to a mass casualty terrorist incident: A mixed methods study. *International Journal of Disaster Risk Reduction*, *46*. https://doi.org/10.1016/j.ijdrr.2020.101503

Slovic, P. (2002). Terrorism as hazard: A new species of trouble. *Risk Analysis*, *22*(3), 425–426.

Sparks, L., Kreps, G. L., Botan, C., & Rowan, K. E. (2005). Responding to terrorism: Translating communication research into practice. *Communication Research Reports*, *22*(1), 1–5. https://doi.org/10.1080/0882409052000343462

Spence, P. R., Lachlan, K. A., Westerman, D., Lin, X., Harris, C. J., Sellnow, T. L., & Sellnow-Richmond, D. D. (2017). Exemplification effects: Responses to perceptions of risk. *Journal of Risk Research*, *20*(5), 590–610. https://doi.org/10.1080/13669877.2015.1100658

Stene, L. E., Vuillermoz, C., Overmeire, R. V. et al. (2022). Psychosocial care responses to terrorist attacks: A country case study of Norway, France and Belgium. *BMC Health Services Research*, *22*(390). https://doi.org/10.1186/s12913-022-07691-2

Stevens, G., Agho, K., Taylor, M., Barr, M., Raphael, B., & Jorm, L. (2009). Terrorism in Australia: Factors associated with perceived threat and incident-critical behaviours. *BMC Public Health*, *9*(91), 1–9. https://doi.org/10.1186/1471-2458-9-91

Sumiala, J., Valaskivi, K., Tikka, M., & Huhtamäki, J. (2018). *Hybrid Media Events. The Charlie Hebdo Attacks and Global Circulation of Terrorist Violence*. Emerald.

TE-SAT (2023). *European Union terrorism situation and trend report 2023.* https://www.europol.europa.eu/cms/sites/default/files/documents/European%20Union%20Terrorism%20Situation%20and%20Trend%20report%202023.pdf (accessed December 12, 2023)

Tikka, M., Sumiala, J., Harju, A. & Valaskivi, K. (2020). Weaponization of liveness: How live streaming activates hybrid media events of extreme violence. *Selected Papers of Internet Research.* Paper presented at AoIR 2020: The 21st Annual Conference of the Association of Internet Researchers. Virtual Event: AoIR. https://spir.aoir.org/ojs/index.php/spir/article/view/11349/9918 (accessed December 12, 2023)

Tikka, M., Ahsanullah, R., Varanasi, U., Härmä, V., Sawhney, N., & Leinonen, T. (2023). Contextual inquiry of affordances for collaboration in crises. Lessons from the Finnish context. In J. Radianti, I. Dokas, N. Lalone, & D. Khazanchi, Eds., *Proceedings from the 20th International ISCRAM Conference* (pp. 33–42). University of Nebraska at Omaha. http://dx.doi.org/10.59297/FCIG6875

Ulmer, R. R., & Sellnow, T. L. (2002). Crisis management and the discourse of renewal: Understanding the potential for positive outcomes of crisis. *Public Relations Review, 28*(4), 361–365. https://doi.org/10.1016/S0363-8111(02)00165-0

Valaskivi, K., Sumiala, J., & Tikka, M. (2022). Ambivalent rituals of belonging: (Re)theorising hybrid, violent media events. *Nordic Journal of Media Studies, 4*(1), 81–98. https://doi.org/10.2478/njms-2022-0005

Veil, S., Reynolds, B., Sellnow, T. L., & Seeger, M. W. (2008). CERC as a theoretical framework for research and practice. *Health Promotion Practice, 9*(4 suppl), 26S–34S. https://doi.org/10.1177/1524839908322113

Vos, M., Schoemaker, H., & Luoma-aho, V. L. (2014). Setting the agenda for research on issue arenas. *Corporate Communications, 19*(2), 200–215. https://doi.org/10.1108/CCIJ-08-2012-0055

Walzer, M. (1977). *Just and Unjust Wars.* Basic Books.

Weick, K. E. (1993). The collapse of sensemaking in organizations: The Mann Gulch disaster. *Administrative Science Quarterly, 38*(4), 628–652.

Wolbers, J. (2022). Understanding distributed sensemaking in crisis management: The case of the Utrecht terrorist attack. *Journal of Contingencies & Crisis Management, 30*(4), 401–411. DOI: 10.1111/1468-5973.12382.

Wood, M. M., Mileti, D. S., Kano, M., Kelley, M. M., Regan, R., & Bourque, L. B. (2012). Communicating actionable risk for terrorism and other hazards. *Risk Analysis, 32*(4), 601–615. https://doi.org/10.1111/j.1539-6924.2011.01645.x

Wray, R. J., Kreuter, M. W., Jacobson, H., Clements, B., & Evans, R. G. (2004). Theoretical perspectives on public communication preparedness for terrorist attacks. *Family & Community Health, 27*(3), 232–241.

Wray, R. J., Becker, S. M., Henderson, N., Glik, D., Jupka, K., Middleton, S., Henderson, C., Drury, A., & Mitchell, E. (2008). Communicating with the public about emerging health threats: Lessons from the pre-event message development project. *American Journal of Public Health, 98*(12), 2214–2222.

Author's Bio

Aino Ruggiero is a post-doctoral researcher at the Humanitarian Logistics and Supply Chain Research Institute, Department of Marketing, within the Hanken School of Economics in Helsinki, Finland. Focusing on crisis communication in the context of terrorism, she received her PhD from the University of Jyväskylä. She is currently working on the EU-funded H2020 project CORE (sCience & human factOr for Resilient sociEty). Her research focuses on governmental crisis communication, disaster risk governance, societal preparedness and resilience, and complex crises. Her work has been published in the *Journal of Contingencies and Crisis Management*, among others.

Minttu Tikka is a post-doctoral researcher in the Department of Computer Science at Aalto University in Espoo, Finland. She received her PhD from the University of Helsinki on crisis communication in the context of citizen participation. At present, she is working on the Crisis Narratives project funded by the Research Council of Finland; she has recently published articles on collaboration in crises and digital media ethnography to aid in studying violent attacks. She is a co-author of the book *Hybrid Media Events: The Charlie Hebdo Attacks and the Global Circulation of Terrorist Violence*, which was published by Emerald in 2018.

6

Paradigms of Risk and Crisis Communication and the Threat of Misinformation and Disinformation

Michael J. Palenchar[1] and Robert L. Heath[2]
[1] Tombras School of ADPR, University of Tennessee, Knoxville, TN, USA
[2] Valenti School of Communication, University of Houston, Houston, TX, USA

Risk and crisis communication has become ubiquitous, pervading and infusing various fields of scholarly research and professional practice as an increasingly important scientific component of rhetorical debates concerning health, safety, and environment among every facet of societal risk governance and individual decision-making. This line of research and practice, and understanding the foundational paradigms of both risk and crisis communication, is more important than ever. For example, the United Nations Office for Disaster Risk Reduction (UNDRR, 2022) released their Global Assessment Report on Disaster Risk Reduction (GAR2022) entitled *Our World at Risk: Transforming Governance for a Resilient Future*. They highlighted in its executive summary that "Despite progress, risk creation is outstripping risk reduction. Disasters, economic loss and the underlying vulnerabilities that drive risk, such as poverty and inequality, are increasing just as ecosystems and biospheres are at risk of collapse. Global systems are becoming more connected and therefore more vulnerable in an uncertain risk landscape" (p. 1).

By the dawn of the twentieth century, Beck (1992) had argued that modern society had become a risk society, and the work of anthropologist Mary Douglas (1992) could be used to reason that the nature of society is its organization for purposes of collective management of risk. The current versions of risk and crisis communication feature complex social relations operating within community infrastructures. Within this process, risk and crisis communication requirements are often a political response to popular demands; they are likely to be multi-vocal rather than univocal.

By the latter part of the twentieth century, both risk and crisis communication had become foundational human communication and human behavior areas of scholarly examination and professional practice. The resulting research produced several risk and crisis communication paradigms that are summarized in this chapter. This analysis builds on the theme that risks are probabilistic events that can result in various harms and benefits caused by risk creators, borne by risk bearers, and intervened by risk mitigators and arbiters (e.g., Heath & O'Hair, 2009; Palmlund, 2009). The amount of benefit or magnitude of harm is a focal point that

The Handbook of International Crisis and Risk Communication Research, Second Edition.
Edited by Andreas Schwarz, Matthew W. Seeger, and Sora Kim.

can be shared, mitigated, and judged to be fair and/or equal, or unfair and/or unequal. By the dawn of the twenty-first century, it could be argued that risk and crisis were intimately associated, and crisis could be conceptualized as the manifestation of risk.

However, risk and the manifestations of risks in crisis events are currently being bombarded by a post-truth communication environment of fake news and intentionally misleading information. A growing threat that underlies all the following discussed paradigms in this chapter is this rapidly expanding role of misinformation and disinformation in identifying and addressing risk.

According to the World Economic Forum's (2024) *Global Risks Perception Survey 2023–2024*, misinformation and disinformation emerged as the most severe global risk anticipated over the next two years, further widening societal and political divides. "The disruptive capabilities of manipulated information are rapidly accelerating, as open access to increasingly sophisticated technologies proliferates and trust in information and institutions deteriorates. In the next two years, a wide set of actors will capitalize on the boom in synthetic content, amplifying societal divisions, ideological violence and political repression – ramifications that will persist far beyond the short term" (p. 18). In addition:

> "Beyond elections, perceptions of reality are likely to also become more polarized, infiltrating the public discourse on issues ranging from public health to social justice. However, as truth is undermined, the risk of domestic propaganda and censorship will also rise in turn. In response to mis- and disinformation, governments could be increasingly empowered to control information based on what they determine to be "true." Freedoms relating to the internet, press and access to wider sources of information that are already in decline risk descending into broader repression of information flows across a wider set of countries (p. 8)."

Thus, if risk [and crises] are viewed from the lens of chance as a future outcome (Cho et al., 2015), which is generally understood to be negative, "this deceptively simple notion is interesting because it tells us that risk is an idea rather than a thing – specifically an idea about the future" (p. 65). As such, ongoing examination and critical evaluation of society's conversations about those "ideas" related to risk and crises are more important than ever, and understanding the paradigms that guide such research and practice is a critical component.

In such cases, individual and community efficacy is a key variable. In the case of risk and crisis, a central question is whether people are prepared and able to respond in ways that are responsible to other interests, whether based on valid claims or misinformation or disinformation campaigns. The various paradigms of risk and crisis communication address these core concerns and challenges from at times vastly different axiological, ontological, epistemological, and methodological orientations. With this foundation in mind, consideration can be given to the paradigms of risk and crisis communication, asking a key question: How well do risk and crisis communication research and practice affect individual self-efficacy, perceptions of personal and expert efficacy, and collective efficacy, and to what extent is that threatened by misinformation and disinformation.

Risk Communication Paradigms

While various scholars in eclectic disciplines have defined various typologies of risk communication paradigms and risk communication research orientations, this chapter collapses the past 45+ years of research into four broadly defined paradigms of risk communication: risk perception/expressed preference, mental models, critical/cultural studies, and infrastructural risk communication. Each of these research orientations is affected by all of the factors of the other three, shaped by social-amplification processes, and driven by dialogic and discursive approaches to the co-creation of meaning that currently is being discussed under the principle of deliberative democracy.

Risk Perception/Expressed Preference Paradigm

Risk perception/expressed preference is based on decades of risk perception and risk analysis research. One of the primary research lines within this paradigm is research concerning the discrepancy between scientists and policymakers' perspectives on risk as compared to potential and actual risk bearers' perceptions of, for example, environmental and technological risks. In this analysis, it features attitudinal and cognitive processes through which risks are interpreted. Analysis, especially by Vincent Covello and by Paul Slovic, addresses the perceptual patterns individuals use, idiosyncratically, in their perception and assessment of risks.

This paradigm presumes that key variables about the nature of risks as well as demographics predict levels of risk tolerance. This paradigm features concepts such as dread, unknown, involuntary, unfamiliar, uncontrollable, focused in time and space, fatal, unfair, memorable, delayed, artificial, and undetectable, and results from the work of psychologists, economists, sociologists, anthropologists, and experts on public relations and communication studies, and marketing. Typical of such research, Fischhoff et al. (1978) found that experts based their risk perspectives on probabilities of fatality, while lay people's evaluations are more based on perceived characteristics of the hazard.

Mental Models Paradigm

Integrating decision theory and behavioral research, the *mental models* approach is grounded in a sound science hegemony featuring cognitive psychology and artificial intelligence (AI). Mental modeling proposes that risk-bearers form their own interpretation of a risk event based on the construction and clarification of the information within their own cognitive framework. Successful integration of risk assessment information with existing beliefs requires creating coherent mental models that allow people to make sense of or in a way "add up" what they read and hear and how they make consistent inferences regarding bearing risks.

Morgan et al. (2002) offered one of the most insightful explanations of this paradigm. It starts with a scientific assessment of the likelihood, cause, impact, and most responsible response to risk. It uses science to presume the level of risk, the entities most likely to be benefited or harmed, and the best assessment of what should be done, by whom, and in what way to mitigate and/or prevent risk or its impact.

Risk management and communication proceeds to determine the extent to which key stakeholders agree or disagree/understand, or don't understand the risk and its causes, conditions, and best-case responses. The success of this process is grounded with "it's ability to improve the understanding of those who attend to the communications that it produces" (Morgan et al., 2002, p. 14). Thus, the compelling question in this paradigm is what must be done and said to bring the judgment of stakeholders into concurrence with that of sound science.

Critical and Cultural Paradigm

Critical and cultural scholarship, built from the origins in the Frankfurt School in the 1920s and 1930s and Western Marxism, has increased over the past three decades within risk and crisis communication. Many voices have advanced this dialogue and sought to correct the disregard for risk themes such as socioeconomic status, hegemony, and power differentials, especially historically constructed power relations.

Cultural theory, based on the work of Durkheim and Fleck among others, argues that individual's values and beliefs need to be interpreted and given voice in the social contexts of various risks; the social constructions of culture have a strong influence on cognition. For risk, this can include rituals related to sensemaking and how social classifications impose order on the complexity of risk and crisis and enable collective social action.

Douglas (1992), Beck (1992), and Rayner (e.g., Tansey & Raymer, 2009) have argued that people's perceptions and value judgments cannot be slighted in the assessment, management, and communication of risk. At the heart of such battles is the right of scientists (however soundly and wisely) to exclusively or even predominantly determine levels of risk, best-case scenarios for mitigation and management, and the private and public policy that derive from scientific analysis. Critical studies presume that legitimization is provided by civil society; political institutions (an industry is political) must judge policies and actions to be rational insofar as they align with social norms (Habermas, 1976). Habermas' ideal, the public aspect of civil society, asks that issues such as acceptable risk and responsible actions be determined by open discourse free of strategic intent and narrow self-interest; thus risk decisions should be collaboratively negotiated.

Infrastructural Risk Communication Paradigm

Infrastructural risk communication works to incorporate the best of the other paradigms. It is dialogic and discursive and presumes the need for effective decision-making institutions and co-created meanings that arise from risk democracy. In association with various experts and policymakers, individual voices of risk bearers must be brought together to create systems and shared perspectives that appropriately assess, mitigate, and respond to risks that may be unevenly borne throughout any community or larger society. This paradigm posits that individual and community efficacy are principal loci for examining and ascertaining whether a community's risk infrastructure is suitably systematized to plan and communicate about various risks in ways that make it resilient.

Risk assessors and communicators realize that each key public makes an idiosyncratic response to each risk based on its unique decision heuristic (Palenchar et al., 2011), including its value set. A fully functioning society is aware of risk and does its best to be aware of, assess, and discuss important matters as it develops plans tailored to particular risk-bearing communities and their individual and group unique risk decision heuristics (2011). This view, including Kasperson's social amplification of risk theory, reasons that structures, functions, and discursive strategies can and must lead to community assessments of risk and crisis based on expert opinions and individual senses of efficacy (see also Heath & Palenchar, 2009).

Collaborative processes are made real, as are the social constructions that arise from them, as organizations enact community right to know as means by which they are variously transparent on matters of risk and crisis. Media of various kinds, including social media, are important channels/contexts in which information is shared, knowledge is formed, and enlightened choices are achieved. Similarly, there are many structures and functions devoted to risk collaborative decision-making: meetings, hearings, conferences, structured debate (legislative, administrative, and judicial), protests, and boycotts. Thus, the challenge of risk management is to help individuals and communities to be resilient in the face of risk.

Crisis Communication Paradigms

Early crisis communication paradigms emphasized source-based explanations aimed at reputation and image management and repair. They included the classic paradigm of apologia, a complex of discourse options by which atonement is championed as a resource for recovery. From this organization as an agency approach, and similar to risk communication, crisis communication has moved more toward a collaborative perspective based on relationships and socially-constructed meanings of crisis generators, arbiters, and bearers to address crisis mitigation. One view sees the preferred outcome of crisis response as a successful return of communities and businesses, whereas another view focuses on lessons learned and cultural understandings and change management to mitigate the health, safety, and environmental damages of future crisis events.

If crises are manifested risks, then organizations can be evaluated by the quality of their risk management, which can aid in preventing a crisis or in understanding the conditions and preparation requirements to reduce its impact. Societal thoughtfulness depends on the amount and type of communication engagement with various stakeholders, including often-ignored, marginalized publics. In this discussion, vast amounts of global research into crisis situations can be roughly organized, though with considerable overlap, into two paradigms of crisis communication: restorative/status-quo and transformative/change-growth-oriented.

Restorative/Status-Quo Crisis Communication

Restorative/status-quo crisis communication is concerned with managing organizational, and most often corporate, reputation during a crisis; ostensibly ensuring business continuity. This research perspective is concerned about mitigating the risks associated with crises, including managing the health, safety, and environmental impacts of the crisis event, including loss of life. It includes building crisis communication plans, conducting environmental scanning, and being as fully prepared to communicate through all available media during a crisis event to manage the return to normalcy of business operations, organizational culture, and reputation; the major test of such strategies can be as instrumental as the uninterrupted purchasing of products and services while also limiting regulatory and policy interventions in the aftermath of a poorly managed crisis.

At the same time, the traditional categorization of crisis communication theories and models follows an assumed crisis stage pattern of pre-crisis, crisis event, and post-crisis, upon which much of the literature has developed. Within this structure, theories of communication related to crisis development and warning dominate the pre-crisis focus, which include failures of communication associated with the onset of the crisis event and warnings, including evacuations, that are central tools in limiting harm. Theories of communication related to mediated crises, emergency response, influence communication research, and crisis outcomes dominate the crisis event literature, including efforts to characterize and explain the role of mass communication, including social media, during a crisis event.

Advocates of this paradigm recommend that crisis responders know how various processes, before, during, and after a crisis, can affect how it plays out (Heath, 2010). According to Heath, one of the key challenges is to provide insights that can be applied effectively and ethically under pressures of limited time and severe scrutiny of the organization's legitimacy.

Transformative/Change-Growth Oriented Crisis Communication

Theories of communication related to the broader issues of influence, ethics, and community/organizational change management include persuasion and rhetorical approaches to dialogue and discursiveness. They are centrally interested in the social constructions surrounding questions of good and bad, fairness and equity, and the role power plays in discourse and resource management.

Cultural and critical perspectives dwell on issues of legitimacy, renewal, lessons learned, and organizational change needed to better manage risks. Theories related to organizational change, sensemaking, and organizational legitimacy related to crisis outcomes that make society more fully functioning are transformative paradigms. In this regard, one can think in terms of the discourse of renewal, chaos theory and emergent self-organization, complexity theory, and communication and community resilience.

Such discourse resources investigate the wisdom of wanting to maintain the status quo. It examines corporate social responsibility, the concept of responsible communication and right to know, and the exploration into significant choices provoked by the ethics of each caring community. Presuming the need for change management, it can envision the advantage of better ways to manage the health, safety, and environmental implications of crisis events.

As content and theme, it offers insights that help to better understand the crisis response infrastructure. As such, it can presume that an organization is not the only entity that is suffering crisis. In fact, "that" crisis really creates and is defined by the crises that other entities in a community are experiencing. Change rather than restoration may be required.

Most empirical studies within the crisis communication field focus on communication as it is practiced within Western liberal democratic societies and is the dominant interest of the restorative/status-quo crisis communication paradigm of crisis communication (previously explained). However, many scholars from the transformative/change-growth oriented crisis communication perspective argue that such empirical studies have become a hegemonic influence on attempts within the academy to theorize crisis communication. Critical crisis communication scholars, as well as risk communication scholars, as noted in the previous section, question whether the theory building and ensuing crisis communication models, developed in these dominantly studied contexts and societies have an application to the far more numerous other countries and cultures, as well as study about related power resources in relationship to crisis recovery and renewal.

Misinformation and Disinformation in the Social Construction of Risk and Crisis Communication

The profound advancement of both the research domain and practical application of risk and crisis communication has been one of the most crucial expansions of communication science in the past 40+ years (Palenchar & Heath, 2024). However, this advancement is being thwarted by post-truth, fake news, and individual and organized group disinformation and misinformation efforts and campaigns. Whether it takes place in text-based narratives or deep fake videos and/or through AI-generated content, "one of the hallmarks of post-truth politics is the level of heated emotion and sheer noise it produces. This noise sucks audience time and attention, making fake news a highly effective form of misdirection in today's public sphere. It helps to enforce our silence by redirecting public attention away from controversial issues" (Bourne & Edwards, 2021, p. 605).

Numerous contemporary events have changed how risk discourse is conducted and covered by social and legacy media, interpreted by potential risk bearers, and advanced by various interests, including: the 9/11 truth movement, or "truthers," gun lobbies that discredit data on gun violence, anti-vaccination movements citing disproved research, and the 2021 U.S. Capital uprising conspiracies. These events, among many others, demonstrate how misinformation plays an increasingly large and problematic role in the political and social discourse surrounding risk events in the United States and throughout the world. Elizabeth Williamson, former New York Times editorial board member, in her book ***An American Tragedy and the Battle for the Truth*** "argues, in a narrative fueled by moral indignation, that Sandy Hook set our society into the land of 'alternative facts' four years before Kellyanne Conway coined that phrase" (Kolker, 2022, para. 3).

Currently, anyone from state-backed propagandists to trolls can access AI technologies to create deep fake videos (Schwartz, 2018). AI technologies can alter what a speaker says in an existing video, combine two disparate videos, or create artificial video material from scratch. Easy-to-use interfaces to large-scale AI models have already enabled an explosion in falsified information and so-called "synthetic" content, from sophisticated voice cloning to counterfeit websites (World Economic Forum, 2024).

To combat growing risks, governments are beginning to roll out new and evolving regulations to target both hosts and creators of online disinformation and illegal content (Breton, 2023). Nascent regulation of generative AI will likely complement these efforts. For example, requirements in China to watermark AI-generated content may help identify false information, including unintentional misinformation through AI hallucinated content (Huw & Hine, 2023). Generally, however, the speed and effectiveness of regulation is unlikely to match the pace of development (World Economic Forum, 2024). Disinformation, such as deep fake video, can thus skew information and manipulate beliefs, creating wider chasms between communities and between the powerful and the marginalized (Schwartz, 2018).

The UNDRR (2022) report specifically discussed the challenges and advancements of risk communication related to misinformation. "Misinformation and anti-vaccination campaigns reduced trust in public health measures, but there were also many effective scientific communicators in the media and successful collaborations focusing on specific communities" (p. 2). However, these issues have historically been a concern within risk and crisis communication research. Plough and Krimsky (1987) had similar thoughts in their essay and summed it up as well as the field can some three-plus decades earlier. "The emergence of risk communication as a research theme cannot be fully appreciated or accounted for without understanding its link to a set of issues that symbolize the discord between scientific experts and the public around the issue of risk. These tensions are played out in disputes between different research traditions on fundamental questions regarding the perception of risk and the essential nature of human rationality" (p. 4).

From their perspective at the time, individuals and organized groups were becoming increasingly aware "that getting a message across to government in disputes over health and environmental hazards is essentially a political activity. On the other hand, experts in risk analysis have come to appreciate the gap between their analytically derived conclusions and the conceptions of popular culture" (Plough & Krimsky, 1987, p. 4). In their final analysis, "those who control the discourse on risk will most likely control the political battles as well" (p. 4).

Robert Califf, the Food and Drug Administration Commissioner, noted in 2022, "the issue that keeps him [me] up at night [...] is the proliferation of false and misleading health information, particularly online – and the distrust in institutions, data and expertise that it has wrought" (cited in Chapman, 2022, May 2, para. 1). Califf argued that "misinformation is now our leading cause of death" (para. 3), referring to resistance to Covid-19 vaccinations, the number of people taking the anti-parasite drug Ivermectin as a defense option against Covid-19, and the increasing use of electronic cigarettes. "Historically, the FDA has been relatively quiet and puts out definitive information through guidance or labels or regulatory actions [...] that would be transmitted to consumers and patients through trusted intermediaries [...] But the world has changed at this point" (para. 4).

In a disillusioned and dissatisfied society, such misinformation can and has found some purchase; intentionally manufactured ideas through misinformation (Palenchar & Heath, 2024). In reaction to the GAR2022 report, "In a world of dis- trust and misinformation, this [overhaul in how we speak about risk] is a key to moving forward [...] We can move forward to reduce the underlying drivers of risk: Inequality, poverty and most significantly climate change" (Borenstein, 2022, para. 15).

The role of misinformation and disinformation requires researchers and practitioners to return focus to a fundamental perspective or paradigm within both fields – social construction. The social construction of reality theory (Berger & Luckmann, 1967) contends that reality is socially constructed and that the sociology of knowledge must scrutinize the manner in which this occurs. In essence, people conceive their own distinctive social reality through contact and interaction with others. Building on the work of Alfred Schutz, Berger and Luckmann argued that the reasonableness of knowledge in everyday life presents itself as a reality interpreted by individuals and subjectively meaningful for them as a rational and coherent perspective.

Two key publications grounded the discussion of a risk constructionist perspective, including Douglas and Wildavsky's *Risk and Culture* (1983) and Johnson and Covello's *The Social and Cultural Construction of Risk* (1987). For risk and crisis communication scholars and practitioners, the social construction of reality theory raises questions about whether the differences among key stakeholders' realities may not be understood in relation to various differences between the multiple publics and stakeholders, including their unintentional and intentional misinformation and disinformation efforts. Though not directly naming these fields, Seibold and Spitzberg (1982) contended that communication cannot be considered and realized without an appreciation for the interpretations that communicators bring to symbolic discourse.

> "Without attention to the ways in which actors represent and make sense of the phenomenal world, construe event associations, assess and process the actions of others, and interpret personal choices in order to initiate appropriate symbolic activity, the study of human communication is limited to mechanistic analysis (p. 87)."

In a sense, what individuals and societies choose to call risky is largely determined by the social and cultural construction of perceptions rather than some objective nature. Ultimately, the social construction of reality theory argues against a purely objective sense of perception (Palenchar, 2013). According to Kent (1993), knowledge is not something that exists only in our heads and is learned from informative communication; rather, "the production of discourse … comes into being through social interaction, because discourse can be recognized as discourse only after it becomes part and parcel of the normative conventions that form the social communities in which we all must live and work" (p. 79).

Within this constructionist approach, which is less focused on traditional functional or normative understandings, "the new framework was not concerned with how problems were functional or otherwise. Social problems needed to be seen less as a condition or more as an activity" (Spector & Kitsuse, 1987, p. 73). This perspective's aim is to "shift the focus of analysis from the causes of objective social conditions to the processes by which members of a society define those conditions as problems" (p. 59).

According to Cho et al. (2015), in their discussion about Spector and Kitsuse's research about constructing social problems and risk, risk analysis and communication research examine claims (rhetoric used to define social problems and promote policy solutions) and claim makers (those who advance these claims). "Being centrally concerned with the process of claims-making activities, objective conditions are principally of interest with regard to assertations made about them rather than their actual validity" (p. 59).

Conclusion

The previous version of this chapter suggested that the main product of risk and crisis communication is not necessarily the quality of information or access to it, but the quality of the social relationship needed to engage in transparent and risk-bearer focused decision-making. However, in light of the current social and political climate, the increasing role of intentional misinformation and disinformation requires a second look at the role that information quality plays in risk assessment and resulting behaviors.

This review of these paradigms notes that there is a serious problem underlying most message strategy and influence research in that there is an assumption that risk and crisis communication strategies achieve universal impact with multiple publics while ignoring, or at least failing to acknowledge, the extent that individual and group's social construction of risk plays into their understanding of the world and associated risks around them. The ultimate challenge to future research lies in both the managerial biases in the assignment of risk manifestation during crises and the paradoxes of the positive and negative which warn that socially constructed shapes get shifted, ethics twisted, and matters of responsibility and support/opposition get distorted, often intentionally, through misinformation and disinformation.

A large amount of risk and crisis communication research comes from the traditional theoretical position known as objectivism. This perspective operates on the assumption that awareness, knowledge, behavioral intentions, and behaviors are a given in nature, essentially uncontaminated by social factors. On the other hand, according to Palenchar (2013) and Palenchar and Heath (2024), a social constructionist orientation is a generally accepted and growing perspective in risk and crisis communication, arguing that risk and crisis claims are subject to social interpretation and negotiation. From a rhetorical perspective to risk discourse, it is through dialogue that participants identify, create, and manage meaning by the rhetorical processes of statement and counterstatement.

It is difficult to conceptualize and engage in risk and crisis communication without framing such activities in the spirit of the fully functioning society theory of public relations (Heath, 2006). This theory reasons that the role and challenge of public relations is to constantly address ways that organizational management, including public relations, can work together to make society more fully functioning by serving citizens' needs and facilitating collaborative decision-making; dialogue – the rubrics of deliberative democracy. The infrastructures of deliberation must be strong and open to all voices and committed to reflective management and service to the public interest. The infrastructures of deliberation must also address efficacy in countering individual efforts and organized campaigns of misinformation and disinformation.

References

Beck, U. (1992). *Risk Society: Towards a New Modernity.* London, UK: Sage.

Berger, P. L., & Luckmann, T. (1967). *The Social Construction of Reality: A Treatise in the Sociology of Knowledge.* Doubleday.

Borenstein, S. (April 25, 2022). UN says worse disasters yet to come. *Associated Press.* https://apnews.com/article/climate-science-united-nations-natural-disasters-fa1d16ad7d59c7629bb1a9a955a494b

Bourne, C., & Edwards, L. (2021). Critical reflections on the field. In C. Valentini, Ed., *Public Relations.* De Gruyter Mouton. https://doi.org/10.1515/9783110554250

Breton, T. (2023, October 18). *Fighting disinformation and dissemination of illegal content in the context of the Digital Services Act and in times of conflict.* Speech delivered at the European Commission, Brussels. https://ec.europa.eu/commission/presscorner/detail/en/SPEECH_23_5126

Chapman, H. (May 2, 2022). "Misinformation is now our leading cause of death", FDA boss says. *Kentucky Health News.* https://ci.uky.edu/kentuckyhealthnews/2022/05/02/misinformation-is-now-our-leading-cause-of-death-fda-boss-says/

Cho, H., Reimer, T., & McComas, K. A. (2015). *The SAGE Handbook of Risk Communication.* Sage.

Douglas, M. (1992). *Risk and Blame.* Routledge.

Douglas, M., & Wildavsky, A. (1983). *Risk and Culture: An Essay on the Selection of Technological and Environmental Dangers.* University of California Press.

Fischhoff, B., Slovic, P., Lichtenstein, S., Read, S., & Combs, B. (1978). How safe is safe enough? A psychometric study of attitudes towards technological risks and benefits. *Policy Sci, 8,* 127–152.

Habermas, J. (1976). *Legitimation Crisis.* T. McCarthy, Trans. Heinemann.

Heath, R. L. (2006). Onward into more fog: Thoughts on public relations' research directions. *J Public Relat Res, 18,* 93–114.

Heath, R. L. (2010). Introduction. In W. T. Coombs, & S. J. Holladay, Eds., *The Handbook of Crisis Communication* (pp. 1–14). Wiley-Blackwell. http://doi.org/10.1002/9781444314885.ch

Heath, R. L., & O'Hair, H. D. (Eds.). (2009). *Handbook of Risk and Crisis Communication.* Routledge.

Heath, R. L., & Palenchar, M. J. (2009). *Strategic Issues Management* (2nd ed.). Sage.

Huw, R., & Hine, E. (September 27, 2023). The future of AI policy in China. *East Asia Forum.* https://www. eastasiaforum.org/2023/09/27/the-future-of-ai-policy-in-china/

Johnson, B. B., & Covello, V. T. (1987). *The social and cultural construction of risk.* Springer.

Kent, T. (1993). Formalism, social construction, and the problem of interpretive authority. In N. R. Blyler, & C. Thralls, Eds., *Professional Communication: The Social Perspective* (pp. 79–91). Sage.

Kolker, R. (March 8, 2022). The long shadow of Sandy Hook. *New York Times*. https://www.nytimes.com/2022/03/08/books/review/sandy-hook-elizabeth-williamson.html/

Morgan, M. G., Fischhoff, B., Bostrom, A., & Atman, C. J. (2002). *Risk Communication: A Mental Models Approach*. Cambridge University Press.

Palenchar, M. J. (2013). Social construction of reality theory. In R. L. Heath, Ed., *Encyclopedia of Public Relations* (Vol. 2, 2nd ed., pp. 839–841). Sage.

Palenchar, M. J., & Heath, R. L. (2024). Communicating safety and risk: Advancement in a field of constant uncertainty. In T. L. Sellnow, & D. D. Sellnow, Eds., *Communicating Risk and Safety* (pp. 14–31). De Gruyter Mouton. https://doi.org/10.1515/9783110752427

Palenchar, M. J., Hocke, T., & Heath, R. L. (2011). Risk communication and corporate social responsibility: The essence of sound management for risk bearers, generators and arbiters. In O. Ihlen, J. Bartlett, & S. May, Eds., *Handbook of Communication and Corporate Social Responsibility* (pp. 188–207). Wiley-Blackwell.

Palmlund, I. (2009). Risk and social dramaturgy. In R. L. Heath, & H. D. O'Hair, Eds., *Handbook of Risk and Crisis Communication* (pp. 192–204). Routledge.

Plough, A., & Krimsky, S. (1987). The emergence of risk communication studies: Social and political context. *Sci Technol Hum Values*, *12*(2), 4–10.

Schwartz, O. (2018). You thought fake news was bad? Deep fakes are where truth goes to die. *The Guardian*. https://www.theguardian.com/technology/2018/nov/12/deep-fakes-fake-news-truth

Seibold, D. R., & Spitzberg, B. H. (1982). Attribution theory and research: Review and implications for communication. In B. Dervin, & M. J. Voigt, Eds., *Progress in the Communication Sciences* (Vol. 3, pp. 85–125). Ablex.

Spector, E., & Kitsue, J. I. (1987). *Constructing Social Problems* (2nd ed.). Aldine de Gruter.

Tansey, J., & Raymer, S. (2009). Cultural theory and risk. In R. L. Heath, & H. D. O'Hair, Eds., *Handbook of Risk and Crisis Communication* (pp. 53–79). Routledge.

United Nations Office for Disaster Risk Reduction (UNDRR) (2022). *Global assessment report on disaster risk reduction. Our world at risk: Transforming governance for a resilient future*. https://www.undrr.org/gar2022-our-world-risk#container-downloads

World Economic Forum (2024). *The global risks report 2024* (19th edn.). https://www.weforum.org/publications/global-risks-report-2024/

Author's Bio

Michael J. Palenchar (PhD, University of Florida), associate professor (and former associate dean) in the Tombras School of Advertising and Public Relations at the University of Tennessee, has published extensively in journals and book chapters and has presented his research around the world to both industry and the academy. He conducts research in the areas of risk and crisis communication and issue management. He is the co-author with Robert L. Heath on *Strategic Issues Management* (2nd ed.).

Robert L. Heath (PhD, University of Illinois, 1971), professor emeritus at the University of Houston, is the author or editor of 25 books, handbooks, and master collections, and 294 articles in major journals, chapters in leading edited books, and encyclopedia entries. In addition to strategic issues management, he has written on rhetorical theory, social movements/grassroots activism, communication theory, public relations, strategic communication, organizational rhetoric, crisis communication, risk communication, terrorism, corporate social responsibility, investor relations, engagement, public interest, and reputation management. His most recent books are the *International Encyclopedia of Strategic Communication*, the *Handbook of Organizational Rhetoric and Communication*, and *Public Relations Theory: Capabilities and Competencies*.

7

Strategic Communication in Global Health Crises

Are (Trans)National Institutions Up to the Task?

Martin Löffelholz[1] and Yi Xu[2]

[1] Institut für Medien und Kommunikationswissenschaft, Technische Universität Ilmenau, Ilmenau, Germany

[2] Institut für Kommunikationswissenschaft, Friedrich Schiller University Jena, Jena, Germany

Mitigating Cross-Border Health Crises Requires Effective Communication

Two days after Dr. Tedros Adhanom Ghebreyesus, Director-General of the World Health Organization (WHO), declared the Mpox outbreak in the Democratic Republic of Congo and other African countries a "public health emergency of international concern" (PHEIC) on August 14, 2024 (WHO, 2024a), the European Centre for Disease Prevention and Control (ECDC) urged its member states to issue travel advisories for people visiting or returning from affected regions (ECDC, 2024). WHO and ECDC acted after the African Center for Disease Control and Prevention (AfricaCDC) declared the Mpox outbreak a "public health emergency of continental security" on August 13, 2024 (AfricaCDC, 2024), the first such declaration since the agency was established in 2017. At first glance, it appears that transnational health authorities around the world responded quickly and in a coordinated fashion to the recent outbreak of a dangerous virus. But are intergovernmental institutions, working with national governments and other actors, really up to the task of responding to and communicating transnational health crises in ways that mitigate their serious consequences?

In our globalized world of international travel, increased tourism and migration, and interconnected trade, health crises like the Mpox outbreak can easily cross borders. These events pose a serious threat to large populations, dramatically increasing demand for health services and potentially overwhelming even the most advanced health systems, resulting in significantly higher morbidity and mortality (Sampath et al., 2021). Health emergencies can arise from a variety of causes, including infectious diseases, natural disasters, nuclear or chemical accidents, bioterrorism, environmental hazards, and, last but not least, what has been called an "infodemic," the rapid spread of information, "including false or misleading information in

The Handbook of International Crisis and Risk Communication Research, Second Edition.
Edited by Andreas Schwarz, Matthew W. Seeger, and Sora Kim.

digital and physical environments during a disease outbreak" (WHO, 2022). In addition to the Mpox outbreak (and many less far-reaching crises), the WHO has identified seven PHEICs since 2005, the year in which the organization was urged to strengthen its International Health Regulations (WHO, 2008) following the disastrous response to the SARS outbreak of 2002 (Fidler, 2004; Menon & Goh, 2005): the H1N1 pandemic (2009–2010), the spread of polio (since 2014), the West African Ebola outbreak (2013–2016), the Zika virus epidemic (2015–2016), the Kivu Ebola epidemic (2018–2020), and, still deeply embedded in the world's collective memory, the truly global COVID-19 pandemic (WHO, 2024b).

According to WHO's revised International Health Regulations, countries are required to respond promptly to any PHEIC (WHO, 2008). However, the global nature of these crises can complicate efforts to mitigate their effects, as different countries tend to have varying levels of preparedness, resources, and policies (Esra et al., 2020). The risks associated with transnational health crises are often compounded by factors such as population density, poor health infrastructure, and the speed of modern transportation. Environmental change, political instability, and conflict can exacerbate these risks. Transnational health crises are complex events that pose significant risks to global security and require a coordinated international response, a robust public health infrastructure (Michaud et al., 2024), and effective communication strategies (Ataguba & Ataguba, 2020; King & Lazard, 2020; Löffelholz et al., 2024; Miller et al., 2021; Schleicher et al., 2024; Tomić et al., 2024; Voges et al., 2023; Xu & Löffelholz, 2024).

Against this backdrop, this chapter first describes the multifaceted institutional framework that has evolved to contain, mitigate, and manage transnational health crises (Gostin et al., 2023; Jones & Hameiri, 2022; Schleicher et al., 2024). Drawing on key literature and findings from two large-scale empirical studies of how government actors in Europe and the United States communicated during the COVID-19 pandemic (Löffelholz et al., 2024; Xu & Löffelholz, 2024), we then analyze both communication strategies for managing public health crises and contextual factors that influence the selection and design of these strategies in health emergencies. The chapter concludes with implications for future research.

The "Fragmented Array" of Health Crisis Response

Addressing cross-border health crises requires the collaboration of multiple actors operating at different levels of governance, from the global to the local, from intergovernmental organizations and national governments to non-state actors and the private sector (Gostin et al., 2023). Non-state actors, including civil society organizations (e.g., Doctors Without Borders) and philanthropy (e.g., the Bill and Melinda Gates Foundation), play a critical role in filling gaps in public health services, particularly in regions where government resources are limited. They often act as intermediaries, providing direct health services and advocating for and helping to implement public health goals on behalf of vulnerable populations (Gostin, 2014; Kirton, 2017). Meanwhile, the private sector, which comprises not only pharmaceutical companies (e.g., Pfizer and BioNTech), but also healthcare providers and technology companies, contributes by developing and distributing vaccines, drugs and medical technologies, and providing logistical support during health crises, typically motivated by both public health needs and market incentives. Examples of public-private partnerships include the Global Fund to Fight AIDS, the Vaccine Alliance (Gavi), and the Coalition for Epidemic Preparedness Innovations (Gostin et al., 2023).

At the center of this "fragmented array of governmental, non-governmental and intergovernmental agencies" (Jones & Hameiri, 2022) appears to be the WHO, as the specialized agency of the United Nations charged with coordinating international public health efforts. Some scholars even refer to the organization as the "leader in global health" (Gostin et al., 2023) because its constitution states that it should "act as the directing and coordinating authority on international health work" (WHO, 1946). In fact, the WHO works closely with the ECDC (https://www.ecdc.europa.eu/en/), the AfricaCDC (https://africacdc.org), other intergovernmental health organizations, and national actors who rely on the WHO for advice, technical support, and international coordination during global health emergencies (Gostin et al., 2023). However, after the SARS outbreak in 2002, it became clear that successful global health governance is only possible if nation states agree on common rules for dealing with cross-border health crises (Fidler, 2004; Menon & Goh, 2005). As a result, the WHO adopted its International Health Regulations to ensure that information about the discovery of dangerous pathogens in a particular country is shared early so that the global community can respond in an appropriate and coordinated manner (WHO, 2008).

Soon, however, it became apparent that this agreement, while consensual, was not enough. During the spread of H1N1 in 2009, the Ebola outbreak in 2014, and the recent COVID-19 pandemic, especially in the first months after its outbreak and then again after the first vaccines became available, the world learned the hard way that the challenge of balancing global health governance and national sovereignty is far from resolved (Jones & Hameiri, 2022). Not only do national governments retain primary responsibility for the health of their populations by implementing and enforcing health policies within their jurisdictions. They also prioritized their own interests (e.g., "vaccine nationalism") and even exerted pressure on the WHO, for example, when discussing the cause of the COVID-19 pandemic, which compromised the clarity and neutrality of its messages. Thus, despite a common interest in mitigating the impact of the crisis, global health governance largely failed during the COVID-19 pandemic because of self-serving nationalism, international conflicts (e.g., between the United States and China), WHO's subordination to major donors, and inadequate resources for intervention (Jones & Hameiri, 2022; Sohrabi et al., 2020).

In sum, the effectiveness of the WHO in particular and intergovernmental health institutions in general is tied to the willingness of national actors to support and implement recommended policies (Gostin et al., 2023). Indeed, "the resilience of 'global' health governance depends overwhelmingly on what happens at the national and subnational levels" (Jones & Hameiri, 2022, p. 2075). This conclusion is supported by our three-year analysis of press releases issued by governments and public health institutions in six European countries and the United States during the COVID-19 pandemic (Löffelholz et al., 2024). We found that intergovernmental organizations, including the WHO, were mentioned relatively infrequently in press releases in all countries analyzed, while national institutions were the dominant actors, with little variation across countries (Figure 7.1).

In this quantitative content analysis, we analyzed a total of 6,598 press releases on COVID-19 published by national governments and public health institutions between January 1, 2020 and December 31, 2022. The codebook is based on the IDEA model (Sellnow & Sellnow, 2019) and theoretical considerations with regard to strategic political communication (Löffelholz et al., 2024). The results also support the findings of other studies that suggest that the often-used term "national government" is not sufficient to understand how political communication in the public sector (Strömbäck & Kiousis, 2011), especially in crisis situations (Liu & Horsley, 2007), is planned and implemented within countries. Not only in health crises, communication needs to be coordinated within a complex institutional framework that includes the vertical levels of government (national, regional, and local) and various horizontal structures (Hyland et al., 2021; Kim & Kreps, 2020; Liu et al., 2020; Mori et al., 2020; Schleicher et al., 2024). Such structures in the public sector include, but are not limited to, cooperation and/or competition between ministries at the national or regional level and coordination and/or competition between policy-driven government actors (e.g., ministries and prime minister's offices) and science-driven, publicly-funded institutions such as the U.S. Centers for Disease Control and Prevention (CDC), the U.K. National Health Service (NHS), and the German Robert Koch Institute (RKI).

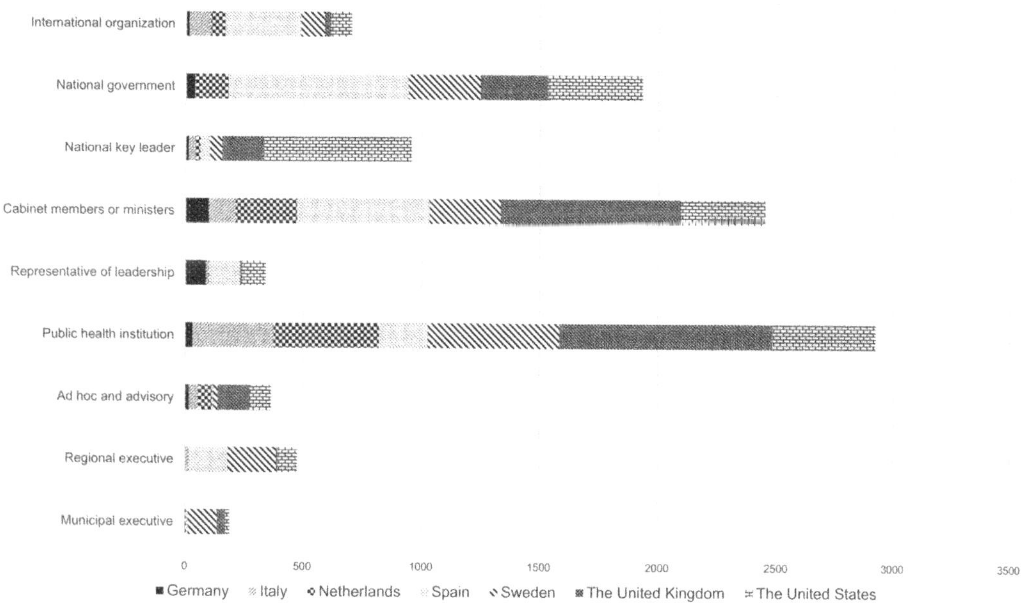

Figure 7.1 Main actors in press releases published by governments and health institutions (2020–2022). *Note*: N_{total} = 6,598 press releases ($N_{Germany}$ = 220, N_{Italy} = 481, $N_{Netherlands}$ = 724, N_{Spain} = 1,530, N_{Sweden} = 866, $N_{United\ Kingdom}$ = 1,622, $N_{United\ States}$ = 1,155).

As a result, a major challenge to adequately managing protracted health crises is ensuring the coherence of communication efforts across different levels and subdivisions of government (Biernacka-Ligieza, 2021; Schleicher et al., 2024). Other difficulties that hampered rapid responses to the COVID-19 pandemic arise from complex government decision-making and information processes, such as lengthy chains of command and control, both overly hierarchical internal and lack of interagency collaboration (Gregory et al., 2021; Schleicher et al., 2024), and conflicts of authority (Biernacka-Ligieza, 2021). These problems are exacerbated when government institutions lack sufficient resources, such as funding, technical infrastructure, or adequately trained staff, which can lead, for example, to misinterpretation of legal provisions or shifting of responsibilities to other levels or subdivisions of government (Biernacka-Ligieza, 2021). Overall, given the complex and not always consistent institutional framework of global and national health governance and the multiplicity of issues involved, it is not surprising that government communication strategies to mitigate the impact of transnational health crises rarely follow a unified approach. As the COVID-19 pandemic painfully demonstrated, the communicative management of such protracted health crises still needs to be further optimized, and it is clear that more research is needed to better prepare the world for future health emergencies.

Strategic Government Communications in Times of Multiple Health Crises

Given the far-reaching consequences of cross-border health crises, not only for millions of people but also for entire sociopolitical systems and economies, researchers have conducted a large number of empirical studies to better understand how (strategic) communication can help prevent or at least better manage crises. Examples of such studies include analyses of government risk communication during the 2002 SARS outbreak (Fidler, 2004; Menon & Goh, 2005), health organization communication during the avian influenza (Avery &

Kim, 2009), government and health organization communication during the 2009 H1N1 pandemic (Lee & Basnyat, 2013), health organization information about the spread of the Ebola virus, and related audience engagement on social media (Guidry et al., 2017), government dialogic competence during the MERS outbreak (Yang, 2018), and international organization and national government communication during the COVID-19 pandemic (Diers-Lawson et al., 2021; Löffelholz et al., 2024; Mello et al., 2023; Schleicher et al., 2024; Tagliacozzo et al., 2023; Xu & Löffelholz, 2024).

These and other studies have produced a large number of findings, but the results tend to be unconnected and therefore do not provide a comprehensive understanding of how government communication strategies aimed at mitigating the impact of public health crises are prepared and work in detail. Given the mosaic-like state of research fostered by the COVID-19 pandemic (Croucher & Diers-Lawson, 2023; Löffelholz, 2022; Löffelholz et al., 2023), it also seems that the traditional approach of analyzing the different phases of a single crisis is not really appropriate for studying health crises that last for years, affect the whole world, and are handled in different ways by governments around the globe. The COVID-19 pandemic was not just one prolonged crisis but a multitude of crises, some of which were interrelated, some of which developed separately, and some of which arose because a particular crisis was not adequately managed and new problems arose. This may be the main reason why it is difficult to provide an evidence-based holistic assessment of government communication in protracted health crises such as pandemics through empirical studies. The complexity and especially the interconnectedness of such a variety of crises may require a different form of empirical analysis that is not based on (small-scale) individual studies that cannot take into account all relevant political, legal, economic, health, societal, and communication aspects. Nevertheless, we believe that several theoretical approaches, such as the Extended Parallel Process Model (EPPM) (Basil & Witte, 2012), the Crisis and Emergency Risk Communication (CERC) model (Reynolds et al., 2002), and the IDEA model (Sellnow & Sellnow, 2019), which have been developed to analyze (health) risk and crisis communication, are still useful, even in health emergencies that are prolonged, involve different types of sub-crises, and affect many countries at the same time.

The EPPM has been widely used as a theoretical framework for designing and evaluating the effectiveness of health risk communication (Basil & Witte, 2012). The model postulates that when people are exposed to fearful messages, they typically engage in two cognitive appraisal processes: first, threat, which assesses the severity and one's vulnerability or susceptibility to the disease; and second, efficacy, which assesses one's ability to overcome the threat by taking recommended actions (Witte, 1992, 1994). The effectiveness and theories of fear appeals have been extensively studied across a wide range of health-related topics, including smoking, cancer prevention, HIV/STDs, alcohol/drug use, dental hygiene, driving safety, and environmental issues (Tannenbaum et al., 2015). A review of 60 years of research on fear appeals concluded that emphasizing self-efficacy is more important than presenting threatening health information in promoting protective behaviors (Ruiter et al., 2014). Another interesting general finding is based on a meta-analysis of 127 articles, which found that the effectiveness of fear appeals tends to increase when the message emphasizes the severity of the threat, portrays one's vulnerability, and recommends effective behavioral responses (Tannenbaum et al., 2015).

The CERC model for describing effective messages tailored to an infectious disease outbreak was developed by the CDC in the United States (Reynolds et al., 2002). The corresponding CDC manual serves as a comprehensive effort to build crisis response capacity among public health agencies, with a five-stage model of crisis development: pre-crisis, initial event, maintenance, resolution, and evaluation (Reynolds & Seeger, 2005). To better assist health communicators, the CERC model was published in a series of manuals by the U.S. Department of Health and Human Services. Later, Veil et al. (2008) proposed six suggestions from the CERC model for future research related to communicating uncertainty, two-way communication, strategies, the relationship between risk and crisis, enhancing self-efficacy, and audience diversity. Through a systematic review, Miller et al. (2021) concluded that the CERC model has been widely applied not only to general types of crises (e.g., natural disasters, weather-related crises, and drought) but also to infectious diseases (e.g., SARS, Ebola, H1N1, and Zika). However, the theoretical underpinnings of the CERC model have rarely been tested, and few researchers have used the conceptual ideas of Veil et al. (2008), although their suggestions are intended to clarify the underlying assumptions of the model rather than to state theoretical principles.

One of the main limitations of both the EPPM and CERC models is that they have been predominantly tested in the United States, while empirical evidence from other cultural contexts is still lacking (Diers-Lawson et al., 2021; Miller et al., 2021). Based on both the EPPM and CERC models, Mello et al. (2023) examined how the WHO and the CDC used their Instagram accounts to communicate COVID-related information. They found that threat information was limited, whereas efficacy appeals and action cues were abundant. The CDC relied more heavily on self-efficacy and response efficacy, while the WHO appealed more frequently to collective efficacy. Neither visually incorporated behaviors nor scientific evidence or experts appeared to be frequent (Mello et al., 2023).

Finally, the IDEA (Internalization, Distribution, Explanation, and Action) model has been recommended as an effective approach for creating instructional risk and crisis messages (Sellnow & Sellnow, 2019). Internalization incorporates key message elements to motivate recipients to engage in self-protective behaviors, for example, by addressing the timeliness, relevance, compassion, proximity, and impact of the health crisis; Distribution is concerned with providing access to diverse sources and communication channels to reach diverse audiences, especially at-risk audiences; Explanation is concerned with translating scientific information in an easily understandable manner and considering strategies to gain people's support and trust in the institution; Action includes mobilizing appropriate protective behaviors, compliance actions, and assigning responsibility to maximize the effectiveness of instructional crisis messages. By reviewing risk and crisis communication theories that have been used to study health crises, pandemics, and COVID-19, Diers-Lawson et al. (2021) summarized factors that influence information seeking, risk perceptions, and self-protective behaviors. As a stakeholder-centered model of crisis communication, the IDEA model has been tested in various crisis situations and societal contexts (Diers-Lawson et al., 2021; Schwarz et al., 2024).

Building on the IDEA model (Sellnow & Sellnow, 2019) and suggestions by a research group from the Karlsruhe Institute of Technology (Boy et al., 2024), we identified five messaging strategies for the purpose of instructional crisis communication. Our empirical results show how governments and public health institutions communicated strategically to achieve their goals through instructional crisis messages in their press releases during the COVID-19 pandemic. Press releases have long been used as a tool to communicate information from organizations or institutions to multiple target audiences (Catenaccio, 2008). In the context of the COVID-19 pandemic, institutional press releases are not only meant to subsidize the media agenda and target journalists who take them as responsible and legitimate sources for retelling the news to a wider audience (Boumans, 2018). Rather, in times of health crises, press releases issued by governments and health institutions are intended to incorporate effective instructional crisis messages, disseminate preventive knowledge, and mobilize appropriate actions to be taken by the public.

We found that the *informing strategy* was mainly used by governments and health institutions in press releases to inform their audiences, report changes in the pandemic, and announce decisions. The *explaining strategy* is also often used to verify the evolution of the pandemic, justify protective measures and policy decisions, argue for public support, and provide a narrative. This strategy is more pronounced in the institutional press releases of Spain, Germany, and Sweden. In contrast, the *mobilization strategy* refers to attracting the attention of the audience, motivating appropriate protective action, mandating mandatory measures, and warning of negative consequences. In general, this strategy is used much less in institutional press releases, although it is more prominent in the Dutch and Swedish contexts than in other countries. While risk and crisis communication scholars have repeatedly emphasized the importance of cues to action in messages (Basil & Witte, 2012; Reynolds & Seeger, 2005; Ruiter et al., 2014; Sellnow & Sellnow, 2019), governments and health institutions tended not to adopt these recommendations in their press releases. The *emotionalizing strategy*, although rarely visible in institutional press releases, aims to elicit certain emotions in the audience by expressing compassion and sympathy, promoting psychological well-being, increasing trust in institutions, and ensuring loyalty to official crisis management (Figure 7.2).

In addition, the *interactive strategy* rarely appears in press releases to interactively consult with the media and the public, thank individuals or organizations, welcome evaluations, and encourage feedback, no matter how critical or contradictory opinions. The lack of interactivity is consistent with existing research that criticizes the lack of engagement and unavailable

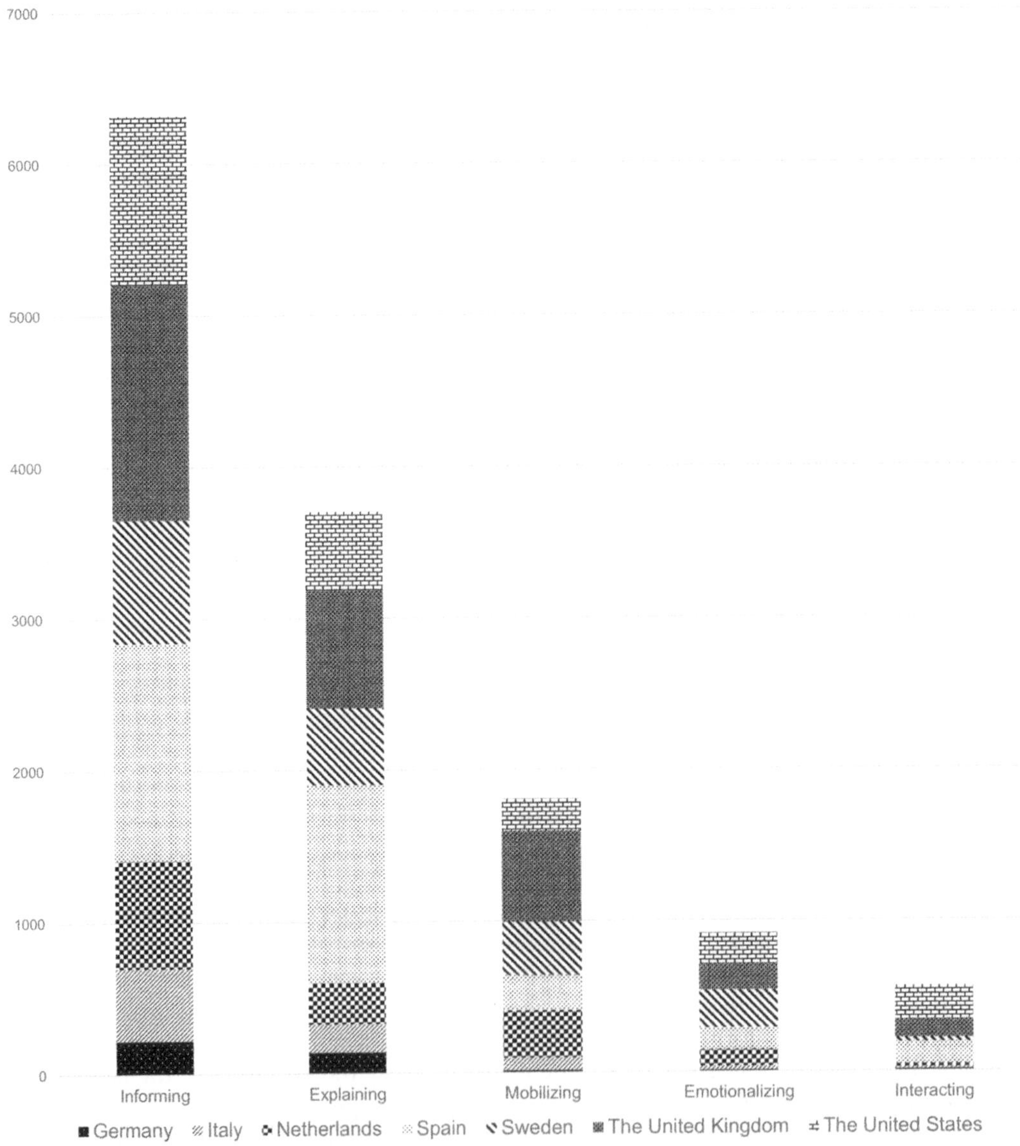

Figure 7.2 Main strategies in press releases published by governments and health institutions (2020–2022). *Note*: N_{total} = 6,598 press releases ($N_{Germany}$ = 220, N_{Italy} = 481, $N_{Netherlands}$ = 724, N_{Spain} = 1,530, N_{Sweden} = 866, $N_{United\ Kingdom}$ = 1,622, $N_{United\ States}$ = 1,155).

channels for two-way communication with the public sector (Guidry et al., 2017; Liu & Horsley, 2007; Tagliacozzo et al., 2023).

Risk Cultures and Political Systems Shape How Health Crises are Communicated

The public sector environment has specific constraints and opportunities that differentiate political public relations from corporate public relations (Strömbäck & Kiousis, 2011). The unique characteristics of the public sector environment include: internal and external politics, serving the public interest, legal constraints, media and public scrutiny, lack of management support for public relations practitioners, poor public perception of government communication, lagging professional development, and the power distribution of federalism (Liu & Horsley, 2007).

Because protracted health crises often have societal impacts on an international or global scale, a cross-national or cross-cultural comparative perspective can enrich our understanding of government risk and crisis communication by identifying similarities and differences with those of other systems. Comparative studies have the potential to test and generalize existing theoretical frameworks (Esser & Hanitzsch, 2012) and provide insights into the influence of contextual factors on crisis communication strategies and outcomes. However, the lack of representation of different cultural perspectives is an emerging agenda in risk and crisis communication research, as empirical studies primarily focus on case studies within a specific national context (Diers-Lawson et al., 2021). In the midst of prolonged health crises, such as the COVID-19 pandemic, we propose the following contextual factors that have the potential to shape governmental and health institutional risk and crisis communication: risk cultures, political systems, and media systems.

A cultural perspective allows us to see how different communities relate perceived risks and crises to moral culpability (Douglas & Wildavsky, 1982). The typology of risk cultures (Cornia et al., 2016) suggests three dimensions of how sociocultural contexts influence risk perceptions: disaster framing, trust in institutions, and attribution of responsibility. Based on empirical evidence, the framework suggests that in individual-oriented risk cultures (e.g., the Netherlands, the United Kingdom, and the United States), citizens are highly self-reliant in risk preparedness and crisis mitigation. In state-oriented risk cultures (e.g., Germany and Sweden), state institutions are expected to deal with risk and crisis management, while trust in their effectiveness is high. In fatalistic risk cultures (e.g., Italy and Spain), risks are perceived as unpredictable, and neither the state nor the citizens are capable of risk prevention. An intercultural comparative perspective should be trivial if we consider the distribution of power in relation to the pattern of risks or crises that have occurred.

The level of political autonomy is another factor that shapes how the public sector manages crisis response and communication. In consensual democracies, such as Germany and Sweden, the parliament is formally dominant over the executive of the multiparty coalition government (Lijphart, 2012; Schmidt, 2015). In majoritarian democracies, such as the United Kingdom and the United States, the political sphere is dominated by two parties (Lijphart, 2012). The patterns of democracy may lead to different approaches in which governments consider legitimacy and compliance measures in a health crisis. Furthermore, in countries such as Spain, Sweden, the United Kingdom, and the Netherlands, districts and local authorities enjoy a high degree of autonomy (Schmidt, 2015). In contrast, the United States and Germany follow a federalist system in which subdivisions (states) govern issues of regional or local concern alongside the overarching national government (Schmidt, 2015). These differences are factors that potentially shape the national government's communication of the proximity of the crisis, the level of impact, and the protective or obligatory cues for action.

The type of media system can influence news coverage and, in turn, how governments communicate with the news media (Hallin & Mancini, 2004, 2017). Among other factors, the polarized pluralist model (e.g., Italy and Spain) is characterized by strong state intervention, the democratic corporatist model (e.g., Germany, the Netherlands, and Sweden) by strong public broadcasting, and the liberal model (e.g., the United Kingdom and the United States) by market-oriented journalism.

Taking the COVID-19 pandemic communication as an example, several studies have used a cross-national comparative approach to examine crisis communication by governments and public health institutions (e.g., Johansson et al., 2023; Tagliacozzo et al., 2023; Xu & Löffelholz, 2024). For example, drawing on a cultural theory of risk, Dimitrijevska-Markoski and Nukpezah (2023) examined how the cultural biases (hierarchy, individualism, egalitarianism, and fatalism) of local government officials affected their risk perceptions and support for the COVID-19 mitigation measures in the United States. Results indicated that officials with egalitarian and hierarchical cultural biases reported higher support for the adoption of COVID-19 mitigation measures, while those with individualistic cultural biases reported lower support.

In a cross-national comparative study, we identified three patterns of multimodal crisis messages (the person-oriented protection pattern, the state-oriented instruction pattern, and the politicizing crisis pattern) through a content analysis of 2,140 Instagram posts published by governments and health institutions in Germany, Türkiye, the United Kingdom, and the United States between 2020 and 2021 (Xu & Löffelholz, 2024). The results showed that both risk cultures and political systems significantly shaped the formation of crisis messages, but risk cultures tend to have a more significant effect. The individual-oriented risk culture shaped the instructive crisis messages in the contexts of the United Kingdom and the United States, while the state-oriented risk culture influenced the formation of crisis messages in Germany. The politicizing crisis message pattern, mainly found in Turkish Instagram posts, was shaped by both the country's fatalistic risk culture and its partial majoritarian democracy with authoritarian tendencies. The United Kingdom's devolved governments were likely to influence the emphasis on crisis proximity at the regional level. In contrast, the federalism of Germany and the United States led to an emphasis on national proximity and institutional responsibility.

Cross-Sector Collaboration, Policy-Science Relationships, and Recipient-Centeredness

This chapter has discussed the challenges and strategies for mitigating cross-border health crises, emphasizing the need for effective communication and collaboration among international, national and nongovernmental actors, and the complexity of managing these crises due to globalization, differences in national preparedness, and complex institutional frameworks that require coordination among different levels of government. The WHO and regional bodies such as the ECDC and the AfricaCDC play a central role in declaring and managing health emergencies. However, the effectiveness of their efforts is often hampered by national sovereignty, differing levels of preparedness, and the prioritization of national interests over global cooperation. The response to health crises involves a fragmented array of governmental, nongovernmental and intergovernmental organizations, with the WHO at the center. However, the effectiveness of intergovernmental institutions depends on the willingness of national governments to support and implement international recommendations. Despite a common interest in mitigating crises, global health governance has often failed because of nationalism, international conflict, and inadequate resources.

In addition, we have discussed various theoretical models of crisis communication, such as the EPPM, the CERC model, and the IDEA model. These models provide frameworks for designing effective health risk communication, but their applicability varies in different cultural and national contexts. During health crises such as the COVID-19 pandemic, governments and public health organizations various strategies in their press releases, including informing, explaining, mobilizing, emotionalizing, and interacting with the public. However, the effectiveness of these strategies varies, and there is a notable lack of interactivity and engagement with the public. The public sector environment, characterized by legal constraints, media scrutiny, and federalism, influences how governments communicate during health crises. Comparative studies across national contexts are recommended to better understand these influences and improve crisis communication strategies. In conclusion, the evaluation of governmental and institutional crisis communication is crucial for improving preparedness and effectiveness in managing future public health crises. This evaluation has highlighted several key areas for enhancement and future research:

- First, health communication executives need to refine their decision-making processes by regularly assessing risks and integrating diverse, representative perspectives into their teams. This approach will help them avoid the pitfalls of over-reliance on past experiences, as seen during the COVID-19 pandemic. Future research could explore the development of frameworks that guide executives in adapting their strategies to emerging health crises.
- Second, improving cross-sector collaboration and effectively balancing the relationship between politics and science are vital for a cohesive and coordinated response to public health emergencies. Research should investigate the mechanisms that facilitate better cooperation between institutions, focusing on how these partnerships can be strengthened and maintained during protracted crises.
- Third, the public sectors must adopt a more recipient-oriented approach, prioritizing timely, transparent communication that engages a wide range of audiences, particularly at-risk groups. This shift requires further research into the most effective communication strategies that address the diverse needs of different populations, ensuring that critical information reaches those who need it most.
- Finally, the strategic use of visual communication is essential in mitigating the effects of an infodemic (King & Lazard, 2020). Therefore, more research is needed on the effective use of graphical images, data visualizations, and illustrative visuals to improve the quality of health communication during crises. Future studies should focus on developing guidelines for the strategic deployment of visuals that enhance message clarity and reduce misinformation (Xu & Löffelholz, 2024).

By addressing these areas and pursuing these avenues of research, institutions can significantly improve their preparedness and responsiveness for future public health challenges.

References

AfricaCDC (African Center for Disease Control and Prevention) (2024). *Africa CDC declares Mpox a public health emergency of continental security, mobilizing resources across the continent.* Retrieved August 20, 2024 from https://africacdc.org/news-item/africa-cdc-declares-mpox-a-public-health-emergency-of-continental-security-mobilizing-resources-across-the-continent/

Ataguba, O., & Ataguba, J. (2020). Social determinants of health: The role of effective communication in the COVID-19 pandemic in developing countries. *Global Health Action, 13/1.* http://doi.org/10.1080/16549716.2020.1788263

Avery, E. J., & Kim, S. (2009). Anticipating or precipitating crisis? Health agencies may not be heeding best practice advice in avian flu press releases. *Journal of Public Relations Research, 21*(2), 187–197.

Basil, M., & Witte, K. (2012). Health risk message design using the extended parallel process model. In H. Cho, Ed., *Health Communication Message Design: Theory and Practice* (pp. 41–58). Thousand Oaks, CA: Sage.

Biernacka-Ligieza, I. (2021). The significance of digital media in local public space crisis management: The case of Poland, the United Kingdom and Italy. *Journal of Arab & Muslim Media Research, 14*, 47–70.

Boumans, J. (2018). Subsidizing the news? Organizational press releases' influence on news media's agenda and content. *Journalism Studies, 19*(15), 2264–2282.

Boy, B., Bucher, H.-J., & Mayer, J. (2024). Soziale Medien in der Krisenkommunikation. Herausforderungen und Chancen für den Bevölkerungsschutz. In Bundesamt für Bevölkerungsschutz und Katastrophenhilfe, Ed., *Forschung für den Bevölkerungsschutz. Kongressband I* (pp. 55–57). Bonn, Berlin: BBK.

Catenaccio, P. (2008). Press releases as a hybrid genre: Addressing the informative/promotional conundrum. Pragmatics. *Quarterly Publication of the International Pragmatics Association (IPrA), 18*(1), 9–31.

Cornia, A., Dressel, K., & Pfeil, P. (2016). Risk cultures and dominant approaches towards disasters in seven European countries. *Journal of Risk Research, 19*(3), 288–304.

Croucher, S., & Diers-Lawson, A. (Eds.). (2023). *Pandemic Communication*. London: Routledge.

Diers-Lawson, A., Johnson, S., Clayton, T., Kimoto, R., Tran, B. X., Nguyen, L. H., & Park, K. (2021). Pandemic communication: Information seeking, evaluation, and self-protective behaviors in Vietnam and the Republic of Korea. *Frontiers in Communication, 6*, 1–22.

Dimitrijevska-Markoski, T., & Nukpezah, J. A. (2023). COVID-19 risk perception and support for COVID-19 mitigation measures among local government officials in the US: A test of a cultural theory of risk. *Administration and Society, 55*(3), 351–380.

Douglas, M., & Wildavsky, A. (1982). *Risk and Culture: An Essay on the Selection of Technological and Environmental Dangers*. Berkeley, CA: University of California Press.

ECDC (European Centre for Disease Prevention and Control) (2024). *ECDC recommends enhancing preparedness as more imported cases of clade I mpox highly likely*. Retrieved August 18, 2024 from https://www.ecdc.europa.eu/en/news-events/ecdc-recommends-enhancing-preparedness-more-imported-cases-clade-i-mpox-highly-likely

Esra, R., Jamieson, L., Fox, M. P., Letswalo, D., Ngcobo, N., Mngadi, S., Estill, J., Meyer-Rath, G., & Keiser, O. (2020). Evaluating the impact of non-pharmaceutical interventions for SARS-CoV-2 on a global scale. *medRxiv*, preprint (5 August 2020), http://doi.org/10.1101/2020.07.30.20164939

Esser, F., & Hanitzsch, T. (2012). On the why and how of comparative inquiry in communication studies. In F. Esser, & T. Hanitzsch, Eds., *The Handbook of Comparative Communication Research* (pp. 3–22). New York, NY: Routledge.

Fidler, D. (2004). Germs, governance, and global public health in the wake of SARS. *The Journal of Clinical Investigation, 113*(6), 799–804. http://doi.org/10.1172/JCI21328

Gostin, L. (2014). *Global Health Law*. Cambridge, MA: Harvard University Press.

Gostin, L., Friedman, E., & Finch, A. (2023). The global health architecture: Governance and international institutions to advance population health worldwide. *The Milbank Quarterly, 101*(S1), 734–769. http://doi.org/10.1111/1468-0009.12627

Gregory, A., Nichols, B., & Underwood, J. (2021). The lived experience of UK health communication professionals during the Covid-19 pandemic. *Journal of Communication Management, 25*, 105–124.

Guidry, J. P. D., Jin, Y., Orr, C. A., Messner, M., & Meganck, S. (2017). Ebola on Instagram and Twitter: How health organizations address the health crisis in their social media engagement. *Public Relations Review, 43*(3), 477–486.

Hallin, D. C., & Mancini, P. (2004). *Comparing Media Systems: Three Models of Media and Politics*. Cambridge University Press.

Hallin, D. C., & Mancini, P. (2017). Ten years after comparing media systems: What have we learned? *Political Communication, 34*(2), 155–171.

Hyland-Wood, B., Gardner, J., Leask, J., & Ecker, U. (2021). Toward effective government communication strategies in the era of COVID-19. *Humanities and Social Sciences Communications, 8*(30). http://doi.org/10.1057/s41599-020-00701-w

Jones, L., & Hameiri, S. (2022). Explaining the failure of global health governance during COVID-19. *International Affairs, 98*(6), 2057–2076. http://doi.org/10.1093/ia/iiac231

Johansson, B., Ihlen, Ø., Lindholm, J., & Blach-Ørsten, M. (2023). *Communicating a Pandemic. Crisis Management and Covid-19 in the Nordic Countries.* Nordicom, Sweden: University of Gothenburg.

Kim, D., & Kreps, G. (2020). An analysis of government communication in the United States during the COVID-19 pandemic: Recommendations for effective government health risk communication. *World Medical & Health Policy, 12*(4), 398–412.

King, A. J., & Lazard, A. J. (2020). Advancing visual health communication research to improve infodemic response. *Health Communication, 35*(14), 1723–1728.

Kirton, J. J. (Ed.). (2017 [2009]). *Global Health.* London: Routledge.

Lee, S. T., & Basnyat, I. (2013). From press release to news: Mapping the framing of the 2009 H1N1 A influenza pandemic. *Health Communication, 28*(2), 119–132.

Lijphart, A. (2012). *Patterns of Democracy.* New York, NY: Yale University Press.

Liu, B., & Horsley, J. S. (2007). The government communication decision wheel: Toward a public relations model for the public sector. *Journal of Public Relations Research, 19*(4), 377–393.

Liu, B., Iles, I., & Herovic, E. (2020). Leadership under fire: How governments manage crisis communication. *Communication Studies, 71*(1), 128–147.

Löffelholz, M. (2022). Von Tschernobyl zur Corona-Infodemie. Entwicklung, Ergebnisse und Herausforderungen der Risiko- und Krisenkommunikationsforschung [From Chernobyl to the Corona Infodemic. Development, Results and Challenges of Risk and Crisis Communication Research]. In M. Beuthner, U. Bomnüter, & J. Kantara, Eds., *Risiken, Krisen, Konflikte. Herausforderungen und Perspektiven medialer Vermittlungen [Risks, Crises, Conflicts. Challenges and Perspectives of Media Mediation]* (pp. 27–48). Wiesbaden: Springer Gabler.

Löffelholz, M., Estella, P., & Xu, Y. (2023). COVID-19 as catalyst of Global Risk Society. Institutionalization, de-westernization, and datafication of crisis communication research. In N. Yamamoto, Ed., *The COVID-19 Pandemic and Risks in East Asia* (pp. 14–40). Milton Park, Abingdon, Oxon: Routledge.

Löffelholz, M., Xu, Y., & Estella, P. (2024). *Government communication in protracted crises: A comparative long-term analysis of press releases from six European countries and the USA on coping with the Covid-19 pandemic (2020–2022).* Paper presented at the 13th International Crisis and Risk Communication Conference, 11–13 March 2024, Orlando, USA.

Mello, S., Glowacki, E., Fuentes, I., & Seabolt, J. (2023). Communicating COVID-19 risk on Instagram: A content analysis of official public health messaging during the first year of the pandemic. *Journal of Health Communication, 28*(1), 38–52.

Menon, K. U., & Goh, K. T. (2005). Transparency and trust: Risk communications and the Singapore experience in managing SARS. *Journal of Communication Management, 9*(4), 375–383.

Michaud, A., Goldsmith, Z., & Stawicki, S. (2024). Introductory chapter: Contemporary considerations and developments in global health security. In A. Michaud, S. Stawicki, & R. Izurieta, Eds., *Global Health Security: Contemporary Considerations and Developments* (pp. 3–16). London: InTechOpen.

Miller, A. N., Collins, C., Neuberger, L., Todd, A., Sellnow, T. L., & Boutemen, L. (2021). Being first, being right, and being credible since 2002: A systematic review of Crisis and Emergency Risk Communication (CERC) research. *Journal of International Crisis and Risk Communication Research, 4*(1), 1–27.

Mori, E., Barabaschi, B., Cantoni, F., & Virtuani, R. (2020). Local governments' communication through Facebook. Evidences from COVID-19 pandemic in Italy. *Journal of Public Affairs, 21*(4), 1–14. http://doi.org/10.1002/pa.2551

Reynolds, B., Hunter-Galdo, J., & Sokler, L. (2002). *Crisis and Emergency Risk Communication.* Atlanta, GA: Centers for Disease Control and Prevention.

Reynolds, B., & Seeger, M. (2005). Crisis and emergency risk communication as an integrative model. *Journal of Health Communication, 10*(1), 43–55.

Ruiter, R. A., Kessels, L. T., Peters, G. J. Y., & Kok, G. (2014). Sixty years of fear appeal research: Current state of the evidence. *International Journal of Psychology, 49*(2), 63–70.

Sampath, S., Khedr, A., Qamar, S., Tekin, A., Singh, R., Green, R., & Kashyap, R. (2021). Pandemics throughout the history. *Cureus, 13*(9), e18136. http://doi.org/10.7759/cureus.18136

Schleicher, K., Radechovsky, J., & Löffelholz, M. (2024). Krisenkommunikation staatlicher Institutionen. Studienergebnisse und zentrale Erkenntnisse aus der COVID-19-Pandemie [Crisis communication by state institutions. Study results and key findings from the COVID-19 pandemic]. In J. Meißner, & A. Schach, Eds., *Professionelle Krisenkommunikation: Basiswissen, Impulse und Handlungsempfehlungen für die Praxis [Professional Crisis Communication: Basic Knowledge, Impulses and Recommendations for Practical Action]* (pp. 131–154). Wiesbaden: Springer Fachmedien. http://doi.org/10.1007/978-3-658-43639-1_9

Schmidt, M. G. (2015). The four worlds of democracy: Commentary on Arend Lijphart's revised edition of Patterns of Democracy (2012). In V. Schneider, & B. Eberlein, Eds., *Complex Democracy: Varieties, Crises, and Transformations* (pp. 29–49). Cham, Switzerland: Springer.

Schwarz, A., Sellnow, D. D., Sellnow, T. D., & Taylor, L. E. (2024). Instructional risk and crisis communication at higher education institutions during COVID-19: Insights from practitioners in the global south and north. *Journal of International Crisis and Risk Communication Research, 7*(1), 1–47. https://doi.org/10.56801/jicrcr.V7.i1.1

Sellnow, D. D., & Sellnow, T. L. (2019). The IDEA model for effective instructional risk and crisis communication by emergency managers and other key spokespersons. *Journal of Emergency Management (Weston, Mass.), 17*(1), 67–78.

Sohrabi, C., Alsafi, Z., O'neill, N., Khan, M., Kerwan, A., Al-Jabir, A., & Agha, R. (2020). World Health Organization declares global emergency: A review of the 2019 novel coronavirus (COVID-19). *International Journal of Surgery, 76*, 71–76.

Strömbäck, J., & Kiousis, S. (Eds.). (2011). *Political Public Relations: Principles and Applications.* New York, NY: Routledge.

Tagliacozzo, S., Albrecht, F., & Ganapati, N. E. (2023). Public agencies tweeting the COVID-19 pandemic: Cross-country comparison of must have and forgotten communication topics. *Frontiers in Communication, 8*, 1–13.

Tannenbaum, M. B., Hepler, J., Zimmerman, R. S., Saul, L., Jacobs, S., Wilson, K., & Albarracín, D. (2015). Appealing to fear: A meta-analysis of fear appeal effectiveness and theories. *Psychological Bulletin, 141*(6), 1178–1204.

Tomić, Z., Vegar, V., & Radalj, M. (2024). Crisis communication in healthcare. *Medicina Academica Integrativa*, 1(1), 11–25. Retrieved August 20, 2024 from https://pauk.sum.ba/ojs/mai/article/view/4

Veil, S., Reynolds, B., Sellnow, T. L., & Seeger, M. W. (2008). CERC as a theoretical framework for research and practice. *Health Promotion Practice, 9*(4_suppl), 26S–34S.

Voges, T. S., Jin, Y., Eaddy, L. L., & Spector, S. (2023). Effective communication management in a public health crisis: Lessons learned about COVID-19 pandemic through the lens of health communication executives. *Journal of Communication Management, 27*(1), 64–83.

WHO (World Health Organization). (1946). *Constitution of the World Health Organization.* Retrieved August 20, 2024 from https://apps.who.int/gb/bd/PDF/bd47/EN/constitution-en.pdf

WHO (World Health Organization). (2008 [2005]). *International Health Regulations.* 2nd edn., Reprint Geneva: WHO Press.

WHO (World Health Organization) (2022). *Infodemic.* Retrieved March 6, 2023 from https://www.who.int/health-topics/infodemic

WHO (World Health Organization) (2024a). *WHO Director-General declares mpox outbreak a public health emergency of international concern.* Retrieved August 24, 2024 from www.who.int

WHO (World Health Organization) (2024b). *Emergencies.* Retrieved August 23, 2024 from https://www.who.int/emergencies/situations

Witte, K. (1992). Putting the fear back into fear appeals: The extended parallel process model. *Communication Monographs, 59*(4), 329–349.

Witte, K. (1994). Fear control and danger control: A test of the extended parallel process model (EPPM). *Communication Monographs, 61*(2), 113–132.

Xu, Y., & Löffelholz, M. (2024). Multimodal crisis messaging in times of pandemic: Comparing Instagram posts published by governments and public health institutions in Germany, Türkiye, the UK, and the USA. *International Journal of Communication, 18*, 4003–4030.

Yang, S. U. (2018). Effects of government dialogic competency: The MERS outbreak and implications for public health crises and political legitimacy. *Journalism and Mass Communication Quarterly, 95*(4), 1011–1032.

Author's Bio

Dr. Martin Löffelholz is Professor of Media Studies and Head of the International Crisis Communication Research Group at the Technische Universität Ilmenau, Germany, and former President of the Swiss German University in Jakarta, Indonesia. Since 2021, he has been the spokesperson of the DECIPHER research consortium, which analyzes the crisis communication strategies of governments in Europe and the United States. He has conducted numerous research projects, and he is (co-)author or (co-)editor of more than 400 publications, including 22 books. His research has been published in journals such as *Journalism Theory*, *Journalism Practice*, *International Journal of Communication*, *Brazilian Journalism Research*, *Equid Novi*, and *Journalism Studies*, among others. Martin has taught in more than 30 countries, mainly in the areas of crisis and war communication, political and intercultural communication, journalism, and regional cooperation. He is a recipient of the International Crisis and Risk Communication Association's *Award for Excellence in Connecting Research to Practice.*

Dr. Yi Xu is a postdoctoral researcher at the Institute for Communication Science, Friedrich Schiller University Jena, Germany. She received her PhD from the Technische Universität Ilmenau, Germany in 2023. Her research interests include multimodal framing, risk and crisis communication, visual political communication, journalism studies, and public diplomacy. From 2021 to 2024, Yi worked for the DECIPHER research project, which concentrated on cross-national comparative studies of risk and crisis communication by governments and public health institutions in Europe and the United States during the COID-19 pandemic. Her research focuses on instructive crisis messages, crisis communication strategies, framing, and newsworthiness in institutional press releases and social media posts. Her work has appeared in journals such as the *International Journal of Communication, Journalism Practice, Journalism & Mass Communication Quarterly*, and *Journalism Studies.* In 2022, she received the Top Student Paper Award from the Visual Communication Studies Division of the International Communication Association.

8

International Organizational Crisis Communication

A Simple Rules Approach to Managing Crisis Complexity

Andrew S. Pyle[1], Ryan P. Fuller[2], and Robert R. Ulmer[3]

[1] Department of Communication, Clemson University, Clemson, SC, USA
[2] Department of Management & Organizations, College of Business, California State University-Sacramento, Sacramento, CA, USA
[3] Greenspun College of Urban Affairs, University of Nevada Las Vegas, Las Vegas, NV, USA

Introduction

While it has long been well known and accepted that organizational crisis communication is a topic of global significance, events such as the COVID-19 pandemic have brought into stark relief the impact that global crises can have on organizations, communities, nations, and international systems (Jong, 2020; Noar & Austin, 2020). The pandemic is a recent, relevant example of how a crisis (or series of crises) can have a lasting impact on physical and mental health, social norms, and work practices (Gilbert & Bever, 2023). Organizations increasingly have international reach and impact but are also shaped by a range of difficult-to-predict global pressures. Consider the global effects on national economies, energy prices, and food prices following Russia's invasion of Ukraine in 2022 (Lawless, 2023). Following the invasion, digital diplomacy efforts by Ukraine and its allies led to global organizations such as McDonald's and Coca-Cola being pressured by consumers to withdraw their business interests from Russia (Boatwright & Pyle, 2023).

Crises in global organizations create international consequences. Organizations, their leaders, and their employees are charged with meeting the communication demands of diverse international stakeholders during crises. For these reasons, research on crisis communication is increasingly focused on how to manage crises, including those with international reach. Crisis communication research and practice has reached a critical moment. The challenge for crisis communication scholars is to develop theory and practice that will meet the needs of diverse communities, cultures, nations, and regions. A critique of crisis communication research raised in the previous edition of this text was how frequently crisis communication research

The Handbook of International Crisis and Risk Communication Research, Second Edition.
Edited by Andreas Schwarz, Matthew W. Seeger, and Sora Kim.

provides only descriptive accounts of how organizations communicate (see, e.g., Benoit, 1995; Coombs, 2011, 2016; Fearn-Banks, 2011; Frandsen & Johansen, 2010; Gilpin & Murphy, 2008; Hearit, 2006), as well as a call for more literature focusing on international crisis communication, particularly with theoretical approaches suited specifically to the study of international crisis communication.

In this chapter, we review the simple rules process for meeting the knowledge and skill demands of international organizational crisis communication originally explored in the previous edition of this handbook (Ulmer & Pyle, 2021). We argue here that simple rules, which are a part of complexity theory research and practice, are a practical way to meet the demands faced by global organizations in crisis (Sull & Eisenhardt, 2012, 2015). First, we review organizational crisis communication literature, focusing specifically on intercultural and international organizational crisis communication. Second, we provide a roadmap for considering a simple rules approach for creating research and practice in international organizational crisis communication. Finally, we consider relevant cases, highlighting the value of this approach for effective international organizational crisis communication.

International Organizational Crisis Communication

Organizational Crisis Communication Theories

Organizational crises are dynamic and complex. Crisis communication scholars have devoted much effort to analyzing organizational crisis management. This research may be organized according to frameworks that describe the impact of crisis types on communication and that describe the developmental stages of crisis and communication (for a comprehensive overview of frameworks and approaches, see Sellnow & Seeger, 2021). These developmental approaches include descriptions of the role communication plays at each stage. Theories have also explored communication and the management of organizational crises, including decision-making and leadership, and ethical issues in organizational crisis communication (Seeger et al., 2003, 2012).

The current state of theory in organizational crisis communication is generally bifurcated. On one side is theory and research that tends to emphasize the critical nature of an organization's image or reputation in crisis communication (Benoit, 1997; Coombs & Halladay, 2002; Hearit, 2006). These cluster together under theories of image repair, corporate apologia, and situational crisis communication. Image repair literature, for example, explains how post-crisis communication strategies can be used to repair the image of an organization following a crisis (Benoit, 1997). The apologia literature examines how organizations can and should apologize for transgressions or attacks that result in crises and negatively impact an organization's image (Hearit, 2006). Situational crisis communication theory "evaluates the reputational threat posed by the crisis situation and then recommends crisis response strategies based upon the reputational threat level" (Coombs, 2011, p. 138). In each case, these theories describe communication strategies and guidance for repairing the image or reputation of the organization in the aftermath of a crisis. These approaches also, arguably, represent the dominant research tradition in organizational crisis communication.

Much of the literature in this area has historically been U.S.-centric and relied too heavily on the potentially narrow viewpoint of scholars from one cultural context. In recent years, crisis communication scholarship has expanded rapidly across multiple cultural contexts with cutting-edge crisis research coming from around the globe. A well-established example of this work is the scholarship of Frandsen and Johansen on their ***multivocal approach*** to organizational crisis communication via their ***rhetorical arena model*** (also referred to as "rhetorical arena theory," see Frandsen & Johansen, 2009, 2010, 2011, 2016, 2022). Frandsen and Johansen's model presents the notion that there are multiple valuable voices that come into play in the rhetorical space that is created when crises occur. The model specifically examines voices that are in conflict with one another and has been employed to study areas such as organizational resilience and employee performance (Kim, 2020); fighting crisis misinformation (Jin et al., 2020); and social media influence in crisis (Schwarz, 2012; Zhao et al., 2018). In line with other scholarship in this area, rhetorical arena theory focuses on organizational image and reputation. Per Mayfield et al. (2020), "rhetorical arena theory contends that organizational reputation can improve after a crisis occurs by incorporating the voices of diverse stakeholders in crisis communication" (p. 203).

This research has a rich and long-standing tradition within the field of crisis communication. This research tradition is important because it illustrates how many organizations respond to crises: with denials of responsibility, minimization of the crisis, and shifting the blame away from the crisis-stricken organization in order to reduce attributions of responsibility for the crisis or to protect the image of the organization. Multiple reviews and meta-analyses have identified image and reputation-focused theories as the predominant thought leadership in the field of organizational crisis communication (Arendt et al., 2017; Cheng et al., 2022; Ha & Riffe, 2015; Ma & Zhan, 2016; Manias-Muñoz et al., 2019).

On the other side of the bifurcation in crisis communication theory, there are theories that emphasize the importance of open, honest communication and developing strong stakeholder relationships (Botan, 1993, 1997; Olaniran & Williams, 2001; Olaniran et al., 2012; Ulmer et al., 2023). These theories emphasize the importance of building and maintaining strong stakeholder relationships, communicating openly and honestly, and promoting renewal rather than attempting to protect the image or reputation of the organization. While the theories listed above tend to be descriptive, theories such as Ulmer et al.'s (2023) discourse of renewal theory take a normative stance on crisis theory, suggesting knowledge, principles, and practices for organizational actors to follow before, during, and after a crisis event (see Pyle et al., 2020 for a comprehensive review of the development and application of the discourse of renewal). Theories on both sides of the bifurcation have been utilized to examine, understand, and evaluate crisis events.

Existing International and Intercultural Crisis Communication Research

The first edition of the *Handbook of International Crisis Communication Research* pointed out the relatively thin body of literature on organizational international and intercultural crisis communication (Falkheimer & Heide, 2006; Frandsen & Johansen, 2010; Lee, 2005). Since that time, more work has been done in this area (e.g., Coombs & Laufer, 2018; Lehmberg & Hicks, 2018; Pyle, 2018; Zhao, 2022). However, a recent Delphi study of crisis communication experts across the world (Manias-Muñoz et al., 2019) reported that the discipline is more established in North America and most theories of crisis communication have been developed by U.S. scholars. The discipline has seen application in studies internationally, but this continues to be an area for needed growth. Most of the intercultural crisis communication research to date has involved case studies on the management of a particular crisis event by an organization in a specific cultural context, as opposed to a cross-cultural examination of multiple cultural contexts. These include episodes such as the Bhopal-Union Carbide disaster, the Chernobyl radiological event, or the Fukushima-Daiichi disaster. There has also been some tangential research in related fields, such as risk communication and management that is applicable to intercultural crisis communication.

Case studies. According to Frandsen and Johansen's (2010) review of intercultural crisis research, most studies up to that point focused on the impact of a crisis on organizations based on their organizational and national cultures. For example, Pinsdorf (2004) studied the impact of disparate national cultures on crises in airline companies. These organizations must manage distinct, sometimes volatile differences of various national cultures both internally with their employees and externally with their customers. Lee (2005) has conducted research on the impact of consumers on organizational crisis events in Hong Kong, attempting to learn how consumers respond to organizational statements following various types of plane crash scenarios.

Taking a more cross-cultural approach, Fearn-Banks (2011) explored the international response to the growing HIV/AIDS epidemic in sub-Saharan Africa. Fearn-Banks's study critiques the crisis responses carried out by organizations in six different African countries. Another effort at exploring cross-cultural crisis management was Hearit's (2006) study of the apology after an American nuclear-powered submarine collided with a Japanese fishing boat, resulting in the deaths of nine of the fishing boat passengers. More recently, Lehmberg and Hicks (2018) examined how multinational corporations could adopt a "glocalization" approach, or leveraging global resources while remaining responsive to the needs and interests of local customers around the world. They argue that the process of glocalization which has helped corporations like McDonald's become internationally successful can also help crisis communicators be more successful in a global context. Connecting once again to Frandsen and Johansen's (2022) rhetorical arena theory, Zhao and Valentini (2022) examined the political factors that informed stakeholder perceptions of the crisis faced by the National Basketball Association in China in 2019. The authors found a great deal of politically divided rhetoric, along with a shift in the organization's stance as the crisis unfolded. The case study captured the intricacies of a cross-cultural, politically complex conflict building into an extended crisis.

Literature outside the communication discipline. Varley (2009) conducted a comprehensive case study of the 2003 outbreak of SARS in Toronto. Varley approached the case study from a public administration perspective, studying and reflecting on the response to the outbreak from the point of view of a governmental agency. The review of the case provides important insights into the functioning of a health system in Canada as compared to a similar response in the United States. Scholars studying crisis negotiation and hostage negotiation have done interesting cross-cultural research on managing negotiations across cultural boundaries (Hammer, 1997; Hammer & Weaver, 1994). Scholars such as Caprioli and Boyer (2001) have also done important conflict management research across cultural contexts, specifically on the role of gender differences and their impact on violence in international crisis events. In the management literature, we also see scholars exploring organizational crisis response, such as Bundy et al.' (2017) work that sought to bridge the gaps between organizational behavior, public relations, and corporate communication; or the work of Williams et al. (2017), who focused on bridging crisis management with resilience research.

Lastly, there is a body of research that goes beyond the typical focus on corporate communication in crises. Political science scholars such as Gelpi (2001) have studied the impact of international crises on governmental entities and have studied why democracies have historically fared better during crisis events than other types of governments. Outside of the governmental sector, scholars such as Chapman et al. (2022a, 2022b) and Scurlock et al. (2020) have examined the responses of nonprofit organizations to scandals. Outside of scandals, Manoli and Anagnostou (2022) examined FIFA's response to the COVID-19 pandemic. Across these disciplines, scholars are conducting important research and advancing their respective fields, but there remains a dearth of international crisis research in the field of communication.

Need for More Research

Questions about the generalizability of organizational crisis communication work across contexts remain open. International and intercultural organizational crisis communication, therefore, needs to be studied in greater depth. Geert Hofstede's work on *cultural value dimensions* (Hofstede, 1982, 1983; Hofstede & Bond, 1984) has been widely applied to organizational contexts (Hofstede et al., 2010). Despite the focus on organizational contexts,

Hofstede does not describe his work as organizational crisis communication research. Lindsley and Braithwaite (1996) studied cross-cultural conflict in organizational contexts, which is important, as conflict is generally one facet of crisis communication, but they did not explore crisis contexts specifically. Cohen (1987) examined Egyptian-American diplomatic relations, which is another important facet of cross-cultural crisis communication, but the study took place in non-crisis contexts. Saphiere (1996) explored types of behaviors that were productive for global business teams working together on specific projects. Crisis communication scholars can learn from these productive practices, but this study did not explore the implications of working together in crisis contexts. Scholars such as Redmond and Bunyi (1993) have also worked with students to make sense of how people from various cultures process and manage the stress of studying in a foreign country and culture.

Additionally, out of management, organizational psychology, business, and systems scholarship, we see important work related to organizational resilience. Somers (2009) argued that organizational structures and processes could create an environment where organizations would be more likely to demonstrate resilience during and after a crisis. This work followed on the heels of Vogus and Sutcliffe's (2007) theorizing about the importance of resilience building for organizations in crisis. More than a decade later, Duchek (2020) argues that organizations are still struggling to build resilience ahead of facing crises.

All of these areas are important and can help inform crisis communication scholars, but there is still a gap in the literature specifically relating to the study of intercultural crisis communication. For this reason, we propose the complexity theory-inspired simple rules approach to close this gap in studying and conducting crisis communication research, particularly in international and intercultural contexts. Since 2018, the *Journal of International Crisis & Risk Communication Research* has contributed to a growing body of research drawing in scholars from around the globe and expanding the literature well beyond the previous primarily case-based scholarship. In the past five years, scholars from around the world have examined crisis communication dynamics ranging from the Swedish response to the COVID-19 pandemic (Loubere et al., 2023) to public concerns about risk messaging in Singapore (Chen et al., 2021). The scholarship called for by this publication of this and similar internationally focused outlets is helping to answer the call for an increase in international, intercultural crisis communication research. While these and many other approaches in management, organizational theory, and organizational communication in individual, transcultural, and multicultural contexts are valuable, there is a need for this work to continue to grow and develop in the next decade. To develop both crisis communication research and practice, we build upon the simple rules approach. Toward that end, we explain the approach emerging out of complexity science, describe the value added to communication research and practice, and provide case exemplars of international organizations illustrating simple rules or failure to adopt simple rules.

Simple Rules: An Approach to Engaging Dynamic and Complex Contexts

Complexity science developed the idea of a "simple rules" approach for managing complex situations (Epstein, 1995; Sull & Eisenhardt, 2012, 2015). Complex adaptive environments do not need elaborate systems to be managed or understood. Rather, complex systems are better understood by the application and engagement of simple, flexible rules. For instance, water systems such as the oceans, rivers, lakes, and streams are often described as complex, adaptive, and dynamic systems. However, the single rule that water seeks to find its own level is central to understanding water systems. Taken further, in nature, ants and bees do not engage in complex strategic planning initiatives to produce what appear to be elaborate anthills and beehives. Rather, complexity-inspired research suggests that these insects perform a few genetically coded flexible rules iteratively with feedback from their environment to accomplish their goals.

Simple rules are not best practices (Seeger, 2006). Best practices are often described as universal truths or specific guideposts without much room for flexibility in their application. What simple rules call for are a very limited number of flexible guideposts for action followed by sophisticated, iterative responses and communication activities designed to engage the environment and adapt. Where best practices can be described as a process of thinking your way into new ways of acting, simple rules involve a process of not following rules or best practices but acting your way into new ways of thinking (Pascale et al., 2010). Crisis management cannot follow a uniform or consistent response plan due to the nature of the people involved, the conditions of the crisis, or the context of the events. Similarly, best practices generally do not develop from the application of simple rules. What works for one organization due to its expertise, values, communication competence, and the feedback it receives during the process is unique. In addition, best practices do not provide the flexibility or adaptability associated with simple rules.

A common problem in international crisis communication is meeting the communication needs of diverse international stakeholders. Crisis stakeholders are often diverse, and autonomous, each making decisions based upon their own understanding of local circumstances and feedback. By providing simple communication rules to guide messages with stakeholders and incorporating feedback as the crisis unfolds, we can shape communication practices without trying to force a "one size fits all" approach. Similarly, in order to meet the complexity of international organizational crisis communication, we need to be clear about what simple rules are most useful.

Simple Rules for Managing the Complexity of International Crisis Communication

A simple rules approach to international crisis communication involves first addressing the context and purpose of the event. An initial value position or assumption is that the ultimate goal of crisis communication is not to protect the image of an organization or to get the organization out of legal trouble. Rather, the goal is to enhance stakeholder sensemaking about the crisis: to promote safety and wellbeing, create understanding among those stakeholders involved, and resolve the event for the organization and its stakeholders.

The following list (see Table 8.1) describes a simple rules approach to organizational crisis communication. The list also represents examples in the research of very general guidelines for organizational crisis communication that generated useful, productive, and constructive crisis responses.

Table 8.1 Four simple rules for engaging in international organizational crisis communication.

Things organizations should do	*Things organizations should not do*
Be honest	Try to protect its image
Be open	Withhold information
Be relationship focused	Avoid conflict
Be authentic	Control or spin information

Simple Communication Rules Organizations Should Follow During a Crisis

This simple rules approach helps address the gap in existing intercultural organizational crisis literature by suggesting an adaptive, flexible system for approaching crisis communication. The simple rules approach is flexible enough to accommodate multiple disparate international and cultural contexts and helps move away from reliance on past theoretical perspectives and concepts.

Being honest involves providing information to stakeholders that enables them to make significant choices about how to protect themselves from the crisis (Nilsen, 1974). Significant choice provides clear guidelines for honesty in crisis communication and has been discussed extensively in the crisis communication literature as a way to assess the ethicality of crisis communication (Ulmer & Sellnow, 1997; Ulmer et al., 2023). In the early stages of the COVID-19 pandemic, the CDC came under fire for unclear and inaccurate messaging (Chow, 2021). The inconsistent messages coming out of the CDC when many details about the virus and how it spreads resulted in a short-term decrease in trust for the CDC and its directions on how best to respond to the pandemic. Another example of the importance of significant choice is the response by Taiwanese company King Car following the melamine contamination crisis in 2008 (Ku, 2009). King Car discovered that their products had been contaminated, so they immediately recalled the affected products, established a new level of testing, and apologized to the public about the contamination. This response not only saved lives, it resulted in an increased level of public trust in the organization and allowed the company to be more successful following the crisis.

Being open is critical to any crisis response. Openness involves being mindful about evidence surrounding the crisis, the impact of the crisis, responsibility for the crisis, and how your stakeholders will be impacted by the crisis. Mindfulness, according to Langer (1989), is a process of ongoing adaptation to the ever-changing world around us. Consider Ostermann's (2002) example of German police officers learning to manage difficult negotiations with individuals from other countries, cultures, and belief systems. One case involving a suicidal Turkish police officer required the negotiator to learn more about the officer's culture to connect with her on a personal and cultural level. The negotiator was able to suggest a course of action that was in line with the officer's cultural norms, which provided the officer with an option other than suicide. It was the negotiator's mindfulness regarding the Turkish officer's cultural heritage that contributed to successfully resolving the situation. Openness allows organizations to function more effectively in dynamic, complex contexts. Openness also involves communicating with uncertainty during highly evolving and dynamic crises. Evidence supports the necessity of ambiguous communication during highly complex crises (Ulmer et al., 2023). Organizations should also be open to engaging stakeholders in communication about the crisis and to initiate communication with stakeholders as early as possible. Openness, then, is about being accessible and engaged with stakeholders early and throughout the crisis.

Crisis communication is about managing relationships as much as it is about designing messages for stakeholders. During a crisis, organizations should manage positive, negative, and ambivalent stakeholder relationships. Managing relationships is about building consensus, managing difference, and coordinating relationship building among diverse stakeholder networks, often at the same time. It is easy to engage in name-calling and to pull away from angry or demanding stakeholders during a crisis. Conversely, relationship building is about rising above differences, working to manage conflict constructively, and developing communication patterns that result in respectful, honest, debate, discussion, and communication. One example of the value of focusing on relationships is the findings of Diers-Lawson et al. (2021) on stakeholder responses to data breaches. In their study of organizational responses to data breaches, they found that the typical response to data breach management was a reactive crisis management response. In their experiment, they determined that pre-crisis proactive relationship building was more effective for stakeholder engagement and long-term relational health between stakeholders and the organization. Their findings challenged much of what had been assumed in crisis communication literature regarding the value of reactive crisis response strategies.

Authenticity involves the organization knowing its values, its strengths and weaknesses, and communicating in a provisional rather than strategic manner. Crisis communication is a form of communication that must be understandable, clear in terms of its purpose, and genuine. When the people representing organizations try to strategically manipulate information and are not authentically communicating about the crisis, they come off as lacking empathy and understanding about the crisis. These individuals also lose credibility over time. As Cheney and Christensen (2001) point out, "the cumulative effect of… organizational messages perceived by some public to be untruthful or inauthentic can be a wide and deep breach of trust" (p. 260). The concept of authenticity links to Davis's (1960) concept of the "Iron Law of Responsibility" (p. 71). He calls for the social responsibility of businessmen (or organizations) to match or complement their social power. Davis argues that "*continued vitality of business depends upon its vigorous acceptance of socio-human responsibilities along with socio-economic responsibilities*" (p. 74, italics in the original). Being authentic involves clearly communicating your values, what you are experiencing, being empathic about what everyone is going through, and down to earth about how the organization plans to learn from and move beyond the crisis.

Simple Communication Rules Organizations Should Not Follow During a Crisis

The following section examines the rules that organizations should not follow in international crisis communication if they are to be successful. The first simple rule to avoid is focusing on protecting the image of the organization. The image or reputation of the company is held in others. Trying to make people think anything is a counterproductive enterprise. For this reason, organizations that willfully try to protect an image are not likely to enhance sensemaking about the crisis. Organizations that are focused on protecting their image most often use communication strategies to absolve themselves from blame, minimize the crisis, or over reassure the public about the impact of the crisis. These communication "strategies" do not produce constructive approaches to crisis communication. Consider, for example, the early response of Exxon following the Exxon-Valdez oil spill. Rather than accepting responsibility for the event, the organization immediately placed blame on the captain of the ship and attempted to separate itself from direct responsibility (Mauer, 1989). The decision to shunt blame onto two employees rather than accepting even some small amount of responsibility initiated a post-crisis media storm that left Exxon weaker, and with a marred reputation rather than a renewed one, for years to come. When the sole focus of the organization is protecting its reputation, a negative outcome is likely. In contrast to the Exxon response, Ulmer and Pyle (2021) examined local-level communication efforts during the response to the Deepwater Horizon oil spill. While there are well-established critiques of BP's communication efforts on an international platform, Ulmer and Pyle found evidence of concerted efforts to build relationships with local leaders and to help foster trust for a more effective disaster response.

Withholding information leads to counter-productive crisis communication. Organizations that withhold information are often plagued by inaction and the inability to initiate communication with stakeholders following a crisis. One example of the danger of withholding information from stakeholders is the Enron crisis of the early 2000s (Lyon, 2008; Seeger & Ulmer, 2003; Ulmer, 2001). Over the course of several months, it became clear that Enron executives had acting unethically and had withheld vital internal information from key stakeholders (Oppel & Eichenwald, 2002). Additionally, Arthur Andersen, the firm in charge of auditing Enron, was complicit with the deception and attempted to destroy incriminating documents after the investigation into Enron's dealings began (Oppel & Eichenwald, 2002). Eventually, the decision to withhold information led to the dissolution of both Enron and Arthur Andersen. Withholding information also fails to meet the requirement of enhancing sensemaking for stakeholders following a crisis. To engage stakeholders in constructive communication practices organizations must not withhold information about the crisis. Clementson and Xie (2021) studied this dynamic in the context of an organizational spokesperson engaging in evasive messaging, or "spin," during a media interview. They found that evasive communication strategies and spin led to the spokesperson's perception as untrustworthy, which translated to negative impressions of the organization. This held up across multiple experiments, confirming the importance of transparency in organizational crisis communication efforts.

Organizations that avoid conflict are not able to produce constructive crisis responses. An important part of any crisis response is the ability of the people communicating to construct positive outcomes from conflict. Finding ways to collaborate, manage differences, listen, and build consensus is crucial to crisis communication. Both within and outside of the organization there is going to be conflict that must be resolved. One sobering example of dangerous conflict avoidance is the Peanut Butter Corporation of America's (PCA) long-term avoidance of clearly determined salmonella contamination in their products (Goetz, 2013). Stewart Parnell, the president of PCA ignored, avoided, and lied to evade conflict and questioning related to salmonella contaminations until the Food and Drug Administration finally traced the contamination to PCA in 2009 (Goetz, 2013). Had Parnell chosen to address the issues head-on at their outset, in the same way Schwan's managed its salmonella outbreak in 1994 (Sellnow et al., 1998), perhaps PCA would not have been shut down in 2009. Organizations that pull back from conflict, resist engaging in constructive conflict practices, or engage in conflict unproductively are not likely to communicate effectively during the crisis.

Organizations that spin information following a crisis are not contributing to the sensemaking abilities of their stakeholders. Spinning facts or details following a crisis leads to less clarity and understanding by external organizational audiences. Organizations that produce communication practices designed to be opaque rather than transparent are not contributing to stakeholder sensemaking or understanding; rather, these types of communication policies often lead to or exacerbate crisis situations. Consider the decision by Ford automakers to continue producing the Pinto even after they received evidence that a design flaw could lead to dangerous fires in rear-impact collisions (*New York Times*, 1977). The decision to continue producing the Pinto without fixing the flaw or conducting a recall resulted in multiple deaths and a loss of nearly half a billion dollars to Ford Motor Company (Peterson, 1980). In a more recent example of automotive malfeasance, Volkswagen was sanctioned in 2015 for an extensive emissions scandal (Hotten, 2015). Volkswagen had installed small devices in their diesel vehicles that masked their emissions output when tested by governmental environmental assessors. According to a report published in 2019, despite having rebounded to their prior sales levels, Volkswagen has continued to face difficulties related to decreased organizational trust, increased scrutiny, and additional challenges from policymakers (Jung & Sharon, 2019). Organizations that spin facts or details surrounding the crisis are more often called out for a lack of transparency as well as a lack of trustworthiness as a source for crisis information. For these reasons, organizations should not control or spin information concerning the crisis.

Conclusion

The field of organizational crisis communication faces a critical juncture. The field is diverse and includes a wide array of approaches from many disciplines. A broader, more general, and flexible approach will help improve both the research and practice of organizational crisis communication, particularly in international contexts. Simple rules is one such approach.

Furthermore, a simple rules approach will meet the even more dynamic, fluid, and complex needs of international organizational communication.

The simple rules approach is an action-, communication-, and process-centered approach rather than a strategy-focused approach to crisis communication. The results of this approach largely depend upon the rules used and the quality of the interactions. Similar to other dynamic, complex systems, the interactions and the quality and sophistication of the application of the simple rules approach will have a profound impact on this crisis response. For this reason, the simple rules approach is designed for a wide variety of crisis settings and contexts.

More research is needed to describe and explain the character and quality of the dynamic, ongoing organizational communication processes associated with utilizing the simple rules approach. For example, case studies that address the application of simple rules in crisis communication. Also needed is more examination of which simple rules are most effective for organizations in international contexts. Other studies should address the role of knowledge development and skill building in complexity science. Furthermore, this approach calls for revisiting our methods for understanding crisis communication along with our standards for assessing the efficacy of crisis communication. A better understanding of these approaches will ultimately lead to the communication practices that promote safer, more resilient, and transformative organizations and communities around the world.

References

Arendt, C., LaFleche, M., & Limperopulos, M. A. (2017). A qualitative meta-analysis of apologia, image repair, and crisis communication: Implications for theory and practice. *Public Relations Review*, *43*(3), 517–526.

Benoit, W. L. (1995). *Accounts, Excuses and Apologies.* Albany, NY: State University of New York Press.

Benoit, W. L. (1997). Image repair discourse and crisis communication. *Public Relations Review*, *23*, 177–186. http://dx.doi.org/10.1016/S0363-8111(97)90023-0

Boatwright, B. C., & Pyle, A. S. (2023). "Don't Mess with Ukrainian Farmers": An examination of Ukraine and Kyiv's official Twitter accounts as crisis communication, public diplomacy, and nation building during Russian invasion. *Public Relations Review*, *49*(3), 102338. http://doi.org/10.1016/j.pubrev.2023.102338

Botan, C. (1993). A human nature approach to image and ethics in international public relations. *Journal of Public Relations Research*, *5*(2), 71–81. http://doi.org/10.1207/s1532754xjprr0502_02

Botan, C. (1997). Ethics in strategic communication campaigns: The case for a new approach to public relations. *Journal of Business Communication*, *34*(2), 188–202. http://doi.org/10.1177/002194369703400205

Bundy, J., Pfarrer, M. D., Short, C. E., & Coombs, W. T. (2017). Crises and crisis management: Integration, interpretation, and research development. *Journal of Management*, *43*(6), 1661–1692. http://doi.org/10.1177/0149206316680030

Caprioli, M., & Boyer, M. A. (2001). Gender, violence, and international crisis. *Journal of Conflict Resolution*, *45*(4), 503–518. http://doi.org/10.1177/0022002701045004005

Chapman, C. M., Hornsey, M. J., Gillespie, N., & Lockey, S. (2022a). Nonprofit scandals: A systematic review and conceptual framework. *Nonprofit and Voluntary Sector Quarterly*. http://doi.org/10.1177/08997640221129541

Chapman, C. M., Hornsey, M. J., Mangan, H., Gillespie, N., Macchia, S. L., & Lockey, S. (2022b). Comparing the effectiveness of post-scandal apologies from nonprofit and commercial organizations: An extension of the moral disillusionment model. *Nonprofit and Voluntary Sector Quarterly*, *51*(6), 1257–1280. http://doi.org/10.1177/08997640211062666

Chen, X. K., Ang, A., Lee, J. Y., Wong, J., Seng, N. L., Ong, G., & Khader, M. (2021). Identifying the public's psychological concerns in response to COVID-19 risk messages in Singapore. *Journal of International Crisis and Risk Communication Research*, *4*(2), 309–334.

Cheney, G., & Christensen, L. T. (2001). Organizational identity. In F. M. Jablin, & L. L. Putnam, Eds., *The New Handbook of Organizational Communication: Advances in Theory, Research, and Methods* (pp. 231–269). Thousand Oaks, CA: Sage.

Cheng, Y., Funkhouser, C., Raabe, T., & Cross, R. (2022). Examining organization-public relationships in crises: A thematic meta-analysis of updated literature from 1997 to 2019. *Journal of Contingencies & Crisis Management, 30*(2), 148–160.

Chow, D. (April 6, 2021). CDC's messaging problem highlights pandemic's uncertain future. *NBC News.* https://www.nbcnews.com/science/science-news/cdcs-messaging-problem-highlights-pandemics-uncertain-future-rcna602

Clementson, D. E., & Xie, T. (2021). On the merits of transparency in crisis: Effects of answering vs. evading through the lens of deception theory. *International Journal of Strategic Communication, 15*(1), 1–17.

Cohen, R. (1987). Problems of intercultural communication in Egyptian-American diplomatic relations. *International Journal of Intercultural Relations, 11*, 29–47. https://doi.org/10.1016/0147-1767(87)90030-7

Coombs, W. T. (2011). *Ongoing crisis communication: Planning, managing, and responding* (3rd ed.). Thousand Oaks, CA: Sage.

Coombs, W. T. (2016). Reflections on a meta-analysis: Crystallizing thinking about SCCT. *Journal of Public Relations Research, 28*(2), 120–122.

Coombs, W. T., & Halladay, S. J. (2002). Helping crisis managers protect reputational assets: Initial tests of the situational crisis communication theory. *Management Communication Quarterly, 16*, 165–186. https://doi.org/10.1177/089331802237233

Coombs, W. T., & Laufer, D. (2018). Global crisis management–current research and future directions. *Journal of International Management, 24*(3), 199–203.

Davis, K. (1960). Can business afford to ignore social responsibilities? *California Management Review, 2*(3), 70–76.

Diers-Lawson, A., Symons, A., & Zeng, C. (2021). Building crisis capacity with data breaches: the role of stakeholder relationship management and strategic communication. *Corporate Communications: An International Journal, 26*(4), 675–699.

Duchek, S. (2020). Organizational resilience: a capability-based conceptualization. *Business Research, 13*(1), 215–246. http://doi.org/10.1007/s40685-019-0085-7

Epstein, R. (1995). *Simple rules for a complex world.* Cambridge, MA: Harvard University Press.

Falkheimer, J., & Heide, M. (2006). Multicultural crisis communication: Towards a social constructionist perspective. *Journal of Contingencies and Crisis Management, 14*(4), 180–189. https://doi.org/10.1111/j.1468-5973.2006.00494.x

Fearn-Banks, K. (2011). *Crisis communications: A casebook approach* (4th ed.). New York, NY: Routledge.

Frandsen, F., & Johansen, W. (2009). Institutionalizing crisis communication in the public sector: An explorative study in Danish municipalities. *International Journal of Strategic Communication, 3*(2), 102–115. http://doi.org/10.1080/15531180902805460

Frandsen, F., & Johansen, W. (2010). Crisis communication, complexity, and the cartoon affair: A case study. *The Handbook of Crisis Communication*, 425–448. http://doi.org/10.1002/9781444314885.ch21

Frandsen, F., & Johansen, W. (2011). The study of internal crisis communication: Towards an integrative framework. *Corporate Communications: An International Journal, 16*(4), 347–361. http://doi.org/10.1108/13563281111186977

Frandsen, F., & Johansen, W. (2016). *Organizational Crisis Communication: A Multivocal Approach.* Sage.

Frandsen, F. & Johansen, W. (2022). Rhetorical arena theory: Revisited and expanded, ch. 12. In W. T. Coombs & S. J. Holladay (Eds.), *The Handbook of Crisis Communication* (2nd ed.), 169–181. Wiley Blackwell.

Gelpi, C. F. (2001). Winners or losers? Democracies in international crisis, 1918–94. *American Political Science Association, 95*(3), pp. 633–647. Cambridge University Press.

Gilbert, C., & Bever, L. (March 11, 2023). Gyms, pets and takeout: How the pandemic has shifted daily life. *Washington Post.* Retrieved from https://www.washingtonpost.com/wellness/interactive/2023/pandemic-changes-daily-life/

Gilpin, D. R., & Murphy, P. J. (2008). *Crisis Management in a Complex World.* New York: Oxford University Press.

Goetz, G. (February 22, 2013). Peanut Corporation from inception to indictment: A timeline. *Food Safety News.* Retrieved from http://www.foodsafetynews.com/2013/02/peanut-corporation-of-america-from-inception-to-indictment-a-timeline/#.U8_83fk7vLk

Ha, J. H., & Riffe, D. (2015). Crisis-related research in communication and business journals: An interdisciplinary review from 1992 to 2011. *Public relations review, 41*(4), 569–578.

Hammer, M. R. (1997). Negotiating across the cultural divide: Intercultural dynamics in crisis incidents. In *Dynamic Processes of Crisis Negotiation: Theory, Research and Practice* (pp. 105–114). Westport, CT: Praeger.

Hammer, M. R., & Weaver, G. R. (1994). Cultural considerations in hostage negotiations. In G. R. Weaver, Ed., *Culture, Communication, and Conflict: Readings in Intercultural Relations* (pp. 499–510). Needham Heights, MA: Ginn.

Hearit, K. M. (2006). *Crisis Management by Apology: Corporate Response to Allegations of Wrongdoing*. Mahwah, NJ: Lawrence Erlbaum Associates.

Hofstede, G. (1982). Dimensions of national cultures. In R. Rath, H. S. Asthana, D. Sinha, & J. B. H. Sinha, Eds., *Diversity and Unity in Cross-Cultural Psychology*. Swets and Zeiglinger: Lisse, Netherlands.

Hofstede, G. (1983). National cultures in four dimensions: A research-based theory of cultural differences among nations. *International Studies of Management and Organization, 13*(1/2), 46–74. http://doi.org/10.2307/40396953

Hofstede, G., & Bond, M. H. (1984). Hofstede's cultural dimensions: An independent validation using Rokeach's value survey. *Journal of Cross-Cultural Psychology, 15*(4), 417–433. http://doi.org/10.1177/0022002184015004003

Hofstede, G., Hofstede, G. J., & Minkov, M. (2010). *Cultures and Organizations: Software of the Mind*. New York, NY: McGraw-Hill.

Hotten, R. (December 10, 2015). Volkswagen: The scandal explained. *BBC News*. https://www.bbc.com/news/business-34324772

Jin, Y., van der Meer, T. G., Lee, Y. I., & Lu, X. (2020). The effects of corrective communication and employee backup on the effectiveness of fighting crisis misinformation. *Public Relations Review, 46*(3), 101910. http://doi.org/10.1016/j.pubrev.2020.101910

Jong, W. (2020). Evaluating crisis communication. A 30-item checklist for assessing performance during COVID-19 and other pandemics. *Journal of Health Communication, 25*(12), 962–970. http://doi.org/10.1080/10810730.2021.1871791

Jung, J. C., & Sharon, E. (2019). The Volkswagen emissions scandal and its aftermath. *Global Business and Organizational Excellence, 38*(4), 6–15. http://doi.org/10.1002/joe.21930

Kim, Y. (2020). Organizational resilience and employee work-role performance after a crisis situation: Exploring the effects of organizational resilience on internal crisis communication. *Journal of Public Relations Research, 32*(1–2), 47–75. http://doi.org/10.1080/1062726X.2020.1765368

Ku, F. (2009). Organizational renewal: A case study of king car's crisis communication strategies. Unpublished Master's Thesis. University of Arkansas at Little Rock.

Langer, E. J. (1989). Minding matters: The consequences of mindlessness–mindfulness. *Advances in Experimental Social Psychology, 22*, 137–173. Academic Press

Lawless, J. (February 22, 2023). Global impact: 5 ways war in Ukraine has changed the world. *Associated Press*. Retrieved from https://tinyurl.com/yzbbnjfe

Lee, B. K. (2005). Crisis, culture, community. *Communication Yearbook, 29*(1), 275–309.

Lehmberg, D., & Hicks, J. (2018). A 'glocalization' approach to the internationalizing of crisis communication. *Business Horizons, 61*(3), 357–366.

Lindsley, S. L., & Braithwaite, C. A. (1996). "You should 'wear a mask'": Facework norms in cultural and intercultural conflict in maquiladoras. *International Journal of Intercultural Relations, 20*(2), 199–225. http://doi.org/10.1016/0147-1767(96)00002-8

Loubere, N., O'Shea, P., & Göransson, M. B. (2023). Mediating official misinformation during the Covid-19 pandemic: The case of mask scepticism in Sweden's public broadcasting health communication. *Journal of International Crisis and Risk Communication Research, 6*(2), 53–111.

Lyon, A. (2008). The mis/recognition of Enron executives' competence as cultural and social capital. *Communication Studies, 59*(4), 371–387. http://doi.org/10.1080/10510970802467411

Ma, L., & Zhan, M. (2016). Effects of attributed responsibility and response strategies on organizational reputation: A meta-analysis of situational crisis communication theory research. *Journal of Public Relations Research, 28*(2), 102–119.

Manias-Muñoz, I., Jin, Y., & Reber, B. H. (2019). The state of crisis communication research and education through the lens of crisis scholars: An international Delphi study. *Public Relations Review, 45*(4), 101797.

Manoli, A. E., & Anagnostou, M. (2022). Operational crisis communication management: A content analysis of FIFA's communication during Covid-19. *Sport Management Review*. http://doi.org/10.1080/14413523.2022.2059992

Mauer, R. (March 27, 1989). Unlicensed mate was in charge of ship that hit reef, Exxon says. *The New York Times*. Retrieved from http://tinyurl.com/k86epdk

Mayfield, M., Mayfield, J., & Walker, R. (2020). *Fundamental Theories of Business Communication: Laying a Foundation for the Field*. Springer Nature.

New York Times. (August 10, 1977). Ford Pinto scored in coast magazine on Peril from fire. Retrieved from http://query.nytimes.com/gst/abstract.html?res=9E06E5DC1F38E036A05752C1A96E9C946690D6CF

Nilsen, T. R. (1974). *Ethics of Speech Communication* (2nd ed.). Indianapolis, IN: Bobbs-Merrill.

Noar, S. M., & Austin, L. (2020). (Mis) communicating about COVID-19: Insights from health and crisis communication. *Health Communication*, *35*(14), 1735–1739. http://doi.org/10.1080/10410236.2020.1838093

Olaniran, B., & Williams, D. (2001). Anticipatory model of crisis management. In R. Heath, Ed., *Handbook of Public Relations* (pp. 487–500). Thousand Oaks, CA: Sage.

Olaniran, B. A., Scholl, J. C., Williams, D. E., & Boyer, L. (2012). Johnson and Johnson phantom recall: A fall from grace or a re-visit of the ghost of the past. *Public Relations Review*, *38*(1), 153–155. http://doi.org/10.1016/j.pubrev.2011.08.001

Oppel, R. A., & Eichenwald, K. (January 16, 2002). Enron's collapse: The overview. *The New York Times*. Retrieved from http://www.nytimes.com/2002/01/16/business/enron-s-collapse-overview-arthur-andersen-fires-executive-for-enron-orders.html?module=Search&mabReward=relbias%3Ar%2C%7B%222%22%3A%22RI%3A14%22%7D

Ostermann, B. M. (2002). Cultural differences make negotiations different: Intercultural hostage negotiations. *Journal of Police Crisis Negotiations*, *2*(2), 11–20.

Pascale, R., Sternin, J., & Sternin, M. (2010). *The Power of Positive Deviance: How Unlikely Innovators Solve the World's Toughest Problems*. Harvard, MA: Harvard Business Review Press.

Peterson, I. (July 30, 1980). $467.9 Million loss, a company record reported by Ford. *The New York Times*. Retrieved from http://www.lexisnexis.com.mutex.gmu.edu/hottopics/lnacademic/

Pinsdorf, M. K. (2004). *All Crises are Global: Managing to Escape Chaos*. New York: Fordham University Press.

Pyle, A. S. (2018). Intercultural crisis communication: Examining the experiences of crisis sojourners. *Journal of Applied Communication Research*, *46*(3), 388–407. http://doi.org/10.1080/00909882.2018.1467031

Pyle, A. S., Fuller, R. P., & Ulmer, R. R. (2020). Discourse of renewal: State of the discipline and a vision for the future. The handbook of applied communication research, 343–361.

Redmond, M. V., & Bunyi, J. M. (1993). The relationship of intercultural communication competence with stress and the handling of stress as reported by international students. *International Journal of Intercultural Relations*, *17*, 235–254. http://doi.org/10.1016/0147-1767(93)90027-6

Saphiere, D. M. H. (1996). Productive behaviors of global business teams. *International Journal of Intercultural Relations*, *20*(2), 227–259. http://doi.org/10.1016/0147-1767(95)00043-7

Schwarz, A. (2012). How publics use social media to respond to blame games in crisis communication: The Love Parade tragedy in Duisburg 2010. *Public Relations Review*, *38*(3), 430–437. http://doi.org/10.1016/j.pubrev.2012.01.009

Scurlock, R., Dolsak, N., & Prakash, A. (2020). Recovering from sandals: Twitter coverage of Oxfam and save the children scandals. *VOLUNTAS: International Journal of Voluntary and Nonprofit Organizations*, *31*, 94–110. http://doi.org/10.1007/s11266-019-00148-x

Seeger, M. W. (2006). Best practices in crisis communication: An expert panel process. *Journal of Applied Communication Research*, *34*, 232–234. http://doi.org/10.1080/00909880600769944

Seeger, M. W., & Ulmer, R. R. (2003). Explaining Enron communication and responsible leadership. *Management Communication Quarterly*, *17*(1), 58–84. http://doi.org/10.1177/0893318903253436

Seeger, M. W., Sellnow, T. L., & Ulmer, R. R. (2003). *Communication and Organizational Crisis*. Westport, CT: Greenwood Publishing Group.

Seeger, M. W., Sellnow, T. L., & Ulmer, R. R. (2012). Communication, organization, and crisis. *Communication Yearbook*, *21*, 231.

Sellnow, T. L., & Seeger, M. W. (2021). *Theorizing Crisis Communication* (2nd ed.). Hoboken, NJ: John Wiley & Sons.

Sellnow, T. L., Ulmer, R. R., & Snider, M. (1998). The compatibility of corrective action in organizational crisis communication. *Communication Quarterly*, *46*, 60–74. http://doi.org/10.1080/01463379809370084

Somers, S. (2009). Measuring resilience potential: An adaptive strategy for organizational crisis planning. *Journal of Contingencies & Crisis Management*, *17*(1), 12–23. http://doi.org/10.1111/j.1468-5973.2009.00558.x

Sull, D., & Eisenhardt, K. M. (2012). Simple rules for a complex world. *Harvard Business Review*, *90*(9), 68–74.

Sull, D., & Eisenhardt, K. M. (2015). *Simple Rules: How to Thrive in a Complex World*. Houghton Mifflin Harcourt.

Ulmer, R. R. (2001). Effective crisis management through established stakeholder relationships: Malden Mills as a case study. *Management Communication Quarterly*, *14*, 590–615. http://doi.org/10.1177/0893318901144003

Ulmer, R. R., & Pyle, A. S. (2021). Finding renewal in the midst of disaster: The case of the deepwater horizon oil spill. *Public Relations Review*, *47*(1), 102001.

Ulmer, R. R., & Sellnow, T. L. (1997). Strategic ambiguity and the ethic of significant choice in the tobacco industry's crisis communication. *Communication Studies*, *48*, 215–233. http://doi.org/10.1080/10510979709368502

Ulmer, R. R., Sellnow, T. L., & Seeger, M. W. (2023). *Effective Crisis Communication: Moving from Crisis to Opportunity* (5th ed.). Thousand Oaks: Sage.

Varley, P. (2009). SARS in Toronto: Emergency response system under duress. In A. M. Howitt, & H. B. Leonard, Eds., *Managing Crises: Responses to Large-Scale Emergencies*. Washington, DC: CQ Press.

Vogus, T. J., & Sutcliffe, K. M. (2007). Organizational resilience: Towards a theory and research agenda. In *2007 IEEE International Conference on Systems, Man and Cybernetics* (pp. 3418–3422). IEEE. October,

Williams, T. A., Gruber, D. A., Sutcliffe, K. M., Shepherd, D. A., & Zhao, E. Y. (2017). Organizational response to adversity: Fusing crisis management and resilience research streams. *Academy of Management Annals*, *11*(2), 733–769. http://doi.org/10.5465/annals.2015.0134

Zhao, H. (2022). When organizational crises meet nationalism: Crisis communication of multinational corporations in the Chinese context. *Public Relations Review*, *48*(3), 102198.

Zhao, H., & Valentini, C. (2022). Navigating turbulent political waters: From corporate political advocacy to scansis in the case of NBA-China crisis. *Journal of Public Relations Research*, *34*(1–2), 64–87. http://doi.org/10.1080/1062726X.2022.2064288

Zhao, X., Zhan, M., & Liu, B. F. (2018). Disentangling social media influence in crises: Testing a four-factor model of social media influence with large data. *Public Relations Review*, *44*(4), 549–561. http://doi.org/10.1016/j.pubrev.2018.08.002

Authors' Bio

Andrew S. Pyle is Associate Professor of Communication in the Department of Communication at Clemson University. He studies the intersection of crisis communication and intercultural communication. Much of his current research focuses on the challenges emergency responders face when deploying to diverse cultural contexts. He also studies how organizations utilize social media platforms to engage key stakeholders during and after crisis events. He teaches courses in Public Relations and Intercultural Communication.

Ryan P. Fuller is Associate Professor of Management in the Department of Management and Organizations at California State University, Sacramento. His research focuses on communication practices that support pre-crisis preparedness and crisis responses of organizations.

Robert R. Ulmer is Professor of Communication Studies and Dean of the Greenspun College of Urban Affairs at UNLV. His interests focus on creating renewal, growth, and opportunity through effective risk and crisis communication. He has published 6 books and over 50 articles on the topic and secured numerous grants and contracts to support his research. He has served as a consultant, working with a wide variety of organizations on how to effectively prepare for and manage risk and crises effectively.

9

Political Crises

Bengt Johansson and Orla Vigsø
Department of Journalism, Media, and Communication, University of Gothenburg, Gothenburg, Sweden

Political dimensions have traditionally not been a central aspect of crisis communication research, and political crises are, if not neglected, at least subordinated in crisis communication and crisis management research. Politics cannot be separated from crisis since political actors are crisis actors and political decisions are central for risk and crisis preparedness as well as for crisis management (Auer, 2016; Johansson & Vigsø, 2020). During the last decade, there has been a growing awareness of the political dimensions of crisis communication, both in terms of acknowledging that organizational and societal crises include political dimensions but also a growing interest in political crises as such (Boin et al., 2017; Salomonsen & t'Hart, 2020).

Political crises focus primarily on political power and how it is used, which makes concepts like responsibility, accountability, and blame central (Frandsen & Johansen, 2020). This will have consequences for the strategic management of a crisis and the strategic communication, as different things are at stake in a political crisis compared to other types of crises. In all of the aspects dealt with below, one must also take into account the role of risk and risk assessment, as the actors are aware of how potential crises can harm their position. The crisis theories deal with the situation where a crisis has manifested itself, but the strategic management from all actors also includes the prevention of crises as risks are assessed and measures taken to try and avoid future damaging situations.

The main part of this chapter will cover four research areas of political crises and crisis communication: *the politics of crisis management, political scandals, the rhetoric of political leaders*, and *interstate crisis communication*, this to give an overview of how political crises can be related to crisis communication research. Some of these research traditions are well-known for crisis communication scholars while others are more researched in fields less connected to crisis communication. However, we will begin with defining political crises and how they relate to public and corporate crises, thereafter, we present a framework of political arenas to understand the dynamics of how crisis communication in a political crisis must be understood.

Three Subfields of Crisis Management

Frandsen and Johansen (2020) distinguish between public crisis management, political crisis management, and corporate crisis management. These subfields represent "group of actors who solve crisis-related tasks for specific sectors of society defined as an interinstitutional system"

The Handbook of International Crisis and Risk Communication Research, Second Edition.
Edited by Andreas Schwarz, Matthew W. Seeger, and Sora Kim.

(p. 59). Further, these subfields are defined by their respective histories and legal frameworks, vocabulary, and understanding of communication, organization, and management, their key actors, and the specific tasks they solve. It is important to stress that they are at the same time separated and interrelated. Thus, political dimensions are both central in political crises and often relevant in public and corporate crises. Public crisis management during pandemics or disasters has a clear connection with the political system, both because crisis preparedness and legislation are responsibilities for political actors, and because crisis response and accountability failure can have political dimensions. The same is true for corporate crisis management, where legislation often frames different kinds of corporate crises such as accidents or environmental pollution.

If limiting the scope to political crises, a central question is what constitutes a political crisis. Rosentahl and colleagues (1989, p.10) define it as when *"policymakers experience a serious threat to the basic structures or fundamental values and norms of a system, which under time pressure and highly uncertain circumstances necessitates making vital decision."* This definition argues that a political crisis basically is a perceptual crisis, and as Salomonsen and t'Hart (2020) argue, it is also highly dependent on political and historical context. Another more specified definition is offered by Edelman (1977), who argues that political crises are not only perceptual but affective categories and can involve multiple levels of conflict. Further, they disrupt our images and assessments of norms and routines. However, they are not only threats but also opportunities for mobilization of the publics and (self-)dramatization of politicians. Auer (2016, p. 123) also proposes a definition which includes many of the above-mentioned aspects but even acknowledges the limited time for response and that crisis include opposing parties fighting over crisis frames, such as states, political organizations, and individual political actors. Her definition proposes that: "A political crisis is a situation in which a political entity perceives a higher-than-normal threat to one or more of its core values and finite time for response triggered by the behavioral change of another entity and that is characterized by disruptive interaction between the opposing entities."

Apart from these formal definitions, some more aspects can help clarify the characteristics of political crises. A crucial aspect is to what extent the political crisis is *situational* or *institutional* and if it is *urgent* (happens suddenly) or *creeping* (a slowly increasing threat) (Salomonsen & t'Hart, 2020). Situational crises are exogenous, like natural disasters, which are beyond the responsibility of political system actors. Institutional crises are, on the other hand, mistakes made by political institutions, like corruption or scandals. These can be combined in different ways, where urgent and situational crises can be exemplified by the COVID-19 pandemic. An urgent and institutional crisis is the exposure of wrongdoings like any type of political scandal. Climate change or demographic challenges can illustrate creeping and situational crises, while the political system's failure to solve societal challenges is a creeping and institutional crisis. Central in this typology are questions of accountability and responsibility, where institutional crises to a high degree accentuate such claims, while political system actors and organizations are less vulnerable during situational crises as they can be seen as victims (Coombs, 2011). However, a significant aspect is how a situational crisis can turn into an institutional crisis. Even if political system institutions might not be responsible for the situational crisis, they are responsible for crisis response and crisis management. Mismanaged crisis response can then turn into an institutional crisis, which resembles what also is called a "double crisis" (Frandsen & Johansen, 2010). There are many examples of how mismanaged crisis response has turned into a political crisis with accountability claims. Critique against how the government in both the United Kingdom (Lawson & Lugo-Ocando, 2022) and Brazil (Soares et al., 2021) handled the COVID-19 pandemic are examples of this, and criticism against the Norwegian police after the Breivik terrorist attack in 2011 is another (Falkheimer, 2014). The latter is important, as the notion of political actors should not be limited to politicians. Salomonsen and t'Hart (2020) point out that bureaucrats and civil servants should be included when discussing political crises, not at least since political administrative organizations like government agencies often are those being responsible for the crisis response.

Another aspect connected to accountability is the distinction between *operational* and *political* closure. From a government perspective, the ideal is the simultaneous presence of both, where the accountability questions and the public debate are over at the same time as the crisis at hand is dealt with operationally. Boin et al. (2017) describe the ending of WWII as an example of such a closure. From a Western perspective, the AIDS epidemic was a politically closed crisis in the 1990s, but operationally it is still ongoing. An operationally closed but politically open crisis could be the aftermath of how different terrorist attacks, school shootings, accidents, or disasters have been dealt with, where the political debate continues long after the crisis has ended operationally. A crisis without both operational and political closure is exemplified by Boin and colleagues by the 9/11 terrorist attack.

Political Arenas – Stakeholders, Interest Groups, and Voters

A way to a deeper understanding of the complexity of crisis communication in political crises is to use the concept of arenas, which politicians need to manage and communicate with simultaneously during a crisis. The political scientist Sjöblom (1968) proposed the arena framework to understand party strategies in a multiparty system, but this framework works to understand strategic communication during a political crisis as well, where politicians need to address different audiences to control political power.

The electoral arena (voters) is of course central to withhold political power, and the objective on this arena is to maximize voter support, both of which are related to electoral success. In today's permanent election campaigns, however, it is also a question of support in opinion polls. A possible loss of reputation and trust among the general public because of a political crisis is of great significance, both to the individual politician and to the political party. Due to the crisis, the party will often demand that the responsible politician resigns, or persuade him/her to do so, so that the popular support for and trust in the party is not damaged. Crisis communication in a political crisis is therefore also addressed to the *internal arena*. The strategic communication within the internal arena is directed towards securing or strengthening the relative position of the sender, be it an individual or a group of individuals. The internal arena is delicate during a crisis. The position of those responsible for the crisis is weakened, and competitors inside the party might see their chance to move upward in the party hierarchy.

Further, in a political crisis, the *parliamentary arena* is crucial as it sets the scene for the "everyday politics" of negotiations, debates, committee meetings, and so on. In a political crisis, other parties in parliament might take the opportunity to address criticism and obstruct work inside the parliament. Negotiations, committee meetings, and other aspects of everyday work can also be used strategically. Other scholars have added *public administration* as another arena in which politicians act strategically. During a political crisis, this arena can become central, not at least if the crisis involves government agencies or authorities on a regional or local level. Other possible arenas to include in a political crisis is the *civil society arena*, where trade organizations, cooperations, trade unions, NGOs, and other organizations might feel forced to address the public depending on their involvement in the crisis.

Strömbäck and Esser (2017) propose that the *media arena* should be considered as a strategic arena. However, we argue that the media arena is not an arena like the above mentioned, but instead it is used predominantly to influence the other arenas, which of course makes it central when managing a political crisis. From a political actor perspective, the media image is often seen as mirroring the public's perceptions of the attitudes and behavior of the actors in different arenas, including the electoral and civil society arenas. Political responses during a crisis are reactions to accusations or allegations by the media, and the response from the organization, in its turn, informs and influences the perception of the behavior among the voters and actors in other arenas. The media then takes up the perception of the public, the angry voices of "the common people," the victims, or other people affected by what the political actors responsible for handling the crisis are doing. It is at this stage that a general moral outrage may arise due to the perception of the behavior as transmitted by the media and the perception of the response of the organization as transmitted by the media. If moral outrage is widespread at this point, the organization faces a scandal, which might turn into a crisis if it results in any form of damaging action from the public and/or a damaging loss of trust in the organization.

The arena framework is based on democracy, where free speech, independent media, and a strong civil society are the pillars on which the political system rests. An important question is of course if political crises are relevant in more authoritarian regimes. Research shows that political crisis can occur even in strong authoritarian regimes like China, where a mismanaged natural disaster or corruption can have political consequences, be it that the reactions from citizens and civil society are more limited as repression from the state is much stronger (Chan, 2013).

Four Research Traditions of Political Crisis and Crisis Communication

In the following section, we will present four different research traditions dealing with political crises: the politics of crisis management, political scandals, the rhetoric of political leaders, and interstate crisis communication. In each section, we will present a definition of the field, key concepts, and important findings, with a special emphasis on their relation to strategic aspects.

The Politics of Crisis Management

This tradition has been developed around the two research centers, the Leiden University Crisis Research Center (CRC), and the Center for Crisis Management Research and Training (CRISMART) (Frandsen & Johansen, 2020). Their research has mainly been occupied with how political leaders manage political crises, and communication is seen as an integrated part of crisis management. The basic normative assumption for this research tradition is that public leaders have a special responsibility to help safeguard society from the adverse consequences of a crisis (Boin et al., 2017). Citizens also expect their leaders to mitigate a crisis and hold them accountable for both crisis preparedness and decision-making during a crisis. The arena framework is central to the politics of crisis management, as crises will amplify divisions in society, but also between organizations, groups, and individuals within the government.

The management of political crises is evaluated in a crisis cycle of five stages, where the first one deals with to what extent leaders are able to detect a crisis and understand what happens (sense making), the second if critical decisions are taken by the right people (decision making), the third focuses on how the crisis is framed and communicated to the citizens (meaning making), the fourth phase on how accountability processes are dealt with (terminating), and the fifth and last (learning) on how and what is learned and implemented from a political crisis.

Central in all these five phases of a political crisis is the question of legitimacy, and as the core relationship in a political crisis is the relations with the voters, all these phases are determined by how a successful or mismanaged crisis will affect citizens' support for and trust in their leaders.

A somewhat different perspective inside this tradition is the crisis exploitation theory (Salomonsen & t'Hart, 2020). All leaders – corporate, organizational, and public leaders – deal with crisis framing and responsibility, but according to the crisis exploitation theory, political leaders have an interest in labeling a situation as a crisis and using it as a political weapon. This diverges politicians from other leaders. A central point here is the frame contest perspective, with political actors using different frames and counter-frames to create a beneficial narrative. During the COVID-19 pandemic, which was also a political crisis, we saw numerous examples of how politicians tried to frame the crisis and the chosen strategy in a way which was beneficial to themselves in relation to the voters.

As already pointed out, responsibility and accountability are important concepts in the politics of the crisis management tradition. Consequently, blame, blame risk, blame avoidance, and similar concepts have become the cornerstones of the politics of crisis management. A central thought is that voters have a negative bias, meaning that they are more sensitive to losses than gains, which is why politicians' main drive is to avoid blame for unpopular decisions rather than gaining credit for popular decisions (Weaver, 1986). Researchers inside the tradition of politics of crisis management have developed lists of blame strategies, including many of the aspects which are taken up by image repair theory.

Political Scandals

When looking into crisis communication, one will inevitably come across the concept of scandal. Even if crisis and scandal seem to have a lot in common, it is necessary for researchers to keep them apart; not all crises are scandals, and even if a scandal may lead to a crisis, it is a crisis of a particular kind. When talking about the political sphere, a key factor in a scandal is that the public demands accountability and that the scandalized takes responsibility (Johansson & Vigsø, 2020).

Scandals deal with transgressions of social norms or moral codes, but these transgressions are not sufficient to create a scandal. The inappropriate actions must be revealed and become known to someone else, something which always happens through the media, turning the media audience into "the public." Furthermore, the actions need to arouse a feeling of offense and indignation among those who hear about them. In addition, the disclosure and publicly expressed criticism must pose a threat to the reputation of the individual/organization who committed the transgression (Thompson, 2000). Furthermore, political scandals can be both personal and institutional, and while some researchers claim that in order for a scandal to be political, it has to involve political institutions, political processes, or decisions, most research on political scandals includes both institutional and personal scandals (Allern & Pollack, 2012).

A great deal of research in political scandals takes as its starting point Thompson's (2000) distinction between three types of political scandals: the sexual-political scandal, the financial-political scandal, and the power scandal. Even if Thompson pays attention to the importance of mediated visibility, a fourth type of scandal – the talk scandal – has been proposed by Ekström and Johansson (2008, 2019) to capture the role of mediated talk (see also Allern & Pollack, 2012). The talk scandal focuses on how utterances by politicians create scandals, originating in speech acts where discursive norms and codes are transgressed. The central question is what people in a certain position are allowed to say and how they should behave in public talk and discourses.

Considerable attention has been paid to the impacts of the 24/7 news cycle on scandals, with the breakthrough of social media, this has increased even more rapidly (Burkenhardt, 2018). Predictions of range and effects are more difficult and scandal management strategies must be decided during a short time span. An upside for scandalized politicians is that social media are a resource for how the scandal is framed, as politicians and supporters can question the scandal frame and use crisis management strategies more effectively (Boin et al., 2017).

An important question is of course if there is any empirical support of these scandal consequences or if they are just theoretical assumptions. Von Sikorski (2018) presents a review of different kinds of effects found in previous scandal research, indicating that scandals have a negative effect on evaluations of political candidates. But there are results suggesting the opposite, especially when the accusations are seen as politically biased instead of objective. In general, politicians with a good reputation in terms of being competent politicians seem to be less damaged when being scandalized.

Politicians' reactions to the accusations have also been the subject of study, and so far there seems to be no consensus on a best strategy. As with negative news in general, we find research supporting a decline in voter turnout when scandals are present during a campaign, while other results instead indicate mobilization effects and increased voter turnout. In relation to political trust, there seems to be a correlation between scandals and political trust, but the relationship is conditioned by other factors like partisanship. However, if several politicians and parties are involved in scandals, this can affect citizens' trust in institutions and the political process and strengthen a dissatisfaction with democracy.

The Rhetoric of Political Leaders

Rhetoric has played an important role in crisis communication research, and focus has been on the strategies of apologia, that is the response to accusations (of which an apology is but one of several). Some of the most quoted studies and theories have been made by William Benoit (1995), Keith Michael Hearit (2005), Dan Pyle Millar and Robert L. Heath (2004), but the theories of course date back to the Greeks and Romans, for instance the work *Ad Herennius* attributed to Cicero (1989). The re-awoken interest in apologia was to a large extent due to B.L. Ware and Wil A. Linkugel, who in 1973 stressed the fact that apologia strategies cannot be studied without paying attention to the characteristics of the accusations (kategoria). Different accusations call for different apologias, and this spurred an interest in trying to determine which kind of apologia was most suited, i.e. most effectful, to a specific audience at a specific time as a response to specific accusations. However, the most cited and acknowledged accounts of audiences in contemporary rhetorical research.

> "[...] all have one thing in common: They are speculative, theoretical constructions of the audience. Audiences are either perceptions of the speaker, implied by the text, left out by the text or constituted by the rhetoric. While all these accounts are essential theoretical contributions to our field, none of them deals with actual audiences or takes into consideration any kind of real reception or factual response given by an existing audience. Even though there has been some rhetorical research attending to actual audiences, studying reception [...] and especially using ethnographic approaches [...], rhetorical scholars have mostly limited themselves to textual analysis and rhetorical criticism." (Kjeldsen, 2018, p. 4)

Research has to a large extent focused on corporate crises, but political leaders' rhetoric has been studied, often in combination with large-scale crises like 9/11, Fukushima, and not least COVID-19. What is interesting in relation to political crises is the fact that the goal of the rhetoric differs depending on what sort of crisis we are dealing with. If there is an accusation against a political actor (Prime Minister, minister, or party), apologia is of course an important part, but in situations where a crisis is a threat to the public or where civilians have been victims of events like natural disasters, political leaders are expected to deliver a different discourse. The rhetorical system of genres includes three genres for different situations: the judicial genre which has to do with accusations and defense (like the apologia), the deliberative genre, which is the classic political discourse of speaking in favor of or against suggestions for future decisions, and the demonstrative genre. This genre deals with "what is," demonstrating that this is the case, this is how reality is. The goal of this genre is to produce a feeling of shared beliefs and values in the public, to strengthen the cohesion in a group, and it is thus of paramount importance to politicians in times of crisis.

Political leaders address their subjects with the intent to strengthen the feeling of unity, of a shared belief in who we are and what we believe in (our doxa), and our belief in the leaders and public servants who are dealing with the consequences of the crisis. This has been studied in relation to 9/11 (Bligh et al., 2004), the Gulf Crisis (Wallace et al., 1993), and COVID-19 (Bjørkdahl et al., 2021). Bjørkdahl et al. (2021) conducted a comparative study of Scandinavian Prime Ministers' public speeches and concluded that despite the differences, what unites them is an appeal to solidarity. This is a good example of the need to consider the cultural context when assessing the success or failure of political crisis rhetoric; every rhetorical effort is contextual, and its reception is dependent on the ability of the speaker to address the expectations and doxa of the public.

Interstate Crisis Communication

Auer (2016) points out how intestate crises have been neglected in crisis communication research. Interstate conflicts are usually a topic for political science and international relations research, even if there are a few examples of crisis communication research dealing with crises involving two states, such as the crisis of the Muhammad drawings in 2005 when the Danish newspaper Jyllands-Posten published 12 cartoons depicting the prophet Muhammad, leading to an international conflict between Denmark and Muslim countries (Lindholm & Olsson, 2011). Auer (2016) argues that this is a missed opportunity for crisis communication research to understand how state decision-makers and citizens behave in different phases of such crises, how the crisis is framed and constructed by different parties, and which information is needed and communicated to increase the possibilities of managing such crises.

Interstate crises can be defined as a foreign policy crisis, which was defined by Brecher (1993, p. 3) as arising from the highest-level political policy decision makers' perception of (1) threat to one or more values, (2) finite time for response, and (3), heightened probability of involvement in military hostilities. Research of interstate conflicts generally does not only study the attacked political entity but also the attacker, giving a more holistic view of the situation. It thus fits well with the arena framework described previously, but also with the rhetorical arena theory (RAT) (Frandsen & Johansen, 2020), which acknowledges the need to understand competing voices during a crisis. Just like other political crises, interstate conflict is a matter of political power, where the attacked tries to restore government power, support, and popularity, or increase economic welfare. The attacker might want to increase awareness of group demands, get them accepted, or even cause a regime change (Auer, 2016).

Crisis management strategies in interstate conflicts can include sanctions, threats, and even violence. The clearest examples of a crisis communication perspective are negotiation and mediation, but several communicative strategies to avoid blame, such as denial and bolstering, are found in the literature. Apology is also a common strategy, even if partial apologies seem to be more widespread, where politicians allude to their responsibility but do not formally apologize (Liu, 2007).

The researchers also profile the state that is most likely to initiate a foreign policy crisis: "a new or recent independent member of the global system; with an authoritarian regime; contiguous to, and more powerful than, its adversary; and experiencing domestic instability" (Brecher, 1993, p. 549).

In research on interstate conflicts, the audience is often not taken into account, but perceptions of audience reactions can be used, especially by the attacker and accuser, as we described it in relation to the previous types of political crises. In the already mentioned Muhammad cartoon crisis, orchestrated public outrage in Muslim countries played an important role when legitimizing attacks on Denmark and its government.

Theories on public diplomacy as a form of strategic communication focus on soft power in interstate relations, and Signitzer and Coombs (1992) define it as "the way in both government and private individuals and groups influence directly or indirectly those public attitudes and opinions which bear directly on another government's foreign policy decisions" (p. 138).

In sum, public diplomacy serves as an ongoing crisis management technique in all crisis phases: it supports development cooperation, aims at generating mutual understanding, it builds reputational capital, and reaches out to the (foreign) public. Hence, it supports crisis communication strategies as well as traditional diplomacy (Auer, 2016).

Conclusions

In this chapter, we have presented different traditions of political crises – ***the politics of crisis management, political scandals, the rhetoric of political leaders***, and ***interstate crisis communication***. Risk and crisis communication research would benefit from taking these traditions into consideration to further develop theories and practices of strategic communication to manage crises, as the political dimension almost always is prevalent in contemporary crises.

Political crises are about political power, dealing with individuals as voters. Political leaders are given the mandate to represent voters and are in an accountability relation to them. This relationship between the audience and those in power is thus different compared to other crises, such as public crises or corporate crises, where the relation to the audience is in their role as citizens or customers. The audience relation is also different as there are strong ideological ties between the "ruler and the ruled" in political crises, which creates an opportunity to exploit a crisis, either by defining a situation as being a crisis or by politicians self-scandalizing themselves to gain support from specific segments of voters. Compared to other types of crises, both the attacker and the attacked are central to understand the dynamics and the strategic management of the political crisis. One could argue that the strategic dimension, where political power is at play, therefore is stronger in a political crisis compared to public or corporate crises. What also increases the complexity of political crises is the need to strategically manage the crisis in different arenas – electoral, internal, parliamentary, and public administration – simultaneously using the media arena to reach and influence all arenas in situations characterized by uncertainty and a need to make decisions under time pressure.

References

Allern, S., & Pollack, E. (2012). Mediated scandals. In S. Allern, & E. Pollack, Eds., *Scandalous! The Mediated Construction of Political Scandals on Four Nordic Countries* (pp. 9–28). Nordicom: University of Gothenburg.

Auer, C. (2016). Conceptualizing political crisis and the role of public diplomacy in crisis communication research. In A. Schwarz, M. Seeger, & C. Auer, Eds., *The Handbook of International Crisis Communication Research* (pp. 119–132). Wiley-Blackwell.

Benoit, W. (1995). *Accounts, Excuses, and Apologies: A Theory of Image Restoration Strategies*. State University of New York Press.

Bjørkdahl, K., Kjeldsen, J. E., Villadsen, L., & Vigsø, O. (2021). Argumentum ad solidaritatem: Rhetorical leadership strategies in Scandinavia during COVID-19. In M. Lewis, E. Govender, & K. Holland, Eds., *Communicating COVID-19* (pp. 163–183). Palgrave Macmillan. https://doi.org/10.1007/978-3-030-79735-5_9

Bligh, M. C., Kohles, J. C., & Meindl, J. R. (2004). Charisma under crisis: Presidential leadership, rhetoric, and media responses before and after the September 11th terrorist attacks. *The Leadership Quarterly*, *15*(2), 211–239. https://doi.org/10.1016/j.leaqua.2004.02.005

Boin, A., t'Hart, P., Stern, E., & Sundelius, B. E. (2017). *The Politics of Crisis Management: Public Leadership Under Pressure*. Cambridge University Press.

Brecher, M. (1993). *Crises in World Politics: Theory and Reality.* Pergamon Press.
Burkenhardt, S. (2018). Scandals in the network society. In A. Haller, H. Michael, & M. Kraus, Eds., *Scandalogy. An Interdisciplinary Field* (1st ed., pp. 18–44). Herbert von Halem.
Chan, H. Y. (2013). Crisis politics in authoritarian regimes: How crises catalyse changes under the state–society interactive framework. *Journal of Contingencies & Crisis Management, 21*(4), 200–210.
Cicero (attributed to) (1989). *Ad Herennium.* Translated by Harry Caplan. Harvard University Press.
Coombs, T. W. (2011). Political public relations and crisis communication. In J. Strömbäck, & S. Kiousis, Eds., *Political Public Relations. Principles and Application* (pp. 214–234). Routledge.
Edelman, M. J. (1977). *Political Language: Words that Succeed and Policies that Fail.* Academic Press.
Ekström, M., & Johansen, B. (2008). Talk scandals. *Media, Culture and Society, 30*(1), 61–79.
Ekström, M., & Johansson, B. (2019). Talk scandals: The power of mediated talk. In H. Tumber, & S. Waisboard, Eds., *Routledge Companion to Media and Scandal* (pp. 183–192). Routledge.
Falkheimer, J. (2014). Crisis communication and terrorism: The Norway attacks on 22 July 2011. *Corporate Communications: An International Journal, 19*(1), 52–63. https://doi.org/10.1108/CCIJ-08-2012-0053
Frandsen, F., & Johansen, W. (2010). Crisis communication, complexity, and the cartoon affair: A case study. In W. T. Coombs, & S. J. Holladay, Eds., *The Handbook of Crisis Communication* (pp. 425–448). Wiley-Blackwell.
Frandsen, F., & Johansen, W. (2020). Reframing the field: Public crisis management, political crisis management, and corporate crisis management. In F. Frandsen, & W. Johansen, Eds., *Crisis Communication* (pp. 461–476). De Gruyter Mouton.
Hearit, K. M. (2005). *Crisis Management by Apology.* Routledge.
Johansson, B., & Vigsø, O. (2020). Crisis communication and the political scandal. In F. Frandsen, & W. Johansen, Eds., *Crisis Communication* (pp. 439–460). De Gruyter Mouton.
Kjeldsen, J. E. (2018). Audience analysis and reception studies of rhetoric. In J. E. Kjeldsen, Ed., *Rhetorical Audience Studies and Reception of Rhetoric* (pp. 1–42). Palgrave/Macmillan.
Lawson, B. T., & Lugo-Ocando, J. (2022). Political communication, press coverage and public interpretation of public health statistics during the coronavirus pandemic in the UK. *European Journal of Communication, 37*(6), 646–662. http://doi.org/10.1177/02673231221099407
Lindholm, K., & Olsson, E.-K. (2011). Crisis communication as a multilevel game: The Muhammad Cartoons from a crisis diplomacy perspective. *International Journal of Press/Politics, 16*(2), 254–271. https://doi.org/10.1177/1940161210391785
Liu, B. F. (2007). President Bush's major post-Katarina speeches: Enhancing image repair discourse theory applied to the public sector. *Public Relations Review, 33*(1), 40–48.
Millar, D. P., & Heath, R. L. (2004). *Responding to Crisis. A Rhetorical Approach to Crisis Communication.* Lawrence Erlbaum.
Rosenthal, U., Charles, M. T., & t' Hart, P. (1989). *Coping with Crises: The Management of Disasters, Riots and Terrorism.* Thomas.
Salomonsen, H. H., & t'Hart, P. (2020). Communicating and managing crisis in the world of politics. In F. Frandsen, & W. Johansen, Eds., *Crisis Communication* (pp. 59–102). De Gruyter Mouton.
Signitzer, B. H., & Coombs, T. (1992). Public relations and public diplomacy: Conceptual convergences. *Public Relations Review, 18*(2), 137–147. https://doi.org/10.1016/0363-8111(92)90005-J
Sjöblom, G. (1968). *Party Strategies in a Multiparty System.* Studentlitteratur.
Soares, F. B., Recuero, R., Volcan, T., Fagundes, G., & Sodré, G. (2021). Research note: Bolsonaro's firehose: How Covid-19 disinformation on WhatsApp was used to fight a government political crisis in Brazil. *The Harvard Kennedy School Misinformation Review, 2*(1). https://doi.org/10.37016/mr-2020-54
Strömbäck, J., & Esser, F. (2017). Political public relations and mediatization: The strategies of news management. In P. van Aelst, & S. Walgrave, Eds., *How Political Actors Use the Media. A Functional Analysis of the Media's Role in Politics* (pp. 63–83). Palgrave.
Thompson, J. B. (2000). *The Political Scandal. Power and Visibility in the Media Age.* Polity Press.
Von Sikorski, C. (2018). The content and effects of political scandals: A synopsis. In A. Haller, H. Michael, & M. Kraus, Eds., *Scandalogy. An Interdisciplinary Field* (pp. 135–154). Herbert von Halem.

Wallace, M. D., Suedfeld, P., & Thachuk, K. S. (1993). Political rhetoric of leaders under stress in the gulf crisis. *The Journal of Conflict Resolution*, *37*(1), 94–107.
Weaver, R. K. (1986). The politics of blame avoidance. *Journal of Public Policy*, *6*(4), 371–398.

Author's Bio

Bengt Johansson, PhD, is a professor in journalism and mass communication at the University of Gothenburg, Sweden. His research focuses on different aspects of risk and crisis communication as well as political communication. Johansson has in risk and crisis communication a special interest in citizen perspectives of crisis communication and has published studies on information-seeking, crisis response, and crisis preparedness during different crises. Among his latest publications are the edited volume Communicating a Pandemic, Crisis management in the Nordic countries (Nordicom, with O. Ihlen, J. Lindholm, & M. Blach-Ørsten), No heat, no electricity, no water. oh no!: an IDEA model experiment in instructional risk communication (*Journal of Risk Research*, with D.R. Lane, D.D. Sellnow, & T.W. Sellnow) and When the rally-around-the-flag effect disappears (*Journal of Election, Public Opinion and Parties*, with D. Hopmann & A. Shehata).

Orla Vigsø, is a professor in media and communication studies, at the University of Gothenburg, Sweden. PhD in Scandinavian languages from Uppsala, Sweden, with a thesis on election posters. Professor of Rhetoric at Södertörn University before moving to Gothenburg. He has published works on rhetoric, political communication, visual communication and crisis communication, and participated in several projects funded by the Swedish Contingency Agency, e.g., Rhetorical Aspects of Crisis Communication. Recent publications include *Kriskommunikation* (*Crisis Communication*) 2016; Argumentum ad solidaritatem: Rhetorical Leadership Strategies in Scandinavia During COVID-19 (with Bjørkdahl, K., Kjeldsen, J.E., & Villadsen, L.) in M. Lewis, E. Govender, & K. Holland (Eds.) *Communicating COVID-19. Interdisciplinary Perspectives*; Pandemic Rhetoric, in S.M. Croucher & A. Diers-Lawson (Eds.) *Pandemic Communication* 2023.

Part III

The Role of Legacy Media and Social Media in International Crises and Risks

10

War Reporting in an Evolving Media Landscape

Perspectives and Prospects

Aynur Sarısakaloğlu and Pauline Gidget Estella
Department of Media Studies, Institute of Media and Communication Science, Technische Universität Ilmenau, Ilmenau, Germany

Introduction

The most recent headlines were distressing to say the least: a quickly rising death toll in the decades-long Israel-Palestine War, bloodshed in the civil war in Sudan, and yet another set of casualties in the Russia-Ukraine War that has claimed thousands of civilian lives. In fact, the number of highly violent conflicts (wars and limited wars), as well as the number of states experiencing armed conflicts, have increased compared to 2021 (Heidelberg Institute for International Conflict Research, 2023, p. 4; see also Stockholm International Peace Research Institute, 2023). Undoubtedly, the world has not become more peaceful, lending credence to the claim of novelist Cormac McCarthy (1985): "War was always here. Before man was, war waited for him. The ultimate trade awaiting its ultimate practitioner" (p. 259).

In wars or conflicts, journalism plays a role in how people make sense of the event, and reportage can even contribute to the development of conflicts (Hoxha & Hanitzsch, 2018; see also Philo, 2002; Quandt et al., 2014). This chapter concerns itself with war reporting, in particular how the media has shaped narratives related to wars and the factors that influence the process. It also covers contemporary issues in the field, especially in the time of social media and artificial intelligence. The following sections will delve into some central concepts and provide a brief historical overview on war journalism. The factors affecting reportage will then be discussed, as well as the characteristics and critique of war coverage. The final section focuses on the interplay between technological trends and war reporting.

Re-Imagining War Journalism: War, Crisis, and Mediatization

Literature offers several ways of conceptualizing war as a crisis or in relation to crisis. For instance, Brecher (1996) wrote that war can be a "continuation of crisis by other means" and crises can be either be the catalyst or a consequence of war (p. 128; see also Löffelholz, 2004).

The Handbook of International Crisis and Risk Communication Research, Second Edition.
Edited by Andreas Schwarz, Matthew W. Seeger, and Sora Kim.

War does not replace or terminate a crisis; rather, war accentuates crisis (Brecher, 1996). Wars can also create "cosmology episode[s]," a term coined by Weick (1997) to describe "[s]udden losses of meaning" following an event that disrupts how one makes sense of the universe (p. 213; see also Frandsen & Johansen, 2023; Orton & O'Grady, 2016). In such episodes, what is at stake are "fundamental societal and material values" as well as the legitimacy of war policy and even governance in general (Nohrstedt, 2016, p. 204). Following the collapse of meaning and order, a period of transformation usually takes place in which new systems of meaning-making are established (Orton & O'Grady, 2016, p. 11). The meaning-making that comes with war largely occurs by and through media coverage, "a central resource for the public understanding of conflicts" (Hoxha & Hanitzsch, 2018, p. 46). Using Cottle's (2009) distinction between mediatization and mediation as a departure point, Nohrstedt (2016) wrote that crises can be "created in and by the media" (mediatization; see also Esser et al., 2005), as opposed to crises being covered by the media (mediation) (p. 205). In a so-called "threat society," wars are mediatized in a manner that designates certain groups as carriers of threat ("Othering"), often as a tool for political ambitions (Nohrstedt, 2016, p. 205).

Indeed, there is much to say about the portrayal (or construction) of wars or conflicts in the media. This manifests even in the act of pinning down the definition of war journalism itself. For many, war reporting is simply the practice of gathering, selecting, producing, and disseminating information related to wars or war-related events (Staiger, 2004). However, for some scholars, the term carries specific connotations that must be taken into consideration. For example, leveling a critique against its ontology, some argued that sensationalism, one-sidedness, and an elitist orientation characterize war journalism, which tends to use "the language of military triumph" with "an action orientation urging violence" (Gouse et al., 2019, p. 436; see also Lee & Maslog, 2005). As an anti-thesis, the concept of peace journalism was proposed: Journalists should report on war in a way that promotes conflict resolution by shedding light on causes and possible solutions, "giving voice to all parties through responsible, empathetic journalism" (Gouse et al., 2019, p. 435; see also Galtung, 1998).

Through the years, one could observe how the nature of war journalism changed along with political and technological shifts (Dominikowski, 2004; Jungblut, 2020a; Nohrstedt, 2016). Dominikowski (2004) mapped the key developments in war journalism through the historical periods from antiquity to the Gulf War in the early 2000s. Within this vast landscape of media and warfare, several pivotal junctures come to the fore (Dominikowski, 2004, p. 61, translated by authors): In the period of antiquity, war reporting is mainly done by messengers and field commanders, who relayed information primarily for managing public sentiment on a smaller scale. The advent of mass media and mass warfare in the early nineteenth century paved the way for the first independent war correspondents as well as the first "press war" (Crimean War). The period between 1860 and 1914 was the so-called "Golden Age," when new technologies such as photography and telegraphy stretched the possibilities of immediacy, with war being depicted in the press as a "distant, foreign adventure." It was during the First World War that a massive propaganda apparatus was used for "psychological warfare," coupled with censorship and press control, which only intensified in the Second World War with the widespread use of radio, film, and new media. A few decades after, the Vietnam War broke out and lasted from the 1950s to 1970s. This was the first "war in the living room," as television was the primary gateway to information. The capability for real-time reporting through satellite technology was made possible during the Falklands War (1982) and the Kosovo War (1998–1999), although the media was kept away from the battlefield. By the early 2000s, "information warfare" started to become part and parcel of modern warfare, as exemplified by the information and public relations management in the 2003 Gulf War (Dominikowski, 2004).

As discussed in a plethora of studies, the internet coming-of-age starting the early 2000s radically changed the practice of journalism as new forms of reporting and information exchange emerged. The advantages that come with the technological upheavals (e.g., multi-modal presentation forms and innovative information-gathering), as well as the challenges (e.g., algorithmic bias and ethical concerns), also apply to war and conflict reporting. At the same time, the evolution of the internet also provided political actors with new methods and channels for managing public sentiment, or new venues for propaganda (Gohdes, 2018). Leaders in autocracies have co-opted social media to manipulate public discourse and mobilize their supporters, making it a tool for maintaining the political status quo (Gunitsky, 2015). Indeed, with the digital and algorithm-based transformation of the media landscape, war journalism and information warfare, as well as the corresponding scholarship, must be reimagined. To do so, it is necessary to understand trends in and critiques of war coverage, which in turn requires familiarity with the factors affecting war reporting.

Layers of Influence: Factors Affecting War Reporting as a Practice

Several scholars proposed frameworks for understanding the different factors shaping war reporting, and these frameworks have conceptual overlaps with each other. Based on the results of the INFOCORE project, which examined the role of media in armed conflict across six countries, different actors and communicators are involved in war reporting through social processes that are influenced by "systemic, thematic and/or conflict-specific" factors (Fröhlich, 2018b, p. 288). These processes then make each war/conflict unique with respect to coverage. The contextual factors can be likened to what Bilke (2008) called as "societal structural and cultural dimensions" in war reporting (p. 141, translated by authors). In her work, Bilke (2008) then identified the influencing factors in war reporting: "security policy information management," "public relations and propaganda," "media organization structures," and "motives and self-perception of journalists" (p. 144, translated by authors). Bläsi (2004) also identified the same set of factors influencing conflict coverage but also included political climate, conflict situation on the ground, lobbies, and the audience.

Hanitzsch (2007), meanwhile, organized the influencing factors into micro-, meso-, and macro-levels within a heuristic integrative model. Like the works of Bilke (2008) and Bläsi (2004), the model takes into account individual characteristics, training, and personal background (micro-level), as well as editorial structures, workflows, criteria for news selection, and other organizational routines (meso-level). At the macro-level, the elements to be considered also include contextual factors (e.g., political climate), similar to what was discussed in the previous paragraph, but Hanitzsch's model also emphasizes the normative requirements of different functional or performance systems (journalism, public relations, and security policy), as well as the relationships between such systems. The model shares some assumptions with Shoemaker and Reese's (1991, 1996, 2014) oft-cited "Hierarchy of Influences" model, which describes the levels of influence on journalistic production: individual characteristics, professional routines, organizational structures, societal institutions, and ideological, cultural, economic, and political factors.

Multiple studies on war reporting lay the evidence for the influence of the abovementioned factors. For instance, Löffelholz (2004) wrote on the strategy of embedding journalists in military forces, in which reporters were allowed to accompany troops at the battlefield, eventually affecting the independence of journalists through emotional proximity. In this way, "embedded journalism" does not blatantly undermine the non-deterministic nature of media-military relationships in democratic societies, even though it compromises journalistic autonomy in the process (Löffelholz, 2004, p. 22). The consensus among political elites (or lack thereof), such as parliamentary consensus in support for or against war, was also described as an influencing variable in what is known as the indexing theory (Bennett, 1990), albeit other works called for refinement of the theory as some elite voices were found to be more visible than others (Althaus et al., 1996). In terms of organizational structures and resources,

Vandevoordt (2017) wrote that media organizations with economic capital can afford to station correspondents permanently in crisis zones or conflict areas, as opposed to hiring parachute journalists, who in most cases lack the language skills and contextual knowledge, translating to lapses in reporting such as missing (but necessary) contextualization (Fondren et al., 2019; Musa & Yusha'u, 2013). Last, when it comes to professional routines and norms, journalists in general may tend to prefer certain frames as their peers usually do, or follow a codified set of professional guidelines, as in the case of conflict reporting by German journalists who are inclined toward producing negative or less solution-oriented content (Zillich et al., 2011).

Furthermore, threats to safety obviously put pressure on the journalistic enterprise, as lives are also at stake in war reporting. Slavtcheva-Petkova et al. (2023) identified four dimensions of threats against the occupational and infrastructural safety of journalists, any of which are present in war or conflict situations: physical dimension (e.g., assault), psychological (e.g., psychological effect of acts such as verbal aggression and hate speech), digital (e.g., threats to digital privacy), and financial (e.g., threat to job stability). These threats to safety test the adherence to ethical guidelines and ultimately compromise journalists' normative understanding of roles (Slavetcheva-Petkova et al., 2023). As Mercier (2005) said, the media is involved in war and conflict "either as targets (war on the media) or as an auxiliary (war thanks to the media)" (p. 649).

"Othering" and War-Mongering: State of the Art and Issues in Media Coverage

Scholarship on war reporting has expanded significantly in recent decades, but it is also highly fragmented as it is highly diverse (Robinson et al., 2017). The field was already diverse in the early 2000s, as Löffelholz (2004) found in his appraisal of the state of research, with works referring to each other only occasionally. Löffelholz (2004) also observed that contexts specific to each environment profoundly shape war reporting, so "one cannot speak of globally homogenized crisis and war reporting in general" (p. 29, translated by authors). Therefore, scoping the field becomes complex as it considers not only the contexts that shape reporting, which vary across environments but also the different theoretical perspectives and methodological approaches from a wide range of disciplines, from political science to communication to international relations. As an object of study, war reporting has been examined as a tool for legitimizing war, as both an enabler and threat to peace-building, or as an instrument for those responding to humanitarian crises (Robinson et al., 2017). The literature shows the many roles the media take before, during, and after conflicts (Fröhlich, 2018a). Fröhlich (2018b) cited the following reasons for the diversity and fragmentation of research: (1) globalization of war and communication, (2) technological advancement, and (3) new and rapidly changing dynamics between media content creation and public opinion. The near-monopoly of Western media in global news is also being challenged. This is seen in the rise of Al-Jazeera, which established itself as an alternative to Western news organizations, especially when it comes to conflict reporting, described as part of a shift away from "US cultural hegemony" (Seib, 2005, p. 601). Nevertheless, there are still recurring tendencies in the study of war journalism, especially in the area of media or journalism research. Many studies, in particular content analyses, focused on "how the media legitimize or delegitimize wars," followed by a critique of the media (Eilders & Hagen, 2005, p. 208, translated by authors). As for the theoretical approaches, the news values theory (see Harcup & O'Neil, 2017), the framing approach (see Entman, 1993), and agenda-setting (see McCombs et al., 2014) are often used as lenses.

Visibility of Conflict in the Media

Conflict-related events are considered newsworthy in general (Harcup & O'Neill, 2017), but not all wars or conflict situations are on the same level in terms of media attention. In fact, based on a content analysis of conflict coverage, many conflicts in the world are not reported by the media, and it is even the deadliest conflicts that are often ignored (Hawkins, 2011). Decades ago, scholars already tried to explain the amount and focus of media attention in cross-border conflict reporting. For Chang et al. (1987), the character of reportage can be examined through a context-oriented approach or an event-oriented one. The first one looks at how contextual factors (e.g., economic relations and geographical proximity) determine the nature of reporting, while the second looks at intrinsic characteristics of international events, such as the negative nature or the degree of deviance (Chang et al., 1987). This aligns with Löffelholz's (1993) observation: The newsworthiness of war-related events is largely a matter of context, characterized by factors like the involvement of the country and the "elite nations," domestic relevance or connection to local circumstances, and "cultural, political, and economic distance" (p. 19, translated by authors). The findings of more recent studies also point to the existence of context-related determinants, some of which were found to have a stronger effect than others. Zillich et al. (2011) revealed that in German conflict reporting, the status of the event nation matters, as well as the level of damage and aggression, involvement of the public (reach), and perceived benefit of the public. The level of public involvement was identified as the most important news factor, with the relevance of other factors depending on the phase of the conflict (Zillich et al., 2011). In another study, geographical proximity was determined to have the strongest effect on news selection, such that a greater distance from the event nation meant less reporting on the conflict (Zerback & Holzleitner, 2018; see also Heimprecht, 2017). Furthermore, media attention increases when transnational organizations impose sanctions or when the nuclear arms or the military of the reporting nation is involved (Zerback & Holzleitner, 2018).

Indeed, national images and relationships among countries can play a role in conflict reporting, reflecting colonial vestiges and structures of geopolitics. An analysis of *The New York Times* international news revealed that low-income countries were portrayed as sites of conflict more frequently than middle and high-income countries (Sobel et al., 2020). Moreover, foreign news on conflict tends to be nation-centric – coverage of conflicts "in less developed countries may have little newsworthiness without a signal of its relevance" (Sobel et al., 2020, p. 183). Such a tendency may lead the audience to associate low-income nations with conflict as opposed to more developed regions, perpetuating stereotypes of countries that are already marginalized to begin with. The findings of Sobel et al. (2020) are congruent with the view held by many media scholars: Western media disproportionately emphasize "bad news" related to developing regions, and positive developments receive less attention (Asante, 2013). This becomes a bigger cause for concern when situated within a broader historical context: In the past three decades, stereotypes and domestication increased in international news published by well-known news organizations despite increased globalization and the rise of transnational publics (Tanikawa, 2019). Fengler et al. (2020), meanwhile, revealed that Russia's politics is reflected in how newspapers from 13 different countries covered the conflict in Ukraine. They observed that "Russia dominated the news agenda" and that Russian actors "shaped coverage in Europe far more than European actors and institutions" (Fengler et al., 2020, p. 411). Attention to the conflict also varies across the 13 countries, depending on trade, cultural and geographical distance, domestication, and scarcity of newsroom resources, particularly in Eastern Europe (Fengler et al., 2020).

Jungblut (2020b) expanded the discourse on conflict reporting by including the impact of strategic communication on news production. He conducted an automated content analysis of over 83,000 texts from strategic communicators and media outlets and discovered that visibility in conflict reporting is primarily driven by elite status and ethnocentrism. This finding confirms those of earlier studies, some of which were discussed in this section. However, framing is a different issue: the study found that journalistic framing depends more on context and is relatively more independent from strategic communication and elite voices (Jungblut, 2020b).

Coverage by Conflict Phase

War reporting is fundamentally event-driven, and studies have shown how media coverage and the conflict itself can be viewed as multi-phase (Löffelholz, 2004; Miltner & Waldherr, 2013; Savarese, 1993). Gilboa (2009), for one, emphasizes the importance of considering both the pre-phases and post-phases of an international conflict. Applying a functional approach to international conflicts, he identified four phases: "(1) onset-prevention, (2) escalation management, (3) de-escalation-resolution, and (4) termination-reconciliation" (p. 93). The first phase, onset-prevention, is marked by the emergence of the conflict, usually in the form of "hostile verbal and behavioral exchanges," and may escalate to violence if prevention measures do not succeed (Gilboa, 2009, p. 93). The second phase is about managing the conflict, reducing the violence to levels that are considered more tolerable, such as declaring a ceasefire, while the third refers to reaching a formal agreement to end hostilities. The last phase, termination-reconciliation, covers not just conflict resolution but also ways to overcome psychological and cognitive barriers to peace. Studies on conflict coverage can then benefit from phase models to describe and predict media attention, or can arrive at phase models based on patterns in media attention. According to Zillich et al. (2011), the phase model of Gilboa (2009) allows for an analysis of news factors across the development and resolution of the conflict. The phases can also vary according to the duration and predictability of the conflict, based on the results of Miltner and Waldherr's (2013) study on the 2006 Lebanon war coverage. Their research indicates that in the case of a highly visible, short, and unexpected war, reporting will begin only after the outbreak of the war and the escalation of violence, "increase rapidly and persist at a high level for a short time period, then decline sharply, and will remain at levels higher than" those in the pre-war period (Miltner & Waldherr, 2013, pp. 275–276; translated by authors). In contrast, reporting on predictable and longer wars may start before the war breaks out, followed by an initial peak and consecutive peaks in the latter period (Miltner & Waldherr, 2013).

Critique of Themes and Frames in War Reporting

Within and beyond academic literature, the media has been criticized for its serious lapses in conflict reporting. The media have been criticized for promoting biased, ethnographic views against out-groups, spreading falsehood and casting doubt on truthful claims, or inciting or justifying violence (Baden & Meyer, 2018). They also identified the three main ways by which the media represents conflict: (1) providing evidential claims, such as assessment of the situation and describing a prognosis, (2) "interpretative frames," which can take the form of "ethnocentric narratives," and (3) conveying an agenda for action, such as highlighting ways of involvement or endorsing a specific policy (Baden & Meyer, 2018, p. 35).

Various studies have dealt with instances of stereotyping, uncritical use of official sources, and "friend-enemy polarization" (Löffelholz, 2004, p. 33, translated by authors). Such journalistic tendencies are obviously problematic if viewed from a normative perspective and can bolster a war-mongering agenda. In many cases, war reporting exhibited an ethnocentric bias, relying solely on sources from one side and sidelining perspectives from out-groups often perceived as threats or the enemy (Baden & Tenenboim-Weinblatt, 2018). By helping foster an "Us versus Them" mentality, the media has become "facilitators of Otherism" and the purveyors of orientalist Muslims-as-terrorist narratives (Nohrstedt, 2016, p. 135). Orientalism, introduced by Edward Said (1978) in the 1970s, refers to the Western depiction of the Orient as violent, primitive, sometimes romanticized, but always as inferior to the Occident (West). Ever since its introduction, the concept has been used time and again in postcolonial critique, literary criticism, and other related fields.

What could explain these problematic tendencies in the media? For Eilders and Hagen (2005), such tendencies stemmed from the cultural or engagement-driven perspectives of practitioners. This could indeed be the case if one looks into the findings of Maslog et al. (2006), who examined the role of religion in war coverage. They analyzed the newspaper coverage of the Iraq War in five Asian countries and discovered that, based on sourcing and framing, non-Muslim countries tend to support the US-led coalition as protagonists in the war, while Muslim countries tend to support the Iraqis. Moreover, stories from international wire services tend to have a more pronounced war journalism framing than those from newspaper correspondents. The tendency toward war journalism framing can also be explained by a profit motive. Reports on South Kaduna conflicts, for example, lacked context and were sensationalized to sustain audience attention "at the expense of accuracy and professionalism" (Ishaku, 2021, p. 295).

The findings of Maslog et al. (2006) on war journalism bring the discussion back to the dichotomy between war and peace journalism, which was already mentioned briefly in an earlier section. Empirical studies offer the evidence base for critiquing the emphasis on "bad news" – violence and other negative frames – in conflict reporting, with little attention given to positive developments, such as peace negotiations (Baden & Tenenboim-Weinblatt, 2018; Gouse et al., 2019; Lee & Maslog, 2005). This characterizes war journalism, which underscores militarist victory and has an elitist orientation, promoting violence as a means to resolve conflicts (Gouse et al., 2019; Lee & Maslog, 2005). As mentioned, the concept of peace journalism was created as a corrective to war journalism. Peace journalism, described as a new form of journalism, provides space for other voices apart from official sources, uncovers the causes of the conflict, and contributes to prevention and resolution (McGoldrick, 2000; see also Galtung, 2002). Critics, however, argued that peace journalism assigns a political and military responsibility to journalists who are expected to be objective, but for several scholars, social responsibility is at the core of peace journalism, a tool for preventing and resolving violent conflicts (Hanitzsch, 2004; Vincent & Galtung, 1993). It is worth noting that the media portrayal of conflicts and wars is often examined through the lens of peace and war journalism perspective, employing content analysis and framing analysis (Fahmy & Eakin, 2014; Gouse et al., 2019; Lacasse & Forster, 2012; Lee & Maslog, 2005; Neumann & Fahmy, 2016; Zillich et al., 2011). An analysis of war/peace journalism framing revealed that most of the studies look at the degree of elite-orientedness versus people-orientedness, while also highlighting ample opportunities to expand the field by exploring "cultural and structural violence as viable inequalities" (Gouse et al., 2019, p. 444).

It is clear from extant literature that journalistic framing speaks a lot about the intentions of reporters, influenced by their sensibilities or lack of expertise in war zones or other entanglements (Eilders & Hagen, 2005; Mueller, 1973). By making "salient some aspects of a perceived reality," as Entman (1993) described it, reporting in many cases has been instrumentalized for war propaganda. In this regard, it becomes crucial to also look at visual framing analysis, as online news content is becoming more and more multi-modal (Hangloo & Arora, 2022). It is therefore not surprising that there is a growing scholarly interest in how visual elements (e.g., images and videos) are deliberately selected and presented (Fahmy, 2010; Makhortykh & Sydorova, 2017; Manor & Crilley, 2018; Schwalbe & Dougherty, 2015; Schwalbe et al., 2008). Visuals are powerful tools in conveying ideological messages (Messaris & Abraham, 2001), as evidenced by several studies, such as the work of Schwalbe and Dougherty (2015) on the 2006 Lebanon war coverage. The authors of the study concluded that visuals evoke an emotional response and are also processed more quickly than text (Schwalbe & Dougherty, 2015). With the internet facilitating the rapid and widespread distribution of images, this significantly amplifies the reach and impact of journalistic war framing and war propaganda.

Paradigm-Shifters: War Reporting and New Technologies

This section expounds on how technological innovations have transformed the (war) communication ecology, opening new avenues for study while also posing challenges for research. Social media platforms, particularly Facebook, Instagram, X, and YouTube, have become central to the mediatization of conflict, with an increasing number of people relying on these platforms for news rather than direct access to publisher's websites, and journalists increasingly incorporating them into their practices (Newman, 2023). It is now the time of the so-called "participative war," where everyone within or beyond conflict zones can express their thoughts and share their stories, contributing to the public discourse (Merrin, 2019, p. 215). Individuals can actively shape and spread conflict frames, thereby influencing the escalation or de-escalation of the conflict (Fröhlich, 2018b). At the same time, political actors and state functionaries have exploited social media channels for spreading war propaganda and galvanizing public support (Astuti et al., 2022). Manor and Crilley's (2018) article offers an illustrative example: The authors analyzed 795 tweets published by the Israeli Ministries of Foreign Affairs during the 2014 Gaza War, and they found that the institution used a series of frames that promoted Israeli strategic narratives. As the conflicts in Libya, Syria, and Ukraine have shown, social media strategy has become part of "hybrid warfare strategies," which now characterize modern warfare (Svetoka 2016, p. 4).

Social media also serves as a platform where deepfake videos and disinformation persist as part of war propaganda, which has been particularly evident in the viral spread of disinformation during the Russia-Ukraine War. Social bots on X or Facebook were also employed to spread disinformation systematically, with their behavior becoming increasingly sophisticated to imitate human patterns and create convincing social networks (Ferrara et al., 2016). For instance, the Russian propaganda campaign deployed bots on a massive scale to spread disinformation at the beginning of the Ukraine invasion in 2022 (Geissler et al., 2023). Such developments pose challenges for researchers, who have to deal with datasets that may include inauthentic behavior from non-human actors (Ferrara et al., 2016). Furthermore, there is a need for innovative techniques to better describe the effects of content conveyed through a wide range of visual media (Knüpfer & Entman, 2018). The same applies to datasets on social media, which can be too massive for traditional content or thematic analyses.

Automation and artificial intelligence (AI) systems, meanwhile, offer opportunities for enhancing the practice, but the technology also comes with potential pitfalls. The use of AI tools can allow journalists to efficiently process vast amounts of data (e.g., social media posts, press releases), identify relevant topics automatically, verify news content, generate news stories quickly, and translate news stories to multiple languages, among others (Diakopoulos, 2019; Sarısakaloğlu, 2024). Algorithm-driven distribution technologies, such as news recommender systems, can also help facilitate constructive war reporting by countering journalistic self-censorship and exposing readers to diverse perspectives (Bastian et al., 2019). However, while it can stretch possibilities for reporting and free the journalist from routine tasks, the ethical judgment and contextual understanding of human journalists are still necessary, as the quality may suffer from algorithmic biases, lack of context, and poor sourcing (Sarısakaloğlu, 2022a).

The use of drones and Virtual Reality (VR) technologies in journalism has gained considerable attention as well. Drones, with their real-time reporting capabilities, can be used in war reporting to capture high-quality images and detailed perspectives, especially in conflict zones that are far too dangerous for journalists. As such, the use of drones can help strengthen the credibility of journalists, which is crucial in the current media landscape, as content is seen as authentic or untampered. However, legal and ethical issues have to be considered, such as compliance with laws and regulations, especially those concerning privacy. There are also ethical concerns surrounding the use of VR technologies (Sarısakaloğlu, 2023; Sarısakaloğlu & Tribusean, 2024), as some question the shift from the journalistic role of documenting events to crafting scenes akin to filming (Mehendale, 2020). As an immersive multimodal form of reporting, VR journalism (or immersive journalism) recreates events for audiences to experience, typically with the aim of fostering empathy (Sarısakaloğlu & Tribusean, 2024). A popular example would be de la Peña's (2014) "Project Syria," which reconstructed scenes from the Syrian Civil War. However, immersive journalism "treads a hazy ground between fact and fiction" (Mehendale, 2020) and, in its intention to create empathy, can even be used for propaganda.

Conclusion

This chapter delved into the mediatization of war and other violent conflicts, starting with the factors that affect the production and the content of war reporting. Critical perspectives on journalistic framing were discussed in length, as well as how new technologies offer opportunities and challenges for practice and research. As information warfare becomes an integral part of modern conflict and as new technologies allow both massive deception and audience empowerment, scholarship has to keep pace with innovative and more critical approaches. Additionally, an area of considerable significance requiring in-depth exploration is the integration of AI technologies in war reporting and the potential implications thereof. Strikingly, there exists a conspicuous lack of research in this domain, creating a substantial gap that needs to be addressed.

References

Althaus, S. L., Edy, J. A., Entman, R. M., & Phalen, P. (1996). Revising the indexing hypothesis: Officials, media, and the Libya crisis. *Political Communication*, *13*(4), 407–421. https://doi.org/10.1080/10584609.1996.9963128

Asante, M. K. (2013). The Western media and the falsification of Africa: Complications of value and evaluation. *China Media Report Overseas*, *9*(4), 64–70.

Astuti, Y. D., Attaymini, R., & Dewi, M. S. R. (2022). Digital media and war: Social media as a propaganda tool for the Russia-Ukraine conflict in the post-truth era. *Proceedings of the Annual International Conference on Social Science and Humanities (AICOSH)*, 19–27. https://doi.org/10.2991/978-2-494069-87-9_4

Baden, C., & Meyer, C. O. (2018). Dissecting media roles in conflict a transactionist process model of conflict news production, dissemination and influence. In R. Fröhlich, Ed., *Media in War and Armed Conflict: The Dynamics of Conflict News Production and Dissemination* (pp. 23–48). New York: Routledge.

Baden, C., & Tenenboim-Weinblatt, K. (2018). The search for common ground in conflict news research: Comparing the coverage of six current conflicts in domestic and international media over time. *Media, War & Conflict*, *11*(1), 22–45. https://doi.org/10.1177/1750635217702071

Bastian, M., Makhortykh, M., & Dobber, T. (2019). News personalization for peace: how algorithmic recommendations can impact conflict coverage. *International Journal of Conflict Management*, *30*(3), 309–328. https://doi.org/10.1108/IJCMA-02-2019-0032

Bennett, W. L. (1990). Toward a theory of press–state relations in the United States. *Journal of Communication*, *40*, 103–125. https://doi.org/10.1111/j.1460-2466.1990.tb02265.x

Bilke, N. (2008). *Qualität in der Krisen- und Kriegsberichterstattung: Ein Modell für einen konfliktsensitiven Journalismus.* Wiesbaden: VS Verlag für Sozialwissenschaften.

Bläsi, B. (2004). Peace journalism and the news production process. *Conflict & Communication online*, *3*(1/2), 1–12.

Brecher, M. (1996). Introduction: Crisis, conflict, war – State of the discipline. *International Political Science Review*, *17*(2), 127–139. https://doi.org/10.1177/019251296017002001

Chang, T.-K., Shoemaker, P. J., & Brendlinger, N. (1987). Determinants of international news coverage in the US media. *Communication Research*, *14*(4), 396–414.

Cottle, S. (2009). *Global Crisis Reporting. Journalism in the Global Age*. Maidenhead: Open University Press.

de la Peña, N. (2014). Project Syria: An immersive journalism experience. *YouTube Video*, *4*, 13. www.youtube.com/watch?v=jN_nbHnHDi4 (accessed January 14, 2025)

Diakopoulos, N. (2019). *Automating the News: How Algorithms are Rewriting the Media*. Cambridge and London: Harvard University Press.

Dominikowski, T. (2004). Massenmedien und Massenkrieg: Historische Annäherungen an eine unfriedliche Symbiose. In M. Löffelholz, Ed., *Krieg als Medienereignis II: Krisenkommunikation im 21. Jahrhundert* (pp. 59–80). Wiesbaden: VS Verlag für Sozialwissenschaften.

Eilders, C., & Hagen, L. M. (2005). Kriegsberichterstattung als Thema kommunikationswissenschaftlicher Forschung. *Medien & Kommunikationswissenschaft*, *53*(2–3), 205–221.

Entman, R. M. (1993). Framing. Toward clarification of a fractured paradigm. *Journal of Communication*, *43*(4), 51–58. https://doi.org/10.1111/j.1460-2466.1993.tb01304.x

Esser, F., Schwabe, C., & Wilke, J. (2005). Metaberichterstattung im Krieg. Wie Tageszeitungen die Rolle der Nachrichtenmedien und der Militär-PR in den Irakkonflikten 1991 und 2003 framen. *Medien & Kommunikationswissenschaft*, *53*, 314–332.

Fahmy, S. (2010). Contrasting visual frames of our times: A framing analysis of English- and Arabic-language press coverage of war and terrorism. *International Communication Gazette*, *72*(8), 695–717.

Fahmy, S., & Eakin, B. (2014). High drama on the high seas: Peace versus war journalism framing of an Israeli/Palestinian-related incident. *International Communication Gazette*, *76*(1), 86–105.

Fengler, S., Kreutler, M., Alku, M., Barlovac, B., Bastian, M., Bodrunova, S. S., Brinkmann, J., Dingerkus, F., Hájek, R., Knopper, S., Kus, M., Láb, F., Lees, C., Litvinenko, A., Medeiros, D., Orlova, D., Ozolina, L., Paluch, A., Nicoleta Radu, R., Stefanikova, S., Veldhoen, H., & Zguri, R. (2020). The Ukraine conflict and the European media: A comparative study of newspapers in 13 European countries. *Journalism*, *21*(3), 399–422. https://doi.org/10.1177/1464884918774311

Ferrara, E., Varol, O., Davis, C., Menczer, F., & Flammini, A. (2016). The rise of social bots. *Communications of the ACM*, *59*(7), 96–104. https://doi.org/10.1145/2818717

Frandsen, F., & Johansen, W. (2023). Geo-political conflict. In *Presentation at Crisis 7th International Crisis Communication Conference Organized by the European Communication Research and Education Association (ECREA)*. Sweden: Gothenburg.October 6.

Fondren, E., Hamilton, J. M., & McCune, M. M. (2019). Parachute journalism. In T. P. Vos, & F. Hanusch, Eds., *The International Encyclopedia of Journalism Studies*. Wiley & Sons. https://doi.org/10.1002/9781118841570.iejs0178

Fröhlich, R. (2018a). Introduction – Media's role in the creation of knowledge and images of wars: More relevant and more complicated than ever. In R. Fröhlich, Ed., *Media in War and Armed Conflict: The Dynamics of Conflict News Production and Dissemination* (pp. 2–22). New York: Routledge.

Fröhlich, R. (2018b). The integration of findings: Consequences of empirical results for the advancement of theory building. In R. Fröhlich, Ed., *Media in War and Armed Conflict: The Dynamics of Conflict News Production and Dissemination* (pp. 287–309). New York: Routledge.

Galtung, J. (1998). High road, low road: Charting the course for peace journalism. *Trade Two*, *7*, 7–10.

Galtung, J. (2002). Peace journalism – a challenge. In W. Kempf, & H. Luostarinen, Eds., *Journalism and the New World Order: Studying the War and the Media* (pp. 260–280). Gothenburg: Nordicom.

Geissler, D., Bär, D., Pröllochs, N., & Feuerriegel, S. (2023). Russian propaganda on social media during the 2022 invasion of Ukraine. *EPJ Data Science*, *12*(35), 1–20. https://doi.org/10.1140/epjds/s13688-023-00414-5

Gilboa, E. (2009). Media and conflict resolution: A framework for analysis. *Marquette Law Review*, *93*, 87–110.

Gohdes, A. R. (2018). Studying the internet and violent conflict. *Conflict Management and Peace Science*, *35*(1), 89–106. https://doi.org/10.1177/0738894217733878

Gouse, V., Valentin-Llopis, M., Perry, S., & Nyamwange, B. (2019). An investigation of the conceptualization of peace and war in peace journalism studies of media coverage of national and international conflicts. *Media, War & Conflict, 12*(4), 435–449. https://doi.org/10.1177/1750635218810917

Gunitsky, S. (2015). Corrupting the cyber-commons: Social media as a tool of autocratic stability. *Perspectives on Politics, 13*(1), 42–54. https://www.doi.org/10.1017/S1537592714003120

Hangloo, S., & Arora, B. (2022). Combating multimodal fake news on social media: Methods, datasets, and future perspective. *Multimedia Systems, 28*, 2391–2422. https://doi.org/10.1007/s00530-022-00966-y

Hanitzsch, T. (2007). Kriegskorrespondenten entmystifiziert'. In B. Korte, & H. Tonn, Eds., *Kriegskorrespondenten: Deutungsinstanzen in der Mediengesellschaft* (pp. 39–58). Wiesbaden: VS Verlag für Sozialwissenschaften.

Hanitzsch, T. (2004). Journalists as peacekeeping force? Peace journalism and mass communication theory. *Journalism Studies, 5*(4), 483–495.

Harcup, T., & O'Neill, D. (2017). What is news? *Journalism Studies, 18*(12), 1470–1488. https://doi.org/10.1080/1461670X.2016.1150193

Hawkins, V. (2011). Media selectivity and the other side of the CNN Effect: The consequences of not paying attention to conflict. *Media, War & Conflict, 4*(1), 55–68.

Heidelberg Institute for International Conflict Research (2023). *Conflict barometer 2022.* Retrieved from https://hiik.de/wp-content/uploads/2023/05/CoBa_2022_00_01.pdf (accessed January 14, 2025)

Heimprecht, C. (2017). *Determinanten der Auslandsberichterstattung: Eine Mehrebenenanalyse des internationalen Nachrichtenflusses.* Wiesbaden: Springer VS.

Hoxha, A., & Hanitzsch, T. (2018). How conflict news comes into being: Reconstructing 'reality' through telling stories. *Media, War & Conflict, 11*, 46–64.

Ishaku, J. (2021). Peace journalism or war journalism? An analysis of newspaper coverage of ethno-religious conflicts in Southern Kaduna, Nigeria (2020–2021). *International Journal of Communication Research, 11*(4), 295–313.

Jungblut, M. (2020a). Kriegs- und Konfliktberichterstattung im digitalen Zeitalter. In I. Borucki, K. Klein-von-Königslow, S. Marschall, & T. Zerback, Eds., *Handbuch Politische Kommunikation.* Wiesbaden: Springer VS. https://doi.org/10.1007/978-3-658-26233-4

Jungblut, M. (2020b). *Strategic communication and its role in conflict news a computational analysis of the international news coverage on four conflicts.* Wiesbaden: Springer VS.

Knüpfer, C. B., & Entman, R. M. (2018). Framing conflicts in digital and transnational media environments. *Media, War & Conflict, 11*(4), 476–488. https://doi.org/10.1177/1750635218796381

Lacasse, K., & Forster, L. (2012). The war next door: Peace journalism in US local and distant newspapers' coverage of Mexico. *Media, War & Conflict, 5*(3), 223–237. https://doi.org/10.1177/1750635212447907

Lee, S. T., & Maslog, C. C. (2005). War or peace journalism? Asian newspaper coverage of conflicts. *Journal of Communication, 55*(2), 311–329.

Löffelholz, M. (2004). Krisen- und Kriegskommunikation als Forschungsfeld. In M. Löffelholz, Ed., *Krieg als Medienereignis II: Krisenkommunikation im 21. Jahrhundert* (pp. 13–55). Wiesbaden: VS Verlag für Sozialwissenschaften.

Löffelholz, M. (1993). Krisenkommunikation: Probleme, Konzepte, Perspektiven. In M. Löffelholz, Ed., *Krieg als Medienereignis: Grundlagen und Perspektiven der Krisenkommunikation* (pp. 11–32). Opladen: Westdeutscher Verlag.

Makhortykh, M., & Sydorova, M. (2017). Social media and visual framing of the conflict in Eastern Ukraine. *Media, War and Conflict, 10*(3), 359–381. https://doi.org/10.1177/1750635217702539

Manor, I., & Crilley, R. (2018). Visually framing the Gaza War of 2014: The Israel Ministry of Foreign Affairs on Twitter. *Media, War & Conflict, 11*(4), 369–391. https://doi.org/10.1177/1750635218780564

Maslog, C. C., Lee, S. T., & Kim, H. S. (2006). Framing analysis of a conflict: How newspapers in five Asian countries covered the Iraq War. *Asian Journal of Communication, 16*(1), 19–39. https://doi.org/10.1080/01292980500118516

McGoldrick, A. (2000). Zur Rolle von Medien in Konflikten. In Friedrich-Ebert-Stiftung, Ed., *Medien im Konflikt – Mittäter oder Mediatoren?* Bonn: Friedrich-Ebert-Stiftung. Retrieved from https://library.fes.de/pdf-files/iez/00960.pdf (accessed January 14, 2025)

McCarthy, C. (1985). *Blood Meridian.* New York: Vintage.
McCombs, M. E., Shaw, D. L., & Weaver, D. H. (2014). New directions in agenda-setting theory and research. *Mass Communication and Society, 17*(6), 781–802. https://www.10.1080/15205436.2014.964871
Mehendale, S. G. (2020). Reviewing ethical concerns about immersive journalism. *Media Ethics, 32*(1). Retrieved from: https://www.mediaethicsmagazine.com/index.php/browse-back-issues/215-fall-2020-vol-32-no-1/3999319-reviewing-ethical-concerns-about-immersive-journalism (accessed January 14, 2025)
Mercier, A. (2005). War and media: Constancy and convulsion. *International Review of the Red Cross, 87*(860), 649–659. https://doi.org/10.1017/S1816383100184486
Merrin, W. (2019). *Digital War: A Critical Introduction.* New York, NY: Routledge.
Messaris, P., & Abraham, L. (2001). The role of images in framing news stories. In S. D. Reese, O. H. Gandy, & A. E. Grant, Eds., *Framing Public Life: Perspectives on Media and Our Understanding of the Social World* (pp. 215–226). Mahwah, NJ: Lawrence Erlbaum.
Miltner, P., & Waldherr, A. (2013). Themenzyklus der Kriegsberichterstattung: Ein Phasenmodell. *Publizistik, 58*, 267–287.
Musa, A. O., & Yusha'u, M. J. (2013). Conflict reporting and parachute journalism in Africa: A study of CNN and Al Jazeera's coverage of the Boko Haram insurgency. *Journal of Arab & Muslim Media Research, 6*, 251–267. https://doi.org/10.1386/jammr.6.2-3.251_1
Mueller, J. E. (1973). *War, presidents and public Opinion.* New York: John Wiley & Sons.
Neumann, R., & Fahmy, S. (2016). Measuring journalistic peace/war performance: An exploratory study of crisis reporters' attitudes and perceptions. *International Communication Gazette, 78*(3), 223–246.
Newman, N. (2023). *Reuters Institute digital news report 2023.* Retrieved from https://reutersinstitute.politics.ox.ac.uk/sites/default/files/2023-06/Digital_News_Report_2023.pdf (accessed January 14, 2025)
Nohrstedt, S. A. (2016). The role of the media in the discursive construction of wars. In A. Schwarz, M. W. Seeger, & C. Auer, Eds., *The Handbook of International Crisis Communication Research* (pp. 135–144). Chichester, UK: John Wiley & Sons.
Orton, J. D., & O'Grady, K. A. (2016). Cosmology episodes: a reconceptualization. *Journal of Management, Spirituality & Religion, 13*(3), 226–245. https://doi.org/10.1080/14766086.2016.1159975
Philo, G. (2002). Television news and audience understanding of war, conflict and disaster. *Journalism Studies, 3*(2), 173–186. https://doi.org/10.1080/14616700220129955
Quandt, T., Wilke, J., Heimprecht, C., & Pape, T. (2014). *Fernsehwelten: Auslandsnachrichten im deutschen Fernsehen.* Wiesbaden: Springer VS.
Robinson, P., Seib, P., & Fröhlich, R. (2017). Introduction: Media, conflict and security. In P. Robinson, P. Seib, & R. Fröhlich, Eds., *Routledge Handbook of Media, Conflict and Security* (pp. 1–5). New York: Routledge.
Said, E. (1978). *Orientalism.* New York, NY: Vintage Books.
Sarısakaloğlu, A. (2023). Virtuelle Realität im Journalismus: Potenziale und Herausforderungen der partizipativ-immersiven Dimension der Berichterstattung. *Communicatio Socialis, 56*(4), 460–470. https://doi.org/10.5771/0010349720234460
Sarısakaloğlu, A. (2022a). Algorithmisierung des Journalismus. Chancen und Herausforderungen künstlicher Intelligenzsysteme in sozio-technischen Newsrooms. *Communicatio Socialis, 55*(3), 308–319. https://doi.org/10.5771/0010-3497-2022-3-308
Sarısakaloğlu, A. (2024). Künstliche Intelligenz und Journalismus. In M. Löffelholz, & L. Rothenberger, Eds., Handbuch Journalismustheorien (pp. 437–449). Wiesbaden: Springer VS. https://doi.org/10.1007/978-3-658-32151-2_30
Sarısakaloğlu, A., Tribusean, I. (2024). Virtuelle Realität und Journalismus. In M. Löffelholz, & L. Rothenberger, Eds., Handbuch Journalismustheorien (pp. 427–436). Wiesbaden: Springer VS. https://doi.org/10.1007/978-3-658-32151-2_58
Savarese, R. (1993). The European Press and Saladin the fierce. *European Journal of Communication, 8*(1), 53–75.
Schwalbe, C. B., & Dougherty, S. M. (2015). Visual coverage of the 2006 Lebanon War: Framing conflict in three US news magazines. *Media, War & Conflict, 8*(1), 141–162. https://doi.org/10.1177/1750635215571204

Schwalbe, C. B., Silcock, W., & Keith, S. (2008). Visual framing of the early weeks of the U.S.-led invasion of Iraq: Applying the master war narrative to electronic and print images. *Journal of Broadcasting & Electronic Media*, *52*(3), 448–465.

Seib, P. (2005). Hegemonic no more: Western media, the rise of Al-Jazeera, and the influence of diverse voices. *International Studies Review*, *7*(4), 601–615.

Shoemaker, P. J., & Reese, S. D. (2014). *Mediating the message in the 21st century: A media sociology perspective*. New York: Routledge.

Shoemaker, P. J., & Reese, S. D. (1991, 1996). *Mediating the message: Theories of influences on mass media content*. New York: Longman.

Stockholm International Peace Research Institute (2023). *SIPRI yearbook 2023. Armaments, disarmament and international security. Summary*. Retrieved from https://www.sipri.org/sites/default/files/2023-06/yb23_summary_en_1.pdf (accessed January 14, 2025)

Slavtcheva-Petkova, V., Ramaprasad, J., Springer, N., Hughes, S., Hanitzsch, T., Hamada, B., Hoxha, A., & Steindl, N. (2023). Conceptualizing journalists' safety around the globe. *Digital Journalism*, *11*(7), 1211–1229. https://www.doi.org/10.1080/21670811.2022.2162429

Sobel, M. R., Kim, S., & Riffe, D. (2020). The world at war: Three and a half decades of New York Times conflict coverage. *Media, War & Conflict*, *13*(2), 170–187. https://doi.org/10.1177/1750635219828763

Staiger, J. (2004). Selbstorganisation, Nicht-Linearität, Viabilität. Eine konstruktivistisch-sozialsystemische Perspektive auf Kriegsberichterstattung. In M. Löffelholz, Ed., *Krieg als Medienereignis II: Krisenkommunikation im 21. Jahrhundert* (pp. 145–168). Wiesbaden: VS Verlag für Sozialwissenschaften.

Svetoka, S. (2016). *Social media as a tool of hybrid warfare*. Riga: NATO Strategic Communications Centre of Excellence. Retrieved from https://stratcomcoe.org/cuploads/pfiles/public_report_social_media_hybrid_warfare_22-07-2016-1.pdf (accessed January 14, 2025)

Tanikawa, M. (2019). Is "global journalism" truly global? *Journalism Studies*, *20*(10), 1421–1439. https://doi.org/10.1080/1461670X.2018.1520610

Vandevoort, R. (2017). Why journalists covered Syria the way they did: On the role of economic, social and cultural capital. *Journalism*, *18*(5), 609–625. https://www.doi.org/10.1177/1464884915620271

Vincent, R., & Galtung, J. (1993). Krisenkommunikation morgen. Zehn Vorschläge für eine andere Kriegsberichterstattung. In M. Löffelholz, Ed., *Krieg als Medienereignis. Grundlagen und Perspektiven der Krisenkommunikation* (pp. 177–210). Opladen: Westdeutscher Verlag.

Weick, K. E. (1997). Cosmos vs. chaos: Sense and nonsense in electronic contexts. In L. Prusak, Ed., *Knowledge in Organizations* (pp. 213–226). Boston: Butterworth-Heinemann.

Zillich, A. F., Göbbel, R., Stengel, K., Maier, M., & Ruhrmann, G. (2011). Proactive crisis communication? News coverage of international conflicts in German print and broadcasting media. *Media, War & Conflict*, *4*(3), 251–267. https://doi.org/10.1177/1750635211420629

Zerback, T., & Holzleitner, J. (2018). Under-cover: The influence of event- and context-traits on the visibility of armed conflicts in German newspaper coverage (1992–2013). *Journalism*, *19*(3), 366–383. https://doi.org/10.1177/1464884916683552

Author's Bio

Dr. Aynur Sarısakaloğlu is a postdoctoral researcher and lecturer at the Institute of Media and Communication Science at Technische Universität Ilmenau, Germany. She earned her Bachelor's, Master's, and PhD degrees in Communication Science from the Paris Lodron University of Salzburg. She was an assistant professor at the Department of Communication at the Turkish-German University in Istanbul. She worked as a research assistant and a project assistant at the Paris Lodron University of Salzburg. She was a visiting scholar at the University of San Francisco. Preferring an interdisciplinary approach to research and teaching, her main interests include artificial intelligence in communications, journalism research, and intercultural communication. Her recent research focuses on the transformation of journalism induced by artificial intelligence and automation systems, including the use of new technologies in war journalism.

Dr. Pauline Gidget Estella is a postdoctoral researcher and lecturer at the Technische Universität Ilmenau in Germany. She is also a former assistant professor at the University of the Philippines and a former visiting lecturer at the Turkish-German University. Pauline had worked in international comparative research projects, such as the DECIPHER project, a comparative study examining COVID-19-related crisis communication in Europe and the U.S., funded by the German Research Foundation. She has served as a consultant for research in international organizations like the European Journalism Centre and Asia Pacific Research Network. She was also one of the technical consultants advising the Philippine Department of Education in crafting its special journalism curriculum. Her research interests lie on the areas of journalism education, Global South studies, digital mis- and disinformation, and crisis communication.

11

Terrorism, Lone Wolf Shootings, School Shootings, and the Role of (Social) Media

Liane Rothenberger[1] and Melanie Verhovnik-Heinze[2]
[1] School of Journalism, Catholic University of Eichstätt-Ingolstadt, Eichstätt, Germany
[2] Faculty of Business, Ansbach University of Applied Science, Ansbach, Germany

Introduction

This chapter focuses on media organizations, journalism, and, in particular, social media and how they report on and interrelate with the crisis types "terrorism" and "lone wolf/school shootings." We will explore the questions of what characteristics of (social media) journalism and (social) media organizations are relevant and/or affected within the context of a terrorism or school shooting event and how the media respond, for example, with a certain framing. First, we need to a) define terrorist attacks and school shootings and b) explain why we are considering these acts together in the context of media and their coverage. In contrast to rampage or employee shootings, for example, both school shootings and lone wolf shootings have common features, especially in the planning and preparation as well as in the linking of the acts to a certain ideology. Therefore, they are much more similar to terrorist attacks than rampages (as they are nevertheless often called) or can even be classified as such. Terrorism is considered a form of strategic communication, and we find this form in whole or in part in lone wolf terrorist and school shootings as well. An important characteristic of these acts is that the perpetrators plan for media coverage and present themselves as if they were on a stage, both before and during the act, and that they themselves become active in the media, for example, by sending messages to media organizations (videos, photographs, pamphlets, etc.), announcing their act via (social) media, or even streaming it live. Thus, this chapter refers, on the one hand, to attacks by terrorist groups, to lone wolf shootings that are terrorist in nature – that is, involve offenders who operate individually or in dyads, with no formal ties to terrorist organizations or networks, but are influenced by an extremist ideology (e.g., Christchurch, 2019; Orlando, 2016; Oslo/Utøya, 2011) – and to school shootings in which students target their current or former schools or individuals in that school.

This chapter offers a risk and crisis communication approach to terrorism and school shootings. First, we will ask how far and in which regard terrorism or school shootings can be constituted or constitute a risk or crisis. In this context, we look at how media reacts to these crisis events and shapes the coverage, especially labeling and framing. Second, we look at how far the media are part of the perpetrators' strategies, especially including social media communication. Third, we look at contagious effects of the coverage before discussing existing media guidelines. The chapter terminates with a conclusion and outlook for future work.

The Handbook of International Crisis and Risk Communication Research, Second Edition.
Edited by Andreas Schwarz, Matthew W. Seeger, and Sora Kim.

Terrorism and School Shootings as Crisis and Risk

Nossek and Berkowitz (2006) speak explicitly of terrorism as "crisis"; Sellnow et al. (2009) consider terrorist hoaxes as "risks." Many taxonomies of crisis also include terrorism as one crisis type. Some authors speak of "mass shooting crisis" (e.g., Lee et al., 2022) or include both terrorist acts and mass/school shootings in their sample on crises (e.g., Reuter & Kaufhold, 2017). If we assume that terrorism and school shootings are crises, we have to ask whether the existence of terrorist groups or perpetrators, the terrorist attack or shooting, or the aftereffects constitute the crisis. It could also be considered that terrorism and school shootings in themselves are not a crisis but only provoke crises for society and governments and for the media and its audiences. However, they would yet constitute a permanent risk.

Usually, the main focus within conventional crisis communication research is on private organizations and their efforts to regain a stakeholder group's confidence. Here, the situation is different: The overall goal of terrorists is to sow fear and mistrust in society. The media, for their part, are interested in gaining and maintaining their audiences' trust and interest. If a crisis is defined as a threatening situation with high impact on the emotional and organizational level, as a disruption in the ordinary flow of daily life, we have to reflect that the existence of terrorist groups or lone offenders is not obviously always a crisis. Only certain forms constitute crisis, that is, when the perpetrators are actively committing terrorist attacks or school shootings, when announcing deeds or distributing propaganda that may affect a large scale. Media have to deal with reporting on such crises. They can do that in various ways: focusing on the event, interviewing victims, or allotting space to describe the causes and political circumstances in which a terrorist group or a lone offender came into being. Regarding the quantity of articles and agenda setting of terrorist attacks and school shootings provided by the media, researchers have described the relationship between terrorism and media as "symbiotic" or "parasitic." We will address this argument again later.

Grounding terrorism-media-research in crisis communication, we direct our view to the purpose that underlies such organizations. Their aim is to create chaos, crisis, disruption, and harm for which they apply a variety of strategies (Kydd & Walter, 2006). They sow fear in the wider public and thus call attention to their cause and their felt mistreatment while trying to undermine social political institutions. They have a "good versus evil" view of the world, most times built upon a sophisticated ideology. School shooters often seek revenge on those they believe mistreated them and seek fame. Publicity and media coverage are an essential part of the strategy of both kinds of perpetrators.

A concrete terrorist attack or school shooting is an event that the media will not ignore because of its dominant news values, above all negativity, surprise, and conflict. This is why we can call it a "*coercive media event* or *coercion*" (Weimann & Winn, 1994, p. 92). Even though reporters seem to have no other choice than covering the event, they still have the choice of how to frame it. Recalling Iyengar (1991), we differentiate between episodic framing that describes stories that focus on one specific event and a short timeframe and thematic framing that offers a wider context and background information. With regard to crisis and risk communication, we consider crises rather in an episodic and risks than in a thematic framing. This can have an effect on attribution of responsibilities (Boukes, 2021), for example, especially in the context of counterterrorism measures.

Another crucial point in reporting is the labeling of the attack, perpetrator, or group. Here, research shows that different labeling can lead to different normative associations and further to different extents in how far recipients support or disapprove of countermeasures (for an overview, see Rothenberger & Hase, 2023, p. 140). In addition to textual framing, visual framing is of great importance. As Moeller (1999, p. 37) states that "Crisis coverage demands pictures" and "If a story doesn't have a visual hook, an audience will often ignore it," we also find that news stories with photographs receive more attention from audiences than news stories without photographs (Adam et al., 2007). Here, reporters have the duty of not providing the perpetrator(s) with too much publicity and a "heroic" aura. In the same way, the victims should be treated with respect in media visuals.

Media as Part of the Perpetrators' Strategies

Research regarding terrorism and media emanates from diverse disciplinary traditions (Rothenberger, 2023). However, most authors share one common opinion: "Terrorism and the media are entwined in an almost inexorable, symbiotic relationship" (Miller, 1982, p. 13). Terrorism provides the mass media with spectacular stories, and the mass media give the terrorists the attention and awareness level on which they depend. The terrorist groups' and the lone offender's strategy in regard to the media is this: The occurrences are of such great and far-ranging importance that the journalists cannot ignore them, in particular since there is a keen public interest, and the attacks are definitely newsworthy. There is the risk, however, that perpetrators are offered a platform which has never been available to them before.

Schaffert does not see a symbiosis between terrorism and the media, but argues for "parasitism" (Schaffert, 1992, p. 75), since in the end, if the terrorists should reach their goal with the assistance of the media and come into power, they would obtain control of the media system. "The often-declared symbiotic relationship between the media and terrorists, when viewed in its entirety, is a myth. The correct label for that relationship is parasitic, not symbiotic" (Schaffert, 1992, p. 76). The terrorists exploit the media's function of distribution. Only then, terrorists can sow threat in their actual target group: the wider society, beyond the directly affected victims. In this context, terrorism in particular must be understood as a communication strategy – committed from an ideological background and in order to achieve certain political goals, terrorism is primarily intended to spread fear. Fear is the breeding ground on which terrorists seek opportunities to push through their goals, and fear can only develop if a broad mass learns of an attack – primarily through the media.

Another motivation of perpetrators lies in the possibility of becoming famous and – even posthumously – being named at the same time as their role models (perpetrators of previous acts). In the context of school shootings, this aspect has been well studied. As Muschert summarizes, "many shooters have been quite media-savvy, and have consciously used media to convey messages. School shooters are quite certain that they are acting on a public stage, and in fact intend to seize this mediatized stage" (2013, p. 168). The fact that media and media structures provide platforms for perpetrators is not new. In the last twenty years, terrorist organizations have become increasingly professionalized in terms of their media presence in general, but also in terms of their own media productions and relationships. As early as 1999, almost all of these organizations were active on the Internet (Weimann, 2008); in just a few years, organizations such as Al-Qaeda and the Taliban in Afghanistan or the so-called Islamic State (IS) built up extensive media structures. Winter (2016) provides an overall picture of IS media operations, which comprise agencies and production of highly professional propaganda films, but propaganda is only one part of this media strategy. The A'maq News Agency, which is officially independent but always acts in the interests of the so-called IS, proclaims attacks for itself and disseminates them in IS-like language and in breaking news style. In an article in the *New York Times*, Callimachi (2016) describes in this context how the reports from A'maq became a "must-read" – also for classical media and their representatives, since the agency with its direct connection to the so-called IS became an important source of information. The terrorists (mis)use the media as the transmitter of their *propaganda of the deed*. Apart from all other media channels, the dissemination of propaganda is particularly effective via social media, as it spreads extremely quickly through the actions of users – both in crisis communication in the context of an attack and in the perpetrators' media strategy. In the next section, we will follow this in more detail.

The Role of Social Media

Concerning risk and crisis communication in general, social media has changed the landscape of how people receive information. For example, as Hu et al. (2012, p. 2751) state, there are instances like the killing of Osama Bin Laden, when Twitter had been more effective in dispersing information of national interest more rapidly than conventional news sources. Extremists also recognized the potential of social media in terms of their goals of dissemination of propaganda and recruitment of new supporters. Furthermore, analyses of many lone wolf attacks show that they received instructions via instant messaging services right up to the very end. Organizations such as the so-called IS since long were very active on platforms such as Twitter, as part of a media decentralization strategy, by handing over much of the propaganda work to members or supporters. Berger and Morgan (2015), for example, showed that 46,000 IS-supporting accounts were active in December 2014. Government pressure on private companies to minimize the presence of extremist networks on these platforms through account blocking and posting deletion has reduced their visibility. In particular, other providers and services like the text messaging service Telegram became the focus of terrorist organizations, as they regulate the content of their platforms less or not at all (Neumann et al., 2018, p. 9).

Social media has also played a crucial role in the process of school shooters getting nationwide or even worldwide public attention. Related to contagious effects (see following sections), the use of social media seems to be a relevant factor. Garcia-Bernardo et al. (2018, p. 6) found that the probability of a school shooting doubles when tweets mentioning the words "school" and "shooting" increase from 10 tweets per million to 50 tweets per million during the preceding week. The analysis of such acts has shown that the perpetrators use social media platforms over a long period of time to exchange information with a (fan) community, for example, about previous acts, perpetrators, and motives. The perpetrators also use social media to do research about those topics. There is evidence that two Finish school shooting perpetrators (Tuusula, 2007; Kauhajoki, 2008) were in online contact before their shootings (Bondü, 2012), and so-called imageboards (e.g., 4chan and 8kun) are repeatedly part of investigations, after announcements of acts or also because the perpetrators were demonstrably active there. Through photographs, status updates, or anonymous postings on message boards, shooters leave digital legacies – often not in their native language, but in English to reach a larger, mostly undefined public.

Brenton Tarrant, an Australian far-right extremist, took advantage of Facebook's Achilles heel by livestreaming his terrorist attack in Christchurch, where he fatally shot 51 people in two mosques. Some 200 Facebook users watched the terrorist attack in Christchurch broadcast by the perpetrator in real time – but no one reported it as problematic content. The extremely violent content went viral within minutes, and it took 29 minutes after the video began and 12 minutes after the live broadcast ended before the first user report was made (Meta, 2019). The new features of social media, allowing every user to spread his or her own news in the desired style, show on the one hand that perpetrators are no longer dependent on the reporting of traditional media to the same extent as before in order to reach a wider public. On the other hand, the traditional media have little or no opportunity to ignore such "coercive events," but must report them, which means further attention for the perpetrators. The way in which this reporting is done is therefore all the more important.

Contagious and Incentivizing Effects on Would-be Mass Killers

Traditional media play a major role in crisis communication around terrorist attacks or shootings because they have not only an informative but above all a contextualizing and explanatory function, which appears to be particularly important in view of the public upheaval. However, it is problematic that terror is also "nourished" by reporting, and the analysis of school shootings in particular shows that different perpetrators very strongly refer to each other and incorporate many details from the media coverage into their own acts. Research increasingly discusses contagious and incentive effects of media coverage on copycats. It is not so much the short-term contagion effects, that are also discussed (e.g., Garcia-Bernado et al., 2018; Kissner, 2016; Towers et al., 2015), but rather effects in the broader (later) aftermath, for which detailed reporting plays a role. The Columbine shooting of 1999 – which, incidentally, was not planned by the two perpetrators as a shooting, but as a bombing in imitation of the terrorist Oklahoma attack – exhibits a remarkable iconicity in this regard; not least because the first time there was live reporting during the shooting. The shooting was a media spectacle that 68% of Americans followed "very closely" and 92% "very or fairly closely" (Pew Research Center for the People and the Press, 1999) and 1999 was the second consecutive year that a school shooting had been "Top Story of the Year." Subsequent shootings show that their perpetrators were intensely preoccupied with it. For example, the perpetrator of the Virginia Tech Shooting 2007 staged himself as an avenger of injustice and successor of Columbine. He sent a package of pictures, text, and video to the NBC television network, whereupon the television networks excerpted his hate messages (for more examples, see Verhovnik, 2015).

With respect to terrorism, the contagion hypothesis is discussed, for which there are both supporting (Schmid & de Graaf, 1982; Weimann, & Winn, 1994) and negative views (e.g., Picard, 1991; Schlesinger et al., 1984). The theory was developed as a result of a series of attacks between 1960 and 1980. Initially, there was a series of spectacular airplane hijackings and then attacks on embassies, and in recent years, it has been vehicles used as weapons. The media coverage is considered a relevant factor in this theory, because the sequence of events is very similar and because some of the acts are committed on very different continents. Media coverage does not lead directly to other acts but could inspire people who are already contemplating committing such an act. In this context, media can initiate the course of action – a detailed description of the action is provided by a script. The number of dead and injured becomes an ambitious yardstick (e.g., Sitzer, 2013, p. 300). While in many places, police tactics in school shootings have been changed as a result of experience, media and journalists are still – apparently – more or less unprepared for these events and act according to their own motives instead of presenting reliable information (cf. Verhovnik, 2009).

Guidelines and Censorship – Yes or No?

This leaves the question of how the media deal with this "burden" of obviously or at least of potentially being an accessory to terrorism. Biernatzki (2002) introduces two models of the relationship between terrorism and the media: the "culpable media model," in which the media play a culpable part in the relationship and the "vulnerable media model," which presents the media as victim and not as an accessory to terrorism and which does not see any limitation in news coverage as a resort or solution for an alleviation or reduction of terrorist activities. On the contrary, the media could play an active role in the struggle against terrorism here: "The media can be enemies of the terrorists, carrying counterterrorist propaganda and using criticism and innuendo to discredit the terrorists' motives and goals as well as their methods" (Biernatzki, 2002, p. 22).

Ross determines six basic difficulties in connection with reporting about terrorism (cf. Ross, 2007, pp. 217–218) that sometimes interfere with traditional journalistic norms and values:

1. Selectivity and self-censorship for fear of reprisals – either by the state or by the terrorists;
2. Reluctance of the editors, who sometimes hesitate to bring to the public a story or photographs ready for publication;
3. Not enough specialists who are sufficiently familiar with the field of terrorist groups and tactics to professionally report about them;
4. Strategically spread misinformation by the national security authorities, which leads to incorrect or news coverage following a certain tendency;
5. The risk of endangering anti-terrorist actions or, in the worst case, hostages, as a result of the news coverage;
6. The bias toward sensationalism: exaggeration of events to win new readers.

Due to the combination of these interferences and the difficulties which exist in crisis reporting and with the terrorists' or school shooters' media strategies, one has to admit that even elaborated guidelines could only help to reduce journalists' insecurity in dealing with such a situation but cannot at all hinder nor prevent the underlying dilemma.

Given the media's symbiotic or parasitic function in relation to terrorism and based on research findings on possibly contagious and incentivizing effects, it seems appropriate to reflect on whether (a) censorship and regulation of news coverage by the state or (b) the voluntary self-restraint of and guidelines for the media can be necessary or helpful in this context. Numerous authors have dealt with censorship and regulation of news coverage by the state in the past, often in the context of specific media channels (cf. Soria & Giner, 1990; Wilkinson, 1997). Today, the discussion is more topical than ever, since content does not circulate as it used to, but persists to a large extent, especially on the Internet. This does not only affect traditional media but also affect private news sites, blogs, or social media. As already described, governments have been exerting increased pressure on private companies, especially since 2014, to monitor content presented on their platforms more closely and to take action in the event of violations of standards. As a result, Facebook, Microsoft, Twitter, and YouTube, for example, founded the Global Internet Forum to Counter Terrorism in 2017, to combine their efforts to remove terrorist content from their platforms (cf. gifct.org, 2023). As mentioned above, the restrictive efforts of some media providers, especially in the social media sector, already led to a reduced visibility of terrorist groups, but primarily, they seem to lead to a change in the groups' use of these media. However, aggressive negative measures may even be reinterpreted by the groups as positive ones. With regard to the measures taken against IS's online presence on Twitter, Pearson concludes in her study on the psychological effect of account blocking that this had become an "integral" part of the online identities of IS's extremist followers (Pearson, 2018, p. 850).

In democratic countries, there are usually voluntary self-restraint of and guidelines for the media, in which sensationalist reporting in particular is denounced and suggestions are made as to how the balance between the duty and right to inform and ethically sensitive reporting can be achieved. In the aftermath of major attacks, there are always examples of concrete measures or self-declarations that media implement (e.g., Le Monde in France, in the aftermath of the Nice attack in 2016). While other media companies and their editorial departments reject such measures with reference to their duty to show names and images of perpetrators, these initiatives draw attention to a long-standing dilemma. In the end, the unpleasant predicament of deciding for or against certain publications remains the responsibility of the media, which face an uncomfortable choice: "If they censor the terrorist news they are infringing on the public's right to know. If they give extensive coverage they might terrorize the public and become allies of the terrorists. If they follow the government line they might become a propaganda and police tool" (Schmid & de Graaf, 1982, p. 98).

A relatively old implication is still relevant and more in demand than ever. Chaliand goes beyond the normative requirements for organizations or press owner associations by demanding: "It is high time that every newspaper, magazine and television channel had one person responsible for all events connected with terrorism" (Chaliand, 1987, p. 122). However, there are still hardly any such terrorism experts or experts concerning shootings in the editorial departments.

Conclusion and Outlook

A synthesis of the scientific discussion reveals that the relationship between the media and the perpetrator of a shooting or terrorist attack is considered, analyzed, and interpreted almost solely from a normative Western democratic perspective (and this also applies to this contribution) that demands the media to, on the one hand, adhere to their duty to supply information, and on the other hand, not to play into the terrorists' hands. In future research, this limitation should be broken up more and more frequently, for example, by interviewing journalists and editors and conducting international comparative content analyses. Self-presentations by terrorist groups on the web such as in online media, forums, and blogs are all potential foci for new research. In particular, the treatment of new media in the context of terrorism crisis is lacking in literature. Terrorism nowadays almost always crosses boundaries; it is an international crisis affecting international audiences and demanding international responses in a globalized world with an international media agenda. Of course, journalists do not want to follow or transfer the terrorists' propaganda, but the very fast coverage does not leave much time for investigation.

Even though this article did not suggest solutions to the terrorism-media dilemma in a normative way, it has demonstrated that the media form part of the terrorists' crisis strategy and are a necessary step on their way to reach their goals. The crisis-inducing terrorist organizations stage their events in order to spread fear through the media. The governments' responses are also communicated through the media, and thus, they function as a linkage or mediator between these two actors.

References

Adam, P. S., Quinn, S., & Edmonds, R. (2007). *Eyetracking the News: A Story of Print and Online Reading*. Poynter Institute.

Berger, J. M., & Morgan, J. (2015). The ISIS Twitter census: Defining and describing the population of ISIS supporters on Twitter. *The Brookings Project on U.S. Relations with the Islamic World*. www.brookings.edu/wp-content/uploads/2016/06/isis_Twitter_census_berger_morgan.pdf

Biernatzki, W. E. (2002). Terrorism and mass media. *Communication Research Trends*, *21*(1), 3–27.

Bondü, R. (2012). *School Shootings in Deutschland Internationaler Vergleich, Warnsignale, Risikofaktoren, Entwicklungsverläufe*. Dissertation, Freie Universität Berlin.

Boukes, M. (2021). Episodic and thematic framing effects on the attribution of responsibility: The effects of personalized and contextualized news on perceptions of individual and political responsibility for causing the economic crisis. *The International Journal of Press/Politics.*, *27*(2), 374–395. https://doi.org/10.1177/1940161220985241

Callimachi, R. (2016). A news agency with scoops directly from ISIS, and a veneer of objectivity. *The New York Times Online*. January, 14th. https://www.nytimes.com/2016/01/15/world/middleeast/a-news-agency-with-scoops-directly-from-isis-and-a-veneer-of-objectivity.html

Chaliand, G. (1987). *Terrorism. From Popular Struggle to Media Spectacle*. Saqi Books.

Garcia-Bernardo, J., Qi, H., Shultz, J. M., Cohen, A. M., Johnson, N. F., & Dodds, P. S. (2018). *Social media appears to affect the timing, location, and severity of school shootings.* https://pdodds.w3.uvm.edu/teaching/courses/2013-01UVM-300/output/files/2015/garcia-bernardo2015a.pdf

Global Internet Forum to Counter Terrorism (2023). *Preventing terrorists and violent extremists from exploiting digital platforms.* https://gifct.org/

Hu, M., Liu, S., Wei, F., Wu, Y., Stasko, J., & Ma, K.-L. (2012). Breaking news on Twitter. *Proceedings of the SIGCHI Conference on Human Factors in Computing Systems,* 2751–2754.

Iyengar, S. (1991). *Is Anyone Responsible? How Television Frames Political Issues.* The University of Chicago Press.

Kissner, J. (2016). Are active shootings temporally contagious? An empirical assessment. *Journal of Police and Criminal Psychology, 31*(1), 48–58.

Kydd, A. H., & Walter, B. F. (2006). The strategies of terrorism. *International Security, 31*(1), 49–80.

Lee, J., Britt, B. C., & Kanthawala, S. (2022). Taking the lead in misinformation-related conversations in social media networks during a mass shooting crisis. *Internet Research, 33*(2), 638–663. https://doi.org/10.1108/INTR-02-2021-0120

Meta (2019). *Update on New Zealand.* https://about.fb.com/news/2019/03/update-on-new-zealand/ (accessed March 18, 2019)

Miller, A. H. (1982). *Terrorism, the Media and the Law.* Dobbs Ferry, NY: Transnational Publishers.

Moeller, S. D. (1999). *Compassion Fatigue: How the Media Sell Disease, Famine, War and Death.* Routledge.

Muschert, G. W. (2013). School shootings as mediatized violence. In N. Böckler, T. Seeger, P. Sitzer, & W. Heitmeyer, Eds., *School Shootings. International Research, Case Studies, and Concepts for Prevention* (pp. 265–281). Springer.

Neumann, P., Winter, C., Meleagrou-Hitchens, A., Ranstorp, M., & Vidino, L. (2018). *Die Rolle des Internets und sozialer Medien für Radikalisierung und Deradikalisierung. PRIF Report* (p. 10). Peace Research Institute Frankfurt.

Nossek, H., & Berkowitz, D. (2006). Telling "our" story through news of terrorism. Mythical news-work as journalistic practice in crisis. *Journalism Studies, 7*(5), 691–707.

Pearson, E. (2018). Online as the new frontline: Affect, gender, and ISIS-take-down on social media. *Studies in Conflict & Terrorism, 41*(11), 850–887.

Pew Research Center for the People and the Press (1999). *Columbine shooting biggest news draw of 1999.* https://www.pewresearch.org/politics/1999/12/28/columbine-shooting-biggest-news-draw-of-1999/

Picard, R. (1991). *Media Portrayals of Terrorism: Functions and Meanings of News Coverage.* Ames: Iowa State University Press.

Reuter, C., & Kaufhold, M.-A. (2017). Fifteen years of social media in emergencies: A retrospective review and future directions for crisis Informatics. *Journal of Contingencies & Crisis Management, 26*(1), 1–17.

Ross, J. I. (2007). Deconstructing the terrorism news media relationship. *Crime, Media, Culture, 3*(2), 215–225.

Rothenberger, L. (2023). *Terrorism as Communication. Stocktaking, Explanations and Challenges.* Palgrave Macmillan.

Rothenberger, L., & Hase, V. (2023). Content analysis in the research field of terrorism coverage. In F. Oehmer, S. H. Kessler, E. Humprecht, K. Sommer, & L. C. Herrero, Eds., *Standardisierte Inhaltsanalyse in der Kommunikationswissenschaft – Standardized content analysis in Communication Research* (pp. 137–146). Springer. https://doi.org/10.1007/978-3-658-36179-2_12

Schaffert, R. W. (1992). *Media Coverage and Political Terrorists: A Quantitative Analysis.* Praeger.

Schlesinger, P., Murdock, G., & Elliott, P. (1984). *Televising Terrorism: Political Violence in Popular Culture.* Charles Scribner's Sons.

Schmid, A. P., & de Graaf, J. (1982). *Violence as Communication: Insurgent Terrorism and the Western News Media.* Sage.

Sellnow, T. L., Littlefield, R. S., Vidoloff, K. G., & Webb, E. M. (2009). The interacting arguments of risk communication in response to terrorist hoaxes. *Argumentation and Advocacy, 45*(3), 135–150.

Sitzer, P. (2013). The role of media content in the genesis of school shootings: The contemporary discussion. In N. Böckler, T. Seeger, P. Sitzer, & W. Heitmeyer, Eds., *School Shootings. International Research, Case Studies, and Concepts for Prevention* (pp. 283–307). Springer.

Soria, C., & Giner, J. A. (1990). El secuestro terrorista de los medios de información. In C. Soria, Ed., *Prensa, Paz, Violencia y Terrorismo: La crisis de credibilidad de los informadores* (pp. 51–68). Pamplona: Ediciones Universidad de Navarra.

Towers, S., Gomez-Lievano, A., Khan, M., Mubayi, A., & Castillo-Chavez, C. (2015). Contagion in mass killings and school shootings. *PLoS One, 10*(7), e0117259. https://doi.org/10.1371/journal.pone.0117259

Verhovnik, M. (2009). Chaos vom Feinsten. Berichterstattung zum Amoklauf in Winnenden. *Communicatio Socialis, 42*(3), 288–292.

Verhovnik, M. (2015). *School Shootings. Interdisziplinäre Analyse und empirische Untersuchung der journalistischen Berichterstattung*. Nomos.

Weimann, G., & Winn, C. (1994). *The Theater of Terror. Mass Media and International Terrorism*. Longman.

Weimann, G. (2008). The psychology of mass-mediated terrorism. *American Behavioral Scientist, 52*(1), 69–86.

Wilkinson, P. (1997). The media and terrorism: A reassessment. *Terrorism and Political Violence, 9*(2), 51–64.

Winter, C. (2016). *An integrated approach to Islamic State recruitment*. Australian Strategic Policy Institute. https://css.ethz.ch/content/dam/ethz/special-interest/gess/cis/center-for-securities-studies/resources/docs/An%20integrated%20approach%20to%20Islamic%20State%20recruitmen.pdf

Author's Bio

Liane Rothenberger, Dr. phil. habil., holds the professorship of Media and the Public with specialization in migration at the Catholic University of Eichstätt-Ingolstadt, Germany. From 2008 to 2021, she worked at Technische Universität Ilmenau in the research group of media studies. Her research focuses on journalism, migration, crisis communication, and intercultural communication.

Melanie Verhovnik-Heinze, Dr. phil., holds the professorship of Digital Media Practice with a focus on social media at the Ansbach University of Applied Sciences. She previously headed the Transfer Service Center at the Leibniz Institute for Research and Information in Education in Frankfurt, and before that, she worked in the research department of the State Office of Criminal Investigation of Lower Saxony. Her research interests lie in the areas of social media, radicalization, media psychology, and transfer.

12

Environmental Risk Communication

The Challenges to Progressively Affecting Behavior

Michael J. Palenchar and Carla White
Tombras School of ADPR, University of Tennessee, Knoxville, TN, USA

The study and effective practice of environmental risk communication (ERC) has never been more imperative; it is essential to the survival of this planet, its human and animal inhabitants, and other life forms and living material. According to the United Nations Office for Disaster Risk Reduction (2022), a total of 321 major disasters (excluding epidemic disasters) occurred worldwide in 2022, affecting 118 countries and regions. Among all these disasters, 51% were caused by floods, 21% by storms (typhoons and hurricanes), 9% by earthquakes, 6% by droughts, 5% by landslides, 5% by wildfire disasters, 2% by extreme temperatures, and 1% by volcanic eruptions.

Its recommendation focused on three comprehensive blueprints that involve the field of ERC: (1) measure what we value, (2) design systems to factor in how human minds make decisions about risk, and (3) reconfigure governance and financial systems to work across silos and design in consultation with affected people. According to their report, "Despite progress, risk creation is outstripping risk reduction. Disasters, economic loss and the underlying vulnerabilities that drive risk, such as poverty and inequality, are increasing just as ecosystems and biospheres are at risk of collapse. Global systems are becoming more connected and therefore more vulnerable in an uncertain risk landscape" (p. 1).

Other reports that indicate similar increases in global and regional disasters and stress similar concerns include the International Federation of Red Cross and Red Crescent Societies, the United States Geological Survey, the National Oceanic and Atmospheric Administration, and the Global Disaster Alert and Coordination System, which was created in 2004 as a joint effort between the United Nations and the European Commission to address significant gaps in data collection and analysis during the early phase of major sudden-onset disasters, often caused by weather-related events that have been more impactful in recent years due to climate change and other weather pattern changes.

There is a myriad of environmental, health, and safety issues and concerns, as well as an eclectic range of communication theories and frameworks, associated with ERC research in developing effective approaches to either disseminate information to or engage in dialogue with risk bearers to address the current environmental crisis. This book chapter provides a brief overview of ERC with a focus on three, among the many, challenges that ERC researchers and practitioners face in developing effective risk communication campaigns based on sound risk management practices that can mitigate climate change.

The Handbook of International Crisis and Risk Communication Research, Second Edition.
Edited by Andreas Schwarz, Matthew W. Seeger, and Sora Kim.

These challenges include the following: (1) the failure of traditional science communication based on information exchange, (2) uncertainty and the challenge of wrongly disputed (intentional or unintentional) risks during an ongoing crisis, and (3) the fundamental dilemma of all risk communication efforts. While there is no consensus on the next direction of ERC scholarship to guide practitioners, the chapter will briefly identify some promising frameworks that continue to deserve attention from the academic community as well as those on the front line of engaging in dialogue concerning the mitigation of climate change.

Environmental Risk Communication

ERC is the exchange of information related to environmental risks among individuals, communities, and organizations. Most often, ERC aims to inform, educate, and encourage behaviors and decision-making to better manage the risk at hand (Renn, 2020). Topics are complex as it often highlights an interconnectedness between the natural, scientific, and business world (Gurabardhi et al., 2005), along with other sociocultural, political, ideological, and communicative issues and concerns.

A notable example of ERC's complexity existed during the recent COVID-19 pandemic, when researchers discovered that air quality had a significant impact on the worsening of symptoms (Ali & Islam, 2020). This launched a broad ERC effort among government and public health departments like the World Health Organization and the U.S. Centers for Disease Control and Prevention (e.g., Gupta-Smith, 2020). In addition to providing up-to-date health information, these organizations also distributed guidelines on air quality, information about pollution, and the potential for environmental impact on individual's health status during the pandemic. According to Qiu and Chu (2019), the public health sector often assumes responsibility for the dissemination of ERC for issues relating to air quality, water contamination, and food safety. Other common areas of practice for ERC surround topics like pollution, chemical spills, industrial emissions, natural disasters, emergency preparedness, and climate change.

Historically, the ERC field dramatically shifted following the advent and use of nuclear bombs beginning in the 1940s. The development of nuclear weapons and their subsequent testing created a new context for possible catastrophic environmental and health impacts due to human action (Abe, 2013).

This development of existential risk that threatens all of humanity shifted ERC focus to include global and long-lasting impacts. The need to standardize procedures related to nuclear risk also forecasted the importance of formal, transparent, clear, and accessible risk communication plans that are still relied upon in modern practice (Renn, 2020). The National Research Council (1983) highlighted the rapid evolution of ERC as a top priority for governments, scientists, and policymakers in an effort to properly inform and manage public risk. It formalized risk management procedures, promoted stakeholder engagement, and prioritized transparency in risk communication, which all remain central in current risk management and risk communication procedures (Covello, 2020).

ERC as a distinct field evolved over the second half of the twentieth century in response to the public's growing awareness of environmental issues and several high-profile environmental disasters and risk communication failures, including the following: (1) the 1978 Love Canal environmental crisis in Niagara Falls, New York, where residents' homes, schools, and playgrounds were built upon a former chemical waste dump that led to widespread negative health effects; (2) the 1984 Bhopal Union Carbide chemical plant explosion that is considered one of the worst industrial accidents that caused thousands of deaths (various estimates range from thousands to tens of thousands). This disaster underscored the importance of risk communication before, during, and after industrial crisis events; and (3) the 1986 Chernobyl nuclear reactor meltdown that had lasting implications for how governments communicate with its citizens about such risks and associated health, safety, and environmental implications.

Overall, these and other man-made and natural disasters that included severe environmental impacts increased scrutiny into ERC research and practices. It also led to great advocacy for right to know research and education for communities that live near major sources of industrial risk (Palenchar & Motta, 2012).

To effectively mitigate environmental risk, it is imminent that ERC practitioners actively informs and engages prominent stakeholders, relevant publics, and active decision-makers (Lundgren & McMakin, 2013). When communicating environmental hazard and risk, communicators often focus on improving the scope of understanding related to potential threats in order to best facilitate informed decision-making. For example, during a 2018 severe water crisis caused by a prolonged drought in South Africa, governmental agencies in Cape Town launched an ERC plan designed to update residents on current water levels. The ERC plan also proposed strict water usage recommendations for households to ensure the continued safety of all community members (City of Cape Town, 2018).

Despite the City of Cape Town providing actionable documentation to its residents during the drought, a qualitative investigation of a neighboring city, Stellenbosch, revealed that most residents in the Western Cape region were unfamiliar with the concept of climate change. This particular area was even more susceptible to drought and other climate-related threats due to its proximity to the sea, rising tide levels, and lessening biodiversity (Mahl et al., 2020). This particular study informs the need for more prolific ERC in rural and remote regions, especially those susceptible to climate-related crises.

In many cases, the inclusion of actionable items and recommendations in risk communication strategy leads to more favorable outcomes for the health and well-being of impacted or at-risk individuals and environments (Renn, 2020). Promoting actions related to the adaptation to or mitigation of risk have long been relied upon in the study of ERC. Communicating actions that help to build resilience among publics and the promotion of behaviors or decisions that aim to reduce risk are most commonly relied upon in current ERC practice (Castaños & Lomnitz, 2008).

ERC's Evolution

There are numerous ERC research lines that continue to evolve in scholarship and practice. Each approach provides a framework to best address threats and communicate effectively in a variety of contexts based on current trends surrounding risk communication. Early ERC research focused heavily on a one-way flow of information, under the assumption that all individuals would be better prepared and informed for managing and accepting risk.

However, in the 1990s, research began to address discrepancies within the public perception of risk (e.g., Heath & Palenchar, 2009; Slovic, 2016). Researchers began to note the impact of cultural and social values, along with personal experiences, in how it impacted individuals' understandings and perceptions of risk. Therefore, a shift in the dominant epistemological lens from which risk was studied allowed for a more sociopsychological, cultural, and social construction approach.

This change brought an increased focus on creating opportunities for dialogue among risk bearers, risk arbiters, and risk-generating organizations, along with those creating ERC strategies, to learn more about individual characteristics and group dynamics that influence risk perception. The call for more tailored risk communication for different stakeholder groups and mediums has resulted in a more participatory risk management culture. Involving a variety of actors and collaborating with opinion leaders and influencers across a variety of channels may assist in the overall management of environmental risk.

Information dissemination relates to the specificities of the risk at hand, for example, what is the nature of the risk? How can ERC provide timely, up-to-date information related to the risk? In the practice of information dissemination, it is recommended that all relevant information pertaining to the risk should be shared (Holland et al., 2021). This means that if background information is required to best articulate a potential or current risk, communication strategies should include supporting evidence and information to provide context for the public.

When sharing pertinent information related to hazard and risk, it is recommended that potential impacts and uncertainties are disclosed. Despite the potential for negative public response rooted in fear or uncertainty, evidence suggests that it is better to inform publics of all potential outcomes to best prepare for and respond to issues related to ERC. Heath and Palenchar's (2009) longitudinal study of communities dominated by manufacturing facilities showed an increase in support and in trust of risk-generating organizations, along with less perceived risk, when it informs the public about the risk uncertainties, potential consequences, and risk mitigation efforts. Even if no crisis or pressing threat is present, it has been found that organizations that promote transparency in communicating the intricacies of ERC (e.g., educating about the risk and also preparing for all possible outcomes) have been shown to lead to higher levels of organizational trust and satisfaction among affected publics (Holland et al., 2021).

Stakeholder engagement is also a central component of successful ERC (Renn, 2020). Without the involvement of various publics and stakeholders, organizations, industry leaders, and governmental agencies (i.e., risk bearers, risk generators, and risk arbiters), ERC strategies would fail to represent a diversified outlook on proactive, active, or retrospective risks. Since each stakeholder group provides a unique set of experiences, backgrounds, knowledge, and beliefs, ERC plans should account for the idiosyncratic ways in which different individuals and groups perceive and understand risk (Covello, 2020).

For example, as result of climate change and increasing occurrences of extreme weather events, the National Center for Environmental Information (n.d.) and other U. S. agencies like the Federal Emergency Management Agency have developed an ERC campaign to educate publics across the United States on preparedness and response to weather threats based on their geographical location through a variety of interactive web tools, printable flyers, among other tactics.

However, this is only the start. Gaps in ERC effectiveness related to extreme weather events were previously highlighted during the catastrophic damages to the U. S. Gulf Coast after Hurricane Katrina in 2005. Failures in timely and accurate messaging during the storm caused confusion about evacuation orders, the severity of the risks, and different messaging from various authorities contributed to chaos and confusion (Rodríguez et al., 2007).

A unified voice in real time was desperately needed as the impact from the storm left thousands of people in immediate danger. After Hurricane Katrina, standardized response strategies became prevalent in ERC to best deploy clear, timely, and consistent messaging to impacted communities. Another key contribution to the field of ERC made from the lessons of Hurricane Katrina is the critical need to better address vulnerable populations and communities (Eisenman et al., 2007).

Over the past decade, leveraging new technologies and social media have become an increasing focus for ERC scholars and practitioners in recent years. Social media fundamentally changed the way, especially how ERC is communicated in terms of timeliness and global reach (Malecki et al., 2020). The rise of social and digital platforms has become even more essential for environmental risk communicators to have a diverse understanding of both communication channels and varying audiences (Silver, 2019). It has also allowed for organizations to more easily participate in dialogue with its stakeholders. While social media has assisted in ERC's participatory and timely nature, it has presented some challenges related to trust and credibility (Shahbazi & Bunker, 2024), among other issues.

Additional ERC Frameworks

In addition to the knowledge deficit model, which will be discussed in detail later in the chapter, there are numerous other ERC frameworks to guide researchers and practitioners. While a detailed list is beyond the scope of this chapter, here are a few of the more prominent approaches:

- *Technical-scientific framework* focuses on the quantifiable assessment of risk using scientific data and methodologies. It conveys risks based on statistical probabilities, toxicological findings, and exposure levels, presuming that public concerns will be assuaged by accurate evidence and information.
- *Public relations framework* focuses more on managing the organization's reputation and relationships with stakeholders. Communication strategies aim to present environmental risks in a way that manages public trust and minimizes potential repercussions against individuals, organizations, or industries, while at the same time mitigating health, safety, and environmental risks for risk bearers and others effected by natural disasters.
- *Discourse-based framework* considers how language and social interactions influence public perception and understanding of environmental risks. This approach acknowledges that various stakeholders may interpret the same information differently based on cultural values, beliefs, and prior knowledge.
- *Participatory framework* advocates for involving community members in decision-making processes about environmental risks affecting them. It promotes transparency, dialogue, and collaboration among experts, policymakers, key stakeholders, and the public to empower communities, adjust for comprises, and form consensus.
- *Psychological framework l*ooks at individual psychological factors that affect risk perception such as heuristics (mental shortcuts), emotions and biases, and personal values that influence an individual's reaction and response to communicated risks.
- *Social amplification of risk framework (SARF)* examines how risk events resound through society, influencing public perception beyond what is reasonable by scientific evidence alone. It considers media portrayal, cultural beliefs, personal experiences, and social discourse as amplifiers or attenuators of perceived risk (Kasperson et al., 1988).
- *Infrastructural approach to risk communication* incorporates other frameworks strengths. It is dialogic and discursive. Assorted and diverse experts, policymakers, risk arbiters and advocates, and individual voices of risk bearers must be brought together to create systems and shared perspectives that appropriately assess, mitigate, and respond to risks, which are routinely and unevenly experienced throughout any community or larger society. This approach argues that individual and community efficacy are principal loci for examining and ascertaining whether a community's risk infrastructure is suitably structured to plan and communicate about various risks in ways that make it resilient (Heath & Palenchar, 2016).

Each of these frameworks and theories offers unique insights into how people perceive, understand, and communicate about environmental risks. While some emphasize objective data or expert opinion, others prioritize social dynamics or individual psychology. Effective ERC often requires integrating aspects from multiple frameworks to comprehensively address diverse stakeholder concerns.

Three Major ERC Challenges

Information Exchange

A historically dominant approach to ERC is based on a scientific information exchange model of communication. This model has been the predominant orientation to creating and disseminating scientific information, including ERC. As previously discussed in this chapter, the information exchange model is similar to the technical-scientific framework that focuses on the one-way dissemination of quantifiable assessment of risk using scientific data and methodologies. As noted in the ERC section of this chapter, this approach has had limited success in addressing complicated issues that affect people and the environment.

Within this ERC approach, the knowledge deficit model has been the mainstay of environmental and other scientific communication research and practice. The knowledge deficit model of science communication assumes a lay public with a limited knowledge and understanding of science and its process. Fundamentally, the scientist is the expert who provides and sometimes explains and engages in dialogue, about the scientific data to drive public discourse and public policy to mitigate environmental risk.

Grant (2023) provided a strong summary about this model:

> The knowledge deficit model represents a key boundary concept in the modern discussion of science communication. In essence, the model asserts an epistemic priority for science and scientific information; that scientific knowledge should be paramount in making decisions on science-related issues, that his knowledge should be communicated from scientists to audiences who do not have this knowledge, that scientists should be in control of this communication flow, that the nonscientific audiences receiving this knowledge will be grateful for this, and they will make better decisions as a result. (para 1)

The knowledge deficit model has three parts: product, process, and remedy (Suldovsky, 2016). The fundamental challenge to this model relates to the product (scientific knowledge) and the disparity between understanding (apply scientific knowledge to adjust behavior) and the general public. Thus, scientists and communication professionals transfer scientific knowledge, but in order to be effective, the targeted stakeholders must have scientific literacy.

Process, the second element, concerns a lack of knowledge about the process of science that often leads to distrust among the public, public policymakers, and related risk generators and risk arbiters; often due a lack of transparency about the scientific process. The third part, remedy, focuses on crossing this bridge between product and process by improving science communication. According to Suldovsky (2016), the knowledge deficit model addresses the fractured relationship between science and society. "As long as science communication research and practice are founded upon the desire to resolve a problematic gap through the use of (often) one-directional communication, the public deficit will have an integral role within that process" (p. 417).

The deficit model has been heavily criticized, among other things, for its implicit assumption that scientific expertise and worldview are dominant over other forms of knowledge (Jasanoff, 2011). Indeed, several studies conducted both in Europe and the United states indicated that the majority of scientists still adhere to a so-called deficit model when interacting with nonscientist publics (Dudo & Besley, 2016).

One reason advocated by Suldovsky (2016) for the persistence of the deficit model is that the scientific process itself is "inextricably linked to knowledge acquisition" (p. 419). This process propagates an elitist, hierarchical model of knowledge dissemination – limiting the positive effects of ERC in mitigating risk.

However, ERC is interdisciplinary in nature and eclectic in its foundation of incorporating all aspects of human behavior, while it takes into account many other uncertainties when applied to the public, such as ethics, moral, ideological, cultural, and social implications. Ultimately, all these elements related to science affect how ERC researchers and practitioners study and engage in dialogue about the catastrophic risk of the increasing number of natural disasters related to climate change and its associated political, cultural, and economic issues.

It is therefore partly a question of morality to inscribe scientific evidences in precautionary or sound policy: Organizational interpretations of prudence are sensitive to self-interest but also to culture (Rayner, 1992). However, when these choices over- or under-represent a risk uncertainty, the interest of the community ought to override it. Reincke et al. (2020) concisely summarized this challenge: "The 'one-way' expert model of science communication is out of date. The new dialogue model requires from scientists more than just providing expert knowledge to the publics" (p. 1).

Overall, the major criticism of this model is that it oversimplifies complex issues based on a communication model that is a linear between knowledge and acceptance. It fails to address cultural values, personal beliefs, identity, trust in information sources, trust in policymakers, and the broad category of emotional responses. The field has evolved, as noted earlier in the chapter, but too many practitioners and organizations rely on this model for ERC campaigns and responses.

Misinformation/Disinformation (Uncertainty) During a Crisis

The profound advancement of both the research domain and practical application of risk and crisis communication has been one of the most crucial expansions of communication science in the past 40-plus years (Palenchar & Heath, in press). However, this advancement is being thwarted by post-truth, fake news, and individual and organized group disinformation and misinformation efforts and campaigns, along with the ease of digital alteration and artificial intelligence (Palenchar, 2024). Regardless, according to Bourne and Edwards (2021), "one of the hallmarks of post-truth politics is the level of heated emotion and sheer noise it produces. This noise sucks audience time and attention, making fake news a highly effective form of misdirection in today's public sphere. It helps to enforce our silence by redirecting public attention away from controversial issues" (p. 605).

Numerous contemporary events, as described earlier in this chapter, demonstrate how misinformation and disinformation plays an increasingly dominant and complicating role in the political and social discourse surrounding environmental risk events throughout the world. Stemming from incidents like The Oregon Petition and Climategate, mistrust in climate science continues to be a prevalent issue in the ERC field.

For example, in the late 1990s, a petition refuting the impacts and dangers of global warming allegedly containing the signatures of approximately 30,000 scientists circulated through traditional media. However, it was later discovered that most of the names on this document were not scientists or climate experts but rather members of the general public. The petition was not based on peer-reviewed research; however, it still has lasting effects on broad levels of skepticism toward climate change (Grandia, 2009).

On a similar note, in 2009, a group of scientists were hacked, which the occurrence was later deemed Climategate. Their research was selectively shared across media channels by hackers in an effort to portray data manipulation. This led to widespread mistrust in the area of climate change despite the research being mis-portrayed (McKie, 2019).

While the Paris Agreement in 2015 assisted in the global legitimization of climate change (United Nations, n.d.), additionally and just as importantly, it encouraged transparency and accountability from politicians and global government bodies. Despite the agreement, global warming continues to be discussed as a hoax across current social media channels by various opinion leaders, conspiracy theorists, and political figures. This establishes large barriers for the successful dissemination of and dialogue related to ERC.

Brulle (2018) claimed the increased delegitimization of science through misinformation is due to the rise of the conservative movement and associated research centers that contribute to the devaluing of science by disputing the scientific basis for federal regulations, such as the Clean Air Act or the National Environmental Policy Act. "This has created an anti-science intellectual climate in the conservative movement that has been promulgated via the right-wing media and conservative intellectuals and political elites" (p. 255–256).

These active media settings where misinformation related to environmental risk is discussed provide a complex medium for climate experts and organizations to discuss the current environmental crisis. When the sharing of scientific conclusions leads to public mistrust and confusion, it becomes extremely difficult to mobilize public support for risk management or action. Researchers and practitioners engaging in ERC strategy and dissemination play an important role in combating misinformation, and increasing trust and digital literacy, among their target audiences to achieve desired outcomes.

The Fundamental Dilemma of Risk Communication

The dilemma of ERC is in some ways obvious and ostensibly uncomplicated to manage. The fundamental dilemma of the ERC and other risk communication, however, is considerably more convoluted: ***why is it that the risks that cause detriment to people and populaces and the risks that distress those same individuals and groups are often utterly different*** (Palenchar, 2024)?

Environmental risk assessment detects and categorizes potential risks and its likelihood to impact health and safety, economic issues or manufacturing production, or any range of human ambitions and activities that affect the environment. With that scientifically identified assessment of risks, ERC researchers and practitioners share the findings with people and organizations responsible for managing and mitigating the risks, with risk arbiters, and most importantly risk bearers. Identify, share, discuss, manage, and adjust behaviors and actions: simple (Palenchar, 2024).

Then, why is it so challenging. In 1988, Krimsky and Plough had similar thoughts in their essay and summed it up as well as we can some 35-plus years later:

> The emergence of risk communication as a research theme cannot be fully appreciated or accounted for without understanding its link to a set of issues that symbolize the discord between scientific experts and the public around the issue of risk. These tensions are played out in disputes between different research traditions on fundamental questions regarding the perception of risk and the essential nature of human rationality (p. 4).

The emergence of ERC cannot be fully appreciated for or accounted for without understanding its link to a set of issues that symbolize the discord between scientific experts and the public around the issue of risk. These tensions are played out in disputes between different research traditions on fundamental questions regarding the perception of risk and the essential nature of human rationality (Krimsky & Plough, 1988), while also mixing in misinformation and disinformation. As such, disputes over ERC are essentially a political, cultural, and social activity wrapped around scientific-based information that is not often presented in an effective manner or dialogic approach.

Regrettably, this fundamental ERC dilemma has not changed since the early days of issues management, crisis communication, and risk communication research and its practice. Risk assessment and managed ERC are in many ways considered the responsibilities of the educated elites to create a public understanding of science; a technical rationale understanding of science. This view of success has been, unfortunately, consistent over the 40-plus year of the field of risk communication studies and practice (Palenchar, 2024). According to Plough and Krimsky (1987), "The success of risk communication is measured by the degree to which popular attitudes reflect the technical rationality of risk and the extent that popular behavior conforms to technocratic values. A lack of convergence is attributed to a failure of risk communication" (p. 8). This same lens of success has deemed lacking much ERC.

Conclusion

More than six decades ago, Rachel Carson (1962) challenged individuals, organizations, and governments to more lucidly focus attention on the wonders and realities of the world in which people live in order to have less desire to behave in ways that could lead to its devastation. In response to this challenge and as researchers and practitioners of the means and processes of social influence and behavioral change, ERC scholars and practitioners can and should serve the vital social role of bringing ethical concerns to bear on the lines of scientific investigation, applications of such investigation, the formation of personal and public policy, and its subsequent communication efforts.

ERC integrates a focus on the probative force of various facts in the context of symbolic processes that result from the dynamics of a functional or a dysfunctional communication infrastructure. As such, the role of ERC, and the essence of its analysis and pedagogy, is to increase the quality of enlightened decision-making so that societies can be more fully functional in their identification, assessment, and management of risks (Heath et al., 2007).

Ultimately, risk communication [including ERC] serves as a place for the sort of normative hand-wringing that has characterized communication studies since the age of Plato and Aristotle (Heath et al., 2017). The central universal question of how can people know (ever more challenged by misinformation and disinformation campaigns) and how can individuals and organizations collectively engage in dialogue and effect action in protecting the environment in ways that improve society, the environment, and thus the overall human condition remains a continuing challenge. Researchers must do more than merely describe the conditions studied; they are obligated to develop and add to normative theory because they are expected to help society be more fully functional (Heath, 2006; Heath et al., 2007) despite current obstacles such as misinformation and disinformation, and mistrust in science.

References

Abe, Y. (2013). Risk assessment of nuclear power by Japanese newspapers following the Chernobyl nuclear disaster. *International Journal of Communication*, *7*, 22. https://ijoc.org/index.php/ijoc/article/view/1848

Ali, N., & Islam, F. (2020). The effects of air pollution on covid-19 infection and mortality – A review on recent evidence. *Frontiers in Public Health*, *8*. https://doi.org/10.3389/fpubh.2020.580057

Bourne, C., & Edwards, L. (2021). Critical reflections on the field. In C. Valentini, Ed., *Public relations* (pp. 601–614). De Gruyter Mouton. https://doi.org/10.1515/9783110554250

Brulle, R. J. (2018). Critical reflections on the march for science. *Sociological Forum*, *33*(1), 255–258. https://doi.org/10.1111/socf.12398

Carson, R. (1962). *Silent Spring*. Houghton Mifflin.

Castaños, H., & Lomnitz, C. (2008). Review of the book risk governance: Coping with uncertainty in a complex world by Ortwin Renn. *Natural Hazards*, *48*(2), 313–314. https://doi.org/10.1007/s11069-008-9286-7

City of Cape Town (2018). *Level 3 Water Restrictions.* City of Cape Town. https://resource.capetown.gov.za/documentcentre/Documents/Procedures%2C%20guidelines%20and%20regulations/Water%20restrictions%20FAQs.pdfNovember 30.

Covello, V. T. (2020). Strategies for overcoming challenges to effective risk communication. In R. L. Heath, & D. H. O'Hair, Eds., *Handbook of Risk and Crisis Communication* (pp. 143–167). Routledge.

Dudo, A., & Besley, J. C. (2016). Scientists' prioritization of communication objectives for public engagement. *PLoS One, 11*, e0148867. https://www.ncbi.nlm.nih.gov/pmc/articles/PMC7506985/#embr202051278-bib-0004
Eisenman, D. P., Cordasco, K. M., Asch, S., Golden, J. F., & Glik, D. (2007). Disaster planning and risk communication with vulnerable communities: Lessons from Hurricane Katrina. *American Journal of Public Health, 97*, 109–115. https://doi.org/10.2105/AJPH.2005.084335
Grandia, K. (August 22, 2009). The 30,000 global warming petition is easily-debunked propaganda. *The Huffington Post.* https://www.huffpost.com/entry/the-30000-global-warming_b_243092
Grant, W. J. (November 22, 2023). The knowledge deficit model and science communication. *Oxford Research Encyclopedia.* https://doi.org/10.1093/acrefore/9780190228613.013.1396
Gupta-Smith, V. (October 22, 2020). Air pollution & COVID-19 (No. 9) [Audio podcast episode]. In *Science in 5.* Department of Communications (DCO) at World Health Organization. https://www.who.int/podcasts/series/science-in-5/episode--9---air-pollution---covid-19
Gurabardhi, Z., Gutteling, J. M., & Kuttschreuter, M. (2005). An empirical analysis of communication flow, strategy and stakeholders' participation in the risk communication literature 1988–2000. *Journal of Risk Research, 8*(6), 499–511. https://doi.org/10.1080/1366987050064192
Heath, R. L. (2006). Onward into more fog: Thoughts on public relations research directions. *Journal of Public Relations Research, 18*(2), 93–114.
Heath, R. L., & Palenchar, M. J. (2009). Strategic issues management. *Organizations and public policy challenges* (2nd ed.). Sage.
Heath, R. L., & Palenchar, M. J. (2016). Paradigms of risk and crisis communication in the 21st century. In A. Schwarz, M. Seeger, & C. Auer, Eds., *The Handbook of International Crisis Communication Research* (pp. 437–446). Wiley-Blackwell.
Heath, R. L., Palenchar, M. J., Proutheau, S., & Hocke, T. (2007). Nature, crisis, risk, science, and society: What is our ethical responsibility? *Environmental Communication: A Journal of Nature and Culture, 1*(1), 34–48.
Holland, D., Seltzer, T., & Kochigina, A. (2021). Practicing transparency in a crisis: Examining the combined effects of crisis type, response, and message transparency on organizational perceptions. *Public Relations Review, 47*(2), 102017. https://doi.org/10.1016/j.pubrev.2021.102017
Jasanoff, S. (2011). Constitutional moments in governing science and technology. *Science and Engineering Ethics, 17*, 621–638.
Kasperson, R. E., Renn, O., Slovic, P., Halina, S., Emel, J., Gobel, R., Kasperson, X., & Ratick, S. (1988). The social amplification of risk: A conceptual framework. *Risk Analysis, 8*(2), 177–187.
Krimsky, S., & Plough, A. (1988). *Environmental Hazards: Communicating Risks as a Social Process.* Praeger.
Lundgren, R. E., & McMakin, A. H. (Eds.). (2013). *Risk Communication.* Wiley. https://doi.org/10.1002/9781118645734
Mahl, D., Guenther, L., Schäfer, M. S., Meyer, C., & Siegen, D. (2020). "We are a bit blind about it": A qualitative analysis of climate change-related perceptions and communication across South African communities. *Environmental Communication, 14*(6), 802–815. https://doi.org/10.1080/17524032.2020.1736116
Malecki, K. M. C., Keating, J. A., & Safdar, N. (2020). Crisis communication and public perception of COVID-19 risk in the era of social media. *Clinical Infectious Diseases, 72*(4), 697–702. https://doi.org/10.1093/cid/ciaa758
McKie, R. (November 9, 2019). Climategate 10 years on: What lessons have we learned? *The Guardian.* https://www.theguardian.com/theobserver/2019/nov/09/climategate-10-years-on-what-lessons-have-we-learned
National Centers for Environmental Information (n.d.). *Natural hazards interactive map.* https://www.ncei.noaa.gov/products/natural-hazards
National Research Council (1983). *Improving Risk Communication.* US Committee on Risk Perception and Communication.
Palenchar, M. J. (2024). Communicating safety and risk: Advancement of a field in constant uncertainty. In T. Sellnow, & D. Sellnow, Eds., *Handbook of Communicating Safety and Risk.* Mouton de Gruyter.
Palenchar, M. J., & Heath, R. L. (in press). Environmental risk communication: The challenges to progressively affecting behavior. In A. Schwarz, M. Seeger, & S. Kim, Eds., *The Handbook of International Crisis Communication Research* (2nd ed.). Wiley Blackwell.

Palenchar, M. J., & Motta, B. H. (2012). Environmental risk communication: Right to know as a core value for behavioral change. In L. Ahern, & D. S. Bortree, Eds., *Exploring Contemporary Issues in Environmental Communications.* Peter Lang.

Plough, A., & Krimsky, S. (1987). The emergence of risk communication studies: Social and political context. *Science, Technology & Human Values, 12*(2), 4–10.

Qiu, W., & Chu, C. (2019). Clarification of the concept of risk communication and its role in public health crisis management in China. *Disaster Medicine and Public Health Preparedness, 13*(5–6), 834–836. https://doi.org/10.1017/dmp.2019.10

Rayner, S. (1992). Cultural theory and risk analysis. In S. Krimsky & D. Golding (Eds.), Social theories of risk, 83–115. Praeger.

Reincke, C. M., Bredenoord, A. L., & van Mil, M. H. W. (2020). From deficit to dialogue in science communication. *EMBO Reports, 21*(9). https://doi.org/10.15252/embr.202051278August 4.

Renn, O. (2020). Risk governance: Coping with uncertainty in a complex world. *Natural Hazards, 48*(2), 313–314. https://doi.org/10.1007/s11069-008-9286-7

Rodríguez, H., Quarantelli, E. L., & Dynes, R. R. (Eds.). (2007). *Handbook of Disaster Research.* Springer. https://doi.org/10.1007/978-0-387-32353-4

Shahbazi, M., & Bunker, D. (2024). Social media trust: Fighting misinformation in the time of crisis. *International Journal of Information Management, 77*, 102780. https://doi.org/10.1016/j.ijinfomgt.2024.102780

Silver, A. (2019). The use of social media in crisis communication. *Risk Communication and Community Resilience, 267–282.* https://doi.org/10.4324/9781315110042-20

Slovic, P. (2016). *The Perception of Risk.* Routledge.

Suldovsky, B. (2016). In science communication, why does the idea of the public deficit always return? Exploring key influences. *Public Understanding of Science, 25*(4), 415–426. https://doi.org/10.1177/0963662516629750

United Nations (n.d.). *What is the Paris Agreement?* The United Nations. https://unfccc.int/process-and-meetings/the-paris-agreement

United Nations Office for Disaster Risk Reduction (2022). *Global Assessment Report on Disaster Risk Reduction. Our world at risk: Transforming governance for a resilient future.* Geneva: United Nations Office for Disaster Risk Reduction. ISBN: 9789212320281. https://www.undrr.org/gar/gar2022-our-world-risk-gar#container

Author's Bio

Michael J. Palenchar (PhD, University of Florida) is an associate professor in the Tombras School of Advertising and Public Relations at the University of Tennessee, has published extensively in journals and book chapters, and has presented his research around the world to both industry and the academy. He conducts research in the areas of risk and crisis communication and issue management. He is the co-author with Robert L. Heath of the book *Strategic Issues Management* (2nd ed.).

Carla White is a PhD student at the University of Tennessee-Knoxville. Her research focuses on the intersection between public relations, internal workplace systems, and health communication. Her previous work has been published in academic journals including *Critical Studies in Media Communication*, *Management Communication Quarterly*, and *Communication Quarterly*. She completed her Master of Arts in Communication, Technology, and Society at Clemson University where she was awarded the Graduate Researcher award in 2022.

13

Missed Risk and Crisis Communication Opportunities During the COVID-19 Pandemic

Brooke Fisher Liu[1] and Cynthia Baur[2]

[1] Department of Communication, University of Maryland, College Park, MD, USA

[2] Department of Behavioral and Community Health, Horowitz Center for Health Literacy, School of Public Health, University of Maryland, College Park, MD, USA

Globally, more than 6.7 million reported deaths due to COVID-19 have been recorded as of January 2023 (WHO, 2023), with millions of additional unreported deaths (Adam, 2022). According to experts, many of these deaths were preventable if governments and their partners had responded quicker, provided more clear data and messaging, created inclusive communication from trusted sources, partnered with the media, and invested in testing technology earlier (National Academies, 2021; Noar & Austin, 2020). Other missteps included slow responses to misinformation; underestimating vaccine hesitancy; inconsistent global coordination; inequitable distributions of supplies, vaccines, and treatments; and inadequate message testing (DiSalvo et al., 2021; Fischhoff, 2021; LaFraniere & Weiland, 2022; Lazarus et al., 2022; National Academies, 2021). For these mistakes and others, the Director of the U.S. Centers for Disease Control and Prevention (CDC) stated "in our big moment, our performance did not reliably meet expectations" (Edwards, 2022, para. 4).

One critical area for improvement in responding to the COVID-19 pandemic is risk and crisis communication (e.g., Fischhoff, 2021; Lazarus et al., 2022; Noar & Austin, 2020; Sauer et al., 2021). In a Delphi study of 386 academic, health, governmental and non-governmental, and other experts, Lazarus et al. (2022) identified ten recommendations for ending COVID-19 as a public health threat; two pertain to communication, including combating "false information proactively based on clear, direct, culturally responsive messaging that is free from unnecessary scientific jargon" and using "the preferred means of access and communication for different populations" (p. 337). Most of these after-action and scholarly recommendations about COVID-19 communication reflect best practices in risk and crisis communication (Liu et al., 2022; Schoch-Spana et al., 2021; Seeger, 2006), including the U.S. CDC's crisis and emergency risk communication (CERC) guidance (CDC, 2018). Best practices consolidate bodies of evidence and established practices that convey the state of the science and what works in the field.

These best practices include taking a process approach to crises, engaging in pre-event planning, leading with an ethic of care, and meeting publics' information needs. Other best practices are communicating with transparency, collaborating with credible sources, forming partnerships with publics, listening and acknowledging publics' concerns, empowering publics,

The Handbook of International Crisis and Risk Communication Research, Second Edition.
Edited by Andreas Schwarz, Matthew W. Seeger, and Sora Kim.

collaborating with key partners to disseminate information like the media, and accepting uncertainty along with helping publics accept uncertainty (Liu et al., 2022; Seeger, 2006). Additional best practices include responding quickly with credibility and promoting action (Sauer et al., 2021) and using plain language (Rudd & Baur, 2020). Despite being well-known, best practices in risk and crisis communication appear to have been largely ignored during the COVID-19 pandemic; best practices also were underutilized during past outbreaks such as Zika and severe acute respiratory system (SARS; Avery, 2019; Noar & Austin, 2020; Sauer et al., 2021; Toppenberg-Pejcica et al., 2019). In this chapter, we discuss four primary missed opportunities to apply risk and crisis communication best practices in the U.S. COVID-19 response. We conclude with key lessons learned and suggestions for future research.

Missed Opportunity: Follow Crisis and Emergency Risk Communication Principles

At the heart of risk and crisis communication models and frameworks is the recognition that humans must respond to situations with less than full and perfect information and therefore are dealing with uncertainties and probabilities when deciding how to respond (CDC, 2018; Veil et al., 2008). These uncertainties and probabilities include who is most affected by a risk or crisis, how serious and long-lasting the risk or crisis might be, and the most protective behaviors to take under different circumstances. Therefore, the best practice is to be responsive yet cautious in an outbreak's early days and be clear about what is known and unknown and what is being investigated to maintain credibility over an unfolding situation (CDC, 2018; Veil et al., 2008).

Almost all recent global health emergencies have been novel in human exposure and effects in some way, and novelty generates many uncertainties and surprises. Examples include the 2014–2016 Ebola outbreak in West Africa that spread more rapidly and to more people than prior Ebola outbreaks. The 2015–2016 Zika outbreak in the Americas surprised public health professionals by being both a mosquito-borne and sexually transmitted disease. SARS and Middle East respiratory syndrome (MERS), prior coronavirus outbreaks, were novel viruses for humans but were contained in relatively short time periods. COVID-19, the first coronavirus-based pandemic, is one of the latest and most widespread of novel and, therefore, uncertain health risks that we must continually assess and respond to.

The CERC framework was part of the U.S. CDC's after-action steps for the novel events of the 9/11 terrorist attacks and the human anthrax attacks in the USA (CDC, 2012; Veil et al., 2008). CERC's six principles are be first, be right, be credible, express empathy, promote action, and show respect (CDC, 2018). In a 2008 article explaining the theoretical basis for CERC, the authors placed the uncertainty inherent in risk and crises and managing uncertainty as core to the six CERC principles (Veil et al., 2008). The authors proposed CERC as an uncertainty management strategy that helps people make sense of complex situations and decide the best ways to reduce harm.

Early official statements about COVID-19 often did not reflect best practices to address COVID-19 uncertainties. For example, while confirming human-to-human transmission on January 30, 2020, CDC Director Dr. Robert Redfield was quoted in a press release: "We understand that this may be concerning, but based on what we know now, we still believe the immediate risk to the American public is low" (CDC, 2020, para. 4). This press release invoked SARS and MERS (other coronavirus outbreaks) with the reminder that SARS and MERS transmission was limited to close contacts. Given that no one was sure in January 2020 if COVID-19 transmission also required close contact, Redfield should have also addressed what CDC, World Health Organization (WHO), and other agencies were investigating about transmission and how they would confirm if the risk would remain low. A second example is from a March 11, 2020, statement from the WHO Director General who assured the world that COVID-19 could still be contained with standard public health measures, even though the virus was spreading in enough countries to be declared a pandemic, the exact pathways for human to human transmission were not confirmed, and society-wide shutdowns were imminent (WHO, 2020). Initial comparisons between seasonal influenza and COVID-19 created uncertainty rather than reassurance about COVID's riskiness and undermined officials' credibility even though the COVID-19 event still had many years to unfold (Blake, 2020).

COVID-19's uncertainties were so numerous that they prompted a series of evolving policy decisions with far-reaching implications for public understanding and adherence. Short-term stay at home orders turned into closed workplaces, schools, and public spaces, such as government offices, restaurants, and theaters. Ambiguous or discouraging messages from officials about the value of wearing face masks became mandatory mask orders. Universal health behavior and vaccination recommendations became more targeted as specific population groups, such as healthcare workers, workers in public-facing jobs, and adults 65 years and older, emerged as among the most vulnerable (Noar & Austin, 2020). Although these policy changes might align with changing scientific knowledge, the CERC principle to be transparent and tell people what you know, do not know, and what you are doing to find out new information was often not applied when presenting mandatory policies or categorizing policy decisions. For example, years before COVID-19, researchers tested the term "emergency use authorization" for a new vaccine or therapy with the U.S. public and reported the term reinforces uncertainty and does not aid transparency in explaining vaccine review and approval (Quinn et al., 2021).

Failure to manage situational and informational uncertainties can have immediate, significant negative effects. In their review of Ebola, Zika, and yellow fever outbreak risk communication, Toppenberg-Pejcica et al. (2019) stated that during the Ebola response, inaccurate official statements about the role of bushmeat undermined trust and caused unnecessary confusion and a loss of spokesperson credibility. Noar and Austin (2020) observed that early in the U.S. COVID-19 response, conflicting and confusing government messages were common and heavily reported by the media, but were an unforced error.

In COVID-19, one immediate effect was a media narrative about public confusion. Headlines and stories reported on public confusion as well as reinforced a perception that officials were poor communicators whose actions confused the public. Public opinion research reinforced the confusion narrative (National Public Radio, 2021; Segal, 2022). The Pew Research Center reported that U.S. public confusion increased rather than decreased as the outbreak response continued and officials continued to communicate their recommendations (Tyson & Funk, 2022). Moreover, public ratings of public health officials' job performance declined from 2020 to 2022 (Tyson & Funk, 2022). Ongoing public uncertainty about the value and safety of COVID-19 vaccines can be linked to trust in public officials and their messages.

Missed Opportunity: Include Communication Experts at the Decision-making Table

During public health crises, including pandemics, a common failure is not bringing risk and crisis communication scientists to the decision-making table. In an expert consensus study on readying populations for COVID-19 vaccination, Schoch-Spana et al. (2021) advocated for "embedding rapid social, behavioral, and communication science within the COVID-19 response, helping to deliver timely data and empirically-based advice" (p. 6007). The National Academies of Sciences, Engineering, and Medicine created the Societal Experts Action Network (SEAN) to offer "timely, actionable guidance to the critical and complex questions facing decision makers" about a range of COVID-19 issues (National Academies, n.d., para 1). The SEAN issued multiple public reports, including several focused on COVID-19 communication, but without an evaluation of the reports' dissemination and uptake, it is unknown whether this approach to marshaling communication expertise was effective in helping members of the public understand the science behind the pandemic and interpret government responses. Also unknown is to what extent efforts from SEAN and similar academic groups informed media coverage of the pandemic.

Indeed, risk and crisis communication expertise may be available to decision-makers, official spokespersons, and the media and yet go unused. Research during the COVID-19 response reveals that the recommendation to include social, behavioral, and communication scientists was not well adopted. In a study of higher education institutions' responses to the pandemic, Liu et al. (2022) discovered that risk and crisis communication scholars, as well as other social and behavioral scientists, rarely were consulted despite that many of the institutions had ready access to these experts. Fischhoff (2021) noted that a failure during the COVID-19 response was a lack of message testing, which communication and other social and behavioral scientists could conduct in collaboration with government and media partners. One model is the way health departments partnered with academia and industry for help with COVID-19 data tracking and reporting activities (DiSalvo et al., 2021).

Some institutions may not consult with communication and other scientists because of a more fundamental issue: a lack of in-house communication expertise. Social and behavioral scientists historically are not well represented in government agencies or well-funded, though progress has been made in recent years (Baird, 2015; Sanders et al., 2018; Schoch-Spana et al., 2021). Avery (2017, 2019) found that during the Zika outbreak, U.S. public health agencies' preparedness and their capacity to engage in social media monitoring were significantly different depending upon the size of the communities they served. Those serving larger communities were better prepared and engaged in more social media monitoring to improve their crisis responses. Small health departments may be overwhelmed with the volume of public information requests and not have dedicated, trained communication staff. For example, the University of Maryland School of Public Health supported local health departments by sponsoring community conversations about COVID-19 and providing public messages and materials that local health departments disseminated. Without necessary in-house expertise and external partners, we suspect that organizations will miss opportunities to maximize risk and crisis communication effectiveness.

Another challenge may be that, although some government agencies have the requisite risk and crisis communication expertise, those experts may not be the decision-makers when it comes to the public health agenda (Avery, 2019). Although CDC has many dedicated, experienced communication staff, created the CERC framework, and must meet Federal Plain Writing Act requirements, former CDC Director Rochelle Walensky publicly admitted the agency did not communicate clearly or effectively with the public (CDC, 2022). The CDC was criticized for guidance and messages about masking, testing, isolation, and vaccinations because they were confusing and often lacked a clear rationale and action steps (Stanley-Becker et al., 2021; Tyson & Funk, 2022). These missteps do not align with CERC principles to be right, be credible, or promote action, nor the plain language principle to organize information to serve the reader or listener. Even more disturbing is that 20 years ago, CDC's own communication staff came to similar conclusions about the mismatch between communication expertise and guidance and the agency's anthrax attack response (Freimuth, 2003).

A full public accounting is needed of how CDC communication staff were deployed during the COVID-19 response and why communication execution strayed so far from CDC's own best practices. A model is the *Journal of Health Communication* special issue that CDC's communication staff did as an "after-action" communication report on the anthrax attacks (Freimuth, 2003). Importantly, such public accounting needs to include wide dissemination of findings. Social media, such as Twitter, were essential during the COVID-19 pandemic for officials and researchers to disseminate timely information about case rates and research findings at a faster rate than traditional media (Bergstrom, 2022; Villasenor, 2022) – despite the well-documented issues with social media also proliferating misinformation (see the following section).

Missed Opportunity: Faster Recognition of and Response to the Power of Misinformation

A well-identified misstep in COVID-19 communication was government and social media companies' delayed recognition of the power of misinformation, leading the WHO (2021) to declare COVID-19 an "infodemic." Misinformation is a "health-related claim of fact that is currently false due to a lack of scientific evidence" (Chou et al., 2018, p. 2417) or conflicts "with the best available evidence," (Krause et al., 2020, p. 1053) given expert consensus at the time (Vraga & Bode, 2020). COVID-19 and vaccination misinformation took hold quickly because the ground had been well prepared by ongoing misinformation and disinformation campaigns about other topics, including other vaccines. Broniatowski et al. (2018) found vaccine misinformation data from online trolls, bots, and "content polluters" (p. 1378) in Twitter data from 2014 to 2017. Once the scope of the COVID-19 misinformation problem became obvious, many governments were too slow to respond and, when they did, it was too late to counteract many publics' established low risk perception, polarization, and noncompliance with recommended preventative behaviors (Chung & Jones-Jang, 2022; Lazarus et al., 2022).

Timely strategies for combating misinformation include two broad categories: simple rebuttal and factual elaboration. A simple rebuttal is a brief argument that refutes myths, whereas factual elaboration contains sufficient details to explain why misinformation is false (van der Meer & Jin, 2020). Yet, there is insufficient evidence to guide deployment of these two strategies. In a systematic review and meta-analysis of interventions to mitigate COVID-19 misinformation, Janmohamed et al. (2021) found that "mitigation does not successfully or necessarily reduce the influence of misinformation" (p. 851).

Of course, governments must be trustworthy, authoritative sources in order to be believed or to credibly counteract misinformation. A troubling fact from COVID-19 is that governments themselves often have been sources of misinformation (Lazarus et al., 2022). COVID-19 misinformation was politically useful and deployed by various actors for ideological purposes. Singh and Banga (2022) identified a number of extreme instances of COVID-19 misinformation including Indian politicians claiming that drinking cow urine could cure COVID-19, recommendations to use aspirin dissolved in hot honey to combat COVID-19 in Brazil, and consuming rubbing alcohol to prevent COVID-19 in Turkey. In an extreme U.S. example, President Trump endorsed the use of hydroxychloroquine to combat COVID-19 without scientific evidence for this endorsement (Singh & Banga, 2022). Other examples are less extreme but present a picture of frequent conflicting government messages that contributed to public confusion about how to mitigate COVID-19. For instance, early in the pandemic, the U.S. government recommended against widespread use of face masks primarily attributed to mask shortages for healthcare workers; later, the CDC recommended wearing face masks, but by then wearing face masks had become heavily politicized (Noar & Austin, 2020).

Missed Opportunity: Audience-specific Messaging

A final misstep in COVID-19 communication was a lack of audience-specific messaging from government officials and the media. A hallmark of effective risk and crisis communication is listening to audiences' specific needs and concerns and incorporating that feedback in messages (Liu et al., 2022; Seeger, 2006). Guest and Peckman (2022) observed that "early messaging emphasized the role of social distancing for all populations"; they further noted that "as attention to the pandemic waned, messaging evolved into generalizable claims regarding large swaths of the population" (p. 11). In contrast to generalized messaging, researchers discovered that COVID-19 vaccine messages that recognized past unethical treatment of Blacks in U.S. medical research and emphasized current safeguards were associated with significantly less vaccine hesitancy among Black participants than the experimental control condition (Dhanani & Franz, 2022). If such research had been done before the pandemic and then deployed early in the pandemic, COVID-19 messaging would undoubtedly have resonated more directly with intended audiences.

Distressingly, some instances of audience-specific messaging were marginalizing. Researchers identified issues with ageism in COVID-19 messaging reported in the mass media, such as encouraging stereotypes about older adults as frail (Guest & Peckman, 2022). These stereotypes contributed to a sense of isolation and led to some older adults being less likely to discuss COVID-19 with their healthcare providers (Guest & Peckman, 2022; McDarby et al., 2022). Liu et al. (2021) alluded to issues with classism in higher education COVID-19 messages about virtual work opportunities only for certain categories of employees, such as faculty, but not campus cleaning staff. Early use of the term *Chinese virus* on social media and in mass media to refer to COVID-19 has been linked to a rise in anti-Asian sentiment online, decline in support for Asian-owned businesses, and hate crimes against Asians (Hswen et al., 2021; Tessler et al., 2020). Other COVID-19 government and mass media messaging placed too much emphasis on obesity as a COVID-19 risk factor, encouraging "weight bias stigma" and "promoting unhealthy weight control behaviors" (Pearl & Schulte, 2021, p. 181). These examples show a clear pattern of failure to avoid stereotypes and stigmatization and consider audiences' unique needs and concerns, which are imperative for effective public health messages.

Lessons Learned about Applying Risk and Crisis Communication Best Practices

Our assessment is that despite having well-established best practices, failures in four key areas undermined an effective risk and crisis communication response for COVID-19 in the USA and elsewhere. We present numerous examples that show risk and crisis communication best practices were not followed with predictably poor results for public understanding, officials' credibility, and disease mitigation goals. Both communicators and those who review and approve public messages and materials must know and use these best practices in future pandemics if we hope to have better outcomes.

The lessons learned from the missed opportunities analysis should not surprise communication scientists, but we hope they will help public health communicators on the front lines of future responses. Communicators can make the case that using best practices will increase the chances that messages and materials will be more effective, thereby contributing to an overall more successful response. For example, the porcine epidemic diarrhea virus (PEDV) case study by Sellnow et al. (2017) demonstrates the positive results when key partners apply many crisis communication best practices. Although Sellnow and colleagues do not speculate if the crisis was shortened by best practices, their report indicates that the communication best practices were critical to minimizing damage from the PEDV outbreak. In the spirit of learning from every failure, we offer five lessons and some research ideas to prepare before the next pandemic and to recover from the COVID-19 pandemic.

Lesson 1: Refocus on Addressing Situational Uncertainties and Risk Communication

The CDC Clear Communication Index, a best practice tool based on health literacy principles, has multiple items about clearly explaining who is at risk and why; the likelihood and severity of harm; and feasible, concrete action steps that reduce harm (CDC, 2021). When people cannot find information to answer their questions or do not understand what they find, they fill in with what they know or is easily available to them, including information on social media and legacy media that may not be accurate. In a situation as new and evolving as COVID-19, whatever people fill in for themselves will likely not align with scientific knowledge, especially if that knowledge is changing rapidly. Monitoring and responding to uncertainties with fact-based messages can help people anticipate what is coming and understand the limits of scientific and medical knowledge. It is especially important for governments and the mass media to communicate levels of risk with "appropriate tentativeness" and context in the early stages of a pandemic (Ratcliff et al., 2022, p. 17).

Lesson 2: Recognize the Centrality of Effective Risk and Crisis Communication

"After-action" reports have long been standard practice after an outbreak response (Savoia et al., 2012), and COVID-19 after-action reports should explain if and how communicators were used in the response and barriers to the use of risk and crisis communication best practices. It is equally imperative for risk and crisis communication scholars and those in allied fields to continue to advocate for our knowledge base, including serving on government advisory boards, collaborating with governments on research, engaging in public outreach, and working with the media to support pandemic coverage.

Lesson 3: Focus on Accurate Information, Maintain Consistency, and Acknowledge and Correct Inaccurate Information

Inaccurate, inconsistent, and unclear information weakened the COVID-19 response. Governments must develop routine systems and structures to monitor misinformation, predominately on social media, and collaboratively respond in a quick and accurate way. Also, COVID-19 shows the value of anticipatory work, including developing and testing messages in advance to combat frequent forms of misinformation during pandemics, such as causes of and treatments for infectious diseases (Singh & Banga, 2022; Tan et al., 2015). Such pretested messages could be rapidly updated and deployed to prebunk or correct misinformation online during future pandemics. As noted before, establishing partnerships with risk and crisis communication scientists can support rapid message development and testing during public health emergencies. The partnerships should reflect diverse crisis response team members, advisory committees with diverse members, and working with diverse partner groups to avoid messaging missteps. Equally important is working with journalists to rapidly combat misinformation.

Lesson 4: Avoid Marginalizing Messaging

We previously documented numerous instances of COVID-19 messaging that was marginalizing for diverse audiences including Asians, Blacks/African-Americans, older adults, and those at risk for obesity. Best practices in risk and crisis communication have long emphasized the importance of meeting audiences' information needs, forming partnerships with key audiences, and empowering these audiences (Liu et al., 2021; Seeger, 2006). Yet, these best practices were absent in much COVID-19 government messaging and media coverage, leading to disturbing outcomes like hate crimes, isolation, and depression (Guest & Peckham, 2022; Tessler et al., 2020). It is imperative that future responses to pandemics avoid marginalizing messaging and, instead, embrace targeted messages that resonate with key audiences and provide positive action steps. It is too soon to know the full impacts of the COVID-19 marginalizing messaging, but it is clear that distrust in public health authorities and science has strengthened during the pandemic (Best et al., 2021). The ethical and the practical approach for public health communicators is to recognize and avoid issuing messages that might be marginalizing rather than engaging in the lengthy, costly exercise of doing damage control and attempting to rebuild trust, as further discussed below.

Lesson 5: Message Testing Must Be in Place Prior to an Event

Experts have noted that a primary risk and crisis communication failure during COVID-19 has been a lack of message testing (e.g., Fischhoff, 2021). Message testing is essential to ensure that risk and crisis communication has the desired impacts while avoiding unintended consequences. Early analysis of COVID-19 messaging reveals that many messages were confusing and polarizing and did not lead to desired outcomes like intentions to vaccinate (Dhanani & Franz, 2022; Noar & Austin, 2020, Ratcliff et al., 2022). While governments established advisory groups like the SEAN in the USA to provide guidance (National Academies, n.d., para 1), such guidance is not a substitute for formal message testing through methods like focus groups and experiments. Ideally, this message testing should occur before a pandemic so that scientifically validated messages can be immediately deployed. Risk and crisis communication researchers can help by developing and testing audience-specific messages.

New messages will also need to be developed and deployed during future pandemics, and establishing a message testing infrastructure before an event will be essential to accomplish this goal. We argue that such an infrastructure needs to be more than a funding program to support event-specific research, such as the National Science Foundation's Rapid Response COVID research awards (Natural Hazards Center, n.d.). Instead, considerable investment is needed in building sustainable long-term funding for risk and crisis communication research long before public health emergencies emerge, as others also have argued (Schoch-Spana et al., 2021). One example is the pandemic-focused research centers that have emerged during COVID-19 such as Brown University's Pandemic Center, the Michigan Center for Infectious Disease Threats, and the University of Maryland Pandemic Readiness Institute. If sustained, these centers will be prime resources for helping frontline responders test and deploy messages before and during future public health emergencies.

Future Research

Much new research is necessary to inform new best practices to reflect the COVID-19 experience. Research on effective misinformation strategies is a priority. As previously noted, timely strategies for combating misinformation include two broad categories: simple rebuttal and factual elaboration (van der Meer & Jin, 2020). Yet, there is insufficient evidence to guide deployment of these two strategies. More work is needed to understand effective correction strategies for combating pandemic misinformation, including the optimal timing of such strategies. In a scoping review of emerging COVID-19 health communication research, Lin and Nan (2022) further noted a dearth of research on diverse populations, such as racial/ethnic minorities and other disadvantaged groups, including how to correct misinformation targeted at these groups. Another area for future research is testing and deploying prebunking messages before misinformation occurs. Prebunking is a form of a forewarning designed to "neutralize potential misinformation before it is encoded" (Cook et al., 2017, p. 4).

Also of high priority is research testing messages to communicate pandemic uncertainty. In a scoping review of the literature on uncertainty communication and COVID-19, Ratcliff et al. (2022) concluded "We do not believe the current body of scholarship points toward specific evidence-based recommendation for communication just yet" (p. 25). They further posited "it could be that during the pandemic, individuals grow fed up with living in a constant state of uncertainty" (pp. 25–26). Initial research on message features like accuracy nudges are promising (Pennycook et al., 2020), but significant additional research is needed given the potential long duration and high uncertainty during pandemics.

A third high priority area for future research is developing and testing messages with diverse audiences. COVID-19 revealed widespread marginalizing messaging. Partnerships with community organizations such as the Maryland Barbers and Stylists United for Health (University of Maryland School of Public Health, n.d.) have demonstrated promise for building trust to make informed decisions during pandemics, but research is needed to harness the full power of community health workers embedded in these organizations. University-based communication teams, such as those based in the University of Maryland Horowitz Center for Health Literacy from 2021 to 2023, can partner with local health departments and nonprofit organizations to customize messages and materials in multiple languages and formats and revise based on public feedback.

Conclusion

The U.S. government ended its COVID-19 emergency in May 2023, closing a three-year pandemic period that witnessed a coronavirus becoming a leading cause of death in the USA (Ortaliza et al., 2022; Pager & Sun, 2023). COVID-19 also heralded an amplification of mental health problems, extreme employee disconnection with their workplaces, rampart misinformation online, and heightened distrust in government officials (Edelman, 2023; Sauerwein, 2022; Shipman et al., 2023). The full effects of the pandemic are yet to be known. What is known is that preventable missteps in risk and crisis communication left people confused and uncertain, amplifying negative COVID-19 outcomes. We hope this chapter serves as a rallying call for the research community to partner with public health authorities and other first responders to begin planning now and avoid catastrophic communication failures during future pandemics and other public health emergencies.

References

Adam, D. (2022). The pandemic's true death toll: Millions more than official counts. *Nature, 601*, 312–315.

Avery, E. J. (2017). Public information officers' social media monitoring during the Zika virus crisis, a global health threat surrounded by public uncertainty. *Public Relations Review*, *43*(3), 468–476. https://doi.org/10.1016/j.pubrev.2017.02.018

Avery, E. J. (2019). The effects of community size, control over agenda, and contextual variables on Zika virus preparation of public health information officers at local public health departments. *Journal of International Crisis and Risk Communication Research*, *2*(1), 97–119. https://doi.org/10.30658/jicrcr.2.1.5

Baird, B. (2015). Informing public policy with social and behavioral science. *Issues in Science and Technology*, *31*(3). https://issues.org/perspective-informing-public-policy-with-social-and-behavioral-science

Bergstrom, C. T. (November 19, 2022). Twitter was influential in the pandemic. Are we better for it? *New York Times*. https://www.nytimes.com/2022/11/19/opinion/pandemic-twitter.html

Best, A. L., Fletcher, F. E., Kadono, M., & Warren, R. C. (2021). Institutional distrust among African Americans and building trustworthiness in the COVID-19 response: Implications for ethical public health practice. *Journal of Health Care for the Poor and Underserved*, *32*(1), 90–98. https://doi.org/10.1353/hpu.2021.0010

Blake, A. (March 11, 2020). Anthony Fauci undercuts Trump on the flu and other coronavirus assertions. *Washington Post*. https://www.washingtonpost.com/politics/2020/03/11/anthony-fauci-undercuts-trump-flu-other-coronavirus-assertions/

Broniatowski, D. A., Jamison, A. M., Qi, S., AlKulaib, L., Chen, T., Benton, A., Quinn, S. C., & Dredze, M. (2018). Weaponized health communication: Twitter bots and Russian trolls amplify the vaccine debate. *American Journal of Public Health*, *108*(10), 1378–1384. https://doi.org/10.2105/AJPH.2018.304567

Centers for Disease Control and Prevention (2012). *Crisis and emergency risk communication*. https://emergency.cdc.gov/cerc/

Centers for Disease Control and Prevention (2018). *Crisis and emergency risk communication*. https://emergency.cdc.gov/cerc/

Centers for Disease Control and Prevention (January 30, 2020). *CDC confirms person-to-person spread of new coronavirus in the United States* [Press release]. https://www.cdc.gov/media/releases/2020/p0130-coronavirus-spread.html

Centers for Disease Control and Prevention (2022). *CDC moving forward*. https://www.cdc.gov/about/organization/cdc-moving-forward.html

Centers for Disease Control and Prevention (2021). *The CDC Clear Communication Index*. https://www.cdc.gov/ccindex/index.html

Chou, W. Y. S., Oh, A., & Klein, W. M. (2018). Addressing health-related misinformation on social media. *JAMA: The Journal of the American Medical Association*, *320*(23), 2417–2418. https://doi.org/10.1001/jama.2018.16865

Chung, M., & Jones-Hang, M. S. (2022). Red media, blue media, Trump briefings, and COVID-19: Examining how information sources predict risk preventative behaviors via threat and efficacy. *Health Communication*, *37*(14), 1707–1714. https://doi.org/10.1007/s12103-020-09541-5

Cook, J., Lewandowsky, S., & Ecker, U. K. H. (2017). Neutralizing misinformation through inoculation: Exposing misleading argumentation techniques reduces their influence. *PLoS One*, *12*(5), e0175799. https://doi.org/10.1371/journal.pone.0175799

DiSalvo, K., Hughes, B., Bassett, M., Benjamin, G., Fraser, M., Galea, S., Gracia, N., & Howard, J. (2021). *Public health COVID-19 impact assessment: Lessons learned and compelling needs*. NAM Perspectives. Discussion paper. National Academy of Medicine. https://doi.org/10.31478/202104c

Dhanani, L., & Franz, B. (2022). An experimental study of the effects of messaging strategies on vaccine acceptance and hesitancy among Black Americans. *Preventive Medicine Reports*, *27*(3), 101792. https://doi.org/10.1016/j.pmedr.2022.101792

Edelman (2023). *Edelman trust barometer: Navigating a polarized world*. https://www.edelman.com/trust/2023/trust-barometer

Edwards, E. (August 17, 2022). CDC director calls for drastic changes to the agency following pandemic missteps. *NBC News*. https://www.nbcnews.com/health/health-news/cdc-director-calls-drastic-changes-agency-rcna43536

Fischhoff, B. (October, 2021). The covid communication breakdown. *Foreign Affairs*. https://www.foreignaffairs.com/articles/united-states/2021-10-04/covid-communication-breakdown

Freimuth, V. (2003). Epilogue to the special issue on anthrax. *Journal of Health Communication*, *9*(supl), 148–151. https://doi.org/10.1080/713851979

Guest, M. A., & Peckham, A. (2022). Identifying better communication practices for older adults during the next pandemic: Recommendations from the COVID-19 experience. *Journal of Communication in Healthcare*, *15*(1), 11–14. https://doi.org/10.1080/17538068.2022.2029104

Hswen, Y., Xu, X., Hing, A., Hawkins, J. B., Brownsten, J. S., & Gee, G. C. (2021). Association of "#covid19" versus "#chinesevirus" with anti-asian sentiments on Twitter: March 9–23, 2020. *American Journal of Public Health*, *11*(5), 956–964. https://doi.org/10.2105%2FAJPH.2021.306154

Janmohamed, K., Walter, N., Nyhan, K., Kloshnood, K., Tucker, J. D., Sangngam, N., Altice, F. L., Ding, Q., Wong, A., Schwitzky, Z. M., Bauch, C. T., De Choudhury, M., Papakyriakopoulos, O., & Jumar, N. (2021). Interventions to mitigate COVID-19 misinformation: A systematic review and meta-analysis. *Journal of Health Communication: International Perspectives*, *26*(12), 846–857. https://doi.org/10.1080/10810730.2021.2021460

Krause, N. M., Freiling, I., Beets, B., & Brossard, D. (2020). Fact-checking as risk communication: The multi-layered risk of misinformation in times of COVID-19. *Journal of Risk Research, 23*(7–8), 1052–1059. https://doi.org/10.1080/13669877.2020.1756385

LaFraniere, S., & Weiland, N. (August 17, 2022). Walensky, citing botched pandemic response, calls for C.D.C. reorganization. *New York Times*. https://www.nytimes.com/2022/08/17/us/politics/cdc-rochelle-walensky-covid.html

Lazarus, J. V., Romero, D., Kopka, C. J., Karim, S. A., Abu-Radddad, L., Almeida, G., Baptista-Leite, R., Baracoas, J. A., Barreto, M. L., Bar-Yam, Y., Bassat, Q., Batista, C., Bazillian, M., Chiou, S.-T., del Rio, C., Dore, G., Gao, G. F., Gostin, L. O., & Hellard, M. . .El-Mogabdes, A. (2022). A multinational delphi consensus to end the COVID-19 public threat. *Nature, 611*, 332–345. https://doi.org/10.1038/s41586-022-05398-2

Lin, T., & Nan, X. (2022). A scoping review of emerging COVID-19 health communication research in communication and media journals. *Health Communication*. https://doi.org/10.1080/10410236.2022.2091916

Liu, B. F., Lim, J. R., Shi, D., Edwards, A., Islam, K., Sheppard, R., & Seeger, M. (2022). Evolving best practices in crisis communication: Examining U.S. higher education's responses to the COVID-19 pandemic. *Journal of International Crisis and Risk Communication Research, 4*(3), 451–484. https://doi.org/10.30658/jicrcr.4.3.1

Liu, B. F., Shi, D., Lim, J. R., Islam, K., Edwards, A. L., & Seeger, M. (2021). When crisis hits home: How U.S. higher education leaders navigate values during uncertain times. *Journal of Business Ethics, 179*(2), 353–368. https://doi.org/10.1007/s10551-021-04820-5

McDarby, M., Ju, C. H., Picchiello, M. C., & Carpenter, B. D. (2022). Older adults' perceptions and experiences of ageism during the COVID-19 pandemic. *Journal of Social Issues, 78*(4), 939–964. https://doi.org/10.1111/josi.12557

National Academies of Sciences, Engineering, and Medicine (2021). *Lessons from COVID-19 on executing communications and engagement at the community level during a health crisis*. https://doi.org/10.17226/26340

National Academies of Sciences, Engineering, and Medicine (n.d.). *About: Societal experts action network*. https://www.nationalacademies.org/our-work/societal-experts-action-network/about

National Public Radio (August 2, 2021). *New phase of pandemic met with confusion and exhaustion*. https://www.npr.org/2021/08/02/1023907905/new-phase-of-pandemic-met-with-confusion-and-exhaustion

Natural Hazards Center (n.d.). NSF RAPID COVID-19 awards. https://hazards.colorado.edu/resources/recent-awards/nsf-rapid-COVID-19-awards

Noar, S., & Auston, L. (2020). (Mis)communicating about COVID-19: Insights from health and crisis communication. *Health Communication, 35*(14), 1735–1739. https://doi.org/10.1080/10410236.2020.1838093

Ortaliza, J., Amin, K., & Cox, C. (November, 2022). COVID-19 leading cause of death ranking. *Kaiser Family Foundation*. https://www.kff.org/coronavirus-covid-19/issue-brief/covid-19-leading-cause-of-death-ranking/

Pager, T., & Sun, L. H. (January 31, 2023). Biden to end Covid national emergencies in May. *Washington Post*. https://www.washingtonpost.com/politics/2023/01/30/biden-end-covid-health-emergencies-may-11/

Pearl, R. L., & Schulte, E. M. (2021). Weight bias during the COVID-19 pandemic. *Current Obesity Reports, 10*(2), 181–190. https://doi.org/10.1007/s13679-021-00432-2

Pennycook, G., McPhetres, J., Zhang, Y., Lu, J. G., & Rand, D. G. (2020). Fighting COVID-19 misinformation on social media: Experimental evidence for a scalable accuracy-nudge intervention. *Psychological Science, 31*(7), 770–780. https://doi.org/10.1177/0956797620939054

Quinn, S. C., Jamison, A. M., & Freimuth, V. (2021). Communicating effectively about emergency use authorization and vaccines in the COVID-19 pandemic. *American Journal of Public Health, 111*(3), 355–358. https://doi.org/10.2105/AJPH.2020.306036

Ratcliff, C. L., Wicke, R., & Harvill, B. (2022). Communicating uncertainty to the public during the COVID-19 pandemic: A scoping review of the literature. *Annals of the International Communication Association, 46*(4), 260–289. https://doi.org/10.1080/23808985.2022.2085136

Rudd, R., & Baur, C. (2020). Health literacy and early insights during a pandemic. *Journal of Communication in Healthcare, 13*(1), 13–16. https://doi.org/10.1080/17538068.2020.1760622

Sanders, M., Snijners, V., & Hallsworth, M. (2018). Behavioral science and policy: Where are we now and where are we going? *Behavioral Public Policy*, *2*(2), 144–167. https://doi.org/10.1017/bpp.2018.17

Sauer, M. A., Truelove, S., Gerste, A. K., & Limaye, R. J. (2021). A failure to communicate? How public messaging has strained the COVID-19 response in the United States. *Health Security*, *19*(1), 65–74. http://doi.org/10.1089/hs.2020.0190

Sauerwein, K. (2022). *COVID-19 Survivors Face Increased Mental Health Risks Up To a Year Later.* Washington University School of Medicine in St. Louis. https://medicine.wustl.edu/news/covid-19-survivors-face-increased-mental-health-risks-up-to-a-year-later/February 16,

Savoia, E., Agboola, F., & Biddinger, P. D. (2012). Use of after action reports (AARs) to promote organizational and systems learning in emergency preparedness. *International Journal of Environmental Research and Public Health*, *9*(8), 2949–2963. https://doi.org/10.3390/ijerph9082949

Schoch-Spana, M., Brunson, E. K., Long, R., Ruth, A., Ravi, S. J., Trotochaud, M., Borio, L., Brewer, J., Buccina, J., Conell, N., Hall, L. L., Kass, N., Kirkland, A., Konnin, L., Larson, H., Liu, B. F., Omer, S. B., Orenstien, W., Poland, G., & A. . ..White, A. (2021). The public's role in COVID-19 vaccination: Human-centered recommendations to enhance pandemic vaccine awareness, access, and acceptance in the United States. *Vaccine*, *39*(4), 6004–6012. https://doi.org/10.1016/j.vaccine.2020.10.059

Seeger, M. W. (2006). Best practices in crisis communication: An expert panel process. *Journal of Applied Communication Research*, *34*(3), 232–244. https://doi.org/10.1080/00909880600769944

Segal, E. (January 8, 2022). Mixed messages and sudden policy changes sow confusion, opposition to covid guidelines. *Forbes*. https://www.forbes.com/sites/edwardsegal/2022/01/08/mixed-messages-and-sudden-policy-changes-sow-confusion-opposition-to-covid-guidelines/?sh=368be5797453

Sellnow, T. L., Parker, J. S., Sellnow, D. D., Littlefield, R. S., Helsel, E. M., Getchell, M. C., Smith, J. M., & Merrill, S. C. (2017). Improving biosecurity through instructional crisis communication: Lessons learned from the PEDv outbreak. *Journal of Applied Communications*, *101*(4). http://doi.org/10.4148/1051-0834.1298

Shipman, K., Burrell, D. N., & Pherson, A. H. M. (2023). An organizational analysis of how managers must understand the mental health impact of teleworking during COVID-19 on employees. *International Journal of Organizational Analysis*, *31*(4), 1081–1104. https://doi.org/10.1108/IJOA-03-2021-2685

Singh, N., & Banga, G. (2022). Media and information literacy for developing resistance to 'infodemioc': Lessons to be learnt from the binge of misinformation during COVID-19 pandemic. *Media, Culture and Society*, *44*(1), 161–171. https://doi.org/10.1177/01634437211060201

Stanley-Becker, I., Guarino, B., Sellers, F. S., Cha, A. E., & Sun, L. H. (May 14, 2021). CDC's mask guidance spurs confusion and criticism, as well as celebration. *Washington Post*. https://www.washingtonpost.com/health/2021/05/14/cdc-mask-update-decision-confusion/

Tan, A. S., Lee, C. J., & Chae, J. (2015). Exposure to health (mis) information: Lagged effects on young adults' health behaviors and potential pathways. *Journal of Communication*, *65*(4), 674–698. https://doi.org/10.1111/jcom.12163

Tessler, H., Choi, M., & Kao, G. (2020). The anxiety of being Asian American: Hate crimes and negative biases during the COVID-19 pandemic. *American Journal of Criminal Justice*, *45*(4), 636–646. https://doi.org/10.1007/s12103-020-09541-5

Toppenberg-Pejcica, D., Noyes, J., Allen, T., Alexander, N., Vanderford, M., & Gamhewage, G. (2019). Emergency risk communication: Lessons learned from a rapid review of recent gray literature on Ebola, Zika, and Yellow Fever. *Health Communication*, *34*(4), 437–455. https://doi.org/10.1080/10410236.2017.1405488

Tyson, A., & Funk, C. (2022). Increasing public criticism, confusion over COVID-19 response in U.S. *Pew Research Center*. https://www.pewresearch.org/science/2022/02/09/increasing-public-criticism-confusion-over-covid-19-response-in-u-s/

van der Meer, T. G. L. A., & Jin, Y. (2020). Seeking formula for misinformation treatment in public health crises: The effects of corrective information type and source. *Health Communication*, *35*(5), 560–575. https://doi.org/10.1080/10410236.2019.1573295

Veil, S., Reynolds, B., Sellnow, T. L., & Seeger, M. W. (2008). CERC as a theoretical framework for research and practice. *Health Promotion Practice*, *9*(4), 26S–34S. http://doi.org/10.1177/1524839908322113

Villasenor, J. (2022). The vital role of Twitter in responding to Covid. *Brookings Institution*. https://www.brookings.edu/blog/techtank/2022/01/04/the-vital-role-of-twitter-in-responding-to-covid/

Vraga, E. K., & Bode, L. (2020). Defining misinformation and understanding its bounded nature: Using expertise and evidence for describing misinformation. *Political Communication*, *37*(1), 136–144. https://doi.org/10.1080/10584609.2020.1716500

University of Maryland School of Public Health (n.d.). *Maryland barbers and stylists united for health*. https://sph.umd.edu/research-impact/research-centers/maryland-center-health-equity/projects-maryland-center-health-equity/maryland-barbers-and-stylists-united-health

WHO (2020). *WHO Director-General's opening remarks at the media briefing on COVID-19 – 11 March 2020*. www.who.int/director-general/speeches/detail/who-director-general-s-opening-remarks-at-the-media-briefing-on-covid-19---11-march-2020

WHO (2021). *Infodemic*. https://www.who.int/health-topics/infodemic#tab=tab_1

WHO (January, 2023). *WHO coronavirus (COVID-19) dashboard*. https://covid19.who.int/

Author's Bios

Brooke Fisher Liu is a professor in the Department of Communication at the University of Maryland. She earned a PhD in mass communication from the University of North Carolina at Chapel Hill. Dr. Liu's risk and crisis communication research has been supported by a variety of U.S. government agencies including the Food and Drug Administration, National Science Foundation, Department of Homeland Security, and the National Oceanic and Atmospheric Administration. She is the cofounder and former editor of the *Journal of International Crisis and Risk Communication Research*. With Dr. Cynthia Baur, Dr. Liu founded and directs the University of Maryland Pandemic Readiness Initiative.

Cynthia Baur is a professor in the Department of Behavioral and Community Health at the University of Maryland. She is also the Endowed Chair and Director of the Herschel S. Horowitz Center for Health Literacy. Dr. Baur earned her PhD in communication from the University of California, San Diego. Her health literacy and risk communication research has been supported by the U.S. CDC, the Food and Drug Administration, National Institutes of Health, the federal Office of Minority Health, and the Maryland Department of Health. Before becoming UMD faculty, Dr. Baur spent almost 20 years leading health communication and health literacy initiatives at the U.S. Department of Health and Human Services and the CDC.

14

The Role of Legacy Media and Social Media in International Organizational Risk and Crisis Communication

Yan Jin and Toni G.L.A. van der Meer
Grady College of Journalism and Mass Communication,
University of Georgia, Athens, GA, USA
Amsterdam School of Communication Research (ASCoR),
University of Amsterdam, Amsterdam, The Netherlands

Introduction

In an Arthur W. Page Society report (2023) based on perspectives shared by chief communication officers, trust and division were identified as among the major challenges confronting global businesses, manifested in (1) trust in business, government, and media; (2) political polarization; (3) racism/diversity, equity, and inclusion (DEI); and (4) misinformation (Page Society, 2023). These challenges reflect large-scale risks and crises confronting organizations across sectors and beyond borders, shedding light to "sticky crisis" challenges (Jin et al., 2021). At the center of the creation and amplification of these challenges are global media and the communication eco-system, crossing over legacy media, social media, and emerging digital technology.

Sticky crises are severe, recurring, and complex crises that cause ripple effects, resulting in ancillary crises simultaneously and impacting organizations and industries alike (Reber et al., 2021). According to Reber et al. (2021): "Sticky crises demand not only a near-instant response, but they may require crisis communicators to see possibilities, understand the potential breadth and scope of an emerging crisis, and be ready to change strategy and tactics quickly" (p. 7). Thus, communication processes, which flow through platforms provided by legacy and social media, can determine the development of crisis situations and how "sticky" they turn out to be. Accordingly, in a posited model of managing sticky crisis (Jin, 2021; see Figure 14.1), understanding the media environment is essential for effective and ethical organizational risk and crisis communication, domestically and globally. In this chapter, we discuss the state-of-art-research insights on the role of legacy media and social media in organizational risk and crisis communication, as well as influences and challenges exerted by and associated with modern digital platforms and emerging technologies.

The Handbook of International Crisis and Risk Communication Research, Second Edition.
Edited by Andreas Schwarz, Matthew W. Seeger, and Sora Kim.

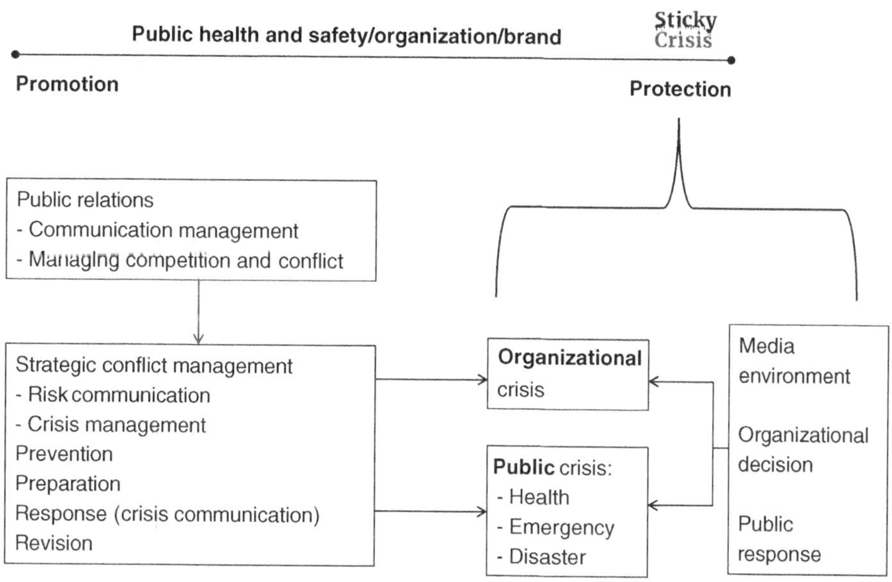

Figure 14.1 Sticky Crisis Management. *Source*: Jin (2021).

The Role of Legacy Media in Organizational Risk and Crisis Communication

Legacy media, composed by journalism and media organizations, has continued to exert its influences in organizational risk and crisis communication (van der Meer, 2018), the process of which is amplified via mediatization of organizations and influenced by culture, politics, dynamics, resources, and dependencies in different media systems embedded in different national settings and international media.

Mediatization and Organizational Risks and Crises

With the mediatization of organizations over time, risks and crises related to organizations have become more and more communicative events. Mediatization theory argues that media have become increasingly institutionalized within our society and that different levels of society have gradually adjusted to the logic of the media (Strömbäck, 2008). Initially, mediatization was applied to understand how political processes have become impacted by media. As a long-term and multi-phase process, media logic is argued to govern political actors. Research in the corporate communication realm has argued that the theory can also be applied to the context of organizations (Fredriksson & Pallas, 2021; Ihlen & Pallas, 2014; Pallas & Fredriksson, 2013). With becoming deeper integrated into organizational processes, media crucially shape the environment of these organizations and organizational events are formed and framed according to the preferences of the media.

How Journalism and Media Organizations Influence Organizational Risks and Crises

With the process of mediatization, organizational practices have become more widely visible to publics across the world. This plays out on two levels: (1) organizations have become more visible and therewith organizational crises have become more newsworthy; and (2) organizations are increasingly under scrutiny from a larger and more diverse public.

First, in search for new news events, media are eager to report on anything that goes wrong – highlighting the well research negativity bias in news (Harcup & O'Neill, 2001; Soroka et al., 2019; van der Meer, 2018). News values like negativity, dramatization, or well-known actors (Galtung & Ruge, 1965) make organizational crisis situations, especially when happening at internationally known organizations, highly newsworthy events. Accordingly, news media are often the main source of crisis information and offer the platform for negotiating crisis understanding (van der Meer, 2018). Being on the media agenda, and therewith in the eye of the public, changes and shapes the way such organizational crisis events evolve. The communication around such events takes on a more central role. The different needs of different types of media and publics need to be taken into account. For example, not only communication with local media is essential, ignoring more (inter)national media could further escalate the crisis situation when the definition of the situation and the level of responsibility is not clearly communicated (Cornelissen et al., 2009). In addition, when organizational crises become mediated events, they are also shaped and framed by communicative processes in the media.

In combination with other actors, the interplay with the news media determines how a crisis is defined, which in turn shapes how the public understands the situation at hand and largely determines the development of the crisis. Some scholars go as far as stating that crises and the development of them are constituted in communication (Schultz et al., 2012). This highlights also the lack of control organizations have over risk and crises. Communication is always formed in the interplay with other actors, and, with a credibility disadvantage due to the mere occurrence of an organizational crisis, organizations often have less leverage in frame negotiations. Thus, organizational external crises can often be described as a mediatized situation. The communication of relevant stakeholder and the general evolvement of the situation are to a certain degree shaped by and molded to the demands of news media in their crisis coverage (Ihlen & Pallas, 2014).

Second, besides organizational crisis being increasingly mediatized events, organizations are more in the public eye these days. With the combination of the media's significant role in today's society and organizations' increased visibility, it can be observed that organizations are under more public and media scrutiny than before (van der Meer & Jonkman, 2021). Being constantly monitored creates additional risks for organizations to end up in external crises. With their increased media visibility comes increased focus on organizations societal responsibility. We have seen numerous corporate social responsibility (CSR) activities initiated by organizations for reputational improvement (Aksak et al., 2016), but nowadays organizations are increasingly pressured externally to engage with societal causes, not to just increase their reputation but to maintain their legitimacy in the eyes of their key stakeholders (van der Meer & Jonkman, 2021).

Organizations' so-called license to operate, the level to which corporations meet and engage with expectations of society (Gunningham et al., 2004), needs to be constantly renewed against what societies find acceptable. This form of organizational legitimacy is not a given, but something that is constantly subject to change and that requires an ongoing active maintenance of stakeholder approval (Moffat et al., 2016; Prno & Slocombe, 2012). When public and media debates increasingly involve sociopolitical issues, we see that these norms and standards are also used to judge the organization and its activities. As a form of soft regulation, stakeholder communicatively negotiates whether organizations fulfill their ethical standards, which goes beyond mere profitability and relates more to their wider contribution to society. Accordingly, with growing social visibility and responsibility of corporations through mediatization, organizations get inherently related to public and media issues which have become more political recently. Therefore, it is increasingly difficult for organizations to escape their societal role and refrain from engaging with such sociopolitical issue high on the agenda. This arguably results in the politicization of corporations and their environment since corporate communication and sociopolitical issues have become inherently intertwined (van der Meer & Jonkman, 2021).

Indeed, with the polarization that manifests in numerous debates, we see that organizations increasingly speak out on issues but at the same time struggle with deciding what stakeholder groups to side with and how to maintain their legitimacy in the eye of all of society (Kim et al., 2020; Rim et al., 2020). Especially when organizations operate internationally, this can be a challenging task. With different cultures across countries come different norms and values. In addition, the societal debates might differ per country or society, in terms of what topic gains most attention or what the majority standpoint on polarizing issues is. When an organization successfully sides with a certain stakeholder group on a sociopolitical issue in one country, this might be differently perceived in another country that the organization is active in.

Big tech companies are in a way a catalyst for this. They operate more transnational, and therewith bring the whole world together, which means that sociopolitical issues and (polarizing) debates become more visible to everyone and organizations' stakeholders gain a larger stage to call out organizations for their wrongdoing or lack of involvement with society.

The present opportunities and challenges include how the big tech companies collaborate with other organizations, such as global government agencies, multinational companies, and nongovernmental organizations (NGOs) in addressing global risk and crisis issues such as artificial intelligence (AI; Shivaram, 2023).

The Role of Social Media in Shaping Organizational Risk and Crisis Communication

Social media, along with other emerging digital technologies, has capitalized on the rise of opinion leaders and their influences via various channels among social networks, shaping discourse, and public sentiments on risk and crisis information. It also exerts unprecedented power in the organizational decision-making process in an increasingly competitive and conflicting international media environment, ranging from risk and crisis information generation, consumption, to transmission, which has been shed light on by the social-mediated crisis communication (SMCC) model based on its conceptual framework and empirical evidences accumulated over a decade (Jin et al., 2022). The SMCC model is focused not only on how a crisis is triggered and/or amplified on social media but also on how crisis information is generated, consumed, and transmitted via the interactions and interconnectedness of various sources and channels, crossing over legacy media and social media.

Organizational Risk and Crisis Information Generation, Consumption, and Transmission

Research on organizational risk and crisis information on social media has largely focused on organizational message response strategies (Cheng, 2018), primarily incorporating image repair theory (e.g., Benoit, 1997), situational crisis communication theory (SCCT) (e.g., Coombs, 2019), dialogic communication (Taylor & Kent, 2007), and crisis and risk narratives (e.g., Liu et al., 2020). The five different criteria posited by the SMCC model for organizations to consider in communicating about crisis information to their stakeholders via social media, as a trusted crisis information source/authority, include crisis origin, crisis type, organizational infrastructure, message strategy, and crisis message form (Austin & Jin, 2017), which are also applicable to organizational risk communication practice.

At the stage of the initial risk and crisis information generation, crisis origin (internal or external) and crisis type (as informed by SCCT) guide the development of the message strategy (e.g., to generate one unified message or many different localized and tailored messages connecting to broader messaging themes) (Jin et al., 2022). Findings from the SMCC-based experiments (e.g., Jin et al., 2014; Liu et al., 2016) indicate that (1) for risks and crises of more internal origin, organizations might consider using more accommodative strategies via social media; (2) organizations in risks and crises of more external origin might consider using more defensive strategies, according to the publics' likelihood of attributing more or less organizational responsibility in a SMCC situation. As Jin et al. (2022) pointed out, it is also critical for organizations to proactively combat misinformation, disinformation, and rumors at the risk and crisis information generation stage by using different corrective communication strategies on social media (Jin et al., 2020; van der Meer & Jin, 2020). When an organization is under attack by misinformation spread by third-party groups on social media, employee support on social media in conjunction of organizational crisis misinformation debunking messaging was found to be especially beneficial in lessening reputational damage and lowering perceived organizational crisis responsibility (Jin et al., 2020).

Social listening (i.e., listening to publics' concerns) and engagement (i.e., engaging in dialogue) become increasingly essential (Veil et al., 2011). As Reuter and Kaufhold (2018) highlighted, using social media during crises helps organizations gain on-the-ground data points, keep up-to-date on breaking crisis developments, and understand publics' perspectives and viewpoints. By consuming messages from other sources about risk and crisis information that originated, spread, or amplified on social media, organizations can proactively monitor social media (including legacy media's social media outlets) in the full cycle of risk communication and crisis management, which can help them develop more effective risk communication and crisis response strategies (Ruggiero & Vos, 2014). Such monitoring activities can also support organizations with mapping their political environment and determining whether they should engage with certain sociopolitical issues high on the agenda of their key stakeholders to avoid being called out for lack of societal involvement and demonstrated responsibility.

In the context of health risk and crisis communication, public information officers (PIOs) in health organizations who monitored social media during the Zika virus reported that they were better prepared for crisis response and achieved better crisis management outcomes (Avery, 2017). Vijaykumar et al. (2015) proposed the risk amplification through media spread (RAMS) model, one of the first health risk and crisis communication models developed based on the SMCC model to advancing the understanding of how infectious disease outbreak (IDO) information is communicated by public health authorities to at-risk individuals and communities. To evaluate the RAMS model, Jin et al. (2019) conducted in-depth interviews with PIOs in the United States (at state and national levels) and reported that that PIOs and their health organizations need to strategically integrate legacy and social media in conducting infectious disease communication. The finding was also echoed in a recent study exploring how health communication executives reflected on their practice in managing COVID-19 risk and crisis communication (Voges et al., 2023).

When it comes to transmitting risk and crisis information, organizations use a variety of formats, through different sources and channels, to reach stakeholders directly and indirectly. Among various sources of risk and crisis information, prior research found that publics responded most positively to information received (1) directly from the organization in crisis as a source via news media (Liu et al., 2013) and (2) from employees as sources of crisis information, who advocate for the organization (Opitz et al., 2018). Source credibility (van Zoonen & van der Meer, 2015) and trust (Lu & Jin, 2020) are essential factors to go with the timing (i.e., getting the risk and crisis information out quickly from the trusted authority and/or the crisis-affected organization source) of crisis message transmission (Claeys et al., 2013) in order to achieve better reputation restoration and generate more intended organizational risk and crisis communication outcomes.

Best practices for organizations to use different forms of communication and matching messages to the most appropriate forms in times of risk and crisis have been recommended based on research findings, including (1) using social media to obtain more insider information and check in with friends and family during crises (Austin et al., 2012) and (2) using social media in natural disasters to provide timely and unfiltered information to individuals, facilitating them in learning about the magnitude of the event, checking in on family/friends, connecting with their communities, fostering emotional support/healing, and facilitating cognitive, affective, and behavioral coping processes continue (Fraustino et al., 2017).

Among other factors, media (legacy and social) fatigue needs to be addressed and managed by organizations intending to engage key stakeholders with organizational content generation, consumption, and transmission via a variety of communication efforts (Jin et al., 2022). Posited by Seo et al. (2019) as an organizational business strategy, organizations need to adapt to the continuation of rapid changes in social-mediated and technology-enhanced digital communications so as to gain or maintain competitive advantage in the practice of business communication according to stakeholders' expectations. One of the paramount issues facing communicators is stakeholders' social media fatigue, which can lead to online disengagement and social media strategy ineffectiveness.

Based on a systematic review of research literature and a deep dive in the professional reports regarding corporate communication and social media strategies, Seo et al. (2019) provided a conceptual model for organizations to tackle the challenge of stakeholder social media fatigue. The approaches they recommended include (1) developing alternative social media strategies capitalizing on the impact of vicarious interaction and (2) building positive vicarious interaction experience by cultivating meaningful corporate-influencer-stakeholder (parasocial) relationships. Although this model for overcoming stakeholder social media fatigue is proposed for general organizational business communication (not risk or crisis communication specific), the emphasis on organization-influencer-stakeholder online (social and parasocial) relationship building can play an essential role for proactive risk and crisis communication in an interconnected world that is co-constructed by legacy media, social media, and emerging technology such as AI.

Impact of Organizational Operators of Social Media Platforms and Algorithms

In a review of the SMCC model, Jin et al. (2022) summarized advanced knowledge on how organizations might harness social media to effectively prepare for and respond to risks and crises, as well as cautioned the urgency of understanding the potential dark side of social media and emerging technology such as AI, which introduce novel risks in crisis management (Guthrie & Rich, 2022) and can trigger/amplify sticky crises.

Most recently, as disinformation (false information designed with the intention to mislead) becomes a risk or crisis issue itself, it is critical for organizations to reassess organizational or institutional operators of their social media platforms and algorithms so as to be proactive in anticipating and preparing for potential significant damage disinformation might have on organizational operation and reputation (Karinshak & Jin, 2023). To advance a theory-driven, evidence-based research and practice in communication management that advises how organizations might effectively and proactively manage AI-driven organizational risks and crises, Karinshak and Jin (2023) conducted a review of disinformation literature in security and computer science to (1) identify how previously introduced technologies have affected disinformation and (2) build a systematic and coordinated approach for sustainable counter-disinformation efforts for organizations to consider employing in the management of AI-driven disinformation risks and crises.

The initial conceptual framework for organizational disinformation readiness Karinshak and Jin (2023) proposed is primarily for the corporate sector. However, it can be adapted to different organizational types and tailored toward different media and organizational communication ecosystems. The essence of this new framework includes (1) technologies affecting disinformation attacks and counterattacks and (2) approaches organizations can take to proactively prepare and equip their communication teams to better protect businesses and stakeholders. It provides organizations actor-level and content-level perspectives for influence and discusses their implications for disinformation management system building within organizations with the capacity and agility to detect risks and mitigate crises driven by evolving AI technologies.

As Karinshak and Jin (2023) emphasized, risk and crisis communication efforts according to this new organizational disinformation management framework will not be able to rely solely on detection strategies (e.g., via risk and crisis information monitoring and social-listening techniques), as AI-created content quality becomes more and more convincing (and ultimately, indistinguishable); instead, future disinformation management efforts will need to rely on *content influence* rather than volume (due to emerging capabilities for automated production of disinformation). Capitalizing on preexisting media presence and preparation, as well as built into existing response timing and message engagement strategy, a set of organizational counter-disinformation, risk/crisis mitigation strategies are recommended by Karinshak and Jin (2023) based on the literature: (1) proactively developing a strong online presence and content following (Melchior & Oliveira, 2022); (2) developing a strategic response plan with a focus on prebunking that provides users with a warning prior to exposure to disinformation in order to diminish its persuasiveness (Boman, 2021; Boman & Schneider, 2021; Lewandowsky & Van Der Linden, 2021); and (3) quickly and publicly addressing disinformation with compelling corrective content (Jin et al., 2020).

As Karinshak and Jin (2023) further noted, it is critical to have non-malicious content creators' support of an organization's risk and crisis response (as opposed to the misleading content regarding the risk/crisis). From the standpoint of strategic conflict management, organizations and malicious actors (against the organizations on focal risk/crisis issues) are competing for the support of influential non-malicious voices, affected by how the focal information is then perceived and disseminated by and among stakeholders. Therefore, it is essential for the organizational content to establish its presence in trusted, diverse sources across platforms and channels, constantly and consistently fostering stakeholder engagement by strengthening both digital and non-digital (online and offline, via legacy and social media) communication efforts to relevant influencers, via strategies such as "(1) following and understanding trends on social media platforms; (2) differentiating and optimizing content for each social media platform (as the characteristics of impactful content differ on Facebook and TikTok); (3) creating content that is visually effective (with a strong sense of aesthetics) and digestible (with a clear purpose); and (4) fostering engagement (such as comments) through a question or call to action" (Karinshak & Jin, 2023, p. 554).

Future Research and Conclusion

In sum, legacy media and social media (in its current and emerging forms) support and disrupt the communication channels and information content, forming the backbone of risk communication and crisis management. Confronted by challenging and complex risk and crisis issues, it is essential for scholars and practitioners to advance organizational risk and crisis communication theory and practice based on the enhanced understanding of the role of legacy media, social media, and emerging technology, domestically and internationally. Future research questions and practice directions identified by scholars and practitioners (Crisis Communication Think Tank [CCTT], 2023) include (1) Have AI, VR, and the metaverse changed our inherited blueprint for risk communication and crisis management? And (2) how do organizations and stakeholders perceive these newly constructed realities?

To tackle these questions, international risk and crisis communication professionals and industry leaders across sectors need to routinely examine the state of the field. It is critical to determine how social and technological advancements result in new realities and uncover how these realities manifest via societal and organizational functions (CCTT, 2023). Approaches and new questions shared by the CCTT (2023) include the following:

First, to lay the foundation of future crisis management theoretically and practically: When tackling current and future risks and crises, what are the foundational elements that continually prove to be successful? How can we build upon this bedrock while creating space for a new approach to crisis management? Mapping the foundation of risk and crisis communication will allow practitioners to explore organizational standings by identifying where crisis management is now and where it might be in the future. The theoretical and practical discussions among scholars and practitioners will open with the classic question of "where does crisis management fit within an organization" and sets the stage for "how do social and technological changes influence crisis management within an organization?"

Second, to conceptualize a new framework for risk communication and crisis management: How has risk communication and crisis management evolved across industries and different organization types (e.g., corporations, NGOs, and governments)? How do we continue to manage diverse, multidisciplinary perspectives? Organizations will always face crises. To this end, sticky crisis management is essential. New research and practical insights shall inspire a conversation of truths – determining which foundational elements truly stand the various tests of time, as well as social and technological challenges. Practitioners need to reflect on crisis communication elements and truths: the outdated, the longstanding, and the aspirational. How has risk and crisis communication changed over time and in different parts of the world with diverse cultures and voices?

Third, to build into alternate universes: When unseen constructs exist in an ever-evolving virtual world, it is our responsibility to develop a new way of thinking toward international organizational risk and crisis communication. Technology will always evolve, resulting in opportunities and challenges for practitioners of risk communication and crisis management. These evolutions, however, can influence our fundamental understanding of the reality of how risks and crises exist. Advanced research in these arenas will help us address some of these complex questions changing communication practice globally.

Last but not least, to contend with the intangible effectively and ethically: How do we theorize and practice effective and ethical organizational risk and crisis communication when reality is fluid within space and time? Risk and crisis communication, as well as its place within organizational management, is tied together to understand how old, current, and future practices might exist if we view space and time as elastic. We might need to allow ourselves to reconcile potential contradictions and understand how fundamental truths may or may not apply if we enter the new dimensions of alternative realities.

Looking ahead, to advance our knowledge in answering the emerging challenges confronting crisis and risk scholars and practitioners alike, communication professionals and industry leaders across sectors need to routinely examine the state of the field. They constantly should (1) determine how social and technological advancements result in emerging landscapes of international organizational risk and crisis communication and (2) uncover how these landscapes and media-constructed realities manifest via societal, cultural, and organizational functions.

References

Aksak, E. O., Ferguson, M. A., & Duman, S. A. (2016). Corporate social responsibility and CSR fit as predictors of corporate reputation: A global perspective. *Public Relations Review*, *42*(1), 79–81. https://doi.org/10.1016/j.pubrev.2015.11.004

Arthur W. Page Society (January 12, 2023). *The CCO's distinct outlook on 2023*. https://page.org/blog/the-cco-s-distinct-outlook-on-2023

Austin, L., & Jin, Y. (2017). Social media and crisis communication: Explicating the social-mediated crisis communication model. In A. Dudo, & L. A. Kahlor, Eds., *Strategic Communication: New Agendas in Communication* (pp. 163–186). Routledge.

Austin, L., Liu, B. F., & Jin, Y. (2012). How audiences seek out crisis information: Exploring the social-mediated crisis communication model. *Journal of Applied Communication Research, 40*(2), 188–207. https://doi.org/10.1080/00909882.2012.654498

Avery, E. J. (2017). Public information officers social media monitoring during the Zika virus crisis, a global health threat surrounded by public uncertainty. *Public Relations Review, 43*(3), 468–476. https://doi.org/10.1016/j.pubrev.2017.02.018

Benoit, W. (1997). Image repair discourse and crisis communication. *Public Relations Review, 23*(2), 177–186. https://doi.org/10.1016/S0363-8111(97)90023-0

Boman, C. D. (2021). Examining characteristics of prebunking strategies to overcome PR disinformation attacks. *Public Relations Review, 47*(5), 102105. https://doi.org/10.1016/j.pubrev.2021.102105

Boman, C. D., & Schneider, E. J. (2021). Finding an antidote: Testing the use of proactive crisis strategies to protect organizations from astroturf attacks. *Public Relations Review, 47*(1), 102004. https://doi.org/10.1016/j.pubrev.2020.102004

Cheng, Y. (2018). How social media is changing crisis communication strategies: Evidence from the updated literature. *Journal of Contingencies & Crisis Management, 26*(1), 58–68. https://doi.org/10.1111/1468-5973.12130

Claeys, A.-S., Cauberghe, V., & Leysen, J. (2013). Implications of stealing thunder for the impact of expressing emotions in organizational crisis communication. *Journal of Applied Communication Research, 41*(3), 293–308. https://doi.org/10.1080/00909882.2013.806991

Coombs, W. T. (2019). *Ongoing Crisis Communication: Planning, Managing, and Responding* (5th ed.). Sage.

Cornelissen, J. P., Carroll, C., & Elving, W. J. L. (2009). Making sense of a crucial interface: Corporate communication and the news media. In C. Chouliaraki, & M. Morsing, Eds., *Media, Organisation and Identity* (pp. 1–22). Palgrave McMillan.

Crisis Communication Think Tank (2023). *Crisis Management Keystone.* Grady College of Journalism and Mass Communication, University of Georgia.

Fraustino, J. D., Liu, B. F., & Jin, Y. (2017). Social media during disasters: A research synthesis and road map. In L. Austin, & Y. Jin, Eds., *Social Media and Crisis Communication* (pp. 283–295). Routledge.

Fredriksson, M., & Pallas, J. (2021). Public sector communication and mediatization. In V. Luoma-aho, & M. J. Canel, Eds., *The Handbook of Public Sector Communication* (pp. 167–179). Wiley Blackwell. https://doi.org/10.1002/9781119263203.ch11

Galtung, J., & Ruge, M. H. (1965). The structure of foreign news: The presentation of the Congo, Cuba and Cyprus crises in four Norwegian newspapers. *Journal of Peace Research, 2*(1), 64–90.

Gunningham, N., Kagan, R. A., & Thornton, D. (2004). Social license and environmental protection: Why businesses go beyond compliance. *Law & Social Inquiry, 29*(2), 307–341. https://doi.org/10.1111/j.1747-4469.2004.tb00338.x

Guthrie, W. S., & Rich, J. (2022). New technology, big data, and artificial intelligence. In Y. Jin, & L. Austin, Eds., *Social Media and Crisis Communication* (2nd ed., pp. 180–192). Routledge.

Harcup, T., & O'neill, D. (2001). What is news? Galtung and Ruge revisited. *Journalism Studies, 2*(2), 261–280.

Ihlen, Ø., & Pallas, J. (2014). Mediatization of corporations. In K. Lundby, Ed., *Handbook on Mediatization of Communication* (pp. 423–442). De Gruyter Mouton. https://doi.org/10.1515/9783110272215.423

Jin, Y. (July 3, 2021). Managing the (un)controlled burn: Crisis fighters' ongoing battle against pandemic-infodemic dual threat. Presented at the panel, "How Public Relations Contributed to Fighting the Pandemic: Lessons from the Application of Crisis and Risk Communication" (Chairs: W. T. Coombs and S. J. Holladay). *BledCom 2021 (the 28th International Public Relations Research Symposium)* [virtual].

Jin, Y., Austin, L., & Liu, B. F. (2022). Social-mediated crisis communication research: How information generation, consumption, and transmission influence communication processes and outcomes.

In W. T. Coombs, & S. Holladay, Eds., *The Handbook of Crisis Communication* (2nd ed., pp. 151–167). Wiley.

Jin, Y., Austin, L., Vijaykumar, S., Jun, H., & Nowak, G. (2019). Communicating about infectious disease threats: Insights from public health information officers. *Public Relations Review*, *45*(1), 167–177. https://doi.org/10.1016/j.pubrev.2018.12.003

Jin, Y., Liu, B. F., & Austin, L. (2014). Examining the role of social media in effective crisis management: The effects of crisis origin, information form, and source on publics crisis responses. *Communication Research*, *41*(1), 74–94. https://doi.org/10.1177/0093650211423918

Jin, Y., Reber, B. H., & Nowak, G. (2021). *Advancing Crisis Communication Effectiveness: Integration of Public Relations Scholarship and Practice*. Routledge.

Jin, Y., van der Meer, T., Lee, Y.-I., & Lu, X. (2020). The effects of corrective communication and employee backup on the effectiveness of fighting crisis misinformation. *Public Relations Review*, *46*(3), 101910. https://doi.org/10.1016/j.pubrev.2020.101910

Karinshak, E., & Jin, Y. (2023). AI-driven disinformation: A framework for organizational preparation and response. *Journal of Communication Management 27*(4), 539–562. https://doi.org/10.1108/JCOM-09-2022-0113

Kim, J. K., Overton, H., Bhalla, N., & Li, J. Y. (2020). Nike, Colin Kaepernick, and the politicization of sports: Examining perceived organizational motives and public responses. *Public Relations Review*, *46*(2), 101856.

Lewandowsky, S., & Van Der Linden, S. (2021). Countering misinformation and fake news through inoculation and prebunking. *European Review of Social Psychology*, *32*(2), 348–384. https://doi.org/10.1080/10463283.2021.1876983

Liu, B. F., Fraustino, J. D., & Jin, Y. (2016). Social media use during disasters: How information form and source influence intended behavioral responses. *Communication Research*, *43*(5), 626–646. http://dx.doi.org/10.1177/0093650214565917

Liu, B. F., Austin, L., Lee, Y.-I., Jin, Y., & Kim, S. (2020). Telling the tale: The role of narratives in helping people respond to crises. *Journal of Applied Communication Research*, *48*(3), 328–349. https://doi.org/10.1080/00909882.2020.1756377

Liu, B. F., Jin, Y., & Austin, L. (2013). The tendency to tell: Understanding publics communicative responses to crisis information form and source. *Journal of Public Relations Research*, *25*(1), 51–67. https://doi.org/10.1080/1062726X.2013.739101

Lu, X., & Jin, Y. (2020). Information vetting as a key component in social-mediated crisis communication: An exploratory study to examine the initial conceptualization. *Public Relations Review*, *46*(2), 101891. https://doi.org/10.1016/j.pubrev.2020.101891

Melchior, C., & Oliveira, M. (2022). Health-related fake news on social media platforms: A systematic literature review. *New Media & Society*, *24*(6), 1500–1522. https://doi.org/10.1177/14614448211038762

Moffat, K., Lacey, J., Zhang, A., & Leipold, S. (2016). The social license to operate: A critical review. *Forestry: An International Journal of Forest Research*, *89*(5), 477–488. https://doi.org/10.1093/forestry/cpv044

Opitz, M., Chaudhri, V., & Wang, Y. (2018). Employee social-mediated crisis communication as opportunity or threat? *Corporate Communications: An International Journal*, *23*(1), 66–83. http://dx.doi.org/10.1108/CCIJ-07-2017-0069

Pallas, J., & Fredriksson, M. (2013). Corporate media work and micro-dynamics of mediatization. *European Journal of Communication*, *28*(4), 420–435.

Prno, J., & Slocombe, D. S. (2012). Exploring the origins of 'social license to operate' in the mining sector: Perspectives from governance and sustainability theories. *Resources Policy*, *37*(3), 346–357. https://doi.org/10.1016/j.resourpol.2012.04.002

Reber, B. H., Yarbrough, C. R., Nowak, G. J., & Jin, Y. (2021). Complex and challenging crises: A call for solutions. In Y. Jin, B. H. Reber, & G. J. Nowak, Eds., *Advancing Crisis Communication Effectiveness: Integration of Public Relations Scholarship and Practice* (pp. 3–16). Routledge.

Reuter, C., & Kaufhold, M.-A. (2018). Fifteen years of social media in emergencies: A retrospective review and future directions for crisis informatics. *Journal of Contingencies & Crisis Management*, *26*(1), 41–57. https://doi.org/10.1111/1468-5973.12196

Rim, H., Lee, Y., & Yoo, S. (2020). Polarized public opinion responding to corporate social advocacy: Social network analysis of boycotters and advocators. *Public Relations Review*, *46*(2), 101869.

Ruggiero, A., & Vos, M. (2014). Social media monitoring for crisis communication: Process, methods and trends in the scientific literature. *Online Journal of Communication and Media Technologies*, *4*(1), 105–130. https://doi.org/10.29333/ojcmt/2457

Schultz, F., Kleinnijenhuis, J., Oegema, D., Utz, S., & Van Atteveldt, W. (2012). Strategic framing in the BP crisis: A semantic network analysis of associative frames. *Public Relations Review*, *38*(1), 97–107.

Seo, Y., Primovic, M., & Jin, Y. (2019). Social media strategies for overcoming stakeholder social media fatigue: A trialogue approach. *Journal of Business Strategy*, *40*(6), 40–48. https://doi.org/10.1108/JBS-04-2019-0071

Shivaram, D. (2023). The White House and big tech companies release commitments on managing AI. *NPR*. https://www.npr.org/2023/07/21/1188831773/the-white-house-and-big-tech-companies-release-commitments-on-managing-ai

Soroka, S., Fournier, P., & Nir, L. (2019). Cross-national evidence of a negativity bias in psychophysiological reactions to news. *Proceedings of the National Academy of Sciences*, *116*(38), 18888–18892.

Strömbäck, J. (2008). Four phases of mediatization: An analysis of the mediatization of politics. *The International Journal of Press/Politics*, *13*(3), 228–246. https://doi.org/10.1177/1940161208319097

Taylor, M., & Kent, M. L. (2007). Taxonomy of mediated crisis responses. *Public Relations Review*, *33*(2), 140–146. https://doi.org/10.1016/j.pubrev.2006.11.017

van der Meer, T. G. L. A. (2018). Public frame building: The role of source usage in times of crisis. *Communication Research*, *45*(6), 956–981. https://doi.org/10.1177/0093650216644027

van der Meer, T. G. L. A., & Jin, Y. (2020). Seeking formula for misinformation treatment in public health crises: The effects of corrective information type and source. *Health Communication*, *35*(5), 560–575. https://doi.org/10.1080/10410236.2019.1573295

van der Meer, T. G. L. A., & Jonkman, J. G. (2021). Politicization of corporations and their environment: Corporations' social license to operate in a polarized and mediatized society. *Public Relations Review*, *47*(1), 101988. https://doi.org/10.1016/j.pubrev.2020.101988

van Zoonen, W., & van der Meer, T. (2015). The importance of source and credibility perception in times of crisis: Crisis communication in a socially mediated era. *Journal of Public Relations Research*, *27*(5), 371–388. http://dx.doi.org/10.1080/1062726X.2015.1062382

Veil, S. R., Buehner, T., & Palenchar, M. J. (2011). A work-in-process literature review: Incorporating social media in risk and crisis communication. *Journal of Contingencies & Crisis Management*, *19*(2), 110–122. https://doi.org/10.1111/j.1468-5973.2011.00639.x

Vijaykumar, S., Jin, Y., & Nowak, G. J. (2015). Social media and the virality of risk: The risk amplification through media spread (RAMS) model. *Journal of Homeland Security and Emergency Management*, *12*(3), 653–677. https://doi.org/10.1515/jhsem-2014-0072

Voges, T. S., Jin, Y., Eaddy, L. L., & Spector, S. (2023). Effective communication management in a public health crisis: Lessons learned about COVID-19 pandemic through the lens of health communication executives. *Journal of Communication Management*, *27*(1), 64–83. https://doi.org/10.1108/JCOM-12-2021-0137

Author's Bio

Yan Jin (PhD, University of Missouri-Columbia) is the C. Richard Yarbrough Professor in Crisis Communication Leadership and Professor of Public Relations at the Grady College of Journalism and Mass Communication, University of Georgia (UGA). She serves as Director of CCTT and Associate Director of Center for Health & Risk Communication at UGA. She has authored more than 120 peer-reviewed journal articles and over 40 book chapters. She is the lead editor of the Routledge books Advancing Crisis Communication Effectiveness: Integrating Public Relations Scholarship with Practice and Social Media and Crisis Communication (2nd edition) (2022). Dr. Jin received the 2014 Krieghbaum Under-40 Award from the Association for Education in Journalism and Mass Communication (AEJMC). In 2019, Dr. Jin received the Kitty O. Locker Outstanding Researcher Award from the Association for Business

Communication (ABC). Serving as principal investigator (PI), Co-PI, co-investigator (CI), or lead researcher, Dr. Jin has contributed to public relations, crisis communication, strategic conflict management, health and risk communication projects funded by the U.S. FDA, the National Institutes of Health (NIH), Arthur W. Page Center for Integrity in Public Communication, and WhatsApp Research Awards for Social Science and Misinformation.

Toni G.L.A. van der Meer (PhD, 2016) is an Associate Professor in Communication Science at the Amsterdam School of Communication Research (ASCoR), University of Amsterdam and specifically part of the program group Corporate Communication. His research broadly focuses on disruptions in communication. More specific topics relate to crisis communication of corporations, biases in media coverage and processing of information, and the impact of misinformation. His work is published in numerous scientific journals and frequently presented to communication professionals or covered in the news media. He is a board member in the institutional research ASCoR board and serves as a partner for the international part of the CCTT. His research has been funded by, for example, an individual Veni grant from the Dutch Science Foundation (NWO), Facebook grant, and the U.S. FDA.

15

Political Crisis Communication and the Rhetorical Arena

An Analysis of President Zelensky's War Addresses and Social Media Use

Elin Strand Larsen[1] and Øyvind Ihlen[2]

[1] Department of Computer Science and Communication, Faculty of Computer Science, Engineering and Economics, Østfold University College, Halden, Norway

[2] Department of Media and Communication, Faculty of Humanities, University of Oslo, Oslo, Norway

Introduction

On February 24, 2022, Russia invaded Ukraine (KyivIndependent, 2022) and set off the largest international political crisis in decades. "International political crises" generally describe situations where the stability of a country is threatened, and the conflict potentially spills over into neighboring countries or the global community. Examples include coups, civil wars, terrorist attacks, mass protests, and other forms of instability that can have significant economic, social, and political impacts and require coordinated responses from multiple countries and international organizations. An international political crisis is thus typically an immensely complicated affair with a plethora of stakeholders with different interests and perspectives. Communication tends to take place on several different arenas also using different technologies.

In this chapter, we discuss how legacy media and social media might fuel an international crisis, but also how crisis communication can utilize such media. We relate this to the theory of mediatization where political authorities, even in crisis, must adjust their crisis communication to a media logic (Hjarvard, 2008; Lundby, 2014), and the very same media also judges their performance in crisis (Hajer, 2009). Both political communication and crisis communication take place in a hybrid media system where "older and newer media logics in the fields of media and politics blend, overlap, intermesh and coevolve" (Chadwick, 2017, p. 5). Journalists use social media to find stories to cover or follow a crisis as it evolves. They also use social media to present news stories and attract audiences to their news channels. Politicians might be caught up in a crisis through social media, but they also use social media as a platform to talk both to journalists and directly to the public during a crisis. To bring this notion of a hybrid media system closer to the field of crisis studies, we rely on one particular model of

The Handbook of International Crisis and Risk Communication Research, Second Edition.
Edited by Andreas Schwarz, Matthew W. Seeger, and Sora Kim.

crisis communication, namely the rhetorical arena model (Johansen & Frandsen, 2007). As will be explained later, the latter model focuses on the complexity and many actors involved in a crisis, as well as the context, media, genre, and text of crisis communication. To aid our discussion, we draw on observations and a selection of research articles analyzing the war addresses and social media use of the President of Ukraine, Volodymyr Zelensky, following the Russian invasion in 2022. First, however, we start by giving a definition of what constitutes an international political crisis and discuss the characteristics of political crisis communication.

Defining Political Crisis and Political Crisis Communication

In the last decade, we have seen a significant increase in the number of international political crises, from the Arab Spring in 2011 (AlJazeera, 2020) to the storming of the U.S. Capitol in 2021 (Duignan, 2023) and the Brazilian congress attack in 2023 (Picheta, 2023); from the political assassination of Saudi dissident, Jamal Khashoggi in 2018 (BBC, 2021), to the killing of Sikh activist, Hardeep Singh Nijjar in 2023 (Singh, 2023); from the Russian invasion of Ukraine in 2022 (KiyivIndependent, 2022) to the Israel-Palestine conflict turning into a full-scale war in 2023 (APNews, 2023). Most crises have a political dimension, or in other words, crises are political at heart: "When events and episodes are widely experienced as a crisis, [political] leadership is expected. If incumbent elites fail to step forward, others might well seize the opportunity to fill the gap" (Boin et al., 2017, p. 13).

A frequently cited definition of political crisis points to how it is a "serious threat to the basic structures or the fundamental values and norms of a social system, which – under time pressure and highly uncertain circumstance – necessitates making critical decisions" (Rosenthal et al., 1989, p. 10). According to Auer (2016), "a political crisis is a situation in which a political entity perceives a higher-than-normal threat to one or more of its core values and finite time for response triggered by the behavioural change of another entity and that is characterized by disruptive interaction between the opposing entities" (Auer, 2016, p. 191). The political entity can be a politician, an organization or a state, and the core values range from family and health to security and sustainability. Political entities or actors differ from private companies in that they are elected by a public vote. To be able to make decisions that influence the lives of their constituents, they need legitimacy and trust (Benoit, 2015, p. 63). Hence, our chosen illustrative case – the war in Ukraine and President Zelensky's crisis response – serves as a useful example. Without the trust of the Ukrainian people, it would be difficult to – literally – rally the troops against the invaders.

Conventionally speaking, an international political crisis occurs when tensions grow between two or more countries and might escalate to economic sanctions or outright aggression, like we see in the Ukraine war. Still, what is considered a political crisis varies from country to country, as well as from time period to time period. Sometimes, a crisis might erupt unexpectedly with hard-to-predict ripple effects on different levels and in different geographical regions. A prime example is from 2005, when a Danish newspaper published satirical cartoons picturing the prophet Muhammad. Danish imams reacted and ensuing protests in several Muslim countries targeted Danish corporations, and Western embassies were attacked (Frandsen & Johansen, 2010). Ambassadors from Turkey, Saudi Arabia, Iran, Pakistan, Egypt, Indonesia, Algeria, Bosnia and Herzegovina, Libya, Morocco, and the Head of the Palestinian General Delegation expressed their concerns to the Danish Prime Minister, illustrating the extent to which the incident was elevated to the highest political level (Hervik, 2012).

Another, more recent example of an international political crisis started on October 7, 2023, with the terrorist attack of Hamas on Israel, killing more than 1,400 people and taking at least 240 hostages (BBC, 2023). Israel responded to the attack by declaring war, launching air strikes, and blocking the supply chain of water, food, and fuel to the Gaza population. According to the Gaza Health Ministry, more than 8000 Palestinians were killed in the first three weeks of the war (APNews, 2023). The tension between Israelis and Palestinians is not new, but the sudden escalation of the conflict made headlines and caused concern all over the world. In the UN, the Security Council voted four times, before they on October 27, 2023, finally agreed on a resolution calling for an "immediate, durable and sustained humanitarian truce leading to a cessation of hostilities" (UnitedNations, 2023). Israel refused to accept the UN resolution and argued for their right to defend themselves against Hamas. The 20-day deadlock of the UN, over a resolution calling for humanitarian pause in Gaza, showed very clearly the many different, strong, and opposing voices of this political and humanitarian crisis. We will return to these opposing voices in our analysis of Zelensky's address to the Israeli Knesset.

Crisis communication is an essential part of political communication. A study of U.S. presidents and crisis communication, Bostdorff (2022) shows that crises pose threats, but also offer political opportunities: "The benefits of handling a crisis successfully are far greater for presidents since leadership is their profession" (Bostdorff, 2022, p. 247). Zelensky also followed the essentials elements of strategic presidential crisis management in that he presented a "compelling narrative," employed "engaging imagery," and reinvigorated his message with "new material in order to maintain attention and support" (Bostdorff, 2022, pp. 255–256). We will return later to discuss exactly how the Ukraine President did this.

Another study presents the ineffective crisis response of President George W. Bush in responding to Hurricane Katrina in 2005 (Benoit & Henson, 2009). Using the Theory of Image Repair (Benoit, 2015) as a critical method and a televised speech by Bush from Jackson Square in New Orleans two weeks after the storm as a case, the study shows that the president employed three strategies: bolstering, defeasibility, and corrective action, but the crisis response did little to help his reputation. The study concludes that "presidents should think carefully before they admit that they [lack] the ability to solve or prevent a problem" (Benoit & Henson, 2009, p. 45), since the people "want to believe that [our president] can protect us from threats and dangers" (Benoit & Henson, 2009, p. 44). The support of Zelensky's decision to stay in Ukraine after the Russian invasion confirms this important belief.

While other studies focus on successful presidential crisis response, like Ronald Reagan's public address following the explosion of the space shuttle Challenger in 1986 (Mister, 1986) and his many speeches and news conferences related to the Iran-Contra affair between 1986 and 1987 (Benoit et al., 1991). In the Challenger tribute, Reagan succeeded in both obeying to the generic constraints of the eulogy and adjusting his rhetoric to the situational demands of a nation in shock after witnessing the explosion on live television. He honored the deceased astronauts by portraying them as heroes and revived the nation's commitment to the space program (Mister, 1986). In the Iran-Contra affair, Reagan's rhetoric developed through three phases: First, he denied selling arms to Iran in exchange for the release of American hostages; then, he justified his actions based on his good intentions; and last, he admitted mistakes and offered corrective action to prevent this from happening again. The study concludes that while "Reagan's approval ratings never regained the heights of pre-Iran-Contra popularity," his public image was still good after his "speech of March 4, 1987, when he [admitted] trading arms for hostages" (Benoit et al., 1991, p. 290).

W. Timothy Coombs (2019) presents eight propositions to mark the differences between corporate crisis communication and crisis communication used by political crisis managers. According to Coombs, political crisis managers are more likely than corporate crisis managers to contest crisis responsibility (1). Furthermore, political crisis managers are also much more likely to engage in framing battles (2), to manage outside crises and attempt to harness the role of a hero during a crisis (3). Political crisis managers do not, in the same way as corporate crisis managers, risk intensifying damage from a crisis if their crisis response does not meet the stakeholder expectations (4), and they are more likely to use crisis exploitation than corporate crisis managers (5 and 6). Finally, political crisis managers more often use crisis auto-communication

(7) – sending out messages intended for calming their supporters, but also more likely to seek to stoke crisis anxiety (8) – as a way to use the crisis to pursue political objectives (Coombs, 2019, pp. 212–221). In our case, we can see how Zelensky used the crisis to argue for the importance of Ukraine's membership in the North Atlantic Treaty Organization (NATO; Edwards, 2023) and the European Union (EU; Treisman, 2022).

Finn Frandsen and Winni Johansen (2020) argue that we need to reframe the field of crisis management and crisis communication and propose a new model of three interrelated subfields; public crisis management, political crisis management, and corporate crisis management (Frandsen & Johansen, 2020, p. 61). Political crisis management is the most relevant subfield for our study of President Zelensky's war addresses and social media use. The most prominent political crisis communication and management theories focus on framing contests and crisis exploitations (Frandsen & Johansen, 2020, pp. 82–83; Salomonsen & Hart, 2020, p. 441). A political crisis can be seen as a "contest between frames and counter-frames fighting against each other to have their interpretation accepted as the dominant narrative" (Frandsen & Johansen, 2020, p. 83), and the winners of the framing contest can sometimes use the crisis to gain political support – nationally and internationally – for "public office-holders and public policies" (Salomonsen & Hart, 2020, p. 452). One thing however, public, political, and corporate crisis management all have in common, is the multiple actors involved in the crisis and crisis communication; hence, in the remaining discussion, we turn to the so-called rhetorical arena model.

The Rhetorical Arena

The rhetorical arena model developed by Winni Johansen and Finn Frandsen (2007) can be a useful tool to analyze how the media as well as the multiple other actors involved in a crisis form different relationships as they communicate to each other, with each other, against each other, past each other, and about each other. The model is based both on a rhetorical or text-oriented approach (Benoit, 2015) and on a strategic or context-oriented tradition (Coombs, 2012). The model calls attention to how a crisis is a complex situation that frequently involves more than one message, one sender, and one receiver. Thus, there is a need for an enlarged perspective going beyond studies of single organizations when analyzing crisis communication. The rhetorical arena model consists of two different perspectives: the macro component – the arena itself with the multiple actors involved in a crisis – and the socio-rhetorical micro component – the context, media, genre, and text of the crisis communication used by the many senders and receivers (Johansen & Frandsen, 2007, p. 284).

In an expanded version of the model, Frandsen and Johansen (2022) argue that the framework can also be used for an analysis of political crisis communication:

> In a political crisis, for instance, the voice of politicians of different political affiliations who have different and conflicting standpoints are of course central, but voices such as citizens (voters), civil servants, communication advisers, experts, media, companies and industries, NGO's, etc. will also typically interfere in the arena (Frandsen & Johansen, 2022, p. 173).

The rhetorical arena is not the same as a public sphere, argue Frandsen and Johansen (2010). While much of what has been studied of crisis communication takes place in public, the rhetorical arena also includes semipublic and private arenas, in addition to the public space. In an expansion of the theory, they also argue that the rhetorical arena can include a set of sub-arenas, defined as "a dynamic social space that opens during a crisis, where only a distinct part of the voices in a larger rhetorical arena communicate to, with, from, against or past one other, to a large extent, about a crisis in a specific, delimited part of the larger arena" (Frandsen & Johansen, 2022, p. 176). A sub-arena in our study would be the organization of and communication between the different troops defending the Ukraine border. In our case, the study of Zelensky's war addresses will mostly be focused on the public arena as represented by legacy media and his use of social media to reach a semipublic sub-arena.

Using the rhetorical arena model, we also need to keep in mind that the relationships within the arena are not based on equality. Zelensky has more economic, political, and symbolic capital than many of the other voices involved in the crisis communication. In a position as president, he has more power and access to the media, than most other actors of the arena. Still, the communication and portrayal of the president, especially in social media, are aimed to present Zelensky as equal to his people – in the way he dresses, talks, and situates himself in the streets of Kyiv, the Ukrainian capital.

In addition to the macro perspective providing an overview of all the different actors and voices involved in the rhetorical arena, Frandsen and Johansen (2010, 2007) also present a micro perspective focusing on the characteristics of each communicative process. The rhetorical arena micro perspective includes three elements – sender, crisis communication, and receiver – and four parameters of mediation – context, media, genre, and text. First, the context of the crisis communication involves both *where* the crisis is taking place and how the public interpret the crisis. Two very different frames of the crisis were presented by the Ukrainian and Russian President Vladimir Putin; while Zelensky consequently referred to the crisis as a war, Putin first presented the invasion as a military special operation to "demilitarize and denazify" Ukraine (Putin, 2022b). Using the word war was banned in Russian media from the beginning, and the Russian President himself did not refer to the situation as a war until December 23, 2022, in a press conference almost a year after the invasion (Putin, 2022a).

The second parameter is the media, both the choice of written and oral crisis communication and the media channels used to distribute the crisis messages. Since the choice between writing or oral communication seems a bit outdated in today's media age, we would like to focus on the channels of crisis communication – especially the news and social media channels. Social media can accentuate a crisis (Austin & Jin, 2018; Freberg & Palenchar, 2013). On social media, we usually find three types of publics present in a crisis. The influential social media creators (1) are those who create and disseminate crisis communication, social media followers (2) include those who directly consume the crisis information in social media, while the social media inactives (3) gain access to crisis information through word-of-mouth and/or traditional media following social media creators (Austin et al., 2012, p. 192). Journalists from the news media are represented both as social media creators, using social media as another platform to distribute news, and as followers, finding new stories and perspectives to cover based on social media posts. Ordinary people usually use social media for "insider information and checking in with family/friends" (Austin et al., 2012, p. 197) in a crisis, while traditional media is used for education (Austin et al., 2012, pp. 197–198).

A crisis can also generate misinformation circulating in social media. Crisis misinformation can here be understood as "false information about any aspect of an ongoing crisis or any incorrect information that can lead to a crisis according to factual evidence from credible source(s) (Jin et al., 2022, p. 153). The amounts of information and misinformation, as well as the many senders and receivers involved in social media crisis communication, fit well into the rhetorical arena model. We also argue that the risk of crisis misinformation is especially high in an international political crisis like the war in Ukraine.

The third parameter of the rhetorical arena is the genre. According to Frandsen and Johansen (2010), a genre is a group of texts that share "the same communicative purpose" and "common characteristics when it comes to content, structure, and rhetorical strategies" (p. 436). The press release is presented as a typical genre in crisis communication, but in recent crises, the use of press releases is quite rare, compared to social media posts and livestreaming of video. Mastering these new genres requires long social media experience, as well as an ability to create an authentic social media persona.

The fourth and last parameter of the rhetorical arena model is the text – the actual content of the crisis communication. According to Frandsen and Johansen (2010), "the text is a result of the sender's deliberate and undeliberate selection and application of the verbal and visual semiotic resources and rhetorical strategies available or prescribed to him or her" (p. 437). Crisis response can also be studied as a form of narrative where different actors within the rhetorical arena place the crisis within a new or existing narrative (Frandsen & Johansen, 2010; Heath, 2003). It has been argued that "crisis creates a narrative space, a communication vacuum, or a meaning deficit that will be filled by stories told by those who experienced the crisis, crisis managers, journalists, and observers" (Seeger & Sellnow, 2016, p. 13). Among the narratives that often circulate in a crisis, we find blame narratives, renewal narratives, memorial narratives, victim narratives, and hero narratives (Seeger & Sellnow, 2016, p. 14). The hero narrative, with Zelensky as a hero-leader, became a central part of the crisis in Ukraine. The visibility of Zelensky as a symbol and model of stability, calm, and resoluteness helped him emerge as a hero (Seeger & Sellnow, 2016, p. 120; Zachara-Szymańska, 2023). We will return to and discuss the hero narrative later, as well as how Zelensky himself used narratives in his crisis communication.

The Challenges of Crisis Communication

"The fight is here; I need ammunition, not a ride" (UkrEmbLondon, 2022), said Ukrainian President Volodymyr Zelensky when the United States offered him transport to a safe location following the Russian invasion. His early and resolute response, as well as his decision to stay in the country, had an important impact on how the war in Ukraine was framed in both national and international media. His message was meant for not only the Ukrainian citizens but also foreign leaders, NATO, as well as the Kremlin and the Russian people, illustrating the complexity of the many receivers in large crisis, as encapsulated by the rhetorical arena (Frandsen & Johansen, 2010).

As the war progressed, President Zelensky invited himself to talk to NATO, the UN, the U.S. Congress, and the parliament of the European Union, as well as several parliaments in Europe, Asia, and Australia. His live and virtual address to all these different receivers was clearly based on careful consideration and knowledge about the history, culture, and values possessed by the various audiences. When talking to NATO, he focused on how Ukraine "defend all our common values" and that "Russia does not intend to stop in Ukraine" (PresidentofUkraine, 2022c). In his address to the U.K. Parliament, he compared the Ukrainian fight against Russia with the British fight against the Nazis during World War II and reminded them of the Shakespearean question: "To be or not to be?" (PresidentofUkraine, 2022b), while in the German Bundestag he presented the war in Ukraine as a new wall – "Not the Berlin Wall, but in the middle of Europe, between freedom and slavery" (PresidentofUkraine, 2022a).

Zelensky received international support and standing ovation for his many speeches, but in his address to the Israeli Knesset, he also experienced the difficulties of talking to so many receivers at the same time – balancing their diverse views and opposing opinions. In his call for support from Israel, he took a clear position in the Israel-Palestine conflict: "We are in different countries and in completely different conditions. But the threat is the same: for both us and you – the total destruction of the people, state, culture. And even of the names: Ukraine, Israel" (PresidentofUkraine, 2022d) – at the same time distancing himself and losing support from Palestinians. However, the Israelis were not impressed by his comparison of the Russia's invasion to the Holocaust. "Ukrainians have made their choice. 80 years ago. They rescued Jews. [...] People of Israel, now you have such a choice" (PresidentofUkraine, 2022d), Zelensky said, without accepting the part Ukraine played in the Nazi genocide. Zelensky's lacking consideration of historical and geographical context led him eventually to lose the support of both Israelis and Palestinians.

The Successes of Crisis Communication

However, the majority of research on Zelensky's war addresses has focused on his successful crisis communication due to the way he adjusted his communication to each target audience. An analysis of video addresses by Zelensky found that the President's speeches to his nation followed a common pattern of first a summary of recent diplomacy events and results, then addresses to specific groups within the country and last, a call to action. He used pronouns like "we" and "our," but also "I," to demonstrate authority and assume responsibility, and he used a war discourse to underline the seriousness and urgency of the situation (Rybalchenko, 2022, p. 91).

In his addresses to European and Western leaders, he focused on four key points: he stressed that Europe was not providing enough support to Ukraine (1), he emphasized that Ukraine was an integrated part of Europe (2), he called for immediate action from the European countries (3), and he urged for international solidary and protection of Ukraine's sovereignty (4) (Rybalchenko, 2022, p. 77). All of the analyzed addresses to foreign partners belonged to the genre of political speech to a parliament (Rybalchenko, 2022, p. 80), and the author argues that Zelensky successfully made use of hand-tailored metaphors and references to historical figures for each country, as well as emotional appeals to sway the different audiences (Rybalchenko, 2022, pp. 80–85).

The concept of "imagefare,", as opposed to warfare, has also been launched in connection with the Ukraine war (Yarchi, 2022). Imagefare is defined as follows:

> The use, or misuse, of images as a guiding principle or a substitute for traditional military means to achieve political objectives. The actors involved in the conflict attempt to pro-mote their preferred messages through the media in an attempt to gain the public's support and, ultimately, achieve their political goals (Yarchi, 2022, p. 5).

According to the latter study, the image war strategy of Ukraine was aimed at three different target audiences: the Russian people, the international community, and the Ukrainian people. Zelensky addressed the Russian people directly in many of his speeches. The Ukrainian Ministry of Defence also reached out to mothers of captured Russian soldiers, in a way to influence the Russian perception of the war. The international community was told that the Russian aggression posed a threat to Europe as a whole, while the domestic audience was praised for their bravery and steadfastness (Yarchi, 2022). This brings us to the images and narratives presented by Zelensky.

The Images and Narratives of Crisis Communication

Zelensky used his communication skills as a weapon of war. A study of the speeches made by Zelensky during the first 50 days of war shows how the Ukraine narrative was made dominant in the international media – limiting the pro-Russian agenda. The successful communication strategies of Zelensky also had a political effect when it came to the increased sanctions against Russia, as well as the number of weapons supplied to the Ukraine; "Zelens'kyi became one of the best-known and most respected politicians globally" (Dyczok & Chung, 2022, p. 156).

The notion of heroic leadership and how Zelensky managed to portray himself as a hero-leader during the Ukraine war has also been highlighted. Before the war, Zelensky was seen as a celebrity populist, using his public role and fame as an actor to gain political power and influence, but with the Russian invasion "Zelensky accepted the challenge of history and overnight rebuild his authority and united the nation in a huge unexpected scale of resistance by embracing a leadership style that has been globally recognised as heroic" (Zachara-Szymańska, 2023, p. 199).

In line with the rhetorical arena model, it has been argued that Zelensky made use of both message and media "as a tool of war, along with tanks, drones and rockets" (Zachara-Szymańska, 2023, p. 199). Zelensky's message was grounded in the mythical story of David versus Goliath and Ukraine taking the responsibility for European safety. When it came to media, Zelensky relied on real-time addresses to political leaders, as well as ordinary people. According to *The Economist*, the invasion of Ukraine was not the first social media war, but it was the most viral (The Economist in Zachara-Szymańska, 2023, p. 201).

Crisis Communication on Instagram

In addition to Zelensky's war addresses to parliaments around the world, all posted on his official website, he utilized social media in his communication to internal and external publics – through Facebook, YouTube, Instagram, Telegram, and Twitter. His use of social media to communicate in war times was not a new feature of the president's communication strategy. Social media presence and dialogue with Ukrainian voters was a central part of his 2019 election campaign. He prioritized the digital sphere over traditional media and actively involved voters in the creation of his political program (Plazas-Olmedo & López-Rabadán, 2023). His background as an actor, playing the part of an ordinary man becoming president, helped his campaign message of being the outsider in a time of growing distrust in traditional Ukraine politicians. He promised to put an end to corruption and set the country free from oligarchs (Rybalchenko, 2022). It was a natural choice for the president to continue and even expand his communication in social media after the Russian invasion.

An analysis of videos posted on Instagram found that "political spectacularization, or politainment, was a clearly identifiable style in the publications of President Zelensky during the Russian-Ukrainian war" (Plazas-Olmedo & López-Rabadán, 2023, p. 197). The spectacularization of his Instagram communication was found in his figure being present in most of the videos, as well as the staged spontaneity and amateurism of the Instagram posts. He held his own mobile phone as he recorded the messages, often in the streets of Kyiv, without filters and with reduced image quality. At the same time, and in contrast to the amateur video recordings, he added subtitles "to carry the message to a global audience beyond Ukraine's borders" (Plazas-Olmedo & López-Rabadán, 2023, p. 199).

Another study of Zelensky's Instagram communication during the first 40 days of crisis shows that the president optimized the social network's resources and displaced authentic leadership through his creation of original content adapted to Instagram, his use of military clothes, and his video selfies from the attacked cities of Ukraine. Compared to the leadership approach of other European leaders during the COVID-19 crisis summarized as "do as I say but not as I do," Zelensky managed to implement a successful communication strategy during the Ukraine war described as "do as I do" (Sánchez-Castillo et al., 2023, p. 620).

Crisis Communication on Twitter/X

An analysis of the frames Zelensky employed on Twitter (rebranded to X in July 2023) found that the most prevalent ones related to dialogue, solidarity, Russian aggression, countermeasure, and defense (Nisch, 2023). There was also a consistently positive sentiment in most of the frames, even in those related to Russian aggression and suffering. A conclusion from this study was that the "prominence of certain frames and the consistently positive sentiment throughout the observation period reflected the strategic communication employed by Zelensky in fostering hope, solidarity and resilience during a crisis" (Nisch, 2023, p. 12).

Not only Zelensky but also NATO and other European public institutions like the European Union and OSCE used Twitter to communicate during the crisis in Ukraine (Tasente, 2023).

The Twitter posts included direct statements, condemnations of the crisis in Ukraine, and expressions of concern about the war violence. According to Tasente (2023), the European institutions implemented effective communication strategies and their Twitter messages were timely and accurate. The use of images and videos, hashtags, and retweets of articles from reliable sources were an important part of their successful Twitter communication; "These tactics ensured that their messages were heard and amplified across the platform, enabling them to convey the information to a wide audience" (Tasente, 2023, p. 205).

However, Zelensky also experienced the challenge of massive creation and distribution of crisis misinformation in social media (Jin et al., 2022) during the first days of the Ukraine war. One of these online stories, directly affecting the trustworthiness of Zelensky, was a claim that he had fled Ukraine shortly after the Russian invasion (VoxCheckTeam, 2022). Zelensky responded to the misinformation by giving interviews, holding press conferences, shooting, and publishing videos from Kyiv. In the war's first days he filmed himself and his defense and communication team in the streets of Kyiv, saying: "Good evening, everyone. Faction leader is here. Head of the Presidential Office is here. Prime Minister Shmyhal is here. Podolyak is here. The President is here. Our troops are here. Citizens are here. All of us are here protecting our independence, our country, and it will continue to be this way" (Zelensky, 2022).

Conclusion

The aim of this chapter was to analyze how legacy media and social media might fuel an international political crisis, but also how political leaders can utilize such media to manage a crisis. We have made use of the rhetorical arena model (Johansen & Frandsen, 2007) and integrated other research focusing more specifically on social media use in crisis. The rhetorical arena model addresses the challenges, but also the possible successes when talking to many different receivers at the same time – balancing their diverse views and opposing opinions. The model, as such, works as a useful heuristic to grasp this type of complicated international crisis, but can arguably also be used to analyze risk communication addressing multiple actors and forms of mediation.

The micro perspective of the rhetorical arena includes four central parameters: context, media, genre, and text (Frandsen & Johansen, 2010; Johansen & Frandsen, 2007). The context of crisis communication in an ongoing war is complex and hard to navigate. Following the Russian invasion, Zelensky had the option to accept the American offer of transport to a safe location, but he refused to leave Ukraine. With his war addresses from secret locations to all parliaments of the world, his mobile phone recorded messages from the streets of Kyiv, and later, his invitations to foreign leaders to visit his war-torn country offered a physical and symbolic context strengthening his message of sovereignty, resistance, and need for support.

In our analysis of the media and genre of Zelensky's crisis communication, we see that his presence and daily dialogue to this day, with international leaders and Ukraine citizens, have proven to be successful in gaining support and fostering hope, solidarity, and resilience during the crisis. Because of his prior use, network of followers and knowledge about how to communicate in social media, it was natural for Zelensky to continue to share his messages through channels like Facebook, YouTube, Instagram, Telegram, and Twitter. In the way he dressed and held his own mobile phone as he talked to his people, he created an authentic social media persona, but also adding subtitles to carry the messages to an international audience. Legacy media also turned to social media for information and helped carry the president's message even further – often with more credibility. However, social media also pose a challenge for crisis communication in a political crisis. Further research should be conducted to provide a better understanding of crisis misinformation in social media, as we also could see happening in the Ukraine war.

Last, the text parameter of crisis communication, with a focus on the crisis narratives of the Ukraine war, as well as the narratives told by Zelensky himself. Studies show how the Ukraine President from the beginning was presented as a hero-leader – a former actor stepping up, taking charge, and accepting responsibility from the very beginning of the crisis. In the way he demonstrated personal calm and strength, Zelensky became a hero (Seeger & Sellnow, 2016, p. 120) in this war narrative. Zelensky himself drew on narratives in his multiple war addresses to parliaments and Western leaders. The different narratives told were based on careful consideration and knowledge about the history, culture, and values possessed by the various audiences. Part of Zelensky's success was based on his ability to tie the narrative of Ukraine together with the history of each nation he addressed, but when talking to the Israeli Knesset, he also experienced the challenge of telling the same story to a very divided audience.

In conclusion, we see how crisis communication is an essential part of political communication. While the ongoing war in Ukraine is neither a typical nor ordinary crisis, it still serves as a case to test, elaborate, and add to the rhetorical arena model in analyzing political crisis communication in an international context. Our analysis provides a larger understanding of the complexities of political crisis communication, with the multiple actors involved and their diverse views and opposing opinions, but also the opportunities for strategic social media use and framing the narrative of the crisis.

In our case of Zelensky's many war addresses and use of social media, we also recognize how the hybrid media system (Chadwick, 2017) and mediatization play out in an international political crisis. Political authorities, even in crisis, must adjust to the logic of the media institution (Hjarvard, 2008; Lundby, 2014), and the way political leaders perform is also judged by the media – bolstering their authority or leading to their failure (Hajer, 2009). This constitutes a new situation for political crisis communicators in the media age. Further research needs to take into account the political authorities' ability to utilize social media and collaborate with legacy media for effective crisis communication.

References

AlJazeera (December 17, 2020). *What is the Arab Spring, and how did it start?* https://www.aljazeera.com/news/2020/12/17/what-is-the-arab-spring-and-how-did-it-start

APNews (2023). *Gaza receives largest aid shipment so far as deaths top 8,000 and Israel widens military offensive.* Retrieved October 30 from https://apnews.com/article/israel-hamas-war-news-10-29-2023-de1a7d660ba2f6d80b3d7aeaae5bb0f3

Auer, C. (2016). Conceptualizing political crisis and the role of public diplomacy in crisis communication research. In A. Schwarz, M. W. Seeger, & C. Auer, Eds., *The Handbook of International Crisis Communication Research* (pp. 119–132). https://doi.org/https://doi.org/10.1002/9781118516812.ch12

Austin, L., Fisher Liu, B., & Jin, Y. (2012). How audiences seek out crisis information: Exploring the social-mediated crisis communication model. *Journal of Applied Communication Research, 40*(2), 188–207. https://doi.org/10.1080/00909882.2012.654498

Austin, L. L., & Jin, Y. (2018). *Social Media and Crisis Communication.* Routledge.

BBC (February 24, 2021,). *Jamal Khashoggi: All you need to know about Saudi journalist's death.* https://www.bbc.com/news/world-europe-45812399

BBC (November 2, 2023). *What is happening in Israel and Gaza, and what is Hamas?* https://www.bbc.com/news/world-middle-east-67039975

Benoit, W. L. (2015). *Accounts, Excuses, and Apologies: Image Repair Theory and Research.* SUNY Press.

Benoit, W. L., Gullifor, P., & Panici, D. A. (1991). President Reagan's defensive discourse on the Iran-Contra affair. *Communication Studies, 42*(3), 272–294. https://doi.org/10.1080/10510979109368342

Benoit, W. L., & Henson, J. R. (2009). President Bush's image repair discourse on Hurricane Katrina. *Public Relations Review, 35*(1), 40–46. https://doi.org/10.1016/j.pubrev.2008.09.022

Boin, A., Hart, P., & t., Stern, E., & Sundelius, B. (2017). *The Politics of Crisis Management: Public Leadership Under Pressure* (2nd ed.). Cambridge University Press.

Bostdorff, D. M. (2022). US Presidents and crisis communication. In W. T. Coombs, & S. J. Holladay, Eds., *The Handbook of Crisis Communication* (pp. 247–260). https://doi.org/https://doi.org/10.1002/9781119678953.ch17

Chadwick, A. (2017). *The Hybrid Media System: Politics and Power* (2nd ed.). Oxford University Press.

Coombs, W. T. (2012). *Ongoing Crisis Communication: Planning, Managing, and Responding* (3rd ed.). Sage.

Coombs, W. T. (2019). Political public relations and crisis communication: A public relations perspective. In J. Strömbäck, & S. Kiousis, Eds., *Political Public Relations: Principles and Applications* (2nd ed.). Routledge.

Duignan, B. (November 4, 2023). *January 6 U.S. Capitol attack.* https://www.britannica.com/event/January-6-U-S-Capitol-attack

Dyczok, M., & Chung, Y. (2022). Zelens′kyi uses his communication skills as a weapon of war. *Canadian Slavonic Papers, 64*(2–3), 146–161. https://doi.org/10.1080/00085006.2022.2106699

Edwards, C. (July 13, 2023). What Zelensky wanted from NATO – And what he got. *CNN.* https://edition.cnn.com/2023/07/13/europe/zelensky-nato-vilnius-explainer-intl/index.html

Frandsen, F., & Johansen, W. (2010). Crisis communication, complexity, and the cartoon affair: A case study. In W. T. Coombs, & S. J. Holladay, Eds., *The Handbook of Crisis Communication* (pp. 425–448). https://doi.org/https://doi.org/10.1002/9781444314885.ch21

Frandsen, F., & Johansen, W. (2020). Reframing the field: Public crisis management, political crisis management, and corporate crisis management. In F. Finn, & J. Winni, Eds., *Crisis Communication* (pp. 59–102). De Gruyter Mouton. https://doi.org/doi:10.1515/9783110554236-003

Frandsen, F., & Johansen, W. (2022). Rhetorical arena theory. W. Timothy Coombs, Sherry J. Holladay In *The Handbook of Crisis Communication* (pp. 169–181). https://doi.org/https://doi.org/10.1002/9781119678953.ch12

Freberg, K., & Palenchar, M. J. (2013). Convergence of digital negotiation and risk challenges: Strategic implications of social media for risk and crisis communications. In *Social Media and Strategic Communications* (pp. 83–100). Springer.

Hajer, M. A. (2009). *Authoritative Governance: Policy-Making in the Age of Mediatization.* Oxford University Press.

Millar, D.P., & Heath, R.L. (Eds.) (2003). Telling a story: A narrative approach to communication during crisis. *Responding to Crisis: A Rhetorical Approach to Crisis Communication* 1 (pp. 167–187). Routledge https://doi.org/10.4324/9781410609496

Hervik, P. (2012). *The Danish Muhammad cartoon conflict.* https://www.diva-portal.org/smash/get/diva2:1404786/FULLTEXT01.pdf

Hjarvard, S. (2008). The mediatization of society: A theory of the media as agents of social and cultural change. *Nordicom Review, 29*(2), 102–131. https://doi.org/10.1515/nor-2017-0181

Jin, Y., Austin, L., & Liu, B. F. (2022). Social-mediated crisis communication research. In W. T. Coombs, & S. J. Holladay, Eds., *The Handbook of Crisis Communication* (pp. 151–167). https://doi.org/https://doi.org/10.1002/9781119678953.ch11

Johansen, W., & Frandsen, F. (2007). *Krisekommunikation: når virksomhedens image og omdømme er truet.* Samfundslitteratur.

KyivIndependent (February 24, 2022). *Putin declares war on Ukraine.* https://kyivindependent.com/putin-declares-war-on-ukraine/

Lundby, K. (2014). *Mediatization of Communication* (Vol. 21). Germany: De Gruyter. https://doi.org/10.1515/9783110272215

Mister, S. M. (1986). Reagan's challenger tribute: Combining generic constraints and situational demands. *Central States Speech Journal, 37*(3), 158–165. https://doi.org/10.1080/10510978609368215

Nisch, S. (2023). Invasion of Ukraine: Frames and sentiments in Zelensky's Twitter communication. *Journal of Contemporary European Studies*, 1–15. https://doi.org/10.1080/14782804.2023.2198691

Picheta, R. (January 9, 2023). *The violent attack on Brazil's government was months in the making. Here's what you need to know.* https://edition.cnn.com/2023/01/09/americas/brazil-congress-attack-explained-intl/index.html

Plazas-Olmedo, M., & López-Rabadán, P. (2023). Selfies and Speeches of a President at War: Volodymyr Zelensky's Strategy of Spectacularization on Instagram [celebritization; Instagram; politainment; political communication; pop politics; social media; spectacularization; Ukraine; war; Zelensky]. *2023. Media and Communication*, *11*(2), 15. https://doi.org/10.17645/mac.v11i2.6366

PresidentofUkraine (March 17, 2022a). *Address by President of Ukraine Volodymyr Zelenskyy to the Bundestag*. https://www.president.gov.ua/en/news/promova-prezidenta-ukrayini-volodimira-zelenskogo-u-bundesta-73621

PresidentofUkraine (March 8, 2022b). *Address by the President of Ukraine to the Parliament of the United Kingdom*. https://www.president.gov.ua/en/news/zvernennya-prezidenta-ukrayini-volodimira-zelenskogo-do-parl-73441

PresidentofUkraine (March 24, 2022c). *Speech by President of Ukraine Volodymyr Zelenskyy at the NATO Summit*.https://www.president.gov.ua/en/news/vistup-prezidenta-ukrayini-volodimira-zelenskogo-na-samiti-n-73785

PresidentofUkraine (March 20, 2022d). *Speech by President of Ukraine Volodymyr Zelenskyy in the Knesset*. https://www.president.gov.ua/en/news/promova-prezidenta-ukrayini-volodimira-zelenskogo-v-kneseti-73701

Putin, V. (December 23, 2022a). *For first known time in public, Putin calls fighting in Ukraine a 'war'. CNN*. https://edition.cnn.com/2022/12/22/europe/putin-uses-word-war-fighting-ukraine-russia-intl-hnk/index.html

Putin, V. (February 24, 2022b). *Putin orders 'demilitarisation and denazification of Ukraine', demands Ukrainian forces surrender*. Retrieved February 24 from https://www.youtube.com/watch?v=5jSMj-lLdeo

Rosenthal, U., Charles, M. T., Hart, P., & t. (1989). *Coping with Crises: The Management of Disasters, Riots, and Terrorism*. Springfield, Ill., U.S.A: C.C. Thomas.

Rybalchenko, O. (2022). *"I need ammunition, not a ride": Political Discourse Analysis of Zelenskyy's war addresses to the Ukrainian and international community* Ca'Foscari University of Venice]. http://dspace.unive.it/bitstream/handle/10579/23324/997213-1271335.pdf?sequence=2

Salomonsen, H. H., & Hart, P. T. (2020). Communicating and managing crisis in the world of politics. In F. Frandsen, & W. Johansen, Eds., *Crisis Communication* (pp. 439–460). https://doi.org/doi:10.1515/9783110554236-003

Sánchez-Castillo, S., Galán-Cubillo, E., & Drylie-Carey, L. (2023). Unmuting leadership: The impact of Zelensky's social media strategy at the inset of the Ukrainian War. *Journal of Risk Research*, *26*(6), 610–624. https://doi.org/10.1080/13669877.2023.2194900

Seeger, M. W., & Sellnow, T. L. (2016). *Narratives of Crisis: Telling Stories of Ruin and Renewal*. Stanford Business Books.

Singh, K. (September 19, 2023). *Hardeep Singh Nijjar death: A timeline of recent India-Canada tensions*. https://www.reuters.com/world/canada-probe-indias-role-sikh-separatists-murder-strains-ties-further-2023-09-18/

Tasente, T. (2023). Online communication of European public institutions and NATO during the crisis in Ukraine (February 24, 2022–December 24, 2022). *Technium Social Sciences Journal*, *39*(1), 195–206. https://ideas.repec.org/a/tec/journl/v39y2023i1p195-206.html

Treisman, R. (February 28, 2022). *Ukraine wants to join the EU. Here's how that would work*. https://www.npr.org/2022/02/28/1083528087/ukraine-european-union

UkrEmbLondon (February 26, 2022). *The fight is here; I need ammunition, not a ride*. Retrieved February 26 from https://twitter.com/UkrEmbLondon/status/1497506134692970499?lang=nb

UnitedNations (2023). *Gaza crisis: General Assembly adopts resolution calling for 'humanitarian truce', civilian protection*. Retrieved October 27 from https://news.un.org/en/story/2023/10/1142932

VoxCheckTeam (March 14; 2022). FAKE: Volodymyr Zelensky fled Ukraine after russian invasion. *Vox Ukraine*. Retrieved March 14 from https://voxukraine.org/en/fake-volodymyr-zelensky-fled-ukraine-after-russian-invasion

Yarchi, M. (2022). The image war as a significant fighting arena – Evidence from the Ukrainian Battle over perceptions during the 2022 Russian invasion. *Studies in Conflict & Terrorism*, 1–13. https://doi.org/10.1080/1057610X.2022.2066525

Zachara-Szymańska, M. (2023). The return of the hero-leader? Volodymyr Zelensky's international image and the global response to Russia's invasion of Ukraine. *Leadership*, *19*(3), 196–209. https://doi.org/10.1177/17427150231159824

Zelensky, V. (February 25, 2022). Volodymyr Zelensky takes to the streets to rally people against Russian invaders. *The Telegraph*. Retrieved February 25 from https://www.youtube.com/watch?v=0En27IsHaL0

Author's Bio

Dr. Elin Strand Larsen is an associate professor at the Department of Computer Science and Communication at Østfold University College. She earned her PhD in media and journalism from the University of Oslo with a dissertation, titled *When women have to apologize … Mediated Scandals, Female Politicians and Rhetorical Defence Strategies* (2014). She is co-head of the research group Area*S* and co-editor of multiple anthologies on concepts like borders, alliances and, trust in the digital society. Her research interests include fake news and fact-checking, political scandals, female politicians, crisis communication, and apologia.

Dr. Øyvind Ihlen is professor at the Department of Media and Communication, University of Oslo and co-director of POLKOM – Centre for the Study of Political Communication. Ihlen has over 160 publications, including *Public Relations and Social Theory: Key Figures and Concepts* (2009, 2nd expanded edition 2018), the award-winning edited *Handbook of Communication and Corporate Social Responsibility* (2011), and *Handbook of Organizational Rhetoric* (2018). In the period 2019–2023, he headed a 1.2 million Euro project on COVID-19, funded by the Norwegian Research Council.

Part IV

The Role of Audiences, Citizens, and Victims in International Crises and Risks

16

War, Media, and Public Opinion

A Battle for Hearts and Minds

Michel M. Haigh
School of Journalism and Mass Communication, Texas State University, San Marcos, TX, USA

Introduction

Crisis is a word people use to characterize situations that are "extraordinary, volatile, and potentially far-reaching in their negative implications" and people rely on and are influenced by the mass media to make sense of it (Boin & 't Hart, 2007, p. 53). Crisis is often applied to "situations that are unwanted, unexpected, unprecedented, and almost unmanageable and that cause widespread disbelief and uncertainty" (Boin, 2004, p. 167). When people examine a crisis, they often look at how the government and international partners handle the situation (Boin, 2004). Boin and 't Hart (2007) state that a crisis occurs when a nation recognizes a threat (e.g., the Cuban Missile Crisis). One of the most common crises/threats facing countries today is war. As of 2023, there are more than 70 worldwide outbreaks of crisis (Wars in the World, 2025).

The relationship between the press and the military can be turbulent. The public relies on the media to ask the tough questions needed to gain information about war in order to make up its mind about war (Aday et al., 2005). During times of war, not only is the battle being fought on the actual battlefield, but it is also being fought through the war of information. Governments, the military, the media, and enemies of the state rely on mediated forms of communication to influence public support for war. The Crimean War starting in 1853 was the first war to be systematically photographed. During the World War 1, the British War Office relied on cinema to influence public support for war by mixing documentary footage with staged reenactments to produce a film. The Vietnam War was one of the first times the public could see combat footage on their nightly news on a regular basis. The role of social media was well documented during the Arab Spring uprisings (von Tunzelmann, 2022). It is not clear what drives public support for war, but time does provide some insights.

For example, twenty years after the United States invaded Iraq, it is easy to see the impact false information had on influencing the public to support the war (Doherty & Kiley, 2023). The Bush administration blamed the media for eroding public support of the Iraq War. Then President George W. Bush stated the stories about Iraq were negative and did not depict progress in Iraq, which led to a decline in public support (Cloud, 2005). The role of social media was in its infancy at that time. However, in February 2022 when Russia invaded the Ukraine,

The Handbook of International Crisis and Risk Communication Research, Second Edition.
Edited by Andreas Schwarz, Matthew W. Seeger, and Sora Kim.

social media provided an unfiltered view of what was taking place (von Tunzelmann, 2022). The Global Attitudes Survey conducted in spring 2022 found 90% of adults living in 18 different countries had little public support for Russia or Vladimir Putin after the invasion of Ukraine. Attitudes toward Putin and Russia were negative before the war, but there was a double-digit decline after the invasion (Gramlich, 2023).

This chapter examines several models researchers use to explain public support for war. One model indicates casualties drive public support for war (Mueller, 1971, 1973, 1994), another model shows support for war is determined on beliefs about the rightness or wrongness of going to war and the ability to win the battle (Feaver & Gelpi, 2004; Gelpi et al., 2005–2006), the rhetoric of political elites, and how the story is framed in the media (Aday, 2010; Feaver & Gelpi, 2004; Gelpi et al., 2005–2006). There is a gap between a government and its citizens (Boin, 2004). The government needs to bridge the "gap," especially in times of war. "Stakeholders [citizens] differ in the assumptions they make about the world. When these differences surface, they provide us with a very important resource to use in defining problems," (Mitroff et al., 2004, p. 175). In times of war, governments in countries with a free press system need citizens to show support for military actions because the threat may not be eminent (e.g., President George W. Bush and weapons of mass destruction in Iraq). In the end, winning the hearts and minds of the public is what is important in international crisis, and this is usually determined by public opinion.

Casualties and Public Opinion

The literature concerning public opinion and war is considerable (Feaver & Gelpi, 2004). A significant topic of this literature concerns the impact of casualties in forming public opinion toward war. Feaver and Gelpi (2004) state politicians and military leaders believe "the US public is especially casualty phobic (meaning that public support for a mission will evaporate at the first sign of casualties) is a myth" (p. 7). However, they conclude the public accepts casualties if death is necessary to accomplish a mission being pushed by political leaders (Feaver & Gelpi, 2004; Larson, 1996). Schwarz (1994) argues the public supports casualties at the start of a conflict because they want to rally around the flag and support the mission – much like the press does at the beginning of a conflict.

Human costs of war are known as the following: casualty sensitivity, casualty aversion, casualty shyness, casualty tolerance, and casualty phobia (Feaver & Gelpi, 2004). Feaver and Gelpi (2004) state casualty sensitivity and casualty tolerance refer to public tolerance of casualties in order to achieve a positive end result. Individuals have a casualty limit, and they might express different levels of casualty sensitivity for different military engagements (Feaver & Gelpi, 2004). They reserve the term "casualty aversion" to refer to policies "political leaders and the military implement in order to lower casualties, perhaps in response to a strong casualty sensitivity or even a casualty phobia" (Feaver & Gelpi, 2004, p. 99).

Casualty shyness has a great deal to do with how the public interprets events when confronted with images of war, and how the policymakers and political pundits frame them (Dauber, 2001). It is assumed public opinion is influenced by the visual images of combat operations (Gartner & Segura, 1998; Perlmutter, 1999). For example, during World War II, President Franklin Roosevelt imposed a ban on such photos but later relented saying the photos could galvanize support for the war (Perlmutter, 1999). During the Gulf War, President George H. W. Bush banned photos showing the remains of dead soldiers arriving at Dover Air Force Base. President Bill Clinton lifted the ban only to have it reinstated by President George W. Bush (Milbank, 2003).

President Barack Obama and Secretary of Defense Robert Gates lifted the ban in favor of having the families decide on a case-by-case basis if the photos should be taken (National

Press Photographers Association, 2009). This is known as the "Dover test." Senator John Glenn asked, "Will public opinion and will support in the Congress still be there when the body bags or coffins start coming back through Dover, Delaware?" (Penrod, 2004, p. 7). In the case of the Iraq War, President George W. Bush did not pass the Dover test. "President Bush's exceptional support following 9/11 has turned into near-record levels of disapproval… The standard answer asserts that this unprecedented drop is the result of the Iraq War and its American casualties" (Gartner, 2008a, p. 95). Now that casualty sensitivity, casualty aversion, casualty shyness, and casualty tolerance have been defined and discussed, several theories examining the influence of casualties on public support for war are examined.

Mueller's Hypothesis – Log of Cumulative Casualties

The casualty intolerance hypothesis states the public will not support the use of military force if the conflict results in considerable American casualties (Burk, 1999). This hypothesis suggests Americans do not want to get involved in international conflicts when people die. Burk (1999) developed this idea based on Mueller's (1971, 1973) research stating public support for war is inversely related to cumulative casualties. Mueller (1971) compared the support for the Korean and Vietnam Wars to World War II. He stated Vietnam and Korea provided a good comparison because:

> "The enemy is less obviously 'evil,' progress in battle is more difficult to measure and comprehend, the American entrance into the war is less easily rationalized, and the end of the war is more likely to prove puzzling and unsatisfying" (p. 385).

Mueller (1971) concluded, "*Americans, in aggregate, reacted in similar ways to the two wars* … they are sensitive to relatively small losses in the early stages, but only to large losses in later stages" (emphasis original, p. 367). Both wars had similar amounts of public support at the start and support declined as a function of American casualties (Mueller, 1971). Support for the Vietnam War finally declined past the point of support for the Korean War, but this was because the war lasted longer and the number of casualties increased. Mueller (1994) finds support for a similar public reaction to casualties in the Gulf War.

Mueller (2005) states only in three wars – Vietnam, Korea, and Iraq – has the US military suffered more than 300 deaths during sustained ground combat. In all three wars, "public opinion became a key factor … as casualties mount, support decreases. Broad enthusiasm at the outset invariably erodes" (p. 44). Support for the Iraq War declined at quicker rates than it did for either the Vietnam or Korean Wars (Mueller, 2005). He argues the "Dover Test" was the reason the Bush administration and the military thought support for the Iraq War declined. Both parties tried "to keep Americans from seeing pictures of body bags or flag-draped coffins" in order to stop the decline in public support for the war (Mueller, 2005, p. 46). Progress in Iraq was shown through the Iraqi elections and the capture of Saddam Hussein. These two events increased support, briefly, for the Iraq War, but then support declined back to the level it was before the positive event and continued its decline (Mueller, 2005).

Mueller (2002a, b) argues the public pays little attention to international affairs and employs a cost-benefit analysis when examining foreign affairs. Americans support the loss of lives when "the enemy was a threat like international communism or the country that bombed Pearl Harbor," but when American life is lost to "police small, distant, unthreatening … troubled countries," the public shows little support (Mueller, 2002a, p.160). After military intervention, there is a "rally around the flag effect" (Mueller, 1973) where the president's approval rating increases, but then the public focuses on what is going on at home, so foreign policy is not as important when evaluating the president's performance (Mueller, 2002a, b).

Public support is tied to military casualties. Mueller (1971, 1973, 1994) examined the total number of US deaths. However, a number of scholars argue the public does not know the total number of casualties at any one time, so it is better to examine marginal casualties when trying to predict public support for war.

National, Local, and Marginal Casualties

The public tries to assess if the country will win the war and then performs a cost-benefit analysis of the war (Gartner, 1997). If there are reports of a large amount of casualties in a recent battle/event, this lowers individuals' estimates the victory outweighs the benefits of the loss of life. Research examining support for Vietnam found the log of national casualties and the loss of local military personnel influenced individuals' attitudes on war (Gartner et al., 1997).

In 1998, Scott Gartner and Gary Segura constructed their own theory about casualties and public opinion and commented on Mueller's (1971, 1973) hypothesis of the log of cumulative casualties and public opinion. Gartner and Segura (1998) stated, "we think that the level of recent, marginal casualties is critical in predicting the direction and magnitude of change in the level of opposition at home" (p. 279). Gartner and Segura (1998) argue the use of marginal casualties captures "effects of pivotal events and shocks and does not artificially homogenize different conflicts" (p. 279). "Marginal" is defined as those casualties above and beyond what is experienced in normal operations. It could be casualties resulting from a single catastrophic event or higher than the usual casualties suffered in an ordinary combat event. Their model includes marginal and cumulative casualties and controls for the length of conflict and change of administration. Marginal casualties accumulating at an increasing rate are critical in predicting the direction and magnitude of change in the level of opposition at home (Gartner & Segura, 1998).

Gartner and Segura (1998) argue, "marginal casualties are a better predictor of opposition during periods of escalation or continuous fighting, but cumulative casualties are more likely to serve that purpose during periods of de-escalation" (p. 286). They found the use of cumulative casualties was a better predictor of support for the Korean War because it was a war of de-escalation and the number of marginal casualties declined. When compared to Vietnam, the use of marginal casualties was a better predictor of support for the war when compared to using cumulative casualty numbers like Mueller (1973) did. Marginal casualties work better because there were more events. Gartner and Segura (1998) conclude, "After the rally effect in the opening days of a conflict, the events and costs of a war invariably lead to a decline in support" (p. 296). Larson's (1996) study of Panama, Somalia, and the Gulf War concluded "the log of casualties seems to explain rather well the declining support for many other operations" (p. 8).

Casualty trends are the rate of change of recent casualties (Gartner, 2008a), so one might compare the numbers across months. These trends influence individuals' attitudes and election results (Gartner & Segura, 2000; Gartner et al., 2004) and how individuals interpret future casualties (Gartner, 2008a). Gartner (2008a) conducted multiple experiments and found higher monthly casualty rates, increasing casualty trends, and an interaction between the two led to the decline of public support. Gartner (2008a) calls this the "rational expectations theory of casualties." Gartner (2008b) examined 9/11 and the Iraq War and found individuals who had a personal tie to a victim (military or civilian) were more likely to disapprove of President George W. Bush. Feaver and Gelpi (2004) expanded on this hypothesis and included the media in the battle for public support. They argue casualty numbers matter as well as how casualties are framed by the media and interpreted by the public.

Media, Casualties, and Public Opinion

Feaver and Gelpi (2004) consider communication as a moderator in their model for public support of war. "If policy makers can make the case that the operation is important, then we would expect the public to show a willingness to shoulder greater cost" (p. 146). If communication about the war "demonizes" the enemy, then support for the war increases (Feaver & Gelpi, 2004). The measures determining public support for war "come closer to the winning-the-hearts-and-minds idea that most experts (and Bush administration rhetoric) would identify as the critical factor" (Gelpi et al., 2005–2006, p. 44). The public relies on the media because they have no direct experience with military operations, so they form attitudes based on the information provided by the news media and politicians (Gelpi, 2010).

Casualty tolerance depends on the decision of going to war (was it the right one?) and the expectations about winning (Gelpi et al., 2005–2006). The American public cannot accurately state the cumulative casualty numbers so there must be more driving public support for war than Mueller's hypothesis (Berinsky & Druckman, 2007; Boettcher & Cobb, 2006). Support for the war depends on the frame of the story, political ideology, and attitudes, as well as individual attitudes about casualties of war (Boettcher & Cobb, 2006).

The media impact is exaggerated ("the CNN effect"). The CNN effect "essentially assumes people are so unimaginative that they react only when they see something visualized" (Mueller, 2002a, p. 156). For example, some blamed television images for the declining support for the Vietnam War. Vietnam was known as the television war because it was the first time the public saw the uncensored images of war. However, television images did not reduce support for the Vietnam War until casualty numbers surpassed those of the Korean War (Mueller, 1971).

Pfau et al. (2008) compared the impact of network television news reports of combat operations of the Iraq war (with and without graphic combat footage) on viewers. They found broadcast news stories showing visual footage of combat did not elicit greater emotional responses than the same story packaged as a "reader" (story without visuals). However, participants who viewed television news stories showing visual footage of combat had less pride in the US military than those watching a "reader." The visual footage of combat reduced viewers' support for military presence in Iraq (Pfau et al., 2008).

Similar results are found when examining print stories and photos of casualties. Pfau et al. (2006) examined print photographs of the Iraq War and how these photos may impact public support for the war. News stories showing a photograph plus caption elicited more negative emotions (e.g., puzzlement, anger, and sadness) than stories about casualties without a photo. They also found stories without photos and stories with a photo reduce readers' support for continued US military presence in Iraq.

Aday (2010) tried to parse out the impact media has on shaping public opinion about foreign affairs and war. He concluded the media have less influence on public support when they "report negative or controversial news than they do when they are parroting elite consensus and reflecting patriotic fervor" (p. 458).

Hansen, Haigh, and Pfau (2006) aligned public opinion polls about Iraq with a content analysis of media coverage. They found when the tone of the television news coverage is positive and the number of casualties increases, public support for the war declines less compared to when the television news coverage is negative in tone and the number of casualties increases. For every 250 US military casualties in Iraq, the tone of television news coverage was about 14% more positive, confirming Mueller's (1994) hypothesis the media tend to be cheerleaders and do not want to concentrate on the negatives of war (Hansen et al., 2006).

Support for the war erodes with positive coverage but at a slower rate than when the coverage is negative, supporting Feaver and Gelpi's (2004) theory. This effect was only found for television news and not for print news stories. Hansen, Haigh, and Pfau (2006) find when newspaper stories were more positive, the decline in support for the war lessens (significantly) compared to negative coverage. Newspaper readers have stronger attitudes about the war and are not as easily swayed by the news content (Wenmouth et al., 1982).

Social Media, Disinformation, and Public Support for War

The media landscape has changed with the evolution of social media and the Internet (Baum & Potter, 2019). Most of the traditional models of looking at public support for war relied on traditional news media. For example, the Vietnam War was one of the first wars to have nightly footage of combat coverage, but CNN changed how the public consumed broadcast news coverage of war during the Gulf War. Before cable news, individuals were getting their news from the same places and surveying the media to make up their minds. With the rise of cable news, media consumers no longer surveyed the media for information to make decisions, but rather relied on media that already supported their political viewpoints. The Internet led to even more fragmentation. Social media has followed the same pattern. Social media was supposed to bring people back together and put an end to the hyper-fragmentation because people would be exposed to varying points of view in their newsfeeds, but that has not been the case (Baum & Potter, 2019). Social media has led to an increase of disinformation. Baum and Potter (2019) state the Internet and social media broke the "gatekeeper" function found in traditional forms of media. Without the gatekeeper function, it is estimated 40% of the news shared on social media is untruthful (Ruby, 2023). Cadwalladr (2017) noted any topic can be weaponized. The story can start with the mainstream media and turned into something that turns into a "suicide bomb at the heart of our information system" (Cadwalladr, 2017).

Social media provides another avenue for the public, governments, and the military to garner public support for war. Social media has been a place for activists to share news, recruit, and organize (Specia, 2022).

> "Social media advances on earlier technologies by radically increasing the speed of information delivery and the size of its audience, and by empowering individuals to share their own versions of events – for better or worse," (von Tunzelmann, 2022, "para 10).

Bradshaw and Howard (2018) found in countries with an authoritarian government, online, highly organized disinformation propaganda campaigns were coming from the government (e.g., Vietnam, Russia, China, Iran, North Korea). In countries with a democratic government, the propaganda efforts were less formal and not as well organized and were run by political parties (e.g., Mexico, Poland, Taiwan, the United Kingdom, the United States). The Russian invasion of the Ukraine will provide a current case study of social media and war.

The Ukraine War: A Case Study

The Ukraine War serves as a good case study to examine the relationship between public opinion, the military, the press, and the political elite. Russia's war in Ukraine has been playing out online using propaganda, fake social media accounts, and manipulated videos and images (Bond, 2023). Social media is providing people all over the world a first-hand, real-time account of the war. Johnson (2022, para 2 and 3), states, "people in Ukraine are posting combat footage on Reddit for engagements that are still ongoing. . .a large-scale modern war will be live-streamed, minute by minute, battle by battle, death by death, to the world."

In 2014, Russia annexed Crimea, a part of the Ukraine. Masters (2023) noted Russia's aggression toward the Ukraine triggered the "greatest security crisis in Europe since the Cold war" (p. 2). Ukraine was the second-most populous and powerful of the fifteen Soviet republics when it severed ties in 1991. The country set a path that aligned more closely with Western institutions. It wanted to join the North Atlantic Treaty Organization (NATO). However, the country has two groups – one group wants to be aligned more closely with Europe, and the Russian-speaking community in the east wants to align with Russia (Masters, 2023). These internal struggles have been occurring since 1991. When Russia annexed Crimea in 2014, it was the first time since World War II a territory was annexed. There was no bloodshed. Russian military basically took over the Ukrainian military bases and key military facilities without any resistance (Berzins, 2020).

In February 2022, Russia invaded Ukraine. It is the "bloodiest conflict in Europe since World War II" (Masters, 2023). Those in the West see Russia's invasion as Putin's resentment toward NATO. Putin argues the United States and NATO promised not to expand the alliance to former Soviet countries. However, several former Soviet Baltic republics joined NATO in 2004 including Estonia, Latvia, and Lithuania. NATO then noted it planned on expanding to the Ukraine and Georgia (Masters, 2023). It is estimated more than 10,500 civilians have died in the war (Statista, 2024).

The war has led to one of the largest disinformation campaigns. When examining the pro-Russia narratives, tweets justifying the invasion justified Russia's invasion because of the NATO expansion. It portrayed the invasion as a reasonable and expected consequence. One narrative portrays NATO as an aggressor in the Ukraine War. This narrative claims NATO tried to install a new government in the Ukraine, another was NATO troops stationed in Eastern Europe were to provoke Russia. Finally, the narrative promoted a distrust in institutions and elites. The narrative tells people not to trust the media or international institutions because they work for NATO (Boucher et al., 2022). Some of the Russian disinformation campaigns show Ukraine's government officials as Satanists and terrorists (Bond, 2023).

Social media was not only being used to spread disinformation about the conflict; it was also used to provide real-time updates. Individuals could find footage of airstrikes, ground battles, and civilian casualties. Most of the information was not coming from traditional media sources. There were specific social media accounts devoted to analyzing Russian and Ukrainian military positions, the strength of units, and the front line (Johnson, 2022).

The use of social media and the presence of disinformation and propaganda have not swayed public support for the Russian invasion of the Ukraine. Ninety percent of adults living in 18 countries had little support for Russia invading Ukraine. Attitudes toward Putin and Russia were negative before the war, but there was a double-digit decline after the invasion (Gramlich, 2023). However, several public opinion polls in Russia indicate Russians still support the war in the Ukraine (Rogov, 2023). The Levada Center, Russia's independent pollster, found support for the war was between 74 and 76% from April to August 2022. It dropped slightly to 71–74% from September to December 2022. Public support is increasing around the one-year anniversary of the start of the war. However, The Chronicle, a new polling startup, only saw support for the war range from 59 to 66%. The Russian Field, another new polling group, found support ranged from 66 to 68%. The Levada Center conducts their polls face-to-face while The Chronicle and The Russian Field conduct their polls over the phone.

When reviewing who supports the war, those aged 18–45 who tend to rely on the Internet and social media are no longer showing as much support (Rustamova & Tovkaylo, 2022). Russia has gained support in Africa, Latin America, and southeast Asia using narratives that encourage a distrust of Western society. The support is shown when the countries abstain from voting on U.N. resolutions (Bond, 2023). As the war starts its second year, the messages may change. The "rally-around-the-flag" effect at the start of war (Gartner & Segura, 1998) may not occur as the war drags on. Also, the role of casualties in this war can influence public opinion. In the past, research has looked at the loss of military members – and the loss of civilians have been greater in this war.

Conclusion

It is important to understand the relationship between the military and the media because it impacts how the story is told and the information the public has to form attitudes about the war. Berinsky (2009) states scholars cannot ignore the impact of domestic politics in support for foreign policy during times of crisis. When political leaders differ in support for war, the public follows suit. There are many variables to consider when parsing out public support for war. Casualties, media frames, disinformation circulating on social media, information circulating on social media, and political rhetoric all impact public support for war.

References

Aday, S. (2010). Leading the charge: Media, elites, and the use of emotion in stimulating rally effects in wartime. *Journal of Communication*, *60*(3), 440–465. http://doi.org/10.1111/j.1460-2466.2010.01489.x

Aday, S., Livingston, S., & Herbert, M. (2005). Embedding the truth: A cross-cultural analysis of objectivity and television coverage of the Iraq War. *The Harvard International Journal of Press/Politics*, *10*(1), 3–21. http://doi.org/10.1177/1081180X05275727

Baum, M., & Potter, P. (2019). Media, public opinion, and foreign policy in the age of social media. *Journal of Politics*, *81*(2), 747–756. http://doi.org/10.1086/702233

Berinsky, A. J., & Druckman, J. N. (2007). The polls – review: Public opinion research and support for the Iraq War. *Public Opinion Quarterly*, *71*(1), 126–141. https://doi.org/10.1093/poq/nfl049

Berinsky, A. J. (2009). *In Time of War: Understanding American Public Opinion from World War II to Iraq*. Chicago: University of Chicago Press.

Berzins, J. (2020). The theory and practice of new generation warfare: The case of Ukraine and Syria. *The Journal of Slavic Military Studies*, *33*(3), 355–380. http://doi.org/10.1080/13518046.2020.1824109

Boettcher, W. Q., & Cobb, M. D. (2006). Echoes of Vietnam? Casualty framing and public perceptions of success and failure in Iraq. *Journal of Conflict Resolution*, *50*(6), 831–854. http://doi.org/10.1177/0022002706293665

Boin, A. (2004). Lessons from crisis research. In B. Dayton (ed.), *Managing crisis in the twenty-first century. International Studies Review*, *6*(1), 165–174.

Boin, A., & 't Hart., P (2007). The crisis approach. In H. Rodriguez, E. L. Quarantelli, & R. R. Dynes, Eds., *Handbook of Disaster Research* (pp. 42–54). New York.

Bond, S. (February 28, 2023). How Russia is losing – and winning – the information war in Ukraine. *National Public Radio*. Available at: https://www.npr.org/2023/02/28/1159712623/how-russia-is-losing-and-winning-the-information-war-in-ukraine (accessed April 1, 2023)

Boucher, J., Edwards, J., Kim, J., Badami, A., & Smith, H. (2022). Disinformation and Russia-Ukrainian war on Canadian social media. *The School of Public Policy Publications*, *15*(1). Available at: https://journalhosting.ucalgary.ca/index.php/sppp/article/view/75449

Bradshaw, S., & Howard, P. (2018). The global organization of social media disinformation campaigns. *Journal of International Affairs*, *71*(1.5), 23–32. https://www.jstor.org/stable/26508115

Burk, J. (1999). Public support for peacekeeping in Lebanon and Somalia: Assessing the casualties hypothesis. *Political Science Quarterly*, *114*(1), 53–78. http://doi.org/10.2307/2657991

Cadwalladr, C. (February 26, 2017). Robert Mercer: The big data billionaire waging war on mainstream media. *The Guardian*. Available at: https://www.theguardian.com/politics/2017/feb/26/robert-mercer-breitbart-war-on-media-steve-bannon-donald-trump-nigel-farage (accessed April 1, 2023)

Cloud, D. S. (December 6, 2005). Rumsfeld says the media focus too much on negatives in Iraq. *New York Times*, p. 10.

Dauber, C. (2001). Image as argument: The impact of Mogadishu on military intervention. *Armed Forces and Society*, *27*(2), 205–229. http://doi.org/10.1177/0095327X0102700203

Doherty, C., & Kiley, J. (March 14, 2023). Beliefs bolstered U.S. public support for war in Iraq. *Pew Research Center*. Available at: https://www.pewresearch.org/politics/2023/03/14/a-look-back-at-how-fear-and-false-beliefs-bolstered-u-s-public-support-for-war-in-iraq/ (accessed April 1, 2023)

Feaver, P. D., & Gelpi, C. (2004). *Choosing Your Battles: American Civil-Military Relations and the Use of Force*. Princeton University Press.

Gartner, S. S. (1997). *Strategic Assessment in War*. Yale University Press.

Gartner, S. S., & Segura, G. M. (1998). War, casualties, and public opinion. *The Journal of Conflict Resolution*, *42*(3), 278–300. http://doi.org/10.1177/0022002798042003004

Gartner, S. S. (2008a). The multiple effects of casualties on public support for war: An experimental approach. *American Political Science Review*, *102*(1), 95–106. http://doi.org/10.1017/S0003055408080027

Gartner, S. S. (2008b). Ties to the dead: Connections to Iraq War and 9/11 casualties and disapproval of the president. *American Sociological Review*, *73*(4), 690–695. http://doi.org/10.1177/000312240807300408

Gartner, S. S., & Segura, G. M. (2000). Race, casualties, and opinion in the Vietnam War. *The Journal of Politics*, *62*(1), 115–146. http://doi.org/10.1111/0022-3816.00006

Gartner, S. S., Segura, G. M., & Barratt, B. (2004). War casualties, policy positions, and the fate of legislators. *Political Research Quarterly*, *57*(3), 467–477. http://doi.org/10.1177/106591290405700311

Gartner, S. S., Segura, G. M., & Wilkening, M. (1997). All politics are local: Local losses and individual attitudes toward the Vietnam War. *Journal of Conflict Resolution*, *41*(5), 669–694. http://doi.org/10.1177/0022002797041005004

Gelpi, C. J. (2010). Performing on cue? The formation of public opinion toward war. *Journal of Conflict Resolution*, *54*(1), 88–16. http://doi.org/10.1177/0022002709352845

Gelpi, C. J., Feaver, P. D., & Reifler, J. (2005–2006). Success matters: Casualty sensitivity and the war in Iraq. *International Security*, *30*(3), 7–46. http://doi.org/10.1162/isec.2005.30.3.7

Gramlich, J. (February 23, 2023). What public opinion surveys found in the first year of the war in Ukraine. *Pew Research Center*. Available at: https://www.pewresearch.org/fact-tank/2023/02/23/what-public-opinion-surveys-found-in-the-first-year-of-the-war-in-ukraine/ (accessed April 1, 2023)

Hansen, G., Haigh, M. M., & Pfau, M. (2006). *Examining media coverage and casualty intolerance for post invasion Iraq*. Paper presented at the National Communication Association annual meeting in San Antonio, TX.

Johnson, D. (February 24, 2022). Ukraine could be the most documented war in human history. *Slate*. Available at: https://slate.com/technology/2022/02/ukraine-russia-livestream-google-maps.html (accessed April 1, 2023)

Larson, E. (1996). *Ends and means in the democratic conversation: Understanding the role of casualties in support for U.S. military operations*. Unpublished PhD dissertation, RAND Graduate School.

Masters, J. (February 14, 2023). *Ukraine: Conflict at the crossroads of Europe and Russia. Council on Foreign Relations*. Available at: https://www.cfr.org/backgrounder/ukraine-conflict-crossroads-europe-and-russia (accessed 22 January 2025).

Milbank, D. (October 21, 2003). Curtains order for media coverage of returning coffins. *The Washington Post*. Available at: https://www.washingtonpost.com/archive/politics/2003/10/21/curtains-ordered-for-media-coverage-of-returning-coffins/13375c81-187e-4f91-a565-2ce8f3bf3549/

Mitroff, I. I., Alpaslan, M. C., & Green, S. E. (2004). Crises as ill-structured messes. In B. Dayton (Ed.), *Managing crisis in the twenty-first century. International Studies Review*, *6*(1), 175–182.

Mueller, J. E. (1971). Trends in popular support for the Wars in Korea and Vietnam. *The American Political Science Review*, *65*(2), 358–375. http://www.jstor.org/stable/1954454

Mueller, J. (1973). *War, Presidents, and Public Opinion*. John Wiley & Sons.

Mueller, J. (1994). *Policy and Opinion in the Gulf War*. University of Chicago Press.

Mueller, J. (2002a). American foreign policy and public opinion in a new era: Eleven propositions. In B. Norrander, & C. Wilcox, Eds., *Understanding Public Opinion* (2nd ed., pp. 149–172). CQ Press.

Mueller, J. (2002b). Public support for military ventures abroad: Evidence from the polls. In J. N. Moore, & R. F. Turner, Eds., *The Real Lessons of the Vietnam War: Reflections Twenty-Five Years After the Fall of Saigon* (pp. 173–219). Carolina Academic Press.

Mueller, J. (2005). The Iraq syndrome. *Foreign Affairs*, *84*(6), 44–54. Retrieved from http://www.jstor.org/stable/20031775 (accessed December 9, 2015). http://doi.org/10.2307/20031775

National Press Photographers Association (February 26, 2009). https://nppa.org/news/946 (accessed November 19, 2014)

Penrod, G. (2004). Letting loose the images of war. *News Media & the Law*, *28*(3), 7–9.Summer.

Perlmutter, D. D. (1999). *Visions of War. Picturing Warfare from the Stone Age to the Cyberage*. New York. St. Martin's Press.

Pfau, M., Haigh, M. M., Fifrick, A., Holl, D., Tedesco, A., Cope, J., Nunnally, D., Schiess, A., Preston, D., Roszkowski, P., & Martin, M. (2006). The effects of print news photographs of the images of war. *Journalism and Mass Communication Quarterly*, *83*(1), 150–168. http://doi.org/10.1177/107769900608300110

Pfau, M., Haigh, M. M., Shannon, T., Tones, T., Mercurio, D., Williams, R., Binstok, B., Diaz, C., Dillard, C., Browne, M., Elder, C., Reed, S., Eggers, A., & Melendez, J. (2008). The influence of television depictions of the images of war. *Journal of Broadcasting & Electronic Media*, *52*(2), 303–322. http://doi.org/10.1080/08838150801992128

Rogov, K. (March 17, 2023). Having it both ways: Russians both support and oppose the war. *The Kennan Institute*. Available at: https://www.wilsoncenter.org/blog-post/having-it-both-ways-russians-both-support-and-oppose-war

Ruby, D. (February 15, 2023). 68+ Global fake news statistics for 2023. *Demandsage*. Available at: https://www.demandsage.com/fake-news-statistics/ (accessed April 1, 2023)

Rustamova, F., & Tovkaylo, M. (December 9, 2022). What secret Russian state polling tells us about support for the war. *The Moscow Times*. Available at: https://www.themoscowtimes.com/2022/12/06/what-secret-russian-state-polling-tells-us-about-support-for-the-war-a79596

Schwarz, B. (1994). *Casualties, Public Opinion, and U.S. Military Intervention: Implications for U.S. Regional Deterrence Strategies*. Santa Monica, CA: Rand.

Specia, M. (March 25, 2022). 'Like a weapon': Ukrainians use social media to stir resistance. *The New York Times*. Available at: https://www.nytimes.com/2022/03/25/world/europe/ukraine-war-social-media.html (accessed April 1, 2023)

Statista (2024). Russia-Ukraine war 2022-2024 – statistics & facts. Available at: https://www.statista.com/topics/9087/russia-ukraine-war-2022/#topicOverview (accessed 22 January 2025).

Wars in the World (2025). Available at: http://www.warsintheworld.com/ (accessed January 22, 2025).

von Tunzelmann, A. (April 25, 2022). The big idea: Can social media change the course of war? What we see online can reveal world effects, for good or ill. *The Guardian*. Available at: https://www.theguardian.com/books/2022/apr/25/the-big-idea-can-social-media-change-the-course-of-war (accessed April 1, 2023)

Wenmouth, W., Jr, Shapiro, M., & Cutbirth, C. (1982). *Political framing and agenda setting in the 1980 presidential campaign*. Paper presented at the International Communication Association.

Author Bio

Michel M. Haigh has been a professor at Texas State since July 2017. She served as the graduate program advisor/director until 2023, and teaches in the Public Relations program. She was a member of the ad/pr faculty at Penn State from 2006 to 2017 where she taught a variety of public relations courses.

Haigh earned her undergraduate degrees at South Dakota State University (ag journalism and speech communication). She earned a master's in agricultural education with an emphasis on agricultural communications at Texas Tech University. Haigh earned a Ph.D. in communication studies at the University of Oklahoma in 2006. She has co-authored more than 40 conference presentations, seven of which have been recognized with the "Top Paper" award. She has published more than 35 articles and book chapters. in journals such as *Journalism & Mass Communication Quarterly*, *Journal of Broadcasting & Electronic Media*, *Communication Monographs*, *Communication Research*, *Newspaper Research Journal*, and *Communication Quarterly*.

Haigh currently serves as the Broadcast Education Research Committee chair. She routinely serves as a site-team member for the Accrediting Council on Education in Journalism and Mass Communications (ACEJMC) and serves on the ACEJMC council. In 2014, Haigh was named to NerdScholar's "40 under 40" list of "professors who inspire," and was the recipient of the 2014 Excellence in Teaching Award from the College of Communications Alumni Society Board at Penn State University. In 2015, she was recognized with the Excellence in Teaching Award from The National Society of Leadership and Success.

17

Communicating Terrorism

Meaning-Making and Crisis

Ruth DeFoster
Hubbard School of Journalism and Mass Communication,
University of Minnesota, Minneapolis, MN, USA

Introduction

One of the most visible forms of risk in the twenty-first century is a phenomenon that is instantly recognizable but hard to define: terrorism. And while the subjectivity of scholarly and policy definitions of terrorism has made the adoption of a universally agreed-upon definition for terrorism impossible, understanding both the history of terrorism and its application in crisis communication, media, and public policy is crucial for professional communicators.

While the risk of being injured or killed in a terrorist attack varies based on country of residence and conflict, the likelihood that anyone outside an active war zone will be killed by an act of terror is infinitesimally small – in the United States, for example, the annual fatality rate is about one in 50 million, or six Americans a year (Mueller & Stewart, 2021). However, the global *response* to terror is enormous compared to the risk – extensive and sweeping security measures that have significantly curtailed both privacy and civil rights, decades of war in the Middle East, and a media environment that often continues to uncritically replicate inaccurate and Orientalist explanations for the problem of terror. The choices made by government and police entities, journalists, and organizations to communicate terrorism can affect democratic institutions, the individual emotional well-being of citizens, and electoral behavior (Nussio et al., 2021).

This chapter will review the meaning and history of terrorism; it will then present an overview of key research on how terror events are communicated to audiences by governments, police forces, and the media. It will review common symbolic framing devices for terror and the ways that audiences use crisis communication to make sense of terror.

What is Terrorism?

In 1964, US Supreme Court Justice Potter Stewart was in the midst of a tricky case. *Jacobellis vs. Ohio* hinged on whether the 1958 film *Les Amants* contained obscene material not protected by the First Amendment. The nine justices agreed – with only two dissenting – that the film was not obscene, and did not contain, as its opponents alleged, "hard-core pornography." But the justices could not agree on the reason why. Ultimately, the most memorable line from the *Jacobellis*

The Handbook of International Crisis and Risk Communication Research, Second Edition.
Edited by Andreas Schwarz, Matthew W. Seeger, and Sora Kim.

decision came from Stewart, who famously wrote that while he may not be able to articulate exactly what constitutes pornography, "I know it when I see it" (Jacobellis v. Ohio, 1964).

Today, a similar standard is unconsciously and broadly applied to the cultural idea of terrorism. In popular use, the term "terrorism" has almost no definitional precision. As terrorism scholar Brian Jenkins succinctly observed in 1981, "terrorism is what the bad guys do" (Holtzhausen & Zerfass, 2015).

Even after decades of study, there remains little consensus on how to define the term among the myriad scholars and policymakers who study the phenomenon. As a result, comprehensive definitions of terrorism are slippery at best.

Audiences' and stakeholders' perceptions of terrorism have been powerfully influenced by decades of news media coverage of terror, as well as representations of terrorism in popular culture. These powerful influences, combined with the subjectivity and ambiguity of terror as a legal and political concept, have produced an environment in which audiences have the implicit and vague sense that they know "terrorism" when they see it.

This imprecision makes the formalized study of terrorism difficult. Which acts qualify as acts of terror? How can policymakers and scholars identify broad, international trends in terrorism when the question of which acts qualify is hotly contested by myriad groups across the political spectrum?

There are several elements that recur often in academic and policy attempts to define terrorism. Specifically, most definitions of terrorism include references to either the threat or action of *violence or force* by non-state actors in the pursuit of a *political end* (Schmid & Jongman, 2005; Schmid, 2011).

For example, the Global Terrorism Database (GTD), maintained by the National Consortium for the Study of Terrorism and Responses to Terrorism (START) at the University of Maryland, defines terrorism as acts by non-state actors "involving the threatened or actual use of illegal force or violence to attain a political, economic, religious or social goal through fear, coercion or intimidation" (Lee, 2004; START, 2022).

Hoffman (2006) succinctly summarizes many definitions that emphasize the inherently political nature of terrorism:

> "Terrorism, in the most widely accepted contemporary usage of the term, is fundamentally and inherently political. It is also ineluctably about power: the pursuit of power, the acquisition of power, and the use of power to achieve political change. Terrorism is thus violence—or, equally important, the threat of violence—used and directed in pursuit of, and in service of, a political aim (p. 13)."

One thing upon which terrorism scholars agree is that the landscape of terror has evolved radically over the past two centuries, fueled by a deeply reciprocal relationship with advances in media and technology. In the mid-twentieth century, as communication became instantaneous and news and information began to flow globally, so terrorism evolved from its roots as a form of regional anti-government protest to its current role as an international phenomenon driven by a very different strain of apocalyptic extremism.

The History of Terrorism

The earliest references to terrorism in the modern sense of the word can be traced to the French Revolution, when revolutionary leader Maximilien Robespierre famously asserted that "terror is nothing but justice, prompt, severe and inflexible. It is therefore an emanation of virtue" (Palmer, 1959). In the late eighteenth century, however, French citizens' perceptions of "terror" revolved around the oppression of a tyrannical government they felt compelled to overthrow. Terror was imagined as a state tool, rather than a revolutionary activity, and in enacting the *regime de terreur* in response, revolutionaries justified public beheadings and other forms of mob justice with the promise of a better, more egalitarian, society (Hoffman, 2006).

Rapoport (2001, 2008) identified four major eras, or "waves" of terror. The first wave spans the anarchist movement of the late nineteenth to early twentieth centuries, the second is marked by the state violence and anti-colonial violence of the early twentieth century, and the third wave marks the period during the mid- to late twentieth century when airline hijackings, kidnappings, and bombings became common. The fourth wave extends from the 1990s to the present, typified by attacks like those of September 11, 2001.

The First Wave

One of the first groups identified by scholars as a true terrorist organization is Narodnaya Volya ("People's Will" or "People's Freedom"), a nineteenth-century Russian group opposed to Tsarist rule. Narodnaya Volya applied the philosophy of "propaganda by deed," a theory put forth by an Italian republican extremist named Carlo Pisacane who asserted that violence was sometimes necessary to draw attention to a just cause (DeFoster, 2017). This philosophy went on to inspire many terrorist ideologies of the time and was reflected in the late nineteenth-century anarchist movement, which normalized assassinations and do-it-yourself (DIY) or "how-to" instructions for violence.

The Second Wave

By the 1920s and the early 1930s, anti-anarchist sentiment was pervasive in Western societies, and most references to terror during this early era refer to these revolutionary, separatist, or anarchist groups. But by the mid-1930s, the global political climate began to shift, and with it, the meaning of terrorism did as well. Rapoport (2001) described terror during this second wave as being driven by nationalistic and anti-colonial movements: As countries ruled by colonial powers sought freedom and independence, terrorism emerged as a means to resist colonial rule. But there is another element to this second wave as well: a period that predates the wave of high-profile acts committed by groups like the Irish Republican Army or the Palestine Liberation Organization (PLO) in the mid-twentieth century.

The 1930s and the 1940s saw an enormous rise in authoritarianism across the world, with totalitarian governments emerging in Spain, Italy, Russia, Japan, and Germany. In newspaper coverage and writing from this era, the term "terror" is largely used to describe the practices of mass repression or murder employed by the *state*, rather than subnational or revolutionary violence directed at governments themselves. In contemporary newspaper reports in Spain and the United Kingdom, for example, the use of firing ranges to execute political prisoners in Franco's Spain was described as an "act of terror" (DeFoster, 2017).

The Third Wave

But by the 1960s, with the advent of the third wave of terrorism, the practice and use of terror shifted again, entering the modern era and targeting a global audience. It is no coincidence that the dawn of the third wave, which began in the late 1960s and lasted until the end of the 1980s, coincided with the launch of the first commercial satellites, allowing news and communication to flow instantly to any corner of the globe and opening new pathways to instant visibility for terrorist organizations. This period saw many shifts in the practice and study of terrorism – it was marked primarily by kidnappings, bank robberies, and airline hijackings, which were so prevalent that the third wave is also sometimes called the "hijacking era."

During the third wave, organizations like the PLO and its many subsidiaries, such as the Black September Organization (BSO) or the Popular Front for the Liberation of Palestine, carried out high-profile attacks that were aimed at maximizing media coverage for a new international audience. For example, in 1972, the murder of 11 Israeli athletes at the Olympics in Munich at the hands of the BSO garnered enormous, unprecedented global media coverage.

One element that set the third wave apart from the fourth is that while the use of violence was certainly pervasive during this era, violence itself was not typically seen as the end goal of terrorist acts. Rather, most scholars agree that the primary goal during this era was for visibility and media coverage; terror was a tool used to shine a spotlight on a cause (Hoffman, 2006; Lesser & Jenkins, 1999). By the fourth wave, however, this began to change.

The Fourth Wave

The fourth wave of terrorism, spanning the early 1990s to the present, is defined and motivated by extremist religious ideologies. It is typified by the acts of terrorist groups like al-Qaeda and the Islamic State group, more commonly known as the Islamic State of Iraq and Syria (ISIS), militant extremist Islamist organizations that became central purveyors of anti-Western terror during this period. This shift toward religious extremism as a source for terror is also reflected in the Christian Identity movement in the United States, producing terrorists like Timothy McVeigh, and in groups like Aum Shinrikyo, a Hindu/Buddhist sect that committed the subway sarin gas attack in Tokyo in 1995.

The fourth wave shares the third wave's focus on *international* terror – choosing high-profile targets and enjoying a reciprocal relationship with the mass media. But the fourth wave of terror also reversed one important historical assumption about terrorism – the idea that violence was a tool to be used in the service of some other goal (awareness, policy change) rather than the end goal in itself. This ideological and practical shift reflects the shift in terrorist organizations themselves; groups like al-Qaeda and ISIS are not motivated by the awareness of a political plight or even specific political demands. Rather, these groups are apocalyptic death cults, whose members believe that within their lifetime they will emerge as leaders of a "final caliphate" that requires the slaughter of their enemies. For many fourth-wave terrorist groups, death and suffering *are* the end goal, and terrorist organizations largely use online recruitment to appeal to young, disaffected men to whom these violent appeals are effective.

Two of the most notable terrorist events of the fourth wave both involved New York City's World Trade Center: first, an attack in 1993 that killed seven and injured over a thousand. The leader of the group al-Qaeda, a wealthy, Western-educated Saudi elite named Osama bin Laden, rocketed to infamy overnight after he claimed responsibility for the attack. Second, by 2001, the group had managed to form a much more ambitious plan, carrying out a devastating attack that felled both World Trade Center towers, damaged the US Pentagon building, and directly resulted in the deaths of nearly 3,000 people.

The effects of the September 11 attacks in terms of the evolution of the term "terrorism" cannot be overstated. September 11 prompted the United States to launch the "War on Terror," with the ostensible goal of both eliminating global terrorism and holding accountable those responsible for the attacks. With the aid of several countries, including (but not limited to) Canada, the United Kingdom, France, Germany, and Australia, the US military embarked on long-term and enduring military operations in Afghanistan and later Iraq, while across the world, sweeping anti-terrorism laws were enacted, many of which significantly infringed on citizens' established civil liberties (Whitaker, 2007).

Terror in the Twenty-First Century

According to the GTD, the number of terrorist attacks in Western Europe has gone down in the years since 2004, while the number of attacks overall (but especially in South Asia, the Middle East, and North Africa) has risen during the same period before tapering off slightly in 2016 (START, 2022). However, a general increase in global terror is not a foregone conclusion to draw from these data. For one thing, open-source databases like the GTD draw their data from publicly available Internet materials, including messages, web posts, and news reports, which have increased exponentially in availability and volume in the years since 2004, enabling many more incidents to be counted that would have been missed prior to 2004. Additionally, many events listed in the GTD database have not been vetted correctly. For example, the terrorism database still lists a 2020 incident consisting of a now-debunked hoax in which a Minnesota man set fire to his own garage and framed it as an act of terror by the activist group Black Lives Matter. He later pled guilty to arson in an attempt at insurance fraud (Bella, 2022).

The U.S. State Department currently recognizes 68 official foreign terrorist organizations, many of which are offshoots of ISIS, al-Qaeda, and Ansar al-Sharia (U.S. Dept. of State, 2023). Interestingly, however, while the United States recognizes foreign terrorist organizations – a designation that criminalizes association with these groups in specific ways – there is no comparable list of officially recognized *domestic* terrorist organizations. Additionally, there is no federal criminal charge for domestic terrorism in the United States, although some terrorism-related sentencing enhancements can be applied after conviction.

In recent years, many analyses of Western terror have linked violent incidents to right-wing extremism. The Anti-Defamation League (ADL), which publishes biannual analyses of domestic murder and extremism in the United States, has found an overwhelming turn toward terrorist attacks perpetrated by right-wing extremists and white supremacists, largely in the form of mass shootings (ADL, 2018, 2022).

In 2020, the US Department of Homeland Security released a report listing white supremacists as the gravest immediate terror threat in the United States, elevating the risk to the same level as foreign groups like ISIS:

> "Lone offenders and small cells of individuals motivated by a diverse array of social, ideological, and personal factors will pose the primary terrorist threat to the United States. Among these groups, we assess that white supremacist extremists – who increasingly are networking with likeminded persons abroad – will pose the most persistent and lethal threat." (U.S. Dept. of Homeland Security, 2020, p. 17)

Communicating Terrorism

Terrorist attacks are highly visible, extremely newsworthy events, which are irresistible to news media. Terrorist organizations also rely on media coverage for both visibility and recruitment. There are many key entities that communicate terror to global audiences: state entities (including the separate groups of governments and police forces, who are motivated to quell panic and manage crises by assuring audiences of their safety and security), journalists, and terror organizations themselves (Cristòfol et al., 2020; Liu et al., 2020). Stakeholders' audiences may include citizens, the professional media, emergency personnel, and policymakers.

Governments and political leaders play an important communication role in moments of crisis, using public diplomacy to pass on important information about risks to citizens. According to Tuch (1990), public diplomacy is defined as "a government's process of communication with foreign publics in an attempt to bring about understanding for its nation's ideas and ideals, its institutions and culture, as well as its national goals and policies" (p. 3). The role of public diplomacy is particularly crucial in communicating about terrorism, as governments seek to mitigate negative attitudes or fears among international audiences (Seib, 2012). During crises, audiences seek information from both the media and the state to attempt to understand tragic events like terrorist attacks (An & Gower, 2009).

DuBrin (2013) describes this state communication process as "crisis leadership," defined as "the process of leading group members through a sudden and largely unanticipated, intensely negative, and emotionally draining circumstance" (p. 3). The most important factors in successful crisis leadership include humility, flexibility, crisis perceptiveness, presence, and cooperation (Liu et al., 2020).

For individual leaders like city mayors, governors, or heads of state, the most successful crisis communication strategies involve strategic communication (restoration of perceived public safety, the alleviation of fear) and a humanistic, issue-based approach (Williams et al., 2017). Naturally, culture, context, and decision-making strategies all play important roles in determining individual governments' or leaders' crisis communication decision-making following acts of terrorism. For example, Spanish Prime Minister José María Aznar's public communication after the 2004 Madrid train bombing prompted weeks of protest and hasty electoral defeat in the elections four days later, thanks to significant errors in judgment that included early hasty misinformation and messages scapegoating the Basque ethnic group for the attack. A few years later, Norwegian Prime Minister Jens Stoltenberg employed a different approach following a devastating terror attack in 2011. By emphasizing national unity through calm, measured, and carefully planned statements, Stoltenberg was able to prompt Norwegians to rally around the flag and to increase support for himself and his party in the process (Sinkkonen, 2016).

Messages from police sources also play a crucial role in communicating information about terrorism. However, because police sources play a different and timelier role in preventing and responding to terror attacks, police and government communicators must balance symbols and actions in different ways. In communication following terror incidents, political leaders have found success emphasizing symbolism around collective unity and healing. For police sources, however, audiences are less receptive to these kinds of symbolic messages, leading to criticism of police organization and management related to their perceived failure to stop terror attacks (Christensen et al., 2013).

In a meta-analysis of 45 studies examining police communication in the wake of public crises, Hine and Bragias (2021) examined how police communication during moments of exceptional crisis often results in confused or inconsistent messaging. Two main themes emerged in the most *effective* examples of police communication across the literature – first, the importance of a decentralized communication structure, and second, the importance of shared mental models that create unified understandings of crisis situations before information is communicated to the broader public.

In the context of terrorism, Iyengar (1991) found that when terrorism is framed by journalists and state actors as an individual event, audiences were more likely to blame the individual perpetrators. However, when terrorism is framed as a broader, systemic problem, audiences were more likely to blame society as a whole. Other common organizational control frames of terror include the *leadership frame,* which emphasizes the role of a strong, central organization (Fisher Liu, 2009), the *container frame,* which focuses on the lack of control during a crisis moment (Hearit, 2008), and finally the *collaboration frame,* which emphasizes coordination and communication between government and non-governmental organizations during and after crises. Communication from official and state actors is a crucial source for professional communicators, and journalists often over-rely on official sources, replicating official narratives (Iyengar, 1991).

For journalists, one of the most distinctive features of crisis reporting is the need to produce information quickly, which can lead to hasty decisions, especially on social media, that can snowball into misinformation or real harm. Ghersetti and Johansson (2021) found that journalists are more willing than the general public to embrace complex ethical quandaries related to crisis journalism, but when it comes to the ethics of publishing information about perpetrators and victims, the opposite is true: Citizens seem to value the dissemination of information over personal integrity, which poses a challenge for news organizations that must balance timeliness with journalistic ethics.

The Symbolism of Terror

The 20-year war in Afghanistan and the U.S.-led invasion of Iraq had profound ripple effects on the global community. Not only did these wars radically reshape the geopolitical landscape in the Middle East, but they also strained many global alliances and left a power vacuum in Iraq and Afghanistan that ironically allowed groups like ISIS to flourish and expand their influence through successful recruiting. The events of September 11, and the iconography and ideologies of the wars that followed, also profoundly influenced cultural depictions of terrorism. As Jenkins (1975) wrote, "terrorism is a theater," and no terrorist event has ever proven more theatrical on a broader scale than the September 11 attacks.

Terrorist organizations have always had a reciprocal, symbiotic relationship with the news media. During the third wave of terror, Walter Laqueur (1977) called terrorists the "super entertainers of our time," who offer the mass media irresistible and highly newsworthy fodder that interests audiences. In 1985, British Prime Minister Margaret Thatcher, whose own tenure in the United Kingdom was marked by prolonged disputes over the subject of televising terrorism, presciently described media publicity as the "oxygen" on which terrorist organizations depend to survive, arguing that democratic nations must find a way to "starve" terrorists of this life force (Hoffman, 2006).

In the United States and Western Europe, the post-September 11 media landscape was marked by round-the-clock coverage of these highly visible attacks. At this pivotal point in history, news practitioners had an obligation to present the public with complete, nuanced, unbiased coverage of the fallout from the attacks and the invasions of Iraq and Afghanistan. Instead, many journalists and media organizations took a passive, uncritical approach, echoing nationalistic talking points and repeating military claims – such as the ostensible existence of weapons of mass destruction in Iraq – at face value. Many news organizations also under-reported or delegitimized protest movements and emphasized danger, fear, victimhood, and risk over nuance and objectivity (Bonn, 2010; DiMaggio, 2010; Van der Veer & Munshi, 2004).

News media coverage of the idea of terrorism during the decade following September 11 was also marked powerfully by anti-Muslim bias, producing work that created a "uniquely menacing" image of Islam (Vultee, 2009). And as live news coverage of the September 11 attacks themselves wound down over the ensuing weeks and months, fictional media picked up the slack, featuring pervasive and all-encompassing storylines that echoed political narratives legitimizing the war as a necessary evil (Alsultany, 2012). These representations had the effect of dramatically refiguring the way audiences imagined the idea of *terror* – what terror means, who terrorists are, and what terrorists look like.

In the years since September 11, several themes have emerged in media representation that communicates terrorism. First, marked framing differences have been observed in Western vs. non-Western countries. In the United States, media narratives in the immediate aftermath of September 11 largely cleaved to official government talking points. American news media uncritically replicated claims about weapons of mass destruction in Iraq and cheered the war effort on, bolstering nationalistic fervor for the war (DiMaggio, 2010; Reese & Lewis, 2009).

Other countries have taken a different approach. In Spain, for example, following the Madrid bombing of 2004, the Spanish media outright rejected the government's framing of the event, setting off a battle among major newspapers over how to understand the attacks, as public opinion remained deeply suspicious of the Spanish government (Canel, 2012). In Russia, media framing of terror events tends to mirror the country's contentious relationship with the West, casting doubt on US military claims (such as the assassination of Osama bin Laden in 2011) and offering more humanizing depictions of terrorists than seen in other countries (Khakimova Storie et al., 2014).

Second, in both news and entertainment media, September 11 marked a radical shift in the way terrorism was depicted. Before September 11, depictions of terrorism in both news and entertainment media were considerably more varied – one often-seen trope in American films in the 1990s involved depictions of terrorists as Soviets, rather than Arabs or Muslims. But after September 11, this shifted. Film and television depictions of terrorism after September 11 framed terrorism as a uniquely Muslim phenomenon that originated exclusively in the Middle East.

How do Audiences Make Sense of Terror?

The lasting effects of these trends in representation and communication are clear in the West. A series of surveys ranging from 2014 to 2020 from the Pew Research Center asked Americans to rate religious groups on a scale ranging from 0 to 100, with 0 representing the most negative view and 100 representing the most positive view. In these surveys, Muslims are consistently ranked among the most negatively, along with atheists (Pew, 2021a). And even 20 years after September 11, Americans of all sides of the political spectrum continue to rank terrorism as a top risk and national priority, with 72% of Republicans (and 32% of Democrats) reporting they believe Islam is more likely than other religions to encourage this kind of violence (Pew, 2021b).

On a broad scale, terrorist attacks in the global West often result in a rally-around-the-flag effect – citizens report more trust in government, higher levels of identification with national identity, prejudice against outsiders, and emotions like fear and anger following terror attacks (Nussio, 2020). These shifts in attitude and emotion, described by Hall and Ross (2015) as an "affective wave," can prompt changes in voter behavior, political attitudes, and profound policy shifts around immigration, civil liberties, and even war (Bove et al., 2020; Montalvo, 2010; Pearce et al., 2013; Vasilopoulos et al., 2019). In the United States, the September 11 attacks prompted a large rise in presidential approval (Hetherington & Nelson, 2003), Americans' increased preference for authoritarian policies (Davis & Silver, 2004; Kearns & Young, 2018), more reported prejudice toward racial and religious outgroups (Hitlan et al., 2007), and heightened stress and anxiety (Huddy et al., 2003).

Nussio (2020) has also found that European audiences have become "desensitized" to terror events, finding elevated levels of reported anger, sadness, and fear in the days following highly reported and communicated terror attacks. This may be rooted in *mortality salience,* a concept from terror management theory that posits that people resort to culturally derived meaning systems when confronted with their own mortality, becoming more in-group oriented and less favorable to cultural out-groups (Das et al., 2009; Hitlan et al., 2007).

Even as audiences may have become somewhat inured to messages about terror, terror attacks – and the enormous wave of reporting, communication, and cultural interest that accompany them – dramatically increase the likelihood that individuals report perceiving terrorism as an important issue. This is true across Europe and the United States, with some effects larger than others. Following an attack in Utrecht in 2019, for example, the percentage of citizens of the Netherlands who reported that terror was a pressing issue rose 11 points. Following the 2015 Paris attack, the percentage rose 35 points. Even relatively small attacks resulted in huge percentage spikes – the 2013 London attacks and 2018 Carcassonne attacks increased attention to terror by 13 points in the United Kingdom and 19 points in France (Nussio et al., 2021).

Conclusion

Terrorism poses a very small risk of victimization for most global audiences but remains nonetheless a major source of public fear. As terrorism and the threat of terrorism evolve, audiences' experiences and perceptions of terror have evolved alongside it. As Jenkins (1975) observed, the idea of terrorism as "theater" places the phenomenon of terror squarely in the wheelhouse of the mass media and communication strategy.

In countries like the United States, the risk of being killed by garden-variety gun violence vastly outstrips the risk of being killed in a terror attack. In 2021, 48,830 people died from gun-related injuries in the United States, the highest number of annual gun deaths recorded in American history (Pew, 2023). However, the American policy response to this epidemic of senseless violence remains sluggish at best, especially compared to the outsized policy response that many Western countries implemented to target the problem of international terrorism. For audiences, the cultural iconography of "terror" instills a sense of urgency and risk that the everyday drumbeat of preventable gun violence does not.

According to the GTD, of the 22,847 annual global deaths from terrorism included in their database – which uses very broad criteria for inclusion – 97% occurred in the Middle East, Africa, or South Asia. And even in the country with the most terror-related fatalities, Iraq, only about .003% of the Iraqi population of 43.5 million are killed by terror attacks each year (START, 2022). For most of the world, the risk of being killed or injured in a terrorist incident is so small as to be statistically almost nonexistent. For communicators in all parts of the world, using the "terrorism" label too broadly and without regard for a broader understanding of statistical danger can make it difficult for citizens and media audiences to assess the true risk to themselves and their communities.

Future research may further explicate and compare the most effective and appropriate crisis communication strategies for state, media, police, and organizational sources. As communication about crisis and risk increasingly moves into algorithmic spaces, it will also be important to examine the algorithmic mechanisms behind the spread of terror-related messaging on social media.

In crisis situations, established organizational principles and forms often either prove inadequate or are overstepped, leading to disjointed and inconsistent information communicated to audiences (Christensen et al., 2013). Political leaders often frame terrorist attacks in ways that deliberately exploit fear as a mechanism to pass exceptional policies or bolster the strength of their campaign or party (Sinkkonen, 2016), but this often has the effect of creating nationalistic insularity and suspicion of outsiders among audiences. As Furedi (2007) wrote, "acts of terrorism succeed insofar as the target society responds in the way perpetrators of these deeds intended" (p. 171). For professional communicators, preparedness, an understanding of history, shared mental models, and flexibility are keys to avoid the pitfalls of fear-oriented messaging in times of crisis.

References

Alsultany, E. (2012). *Arabs and Muslims in the Media: Race and Representation After 9/11*. New York University Press.

An, S. K., & Gower, K. K. (2009). How do the news media frame crises? A content analysis of crisis news coverage. *Public Relations Review*, *35*(2), 107–112.

Anti-Defamation League (January 18, 2018). *Murder and extremism in the United States in 2018*. https://www.adl.org/resources/report/murder-and-extremism-united-states-2018

Anti-Defamation League (February 22, 2022). *Murder and extremism in the United States in 2022*. https://www.adl.org/resources/report/murder-and-extremism-united-states-2022

Bella, T. (July 13, 2022). Trump supporter charged with faking politically motivated arson at own home. *The Washington Post*. https://www.washingtonpost.com/nation/2022/07/13/trump-supporter-arson-charges-molla/

Bonn, S. A. (2010). *Mass Deception: Moral Panic and the U.S. War on Iraq*. Rutgers University Press.

Bove, V., Böhmelt, T., & Nussio, E. (2020). Terrorism abroad and migration policies at home. *Journal of European Public Policy*, *28*(2), 190–207.

Canel, M. J. (2012). Communicating strategically in the face of terrorism: The Spanish government's response to the 2004 Madrid bombing attacks. *Public Relations Review*, *38*(2), 214–222.

Christensen, T., Laegreid, P., & Rykkja, L. H. (2013). After a terrorist attack: Challenges for political and administrative leadership in Norway. *Journal of Contingencies & Crisis Management, 21*, 167–177.
Cristòfol, F. J., de Eugenio-Vela, J. S., & Paniagua-Rojano, F. J. (2020). Active listening in the management of crisis communication: Case study of the 2017 terrorist attack in Barcelona. *Communications Society, 33*(4), 61–74.
Das, E., Bushman, B. J., Bezemer, M. D., Kerkhof, P., & Vermeulen, I. E. (2009). How terrorism news reports increase prejudice against outgroups. *Journal of Experimental Social Psychology, 45*(3), 453–459.
Davis, D. W., & Silver, B. D. (2004). Civil liberties vs. security: Public opinion in the context of the terrorist attacks on America. *American Journal of Political Science, 48*(1), 28–46.
DeFoster, R. (2017). *Terrorizing the Masses: Identity, Mass Shootings, and the Media Construction of Terror.* Peter Lang.
Dimaggio, A. R. (2010). *When Media Goes to War: Hegemonic Discourse, Public Opinion, and the Limits of Dissent.* Monthly Review Press.
DuBrin, A. J. (2013). Personal attributes and behaviors of effective crisis leaders. In A. J. DuBrin, Ed., *Handbook of Research on Crisis Leadership in Organizations* (pp. 3–22). Cheltenham, UK: Edward Elgar Publishing Inc.
Fisher Liu, B. (2009). An analysis of US government and media disaster frames. *Journal of Communication Management (London, England), 13*(3), 268–283.
Furedi, F. (2007). *Invitation to Terror: The Expanding Empire of the Unknown.* Continuum.
Ghersetti, M., & Johansson, B. (2021). To publish or not to publish? Assessing journalism ethics in news about a terrorist attack. *Journalism Studies, 22*(13), 1814–1831.
Hall, T. H., & Ross, A. A. G. (2015). Affective Politics after 9/11. *International Organization, 69*(4), 847–879. https://doi.org/10.1017/S0020818315000144
Hearit, K. (2008). Encephalitis outbreaks and public communication exigencies. In M. W. Seeger, T. L. Sellnow, & R. R. Ulmer, Eds., *Crisis Communication and the Public Health.* Hampton Press.
Hetherington, M. J., & Nelson, M. (2003). Anatomy of a Rally effect: George W. Bush and the war on terrorism. *PS: Political Science & Politics, 36*(1), 37–42.
Hine, K. A., & Bragias, A. (2021). Effective communication during major crises: A systematic literature review to identify best practices for police. *Police Practice and Research, 22*(5), 1492–1507.
Hitlan, R. T., Carrillo, K., Zárate, M. A., & Aikman, S. N. (2007). Attitudes toward immigrant groups and the September 11 terrorist attacks. *Peace and Conflict: Journal of Peace Psychology, 13*(2), 135–152.
Hoffman, B. (2006). *Inside Terrorism* (Rev. and expanded ed. Columbia University Press.
Holtzhausen, D. R., & Zerfass, A. (Eds.). (2015). *The Routledge Handbook of Strategic Communication.* Routledge.
Huddy, L., Feldman, S., Lahav, G., & Taber, C. (2003). Fear and terrorism: Psychological reactions to 9/11. In *Framing Terrorism: The News Media, the Government, and the Public* (pp. 255–278). London, United Kingdom: Routledge.
Iyengar, S. (1991). *Is Anyone Responsible? How Television Frames Political Issues.* University of Chicago Press.
Jacobellis v. Ohio, 378 U.S. 184 (1964)
Jenkins, B. M. (1975). *International Terrorism: A New Mode of Conflict.* Crescent Publications.
Kearns, E. M., & Young, J. K. (2018). "If Torture is wrong, what about 24?" Torture and the hollywood effect. *Crime & Delinquency, 64*(12), 1568–1589.
Khakimova Storie, L., Madden, S. L., & Liu, B. F. (2014). The death of bin Laden: How Russian and U.S. media frame counterterrorism. *Public Relations Review, 40*(3), 429–439.
Laqueur, W. (1977). *Terrorism.* Little, Brown.
Lee, J. (2004). Exploring global terrorism data: a web-based visualization of temporal data. *Global Terrorism Database.* https://www.start.umd.edu/gtd/datarivers/JoonghoonLee.pdf
Lesser, I. O., & Jenkins, B. M. (1999). *Countering the New Terrorism.* Rand.
Liu, B. F., Iles, I. A., & Herovic, E. (2020). Leadership under fire: How governments manage crisis communication. *Communication Studies, 71*(1), 128–147.
Montalvo, J. G. (2010). Voting after the bombings: A natural experiment on the effect of terrorist attacks on democratic elections. *Review of Economics and Statistics, 93*(4), 1146–1154.
Mueller, J., & Stewart, M. G. (2021). Terrorism and bathtubs: Comparing and assessing the risks. *Terrorism and Political Violence, 33*(1), 138–163.
Nussio, E. (2020). Attitudinal and emotional consequences of Islamist terrorism. Evidence from the Berlin attack. *Political Psychology, 41*(6), 1151–1171.

Nussio, E., Bohmelt, T., & Bove, V. (2021). Do terrorists get the attention they want? Comparing effects of terrorism across Europe. *Public Opinion Quarterly*, *85*(3), 900–912.
Palmer, R. R. (1959). *The Age of the Democratic Revolution*. Princeton University Press.
Pearce, J. M., Rubin, G. J., Selke, P., Amlôt, R., Mowbray, F., & Rogers, M. B. (2013). Communicating with the public following radiological terrorism: Results from a series of focus groups and national surveys in Britain and Germany. *Prehospital and Disaster Medicine*, *28*(2), 110–119.
Pew Research Center (2021a). *Muslims are a growing presence in U.S., but still face negative views from thepublic.*https://www.pewresearch.org/short-reads/2021/09/01/muslims-are-a-growing-presence-in-u-s but still face-negative-views-from-the-public/)
Pew Research Center (2021b). *Two decades later, the enduring legacy of 9/11*. https://www.pewresearch.org/politics/2021/09/02/two-decades-later-the-enduring-legacy-of-9-11/#views-of-muslims-islam-grew-more-partisan-in-years-after-9-11
Pew Research Center (2023). *What the data says about gun deaths in the U.S.* https://www.pewresearch.org/short-reads/2023/04/26/what-the-data-says-about-gun-deaths-in-the-u-s/
Rapoport, D. C. (2001). The fourth wave: September 11 in the history of terrorism. *Current History (1941)*, *100*(650), 419–424.
Rapoport, D. C. (2008). Before the bombs there were the mobs: American experiences with terror. *Terrorism and Political Violence*, *20*(2), 167–194.
Reese, S. D., & Lewis, S. C. (2009). Framing the war on terror: The internalization of policy in the US press. *Journalism*, *10*(6), 777–797.
Schmid, A., & Jongman, A. (2005). *Political Terrorism: A New Guide to Actors, Authors, Concept, Databases, Theories and Literature*. Transaction Publishers.
Schmid, A. P. (2011). *The Routledge Handbook of Terrorism Research*. Routledge.
Seib, P. (2012). Public diplomacy versus terrorism. In D. Freedman, Ed., *Media and Terrorism: Global Perspectives*. SAGE.
Sinkkonen, T. (2016). Can political leaders make a difference? Norwegian versus Spanish experiences in responding to terrorist attacks. *Studies in Conflict & Terrorism*, *39*(4), 326–341.
START (National Consortium for the Study of Terrorism and Responses to Terrorism). (2022). *Global terrorism database 1970–2020* [data file]. https://www.start.umd.edu/gtd
Tuch, H. N. (1990). *Communicating with the World: U.S. Public Diplomacy Overseas*. St. Martin's Press.
U.S. Department of Homeland Security (October, 2020). *Homeland threat assessment*. https://www.dhs.gov/sites/default/files/publications/2020_10_06_homeland-threat-assessment.pdf
U.S. Department of State (June, 2023). *Designated foreign terrorist organizations*. https://www.state.gov/foreign-terrorist-organizations/
van der Veer, P., & Munshi, S. (2004). *Media, War, and Terrorism: Responses from the Middle East and Asia*. Routledge.
Vasilopoulos, P., Marcus, G. E., Valentino, N. A., & Foucault, M. (2019). Fear, anger, and voting for the far right: Evidence from the November 13, 2015 Paris terror attacks. *Political Psychology*, *40*(4), 679–704.
Vultee, F. (2009). Jump back Jack, Mohammed's here. *Journalism Studies*, *10*(5), 623–638.
Whitaker, B. E. (2007). Exporting the patriot act? Democracy and the "war on terror" in the third world. *Third World Quarterly*, *28*(5), 1017–1032.
Williams, G. A., Woods, C. L., & Staricek, N. C. (2017). Restorative rhetoric and social media: An examination of the Boston Marathon bombing. *Communication Studies*, *68*(4), 385–402.

Author Bio

Ruth DeFoster is an assistant professor at the Hubbard School of Journalism and Mass Communication at the University of Minnesota. Her research on terrorism, mass shootings, gun violence, tragedy, and identity has been published in *Health Communication, Contemporary Drug Problems, Journal of Communication Inquiry, Communication, Culture & Critique*, and *SAGE Research Methods Cases*. Ruth is the author of the 2017 book *Terrorizing the Masses: Identity, Mass Shootings, and the Media Construction of Terror* (Peter Lang) the 2024 book *Catholic Horror on Television: Haunting Faith* (Lexington) and the forthcoming book *The Fear Knot: How Science, History and Culture Shape Our Fears, and How to Get Unstuck* (Prometheus).

18

Reoccurring Challenges and Emerging Threats

Crises and the New Millennium

Patric R. Spence[1] and Kenneth A. Lachlan[2]

[1] University of Central Florida, Orlando, FL, USA
[2] University of Connecticut, Storrs, CT, USA

Introduction

Disasters don't read maps. They don't require passports, observe language differences, or consider cultural divisions. They don't recognize man-made borders or checkpoints. An earthquake in the US state of Alaska can produce infrastructure damage to energy production in Canada. A volcano eruption in Iceland can create air quality problems in Sweden and air traffic problems around the globe. Smog in China impacts agriculture in South Korea. The outbreak of an infectious disease in Japan is just hours away from becoming an outbreak in Sao Paulo or all of South America. Because of the speed and novelty involved with disasters and pandemics, emergency managers, crisis practitioners, and first responders need to be aware that the decisions made, recommendations provided, and actions taken not only have consequences domestically but also abroad. A decision to withhold information early in a crisis has the potential to increase the harm, severity, and duration of that event. Alternatively, providing information too soon, before accurate information avails itself, may not only cause various publics to take unnecessary actions but also ultimately may make them distrustful of following recommendations in the future. With the nature of communicating within the events of a disaster or pandemic being delicate and precise, the following chapter will discuss audience needs, communication patterns, and behaviors associated with such events.

Information Seeking

In an ideal world, public health messages concerning natural disasters and pandemics would meet the public's need for control. A sizable body of research has argued that under similar conditions, risk messages need to offer tangible behavioral recommendations that individuals can use to reduce their susceptibility to risk. Inaccurately communicating the risks associated with disasters and pandemics will inhibit individuals in their attempts to make potentially life-saving decisions. Of equal importance is the message strategy utilized by the message producer; even the best advice will not be acted upon if it is not received, and the failure to reach those audiences who are mostly at risk has the potential to be highly problematic. Further, the information campaigns associated with these types of large-scale disasters should (to some

The Handbook of International Crisis and Risk Communication Research, Second Edition.
Edited by Andreas Schwarz, Matthew W. Seeger, and Sora Kim.

extent) reassure audiences that following the outlined recommendations will lead to a reduction in risk, thereby reassuring them to some degree.

A long history of research has indicated that during high-risk events, the mass media will become the primary resource upon which those affected rely for information that can be used to restore order (Brashers *et al.*, 2000; Lachlan et al., 2024; Lachlan et al., 2009; Murch, 1971; Spence et al., 2005, 2006). This fundamental compulsion to obtain information brings a sense of order, reduces uncertainty, and engenders a sense of control (Berger, 1987; Brashers et al., 2000). Obtaining information leads to several behavioral responses, including vicarious learning of behaviors that may be helpful under the circumstances (Seeger et al., 2003).

This response is theoretically consistent with a large body of work in the social psychology literature. Under conditions of extreme stress, such as those imposed by a natural disaster, individuals have a fundamental compulsion to collect information (Berlyne, 1960; Heath & Gay, 1997). This drive is especially strong when individuals are highly involved in the event, including those in which the potential harm or reward may be great (Brashers et al., 2000; Heath & Gay, 1997).

Audiences will typically gravitate toward trusted sources of information during disasters and will engage in repeated surveillance as the parameters of the event change. Mass media is usually relied upon (Murch, 1971), as it is typically viewed as more timely and reliable than interpersonal or observational means of information acquisition (Heath et al., 1995). At this point, primacy becomes a central consideration. Initial alerts set audience expectations for subsequent updates (CDC, 2002). Though audiences will continue to scan for updates, these initial messages must be as accurate as possible given the information available and must be placed in a manner that they reach those most affected.

One useful means of determining ideal message placement can be derived from media dependency theory (MDT) (Ball-Rokeach & DeFleur, 1976). MDT predicts that audiences have very specific preferences for information acquisition. It also asserts that these dependencies will be far stronger when audiences are highly invested in the information or find themselves surrounded by conflict and ambiguity (DeFleur & Ball-Rokeach, 1989). Natural disasters and pandemics are consistent with these conditions. A substantive body of research has supported this assertion and indicated that media dependencies are closely tied to subsequent behavior after a disaster (Hindman & Coyle, 1999; Loges, 1994; Lowrey, 2004). During a disaster, domestic audiences will not be the only audiences interested in the disaster events and information broadcast. In an increasing global society, several external audiences will be monitoring information and updating that information. Recognizing this and understanding that these external audiences will have their own dependencies will allow for an increased sharing of information. This can be seen as a means of supplementing existing formal information-sharing networks already in place.

This advice is, of course, predicated on the assumption that the audiences in question will have access to their preferred medium. They may not. Physical and social factors associated with crises and pandemics may inhibit the capacity of those affected to reach their preferred information sources (see Lachlan et al., 2021; Lachlan et al., 2007). Extended into an international context, those in several areas of the globe may be further inhibited by poverty, language barriers, and inadequate communication infrastructure. Without information from preferred sources, individuals will seek out whatever information is available, regardless of its accuracy, timeliness, or usefulness.

Secondary Audience Reactions

Audiences not directly impacted by a disaster or pandemic will still use the media for various gratifications. Negative consequences associated with media exposure to extreme events are also common and well researched (Hoven *et al.*, 2005; Pfefferbaum *et al.*, 2001; Saylor *et al.*, 2003). These findings have allowed some researchers to claim that media coverage itself may merit consideration as a form of exposure to extreme events (Ahern *et al.*, 2004). For example, individuals who viewed more television images of the September 11 terrorist attacks were more likely, even after four months, to report post-traumatic stress disorder (PTSD) symptoms (Ahern *et al.*, 2004) along with other negative emotional responses (Lachlan et al., 2009), and similar emotional responses were found for those in close geographic proximity to the event (Spence *et al.*, 2005). Such results suggest that those not directly exposed to a disaster can be impacted emotionally (Galea *et al.*, 2003; Liverant et al., 2004). Although information seeking may reduce uncertainty and anxiety during extreme events, it has also been shown to have the ability to increase such emotions. These findings can be explained through exemplification theory.

Exemplification theory (Zillmann, 1999, 2002) describes the influence of media portrayals that are most likely to drive people's judgments and subsequent reactions to the nonmediated world. The theory draws upon evolutionary principles and three cognitive mechanisms (quantification, representativeness, and availability heuristics). It postulates that concrete, iconic, and emotionally arousing exemplars influence perceptions to a greater degree than abstract, symbolic, and emotionally inconsequential exemplars and base-rate information. Exemplars refer to selective samples representing a population of all possible occurrences that include some shared focal characteristic(s) of that population (Zillmann, 1999, 2002). People tend to use heuristics as cognitive shortcuts to help process information, and one of these is exemplified properties from media portrayals of issues. According to exemplification theory, information is evaluated in a subjective and biased manner, rather than in a detailed systematic way (Busselle & Shrum, 2003).

Exemplars are especially likely to have an impact if they are attentionally favored, emotionally interesting, and heuristically available, as these are the exemplars most likely to be stored and retrieved from memory. Previous studies have examined the effects of these exemplars in various media news contexts. Salient, atypical, concrete, iconic, and emotionally arousing exemplars, which are representative of natural disasters, are found to have more effect on audience attitudes and perceptions than abstract, symbolic, and emotionally inconsequential exemplars.

Westerman, Spence, and Lachlan (2009) outlined just how exemplars in media portrayals could cause overestimations of threat and severity of the risks associated with natural disasters. In the aftermath of a natural disaster, the public will use the media to obtain information concerning potential risks. However, the same sources the public turns to as a means to reduce fear, harm, and uncertainty also have the potential to elevate fear through exemplification effects. Thus, secondary audiences, not directly affected by a natural disaster, can still be influenced by media portrayals and have negative reactions to the event. A disaster in the Philippines can create real psychological effects for individuals in Hawaii. Therefore, attending to such secondary audience needs is important. (For a more complete review of exemplification theory, see Spence et al., 2017; Spence et al, 2024.)

Addressing Variability in Psychological Responses

A sizable body of research in the information-seeking tendencies and psychological responses associated with crises and disasters has offered evidence of variability in response. These psychological responses follow a consistent, replicated pattern across numerous studies, and demographic indicators may be used to accurately predict audience responses. For example, there is evidence of differences across cultures in terms of information desired, perceived accuracy, and comprehension and subsequent behavioral and psychological responses.

Evidence from North American audiences indicates that under the conditions of crisis, members of underrepresented cultural groups indicate less worry concerning environmental risks. These differences hold even when there is control over income and education

(Hohm, 1976; Van Ardosol et al., 1965). This same canon of research offers that underrepresented groups are less likely to accept information without further confirming it via interpersonal networks (Spence et al., 2007), thus impeding response time (Fothergill et al., 1999; Lindell & Perry, 2004).

There may also be a great deal of language variability across and within varying cultural groups creating difficulties in the processing of emergency messages. Extended into an international context, this is especially worrisome for crises and disasters that take place in nations in which multiple languages are spoken. Government agencies and emergency managers in international contexts should gain a sense of the best outlets for emergency messages in reaching various language subgroups during disaster and pandemic.

Vulnerability to a natural disaster or pandemic is the result of several factors, including physical proximity to a risk, individual characteristics such as education, financial assets, constraints, physical abilities, and choices made by an individual. It involves both environmental and social components such as structural issues, gender, race, socioeconomic status, occupation, resources, social dependence, and social networks. Moreover, issues such as home location can also be related to crisis vulnerability. It is widely accepted that throughout the world the most vulnerable to a disaster include ethnic minorities, lower-income groups, the young and the elderly, people with disabilities, and female-headed households. Therefore, the proportion of risk usually falls unevenly on different populations.

Migration

The world is a smaller place, and populations are more mobile than ever before. In the event of disaster or pandemic, immigration status can create a unique set of obstacles. This can be true for a person who has migrated for work or a person forced to migrate due to the effects of a disaster or to escape a pandemic. For example, access to health care can be difficult. Many undocumented immigrants do not seek health care through traditional means because they are either unaware of what they are eligible for, or they are fearful because of their immigration status. One study which examined the fear of immigration authorities and tuberculosis noted that almost half of those who cited fear of immigration authorities delayed seeking health care for more than 60 days (Asch et al., 1994). Such a delay in the immediate aftermath of any type of disaster or pandemic could result in dire human costs, both to the individual who chooses not to seek health care and to their immediate community. Rather, it is more likely for recent immigrants, particularly those with ties to an ethnic community, to receive health care from a member of their social network.

Alongside immigration is the question of language, which will also be a barrier in communication, as many immigrants live in countries where their first language is not the dominant language. In the United States, for example, crisis and emergency messages are often broadcast only in English, leaving many other language groups vulnerable (Aguirre, 1988). One study conducted after Hurricane Katrina noted that nearly a third of New Orleans Spanish-speaking residents spoke English "less than very well" (Hilfinger-Messias & Lacy, 2007), leaving them without comprehensive knowledge of the risks associated with the storm. Increased immigration throughout the world raises questions about the need for bilingual warnings and adequate preparations to reach all audiences.

Knowledge Gaps

In addition to the predictable patterns of psychological response and information seeking that can be detected across ethnicity and gender, there are socioeconomic factors that may play a role in information acquisition and response. The knowledge gap hypothesis

(Tichenor et al., 1970) offers that over time, people from higher socioeconomic status and higher education level will acquire and retain more information than those from lower levels of each variable.

A few studies have focused specifically on knowledge gaps, risks, and disasters. For example, one study attempted to examine knowledge gap processes related to drinking water contamination (Kahlor et al., 2004). Under these conditions of high risk and ambiguity (as described earlier), knowledge gap processes held and were equally strong as in studies exploring relatively benign phenomena. Those with stronger educational background acquired and retained more information concerning the contamination than did those with a limited education. Further, wealthier respondents were more aware of the means by which the parasitic contamination took place.

Building upon this and other studies, Lachlan et al. (2007) sought to examine information-seeking patterns and crisis preparation surrounding those affected by Hurricane Katrina. The findings of their study lend further support to the notion that knowledge gaps are a critical consideration in terms of message acquisition and response during disasters and pandemics. They found further support for knowledge gaps but added initial evidence that these gaps may not be predicted perfectly by socioeconomic status. Spence et al. (2011) then replicated this study two years later and found evidence of knowledge gaps across cultural groups that were evident *even when controlling for socioeconomic status.* The authors offer that this may be an indication of a deeper concern when reaching diverse audiences: underlying distrust in centralized information from government agencies. It is not difficult to imagine that members of these communities would resist information provided by government relief organizations, given previous failures to accurately address their needs. It may be the case that during disasters and pandemics, emergency responders and government agencies need to consider their relationships with varying communities and the impact that cultural and political history may have on the levels of trust and subsequent information processing and response.

Specific Channels

Throughout the world, information consumers have many technologies which can deliver news instantaneously. Examples range from technologies with mass adoption such as television and radio to newer technologies, such as social networking devices. Portable devices such as phones or the numerous types of tablets available are capable of searching the Internet, displaying news channels, and sending and receiving text messages and standard voice communication. Yet, despite the proliferation of information technologies, radio and television have remained vital to the public in times of crisis (Carey, 2003).

Disasters can produce circumstances in which many forms of electronic communication are unable to work. For example, it is difficult for mobile phone carriers and television stations to continue to operate during a power outage, whereas, throughout the world, radio stations can continue to broadcast on generator power. Inside homes, battery-powered radios are a fairly common household device and radios that can be operated on hand crank power are not only marketed specifically for disaster preparedness, but have proliferated around the world, in many areas as the most commonly used home radio. Radio as a medium has several advantages for disasters that make it a turned to medium, worldwide (Spence et al., 2009).

Results from a sample of radio stations in the United States indicated a relationship between market size and disaster preparedness and perceptions about civic responsibility and perceptions about the public. It was found that radio stations in smaller markets indicated they were better prepared to handle a crisis, perceived a higher level of civic responsibility to report on crises, and were more likely to report, believing that citizens would respond to a crisis or emergency in a pro-social manner (Spence et al., 2009).

A follow-up study was conducted with radio stations that directly broadcast to areas impacted by the 2008 flooding in the Midwestern United States (Spence et al., 2011). Results from that study indicated that while radio stations in disaster-prone regions may be more aware of their responsibilities to the public than those in more stable locations, stations were still reluctant to coordinate with public officials. The authors also note that, similar to their first study, stations in larger markets tended to perceive less civic responsibility than those in smaller markets, lending support to an argument that radio stations that reach the greatest number of people may be both unwilling and unable to effectively communicate with the public during a disaster.

In respect to those results, radio stations, regardless of market size, should be expected to aid in the communication and coordination needs of communities during a disaster. Local stations often replace regular programming with continuous live coverage during a disaster (Sellnow & Seeger, 2001; Singer & Green, 1972). Radio can also be used as a mechanism for recruiting volunteers and coordinating disaster logistics (Scanlon et al., 1985; Sellnow & Seeger, 2001). For example, in 1994 Louisville, Kentucky, in the United States, was hit with a record snowfall that shut the city down for almost a week. WHAS 840-AM radio made an effort to coordinate local response efforts, such as mobilizing individuals with 4 × 4 vehicles. Another instance occurred when WHAS broadcast a story about a local 3-year-old girl in need of a liver transplant. A donor was found in the city of Omaha, Nebraska, United States (almost 700 miles/1120 km away). Because of the record snowfall, the streets of Louisville were covered with 16 in. of snow and the local airport was closed. After WHAS broadcast the story, over 200 people showed up with snow shovels to clear a spot in a church parking lot near the home of the 3-year-old, allowing a helicopter to land, and a volunteer showed up to plow a local runway. "On a day when most folks couldn't get down the block, Michelle got to Omaha in time" (Dorsey, 1994). Radio was a needed and effective medium for coordination during the storm. As one newspaper account stated, "try to imagine life without WHAS radio, which wasn't just an essential information source. It was a source of comfort and contact for everyone isolated by the storm" (Dorsey, 1994). With other media being brittle in a disaster, radio is unique in its capacity to continue functioning under extremely trying conditions, and evidence suggests that it continues to do so (Spence & Lachlan, 2023). This includes the issues of geography and the use of social media technologies by radio stations (see Spence et al., 2023).

As mentioned earlier, language can be an issue with the potential to impact disaster response. In the United States, with the exception of a few markets, major television stations only provide English language programming; even in those markets that provide bilingual programming, stations are often unprepared for bilingual broadcasts of emergency messages. A study conducted after Hurricane Katrina found that Latino respondents indicated that they were not "prepared and/or did not anticipate the potential strength of the storm and the implications of staying put or evacuating" (Hilfinger-Messias & Lacy, 2007, p. 491). Thus, local radio outlets also have a role in being prepared to broadcast disaster messages in multiple languages and address the limitations of emergency response if the demographics of the local community call for such preparations.

The presence of a risk and subsequent disaster raises an important issue for the consumption of social media. As noted by Westerman et al. (2009), there are several possibilities for the future use of new media devices, and the use of such devices for production and delivery of information will continue to grow. Emergency practitioners should view this technology as a viable medium for crisis communication. Studying and adapting to the technology now may allow for easier adaptation to micro-media technologies of the future.

Often, the frontlines of information come from eyewitnesses who are reporting on up-to-the-second events. In many cases, even traditional mass media sources such as major news outlets obtain, borrow, and report information from these sources prior to breaking news.

Technological challenges in areas afflicted by crises (i.e., down satellite connections) may slow official news correspondent reports; however, social media reports may be much more swiftly distributed. For example, during the January 2010 Haitian earthquake, social media played a key role in disseminating information about this tragedy (Bunz, 2010).

However, the use of many new media technologies is not standardized from disaster event to disaster event; therefore, much research is needed on the topic. For example, in the event of a pandemic, citizen journalism and reports from around the world may be sought by a larger worldwide public. New forms of media may not only be used to seek out information but also be used to collect and transmit information. The continued growth of new media technologies has created an environment where information consumers are now far less obligated or concerned about what passes through traditional gatekeepers. New media technologies now allow information producers and consumers to bypass gatekeepers and obtain information from the primary source. Because information provided in newer, online channels often suffers from a relative lack of professional gatekeepers to monitor content and, thus, lacks some of these traditional markers used to determine source credibility, consumers become more responsible for making decisions about the perceived credibility of information online (Westerman et al., 2012, 2013; Spence et al., 2013b). The gates within such new media environments are now located not only with the information providers but also with the information seeker, who in the new media environment is acting as their own gatekeeper (Kovach & Rosenstiel, 1999). This fundamental change has created a shift from the traditional notion of "gatekeeping" to what Bruns (2008) has referred to as "gatewatching." Gatewatchers, unable to control the gates through which information passes, instead keep a constant eye at the gates and communicate those gates to information consumers, who then make the choice about the topic relevance. Therefore, gatewatchers fundamentally promote or diffuse news through making sources or stories known to others in the new media environment. Rather than publishing unique information, they make others' information known and add to it. This can be seen in environments such as Facebook where a user publishes a link and then comments or on Twitter where a user reposts a link. At the same time, there is some degree of evidence that social media content associated with legacy news brands may be more likely to be retransmitted and that social media content from these brands is viewed with a high degree of credibility (see Rainear et al., 2021).

Studying how information consumers and information providers use new media during disasters requires a broad approach. Social information processing theory (SIPT) suggests that people use whatever information a channel affords them in order to make judgments about another communicator (Walther, 1992). A central assumption of SIPT is that people have the same goals online as they do offline, an assumption that should hold true during a disaster or pandemic. SIPT suggests that in order to accomplish that goal, if a channel does not allow for the usual cues used, then an information consumer will adapt their perceptions based upon the channel affordances.

For example, in a health-related disaster such as a pandemic, people may turn to new media because of the fear associated with travel alongside of familiarity of use. Studies examining the role of social media and risk information seeking are beginning to emerge. In a health information-seeking study by Spence et al. (2013a) that examined the role of user-generated cues (ethnicity) and credibility on social media, results suggest that African American avatars on social media (Facebook) were found to be highly credible when promoting a health news story germane to the African American community. Another series of follow-up studies examined the role of communicated ethnicity in social media through both user-generated cues and other-generated cues (Spence et al., 2013a; Spence et al., 2013b). Although the studies did not directly measure information seeking and risk communication, they do provide evidence of how social media can and is used for such purposes.

Measurement and Research in Disasters and Pandemics

One of the greatest challenges facing the future of risk research deals with measurement and methods. The unique circumstances posed by large-scale disasters create difficulties for disaster researchers in obtaining valuable and useful data. The perfect conditions and controls found in experimental research and tightly controlled survey work are often simply not possible under these circumstances. For example, the site of a disaster or accident may be restricted in terms of access, and the conditions surrounding a disaster may present very real dangers to researchers and subjects alike (Spence & Lachlan, 2010). Government officials and first responders may justifiably be more concerned with relief efforts than with coordinating with researchers, and the delays in data collection created by these impediments may lead to memory deterioration and inaccurate recall of disaster events (Seeger & Gouran, 2007; Tourangeau et al., 2002).

Given these limitations, it has been argued that imperfect designs may be completely acceptable under conditions of crisis and disaster. For instance, randomized sampling is likely impossible given the constraints imposed by large-scale crises and disasters. By the same token, disaster researchers may find themselves sacrificing randomization in the name of ecologically valid data, which may be a trade-off that is worth pursuing. Disaster researchers may wish to consider simply limiting the expressed generalizability of their sample to the population from which they were actually drawn. It may also be advisable to shift the units of analysis under consideration from individuals to groups (Sawilowsky, 2007). Another solution is to conduct a census; when working with larger units of analysis, one may be able to obtain a sample that includes all relevant locals under consideration.

There are also methodological safeguards that can be taken in terms of data analysis to compensate for non-randomized sampling. For example, there are statistical tests and procedures that are designed specifically for non-normalized distributions, such as those derived from non-random samples. These non-parametric tests tend to involve median comparisons as opposed to mean comparisons or correlations. Some have advocated the use of the Kolmogorov–Smirnov test to check for normality, followed by Wilcoxon–Mann–Whitney or Kruskal–Wallis instead of *t* and analysis of variance (ANOVA), respectively (Spence & Lachlan, 2010).

Despite the challenges posed by collecting data under the conditions of crisis, there exists a growing body of research that aims to develop measurement systems for psychometric constructs under these conditions. Recent efforts to develop a measurement system for public response have revolved around Peter Sandman's (1998, 2003) suggestions that crisis and risk communication can attempt to produce levels of both knowledge acquisition and affective response that will lead to ideal outcomes for audiences. Sandman and colleagues express this notion through the formula: Risk = hazard + outrage. When audiences do not comprehend a risk, then they must be informed accordingly. Once an audience understands the risk, enough negative affect must be induced to engender a response, but not so much as to lead to poor behavior, hopelessness, or despair.

Sandman and colleagues go on to further describe hazard as the technical assessment of a risk and outrage as the cultural assessment (Sandman et al., 1998; Sandman et al., 1987). Depending on the specific parameters of a given disaster or pandemic, the correlation between hazard and outrage might actually be quite low or even inverse.

Recently, efforts have been made to develop measurement tools that can evaluate audience responses along these axes, in order to provide crisis communication practitioners with an understanding of the relative levels of hazard and outrage that may be experienced by the audience. Lachlan and Spence (2007) made the first attempt at developing instrumentation measuring Sandman's (1998) model in a survey administered to Katrina refugees who had been relocated to various parts of the United States. This developed into a thirteen-item measure, using five-point semantic differential scales to tap hazard and outrage. Three separate factor analysis models offered support for the two-factor model of hazard and outrage first proposed by Sandman (1998), and a series of analyses indicated variability in these responses across demographic markers.

Though the authors argue that Sandman's model can be measured empirically in both laboratory and field research, they add that the items developed in the initial study were situationally specific and may not be applicable to very many other disasters. In response, they further refined and developed this measure, in both laboratory and field settings, and created a measure that could be adapted to multiple crises and disasters, with the alteration of only a few words (Lachlan & Spence, 2010). Through two laboratory experiments and one field test, they arrived first at a 32-item measure of the hazard and outrage constructs and then a reduced 16-item measure. Through a series of multilevel modeling (MLM) analyses, they found the measurement system to be both useful and heuristic. It is also important to note that issues of culture are often under-studied and even ignored in measurement design, although outside of the scope of this chapter, it is an area that needs more attention in psychometric research.

Conclusion

Disasters and potential pandemics are receiving increased attention from the social science community. Across this developing body of research, specific and predictable patterns of audience behavior can be seen. This includes information seeking, stress responses, and exemplification. Perhaps more importantly, a strong and consistent evidence of variability in responses across subpopulations with different demographic and psychographic characteristics is evident. These differences in response are compounded when considered alongside the discrepancies in informational access that can be reasonably predicted across diverse audiences. These conclusions may have particular significance when considered in light of global risks and large-scale events that transcend national boundaries. While faced with a number of challenges, disaster researchers should continue to explore audience-based research that produces tangible, applicable data that can be used by emergency managers and government agencies under a variety of disaster circumstances and with a diverse set of cultural contexts.

References

Aguirre, B. E. (1988). The lack of warnings before Saragosa tornado. *International Journal of Mass Emergency and Disasters, 6*, 581–587.

Asch, S. M., Leake, B., & Gelberg, L. (1994). Does fear of immigration authorities deter tuberculosis patients from seeking care? *Western Journal of Medicine, 161*, 373–376.

Ahern, J., Galea, S., Resnick, H., & Vlahov, D. (2004). Television images and probable posttraumatic stress disorder after September 11. *Journal of Nervous and Mental Disease, 192*, 217–226.

Ball-Rokeach, S. J., & DeFleur, M. L. (1976). A dependency model of mass media effects. *Communication Research, 3*, 3–21.

Berger, C. R. (1987). Communicating under uncertainty. In M. E. Roloff, & G. R. Miller, Eds., *Interpersonal Processes: New Directions for Communication Research* (pp. 39–62). Newberry Park, CA: Sage.

Berlyne, D. E. (1960). *Conflict, Arousal and Curiosity.* New York: McGraw-Hill.

Brashers, D. E., Neidig, J. L., Haas, S. M., Dobbs, L. K., Cardillo, L. W., & Russell, J. A. (2000). Communication in the management of uncertainty: The case of persons living with HIV or AIDS. *Communication Monographs, 67*, 63–84.

Bruns, A. (2008). *The active audience: Transforming journalism from gatekeeping to gatewatching.* In C. Paterson, & D. Domingo, Eds., *Making Online News: The Ethnography of New Media Production.* New York: Peter Lang.

Bunz, M. (January 14, 2010). In Haiti earthquake coverage, social media gives victim a voice. *The Guardian*. Retrieved from http://www.theguardian.com/media/pda/2010/jan/14/socialnetworking-haiti (accessed December 9, 2015)

Busselle, R. W., & Shrum, L. J. (2003). Media exposure and the accessibility of social information. *Media Psychology, 5*, 255–282.

Carey, J. (2003). The functions and uses of media during the September 11 crisis and aftermath. In A. M. Noll, Ed., *Crisis communications: Lessons from September 11* (pp. 1–16). New York: Rowman & Littlefield.

CDC [=Centers for Disease Control and Prevention] (2002). *Crisis and Emergency Risk Communication*. Atlanta, GA: CERC.

DeFleur, M. L., & Ball-Rokeach, S. (1989). *Theories of Mass Communication* (5th ed.). White Plains, NY: Longman.

Dorsey, T. (January 21, 1994). A CITY OF VOLUNTEERS . . . So much attention is paid to the troublemakers of the world that it's easy to get the impression that the world is a terrible place. *The Courier-Journal*, Louisville.

Fothergill, A., Maestas, E. G. M., & Darlington, J. D. (1999). Race, ethnicity, and disasters in the United States: A review of the literature. *Disasters, 23*(2), 156–173.

Galea, S., Vlahov, D., Resnick, H., Ahern, J., Susser, E., Gold, J., Bucuvalas, M., & Kilpatrick, D. (2003). Trends of probable post-traumatic stress disorder in New York City after the September 11 terrorist attacks. *American Journal of Epidemiology, 158*, 514–524.

Heath, R. L., & Gay, C. D. (1997). Risk communication: Involvement, uncertainty, and control's effect on information scanning and monitoring by expert stakeholders in SARA Title III. *Management Communication Quarterly, 10*, 342–372.

Heath, R. L., Liao, S., & Douglas, W. (1995). Effects of perceived economic harms and benefits on issues involvement, use of information sources, and actions: A study in risk communication. *Journal of Public Relations Research, 7*, 89–109.

Hilfinger-Messias, D. K., & Lacy, E. (2007). Katrina-related health concerns of Latino survivors and evacuees. *Journal of Health Care for the Poor and Underserved, 18*, 443–464.

Hindman, D. B., & Coyle, K. (1999). Audience orientations to local radio coverage of a natural disaster. *Journal of Radio Studies, 6*(1), 8–26.

Hohm, C. (1976). A human-ecological approach to the reality and perception of air pollution: The Los Angeles case. *The Pacific Sociological Review, 19*, 21–44.

Hoven, C. W., Duarte, C. S., Lucas, C. P., Wu, P., Mandell, D. J., Goodwin, R. D., Cohen, M., Balaban, V., Woodruff, B. A., Bin, F., Musa, G. J., Mei, L., Cantor, P. A., Aber, J. L., Cohen, P., & Susser, E. (2005). Psychopathology among New York City public school children 6 months after September 11. *Archives of General Psychiatry, 62*, 545–552.

Kahlor, L. A., Dunwoody, S., & Griffin, R. J. (2004). Accounting for the complexity of causal explanations in the wake of an environmental risk. *Science Communication, 26*(1), 5–30.

Kovach, B., & Rosenstiel, T. (1999). *Warp Speed: America in the Age of Mixed Media*. New York: Century Foundation Press.

Lachlan, K. A., DiCairano, J., & Spence, P. R. (2024). Looking beyond the television: Variability in information seeking patterns and mitigation behaviors during Hurricane Ian. *Progress in Disaster Science, 23*, 100336. https://doi.org/10.1016/j.pdisas.2024.100336

Lachlan, K. A., Gilbert, C., Spence, P. R., & Hutter, E. (2021). Frozen while I scan: Examining the impact of media dependencies, socioeconomic status, and rumination on preparation behaviors related to Hurricane Dorian. *Journal of Contingencies and Crisis Management*. https://doi.org/10.1111/1468-5973.12362

Lachlan, K. A., & Spence, P. R. (2007). Hazard and outrage: Developing, validating, and testing a psychometric instrument in the aftermath of Katrina. *Journal of Applied Communication Research, 35*, 109–123. https://doi.org/10.1080/00909880601065847

Lachlan, K. A., & Spence, P. R. (2010). Communicating risks: Examining hazard and outrage in multiple contexts. *Risk Analysis, 30*(12), 1872–1886. https://doi.org/10.1111/j.1539-6924.2010.01511.x

Lachlan, K. A., Spence, P. R., & Eith, C. A. (2007). Access to mediated emergency messages: Differences in crisis knowledge across age, race, and socioeconomic status. In K. A. Bates, & R. S. Swan, Eds., *Through the Eye of Katrina: Social Justice in the United States* (pp. 203–219). Durham, NC: Carolina Academic Press.

Lachlan, K. A., Spence, P. R., & Seeger, M. W. (2009). Terrorist attacks and uncertainty reduction: Media use after September 11. *Behavioral Sciences of Terrorism and Political Aggression*, *1*, 101–110. https://doi.org/10.1080/19434470902771683

Lindell, M. K., & Perry, R. W. (2004). *Communicating Environmental Risk in Multiethnic Communities.* Thousand Oaks, CA: Sage.

Liverant, G. I., Hofmann, S. G., & Litz, B. T. (2004). Coping and anxiety in college students after the September 11th terrorist attacks. *Anxiety, Stress, and Coping*, *17*, 127–139.

Loges, W. E. (1994). Canaries in the coal mine: Perceptions of threat and media system dependency relations. *Communication Research*, *21*(1), 5–23.

Lowrey, W. (2004). Media dependency during a large-scale social disruption: The case of September 11. *Mass Communication and Society*, *7*(3), 339–357.

Murch, A. W. (1971). Public concern for environmental pollution. *Public Opinion Quarterly*, *35*, 100–106.

Pfefferbaum, B., Nixon, S. J., Tivis, R. D., Doughty, D. E., Pynoos, R. S., Gurwitch, R. H., & Foy, D. W. (2001). Television exposure in children after a terrorist incident. *Psychiatry*, *64*, 202–211.

Rainear, A., Lachlan, K. A., & Xu, Z. (2021). Storms of a feather tweet together: An exploratory study examining Houston-area emergency management communication on Twitter in Hurricane Harvey. *Journal of Emergency Management*, *20*(1), 53–60.

Sandman, P. M. (2003, April). Four kinds of risk communication. *The Synergist*, 26–27.

Sandman, P. M., Weinstein, N. D., & Hallman, W. K. (1998). Communications to reduce risk underestimation and overestimation. *Risk Decision and Policy*, *3*(2), 93–108.

Sandman, P. M., Weinstein, N. D., & Klotz, M. L. (1987). Public response to the risk from geological radon. *Journal of Communication*, *37*(3), 93–108.

Sawilowsky, S. S. (2007). ANCOVA and quasi-experimental design: The legacy of Campbell and Stanley. In S. S. Sawilowsky, Ed., *Real Data Analysis* (pp. 213–238). Charlotte, NC: Information Age.

Saylor, C. F., Cowart, B. L., Lipovsky, J. A., Jackson, C., & Finch, A. J., Jr. (2003). Media exposure to September 11: Elementary school students' experiences and posttraumatic symptoms. *American Behavioral Scientist*, *46*, 1622–1642.

Scanlon, J., Alldred, S., Farreli, A., & Prawick, A. (1985). Coping with the media in disasters: Some predictable problems. *Public Administration Review*, *45*, 123–133.

Seeger, M., & Gouran, D. (2007). Introduction to special issue on the 2005 Atlantic hurricane season. *Journal of Applied Communication Research*, *25*, 1–8.

Seeger, M., Sellnow, T., & Ulmer, R. (2003). *Communication and Organizational Crisis.* Westport, CT: Praeger.

Sellnow, T. L., & Seeger, M. (2001). Exploring the boundaries of crisis communication: The case of the 1997 Red River Valley flood. *Communication Studies*, *52*, 153–168.

Singer, B., & Green, L. (1972). *The Special Functions of Radio During a Community Emergency.* Toronto: The Copp-Clark Publishing Company.

Spence, P. R., Lin, X., Lachlan, K. A., & DiCairono, J. (2024). Exemplification in communication research: Three studies examining the theory. *Communication Studies*, *76*, 72–88. https://doi.org/10.1080/10510974.2024.2398222

Spence, P. R., Lachlan, K. A., & Edwards, A. L. (2023). We interrupt this program, this is an emergency: Revisiting the role of radio in a crisis. *Journal of Radio & Audio Media*, *30*(2), 680–701. https://doi.org/10.1080/19376529.2021.2023539

Spence, P. R., & Lachlan, K. A. (2010). Disasters, crises, and unique populations: Suggestions for survey research. *New Directions for Evaluation*, *2010*(126), 95–106. https://doi.org/10.1002/ev.332

Spence, P. R., & Lachlan, K. A. (2023). We interrupt this program, this is an emergency: Revisiting the role of radio in a crisis. *Journal of Radio and Audio Media*. https://doi.org/10.1080/19376529.2021.2023539

Spence, P. R., Lachlan, K. A., & Burke, J. (2011). Differences in crisis knowledge across age, race, and socioeconomic status during Hurricane Ike: A field test and extension of the knowledge gap hypothesis. *Communication Theory*, *21*(3), 261–278. https://doi.org/10.1111/j.1468-2885.2011.01385.x

Spence, P. R., Lachlan, K. A., & Griffen, D. R. (2007). Crisis communication, race, and natural disasters. *The Journal of Black Studies*, *37*, 539–554. https://doi.org/10.1177/0021934706296192

Spence, P. R., Lachlan, K. A., McIntyre, J. J., & Seeger, M. (2009). Serving the public interest in a crisis: Radio and its unique role. *Journal of Radio & Audio Media*, *16*(2), 144–159. http://doi.org/10.1080/19376520903277005

Spence, P. R., Lachlan, K. A., St. Spates, A., & Lin, X. (2013a). Intercultural differences in responses to health messages on social media from spokespeople with varying levels of ethnic identity. *Computers in Human Behavior*. http://dx.doi.org/ 10.1016/j.chb.2012.12.013

Spence, P. R., Lachlan, K. A., Westerman, D., & Spates, S. A. (2013b). Where the gates matter less: Ethnicity and perceived source credibility in social media health messages. *Howard Journal of Communications*, *24*(1), 1–16. http://doi.org/10.1080/10646175.2013.748593

Spence, P. R., McIntyre, J. J., Lachlan, K. A., Savage, M. E., & Seeger, M. W. (2011). Serving the public interest in a crisis: Does local radio meet the public interest? *Journal of Contingencies & Crisis Management*, *19*(4), 227–232. http://doi.org/10.1111/j.1468-5973.2011.00650.x

Spence, P. R., Westerman, D., Skalski, P. D., Seeger, M., Sellnow, T. L., & Ulmer, R. R. (2006). Gender and age effects on information-seeking after 9/11. *Communication Research Reports*, *23*(3), 217–223. http://doi.org/10.1080/08824090600796435

Spence, P. R., Westerman, D., Skalski, P. D., Seeger, M., Ulmer, R. R., Venette, S., & Sellnow, T. L. (2005). Proxemic effects on information seeking after the September 11 attacks. *Communication Research Reports*, *22*(1), 39–46. http://doi.org/10.1080/0882409052000343507

Spence, P. R., Westerman, D., & Rice, R. R. (2017). Exemplification theory in health and risk messaging. In J. Nussbaum, Ed., *Oxford Research Encyclopedia of Communication*. https://doi.org.10.1093/acrefore/9780190228613.013.526

Tichenor, P. J., Donohue, G. A., & Olien, C. N. (1970). Mass media flow and differential growth in knowledge. *Public Opinion Quarterly*, *34*, 159–170.

Tourangeau, R., Rips, L. J., & Rasinski, K. (2002). *The Psychology of Survey Response*. London: Cambridge University Press.

Van Ardosol, M., Sabagh, G., & Alexander, F. (1965). Reality and the perception of environmental hazards. *Journal of Health and Human Behavior*, *5*, 144–153.

Walther, J. B. (1992). Interpersonal effects in computer-mediated interaction: A relational perspective. *Communication Research*, *19*(1), 52–90. http://doi.org/10.1177/009365092019001003

Westerman, D., Spence, P. R., & Lachlan, K. A. (2009). Telepresence and the exemplification effects of disaster news. *Communication Studies*, *60*(5), 542–557. http://doi.org/10.1080/10510970903260376

Westerman, D., Spence, P. R., & Van Der Heide, B. (2012). A social network as information: The effect of system generated reports of connectedness on credibility on Twitter. *Computers in Human Behavior*, *28*, 199–206.

Westerman, D. W., Spence, P. R., & Van Der Heide, B. (2013/2014). Social media as an information source: Recency of updates and credibility of information. *Journal of Computer Mediated. Communication*, *19*(2), 171–183.

Zillmann, D. (1999). Exemplification theory: Judging the whole by some of its parts. *Media Psychology*, *1*(1), 69–94. http://doi.org/10.1207/s1532785xmep0101_5

Zillmann, D. (2002). Exemplification theory of media influence. In J. Bryant, & D. Zillmann, Eds., *Media Effects: Advances in Theory and Research* (2nd ed., pp. 213–245). Mahwah, NJ: Lawrence Erlbaum Associates.

Author's Bio

Patric R. Spence (PhD, Wayne State University) is Professor in the Nicholson School of Communication and Media at the University of Central Florida. He is also a member of the Communication and Social Robotics Labs (www.combotlabs.org).

Kenneth A. Lachlan (PhD, Michigan State University) is Professor and Head of the Department of Communication at the University of Connecticut. He holds research affiliations with UConn's Institute for Collaboration on Health, Intervention and Policy, and the Sustainable Global Cities Initiative and served as the Editor-in-Chief of Communication Studies from 2016 to 2018. His research interests include the functions and effects of social media during crises and disasters, community-level risk mitigation interventions, and the role of cognitive processing styles in responding to emergency messages.

19

The Role of Audiences, Citizens, and Victims in International Crises

Addressing Public Health Crises and Pandemics

Annemarie Wiedicke[1] and Constanze Rossmann[2]
[1] Institute for Media Research, Chemnitz University of Technology, Chemnitz, Germany
[2] Department of Media and Communication, University of Munich, Munich, Germany

Over the last years, infectious diseases have been traveling across international borders faster than ever before (Chon & Park, 2019), leading to major public health crises such as the A/H1N1 pandemic in 2009/2010, the Ebola outbreak in Western Africa in 2014, or, most recently, the COVID-19 pandemic (Karlsen & Kruke, 2018; Tandoc & Lee, 2022). Notably, with more than 767 million confirmed cases and nearly 7 million deaths worldwide (status: July 2023), the latter has been characterized as the most significant public health event of the century (WHO, 2023). Given the rapid changes, unknown risks, and high mortality that often occur during such events (Link, 2021; Tang & Zou, 2021), accurate and timely information is of major importance for international audiences. Not only can they help the public to understand the situation, develop adequate risk perceptions, and cope with its uncertainties, but also they empower individuals to make informed decisions about preventive behaviors (Link, 2021; Tandoc & Lee, 2022). In consequence, public communication during public health crises mainly serves three functions: (1) providing information about risks, symptoms, or treatment of a disease; (2) enabling the public to evaluate risks and deal with the threats; and (3) encouraging the public to take appropriate preventive action and increase compliance with healthcare as well as political and social interventions (Rossmann et al., 2018, p. 358). At the same time, crisis communication faces a variety of issues (Link, 2021), including the spread of misinformation among publics (Bin Naeem & Kamel Boulos, 2021), the challenge of raising awareness and concern without creating panic (Rossmann et al., 2018; Seeger et al., 2010), as well as audiences' information overload (Bawden & Robinson, 2009) and message fatigue (Guan et al., 2022; Hwang et al., 2022).

In this chapter, we provide an overview of current research on audiences of communication in public health crises and pandemics. Firstly, we identify major audiences and their role during such events. Furthermore, we discuss people's information behaviors and information processing. Moreover, we portray media and (digital) health literacy as important determinants of how publics obtain and comprehend information from various sources. We then address the

The Handbook of International Crisis and Risk Communication Research, Second Edition.
Edited by Andreas Schwarz, Matthew W. Seeger, and Sora Kim.

media's impact on audiences' risk perceptions, before depicting specific challenges for communication in public health crises and pandemics. Finally, we shed light on possible areas for future research.

Major Audiences

To date, communication research on public health crises and particularly pandemics from an audience-oriented perspective mostly focuses on the *general public* (Chu et al., 2022). This is hardly surprising: Such events mostly affect wide parts of society, often beyond international borders (Berg et al., 2021). Moreover, in order to manage public health crises, not only international authorities – such as the World Health Organization (WHO) – but also national institutions – such as the Centers for Disease Control and Prevention (CDC) in the United States – often depend on engaging the general public in specific preventive or protective behaviors (Koh et al., 2020). While in the following we focus on the general public's role as the *audience*, it should be noted that its members are *not* merely the recipients of communication in public health crises. In fact, they often actively *contribute* to crisis communication, too: For instance, throughout the course of the COVID-19 pandemic, social media users have taken part in all stages of knowledge transmission, including knowledge about COVID-19 morbidity, interventions, spreading rumors or conspiracy theories, and reporting stigma (Islam et al., 2020, p. 1621).

Besides the general public, *journalists* are also an important audience of communication in public health crises (Holmes et al., 2009). More specifically, it is their task to (1) gather and distribute accurate information; (2) act as a conduit for communication between policymakers, medical or scientific experts, and the public; and finally (3) monitor the performance of institutions and authorities in managing the public health response during a crisis (Lubens, 2015; Perreault & Perreault, 2021). Thus, they are not merely the transmitters of information but also gatekeepers and interpreters (Rossmann et al., 2018). Against this background, current research discusses a variety of issues, such as the question of how the role perceptions of journalists shift during public health crises (Klemm et al., 2019), the role of news media as amplification stations (e.g., Rossmann et al., 2018; Zhao & Wu, 2021), or the specific challenges arising for journalists when they cover crises such as the COVID-19 pandemic. These include attempting to maintain objectivity during the times of growing politicization and polarization (Hart et al., 2020; Holland et al., 2014; Perreault & Perreault, 2021) and dealing with a flow of mis- and disinformation in a time of enhanced public demand for reliable facts (e.g., Lwin et al., 2021; Sarelska & Jenkins, 2022; Sharma et al., 2020).

In addition, *healthcare professionals,* such as doctors, nurses (e.g., Bautista et al., 2021; Lubens, 2015), and *policymakers* (e.g., Lubens, 2015; Rufai & Bunce, 2020), are pointed out as significant audiences during public health crises and pandemics. To our knowledge, there is no study (so far) examining how policymakers seek or perceive communication in these events, despite it affecting their decision-making processes regarding crisis response (Hyland-Wood et al., 2021). However, there is a growing body of research explicitly addressing healthcare professionals as audiences during public health crises (e.g., Li & Khan, 2022; Peres et al., 2020; Wang et al., 2020). For instance, results from Taiwan show that during the COVID-19 pandemic healthcare professionals have not only relied on other sources of information than non-healthcare workers but also have dealt with this information differently (Wang et al., 2020) – thus confirming the need for more in-depth research on specific audiences of crisis communication during public health crises, rather than just focusing on the general public.

Although these diverse audiences are characterized by different needs and may also face specific challenges during public health crises and pandemics, they all have to deal with *uncertainty* as central and inevitable feature of such events (Afifi et al., 2012; Chu et al., 2022).

Coping with Uncertainty During a Public Health Crisis

When people experience a high degree of uncertainty (Chon & Park, 2019), they tend to cope through *information seeking*, i.e., "a deliberate, purposeful process in which individuals actively aim to change their state of knowledge by searching for information about a specific topic" (Lewis, 2017, p. 1). During public health crises, information seeking has been shown not only to reduce uncertainties but also to foster empowerment and adaption to the crisis on a cognitive, behavioral, and affective level and support individuals' sensemaking as well as decision-making about preventive behaviors (Li et al., 2022b; Link et al., 2022; Tandoc & Lee, 2022).

Sources, Seeking, and Processing of Risk Information

According to a scoping review of 149 studies on audiences' information seeking during five major outbreaks of infectious diseases spanning different regions and populations, people tend to rely on multiple sources during these events, with major sources differing among international audiences (Majid et al., 2020). For instance, traditional media sources (especially television) and public organizations have been shown to be the preferred sources of information regarding COVID-19 in several European countries (Dreisiebner et al., 2022; Soroya et al., 2021) and the United States (Ali et al., 2020). In sub-Saharan Africa (Osuagwu et al., 2023), such information was mostly sought from television and social media. Findings from Taiwan (Wang et al., 2020) and Jordan (Olaimat et al., 2020), in turn, point out social media and the Internet in general as main sources of COVID-19-related information. On an individual level, personal characteristics, such as age and gender, as well as political orientation and profession (e.g., working in healthcare or not), have been shown to determine which information sources individuals use during public health crises (e.g., Ali et al., 2020; Dreisiebner et al., 2022; Wang et al., 2020).

Besides examining *where* people get their information from, an increasing number of studies have addressed the factors that explain *why* they seek and *how* they process information during public health crises and pandemics (e.g., Hubner & Hovick, 2020; Li & Zheng, 2022; Zhou & Roberto, 2022; Zhou et al., 2023). Theoretically, research in this context often draws on the *risk information seeking and processing (RISP) model* (Griffin et al., 1999) and the *planned risk information seeking model (PRISM)* (Kahlor, 2010).

Based on the *heuristic–systematic model* (Eagly & Chaiken, 1993) and the *theory of planned behavior* (Ajzen, 1991), the RISP model addresses the social, psychological, and communicative factors that drive health risk information seeking and systematic processing in specific thematic contexts (Yang et al., 2014). According to the model, information seeking is motivated by (1) individual characteristics, such as an individual's need for cognition or demographics; (2) individuals' informational subjective norms, i.e., the perceived social pressure to perform a search; and (3) perceived current knowledge respectively knowledge insufficiency. The RISP model further includes (4) perceived hazard characteristics comprising individuals' risk perception; (5) affective responses to the risk, such as worries; (6) beliefs about the usefulness of information in various channels (known as channel beliefs); and (7) one's abilities to seek information, known as perceived information-gathering capacity (Griffin et al., 2012; Link, 2021). Overall, the model has been shown to have excellent explanatory power in analyses with risk information seeking and systematic processing as the outcome variables (Yang et al., 2014), most recently in the context of the COVID-19 outbreak in China (Li & Zheng, 2022) and throughout the COVID-19 pandemic in Taiwan (Li et al., 2022b) and the United States (Zhou & Roberto, 2022; Zhou et al., 2023).

The PRISM (Kahlor, 2010) integrates prior models of health and risk information seeking, including the RISP model (Griffin et al., 1999). Rather than focusing on information seeking within specific health risk contexts, the PRISM aims at explaining health risk information-seeking habits across thematic contexts (Kahlor, 2010), such as climate change and health (Hubner & Hovick, 2020). Given that climate change increases the likelihood of infectious disease outbreaks and epidemics, and thus of public health crises (Marani et al., 2021), the PRISM proves particularly useful in this context (Hubner & Hovick, 2020). In this model, (1) perceived knowledge insufficiency, i.e., desiring more knowledge than one currently has, is considered a key driver of planned information seeking. Additional predictors of individuals' information-seeking intention (and perceived knowledge insufficiency) according to the PRISM are (2) perceived risk via (3) affective risk response, such as worries; (4) seeking-related subjective norms, i.e., individuals' perceptions of others' expectations regarding their information seeking; (5) attitudes toward seeking; and (6) perceived seeking control, which is similar to the perceived information-gathering capacity in the RISP model (Griffin et al., 2012). Finally, the PRISM includes (7) perceived knowledge as a predictor of knowledge insufficiency (Hubner & Hovick, 2020; Kahlor, 2010). Recent studies provide support for the model for predicting individuals' information-seeking intention and systematic processing during infectious disease outbreaks, specifically the Zika virus outbreak in Florida in 2015/2016 (Hubner & Hovick, 2020) as well as the COVID-19 outbreak in China in early 2020 (Liu et al., 2021).

Integrating both RISP model and PRISM with two concepts of information retrieval, namely information seeking and scanning, i.e., information retrieval during routine media use, Rossmann et al. (2021) showed that this integrated model was well able to explain information retrieval and processing in the early phase of COVID-19 as well.

However, information seeking is not the only behavioral response to uncertainty during a public health crisis (Li, 2023; Link et al., 2022).

Information Avoidance and Information Overload

More specifically, ***information avoidance***, i.e., the purposeful decision to "prevent or delay the acquisition of available but potentially unwanted information" (Sweeny et al., 2010, p. 341), is also an active and conscious strategy to cope with such events (Li, 2023; Link et al., 2022). Still, until recently, it has received less scholarly attention compared to information seeking (Link, 2021). Now, there is a growing number of studies indicating information avoidance behaviors during the COVID-19 pandemic (e.g., Bruin et al., 2021; Kim et al., 2020; Link, 2022; Link et al., 2022; Siebenhaar et al., 2020). According to a meta-analysis by Li (2023), research on predictors of information avoidance in this context mostly draws from three theoretical frameworks, including the RISP model (Griffin et al., 1999) as well as the ***comprehensive model of information seeking (CMIS)*** (Johnson & Meischke, 1993) and the ***stimulus–organism–response (S-O-R) framework*** (Mehrabian & Russell, 1974). While perceived efficacy (i.e., individuals' perceived ability and control to perform information behaviors under salient threat) and informational subjective norms showed small but negative effects on COVID-19-related information avoidance, channel belief (i.e., belief about the usefulness of information from a specific media channel) and ***information overload*** have been shown to be the strongest antecedents of such behavior (Li, 2023).

Information overload "occurs when a recipient has insufficient cognitive capacity to handle a large amount of information properly and effectively" (Jia et al., 2022, p. 2). Similarly to information avoidance, information overload has received increased scholarly attention throughout the course of the COVID-19 pandemic (e.g., Bruin et al., 2021; Hong & Kim, 2020; Jia et al., 2022; Soroya et al., 2021; Wang et al., 2022). Importantly, information overload is associated with various unintended negative effects of communication during public health crises: These include negative emotions (Gardikiotis et al., 2021; Wang et al., 2022) as well as greater heuristic and less systematic processing, which leads to people being less likely to enact prevention behaviors (Hong & Kim, 2020). Thus, information overload poses a serious challenge for crisis management (Gardikiotis et al., 2021).

Overall, public health crises and pandemics force individuals to "navigate complex media environments filled with frequently changing and varyingly credible information to acquire and apply health information during times of uncertainty" (Weintraub Austin et al., 2021, p. 239). In these contexts, individuals' *media* and *(digital) health literacy* present critical abilities (Okan et al., 2020).

Media and (Digital) Health Literacy

Media literacy refers to "individuals' ability to obtain, interpret, critically think about information, and improve daily life and social development" (Li et al., 2022a, p. 2). More specifically, media literacy supports individuals' *decision-making* through enhanced *critical thinking* about media content, which includes "interpreting the meaning of stylistic characteristics, assessing content accuracy and completeness, assessing the source's implied values, and understanding the context in which the message has been shared" (Weintraub Austin et al., 2021, p. 239). *(Digital) health literacy*, in turn, describes an "individuals' ability to access, understand, appraise, and apply health information" (from online environments) (Okan et al., 2020, p. 1; Patil et al., 2021, p. 2).

Both concepts are well established in health communication and public health research (e.g., Levin-Zamir & Bertschi, 2018; Sørensen et al., 2012) and have gained increasing attention as important determinants of how publics obtain, comprehend, and, in consequence, act on information from various sources in public health crises and pandemics (e.g., Bin Naeem & Kamel Boulos, 2021; Chen & Wang, 2021; Li et al., 2022a). For instance, findings from the COVID-19 pandemic not only indicate high levels of *media literacy* among different audiences (Li et al., 2022a; Weintraub Austin et al., 2021). They also confirm the significance of media literacy skills "for building both an accurate knowledge base and the necessary willingness to apply that information in social contexts" (Weintraub Austin et al., 2021, p. 248). Specifically, media literacy has been shown to promote the application of recommended protective behaviors during the COVID-19 pandemic in China (Li et al., 2022a) as well as the United States (Weintraub Austin et al., 2021).

Conversely, the current discourse on individuals' health literacy and its role in the context of public health crises is less optimistic. On the one hand, health literacy can facilitate individuals to distinguish between valid and non-valid information (Okan et al., 2020). It supports people in navigating information sources and empowers them to make informed health decisions and practice preventive behaviors in times of uncertainty (Patil et al., 2021; Sørensen et al., 2012). On the other hand, population-based studies on health literacy indicate that great proportions of Asian (Duong et al., 2017), European (Sørensen et al., 2015), Latin (Arrighi et al., 2022), and North American (Lopez et al., 2022) publics show difficulties in dealing with health-related information (Okan et al., 2020). Since low levels of health literacy are strongly associated with poorer health outcomes and poorer use of healthcare services (Berkman et al., 2011), it is not surprising that this issue has been repeatedly referred to as a major concern during public health crises by both health authorities and scientists (e.g., Paakkari & Okan, 2020; Patil et al., 2021). For instance, according to Chen and Wang (2021), individuals with low health literacy were less likely to seek and share crisis information during the Quanjian[1] crisis in China, thus possibly enforcing health inequalities. Furthermore, the low levels of (digital) health literacy have been shown to contribute significantly to the spread of COVID-19-related misinformation (Bin Naeem & Kamel Boulos, 2021).

In sum, individuals' media and (digital) health literacy are crucial competencies when it comes to both (1) acquiring and applying health information and (2) adapting behaviors accordingly (Paakkari & Okan, 2020; Weintraub Austin et al., 2021). Thus, they play a vital

[1] Quanjian had been one of the biggest healthcare product companies in China. On December 25, 2018, it was reported that the company sold a healthcare product that caused the death of a 4-year-old girl (Chen & Wang, 2021).

role in overcoming public health crises. This also holds true for audiences' *risk perceptions* (Cipolletta et al., 2022). More specifically, the effective management of such crises relies on audiences' *accurate* perceptions of risk (Zhou, 2022).

Risk Perception and the Impact of Media Use

As indicated earlier, one of the main tasks of communication in a public health crisis is to raise awareness and concern and thus enable the public to deal with arising threats – without, however, creating panic or inducing irrational behavior (Rossmann et al., 2018; Seeger et al., 2010). In consequence, audiences' risk perceptions have been described "as a primary building block" of effective crisis communication during such events (Rogers & Pearce, 2016, p. 36). Conceptually, *risk perception* is multidimensional, entailing referential, cognitive, affective, and behavioral components (Coleman, 1993). In the context of public health crises and pandemics, risk perception has been referred to as a person's subjective assessment of the actual or potential threat to their life or, more broadly, their well-being (Lohiniva et al., 2022). Past crises have shown that the success of policies to slow down the spread of infectious diseases depends partly on the public's recognition of the relative risks (Slovic, 2000; Zhou, 2022). On the one hand, people who perceive greater risks are more likely to adopt preventive behaviors (Bruine de Bruin & Bennett, 2020; Dryhurst et al., 2020). Still, higher risk perception has also been shown to negatively affect people's psychological states (Cipolletta et al., 2022; Lam et al., 2020; Zhong et al., 2021). On the other hand, lower risk perception may prevent people from adopting preventive behaviors (Cipolletta et al., 2022; Wright, 2021). In consequence, establishing *accurate* risk perceptions among audiences is of great significance for an effective communication in a public health crisis (Dryhurst et al., 2020; Zhou, 2022).

Audiences' perception of risks during public health crises and pandemics has been proven to depend on a variety of factors (Zhou, 2022). Specifically, according to the findings from the COVID-19 pandemic, (1) personal experience with the virus; (2) individualistic and prosocial values; (3) hearing about the virus from friends and family; (4) trust in government, science, and medical professionals; (5) personal knowledge of government strategy; and (6) personal and collective efficacy significantly predict the risk perceptions of audiences across countries and continents (Dryhurst et al., 2020). In addition, mass media have long been considered to be the vital shapers of the public's risk perceptions (Oh et al., 2021; Snyder & Rouse, 1995), especially when individuals lack firsthand experience or knowledge of a health hazard (Oh et al., 2021).

Research examining associations between individuals' media use and risk perceptions during public health crises draws on a variety of theoretical frameworks (Heydari et al., 2021), including the *social amplification of risk framework (SARF)* (Kasperson et al., 1988). The SARF theorizes how and why risks or risk events are amplified and thus may result in public worries (Rossmann et al., 2018). In doing so, it integrates different psychological, social, institutional, and cultural processes, suggesting that these processes affect information flow and risk perception "in ways that may amplify or attenuate public responses to the risk or risk event" (Kasperson et al., 1988, p. 177). Specifically, the framework assumes amplification respectively attenuation processes at two stages: (1) the transfer of information about the risk, i.e., the communication of risks by scientists, in press releases and news media coverage, and interpersonal communication between laymen; and (2) the response mechanisms of society, i.e., the audiences' interpretation and perception processes (Kasperson et al., 1988; Rossmann et al., 2018).

Regarding the media's impact on audiences' risk perception, current research provides conflicting results (Cipolletta et al., 2022). On the one hand, amplification processes have been repeatedly identified during public health crises and pandemics, especially in association with social media use: during the Middle East respiratory syndrome outbreak in South Korea in 2015 (Oh et al., 2021), the Zika outbreak in the United States in 2016 (Lee et al., 2020), and the COVID-19 pandemic in China (Zhao & Wu, 2021; Zhou, 2022). Other data from China point out the news media's role in amplifying risk perceptions regarding COVID-19 (Zhao & Wu, 2021). Finally, amplification of COVID-19-related risks was also found in Greece, as the consequence of media attention in general (Gardikiotis et al., 2021). On the other hand, there is evidence of risk ***attenuation*** processes, e.g., during the early stages of the COVID-19 pandemic in the United States (Zhang & Cozma, 2022) or as a result of obtaining COVID-19-related information from conservative media or the press briefings held by the Trump White House (Chung & Jones-Jang, 2022).

Nazione et al. (2021), however, did not find exposure to news, social media, or health websites to significantly predict risk perceptions at the beginning of the COVID-19 pandemic in the United States. Therefore, more (longitudinal) research is needed to understand causal relationships between the use of specific information channels, the channels' (amplifying or attenuating) characteristics, and audiences' risk perceptions during the different stages of public health crises.

Nevertheless, establishing accurate risk perceptions among audiences is not the only challenge that communication during public health crises and pandemics faces. Rather, in recent years, the *overabundance of information* – both valid and invalid – has been frequently addressed as a major issue in these contexts (e.g., Islam et al., 2020; Siebenhaar et al., 2020).

Infodemics and Their Consequences

Recent public health crises, particularly the COVID-19 pandemic, have also been characterized as "infodemics" (e.g., Islam et al., 2020, p. 1621; Siebenhaar et al., 2020, p 1). The term *infodemic*, or "information epidemic," describes the rapid spread and amplification of vast amounts of both valid and invalid information through the Internet or other communication channels (Okan et al., 2020). Since the beginning of the COVID-19 pandemic, both the production and consumption of information have increased rapidly and significantly (Okan et al., 2020). Thus, whether through active information seeking or routine information exposure (i.e., information scanning; Lewis, 2017), people have been inundated with messages about COVID-19 from a variety of communication channels (Guan et al., 2022; Koh et al., 2020). In consequence, early into the pandemic, Koh et al. (2020) warned that repeated messages carrying, for example, reminders of social distancing and hygiene practices and potential COVID-19 complications can result in *message fatigue*. Similarly, the excessive and continuous news coverage during a public health crisis such as the COVID-19 pandemic may lead to *issue fatigue* (e.g., Gurr et al., 2022; Metag & Arlt, 2016).

Message and Issue Fatigue

Message fatigue has been characterized as a state of exhaustion and boredom after prolonged and repeated exposure to persuasive messages promoting the same health behaviors (Guan et al., 2022; So & Popova, 2018). Emerging research in this field has pointed out various negative consequences arising from message fatigue, including increased desensitization (Keating & Galper, 2021) and decreased message effectiveness (Martinez Gonzalez et al., 2021; Reynolds-Tylus et al., 2021). During the COVID-19 pandemic, message fatigue resulted in inattention and reactance toward messages promoting similar prevention measures (Ball & Wozniak, 2022; Guan et al., 2022; Hwang et al., 2022; Jia et al., 2022) and, in consequence, decreased behavioral intentions for wearing masks, social distancing, and washing hands (Guan et al., 2022). Moreover, similarly to information overload, message fatigue has been shown to lead to information avoidance (Guan et al., 2022).

While the concept of message fatigue draws on ***persuasive*** information promoting specific behaviors distributed via a variety of communication channels (Guan et al., 2022; Gurr et al., 2022), the concept of ***issue fatigue*** explicitly focuses on unintended negative consequences of excessive and continuous news coverage on a particular topic (e.g., Gurr et al., 2022; Metag & Arlt, 2016). Specifically, issue fatigue describes a state in which recipients are not only increasingly annoyed with a certain issue but may also actively avoid further information on this matter (Metag & Arlt, 2016; Schumann, 2018). Since information on public health crises and pandemics is widely distributed via news coverage (Dreisiebner et al., 2022; Rossmann et al., 2018), issue fatigue – similar to message fatigue – can pose severe public health challenges in dealing with global health crises (Koh et al., 2020). Nevertheless, there is a lack of research regarding issue fatigue among audiences during public health crises.

However, as indicated above, the term infodemic refers not only to the spread of ***accurate*** information: Since the onset of the COVID-19 pandemic, researchers and public health authorities, including the WHO, have repeatedly addressed the rapidly spreading ***misinformation*** as a major public health issue (e.g., Kim et al., 2020; Islam et al., 2020; Lee et al., 2021).

Misinformation and Misperceptions

In general, ***misinformation*** is defined as "information considered incorrect based on the best available evidence from relevant experts at the time" (Vraga & Bode, 2020, p. 136), often including fake news, rumors, conspiracy theories, claims about magical cures, and stigmatizing and racist claims (Islam et al., 2020; Rathore & Farooq, 2020). Thus, misinformation refers to the information itself, while the term ***misperception*** refers to the beliefs that people hold (Vraga & Bode, 2020, p. 136). Interestingly, the prevalence and sharing of COVID-19 misinformation do not follow any geographical pattern (Al-Zaman, 2022; Rocha et al., 2021). Regarding the sources of misinformation, social media poses a particular challenge to public health authorities and crisis communication, as it not only produces a lot of misinformation but also offers ways to spread it quickly (Al-Zaman, 2022; Shobowale, 2021). Still, other sources, including traditional news media, have also been shown to mainstream and amplify misinformation during the COVID-19 pandemic (Dhawan et al., 2021).

As for effects on audiences, misinformation has been associated with a variety of negative consequences. These include COVID-19 misperceptions (Lee et al., 2021; Meppelink et al., 2022), which negatively influenced the perceived severity, susceptibility, self-efficacy, and efficacy of preventive measures taken by governments (Dhawan et al., 2021; Meppelink et al., 2022). Moreover, COVID-19 misinformation has been shown to lead to information avoidance (Kim et al., 2020) as well as negative emotions, such as fear (Rocha et al., 2021). Thus, current research underlines the crucial role of media consumption, misinformation, and misperceptions in shaping audiences' beliefs as well as their emotional and behavioral responses in a public health crisis (Dhawan et al., 2021; Meppelink et al., 2022). Against this background, the significance of media and (digital) health literacy during such events becomes even more evident (Bin Naeem & Kamel Boulos, 2021; Singh & Banga, 2022): According to a systematic review by Rocha et al. (2021), the susceptibility to interact with fake news is higher among elder publics, which is associated with the lower levels of media literacy among these groups. In addition, low health literacy correlates with high susceptibility to both COVID-19 misinformation and conspiracy theories (Cheng & Nishikawa, 2022).

Overall, there is a growing body of research on audiences' role during public health crises and pandemics. In particular, the recent COVID-19 pandemic is generating more and more studies in this field – thus not only redefining how we understand audiences in public health crises and pandemics but also pointing out a variety of challenges for public health authorities as well as communication research. Therefore, more research in various areas is needed to successfully encounter future crises and pandemics.

Areas of Future Research

As indicated earlier, research on communication during public health crises and pandemics mainly focuses on its impact on the general public. However, given the differences in, for instance, their information behaviors, information processing, risk perceptions, and susceptibility to misinformation, studies need to address specific audiences during such events. In addition, researchers need to pay greater attention to the differences in media forms and information sources: Past research on the effects of media exposure to viral outbreaks and other crises has typically focused on either a specific media platform or overall media exposure. In consequence, there is little evidence on the distinct impacts of media platforms and their specific characteristics in these situations (Chung & Jones-Jang, 2022). This is particularly important when it comes to preventing unintended negative effects of communication in a public health crisis, such as information overload, inaccurate perceptions, and message respectively issue fatigue. Finally, more research is needed on how to successfully combat misinformation during such events (Janmohamed et al., 2021).

References

Afifi, W. A., Felix, E. D., & Afifi, T. D. (2012). The impact of uncertainty and communal coping on mental health following natural disasters. *Anxiety, Stress, and Coping*, *25*(3), 329–347. https://doi.org/10.1080/10615806.2011.603048

Ajzen, I. (1991). The theory of planned behavior. *Organizational Behavior and Human Decision Processes*, *50*, 179–121.

Ali, S. H., Foreman, J., Tozan, Y., Capasso, A., Jones, A. M., & DiClemente, R. J. (2020). Trends and predictors of COVID-19 information sources and their relationship with knowledge and beliefs related to the pandemic: Nationwide cross-sectional study. *JMIR Public Health and Surveillance*, *6*(4). https://doi.org/10.2196/21071

Al-Zaman, M. S. (2022). Prevalence and source analysis of COVID-19 misinformation in 138 countries. *IFLA Journal*, *48*(1), 189–204. https://doi.org/10.1177/03400352211041135

Arrighi, E., Ruiz de Castilla, E. M., Peres, F., Mejía, R., Sørensen, K., Gunther, C., Lopez, R., Myers, L., Quijada, J. G., Vichnin, M., & Pleasant, A. (2022). Scoping health literacy in Latin America. *Global Health Promotion*, *29*(2), 78–87. https://doi.org/10.1177/17579759211016802

Ball, H., & Wozniak, T. R. (2022). Why do some Americans resist COVID-19 prevention behavior? An analysis of issue importance, message fatigue, and reactance regarding COVID-19 messaging. *Health Communication*, *37*(14), 1812–1819. https://doi.org/10.1080/10410236.2021.1920717

Bautista, J. R., Zhang, Y., & Gwizdka, J. (2021). Healthcare professionals' acts of correcting health misinformation on social media. *International Journal of Medical Informatics*, *148*, 104375. https://doi.org/10.1016/j.ijmedinf.2021.104375

Bawden, D., & Robinson, L. (2009). The dark side of information: Overload, anxiety and other paradoxes and pathologies. *Journal of Information Science*, *35*(2), 180–191. https://doi.org/10.1177/0165551508095781

Berg, S. H., O'Hara, J. K., Shortt, M. T., Thune, H., Brønnick, K. K., Lungu, D. A., Røislien, J., & Wiig, S. (2021). Health authorities' health risk communication with the public during pandemics: A rapid scoping review. *BMC Public Health*, *21*(1), 1401. https://doi.org/10.1186/s12889-021-11468-3

Berkman, N. D., Sheridan, S. L., Donahue, K. E., Halpern, D. J., & Crotty, K. (2011). Low health literacy and health outcomes: An updated systematic review. *Annals of Internal Medicine*, *155*(2), 97–107. https://doi.org/10.7326/0003-4819-155-2-201107190-00005

Bin Naeem, S., & Kamel Boulos, M. N. (2021). Covid-19 misinformation online and health literacy: A brief overview. *International Journal of Environmental Research and Public Health*, *18*(15). https://doi.org/10.3390/ijerph18158091

Bruine de Bruin, W., & Bennett, D. (2020). Relationships between initial COVID-19 risk perceptions and protective health behaviors: A national survey. *American Journal of Preventive Medicine*, *59*(2), 157–167. https://doi.org/10.1016/j.amepre.2020.05.001

Chen, J., & Wang, Y [Yuan] (2021). Health literacy and information seeking and sharing during a public health crisis in China. *Asian Journal of Communication*, *31*(3), 216–235. https://doi.org/10.1080/01292986.2021.1917636

Cheng, J. W., & Nishikawa, M. (2022). Effects of health literacy in the fight against the COVID-19 infodemic: The case of Japan. *Health Communication*, *37*(12), 1520–1533. https://doi.org/10.1080/10410236.2022.2065745

Chon, M.-G., & Park, H. (2019). Predicting public support for government actions in a public health crisis: Testing fear, organization-public relationship, and behavioral intention in the framework of the situational theory of problem solving. *Health Communication*, *36*(4), 476–486. https://doi.org/10.1080/10410236.2019.1700439

Chu, T. H., Yeo, T. E. D., & Su, Y. (2022). Effects of exposure to COVID-19 news and information: A meta-analysis of media use and uncertainty-related responses during the pandemic. *Journalism and Mass Communication Quarterly*, *99*(1), 89–112. https://doi.org/10.1177/10776990211068857

Chung, M., & Jones-Jang, S. M. (2022). Red media, blue media, trump briefings, and COVID-19: Examining how information sources predict risk preventive behaviors via threat and efficacy. *Health Communication*, *37*(14), 1707–1714. https://doi.org/10.1080/10410236.2021.1914386

Cipolletta, S., Andreghetti, G., & Mioni, G. (2022). Risk perception towards COVID-19: A systematic review and qualitative synthesis. *International Journal of Environmental Research and Public Health*, *19*(8), 4649. https://doi.org/10.3390/ijerph19084649

Coleman, C.-L. (1993). The influence of mass media and interpersonal communication on societal and personal risk judgments. *Communication Research*, *20*(4), 611–628. https://doi.org/10.1177/009365093020004006

de Bruin, K., de Haan, Y., Vliegenthart, R., Kruikemeier, S., & Boukes, M. (2021). News avoidance during the COVID-19 crisis: Understanding information overload. *Digital Journalism*, *9*(9), 1286–1302. https://doi.org/10.1080/21670811.2021.1957967

Dhawan, D., Bekalu, M., Pinnamaneni, R., McCloud, R., & Viswanath, K. (2021). Covid-19 news and misinformation: Do they matter for public health prevention? *Journal of Health Communication*, *26*(11), 799–808. https://doi.org/10.1080/10810730.2021.2010841

Dreisiebner, S., März, S., & Mandl, T. (2022). Information behavior during the COVID-19 crisis in German-speaking countries. *Journal of Documentation*, *78*(7), 160–175. https://doi.org/10.1108/JD-12-2020-0217

Dryhurst, S., Schneider, C. R., Kerr, J., Freeman, A. L. J., Recchia, G., van der Bles, A. M., Spiegelhalter, D., & van der Linden, S. (2020). Risk perceptions of COVID-19 around the world. *Journal of Risk Research*, *23*(7–8), 994–1006. https://doi.org/10.1080/13669877.2020.1758193

Duong, T. V., Aringazina, A., Baisunova, G., Nurjanah Pham, T. V., Pham, K. M., Truong, T. Q., Nguyen, K. T., Oo, W. M., Mohamad, E., Su, T. T., Huang, H.-L., Sørensen [Kristine], K., Pelikan, J. M., van den Broucke, S., & Chang, P. W. (2017). Measuring health literacy in Asia: Validation of the HLS-EU-Q47 survey tool in six Asian countries. *Journal of Epidemiology*, *27*(2), 80–86. https://doi.org/10.1016/j.je.2016.09.005

Eagly, A. H., & Chaiken, S. (1993). *The Psychology of Attitudes*. Harcourt Brace Jovanovich.

Gardikiotis, A., Malinaki, E., Charisiadis-Tsitlakidis, C., Protonotariou, A., Archontis, S., Lampropoulou, A., Maraki, I., Papatheodorou, K., & Zafeiriou, G. (2021). Emotional and cognitive responses to COVID-19 information overload under lockdown predict media attention and risk perceptions of COVID-19. *Journal of Health Communication*, *26*(6), 434–442. https://doi.org/10.1080/10810730.2021.1949649

Griffin, R. J., Dunwoody, S., & Neuwirth, K. (1999). Proposed model of the relationship of risk information seeking and processing to the development of preventive behaviors. *Environmental Research*, *80*(2), 230–245. https://doi.org/10.1006/enrs.1998.3940

Griffin, R. J., Dunwoody, S., & Yang, Z. J. (2012). Testing the robustness of a risk information processing model. *Communication Yearbook*, *36*, 323–362.

Guan, M., Li, Y., Scoles, J. D., & Zhu, Y. (2022). Covid-19 message fatigue: How does it predict preventive behavioral intentions and what types of information are people tired of hearing about? *Health Communication*, *1–10*. https://doi.org/10.1080/10410236.2021.2023385

Gurr, G., Schumann, C., & Metag, J. (2022). Negative effects of long-lasting media attention to public issues on recipients: Conceptualizing issue fatigue. *Studies in Communication Sciences*, *22*(2). https://doi.org/10.24434/j.scoms.2022.02.007

Hart, P. S., Chinn, S., & Soroka, S. (2020). Politicization and polarization in COVID-19 news coverage. *Science Communication*, *42*(5), 679–697. https://doi.org/10.1177/1075547020950735

Heydari, S. T., Zarei, L., Sadati, A. K., Moradi, N., Akbari, M., Mehralian, G., & Lankarani, K. B. (2021). The effect of risk communication on preventive and protective behaviours during the COVID-19 outbreak: Mediating role of risk perception. *BMC Public Health*, *21*(1). https://doi.org/10.1186/s12889-020-10125-5

Holland, K., Sweet, M., Blood, R. W., & Fogarty, A. (2014). A legacy of the swine flu global pandemic: Journalists, expert sources, and conflicts of interest. *Journalism*, *15*(1), 53–71. https://doi.org/10.1177/1464884913480460

Holmes, B. J., Henrich, N., Hancock, S., & Lestou, V. (2009). Communicating with the public during health crises: Experts' experiences and opinions. *Journal of Risk Research*, *12*(6), 793–807. https://doi.org/10.1080/13669870802648486

Hong, H., & Kim, H. J. (2020). Antecedents and consequences of information overload in the COVID-19 pandemic. *International Journal of Environmental Research and Public Health*, *17*(24). https://doi.org/10.3390/ijerph17249305

Hubner, A. Y., & Hovick, S. R. (2020). Understanding risk information seeking and processing during an infectious disease outbreak: The case of Zika virus. *Risk Analysis*, *40*(6), 1212–1225. https://doi.org/10.1111/risa.13456

Hwang, Y., So, J., & Jeong, S.-H. (2023). Does COVID-19 message fatigue lead to misinformation acceptance? An extension of the risk information seeking and processing model. *Health Communication*, *38*(12), 2742–2479. https://doi.org/10.1080/10410236.2022.2111636

Hyland-Wood, B., Gardner, J., Leask, J., & Ecker, U. K. H. (2021). Toward effective government communication strategies in the era of COVID-19. *Humanities and Social Sciences Communications*, *8*(1). https://doi.org/10.1057/s41599-020-00701-w

Islam, M. S., Sarkar, T., Khan, S. H., Mostofa Kamal, A.-H., Hasan, S. M. M., Kabir, A., Yeasmin, D., Islam, M. A., Amin Chowdhury, K. I., Anwar, K. S., Chughtai, A. A., & Seale, H. (2020). Covid-19-related infodemic and its impact on public health: A global social media analysis. *The American Journal of Tropical Medicine and Hygiene*, *103*(4), 1621–1629. https://doi.org/10.4269/ajtmh.20-0812

Janmohamed, K., Walter, N., Nyhan, K., Khoshnood, K., Tucker, J. D., Sangngam, N., Altice, F. L., Ding, Q., Wong, A., Schwitzky, Z. M., Bauch, C. T., Choudhury, M. de, Papakyriakopoulos, O., & Kumar, N. (2021). Interventions to mitigate COVID-19 misinformation: A systematic review and meta-analysis. *Journal of Health Communication*, *26*(12), 846–857. https://doi.org/10.1080/10810730.2021.2021460

Jia, X., Ahn, S., & Carcioppolo, N. (2022). Measuring information overload and message fatigue toward COVID-19 prevention messages in USA and China. *Health Promotion International*. Advance online publication. https://doi.org/10.1093/heapro/daac003

Johnson, J. D., & Meischke, H. (1993). A comprehensive model of cancer-related information seeking applied to magazines. *Human Communication Research*, *19*, 343–367.

Kahlor, L. (2010). Prism: A planned risk information seeking model. *Health Communication*, *25*(4), 345–356. https://doi.org/10.1080/10410231003775172

Karlsen, A., & Kruke, B. I. (2018). The role of uncertainty during the Ebola pandemic in Western Africa (2014–2016). *Journal of Extreme Events*, *5*(1), 1–18. https://doi.org/10.1142/S2345737618500094

Kasperson, R. E., Renn, O., Slovic, P., Brown, H. S., Emel, J., Goble, R., Kasperson, J. X., & Ratick, S. (1988). The social amplification of risk: A conceptual framework. *Risk Analysis*, *8*(2), 177–187. https://doi.org/10.1111/j.1539-6924.1988.tb01168.x

Keating, D. M., & Galper, E. (2021). An examination of how message fatigue impacts young adults' evaluations of utilitarian messages about electronic cigarettes. *Communication Research Reports*, *38*(2), 90–102. https://doi.org/10.1080/08824096.2021.1885372

Kim, H. K., Ahn, J., Atkinson, L., & Kahlor, L. A. (2020). Effects of COVID-19 misinformation on information seeking, avoidance, and processing: A multicountry comparative study. *Science Communication*, *42*(5), 586–615. https://doi.org/10.1177/1075547020959670

Klemm, C., Das, E., & Hartmann, T. (2019). Changed priorities ahead: Journalists' shifting role perceptions when covering public health crises. *Journalism*, *20*(9), 1223–1241. https://doi.org/10.1177/1464884917692820

Koh, P. K.-K., Chan, L. L., & Tan, E.-K. (2020). Messaging fatigue and desensitisation to information during pandemic. *Archives of Medical Research*, *51*(7), 716–717. https://doi.org/10.1016/j.arcmed.2020.06.014

Lam, S. C., Arora, T., Grey, I., Suen, L. K. P., Huang, E. Y., Li, D., & Lam, K. B. H. (2020). Perceived risk and protection from infection and depressive symptoms among healthcare workers in Mainland China and Hong Kong during COVID-19. *Frontiers. Psychiatry*, *11*, 686. https://doi.org/10.3389/fpsyt.2020.00686

Lee, J., Choi, J., & Britt, R. K. (2021). Social media as risk-attenuation and misinformation-amplification station: How social media interaction affects misperceptions about COVID-19. *Health Communication*, 1–11. https://doi.org/10.1080/10410236.2021.1996920

Lee, J., Kim, J. W., & Chock, T. M. (2020). From risk butterflies to citizens engaged in risk prevention in the Zika virus crisis: Focusing on personal, societal and global risk perceptions. *Journal of Health Communication*, *25*(9), 671–680. https://doi.org/10.1080/10810730.2020.1836089

Levin-Zamir, D., & Bertschi, I. (2018). Media health literacy, eHealth literacy, and the role of the social environment in context. *International Journal of Environmental Research and Public Health*, *15*(8). https://doi.org/10.3390/ijerph15081643

Lewis, N. (2017). Information seeking and scanning. In P. Rössler, C. A. Hoffner, & L. van Zoonen, Eds., *The International Encyclopedia of Media Effects* (pp. 1–10). Wiley.

Li, J. (2023). Information avoidance in the age of COVID-19: A meta-analysis. *Information Processing & Management*, *60*(1), 103163. https://doi.org/10.1016/j.ipm.2022.103163

Li, J., & Zheng, H. (2022). Online information seeking and disease prevention intent during COVID-19 outbreak. *Journalism and Mass Communication Quarterly*, *99*(1), 69–88. https://doi.org/10.1177/1077699020961518

Li, Q., Zheng, Y., Zhang, J., & Geng, R. (2022a). Self-efficacy, proxy efficacy, media literacy, and official media use in COVID-19 pandemic in China: A moderated mediation model. *Frontiers in Psychology*, *13*. https://doi.org/10.3389/fpsyg.2022.847522

Li, S.-C. S., Lo, S.-Y., Wu, T.-Y., & Chen, T.-L. (2022b). Information seeking and processing during the outbreak of COVID-19 in Taiwan: Examining the effects of emotions and informational subjective norms. *International Journal of Environmental Research and Public Health*, *19*(15). https://doi.org/10.3390/ijerph19159532

Li, W., & Khan, A. N. (2022). Investigating the impacts of information overload on psychological well-being of healthcare professionals: Role of COVID-19 stressor. *Inquiry*, *59*. https://doi.org/10.1177/00469580221109677

Link, E. (2021). Information avoidance during health crises: Predictors of avoiding information about the COVID-19 pandemic among German news consumers. *Information Processing & Management*, *58*(6), 102714. https://doi.org/10.1016/j.ipm.2021.102714

Link, E. (2022). Avoidance of interpersonal discussions about the COVID-19 vaccination: Applying the theory of motivated information management. *Health Communication*, 1–11. https://doi.org/10.1080/10410236.2022.2124055

Link, E., Rosset, M., & Freytag, A. (2022). Patterns of online information seeking and avoidance about SARS-CoV-2 and COVID-19. *European Journal of Health Communication*, *3*(1), 53–75. https://doi.org/10.47368/ejhc.2022.103

Liu, M., Chen, Y., Shi, D., & Yan, T. (2021). The public's risk information seeking and avoidance in China during early stages of the COVID-19 outbreak. *Frontiers in Psychology*, *12*, 649180. https://doi.org/10.3389/fpsyg.2021.649180

Lohiniva, A.-L., Pensola, A., Hyökki, S., Sivelä, J., & Tammi, T. (2022). COVID-19 risk perception framework of the public: An infodemic tool for future pandemics and epidemics. *BMC Public Health*, *22*(1). https://doi.org/10.1186/s12889-022-14563-1

Lopez, C., Kim, B., & Sacks, K. (2022). *Health literacy in the United States: Enhancing assessments and reducing disparities.*

Lubens, P. (2015). Journalists and public health professionals: Challenges of a symbiotic relationship. *Disaster Medicine and Public Health Preparedness*, *9*(1), 59–63. https://doi.org/10.1017/dmp.2014.127

Lwin, M. O., Lee, S. Y., & [Si Yu], Panchapakesan, C., & Tandoc, E. (2021). Mainstream news media's role in public health communication during crises: Assessment of coverage and correction of

COVID-19 misinformation. *Health Communication, 38*(1), 160–168. https://doi.org/10.1080/10410236.2021.1937842
Majid, U., Wasim, A., Bakshi, S., & Truong, J. (2020). Knowledge, (mis-)conceptions, risk perception, and behavior change during pandemics: A scoping review of 149 studies. *Public Understanding of Science, 29*(8), 777–799. https://doi.org/10.1177/0963662520963365
Marani, M., Katul, G. G., Pan, W. K., & Parolari, A. J. (2021). Intensity and frequency of extreme novel epidemics. *Proceedings of the National Academy of Sciences of the United States of America, 118*(35). https://doi.org/10.1073/pnas.2105482118
Martinez Gonzalez, A., Reynolds-Tylus, T., Quick, B. L., & Skurka, C. (2021). Message fatigue and resistance to anti–binge drinking messages: Examining the mediating roles of inattention and reactance. *Journal of Studies on Alcohol and Drugs, 82*(4), 503–510. https://doi.org/10.15288/jsad.2021.82.503
Mehrabian, A., & Russell, J. A. (1974). *An Approach to Environmental Psychology*. The MIT Press.
Meppelink, C. S., Bos, L., Boukes, M., & Möller, J. (2022). A health crisis in the age of misinformation: How social media and mass media influenced misperceptions about COVID-19 and compliance behavior. *Journal of Health Communication, 27*(10), 764–775. https://doi.org/10.1080/10810730.2022.2153288
Metag, J., & Arlt, D. (2016). Das Konstrukt Themenverdrossenheit und seine Messung: Theoretische Konzeptualisierung und Skalenentwicklung [The construct issue fatigue and its measurement. Theoretical conceptualization and scale development]. *Medien & Kommunikationswissenschaft, 64*(4), 542–563.
Nazione, S., Perrault, E., & Pace, K. (2021). Impact of information exposure on perceived risk, efficacy, and preventative behaviors at the beginning of the COVID-19 pandemic in the United States. *Health Communication, 36*(1), 23–31. https://doi.org/10.1080/10410236.2020.1847446
Oh, S.-H., Lee, S. Y., & Han, C. (2021). The effects of social media use on preventive behaviors during infectious disease outbreaks: The mediating role of self-relevant emotions and public risk perception. *Health Communication, 36*(8), 972–981. https://doi.org/10.1080/10410236.2020.1724639
Okan, O., Bollweg, T. M., Berens, E.-M., Hurrelmann, K., Bauer, U., & Schaeffer, D. (2020). Coronavirus-related health literacy: A cross-sectional study in adults during the COVID-19 infodemic in Germany. *International Journal of Environmental Research and Public Health, 17*(15), 1–20.
Olaimat, A. N., Aolymat, I., Shahbaz, H. M., & Holley, R. A. (2020). Knowledge and information sources about COVID-19 among university students in Jordan: A cross-sectional study. *Frontiers in Public Health, 8*, 254. https://doi.org/10.3389/fpubh.2020.00254
Osuagwu, U. L., Mashige, K. P., Ovenseri-Ogbomo, G., Envuladu, E. A., Abu, E. K., Miner, C. A., Timothy, C. G., Ekpenyong, B. N., Langsi, R., Amiebenomo, O. M., Oloruntoba, R., Goson, P. C., Charwe, D. D., Ishaya, T., & Agho, K. E. (2023). The impact of information sources on COVID-19 vaccine hesitancy and resistance in Sub-Saharan Africa. *BMC Public Health, 23*(1), 38. https://doi.org/10.1186/s12889-022-14972-2
Paakkari, L., & Okan, O. (2020). Covid-19: Health literacy is an underestimated problem. *The Lancet Public Health, 5*(5), 249–250. https://doi.org/10.1016/S2468-2667(20)30086-4
Patil, U., Kostareva, U., Hadley, M., Manganello, J. A., Okan, O., Dadaczynski, K., Massey, P. M., Agner, J., & Sentell, T. (2021). Health literacy, digital health literacy, and COVID-19 pandemic attitudes and behaviors in U.S. College students: Implications for interventions. *International Journal of Environmental Research and Public Health, 18*(6). https://doi.org/10.3390/ijerph18063301
Peres, D., Monteiro, J., Almeida, M., & Ladeira, R. (2020). Risk perception of COVID-19 among the Portuguese healthcare professionals and general population. *The Journal of Hospital Infection, 105*(3), 434–437. https://doi.org/10.1016/j.jhin.2020.05.038
Perreault, M. F., & Perreault, G. P. (2021). Journalists on COVID-19 journalism: Communication ecology of pandemic reporting. *American Behavioral Scientist, 65*(7), 976–991. https://doi.org/10.1177/0002764221992813
Rathore, F. A., & Farooq, F. (2020). Information overload and infodemic in the COVID-19 pandemic. *Journal of the Pakistan Medical Association, 70*(5), 162–165.
Reynolds-Tylus, T., Lukacena, K. M., & Truban, O. (2021). Message fatigue to bystander intervention messages: Examining pathways of resistance among college men. *Health Communication, 36*(13), 1759–1767. https://doi.org/10.1080/10410236.2020.1794551

Rocha, Y. M., de Moura, G. A., Desidério, G. A., de Oliveira, C. H., Lourenço, F. D., & de Figueiredo Nicolete, L. D. (2021). The impact of fake news on social media and its influence on health during the COVID-19 pandemic: A systematic review. *Journal of Public Health*, 1–10. https://doi.org/10.1007/s10389-021-01658-z

Rogers, M. B., & Pearce, J. M. (2016). The psychology of crisis communication. In A. Schwarz, M. W. Seeger, & C. Auer, Eds., *The Handbook of International Crisis Communication Research* (pp. 34–44). Wiley Blackwell.

Rossmann, C., Meyer, L., & Schulz, P. J. (2018). The mediated amplification of a crisis: Communicating the A/H1N1 pandemic in press releases and press coverage in Europe. *Risk Analysis, 38*(2), 357–375. https://doi.org/10.1111/risa.12841

Rossmann, C., Stehr, P., Brill, J., Temmann, L. J., Weber, W., & Wendt, K. N. (May 27, 2021). Health information behavior in times of crisis: Determinants of information retrieval and information processing in the context of the SARS-CoV-2 pandemic among younger and older adults. *71st Annual Conference of the International Communication Association, Virtual Conference.*

Rufai, S. R., & Bunce, C. (2020). World leaders' usage of Twitter in response to the COVID-19 pandemic: A content analysis. *Journal of Public Health, 42*(3), 510–516. https://doi.org/10.1093/pubmed/fdaa049

Sarelska, D., & Jenkins, J. (2022). Truth on demand: Influences on how journalists in Italy, Spain, and Bulgaria responded to Covid-19 misinformation and disinformation. *Journalism Practice*, 1–19. https://doi.org/10.1080/17512786.2022.2153075

Schumann, C. (2018). Is topic fatigue an international problem? Four theses. *Global Media Journal, 8*(2), 1–12. https://doi.org/10.22032/dbt.37780

Seeger, M. W., Reynolds, B., & Sellnow, T. L. (2010). Crisis and emergency risk communication in health contexts: Applying the CDC model to pandemic influenza. In R. L. Heath, & D. O'Hair, Eds., *Handbook of Risk and Crisis Communication* (pp. 493–506). Routledge.

Sharma, D. C., Pathak, A., Chaurasia, R. N., Joshi, D., Singh, R. K., & Mishra, V. N. (2020). Fighting infodemic: Need for robust health journalism in India. *Diabetes and Metabolic Syndrome: Clinical Research and Reviews, 14*(5), 1445–1447. https://doi.org/10.1016/j.dsx.2020.07.039

Shobowale, O. (2021). A systematic review of the spread of information during pandemics: A case of the 2020 COVID-19 virus. *Journal of African Media Studies, 13*(2), 221–234. https://doi.org/10.1386/jams_00045_1

Siebenhaar, K. U., Köther, A. K., & Alpers, G. W. (2020). Dealing with the COVID-19 infodemic: Distress by information, information avoidance, and compliance with preventive measures. *Frontiers in Psychology, 11.* https://doi.org/10.3389/fpsyg.2020.567905

Singh, N., & Banga, G. (2022). Media and information literacy for developing resistance to 'infodemic': Lessons to be learnt from the binge of misinformation during COVID-19 pandemic. *Media, Culture and Society, 44*(1), 161–171. https://doi.org/10.1177/01634437211060201

Slovic, P. (2000). *The Perception of Risk.* Routledge.

Snyder, L. B., & Rouse, R. A. (1995). The media can have more than an impersonal impact: The case of AIDS risk perceptions and behavior. *Health Communication, 7*(2), 125–145. https://doi.org/10.1207/s15327027hc0702_3

So, J., & Popova, L. (2018). A profile of individuals with anti-tobacco message fatigue. *American Journal of Health Behavior, 42*(1), 109–118. https://doi.org/10.5993/AJHB.42.1.11

Sørensen, K., Pelikan, J. M., Röthlin, F., Ganahl, K., Slonska, Z., Doyle, G., Fullam, J., Kondilis, B., Agrafiotis, D., Uiters, E., Falcon, M., Mensing, M., Tchamov, K., van den Broucke, S., & Brand, H. (2015). Health literacy in Europe: Comparative results of the European health literacy survey (HLS-EU). *European Journal of Public Health, 25*(6), 1053–1058. https://doi.org/10.1093/eurpub/ckv043

Sørensen, K., van den Broucke, S., Fullam, J., Doyle, G., Pelikan, J., Slonska, Z., & Brand, H. (2012). Health literacy and public health: A systematic review and integration of definitions and models. *BMC Public Health, 12*, 80. https://doi.org/10.1186/1471-2458-12-80

Soroya, S. H., Farooq, A., Mahmood, K., Isoaho, J., & Zara, S.-E. (2021). From information seeking to information avoidance: Understanding the health information behavior during a global health crisis. *Information Processing & Management, 58*(2), 102440. https://doi.org/10.1016/j.ipm.2020.102440

Sweeny, K., Melnyk, D., Miller, W., & Shepperd, J. A. (2010). Information avoidance: Who, what, when, and why. *Review of General Psychology*, *14*(4), 340–353. https://doi.org/10.1037/a0021288

Tandoc, E. C., & Lee, J. C. B. (2022). When viruses and misinformation spread: How young Singaporeans navigated uncertainty in the early stages of the COVID-19 outbreak. *New Media & Society*, *24*(3), 778–796. https://doi.org/10.1177/1461444820968212

Tang, L., & Zou, W. (2021). Health information consumption under COVID-19 lockdown: An interview study of residents of Hubei Province, China. *Health Communication*, *36*(1), 74–80. https://doi.org/10.1080/10410236.2020.1847447

Vraga, E. K., & Bode, L. (2020). Defining misinformation and understanding its bounded nature: Using expertise and evidence for describing misinformation. *Political Communication*, *37*(1), 136–144. https://doi.org/10.1080/10584609.2020.1716500

Wang, J., Huang, X., Wang, Y., Wang, M., Xu, J., & Li, X. (2022). Covid-19 information overload, negative emotions and posttraumatic stress disorder: A cross-sectional study. *Frontiers in Psychiatry*, *13*, 894174. https://doi.org/10.3389/fpsyt.2022.894174

Wang, P.-W., Lu, W.-H., Ko, N.-Y., Chen, Y.-L., Li, D.-J., Chang, Y.-P., & Yen, C.-F. (2020). Covid-19-related information sources and the relationship with confidence in people coping with COVID-19: Facebook survey study in Taiwan. *Journal of Medical Internet Research*, *22*(6). https://doi.org/10.2196/20021

Weintraub Austin, E., Austin, B. W., Willoughby Fitts, J., Amram, O., & Domgaard, S. (2021). How media literacy and science media literacy predicted the adoption of protective behaviors amidst the COVID-19 pandemic. *Journal of Health Communication*, *26*(4), 239–252. https://doi.org/10.1080/10810730.2021.1899345

WHO (2023). *Coronavirus disease (COVID-19) pandemic*. https://www.who.int/emergencies/diseases/novel-coronavirus-2019

Wright, K. B. (2021). Social media, risk perceptions related to COVID-19, and health outcomes. In D. O'Hair, & M. J. O'Hair, Eds., *Communicating Science in Times of Crisis* (pp. 128–148). Wiley.

Yang, J. Z., Aloe, A. M., & Feeley, T. H. (2014). Risk information seeking and processing model: A meta-analysis. *Journal of Communication*, *64*(1), 20–41. https://doi.org/10.1111/jcom.12071

Zhang, X. A., & Cozma, R. (2022). Risk sharing on Twitter: Social amplification and attenuation of risk in the early stages of the COVID-19 pandemic. *Computers in Human Behavior*, *126*, 106983. https://doi.org/10.1016/j.chb.2021.106983

Zhao, S., & Wu, X. (2021). From information exposure to protective behaviors: Investigating the underlying mechanism in COVID-19 outbreak using social amplification theory and extended parallel process model. *Frontiers in Psychology*, *12*, 631116. https://doi.org/10.3389/fpsyg.2021.631116

Zhong, Y., Liu, W., Lee, T.-Y., Zhao, H., & Ji, J. (2021). Risk perception, knowledge, information sources and emotional states among COVID-19 patients in Wuhan, China. *Nursing Outlook*, *69*(1), 13–21. https://doi.org/10.1016/j.outlook.2020.08.005

Zhou, S. (2022). Impact of pandemic proximity and media use on risk perception during COVID-19 in China. *Geomatics, Natural Hazards and Risk*, *13*(1), 591–609. https://doi.org/10.1080/19475705.2021.2003875

Zhou, X., & Roberto, A. J. (2022). An application of the risk information seeking and processing model in understanding college students' COVID-19 vaccination information seeking and behavior. *Science Communication*, *44*(4), 446–474. https://doi.org/10.1177/10755470221120415

Zhou, X., Roberto, A. J., & Lu, A. H. (2023). Understanding online health risk information seeking and avoiding during the COVID-19 pandemic. *Health Communication*, *38*(3), 532–542. https://doi.org/10.1080/10410236.2021.1958981

Author's Bio

Annemarie Wiedicke is a postdoctoral researcher at the Institute for Media Research at the Technical University of Chemnitz, Germany. She earned her PhD in communication science at the University of Erfurt in 2022. In her thesis, she examined journalists' and media's attribution of responsibility for depression and diabetes. Her research focuses on health communication and social media, comprising topics such as journalist and media framing of health issues and their impact on audiences, body image, (de-)stigmatization of mental illness, privacy, and crisis communication. She has co-authored more than 25 conference presentations and has published more than 20 book chapters and peer-reviewed articles in journals such as *Health Communication, The Journal of Health Communication, Journalism Studies,* and *Social Media + Society*.

Constanze Rossmann, PhD, is Professor of Communication at the Department of Media and Communication at LMU Munich. She graduated and completed her habilitation thesis at LMU Munich; she was a guest professor at the universities of Hannover, Mainz, and Zurich and Professor of Communication at the University of Erfurt from 2014 to 2021. She is a co-founder and former speaker of the Health Communication Division within the German Communication Association, an associate editor of the "European Journal of Health Communication," a co-editor of "Studies in Communication and Media," and a co-editor of a German handbook on health communication. In addition, she is the speaker of the research unit "Digital Media in Chronic Disease Self-Management (DISELMA)" funded by the German Research Foundation and an executive board member of the Munich Science Communication Lab funded by the VolkswagenStiftung. Her research focuses on health and crisis communication, especially health-related media use and effects, strategic health communication, and digital health. She has published more than 110 journal articles and book chapters and 10 books (4 monographs and 6 edited books).

20

Domestic and International Audiences of Organizational Risk and Crisis Communication

State of the Art and Cross-Cultural Implications

An-Sofie Claeys[1] and Andreas Schwarz[2]

[1] Department of Translation, Interpreting and Communication, Ghent University, Gent, Belgium

[2] Institute of Media and Communication Science, Technische Universität Ilmenau, Ilmenau, Germany

Organizations that operate across national and cultural boundaries are increasing in number and prominence. This refers in particular to transnational corporations, international nongovernmental organizations, and intergovernmental organizations such as the United Nations or the European Union. These organizations deal increasingly with risks and crises of international scope in terms of either (potential) physical crisis effects or the visibility of such crises due to international news media and social media (Schwarz et al., 2016). Thus, organizations in international contexts must anticipate crises (i.e., risks), respond to crises, and handle post-crisis communication with stakeholders from different countries and/or with heterogeneous cultural backgrounds (Gaither & Curtin, 2007; Gribas et al., 2021; Taylor, 2000). Any attempt by international organizations to strategically manage relationships with stakeholders or to better protect them from threats would need substantial research and knowledge about their information needs, communication habits, culture-specific value orientations, to name only a few relevant aspects. This underlines the importance of both audience-oriented perspectives and cross-cultural comparative research on organizational risk and crisis communication. Risk and crisis communication scholars have addressed the first (Fediuk et al., 2012; Lee, 2004), but the state of the art in this field remains largely ethnocentric (Cheng et al., 2022; Garcia, 2011; Lee, 2005a; Schwarz et al., 2016).

This chapter, therefore, summarizes some of the important frameworks and findings on organizational risk and crisis communication from an audience or stakeholder perspective. We give an overview of how audiences perceive risks, crises, and risk and crisis communication. Variables that are likely to determine their evaluation of risk and crisis are discussed. While crisis communication research initially focused strongly on the role of attributions of responsibility and reputation repair, the field has increasingly investigated other aspects of audience perceptions as well as instructional risk communication to protect risk bearers or crisis

The Handbook of International Crisis and Risk Communication Research, Second Edition.
Edited by Andreas Schwarz, Matthew W. Seeger, and Sora Kim.

stakeholders from harm. Finally, we discuss the extent to which these aspects can be considered culturally contingent or universal, in how they determine the impact of risk, crisis, and subsequent communication on multicultural publics.

The Importance of Responsibility

In a desire to establish how audiences react to crises and to crisis communication, situational crisis communication theory (SCCT) was developed (Coombs, 2007). The theory's basic assumption is that stakeholders attribute a certain degree of crisis responsibility to an organization. The reputational threat of a crisis is mainly a function of perceived crisis responsibility (Coombs & Holladay, 1996). Reputational damage, in turn, is best safeguarded or repaired by accepting as much responsibility as was attributed to the organization by the public (Coombs, 2007). Simply put, organizations that receive a great deal of blame for a given crisis should accept responsibility.

Several studies have examined the propositions made by SCCT. Post-crisis reputation, attitude toward the organization, and attributions of responsibility are the most prominent outcome variables in crisis communication research (Zhou et al., 2022). Studies confirm that the extent to which the public considers an organization responsible influences post-crisis attitudes and behavior (Claeys et al., 2010; Ndone & Park, 2022). Experimental research has also examined the impact of distinct crisis response strategies on stakeholder perceptions. Some studies confirm that a crisis response that matches the crisis type in terms of responsibility acceptance results in the most reputation repair (e.g., Coombs & Holladay, 1996). Other experiments found that accommodating strategies, characterized by a high degree of responsibility acceptance, are more effective throughout (e.g., Claeys et al., 2010).

Despite some inconsistent findings regarding the (limited) impact of crisis response strategies (Ma & Zhan, 2016), SCCT remains the most popular theoretical framework in crisis communication research (Cheng et al., 2022). Several more recent studies confirm the key role played by responsibility attributions. For example, while customer–company relationship and pre-crisis relationship affected American consumers' reaction to a crisis, responsibility attributions were the strongest predictors (Ma, 2018). Two experiments among Belgian consumers confirm the causal relationship between responsibility attributions and post-crisis reputation (Schoofs et al., 2019). Several studies among stakeholders in Singapore likewise found that higher levels of blame result in more negative attitudes toward an organization in crisis (Lwin et al., 2017; Nekmat & Kong, 2019). SCCT has been widely used for case study research as well, for example, a study about a university crisis in Kenya (Muindi & Kiarie, 2021).

Despite the fact that SCCT's propositions have been applied to cases and among samples across the globe, however, crisis communication research remains ethnocentric (Garcia, 2011). Most samples from studies about crisis response strategies are from the United States, followed by Europe, and to a lesser degree Asia and Australia (Zhou et al., 2022). And an overview of global social-mediated crisis communication research confirms that most studies examine American crises (Cheng et al., 2022). To a lesser degree, research has focused on crises from Europe, Asia, and Oceania. Noteworthy, none of the articles about social-mediated crisis communication, even the ones examining crises that originated in Africa (e.g., the 2014 Ebola crisis), focused on that region.

Attributing and Accepting Responsibility Around the Globe

Limited cross-cultural research sheds light on the degree to which the same crisis or crisis response strategy could have different effects across different cultures. A case study of the 1999 Coca-Cola scare in Europe (Taylor, 2000), for instance, concluded that crisis perceptions may differ between countries that vary in terms of Hofstede's (2001) uncertainty avoidance and power distance dimensions. Belgium, Spain, and France reacted particularly strong when Belgian schoolchildren became ill after drinking Coca-Cola, potentially because they scored high on uncertainty avoidance and power distance (Taylor, 2000). Hofstede's (2001) cultural dimensions were also used to explain why the Danish food company Arla Foods struggled to find the right response in the Middle East, after a Danish newspaper published cartoons of the Prophet Muhammad in 2005 (Gaither & Curtin, 2007).

These case studies indicate potential cross-cultural differences and have made scholars aware that perhaps not all audiences interpret organizational crises and crisis responses in exactly the same manner under all circumstances. Noteworthy, the overall connection between responsibility attributions and reputational threat appears to be quite robust. A study that compared samples from the United States, South Korea, and Singapore, for example, confirms that blame attribution predicts consumer boycott universally (Shim et al., 2021). Even though reputational threat seems to be a function of attributed crisis responsibility across cultures, the application as well as the impact of distinct crisis response strategies may differ for several reasons.

While a no-comment response would be considered negatively in a Western society, participants from Hong Kong seem more accepting toward such stonewalling due to the value of keeping silent (Lee, 2004). And while some of the crisis response strategies that are frequently used by Western companies are also used in a non-Western context (i.e., justification, denial), Asian organizations appear to use different strategies as well (e.g., diversion) (Huang et al., 2005). Chinese audiences may also prefer an overall indirect communication style, more so than Western audiences, such as a justification strategy (Huang, 2006).

Other research has examined defensive strategies in particular. Multinationals should be aware of the importance of face, when they consider attacking or threatening strategies in response to crises in Asia (Wen et al., 2012). Blaming Chinese subsidiaries for a crisis is probably not the best strategy for an American multinational company. Blaming individual employees, as a way to deflect organizational blame, may not play well among an Asian audience either (An et al., 2010). In collectivist cultures, a group will more easily feel responsible for mistakes made by individuals (Barkley, 2020). Therefore, audiences in countries like South Korea or Japan may not appreciate when an organization tries to save its own skin by blaming individual employees. In addition to the importance of keeping silent, saving face, and collectivism among Asian audiences, shame avoidance has been documented as an aspect to consider in Arab cultures (Gribas et al., 2021). Defensive crisis response strategies might therefore be less detrimental among Middle Eastern audiences, as compared to the US audiences.

Cross-cultural research has finally shed some light on accommodating crisis response strategies as well. Apologizing has been considered effective for reputation repair in North America, Europe, and Asia (e.g., Claeys et al., 2010; Coombs, 2007; Lee, 2005b; van der Meer & Verhoeven, 2014). The organizational willingness to apologize, however, might differ across countries. Western organizations fear that apologies might incur legal liability (Claeys & Opgenhaffen, 2021; Myers, 2016). Such worries seem less prominent, however, in a Chinese (Zhu et al., 2017), Japanese (Barkley, 2020), or South Korean (Lim, 2020) context. In these collectivist societies, apologies serve to restore social harmony and express concern, even when someone bears no actual blame for a problem (Barkley, 2020).

Covariation

While the explanation of crisis responsibility by stakeholders and its effects on reputation, emotions, and behavioral intentions received considerable attention in SCCT-related research, the explanation of causal attributions in the first place by so-called causal antecedents has not been well explored. This refers to the informational dimensions that stakeholders rely on to decide about the causes of a crisis (e.g., internal or external causes), especially in crisis situations where causal explanations are complex or ambiguous. Causal attribution as reflected by the personal control/locus construct in SCCT has usually been used as the independent variable explaining responsibility. Although Coombs (2004) suggested considering the constructs of crisis history and relationship history as causal antecedents, they were only tested with regard to their impact on responsibility attributions. Thus, they were not considered as independent variables to explain causal attributions in the first place. Social psychologists and subsequently crisis communication scholars have argued that causal attributions and responsibility attributions should be treated as distinct constructs (Lee, 2005a; Schwarz, 2012; Shaver, 1985) because judgments of responsibility also refer, but not only, to the causal contribution of an individual or organization to a crisis outcome. An attribution of responsibility is considered to be a moral judgment and implies, for example, the perception that an actor was aware of the outcome, had the intent to bring about the event, and/or was aware of the moral wrongfulness of a certain action. This means that perceptions of responsibility strongly depend on causality, but the two are not identical (Shaver, 1985). Experimental studies on organizational crisis communication in two different cultural settings, one on Hong Kong consumers' perception of an airline crash (Lee, 2005b) and another on German students' evaluation of a university crisis (Schwarz, 2012), produced some evidence that causality and responsibility are strongly correlated but represent different constructs.

In SCCT, the constructs of controllability and the locus of control were treated as the intentionality of an organizational act. Hence, causal attribution in its original sense and its antecedents did not play an important role in the SCCT framework. For this reason, Schwarz (2008, 2012) extended SCCT by incorporating more systematically Kelley's covariation principle as earlier proposed by Coombs (2004) and the distinction between attributions of causes and responsibility. Kelley (1973) hypothesized that individuals observe persons' behaviors in multiple occasions and explain behavioral outcomes by the causes they covary with over time. When persons attribute causes to certain behavioral outcomes, they roughly refer to three categories according to Kelley: Effects can be attributed either to persons (person attribution), to entities a person is interacting with (entity attribution), or to circumstances of the specific situation (circumstance attribution). Depending on one's viewpoint, person attributions usually would equal internal attributions, whereas entity attributions and circumstance attributions refer to external causes.

Kelley (1973) assumed that such causal attributions are based on three informational dimensions: consensus, distinctiveness, and consistency. Consensus refers to information about a person's behavior toward a certain entity in comparison with other peoples' behaviors with regard to that entity. Distinctiveness refers to information on the person's behavior toward a certain entity in comparison with that person's behavior toward other comparable entities. Information about the person's behavior toward the entity across time or settings is labeled as consistency. The three information dimensions can be perceived as low or high by individual observers of persons or organizations. That means, there are a total of at least eight possible covariation information patterns that influence individuals' or stakeholders' causal perceptions. Social psychologists found substantial support for the importance of covariation information patterns in the process of causal attribution (Försterling, 2001).

Later, the covariation principle was applied to organizational crises (Schwarz, 2012), athlete scandals (Kim et al., 2022), and extreme weather events (McClure et al., 2022). Schwarz (2012) found support for the assumption that stakeholders covary causes to organizations by relying on these information patterns. They predict causal attributions, though with low to moderate effects. Moreover, covariation-based causal attributions were found to have a substantial impact on responsibility attributions and subsequently on evaluations of organizational reputation. However, depending on the crisis scenario, stakeholders seem to weight the three information dimensions differently. This points to a common finding in the broader field of attribution research that the attribution process is not always rational or logical but rather is subject to biases and inconsistencies. In social psychology, certain phenomena such as the correspondence bias and the fundamental attribution error, self-serving attributions, or the underuse of consensus information have been studied extensively. These biases in causal attribution seem to depend substantially on the cultural background of individuals (Choi et al., 1999).

Correspondence bias refers to the finding that individuals tend to attribute the causes of behavior of observed actors to their personal attributes (internal). Under certain conditions, this can lead to a so-called fundamental attribution error. As a result, internal causes are overemphasized, while situational factors and circumstances tend to be neglected. These findings were primarily produced in the context of Western social psychology. Subsequent studies have shown that "[t]he typical finding in cross-cultural comparisons of causal attribution has been that the correspondence bias is weaker, and in some paradigms even nonexistent, in East Asian cultures" (Choi et al., 1999, p. 48). This finding was explained by the difference between individualist and collectivist cultures. According to this, representatives of certain Asian cultures are more situation-centered in their observation and attribution, since they were socialized in an environment that requires them to be more considerate of their social context and relationships. Western cultures on the other hand are more person-centered, meaning that the individuals expect their social environment to be considerate of them, and social behavior is perceived to represent internal dispositions.

Kelley's covariance principle, too, has been subject to cross-cultural research in social psychology. Findings indicate that individuals in Western cultures tend to disregard consensus information as a basis of their causal attributions. In some Asian countries, people are more likely to use consensus information because "high consensus implies powerful situational factors and low consensus implies either weak situational factors or strong dispositional ones" (Choi et al., 1999, p. 51). Again, the common explanation has been the difference between the way people are socialized in collectivist and individualist cultures.

Self-serving attributions describe the tendency of individuals to explain desired behavioral outcomes as caused by internal characteristics (ability) and undesired outcomes as caused by situational factors (Koenig & Dean, 2011). This phenomenon can be explained by individuals' attempt to increase their self-esteem or their perception of control over certain stimuli or tasks. Cross-cultural psychology has produced mixed findings for self-serving attributions across countries by usually comparing the United States with a Southeast Asian country. These self-serving biases seem to occur not at all or only on a small scale with Japanese or Indian participants of experimental studies compared to Western individuals. In some cases, the individuals of collectivist cultures even showed a reverse tendency. Success was attributed to situational factors (e.g., luck), whereas failure was attributed self-critically to internal attributes of that person (e.g., lack of skill). On the other hand, some studies were able to identify self-serving biases also in collectivist cultures. All in all, it seems that the phenomenon is more pronounced in Western contexts (especially the United States) compared to Asian countries (Mezulis et al., 2004). This is again explained by the difference between individualist and collectivist cultures.

These findings raise relevant questions for organizational crisis communication research from an audience perspective. If, for example, fundamental attribution errors are more likely to occur in individualist cultures, then crisis stakeholders in these cultural contexts might be more disposed to attribute causes internally to organizations and blame them more frequently for crisis outcomes compared to collectivist contexts. If validated by future research, this would have important consequences, not only for theory but also for understanding reputation dynamics and the use of crisis response strategies by organizations on an international scale. If, as another example, self-serving attributions can be found on the organizational level and, in addition, differ across cultures in crisis contexts as indicated by social psychology, then this would suggest that Western organizations should be more likely to use denial strategies as crisis response (e.g., scapegoat), while organizations based and "socialized" in collectivist cultures should be more likely to use rebuild strategies (e.g., apology). At least for so-called "victim crises" (organizations are not responsible), tentative evidence showed that Korean organizations used rebuilding strategies more and denial less often compared to American organizations (Lim, 2020). However, whether these differences can be explained by cultural differences or other factors requires further, more systematic research.

Making Room for Emotions

SCCT has always acknowledged the value of emotions and related them to perceptions of organizational crisis responsibility (Coombs, 2007). When an organization is considered responsible, anger is evoked, resulting in a negative behavioral response. When an organization is not considered to blame, sympathy can emerge, resulting in a positive behavioral response. These assumptions have been confirmed in several studies among Western publics. Victim crises indeed increase affective empathy from the audience toward an organization, which reduces reputational damage (Ndone & Park, 2022; Schoofs et al., 2019). Lee (2005b) has suggested that Asian consumers may be less inclined to experience sympathy for organizations as compared to Western audiences. A preventable crisis, for which an organization is considered highly responsible, results in more anger than a victim crisis (Utz et al., 2013). Anger, in turn, leads to more reputational damage (Utz et al., 2013; van der Meer & Verhoeven, 2014).

Whereas SCCT initially focused on anger and sympathy in particular (cf. Coombs, 2007), research later distinguished more broadly between attribution-independent and attribution-dependent emotions (Choi & Lin, 2009b). Emotions such as anger and contempt are associated with the public's attributions of organizational responsibility for the crisis. Fear and anxiety, however, result from the outcome of a crisis and are associated with high uncertainty (Choi & Lin, 2009b; Jin, 2009). Additional research further differentiates between two types of attribution-dependent crisis emotions, namely external-attribution-dependent (i.e., disgust, contempt, and anger) and internal-attribution-dependent (i.e., embarrassment, guilt, and shame) crisis emotions (Jin *et al.*, 2014).

More recently, a distinction has been made between cognitive and emotional reactions to organizational crises (Coombs & Tachkova, 2023). SCCT is based on the assumption that people reflect upon the organizational responsibility in crisis situations. Some crises, however, evoke strong emotional reactions from stakeholders (i.e., moral outrage inducing crises). When a preventable crisis inflicts feelings of injustice, the audience will experience moral outrage rather than mere anger (Coombs & Tachkova, 2019). Crises with strong emotional intensity can lead to emotion-oriented information processing, which likely influences the outcomes of crisis response strategies that have been proposed by SCCT (Coombs & Tachkova, 2023). More research is needed to examine these two types of crisis information processing in different contexts and across different cultures.

Social media are likely to further intensify the importance of emotion in crisis communication theory. People turn to social media in order to fulfill emotional needs in response to a crisis (Jin et al., 2014). At the same time, social media provide organizations with an effective tool to monitor emotional reactions. An emotion detection analysis of public's tweets regarding crises in ten different countries shows that expressions of anger were connected to crisis situations where blame can be attributed (Kusen & Strembeck, 2021). A sentiment analysis of tweets confirms that preventable crises lead to more negative sentiment on social media (Zhao et al., 2020). That same sentiment analysis also found that when organizations respond with sympathy, corrective action, or messages of renewal, as opposed to using strategies focused on responsibility attribution, the audience sentiment on Twitter becomes more positive. Social media therefore provide an interesting manner for organizations to assess how audiences around the world evaluate a crisis and to determine an appropriate response.

The Importance of Sending the Right Message, the Right Way

Organizations should not only select a crisis response strategy that is suitable given the audience's responsibility attributions and emotions, but that response should also be sincere (Schoofs et al., 2023). Studies increasingly indicate that stakeholders are skeptical when they scrutinize the organizational crisis reaction. Stealing thunder, a self-disclosure strategy that has received much support in crisis communication research, is not accepted when the public doubts the company's motivation (Kim & Lee, 2022). Corporate social responsibility messages in response to a crisis are similarly met with public skepticism (Wei & Kim, 2021). When crisis communication efforts raise skepticism, they fail to protect the organizational reputation (Crijns et al., 2017). In order to overcome the audience's skepticism, crisis communicators and their messages must be perceived as sincere.

Crisis communication that is considered sincere is more likely to lead to forgiveness or reputation repair (Choi & Mitchell, 2022; Claeys & Cauberghe, 2014a; Claeys et al., 2013). Experimental research found that an organizational crisis response that conveys emotions, for instance, can increase perceptions of sincerity and as such minimize reputational damage (Claeys et al., 2013; Xiao et al., 2018). The importance of sincerity, however, depends on the stage in the crisis life cycle as well as the type of crisis. If a crisis is ongoing and presents a threat to stakeholders' safety, organizations should primarily communicate in a way that expresses competence (Claeys & Cauberghe, 2014a). During the post-crisis stage, or during reputational crises, sincerity will more likely take the upper hand in determining the audience's assessment of the crisis response.

The prevalence of socially mediated crisis communication, and the use of crisis response videos in particular, has accelerated the importance of sincerity. Influencers use distinct tactics to come across as more sincere in their "YouTube apologies," such as portraying themselves as naturally as possible (e.g., no makeup, wearing a sweatshirt) and conveying the apology as a non-rehearsed, non-scripted message (Choi & Mitchell, 2022). The analyses of comments on crisis response videos reveal that audiences are indeed only forgiving when the apology is considered sincere (Sandlin & Gracyalny, 2018). A focus group study among audience members confirms that sincerity matters most when people evaluate crisis response videos from both public figures and organizational spokespersons (Schoofs et al., 2023). Regardless of the strategy applied, the response will be scrutinized in light of the extent to which it undermines or enhances sincerity. Each of these studies about the importance of sincerity, however, has focused on videos from American, Canadian, Australian, and European messengers and responses from Western audiences. Barkley (2020) argues that a Japanese audience might not value sincerity as much as publics in Western countries. An interesting question for further research is therefore whether the importance of sincerity in crisis communication is universal and which cues audiences from around the world use to question the sincerity of both message and messenger.

Risk Communication

Risks can be understood as probabilistic events that may "result in various harms and benefits caused by risk creators, borne by risk bearers, and intervened by risk mitigators and arbiters" (Heath & Palenchar, 2016, p. 437). The perception of risk is deeply embedded in norms, values, and culture, and thus, it can vary substantially across groups and countries

(Rohrmann, 2013). While a review of the vast literature is beyond the scope of this chapter, risk research repeatedly pointed to findings that suggest the significance of cross-cultural differences in risk perception and some universal agreement about the principal nature of risk across cultural groups and/or countries at the same time (Renn & Rohrmann, 2000). In an attempt to investigate the social response to risk, some scholars proposed a group-grid framework (social cohesiveness and hierarchy) that distinguishes five categories of risk taking. These value clusters separate social groups in societies in terms of perceiving and dealing with risks, named entrepreneurs, egalitarians, hierarchists, atomized individuals, and hermits (Thompson et al., 1990). While the framework was widely criticized, risk researchers agree "that specific culture-based preferences and biases are, indeed, important factors in risk perception" (Renn & Benighaus, 2013, p. 304).

A differentiation of risk culture on the macro-level was proposed by Cornia et al. (2016). They identified three typical risk cultures in Europe depending on the framing of disasters and risks, causal explanations for disasters, people's trust in authorities, the attribution of responsibility for preventing risks, blame, and the framing of risk and crisis management. The resulting ideal risk cultures were individual-oriented (e.g., the Netherlands), state-oriented (e.g., Sweden), and fatalistic (e.g., Italy), which can have important consequences for organizations and their approach to risk communication. While official information channels as well as legacy media can be effective in state-oriented risk cultures, they should be avoided or at least backed up with unofficial channels and an emphasis on informal communication networks in fatalist risk cultures, for example.

Organizations can be creators, bearers, and/or mitigators of risks which, once manifested, can constitute crises (Heath & O'Hair, 2009). Therefore, risk management is a crucial function in organizations to prevent crises, while risk communication serves important functions before as well as during crisis events that can generate further risks (Coombs, 2019). Risk communication was defined by the World Health Organization (2023) as "the real-time exchange of information, advice and opinions between experts or officials and people who face a hazard or threat to their survival, health, or economic or social wellbeing. The purpose of risk communication is to enable people at risk to make informed decisions to mitigate the effects of a threat (hazard) – such as a disease outbreak – and take protective and preventive measures" (para 1).

The fields of risk and crisis communication research have developed separately and still need further integration (Heath & Palenchar, 2016; Schwarz, 2016). Most risk communication research deals with government agencies or scientists/experts in contexts of emergencies (preparedness), public health crises, or emerging technologies, whereas companies have mostly been studied from a reputation management perspective. The role of effective instructional messages in contexts of acute risks has received more attention and often takes an audience-centered perspective (Sellnow et al., 2017). Audiences in their role as risk bearers can be diverse in terms of demographic characteristics as well as culture, which in many contexts warrants the development of culture-sensitive messages of instructional risk communication messages. One of the frameworks of instructional risk communication is the IDEA model according to which effective instructional risk and crisis messages should address ***internalization*** (personal relevance, potential impact, proximity, and timeliness), ***distribution*** (selecting appropriate and trustworthy channels for each target audience), ***explanation*** (explaining the risk and responses to these risks based on credible sources and comprehensible language), and ***action*** (specific actions to take/not to take for self-protection) simultaneously (Sellnow et al., 2017). Research on whether and how the model works in different cultural contexts is still scarce. Some evidence, for example, confirmed the IDEA model's prediction of risk-related learning outcomes in the context of food contamination outbreaks in Sweden (Sellnow et al., 2019) as well as in the context of earthquake preparation in Peru (Farfan, 2020).

Research on fear appeals, which was often based on the extended parallel process model (EPPM; Witte, 1992), showed repeatedly that effective risk messages need to adequately address both threat (severity and susceptibility) and efficacy (response efficacy and self-efficacy) to motivate people to adopt the recommended response (Bostrom et al., 2019; Kok et al., 2018). More nuanced studies of cross-cultural differences in audience perceptions of threat and efficacy are still lacking (Zhang, 2021). An EPPM-based comparison of Chinese and American participants showed, for example, that culture played "a significant role in forming risk perceptions, efficacy perceptions, compliance behaviors during the 2019-nCoV pandemic on both individual and national levels" (Zhang, 2021, p. 12). The authors used Hofstede's cultural orientations and found significant differences depending on cultural dimensions such as collectivism, power distance, long-term orientations, and indulgence. In general, research on the COVID-19 pandemic was an opportunity for studying cross-cultural risk perceptions and self-protective behavior in the context of a comparable threat across the globe. Results suggest that risk perceptions were similarly high and correlated with the motivation for self-protection across countries, while country-specific differences were found for the role of trust in governments or political ideology, for instance (Dryhurst et al., 2020).

Thus, risk perception as well as instructional risk communication can make the difference between safety and harm, occasionally the difference between life and death. These perceptions and the processing of risk messages seem to be somewhat contingent on culture. Given the increasingly global nature of threats as well as the multicultural composition of populations in most countries, more cross-cultural research on risk and crisis communication is needed.

Conclusion

This chapter focused on how audiences perceive and elaborate on risks, crises, and organizational responses to these events. In times of risk and crisis, the primary stakeholders are those who are most affected by the events and who have long-term interests in the organization's operation and influence its reputation (Jin et al., 2007).

In order to prevent, prepare for, and manage crises, organizations should understand how their audiences perceive the crisis on the one hand and the crisis response on the other hand. First, to understand how stakeholders respond to a crisis, organizations must establish attributions of crisis responsibility and public emotions. Research regarding crisis perceptions has long been attribution-centered (Page, 2019). Attributions of responsibility indeed play a consistent part in determining reputational damage. Emotions, although in part related to those attributions of responsibility, have recently taken their place besides responsibility attributions in explaining how the audience responds to a crisis (Coombs & Tachkova, 2019, 2023; Jin, 2014; Jin et al., 2012). Whereas organizations used to rely on traditional media to estimate both responsibility attributions and emotions, social media now allow to monitor these reactions in real time.

When it comes to the audience's evaluation of the organizational crisis response, research has begun to understand that the right response can be given in the wrong manner. Stakeholders expect organizations that are to blame for a crisis, to accept responsibility (cf. Coombs, 2007). But simply saying "sorry" is oftentimes not enough. Stakeholders are skeptical toward organizations in crisis and may especially scrutinize an organizational crisis response when they are highly involved with the crisis (Choi & Lin, 2009a; Claeys & Cauberghe, 2014b). Organizations must therefore consider ways to deliver their response in a sincere manner. Social media influencers seem to look for all sorts of tricks to come across as sincere in their YouTube apologies (Choi & Mitchell, 2022). However, the most effective manner for organizations to come across as sincere may simply be to both behave and communicate in ways that actually prioritize public well-being, as opposed to organizational self-interest.

As risk and crisis communication theory matures, more cross-cultural studies emerge that compare the impact of crises and crisis communication across borders. Such research increasingly goes beyond narrative case studies and post hoc speculations about cultural influences. Scholars are applying more rigid methods of cross-national or cross-cultural comparative research such as quasi-experimental studies (e.g., Guerber et al., 2020) and comparative surveys (e.g., Shim et al., 2021). Nevertheless, these studies are still rare and their findings are difficult to generalize. Attributions and emotions are, however, known in social psychology to differ across cultures in some respect (Choi et al., 1999; Yrizarry *et al.*, 2001). In addition, perceptions and responses to risk vary within and across countries (Cornia et al., 2016; Renn & Rohrmann, 2000).

Hence, the impact of cultural and national context continues to need more substantial research. Such research should further integrate risk and crisis frameworks conceptually and empirically. It should also extend its regional scope beyond North America, Europe, and Asia. Organizations must understand how different audiences around the globe give meaning to risks, crises, and crisis communication. As social media connect all of these audiences, a crisis response directed at stakeholders from one country will easily get picked up by stakeholders from another. Therefore, organizations in general and *transnational* organizations in particular must realize that local communication practitioners are crucial to help assess perception, attribution, and response (Zhu et al., 2017).

References

An, S.-K., Park, D.-J., Cho, S., & Berger, B. (2010). A cross-cultural study of effective organizational crisis response strategy in the United States and South Korea. *International Journal of Strategic Communication*, *4*(4), 225–243. https://doi.org/10.1080/1553118X.2010.515543

Barkley, K. (2020). Does one size fit all? The applicability of situational crisis communication theory in the Japanese context. *Public Relations Review*, *46*(3), 101911. https://doi.org/10.1016/j.pubrev.2020.101911

Bostrom, A., Hayes, A. L., & Crosman, K. M. (2019). Efficacy, Action, and Support for Reducing Climate Change Risks. *Risk Analysis*, *39*(4), 805–828. https://doi.org/10.1111/risa.13210

Cheng, Y., Wang, Y., & Kong, Y. (2022). The state of social-mediated crisis communication research through the lens of global scholars: An updated assessment. *Public Relations Review*, *48*(2), 102172. https://doi.org/10.1016/j.pubrev.2022.102172

Choi, G. Y., & Mitchell, A. M. (2022). So sorry, now please watch: Identifying image repair strategies, sincerity and forgiveness in YouTubers' apology videos. *Public Relations Review*, *48*(4), 102226. https://doi.org/10.1016/j.pubrev.2022.102226

Choi, Y., & Lin, Y.-H. (2009a). Consumer response to crisis: Exploring the concept of involvement in Mattel product recalls. *Public Relations Review*, *35*(1), 18–22. https://doi.org/10.1016/j.pubrev.2008.09.009

Choi, Y., & Lin, Y.-H. (2009b). Consumer responses to Mattel product recalls posted on online bulletin boards: Exploring two types of emotion. *Journal of Public Relations Research*, *21*(2), 198–207. https://doi.org/10.1080/10627260802557506

Choi, I., Nisbett, R. E., & Norenzayan, A. (1999). Causal attribution across cultures: Variation and universality. *Psychological Bulletin*, *125*(1), 47–63. https://doi.org/10.1037/0033-2909.125.1.47

Claeys, A.-S., & Cauberghe, V. (2014a). Keeping control: The importance of nonverbal expressions of power by organizational spokespersons in times of crisis. *Journal of Communication*, *64*(6), 1160–1180. https://doi.org/10.1111/jcom.12122

Claeys, A.-S., & Cauberghe, V. (2014b). What makes crisis response strategies work? The impact of crisis involvement and message framing. *Journal of Business Research*, *67*(2), 182–189. https://doi.org/10.1016/j.jbusres.2012.10.005

Claeys, A.-S., Cauberghe, V., & Leysen, J. (2013). Implications of stealing thunder for the impact of expressing emotions in organizational crisis communication. *Journal of Applied Communication Research*, *41*(3), 293–308. https://doi.org/10.1080/00909882.2013.806991

Claeys, A.-S., Cauberghe, V., & Vyncke, P. (2010). Restoring reputations in times of crisis: An experimental study of the situational crisis communication theory and the moderating effects of locus of control. *Public Relations Review*, *36*(3), 256–262. https://doi.org/10.1016/j.pubrev.2010.05.004

Claeys, A.-S., & Opgenhaffen, M. (2021). Changing perspectives: Managerial and legal considerations regarding crisis communication. *Public Relations Review*, *47*(4), 102080. https://doi.org/10.1016/j.pubrev.2021.102080

Coombs, W. T. (2004). Impact of past crises on current crisis communication – Insights from Situational Crisis Communication Theory. *International Journal of Business Communication*, *41*(3), 265–289. https://doi.org/10.1177/0021943604265607

Coombs, W. T. (2007). Protecting organization reputations during a crisis: The development and application of situational crisis communication theory. *Corporate Reputation Review*, *10*(3), 163–176.

Coombs, W. T. (2019). *Ongoing crisis communication*. In *Planning, Managing, and Responding* (5th ed.). Sage.

Coombs, W. T., & Holladay, S. J. (1996). Communication and attributions in a crisis: An experimental study in crisis communication. *Journal of Public Relations Research*, *8*(4), 279–295. https://doi.org/10.1207/s1532754xjprr0804_04

Coombs, W. T., & Tachkova, E. R. (2019). Scansis as a unique crisis type: Theoretical and practical implications. *Journal of Communication Management*, *23*(1), 72–88. https://doi.org/10.1108/JCOM-08-2018-0078

Coombs, W. T., & Tachkova, E. R. (2023). How emotions can enhance crisis communication: Theorizing around moral outrage. *Journal of Public Relations Research*. Advance online publication. https://doi.org/10.1080/1062726X.2023.2244615

Cornia, A., Dressel, K., & Pfeil, P. (2016). Risk cultures and dominant approaches towards disasters in seven European countries. *Journal of Risk Research*, *19*(3), 288–304. https://doi.org/10.1080/13669877.2014.961520

Crijns, H., Cauberghe, V., Hudders, L., & Claeys, A.-S. (2017). How to deal with online consumer comments during a crisis? The impact of personalized organizational responses on organizational reputation. *Computers in Human Behavior*, *75*, 619–631. http://dx.doi.org/10.1016/j.chb.2017.05.046

Dryhurst, S., Schneider, C. R., Kerr, J., Freeman, A. L. J., Recchia, G., van der Bles, A. M., Spiegelhalter, D., & van der Linden, S. (2020). Risk perceptions of COVID-19 around the world. *Journal of Risk Research*, *23*(7-8), 994–1006. https://doi.org/10.1080/13669877.2020.1758193

Farfan, F. (2020). *Risk communication in the context of earthquakes: Testing the IDEA model in Peru*. Master's thesis, Technische Universität Ilmenau. Ilmenau.

Fediuk, T. A., Coombs, W. T., & Botero, I. C. (2012). Exploring crisis from a receiver perspective: Understanding stakeholder reactions during crisis events. In W. T. Coombs, & S. J. Holladay, Eds., *The Handbook of Crisis Communication* (pp. 635–656). Wiley-Blackwell.

Försterling, F. (2001). *Attribution: An Introduction to Theories, Research and Applications*. Psychology Press.

Gaither, T. K., & Curtin, P. A. (2007). Examining the heuristic value of models of international public relations practice: A case study of the Arla Foods crisis. *Journal of Public Relations Research*, *20*(1), 115–137. https://doi.org/10.1080/10627260701727051

Garcia, C. (2011). Sex scandals: A cross-cultural analysis of image repair strategies in the cases of Bill Clinton and Silvio Berlusconi. *Public Relations Review*, *37*(3), 292–296. https://doi.org/10.1016/j.pubrev.2011.03.008

Gribas, J., DiSanza, J. R., Hartman, K. L., Carr, D. J., & Legge, N. J. (2021). Exploring the effectiveness of image repair tactics: Comparison of U.S. and Middle Eastern audiences. *Communication Research Reports*, *38*(3), 150–160. https://doi.org/10.1080/08824096.2021.1909550

Guerber, A. J., Anand, V., Ellstrand, A. E., Waller, M. A., & Reychav, I. (2020). Extending the situational crisis communication theory: The impact of linguistic style and culture. *Corporate Reputation Review*, *23*, 106–127. https://doi.org/10.1057/s41299-019-00081-1

Heath, R. L., & O'Hair, H. D. (2009). The significance of risk and crisis communication. In R. L. Heath, & H. D. O'Hair, Eds., *Handbook of Risk and Crisis Communication* (pp. 5–30). Routledge.

Heath, R. L., & Palenchar, M. J. (2016). Paradigms of risk and crisis communication in the twenty-first century. In A. Schwarz, & M. W. S. C. Auer, Eds., *The Handbook of International Crisis Communication Research* (pp. 435–446). Wiley Blackwell. https://doi.org/10.1002/9781118516812.ch39

Hofstede, G. (2001). *Culture's Consequences: Comparing Values, Behaviors, Institutions, and Organizations Across Nations* (2nd ed.). Sage.
Huang, Y. (2006). Crisis situations, communication strategies, and media coverage: A multicase study revisiting the communicative response model. *Communication Research, 33*(3), 180–205. https://doi.org/10.1177/0093650206287077
Huang, Y.-H., Lin, Y., & Su, S. (2005). Crisis communicative strategies in Taiwan: Category, continuum, and cultural implication. *Public Relations Review, 31*(2), 229–238. https://doi.org/10.1016/j.pubrev.2005.02.016
Jin, Y. (2009). The effects of public's cognitive appraisal of emotions in crises on crisis coping and strategy assessment. *Public Relations Review, 35*(3), 310–313. https://doi.org/10.1016/j.pubrev.2009.02.003
Jin, Y. (2014). Examining publics' crisis responses according to different shades of anger and sympathy. *Journal of Public Relations Research, 26*(1), 79–101. https://doi.org/10.1080/1062726X.2013.848143
Jin, Y., Liu, B. F., Anagondahalli, D., & Austin, L. (2014). Scale development for measuring publics' emotions in organizational crises. *Public Relations Review, 40*(3), 509–518. https://doi.org/10.1016/j.pubrev.2014.04.007
Jin, Y., Pang, A., & Cameron, G. T. (2007). Integrated crisis mapping: Toward a publics-based, emotion-driven conceptualization in crisis communication. *Sphera Publica, 7*, 81–95.
Jin, Y., Pang, A., & Cameron, G. T. (2012). Toward a publics-driven, emotion-based conceptualization in crisis communication: Unearthing dominant emotions in multi-staged testing of the integrated crisis mapping (ICM) model. *Journal of Public Relations Research, 24*(3), 266–298. https://doi.org/10.1080/1062726X.2012.676747
Kelley, H. H. (1973). The processes of causal attribution. *American Psychologist, 28*(2), 107–128. https://doi.org/10.1037/h0034225
Kim, S.-Y., & Lee, J.-H. (2022). How to maximize the effectiveness of stealing thunder in crisis communication: The significance of follow-up actions and transparent communication. *Corporate Communications: An International Journal, 27*(3), 425–440. https://doi.org/10.1108/CCIJ-04-2021-0047
Kim, D., Lee, J. S., Jang, W. E., & Ko, Y. J. (2022). Does causal reasoning lead to moral reasoning? Consumers' responses to scandalized athletes and endorsements. *International Journal of Sports Marketing and Sponsorship, 23*(3), 465–484. https://doi.org/10.1108/IJSMS-09-2020-0161
Koenig, A. M., & Dean, K. K. (2011). Cross-cultural differences and similarities in attribution. In K. D. Keith, Ed., *Cross-cultural Psychology* (pp. 475–493). Wiley-Blackwell.
Kok, G., Peters, G.-J. Y., Kessels, L. T. E., ten Hoor, G. A., & Ruiter, R. A. C. (2018). Ignoring theory and misinterpreting evidence: The false belief in fear appeals. *Health Psychology Review, 12*(2), 111–125. https://doi.org/10.1080/17437199.2017.1415767
Kusen, E., & Strembeck, M. (2021). Building blocks of communication networks in times of crises: Emotion-exchange motifs. *Computers in Human Behavior, 123*, 106883. https://doi.org/10.1016/j.chb.2021.106883
Lee, B. K. (2004). Audience-oriented approach to crisis communication: A study of Hong Kong consumers' evaluation of an organizational crisis. *Communication Research, 31*(5), 600–618. https://doi.org/10.1177/0093650204267936
Lee, B. K. (2005a). Crisis, culture, community. In P. J. Kalbfleisch, Ed., *Communication Yearbook 29* (pp. 275–309). Routledge.
Lee, B. K. (2005b). Hong Kong consumers' evaluation in an airline crash: A path model analysis. *Journal of Public Relations Research, 17*(4), 363–391. https://doi.org/10.1207/s1532754xjprr1704_3
Lim, J. R. (2020). How organizations in different cultures respond to crises: Content analysis of crisis responses between the United States and South Korea. *International Journal of Strategic Communication, 14*(4), 294–316. https://doi.org/10.1080/1553118X.2020.1812613
Lwin, M. O., Pang, A., Loh, J.-Q., Peh, M. H.-Y., Rodriguez, S. A., & Zelani, N. H. B. (2017). Is saying 'sorry' enough? Examining the effects of apology typologies by organizations on consumer responses. *Asian Journal of Communication, 27*(1), 49–64. https://doi.org/10.1080/01292986.2016.1247462
Ma, L. (2018). How to turn your friends into enemies: Causes and outcomes of customers' sense of betrayal in crisis communication. *Public Relations Review, 44*(3), 374–384. https://doi.org/10.1016/j.pubrev.2018.04.009

Ma, L., & Zhan, M. (2016). Effects of attributed responsibility and response strategies on organizational reputation: A meta-analysis of situational crisis communication theory research. *Journal of Public Relations Research*, *28*(2), 102–119. https://doi.org/10.1080/1062726X.2016.1166367

McClure, J., Noy, I., Kashima, Y., & Milfont, T. L. (2022). Attributions for extreme weather events: Science and the people. *Climatic Change*, *174*(3), 22. https://doi.org/10.1007/s10584-022-03443-7

Mezulis, A. H., Abramson, L. Y., Hyde, J. S., & Hankin, B. L. (2004). Is there a universal positivity bias in attributions? A meta-analytic review of individual, developmental, and cultural differences in the self-serving attributional bias. *Psychological Bulletin*, *130*(5), 711–747. https://doi.org/10.1037/0033-2909.130.5.711

Muindi, B., & Kiarie, C. (2021). University crises in Africa: A situational crisis communicaiton theory case study of Daystar University, Kenya. *Communicatio*, *47*(2), 79–95. https://doi.org/10.1080/02500167.2021.1976239

Myers, C. (2016). Apology, sympathy, and empathy: The legal ramifications of admitting fault in U.S. public relations practice. *Public Relations Review*, *42*(1), 176–183. https://doi.org/10.1016/j.pubrev.2015.10.004

Ndone, J., & Park, J. (2022). Crisis communication: The mediating role of cognitive and affective empathy in the relationship between crisis type and crisis response strategy on post-crisis reputation and forgiveness. *Public Relations Review*, *48*(1), 102136. https://doi.org/10.1016/j.pubrev.2021.102136

Nekmat, E., & Kong, D. (2019). Effects of online rumors on attribution of crisis responsibility and attitude toward organization during crisis uncertainty. *Journal of Public Relations Research*, *31*(5-6), 133–151. https://doi.org/10.1080/1062726X.2019.1644644

Page, T. G. (2019). Beyond attribution: Building new measures to explain the reputation threat posed by crisis. *Public Relations Review*, *45*(1), 138–152. https://doi.org/10.1016/j.pubrev.2018.10.002

Renn, O., & Benighaus, C. (2013). Perception of technological risk: Insights from research and lessons for risk communication and management. *Journal of Risk Research*, *16*(3–4), 293–313. https://doi.org/10.1080/13669877.2012.729522

Renn, O., & Rohrmann, B. (2000). Cross-cultural risk perception: State and challenges. In O. Renn & B. Rohrmann (Eds.), *Cross-Cultural Risk Perception: A Survey of Empirical Studies* (pp. 211–233). Springer US. https://doi.org/10.1007/978-1-4757-4891-8_6

Rohrmann, B. (2013). *Comparisons of risk perception in different cultures: Profile and synopsis of a social science research venture conducted in 9 countries*. http://www.rohrmannresearch.net/pdfs/Rohrmann%5B%5DReportCRD-SynopsisRiskPerceptionResearch-Final-260713.pdf.

Sandlin, J. K., & Gracyalny, M. L. (2018). Seeking sincerity, finding forgiveness: YouTube apologies as image repair. *Public Relations Review*, *44*(3), 393–406. https://doi.org/10.1016/j.pubrev.2018.04.007

Schoofs, L., Claeys, A.-S., De Waele, A., & Cauberghe, V. (2019). The role of empathy in crisis communication: Providing a deeper understanding of how organizational crises and crisis communication affect reputation. *Public Relations Review*, *45*(5), 101851. https://doi.org/10.1016/j.pubrev.2019.101851

Schoofs, L., Claeys, A.-S., & Koppen, E. (2023). "Say it like you mean it": An exploration of how members of the public perceive audiovisual crisis responses. In W. T. Coombs, & S. J. Holladay, Eds., *The Handbook of Crisis Communication* (2nd ed., pp. 391–404). John Wiley & Sons Ltd.

Schwarz, A. (2008). Covariation-based causal attributions during organizational crises: Suggestions for extending Situational Crisis Communication Theory (SCCT). *International Journal of Strategic Communication*, *2*(1), 31–53. https://doi.org/10.1080/15531180701816601

Schwarz, A. (2012). Stakeholder attributions in crises: The effects of covariation information and attributional inferences on organizational reputation. *International Journal of Strategic Communication*, *6*(2), 174–195. https://doi.org/10.1080/1553118X.2011.596869

Schwarz, A. (2016). Crisis communication research in Germany. In A. Schwarz, M. Seeger, & C. Auer, Eds., *The Handbook of International Crisis Communication Research* (pp. 357–372). Wiley Blackwell. https://doi.org/10.1002/9781118516812.ch33

Schwarz, A., Seeger, M. W., & Auer, C. (2016). Significance and structure of international risk and crisis communication research: Toward an integrative approach. In A. Schwarz, M. W. Seeger, & C. Auer, Eds., *The Handbook of International Crisis Communication Research* (pp. 1–10). Wiley Blackwell. https://doi.org/10.1002/9781118516812.ch1

Sellnow, D. D., Johansson, B., Sellnow, T. L., & Lane, D. R. (2019). Toward a global understanding of the effects of the IDEA model for designing instructional risk and crisis messages: A food contamination experiment in Sweden. *Journal of Contingencies & Crisis Management*, *27*(2), 102–115. https://doi.org/10.1111/1468-5973.12234

Sellnow, D. D., Lane, D. R., Sellnow, T. L., & Littlefield, R. S. (2017). The IDEA model as a best practice for effective instructional risk and crisis communication. *Communication Studies*, *68*(5), 552–567. https://doi.org/10.1080/10510974.2017.1375535

Shaver, K. G. (1985). *The Attribution of Blame: Causality, Responsibility, and Blameworthiness*. Springer.

Shim, K., Cho, H., Kim, S., & Yeo, S. L. (2021). Impact of moral ethics on consumers' boycott intentions: A cross-cultural study of crisis perceptions and responses in the United States, South Korea, and Singapore. *Communication Research*, *48*(3), 401–425. https://doi.org/10.1177/0093650218793565

Taylor, M. (2000). Cultural variance as a challenge to global public relations: A case study of the Coca-Cola scare in Europe. *Public Relations Review*, *26*(3), 277–293. https://doi.org/10.1016/S0363-8111(00)00048-5

Thompson, M., Ellis, R. J., Wildavsky, A., & Wildavsky, M. (1990). *Cultural Theory*. Routledge.

Utz, S., Schultz, F., & Glocka, S. (2013). Crisis communication online: How medium, crisis type and emotions affected public reactions in the Fukushima Daiichi nuclear disaster. *Public Relations Review*, *39*(1), 40–46. https://doi.org/10.1016/j.pubrev.2012.09.010

van der Meer, T. G. L. A., & Verhoeven, J. W. M. (2014). Emotional crisis communication. *Public Relations Review*, *40*(3), 526–536. http://dx.doi.org/10.1016/j.pubrev.2014.03.004

Wei, L., & Kim, N. (2021). Attenuating public skepticism: Effects of pre-crisis corporate engagement and post-crisis CSR initiatives on corporate evaluations. *Public Relations Review*, *47*(1), 101999. https://doi.org/10.1016/j.pubrev.2020.101999

Wen, W.-C., Yu, T.-H., & Benoit, W. L. (2012). The failure of 'scientific' evidence in Taiwan: A case study of international image repair for American beef. *Asian Journal of Communication*, *22*(2), 121–139. http://dx.doi.org/10.1080/01292986.2011.642393

Witte, K. (1992). Putting the fear back into fear appeals: The extended parallel process model. *Communication Monographs*, *59*(4), 329–349. https://doi.org/10.1080/03637759209376276

World Health Organization (2023). *Risk communication and community engagement (RCCE)*. Retrieved September 13, 2023 from https://www.who.int/emergencies/risk-communications

Xiao, Y., Hudders, L., Claeys, A.-S., & Cauberghe, V. (2018). The impact of expressing mixed valence emotions in organizational crisis communication on consumer's negative word-of-mouth intention. *Public Relations Review*, *44*(5), 794–806. https://doi.org/10.1016/j.pubrev.2018.10.007

Yrizarry, N., Matsumoto, D., Imai, C., Kooken, K., & Takeuchi, S. (2001). Culture and emotion. In L. L. Adler, & U. P. Gielen, Eds., *Cross-cultural Topics in Psychology* (2nd ed., pp. 131–147). Praeger.

Zhang, X. A. (2021). Understanding the cultural orientations of fear appeal variables: A cross-cultural comparison of pandemic risk perceptions, efficacy perceptions, and behaviors. *Journal of Risk Research*, *24*(3–4), 432–448. https://doi.org/10.1080/13669877.2021.1887326

Zhao, X., Zhan, M., & Ma, L. (2020). How publics react to situational and renewing organizational responses across crises: Examining SCCT and DOR in social-mediated crises. *Public Relations Review*, *46*(4), 101944. https://doi.org/10.1016/j.pubrev.2020.101944

Zhou, Z., Zhang, X., & Ki, E.-J. (2022). Crisis response strategy manipulation: A systematic review and a test of nuances. *Public Relations Review*, *48*(3), 102208. https://doi.org/10.1016/j.pubrev.2022.102208

Zhu, L., Anagondahalli, D., & Zhang, A. (2017). Social media and culture in crisis communication: McDonald's and KFC crises management in China. *Public Relations Review*, *43*(3), 487–492. http://dx.doi.org/10.1016/j.pubrev.2017.03.006

Author's Bio

An-Sofie Claeys (PhD, Ghent University & Royal Military Academy) is an associate professor of corporate communication at the Department of Translation, Interpreting and Communication of Ghent University in Belgium. Her research interests include verbal and non-verbal crisis communication, stealing thunder, empathy, and emotions in crisis communication and decision-making in crisis teams. Her work on organizational crisis communication has been published in journals such as *Journal of Communication*, *Communication Theory*, *Public Relations Review*, *Journal of Public Relations Research*, *Journal of Business Research*, *Journal of Applied Communication Research*, and *Health Communication*.

Andreas Schwarz (PhD, TU Ilmenau, 2009) is a senior researcher in risk and crisis communication at Technische Universität Ilmenau in Germany where he serves as co-director of the International Research Group on Crisis Communication. He was the founding chair of the Crisis Communication Section of the European Communication Research and Education Association (ECREA), 2011–2018. His research interests include cross-cultural risk and crisis communication, crisis response of nongovernmental and higher education organizations, and the science and risk communication of emerging technologies such as artificial intelligence. Schwarz received research grants to study risk communication of COVID-19, crisis communication of child protective services and nonprofit organizations, and perceptions of artificial intelligence or automated mobility. His research has been published in journals like *Health Communication*, *International Journal of Strategic Communication*, *Public Relations Review*, *Journal of Public Relations Research*, and *Science Communication*. He has conducted trainings and consulted on risk and crisis communication for several government agencies, nonprofit organizations, and corporations.

21

Reputational Crisis in Politics

Sergei A. Samoilenko

Department of Communication, George Mason University, Fairfax, VA, USA

In the 2000s, former popular comedian Al Franken remade himself into a high-profile politician after years in the public eye on *Saturday Night Live*. During Donald Trump's presidency, Franken was critical of the Trump administration and championed women's causes. In November 2017, however, talk radio host Leeann Tweeden gave an interview in which she alleged that Franken had forcibly kissed her on a 2006 USO tour during a skit rehearsal.[1] Franken was also photographed appearing to hold his hands above Tweeden's body while she was asleep wearing body armor and a helmet (Rosen, 2017). The story appeared in the media in the aftermath of film producer Harvey Weinstein's sexual scandal and the subsequent downfall of other powerful men. Tweeden's release of the photo caused an immediate reaction from both journalists and politicians. When female colleagues from *Saturday Night Live* and former Senate staffers stepped forward to defend Franken, *Washington Post* editorial writer Molly Roberts dismissed them, writing, "There are plenty of people the Zodiac Killer did not murder." In all, 35 Democratic senators called for Franken to leave office (Mayer, 2019).

A reputational crisis evolves depending on how publics perceive and communicate about the crisis event. Since a high public profile is usually associated with increased public scrutiny, a crisis situation can easily turn into a source of outrage when a political leader falls short of the hopes and expectations of their constituents (Eccles et al., 2007). The key effect of a political crisis is public disappointment and the widespread collapse of expectations due to the actions of public servants (Imhof, 2016). In such a crisis, the media and key audiences demand a response within a compressed timeframe. An official response to the situation that is judged insufficient or inappropriate by key publics can cause a heightened media scandal (Coombs & Tachkova, 2018).

In the Internet age, challenges to reputation are intensifying for three main reasons: the speed with which information can be shared; the volume of information; and the "venom" behind the allegations (Dezenhall, 2014). Dezenhall argues that the political career of Al Franken ended after his crude gesture landed smack in the middle of a "fiasco vortex" – a singular moment when the culture changed, comparable to when a school of fish suddenly turns for no reason discernible to the naked eye. The news cycle subsequently moved too quickly to draw a distinction between "[being] an aging goofball and being a criminal predator." The pressure on Democratic senators was so extreme during that week that there was nothing Franken could have done once the lewd photo emerged: Apologies only work

[1] United Service Organizations is one of the top nonprofit organizations in the U.S. for helping active-duty service members and their families.

The Handbook of International Crisis and Risk Communication Research, Second Edition.
Edited by Andreas Schwarz, Matthew W. Seeger, and Sora Kim.

when audiences want them. In this situation, no apology could have defused the threat to Franken's position because outrage was the end goal of the enterprise. While the Franken photo was not the evidence of an actual assault, it served as a symbol of one in a climate where incontrovertible proof has become difficult to find. In an age, moreover, when the driving media force is to declare a crisis to have been mishandled (to prolong the scandal for consumers), "there is no device to un-ring a bell that the public has demanded be rung loudly" (E. Dezenhall, personal communication, August 15, 2020).

In a tight race, a character attack may be sufficient to cause a substantial drop in the polls, potentially securing victory for the attacker's chosen candidate. At the societal level, the reputational damage incurred can lead to declining confidence in leadership and an erosion of public trust (Imhof, 2016). An online attack may trigger a domino effect, where numerous events occur as a result of a small push. Rivals take advantage of media pitfalls to determine the best timing, content, and channels to employ in launching smear campaigns. Additional reputational risks stem from various types of faux pas, gaffes, and mismanaged performances that are conveniently amplified and capitalized upon by media outlets that largely profit from publishing negative materials.

The focus of this chapter is the reputational crisis in politics. I first discuss the concepts of reputation and reputation management from the perspective of Bourdieu's theory of social fields. I then examine the impacts of digital media and other contemporary challenges to reputation and give an overview of scholarship on the common types of crisis response. My conclusion argues for considering the sociocultural approach when examining reputational crisis situations in the political field.

Character and Reputation

For Bourdieu (1984), society is divided into social fields that are defined by a network of relationships between the orientations and positions held and protected by social actors. All social actors strive for legitimacy to become recognized and thus fully functional in their social environments. The main source of power in social interactions is the accumulated capital represented by resources allowing the exercising of control within the field. Political actors endeavor to acquire administrative control over various types of power such as law, the armed forces, or finances. These struggles in the political field involve the mobilization of supporters around issues and the creation of political products such as a politician's "brand," which constitutes legitimate political authority.

Accumulated capital may take various forms and can be determined by wealth, rank, rare qualifications, or powerful social networks. The amount of valuable field capital is a key criterion for class distinction based on distinguishing signs or properties respected in a given class. Struggles over the appropriation of valuable economic resources, cultural capital, or solid reputation are considered "classification struggles." *Symbolic capital* is considered the most desirable form of capital because both economic and cultural capitals take the form of reputation when they are "grasped through categories of perception" (Bourdieu & Wacquant, 1992, p. 119). This type of capital is constituted by public perceptions of honor, rank, qualification, or status and acquired through "a reputation for competence and an image of respectability and honorability" (Bourdieu, 1984, p. 291). With symbolic capital comes *symbolic power*, which enables social actors to impose categories of thought and perceptions of legitimacy upon collective beliefs (Bourdieu, 1991). Importantly, "the failure to comply with appropriate social expectations is associated with risks of *déclassement* for lack of the qualifications formally required of rightful members" (Bourdieu, 1984, p. 148). Thus, symbolic capital represents superior social status and constitutes a sign of legitimacy and symbolic power in a hierarchy of perceived prestige.

Legitimate actors are expected to comply with norms for self-regulation and social integration and demonstrate cultural alignment with other members of society, as well as support relevant laws, rules, and social values (Bateson, 1972). Individuals are more likely to trust each other if they have a reputation for trustworthiness (Imhof, 2016). *Character* (trustworthiness, ethos) is a core component in the public evaluation of credibility or judgment concerning why someone ought to be believed (O'Keefe, 2002). The moral virtues of character are perceived according to normative ethics and the social role a person is supposed to be playing at a given time according to social commitments and obligations. This is the public image or the impression of honesty and personal integrity that meets the universally accepted standards of appropriateness (Walton, 1999). Legitimate social actors are also required to comply with public expectations across several dimensions, including recognized norms of authenticity and professional qualities. The outcome of these efforts across various contexts leads to the public evaluation of an individual or group's reputation or "the sum of the images the various constituencies have of an organization" (Fombrun, 1996, p. 376).

Sandman (2010) argues that a public figure can have a good and a bad reputation at the same time and be simultaneously loved and hated by different audiences for different reasons. Hence, reputation can be measured in two different dimensions: *positive reputation* (how loved an individual is) and *negative reputation* (how hated that individual is). He argues that it is possible to be both much-loved and much-hated (e.g., Hillary Clinton) at the same time. Importantly, further to this, the public may have more complicated ways of perceiving reputation than simply seeing it as "good" or "bad."

In addition, Sandman (2010) argues that reputation can be compared to a bank balance that can be either depleted or enhanced during major events. Scholarship on corporate reputation seconds this view, noting that organizations with bountiful reputational capital can afford to spend some of this capital in a crisis and still maintain a favorable reputation among their stakeholders (Alsop, 2004). Nonetheless, Thompson (2000) reminds us that *character-based* reputation is a very fragile asset that is intrinsically contestable. Moreover, it can be easily damaged through misuse or offensive transgressions, unlike a *skill-based* reputation.

There is a common belief that a good reputation supplies a buffer against negative public opinion. A study by Seiffert-Brockmann et al. (2018) reveals that the positive perception of character traits and personal values may protect chief executive officers (CEOs) from character attacks and thus shield entire organizations. However, other studies are inconsistent in their findings on this halo effect. Coombs and Holladay (2006) argue that in a crisis, a halo effect works only under the condition of an *extremely* positive prior reputation. Since stakeholders have high expectations of moral consistency, an organization with a good prior reputation can suffer greater moral backlash in a crisis situation that turns into a scandal (a *scansis*) than an organization with a bad prior reputation (Wei & Diddi, 2022).

Political reputation serves as an assurance of good intentions to serve society. During elections, candidates aim to promote their possession of socially approved personal qualities and competencies needed to either reproduce social order or bring about positive change. This involves various forms of strategic self-presentation selected by political actors to form and maintain an appropriate face in relevant contexts (Cupach & Metts, 1994). The appropriate face includes the disposition of character that allows political actors to garner public support and win electoral contests.

The Habitus of Political Reputation Management

The political field is an area involving power disputes in a network of relationships where power is always negotiated and contested by actors with different goals. Pragmatically speaking, political actors engage in relationships with each other to accumulate, conserve, or convert different types of capital (Bourdieu, 1990). Over time, they develop a political ***habitus***, which refers to a set of learned habits, skills, and stratagems. The knowledge of context induces social agents "to orient themselves actively either toward the preservation of the distribution of capital or toward the subversion of this distribution" (Bourdieu & Wacquant, 1992, p. 109). The choice between cooperation and competition in a particular field is dictated by both individual and contextual factors. However, one might expect these factors to overlap and interact with each other (Samoilenko, 2020a). Essentially, opposing goals and interests in obtaining scarce resources promote competition (Tajfel & Turner, 2004). In addition, some social fields can be more conducive to divergence and conflict (e.g., the political field), while others lend themselves to convergence and cooperation (e.g., the cultural field) (Bueno de Mesquita et al., 2001; Zamorano, 2016).

Different contexts provide guidelines for social interaction according to the rules of meaning and action (Pearce & Cronen, 1980). In everyday interactions, all members of society make choices concerning public image that are consistent with approved social norms. As noted above, reputation is a fragile asset that can be easily destroyed during "fateful moments" (Goffman, 1967, p. 237). Building symbolic capital thus requires considerable effort that includes taking measures to court media attention and consulting public relations specialists. In competitive contexts, political actors constantly invest in efforts to maintain and protect their symbolic capital because their status inevitably involves social comparison as part of questioning their authority. Impression management strategies help political actors project the images of competence, induce compliance, or construct impression integrity. When an individual's face is threatened, they will tend to counteract this threat with preventive facework. When face is lost, the individual is motivated to restore it through corrective facework to avoid experiencing discomfort over disrupting the social order (Metts, 2009).

A celebrated public figure who has achieved a powerful social position becomes a potential target for challengers of various kinds. According to Bourdieu (1984), the holders of symbolic capital must protect it from the actions of "pretentious pretenders" who "have a self-image too far out of line" and "ought to cut down their self-image ('climb down')" (p. 254). These ambitious contenders with deficient capital are inclined toward subversion strategies that aim to challenge the authority of the political establishment and influence public opinion in favor of their own acceptance and recognition in the field. They attack those bigger than themselves to appear morally superior and build their own reputations on those of their targets. In 1996, then-comedian and aspiring politician Al Franken published a bestseller, titled ***Rush Limbaugh Is a Big Fat Idiot and Other Observations***, that was critical of the 1990s right-wing political figures such as Pat Buchanan, Bob Dole, Phil Gramm, Newt Gingrich, and particularly radio host Rush Limbaugh. In this book, Franken often makes his points through humor, including the use of graphs with his handwriting superimposed over them. In a subsequent version of his book,

Franken has said that he chose to make the book's title an ***ad hominem*** attack as "an ironic comment on the fact that Rush makes ad hominem attacks all the time" (Franken, 2003, p. 85).

Established political actors often attempt to prevent new challengers from entering the field by challenging the legitimacy of their competitors. Different forms of ***ad hominem*** attacks aimed at intimidating and belittling contenders are popular techniques to maintain power and control (Herbst, 2010). For example, Thompson (2016) interprets the use of nicknames for opponents by former US President George W. Bush as a deliberate rhetorical strategy used to exert his symbolic power and reaffirm his superior position in the field. This behavior inevitably results in the rhetorical consequences of the "punishment of ironic circulation" (p. 44), where a political sobriquet is adopted by the public and later used as mockery. The primary result of these efforts is to decrease the opponent's ability to continue contesting power.

In sum, the application of reputation management strategies is essential to all social interactions. It is especially pronounced in the political field because of that field's competitive nature. Political actors make considerable efforts to build symbolic capital and maintain their desired public image. When this image is threatened, they resort to preventive strategies; when the image is damaged, they restore it through corrective strategies to assure others that they can be trusted. When threats to reputation are not properly addressed, however, a crisis challenge may evolve into a reputational crisis aggravated by political scandal.

Challenges to Political Reputation

In early October 2016, Federal Bureau of Investigation (FBI) criminal investigators seized a laptop belonging to former New York Congressman Anthony Weiner as part of an investigation into a case involving Weiner sending lewd photos to a teenager. On that laptop, investigators discovered emails forwarded to Weiner by his estranged wife, Huma Abedin, vice-chair of Hillary Clinton's 2016 presidential campaign. This prompted FBI Director James Comey to reopen the previously closed investigation into Clinton's use of a private email server, just a few days before the 2016 US presidential election.

As the above incident demonstrates, both offensive transgressions and media misuse can nullify character-based reputations. The Weiner sexting case further entangled Hillary Clinton in an investigation at an inconvenient time. According to Berman (2019), it created another cascade of negative press coverage that altered the outcome of the 2016 election. During the campaign, the FBI's email server investigation received more media coverage than all policy issues combined (Patterson, 2016). Donald Trump's campaign rallies featured regular "lock her up" chants, referring to Clinton. The stories also helped elevate *Breitbart News* and other non-traditional media and attached unprecedented significance to their coverage.

Social media have further changed the norms of public interaction and increased demands for the visibility of public figures. According to Perloff (2021), digital media have rearranged public space, obliterating traditional borders between private and public and revealing the "backstage" behavior of politicians. Direct messaging between candidates and followers adds another level of immediacy and closeness lacking in conventional news coverage. Under Donald Trump's first presidency, Twitter became an official news source and a constant supplier of clickbait content for traditional broadcast news as well as a major carrier of misinformation and collective outrage. Between June 2015, when he declared his intention to run for president, and December 2016, just after he was elected, Donald Trump issued 289 insults via Twitter (Lee & Quealy, 2019). His Twitter strategies also included retweeting favorable fan comments, accentuating contrasts with the political establishment, and celebrity feuding with Megyn Kelly and Rosie O'Donnell that caught the attention of their large Twitter followings and made news (Cornfield, 2017).

Contemporary challenges to political reputation can be attributed to globalization coupled with the rise of social media, the mediatization of politics, declining trust in institutions, and the development of artificial intelligence (AI) technology, among other factors (Samoilenko, 2020b).

In the context of *globalization*, local communities have become more susceptible to international scandals and reputational crises resulting from "the compression of the world" and the heightened "consciousness of the world as a whole" (Robertson, 1992, p. 8). In 2012, a YouTube trailer for the film *Innocence of Muslims* featuring an attack on the character and actions of Islam's Prophet Muhammad resulted in serious reputational damage for the United States. A substandard video composed of hate speech and stereotypical clichés, produced as a prank by an amateur producer, the trailer went viral, fueling public outrage across the world and causing a prominent scandal at the highest level of US and international politics.

Another issue is the *mediatization* of politics, or "the growing intrusion of media logic as an institutional rule into fields where other rules of defining appropriate behavior prevailed" (Esser & Matthes, 2013, p. 177). One critical impact of mediatization is that the production of news content has become ever more dictated by commercial imperatives and consumer expectations, rather than substantive policy issues (Kalb, 2001; Strömbäck, 2008). Since click-bait content centered on scandalous news and rumors has greater value for media producers than traditional or substantive content, issue politics are commonly exploited by political performers who can easily adapt to the soft news format. Since the 2016 US primaries, any content related to Donald Trump has become a hot commodity on the media market, contributing to the economic revival of many traditional media outlets (Samoilenko & Miroshnichenko, 2019).

The *decline of institutional trust* has been a constant for several consecutive years with regard to all metrics: leadership competence; understanding citizen fears and concerns; dissemination of factual information; long-term thinking and planning; accountability; and others (Edelman, 2022). The personalization of politics has desacralized the institutions of power by demystifying the aura of greatness that formerly surrounded traditional politics. With influence being distributed away from traditional institutions, media celebrities and populist figures gain greater political influence than they previously enjoyed. Populist politicians employ incivility to steal the media spotlight, generate hype, and conjure political ratings (Jensen & Bang, 2017). For example, in June 2019, US House Speaker Nancy Pelosi responded to President Trump's *ad hominem* attacks by calling him the "diverter-of-attention in chief" (Roth, 2019).

Finally, AI has gained notoriety in recent years for its utility in organizing smear campaigns (Samoilenko & Suvorova, 2023). Like traditional compromising videos, deepfakes exploit eye-catching topics such as sex (particularly cheating), illegal substance use, inappropriate behavior, or age-related incompetence. Reputational harm becomes more serious when deepfakes promote fake political statements made by imposters or disseminate compromising content. Reputational crises often involve collateral damage and impact perhaps unintended audiences such as the family and friends of the target.

There are multiple factors that determine the effectiveness of crisis prevention and management. Political consultants and campaign managers must have a system in place for identifying issues, detecting warning signs, assessing threats to reputation, and responding to those threats.

Audience-Centric Responses to Reputational Crisis

Prevention

Crises disrupt the normal order of life and are accompanied by a great deal of time pressure and uncertainty associated with the situation (Coombs, 2019). In addition, the stakes of reputational survival for public figures and their organizations become higher than under normal circumstances (Botan, 2018). *Risk management* represents attempts to help individuals and organizations reduce the probability of public outrage that could develop into a reputational crisis. Sandman (1993, p. 1) defines risk using the formula "Risk = Hazard + Outrage," indicating that people assess risks based on the actual *hazard* plus the amount of public *outrage* possible or likely. He suggests that while crisis practitioners define risk by the magnitude of the hazard multiplied by its probability, the public sees risk in all the things it is worried about, including the way this perceived risk is mismanaged by practitioners.

Risk management is especially instrumental in the context of a *challenge crisis*, a situation where the public claims that an organization or its leaders are acting in an irresponsible or immoral manner (Lerbinger, 1997). This type of crisis begins as a threat that, if not properly handled, may escalate into a full-blown reputational crisis. The foundation of risk management is *risk assessment,* which involves a systematic search for warning signs and threats to individual and organizational reputation to predict the likelihood of a crisis developing. As suggested by research on organizational crises, reputational threat is influenced by (1) initial crisis responsibility, (2) crisis history, and (3) prior relational reputation with stakeholders (Coombs, 2019).

During an election campaign, it is important early on to identify any of the candidate's weaknesses that might be exploited by their opponents. As suggested by political consultant Ekaterina Egorova of the firm Political Profiler, psychological profiling helps address some candidates' fundamental vulnerabilities, including the inability to take a punch during debates, sensitivity to criticism, or low self-esteem. Political consultants also conduct a media analysis to detect various stories and rumors circulating and persisting in the minds of the electorate. Expert interviews and focus groups can provide further valuable information and reveal beliefs about the candidate, including aspects such as extramarital affairs, ties with the criminal world, expensive apartments, or various financial gains (E. Egorova, personal communication, May 20, 2023).

In addition, remaining up-to-date with developing social trends (e.g., the #MeToo campaign) allows politicians to relate effectively to public concerns during crucial periods of social change. An expert scan of the political environment can detect critical issues, assess the position of these issues in their life cycle (from emerging to mature), and identify any triggers that might escalate the issue and present reputational risks for public figures. The risk presented by an issue depends on (1) how many publics are concerned or outraged, (2) the probability of issue impact, (3) the probable magnitude of impact, and (4) the number of strategic options available at each new stage of an issue's development (Botan, 2018, p. 142).

The *stealing thunder* approach illustrates the benefits of a quick response in an organization releasing information about wrongdoing or a crisis before the news media. Studies have found that an organization's management is viewed as more credible when it reports a crisis before other sources (Arpan & Roskos-Ewoldsen, 2005). Importantly, a swift and early response allows an organization to generate greater credibility than it would with a slow response. Stealing thunder considerably reduces overall news coverage and increases the percentage of positive stories (Wigley, 2011).

During the 1991–1992 presidential primaries, former State of Arkansas employee Gennifer Flowers scheduled a press conference on a Monday afternoon to declare her adulterous relationship with candidate Bill Clinton. The Clinton campaign had heard of this planned press conference and scheduled an appearance for Bill and Hillary Clinton on the Sunday episode of the popular TV news show, *60 Minutes.* In that episode, the reporter directly asked about the "woman" problem, and the Clintons responded that they were together in marriage as husband and wife. They acknowledged earlier marital problems but stated that these problems were long in the past (Booth-Butterfield, 2009).

Political actors' impression management skills remain crucial. Political leaders who can establish greater authenticity than their rivals are perceived more positively (Cornfield, 2017). In the above-mentioned case, in their first national appearance in the media, the Clintons managed to influence voter attitudes about fidelity, marital privacy, and politics prior to the attack from Gennifer Flowers. By the next day, Flowers' press conference appeared "old news." Many viewers were already inoculated with a different news message and discounted her claims as a cheap attempt to gain "her 15 minutes of fame" (Booth-Butterfield, 2009).

The *inoculation* approach can also give rise to a more advanced and audience-centric pre-crisis plan. The main idea of inoculation theory is that resistance to persuasion can be induced, much like resistance to viral challenges (Compton, 2013). To inoculate a target and generate a protective response, one must expose the target to a weakened dose of a future challenge. Pfau et al. (1990) examined the potential for the direct mail communication channel to confer resistance to the influence of political attack messages among both Republican and Democratic voters in the 1988 presidential campaign (George H. W. Bush vs. Michael Dukakis). Their research found that proper inoculation targeting a voter from either party helped to significantly decrease the impact of subsequent attack messages compared to situations in which a voter had not been inoculated. In addition, inoculation was found to be more effective than a refutation approach in reducing the persuasive effect of attack messages. Research demonstrates that it is also possible to inoculate sources against disseminating misinformation. For example, state legislators who received letters warning of the reputational risk posed by being fact-checked were subsequently found to be less likely to disseminate misinformation than legislators who had not received the warning (Nyhan & Reifler, 2015).

Response

Crises are negative events that create attributions of responsibility and a threat to reputation (Coombs, 2019). The latter occurs when a political actor is accused of being responsible for an action considered offensive by public opinion (Benoit, 2017). Under those circumstances, the perception of crisis translates into a great degree of public outrage due to disappointment in the actions of a political actor or actors, a shared feeling of embarrassment, and a perception of increased risk of social disorder (Coombs & Holladay, 2019; Coombs & Holladay 2020).

Challenges and rumors are two types of crises that rest on the selection of competing crisis stories (Lerbinger, 1997). The importance of believability is heightened when the crisis hinges on stakeholders' choosing between competing versions of the crisis story. In some crises, the version accepted will determine the success of the crisis management effort and affect the amount of damage inflicted. Outrage management requires empathy and the ability to find anchoring frameworks to deal with various publics.

A response to a reputational attack must be anchored in good judgment and enacted with consideration for the consequences of responding and the questions of speed, proportionality, and duration. For example, in May 2020, Democratic presidential nominee Joe Biden responded to US President Donald Trump's attempts to sow doubt about his fitness for office and physical stamina: "In terms of energy, I don't have any problem comparing my energy level to Donald Trump, who I'm really resisting giving a nickname to" (Forgey, 2020). Trump has long branded Biden "Sleepy Joe" in social media posts and remarks at rallies, seizing upon wariness among even some Democrats about the 77-year-old politician's age and mental acuity.

Scandals occur when people come to define the actions or statements of public figures as serious normative violations. A scandal implies a violation of established moral standards, including activities deemed unethical (Wei & Diddi, 2022). According to Coombs and Tachkova (2018), factors that facilitate the eruption of a scandal include inappropriate crisis responses, violation of moral obligations, a strong level of public awareness, and the provocation of moral outrage. Once it arises, a scandal evokes a need for punishment for immoral behavior. Crucially, the media serve to frame the event as a scandal and raise awareness of it through its scandalization. If people accept that framing, this will affect how they relate to the crisis–scandal situation.

There are multiple factors that determine the effectiveness of crisis response. According to Ryan (1982), creating a persuasive defense often begins with identifying attitudes held by different audiences toward the accused. Both reformative and transformative strategies are often considered to address the situation: *Reformative* strategies aim to revise or amend the audience's perceptions of the situation; *transformative* strategies are used to construct new realities and change meanings for the audience (Ware & Linkugel, 1973). Image repair theory (Benoit, 2020) and situational crisis communication theory (Coombs, 2007) offer various options to deal with attacks on reputation.

The apologetic discourse has been analyzed across various contexts, including the rhetoric of presidents and presidential candidates (Blaney & Benoit, 2001; Brummett, 1981; Harrell et al., 1975; Liu, 2007). Some prominent studies concern King Edward VIII's apologia after deciding to marry a commoner (Ryan, 1984), Queen Elizabeth II's statements after Princess Diana's death (Benoit & Brinson, 1999), and Supreme Court Justice Hugo Black's 1937 radio address in which he answered charges that he was a member of the Ku Klux Klan (Carcasson & Aune, 2003). The contrast between political and entertainment image repair suggests that it is riskier for politicians to engage in mortification. Thus, politicians may hesitate to admit fault because constituents may, as a result, develop concerns about their leadership (Benoit, 1997).

An important point to keep in mind is that image repair often occurs in complex situations. In other words, it is not always simply a single attack followed by a single defense. Benoit (2017) argues that although action and character are conceptually very different, audiences often do not make these distinctions. This conflation is known as "nonexplicit assumption" (Walton, 2001, p. 93): When hearing arguments about a misdeed, an audience may naturally draw conclusions about the character of the person who perpetrated that misdeed. Conversely, if someone is demonstrated to have poor character, people might assume that this is accompanied by a greater propensity for reprehensible behavior.

In July 2018, President Donald Trump nominated Judge Brett Kavanaugh to fill a vacant seat on the US Supreme Court. Kavanaugh's nomination provoked a storm of controversy and accusations. The resulting Senate Judiciary Committee hearing, held on September 27, featured testimony by Christine Blasey Ford accusing Kavanaugh of sexual assault and pointed comments by Senate Democrats. Benoit and Stein (2021) suggest that Kavanaugh's perceived responsibility for the offensive act strengthened perceptions that he possessed several offensive traits. Even though Kavanaugh's nomination as an associate justice of the Supreme Court received a confirmatory vote, his accuser's strategy in arguing responsibility, the offensiveness of the alleged events, and poor character traits perceived in Kavanaugh all functioned together to increase the likelihood of people attributing to the jurist further negative actions and traits. Moreover, research suggests that the attack on Kavanaugh was a salient issue in the minds of many voters as they went to the polls during the 2018 midterm elections, in addition to many other contributing factors (including the #MeToo movement).

Post-Crisis Management

Reputation management is equally important after a crisis is over. When the immediate threat of a crisis ends, political campaign management must evaluate the quality of its response and take appropriate actions based on the lessons learned. As suggested above, a good reputation comes from making a promise, delivering on that promise for constituents, and demonstrating ethical behaviors. Importantly, alignment between words and actions builds new trust (Griffin, 2014). However, if a politician does not live up to their promises, no amount of reputation management can help.

Situational crisis communication theory offers recommendations for using crisis response strategies to rebuild damaged post-crisis reputations (Coombs & Holladay, 2002). Follow-up communication is an extension of the crisis recovery phase. At this point, crisis management should respond to public concerns and update audiences on the actions being taken to prevent future crises. This responsibility continues until all crisis-related obligations are fulfilled.

The degree of reputational damage is often in the eye of the beholder. Some targets may appear only "slightly wounded" following smear campaigns and manage to survive. For example, during his presidency, Ronald Reagan was able to deflect reputational crises without lasting or serious damage despite facing multiple embarrassing accusations, especially in the Iran–Contra affair (Benoit et al., 1991).

Crisis management entails vigilance for lurking issues or issues that have already been (at least temporarily) resolved. If a lurking issue reemerges, the public may judge the individual or organization very harshly, either for not learning from the first experience or for not keeping their implied commitment to correct the issue (Coombs, 2019). Essentially, crisis management must, following the conclusion of a crisis situation, resume the actions of the pre-crisis phase both to recover from past crises and to monitor for new issues and threats to reputation.

Conclusions

The topic of the reputational political crisis has great heuristic value for crisis communication scholars. The sociocultural perspective is especially instrumental in situations where reputational crises and scandals require comprehensive analysis in the context of particular intergroup or institutional logic (Craig, 1999). According to this perspective, reputation and social identity are socially constructed and ascribed to individuals by the way others talk about them and are then legitimized via public opinion in the context of a particular group, network, or culture. Culture can help to shape what is defined as a scandal because cultural differences produce variance in what actions count as normative violations – the roots of a scandal. It is also imperative for campaign managers and crisis consultants to assess a candidate's weaknesses in the context of cultural norms, values, and beliefs. For example, in 2017, a series of interviews with French women found that most of them did not consider a politician's private life a reason to vote for or against them (Jordan, 2017). Therefore, the 24-year age gap between French President Emmanuel Macron and his older wife did not become a scandal during the French presidential election. Hence, crisis communication scholars can benefit from studying public reactions to scandals as explained by values, norms, and stereotypes deeply embedded in culture.

In addition, further research is needed to address cultural differences that influence media logic in covering political scandals. Some studies explain the minimal exposure of marital infidelity in Germany and Spain based on the professional position of media neutrality and the strength of party identification, which renders the personal qualities of officeholders less important to voters (Downey & Stanyer, 2013). The media in France, Italy, and the Netherlands, meanwhile, do not incentivize the exposure of sex scandals due to the absence of socially conservative moralizing in politics and the presence of strong privacy protections. However, the commercial logic of the current media system in the United States can make it almost impossible for social and political actors to claim the right to be presumed innocent until proven guilty. Further cross-cultural research exploring media choices in agenda-setting and story-framing in the context of reputational crises will advise practice and contribute to further crisis communication theory building.

References

Alsop, R. J. (2004). *The 18 Immutable Laws of Corporate Reputation: Creating, Protecting, and Repairing Your Most Valuable Asset.* Free Press.

Arpan, L. M., & Roskos-Ewoldsen, D. R. (2005). Stealing thunder: Analysis of the effects of proactive disclosure of crisis information. *Public Relations Review, 31*(3), 425–433.

Bateson, G. (1972). *Steps to an Ecology of Mind.* Chandler Publishing Company.

Benoit, W. L. (1997). Hugh Grant's image restoration discourse: An actor apologizes. *Communication Quarterly, 45*(3), 251–267.

Benoit, W. L. (2017). Criticism of actions and character: Strategies for persuasive attack. *Extended Relevant Rhetoric, 8*, 1–17. https://bit.ly/2Y0rqvC

Benoit, W. L. (2020). Image repair theory. In F. Frandsen, & W. Johansen, Eds., *Crisis Communication* (pp. 106–119). De Gruyter Mouton.
Benoit, W. L., & Brinson, S. L. (1999). Queen Elizabeth's image repair discourse: Insensitive royal or compassionate queen? *Public Relations Review*, *25*, 145–156.
Benoit, W. L., & Stein, K. A. (2021). Character assassination on Judge Brett Kavanaugh in his 2018 supreme court confirmation hearing. *Journal of Applied Social Theory*, *1*(3), 7–30.
Benoit, W. L., Gullifor, P., & Panici, D. A. (1991). Reagan's discourse on the Iran-Contra affair. *Communication Studies*, *42*, 272–294.
Berman, M. (November 26, 2019). *The most important politician of the 2010s*. https://bit.ly/2VaHBmP
Blaney, J. R., & Benoit, W. L. (2001). *The Clinton Scandals and the Politics of Image Restoration*. Praeger.
Booth-Butterfield, S. (2009). *The Complete Idiot's Guide to Persuasion*. Alpha Books.
Botan, C. H. (2018). *Strategic Communication: Theory and Practice*. Wiley-Blackwell.
Bourdieu, P. (1984). *Distinction: A Social Critique of the Judgement of Taste*. Routledge.
Bourdieu, P. (1990). *The Logic of Practice*. Stanford University Press.
Bourdieu, P. (1991). *Language and Symbolic Power*. Polity Press.
Bourdieu, P., & Wacquant, L. J. D. (1992). *An Invitation to Reflexive Sociology*. University of Chicago Press.
Brummett, B. (1981). Gastronomic reference, synecdoche, and political images. *The Quarterly Journal of Speech*, *67*(2), 138–145.
Bueno de Mesquita, B., Morrow, J. D., Siverson, R., & Smith, A. (2001). Political competition and economic growth. *Journal of Democracy*, *12*(1), 58–72.
Carcasson, M. N., & Aune, J. A. (2003). Klansman on the court: Justice Hugo Black's 1937 radio address to the nation. *The Quarterly Journal of Speech*, *89*(2), 154–170.
Compton, J. (2013). Inoculation theory. In J. P. Dillard, & L. Shen, Eds., *The SAGE Handbook of Persuasion: Developments in Theory and Practice* (2nd ed., pp. 220–236). Sage.
Coombs, W. T. (2007). Protecting organization reputations during a crisis: The development and application of situational crisis communication theory. *Corporate Reputation Review*, *10*(3), 163–177.
Coombs, W. T. (2019). *Ongoing Crisis Communication. Planning, Managing, and Responding* (5th ed.). Sage.
Coombs, W. T., & Holladay, S. J. (2002). Helping crisis managers protect reputational assets: Initial tests of the situational crisis communication theory. *Management Communication Quarterly*, *16*(2), 165–186.
Coombs, W. T., & Holladay, S. J. (2006). Unpacking the halo or reputational capital: Reputation and crisis management. *Journal of Communication Management*, *10*(2), 123–137.
Coombs, W. T., & Holladay, S. J. (2019). How scandal varies by industry: The Effect of industry culture on scandalization of behaviors. In A. Haller, & H. Michael, Eds., *Scandalogy 2. Cultures of Scandals – Scandals in Culture* (pp. 144–162). Herbert von Halem Verlag.
Coombs, T., & Holladay, S. (2020). Corporate character assassination and crisis communication. In S. A. Samoilenko, M. Icks, J. Keohane, & E. Shiraev, Eds., *Routledge Handbook of Character Assassination* (pp. 225–235). Routledge.
Coombs, W. T., & Tachkova, E. R. (2018). Scansis as a unique crisis type: Theoretical and practical implications. *Journal of Communication Management*, *23*(1), 72–88.
Cornfield, M. (2017). Empowering the party-crasher: Donald J. Trump, the first 2016 GOP presidential debate, and the Twitter marketplace for political campaigns. *Journal of Political Marketing*, *16*(3–4), 212–243.
Craig, R. T. (1999). Communication theory as a field. *Communication Theory*, *9*(2), 119–161.
Cupach, W. R., & Metts, S. (1994). *Facework*. Sage.
Dezenhall, E. (2014). *Glass Jaw*. Twelve.
Downey, J., & Stanyer, J. (2013). Exposing politicians' peccadilloes in comparative context: Explaining the frequency of political sex scandals in eight democracies using fuzzy set qualitative comparative analysis. *Political Communication*, *30*(3), 495–509.
Eccles, R. G., Newquist, S. C., & Schatz, R. (2007). Reputation and its risks. *Harvard Business Review*, *85*(2), 104.
Edelman (2022). *The 2022 Edelman trust barometer*. https://www.edelman.com/trust/2022-trust-barometer

Esser, F., & Matthes, J. (2013). Mediatization effects on political news, political actors, political decisions, and political audiences. In H. Kriesi, S. Lavenex, F. Esser, J. Matthes, M. Bühlmann, & D. Bochsler, Eds., *Democracy in the Age of Globalization and Mediatization* (pp. 177–201). Palgrave Macmillan.

Fombrun, C. J. (1996). *Reputation. Realizing Value from the Corporate Brand.* Harvard Business School Brand.

Forgey, Q. (May 13, 2020). Biden: 'I don't have any problem comparing my energy level to Donald Trump.' *Politico.* https://www.politico.com/news/2020/05/13/biden-trump-president-254514

Franken, A. (2003). *Lies and the Lying Liars Who Tell Them.* Dutton Penguin.

Goffman, E. (1967). Where the action is. In *Interaction Ritual: Essays in Face-to-Face Behavior* (pp. 149–270). Anchor Books.

Griffin, A. (2014). *Crisis, Issues and Reputation Management: A Handbook for PR and Communications Professionals (PR in Practice).* Kogan Page.

Harrell, J., Ware, B. L., & Linkugel, W. A. (1975). Failure of apology in American politics: Nixon on Watergate. *Communication Monographs, 42*(4), 245–261.

Herbst, S. (2010). *Rude Democracy: Civility and Incivility in American Politics.* Temple University Press.

Imhof, K. (2016). Political, social, and economic crises in public communication. In A. Schwarz, M. Seeger, & C. Auer, Eds., *The Handbook of International Crisis Communication Research* (pp. 175–187). Wiley-Blackwell.

Jensen, M. J., & Bang, H. P. (2017). Populism and connectivism: An analysis of the Sanders and Trump Nomination Campaigns. *Journal of Political Marketing, 16*(3–4), 343–364.

Jordan, M. (May 3, 2017). Emmanuel Macron is 39 and his wife is 64. French women say it's about time. *Washington Post.* https://t.ly/bqHu

Kalb, M. (2001). *One Scandalous Story: Clinton, Lewinsky, and Thirteen Days that Tarnished American Journalism.* Free Press.

Lee, J. C., & Quealy, K. (2019). The 598 people, places and things Donald Trump has insulted on Twitter: A complete list. *The. New York Times.* https://goo.gl/287GJoMay 24,

Lerbinger, O. (1997). *The Crisis Manager: Facing Risk and Responsibility.* Lawrence Erlbaum Associates.

Liu, B. F. (2007). President Bush's major post-Katrina speeches: Enhancing image repair discourse theory applied to the public sector. *Public Relations Review, 33*(1), 40–48.

Mayer, J. (July 22, 2019). The case of Al Franken: A close look at the accusations against the former senator. *The New Yorker.* https://bit.ly/3acbzA6

Metts, S. (2009). Impression management. In S. W. Littlejohn, & K. A. Foss, Eds., *Encyclopedia of Communication Theory* (pp. 506–509). Sage.

Nyhan, B., & Reifler, J. (2015). The effect of fact-checking on elites: A field experiment on US state legislators. *American Journal of Political Science, 59*(3), 628–640.

O'Keefe, D. J. (2002). *Persuasion: Theory and Research* (2nd ed.). Sage.

Patterson, T. E. (2016). *News Coverage of the 2016 National Conventions: Negative News, Lacking Context.* Shorenstein Center, Harvard Kennedy School. https://bit.ly/2znkcXT\September 21,

Pearce, W. B., & Cronen, V. E. (1980). *Communication, Action, and Meaning: The Creation of Social Realities.* Praeger.

Perloff, R. M. (2021). *The Dynamics of Political Communication: Media and Politics in a Digital Age* (3rd ed.). Routledge.

Pfau, M., Kenski, H. C., Nitz, M., & Sorenson, J. (1990). Efficacy of inoculation strategies in promoting resistance to political attack messages: Application to direct mail. *Communications Monographs, 57*(1), 25–43.

Robertson, R. (1992). *Globalization: Social theory and global culture.* Sage.

Rosen, C. (November 16, 2017). Seth Meyers slams 'horrifying' Al Franken sexual misconduct photo. *Entertainment.* https://bit.ly/3nn6BEb

Roth, K. (June 11, 2019). House speaker Pelosi to CNN: Trump is 'Diverter-Of-Attention-In-Chief . . . I'm done with him. *International Business Times.* https://bit.ly/2LivAJr

Ryan, H. R. (1982). Kategoria and apologia: On their rhetorical criticism as a speech set. *The Quarterly Journal of Speech, 68*(3), 254–261.

Ryan, H. R. (1984). Baldwin vs. Edward VIII: A case study in *kategoria* and *apologia*. *Southern Speech Communication Journal, 49*(2), 125–134.

Samoilenko, S. A. (2020a). Character assassination as a structurational phenomenon. In S. A. Samoilenko, M. Icks, E. Shiraev, & J. Keohane, Eds., *Routledge Handbook of Character Assassination and Reputation Management* (pp. 45–62). Routledge.
Samoilenko, S. A. (2020b). Character assassination in the context of mediated complexity. In K. Sriramesh, & D. Verčič, Eds., *The Global Public Relations Handbook: Theory, Research, and Practice* (pp. 268–282). New York, NY: Routledge.
Samoilenko, S. A., & Miroshnichenko, A. (2019). Profiting from the "Trump Bump": The effects of selling negativity in the media. In I. E. Chiluwa, & S. A. Samoilenko, Eds., *Handbook of Research on Deception, Fake News, and Misinformation Online* (pp. 375–391). Hershey, PA: IGI Global.
Samoilenko, S. A., & Suvorova, I. (2023). Deepfakes in strategic deception campaigns. In E. Pashentsev, Ed., *The Palgrave Handbook of Malicious Use of AI and Psychological Security* (pp. 507–529). Palgrave Macmillan.
Sandman, P. M. (1993). *Responding to Community Outrage: Strategy for Effective Risk Communication.* American Industrial Hygiene Association.
Sandman, P. M. (December 3, 2010). *Two kinds of reputation management.* www.psandman.com/col/reputation.htm
Seiffert-Brockmann, J., Einwiller, S., & Stranzl, J. (2018). Character assassination of CEOs in crises. Questioning CEOs' character and values in corporate crises. *European Journal of Communication, 33*(4), 413–429.
Strömbäck, J. (2008). Four phases of mediatization: An analysis of the mediatization of politics. *The International Journal of Press/Politics, 13*(3), 228–246.
Tajfel, H., & Turner, J. C. (2004). The social identity theory of intergroup behavior. In J. T. Jost, & J. Sidanius, Eds., *Political Psychology* (pp. 276–293). Psychology Press.
Thompson, J. B. (2000). *Political Scandal: Power and Visibility and in the Media Age.* Polity.
Thompson, J. (2016). From "big time" to "turd blossom": George W. Bush and the rhetoric of the political sobriquet. In S. M. Vanguri, Ed., *Rhetorics of Names and Naming* (pp. 33–48). Routledge.
Walton, D. N. (1999). Ethotic arguments and fallacies: The credibility function in multi-agent dialogue systems. *Pragmatics & Cognition, 7*(1), 177–203.
Walton, D. N. (2001). Enthymemes, common knowledge, and plausible inference. *Philosophy and Rhetoric, 34*(2), 93–112.
Ware, B. L., & Linkugel, W. A. (1973). They spoke in defense of themselves: On the generic criticism of apologia. *Quarterly Journal of Speech, 59*(3), 273–283.
Wei, L., & Diddi, P. (2022). Morality rules: Understanding the role of prior reputation in consequences of scansis. *Public Relations Review, 48*(1), 102147.
Wigley, S. (2011). Telling your own bad news: Eliot Spitzer and a test of the stealing thunder strategy. *Public Relations Review, 37*(1), 50–56. https://doi.org/10.1016/j. pubrev.2011.01.003
Zamorano, M. M. (2016). Reframing cultural diplomacy: The instrumentalization of culture under the soft power theory. *Culture Unbound, 8*(2), 165–186. http://doi.org/10.3384/cu.2000.1525.1608165

Author Bio

Sergei A. Samoilenko is an assistant professor and co-founder of the Research Lab for Character Assassination and Reputation Politics (CARP) in the Department of Communication at George Mason University. He authored and co-authored numerous books and publications on character assassination and reputation management, political and crisis communication, and post-socialist issues. His latest book project includes two anthologies – *Media and Public Relations Research in Post-Socialist Societies* and *Communication Theory and Application in Post-Socialist Contexts* – published by Lexington Books. https://orcid.org/0000-0002-8607-3053.

Part V

The State of Crisis and Risk Communication Research Around the Globe

Crisis and Risk Communication Research in Africa

22

Crisis Communication in East Africa
The State of Research and Implications for Practice

Angella Napakol[1], Aisha Sembatya Nakiwala[2], and Marjorie Kyomuhendo[2]

[1] School of Journalism, Media and Communication, Uganda Christian University, Mukono, Uganda

[2] Department of Journalism and Communication, Makerere University, Kampala, Uganda

Introduction

East Africa is a developing region that idealizes democracy. The region is organized into the East African Community, which comprises five countries: Uganda, Kenya, Tanzania, Rwanda, Burundi, and South Sudan. Additionally, the Democratic Republic of the Congo will soon join the community. Being in a transitional state, the region is prone to political upheavals, insurrection, and repressive government actions, which worsen during crises. For example, the police have been criticized for their use of excessive force toward journalists during crises despite discussions and existing policies on media democracy and freedom. In Uganda in 2021, the Inspector General of Uganda Police insisted that journalists are beaten during crises for their safety, to ensure that they do not go where there is risk (Fisayo-Bambi, 2021). However, such high-handedness and resulting tensions also cascade to the general populace, who are sometimes shot to kill by the police. Other forms of crises arise out of natural disasters such as floods, famine, drought, and disease outbreaks. During health pandemics, like the recent COVID-19, the relationship between East African governments and the general public revealed an intricate and convoluted dynamic of trust and mistrust. Although the majority of the public believed that government and traditional news outlets were the trusted sources of information on COVID-19, they did not trust them enough to refrain from blaming them for using COVID-19 as a means to secure donor funding (Napakol et al., 2022). In times of such forms of crises, effective crisis communication is essential. Despite the high incidence of crises and their significant impact on the region's stability and democracy, research on crisis communication in East Africa remains limited.

This chapter aims to provide a review of the literature on risk and crisis communication in the three founding countries of the East African Community: Uganda, Kenya, and Tanzania. The chapter examines the current literature and identifies gaps and opportunities for future research that could enhance risk and crisis communication practices in the region such as the

The Handbook of International Crisis and Risk Communication Research, Second Edition.
Edited by Andreas Schwarz, Matthew W. Seeger, and Sora Kim.

use of new technologies and social media platforms. More specifically, the chapter explores risk communication during pandemics, trust, credibility and risk communication, government response to crisis events, effective crisis management, cultural dynamics, vulnerability and crisis response, as well as multilingualism and crisis communication, among other topics. Ultimately, this chapter contributes to the development of effective crisis communication strategies and practices in the region, with the overall aim of improving the region's resilience to crises and reducing the negative impact of crises on people's lives and well-being.

The Context of Risk and Crisis Communication Research in East Africa

Politically, East African countries have been described as a blend of democratic and authoritarian electoral regimes (Blair et al., 2022; Tripp, 2010). Relatedly, the region's political systems are associated with various crisis communication strategies such as those described by Avraham and Ketterb (2017). Furthermore, political leaders are compelled to act fast when crises are perceived as security threats. For instance, the fast recognition of HIV/AIDS as a threat to state existence influenced Uganda's open communication tactics, helping the country to confront the pandemic in the 1980s (Allen & Heald, 2004; Griffin, 2022). Conversely, the poor handling of the recent disastrous mudslides in Uganda exemplified how timely crisis communication is hampered when political leadership and government capacity to construct adequate responses are lacking (Lin et al., 2020; Napakol et al., 2022). Research also suggests that East African governments still struggle to deploy efficient crisis communication due to the incidence of political upheavals, social discontent, and violence, as demonstrated by the Kenyan post-election unrest of 2008 (Mäkinen & Kuira, 2008).

Governments also occasionally stifle the free flow of information during crises, thereby preventing public access to and utilization of accurate and timely information. For instance, while Kenya and Uganda sensitized citizens about COVID-19 (Adebasi et al., 2021; Kiptinness & Okoye, 2021), Tanzania under Magufuli was wary about the pandemic and therefore gagged open discussion about it. This affected both media coverage and public perception of the pandemic (Lukanda & Walulya, 2021; Paget, 2023). In such cases, peripheral actors, including civic society, assume responsibility for closing the information gap during emergencies. Moreover, the internet, as is shown ahead, now gives impetus to peripheral actors to spread misinformation, which normally obscures crisis communication.

Further, although recent years have brought considerable economic progress, all countries are still economically weak, which greatly impacts crisis communication in the region. The primary sources of income in the region remain agriculture, natural resources, and a low volume of trade, which forces governments and institutional players to consider the economic welfare of the population when disseminating crisis information. Specifically, response to emergencies, including public discussions of risks, catastrophes, and crises, is influenced by people's livelihoods. Consider, for example, that the majority of East Africans live in extreme poverty. Thus, despite their vulnerability to crises, the majority struggle to react promptly to crisis information due to financial constraints (Mafigiri & Schmidt-Sane, 2019). Many cannot afford crisis-mitigation behaviors such as seeking medical treatment. The recent public opposition to COVID-19 communication in the region resulted primarily from restrictions that made it impossible for many to live without daily trade (Atcero & Ayikoru, 2022). It is also argued that the economic impact of crises commonly forces countries in the region into denialism, delayed response, and suppression of open communication regarding outbreaks, as was the case with HIV/AIDS and COVID-19 (Adebasi et al., 2021; Parkhurst, 2001).

In general, the state of risk and crisis communication in East Africa is complex and dynamic, reflecting the challenges of communicating effectively with diverse and dispersed communities in a rapidly changing media landscape. The three countries have faced several risks and crises in recent years, including disease outbreaks, natural disasters, and political instability, and in response, the governments have established several agencies and policies aimed at managing these risks and communicating with the public during crises. In Uganda, the Uganda National Emergency Coordination and Operations Centre (NECOC) was established to coordinate emergency response efforts across different sectors and levels of government (NECOC, 2020). The Ministry of Health (2020) also has a dedicated unit for risk communication and community engagement (RCCE), which is responsible for disseminating health-related information and messages to the public. In Tanzania, risk and crisis communication has received increasing attention in recent years, and the government has taken some steps to improve its risk and crisis communication capabilities. This includes establishing a national disaster management agency and developing a national communication strategy for disaster management. On the other hand, the Kenyan government has an established National Disaster Operations Centre (NDOC) that is responsible for coordinating emergency response efforts. The government also disseminates information through various channels such as social media, radio and television broadcasts, and press releases.

The history of East Africa is significant when discussing risk and crisis communication in this region. East Africa is historically among the world's most violently conflicted regions (Davis et al., 2023). It is also prone to terrorism, diseases, and environmental catastrophes. These incidents often influence what information is conveyed during crises, by whom, when, and the strategies used to disseminate it. Moreover, while such history often presents opportunities for risk and crisis communication, it also causes numerous challenges that require sharp communication strategies. For example, the COVID-19 pandemic revealed the importance of fast and timely information, considering the successive variants that emerged at short intervals. The rampant outbreaks of infectious diseases in the region, particularly Ebola and Cholera, normally require clear information to repel misinformation and combat public fear and speculation.

Culture is also potentially impactful on crisis communication, and cultural practices have been found to influence crisis communication tactics used in the East African region (Mafigiri & Schmidt-Sane, 2019; Mbonye et al., 2014). East African countries are rich and diverse in heritage, with numerous languages, ethnicities, tribes, cultural beliefs, and norms. Different cultures implicate different risk communication methods, resulting sequentially in varied influences on audiences and their decision-making prior to, during, and after crises. Cultural practices and beliefs have been linked to differences in how people in the region respond to health epidemics like the recent COVID-19 and the frequent Ebola outbreaks (Mafigiri & Schmidt-Sane, 2019) and to natural disasters, including flooding and landslides (Lin et al., 2020).

Moreover, cultural dynamics that influence vulnerability to crises and their implications for risk and crisis communication in this region have been extensively discussed. Oluoch and Nyongesa (2013), for instance, instantiate how significant widow inheritance practices still are in HIV/AIDS risk communication in Kenya. Similarly, Mafigiri and Schmidt-Sane (2019) report that in Uganda the deceased must be interred in ancestral lands, making funeral customs an essential component of cultural beliefs. Such beliefs remarkably impact the region's risk communication strategies targeting infectious diseases such as cholera, COVID-19, and Ebola, and it is argued that risk communication in this area must incorporate instructions on how to perform safe burials as opposed to a "stop" behavior approach (Mafigiri & Schmidt-Sane, 2019).

Additionally, due to societal dynamics, it is common for resistance to occur when messages and crisis interventions clash with traditional wisdom (Lin et al., 2020). The region's high multilingualism also means that language plays a significant part in risk and crisis communication. O'Brien and Cadwell (2017) have, for example, discussed the dangers of overdependence on an official language in a multilingual Kenyan society. They argue that while communicating crisis information in multiple languages is intricate, English is also unsuitable for communicating risk information to communities who barely speak it. This is also consistent with the situation in other countries in the region. Nevertheless, there is evidence to show that the region's cultural assets such as language and cultural leaders can also be useful for crisis communication (Blair et al., 2022; O'Brien & Cadwell, 2017). For instance, the Kabaka, a traditional leader in Uganda, was instrumental in motivating his subjects to positively respond to the risk message about the COVID-19 virus (Blair et al., 2022).

Lastly, like elsewhere in Africa, East Africa has experienced exponential growth in digital communication technology, bringing with it new possibilities for communicating about risk, emergencies, and crises. The rapid penetration of mobile telephony and the prevalence of digital tools and social network sites such as Facebook, Twitter, and YouTube have revolutionized the way people in the region receive and share information during and after crises, particularly through increasing the speed, geographical coverage, and formats of risk and crisis communication (Simon et al., 2014).

However, the use of technology in crisis communication in East Africa is often constrained by limited access in rural areas caused especially by the low levels of digital literacy and financial capacity among the population. For instance, in her study of environmental and climate risk communication in Uganda, Nassanga (2019) found that only 33% of respondents received information about the topic despite mobile phone use being 71% among men and 30% among women. Accordingly, Nassanga concluded that the potential of mobile phones for communicating climate risk is yet to be completely realized in Uganda. A similar study revealed that in Kenya, access to crisis news through the Internet was idealistic due to the high Internet costs (Mäkinen & Kuira, 2008), implying the need to increase Internet access for crisis communication. Additionally, the increased use of digital technologies for crisis communication frequently exposes sections of the population to disinformation and infodemics, especially when official channels of communication delay timely and accurate information.

The State of Research in Risk and Crisis Communication in East Africa

Risk and crisis communication encompasses the process of proficiently conveying information, steering perceptions, and responding to unforeseen events that either present an immediate threat or have already evolved into a full-blown crisis. It hinges on the principles of timely and transparent communication, aiming to reduce harm, uphold public trust, and facilitate a successful resolution of the crisis (Sellnow & Seeger, 2013; Sellnow et al., 2019). Significant uncertainty penetrates impacted populations during crises, frequently resulting in a state of chaos as people struggle to find meaning within their typical worldviews (Holmes et al., 2009; Sellnow et al., 2019). These circumstances result in what Sellnow et al. (2019) refer to as a "narrative space" (p. 898). Here, organizations and the media play pivotal roles in filling this void with narratives that help in comprehending the crisis. However, due to the inherent uncertainty, multiple and conflicting interpretations of the crisis frequently surface. Failure on the part of organizations to reconcile these contrasting narratives from various stakeholders often leads to ineffective crisis communication, hindering the achievement of a positive resolution.

Risk and crisis communication in the three selected countries covers a range of topics, including accountability and transparency in crisis (Napakol & Mugunga, 2019), social media and crisis communication, misinformation during a crisis (Napakol et al. 2022), culture and crisis communication (Atcero & Ayikoru, 2022), the use of mobile technology for emergency response (Mbivnjo et al., 2021), community participation in disaster management (Adebasi et al., 2021), disaster and emergency communication (Napakol et al., 2022), social media and crisis, tourism (De Sausmarez, 2013), and health communication (Kiptinness & Okoye, 2021; Mugunga & Napakol, 2020; Muzaale et al., 2018; Napakol et al., 2022; World Health Organisation, 2021). The ensuing discussion of the state of risk and crisis communication is organized around institutional perspectives, media, and audience perspectives.

Institutional Perspectives

While there have been some positive developments in risk and crisis communication in the three countries, there is still considerable work to do in terms of building capacity, improving transparency, engaging communities, and preparedness (Lindley, 2011; Marius et al., 2020). Research has critiqued governments' communication efforts during crises, particularly in terms of timeliness and transparency. In the study of crisis communication response during and after the Bududa mudslides, for instance, the participants argued that "government's instructions ... were at best incomplete or inconsistent and at worst, corrupt" (Napakol et al., 2022, p. 199). Unclear and inconsistent messaging from the government may have contributed to confusion and misinformation among the public. Similar sentiments were expressed in Kenya during the Westgate Shopping Mall attack in 2013, where frailties in managing multiple responder communication were noted (Tomer et al., 2014).

Effective risk and crisis communication is important for organizations in East Africa to manage crises and minimize their impact on operations, stakeholders, and reputation (Spradley, 2017). However, the level of and state of research in risk and crisis communication preparedness and practice vary. During the simulation of the Rift Valley fever outbreak in Kenya and Tanzania in 2019, the World Health Organization (WHO) and found that there was difficulty in information flow, following sample handling procedures, limited technical and preparedness capacity among others. Recommendations were made to train staff, effective dissemination of available operating procedures, and having a clear risk communication and community engagement plan among others.

In the public sector, there have been cases of inadequate risk and crisis communication during emergencies such as natural disasters and disease outbreaks. Ssebunya et al. (2019) found that Kenyan hospitals faced challenges in emergency preparedness and response, including inadequate communication and coordination. In 2019, Atugonza and colleagues found that Tanzanian hospitals were still in early stages of risk and crisis communication development. Kiguli and Mwanika (2018) examined the role of risk communication in controlling the Ebola outbreak in Uganda in 2012. They found that early and effective communication strategies helped to mitigate the impact of the outbreak, albeit challenges in terms of limited resources and the need for robust, targeted messaging.

As was already indicated, the importance of the field of crisis and risk communication is increasingly gaining traction in Uganda. In 2019, a study by Napakol and Mugunga showed how some Ugandan organizations minimized the significance of stakeholder communication. At the time, Crane Bank faced allegations of financial misconduct causing anxiety among its stakeholders. The bank did not comment on the issue neither did it communicate to its stakeholders, especially the investors and consequently, a significant number of depositors began to withdraw their savings in large sums. It was not until the Central Bank stepped in to reassure depositors of the safety of their finances that the panic began to subside.

Crane Bank eventually found itself embroiled in a lengthy legal battle with the state. The bank was eventually taken over by a competitor and although it emerged victorious in the courtroom about five years later, the damage was already done and its premises remain uninhabited. More critically, the crisis had eroded the trust and credibility that the bank once enjoyed. This was primarily due to the initial communication delay and subsequent lackluster, vague, and dismissive communication.

Media/Journalism/Social Media Perspective

East Africa has a diverse media landscape. In addition to traditional communication channels, social media and mobile technology have emerged as important tools for information dissemination during crises. However, journalists face challenges such as censorship and harassment, which limit their ability to report on crises and hold governments accountable (Baruga, 2021). There are concerns about the spread of false information and the need for more effective regulation of online communication. Researchers (Lough, 2022; Ohich, 2015; Sseviiri et al., 2022) have analyzed the use of social media for risk, crisis, and disaster communication and cite challenges of reliability, accuracy, and misinformation. Mugabi and Atwine (2017) examined the role of social media in crisis communication during the 2016 elections in Uganda and found that social media platforms such as Twitter and WhatsApp were widely used for disseminating information and mobilizing voters, but there were concerns about the spread of false information and the potential for violence.

Audience Perspective

Audience perception refers to how people interpret and understand the messages they receive about risks and crises. The way in which messages are framed, the source of the message, and the timing of the message can all affect audience perception (Scheufele & Tewksbury, 2007). In as much as there has been scarce research for audience perspectives in risk and crisis communication research, there has been increased scholarship in the area in the last 10 years (Dolan et al., 2022; Kirabo et al., 2021; Muzaale et al., 2018; Nassanga, 2019; Wabagha, 2014; Walusimbi, 2016; Wanjiru, 2022).

While some groups express confidence in government communication efforts, others are skeptical and rely on alternative sources of information. Kyeyagalire et al. (2020) analyzed public perceptions of risk and communication during the COVID-19 pandemic in Uganda. They found that while the government's communication efforts were generally seen as credible, there were concerns about the adequacy of information provided and the need for more engagement with communities. In recent years, there has been a growing recognition of the importance of community participation in risk and crisis communication, including efforts to involve local leaders, civil society groups, and other stakeholders in emergency planning and response.

Risk Communication in Three East African Countries: The Case of COVID-19

The COVID-19, a contagious respiratory disease that causes mild to acute human illness, set out as a global pandemic causing high mortality and morbidity worldwide (WHO, 2022). As of March 1, 2023, over 758 million cases and over 6.8 million deaths had been reported globally (WHO, 2023). The distribution of cumulative cases from the East Africa region is as follows: Kenya, 342,919 cases and 5,688 deaths; Tanzania, 42,846 cases and 846 deaths; and Uganda, 170,504 cases and 3,630 deaths (Esri Eastern Africa, 2023). A prevalent perception among extant research is that COVID-19 cases could be higher in East Africa but are underestimated partly due to underreporting caused by weak health systems, scarcity of testing, several deaths occurring at home, and people opting for self-medication (Cabore et al., 2022; Olamijuwon et al., 2023).

The importance of risk communication was evident during the COVID-19 pandemic. WHO promptly provided guidelines for RCCE adopted by national governments (WHO, 2020). According to Kakaire and Reader (2022), the COVID-19 outbreak emphasized that proactive and effective communication is the most significant intervention in public health response to outbreaks. In this case study, we document the existent research on how institutions, media, and audiences in Kenya, Tanzania, and Uganda deployed and perceived RCCE strategies to halt the chains of transmission and alleviate the impact of the COVID-19 outbreak.

Risk communication is a significant intervention in any health emergency, entailing the systematic dissemination of information to individuals, communities, and institutions through conventional and contemporary media (DiClemente, 2016; WHO, 2020). Kakaire and Reader

(2022), from an RCCE COVID-19 study in Eastern Africa, concluded that risk communication facilitates informed decision-making and the adoption of preventive behavior and mitigation strategies and prevents duplication and wastage of resources.

Institutional Perspectives

Kenya, Tanzania, and Uganda adopted WHO's comprehensive COVID-19 RCCE guidelines, informed by a "Whole-of-Government, Whole-of Society" approach (WHO, 2022) to prevent infections, save lives, and minimize the pandemic impact. According to Adebesi et al. (2021), Kenya, Tanzania, and Uganda designed their national RCCE strategies guided by seven significant pillars derived from WHO's guidance on RCCE for COVID-19. The pillars included "risk communication systems, internal and partners' coordination, community engagement, public communication, addressing infodemic, and training and capacity building" (Adebesi et al., 2021, p. 139).

All national governments in the three countries initially worked closely with WHO and partners to sensitize and consistently communicate with the public about the pandemic (Adebasi et al., 2021). The key RCCE messages focused on educating the public about the symptoms, means of transmission, and preventive and treatment measures of COVID-19 through adherence to various standard operating procedures (SOPs) (Adebesi et al., 2021; Sarki et al., 2020). Evidence abounds on how the RCCE strategies involved using various traditional and contemporary communication channels to sensitize the public about preventing, containing, and managing the outbreak (Adebisi et al., 2021; Kakaire & Reader, 2022; Nasaba & Nakiwala, 2021; Sarki et al., 2020; Tarimo & Wu, 2020). These channels included radio, television, newspapers, social media, community and stakeholder engagement, government websites, toll-free lines, SMS messaging, music, and group emails, to mention a few. For example in Kenya, Tanzania, and Uganda, public engagement about COVID-19 on government websites and toll-free lines reportedly provided a platform for credible information, linkage to medical assistance, and an avenue for feedback mechanisms. Likewise, the three countries' RCCE approaches leveraged community influencers, community health workers, and religious leaders to boost community engagement (Adebasi et al., 2021).

Sarki and other scholars (2020) singled out Uganda as a role model in executing an effective risk communication national strategy. They credited the Ugandan government's communication approach for being transparent, consistent, and inclusive and for using multipronged communication channels. Sarki et al. (2020) further commended the country's president for his periodic press briefings to manage public perception and deliver situation reports about the pandemic. Equally, the COVID-19 Response Committee, led by Uganda's prime minister, was credited for coordinating the testing, contact tracing, and response in collaboration with the smallest administrative units in the country and other relevant stakeholders. Likewise, contemporary studies (Kakaire & Reader, 2022; Wangari et al., 2021) acknowledge the Kenyan government for its swift response to sustain public awareness of the COVID-19 pandemic and leverage existing partnerships between the Ministry of Health and partners such as UNICEF, the International Federation of Red Cross, and WHO to boost the country's RCCE strategies.

On the contrary, prevalent literature (Adebesi et al., 2021; Article 19, 2021; Mfinanga et al., 2021) reveals that whereas the Tanzanian government initially cooperated with the WHO, the eventual onset of COVID-19 denialism fronted by the then-President John Magufuli, created a boomerang effect in the country's subsequent RCCE approach. The denialism manifested in presidential directives downplaying COVID-19 risks and encouraging the public to embrace prayers and herbal remedies instead of vaccination as antidotes to mitigate the virus. As Yamanis et al. (2021) documented in their study, under President Magufuli, "the minister of Health appeared at a press conference where she drank herbal remedies and stated that the government had no plans to import vaccines" (p. 2). The other denialist manifestations included disregarding SOPs and restricting access to and disseminating COVID-19 risk communication messaging and outbreak updates.

Nonetheless, Tanzania experienced a reversal in its RCCE interventions with a change in political leadership upon the death of President Magufuli, who reportedly died due to COVID-19 during the pandemic (Lee et al., 2023; Yamanis et al., 2021). The incumbent, President Samia Suluhu Hassan, charted a new course in Tanzania's revised COVID-19 national response strategy with vaccination and risk communication as pivotal pillars (Hamisi et al., 2023; Mfinanga et al., 2021; Yamanis et al., 2021).

Away from the political locus, studies show that government institutions in Kenya (Ogola et al., 2022), Tanzania (Hamisi et al., 2023), and Uganda (Mbivnjo et al., 2021) created partnerships with religious, cultural, and community-based organizations to rally their influence in mobilizing the public to adhere to and adopt risk communication guidelines for the prevention and mitigation of the COVID-19 virus.

Media Perspectives

Existing literature reveals that the media in Kenya, Tanzania, and Uganda was heavily invested in reporting about the COVID-19 pandemic. A study on media reportage of COVID-19 in Uganda classified media information about the pandemic as "the biggest story of our time" (African Centre for Media Excellence, 2021, p. 18). The newsworthiness of COVID-19 news in Uganda earned the topic daily front-page coverage between January and December 2020, with stories mainly focusing on the impact of COVID-19 on people, households, businesses, and the economy (African Centre for Media Excellence, 2021). The same report identified unique sources in the news as the president of Uganda and the Ministry of Health officials. The report stated that because of the president's regular appearance in news storylines and nationally televised broadcasts, "he made himself the official spokesperson on COVID-19 matters" (p. 31). The Kenyan media (Kiptiness & Okoye, 2021) and Ugandan media (African Centre for Media Excellence, 2021) mainly depicted the pandemic as a national crisis in their respective countries. They amplified the government's efforts to sensitize citizens on the severity of COVID-19 and the drive to adopt RCCE prevention and mitigation measures. Conversely, the media in Tanzania framed the pandemic as a global problem, creating an impression that Tanzania was less vulnerable to the Coronavirus disease (Kiptiness and Okoye, 2021). In so doing, the Tanzania media fell prey to the president's denialism approach, creating a lacuna in the media's information provided during the crisis. Indeed, a study by Article 19 (2021) further revealed how the president's denialism led to a government crackdown on media houses and the arrest of journalists who attempted to publicize any COVID-19-related information.

Besides mainstream media, social media and online communication during the COVID-19 pandemic permeated societies' healthcare, work, education, and social systems globally in positive and negative ways (Wong et al., 2021). On the positive side, online communication platforms were pivotal in the RCCE strategies in Kenya, Tanzania, and Uganda since they provided relevant information depositories. For example, the three countries' governments had depositories on their dedicated websites with useful information such as COVID-19 trends, guidelines, protocols, and SOPs. Information from these depositories was actively distributed on several social media avenues, transcending geographical and language barriers and with wide audience reach (Wong et al., 2021).

On the negative side, social media's ubiquity implied a lack of robust mechanisms to control COVID-19-related information release, flow, and distribution (Jones & Storer, 2022; Wong et al., 2021), resulting in an infodemic. Sommarvia and other scholars (2023) describe an infodemic as a "second disease that occurs when massive information volumes, particularly with a high prevalence of false information, hinder the public health response" (p. 57). A cross-sectional study (Osuagwu et al., 2021) in different African countries, including Kenya, Tanzania, and Uganda, confirmed that the infodemic partly countered effective risk communication in the abovementioned countries. The study revealed that the respondents' adherence to SOPs was low, given that 19% believed the pandemic was premeditated to reduce the world population, 28% assumed that drinking hot water could alleviate the virus, and 14% thought that white people were more susceptible to COVID-19 than blacks. Therefore, Jones and Storer (2022) and Osuagwu et al. (2021) recommended that RCCE strategies adopt proactive online and community feedback mechanisms to detect and address misinformation and misconceptions in real-time.

In light of counteracting the infodemic, the COVID-19 task forces in Kenya and Uganda adopted the social listening approach in their RCCE strategies. Social listening is the process of monitoring and analyzing conversations to inform strategic activities both online and offline (Sommarvia et al., 2023). In Kenya, RCCE social listening activities were run by interagency collaborators, UNICEF, Red Cross, WHO, Ministry of Health, and other partners, to gather social data from several channels including radio, hotlines, SMS, and social media. Social listening involved monitoring rumors and myths on social media, hotlines, SMS, and radio. The data tracked comprised information on the content of specific COVID-19 rumors or myths shared, metrics of reach and engagement of rumors or myths on social media countrywide, and the most popular COVID-19 social media posts or news articles in the country (Sommarvia et al., 2023). In Uganda, UNICEF, together with the Ministry of Health and partners, deployed a social listening tool known as the U-Report messaging tool. According to Okiror and Namusoke (2022), the U-Report tool used chatbots, the Ministry of Health Call Center, and U-Reporters to identify and address rumors and misinformation about the COVID-19 disease and vaccines. As such, the U-Report tool enabled the development of weekly and monthly reports on rumor tracking that informed subsequent recommendations on how to address false information (Okiror & Namusoke, 2022).

Audience Perspectives

Audiences in the three East African countries generally exhibited awareness of COVID-19 and its prevention measures, a situation largely attributed to widespread health education, media campaigns, and news reports about the pandemic. A study on public awareness and perception toward COVID-19 in Sub-Saharan Africa revealed that most adult respondents in Kenya, Tanzania, and Uganda were knowledgeable about the pandemic and its preventive measures (Ekpenyong et al., 2021). However, the same study revealed that except for health workers, most respondents had a perceived low risk of contracting the disease. Other evidence from Kenya, Tanzania, and Uganda (Jones & Storer, 2022; Kaduka et al., 2023; Mchome et al., 2021; Yamanis et al., 2021) suggests that audience adoption of COVID-19 RCCE guidelines and measures such as wearing masks, social distancing, hand washing, and lockdown was uneven. For instance, a nationwide study (Jones & Storer, 2022) in Uganda revealed that mask-wearing was the most adopted preventive measure (60%) in their locality compared to social distancing and hand washing (40%). Further, Jones and Storer (2022) reported that audience adherence to SOPs seemingly corresponded to the changing rates of infection. In the same vein, Nshakira-Rukundo and Whitehead (2021) reported that the public's COVID-19 risk perceptions in Uganda were influenced by various factors, including the local political climate, economic stress, the extent of proliferation of the COVID-19 infodemic, and citizens' lack of confidence in the government. An example of high-profile politicians in Uganda flouting COVID-19 prevention measures by holding crowded rallies during the peak of the pandemic cast doubt among some audience members about the severity of COVID-19 and the need for preventive measures (Jones & Storer, 2022).

Correspondingly, similar prevailing factors in Kenya reportedly shaped audience perceptions of COVID-19 severity and seriousness. Kaduka et al. (2023) reported that a lack of trust in the national government and political leaders was a barrier to adherence to prevention measures, mainly because politicians allegedly misappropriated funds and did not adhere to COVID-19 restrictions. Despite the mistrust of politicians, audiences identified the Ministry of Health as a trusted information source about the pandemic, together with grassroots leaders, religious leaders, and traditional leaders in Uganda and Tanzania (Jones & Storer, 2022; Mchome et al., 2021). On the contrary, in Kenya and Uganda, low trust in the Ministry of Health was found to cause COVID-19 vaccine hesitancy (Napakol et al., 2022; Osur et al., 2022).

Tanzania was slightly an outlier to its two counterparts, with the audience's low-risk perception attributed to the late President John Magufuli's COVID-19 denialist approach. Whereas President Magufuli's government promoted SOPs such as wearing facemasks and allotting quarantine spaces, President Magufuli downplayed the severity of the virus, calling it an ordinary flu (Hamisi et al., 2023). Accordingly, Magufuli's government instead promoted natural remedies, herbal steams, and exercise as the main COVID-19 interventions, hence delaying the implementation of the WHO's RCCE guidelines (Hamisi et al., 2023; Yamanis et al., 2021). A subsequent change in leadership heralded Tanzania's revaluation of its COVID-19 approach to adopting WHO's recommended RCCE guidelines. However, evidence suggests slow audience turnaround given the continued low-risk perception among the populace (Yamansi et al., 2023).

In conclusion, there is a need for ongoing research and evaluation of communication strategies to improve preparedness and response efforts, as well as collaboration between government agencies, civil society groups, and academic institutions. The use of new media and digital communication technologies ought to be considered as an important opportunity. Thus, in terms of future direction, the above review points to the need for more empirical research on contextual factors such as technology, economics, and the politics of the region and how they impact crisis communication. More research is needed that considers the importance of the region's cultural context in crisis communication as well as the role of new digital technologies to provide more understanding to practitioners and researchers. In terms of practice, training and capacity-building efforts can help organizations develop effective risk and crisis communication plans and protocols that prioritize timely and accurate communication with stakeholders. Ongoing research and evaluation can also help identify best practices and areas for improvement in the three countries and organizations.

References

Adebasi, A. Y., Rabe, A., & Lucero-Prisno, E. D. (2021). Risk communication and community engagement strategies for COVID-19 in 13 African countries. *International Health Promotion Perspectives, 11*(2), 137–147. http://doi.org/10.34172/hpp.2021.18

African Centre for Media Excellence (2021). *Research Report on Ugandan Media Coverage of the Covi-19 Pandemic and Other Public Affairs 2020.*

Allen, T., & Heald, S. (2004). HIV/AIDS policy in Africa: What has worked in Uganda and what has failed in Botswana. *Journal of International Development, 16*, 1141–1154. http://doi.org/10.1002/jid.1168

Article 19 (2021). Tanzania: Briefing on attacks against journalists March 2020–July 2021. Retrieved from https://www.article19.org/wp-content/uploads/2021/11/Covid-Response-Africa-Tanzania.pdf

Atcero, M., & Ayikoru, M. (2022). Digital and language inequalities in disseminating COVID-19-related health campaigns in Uganda: The effects of confinement and social distancing strategies. In Y. Zheng et al., Eds., *Freedom and Social Inclusion in a Connected World* (pp. 310–331). Springer. https://doi.org/10.1007/978-3-031-19429-0_19

Atugonza, R., Batwala, V. J., & Sekimpi, P. (2019). Hospital emergency preparedness and response to bio-emergencies: A situational analysis of two hospitals in Uganda. *BMC Health Services Research, 19*(1), 917. https://doi.org/10.1186/s12913-019-4712-x

Avrahama, E., & Ketterb, E. (2017). Destination image repair while combatting crises: Tourism marketing in Africa. *Tourism Geographics, 19*(5), 780–800. https://doi.org/10.1080/14616688.2017.1357140

Baruga, E. (2021). *An assessment of digital rights and freedoms amidst the COVID-19 pandemic and the 2021 general elections: a case study of Uganda.* Available at SSRN: https://ssrn.com/abstract=3897261. http://dx.doi.org/10.2139/ssrn.3897261

Blair, A. R., Curtice, T., Dow, D., & Grossman, G. (2022). Public trust, policing, and the COVID-19 pandemic: Evidence from an electoral authoritarian regime. *Social Science & Medicine, 305*(3), 115045. https://doi.org/10.1016/j.socscimed.2022.115045

Cabore, J. W., Karamagi, H. C., Kipruto, H. K., Mungatu, J. K., Asamani, J. A., Droti, B., Titi-Ofei, R., Seydi, A. B. W., Kidane, S. N., Balde, T., Gueye, A. S., Makubalo, L., Moeti, M., & R. (2022). COVID-19 in the 47 countries of the WHO African region: A modelling analysis of past trends and future patterns. *The Lancet Global Health, 10*(8), e1099–e1114. http://doi.org/10.1016/S2214-109X(22)00233-9. Epub 2022 Jun 1. PMID: 35659911; PMCID: PMC9159735

Davies, T., Matengu, K., & Hall, J. E. (2023). COVID-19 and the view from Africa. *Religions, 14*(5), 589. https://doi.org/10.3390/rel14050589

de Sausmarez, N. (2013). Challenges to Kenyan tourism since 2008: Crisis management from the Kenyan tour operator perspective. *Current Issues in Tourism, 16*(7–8), 792–809. https://doi.org/10.1080/13683500.2013.785488

DiClemente, R. J., & Jackson, J. M. (2016). Risk communication. In *International Encyclopedia of Public Health* (pp. 378–382). Elsevier Inc. https://doi.org/10.1016/B978-0-12-803678-5.00389-1

Dolan, C., Tshimba, D. N., & Nuwagira, G. (2022). *Social Media and Inclusion in Humanitarian Action – The Case of Refugees in Uganda. HPG Briefing Note.* London, Uganda: ODI. Retrieved from www.odi.org/en/publications/social-media-and-inclusion-in-humanitarian-action-the-case-of-refugees-in-Uganda

Ekpenyong, B.N., Osuagwu, U.L., Miner, C.A,, Ovenseri-Ogbomo, G.O., Abu, E.K., Goson, P.C., Langsi, R., Nwaeze O, Chikasirimobi TG, Charwe DD, Mashige KP, Oloruntoba R, Ishaya T, Agho KE. Knowledge, attitudes, and perceptions of COVID-19 among healthcare and non-healthcare workers in Sub-Saharan Africa: A web-based survey. *Health Security* July–Aug, 2021 Jul-Aug;19(4):393–404. https://doi.org/10.1089/hs.2020.0208. Epub 2021 Jul 2. PMID: 34227870

Esri Eastern Africa (2023). *COVID-19 cases in Eastern Africa.* Retrieved from https://africas-covid-19-hub-esri-ea.hub.arcgis.com/

Fisayo-Bambi, F. (2021). Uganda: Police chief threatens to beat journalists for their own safety. *Africanews.* Retrieved from https://www.africanews.com/2021/01/09/uganda-police-chief-threatens-to-beat-journalists-for-their-own-safety/

Griffin, A. J. (2022). *From epidemic to endemic: Leadership decision-making and policy adaptation in response to chronic health epidemics.* Retrieved from https://scholarworks.unr.edu/handle/11714/8342

Hamisi, N. M., Dai, B., & Ibrahim, M. (2023). Global Health Security amid COVID-19: Tanzanian government's response to the COVID-19 Pandemic. *BMC Public Health, 23*, 205. https://doi.org/10.1186/s12889-023-14991-7

Holmes, B. J., Henrich, N., Hancock, S., & Lestou, V. (2009). Communicating with the public during health crises: Experts' experiences and opinions. *Journal of Risk Research, 12*, 793–807. https://doi.org/10.1080/13669870802648486

Jones, T, & Storer, E, (2022). Key Considerations: Adherence to COVID-19 preventive measures in Greater Kampala, Uganda. *Social Science in Human Rights Action.* Retrieved from https://www.socialscienceinaction.org/resources/key-considerations-adherence-to-covid-19-preventive-measures-in-greater-kampala-uganda/

Kaduka, L., Olale, J., Karamanos, A., Mutai, J., Coultas, C., Ahmed, I., L'esperance, V., Read, U., Dazzan, P., Cruickshank, J. K., Muniu, E., & Harding, S. (2023). Contextually appropriate communication strategies for COVID-19 prevention in Kenya border regions: Evidence from a mixed methods observational study in Busia and Mandera counties. *BMJ Open, 13*(5), Article e062686. https://doi.org/10.1136/bmjopen-2022-062686

Kakaire, C. N., & Reader, S. (2022). Coordinating risk communication and community engagement for a better COVID-19 response in Eastern and Southern Africa. *The Pan Africa Medical Journal, 29*(Suppl 2), 41. http://doi.org/10.11604/pamj.supp.2022.41.2.28150. PMID: 36159024; PMCID: PMC9475045

Kiguli, J., & Mwanika, A. (2018). Ebola in Uganda: The role of risk communication in controlling an epidemic. *Journal of Public Health in Africa, 9*(1), 739. https://doi.org/10.4081/jphia.2018.739

Kiptinness, M. E., & Okoye, J. B. (2021). Media coverage of the novel Coronavirus (COVID-19) in Kenya and Tanzania: Content analysis of newspaper articles in East Africa. *Cogent Medicine, 8*(1), 1956034. https://doi.org/10.1080/2331205X.2021.1956034

Kirabo, L., Namara, M., & Mcneese, N. (2021). The Power of the Blue Tick (): Ugandans' experiences and engagement on Twitter at the onset of the COVID-19 pandemic. *Conference Proceedings.* AfriCHI 2021: 3rd African Human-Computer Interaction Conference: Inclusiveness and Empowerment March 2021, pp. 84–93. https://doi.org/10.1145/3448696.3448746

Kyeyagalire, R., Kang, Y., & Shen, L. (2020). Public perceptions of risk and communication during the COVID-19 pandemic in Uganda. *Journal of Risk Research, 23*(7–8), 1039–1052. https://doi.org/10.1080/13669877.2020.1790689

Lee, J. H., Meek, L. A., & Katumusiime, J. (2023). Contested truths over COVID-19 in East Africa: Examining opposition to public health measures in Tanzania and Uganda. *African Studies Review, 66*(4), 873–898. https://doi.org/10.1017/asr.2023.69

Lin, H. E. K., Khan, S., Acosta, A. L., Aliniz, R., & Olanya, R. D. (2020). The dynamism of post disaster risk communication: A cross-country synthesis. *International Journal of Disaster Risk Reduction, 48*, 101556. https://doi.org/10.1016/j.ijdrr.2020.101556

Lindley, A. (2011). Between a protracted and a crisis situation: Policy responses to Somali refugees in Kenya. *Refugee Survey Quarterly, 30*(4), 14–49. https://doi.org/10.1093/rsq/hdr013

Lough, O. (2022) *Social media and inclusion in humanitarian response.* HPG Working Paper. London: ODI. Retrieved from https://odi.org/en/publications/social-media-and-inclusion-inhumanitarian-response

Lukanda, I., & Walulya, G. (2021). Media framing of COVID-19 in the hybrid democracies of Uganda and Tanzania. *Taiwan Journal of Democracy, 17*(22), 73–96.

Mafigiri, D. K. & Schmidt-Sane, M. (2019). *Strengthening community linkages to Ebola virus disease (EVD) outbreak preparedness in Uganda.* Retrieved from https://www.unicef.org/uganda/reports/strengthening-community-linkages-ebola-virus-disease-evd-outbreak-preparedness-uganda

Mäkinen, M., & Kuira, W. M. (2008). Social media and postelection crisis in Kenya. *The International Journal of Press/Politics, 13*(3), 328–335. https://doi.org/10.1177/1940161208319409

Marius, G., Giulia, P., Pinotti, F., Valdano, E., Poletto, C., Boëlle, P. et al. (2020). Preparedness and vulnerability of African countries against importations of COVID-19: a modelling study. *The Lancet, 395*(10227), 871–877.

Mchome, Z., Mshana, G., Peter, E., Aloyce, D., Kapiga, S., & Stöckl, H. (2021). Women's narratives about COVID-19, preventive practices and sources of information in Northwestern Tanzania. *International Journal of Environmental Research and Public Health, 18*(10), 5261. https://doi.org/10.3390/ijerph18105261. PMID: 34063334; PMCID: PMC8156351

Mbivnjo, E. L., Kisangala, E., Kanyike, M. A., Kimbugwe, D., Okucu, T. D., & Nabukeera, J. (2021). Web-based COVID-19 risk communication by religious authorities in Uganda: a critical review. *Pan African Medical Journal, 40*(63). https://doi.org/10.11604/pamj.2021.40.63.27550

Mbonye, K. A., Wamala, F. J., Nanyunja, M., Opio, A., Makumbi, I., & Aceng, R. J. (2014). Ebola viral hemorrhagic disease outbreak in West Africa – Lessons from Uganda. *African Health Sciences, 14*(3), 495–501. https://doi.org/10.4314/ahs.v14i3.1

Mfinanga, S.G., Mnyambwa, N.P., Minja, D.T., Ntinginya, N.E, Ngadaya, E., Makani, J., & Makubi, A.N. (2021). Tanzania's position on the COVID-19 pandemic. *Lancet. 397*(10284):1542–1543. https://doi.org/10.1016/S0140-6736(21)00678-4. Epub 2021 Apr 14. PMID: 33864748; PMCID: PMC8046415

Ministry of Health Uganda (2020). *Risk communication and community engagement (RCCE) action plan for COVID-19 response in Uganda.* Retrieved from https://www.health.go.ug/cause/risk-communication-and-community-engagement-rcce-action-plan-for-COVID-19-response-in-uganda/

Mugabi, I., & Atwine, B. (2017). Crisis communication and social media: The role of social media in Uganda's 2016 elections. *Journal of Homeland Security and Emergency Management, 14*(4), 565–580. https://doi.org/10.1515/jhsem-2016-0097

Mugunga, A., & Napakol, A. (2020). Using the IDEA model to analyse messages used in Hepatitis B vaccination in Uganda. *Proceedings of the International Crisis and Risk Communication Conference*, Volume 3, pp. 33–36. Orlando FL: Nicholson School of Communication and Media. https://www.doi.org/10.30658/icrcc.2020.8

Muzaale, T., Basheka, B. C., & Auriacombe, C. J. (2018). The efficacy of crisis communication in the management of Ebola fever in the Bundibugyo District, Uganda – 2007/2008. *Administratio Publicia, 26*(1), 42–57.

Napakol, A., Miller, N. A., Sellnow, L. T., Sellnow, D. D., Mugunga, A., & Khaukha, J. (2022). Risk and crisis communication: Considering catastrophic mudslides in Uganda's Bududa district. In H. D. O'Hair, & M. J. O'Hair, Eds., *Communication and Catastrophic Events: Strategic Risk and Crisis Management.* Wiley-Blackwell. ISBN: 978-1-119-75181-6. https://doi.org/10.1002/9781119751847.ch12

Napakol, A., & Mugunga, A. (2019). Do not bank on us! Taking stock of transparency and accountability during crises in Uganda: The case of Crane Bank collapse. *Proceedings of the International Crisis and Risk Communication Conference*, vol. 2, pp. 23–26. Orlando FL: Nicholson School of Communication and Media. https://doi.org/10.30658/icrcc.2019.7

Nasaba, M. R. & Nakiwala, S. A. (2021). Is we they? A cross-cultural study of responses to Covid-19 updates in Uganda, Kenya and Rwanda. JAMS, 13(3), 315–366. https://doi.org/10.1386/jams_00053_1

Nassanga, L. G. (2019). Empowering rural farmers to improve livelihoods through environmental risk communication: A case study of Uganda. In Y. Bamutaze, Ed., *Agriculture and Ecosystem Resilience in Sub Saharan Africa: Livelihood Pathways Under Changing Climate* (pp. 595–612). Springer. https://doi.org/10.1007/978-3-030-12974-3_26

National Emergency Coordination and Operations Centre (NECOC) 2020). Annual State of Disaster Report, 2020. Retrieved from https://necoc.opm.go.ug/ASDR/ASDR%202020.pdf

Nshakira-Rukundo, E., & Whitehead, A. (2021). Changing perceptions about COVID-19 risk and adherence to preventive strategies in Uganda: Evidence from an online mixed-methods survey. *Scientific African, 14*, e01049. https://doi.org/10.1016/j.sciaf.2021.e01049. PMID: 34805650; PMCID: PMC8592851

O'Brien, S., & Cadwell, P. (2017). Translation facilities comprehension of health-related crisis information: Kenya as an example. *The Journal of Specialised Translation, 28*, 23–51.

Ogola, E., Pande, E. O., Dusek, A. et al. (2022). Pivoting during the pandemic: Adapting research priorities to address community engagement with COVID-19 in Western Kenya. *Journal of Global Health Reports, 6*, e2022047. http://doi.org/10.29392/001c.38509

Ochich, M. A. (2015). *The use of social media in risk and crisis communication: a case of Westgate Shopping Mall terror attack.* MA thesis. DaystarDaystar University, Kenya. Retrieved from THE_USE_OF_SOCIAL_MEDIA_IN_RISK_AND_CRISIS_COMMUNICATION-libre.pdf (d1wqtxts1xzle7.cloudfront.net)

Olamijuwon, E., Konje, E., Kansiime, C. et al. (2023). Antibiotic dispensing practices during COVID-19 and implications for antimicrobial resistance (AMR): Parallel mystery client studies in Uganda and Tanzania. *Antimicrobial Resistance and Infection Control, 12*, 10. https://doi.org/10.1186/s13756-022-01199-4

Oluoch, A. E., & Nyongesa, J. W. (2013). Perception of the rural Luo community on widow inheritance and HIV/AIDs in Kenya: Towards developing risk communication messages. *International Journal of Business and Social Science, 4*(1), 213–219.

Okiror, A., & Namusoke, F. (2022). U-Report for risk communication and community engagement-COVID-19 vaccine chat bots, polls and awareness campaigns in Uganda. UNICEF Uganda country office. Retrieved from: https://www.unicef.org/uganda/media/14601/file/U-Report%20for%20Risk%20Communication%20and%20Community%20%20Engagement%20%E2%80%93%20COVID-19%20Vaccine%20chat%20bots,%20polls%20%20and%20awareness%20campaigns%20in%20Uganda.pdf.

Osuagwu, U. L., Miner, C. A., Bhattarai, D., Mashige, K. P., Oloruntoba, R., Abu, E. K., Ekpenyong, B., Chikasirimobi, T. G., Goson, P. C., Ovenseri-Ogbomo, G. O., Langsi, R., Charwe, D. D., Ishaya, T., Nwaeze, O., & Agho, K. E. (2021). Misinformation about COVID-19 in Sub-Saharan Africa: Evidence from a cross-sectional survey. *Health Security, 19*(1), 44–56. https://doi.org/10.1089/HS.2020.0202. PMID: 33606572; PMCID: PMC9347271

Osur, J., Muinga, E., Carter, J., Kuria, S., Hussein, S., & Ireri, E. M. (2022). COVID-19 vaccine hesitancy: Vaccination intention and attitudes of community health volunteers in Kenya. *PLOS Global Public Health.*, *2*(3), e0000233. https://doi.org/10.1371/journal.pgph.0000233. PMID: 36962328; PMCID: PMC10021929

Parkhurst, J. (2001). The crisis of AIDS and the politics of response: The case of Uganda. *International Relations, 15*, 69–87. https://doi.org/10.1177/004711701015006006

Paget, D. (2023). Tanzania: Narrating the eradication of COVID-19. In N. Ringe, & L. Rennó, Eds., *Populists and the Pandemic: How Populists Around the World Responded to COVID-19* (pp. 207–217). London: Routledge.

Sarki, A. M., Ezeh, A., & Stranges, S. (2020). Uganda as a role model for pandemic containment in Africa. *American Journal of Public Health, 110*(12), 1800–1802. https://doi.org/10.2105/ajph.2020.305948

Scheufele, A. D., & Tewksbury, D. (2007). French abstract. *Journal of Communication, 57*(1), 9–20. https://doi.org/10.1111/j.1460-2466.2006.00326_5.x

Seeger, M. W., & Sellnow, L. T. (2016). *Narratives of Crisis: Telling the Stories of Ruin and Renewal.* Stanford, CA: Stanford University Press. https://doi.org/10.1177/0001839216679614

Sellnow, L. T., Sellnow, D. D., Helsel, M. E., Martin, M. J., & Parker, S. J. (2019). Risk and crisis communication narratives in response to rapidly emerging diseases. *Journal of Risk Research, 22*(7), 897–908. http://doi.org/10.1080/13669877.2017.1422787

Sellnow, T. L., & Seeger, M. W. (2013). *Theorizing Crisis Communication.* Wiley-Blackwell.

Sommariva, S., Bon, H. B., De Almeida, S., Mote, J., Brouwers, S., Massimiliano, S., & Natalie, F. (2023). Integrated analysis of online signals and insight generation about digital conversations on COVID-19 vaccines in Eastern and Southern Africa: A longitudinal analysis of social listening data. *BMC Proc, 17*(Suppl 7), 7. https://doi.org/10.1186/s12919-023-00261-2

Ssebunya, B. N., Sekimpi, P., Olum, R., Musoke, D., & Nalwadda, C. (2019). Hospital preparedness for disease outbreaks and natural calamities in Uganda: A case of a national referral hospital. *BMC Research Notes, 12*(1), 286. https://doi.org/10.1186/s13104-019-4329-9

Sseviiri, H., Alencar, A., & Kisira, Y. (2022). Urban Refugees' Digital experiences and social connections during COVID-19 response in Kampala, Uganda. *Media and Communication, 10*(2), 276–286. https://doi.org/10.17645/mac.v10i2.5169

Simon, T., Goldberg, A., Aharonson-Daniel, L., Leykin, D., & Adini, B. (2014). Twitter in the CrossFire: The use of social media in the Westgate Mall Terror Attack in Kenya. *PLoS One, 9*(8), e104136. https://doi.org/10.1371/journal.pone.0104136

Spradley, R. T. (2017). Crisis communication in organizations. In C. R. Scott, & L. K. Lewis, Eds., *The International Encyclopedia of Organizational Communication.* John Wiley & Sons, Inc. http://doi.org/10.1002/9781118955567.wbieoc050

Tarimo, C. S., & Wu, J. (2020). The first confirmed case of COVID-19 in Tanzania: recommendations based on lesson learned from China. *Tropical Medicine and Health, 48*, 25. https://doi.org/10.1186/s41182-020-00214-x

Tomer, S., Avishay, G., Limor, A., Dmitry, L., & Bruria, A. (2014). Twitter in the CrossFire – The use of social media in the Westgate Mall Terror Attack in Kenya. *Plos One.* Retrieved from https://doi.org/10.1371/journal.pone.0104136

Tripp, A. M. (2010). *Museveni's Uganda: Paradoxes of Power in a Hybrid Regime.* Boulder, CO: Lynne Rienner.

Wabagha, L. (2014). *Crisis and emergency risk communication in the Bundibugyo District.* Unpublished MA thesis. Nairobi: University of Nairobi.

Wangari, E. N., Gichuki, P., Abuor, A. A., Wambui, J., Okeyo, S. O., Oyatsi, H. T. N., Odikara, S., & Kulohoma, B. W. (2021). Kenya's response to the COVID-19 pandemic: A balance between minimising morbidity and adverse economic impact. *AAS Open Res, 4*(3). http://doi.org/10.12688/aasopenres.13156.2. PMID: 33709 Tanzania's position on the COVID-19 pandemic

Walusimbi, B. (2016). *Crisis and emergency risk communication during the Ebola Fever Outbreak in Uganda.* Unpublished MA thesis. Kampala: Makerere University.

Wanjiru, L. M. (2022). *The use of social media in crisis communication in an organization: A case of the Kenya Power Company Limited.* Doctoral dissertation. University of Nairobi.

Wong, L.P, Alias, H., Danaee, M., Ahmed, J., Lachyan, A., Cai, CZ., Lin, Y, Hu, Z., Tan, S.Y., Lu, Y, Cai, G, Nguyen, DK, Seheli, F.N, Alhammadi, F., Madhale, M.D, Atapattu, M., Quazi-Bodhanya, T., Mohajer, S., Zimet, GD., & Zhao, Q. (2021).COVID-19 vaccination intention and vaccine characteristics influencing vaccination acceptance: a global survey of 17 countries. *Infectious Diseases of Poverty* 10(1):122. http://doi.org/10.1186/s40249-021-00900-w. PMID: 34620243; PMCID: PMC8496428.

World Health Organization (2020). Risk communication. Retrieved from https://www.who.int/emergencies/risk-communications

World Health Organization (2021). *The United Republic of Tanzania and Kenya's simulation of Rift Valley fever outbreak yields valuable lessons: A case study.* Retrieved from https://apps.who.int/iris/bitstream/handle/10665/339911/9789240018501-eng.pdf?sequence=1

World Health Organization (2022). *Coronavirus disease.* Factsheet. Retrieved from https://www.who.int/health-topics/coronavirus#tab=tab_1

World Health Organization (2023). *Weekly epidemiological update on COVID-19.* Retrieved from https://www.who.int/publications/m/item/weekly-epidemiological-update-on-covid-19---1-march-2023

Yamanis, T., Carlitz, R., & Mollel, H. (2021). Adapting COVID-19-COVID-19 containment in Africa: Lessons from Tanzania. In S. L. Greer, E. J. King, E. Massard de Foseca et al., Eds., *Coronavirus Politics: The Comparative Politics and Policy of COVID-19* (pp. 560–579). Ann Arbor, MI: University of Michigan Press. Available: https://www.press.umich.edu/11927713/coronavirus_politics

Yamanis, T., Carlitz, R., Gonyea, O. et al. (2023). Confronting 'chaos': a qualitative study assessing public health officials' perceptions of the factors affecting Tanzania's COVID-19 vaccine rollout. *BMJ Open, 2023*(13), e065081. https://doi.org/10.1136/bmjopen-2022-065081e

Author's Bio

Angella Napakol, Ph.D., is an Associate Professor in the School of Journalism, Media and Communication and the Director of Academic Affairs in the Division of Academic Affairs at Uganda Christian University. Angella is a Strategic Communication scholar with keen interest in risk and crisis communication and health. Her research and areas of consultancy are disaster/crisis communication, HIV/AIDS, sexual and reproductive health, mental health and currently COVID-19. She has been a consultant on different local and international projects.

Aisha Sembatya Nakiwala, Ph.D., is a Senior Lecturer and Head of the Department of Journalism and Communication, at Makerere University. She is a social change and communication strategist and has worked as a researcher and consultant on several health topics, including Malaria, immunisation, and COVID-19 in Uganda. Her teaching and research focus on communication for social change, communication and gender, and health communication.

Marjorie Kyomuhendo, Ph.D., is a Communication Studies Lecturer in the Department of Journalism and Communication at Makerere University. She has over 20 years of experience in strategic communication work with the government, private sector and development organizations. Her professional interests are in social and behaviour change teaching and research, specifically health communication, development communication, public relations, audience studies and media studies.

23

The Role of Customary Crisis Communication Mechanisms in Ethiopia

Tariku Abas[1] and Zenebe Beyene[2]

[1]Loyola Marymount University, Marymount Institute-TSEHAI Publishers, Los Angeles, CA, USA

[2]University of Mississippi, Media & Communication, Oxford, MS, USA

Introduction

Over the past five years, Ethiopia has experienced a series of crises that have profoundly impacted the nation (Adem, 2020; Gebregziabher et al., 2022; ICG, 2019). These crises range from natural disasters such as droughts and the COVID-19 pandemic (Hagmann & Abdi, 2020) to man-made difficulties like ethnic conflicts and full-scale civil warfare (NRMC, 2020; Tesfaye et al., 2020).

The limited literature on crisis communication within Ethiopia encompasses various themes. These include emergency health crises, where effective risk communication plays a pivotal role in outbreak management (Adera et al., 2022; Taye et al., 2010; Zikargae, 2020); natural disasters, where timely communication of the situation, humanitarian efforts, resource availability, and identified gaps are crucial for mounting effective responses and planning (Marlowe et al., 2022); as well as political crises involving conflicts. In political crises, the role of both state-centric and traditional mechanisms of crisis management and communication are spotlighted as necessary elements for sustainable solutions (Hagmann & Abdi, 2020; NRMC, 2020; Tesfaye et al., 2020). Additionally, cross-border corporate crises such as the 737-MAX crash and its subsequent communication and management, are also explored in the literature (Gebru, 2020; Mohammed, 2020).

This chapter aims to provide an overview of the crisis communication literature in Ethiopia and examines the level of engagement allowed for traditional/customary crisis communication mechanisms in various crisis-hit communities that have functional traditional structures of governance, conflict, and crisis management.

Brief Overview of Crisis Communication Literature in Ethiopia

Crisis communication-related literature in Ethiopia over the past five years appears to be concentrated in three major areas: First, health scares such as COVID-19, cholera, and conflict-induced health crises as seen in the Tigray region in northern Ethiopia (Gebregziabher

The Handbook of International Crisis and Risk Communication Research, Second Edition.
Edited by Andreas Schwarz, Matthew W. Seeger, and Sora Kim.

et al., 2022). Second, natural disasters like droughts and desert locust invasions. Third, various man-made crises and disasters, including conflicts, wars, and the crash of ET302 – 737 MAX.

Overview of Crisis Communication Literature on COVID-19 and 737 MAX Crisis

The COVID-19 Pandemic

The COVID pandemic-related crisis and crisis communication have been examined by different researchers through various thematic approaches. These themes include the pandemic's legal challenges and crisis management and how federal and regional actors attempted to address these challenges through the interpretation of the constitution (Gebregziabher et al., 2022; Mengie, 2021). Other themes explored its psychological effect on women (Kassaw, 2020), political challenges (Zikargae, 2020), and the impact on small businesses (Engidaw, 2022); the approach taken to address the pandemic in a corporate context where there's a designated crisis communication mechanism (Gweh & Bekana 2021), and effects on individuals with special needs (Seid, 2022).

In Ethiopia, the COVID pandemic took center stage when, on April 8, 2020, the government declared a nationwide "public health state of emergency" by invoking Article 93 of the Constitution (Negarit Gazette, 2020). Similar to many other federal countries, both the federal and regional governments have the authority to declare a state of emergency in matters related to public health emergencies. However, the power to establish and implement national standards and basic policy criteria for public health is exclusively vested in the federal government (Gebregziabher et al., 2022, Mekone, 2022). Yet, the lack of clarity regarding the boundaries of regional and federal mandates has led to overlaps and inactions, causing confusion in regional authority. This confusion was particularly evident when the House of Federation (HoF) made a controversial decision regarding the postponement of the national election due to COVID, extending its application to the regional states. This was problematic because the HoF's power is limited to interpreting the federal constitution, and the regional government bodies were beyond its mandate as they are regulated by the regional states' constitutions (Mengie, 2021).

The pandemic, as it impacted elections in over 60 countries and several territories around the world, had political ramifications for Ethiopia (IFES, 2020). The federal government was compelled to postpone the election that had been scheduled for August 29, 2020. This decision extended the terms of the federal and regional councils and executive bodies, including the HoF, by 9–12 months after COVID-19 was no longer considered a threat to public health (Mengie, 2021). This action set off a domino effect of conflict with the Tigray regional state, which refused to accept the Federal Government's decisions and chose to conduct its own elections, further widening the gap between the two parties and eventually leading to a civil war (Davis, 2020; Paravicini, 2020). As both sides seemed determined and entrenched, leaders of the Inter-Religious Council and Elders Consultative Forum of Ethiopia – an independent Council established by Seven dominant religions in the country and fully supported and empowered by government policy (Baleker 2023) – attempted to reconcile the two sides by facilitating negotiations to ease tensions and encouraging face-to-face discussions between officials of the federal and Tigray regional governments to resolve their differences (Ezega, 2020). On their part, the Tigray authorities rejected bilateral talks with the Federal government, instead calling for a comprehensive national dialogue to address the country's faltering transition (ICG, 2020).

The Tigray election proceeded despite the exclusive authority of Ethiopia's National Electoral Board to conduct elections (NEBE) and the authority to establish electoral laws belonging to the federal parliament (Mengie, 2021). However, for some, the postponement under the pretext of constitutional interpretation was considered unconstitutional, and the HoF's decision was technically constitutional in name but political in practice (Salemot, 2021). After the election in the Tigray region, the HoF subsequently declared the Tigray election unconstitutional, and the federal government ceased providing subsidies to Tigray. With no constitutional remedy available, political dialogue and consensus building should have been the only viable path for resolving the crisis (Salemot, 2021). The effort of the Inter-Religious Council and Elders Consultative Forum of Ethiopia was not considered central. On November 4, 2020, Tigray forces attacked Ethiopia's northern military command, triggering a military operation (Mengie, 2021) and exposing the failure of crisis communication capacities of the parties involved.

COVID and Psychology

Literature in crisis communication in Ethiopia also involved psychology and COVID. A study investigating the psychological effects of COVID has revealed that 66.4% of the respondents, primarily females, have experienced moderate to severe psychological conditions, including stress, anxiety, and depression, necessitating immediate mental health crisis intervention (Kassaw, 2020). Another study on risk communication related to COVID assessed the government's administration and risk communication since the outbreak (Zikargae, 2020). The study revealed that despite the implementation of strategies that segmented the population by tailoring risk communication and community engagement activities at all levels, the implementation was not stringent, and the government did not take a heavy-handed approach. The study recommended that the government implement additional strategies to mobilize the public through various communication mechanisms to address socio-cultural, political, and economic factors (Zikargae, 2020).

COVID Crisis in Corporate Setting in Ethiopia

Crisis communication research in Ethiopia also encompasses themes such as Ethiopian Airlines Group and COVID. The special focus on Ethiopian Airlines is justified due to its unique position in the pandemic response within the African aviation industry. Different organizations react differently to crisis situations, which can either lead to their recovery or downfall (Pedersen et al., 2020). Many prominent companies in the airline and travel sectors have faced unprecedented losses in terms of income and revenue due to suspended operations. Amidst a global panic and an exceptional health crisis directly affecting its core operations, and while numerous businesses, especially airlines, travel, and tourism, were at significant risk, Ethiopian Airlines stood out for its crisis management and continued operations (Gweh & Bekana, 2021).

Findings from these studies suggest that the airline's management displayed not only situational awareness but also decisive decision-making during the crisis. As the outcome of a crisis for a company largely depends on its preparedness, proactiveness, and responsiveness (Coombs, 2010a, 2010b), the studies indicate that the leadership not only recognized the adverse impacts of the pandemic but also identified the opportunities it presented and capitalized on them (Gweh & Bekana, 2021). This preparedness is evident in the activation of internal crisis communication mechanisms and the management's decision to shift the business model toward cargo operations during the pandemic (Coombs, 2010a, 2010b; Gweh & Bekana, 2021).

However, health-related crisis communication literature extends beyond COVID. One study, for instance, examines the effectiveness and quality of the risk communication process during a cholera outbreak in the capital, Addis Ababa. This study concludes that gaps existed due to poor documentation, a lack of a data management system, and insufficient attention given to risk communication activities (Adera et al., 2022).

ET-302 737 MAX Crisis

Another theme that many studies have covered centers on the corporate and cross-border crisis associated with the 737 MAX crash, specifically focusing on Ethiopian Airlines crisis communication and management (Mohammed, 2020). Additionally, research explores inter-organizational crisis communication in alignment with theoretical and empirical literature related to aviation crisis communication, comparing Ethiopian Airlines crisis communication with Boeing's regarding the same crash (Gebru, 2020).

The literature examines how the ET-302, 737 MAX Crash, as a test for business partners Ethiopian Airlines and Boeing, has led to an assessment of each other's actions and their partnership agenda through a relational review. They employed distinct strategies and frames, with Ethiopian Airlines taking a more cautious stance while Boeing engaged in denial and defensiveness that later morphed into the rhetoric of renewal (Gebru, 2020). The airline's crisis communication and its execution of strategies were tailored to convey sympathy and provide compensation to the families of the victims. The focus was on safeguarding the company's reputation and brand, aiming to prevent irreversible damage (Temesgen, 2019).

According to these studies, Ethiopian Airlines adopted a coordinated and well-planned approach to crisis communication. This coordination was evident as the government, not the airline, initially announced the tragic news through the Prime Minister. The Office of the Prime Minister, on behalf of the government and people of Ethiopia, extended condolences to the families of those that have lost their loved ones on the crashed Ethiopian Airlines Boeing 737 (Kiruga, 2019). Industry experts note that entrusting the Prime Minister with breaking the news established immediate trust, primarily because the Prime Minister, at the time, had garnered global attention through his extensive reform program, enhancing his credibility (Kiruga, 2019).

Timing is crucial when responding to crises, especially those that capture public attention. In this regard, Ethiopian Airlines demonstrated a high level of responsiveness. Not only did they react swiftly, but they also provided timely and sequentially accurate information (Chaba, 2019). Consequently, Ethiopian Airlines succeeded in presenting the tragedy as a situation where a vulnerable victim, like themselves, encountered issues with a seemingly faultless corporate behemoth such as Boeing. Boeing, known as a top-tier technology provider from a prestigious nation, enjoyed implicit credibility advantages (Gebru, 2020).

Within a week following the crash, Ethiopian Airlines issued approximately six accident bulletins, each containing crucial and well-defined information that built upon the previous ones (Chaba, 2019). Adhering to aviation crisis protocol, the initial two press releases from Ethiopian Airlines provided factual details about the aircraft's schedule and passengers, along with procedural instructions. A subsequent press release acknowledged the absence of survivors and conveyed condolences, with the CEO addressing the situation at the crash site, underscoring the gravity of the tragedy (Gebru, 2020).

Initially, Ethiopian Airlines declared that the airplane was newly delivered to them by Boeing in October 2018. Second, without delving into specifics or engaging in a blame game, they identified the equipment in question as the Boeing 737-8 MAX. Third, they noted that the involved pilot was a senior professional, possessing extensive experience with a cumulative flight time exceeding 8000 hours and a commendable performance record. Furthermore, they subtly indicated that the flight had recently completed a safe journey from Johannesburg prior to its ill-fated voyage to Nairobi (Chaba, 2019).

The airline was also careful and strong in defending its reputation. On March 21 and 22, Ethiopian Airlines criticized the New York Times and the Washington Post for publishing unverified claims and urged everyone to await the results of the ongoing investigations (Kiruga, 2019). Fortunately, these reports played a role in enhancing Ethiopian Airlines' reputation for safety. Alongside their anticipatory rhetorical self-defense, Ethiopian Airlines centered its attention on addressing the emotional impact of the loss (Gebru, 2020). The crisis communication strategies predominantly involved expressions of remorse and efforts to reinforce the airline's image. These strategies aimed to demonstrate sensitivity toward the needs of the victims and their families who suffered losses in the accident. The airline endeavored to maintain positive relationships and prevent the crisis from escalating further (Temesgen, 2019).

Traditional/Customary Crisis Communication Mechanisms in Natural and Man-Made Crisis Situations

Inter-ethnic conflicts in Ethiopia have been on the rise since 2018 (Hagmann & Abdi, 2020). During 2018/2019, these conflicts led to 1229 fatalities and 1393 injuries among various ethnic groups (Gessese, 2020). Consequently, the peaceful coexistence of diverse ethnic groups is being tainted by these conflicts (Alemayehu, 2009; Anteneh, 2013). The conflict landscape is increasingly being infiltrated by fervent ethnic nationalists who exacerbate tensions through the utilization of both mainstream and social media (Gessese, 2020). The majority of these internal ethnic conflicts can be categorized into two primary groups: first, conflicts revolving around administrative boundaries, often related to regional states, districts, or, at times, kebele boundaries; second, disputes arising among minorities who have become the hosts of ethnic majorities in a political structure that emphasizes ethnically defined entities (Hagmann and Abdi, 2020, Debelo & Jirata, 2018).

Nonetheless, similar to many contemporary large-scale violent conflicts, the conflicts in Ethiopia can also be interpreted as outcomes of hybrid socio-political interactions where both state-centric and non-state-centric factors, encompassing traditional and economic aspects, come into play (Boege, 2011). This context necessitates a nuanced approach to crisis communication that acknowledges these dynamics. This implies that the 'formal' state, as well as the 'informal' societal order shaped by tradition, globalization, and the international civil society with its diverse actors such as non-governmental organizations (NGOs), play significant roles. In such a setting, authority, capacity, and legitimacy are shared between the state and non-state actors and institutions engaged at various levels. Within these scenarios, we encounter hybrid political frameworks that substantially differ from the Western model of the state (Abbink, 2003; NRMC, 2020). Communicating disaster risks to communities marked by rich cultural and linguistic diversity presents a crucial challenge to disaster risk reduction (DRR) practices, which are often under-resourced and insufficiently researched (Diers-Lawson & Meibner 2021).

The challenges become more evident in situations where modern crisis management and communication methodologies are recommended without adequately accommodating indigenous mechanisms, as is often the case in many African countries, including Ethiopia. In the cultural heritage of indigenous communities, the institution of traditional leadership has effectively maintained its position and continues to function as the guardian of the culture, customs, origins, and history of its people (Mboh, 2021). Establishing this fact, a recent study conducted by Afrobarometer (2021) reveals that Ethiopians tend to place more trust on their traditional leaders than state institutions and elected officials, and they express a desire to see the influence of these traditional leaders increase. According to the study, more than six out of ten Ethiopians (62%) exhibit a certain level of trust toward traditional leaders, indicating higher trust levels compared to most state institutions and officials. Traditional leaders are perceived as having an impact on resolving local disputes (79%) and governing local communities (60%), but their influence is perceived as lower in areas such as land allocation (42%) or influencing voting choices (36%). The legitimacy of state and international institutions in achieving conflict resolution goals has been subject to debate (Regassa & Jirata, 2018). An overwhelming majority (81%) desire increased influence for traditional leaders, while a majority (61%) prefer that they remain apolitical. In comparison to members of the House of Peoples' Representatives (9%) and local government councilors (12%), over half (52%) believe that traditional leaders frequently or always listen to their constituents (Afrobarometer, 2021). Notably, political leaders (ministers, department heads, or directors) aren't always fully aware of the requisites or consequences of effective communication (Mekasha & Wudneh, 2018).

The effectiveness of communicating and managing extensive crises often hinges on the creation of efficient communication mechanisms. This is evident, for example, in Ethiopia, where citizens prefer religious and traditional leaders over political figures (Afrobarometer, 2021; Tesfaye et al., 2020). Incorporating traditional and customary mechanisms and structures is motivated not only by their potential positive impact in conflict resolution but also due to their relevance when dealing with violent conflicts. These traditional social entities such as extended families, lineages, clans, 'tribes,' religious brotherhoods, and ethnolinguistic groups, become involved in the conflicts themselves, introducing their own objectives into the broader conflict context. These objectives extend beyond modern political ambitions like acquiring political power or economic considerations such as personal gain and profit. Instead, they encompass notions like "honor," "revenge," or the "right to (violent) self-help" (Boege, 2011).

Ethiopia and Traditional Crisis Communication Practices

For decades, traditional leaders have played roles in conflict resolution within indigenous communities (Mboh, 2021), yet the broader conversation surrounding crisis communication frequently neglects their contributions. Although at times courted, supported, and even compensated with state salaries, traditional leaders have also faced restrictions, removals, and imprisonments – often by the very governments they grapple with while adapting to their own changing circumstances (Logan & Yeshtila, 2019). For instance, in Somalia traditional leaders are considered trustworthy in solving inter-clan conflicts because they form the core of Somalia society and the socialization process; however, their input was not taken into consideration in major peace negotiations. The neglect of local wisdom from such negotiations could result in the rejection of the peace agreement by the people (Achieng, 2015).

The situation in Ethiopia is similar. Ethiopia, primarily a rural nation, shares many characteristics common to rural communities in Sub-Saharan Africa, relying on indigenous political structures (Abbink, 2003; Boege, 2011, Debisa, 2022). Throughout much of its history, Ethiopia has been composed of culturally and linguistically diverse groups who have participated in both trade and conflicts for millennia. Over these long-term interactions, indigenous legal traditions have persisted in governing the various groups, their neighboring tribes, clans, and people, and this continuity has extended to the present day (Abbink, 2003). Particularly in most southern regions, various indigenous forms of governance and authority remain influential. These structures encompass segmentary societies (such as the Somali), age-grade societies in the east and south (including Oromo, Konso, Darasa, and Sidama), divine kingdoms (Wolayta, Maale, and Oida), democratic assembly societies (Gamo), and hierarchical chiefdoms in the central and southern regions (like Aari, Bench, and Dizi) (Abbink, 2003). These traditional approaches trace their origins to the pre-contact history of local societies, yet they have consistently evolved over time due to interactions with the external world. It's crucial to understand that the traditional realm is not immutable or static, as custom undergoes constant change (Boege, 2011). This realization bridges the gap between state-centric and customary perspectives.

Considering the significant divergence in community trust toward government and traditional leadership structures, as highlighted by Afrobarometer (2021), an important question arises: should traditional mechanisms play a prominent role in crisis communication and management in Ethiopia? Currently, traditional, non-Western methods of conflict transformation have received limited attention in scholarly research and political application. In many cases, they are disregarded, despite empirical evidence demonstrating their practical relevance, even amidst the era of 'new wars' in a globalized world (Boege, 2011). Traditional leaders have long been engaged in conflict resolution within African indigenous communities, yet their contributions have not been as extensively documented as formal conflict resolution efforts (Mboh, 2021). It has been proposed that due to cultural disparities in the public's communication preferences during crisis situations and the challenges of adequately "translating" communication strategies across cultures, Western-style communication strategies are inadequate for addressing global and transboundary concerns (George Amiso & Kwansah-Aidoo, 2017).

The Culture of Communicating Crisis and Customary Methods

In Ethiopia, since the 1960s, the ascendancy of modernist discourses intertwined with the process of globalization has predominantly shaped the landscape of conflict resolution, especially following the rise to power of the Derg regime. During this period, many customary structures and traditions were branded as antiquated and dispensable, leading to their discouragement. In contrast, the nation has continued to grapple with a parallel history of violence, interethnic conflicts, civil wars (both interstate and intergroup), and sociopolitical upheavals that have unsettled the state and societies for several decades (Regassa & Jirata, 2018).

While crises themselves are not inherently classified as good or bad, they are typically perceived by most as negative. The way crises are perceived can indeed influence their eventual outcomes (Penrose, 2000). Therefore, the community's understanding of the concept of crisis may offer insights into how it could potentially be resolved. For instance, in Amharic, the Ethiopian lingua franca, the term for crisis is "ቀውስ" (qews), which also translates to an "insane" person. While literature exploring the socio-psychological associations and etymology of this term remains limited, it prompts consideration of whether this dual meaning sheds light on the collective psychological tendency toward both crisis and insanity in Ethiopia. For many Ethiopians, their country is perceived as favored by God and thus under His protection at all times. Yet, when instances of insanity or crisis arise, both represent deviations from the norm and have historically been met with suppression, secrecy, and forceful isolation due to the belief that they signify God's disfavor or punishment. Therefore, crises such as pandemics, wars, and conflicts are often interpreted as manifestations of God's wrath upon those afflicted or those connected to them. During a cholera epidemic in the fifteenth century, for example, the conversion to Catholicism by the ruling class was blamed to have triggered God's punishment (Pankhurst, 1972). Even during the COVID-19 pandemic, many held the belief that the virus would not enter Ethiopia due to its status as God's chosen land. Such notions underscore the enduring prominence of Ethiopian exceptionalism among the populous and its profound religious underpinnings (Østebø et al., 2021).

Applying Benoit's image restoration theory,(Benoit, 1997) the response to the crisis mirrors the approach taken toward insanity. Denial and evasion of responsibility are frequent reactions, often leaving matters to divine intervention and seeking divine aid. Praying and surrendering control to God constitute common responses to crises among religious Ethiopians. Crises are not usually publicized or preemptively addressed, as such measures might be viewed as inviting divine retribution. Historical regimes have typically contained and stifled crises, rather than strategizing, communicating, and effectively managing them (Kebede, 1999).

These perspectives could provide insights not only into how crises are perceived but also into how they are communicated and could be resolved. By incorporating local perceptions into crisis management, the facets of crisis communication could gain from contemplating why both forms of crisis – social and personal – are not only labeled with the same term but are also conventionally regarded as divine punishments. In such contexts, open interventions by people are often passive; if and when active measures are pursued, they typically involve the utilization of traditionally accepted tools such as spiritual leaders or traditional authorities (Borkena, 2020; Østebø et al., 2021).

As a result, crises such as pandemics, wars, conflicts, and personal hardships are frequently attributed to the will and anger of God. An Ethiopian proverb encapsulates this mindset: "Better be filled with gratitude for the chronic illness; complaining might worsen it." Over time, interpretations emphasizing divine judgment and retribution have thrived during pandemics. Hence, the interpretations emerging in Ethiopia during the COVID-19 pandemic align with historical consistency (Østebø et al., 2021).

Current State of Customary Crisis Management Mechanisms

A recent study on Ethiopia's communication landscape reveals that many government communication professionals distrust the media, offering limited information when they do decide to share. This is partly due to perceiving the media as adversaries rather than partners. Consequently, information is often delayed, and public relations agents tend to withhold information until prompted by media figures. The study also highlights the government communication personnel's limited capacity and lack of organization (Mekasha & Wudneh, 2018). Unfortunately, the impact of crisis is often worsened due to lack of timely responses once tragedy occurs (Rosenthal, 1997).

Traditional institutions could fill the void. However, they hardly seem to be invited. Traditional institutions are not merely anachronistic relics of the past but rather integral components of the present (Boege, 2011). In recent years, Ethiopia has witnessed a growing interest in indigenous approaches to resolving political and ethnic conflicts and establishing sustainable peace. This can also be perceived as a response to the apparent failure of the state-centric approach, which emphasizes top-down directives (Regassa & Jirata, 2018). Over the past five years, there has been an inclination on the part of the government to engage traditional leaders, community elders, and religious figures and organizations in facilitating discussions, defusing tensions, and actively intervening to reduce violence and promote communication. There are even proclamations establishing the Ethiopian National Dialogue Commission (Negarit Gazette, 2022). Despite these roles of customary dispute resolution mechanisms, the procedural and substantive laws of Ethiopia, including the Constitution itself, exclude their application in criminal matters (Enyew, 2014). The only relevant recognition of their importance is articulated by Article. 34 (5) of the constitution where customary dispute resolution mechanisms are legally authorised to regulate personal and family matters as long as the conflicting parties give their consent to that effect (Enyew, (2014).

For instance, the National Disaster Risk Management Commission (NDRMC), which was under the Office of the Prime Minister and was mandated to coordinate emergency response across various entities, lacks traditional mechanisms of crisis management(Gray & Asmare, 2021).

NDRMC mandates the establishment of disaster risk information management and communication systems supported by technology at all levels of administration, from the federal to regional and local levels (NPSDRM, 2013). Although the policy emphasizes technology as a key means to enhance communication and crisis management processes across the country, it does not address the utilization of tested customary risk management mechanisms. The focus on technology as the primary solution tends to overlook local wisdom.

While technology can expedite certain aspects of communication, it also complicates and potentially bypasses natural crisis management processes. Traditional approaches tend to be process-oriented and context-dependent that can affect the outcome of peacebuilding processes (Boege, 2011). Recent research on Ethiopia's communication landscape highlighted a lack of coordination between the Prime Minister's office and the Government Communication Affairs Office (GCAO), pointing to the need for effective leadership within the communication machinery. Political leaders often lack awareness of effective communication requirements (Mekasha & Wudneh, 2018). Revising this gap will improve the way crises have been communicated and managed.

Conclusion

The literature on crisis communication in Ethiopia highlights a distinct contrast in crisis management approaches between corporate entities and those operating within socio-political spheres. This contrast is exemplified by the crisis management and communication strategies employed by Ethiopian Airlines during both the COVID-19 pandemic and the 737-MAX crash-induced crisis. In these instances, established protocols were promptly activated, resulting in effective crisis management without incurring excessive costs for the company or its customers. There are lessons to be derived from the exemplary preparedness and execution of crisis management by Ethiopian Airlines during the two crises.

Conversely, the political turmoil in the country has consistently revealed a significant disconnect between public expectations and the actions of both the Federal and regional governments. While there is a prevailing inclination to incorporate traditional and customary laws and mechanisms into crisis communication and management at the national level, political institutions tend to rely heavily on top-down crisis communication methods, often relegating local and traditional peace and crisis management mechanisms to peripheral and secondary roles. Both the Federal and regional governments have faltered in proactively engaging crisis management mechanisms, allowing situations to escalate to the detriment of the country and its people.

Finally, the limited studies in this field underscore the neglect of crisis communication research in Ethiopia. These studies reveal the disparity between theory and practical application in crisis communication in the country. This disparity emphasizes the urgent need to reassess the state of crisis communication research in Ethiopia. Conducting comprehensive studies in this area is imperative, as they can inform the review of existing policies and practices, if any. By bridging this gap, Ethiopia can take proactive measures to address the numerous crises it has confronted over the years.

References

Abbink, G. J. (2003). Local leadership and state governance in southern Ethiopia: From charisma to bureaucracy. In *Indigenous Political Structures and Governance in Africa* (pp. 177–207). Ibadan: Sefer Books. Retrieved from https://hdl.handle.net/1887/9692

Achieng, O. M. (2015). *The Role of Traditional Leaders in Conflict Management in Africa: A Case Study of the Somalia National Reconciliation Conference (SNRC) 2000–2010 (Master's Research Project, University of Nairobi).* University of Nairobi Institute of Diplomacy and International Studies (IDIS).

Adem, J. M. (2020). *Blurred Bottom lines of Ethiopian Political Crisis from 20011 to 2020.* The International Institute for Science, Technology and Education (IISTE). ISSN 2224-8951 (Online). https://core.ac.uk/display/287193242?utm_source=pdf&utm_medium=banner&utm_campaign=pdf-decoration-v1

Adera, N. G., Ketema, B., & Girma, E. (2022). Effectiveness and quality of risk communication process in Ethiopia: The case of risk communication during a cholera outbreak in Addis Ababa. *PLoS One, 17*(8), e0265203.

Afrobarometer (2021). *Ethiopians trust traditional leaders more than other institutions, would like to see their influence increase, afrobarometer survey shows.* https://www.afrobarometer.org/articles/

ethiopians-trust-traditional-leaders-more-other-institutions-would-see-their-influence/ (accessed 10 March 2021).

Alemayehu, F. W. (2009). *Conflict Management in the Ethiopian Multi-national Federation: A Critical Examination*. University of Texas at Austin, Suffolk University: LBJ School of Public Affairs. https://papers.ssrn.com/sol3/papers.cfm?abstract_id=1429266

Anteneh, A.2013). *The practice of inter-ethnic conflict transformation in Ethiopia: The case of Amhara-Afar conflict in Kewot and Semurobi Gela Alo Woreda*. Master's thesis, Addis Ababa University, Anthology of Peace and Security Studies. https://www.academia.edu/68766136/Anthology_of_Peace_and_Security_Studies_Volume_4

Baleker, A. R. (2023). *Religion's roles in peacebuilding in Ethiopia: Religion and interfaith engagement in times of conflict and disaster*. https://talkabout.iclrs.org/2023/01/15/religions-roles-in-peacebuilding-in-ethiopia-religion-and-interfaith-engagement-in-times-of-conflict-and-disaster%EF%BF%BC/

Benoit, W. L. (1997). Image repair discourse and crisis communication. *Public Relations Review*, *23*(2), 177–186.

Boege, V. (2011). *Potential and limits of traditional approaches in peacebuilding*. Retrieved from https://berghof-foundation.org/files/publications/boege_handbookII.pdf

Borkena (June, 2020). *Elders intervene to mediate Abiy gov't, de facto state in the north*. https://borkena.com/2020/06/15/ethiopia-elders-intervene-to-mediate-abiy-govt-de-facto-state-in-the-north/

Chaba, R. (March 17, 2019). What can we learn from Ethiopian Airlines crisis communication strategy? *Medium*. https://chaba-rhuwanya.medium.com/what-can-we-learn-from-ethiopian-airlines-crisis-communication-strategy-2b681222f43d

Coombs, W. T. (2010a). Crisis communication: A developing field. In R. L. Heath, Ed., *The Sage Handbook of Public Relations* (pp. 477–488). SAGE S Publications, Inc.

Coombs, W. T. (2010b). Conceptualizing crisis communication. In R. L. Heath, & H. D. O'hair, Eds., *Handbook of Risk and Crisis Communication* (pp. 99–100). Routledge. https://www.google.com/books/edition/Handbook_of_Risk_and_Crisis_Communicatio/rA4HEAAAQBAJ?hl=en&gbpv=1&dq=crisis+communication+pdf&pg=PA99&printsec=frontcover

Davis Jr., K. (2020). *Ethiopia delays elections: Is COVID a valid excuse*. https://www.theafricareport.com/37721/ethiopia-and-cote-divoire-delay-elections-is-covid-a-valid-excuse/

Debisa, N. G. (2022). Building peace by a peaceful approach: The role of Oromo Gadaa system in peacebuilding. *Cogent Social Science*, *8*(2022), 2023254. https://doi.org/10.1080/23311886.2021.2023254

Debelo, A. R., & Jirata, T. J. (2018). "Peace is not a free gift": Indigenous conceptions of peace among the Guji-Oromo in Southern Ethiopia. *Northeast African Studies*, *18*(1–2), 201–230.

Diers-Lawson, A., & Meißner, F. (2021). Editor's essay: Moving beyond Western Corporate perspectives: on the need to increase the diversity of risk and crisis communication research. *Journal of International Crisis and Risk Communication Research*, *4*(1), 165–176. https://doi.org/10.30658/jicrcr.4.1.6

Engidaw, A. E. (2022). Small business and their challenges during COVID-19 pandemic in developing countries. In *Case of Ethiopia*. Woldia University. https://orcid.org/0000-0002-5081-5668

Enyew, E. L.(2014). *Ethiopian customary dispute resolution mechanisms Forms of restorative justice?* https://www.accord.org.za/ajcr-issues/ethiopian-customary-dispute-resolution-mechanisms/

Ezega (June, 2020). *Religious leaders to mediate dispute between federal government and TPLF* https://www.ezega.com/News/NewsDetails/7984/Religious-Leaders-to-Mediate-Dispute-Between-Federal-Government-and-TPLF

Gebregziabher, M., Amde Selassie, F., Esayas, R. et al. (2022). Geographical distribution of the health crisis of war in the Tigray region of Ethiopia. *BMJ Global Health*, *2022*(7), e008475. http://doi.org/10.1136/ bmjgh-2022-008475

Gebru, A. (2020). *International Inter-corporate Crisis Communication: Ethiopian Airlines, Boeing and the 737 Max 8 Tragedy*. Addis Ababa University. https://www.researchgate.net/publication/344862237_International_Inter-corporate_Crisis_Communication_Ethiopian_Airlines_Boeing_and_the_MAX_8_Tragedy

George, A. M., & Kwansah-Aidoo, Kwamena (eds). (2017). *Culture and Crisis Communication Transboundary Cases from Nonwestern Perspectives*. IEEE PCS Professional Engineering

Communication Series. https://www.google.com/books/edition/Handbook_of_Risk_and_Crisis_Communicatio/rA4HEAAAQBAJ?hl=en&gbpv=1&dq=crisis+communication+pdf&pg=PA99&printsec=frontcover

Gessese, A. (2020). *Ethnic Nationalists Abuse of Media: Lessons of Yugoslavia and Rwanda for Ethiopia.* Ethiopia: Department of Journalism and Communication, Bahir Dar University. http://doi.org/10.19044/esj.2020.v16n16p98 http://dx.doi.org/10.19044/esj.2020.v16n16p98

Gweh, G. N., & Bekana, D. M. (2021). Organizational risk management practices in time of crisis: An exploratory case study of ethiopian airlines in the coronavirus pandemic. *Journal of Business and Administrative Studies, 13*(2), 22–29.

Gray, B., & Asmare, E. (2021). *Building resilience in Ethiopia (BRE) study to assess the effectiveness of the National Disaster Risk Management Commission's coordination role in recent disasters in Ethiopia.* https://edrmc.gov.et/sites/default/files/Ref.%20B%20Q12021%20-%20Effectiveness%20of%20NDRMC%27s%20coordination%20role%20in%20past%20disasters_0.pdf

Hagmann, T., & Abdi, M. M. (2020). *Inter-ethnic violence in Ethiopia's Somali Regional State, 2017–2018, Conflict Research Programme Research Memo*, March 2020.

International Crisis Group (ICG) (2020). *Toward an End to Ethiopia's Federal-Tigray Feud Crisis Group Africa Briefing N°160 Addis Ababa/Nairobi//Brussels.* https://www.crisisgroup.org/africa/horn-africa/ethiopia/b160-toward-end-ethiopias-federal-tigray-feud (accessed 14 August 2020).

International Crisis Group (ICG) (2019). *Managing Ethiopia's Unsettled Transition Africa Report N°269 | 21 February 2019 Headquarters.* https://www.crisisgroup.org/africa/horn-africa/ethiopia/269-managing-ethiopias-unsettled-transition

International Foundation for Electoral Systems (IFES) (2020). *Elections postponed due to COVID-19.* https://www.ifes.org/sites/default/files/elections_postponed_due_to_covid-19.pdf

Kassaw, C. (2020). The magnitude of psychological problem and associated factor in response to COVID-19 pandemic among communities living in Addis Ababa, Ethiopia, March 2020: A cross-sectional study design. *Psychology Research and Behavior Management, 13*, 631–640.

Kiruga M. (2019). *Ethiopian Airlines: crisis and communications in Nairobi.* https://www.theafricareport.com/10987/ethiopian-airlines-crisis-and-communications/

Kebede, M. (1999). *Survival and Modernization in.* Ethiopia: Enigmatic Present.

Logan, C., & Yeshtila, B. (2019). *Politics and power in Southern Ethiopia: Imposing, opposing and calling for linguistic unity, language matters to link to this article.* https://doi.org/10.1080/10228195.2018.1553993

Marlowe, J., Jehan, F., Udahemuka, M., Mizero, A., Jaduram, R., Rotstein, J. et al. (2022). Disaster communications with resettled refugees: Six principles of engagement. *International Journal of Disaster Risk Reduction, 67*, 102672.

Mboh, L. (2021). *An investigation into the role of traditional leaders in conflict resolution: The case of communities in the Mahikeng Local Municipality, North West Province, South Africa. African Journal on Conflict Resolution. ACCORD. Cedric de Coning.* Retrieved from https://www.ajol.info/index.php/ajcr/issue/view/21143

Mekasha, M., & Wudneh, T. (2018). *Communication Landscape in Ethiopia: Assessment of Legislative and Operational Environment.* UNDP. https://www.undp.org/sites/g/files/zskgke326/files/2023-03/05-UNDP-Comm%20Media%20Landscape%20Assesment-Draft4.pdf

Mekone, Y. M. (2022). "Public health emergency declarations" in the Ethiopian federal system: Understanding the scope of state and federal emergency declarations and authorities. *Law, Democracy & Development, 26*, 1–27. http://www.scielo.org.za/pdf/ldd/v26/01.pdf

Mengie, L. T. (2021). *COVID-19 Elections in "Ethiopia:" Exploring Constitutional Interpretation Researcher.* South Australia: The University of Adelaide. ORCID ID https://orcid.org/0000-0003-4288-2761

Mohammed, Z. (2020). *Crisis Communication and Management using Social Media: a Crisis Response to Ethiopian Airlines ET302 Crash.* Örebro University School of Humanities, Education & Social Sciences. https://www.diva-portal.org/smash/get/diva2:1466066/FULLTEXT01.pdf

National Policy and Strategy on Disaster Risk Management (NPSDRM) Federal Democratic Republic of Ethiopia (July 2, 2013). *Addis Ababa.* https://www.refworld.org/pdfid/5a2689ea4.pdf

Negarit Gazette of the Federal Democratic Republic of Ethiopia. (2020). *State of emergency proclamation No 3/2020: 26th year no 35 Addis Ababa.* https://www.icnl.org/covid19tracker/covid19

uploads/Ethiopia%20State%20of%20Emergency%20Reg.466%20(Implem.of%20Proc.3.2012%20 State%20of%20Emergency).pdf (accessed 8 April 2020)

Negarit Gazette of the Federal Democratic Republic of Ethiopia (2022). *The Ethiopian National Dialogue Commission establishment proclamation.* https://ethiondc.org.et/wp-content/uploads/2022/12/Ethiopian-National-Dialogue-Commission-Establishment-Proclamation-No.-1265-2021.pdf

NRMC (2020). *Stabilization and recovery support to communities affected by Gedeo-West Guji Displacement.* https://edrmc.gov.et/sites/default/files/2019_Project%20Report_Gedeo%20and %20West%20Guji_FW%26JSB.pdf

Østebø, T., Tronvoll, K., & Østebø, M. T. (2021). God's wrath in the era of the digidemic: Religious interpretations of Covid-19 in Ethiopia. *Journal of the American Academy of Religion, 89*(4), 1334–1359.

Pankhurst, R. (1972). The history of famine and pestilence in Ethiopia prior to the founding of Gondar. *Journal of Ethiopian Studies, 10*(2), 37–64. https://www.jstor.org/stable/41965857

Paravicini, G. (2020). *Ethiopia's Tigray holds regional election in defiance of federal government.* https://www.reuters.com/article/us-ethiopia-politics/ethiopias-tigray-holds-regional-election-in-defiance-of-federal-government-idUSKBN25Z35S

Pedersen, C. L., Ritter, T., & Di Benedetto, C. A. (2020). Managing through a crisis: Managerial implications for business-to-business firms. *Industrial Marketing Management.* https://www.ncbi.nlm.nih.gov/pmc/articles/PMC7273163/

Penrose, J. M. (2000). The role of perception in crisis planning. *Public Relations Review, 26*(2), 155–171. Retrieved from https://go.gale.com/ps/i.do?id=GALE%7CA64333353&sid=googleScholar

Regassa, A., & Jirata, T. J. (2018). "Peace is not a free gift": Indigenous conceptions of peace among the Guji-Oromo in Southern Ethiopia Rhuwany Chaba (2019). *What can we learn from Ethiopian Airlines Crisis Communication Strategy?* https://web.archive.org/web/20230316195028id_/https://www.zora.uzh.ch/id/eprint/231916/9/2018_Regassa_TEXT_11.pdfhttps://chaba-rhuwanya.medium.com/what-can-we-learn-from-ethiopian-airlines-crisis-communication-strategy-2b681222f43d

Rosenthal, U. (1997). *Crises and Crisis Management: Toward Comprehensive Government Decision Making.* The Netherlands: Leiden University, Alexander Kouzmin University of Western Sydney.

Seid, A. A. (2022). *COVID-19 vaccination and disability in Ethiopia: Ensuring no one is left behind.* http://doi.org/10.4314/ejhs.v32i3.25

Salemot, M. A. (2021). *Constitutional silence on election postponement in Ethiopia amidst a pandemic: A critique of constitutional interpretation.* https://www.academia.edu/91470791/Constitutional_silence_on_election_postponement_in_Ethiopia_amidst_a_pandemic_A_critique_of_constitutional_interpretation

Taye, A., Haile Mariam, D., & Murray, V. (2010). Interim report: Review of evidence of the health impact of famine in Ethiopia. *Perspectives in Public Health: SAGE Journals, 130*(5). https://doi.org/10.1177/1757913910379197

Temesgen, D. (2019). *Crisis communication strategies of Ethiopian Airlines Group: A case study of flight 302 accident.*

Tesfaye, M., Hadis, S., Hailu, S., & Getahun, A. (2020). Promoting people's coexistence and interdependencies in North Shoa and Oromo Nationality Zones: An urge for crisis communication and reconciliation. *Abyssinia Journal of Business and Social Sciences., 5*(2), 42–51. ISSN 2707-1340 (Online). https://abjol.org.et/index.php/ajbs/article/view/199

Zikargae, M. H. (2020). *COVID-19 in Ethiopia: Assessment of how the Ethiopian government has executed administrative actions and managed risk communications and community engagement.* Published online December 3, 2020. http://doi.org/10.2147/RMHP.S278234

Author's Bio

Tariku Abas is a professional with extensive experience as an educator, writer, editor, translator, training quality expert, and NGO leader. He holds a Bachelor of Education (B.Ed.) from Bahir Dar University, a Master's degree in Teaching English as a Foreign Language (TEFL)

from Addis Ababa University, and a Master's degree in Creative Writing from Loyola Marymount University in Los Angeles.

With over 20 years of academic experience, Tariku has held teaching and leadership roles at institutions such as St. Mary's University, Ethiopian Aviation University, and Montgomery College-Maryland. His expertise spans language instruction, business communication, and aviation communication. Additionally, he is a certified ICAO language proficiency assessor and aviation internal auditor.

Tariku published his novel *Eyes and Mist* in 2012. In his capacity as a translator and editor, he has contributed to various projects across languages and disciplines.

Tariku is the founder and president of the **GEAT Foundation**, a nonprofit organization committed to enhancing education quality in rural Ethiopia.

Zenebe Beyene is Associate Professor and Coordinator of International Programs in the School of Journalism and New Media at the University of Mississippi. He specializes in media in conflict and post-conflict societies. He has taught, researched, or provided training in Ethiopia, Kenya, Rwanda, Uganda, and the US. Dr. Beyene has served as a consultant for InterNews Network, USAID, UNDP, Voice of America, Pennsylvania University/Carnegie Foundation, Oxford University and Oxford University/UK Embassy in Ethiopia and IDEA International. He has published or co-published work about tolerance and online debate in Ethiopia; the role of TeleCourt in changing conceptions of justice and authority in Ethiopia; the role of ICT in peacebuilding in Africa; Media Use and Abuse in Ethiopia; and From an Emperor to the Derg and Beyond: Examining the Intersection of Music and Politics in Ethiopia, the Role of the Diaspora in Nation Building and Peace-building; Building Peace Through Listening, "International Peace Journalism (PJ) practice: Comparing the levels of PJ awareness among Bangladeshi and Ethiopian journalists." Etc. He co-edited "Listening, Community Engagement and Peace Building" (2023) and was one of the panelists during the Oslo Peace Week in Oslo, Norway, 2019.

24

Culture, Ethnicity, and Religion
A Combustible Mix in Crisis Communication in Nigeria

Amiso M. George[1] and Wole Adamolekun[2]

[1] Department of Strategic Communication, Bob Schieffer College of Communication, Texas Christian University, Fort Worth, TX, USA
[2] Department of Mass Communication, Elizade University, Ilara-Mokin, Nigeria

Introduction

Crisis communication research in Nigeria continues z to evolve, albeit Nigeria is a country affected by a myriad of crises, from political unrest as reported in the 2023 elections, natural disasters, ethnic and religious clashes, health pandemics, and economic crises.

Cultural values and sentiments have often factored into decisions made at organizational and governmental levels in Nigeria, even when the decisions are wrong or negatively impact a large segment of the population. In this chapter on crisis communication in Nigeria, we use Geert Hofstede's theory of cultural dimensions (2011) and Stella Ting-Toomey's face negotiation theory (2005) to examine how culture influences crisis communication in Nigeria, with two significant cases as examples: the COVID-19 response and the catastrophic flooding of 2022. We chose to analyze these cases because they reflect the need for crisis communication research with implication for practitioners in Nigeria.

Nigeria: Country Profile

Nigeria is Africa's most populous country with an estimated population of 219 million (Nigeria Demographics Profile, 2023), comprising more than 250 ethnic groups and occupying a landmass of over 923,768,64 km^2 (CIA Factbook, 2023). Religion plays an important role in the country as 53% classify themselves as Muslim, 46% as Christian, and 06% as adherents of indigenous beliefs (CIA Factbook, 2023)

A former British colony, Nigeria was created from the amalgamation of the northern and southern protectorates in 1914 with Colonial Officer Frederick (Lord) Lugard as governor-general. The country gained independence from Britain in 1960 with Dr. Nnamdi Azikiwe as the first indigenous governor-general (Britannica, 2024).

Nigeria has suffered a series of crises of various types, beginning in 1962 when a violent political strife in the western region led to the declaration of a state of emergency and the

The Handbook of International Crisis and Risk Communication Research, Second Edition.
Edited by Andreas Schwarz, Matthew W. Seeger, and Sora Kim.

invocation of a Federal Emergency Powers Act (EPA No.14, 1962). Ethnicity and religion played important roles in the rash of political crises that culminated in the first military coup in 1966 and subsequently the civil war of 1967–1970. Military rule ended in 1979 when Nigeria adopted a new constitution and elected Alhaji Shehu Shagari as the first civilian president since 1966. Another coup brought the military back to power in 1983, but in the 1999 election, with Olusegun Obasanjo, a former military ruler, as president, the country returned to civilian rule again. Nigeria has experienced relative political peace until the current spate of deadly attacks in parts of northern Nigeria by the militant Islamist group, Boko Haram, which loosely translates to "Western education is forbidden."

Successive governments have tried different approaches to deal with each crisis – from containment through aggressive military response (the 1967–1970 civil war), joint police and military campaigns, and offers of negotiations and police response (Niger Delta militants, Boko Haram, and Indigenous People of Biafra (IPOB), the latter a former breakaway region of Nigeria). Coupled with government crises are those from the financial sector, airline industry, labor movement, and ethnic, religious, or political groups, as well as natural disasters and disease outbreaks.

The Context of Crisis Communication Research in Nigeria

Crisis communication research is still in its infancy in Nigeria. Interviews with Nigeria-based communication scholars conducted in September 2013 in Nigeria and repeated in 2021, on the scant crisis communication research in Nigeria revealed the same reasons given in previous interviews – lack of curriculum and instruction in tertiary institutions that deal with crisis and minimal or no support for scholarship on crisis communication. A review of crisis communication literature supports the assertion of communication scholars interviewed. Some research studies in crisis communication exist. They include the development of strategic models that organizations can use for internal crisis communication (Ihekweazu et al., 2022); government's crisis communication response to health pandemic, such as COVID-19 (Dan-Nwafor, 2020); development of risk and crisis communication campaigns to address health pandemics (Adamu & Mohamad, 2019); and media coverage of crisis stories (Apuke & Omar, 2022). Others include public perceptions of crises, including whether government can be trusted during crises, their understanding of the causes and effects of crises, and their attitudes toward crisis communication (Yunusa et al., 2021), exploring how social media is used to communicate during crises (Ehondor & Unakalamba, 2021), as well as how social media affects how the public perceives a crisis (Soladoye & Ojo, 2020).

Overall, crisis communication research in Nigeria is an important area of study that can help organizations and governments develop more effective crisis communication strategies, improve public perceptions of crises, and ultimately save lives and reduce the impact of crises on communities. With minimal academic input or research into solutions in this crucial area, organizations and the government in Nigeria won't repeat unplanned methods of crisis communication. Unlike academia, the media have covered crisis stories extensively on issues ranging from trust in government during a crisis (Popoola, 2021) to opinion pieces on the need for crisis communication (El-nafaty, 2023). However, most do not provide the kind of in-depth analysis or cultural context for the stories. Additionally, the stories fade from the headlines once the initial attention dissipates. This underpins the need to use the cases mentioned earlier to understand how culture influences crisis communication in Nigeria and the need for more research in the area that would provide lessons for practitioners.

Culture and Crisis Communication in Nigeria

Culture plays a significant role in crisis communication in Nigeria; therefore, Hofstede's theory of cultural dimensions (2011) and Ting-Toomey's face negotiation theory (2005) help to make sense of Nigeria's crisis communication challenges. Hofstede describes how a society's culture influences the values of its members and how those values affect their behavior. His culture-based model uses four dimensions to analyze cultural values: power distance index (PDI), which highlights the strength of social hierarchy; individualism versus collectivism (IDV), whereby in individualism, individuals take care of only themselves and their nuclear families within a social system, and in collectivism, relatives or group members take care of each other in exchange for absolute loyalty; masculinity versus femininity (MAS), which highlights task orientation versus person orientation; and uncertainty avoidance index (UAI), which reflects the level to which members of a society endeavor to cope with anxiety by minimizing uncertainty (Hofstede, 2011).

Face is variously described as the image one projects either of oneself or one's nationality in a public arena. Although the concept of face is believed to have originated from China (Ho, 1976), other cultures have notions of what they consider "face" issues. Ting-Toomey (2005) extends the concept through her development of face negotiation theory, as a way of describing cultural differences in communication and conflict resolution. The theory is grounded in how culture affects people's perception of crises and their reaction to others in their quest to protect the "face" of the person disseminating the crisis information. In a society and culture such as Nigeria, where authority and hierarchy are respected, someone with no authority is less likely to tell the highly placed person that his or her decision or action is wrong, albeit that is changing now. The assumption is that authority figures speak the truth; thus, disagreeing with them publicly shames the authority figure and may incur wrath. Thus, face negotiation theory enables one to understand how crisis information is communicated by the Nigerian government, perceived by its audience, and reported in the media.

Broadly defined as a way of life of a group of people, culture is the cumulative systems of knowledge, beliefs, values, attitudes, behaviors, meanings, experience, hierarchies, religion, concept of time, the universe, roles, relationships, and material objects and possessions acquired, accepted, and shared by a large group of people and transmitted over generations (Samover & Porter, 1994; Samover et al., 2014). It is a structure of knowledge shared by a large group of people (Gudykunst & Kim, 1992, 2003).

In essence, culture is learned, symbolic, shared, adaptive, and integrated as exemplified by the varied definitions. British anthropologist Edward B. Tylor who is believed to have produced the first formal definition of culture states that "Culture … is that complex whole which includes knowledge, belief, arts, morals, law, custom, and any other capabilities and habits acquired by man as a member of society" (Tylor, 1871/1958, p. 1). Other anthropologists define culture as follows: embraces all manifestations of social behavior of a community (Boas, 1930); a form of traditional behavior of a society, race, area, or period of time (Mead, 1937); an acquired system of knowledge, behaviors, attitudes, beliefs, values, and norms shared by a group of people (Smith, 1966); control mechanisms that govern behavior (Geertz, 1973); and rules of conduct from different types of social structure through which each human group has passed (Lévi-Strauss, 1983). Culture becomes important in crisis communication because of interests, drivers, agendas, and emotions of various stakeholders at the time of fear or vulnerability (Minty, 2020).

Crisis is a dangerous event that happens without warning and can potentially threaten an organization in a way that demands quick response. It is a sudden and unexpected event that threatens to disrupt an organization's operations and poses both financial and reputational threats (Coombs, 2022). While some definitions consider crisis as a sudden occurrence, research by the Institute of Crisis Management (ICM) indicates that 86% of 55,000 separate items serious enough to garner media attention were "simmering" and only 14% were "sudden" (Elsasser, 1996, p. 3). Boin et al. (2020) call such the "creeping crisis," one that "creeps up," yet surprises stakeholders. This latter statement captures the nature of the evolution of crises that have plagued Nigeria for decades. Given that most of the crises in Nigeria simmer before they erupt, one would assume that the leadership would have developed ongoing strategies to communicate to its publics in a crisis to maintain order, reputation, and image. The two cases examined reinforce the need for crisis research and an understanding of the impact of culture on crisis communication.

Since its independence in 1960, Nigeria has grappled with the issue of maintaining a "federal character" in all government appointments and decisions. This "federal character," which mandates that candidates for government appointments must represent the ethnic or religious makeup of the country, and resource allocations follow the same pattern, has been problematic. Mismanagement of resources, inadequate resources, and inept governance have all contributed to high unemployment, increased poverty, religious extremism, and violence. These crises issues notwithstanding, any Nigerian government that does not consider the delicate balance of culture, religion, and ethnicity in response to crises, would continue to face the daunting challenge of effective crisis communication in the country.

With limited research on crisis communication in Nigeria, this chapter uses Geert Hofstede's theory of cultural dimensions (2011) and Stella Ting-Toomey's face negotiation theory (2005) to briefly examine how culture influences crisis communication in Nigeria. Although Hofstede's work had been criticized for being Western-centric, some of the concepts still apply. We examine two recent cases: COVID-19 and the 2022 flooding, to highlight the challenges of the government in responding to crisis. These cases and the response to them reflect the ongoing need for crisis communication research in Nigeria, one in which sustainable response strategies based on research are African-centric and incorporate elements of culture, religion, and ethnicity.

Case Study 1: The COVID-19 Response: Challenges

The COVID-19 pandemic in Africa and, specifically, Nigeria posed surprises as the continent posted low numbers of infected people as well as deaths throughout the 12-month-long peak period of the pandemic. Nigeria is home to about 219 million people (Nigeria Demographics Profile, 2023). COVID-19 crept in with the index case of an Italian citizen who arrived in the commercial capital, Lagos, on February 27, 2020, and subsequently processed through contact tracing, isolation, and treatment (NCDC, 2020). Shortly afterward, crisis containment measures kicked in accordance with the World Health Organization (WHO) guidelines. Such actions included closure of the airspace to international travelers from countries that had been identified as prone to the disease and setting up of the presidential task force on COVID-19 with the Nigeria Centre for Disease Control (NCDC) where all the critical agencies were represented. However, the government's actions were inconsistent across the country.

In the heavily populated Muslim Kano State in the northern part of the country, instances of mass deaths arose shortly after COVID-19 was declared a pandemic. Without any scientific basis, the government claimed the deaths were caused by yellow fever, diabetes, hypertension, meningitis, and acute malaria (Campbell, 2020). Yet, most of the affected victims presented COVID-19-like symptoms such as fever, cough, breathing difficulties, and low oxygen saturation levels. As Muslims, their remains were quickly interred according to religious injunctions (Odukoya & Omeje, 2020). This underreporting of victims of the pandemic added to distrust of government, which was already perceived as not transparent with the information it provided to the public (Ohia et al., 2020).

Given the peculiarity of Nigeria and the challenge of inaccurate, incomplete, and invalid data collection and processing, and poor retrieval system, managing a public health emergency such as COVID-19 requires dynamic leadership and proactivity (Tijani et al., 2021). Other relevant issues in managing the pandemic included dealing with a brief strike action by medics during the peak period of the pandemic, creating a dedicated response team and operational response teams (public health and scientists, laws and regulations, and public relations and communications), establishing the facts and data quality, developing relevant internal and external messaging templates pre-crisis, during crisis, and post-crisis, identifying communication channels (digital, broadcast, and print), deciding on a preferred vendor list of needed materials, and outlining a digital communication plan of best practices and guidelines. As these challenges unfolded, the government did not communicate its actions early enough to the public through its normal channel, Twitter (Now, X). Instead, rumors on social media replaced what should have been an opportunity for the government to be transparent (Obi-Ani et al., 2020). Given that Nigeria is a very religious country, equally divided between Islam and Christianity, the government also missed opportunities to engage religious leaders, who are trusted and have large followings, to act as their proxies in amplifying their messaging through their social media and their weekly religious gatherings as early as possible.

Even as some Nigerians believed they were immune from COVID-19 infections because the humidity in the tropics acts as protection or that the pandemic was a conspiracy by national and foreign governments, the government's tepid response did little to assuage the attitudes about COVID-19 cures held by Nigerians. Social media was awash with conspiracy theories and herbal remedies to cure COVID-19 (Obi-Ani et al., 2020); yet, the government focused on tweeting the statistics of COVID-19 from various states of the federation. However, health officials were also on television to discuss some of the actions taken by the government, in what was considered a face-saving tactic. While average Nigerians could criticize the government's action on social media, they did not have the national platform of the traditional media to do so. However, when news broke that some government officials hoarded palliatives meant to be distributed to Nigerians who were experiencing hardship because of the lockdown, people stormed warehouses and carted off food, some of which had expired. Government officials went on television to deny hoarding, claiming that the palliatives were to be distributed during the second wave of COVID-19. It was clear that this was an illustration of Ting Toomey's (2005) face negotiation theory. The officials' communicative behavior, called "facework," was designed to restore their "face" or reputation, which had been tarnished because of the accusation of theft or hoarding of the palliatives (Sanni, 2020).

The lesson learned from the pandemic is that there is a need for coordinated and proactive planning at federal, state, and local government levels to create awareness and intensively work with the people given the high poverty level, high illiteracy, and cultural bias against Western medicine because of failed past campaigns, partially fueled by disinformation (Jegede, 2007). The NCDC partnered with the NNPC-IPPG team, an association of indigenous oil and gas-producing companies, to develop the #TakeResponsibility awareness campaign against the COVID-19 virus, translating the message into the major Nigerian languages and Pidgin English (a mixture of English and local language) and launching them on all media, including social media (Abujah, 2020). While this is commendable, one size does not fit all. What happens to the majority of people who do not belong to the major ethnic groups, who do not speak English or Pidgin English, or who do not own smartphones or television? How do they get the message? In asking the people to take responsibility, were there provisions for people who do not have access to soap or clean water, people who live in multigenerational family homes who cannot socially distance, and those who work in the informal sector economy? While the government asked the public through these campaigns to "take responsibility," top government officials were seen flouting the law (Akpeji & Omolaoye, 2020). Again, the government failed to be transparent, did not have the full buy-in of all its stakeholders, and did not make them feel safe. Additionally, the government did not take full advantage of the role that religion and ethnicity play in the lives of Nigerians. These important cultural markers are relevant to the framework for any kind of risk and crisis communication.

Officials' response to the media exposure of hoarded palliatives was clearly seen by the average Nigerian as face-saving tactic, adding to the mistrust of the government.

COVID-19: Success Factors

The WHO, in association with other international partners, developed a global roadmap with adjustments for socio-cultural, geographic, economic, and other factors to tackle the COVID-19 pandemic. The areas of concern were infection and isolation centers, personal protective equipment (PPE), patient care, personal health care, crisis standard care, law enforcement, operations, contact tracing, constant stakeholder engagement, and funding/giving guidance. As a result of COVID-19's novel status and the immediate global and devastating impact on the economy, sociopolitical life, well-being, employment, security, food security, and every aspect of human existence, even the doubters fell in line and followed the protocols rolled out by the WHO and the various national disease control agencies. The WHO protocols addressed all the areas of concern, including social distancing, use of PPE, contact tracing, care for patients, required preventive hygiene, and patient isolation (WHO, 2020). Again, it is important to note that many of these successes do not include the challenges described earlier.

Throughout the peak period of COVID-19, the government-led NCDC, in tandem with global partners, held weekly press briefings highlighting the status of the disease and updating data, government actions, and the expectations of the populace, given that there was a mandatory lockdown where movements were restricted for months. The briefings were standardized, clear, and consistent, and it made information exchanges better and more effective. As mentioned earlier, the NCDC also developed the #TakeResponsibilty campaign to encourage people to be aware of and take necessary actions for their own health (NCDC, 2020). The experience of the Ebola outbreak and the effective way it was managed gave health workers and even the government the impetus to confront the COVID-19 pandemic, despite the early missteps, using the guidelines of the WHO and best healthcare practices.

Case Study 2: The 2022 Catastrophic Flooding

In 2022, deadly floods inundated several states in Nigeria killing over 600 people and displacing millions more (Ominabo, 2022). Before the 2022 flooding disaster, Nigeria had flooding incidents of great magnitude in 2012 and 2018, with flooding in other years being less catastrophic. The 2022 floods, like the 2012 floods, were instigated by continuous torrential rainfall across the country that lasted many days and the release of excess water from the Lagdo Dam in northern Cameroon along the eastern border of Nigeria. Built in 1972 by China, the dam is Cameroon's major source of electricity generation and irrigation, and whenever it is full to capacity, excess water is released (Oloniniran, 2022). This release causes the waterway and its banks to be swamped, and everything along the axis is exposed to floods. When Cameroon was constructing the dam in 1980, Nigeria agreed to construct a twin dam across the border to receive any excess water from Lagdo, but the Nigerian portion of the project was never executed (McClean, 2022). Initially, there were no problems, but in the last two decades, it has become a tale of horrific periodic flooding. Unfortunately, the knowledge and warnings of flooding have not made the Nigerian government take definitive steps to prevent these floods, but officials would rather reactively manage the consequences by offering palliative measures for those affected and creating camps for internally displaced persons (IDPs) at great costs.

While the government announced humanitarian aid after the floods, it only used Twitter (Now, X) to warn its citizens about the potential impact of the release of water from the Lagdo Dam in the neighboring country of Cameroon and, subsequently, the extent of the flood damage. The government was criticized for its lack of transparency, consistency, accountability, and proportionality of aid disbursed (Adetayo, 2022). Without a clear crisis communication framework in which culture is embedded and the buy-in of the stakeholders is assured, evaluating the effectiveness of a crisis or disaster communication program becomes a challenge.

The government's response to the great floods of 2022 has been criticized variously. Obviously, lessons have not been learned from previous floods. Hofstede's power distance can be seen at play. Power distance describes how people within certain cultures view power relationships – superior/subordinate – and therefore are less likely to criticize those perceived as holding superior positions in the relationships. Even when that is done, it is often tepid. One such criticism, not from disaster victims, is that the government has not taken responsibility to educate its citizens on how to organize and respond to crisis, and the citizens have not demanded that the government do a better job of flood management (Shittu, 2022). The Nigerian National Emergency Agency (NEMA) was on record to have warned the citizens based on the forecast of the Nigerian Meteorological Agency (NiMET) that the year 2023 would experience serious flooding nationwide. Unfortunately, the lack of responsible governance and coordination at all levels, entrenched cultural beliefs (that nothing bad would happen), unheeded warnings, unethical environmental practices, and global warming, combined to create the tragedy that followed the flooding in 27 states of the federation and the 6 geopolitical zones. The central and south zones of the country suffered 662 deaths, more than 3,174 people were injured, and over 2.4 million displaced (Ogune, 2023). Additionally, road infrastructures were wiped out, vast areas of farmland were destroyed, massive disruption of economic activities occurred, food security was threatened, supply chains were disrupted, and over 200,000 homes were partly or wholly submerged (McClean, 2022). The Minister of Humanitarian Affairs, Sadiya Umar Farouq, asserted that the negligent and unethical role played by different branches of government at the state and local levels, as well as citizens' poor responses to government directives, led to the great losses caused by the floods (McClean, 2022). Alluding to the scale of the destructive floods across Nigeria, Matthias Schmale, the United Nations' humanitarian coordinator for the country, said it appeared that the government and its disaster management agencies failed to see the correlation between poor policy formulation, inappropriate communication to stakeholders, and the consequential destruction that accompany flooding (McClean, 2022).

The government showed a lack of care for its citizens in risk and crisis situations. Whenever there is disaster such as flooding, the three tiers of government, emergency agencies, and volunteers quickly mobilize resources for palliatives for victims. However, opaque distribution systems, inflated cost of materials purchased, diversion of relief materials, and outright falsification of data that do not correlate with the reality on ground have often led to victims not getting the help they need. Investigations over the corruption turn attention away from the help that should have been rendered to disaster victims and strategies on how to mitigate future occurrences.

Crisis communication strategies in Nigeria have not been as effective as they could be, because they are dependent on the three tiers of government that have not been particularly proactive in communicating with their disparate audiences or coordinating among themselves. The NEMA and NiMET that had adequate weather data on the impending flooding challenges of the year did not have the personnel and resources to take the necessary steps for a robust public communication campaign to inform the citizenry of the impending danger. At best, they issued statements to the effect that there would be flooding, but they failed to take any action in terms of technical and professional expertise as to what could be done by the citizenry to avoid being impacted by the floods. For example, there was no advanced planning for displaced persons, and no evacuation arrangements were made. Provisions were made for palliatives, but that was often not enough to encourage potential victims to take such decisions as moving away from the danger zones. Even with the abundance of the various communication channels of print, electronic, social media, traditional, and non-traditional, such as religious leaders and Nollywood (movie) stars, there was no evidence the government used any of them in 2022 to warn communities in harm's way.

However, in January 2023, the NEMA, having learned from the 2022 flooding, organized a one-week Strategic Executive Seminar for NEMA staff and stakeholders in collaboration with state governments and other partners to work toward long-term recovery of impacted communities across the nation and prevent future flooding crises. The outcome of the stakeholder's engagement resulted in both NiMET and NEMA independently issuing warnings about the forecast and the reality of the repeat of floods in 2023. It remains to be seen if the concerned government agencies at the federal, state, and local government levels will be proactive and prevent the unfortunate tragedies of 2022 from recurring. The Director-General of NiMeT, Prof. Mansur Bako Matazu, during the public release of the 2023 seasonal climate prediction (SCP), said, "Flood is a natural event and with the increase in climate change activities there will be more floods. This is because climate change is due to increasing temperatures. With increased temperature, the atmosphere will be more pregnant with more water vapour. That means more rain" (Emergency Digest, 2023). Conversely, NEMA believes that the interactions with stakeholders, especially the media, would lead to the development of holistic approaches to disaster and crisis management in Nigeria through public enlightenment, education, training, retraining, and simulation that would support existing senior officers in the discharge of their duties. NEMA recognizes the need to "re-examine some fundamentally new and more efficient approach to disaster management" (Ogune, 2023) given the experience of 2022.

The perennial flooding in Nigeria is also an indication of emerging risks from climate change and a dysfunctional government that seems unable to provide security for its citizenry or employment for the burgeoning youths. Nigeria is dealing with runaway inflation, food insecurity, poverty, and broken-down infrastructure. The Nigerian government operates at the federal, 36 states and 774 local government levels, in addition to the Federal Capital Territory. Whenever there is a flood, it disrupts communities, destroying livelihoods, and infrastructures and upends lives. There must be a framework that should guide the communication actions of the government during risk and crisis events. Attention must be paid to how communities perceive risk and the socio-economic, religious, and cultural factors that cause some Nigerians not to heed warnings of impending disasters until it is too late.

Several lessons can be learnt from these incidences described in the two cases examined.

- An improvement of governance structure that is responsive and responsible to the needs of its citizenry instead of one bogged down by inappropriate appointments, corruption, ineptitude, and unethical practices.
- Nigerians do not trust their government, and thus, are less likely to trust messages (even when useful) that are disseminated by the government. Government must work to build trust with its citizens.

- The multiplicity of government agencies that are charged to ensure that disasters such as floods are contained do not appear to coordinate their efforts. Cooperation in disaster management is essential.
- All the stakeholders ranging from government to the media are handicapped by general economic dislocation and are unable to fund their operations; hence, in disaster situations, communities and local organizations become the first respondents. Therefore, these groups must be trained on how to serve as partners with government agencies designated to serve them during crisis.
- There is a limited database that people can easily access to get needed information on the causes, impacts, and remedies of flooding or other disasters. Even when such databases exist, the average Nigerian would not be interested in looking for such information. It is the duty of the government or appropriate agencies to disseminate this information to them in a timely manner through channels they use and through spokespersons or messengers they trust.
- Understand the important role of religion and people's deep beliefs that God will save them from every disaster, so they will not evacuate when warned to do so.
- Understand the culture of fatalism that would lead people to believe that what is meant to happen will happen; therefore, they will not leave a danger zone until it is too late. Some might even see the disaster as "punishment" for not appeasing their "gods."
- Understand cultural and social factors that impact people's decision not to heed warnings that end up harming them (Okunola et al., 2023). Therefore, it is imperative to work with communities to harness elements of their cultural and social norms in designing effective and sustainable strategies for preparing or mitigating disasters.
- Understand the economic and social reasons for why some Nigerians are perpetual victims of crisis and disasters and work with them to mitigate those factors.

The proactive step taken by NEMA to have a stakeholders conversation in 2023 may indicate that the government and its agencies have begun to recognize the need to be proactive and have a strategic plan that is well laid out to ensure that flooding is contained and prevented from becoming a perennial national crisis. There is an urgent need to review Nigeria's emergency management policy that addresses well-thought-out programs of action, provision of adequate resources (human resources, funding, and equipment), and design of risk management strategies and to specify responsibilities for all stakeholders. Most importantly, there is a need to adapt a systemic approach to crisis and risk communication in Nigeria, one that is also attuned to the social, religious, and cultural needs of the population.

Conclusion

The case studies used as examples in this chapter indicate the need for more crisis communication research in the country. Most important, the cases suggest that if the Nigerian government expects to create a positive image among its people, it must trust Nigerians with accurate and timely information that would enable them to exercise their rights in making appropriate decisions in times of crises. That trust must be extended by listening to them and inviting them as partners in programs that directly affect them. The government must also ensure proper coordination among the various agencies charged with crisis management before a crisis occurs. Such coordination would aid in a seamless response to crisis.

Transparency, empathy, and recognition of the central role that religion, ethnicity, culture, and politics play in the lives of Nigerians are essential. Such an understanding is essential in crafting effective communication messages, disseminated by the right spokespersons, using all the channels that Nigerians prefer to receive information.

While the cases illustrate Hofstede's theory of cultural dimensions and Ting Toomey's face negotiation theory, they highlight the central role of culture in crisis communication in the Nigerian context. For instance, government officials blamed citizens for ignoring flood warnings and building codes, which they attributed to the catastrophic flooding of 2022. However, there were no mentions from officials of the lack of planning on their part, given that floods have hit many parts of the country before the devastating one of 2022. Nigerians watched as the government instituted strict COVID-19 lockdown, while images of government ministers at large gatherings emerged on social media and enraged many Nigerians. Government officials went on national television to justify the hoarding of palliatives meant for Nigerians during the lockdown, but the action was seen as a face-saving tactic. While elements of Hofstede's cultural dimension theory and Ting Toomey's face negotiation theory are illustrated in these two cases, one can argue that they don't hold firm in all circumstances in Nigeria. The government's response to the deadly #EndSars protest, the disputed 2023 presidential election, and the ongoing security issues, which have plagued the country for years, have made the average Nigerian more outspoken than before, challenging authority and recognizing and calling out dubious face-saving tactics adopted by government officials in the face of botched response to crisis. Such responses by the government do not engender confidence, nor do they indicate any semblance of crisis communication strategy that would minimize the negative perception by Nigerians and the international community that suggests that the Nigerian government lacks transparency.

Governments of most countries use research from tertiary institutions and think tanks to inform their decision-making process on public policy issues, including crisis management. Evidence-based solutions derived from research provide an understanding of complex crisis situations and how best to respond to them. Crisis communication must be an important component of a comprehensive crisis management plan and, by extension, a part of a strategic plan for any organization or country. Crisis communication should be part of the curriculum in tertiary institutions as a means of developing a body of research in the field. The research, however, must recognize the role of culture in ways that would engender effective crisis communication practice in Nigeria.

References

Abujah, R. (December 14, 2020). The fight against Covid-19: The journey so far. *The Pointer*. https://www.thepointeronlineng.com/article?artId=2752&art=The_Fight_Against_Covid-19:__The_Journey_So_Far

Adamu, A. A., & Mohamad, B. (2019). Developing a strategic model of internal crisis communication: Empirical evidence from Nigeria. *International Journal of Strategic Communication*. http://doi.org/10.1080/1553118X.2019.1629935

Adetayo, O. (October 25, 2022). Nigerian flood victims decry government's response to disaster. *Al Jazeera*. https://www.aljazeera.com/news/2022/10/25/nigerian-flood-victims-decry-governments-response-to-disaster

Akpeji, C & Omolaoye, S. (May 7, 2020). How politicians flout physical distancing order. *The Guardian*. https://guardian.ng/news/how-politicians-flout-physical-distancing-order/

Apuke, O. D., & Omar, B. (2022). Media and conflict reporting: A content analysis and victims assessment of media coverage of the conflict between farmers and herdsmen in Nigeria. *Secur J*, *35*, 345–366. https://doi.org/10.1057/s41284-020-00280

Nnamdi Azikiwe, President of Nigeria (2024). Britannica. https://www.britannica.com/biography/Nnamdi-Azikiwe

Boas, F. (1930). Anthropology. In E. R. A. Seligman, Ed., *Encyclopedia of the Social Sciences* (Vol. 2, pp. 73–110). New York: Macmillan.

Boin, A., Ekengren, M., & Rhinard, M. (2020). Hiding in plain sight: Conceptualizing the creeping crisis. *Risks, Hazards & Crisis in Public Policy*, *11*, 116–138. https://doi.org/10.1002/rhc3.12193

Campbell, J. (April 29, 2020). Tracking the spread of COVID-19 in Nigeria's largest northern city. *Council for Foreign Relations.* https://www.cfr.org/blog/tracking-spread-covid-19-nigerias-largest-northern-city

Coombs, W. T. (2022). *Ongoing Crisis Communication: Planning, Managing, and Responding* (6th ed.). Thousand Oaks, CA: Sage.

Dan-Nwafor, C. (2020). Nigeria's public health response to COVID-19 pandemic. January to May 2020. *Journal of Global Health, 10*(2), 020399. https://www.google.com/search?client=firefox-b-1-d&q=Nigeria%E2%80%99s+public+health+response+to+COVID-19+pandemic.+January+to+May+2020December.

Ehondor, B., & Unakalamba, C. (2021). Social media for crisis communication in the Coronavirus (COVID-19) outbreak: A study of NCDC. *Journal of Media Research, 14*(2), 45–69. http://doi.org/10.24193/jmr.40.3 July.

El-nafaty, Z. A. (February 8, 2023). The place of crisis communication in Nigeria. *PR Nigeria.* https://prnigeria.com/2023/02/08/the-place-crisis-communication/

Elsasser, J. (1996). Crises not so sudden after all. *Public Relations Tactics, 3*(3), 3.March.

Geertz, C. (1973). *The Interpretation of Cultures.* New York: Basic Books.

Gudykunst, W. B., & Kim, Y. Y. (1992). *Communicating with Strangers: An Approach to Intercultural Communication.* McGraw-Hill.

Gudykunst, W. B., & Kim, Y. Y. (2003). *Communicating with Strangers: An Approach to Intercultural Communication* (4th ed.). McGraw-Hill.

Ho, D. Y. (1976). On the concept of face. *American Journal of Sociology, 81*(4), 867–884.

Hofstede, G. (2011). Dimensionalizing cultures: The Hofstede model in context. *Online Readings in Psychology and Culture, 2*(1). https://doi.org/10.9707/2307-0919.1014

Ihekweazu, V., Ejibe, U., Kaduru, C. et al. (2022). Implementing an emergency risk communication campaign in response to the COVID-19 pandemic in Nigeria: Lessons learned. *BMJ Global Health, 7*, e008846. http://doi.org/10.1136/bmjgh-2022-008846

Jegede, A. S. (2007). What led to the Nigerian boycott of the polio vaccination campaign? *PLoS Med., 3*, e73. http://10.1371/journal.pmed.0040073. PMID: 17388657; PMCID: PMC1831725 March 4.

Lévi-Strauss, C. (1983). *Structural Anthropology II.* Chicago: University of Chicago Press.

McClean, R. (October 17, 2022). Deadly flooding in Nigeria displaces over a million people. *New York Times.* https://www.nytimes.com/2022/10/17/world/africa/nigeria-floods.html

Mead, M. (Ed.). (1937). *Cooperation and Competition Among Primitive Peoples* (p. 17). New York: McGraw Hill.

Minty, E. (2020). Culture in crisis communications. In P. Harris, A. Bitonti, C. S. Fleisher, & A. Skorkjær Binderkrantz, Eds., *The Palgrave Encyclopedia of Interest Groups, Lobbying and Public Affairs.* Cham: Palgrave Macmillan. https://doi.org/10.1007/978-3-030-13895-0_125-1

National Centre for Disease Control (NCDC) (February 28, 2020). *First case of corona virus disease confirmed in Nigeria.* https://ncdc.gov.ng/news/227/first-case-of-corona-virus-disease-confirmed-in-nigeria

Nigeria-Country Factsheet (2023). *CIA World Factbook.* https://www.cia.gov/the-world-factbook/countries/nigeria/factsheets/

Obi-Ani, N. A., Anikwenze, C., & Isiani, M. C. (2020). Social media and the Covid-19 pandemic: Observations from Nigeria. *Cogent Arts & Humanities, 7*, 1. http://doi.org/10.1080/23311983.2020.1799483

Odukoya, O. O., & Omeje, U. A. (2020). COVID-19 pandemic in Nigeria: A case study of Kano State – Challenges and lessons learned. *Journal of Clinical Science* [serial online] [cited 2023 Apr 5], *17*, 91–92. https://www.jcsjournal.org/text.asp?2020/17/4/91/298462

Ogune, M. (2023, January 24). Over 2 million Nigerians displaced by flood in 2022, says NEMA. *The Guardian.* https://guardian.ng/news/over-2-million-nigerians-displaced-by-flood-in-2022-says-nema/

Ohia, C., Bakarey, A. S., & Ahmad, T. (2020). COVID-19 and Nigeria: Putting the realities in context. *International Journal of Infectious Diseases., 95*, 279–281. https://doi.org/10.1016/j.ijid.2020.04.062 June.

Okunola, O. H., Simatele, M. D., & Daramola, O. (2023). To live or to die: Cultural and social factors influencing flood preparedness in Nigerian cities. *African Geographical Review.* http://doi.org/10.1080/19376812.2023.2184841

Oloniniran, G. (October 10, 2022). Flooding: What you must know about Lagdo dam. *The Punch Newspaper*. https://punchng.com/flooding-what-you-must-know-about-lagdo-dam/

Ominabo, W. D. (October 27, 2022). 2002 Flood: A tragedy foretold. *This Day Live*. https://www.thisdaylive.com/index.php/2022/10/27/2022-flood-a-tragedy-foretold/

Popoola, J. (April 6, 2021). 1 in 4 Nigerians don't trust the government to save their lives. And that's a problem. *The Guardian Newspaper*. https://guardian.ng/opinion/1-in-4-nigerians-dont-trust-the-government-to-save-their-lives-and-thats-a-problem/

Samovar, L. A., & Porter, R. E. (1994). *Intercultural Communication: A Reader*. Wadsworth.

Samovar, L. A., Porter, R. E., McDaniel, E. R., & Roy, C. S. (2014). *Intercultural Communication: A Reader* (14th ed.). Cengage Learning.

Sanni, K. (October 26, 2020). Governors deny hoarding CACOVID palliatives; explain storage of looted food items. *Premium Times*. https://www.premiumtimesng.com/news/headlines/423085-governors-deny-hoarding-cacovid-palliatives-explain-storage-of-looted-food-items.html

Shittu, J. (October 12, 2022). The real issues in Nigeria's recent floods. *Premium Times*. https://www.premiumtimesng.com/opinion/559100-the-real-issues-in-nigerias-recent-floods-by-jubril-shittu.html

Smith, G. (Ed.). (1966). *Communication and Culture*. New York: Holt, Rinehart, and Winston.

Soladoye, A. A., & Ojo, A. O. (2020). Impact of social media on police brutality awareness in Nigeria. *International Journal for Management and Modern Education*, *1*(1), 14–27.

Tijani, B., Jaiyeola, T., Oladejo, B., & Kassam, Z. (2021). Improving data integrity in public health: A case study of an outbreak management system in Nigeria. *Glob Health Sci Practice*, *9*(2), 226–233. http://doi.org/10.9745/GHSP-D-21-00240 November 29.

Ting-Toomey, S. (2005). The matrix of face: An updated face-negotiation theory. In W. B. Gudykunst, Ed., *Theorizing About Intercultural Communication* (pp. 71–92). Thousand Oaks, CA: Sage.

Tylor, E. B. (1871/1958). *Primitive Culture*. New York: Harper & Row.

Yunusa, I., Iloanusi, S., Mgbere, O., Iloanusi, N. R., Ajayi, A. I., & Essien, E. J. (2021). Public opinion regarding government response to COVID-19: Case study of a large commercial city in Nigeria. *Pan Afr Med J.*, *38*, 282. http://doi.org/10.11604/pamj.2021.38.282.26361. PMID: 34122709; PMCID: PMC8179992March 17.

Authors' Bio

Amiso M. George (PhD, Ohio University; Accredited in Public Relations (APR); Fellow of the Public Relations Society of America [PRSA]) is professor and the former chair of the Strategic Communication Department at Texas Christian University (TCU), Fort Worth, Texas. She is also chair of the Race and Reconciliation Initiative at TCU. A 2022 Fulbright Scholar at the American University of Central Asia, Bishkek, Kyrgyzstan, she was recognized as the PRSA *2017 Educator of the Year*. She also received the *2017 Bridge Award for Excellence in Strategic Communication Research* from the International Crisis and Risk Communication Conference (ICRCC). George was the director of the public relations program at the Reynolds School of Journalism, University of Nevada, Reno, where she developed and taught the first course in crisis communication. She was a visiting professor of strategic communication at the Swinburne University of Technology, Australia, in 2012, and an external examiner for public relations at Universiti Tunku Abdul Rahman in Malaysia, from 2015 to 2021, and she worked as a broadcast journalist and consultant for universities and nonprofit organizations in the United States, Nigeria, Australia, Malaysia, India, and Pakistan. She has been quoted in local and national media on crisis communication cases. George is co-editor of three books, including *Culture and Crisis Communication: Transboundary Cases from Nonwestern Societies* (Wiley, 2017) and *Crisis Communication: An International Perspective on Hits and Misses* (Routledge/Taylor Francis, 2012). She consults in risk and crisis communication. Contact her at a.george2@tcu.edu. Connect with her on LinkedIn. Follow her on Threads @amisog.

Wole Adamolekun (PhD, University of Abuja, Nigeria) is an associate professor of Mass Communication at Elizade University, Ilara-Mokin, Ondo State, Nigeria. He has over four decades of experience in corporate communications in the downstream petroleum oil sector, micro-credit administration, youth, and social development. While in top management positions, he actively and strategically participated in formulating and executing management policies alongside organizational objectives, communication, and research goals. His last appointment in the public service (2011–2013) was as the general manager (Operations and Corporate Services). In Petroleum Products Pricing Regulatory Agency (PPPRA), he functioned as the chief executive officer. He has authored three books in public relations, co-authored chapters in books, and published several scholarly articles in reputable journals in Nigeria and other countries. He is a Fellow of the Nigerian Institute of Public Relations (FNIPR), Fellow of the Nigerian Institute of Management (FNIM), Fellow of the African Public Relations Association (APRA), and former secretary-general and ranking council member of APRA. He is a senior member of the International Public Relations Association (IPRA); a member of the Chartered Institute of Public Relations (CIPR), United Kingdom; a member of the Public Relations Society of America (PRSA); a board member of the Commission for Public Relations Education (CPRE), United States; and a board member of the Global Alliance (GA) for Public Relations and Communication Management. At Elizade University, he is presently the interim head of the department of mass communication and interim director of academic planning. He has won several professional awards, and he is a global conference facilitator.

Crisis and Risk Communication Research in Asia

25

Crisis Communication Research in South Korea

Soo-Yeon Kim[1] and Sora Kim[2]
[1] College of Media, Arts, and Science, Sogang University in Seoul, Seoul, Korea
[2] School of Journalism and Communication, Chinese University of Hong Kong, Shatin, Hong Kong

Introduction

In 2020, during the first wave of the COVID-19 pandemic, many countries implemented either full or partial lockdowns. South Korea, however, managed the pandemic without imposing any lockdowns. The government implemented innovative measures; they promoted early detection through widespread screening facilities; they quickly contained outbreaks using quarantines and surveillance technology; when infections surged, the government facilitated the treatment of massive numbers of patients by restructuring the hospital system (Kim et al., 2021a). During the first wave, officials tested approximately 20,000 people each day (the highest number per capita in the world), drawing on various types of measures such as drive-through COVID-19 testing. The early detection measures yielded a low fatality rate (0.7%) much lower than the world's average of 3.4% (Bicker, 2020). The Korean government's risk and crisis communication efforts attracted praise from global media, which highlighted its transparency and its rapid communication of information (Ahrens, 2020).

The government's successful management of COVID-19 did not, however, translate into widespread trust from its citizens in its national institutions. In fact, of the 28 countries included in an Edelman Trust Survey in 2023 (Edelman, 2023), South Koreans ranked lowest in their trust toward their nation, businesses, and media. How such low levels of trust came to be is hard to pin down to any one factor? An observer should, however, consider the fact that in the last 30 years Korea has been home to a long string of human-made disasters. In 1994, for instance, 32 people died in the collapse of Seongsu Bridge in Seoul. In Seoul in 1995, 295 people perished in the Sampoong Department Store collapse. In 2014, the Sewol Ferry sank, killing 295 and nine others missing. On the night of October 29, 2022, the Halloween stampede occurred in Itaewon, Seoul, killing more than 150 people. This more recent case deeply shook Korean society, as it took place on one of central Seoul's typical streets. Known to be the most popular area in Korea for Halloween festivities, Itaewon received no special security preparations from the Yongsan district office, whose jurisdiction includes Itaewon. Ultimately, police arrested the head of the Yongsan district office and charged with professional negligence.

The Handbook of International Crisis and Risk Communication Research, Second Edition.
Edited by Andreas Schwarz, Matthew W. Seeger, and Sora Kim.

Given the level of public trust in Korean institutions, it is crucial that we better understand and learn from risk and crisis communication research. Indeed, this would seem vital to helping restore public trust and prevent future crises and missteps. Since the 2000s in South Korea, scholars have significantly increased their crisis and risk communication research (Kim, 2016). In fact, this field has become one of the key areas in the communication field, specifically in public relations (Bae et al., 2021). How a crisis or risk is defined in South Korea is no different from how it is defined elsewhere in the world. Crisis (위기 in Korean) refers to "a situation that arises unexpectedly and poses a significant threat to a variety of stakeholders" (Paek, 2022, p. xi). Risk (위험 in Korean) refers to "the potential hazard of harm to humans" (Paek, 2022, p. xii).

While both crisis and risk communications involve the communication process of imminent or potential negative situations or events, crisis communication research seems to focus more on organizational or institutional management aspects of communication efforts than risk communication research in Korea. Risk communication research, on the other hand, seems to focus more on public perspectives and their interactions with varying risks such as public perceptions of risks and public adoption of preventive measures (Palenchar, 2020; Reynolds & Seeger, 2005). This chapter discusses the current status of risk and crisis communication research in Korea and provides challenges and future directions.

State of Research in Risk and Crisis Communication in South Korea

Following Korea's exposure to the 2015 Middle East respiratory syndrome coronavirus (MERS) outbreak, risk communication research has grown significantly (Yang et al., 2021). However, there has been little research systematically reviewing existing risk communication research in Korea. Thus, to identify its trends, we conducted simple analyses of risk communication research. We used keywords like "risk" or "risk communication" to identify risk communication studies from five peer-reviewed journals – *Journal of Public Relations* (*JPR*), *Korean Journal of Journalism & Communication Studies (KJJCS)*, *Korean Journal of Advertising*, *Korean Journal of Advertising and Public Relations (KJAPR)*, and *Crisisonomy*. These journals were chosen because they were found to be the top five journals that most often published risk communication research according to prior research (Bae & Hu, 2020). A total of 103 journal articles published from 2005 to 2022 were found from this search. *Crisisonomy*, one of the most representative peer-reviewed journals in public administration in Korea, published the largest number of risk communication studies ($n = 36$, 35.0%), followed by *KJJCS* ($n = 30$, 29.1%) and *JPR* ($n = 19$, 18.4%). Twelve studies (11.7%) were published between 2005 and 2010, 31 studies (30.1%) were found between 2011 and 2015, 42 studies (41.0%) were published between 2016 and 2020, and 18 studies (17.6%) were found between 2021 and 2022. It clearly showed that more risk communication research has been published in recent years.

To find salient keywords in the Korean risk communication scholarship, a semantic network analysis was performed using English keywords. Of a total of 557 keywords, the most frequently used was risk perception ($n = 50$). *Risk perception* was followed by *risk communication* ($n = 39$), *risk behavior* ($n = 17$), *particulate matter* (PM; $n = 12$), *emotion* ($n = 10$), *food safety* ($n = 9$), *intention* ($n = 9$), *COVID-19* ($n = 8$), and others (e.g., *MERS*, *risk information seeking and processing* [*RISP*] *model*). The results revealed that risk communication research in Korea significantly focused on publics' risk perception and their behaviors, intentions, and emotions toward a risk. For a theoretical framework in risk communication research, researchers frequently used the RISP model (Griffin et al., 1999), which attempts to find the key factors for individuals to seek and process risk information in a systematic manner.

As to crisis communication research in Korea, it has expanded since the 2000s (Kim, 2016). Recently, several bibliometric studies have examined the development of crisis communication research in major Korean-language, peer-reviewed journals (e.g., Bae & Hu, 2020; Lee & Sohn, 2016; Lee & Sung, 2019). Bae et al. (2021) content-analyzed all articles (n =481) published from 1997 to 2020 in *JPR*, one of Korea's major peer-reviewed, public relations journal. They found that the most frequent topics were crisis, risk, and conflict-related (n = 30, 28.8%), indicating domestic public relations scholars' high interest in crisis and risk communication research.

Another study reviewed 51 crisis communication studies published between 2008 and 2018 in four advertising and public relations peer-reviewed journals (Lee & Sung, 2019). Their study found that the largest number of studies (n = 19, 37.3%) were published in *JPR*. As for popular study topics, the most frequent topic was factors determining effective crisis communication (n =12, 23.5%), followed by evaluation of crisis responses (n =11, 21.6%), crisis preparedness (n =6, 11.8%), social media in crisis management (n =6, 11.8%), and organizational reputation management (n =6, 11.8%). With regard to the methodology, experiments (n =33, 56.9%) were used most frequently, followed by surveys (n =9, 15.5%), in-depth interviews (n =4, 6.9%), mixed methods (n =4, 7.8%), and quantitative content analysis (n = 1, 1.7%). Compared to the earlier findings of Kim (2016), the popularity of the experimental method has continued and increased even more in Lee and Sung (2019).

With regard to study samples, the most popular was that of college students, though utilizing the general public is increasing (Lee & Sung, 2019). The most popular crisis communication theory in Korea over the years has been situational crisis communication theory (SCCT; Coombs, 2007). The second most popular was the attribution theory in Lee and Sung (2019), while it was image restoration theory (Benoit, 1997) in Kim (2016). Although the order differed between the second and the third, both studies identified the same three – SCCT, attribution theory, and image restoration theory – as the most popular theories.

Reflecting the dominance of SCCT in crisis communication scholarship, Bae and Hu (2020) reviewed 148 SCCT-based crisis studies published between 2002 and 2019 in 34 Korean journals. They found that the communication discipline covered the majority of the crisis studies (n = 105, 70.9%), followed by public policy (n = 13, 8.8%), physical education (n = 10, 6.8%), interdisciplinary approach (n =7, 4.7%), and business administration (n =4, 2.7%). As to the publication outlet, *JPR* had the largest number of crisis studies published (n =29, 18.9%), followed by *KJJCS* with 24 studies (16.2%). With regard to methodology, more than half of the studies (n =78, 52.7%) used an experiment, followed by quantitative content analysis (n =31, 20.9%), mixed methods (n = 18, 12.2%), survey (n = 14, 9.5%), and others (n =6, 4.1%). Of the crisis communication strategies being tested in SCCT-related research, the majority focused on testing the accommodative strategy (n =103, 69.6%), followed by denial and offensive strategies (n =86, 58.1%), minimization (n = 54, 36.5%), silence (n = 30, 20.3%), and others (n =10, 6.8%). Of the 275 hypotheses that appeared in 148 studies, 176 were supported (64.0%). Accordingly, this study interpreted that the predictive power of SCCT was 64.0%. Regarding the dependent variables being tested in SCCT-related research, the one used most was evaluation of corporation (n =70, 42.4%), followed by message acceptance (n =46, 27.9%), evaluation of brand (n =11, 6.7%), reputation (n = 10, 6.1%), crisis perception (n =8, 4.8%), and perception of crisis responsibility (n =8, 4.8%).

In the following sections, we further discuss risk and crisis communication research based on the three categories of its *primary* focus – institutional, media, and public perspectives. Research with institutional perspectives refers to studies that *primarily* investigate crisis and risk communication phenomena from institutional or organizational perspectives, focusing on managerial aspects of risk and crisis communication. Such studies include those describing how organizations deal with crisis or risk situations and testing the effectiveness of crisis communication strategies or risk messages; they also describe how to better protect organizational reputation in times of crisis and risks. Research with media perspectives indicates the studies that investigate the phenomena primarily from media perspectives such as how media frame crisis or risk and how media or reporters play roles in crisis and risk communication. Research with public perspectives refers to those primarily investigating how publics make sense of risks and crises and respond to the situations such as uncovering people's cognitive, affective, and behavioral response mechanisms in risks and crises. This categorization is not necessarily mutually exclusive. A good deal of research may entail more than one perspective, and in such cases, the classification is done based on its *primary* focus for easier classification.

Institutional Perspectives

Much of Korean crisis research has been conducted within corporate or organizational contexts, as opposed to individual or national contexts (Lee & Sohn, 2016). Lee and Sohn's (2016) meta-analysis of 43 crisis studies published between 2004 and 2015 showed that the majority ($n = 36$, 83.7%) investigated corporate or organizational crises. In studying organizational crises, however, less than 10% (9.8%) of researchers used samples of crisis managers. This may be attributed to the challenges associated with accessing and collecting crisis managers' perceptions on crisis communication due to the confidential nature of organizational information (Ha & Boynton, 2014). As a result, existing Korean research has often used news media as a source to discover organizational crisis communication practices (Kim, 2016). Because media reports were merely used as a source for collecting organizational perspectives, this chapter houses such research with institutional perspectives rather than media perspectives. Much prior research has used a content analysis method using newspaper articles about corporate crises (e.g., Ha, 2016a; Park & Ha, 2014). Most studies focused on categorizing organizational crisis communication practices by varying levels of crisis responsibilities (i.e., crisis type) rather than by different news media (e.g., Lee & Kim, 2023; Park & Ha, 2014). Park and Ha (2014) content-analyzed 89 corporate crises covered in the news media between 2011 and 2014 and examined the characteristics of corporate crises and crisis strategies used by companies applying Coombs' (2007) typologies. A majority of 87 corporate crises were categorized into either intentional (high responsibility) or accidental (moderate responsibility) crises – each 47.2%, respectively. Only 5.6% were categorized as victim crises (low responsibility). Of the adopted corporate response strategies, the one used most predominantly by in-crisis corporations was apology (58.3%), followed by silence (20.8%), minimization (15.0%), and denial (5.8%). Even in situations where their crisis responsibility was not high, Korean corporations most often used apology (the most accommodative strategy). Interestingly, the second most used strategy was a silence strategy (the most passive strategy).

The frequent adoption of the apology strategy by Korean corporations is often attributed to the publics' anti-*chaebol* sentiment. In Korea, a wide range of industries are dominated by family-owned conglomerates, referred to in Korean as *chaebols*. *Chaebols* flourish in areas such as the mobile phone market, food products, shopping malls, hospitals, and construction. While *chaebols* have contributed to the successful economic development of South Korea, they have faced criticism for the collusion of politics and business and its excessive accumulation of great wealth (Kim & Kim, 2022). The widespread anti-*chaebol* sentiment has made corporations more sensitive to media coverage and public opinion in crisis. This influenced Korean corporations' inclination to most frequently use an apology strategy regardless of crisis type or level of responsibility and to quickly cover up the negative news (Ha, 2016). Although organizational crisis responsibility is one of the most significant factors determining effective crisis communication strategies (Coombs, 2007), Korean corporations typically just apologize, even when they bear little responsibility.

Another stream of research adopting an institutional perspective is to test the effectiveness of crisis response strategies recommended by either SCCT or image restoration theory (e.g., Kim & Kim, 2016; Kwon & Kim, 2018). Given that SCCT has been the predominant theory in Korean crisis scholarship, it is to be expected that a majority of studies have focused on testing the effectiveness of varying crisis-response strategies. Prior research examining the consequences and effectiveness of the crisis-response strategies in the context of Korea generally supported the recommendations of crisis communication theories such as SCCT (Coombs, 2007) and image repair theory (Benoit, 1997). However, a line of research has consistently identified Korea's unique results, which the existing theories cannot explain (Ha, 2019). For example, the findings of Lee and Choi (2020) regarding the effectiveness of apologies in improving public attitude toward an organization – compared to defensive communication strategies – were inconsistent with what SCCT suggested. Korean corporations tend to use the apology strategy most often without considering crisis type or their own organizational characteristics (Ha, 2019). Korean publics have remained persistent in their preference of a sincere apology to other crisis communication strategies. Such persistence is mainly influenced by the country's collectivistic culture and anti-conglomerate sentiment. As a result, organizations often see the apology strategy as a one-size-fits-all solution; they use it uniformly and habitually. This is likely a unique characteristic of Korean crisis communication.

Media Perspectives

Media have played important roles in risk communication research in Korea, whereas there is relatively little research with media perspectives in crisis communication research. A great deal of risk communication research has investigated media framing and news coverage of various risks including PM (e.g., Choi & Choi, 2021) and Ebola virus (e.g., Song & Cho, 2015). Song and Cho (2015) content-analyzed the news reports of Ebola virus on domestic broadcasting media for a year (2014–2015). Of a total of 349 reports, one of the major news channels, YTN, reported the largest number of related news (n =96, 27.5%), followed by JTBC (n =52, 14.8%), MBN (n =44, 12.6%), KBS (n =42, 12%), SBS (n =40, 11.5%), and MBC (n =38, 10.9%). The most used frame was the risk frame (n = 133, 38.1%), followed by policy frame (n =60, 17.2%), medical frame (n =39, 11.2%), and social frame (n =38, 10.1%). Their study emphasized that Korean news media should be careful in delivering the news about risk so as to appear neutral and not arouse too much public anxiety.

In 2021, according to the Korea Press Foundation (2021), the five most popular social media channels were KakaoTalk (a Korean mobile messenger app; 97.2%), YouTube (86.5%), Naver Cafe (70.0%), Instagram (58.5%), and Band (a Korean mobile community app; 53.6%). In particular, domestic scholars have studied the use of YouTube as a source of risk communication (e.g., Choi & Choi, 2021; Chung, 2021), reflecting the widespread use of the platform across all generations. Choi and Choi (2021) compared how the traditional news media – online newspapers and TV news – reported news related to PM differently from YouTube videos for the period between 2010 and 2020. Both traditional and social media channels were similar in terms of delivering content on the causes and health risks of PM. However, compared to traditional news media, YouTube channels tend to concentrate more on personal life issues (e.g., air purifier filters) and deal with more diverse policy issues (e.g., Special Act on the Reduction and Management of Fine Dust). Chung (2021) analyzed YouTube videos (appearing between February and December 2020) to understand COVID-19 pandemic communication and public engagement on social media. Chung's sample included 823 YouTube videos produced by Korean government agencies – Ministry of Health and Welfare, Ministry of the Interior and Safety, and the Korea Disease Control and Preventive Agency (KDCA) – and public comments to the videos (n = 11,399) as well as 1088 YouTube videos uploaded by the general public about COVID-19 and public comments to them (n =89,816). In their communication on YouTube, Korean government agencies tend to focus on increasing public awareness of COVID-19 risks. Korean publics, on the other hand, used YouTube videos for sharing not only government-issued news information of COVID-19 but also sensational or negative news items about COVID-19. Chung's study empirically showed that the Korean government and the general public differed significantly in their risk communication on YouTube during the COVID-19 pandemic. It is noteworthy that the public used social media not only for sharing crisis and risk information from various sources but also for venting their negative emotions or reactions to crises and risks. This finding is not unique to Korea, as similar findings have been identified in existing crisis and risk literature in Western countries (e.g., Kim et al., 2021).

While the majority of existing crisis and risk communication research has focused on organizational crisis communication strategies or media framing in risk communication, some explanatory research has focused on examining contextual factors that could determine the relative impacts of media channels in crisis and risk communication. For instance, Lee and Choi (2020) found that in cases of low crisis responsibility such as a victim crisis (e.g., natural disasters or product tampering), newspaper articles were more effective at improving message acceptance than Instagram and Twitter messages. However, in cases of high responsibility such as a preventable crisis (e.g., organizational misdeeds or human-error accidents), Instagram and Twitter messages were more effective than newspaper articles at improving message acceptance. The authors interpreted this to mean that traditional media can be more effective at delivering fact-based news (e.g., natural disasters), while during times of a preventable crisis that requires immediate responses Twitter's high speed and interactive functions can be more effective.

Public Perspectives

Risk communication scholars in Korea have focused on investigating publics' perceptions of diverse risks including PM (e.g., Cha & Cho, 2019; Kim et al., 2016), food safety (e.g., Kim et al., 2020), COVID-19 (e.g., Chung, 2022; Oh & Kim, 2021), and nuclear power (e.g., Lim & Kim, 2017). The Korean public has been most concerned, notably, about the environmental issue of PM or fine dust. In 2018, according to Statistics Korea (2020), 82.5% of the public viewed PM as the biggest environmental problem. In 2020, it was still considered that way by 72.9% of the public. However, Kim et al. (2016) found that lay people perceived the PM risks including its concepts, causes, impacts, and solutions more superficially and inconsistently than experts did. To effectively communicate PM risks to the general public, the authors warned of information overload and stressed the importance of considering personal characteristics and social contexts.

Since COVID-19, the Korean public's perception of the biggest threat has changed dramatically. According to Statistics Korea (2020), the emergence of unknown diseases (32.8%) was seen as the biggest threat in 2020, a drastic increase from 2018 when it was 2.9%. The pandemic impacted the field of crisis and risk communication research enormously, leading to a surge of studies investigating COVID-19 (e.g., Cho & Kim, 2021; Chung, 2022; Oh & Kim, 2021). Cho and Kim (2021) investigated how Korean publics' age and political orientation affected their risk perceptions and evaluation of Korean government's response to COVID-19. Age had a negative effect on risk perception, with younger respondents (in their 20s) having a more negative view of COVID-19 compared to older respondents (in their 60s). Younger people's negative perception of COVID-19 could be due to the disruption of their social lives and activities such as attending school and social gatherings. Although their research found no impact of publics' political orientation on risk perceptions, Cho and Kim found that political orientation significantly impacted public evaluation of government responses to

COVID-19. Progressives and liberals tend to have a more positive view of government policies related to COVID-19 than their conservative counterparts. Up until May 2022, Korea's ruling party during the COVID-19 pandemic was Korea's Democratic Party.

When it comes to crisis communication research, there has, over the years, been increasing emphasis on public perspectives although institutional perspectives are still dominant. Most crisis communication studies investigating public perspectives are to some extent still related to managerial aspects of organizations (i.e., research with institutional perspectives) such as investigating public perceptions of corporations in crises (e.g., Kim & Kim, 2016), message acceptance (e.g., Lee & Choi, 2020), or evaluation of brand (e.g., Kwon & Kim, 2018) for the purpose of better management of crisis communication. Despite that, an observer can see an increased emphasis on public perspectives, expanding investigations to uncovering the mechanism of publics' affective, cognitive, and behavioral responses to varying crises. For example, Kim and Park (2021) attempted to uncover publics' negative emotions such as anger, disgust, and disappointment in crisis communication. Their study emphasized that what is crucial for reducing public disgust during corporate crises is an organization's sincere communication and responsiveness to societal needs. Their study suggested that Korean corporations should make extra efforts to manage their crisis communication effectively so as to avoid becoming the target of public animosity. Kim and Park argued that such efforts could be crucial to the survival of corporations in Korean society, as instances of public hatred against certain targets have become more frequent due to the popularity of social media and Internet communities.

Case Study: MERS-CoV Outbreak in 2015

In May 2015, doctors in South Korea confirmed the country's first case of MERS. The patient was a 68-year-old man who had traveled to Bahrain and returned to Korea on May 4, developed a fever on May 11, and was admitted to an emergency room on May 18. In response to the first case, the Korea Centers for Disease Control and Prevention (KCDC) released guideline information on the disease, including answers to frequently asked questions, to raise public awareness and help control the spread of the virus. According to the information, the spread of MERS occurs only when individuals have close contact such as sharing the same space with one who is infected. Health officials declared there was no possibility of being infected with MERS by visiting the same medical institution that a patient has already passed through (Chung, 2015). Yet, on May 28, another case was confirmed that undercut that declaration. That is, a new patient was infected by using the same ward after a MERS patient left despite having no close contact with the infected patient.

On May 31, the Minister of Health and Welfare, Moon Hyung-pyo, apologized to the public for causing concern and anxiety, misstating the contagiousness of the virus, and inaccurately reporting the first patient's contact groups (Lee, 2015). The failure to initially contain the first MERS patient resulted in an exponential increase in the infection. That time, the Korean CDC was also accused of withholding from the public information about the outbreak, which contributed to the spread of the disease and caused panic. The KCDC was also criticized for not effectively communicating with hospitals and other government agencies, which led to a lack of proper coordination among them (Ha, 2016).

The first death from MERS occurred on June 1. And the month of June saw the MERS virus spread with astonishing speed. The outbreak's epicenter became the Samsung Medical Center (SMC), a flagship healthcare institution of the Samsung Group. By June 3, the total number of quarantined people exceeded 1000. On June 7, the president of SMC announced that 890 patients and medical staff had possibly been exposed to MERS due to a patient in quarantine who was a source of virus infection (Ock, 2015). On June 14, SMC acknowledged that it had failed to deal with the MERS outbreak and decided to partially close the center for better crisis containment (Jeon & Im, 2015). By June 20, the number of confirmed cases had reached 166, with 25 dead. It was not until June 23 that Samsung Electronics Vice Chairman Lee Jae-yong[1] issued a full apology for SMC's response. Mr. Lee promised that Samsung Group would take steps to improve its crisis management capabilities. Although SMC has its own management team and leadership structure that is separate from Samsung Electronics, Vice Chairman Lee had been involved with the medical center. Due to the extensive negative impact of the SMC crisis on the entire Samsung brand as well as Korean society in general, Mr. Lee stepped in to become the official spokesperson and to show Samsung's group-wide commitment to the crisis. In cultures like South Korea, which are characterized by valuing a high power distance and high uncertainty avoidance, the top figure is desirable as a spokesperson during a crisis (Haruta & Hallahan, 2003). In July, health officials made progress in controlling the outbreak. Given the longest incubation period for the disease was 14 days, on July 28, the prime minister of South Korea declared an end to the outbreak. The final death toll was 38. The Korean government's initial handling of the MERS outbreak was criticized for slow decision-making about releasing information concerning the outbreak and the lack of transparency in announcing the names of hospitals that were treating MERS patients. The failure to act promptly resulted in the loss of an opportunity to control the situation and, worse, contributed to the quick spread of the virus (Jeon, 2016). While both the news media and the public were seeking accurate information about the situation, the Korean government was not well prepared to handle the situation (Jeon, 2016). The entire episode motivated the Korean government to learn from its mistakes. In September 2015, the Ministry of Health and Welfare announced its master plans for the national infectious disease prevention and management system; this included strengthening the disease surveillance system and expanding surge capacity (Yang et al., 2021). The MERS outbreak also exposed weaknesses in the government's risk communication management, serving as a learning tool that underscored the importance of preparedness and transparency in risk communication. After the failure of the MERS outbreak response, South Korea implemented 48 reforms and updated its pandemic preparedness (Ministry of Health and Welfare, 2015). When COVID-19 struck, it became evident that the Korean government had learned valuable lessons from its past mistakes. These lessons encompassed various aspects, including the speed and accuracy of testing capacity, effective tracing of infected patients, providing adequate treatment for patients, and maintaining transparent crisis communication.

Conclusion and Areas of Future Research

This chapter aims to bring together research on domestic crisis and risk communication in South Korea. The majority of crisis communication research seems to focus more on investigating institutional perspectives utilizing experimental methods. In Korea, the predominant crisis communication theory is SCCT. Hence, most crisis communication research with institutional perspectives has focused on testing the effectiveness of varying crisis-response strategies for different crisis types or on describing how organizations responded to varying crises. Even when focusing on public perspectives measuring public perceptions in crisis, most studies

[1] At the time of the crisis, Lee Jae-yong was the top figure in Samsung Electronics as Samsung Electronics' executive chairman, Lee Kun-hee (Jae-yong's father) was in a coma. Lee Jae-yong has been the executive chairman of Samsung Electronics since October 2022.

have paid attention to publics for the purpose of organizational reputation management or determining the effectiveness of institutional crisis strategies. That is, the majority of crisis communication research focuses on the interaction between "organization" and "publics" in times of crisis with more emphasis on institutional perspectives. Nevertheless, little research has adopted crisis managers' perspectives. There is a clear need for future research to gain institutional insights from crisis managers or practitioners. In addition, we call for future research to focus more on "publics" and their interaction with varying "crises" to uncover publics' unique cognitive, affective, and behavioral response mechanisms.

The majority of risk communication research, however, seems to focus on public perspectives such as publics' risk perceptions and behavior responses rather than how organizations manage varying risks. That is, the majority has emphasized the interaction between "publics" and varying "risks" rather than the interaction between "organizations" and "publics." Thus, we call for more research to investigate institutional perspectives such as how organizations can better deal with publics regarding risks. With regard to media perspectives, media framing has been more frequently used in risk communication than in crisis communication. In crisis communication research, media were merely used as the source to collect organizational crisis communication practice. Given this lack of emphasis on media and its interaction with publics, we call for more research to focus on the interaction between "media" and "publics," such as how, in times of crisis, publics utilize legacy and social media.

References

Ahrens, F. (March 16, 2020). In coronavirus crisis, South Korea shows how government PR is done. *PR Week.* https://www.prnewsonline.com/South+Korea-coronavirus-communication

Bae, J., & Hu, J. (2020). PR 이론의 국내발전 상황 진단 상황적 위기커뮤니케이션 논문의 내용 분석을 중심으로 [Evaluation for the development of PR theories in Korea: Content analysis of SCCT research]. *홍보학연구, 24*(6), 33–73. https://www.dbpia.co.kr/Journal/articleDetail?nodeId=NODE10631405

Bae, J., Hu, J., & Yang, S. (2021). 한국 PR 연구의 연구 경향: 『홍보학연구』를 중심으로 [Korean PR research trend: Based on *Journal of Public Relations Research*]. *홍보학연구, 25*(2), 1–34. https://www.dbpia.co.kr/Journal/articleDetail?nodeId=NODE10631416

Benoit, W. L. (1997). Image repair discourse and crisis communication. *Public Relations Review, 23*(2), 177–186. https://doi.org/10.1016/S0363-8111(97)90023-0

Bicker, L. (March 12, 2020). Coronavirus in South Korea: How 'trace, test and treat' may be saving lives. *BBC.* https://www.bbc.com/news/world-asia-51836898

Cha, Y., & Cho, J. (2019). 국내 인터넷 이용자의 미세먼지 위험 예방행위의도에 관한 사회인지접근의 RISP, HBM 적용모형 정보 노출, 주관적 규범, 부정적 감정, 위험 지각의 역할 [A social-cognitive model of applying RISP and HBM model for Korean internet users' behavioral intentions regarding fine-dust risk protection the role of information exposure, subjective norms, negative emotions, and risk perception]. *한국언론학보, 63*(6), 96–142. https://journal.comm.or.kr/xml/22243/22243.pdf

Cho, Y.-L., & Kim, S.-Y. (2021). 공중의 연령과 정치 성향이 코로나19 위험 인식, 위험 정보의 탐색 처리, 정부의 재난 대응 평가에 미치는 영향 [How public's age and political orientation affect COVID-19 risk perceptions, risk information seeking and processing, and evaluation of government's response to COVID-19?]. *한국언론학보, 65*(4), 106–147. http://b8323.nurimedia.co.kr/resource/global/mail/202109/65-4_03.pdf

Choi, H.-L., & Choi, J. (2021). 이슈생성주기에 따른 미세먼지 위험 담론 [The discourse of the fine dust risk according to the issue life cycle]. *광고PR실학연구, 14*(2), 161–192. http://www.earticle.net/Article.aspx?sn=395122

Chung, M. (May 25, 2015). Middle East Respiratory Syndrome (MERS) Q&A. *Financial News.* https://www.fnnews.com/news/201505251549446534

Chung, W. (2021). 코로나19 위험 커뮤니케이션 탐색 연구: 소셜 미디어 의존 이론을 응용한 정부와 일반인 유튜브 콘텐츠와 댓글 내 담론 분석 [The discourse analysis of the YouTube contents and their replies on the Covid-19 risk]. *홍보학연구*, *25*(2), 59–101. https://www.dbpia.co.kr/Journal/articleDetail?nodeId=NODE10631418

Chung, W. (2022). 위험정보 프로세싱(Processing) 다양화에 의한 코로나 예방 실천 행동 연구: 문제해결상황이론을 확장하여[A study of developing customized risk communication in the COVID-19 context by extending the situational theory of problem solving (STOPS)]. *한국광고홍보학보*, *24*(3), 69–103. https://www.dbpia.co.kr/Journal/articleDetail?nodeId=NODE11112934

Coombs, W. T. (2007). *Ongoing Crisis Communication: Planning, Managing, and Responding* (2nd ed.). SAGE.

Edelman. (2023). *Edelman Trust Barometer 2023: Global Report.* https://www.edelman.com/trust/2023/trust-barometer

Griffin, R. J., Dunwoody, S., & Neuwirth, K. (1999). Proposed model of the relationship of risk information seeking and processing to the development of preventive behaviors. *Environmental Research*, *80*(2), S230–S245. https://doi: 10.1006/enrs.1998.3940

Ha, J.-H. (2016a). 기업 위기와 사과 전략 활용에 관한 분석 연구 위기 유형과 사과 시점을 중심으로 [A content analysis of the relations between crisis types and apology response strategies]. *광고연구*, *109*, 76–100. https://www.dbpia.co.kr/Journal/articleDetail?nodeId=NODE06717312

Ha, J.-H. (2019). 효과적 위기 커뮤니케이션을 위한 한국형 사과 전략 모델의 방향 탐색 연구 [A study on crisis-related apology strategies in South Korea]. *홍보학연구*, *23*(2), 1–33. http://www.earticle.net/Article.aspx?sn=354553

Ha, J. H., & Boynton, L. (2014). Has crisis communication been studied using an interdisciplinary approach? A 20-year content analysis of communication journals. *International Journal of Strategic Communication*, *8*, 29–44. https://doi.org/10.1080/1553118X.2013.850694

Ha, K. M. (2016b). A lesson learned from the MERS outbreak in South Korea in 2015. *Journal of Hospital Infection*, *92*(3), 232–234. https://doi: 10.1016/j.jhin.2015.10.004

Haruta, A., & Hallahan, K. (2003). Cultural issues in airline crisis communications: A Japan-US comparative study. *Asian Journal of Communication*, *13*(2), 122–150. https://doi.org/10.1080/01292980309364841

Jeon, J. & Im, I. (June 15, 2015). Samsung Medical Center to partially close, but is it too little too late? *Hankyoreh*. https://english.hani.co.kr/arti/english_edition/e_national/696000.html

Jeon, H. (2016). 메르스 위험 커뮤니케이션 분석: 심층 사례 연구 [An analysis of risk communication: A case study of MERS-CoV in Korea]. *Crisisonomy*, *12*(5), 143–155. https://www.earticle.net/Article/A276315

Kim, E. M., & Kim, N. Y. (2022). *Chaebol* and the political economy of South Korean development, 1945-present. In S. Lim, & J. P. Alsford, Eds., *Routledge Handbook of Contemporary South Korea* (pp. 99–117). Routledge. https://doi.org/10.4324/9781003026150

Kim, H., Choi, J., & Noh, G. Y. (2020). 식품안전 위험인식과 예방적 행동의도에 영향을 미치는 요인에 관한 탐색적 연구 [An exploratory study about the factors influencing risk perception and preventive behavioral intention of food safety]. *한국광고홍보학보*, *22*(2), 156–193. https://www.dbpia.co.kr/Journal/articleDetail?nodeId=NODE09333172

Kim, J.-H., An, J. A.-R., Oh, S. J., Oh, J., & Lee, J.-K. (March 5, 2021a). Emerging COVID-19 success story: South Korea learned the lessons of MERS. *Our World in Data*. https://ourworldindata.org/covid-exemplar-south-korea

Kim, S. (2016). Crisis communication research in South Korea. In A. Schwarz, M. W. Seeger, & C. Auer, Eds., *The Handbook of International Crisis Communication Research* (pp. 292–301). Wiley-Blackwell. https://doi.org/10.1002/9781118516812.ch27

Kim, S., Sung, K.-H., Ji, Y., Xing, C., & Qu, J. (2021b). Online firestorms in social media: Comparative research between China Weibo and USA Twitter. *Public Relations Review*, *47*(1), 102010. https://doi.org/10.1016/j.pubrev.2021.102010

Kim, S.-R., & Kim, S.-Y. (2016). 기업의 이슈소유권, 위기책임성, 위기커뮤니케이션이 공중의 기업에 대한 태도에 미치는 영향 [The effects of corporate issue ownership, crisis responsibility, and crisis communication on publics' attitudes towards a corporation]. *한국광고홍보학보*, *18*(4), 5–37. https://www.dbpia.co.kr/Journal/articleDetail?nodeId=NODE07045001

Kim, S.-Y., & Park, H. (2021). 기업 위기 관리 커뮤니케이션에서 공중의 신뢰 회복과 불신 강화 차원이 부정적 위기 감정에 미치는 영향 [Effects of constructs of repairing trust and strengthening distrust in crisis communication management on public's negative emotions in corporate crisis]. *광고PR실학연구*, *14*(2), 25–65. https://www.dbpia.co.kr/Journal/articleDetail?nodeId=NODE10659056

Kim, Y., Lee, H., Lee, H., & Jang, Y. (2016). 미세먼지 위험에 대한 전문가와 일반인의 인식차이와 커뮤니케이션 단서 탐색 [A study on differences between experts and lay people about risk perceptions toward particular matter]. *커뮤니케이션 이론*, *12*(1), 53–117. https://www.dbpia.co.kr/Journal/articleDetail?nodeId=NODE06639071

Korea Press Foundation (2021). *Social media users in Korea 2021*. https://www.kpf.or.kr/front/board/boardContentsView.do?board_id=246&contents_id=62666fac70c2463c879c3a34fc12b364

Kwon, J.-H., & Kim, S.-Y. (2018). 기업 위기 커뮤니케이션의 전략과 그 전략의 활용 시점이 기업의 고객기반 브랜드자산 및 부정적 조직-공중 관계싱에 미시는 영향 [The effects of crisis communication strategy and timeliness on a corporation's brand equity and negative dimensions of organization-public relationships]. *한국언론학보*, *62*(1), 165–198. https://www.dbpia.co.kr/journal/articleDetail?nodeId=NODE07369604

Lee, J., & Choi, Y. (2020). 지방자치단체 위기 대응에 있어 위기 책임성이 메시지 수용도와 지방자치단체 신뢰도에 미치는 영향 [The impact of crisis responsibility on message acceptance and the trust of local governments]. *홍보학연구*, *24*(5), 66–104. https://www.dbpia.co.kr/Journal/articleDetail?nodeId=NODE10631403

Lee, H. (May 31, 2015). Moon Hyung-pyo "Focusing on national capabilities to prevent the 3rd infection of MERS." *Money Today*. https://news.mt.co.kr/mtview.php?no=2015053111375486912&outlink=1&ref=https%3A%2F%2Fsearch.naver.com

Lee, H.-O., & Sohn, Y. (2016). 국내 위기관리 커뮤니케이션 연구에 대한 메타분석 [A meta-analytic review of crisis communication research in Korea]. *홍보학연구*, *20*(3), 139–172. http://www.earticle.net/Article.aspx?sn=285510

Lee, J., & Sung, M. (2019). *국내 위기관리PR분야 연구 현황에 대한 분석과 고찰 [Status of Crisis Communication Research in Korean Public Relations]* [Paper presentation]. Seoul, Korea: Korean Academic Society for Public Relations Annual Meeting in Spring.May 31.

Lee, Y., & Kim, S. (2023). 신문 기사를 통해 나타난 종교조직의 위기 유형과 대응 전략 : 불교, 천주교, 개신교를 중심으로 [Crisis types and crisis response strategies in religious organizations revealed through newspaper articles]. *한국광고홍보학보*, *25*(1), 5–43. https://www.dbpia.co.kr/journal/articleDetail?nodeId=NODE11209381

Lim, C., & Kim, S. (2017). 원전주변 지역의 원자력 수용성과 신뢰회복 전략 비교 분석 [A comparative study on strategies for trust recovery and acceptance of nuclear power in nuclear power plant areas]. *Crisisonomy*, *13*(11), 133–148. https://www.dbpia.co.kr/Journal/articleDetail?nodeId=NODE09009449

Ministry of Health and Welfare. (September 1,2015). *Measures to reform national infection prevention and control system for the purpose of immediate response to emerging infectious diseases* [Press release]. https://www.mohw.go.kr/eng/nw/nw0101vw.jsp?PAR_MENU_ID=1007&MENU_ID=100701&page=1&CONT_SEQ=326060

Ock, H. (June 7, 2015). Top hospital new source of MERS outbreak. *The Korea Herald*. https://m.koreaherald.com/amp/view.php?ud=20150607000405

Oh, J., & Kim, Y. (2021). 위험 수치 제시 형식과 단위가 코로나 19 예방 행동 의도에 미치는 영향 [The impact of number formats and time frames on the intention to adopt COVID-19 preventive behaviors]. *광고학연구*, *32*(2), 7–39. https://www.dbpia.co.kr/Journal/articleDetail?nodeId=NODE10704924

Paek, H.-J. (2022). *공공 위기 소통 [Public Crisis Communication]*. Communication Books.

Palenchar, M. J. (2020). Historical trends of risk and crisis communication. In R. L. Heath, Ed., *Handbook of Risk and Crisis Communication* (pp. 31–52). Routledge. https://doi.org/10.4324/9781003070726

Park, H., & Ha, J. H. (2014). 위기대응 전략으로서의 사과와 활용 시점에 대한 양적 내용분석 연구: 최근 2년간 국내 기업의 위기 사례를 중심으로 [How have South Korean companies used apology response strategy in crisis situations for recent 3 years?]. *한국광고홍보학보*, *16*(3), 181–218. https://www.dbpia.co.kr/Journal/articleDetail?nodeId=NODE02499863

Reynolds, B., & Seeger, M. W. (2005). Crisis and emergency risk communication as an integrative model. *Journal of Health Communication*, *10*(1), 43–55. https://doi.org/10.1080/10810730590904571

Song, H. R., & Cho, H. M. (2015). 국내언론의 질병관련 위험보도에 관한 특성연구: 에볼라 바이러스에 대한 방송뉴스보도 분석을 중심으로 [Study on the characteristics of the domestic press' disease-related risk reports: Focusing on the news reports of Ebola virus]. *Crisisonomy, 11*(6), 45–68. https://www.dbpia.co.kr/Journal/articleDetail?nodeId=NODE09008779

Stratistics Korea (2020). *2020 Social survey.* http://kostat.go.kr/portal/eng/pressReleases/11/5/index.board?bmode=read&bSeq=&aSeq=372014&pageNo=1&rowNum=10&navCount=10&currPg=&searchInfo=srch&sTarget=title&sTxt=2018

Yang, T., Noh, J., Song, J., Cheong, H., & Kim, W. (2021). How lessons learned from the 2015 Middle East respiratory syndrome outbreak affected the response to coronavirus disease 2019 in the Republic of Korea. *The Korean Journal of Internal Medicine, 36*(2), 271–285. https://doi: 10.3904/kjim.2020.371

Author's Bio

Soo-Yeon Kim is a professor in the College of Media, Arts, and Science at Sogang University in Seoul, Korea. Her research interests are in corporate social responsibility, crisis communication, and public relations ethics. Her work has been published in top-tier journals, such as *Journal of Business Ethics, Journalism & Mass Communication Quarterly*, and *Journal of Mass Media Ethics.* She has received top research paper awards from international communication conferences (International Communication Association (ICA) and Association for Education in Journalism and Mass Communication (AEJMC)) four times.

Sora Kim is a professor in the School of Journalism and Communication and the director of the Corporate Communication MSc program at the Chinese University of Hong Kong. Her research focuses on crisis and corporate social responsibility (CSR) communication. She has published more than 130 publications including refereed international journal articles, conference papers, book chapters, and other publications. Her work has been published in top international journals across communication, business, management, and ethics. She has presented at leading international conferences, received six prestigious top research awards, and secured significant research funding from organizations such as the General Research Fund (GRF)/Research Grants Council (RGC), Toyota Foundation Research Grants, and the Arthur W. Page Center. Sora Kim has been recognized on the Top 2% Scientists list by Stanford University in the subfield of communication and media studies for five consecutive years, from 2020 to 2024.

26

Risk and Crisis Communication Research in Singapore

Augustine Pang, Jerena Ng, and Jason Shi-yang Lim
Lee Kong Chian School of Business, Singapore Management University, Singapore, Singapore

Introduction

Context of Risk and Crisis Communication Research in Singapore

Singapore, a city-state situated near the equator, is a developed business and financial hub (Pang & Yeo, 2012), and has enjoyed high economic growth and social achievements, strong development of infrastructure, low corruption, and strong investments (Lim et al., 2005). Singapore retains its position as the world's leading business environment and the best place for foreign companies to operate (Economist Intelligence Unit, 2023) even after the pandemic. Singapore's competitive and friendly policy toward foreign investments and trade, high technological readiness and start-up ecosystem, and maintenance of investor friendly tax regime (The World Bank, 2019) has catapulted it to the top position for the 15th consecutive year, above Canada and Denmark, according to Economist Intelligence Unit (Chong, 2023). Singapore, which boasts one of the world's highest Gross Domestic Product, is one of the four "Asian Tigers" (Han, 2023) along with Taiwan, Hong Kong, and South Korea. With a population of 5.64 million, Singapore is a multiethnic society consisting of 74.1% Chinese, 13.6% Malays, 9% Indians, and 3.3% comprising other races (Department of Statistics Singapore, 2023). A former British colony, English is its lingua franca even though it has a mixed linguistic, cultural, and religious heritage (Lim et al., 2005).

The media environment in Singapore is highly developed and regulated. The Newspaper and Printing Presses Act (NPPA) was enacted in 1974 (Singapore Statutes Online, 2023) to regulate print media in Singapore in terms of ownership and control of local newspaper companies. The ruling empowered the Government to curb foreign publications that did not report fairly and objectively (National Library Board, n.d.; Lai, 2021). In October 2019, the country introduced the Protection from Online Falsehoods and Manipulation Act (POFMA) to curb fake news ("Protection from Online Falsehoods," 2023). The Act seeks to deter the dissemination of electronic communication of false statements and enact measures to counteract the effects of such misleading communication to the public ("Protection from Online Falsehoods," 2023).

Two media conglomerates dominate the scene. Singapore Press Holdings (SPH) has the largest market share for print media, while MediaCorp, owned by Temasek Holdings, operates

The Handbook of International Crisis and Risk Communication Research, Second Edition.
Edited by Andreas Schwarz, Matthew W. Seeger, and Sora Kim.

most of the radio and local television stations in Singapore including CNA or *Channel NewsAsia* (Tandoc, 2022). *Asian Wall Street Journal, International Herald Tribune and the Economist, Reuters, CNBC Asia and the Dow Jones Group* are some international media with key offices in Singapore, and they complement the local media scene (Pang et al., 2014). The online news landscape is also evolving with local media start-up, mothership.sg, which started in 2014 and connects audiences with highly interactive multimedia content that encourages social sharing; it is one of the most accessed news websites, sharing top spot with *CNA* (Tandoc, 2022). In December 2021, SPH Limited was restructured and became not-for-profit SPH Media Trust (SMT) (Lim, 2022). This was to allow SPH Media to focus on its core competencies – to enhance digital capabilities, deliver high-quality journalism, and to serve as a credible and trusted source of local and international news (Choy, 2021; Ho, 2021). The Government has committed to fund SMT up to $180 million annually in 2022 for the next five years (Goh, 2022; Sun, 2023). This has shown the importance of the news media in nation-building and Singapore's continual adoption of the development press model in a changing media landscape (Lee & Willnat, 2009).

In recent years, Singapore has had crises involving a number of organizations. The Government has been proactive in ensuring these crises are managed well. In Edelman Trust Institute survey in November 2022, 76% of the respondents indicated that they trust the Singapore Government, whereas in some other countries, business leaders enjoyed higher trust than the government ("2023 Edelman Trust Barometer," 2023; Chew, 2016). This is an indicator that the trust level between the Government and citizens has remained strong, and has been the foundation for examining the state of risk and crisis communication research in Singapore.

The aim of this chapter is thus to capture the latest insights on the state of risk and crisis communication research, building on Pang's (2016) crisis communication research in Singapore. This chapter is divided into three sections. The first consolidates the risk and crisis communication research studies. The second discusses the state of research in risk and crisis communication. The third section builds on the prior sections and offers a case study on the research conducted. Last but not least, we offer some suggestions on how research can grow. It is hoped that this chapter can offer the latest comprehensive view of risk and crisis communication research in Singapore and provide an impetus for a more robust exploration for researchers and practitioners. Only studies that have been empirically researched, published, and presented are examined here as these are screened through the rigors of scholarly scrutiny.

As argued by Pang (2016), research on crisis communication in Singapore has been mostly event-based. To contextualize risk and crisis communication research, we categorize them into three themes based on the crisis types posited by the Situational Crisis Communication Theory (SCCT) (Coombs, 2023a). The three crisis clusters, defined by the type of crisis and level of crisis responsibility, in SCCT, are (1) Victim Cluster, (2) Accidental Cluster, and (3) Intentional Cluster (see Table 26.A.1). This section highlights some of the key research done.

Theme 1: Victim Cluster

This refers to crisis with weak attributions of crisis responsibility, and communicating risks in view of public interests should be the main focus of this crisis type. The organization suffers mild reputational threat. Such crises include *natural disasters, rumors, workplace violence,* and *product tampering/malevolence* (Coombs, 2023a).

Some of the research conducted included:

- SARS in 2003;
- Haze crisis in 2013;
- COVID-19 (2020 to present).

SARS hit Singapore in early March 2003 when a traveler who had returned from Hong Kong was later diagnosed with the disease ("Special Feature: Severe," 2003). Singapore – with China, Hong Kong, Canada, and Taiwan – joined the World Health Organization's (WHO) list of SARS-infected nations and was commended by the WHO for its "exemplary" crisis management (Khalik & Wong, 2003, p. 1). Mainstream media was the primary communication tool used by the Singapore Government in times of crises like SARS (Lee & Willnat, 2009). Menon and Goh (2005) argued that beyond the local media, other risk communication tools included dialogue by political leaders with community leaders, business groups, diplomats, religious groups, and trade associations. This was evident in the study conducted by Jin et al. (2006) on the communication of the Government to its various stakeholders during the outbreak of SARS. They found that the Government employed a "proactive advocacy style" (p. 97), making clear its stance on issues so that the stakeholders could follow, in particular setting directions for both quarantined stakeholders and the public who could help in containing the virus. The Government's strong leadership (Jin et al., 2006) won the support of all segments of stakeholders. Chong (2006) examined the blueprint used by health officials, and found five trust-building strategies: openness, participation, competence, care, and fairness. Another study by Jin et al. (2007) found that trust enabled the public to rally behind the Government

Another event examined in this category was the haze crisis in 2013, caused by illegal slash-and-burn farming in Indonesia (O'Callaghan & Fabi, 2013). In mid-June 2013, the haze issue escalated into a crisis when Singapore experienced its worst air quality level (Mayberry, 2019). Studies conducted included citizens' concerns over health issues caused by the haze and rising diplomatic tensions between Singapore and Indonesia (O'Callaghan & Fabi, 2013). Lin (2018) examined online opinion and found that mainstream media remained a credible source of information for citizens, helping to defuse public panic and shed light on what the Government was doing. Those who sought alternate views would transit to online media (Tandoc, 2022). Prasetyo et al.'s (2013) study on the social sensing of the haze crisis and its impact on Singaporeans also found that Government communication played a critical role.

Studies on COVID-19 will be presented in the next section.

Theme 2: Accidental Cluster

This cluster refers to crisis which has low level of attributions of crisis responsibility and the damage to the organization's reputation is moderate. The main focus is to address vulnerabilities arising from the crisis. The crisis types include challenges, technical-error accidents, and technical-error product harm (Coombs, 2023a).

Some of the research conducted included:

- Singapore Airlines' MI185 crash in 1997;
- Singapore Airlines' SQ006 crash in 2000;
- Mass recall of angiotensin II receptor blocker losartan by Singhealth in 2019.

The two air crashes involving the national carrier, Singapore Airlines (SIA), were examined together. On December 19, 1997, MI185 plunged into Palembang, Indonesia. All onboard perished ("104 Feared Dead," 1997). Although the cause of the crash remained unsolved, the airline's poor crisis communication was evident. Pang (2006) found dissatisfactions included stonewalling of information and delay in addressing compensation issues. The airline was accused of being too businesslike and cold. Even before the airline could find full closure to the MI185 crisis, a second disaster occurred on October 30, 2000, at Chiang Kai-shek International Airport in Taipei, Taiwan. During departure to Los Angeles, the plane crashed into a crane on the runway, killing 83 passengers and crew (Goh & Ng, 2000). This time, however, Pang (2006) found SIA well prepared. SIA took responsibility. The Geneva-based International Air Transport Association (IATA) lauded its good management of the crisis ("SIA's handling of crisis praised," 2000, p. 34).

Another crisis in this category involved the recall of angiotensin II receptor blocker (ARB) losartan, a blood pressure medication, by the Singhealth polyclinics (SHP). On March 28, 2019, the Singapore Health Sciences Authority (HSA) announced that nitrosamine impurities were above the acceptable levels in three brands of ARB's losartan products namely *Hyperten*, *Losagen*, and *Losartas* which led to a mass recall of the medication by SHP. One of the three largest public primary health institutions, SHP had prescribed *Losartas* (Ng et al., 2022) for over 32,000 patients. This crisis highlighted the vulnerability of the healthcare sector, especially polyclinics, which manage 40% of the non-communicable diseases in Singapore (Ng et al., 2022). The authors examined SHP's crisis management efforts. Within 14 days, SHP effectively completed the recall from 29,794 patients as it utilized communication formats like SMS and letters, set up a centralized call center, dedicated information counters for inquiries, and also developed collaterals on the tainted product for the public. These actions preserved the institution's reputation.

Theme 3: Intentional Cluster

This refers to crisis which has high levels of attributions of crisis responsibility and severe reputational threat as the organization is blamed and needs to communicate credibility to its stakeholders. In these crisis types, the organization has violated a law/regulation or has undertaken actions deemed inappropriate/unacceptable by stakeholders, and knowingly put them at risk. These crises include human-error accidents, human-error product harm, organizational misdeed with no injuries, organizational misdeed management misconduct, and organizational misdeed with injuries (Coombs, 2023a).

Some of the research conducted included:

- National Kidney Foundation financial scandal in 2005;
- SMRT train disruptions in 2011;
- SMRT train accident with casualties in 2016.

In July 2005, the chief executive officer of the National Kidney Foundation (NKF) T.T. Durai sued SPH for defamation for reporting that NKF had lacked accountability for their funds. Allegations of malpractice as well as financial mismanagement by NKF surfaced during the trial (Foo, 2013), resulting in widespread public outrage, and Government intervention. Lee et al. (2009) found high level of trust between the Government and the public. The Government's open and constant communication about their plan of action, transformation of the charity sector, and successful management of the crisis, helped resolve the crisis.

The other studies in this category involved SMRT Corporation Limited, a multi-modal public transport operator in Singapore. Pang and Appasamy (2019) argued that since its inception in 1987, SMRT had been recognized internationally for its service efficiency. However, since 2011, it had seen its reputation impacted when breakdowns led to disruptions and public inconvenience. SMRT's 24-year history of excellence in public transportation was disrupted (Lim, 2012) with two crises, one on December 15 and the other on December 17, 2011. More than 220,000 commuters were affected by the two events. Trains were stalled in tunnels and passengers had to walk out of them. Commuter anger was fueled by the late arrival of bridging bus services that were supposed to send them to their destinations. Many vented their frustrations on social media. Prime Minister Lee Hsien Loong ordered a Committee of Inquiry (COI), and in July 2012, a 358-page report was submitted.

The first breakdown was caused by a defective part in the tracks, which compromised other mechanical parts that hitherto went undetected, resulting in the second breakdown. The inquiry highlighted SMRT's poor management and lapses in system maintenance (Pang, 2013).

In March 2016, SMRT saw its worst accident involving two employees when they were hit by a train while carrying out track inspection (Tan, 2018). Investigations concluded that critical safety protocols were flouted due to staff negligence. The immediate response strategy of then-CEO Desmond Kuek was to activate the crisis management team, and address the various stakeholders (Pang & Appasamy, 2019), which were next-of-kin, employees, media, and commuters, and to prevent an information vacuum (Pang, 2013). After the accident, the CEO engaged the leadership team to review existing processes, and feedback/concerns from staff via group discussions. This allowed him to emphasize the importance of safety protocol compliance. It also helped in their recovery efforts (Pang & Appasamy, 2019).

What It All Means

Pang and Tan (2018) argued that in crises in Asian countries, three conditions often trigger government intervention:

- severity of crisis,
- organizational ability in handling crises,
- crisis history of organizations. This last condition influences governments' assessment of the second condition.

Pang and Tan (2018) argued, "Of the three conditions, severity of crises and organizational ability in handling crises affect the timing and the levels of the intervention adopted by Asian governments studied (Singapore, Japan, China, Taiwan and South Korea). If the crisis is less severe and organization is able to handle it with minimal support, the governments tend to adopt a supportive level of intervention within the same day. In cases of severe crises involving casualties and the organizations show a high level of incompetency in managing the situation, the Asian governments studied tend to adopt a directive level of intervention immediately" (p. 44).

In Singapore's case, building on Pang (2016), studies on crises often involved:

- Those with national interests and/or international impact,
- Those that attract extensive mainstream coverage and online conversations,
- Reputational damage and/or issues that reflect on competency/management.

State of Research in Risk and Crisis Communication in Singapore: Institutional Perspectives on COVID-19 Research

This section examines how Singapore manages crisis and risk communication from different institutional perspectives – at the state, public, community, and social level – drawing on insights from the research conducted on COVID-19.

When SARS swept through 29 countries, it infected 8,096 people and killed 774 (CDC, n.d.). Singapore recorded 33 deaths with 238 people reportedly infected (Ministry of Health, n.d.). With SARS, revenues from hotel, retail, and tourism industry fell, and the economy contracted by 4.2%, leading the Government to release a S$230-million relief package to help businesses recover (Chew, n.d.). In 2019, a new coronavirus, emerged from Wuhan, China, and Singapore recorded its first COVID-19 case in January 2020. To understand how Singapore managed the pandemic, we looked at research on risk and crisis communication in Singapore at three institutional levels: the state, healthcare, and media.

State as an Institution: Risk and Crisis Communication at the State Level

This category identifies state-level communication as an institution and forms the bedrock of a nation's risk and crisis plan, and studies at this level included the Government's approach in managing the pandemic as well as its responses.

The Singapore Government relied on its institutional memory accumulated from combatting SARS and adopted similar tactics for COVID-19 (Abdullah & Kim, 2020). They initiated a multi-ministry task force, protected its borders, set up temperature-sensing machines in public, instituted quarantines for those who had returned to Singapore, and implemented mass testing and contact tracing (Abdullah & Kim, 2020; Ambikapathy & Abdul Razak, 2022; Khondker, 2021). Ambikapathy and Abdul Razak (2022) examined how the state engaged the public through media briefings and public service advertisements on personal hygiene like washing hands, safe distancing, and observing community protocols.

Khondker (2021) argued that "highly rational bureaucracy" or "structural conditions," terms raised by Abdullah and Kim (2020), allowed the Government to shape public opinion and behaviors. Effective execution of their policies gave the Government "performance legitimacy," and accorded them some measure of success in the early phase of the pandemic (Khondker, 2021). Trust in Government enabled public compliance to the extent that some citizens even turned vigilantes to ensure others followed the rules (Abdullah & Kim, 2020).

These studies also identified fault lines. Abdullah and Kim (2020) contended that the Government failed to consider that the virus was asymptomatic, thus did not impose measures like lockdown immediately. They also ignored the fear that drove panic buying of masks, and used public service advertisements to remind the public that masks were not needed if they were well (Zhang, 2020). Abdullah and Kim (2020) argued that as the pandemic became more unpredictable, Singapore sought to balance "between total economic collapse and managing infection numbers" (p. 774). The authors also argued that Singapore was quick in adopting restrictive measures and embracing "an integrated learning approach" based on its past and current experiences (p. 775).

Healthcare as an Institution: Communicating at the Forefront of Risks

In a health pandemic, healthcare workers are the first line of defense, and as such healthcare institution forms the front and center of crisis management, and would form a critical focal point for crisis and emergency risk communication (CERC) research.

Ow Yong et al. (2020) examined the response plans within an acute hospital, Singapore General Hospital, and found that it was viewed with high trust, and staff appreciated the consistent updates on the evolving situation. The study, however, also identified issues, or "barriers" such as unclear safety instructions and allocation of resources such as "screening hours, and location", no "go-to person" to clarify rules, no "anonymous" channel for feedback and better communication, and low morale due to inadequate staff welfare and unsympathetic supervisors (p. 8). Ow Yong et al. (2020) proposed that for CERC to be effective, leaders should be trained to communicate and translate plans into actions, work with other healthcare institutions, and identify the best communication tool to reach different groups of audience (p. 10). The study also highlighted inadequate staff welfare and lack of empathy, which could lead to mental health issues – a global concern that could impact businesses (WHO, 2022).

Media as an Institution: Communicating and Bridging Divides

At the media level, the research examined how dangerous world beliefs can impact health-preventive behaviors, how mainstream media stand as a gatekeeper of misinformation and fake news, and how Singapore's management of COVID-19 is portrayed by other newspapers from other tourist destinations (Lwin et al., 2021; Thirumaran et al., 2021; Yeo et al., 2022).

While the media landscape is ever-evolving, the media remains critical in parsing messages and serving as a conduit for different government institutions and organizations, as research shows.

Yeo et al. (2022) argued that public health communicators should scan the environment for fake news and misinformation, be proactive, and not reactive in working with the media to deliver fact-driven information. Their study highlighted that even mainstream media was guilty of communicating danger and uncertainties. Lwin et al. (2021) asserted a "knowledge gap" allows "conspiracy theories, rumors, fakes news, and other types of misinformation" to perpetuate (p. 7). As such, the media needs to perform "high complexity rebuttals" to counter them. Yeo et al. (2022) contended that positive news reports help avoid "mass hysteria and panic" (p. 494). However, these studies also proffered that if media was not "critical" or was too compliant with Government bidding, there may not be enough "checks and balances" in governance (Lwin et al., 2021). Abdullah and Kim (2020) argued that had the media been critical, it could have questioned how the virus could spread, since it was asymptomatic.

What It All Means

These studies have shown that risks and crisis communications are critical to the survival of the state and the well-being of its people. Ho (2017) argued that disruptions, which include pandemics are "known knowns or unknown knowns" – variables that can be predicted by modern science. However, the future is often "volatile, uncertain, complex and ambiguous" (Ho, 2017), and as such, nations have to be nimble, learn and adapt their risk and crisis communication accordingly to manage evolving situations. Risk and crisis communication planners should listen for and identify blind spots that are often obfuscated by the sound and fury in an evolving situation and use them to counter every crisis event.

Case Study: Audience Perspective on COVID-19 Communication

As discussed in the previous section, studies on risk and crisis communication have examined how entities like the government, healthcare, and media communicated during COVID-19. This case study is arguably the first to examine the audience perspective, responding to the call to understand reactions to crisis responses (Coombs, 2010a) by understanding stakeholder emotions.

Warnings about the threat of COVID-19 came in early 2020. Singapore had a system of detecting threat levels, known as the Disease Outbreak Response System Condition (DORSCON). The threat levels – green, yellow, orange, and red – depend on the disease condition in other countries, the transmissibility of the disease, how likely will the disease arrive in Singapore, and the impact it will have on Singapore ("What do the different DORSCON levels mean," 2020). At the start, the threat level was yellow, meaning the disease was severe and spreading outside of Singapore but domestically was regarded as mild and under control. On February 7, DORSCON was raised to orange (meaning the disease was severe, spreading from person to person but not spread widely domestically). By then, people had become anxious and were panic-buying food and toilet paper (Pang, 2020). On April 3, 2020, the Government announced a nationwide partial lockdown, known as circuit breaker, that lasted till June 1, 2020. Other measures like restrictions on dining-in, social gatherings, and gathering of large groups in institutions, were introduced in phases, depending on the severity of infections, that lasted till May 2021.

Pang's (2021) study was analyzed through the theoretical lens of the Integrated Crisis Mapping model (ICM) developed by Jin et al. (2012). The model was expanded to understand stakeholders' emotions in a crisis so that organizations can target them in meaningful ways. Four emotions were identified based on Lazarus' (1991) appraisal of emotion – anger, fright, anxiety, and sadness, and these were integrated into the crisis types. For instance, in crises involving technological breakdown, stakeholders are likely to experience anger and sadness. In crises involving psychopathic acts, stakeholders are likely to experience fright and anger. In crises involving transport failure, stakeholders are likely to experience anger and sadness. In all crises, Jin et al. (2012) found anxiety the default emotion.

There was no crisis type of pandemic in the ICM model, so COVID-19 was argued to fall in the category of natural worldwide disaster not caused by organizational negligence. For crises involving natural disasters, stakeholders are likely to experience sadness, fright, and anger. Content analysis of the prestige media in Singapore, *The Straits Times* and *Channel NewsAsia*, from April 2020 to April 2021 (N = 126 articles) found that the four emotions posited in ICM were manifested. The announcements of tightened restrictions in the early stages of the crisis led to anger and anxiety (Tan & Kurohi, 2020). Reports of more strains led to anger. Fright and sadness were also evident when stakeholders experienced helplessness against an unseen virus and a global pandemic. In addition to the four emotions, fear, which was not posited in ICM, was evident. Stakeholders experienced fear when there was an increase in community infections and reports of more strains of the virus. Fear and anxiety at the prospect of potential exposure to the virus was palpable.

Singapore had been lauded for its "gold standard" of managing the virus (Pang, 2020). This study found that in a well-managed situation, stakeholders would still experience negative emotions (Ow Yong et al., 2020). Ministers Gan Kim Yong, Lawrence Wong, and Ong Ye Kung acknowledged the emotional upheavals stakeholders felt and wrote in *The Straits Times*, on June 24, 2021: "But it has been 18 months since the pandemic started, and our people are battle-weary. All are asking: When and how will the pandemic end?" (Gan et al., 2021). Such acknowledgments by crisis communicators in addressing audience perspective augur well in building stronger connections with stakeholders in times of crisis.

**This case study is an abridged version of a fuller article that will be published in the forthcoming book, Media and Crisis Communication (Routledge), edited by W. T. Coombs.*

Areas of Future Research

Based on the discussion thus far, as Pang (2016) argued, there appears to be a lack of systematic thread in risk and crisis communication research in Singapore. The recent studies found were more studies of cases, like COVID-19, than model and theory developing. There also remains a lack of large-scale studies. Moving forward, three areas of research are suggested. First, large-scale studies. The last large-scale study was conducted by Wu and Dai (2001) which examined the crisis preparedness of organizations in Singapore and Hong Kong. For Singapore, their survey of 200 organizations found that many (76%) claimed they had planned for crises, but a little more than half admitted their organizations did not have either a written crisis plan or a crisis management team, even though more than a third (35%) of organizations reported they had a crisis in the past five years. Interviews with practitioners from government, finance, education, consumer, retail, entertainment, and creative industries in 2013 to understand the level of social media crisis preparedness found that organizations in Singapore had increasingly recognized the importance of social media and have incorporated it into their operations. Results showed that few had monitoring teams and systems. "Though almost all interviewees felt it was a relevant concern, not all actually took the step further to have one" (Pang & David, 2017, p. 216). Though these were insightful, larger and more comprehensive studies need to be conducted.

Second, Singapore-centric research. Some have been discussed in the above sections. Others include Pang and Yeo's (2012) study, arguably the first study to assess the state of consultants in offering crisis consultancies in Singapore; and in related topics like Pang and Yeo's (2009) analysis of the state of public relations in Singapore; or Lwin and Pang's (2014) analysis of the history of public relations in Singapore. More is required to build a repository of studies on Singapore, be they in risk and crisis communication fields or other related studies on strategic communication.

Third, as Pang (2016) argued, more needs to be done to build theories that can be used to explain the context in Singapore. Coombs (2010b) argued that for crisis research to grow, more "formal research" (p. 35), like theory-building, ought to be conducted. These theories need not necessarily be new insights, but they can be adaptations of global theories into local contexts. Much of the studies conducted in Singapore have been examined through a Western theoretical lens. Increasingly, calls have been made by leading Asian scholars (Wang & Kuo, 2010) to indigenize these models to the Asian context to consider specific cultural influences in terms of historical, social, cultural, and subcultural contexts. To explore universality, Morris et al. (1999) proposed a four-part process: Stage 1 is the local application of extant theory as basic exploration; Stage 2 is a more advanced approach that involves cross-context comparative research to derive novel constructs or measures unique to a local phenomenon; Stage 3 is developing a novel context-specific theory to complement or supersede the extant theory; and Stage 4 is the integration of the above approaches toward a universal framework that integrates both local and global considerations. A nascent attempt was made in 2011 when Cheng et al. (2011) applied the ICM model to crises in Singapore. They found variances in crisis emotional responses, a further testament that cultural differences could evoke different emotional and cognitive responses to challenging situations (Kim, 2010; Wang, 2009). When more of such studies are conducted, they can collectively and incrementally aid in the development of frameworks that reflect the unique workings of this context.

This chapter has consolidated current risk and crisis communication research in Singapore and offers suggestions on how crisis research can move forward. The potential for research in this field remains bright. The authors hope that this chapter can provide the imprint for future studies to take place.

References

104 feared dead in SilkAir jet crash in Indonesia. (December 20, 1997). *The Straits Times*, p. 1.

Abdullah, W. J., & Kim, S. J. (2020). Singapore's Response to the COVID-19 Outbreak: A critical assessment. *The American Review of Public Administration*, *50*(6-7), 770–775. https://doi.org/10.1177/027507402094245

Ambikapathy, M., & Abdul Razak, N. A. (2022). A comparative analysis of the first phase of COVID-19 pandemic crisis management between Malaysia and Singapore. *Journal of Southeast Asian Studies*, *27*(1). https://doi.org/10.22452/jati.vol27no1.2

Cheng, L. C., Loh, Y., & Pang, A. (2011). Culture and emotion in crisis communication: Indigenization of the Integrated Crisis mapping (ICM) Model. *Proceedings of the 10th Conference on Corporate Communication*, pp. 222–239.

Chew, H. M. (January 19, 2016). Power shutdown at North-South, East-West lines: Past major train disruptions. *The Straits Times*. Retrieved April 29, 2023 from https://www.straitstimes.com/singapore/transport/power-shutdown-at-north-south-east-west-lines-past-major-train-disruptions#:~:text=When%3A%20Dec%2017%2C%202011&text=Prime%20Minister%20Lee%20Hsien%20Loong,seven%20hours%2C%20affecting%2094%2C000%20commuters

Chew, V. (n.d.) Severe acute respiratory syndrome (SARS) outbreak, 2003. *Singapore Infopedia*. https://eresources.nlb.gov.sg/infopedia/articles/SIP_1529_2009-06-03.html

Chong, C. (April 14, 2023). Singapore still leads the way as the world's best place to do business. *The Straits Times*. Retrieved April 17, 2023 from https://www.straitstimes.com/business/singapore-still-leads-the-way-as-the-world-s-best-place-to-do-business#:~:text=Singapore%20still%20leads%20the%20way% 20as%20the%20world's%20best%20place%20to%20do%20business,-Singapore%20had%20perfect&text=SINGAPORE%20%E2%80%93%20Singapore%20has%20retained%20its,to%20a%20leading%20market%20analyst

Chong, M. (2006). A crisis of epidemic proportions: What communication lessons can practitioners learn from the Singapore SARS crisis? *Public Relations Quarterly*, Spring, *51*(11), 6–11.

Choy, N. (December 1, 2021). SPH completes transfer of media business to CLG. *The Business Times*. Retrieved April 29, 2023 from https://www.businesstimes.com.sg/companies-markets/sph-completes-transfer-media-business-clg

Coombs, W. T. (2007). Protecting organization reputations during a crisis: The development and application of Situational Crisis Communication theory. *Corporate Reputation Review*, *10*(3), 163–176. https://doi.org/10.1057/palgrave.crr.1550049

Coombs, W. T. (2010a). Pursuing evidence-based crisis communication. In W. T. Coombs, & S. J. Holladay, Eds., *Handbook of Crisis Communication* (pp. 719–725). Malden, MA: Wiley-Blackwell.

Coombs, W. T. (2010b). Parameters for crisis communication. In W. T. Coombs, & S. J. Holladay, Eds., *Handbook of Crisis Communication* (pp. 17–53). Malden, MA: Wiley-Blackwell.

Coombs, W. T. (2023a). Situational Crisis Communication Theory (SCCT). *The Handbook of Crisis Communication*, 193–204. https://doi.org/10.1002/9781119678953.ch14

Coombs, W. T. (2023b). Ongoing crisis communication (6th ed). Thousand Oaks, CA: Sage.

Department of Statistics Singapore (2023). *Population dashboard*. Retrieved April 27, 2023 from https://www.singstat.gov.sg/find-data/search-by-theme/population/population-and-population-structure/visualising-data/population-dashboard

Economist Intelligence Unit (April 13, 2023). *Singapore retains its position as the world's best business environment for 15 consecutive years*. Retrieved April 17, 2023 from https://www.eiu.com/n/eius-business-environment-rankings/

Edelman.com (2023). *Edelman Trust Barometer Global Report*. Retrieved April 16, 2023 from https://www.edelman.com/sites/g/files/aatuss191/files/2023-01/2023%20Edelman%20Trust%20Barometer%20Global%20Report_Jan19.pdf?trk=organization_guest_main-feed-card_reshare_feed-article-content

Foo, T. (June 25, 2013). National Kidney Foundation financial scandal (2005). *Singapore Infopedia*. Retrieved May 3, 2023 from https://eresources.nlb.gov.sg/infopedia/articles/SIP_2013-07-01_120748.html

Gan, K. Y., Wong, L., Ong, Y. K. (June 24, 2021). Living normally, with Covid-19: Task force ministers on how S'pore is drawing road map for new normal. *The Straits Times*. https://www.straitstimes.com/opinion/living-normally-with-covid-19

Goh, S. N., & Ng, I. (November 2, 2000). SIA crash: 79 dead, no ready answers. *The Straits Times*, p. 1.

Goh, Y. H. (March 4, 2022). SPH Media Trust to get up to $180M a year in government funding for next five years. *The Straits Times*. Retrieved April 29, 2023 from https://www.straitstimes.com/singapore/politics/sph-media-trust-to-get-up-to-180m-a-year-in-government-funding-for-next-five-years

Han, D. (January 14, 2023). Economic growth in the East: Asian Tiger economies. *JSTOR Daily*. Retrieved April 27, 2023 from https://daily.jstor.org/economic-grrrowth-in-the-east-asian-tiger-economies/

Ho, G. (May 6, 2021). SPH to restructure media business into not-for-profit entity to support quality journalism. *The Straits Times*. Retrieved May 3, 2023 from https://www.straitstimes.com/singapore/sph-to-restructure-media-business-into-not-for-profit-entity

Ho, P. (April 17, 2017). *Hunting black swans and taming black elephants: Governance in a complex world, lecture I*. https://www.worldscientific.com/doi/pdf/10.1142/9789813231832_0001

Jin, Y., Pang, A., & Cameron, G. T. (2006). Strategic communication in crisis governance: Singapore's management of the SARS crisis. *Copenhagen Journal of Asian Studies*, *23*, 81–104.

Jin, Y., Pang, A., & Cameron, G. T. (2007). Different means to the same end. *Journal of International Communication*, *13*(1), 39–70. https://doi.org/10.1080/13216597.2007.9674707

Jin, Y., Pang, A., & Cameron, G. T. (2012). Toward a publics-driven, emotion-based conceptualization in crisis communication: Unearthing dominant emotions in multi-staged testing of the Integrated Crisis Mapping (ICM) model. *Journal of Public Relations Research*, *24*, 266–298. http://doi.org/10.1080/1062726X.2012.676747

Khalik, S. & Wong, S.M. (June 1, 2003). SARS-free, not to fine-tune crisis handling. *The Straits Times*.

Khondker, H. H. (2021). State and Covid-19 Response in the Asian Tiger Economies – Hong Kong, Taiwan and Singapore. *Comparative Sociology*, *20*(2021), 695–717. https://doi.org/10.1163/15691330-bja10043 October 25.

Kim, M. (2010). Intercultural communication in Asia: Current state and future prospects. *Asian Journal of Communication*, *20*(2), 166–180.

Lai, L. (May 11, 2021). Newspaper and printing presses act will apply to news entities after restructuring. *The Straits Times*. Retrieved April 17, 2023 from https://www.straitstimes.com/singapore/politics/newspaper-and-printing-presses-act-will-apply-to-news-entities-after

Lazarus, R. S. (1991). *Emotion and Adaption*. New York: Oxford University Press.

Lee, J. M. H., Lee, J. L. Z., & Pang, A. (2009). *Credibility Governance: Singapore Government's Management of Charity Scandal Arising from the National Kidney Foundation (NKF) Crisis*. New Delhi, India. AMIC.

Lee, T., & Willnat, L. (2009). Media management and political communication in Singapore. In *Political Communication in Asia* (pp. 93–111). Routledge Taylor & Francis Group. https://doi.org/10.4324/9780203885680

Lim, L. (January 10, 2012). MRT breakdowns 'exposed gaps' in crisis response. *The Straits Times*, p. A10.

Lim, S., Goh, J., & Sriramesh, K. (2005). Applicability of the generic principles of excellent public relations in a different cultural context: The case study of Singapore. *Journal of Public Relations Research*, *17*(4), 315–340. http://doi.org/10.1207/s1532754xjprr1704_1

Lim, Y. L. (May 14, 2022). Singapore Press Holdings officially delisted, Gerald Yong to take over as CEO from Ng Yat Chung. *The Straits Times*. Retrieved April 29, 2023 from https://www.straitstimes.com/singapore/singapore-press-holdings-officially-delisted-gerald-yong-to-take-over-as-ceo

Lin, T. T. (2018). Communicating haze crisis online: Comparing traditional media news and new media perspectives in Singapore. *Environmental Communication*, *13*(7), 864–878. https://doi.org/10.1080/17524032.2018.1488754

Lwin, M. O., & Pang, A. (2014). History of public relations in Singapore. In T. Watson, Ed., *Asian Perspectives on the Development of Public Relations: Other Voices* (pp. 105–113). Hampshire, England: Palgrave Pivot.

Lwin, M. O., Lee, S. Y., Panchapakesan, C., & Tandoc, E. (2021). Mainstream news media's role in public health communication during crises: Assessment of coverage and correction of Covid-19 misinformation. *Health Communication*, *38*(1), 160–168. https://doi.org/10.1080/10410236.2021.1937842

Mayberry, K. (October 7, 2019). Southeast Asia struggles to tackle haze despite long-term dangers. *Environment News Al Jazeera*. Retrieved April 29, 2023 from https://www.aljazeera.com/news/2019/10/7/southeast-asia-struggles-to-tackle-haze-despite-long-term-dangers

Menon, K. U., & Goh, K. T. (2005). Transparency and trust: Risk communications and the Singapore experience in managing SARS. *Journal of Communication Management*, *9*(4), 375–383. https://doi.org/10.1108/13632540510621614

Ministry of Health (n.d.). *Communicable disease surveillance in Singapore 2003*. https://www.moh.gov.sg/resources-statistics/reports/the-communicable-disease-surveillance-in-singapore-2003

Ministry of Health. (2003). Special feature: Severe acute respiratory syndrome (SARS). *Communicable diseases surveillance in Singapore 2003*. Retrieved April 29, 2023 from https://www.moh.gov.sg/docs/librariesprovider5/resources-statistics/reports/special_feature_sars.pdf

Morris, M. W., Leung, K., Ames, D., & Lickel, B. (1999). Views from inside and outside: Integrating emic and etic insights about culture and justice judgment. *Academy of Management Review*, *24*(4), 781–796.

National Library Board (n.d.). Newspaper and printing presses (Amendment) bill introduced. HistorySG an online resource guide. Retrieved May 2, 2023 from https://eresources.nlb.gov.sg/history/events/34dd0f05-00bc-49c2-9989-5c69e662a50b

Ng, L. P., Oka, P., Lim, C. J. F., Aau, W. K., Koh, E. Y. L., Ee, A. G. L., & Tan, N. C. (2022). Crisis management in the community mass recall of angiotensin II receptor blocker losartan due to nitrosamine impurities. *Proceedings of Singapore Healthcare*, *31*, 201010582211297. https://doi.org/10.1177/20101058221129715

O'Callaghan, J., & Fabi, R. (June 22, 2013). Indonesia fights fires, faces ire as smog blankets Singapore. *Reuters*. Retrieved April 29, 2023 from https://www.reuters.com/article/southeastasia-haze-idUKL2N0EY02820130622

Ow Yong, L. M., Xin, X., Wee, J. M. L., Poopalalingam, R., Kwek, K. Y. C., & Thumboo, J. (2020). Perception survey of crisis and emergency risk communication in an acute hospital in the management of Covid-19 pandemic in Singapore. *BMC Public Health*, *20*, 1919. https://doi.org/10.1186/s12889-020-10047-2

Pang, A. (2006). *Conflict positioning in crisis communication: Integrating contingency stance with image repair strategies.* Doctoral dissertation, University of Missouri-Columbia.

Pang, A. (2013). Dealing with external stakeholders during the crisis: Managing the information vacuum. *Handbook of Research on Crisis Leadership in Organizations*, 209–230. https://doi.org/10.4337/9781781006405.00020

Pang, A. (2016). Crisis communication research in Singapore. *Handbook of International Crisis Communication Research*, 283–291. https://doi.org/10.1002/9781118516812.ch26

Pang, A. (2020). Coping with course delivery in Singapore. *International Communication Research Journal*, *55*(1), 74–75.

Pang, A. (2021). Examining publics' emotion in Covid management and communication: Identifying behavioural manifestations from emotional reactions. *28th International Public Relations Research Symposium (BledCom) (Virtual)*

Pang, A., & Appasamy, L. (2019). *SMRT: Internal Crisis Leadership.* Centre for Management Practice: Singapore Management University. SMU-190007TN https://cmp.smu.edu.sg/case/3906

Pang, A., Nasrath, B., & Chong, A. (2014). Negotiating crisis in the social media environment: Evolution of crises online, gaining credibility offline. *Corporate Communications: An International Journal*, *19*(1), 96–118. http://doi.org/10.1108/CCIJ-09-2012-0064

Pang, A., & David, C. R. (2017). Cultural impediment or reflection of global phenomenon: State of social media crisis preparedness in Singapore. In A. George, & K. Kwansah-Aidoo, Eds., *Culture and Crisis Communication: Transboundary Cases from Nonwestern Perspectives* (pp. 209–224). Institute of Electrical and Electronic Engineers, John Wiley & Sons.

Pang, A., & Tan, P. (2018). Government intervention in corporate crises: An Asian Perspective. *Communication and Media in Asia Pacific*, *1*(1), 34–54.

Pang, A., & Yeo, S. L. (2009). Winning respect: Transformation to professionalization of public relations in Singapore. *Media Asia*, *36*(2), 96–103.

Pang, A., & Yeo, S. L. (2012). Examining the expertise, experience and expedience of crisis consultants in Singapore. *Public Relations Review*, *38*, 853–864. http://doi.org/10.1016/j.pubrev.2012.06.009

POFMA Office (March 10, 2023). Protection from online falsehoods and manipulation act. Retrieved March 27, 2023 from https://www.pofmaoffice.gov.sg/regulations/protection-from-online-falsehoods-and-manipulation-act/

Prasetyo, P. K., Gao, M., Lim, E.-P., & Scollon, C. N. (2013). Social sensing for urban crisis management: The case of Singapore haze. In *Social Informatics. SocInfo 2013. Lecture Notes in Computer Science* (Vol. 8238). Cham: Springer. https://doi.org/10.1007/978-3-319-03260-3_41

The Straits Times (November 7, 2000). SIA's handling of crisis praised. *The Straits Times*, p. 34.

Singapore Statutes Online (April 29, 2023). *Newspaper and Printing Presses Act 1974.* Retrieved April 29, 2023 from https://sso.agc.gov.sg/Act/NPPA1974

Sun, D. (February 23, 2023). SPH Media Trust Committee should be given ample time for thorough investigation: Josephine Teo. *The Straits Times.* Retrieved April 29, 2023 from https://www.straitstimes.com/singapore/politics/sph-media-trust-committee-should-be-given-ample-time-for-thorough-investigation-josephine-teo

Tan, T. M. (March 12, 2018). Engineer who led SMRT trainees onto tracks in 2016 fatal rail accident jailed for 4 weeks. *The Straits Times.* Retrieved April 30, 2023 from https://www.straitstimes.com/singapore/courts-crime/engineer-who-led-smrt-trainees-onto-track-in-2016-fatal-rail-accident-jailed

Tan, T., & Kurohi, R. (April 5, 2020). Anxiety and worry amid Covid-19 uncertainty. *The Straits Times.* https://www.straitstimes.com/singapore/anxiety-and-worry-amid-covid-19-uncertainty

Tandoc Jr, E. C. (June 15, 2022). *Singapore. Reuters Institute for the Study of Journalism.* Retrieved April 29, 2023 from https://reutersinstitute.politics.ox.ac.uk/digital-news-report/2022/singapore

Thirumaran, K., Mohammadi, Z., Pourabedin, Z., Azzali, S., & Sim, K. (2021). COVID-19 in Singapore and New Zealand: Newspaper portrayal, crisis management. *Tourism Management Perspectives*, *38*, 1–11. https://doi.org/10.1016/j.tmp.2021.100812

Wang, G. (2009). Editorial. *Asian Journal of Communication, 19*(4), 359–365.

Wang, G., & Kuo, E. (2010). The Asian communication debate: Culture-specificity, culture-generality, and beyond. *Asian Journal of Communication, 20*(2), 152–165. http://doi.org/10.1080/01292981003693344

World Bank (2019). *The World Bank in Singapore.* Retrieved April 27, 2023 from https://www.worldbank.org/en/country/singapore/overview

Gov.sg (February 6, 2020). *What do the different DORSCON levels mean.* Retrieved May 12, 2020 from https://www.gov.sg/article/what-do-the-different-dorscon-levels-mean

World Health Organization (June 16, 2022). *The impact of COVID-19 on mental health cannot be made light of.* https://www.who.int/news-room/feature-stories/detail/the-impact-of-covid-19-on-mental-health-cannot-be-made-light-of

Wu, W., & Dai, S. (2001). *A comparative study of crisis management planning in Singapore and Hong Kong.* Research Paper Series (National University of Singapore. Faculty of Business Administration), 2001–007. ScholarBank@NUS Repository.

Yeo, S. L., Phua, D. Y., & Hong, Y. Y. (2022). The effects of dangerous world beliefs on Covid-19 preventive behaviors in Singapore: The moderating role of public health communication. *International Journal of Strategic Communication, 16*(3), 485–498. https://doi.org/10.1080/1553118X.2022.2036742

Zhang, J., (April 16, 2020). How S'pore went from 'wear a mask only if you are sick' to 'it is a must to wear masks' in 3 months. *Mothership.* https://mothership.sg/2020/04/covid-19-mask-wearing-explainer-singapore/

26.A Appendix

Table 26.A.1 SCCT crisis types by crisis clusters.

Victim cluster: In these crisis types, the organization is also the victim.
(Weak attributions of crisis responsibility = Mild reputational threat)

Natural disaster: Acts of nature damage such as an earthquake damages the organization.
Rumor: False and damaging information about an organization is being circulated.
Workplace violence: Current or former employee attacks current employees onsite.
Product tampering/Malevolence: External agent causes damage to an organization.

Accidental cluster: In these crisis types, the organizational actions leading to the crisis were unintentional.
(Minimal attributions of crisis responsibility = Moderate reputational threat)

Challenges: Stakeholders claim an organization is operating in an inappropriate manner.
Technical-error accidents: A technology or equipment failure causes an industrial accident.
Technical-error product harm: A technology or equipment failure results in product recall.

Preventable cluster: In these crisis types, the organization knowingly placed people at risk, took inappropriate actions, or violated a law/regulation.
(Strong attributions of crisis responsibility = Severe reputational threat)

Human-error accidents: Human error causes an industrial accident.
Human-error product harm: Human error results in a product recall.
Organizational misdeed with no injuries: Stakeholders are deceived without injury.
Organizational misdeed management misconduct (Coombs, 2007): Violations of laws or regulations by management.
Organizational misdeed with injuries: Stakeholders are placed at risk by management and injuries occur.

Source: Coombs (2023b).

Author's Bio

Augustine Pang, PhD, is Professor of Communication Management (Practice) at the Lee Kong Chian School of Business, Singapore Management University. At SMU, he is appointed as Associate Dean (Partnerships and Engagement and a Member of the University Tribunal. Gus, as he is commonly known, graduated from the Missouri School of Journalism at the University of Missouri, the world's first and foremost journalism school in the United States, specializing in crisis communication and management. His research interests include crisis management, communication and leadership, image/reputation management and repair, media management, and communication management. Gus has published more than 130 refereed journal articles, book chapters, conference proceedings, and case studies. He has also won more than a dozen research awards. He is grateful for the international impact and recognition of his work. In 2021, he was awarded the Lee Kong Chian Fellowship at Singapore Management University. In 2016, he was awarded the coveted Kitty O. Locker Outstanding Researcher award for his body of work in crisis management and communication by the Association for Business Communication (United States). In 2015, he was inducted as a member of the prestigious Arthur W Page Society (United States). Since 2015, he has been an Honorary Fellow in Crisis and Media Communication at Hong Kong Polytechnic University. He had Visiting Professor appointments at Toyo University (Tokyo, Japan), Hong Kong Baptist University, University of Technology, Sydney, and University of Gothenburg. He is an Academic Core Member of the Crisis Communication Think Tank at the University of Georgia (United States).

Jerena Ng, MMC, works as a research assistant at Singapore Management University (SMU). She is a copy editor for an American blue-chip organization, a PR consultancy, and a book project involving an SMU professor in collaboration with a professor at the University of Colorado-Boulder. She has also done work for a professor at Hong Kong Baptist University. She has co-authored a book chapter for the Handbook of Digital Corporate Communication (in press, Edward Elgar Publishing). She also teaches Basic English to adult learners from foreign countries.

Jason Shi-yang Lim, MMC, is currently working at the Agency for Integrated Care in Singapore. The agency coordinates and supports efforts in integrating care for seniors and caregivers to achieve the best care outcomes for them to live well and age gracefully. He graduated from the RMIT University with a Bachelor of Communication (Mass Communication) with distinction and completed his Master of Mass Communication from the Nanyang Technological University Singapore. He has published a book chapter in Social Media and Crisis Communication (Second Edition) edited By Yan Jin and Lucinda Austin for research on Dark Social Influencer Engagement in Brand Communication with other co-authors in 2022.

27

Risk and Crisis Communication Research in China

Yingru Ji and Chang Wan
College of Media and International Culture, Zhejiang University, Hangzhou, China

Introduction

China's rapid modernization and the resulting societal transformations have spawned numerous risks and crises (Hu, 2016; Zeng & Dai, 2015). The interest in research on risk and crisis communication began to surge after the Severe Acute Respiratory Syndrome (SARS) outbreak in 2003 and matured further following significant events like the Wenchuan earthquake and the Sanlu Milk scandal in 2008. Notably, during the COVID-19 pandemic, the importance and impact of risk and crisis communication became even more pronounced. This chapter is dedicated to tracing the evolution of risk and crisis communication over the past two decades. By employing both bibliographic coupling analysis and content analysis, our study systematically reviews 447 articles published in communication journals listed in the Social Science Citation Index (SSCI). Through these analytical methods, this chapter explores how China's socio-cultural context influences risk and crisis communication, offering diverse perspectives for a comprehensive understanding of the field. Our ultimate goal is to provide valuable insights to guide future research in the domain of risk and crisis communication in China.

The Status of Risk and Crisis Communication in China

To delimit a comprehensive overview of research status, this chapter adopts a two-level methodological approach, incorporating both bibliographic coupling analysis and content analysis. This approach was chosen as it is deemed more suitable for thoroughly analyzing a research field (Maseda et al., 2021; Rialti et al., 2019). Moreover, it ensures better adherence to the principles of a systematic review, which emphasizes a replicable, systematic, and transparent protocol (Kraus et al., 2020). Articles were retrieved from the Social Science Citation Index (SSCI) journals by searching the keywords "China crisis communication" and "China risk communication" in the Web of Science (WOS) core collection database with a specific focus on the communication category. A total of 241 articles were yielded for crisis communication and 244 articles were acquired for risk communication. After eliminating duplicates, 447 articles were available for analysis. These articles showed an overall upward trend from 2001 to

The Handbook of International Crisis and Risk Communication Research, Second Edition.
Edited by Andreas Schwarz, Matthew W. Seeger, and Sora Kim.

2023 (refer to Figure 27.1). Notably, the number of articles saw a significant spike from 2020 to 2022, with 192 articles, constituting 42.95% of the total. Key outlets are detailed in Table 27.1.

We conducted a bibliographic coupling analysis using VOSviewer on the 447 articles, employing a minimum citation threshold of 10. This threshold is crucial for identifying significant articles while managing the document count effectively (Zupic & Čater, 2015). Bibliographic coupling analysis, which assesses research theme similarity through shared references, provides more precise insights into the current research frontier compared to co-citation and direct citation methods (Boyack & Klavans, 2010). It helps reveal central topics within the research field by identifying different clusters (Boyack & Klavans, 2010).

The bibliographic coupling analysis revealed eight clusters (see Figure 27.2), each representing a distinct theme. Clusters in close proximity indicate stronger conceptual connections, and node size within each cluster corresponds to document citation weights. Larger nodes signify more highly cited documents. Specifically, the first cluster (red) explored mechanisms

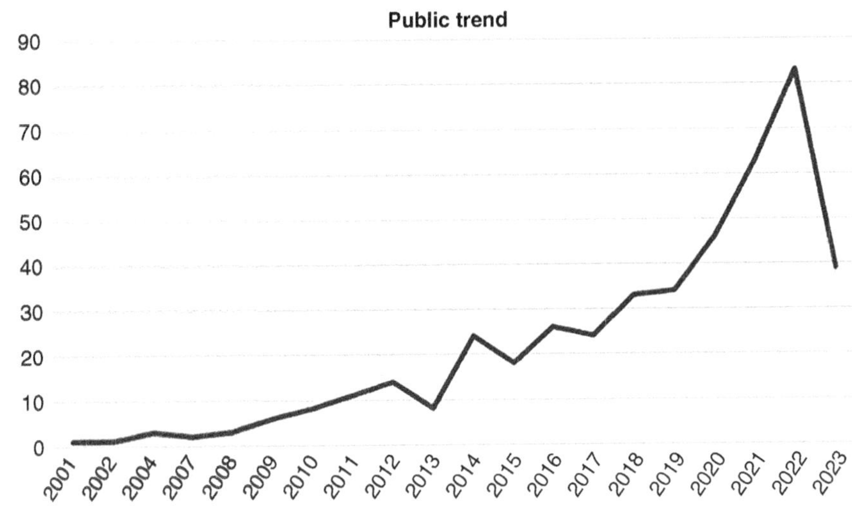

Figure 27.1 The publication trend of all articles. *Note.* The decline in the number of articles in 2023 may be attributed to the early September data collection this year.

Table 27.1 Key outlets of articles (number of articles above 10).

ID	*Journal*	*Number of articles*
1	Public Relations Review	53
2	Chinese Journal of Communication	44
3	Health Communication	43
4	International Journal of Communication	39
5	Asian Journal of Communication	27
6	Journal of Health Communication	24
7	Discourse & Communication	14
8	Environmental Communication: A Journal of Nature and Culture	11
9	Journalism & Mass Communication Quarterly	11
10	New Media & Society	11
11	Science Communication	11
12	Information, Communication & Society	10
13	International Communication Gazette	10
14	Journalism	10

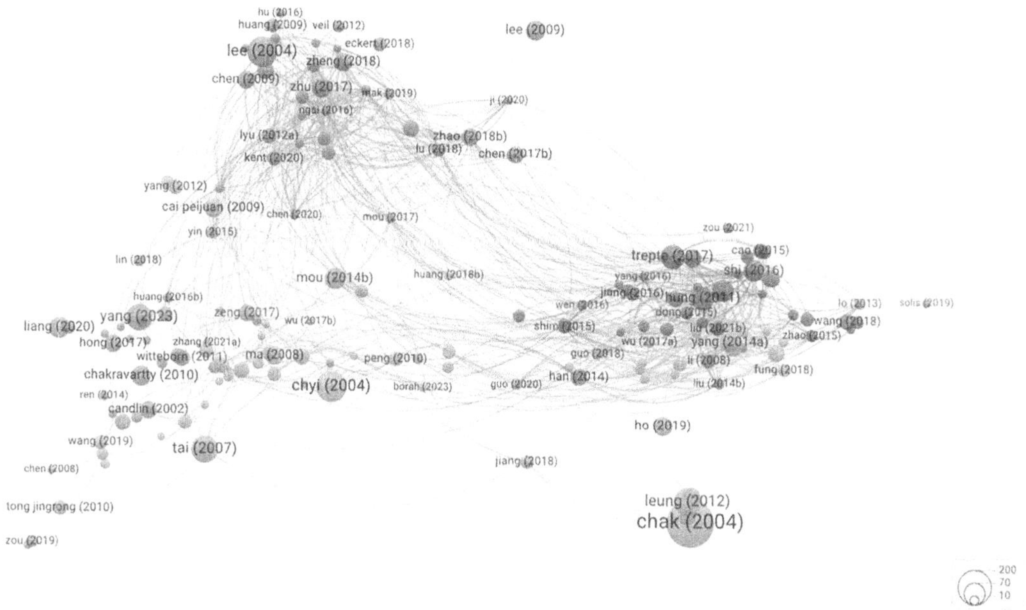

Figure 27.2 Bibliographic coupling network. *Source*: VOSviewer/Centre for Science and Technology Studies, Leiden University, The Netherlands.

underlying protective behavior in risk contexts. The second cluster (green) focused on risk communication from media perspectives, encompassing media use, news frames, and media topics. The third cluster (blue) delved into Chinese crisis communication in the social media era, including research status, response strategies, and narratives. The fourth cluster (yellow) examined how journalists and individuals portrayed risks in China. The fifth cluster (purple) investigated antecedents of information seeking in various risk events. The sixth cluster (cyan) studied the impact of media dependency on risk communication. The seventh cluster (orange) centered on risk communication on social media, including risk perceptions, information processing, and self-efficacy. The eighth cluster (brown) analyzed the role of China's government in crisis communication.

To gain in-depth cluster insights, we conducted content analysis to identify the most representative articles within each cluster, determined by their total link strength, reflecting shared cited references and research theme similarity (Hasumi & Chiu, 2022). We selected the top five articles per cluster based on total link strength, totaling 36 articles (including Clusters 7 and 8 with 4 and 2 articles, respectively). In addition, we added nine more articles to diversify research perspectives, particularly from institutional and media viewpoints, resulting in a total of 45 articles (see Table 27.2). Our codebook, informed by prior research (e.g., Boyd & Furgal, 2018; Cheng & Lee, 2019; Khamitov et al., 2016), guided the coding process, which was conducted by a single coder. An intercoder-reliability test involving a random 10% sample of five articles yielded high-reliability scores ranging from .97 to 1.00 (Krippendorff, 2004).

Among the 45 articles, one-third focused on crisis communication (n = 20), while the remaining articles examined risk communication (n = 25). Six studies included cross-cultural comparisons, with the United States being the most common country in comparative studies (n = 5). In terms of risk and crisis types, over a third of the articles focused on public health risks and crises (n = 15, 33.3%), including events like COVID-19, SARS, and H1N1. Other examined risk types included air pollution (n = 3, 6.7%), food safety (n = 4, 8.9%), and climate change (n = 2, 4.4%). Three studies (6.7%) explored internet-related risks, like internet

Table 27.2 Articles for Content Analysis.

Cluster	*Author and year*	*Article name*	*Total link strength*
1 (Red)	Liu and Yang (2020)	In the wake of scandals: How media use and social trust Influence risk perception and vaccination intention among Chinese parents	82
	Li (2018)	Media exposure, perceived efficacy, and protective behaviors in a public health emergency	71
	Zhang and Yang (2021)	Linking risk perception to breast cancer examination intention in China: Examining an adapted cognitive mediation model	71
	Zheng et al. (2022)	Linking online vaccine information seeking to vaccination intention in the context of the COVID-19 pandemic	52
	Liu et al. (2023)	Associations between COVID-19 information acquisition and vaccination intention: The roles of anticipated regret and collective responsibility	50
2 (Green)	Peng and Tang (2010)	Health content in Chinese newspapers	43
	Wirz et al. (2022)	Media systems and attention cycles: Volume and topics of news coverage on COVID-19 in the United States and China	40
	Mao (2014)	Cosmopolitanism and global risk: News framing of the Asian financial crisis and the European debt crisis	39
	Wang (2017)	Understanding climate change risk perceptions in China: Media use, personal experience, and cultural worldviews	38
	Duan and Takahashi (2017)	The two-way flow of news: A comparative study of American and Chinese newspaper coverage of Beijing's air pollution	37
	Gong and Firdaus (2022)	Is the pandemic a boon or a bane? News media coverage of COVID-19 in China Daily	23
3 (Blue)	Cheng and Lee (2019)	Online crisis communication in a post-truth Chinese society: Evidence from interdisciplinary literature	111
	Cheng (2020)	The social-mediated crisis communication research: Revisiting dialogue between organizations and publics in crises of China	100
	Cheng et al. (2020)	Corporate dialogue in crises of China: Examining dialogic strategies and communicative outcomes in a child abuse scandal	94
	Nagi and Jin (2016)	The effectiveness of crisis communication strategies on Sina Weibo in relation to Chinese publics' acceptance of these strategies	93
	Zhang et al. (2020)	Crisis collective memory making on social media: A case study of three Chinese crises on Weibo	88
	Zhu et al. (2017)	Social media and culture in crisis communication: McDonald's and KFC crises management in China	46
	Kim et al. (2016)	Self-mocking crisis strategy on social media: Focusing on Alibaba chairman Jack Ma in China	14
4 (Yellow)	Mou and Lin (2014)	Communicating food safety via the social media: The role of knowledge and emotions on risk perception and prevention	50
	Yin et al. (2015)	Social media and multinational corporations' corporate social responsibility in China: The case of ConocoPhillips oil spill incident	48
	Huang and Sun (2016)	Dynamic preference revelation and expression of personal frames: How Weibo is used in an anti-nuclear protest in China	29

	Mou (2014)	What can microblog exchanges tell us about food safety crises in China?	23
	Huan (2016)	Journalistic engagement patterns and power relations: Corpus evidence from Chinese and Australian hard news reporting.	23
5 (Purple)	Huang and Yang (2018)	Risk, affect, and policy support: Public perception of air pollution in China	150
	Li and Zheng (2022)	Online information seeking and disease prevention intent during COVID-19 Outbreak	132
	Yang et al. (2014)	A United States-China comparison of risk information–seeking intentions	128
	Yang and Liu (2021)	Information seeking and processing in the context of vaccine scandals	123
	Yang and Huang (2019)	Seeking for your own sake: Chinese citizens' motivations for information seeking about air pollution	118
	Tang and Zou (2021)	Health information consumption under COVID-19 lockdown: An interview study of residents of Hubei Province, China	28
6 (Cyan)	Lyu (2012)	How young Chinese depend on the media during public health crises? A comparative perspective	47
	Tai and Sun (2007)	Media dependencies in a changing media environment: The case of the 2003 SARS epidemic in China	32
	Hu and Zhang (2014)	Channel selection and knowledge acquisition during the 2009 Beijing H1N1 flu crisis: A media system dependency theory perspective	31
	Jiang et al. (2018)	Examining factors influencing Internet addiction and adolescent risk behaviors among excessive internet users	26
	Leung and Lee (2012)	The influences of information literacy, internet addiction and parenting styles on internet risks	16
7 (Orange)	Yang et al. (2016)	Risk perception of food safety issue on social media	81
	Han et al. (2014)	Self–Other Differences in H1N1 Flu Risk Perception in a Global Context: A Comparative Study Between the United States and China	59
	Lo et al. (2013)	Self-efficacy, information-processing strategies, and acquisition of health knowledge	38
	Solis and Wong (2019)	To meet or not to meet? Measuring motivations and risks as predictors of outcomes in the use of mobile dating applications in China	1
8 (Brown)	Ji and Kim (2020)	Crisis-induced public demand for regulatory intervention in the social media era: Examining the moderating roles of perceived government controllability and consumer collective efficacy	54
	Lee (2009)	How the Hong Kong government lost the public trust in SARS: Insights for government communication in a health crisis	1
Others	Li et al. (2022)	Unpacking government social media messaging strategies during the COVID-19 pandemic in China	
	Li et al. (2023)	Does the message frame promote people's willingness to vaccinate when they worry about side effects from the covid-19 vaccine? Evidence from an online survey experiment in China	
	Meadows et al. (2022)	Managing government legitimacy during the COVID-19 pandemic in China: a semantic network analysis of state-run media Sina Weibo posts	
	Ngai et al. (2023)	Exploring the relationship between trust-building strategies and public engagement on social media during the COVID-19 outbreak	
	Pang et al. (2018)	A broad stroke or different strokes for different folks? Examining the subtleties in crisis management approaches in state-owned enterprises and privately owned enterprises in China	

Note. The selection of the top five articles per cluster was based on their total link strength. Furthermore, an additional nine articles were included to provide a diversified range of research perspectives, specifically from institutional and media perspectives. As a result, a total of 45 articles were included in the analysis.

addiction and online dating, while individual risk issues, such as breast cancer, were mentioned once (2.2%). Additionally, six crises (13.3%) resulted from management misconduct, with paracrisis, economic crisis, and technological crisis each being investigated once. Regarding the media setting, approximately half of the research ($n = 20$, 44.4%) was conducted within the realm of digital media. Around one-third of the studies ($n = 12$, 26.7%) were situated in the context of traditional media, specifically newspapers. The remaining articles ($n = 12$, 26.7%) spanned both traditional and digital media as their research context. Only a single article (2.2%) did not specify any particular media context.

Concerning the methodological approaches, the majority of articles utilized quantitative methods, with 19 (42.2%) relying on surveys and 9 (20.0%) employing content analysis. Qualitative methods were used in only six studies (13.3%), while four articles incorporated mixed methods, combining both quantitative and qualitative approaches. Four articles opted for computational content analysis to investigate news coverage and social media posts (e.g., Huang & Sun, 2016; Wirz et al., 2022). More than one-third of the research gathered data from various sources, including the general public ($n = 12$, 26.7%) and students ($n = 4$, 8.9%). About a quarter of the studies focused on media content, encompassing traditional news coverage ($n = 6$, 13.3%) and social media posts ($n = 9$, 20.0%). Some studies targeted specific groups, such as Chinese parents ($n = 2$, 4.4%), Chinese women ($n = 1$, 2.2%), crisis practitioners ($n = 1$, 2.2%), and adolescents ($n = 1$, 2.2%). Nearly half of the research still relied on non-probability sampling methods ($n = 22$, 48.9%), while a few studies reported using probability sampling methods, such as stratified sampling ($n = 8$, 17.8%). Additionally, ten articles (22.2%) collected data for population-based content analysis.

In the realm of theoretical approaches, the majority of research drew upon one or multiple theories ($n = 40$, 88.9%). Of these articles, only a mere seven cited just one theory ($n = 7$, 15.6%). Approximately half of the articles incorporated two theories ($n = 27$, 60.0%), with a handful referencing three theories ($n = 5$, 11.1%), and only one article mentioning five theories ($n = 1$, 2.2%). In the context of crisis communication, several theories were frequently utilized. Situational crisis communication theory (SCCT; Coombs, 2007) appeared in 15.6% of the articles ($n = 7$). The social-mediated crisis communication model (SMCC; Austin et al., 2012) was featured in 8.9% of the articles ($n = 4$), while image repair theory (Benoit, 1997) was employed in 6.7% of cases ($n = 3$). Classical risk communication models, like the risk information seeking and processing (RISP) model (Griffin et al., 1999) and the planned risk information seeking model (Kahlor, 2010), were commonly used ($n = 5$, 11.1%). Additionally, media and communication theories, such as media system dependency theory (Ball-Rokeach, 1985; $n = 5$, 11.1%), framing (Entman, 1993; Iyengar, 1991; $n = 4$, 8.9%), and uses and gratifications theory (Katz et al., 1973; $n = 2$, 4.4%), found application in the research. Scholars (e.g., Ji & Kim, 2020; Li, 2018; Lo et al., 2013) also developed crisis and risk communication frameworks from social psychological theories, including social cognitive theory (Bandura, 1986; $n = 3$, 6.7%), and cognitive theories like cognitive mediation theory (Lo et al., 2013; Zhang & Yang, 2021; $n = 2$, 4.4%).

Risk and Crisis Communication in China: Key Findings

The Socio-Cultural Context of Risk and Crisis Communication in China

Three aspects of the Chinese social-cultural context were discussed in the examined articles: culture ($n = 15$, 33.3%), media system ($n = 18$, 40.0%), and political system ($n = 15$, 33.3%). In terms of the cultural aspect, collectivism, prioritizing the welfare and unity of the group or community over individual interests (Hofstede, 1984), was the most frequently mentioned ($n = 11$, 26.7%). China's collectivist culture emphasizes group identity, harmony, and social norms in risk and crisis communication (Cheng & Lee, 2019; Liu et al., 2023;

Zhu et al., 2017). News often highlights collective efforts, and Chinese individuals rely on peer networks to determine their behavior, valuing consistency with peers (Zhang & Yang, 2021). Additionally, preserving harmony through face-giving is seen as a crucial crisis communication strategy in China (Cheng, 2020). The cultural influence of collectivism can sometimes lead to the downplaying or delayed disclosure of negative information during risk events and crises (Cheng & Lee, 2019). Conservative cultural elements were also mentioned, explaining personal risk and crisis like breast cancer, suggesting that Chinese individuals may inherently associate breasts with sexuality due to a conservative societal ethos (Zhang & Yang, 2021). However, the impact of globalization in recent decades has brought about changes. Traditional cultural traits, including collectivism and conservatism, have evolved (Wang, 2017). Chinese society has become more open to risk-taking, evident in areas like online dating and casual encounters (Solis & Wong, 2019). This shift coincides with a growing recognition of the importance of transparency, timely disclosure, and accountability as crucial elements in the effective management of risks and crises (Li et al., 2022; Zheng, 2023).

China's media landscape is primarily characterized by government supervision and restrictions, which exert a significant influence on media expression and operations, both in traditional and social media platforms (Huang & Yang, 2018; Mou, 2014; Yang & Liu, 2021). Traditional media in China are often state-owned or closely affiliated with the government, which allows the government to influence their editorial decisions and content (Duan & Takahashi, 2017; Gong & Firdaus, 2022). Thus, China's government plays a pivotal role in shaping media coverage of risks and crises. In contrast, government oversight of social media platforms assumes a more guiding role (Cheng, 2020). Social media has emerged as the dominant channel for the public to seek information and express their views on various crises and risks, fostering a bottom-to-top communication approach (Huang & Sun, 2016; Yin et al., 2015). The heavy reliance on social media has significantly transformed organizational-public relationships and dialogues in China (Cheng, 2020; Cheng & Lee, 2019). This evolving media landscape highlights the dynamic interplay between government control and the changing role of social media in public discourse.

The political system in China significantly impacts risk and crisis communication (Cheng, 2020; Hu & Zhang, 2014; Liu et al., 2023). The government is widely perceived as a powerful authority responsible for safeguarding the public's interests and regulating both private and public sectors in China. The government serves as the top management that the public turns to for risk and crisis management and communication (Ji & Kim, 2020). Chinese citizens trust the government to release information, manage risk and crisis situations, and ensure the safety of the population. The government continues to play a crucial role in addressing corporate crises and personal risk issues. Despite the common perception of a centralized government, it is important to note that the Chinese political system includes local governments operating under central authority (Li et al., 2022). This structure leads to varied responses at different government levels during public crises. Typically, the central government formulates guidelines, and local governments implement regulations based on the central government's directives (Li et al., 2022).

Understanding Risk and Crisis Communication in China through Varied Perspectives

Research perspectives vary in their distribution. The majority of articles, nearly two-thirds (n = 26, 57.8%), focused on the audience perspective, delving into individual psychological dynamics and audience frames. A total of nine articles (20.0%) adopted the institutional perspective, examining organizational response strategies to risks and crises. Six articles (13.3%) took a media perspective, analyzing media frames and topics related to risk and crisis events.

Additionally, four articles (8.9%) explored both institutional and audience perspectives. Subsequent sections will discuss these perspectives in greater detail.

Institutional perspective. The majority of crisis and risk communication research in China focuses on government and corporate institutions. The government crisis communication aims to maintain a positive public opinion and protect the government's reputation (Cheng, 2020; Cheng & Lee, 2019). Cheng and Lee (2019) suggest that the government often employs defensive strategies, such as "no comment" and denial. However, crisis response strategies may vary depending on the government's hierarchy. Research by Li et al. (2022) found that the central government tends to adopt advocacy and bolstering strategies to emphasize competence in risk and crisis management and nurture public trust. In contrast, local governments may use instructing and adjusting information strategies during crises like the COVID-19 pandemic, especially in the initial stage of the pandemic (Meadows et al., 2022). In this context, the central government provides emotional support to alleviate public concerns, while local governments focus on providing factual information. Notably, when the central government makes errors, local governments may be held accountable as scapegoats (Li et al., 2022).

In the realm of risk communication, establishing trust through a trust-building strategy is considered crucial (Ngai et al., 2023). Factors such as source credibility, transparency, and actions to reduce uncertainty are prioritized when communicating risks (Ngai et al., 2023). This involves incorporating information from experts, providing access to external sources like the WHO, demonstrating care toward the public, and offering skills and knowledge for coping with risks. Additionally, transparency is recognized as playing a pivotal role in mitigating public perceptions of risk in China (Li et al., 2023). Li et al. (2023) also recommend the use of a loss-framed information strategy, which highlights the consequences of non-adherence to recommended measures, as an effective strategy for encouraging vaccination.

Within the domain of corporate crisis communication, it is worth noting that state-owned and privately-owned companies in China often take divergent paths. According to the findings by Pang et al. (2018), state-owned corporations tend to embrace what's colloquially known as the "barnacle strategy," leaning heavily on government support. In contrast, privately owned enterprises prefer the "third-party endorsement strategy" and are prone to introducing novel topics into the mix. In the era of social media, we've witnessed the emergence of various internet-based crisis response techniques. For instance, Kim et al. (2016) have shed light on the efficacy of self-mocking strategies in dealing with paracrisis, which poses a substantial threat to organizations. Furthermore, the use of emoticons and figurative language resonates with the ethos of social media, effectively conveying emotions and nurturing a sense of intimacy (Cheng, 2020; Kim et al., 2016). These approaches serve to not only amplify public endorsement of the company but also to temper unfavorable public reactions (Cheng, 2020; Kim et al., 2016). Even when companies opt for the same crisis response strategy, they may choose disparate frames and narratives to convey their message via social media. Research indicates that both the Chinese government and corporate entities are notably inclined to utilize "informing" and "corrective action" frames (Zhang et al., 2020). Moreover, Zhang et al. (2020) posit that the government often leans into a narrative of nationalism to underscore its endeavors in navigating crises and securing societal recognition.

Media perspective. Research from media perspectives delves into traditional media coverage of crisis and risk issues, focusing on aspects like media frames, agenda-setting, volume, and topics (Mao, 2014; Peng & Tang, 2010; Wirz et al., 2022). These studies often examine crises linked to societal concerns such as public health, financial crises, air pollution, and food safety (Duan & Takahashi, 2017; Huan, 2016; Mao, 2014; Wirz et al., 2022). Given the government-controlled media system in China, media commonly tailor their information dissemination strategies in accordance with the central government's guidance (Huan, 2016). Comparative research, comparing news topics across various cultural contexts, is common when studying news coverage (e.g., Huan, 2016; Wirz et al., 2022). In addition to well-established media theories like framing and agenda-setting, scholars utilize theories such as issue-attention theory, the hierarchy of influence theory, and the engagement system of the appraisal framework to unveil characteristics of news coverage on crises and risks in China (Duan & Takahashi, 2017; Huan, 2016; Wirz et al., 2022).

As it relates to news frames, research reveals that the attribution of responsibility is the primary frame in reporting crises in China (Mao, 2014). Even during economic crises, the responsibility frame remains the dominant choice for the news media (Mao, 2014). Chinese media accentuate the government's efforts and successes in managing the pandemic by highlighting societal-level scenarios and government measures (Wirz et al., 2022). Similar patterns emerge in risk communication research, where attribution of responsibility frames is commonly used to report environmental risks like air pollution (Duan & Takahashi, 2017). Both causal attribution (the causes of risks and crises) and treatment attribution (responsibility for addressing them) are discussed, with treatment responsibility attributions being more prevalent (Duan & Takahashi, 2017). When conveying treatment responsibility, Chinese media often emphasize the government's commitment to resolving issues with an optimistic tone, rather than presenting specific solutions (Duan & Takahashi, 2017).

As for crisis reporting topics, Chinese media primarily concentrate on societal-level actions and essential supplies during the pandemic (Gong & Firdaus, 2022; Wirz et al., 2022). Researchers argue that Chinese media coverage tends to cast crises in a positive light, emphasizing pro-sociality, cooperation, and pandemic recovery (Gong & Firdaus, 2022). Additionally, Chinese media show a significant interest in international topics, particularly international collaboration in pandemic management, as a way to project a positive national image (Wirz et al., 2022). The government's efforts to display global concern during the COVID-19 pandemic not only reflect China's collectivistic cultural values and promote international cooperation but also signify an intention to cultivate a positive national image (Gong & Firdaus, 2022).

Mainstream media, like People's Daily, remains a focal point of research within the media perspective due to their pivotal role in disseminating credible information and representing the state's stance during crises and risks (Duan & Takahashi, 2017). Mainstream media remains the primary news source in China (Tang & Zou, 2021), with experts, scholars, and government officials serving as the primary information sources (Huan, 2016). Notably, there is an intriguing observation that China Daily has incorporated information from U.S. sources, including official channels such as the U.S. embassy and U.S. NGO sources when reporting risk issues (Duan & Takahashi, 2017). This trend signifies a growing trend toward openness and transparency in Chinese mainstream media (Duan & Takahashi, 2017).

Audience perspective. Two distinct research avenues have been explored, focusing on audiences' underlying psychological mechanisms and their personal expressions on social media. In the context of risk communication, extensive research has delved into the effects of various factors on the public's cognitive, affective, and behavioral responses. Specifically, studies have investigated cognitive aspects such as risk perception (Wang, 2017) and information processing (Yang & Liu, 2021), emotional dimensions including fear and danger control (Li, 2018), and behavioral facets like information-seeking (Li & Zheng, 2022), preventive actions (Mou & Lin, 2014), and vaccination intentions (Liu et al., 2023). Antecedents of risk communication encompass personal factors such as prior experience (Wang, 2017), knowledge (Yang & Liu, 2021), media usage (Mou & Lin, 2014), and self-efficacy

(Lo et al., 2013), along with contextual factors like cultural backgrounds (Wang, 2017), media exposure (Li, 2018), media channels (Han et al., 2014), and parenting styles (Leung & Lee, 2012). Notably, cultural factors play a pivotal role in shaping the audience's responses. For example, research has underscored the significance of collectivism among Chinese audiences, which engenders a strong adherence to social norms, consequently fostering greater concern for issues such as climate change and support for related policies (Wang, 2017; Yang et al., 2014). Hence, risk communication strategies that integrate social norms have proven effective (Yang et al., 2014; Zhang & Yang, 2021). Additionally, collectivism amplifies the perceived collective responsibility of Chinese audiences in risk management, leading to heightened engagement in preventive behaviors, such as vaccination during the COVID-19 pandemic (Liu et al., 2023).

Shifting the focus to corporate crisis communication, Chinese audiences exhibit distinct expectations. They not only anticipate responses from the crisis-affected organizations but also look to the government and collective actors (Ji & Kim, 2020). The public in China places a premium on both accommodating responses from in-crisis entities and government intervention (Ji & Kim, 2020). In addition to evaluating the responsibility of companies in crisis, Chinese audiences consider collective efficacy and government controllability when shaping their responses to preventable crises (Ji & Kim, 2020). Regulatory intervention by the government is a predominant public demand during crises in China, reflecting the perception of the government as a reliable regulator for corporate crises (Ji & Kim, 2020).

Concerning the acceptance of crisis response strategies, scholars have found that accommodating strategies, such as public apologies, prove effective in responding to crises irrespective of their causes (Ngai & Jin, 2016). In collectivistic cultures, organizations are often sensitive to issues of face and hesitant to issue public apologies (Zhu et al., 2017). Consequently, public apologies in China may positively violate audience expectations, reducing their perception of the crisis's severity (Zhu et al., 2017). However, overuse of symbolic accommodating strategies, like apologies, can lead to audience resistance, with the audience perceiving the organization as incapable or unwilling to address the crisis (Ngai & Jin, 2016). Chinese audiences tend to prioritize substantive accommodating crisis response strategies, such as solutions and corrective actions implemented by companies (Ngai & Jin, 2016). Furthermore, Chinese audiences are more likely to accept internet-based crisis response strategies during paracrisis. Kim et al. (2016) found that combining self-mocking strategies with informal and non-verbal language can align with Chinese audience expectations and reduce perceptions of crisis severity.

Notably, social media has emerged as a crucial data source for investigating audience responses to risk and crisis communication in China. Social media platforms serve as a prominent channel for people to express their opinions and emotions during times of crises and risks (Mou, 2014). In terms of personal expression, research reveals that Chinese audiences tend to adopt distinct frames depending on the level of responsibility attribution in a crisis. Informing and corrective action frames are common during accidental crises, while blaming and social issues frames prevail in preventable crises (Zhang et al., 2020). Narrative styles also vary based on the type of crisis. For accidental crises like natural disasters, audiences often employ a nationalist narrative to show support, whereas preventable crises typically invoke power and contestation narratives to express dissatisfaction (Zhang et al., 2020). Moreover, audience responses in risk-related protest activities have garnered scholarly attention. Huang and Sun (2016) found that personal frames centered on personal preference revelation, risk, and distrust are the dominant frames employed by Chinese audiences to convey their disagreements and concerns in anti-nuclear protests. However, these personal frames primarily serve as tools for moderate mobilization and have limited potential to translate into offline activities.

Case Study: 2022 MU5735 Airplane Crash

On March 21, 2022, China Eastern Flight MU5735 tragically crashed almost vertically and erupted in flames in Guangxi Province (CAAC, 2022). The devastating incident claimed the lives of numerous individuals, including 123 passengers and 9 crew members (CAAC, 2022). In the aftermath of the crash, only scattered wreckage, debris, and some human remains were discovered. Despite the recovery of both black boxes, the exact causes of this air disaster are still under investigation. MU5735 has been marked as the most severe indigenous air crash in China over the past three decades, garnering significant global attention (Reuters, 2023).

From an institutional perspective, both the Chinese government and the airline company were involved in responding to the crisis. The Chinese government swiftly formed a dedicated working group to address the situation. The government took on the primary responsibility for managing the crisis. On one front, the military and firefighters were dispatched to search for potential survivors, while, on the other hand, this group provided updates and news regarding the developments of the airplane crash. A catastrophe of this magnitude naturally instilled a public desire for risk mitigation and emotional consolation (Yan & Ge, 2022). The Chinese government, often seen as a paternal figure, was expected to console the public and conduct a thorough investigation. In contrast, China Eastern played a supportive role in crisis management. The airline employed a variety of strategies to support the grieving families, including providing psychological assistance, facilitating compensation settlements, and suspending all Boeing 737 flights for safety concerns. Nonetheless, the company still incurred significant financial losses due to the crisis.

From a media perspective, the air crash ignited intense debates regarding disaster reporting (Fang, 2022; Wang, 2022). An article by *Figure* delved into personal stories of the deceased, sparking controversy (Fang, 2022). Many criticized the report for violating journalistic ethics, accusing it of employing the "death knock," intruding on grief, and invading privacy (Wang, 2022). Journalists were seen as disturbing the victims' families to obtain information and portraying the deceased with highly emotive language to capture public attention. While using human-interest angles in media reports is common to address the emotional needs of the public (Yan & Ge, 2022), there was a growing call for greater empathy toward the victims' families when reporting on such tragic incidents (Wang, 2022). Reports that piece together victim information from fragmented sources can inflict further distress on the affected families. On social media, public sentiment surged on the day of the air crash, characterized by strong emotional and informational needs. These sentiments subsided once official news about the incident was provided (Yue et al., 2023). However, as confirmation emerged that all on board had perished and the black boxes had been recovered, public opinion once again intensified, this time focusing on the causes of the incident (Yue et al., 2023).

From an audience perspective, a sentiment analysis conducted by Yue et al. (2023) revealed that the dominant emotions among the public were neutral, followed by negative emotions, and, lastly, positive emotions related to the rescuers. People demonstrated concern for both the rescue efforts and the truth, displaying significant empathy toward the deceased (Yue et al., 2023). It is imperative for both the government and companies in crisis to offer accommodating and corrective information, including compensation and actions aimed at alleviating public concerns (Coombs, 2007).

Having experienced no major air crashes in nearly 12 years, China now faces a transformed media landscape. In this particular air crash, the government disseminated information primarily through news conferences. While this approach ensures accuracy, it may fall short of meeting the public's need for timely information, potentially fostering the spread of disinformation and rumors. For instance, there were cases of individuals falsely claiming to have been passengers on the ill-fated flight in a bid to gain attention. In light of such a severe air crash, robust discussions are inevitable, prompting the government and social media platforms to consider more effective ways to deliver accurate and timely information to comfort the public and address the issue of rumors.

The media, in turn, confronts substantial challenges stemming from ethical concerns. Journalists often gather fragmented information about victims from their families and friends to piece together their reports. This approach can distort the truth and lead to secondary harm for the families of the victims. Some families even experienced cyberbullying following media reports. Thus, it is incumbent upon the media to reconsider their approach to disaster reporting and strike a balance between the truth and the privacy of the victims.

Conclusion

In this chapter, a systematic review of 447 articles provides a comprehensive overview of risk and crisis communication research in China. Findings revealed a predominant use of quantitative methods, particularly surveys, and the adoption of interdisciplinary theoretical frameworks. Notably, the research illuminated an increasing intersection between risks, crises, and social issues. The socio-cultural context played a pivotal role, with traditional cultural dimensions such as collectivism frequently employed to interpret findings. China's hierarchical political system had distinct effects on government responses, where the central government offered emotional support, while local authorities concentrated on practical measures (Li et al., 2022). The tightly regulated media environment significantly influenced media framing and topic selection, with traditional media often portraying crises in a positive light, emphasizing government's effective risk and crisis management efforts (Gong & Firdaus, 2022). Interestingly, audiences in China, even in corporate contexts, perceived the government as a regulatory authority (Ji & Kim, 2020). Furthermore, audiences actively harnessed social media platforms to voice their opinions and engage with crises and risks.

These findings suggest several potential directions for future research. Firstly, with the evolving social landscape in China, it's important to explore how traditional cultural elements are challenged in a global context and consider the influence of factors like nationalist sentiments in the field of risk and crisis communication (Zhao, 2022). Secondly, emerging methods such as large language models could better analyze social media content in future research. From an institutional perspective, the absence of tailored response strategies for crises and risks linked to social issues requires further investigation (Ji & Wan, 2023). Additionally, research from a media standpoint should delve into the impact of digital media affordances on risk and crisis communication, recognizing digital media as a permanent infrastructure in social and cultural practices rather than a mere research context (van Dijck et al., 2018). Furthermore, researchers may explore how new media technologies, such as generative artificial intelligence, virtual reality and augmented reality, shape risk and crisis communication in the Chinese context (Zerfass et al., 2020). Finally, in addition to assessing the applicability of existing Western theories in China, there's potential to develop indigenous theories rooted in the Chinese context for the field of crisis and risk communication.

References

Austin, L., Liu, B. F., & Yan, J. (2012). How audiences seek out crisis information: Exploring the social-mediated crisis communication model. *Journal of Applied Communication Research, 40*(2), 188–207. https://doi.org/10.1080/00909882.2012.654498

Ball-Rokeach, S. J. (1985). The origins of individual media system dependency: A sociological framework. *Communication Research, 12*(4), 485–510. https://doi.org/10.1177/009365085012004003

Bandura, A. (1986). *Social foundations of thought and action*. Englewood Cliffs.

Benoit, W. L. (1997). Image repair discourse and crisis communication. *Public Relations Review, 23*(2), 177–186. https://doi.org/10.1016/s0363-8111(97)90023-0

Boyack, K. W., & Klavans, R. (2010). Co-citation analysis, bibliographic coupling, and direct citation: Which citation approach represents the research front most accurately? *Journal of the American*

Society for Information Science and Technology, *61*(12), 2389–2404. https://doi.org/10.1002/asi.21419

Boyd, A. D., & Furgal, C. (2018). Communicating environmental health risks with indigenous populations: A systematic literature review of current research and recommendations for future studies. *Health Communication*, *34*(13), 1564–1574. https://doi.org/10.1080/10410236.2018.1507658

CAAC (April 20, 2022). 关于"3•21"东航MU5735航空器飞行事故调查初步报告的情况通报 [Briefing on the preliminary report on the flight accident investigation of "3•21" China Eastern Flight MU5735 aircraft]. http://www.caac.gov.cn/XXGK/XXGK/TZTG/202204/t20220420_212895.html

Cheng, Y. (2020). The social-mediated crisis communication research: Revisiting dialogue between organizations and publics in crises of China. *Public Relations Review*, *46*(1), 101769. https://doi.org/10.1016/j.pubrev.2019.04.003

Cheng, Y., & Lee, C.-J. (2019). Online crisis communication in a post-truth Chinese society: Evidence from interdisciplinary literature. *Public Relations Review*, *45*(4), 101826. https://doi.org/10.1016/j.pubrev.2019.101826

Cheng, Y., Shen, H., & Jiang, Q. (2020). Corporate dialogue in crises of China: Examining dialogic strategies and communicative outcomes in a child abuse scandal. *Public Relations Review*, *46*(1), 101816. https://doi.org/10.1016/j.pubrev.2019.101816

Coombs, W. T. (2007). Protecting organization reputations during a crisis: The development and application of situational crisis communication theory. *Corporate Reputation Review*, *10*(3), 163–176. https://doi.org/10.1057/palgrave.crr.1550049

Duan, R., & Takahashi, B. (2017). The two-way flow of news: A comparative study of American and Chinese newspaper coverage of Beijing's air pollution. *International Communication Gazette*, *79*(1), 83–107. https://doi.org/10.1177/1748048516656303

Entman, R. M. (1993). Framing: Toward clarification of a fractured paradigm. *Journal of Communication*, *43*(4), 51–58. https://doi.org/10.1111/j.1460-2466.1993.tb01304.x

Fang, K. (March 23, 2022). *灾难报道是"吃人血馒头"吗?[Is disaster reporting taking advantage of other's misfortune]. 新闻实验室[News Lab].* https://www.xiaoyuzhoufm.com/episode/623b22fda36f87d90b3ad8b1

Griffin, R. J., Dunwoody, S., & Neuwirth, K. (1999). Proposed model of the relationship of risk information seeking and processing to the development of preventive behaviors. *Environmental Research*, *80*(2), S230–S245. https://doi.org/10.1006/enrs.1998.3940

Gong, J., & Firdaus, A. (2022). Is the pandemic a boon or a bane? News media coverage of COVID-19 in China Daily. *Journalism Practice*, *18*(3), 621–41. https://doi.org/10.1080/17512786.2022.2043766

Han, G. K., Zhang, J. M., Chu, K. R., & Shen, G. (2014). Self–other differences in H1N1 flu risk perception in a global context: A comparative study between the United States and China. *Health Communication*, *29*(2), 109–123. https://doi.org/10.1080/10410236.2012.723267

Hasumi, T., & Chiu, M.-S. (2022). Online mathematics education as bio-eco-techno process: Bibliometric analysis using co-authorship and bibliographic coupling. *Scientometrics*, *127*(8), 4631–4654. https://doi.org/10.1007/s11192-022-04441-3

Hofstede, G. (1984). *Culture's consequences: International differences in work-related values*. SAGE.

Hu, B. (2016). 互联网、公共危机与社会认同 [Internet, public crisis and social identification]. *山东社会科学 [Shandong Social Sciences]*, *4*, 5–12.

Hu, B., & Zhang, D. (2014). Channel selection and knowledge acquisition during the 2009 Beijing H1N1 flu crisis: A media system dependency theory perspective. *Chinese Journal of Communication*, *7*(3), 299–318. https://doi.org/10.1080/17544750.2014.926951

Huan, C. (2016). Journalistic engagement patterns and power relations: Corpus evidence from Chinese and Australian hard news reporting. *Discourse & Communication*, *10*(2), 137–156. https://doi.org/10.1177/1750481315611239

Huang, J., & Yang, Z. J. (2018). Risk, affect, and policy support: Public perception of air pollution in China. *Asian Journal of Communication*, *28*(3), 281–297. https://doi.org/10.1080/01292986.2017.1386220

Huang, R., & Sun, X. (2016). Dynamic preference revelation and expression of personal frames: How Weibo is used in an anti-nuclear protest in China. *Chinese Journal of Communication*, *9*(4), 385–402. https://doi.org/10.1080/17544750.2016.1206030

Iyengar, S. (1991). *Is anyone responsible?* University of Chicago Press.

Ji, Y., & Kim, S. (2020). Crisis-induced public demand for regulatory intervention in the social media era: Examining the moderating roles of perceived government controllability and consumer collective efficacy. *New Media & Society*, *22*(6), 959–983. https://doi.org/10.1177/1461444819874473

Ji, Y., & Wan, C. (2024). Working too much in China's tech industry: Corporate social advocacy as a crisis response strategy to issue-based opinion polarization. *Internet Research*, *34*(2), 320–342. https://doi.org/10.1108/INTR-12-2021-0878

Jiang, Q., Huang, X., & Tao, R. (2018). Examining factors influencing internet addiction and adolescent risk behaviors among excessive internet users. *Health communication*, *33*(12), 1434–1444. https://doi.org/10.1080/10410236.2017.1358241

Kahlor, L. A. (2010). PRISM: A planned risk information seeking model. *Health Communication*, *25*(4), 345–356. https://doi.org/10.1080/10410231003775172

Katz, E., Blumler, J. G., & Gurevitch, M. (1973). Uses and gratifications research. *Public Opinion Quarterly*, *37*(4), 509–523. https://doi.org/10.1086/268109

Khamitov, M., Grégoire, Y., & Suri, A. (2016). A systematic review of brand transgression, service failure recovery and product-harm crisis: Integration and guiding insights. *Journal of the Academy of Marketing Science*, *48*(3), 519–542. https://doi.org/10.1007/s11747-019-00679-1

Kim, S., Zhang, X. A., & Zhang, B. W. (2016). Self-mocking crisis strategy on social media: Focusing on Alibaba chairman Jack Ma in China. *Public Relations Review*, *42*(5), 903–912. https://doi.org/10.1016/j.pubrev.2016.10.004

Kraus, S., Breier, M., & Dasí-Rodríguez, S. (2020). The art of crafting a systematic literature review in entrepreneurship research. *International Entrepreneurship and Management Journal*, *16*(3), 1023–1042. https://doi.org/10.1007/s11365-020-00635-4

Krippendorff, K. (2004). *Content analysis: An introduction to its methodology*. SAGE.

Lee, K. (2009). How the Hong Kong government lost the public trust in SARS: Insights for government communication in a health crisis. *Public Relations Review*, *35*(1), 74–76. https://doi.org/10.1016/j.pubrev.2008.06.003

Leung, L., & Lee, P. S. N. (2012). The influences of information literacy, internet addiction and parenting styles on internet risks. *New Media & Society*, *14*(1), 117–136. https://doi.org/10.1177/1461444811410406

Li, J., Tang, Z., & Gong, Z. (2023). Does the message frame promote people's willingness to vaccinate when they worry about side effects from the COVID-19 vaccine? Evidence from an online survey experiment in China. *Health Communication*, *38*(8), 1688–1696. https://doi.org/10.1080/10410236.2022.2028469

Li, J., & Zheng, H. (2022). Online information seeking and disease prevention intent during COVID-19 Outbreak. *Journalism and Mass Communication Quarterly*, *99*(1), 69–88. https://doi.org/10.1177/1077699020961518

Li, X. (2018). Media exposure, perceived efficacy, and protective behaviors in a public health emergency. *International Journal of Communication*, *12*, 2641–2660.

Li, Y., Chandra, Y., & Fan, Y. (2022). Unpacking government social media messaging strategies during the COVID-19 pandemic in China. *Policy & Internet*, *14*(3), 651–672. https://doi.org/10.1002/poi3.282

Liu, Z., & Yang, J. Z. (2020). In the wake of scandals: How media use and social trust influence risk perception and vaccination intention among Chinese parents. *Health Communication*, *36*(10), 1188–1199. https://doi.org/10.1080/10410236.2020.1748834

Liu, P. L., Ao, S. H., Zhao, X., & Zhang, L. (2023). Associations between COVID-19 information acquisition and vaccination intention: The roles of anticipated regret and collective responsibility. *Health Communication*, *38*(10), 2198–2209. https://doi.org/10.1080/10410236.2022.2059801

Lo, V., Wei, R., & Su, H. (2013). Self-efficacy, information-processing strategies, and acquisition of health knowledge. *Asian Journal of Communication*, *23*(1), 54–67. https://doi.org/10.1080/01292986.2012.725175

Lyu, J. C. (2012). How young Chinese depend on the media during public health crises? A comparative perspective. *Public Relations Review*, *38*(5), 799–806. https://doi.org/10.1016/j.pubrev.2012.07.006

Mao, Z. (2014). Cosmopolitanism and global risk: News framing of the Asian financial crisis and the European debt crisis. *International Journal of Communication*, *8*, 1029–1048.

Maseda, A., Iturralde, T., Cooper, S., & De Castro, G. A. (2021). Mapping women's involvement in family firms: A review based on bibliographic coupling analysis. *International Journal of Management Reviews*, *24*(2), 279–305. https://doi.org/10.1111/ijmr.12278

Meadows, C. Z., Tang, L., & Zou, W. (2022). Managing government legitimacy during the COVID-19 pandemic in China: A semantic network analysis of state-run media Sina Weibo posts. *Chinese Journal of Communication*, *15*(2), 156–181. https://doi.org/10.1080/17544750.2021.2016876

Mou, Y. (2014). What can microblog exchanges tell us about food safety crises in China? *Chinese Journal of Communication*, *7*(3), 319–334. https://doi.org/10.1080/17544750.2014.926952

Mou, Y., & Lin, C. A. (2014). Communicating food safety via the social media: The role of knowledge and emotions on risk perception and prevention. *Science Communication*, *36*(5), 593–616. https://doi.org/10.1177/1075547014549480

Ngai, C. S. B., & Jin, Y. (2016). The effectiveness of crisis communication strategies on Sina Weibo in relation to Chinese publics' acceptance of these strategies. *Journal of Business and Technical Communication*, *30*(4), 451–494. https://doi.org/10.1177/105065191665190

Ngai, C. S. B., Singh, R. G., Lu, W., Yao, L., & Koon, A. C. (2023). Exploring the relationship between trust-building strategies and public engagement on social media during the COVID-19 outbreak. *Health Communication*, *38*(10), 2141–2157. https://doi.org/10.1080/10410236.2022.2055261

Pang, A., Hu, Y., & Woon, E. (2018). A broad stroke or different strokes for different folks? Examining the subtleties in crisis management approaches in state-owned enterprises and privately owned enterprises in China. *Chinese Journal of Communication*, *11*(1), 5–25. https://doi.org/10.1080/17544750.2017.1357641

Peng, W., & Tang, L. (2010). Health content in Chinese newspapers. *Journal of Health Communication*, *15*(7), 695–711. https://doi.org/10.1080/10810730.2010.514028

Reuters (March 21, 2023). *Beijing still seeking answers a year after China Eastern plane crash*. https://www.reuters.com/world/china/china-still-seeking-answers-year-after-plane-crash-2023-03-20/

Rialti, R., Marzi, G., Ciappei, C., & Busso, D. (2019). Big data and dynamic capabilities: A bibliometric analysis and systematic literature review. *Management Decision*, *57*(8), 2052–2068. https://doi.org/10.1108/MD-07-2018-0821

Solis, R. J. C., & Wong, K. Y. J. (2019). To meet or not to meet? Measuring motivations and risks as predictors of outcomes in the use of mobile dating applications in China. *Chinese Journal of Communication*, *12*(2), 204–223. https://doi.org/10.1080/17544750.2018.1498006

Tai, Z., & Sun, T. (2007). Media dependencies in a changing media environment: The case of the 2003 SARS epidemic in China. *New Media & Society*, *9*(6), 987–1009. https://doi.org/10.1177/1461444807082691

Tang, L., & Zou, W. (2021). Health information consumption under COVID-19 lockdown: An interview study of residents of Hubei Province, China. *Health Communication*, *36*(1), 74–80. https://doi.org/10.1080/10410236.2020.1847447

van Dijck, J., Poell, T., & de Waal, M. (2018). *The platform society: Public values in a connective world*. Oxford University Press.

Wang, X. (2017). Understanding climate change risk perceptions in China: Media use, personal experience, and cultural worldviews. *Science Communication*, *39*(3), 291–312. https://doi.org/10.1177/1075547017707320

Wang, Y. (2022). 浅论灾难报道叙事——兼谈《MU5735航班上的人们》伦理问题 [The narrative of disaster report: The ethical issues of *The people on flight MU5735*]. *科技传播 [Public Communication of Science & Technology]*, *14*(15), 90–92.

Wirz, C. D., Shao, A., Bao, L., Howell, E. L., Monroe, H., & Chen, K. (2022). Media systems and attention cycles: Volume and topics of news coverage on COVID-19 in the United States and China. *Journalism and Mass Communication Quarterly*, *99*(4), 1048–1071. https://doi.org/10.1177/10776990211049455

Yan, Y., & Ge, X. (2022). 避险需求和情感抚慰:灾难报道的核心功能及变迁 [Risk aversion and emotional pacification: Core functions of disaster reporting and its changing landscape]. *传媒观察 [Media Observer]*, *5*, 14–20.

Yang, J. Z., & Huang, J. (2019). Seeking for your own sake: Chinese citizens' motivations for information seeking about air pollution. *Environmental Communication*, *13*(5), 603–616. https://doi.org/10.1080/17524032.2017.1397041

Yang, X., Chen, L., & Feng, Q. (2016). Risk perception of food safety issue on social media. *Chinese Journal of Communication*, *9*(2), 124–138. https://doi.org/10.1080/17544750.2015.1111247

Yang, J. Z., & Liu, Z. (2021). Information seeking and processing in the context of vaccine scandals. *Science Communication*, *43*(3), 279–306. https://doi.org/10.1177/1075547020983589

Yang, Z. J., Kahlor, L., & Li, H. (2014). A United States-China comparison of risk information-seeking intentions. *Communication Research*, *41*(7), 935–960. https://doi.org/10.1177/0093650213479795

Yin, J., Feng, J., & Wang, Y. (2015). Social media and multinational corporations' corporate social responsibility in China: The case of ConocoPhillips oil spill incident. *IEEE Transactions on Professional Communication*, *58*(2), 135–153. https://doi.org/10.1109/TPC.2015.2433071

Yue, Y., Shan, C., Peng, C., Zheng, X., Yan, Y., & Gu, Q. (2023). 基于新浪微博数据的东航MU5735坠毁事件舆情热度演化及情感分析 [The evolution and sentiment analysis of the public opinion on the crash of China Eastern Airlines flight MU5735 based on Sina Weibo data]. *计算机时代 [Computer Era]*, *2*, 55–60.

Zeng, F., & Dai, J. (2015). 中国式风险传播:语境、脉络与问题 [Technical risk vs. perceived risk: Communication processes and social amplification of risk]. *西南民族大学学报(人文社会科学版) [Journal of Southwest Minzu University(Humanities and Social Science)]*, *36*(4), 185–189.

Zerfass, A., Hagelstein, J., & Tench, R. (2020). Artificial intelligence in communication management: A cross-national study on adoption and knowledge, impact, challenges and risks. *Journal of Communication Management*, *24*(4), 377–389. https://doi.org/10.1108/JCOM-10-2019-0137

Zheng, H., Jiang, S., & Rosenthal, S. (2022). Linking online vaccine information seeking to vaccination intention in the context of the COVID-19 pandemic. *Science Communication*, *44*(3), 320–346. https://doi.org/10.1177/10755470221101067

Zhang, L., & Yang, X. (2021). Linking risk perception to breast cancer examination intention in China: Examining an adapted cognitive mediation model. *Health Communication*, *36*(14), 1813–1824. https://doi.org/10.1080/10410236.2020.1796283

Zheng, Q. (2023). Restoring trust through transparency: Examining the effects of transparency strategies on police crisis communication in Mainland China. *Public Relations Review*, *49*(2), 102296. https://doi.org/10.1016/j.pubrev.2023.102296

Zhang, X., Nekmat, E., & Chen, A. (2020). Crisis collective memory making on social media: A case study of three Chinese crises on Weibo. *Public Relations Review*, *46*(4), 101960. https://doi.org/10.1016/j.pubrev.2020.101960

Zhao, H. (2022). When organizational crises meet nationalism: Crisis communication of multinational corporations in the Chinese context. *Public Relations Review*, *48*(3), 102198. https://doi.org/10.1016/j.pubrev.2022.102198

Zhu, L., Anagondahalli, D., & Zhang, A. (2017). Social media and culture in crisis communication: McDonald's and KFC crises management in China. *Public Relations Review*, *43*(3), 487–492. https://doi.org/10.1016/j.pubrev.2017.03.006

Zupic, I., & Čater, T. (2015). Bibliometric methods in management and organization. *Organizational Research Methods*, *18*(3), 429–472. https://doi.org/10.1177/1094428114562629

Authors' Bio

Yingru Ji (PhD), an assistant professor in the College of Media and International Culture at Zhejiang University, earned her doctoral degree from the Chinese University of Hong Kong. Her research interests encompass strategic communication, risk and crisis communication, and human–machine communication. Her research has been published in the leading journals in the communication field such as *Communication Research*, *New Media & Society*. Her commitment to excellence and innovation in communication research has been acknowledged through multiple prestigious top paper awards at top-tier international conferences in the communication field such as annual conferences of international communication association (ICA) and Association for Education in Journalism and Mass Communication (AEJMC).

Chang Wan, a doctoral student in the College of Media and International Culture at Zhejiang University. Her research interests include strategic communication, risk and crisis communication, and communication technology. Her research has been published in the leading journals in communication field such as *Communication Research*. She has also presented multiple research papers at the annual conferences of the ICA.

28

Risk and Crisis Communication Research in India

Krishnamurthy Sriramesh[1] and Ganga S. Dhanesh[2]
[1]Advertising, Public Relations, and Design, University of Colorado, Boulder, CO, USA
[2]Department of Communication, University of Maryland, College Park, MD, USA

Introduction

India has experienced a staggering number of natural disasters and man-made crises since the beginning of recorded history. Its geographic location, coupled with the physical, social, and economic vulnerabilities of its residents, makes India one of the most disaster- and crisis-prone countries in the world. The 1737 cyclone in Calcutta that claimed 300,000 lives, the Indian famine of 1896–1897 that led to between 1.25 and 10 million deaths, and the 1970 cyclone in West Bengal, India, and East Pakistan (now Bangladesh) that took 500,000 lives rank among the world's deadliest disasters. The Geneva-based Internal Displacement Monitoring Centre reported that natural disasters – especially heavy floods and cyclones – resulted in 2.5 million internal displacements in the country in 2022 (*The Hindu,* May 18, 2023). In addition to natural disasters, India has also experienced one of the world's deadliest industrial accidents, the leakage of toxic gas from the Union Carbide plant in Bhopal, India, in 1984 that killed 3000 people and injured over 200,000 (Shrivastava, 1987). Though crises such as natural disasters and pandemics cannot be prevented, their devastating impact can be mitigated through effective communication strategies.

Definition of Risk and Crisis Communication in the Indian Context

The sparse literature on risk and crisis communication in India relies almost entirely on Western theoretical frameworks and definitions. Chattaraj et al. (2021) relied almost exclusively on Western notions of the terms including citing the Oxford English Dictionary in offering this definition of *crisis:* "Crisis communication is generally defined as the accumulation and dissemination of information during crisis situations to alleviate the severity of the crisis" (p. 166). Gupta et al. (2022) did not offer a specific definition but classified crises into three categories: ***deliberate act*** by an individual or organization; ***accidental type*** where organizations may be both responsible for, and victims of, the crisis; and ***victim type*** where an organization is the victim of a crisis beyond its control.

The Handbook of International Crisis and Risk Communication Research, Second Edition.
Edited by Andreas Schwarz, Matthew W. Seeger, and Sora Kim.

Sriramesh et al. (2006) offered the following definition in their essay addressing the use of information and communication technologies (ICTs) for risk and crisis communication in the Asia–Pacific region:

> "Simply put, risks often are precursors to crises. That is, a lack of, or inadequate, risk management often may lead to a crisis with grave consequences. It is wiser to avoid a crisis, which requires that we pay attention to risk management (p. 31)."

Several scholars have contended that while risk communication is typically employed in routine or long-term risk events such as communicating risks related to public health, environmental hazards, and warning systems in the case of natural disasters, crisis communication involves time urgency and a dynamic component (Reynolds & Seeger, 2005; Seeger et al., 1998). In this chapter, we follow this distinction between risk and crisis communication.

The terms *crisis* and *disaster* are often used interchangeably in India. India's Disaster Management Act defines disaster as "a catastrophe, mishap, calamity or grave occurrence in any area, arising from natural or manmade causes, or by accident or negligence which results in substantial loss of life or human suffering or damage to, and destruction of, property, or damage to, or degradation of, environment, and is of such a nature or magnitude as to be beyond the coping capacity of the community of the affected area" (Ministry of Home Affairs, 2011, p. 1). This would be quite close to the dominant definitions of the terms used by Western scholars. The High Powered Committee (HPC) on Disaster Management set up by the Government of India in 1999 identified 31 types of disasters, several of which have been classified by mainstream crisis communication scholars as *crises*. The HPC categorized these 31 disasters into five major groups: (1) water and climate disasters; (2) geologically related disasters; (3) chemical, industrial, and nuclear disasters; (4) accident-related disasters; and (5) biologically related disasters (Ministry of Home Affairs, 2011). As is evident in this classification, the term "disaster" covers both natural and man-made events that could potentially entail the involvement of government and government agencies, nongovernmental organizations (NGOs), and corporations in risk and crisis/disaster communication. As a result, we have chosen to stay true to the need to express the terms in the "Indian context" and will use *disaster* as a synonym for *crisis* with a caveat: We will use the term *disaster* to refer to large-scale events that will require the intervention of multiple organizations at all levels, while *crisis* will refer to events that are mostly confronted by a single organization.

In the previous edition, we had noted the distinct paucity of published literature on risk and crisis communication in India. Since then, the body of literature on this topic has grown significantly aided largely by the COVID-19 pandemic. We will review some of the key studies next including our own case study that attempted to assess the role of *culture* (broadly defined) on crisis communication.

Risk and Disaster Communication in India

Institutional (Organizational) Perspective

We had previously noted that most of the research that had adopted an institutional perspective addressed issues related to early warning systems in risk and disaster communication with three main foci: (1) social and community aspects, (2) communication infrastructure, and (3) use of ICTs. The COVID-19 pandemic, which hit India and its economy very hard, helped spur research on risk and disaster communication in India. Scholars have studied various facets of the pandemic and its aftermath that we can classify into the above three foci.

Just three months into the COVID-19 pandemic, Dasgupta et al. (2020) commented on the reopening strategies adopted by India immediately following a nationwide lockdown. The country's central government adopted color-coded activity zones to get a stagnant economy underway.

Sanjeev et al. (2021) analyzed the successful COVID-19 communication by the Kerala state government during the first wave of the pandemic. The authors noted that the "pre-crisis communication" adopted by the government was successful in *inoculating* citizens, thus bolstering the state's capabilities in mitigating the effects of the crisis. The authors lauded the state's efficacious direct communication with stakeholders, leading to better information management, positive framing, and successful adoption of government policies by stakeholders. Based on these, the authors proposed what they called as the *Kerala model* of crisis communication.

Gupta et al. (2022) surveyed 294 public health professionals (PHPs) in India to assess how the World Health Organization's (WHO) reputation was impacted by the way it handled the COVID-19 crisis. The authors concluded that the pandemic had "dented the WHO's reputation among PHPs in India" because of the many mix-ups by the world body. The authors further commented that loss of reputation can prevent "an organization from achieving its stated objectives and enlisting constituent contributions. . ." (p. 9).

A few studies have examined the use of ICTs in risk and disaster communication in India. Mohanty et al. (n.d.) highlighted the crucial role played by ICT systems in early disaster warning, preparedness, and mitigation measures, outlining three key ICT-based initiatives developed to help disaster managers function effectively: (1) India Disaster Resource Network (IDRN); (2) geographical information system (GIS)-based decision support systems; and (3) National Emergency Communication Plan, which aims to keep communication links operational among decision-makers at various levels and operational response teams on the disaster site.

In their analysis of the role of ICTs in the Asia–Pacific region, Sriramesh et al. (2006) described India's role in the Indian Ocean tsunami early warning system coordinated by UNESCO as a result of the 2004 Asian tsunami. The authors identified India as one of 26 countries that have established official Tsunami Warning Focal Points (TWFP) to receive interim advisory information based on seismological and sea level information from the operational centers serving the Pacific in Hawaii and Tokyo (UNESCO, 2006). Samarajiva and Waidyanatha (2009) examined the use of emerging mobile technology in disaster risk reduction in Asian countries including India and found through field testing of wireless technologies and consultations with stakeholders in India, Bangladesh, Malaysia, and Indonesia that mobile phones are a reliable, effective, and affordable solution for alerting last-mile communities even among the poor in developing countries.

The Media/Journalism Perspective

This perspective also received a boost in scholarship as a result of the COVID-19 pandemic. We had reported previously that the Mumbai terror attacks of 2008 garnered domestic and international journalistic attention primarily because the world had been sensitized to terrorism as a present and clear danger after the attack on the World Trade Center in New York. That the terrorists in this incident originated in Pakistan, a country widely seen to be harboring Al-Qaeda and other terror suspects, also contributed to increased international media coverage.

While Allan (2012) explored the role and extent of citizen journalism in crisis news reporting of the Mumbai attacks, Narayana and Kapur (2010) examined the role of mass media, especially live television coverage of the Mumbai terror attack, in shaping public understanding of terrorism. They found from a survey of 325 cable subscribers in Mysuru, India, that the public felt live coverage of terrorism during the Mumbai terror attack showed utter disregard for public interest. However, Kodrich and Laituri (2005) conducted a content analysis of three leading English-language Indian dailies – *The Times of India, The Hindu*, and *The Hindustan Times* – to examine the role of the news media in the formation of an online disaster response community in the aftermath of the 2001 Gujarat earthquake and found that the media played an important role in bringing concerned people together online from all over the world.

Das et al. (2019) offered a survey of disaster communication systems in Europe and the United States and extrapolated how one could adapt those systems to suit the needs of India. The authors lamented the absence of dedicated, harmonized frequency bands for public safety and disaster relief communication in the country, which limits rescue efforts when disasters strike. They also analyzed global standards and regulatory frameworks to draw lessons from those for the Indian environment.

Inspired by the COVID-19 pandemic, De and Shukla (2021) assessed the privacy policies of public apps devoted to the COVID-19 pandemic. At the onset of the pandemic, the country had 63 government-initiated public apps to help cope with the pandemic. Aarogya Setu (bridge to health) was initiated by the Government of India to manage the pandemic including serving as the primary portal for contact tracing with over 100 million downloads by spring 2021. The authors found that only 38% of the apps had an app-specific privacy policy. Further, only one nationwide app articulated a comprehensive privacy policy covering key principles with a high degree of specificity. The authors recommended that the government pay greater attention to privacy issues through specific legislation while also educating beneficiaries about the need to pay attention to their own privacy.

The rest of the sparse research on crisis communication in India consists mostly of case studies of specific crises such as the sacking of employees by Jet Airways (Mehra, 2011) and McDonald's use of oil with beef extract for cooking its fries (Gupte, 2001). In sum, the number of empirical studies on risk and crisis communication in India does not match the size of the economy, the population, or the interest among international investors in this emerging economy.

Audience Perspective

The sparse research on viewing crises from the perspective of the audience has focused on long-term risk communication of (1) public health issues, especially polio eradication and human immunodeficiency virus/acquired immunodeficiency syndrome (HIV/AIDS), and (2) climate change. Obregon *et al.* (2009) reviewed primary and secondary data on polio communication efforts in India and Pakistan between the years 2000 and 2007 and found that communication strategies such as sustained media campaigns, community and social mobilization, and interpersonal communication contributed significantly to reducing polio incidence in these countries. Similarly, Murphy (2012) presented lessons from the polio eradication campaigns in India, Ethiopia, and Angola and argued for the use of research to tailor campaign messages to the context of people's lives, repeatedly delivering the key messages through home visits, involving community leaders and public education, and finally involving children in campaigns to help counter campaign fatigue.

Prior to the COVID-19 pandemic, HIV/AIDS had received the bulk of research attention on communicating public health risks with most of the research focused on identifying the target audience of risk communication campaigns. Go et al. (2003) examined the impact of marital violence on women's ability to protect themselves from HIV/AIDS in two randomly selected slums of metropolitan Chennai and recommended targeting HIV-prevention messages at men in order to reduce women's exposure to the threat of contracting HIV/AIDS. Similarly, Sivaram *et al.* (2005) suggested targeting unmarried men for communication intervention. Godbole and Mehendale (2005) argued that for the effective prevention and control of AIDS in the country, a multidisciplinary approach was imperative, combining action strategies such as early identification and treatment of sexually transmitted diseases with long-term communication strategies such as awareness aimed at behavioral change.

Research focused on communicating climate change risks has mostly emphasized the need to involve local communities in communicating climate change risks. For instance, the advancing capacity to support climate change adaptation ACCCA (2009) report on communicating climate change risks in Africa and Asia including India found that the creative use of indigenous media such as vernacular dramas, songs, and storyboards helped to diminish the difficulties of conveying complex information on climate change. This finding is not unlike experiences from other countries in Asia (Sriramesh, 2004) and Africa (Sriramesh & Verčič, 2009) although those went beyond risk and crisis communication. The report also recommended participatory development and testing of communication material that is relevant to stakeholders and active dialog between local communities and policymakers in developing clear and relevant climate risk communication messages. Prabhakar and Shaw (2008) also emphasized the importance of community-based climate change preparedness planning in addition to the establishment of drought monitoring and early warning systems.

The COVID-19 pandemic caused multiple hardships to people around the world. Countries like India have unique socio-economic characteristics that provided new dimensions of hardship to audiences. Particularly in the new millennium, the Indian economy has thrived on the migration of labor from rural to urban areas. Many of these migrants had traveled far away from home seeking work and economic prosperity. The nationwide lockdown at the onset of the pandemic caused havoc in the lives of migrant labors who had to find ways of returning home as economic activity had ground to a halt. Panwar and Mitra (2020) addressed the plight of migrant labor, which the 2011 census of India had put at 37% of the population. Although the study does not focus on communication, it is relevant because of its policy implications on how especially the government regulates and then communicates to migrants, many of whom are either illiterate or have minimal education. After reviewing theories and models on labor migration, the scholars offered a "new theoretical model of migration and urbanization" that highlighted the importance of better public policies in *agglomeration economies* where organizations and people cluster in predominantly urban economic zones (cities). As these zones often consist of migrant labors, a pandemic poses multiple challenges in communicating with them and assisting them to safety.

Stating that "capacity building and monitoring of response capacity" as being "critical to disaster preparedness," George and Kumar (2022) critiqued what they called as the "absence of a methodological framework" to measure disaster response capacity in the various districts of India. In attempting to provide such a framework, the authors identified four factors of response capacity: resources, budgét, communication and coordination, and engagement (of stakeholders). The final two are very relevant to the field of crisis communication. The authors also noted that creating a disaster preparedness framework for a vast and complex culture such as India is challenging at best.

Chattaraj et al. (2021) analyzed communication by one of the biggest manufacturing industries in India, the Steel Authority of India Limited, during the COVID-19 pandemic. They concluded that employees generally gave a "high level of support" to the communication by senior managers. Junior-level managers, however, felt the need for greater interaction between them and senior managers. Interestingly, the authors found that senior managers responded to the criticism and adopted a "*Mass Contact Exercise*" in an online format including a mobile app.

When one takes an "audience perspective" to crisis communication, or any communication, the critical role of *culture* as a determinant of communication processes is often ignored, thus reducing the efficacy of such research. Critiquing the crisis communication literature for almost totally ignoring culture, we (Dhanesh and Sriramesh, 2018) used a framework that broadly defined culture to include societal, media, political, economic, and activist cultures in global public relations (Sriramesh and Vercic, 2020) and analyzed the reputational crisis that

Nestle India faced when a regional government accused the Swiss company for infusing 7 times the acceptable amount of lead in its popular Maggi noodle brand. Our analysis revealed that Nestle had ignored the relevance of socio-cultural variables to any communication particularly crisis communication. Even though the brand had been in the country for over 30 years establishing itself as one of the five most trusted brands in the country, it failed to understand India's political economy and its delayed reaction to the accusations of the regional government let the crisis escalate to the national level, leading to a ban on the product in the country. The company recalled and incinerated over 37 million US dollars worth of the product even though its own tests had failed to detect the high levels of lead claimed by the regional government. In the end, the regional government could not prove its claim in the court of law and Nestle was vindicated. However, the global brand suffered a total loss of about 500 million in lost sales as well as reputational damage. Not understanding the political economy of the country, the level of activism (often directed at international competitors of local economic interests), the media system of the country (mass media as well as digital media), and the culture of the average Indian all contributed to Nestle suffering both reputational and financial damage.

Case Study: COVID-19 Crisis Communication Strategies of the Government of India

When the WHO declared COVID-19 as a global pandemic on March 11, 2020, India only had a few confirmed cases. When India reported its third death on March 17, the Government of India adopted emergency measures and initiated a public awareness campaign. A dedicated toll-free 24×7 national helpline number was started with specific helpline numbers for each state and union territory. Prime Minister Narendra Modi made the first official address to the nation on the pandemic on March 19, calling on people to impose a voluntary 14-hour *Janata Curfew* (people's curfew) on March 22, followed by a 21-day nationwide lockdown three days later. He used the slogan: ***Koi road par na nik**ale* that used the three syllables of the virus (CO – RO – NA) to produce a similar sounding message in Hindi forbidding people from going out.

After the lockdown was announced, the Ministry of Health and Family Welfare (MoHFW) collaborated with UNICEF and partners to implement COVID-19 risk communication and community engagement (RCCE) plan in early April. RCCE for COVID-19 focused on sharing information among communities, mitigating rumors, and involving communities through two-way communication. Key RCCE strategies included the development of national and state-specific communication strategies, a standardized, contextualized message matrix, layering COVID-19-appropriate messages with COVID-19-sensitive messaging, production of communication material, and use of digital media alongside community media such as radio. India launched the Aarogya Setu (bridge of health) mobile app on April 2, which enabled Bluetooth-based contact tracing, mapping of likely hotspots, and dissemination of COVID-19 information. In a televised address to the nation, the Prime Minister announced the Atmanirbhar Bharat ("self-reliant India") COVID-19 stimulus package of US$260 billion.

After 10 weeks of lockdown, a phased reopening of the economy was initiated on May 31, 2020, following which transmission rates skyrocketed to 1 million cases in July. A dedicated vaccine portal and National Clinical Registry for COVID-19 were launched. The MoHFW published the COVID-19 vaccine communication strategy in December 2020. The strategy aimed to address four key areas. These included providing information on the new COVID-19 vaccines and vaccination processes; addressing vaccine eagerness; and vaccine hesitancy; and maintaining and sustaining COVID-19-appropriate behaviors. Initiatives to counter vaccine hesitancy through media included adverse event following immunization (AEFI) spokesperson training; media sensitization training to highlight positive stories of vaccine beneficiaries; amplifying statements and appeals from those who recovered from AEFI; interviews with experts and scientists on vaccine efficacy; and celebrity engagement. The communication channels included individuals and influencers (including celebrities, faith leaders, and frontline workers); community groups such as village councils, scouts and guides, and school management; and media including social media, community media, mass media, and outdoor media. The materials included games, songs, prayers, pledges, posters, videos, interactive radio programs, tweets, folk song lyrics, community radio programs, TV programs and commercials, ringtones, and mobile games. The COVID-19 vaccine communication strategy was delivered alongside partners including ministries of information and broadcasting and international partners such as UNICEF, United Nations Development Programme (UNDP), United Nations Populations Fund (UNFPA), United States Aid for International Development (USAID), WHO, and Gates Foundation.

As fighting fake news became a critical priority, a National Media Rapid Response Cell was set up to facilitate community engagement and rapid response to news in traditional and social media. The cell enabled real-time monitoring of conversations on COVID-19 vaccination, including fact-checking false and misleading vaccine information. March 2021 saw a sudden spike with a second wave of cases. India surpassed the United States for the highest number of recorded cases in a day on April 22, 2021. The MoHFW in collaboration with the UNICEF organized an online workshop with officials from various communication partners in July 2021, to stress the need to reinforce messaging on COVID-19 appropriate behavior and encourage vaccine uptake. The training session focused on the need to fight fake news and misinformation rampant on social media through increasing awareness of WhatsApp's chatbot, which along with the International Fact-Checking Network (IFCN) connects users to 80 fact-checking applications and Twitter and Facebook's warning systems on labeling misleading information.

A nationwide COVID-19 vaccination campaign *Har Ghar Dastak* (every door knocked on) was implemented from Nov 3 till Dec 31, 2021, and later in June–July 2022, which through multiple rounds of household visits aimed to vaccinate eligible beneficiaries who had missed earlier attempts. The year 2021 ended with the advent of the new COVID-19 variant, Omicron, and the government issuing guidelines to the states, laying emphasis on the test–track–treat–vaccinate strategy.

Analysis of COVID-19 Crisis Communication by the Government of India

In the previous edition of this handbook, we had reported that the terms *crisis* and *disaster* are often used interchangeably in India. Seven years later, it appears that the term *crisis communication* has come into its own almost entirely because of the COVID-19 pandemic. There has been emerging research on COVID-19 crisis communication, exploring leadership crisis communication (Jain et al., 2021; Kaur et al., 2021), fake news and disinformation (Goswami et al., 2022), public response to crisis communication strategies (Lwin et al., 2022), and crisis communication strategies of state governments (e.g., Sanjeev et al., 2021) and corporations (e.g., Chattaraj et al., 2021). The COVID-19 crisis placed inordinate demands on crisis communication managers in the public sector. The following section will analyze the Government of India's response to the crisis using the extended parallel process model (EPPM).

The EPPM (Witte, 1994) offers a framework for effective communication of health- and risk-related messages. According to the EPPM, depending on audiences' perceptions of threat and efficacy, they will engage in non-responses, danger control responses, and fear control responses. Audiences' perception of threat, which motivates them into action, consists of the perceived severity of the threat and perceived susceptibility. As messages influence perceptions of threat, fear appeals will persuade audiences that they are susceptible to dire consequences. Perceived efficacy, which consists of response/plan efficacy and self-efficacy, will then influence whether a subsequent response is adaptive or maladaptive. While response/plan efficacy refers to the perceived effectiveness of the recommended course of action, self-efficacy refers to beliefs about one's ability to perform the recommended action. Depending on a combination of assessing threat and efficacy, audience will engage in non-responses, fear control responses such as ignoring the threat, and danger control responses. Examples of danger control responses for COVID-19 include washing hands, social distancing, and self-isolation.

Based on the tenets of EPPM, Coombs (2020) highlighted six major communicative demands that influenced COVID-19 crisis communication by public sector actors: (1) anxiety, (2) empathy, (3) efficacy, (4) fatigue, (5) reach, and (6) threat and suggested ways in which crisis communicators can address each of these demands. The following section analyzes the Government of India's crisis communication response using this framework.

Anxiety

Crisis communicators have to keep messages simple to address public anxiety, as anxiety tends to produce stress, which in turn negatively affects cognitive abilities and reduces comprehension. The Government of India used short and simple messages, such as *Do Gaj Ki Doori* (six-feet distancing), Help Us to Help You, and #BreakTheStigma. Further, a hub-and-spoke message design is recommended wherein the hub refers to the central repository that contains detailed information, while the spokes refer to the short and simple messages that are disseminated through various channels. The MoHFW had established a dedicated website for COVID-19, and the government had announced a dedicated toll-free 24×7 national helpline number with specific helpline numbers for each state and union territory.

Empathy

Public health crisis communication must convey empathy to assure constituents that you understand their anxiety. An situational crisis communication theory (SCCT)- and discursive theory-based analysis of tweets issued by public sector leaders in India between the four lockdown periods found that leadership communication was primarily focused not only on disseminating crisis management information but also on strengthening followers' resilience and trust through empathetic messages (Jain et al., 2021). Further, the MoHFW initiated campaigns addressing mental health issues using celebrities to break the stigma and discrimination faced by health workers and people affected by COVID-19, emphasizing the need for empathy.

Efficacy

Messages that can convey response and self-efficacy are pivotal in nudging people toward the response of danger control. Message efficacy can be assessed through social media listening and direct contact with audiences. The Government of India incorporated several aspects of response and self-efficacy into its messaging. For instance, the #StayHomeStaySafe and #BreakTheStigma messages highlighted both response and self-efficacy. Further, the establishment of the National Media Rapid Response Cell by the MoHFW responsible for real-time monitoring of conversations on COVID-19 vaccination helped to track the public's response.

Fatigue

In a prolonged public health crisis, the public can become tired of receiving yet another crisis message, to address which creative ways of presenting the messages must be pursued. For instance, MoHFW awareness materials included *ghazals* (a form of poetry) delivered through animated characters; comic books aimed at children that explained the fight against Corona; and rap songs to discourage spitting in public places. Further, the COVID-19 vaccine communication strategy included diverse materials such as games, songs, prayers, pledges, interactive radio programs, folk song lyrics, community radio programs, ringtones, and mobile games to keep the messaging fresh.

Reach

To maximize reach with marginalized constituents, it is critical to create messages in multiple languages, use a mix of traditional and social media platforms, and recruit local community leaders to champion public health communication. The Government of India created messages not only in Hindi and English, India's official languages, but also in regional languages disseminated locally. To amplify reach, the COVID-19 vaccine communication strategy extensively employed influencers including faith leaders and frontline workers; community groups such as village councils, scouts and guides, and school management; and media including social, community, mass, and outdoor.

Threat

It is essential for public health crisis communicators to trigger appropriate threat levels in constituents without unduly increasing fear. The MoHFW initiated a public awareness campaign to inform citizens and debunk false claims that could subdue the perception of threats such as the consumption of garlic would prevent the disease. A key factor that helped to reduce fear was control over fake news (Goswami et al., 2022), and the National Media Rapid Response Cell was set up at MoHFW for fact-checking news. In conclusion, the Indian government's crisis communication response to the public health crisis appears to have followed most of the guidelines recommended for crisis communicators in the public sector (Coombs, 2020; Hyland-Wood et al., 2021; Witte, 1994).

Concluding Thoughts

Systematic research on crisis communication in India has progressed since the last edition of this book, spurred on by the onset of the global COVID-19 pandemic. However, much more work needs to be done so that practitioners can create strategies based on empirical evidence generated from culturally grounded contexts. Although our case study showed that the Indian government appears to have followed most of the guidelines for public sector's communication response to a major health crisis, to move research on crisis communication in India forward, it might be critical to adopt a variety of approaches other than classic approaches to crisis communication such as SCCT and EPPM. The idea of transcultural crisis communication (Bajaj et al., 2021) could be further strengthened with empirical work that assesses the impact of culture on crisis communication. For instance, in India, what were some of the cultural factors that could have propelled the actions of the crisis communicators in the public sector and the responses of the public? This can bolster emergent research on the influence of culture on crisis communication similar to the case study on Nestle's Maggie noodle product line in India (Dhanesh & Sriramesh, 2018). It is vital for the field of crisis communication to adopt the impact of culture (as broadly defined by Sriramesh and Vercic, 2020) to broaden the horizons of the field of crisis communication.

References

ACCCA. (2009). *Communicating climate risks: Insights gained through the ACCCA project*. Retrieved from http://start.org/download/publications/accca09-web.pdf (accessed November 24, 2015)

Allan, S. (2012). Online news reporting of crisis events: Investigating the role of citizen witnessing. In E. Siapera, & A. Veglis, Eds., *The Handbook of Global Online Journalism* (pp. 331–352). Chichester, UK: Wiley-Blackwell.

Bajaj, G., Khandelwal, S., & Budhwar, P. (2021). COVID-19 pandemic and the impact of cross-cultural differences on crisis management: A conceptual model of transcultural crisis management. *International Journal of Cross Cultural Management: CCM, 21*(3), 569–601. https://doi.org/10.1177/14705958211060189

Chattaraj, D., Mohanty, S., & Satpathy, A. (2021). Communicating through a pandemic: Insights on crisis communication from Steel Authority of India Limited, Rourkela Steel Plant. *Vikalpa, 46*(3), 166–176.

Coombs, W. T. (2020). Public sector crises: Realizations from covid-19 for crisis communication. *Partecipazione e Conflitto, 13*(2), 990–1001. https://doi.org/10.1285/i20356609v13i2p990

Dasgupta, U., Jha, C. K., & Sarangi, S. (2020). Procedural rationality in the time of Covid-19. *Economic & Political Weekly, 55*(25), 13–16.

Das, S., Panda, K. G., Sen, D., & Arif, W. (2019). A survey of national disaster communication systems and spectrum allocation – An Indian perspective. *IETE Technical Review*. http://doi.org/10.1080/02564602.2019.1566030

De, S. J., & Shukla, R. (2021). An analysis of privacy policies of public Covid-19 apps: Evidence from India. *Journal of Public Affairs*. http://doi.org/10.1002/pa.2801

Dhanesh, G., & Sriramesh, K. (2018). Culture and crisis communication: Nestle India's noodle case. *Journal of International Management, 24*(3), 204–214.

George, S., & Kumar, P. P. A. (2022). Indicator-based assessment of capacity development for disaster preparedness in the Indian context. *Environment Systems and Decisions, 42*, 417–435. https://doi.org/10.1007/s10669-022-09856-0

Go, V. F., Sethulakshmi, C. J., Bentley, M. E., Sivaram, S., Srikrishnan, A. K., Solomon, S., & Celentano, D. D. (2003). When HIV-prevention messages and gender norms clash: The impact of domestic violence on women's HIV risk in slums of Chennai. *India. AIDS and Behavior, 7*(3), 263–272.

Godbole, S., & Mehendale, S. (2005). HIV/AIDS epidemic in India: Risk factors, risk behaviour and strategies for prevention and control. *Indian Journal of Medical Research, 12*(4), 356–368.

Goswami, M. P., Anjali, R., Raj, A., Puthiyakath, H. H., & Thanvi, J. (2022). Media during pandemic crisis in India: An analysis of people's perception during the first wave of COVID-19. *Journal of Creative Communications*, 97325862210907. https://doi.org/10.1177/09732586221090750

Gupte, S. (2001). McDonald's averts a crisis. *Ad Age Global, 1*(11), 4.

Gupta, S., Pande, N., Arumugham, T., & Sanjeev, M. A. (2022). Reputational impact of Covid-19 pandemic management on World Health Organization among Indian professionals. *Journal of Public Affairs*. http://doi.org/10.1002/pa.2842

Hyland-Wood, B., Gardner, J., Leask, J., & Ecker, U. K. H. (2021). Toward effective government communication strategies in the era of COVID-19. *Humanities & Social Sciences Communications, 8*(1), 1–11. https://doi.org/10.1057/s41599-020-00701-w

Jain, N., Malviya, P., Singh, P., & Mukherjee, S. (2021). Twitter mediated sociopolitical communication during the COVID-19 pandemic crisis in India. *Frontiers in Psychology, 12*, 784907–784907. https://doi.org/10.3389/fpsyg.2021.784907

Kaur et al. (2021). Emotions in leader's crisis communication: Twitter sentiment analysis during COVID-19 outbreak. *Journal of Human Behavior in the Social Environment, 31*(1–4), 362–372.

Kodrich, K., & Laituri, M. (2005). The formation of a disaster community in cyberspace: The role of online news media after the 2001 Gujarat earthquake. *Convergence: The International Journal of Research into New Media Technologies, 11*(40), 40–56.

Lwin, M. O., Sheldenkar, A., Lu, J., Schulz, P. J., Shin, W., Panchapakesan, C., Gupta, R., & Yang, Y. (2022). The evolution of public sentiments during the COVID-19 pandemic: Case comparisons of India, Singapore, South Korea, the United Kingdom, and the United States. *JMIR Infodemiology, 2*(1), e31473. http://doi.org/10.2196/31473

Mehra, P. (2011). Communicating in a crisis and the role of a business leader: The case of jet airways. *Journal of Case Research, 2*(2), 133–147.

Ministry of Home Affairs (2011). *Disaster management in India.* Retrieved from http://ndmindia.nic.in/UNDP-020811.pdf (accessed November 24, 2015)

Mohanty, S., Karelia, H., & Issar, R. (n.d.). *ICT for disaster risk reduction: The Indian experience.* Retrieved from http://www.ndmindia.nic.in/wcdrdocs/ict%20for%20disaster%20risk%20reduction.pdf (accessed November 24, 2015)

Murphy, E. (2012). *Social mobilization lessons from the CORE group polio project in Angola, Ethiopia, and India.* Retrieved from http://www.coregroup.org/storage/Polio_Initiative/smreport-online.pdf (accessed November 24, 2015)

Narayana, U., & Kapur, P. (2010). Media, public attitude and Mumbai terror of 26/11. *Media Asia, 37*(2), 95–102.

Obregon, R., Chitnis, K., Morry, C., Feek, W., Bates, J., Galway, M., & Ogden, E. (2009). Achieving polio eradication: A review of health communication evidence and lessons learned in India and Pakistan. *Bulletin of the World Health Organization, 87*(8), 624–630.

Panwar, N. S., & Mitra, A. K. (2020). COVID-19 crisis and urbanization, migration and inclusive city policies in India: A new theoretical framework. *Journal of Public Affairs.* http://doi.org/10.1002/pa.2249

Prabhakar, S. V. R. K., & Shaw, R. (2008). Climate change adaptation implications for drought risk mitigation: A perspective for India. *Climatic Change, 88,* 113–130.

Reynolds, B., & Seeger, M. W. (2005). Crisis and emergency risk communication as an integrative model. *Journal of Health Communication, 10,* 43–55.

Samarajiva, R., & Waidyanatha, N. (2009). Two complementary mobile technologies for disaster warning. *Info, 11*(2), 58–65.

Sanjeev, M. A., Pande, N., & Kumar, S. P. K. (2021). Role of effective crisis communication by the government in managing the first wave Covid-19 pandemic – A study of Kerala government's success. *Journal of Public Affairs.* http://doi.org/10.1002/pa.2721

Seeger, M. W., Sellnow, T. L., & Ulmer, R. R. (1998). Communication, organization and crisis. In M. E. Roloff, Ed., *Communication Yearbook 21* (pp. 231–276). Thousand Oaks, CA: Sage.

Shrivastava, P. (1987). *Bhopal: Anatomy of a Crisis.* Cambridge, Mass: Ballinger Publishing Company.

Sivaram, S., Johnson, S., Bentley, M. E., Go, V. F., Latkin, C., Srikrishnan, A. K., Celentano, D. D., & Solomon, S. (2005). Sexual health promotion in Chennai, India: Key role of communication among social networks. *Health Promotion International, 20*(4), 327–333. http://doi.org/10.1093/heapro/dai012

Sriramesh, K. (2004). Public relations practice and research in Asia: A conceptual framework. In K. Sriramesh, Ed., *Public Relations in Asia: An Anthology* (pp. 1–27). Singapore: Thomson.

Sriramesh, K., & Verčič, D. (2009). *The Global Public Relations Handbook: Theory, Research, and Practice.* New York: Routledge.

Sriramesh, K., & Vercic, D. (2020). *The Global Public Relations Handbook: Theory, Research, and Practice* (3rd ed.). New York, NY: Routledge.

Sriramesh, K., Wattegama, C., & Abo, J. F. (2006). The role of ICTs in the Asia-Pacific. In F. Libero, Ed., *Digital Review of the Asia-Pacific.* New Delhi: Sage.

UNESCO. (2006). *Indian Ocean tsunami warning and mitigation system IOTWS [Conference paper].* Retrieved from http://www.jodc.go.jp/info/ioc_doc/Technical/146669e.pdf (accessed November 24, 2015)

Witte, K. (1994). Fear control and danger control: A test of the extended parallel process model (EPPM). *Communication Monographs, 61*(2), 113–134. https://doi.org/10.1080/03637759409376328

Author's Bio

Krishnamurthy Sriramesh is a professor of Public Relations at the University of Colorado, Boulder. His extensive teaching experience includes teaching at 10 universities in Asia, Australasia, Europe, and North America. His teaching has been recognized with several awards including Teacher of the Year at the University of Florida and Charles W. Redding Teaching Award at Purdue University. His research program covers topics such as strategic public relations, global public relations, corporate social responsibility, and public relations for development. He has received a number of research awards including the prestigious Pathfinder Award from the Institute of Public Relations in 2004 "for original scholarly research contributing to the public relations body of knowledge." He has also received the 2003 and 2020 PRIDE awards from the National Communication Association (NCA) for "outstanding book/monograph" and the Golden Gator Award for research from the University of Florida. He was appointed as the University Faculty Scholar at Purdue University (2012–2017) as well as the Faculty Fellow at Purdue Institute for Civic Communication (PICC) and was a Page Legacy Scholar of the Arthur W. Page Society in 2016. He has consulted with nonprofits such as the International Institute for Tropical Agriculture (IITA) based in Nigeria and the Global Trade Analysis Project (GTAP). He was a member of the Independent Advisory Committee for Humidtropics – a three-continent agriculture research project for four years. He has co-edited several books and published over 100 research articles and book chapters in addition to presenting over 110 conference papers, seminars, and presentations in over 30 countries. He had served as the assistant editor of *Public Relations Review* (for 11 years) and associate editor of the *Journal of Communication Management* (for 14 years). He is a member of the editorial board of several journals including *Journalism and Mass Communication Quarterly*, *Management Communication Quarterly*, *Public Relations Review*, and *Journal of Communication Management*. He had also served on the Editorial Board of the Digital Review of Asia Pacific (DirAP), *Journal of Communication*, *Journal of Public Relations Research*, and the second edition of the *Encyclopedia of Public Relations*. ORCiD: 0000-0002-5710-026X.

Ganga S. Dhanesh (PhD, National University of Singapore) is an associate professor at the Department of Communication, University of Maryland. Previously, she was an assistant professor at the Department of Communications and New Media, National University of Singapore, and an associate professor and associate dean at the College of Communication and Media Sciences, Zayed University. Dr Dhanesh's prior experience in corporate and nonprofit sectors has informed her extensive research program on corporate social responsibility (CSR) and strategic communication. Her work has appeared in books and journals such as *Business Horizons*, *Management Communication Quarterly*, *Journal of International Management*, *Journal of Public Relations Research*, and *Public Relations Review*. She has won multiple research awards, and a recent bibliometric analysis placed her among the top two most productive scholars on CSR within public relations research. Dhanesh serves as an associate editor for the *Journal of Communication Management* and is on the editorial board of *Business Horizons*, *Public Relations Review*, and *The Journal of Public Relations Research*. Dr. Dhanesh actively consults for national and multinational organizations on strategic communication. She was the founding university lead for the partnership between Zayed University and the UAE chapter of the Unstereotype Alliance, convened by UN Women. Dr. Dhanesh was also a lead researcher for the first Global Capabilities Framework study in the Middle East. She is a regular speaker at industry events and a contributor of thought pieces on strategic communication. Her work has appeared in outlets of the Institute for Public Relations, the European Public Relations Education and Research Association, and the Dubai Chamber of Commerce.

29

Risk Communication Research and Practice in Japan

Mihoko Sakurai
Graduate School of International Management, International University of Japan, Niigata, Japan

The Context of Risk and Crisis Communication in Japan

According to EM-DAT – The International Disaster Database compiled by the Center for Research on the Epidemiology of Disasters (CRED, 2023), nearly 300–400 natural disasters occur around the world every year, with a significant impact also being felt in the daily lives of us living here in Japan. In fact, Japan is highly susceptible to disasters. It is one of the world's 10 most earthquake-prone countries, which is due to the Pacific Ring of Fire, a belt of active volcanoes and earthquake zones around the rim of the Pacific Ocean (WorldAtlas, 2022). The Great East Japan Earthquake in 2011 had the highest magnitude (Mw 9.1) on the Richter scale in Japanese history. On average, around 2,000 earthquakes, including shaking at seismic intensity level one, occur within the country every year. In 2022, 1964 earthquakes[1] were observed (Japan Meteorological Agency, 2022).

Earthquakes are not the only natural threat to the Japanese population. Disasters due to heavy rain, floods, and landslides are also becoming an everyday threat. The annual number of hours with precipitation of 50 mm or more has steadily increased over the statistical period 1976–2016 (Cabinet Office Japan, 2019). While the statistics show no change in trend for the annual number of days with a daily precipitation between 200 and 400 mm over the same period, the number of days with a precipitation of 400 mm or more has been growing. Overall precipitation is predicted to significantly increase in almost all regions and seasons.

Disaster Risk Reduction and Japan

Climate change and the natural disasters that accompany it are at the center of global risk management discussions (World Economic Forum, 2023) and a topic of growing concern in Japan. Disaster risk reduction (DRR) is defined as "preventing new and reducing existing disaster risk and managing residual risk, all of which contribute to strengthening resilience

[1] Including 1282 at magnitude1; 475 at M2; 156 at M3; 36 at M4; 7 at M5-weak; 6 at M5-strong; 1 at M6-weak and 1 at M6-strong.

The Handbook of International Crisis and Risk Communication Research, Second Edition.
Edited by Andreas Schwarz, Matthew W. Seeger, and Sora Kim.

and therefore to the achievement of sustainable development" (United Nations Office for Disaster Risk Reduction, 2017). Looking back on the history of DRR in the Japanese context, there have been three turning points over the past 50 years which affected disaster preparedness and response management activities (Sakurai & Shaw, 2022). The first was the 1959 Isewan Typhoon, which led to the development of the early warning system. The second was the 1995 Great Hanshin Awaji Earthquake, which led to the widespread recognition of the existence of post-disaster volunteers and the need for discussions concerning the importance of mutual aid. The third was the 2011 Great East Japan Earthquake, which raised awareness of the importance of community-based preparedness before a disaster strikes. It was also around this time that digital volunteers became active on the internet.

The need to understand how disasters occur and also how to integrate various disciplines such as psychology, sociology, and engineering in the search for solutions was recognized. Advancements in digital technology have focused attention on the use of that technology to promote mutual aid and help people take action to save lives in the event of a disaster (Sakurai et al., 2014).

Generally, people in Japan are concerned about natural disasters. The author conducted an online questionnaire survey in 2021 asking people to describe their ideal lifestyle. Out of 4,129 respondents, 52.4% responded with "a secure life protected from disasters and crime." Other views which got over 50% of the respondents' answer were "a quiet and hassle-free life," "a life with less worries about money," and "a peaceful and fulfilling retirement." Another survey, which was conducted in June 2022 with 1,000 subjects, had 86.2% of respondents answer that they were interested in preparedness for future natural disasters (Mitsui Sumitomo Insurance Company, 2022). A new public agency, the Digital Agency, was established in 2021. It functions as the Disaster Risk Management team set up under the Group of Service for Citizens. Until then, the Cabinet Office of Japan had been the only organization in charge of disaster management, but its role was solely that of disaster management on behalf of its respective ministries. The Digital Agency was the first instance of an organization established under the header of "disaster" for the affected people at large.

Focus of This Chapter

Once a disaster occurs, whether it is an earthquake or a flood, we need to decide whether to evacuate or not. Communication and behavior related to evacuation are critical because they may affect people's lives profoundly. Therefore, this chapter focuses on both. Risk communication involves both preparedness and the initial response phase when a natural disaster occurs. Preparedness requires increased disaster risk awareness (Ozeki et al., 2017). Initial response relies on a correct understanding of the disaster situation, i.e., situational awareness (Murayama, 2021) and decision-making (Usuda, 2021) appropriate for saving lives. While there are a wide variety of communication actors, this chapter addresses communication between public authorities, i.e., the Japan Meteorological Agency, local government, and the general population.

Among the traditional four stages of disaster management (McLoughlin, 1985; Sakurai & Murayama, 2019), risk communication has a significant impact on the preparedness and response phases (Figure 29.1). Among the range of risk communication activities, situation awareness has the greatest influence on people's attitudes in reacting to a disaster. Situational awareness can be explained along three levels of actions: (1) perception of the critical elements in the environment, (2) comprehension of the situation, and (3) projection of its future status (Endsley, 1988; Murayama, 2021). In order to effectively carry out these three actions in a disaster situation, the correct understanding of disaster risk is crucial. This will guide proper decision-making and evacuation behavior.

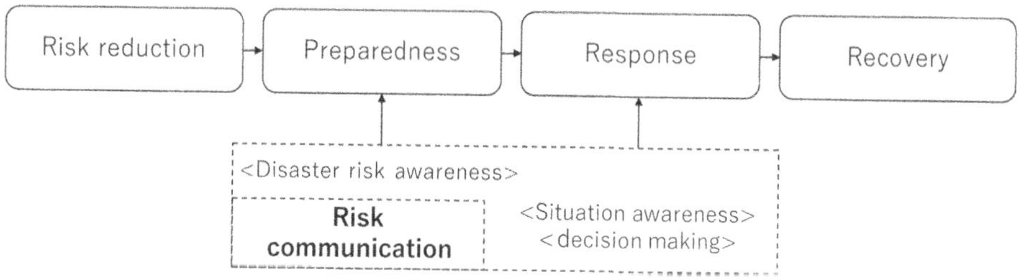

Figure 29.1 Scope of risk communication and stages of natural disaster management.

Issues Around Risk Communication in Japan

There are two major concerns affecting risk communication in Japan when a natural disaster occurs. First, there is the relationship between communication and behavior. As previously noted in one study, public authorities may issue a lot of information, but it does not necessarily lead people to take evacuation action (Nakai & Nakano, 2023). However, behavioral change is imperative and therefore the ultimate goal of DRR and associated risk communication activities (Sakurai & Shaw, 2022). Second, "local" information is difficult to find (Sakurai & Adu-Gyamfi, 2020). The elements of a disaster situation assembled by local governments and other agencies are not immediately communicated to residents. It is extremely difficult to obtain highly localized information on the situation around ourselves, such as whether the roads are passable, whether stores are open, and when infrastructure will be restored, etc.

Among the various types of disasters, this chapter discusses risks associated with earthquakes, floods, and landslides caused by heavy rains, as well as communication which guides action in such situations.

The State of Research in Risk and Crisis Communication

We will look at risk communication in terms of three perspectives, namely, institutional, media, and audience. What will be discussed are institutional issues of risk communication, communication at evacuation centers, reliability of information, attitudes of local government towards social media, and information provision to the general public.

Local Government

Japan's governance structure has three levels: national, prefectural, and local. Although a disaster response plan is a guideline for responses to natural disasters determined at each level of government (Abdolahzadeh et al., 2023), it is local government that has the responsibility of issuing the evacuation order to its residents. Local government acts as the disaster-related central risk information center managing disaster response activities. This effort includes extensive information exchange and communication with national and prefectural governments and even industry and third-party actors. Once a disaster occurs, information overload and confusion may cause havoc in the response. Information collection makes extremely labor-intensive demands on local government officials (Sakurai et al., 2014). Therefore, a standardized data model for effective communication among first responders and other related entities should be in place (Sakurai, 2021). While collecting situational information from various stakeholders, the local government issues an evacuation order and sets up official evacuation centers. Depending on the scale of a disaster, the number of evacuation centers can easily exceed a hundred. For instance, the number of planned evacuation centers in Tokyo is as many as 4,800 (Tokyo Metropolitan Government, 2023).

The management of these evacuation centers is handled by local governments such as wards, cities, towns, and villages.

The importance of a standardized communication structure is often discussed in health care interactions with evacuees. Miyamoto et al. (2023) argue that a logbook could help with recording the medical/clinical status of an evacuee. A logbook could be used by public health nurses, doctors, and volunteers, enabling them to communicate with evacuees much more easily. A standardized, strategic manual for setting up a disaster response management headquarters should be considered for smooth communication among related organizations (Ojima et al., 2023). Ojima et al. (2023) presented a survey result showing that only 36% of prefectural governments have prepared such a manual.

Media and Social Media

Media is one of the essential stakeholders that publicizes evacuation information orders and other related guidance. TV, radio, websites, and social media are the major channels through which people can get information and communicate with local authorities. As shown, however, local information is hard to find on commercial media channels (Sakurai & Adu-Gyamfi, 2020). Local information might cover, for instance, where to evacuate to and details about what is happening in one's own neighborhood. Other frequently asked questions to local government are whether one's household is subject to an evacuation order, what one should do if the house is damaged or a smell of gas has been noticed, what to do if water pipes are leaking, the road is sinking, or a bridge has fallen down. Frightened residents will ask where the water trucks are, when food and other supplies are scheduled to arrive, when roadblocks will be lifted, electricity, gas, and water restored, disaster victim certificates issued, and what is going on at the city office, etc.

Such local information can be found on individual media channels, especially on social media. However, verifying the authenticity of information on those media remains a problem (Tanaka, 2021). An earlier study argues that after the 2011 Great East Japan Earthquake and the Fukushima nuclear accident, Twitter showed a clear division between groups that sent out information based on scientific fact and those that sent out emotional rather than factual statements about radiation risks (Murakami et al., 2023).

From the standpoint of local government, Kawamura et al. (2023) show that local governments which experienced a disaster used SNS much more frequently than those that did not have any disaster experience. Local governments that have not experienced disasters are more likely to use the online homepage of public agencies and news organizations rather than SNS for information gathering. In addition, some municipalities have difficulties in gathering and disseminating situational information through SNS due to the lack of personnel.

People

Evacuation alerts are broadcast to people along five color-coded levels (Figure 29.2). Evacuation orders issued by local government cover Alert Levels 3 to 5. Level 1 and 2 are issued by the Japan Meteorological Agency, which provides information on growing meteorological risk.

Alert Level 5, in black color, calls for "Emergency Safety Measures," which indicates a life-threatening situation where we can no longer safely evacuate. Evacuation action is required before it gets to Level 5. Alert Level 4, in purple, provides "Evacuation Instruction," which tells all residents to evacuate from the affected areas. Alert Level 3, in red, indicates "Evacuation of the Elderly." It asks elderly people, those with disabilities, and others who may need more time to leave, to evacuate the affected areas.

Traditionally, evacuation drills have been part of primary and secondary school education (Sakurai et al., 2020; Shaw et al., 2021). Children learn about the evacuation process and

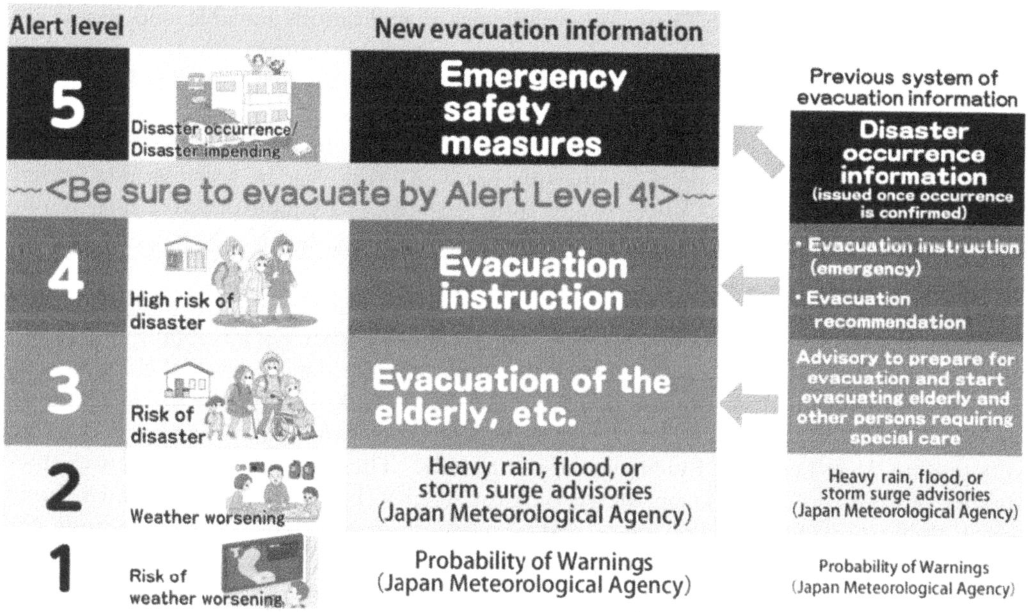

Figure 29.2 Evacuation information. *Source*: Cabinet Office Japan (2023)/Disaster Management, Cabinet Office/CC BY 4.0.

procedures. However, this type of educational opportunity is not officially available to adults and foreigners (Sakurai & Shaw, 2022). In addition, due to language issues, some foreigners remain distant from such information, which causes problems in evacuation behaviors (Kanbara et al., 2016). Also, color coding is not always provided in information from the media, which remains a challenge in how to communicate with people with disabilities (Shek-Noble, 2023; Shimoda, 2023).

Practical Cases of Risk Communication

This section shows how local government and related agencies try to solve risk communication issues. The process follows the traditional stages of disaster management and risk communication described in Figure 29.1.

Risk Communication for Initial Response

Evacuation information is disseminated through various channels. When local government and the Japan Meteorological Agency issue an evacuation order or weather-related advisory/ warning, they both tend to send the details through their social media accounts. Broadcasting companies also transmit that information to the local population through both television and their own social media accounts.

Independently, residents can receive the information directly on their mobile phones in two ways. One way has each cell phone company employ so-called "area mail" or "emergency alert mail," the actual term depending on the company providing the service. When the Japan Meteorological Agency issues a weather-related warning, people in the area where that warning is issued automatically receive a message on their mobile phone. This is not a message through social media, but more likely using SMS. The other way is using a "disaster prevention app." This application is developed by media and the disaster prevention industry and is free to download by everyone. There are several types of applications available, and people can choose which app they want to use. Some of these disaster prevention apps have a function to send push notifications of evacuation information and weather-related advisories or warnings.

According to a survey by the Mobile Society Research Institute, Japan, the percentage of people who install such apps on their smartphones is growing year by year (Mobile Society Research Institute, 2022). The survey results show that 48% of a sample of 9,072 smartphone owners installed one of those apps in 2021. The higher the age, the greater the percentage of people who have installed the app.

Some disaster prevention apps are connected to the "Kikikuru" platform, which is a web-based Geographical Information System (GIS) application. Kikikuru is a mapping tool developed by the Japan Meteorological Agency that indicates the danger level of flooding and landslide disasters by area. Figure 29.3 shows the hazard risk distribution of landslides on August 17, 2023. The map displays evacuation information at each of the five levels. The red areas refer to Alert Level 3, "Evacuation of the Elderly." The yellow area received a weather advisory/warning from the Japan Meteorological Agency. In Figure 29.3, Kikikuru shows Tottori Prefecture, Okayama Prefecture, and Gifu Prefecture with a high risk of landslide disaster. Evacuation information and weather advisories, which are displayed on Kikikuru, can also be sent through some of the disaster prevention apps.

"Area mail" or "emergency alert mail" delivers the same information directly to mobile phones. The advantage of this system is that warnings are delivered automatically without the need to register, as the message is sent from the location of the cellular base station. However, since the advisory/warning or evacuation request is issued to an entire city or district, it is not always clear whether the risk of a disaster is relatively high or low near one's own specific location. While disaster prevention apps generally require user registration, some of them link to the Kikikuru platform and provide detailed hazard risk locations on the map. The color-coded visualization of disaster hazard risk areas allows us to determine at a glance the degree to which a residence or current location is at risk.

Various efforts have been made by local governments across Japan to raise disaster awareness among residents. However, even though municipalities have developed applications that specialize in disaster prevention functions and are "just for disaster prevention," the number of downloads has been slow to increase. Although Japan is much exposed to disasters, it took us

Figure 29.3 Kikikuru created by processing. *Source*: Japan Meteorological Agency (2023).

a decade or so to learn that tools we are not accustomed to using on a daily basis are useless in times of emergency (Sakurai & Chughtai, 2020).

The most popular disaster prevention apps are the ones developed by Yahoo! Japan and NHK (Mobile Society Research Institute, 2022). Both are media companies: Yahoo! Japan is an online media platform, while NHK is the Japanese Public Broadcaster. They provide news and weather information used on a daily basis, facilitating smooth integration of functions during normal times and times of disaster.

Risk Communication for Preparedness

Area mail, emergency alert mail, disaster prevention apps, and Kikikuru are designed to increase people's situation awareness and evacuation behavior. However, in order to approach behavioral change for evacuation, advance preparation is important (Hatori et al., 2023). It means preparation as part of everyday-based activities to facilitate communication between residents and local governments in emergencies and consequently also encourage appropriate evacuation behavior. It means there is a strong need to intensify the degree of disaster risk awareness. Ozeki et al. (2017) suggested five aspects for fostering disaster risk awareness. They are imagination, sense of crisis, awareness of mutual aid, interest, and anxiety (Table 29.1).

An earlier study shows that ongoing disaster risk education using digital technology increases the degree of imagination, the sense of mutual aid, and the interest of participants in disaster events (Sakurai & Shaw, 2022). This technology enables people to get a correct understanding of weather-related advisory/warning and evacuation information, and it encourages behavioral change. Disaster risk education takes various forms. For instance, Hamanaka and Umemoto (2019) developed a card game for raising people's imagination in an emergency and fostering cooperation with community associations. It is named *Areganai! Dohsuru?* in Japanese, which means *I don't have that! What should we do?*

As an everyday-based practice, the Ministry of Land, Infrastructure, Transport and Tourism has prepared "My Timeline." Each local government in Japan publishes a so-called "hazard map," which visualizes local vulnerability to each type of disaster. It looks similar to Kikikuru, but instead of real-time situations, it shows high-risk areas with hazardous topography. A hazard map also shows the location of the official evacuation center in each municipality. This map has long been used for disaster education. However, the previously cited survey shows less than 40% of respondents knew about the existence of such a map (Mobile Society Research Institute, 2022).

To raise awareness of hazard maps, the Ministry has taken the My Timeline initiative. My Timeline is a disaster preparedness sheet in which people, while studying the hazard maps, fill in details such as the distance from their homes to evacuation centers, the time it will take to

Table 29.1 Five aspects of disaster risk awareness.

Aspects of risk awareness	*Description*
1 Imagination	The ability to imagine what might happen, what would be needed and what would constitute a risk if a disaster occurred
2 Sense of crisis	Consideration of the seriousness of a disaster and ability to decide if the current situation is bad
3 Awareness of mutual aid	Consideration of what can be done for others and society in the area affected
4 Interest	The level of interest in disasters and the ability to see them as a personal matter
5 Anxiety	The degree to which one worries about disasters

Source: Adapted from Ozeki et al. (2017).

evacuate, and what emergency supplies are needed for their home. Neighborhood associations and other groups in regional Japan are also taking the initiative in educating the public about disaster preparedness using My Timeline.

My Timeline was originally stated on a sheet of paper, but recently some of the disaster prevention apps have begun to employ My Timeline as one of the app's functions. This digital My Timeline can record contact information and set evacuation centers for each disaster and region. As people receive automatic notifications of weather-related advisories, warnings, and evacuation information via a disaster prevention app, coordinating My Timeline with the app can strengthen people's disaster risk awareness and further enhance situational awareness.

Likewise, disaster prevention applications using emerging technology are getting popular, such as especially drones (Furutani & Minami, 2021), robots (Kuramoto et al., 2023), and VR/AR (Itamiya, 2021), all of which offer promising technology to boost imagination focused on disaster situations.

The seamless, or "phase-free," integration of everyday life and life in a disaster situation also greatly supports preparedness. The phase-free concept has been frequently discussed in recent years (Matsuzaki et al., 2018; Sakai et al., 2023). It is the idea to protect people's lives right across all ordinary phases of daily life and emergencies without any division between the two. This concept was initially discussed in the area of product design. In the context of this paper, it can be interpreted as producing a tight integration of risk preparedness and initial response phases. For instance, when we think about disasters, we inevitably ask ourselves what we might need in such a situation or what preparations we should make in advance. However, the idea is to make effective use of things and strategies that are available on a daily basis and that are also readily in use at the time of a disaster, rather than things and strategies that are set aside to be used "only" at the time of an emergency.

Concluding Remarks

As discussed, there is a large body of research on evacuation behavior, and there has been considerable progress in technology that allows warnings of disaster risk to reach people directly. Yet despite advances in technology, people still lose their lives to natural calamities every year. It looks like awareness is not keeping pace with technological advances. Nevertheless, technology is beginning to bridge the gap between everyday life and disaster situations, and people are beginning to recognize the need for pre-disaster preparedness.

Research and Practice for Risk Communication Issues

The communication efforts described in this chapter, i.e., area/emergency alert mail, disaster prevention apps, and collaboration with Kikikuru, all encourage people to take life-saving actions at the time of a disaster. Although there are initiatives which encourage behavioral change, promoting evacuation intentions in itself is not enough; what is most important are specific evacuation criteria (Hatori et al., 2023). These criteria vary depending on the geography of where people live and their household composition. For example, areas at high risk of landslides and flat areas away from rivers have different levels of landslide risk and flood danger. Time for evacuation will take longer if there are elderly people or children in the family. In order to coordinate the evacuation information following a disaster with one's own specific criteria, we must use the knowledge gained in advance preparation.

In doing so, it is quite important to incorporate the tools provided for advance preparedness into risk communication activities. This chapter introduced My Timeline, a disaster risk education tool using card games and the use of emerging technology to enhance the imagination skills of the participants. It is necessary to place these initiatives within the whole framework of risk communication and emphasize preparedness and response coordination.

The use of Geographical Information System (GIS) in risk communication has made it possible to deliver more detailed local information to residents. Likewise, Kikikuru interactively shows the real-time disaster risk of specific areas on the map, and a couple of disaster management applications employ Web-GIS in order to produce interactive hazard/vulnerability maps of residential areas (Koyama, 2022). Several experiments are ongoing to utilize GIS for displaying evacuation routes using residents' location data (Shimoda, 2023). However, GIS cannot yet show the usability of all potentially nearby roads or the reopening times of any stores. Therefore, the role of local communities in providing such details will become important as communicators of local risk conditions. The importance of local communities has been discussed in the literature. They act as communication hubs for their local residents, emphasizing the importance of everyday practice and neighborhood drills (Sakurai, 2022).

This perspective requires the coordination of advance preparation and post-disaster communication in the response phase. Since relationships of individuals within their local communities are one component of proactive disaster risk awareness (Ozeki et al., 2017), daily-basis risk communication at the local community level should receive more attention. This will not only strengthen individual alertness in disaster response choices but also foster increased attentiveness to practical mutual aid options. On that basis, proactive behavioral change can be expected to grow.

Future Research Areas

As discussed in the previous section, organizations involved in disaster response often lack standardized communication structure. This causes confusion in information management at disaster response sites, including local government offices. As an area for future research, standardized communication protocols and coordination of advance risk preparation and post-disaster communication in the response phase should be considered.

Further research should be done on how to use social media on a local community basis. As stated previously, very "local" information is difficult to get on commercial social media. Local governments also have difficulties in using social media for information gathering due to the lack of personnel. However, local communities and social media are a good match. There is potential for the use of social media in local communities to increase disaster risk awareness and encourage evacuation behavior.

Phase-free thinking relies on the idea of "everydayness" at all times. Risk communication for responding to natural disasters should not be something special and distant from everyday life; rather, it should play a role in emergencies because it does so also in the context of everyday life. While the disaster prevention applications and the message system introduced in this chapter have become pervasive in our daily lives, communication for preparedness and response phases is still conducted separately. I look forward to further research on how to improve the coordination and integration of each communication activity in the future.

References

Abdolahzadeh, F., Bagherian, H., Peyravi, M., Kolivand, P., & Tavakoli, N. (2023). A comparative study of interagency communications and information exchange in disaster response among selected countries [Original Article]. *Journal of Education Health Promotion*, *12*(1), 251–251. https://doi.org/10.4103/jehp.jehp_92_23

Cabinet Office Japan (2019). *White paper on disaster management 2018*. https://www.bousai.go.jp/kaigirep/hakusho/pdf/H30_hakusho_english.pdf

Cabinet Office Japan (2023). *Evacuation information (revised version)*. https://www.bousai.go.jp/oukyu/hinanjouhou/r3_hinanjouhou_guideline/evacuation_en.html

CRED (2023). *EM-DAT: The International Disaster Database*. https://www.emdat.be/

Endsley, M. R. (1988). Situation awareness global assessment technique (SAGAT). *Proceedings of the IEEE 1988 National Aerospace and Electronics Conference.*

Furutani, T., & Minami, M. (2021). Drones for disaster risk reduction and crisis response. In M. Sakurai, & R. Shaw, Eds., *Emerging Technologies for Disaster Resilience: Practical Cases and Theories* (pp. 51–62). Springer Singapore. https://doi.org/10.1007/978-981-16-0360-0_4

Hamanaka, R., & Umemoto, M. (2019). Effects on citizen's disaster preparation behaviors by risk communication using an imagination card game: Verification based on a follow-up survey on the participants (in Japanese). *Journal of Social Safety Science, 35*, 207–215. https://doi.org/10.11314/jisss.35.207

Hatori, T., Moriwaki, R., & Shingu, K. (2023). Disparity between evacuation intention and actual evacuation behavior during a heavy rain induced disaster event in Japan: Exploring the role of everyday awareness of disaster preparedness. *International Journal of Disaster Risk Reduction, 92*, 103729. https://doi.org/https://doi.org/10.1016/j.ijdrr.2023.103729

Itamiya, T. (2021). VR/AR and its application to disaster risk reduction. In M. Sakurai, & R. Shaw, Eds., *Emerging Technologies for Disaster Resilience: Practical Cases and Theories* (pp. 63–79). Springer Singapore. https://doi.org/10.1007/978-981-16-0360-0_5

Japan Meteorological Agency (2022). *Seismic activity in 2022 (in Japanese).* https://www.jma.go.jp/jma/press/2301/12a/2212jishin2022.pdf

Japan Meteorological Agency (2023). *"Kikikuru" risk distribution map.* https://www.jma.go.jp/bosai/risk/#zoom:8/lat:35.427106/lon:136.867676/colordepth:normal/elements:land&hazardmap

Kanbara, S., Lee, H.-J., Ngatu, R. N., Nojima, S., Nagasawa, K., & Yamada, S. (2016). Shortfall of disaster health information for foreign residents in Japan. *Health Science Journal, 10*(2), 1–5. https://www.proquest.com/scholarly-journals/shortfall-disaster-health-information-foreign/docview/1792206061/se-2?accountid=27656

Kawamura, T., Sasaki, Y., & Tomatsu, M. (2023). *Study on information collection and dissemination using SNS by local government in the event of a great disaster (in Japanese)* https://www.hro.or.jp/list/building/result_pdf/R04h/R4_houkoku432.pdf

Koyama, M. (2022). Involving the community to manage natural disasters: A study of Japanese disaster risk reduction practices. In F. Li, Y. Awaya, K. Kageyama, & Y. Wei, Eds., *River Basin Environment: Evaluation, Management and Conservation* (pp. 343–356). Springer Nature Singapore. https://doi.org/10.1007/978-981-19-4070-5_16

Kuramoto, I., Baba, J., & Nakanishi, J. (2023). *Designing a Robot as an Interaction Frontend for Elderly People Living in Aging Mountainous District in Japan.* Cham: Social Computing and Social Media.

Matsuzaki, G., Sato, T., Hada, Y., Nishihara, T., & Meguro, K. (2018). Phase free concept and its expansion for design (in Japanese). *Bulletin of JSSD, 65*, 114–115. https://doi.org/10.11247/jssd.65.0_114

McLoughlin, D. (1985). A framework for integrated emergency management. *Public Administration Review, 45*, 165–172. https://doi.org/10.2307/3135011

Mitsui Sumitomo Insurance Company, L (2022). *Survey results on natural disasters (in Japanese).* https://prtimes.jp/main/html/rd/p/000000013.000090956.html

Miyamoto, J., Hatakeyama, N., & Kanbara, S. (2023). Communication for self-care and the role of a logbook on health risk during a flood disaster. *Health Emergency and Disaster Nursing, 10*(1), 29–40. https://doi.org/10.24298/hedn.2022-0001

Mobile Society Research Institute (2022). *Disaster Prevention and Mitigation Study 2021 (in Japanese).* https://www.moba-ken.jp/project/disaster/disaster20220721.html

Murakami, M., Tsubokura, M., Torii, H., Yuliya, L., Hayashi, T., & Uno, K. (2023). Considering the state of scientific information dissemination during crises in the age of social networking. *Japanese Journal of Risk Analysis, 32*(4), 259–263. https://doi.org/10.11447/jjra.T-22-027

Murayama, Y. (2021). Use of IT for situation awareness for disaster risk reduction (in Japanese). In M. Sakurai, & R. Shaw, Eds., *Emerging Technologies for Disaster Resilience: Practical Cases and Theories* (pp. 145–160). Springer Singapore. https://doi.org/10.1007/978-981-16-0360-0_9

Nakai, F., & Nakano, G. (2023). Community-mediated individual disaster preparedness practices: A case study in Kochi, Japan. *International Journal of Disaster Risk Reduction, 86*, 103532. https://doi.org/https://doi.org/10.1016/j.ijdrr.2023.103532

Ojima, T., Takasugi, T., Haraoka, T., Tonai, S., Miyagawa, S., Ichikawa, M., Hattori, K., Okuda, H., Yi, T.-Y., & Tomio, J. (2023). Required functions of information gathering and processing for health, medical, and welfare coordination headquarters for disasters in Japan. *Prehospital and Disaster Medicine*, *38*(S1), s69–s70. https://doi.org/10.1017/S1049023X23002078

Ozeki, M., Shimazaki, K., & Yi, T. (2017). Exploring elements of disaster prevention consciousness: Based on interviews with anti-disaster professionals. *Journal of Disaster Research*, *12*(3), 631–638.

Sakai, N., Taguchi, J., & Rokukawa, S. (2023). Phase-free satellite data utilization for use in disasters (in Japanese). *AI Data Science Collection of Papers*, *4*(L1), 9–18. https://doi.org/10.11532/jsceiii.4.L1_9

Sakurai, A., Sato, T., & Murayama, Y. (2020). Impact evaluation of a school-based disaster education program in a city affected by the 2011 great East Japan earthquake and tsunami disaster. *International Journal of Disaster Risk Reduction*, *47*, 101632. https://doi.org/10.1016/j.ijdrr.2020.101632

Sakurai, M. (2021). Communication structure, protocol and data model toward resilient cities in Japan. In M. Sakurai, & R. Shaw, Eds., *Emerging Technologies for Disaster Resilience: Practical Cases and Theories* (pp. 83–99). Springer Singapore. https://doi.org/10.1007/978-981-16-0360-0_6

Sakurai, M. (2022). The path to urban sustainability with technology: The case of a Japanese smart town. In R. Shaw, Ed., *Handbook on Climate Change and Disasters* (pp. 538–546). Edward Elgar Publishing. https://doi.org/10.4337/9781800371613.00051

Sakurai, M., & Adu-Gyamfi, B. (2020). Disaster-resilient communication ecosystem in an inclusive society – A case of foreigners in Japan. *International Journal of Disaster Risk Reduction*, *51*, 101804. https://doi.org/https://doi.org/10.1016/j.ijdrr.2020.101804

Sakurai, M., & Chughtai, H. (2020). Resilience against crises: COVID-19 and lessons from natural disasters. *European Journal of Information Systems*, *29*(5), 585–594. https://doi.org/10.1080/0960085X.2020.1814171

Sakurai, M., & Murayama, Y. (2019). Information technologies and disaster management – Benefits and issues. *Progress in Disaster Science*, *2*, 100012. https://doi.org/https://doi.org/10.1016/j.pdisas.2019.100012

Sakurai, M., & Shaw, R. (2022). The potential of digitally enabled disaster education for sustainable development goals. *Sustainability*, *14*(11), 6568. https://www.mdpi.com/2071-1050/14/11/6568

Sakurai, M., Watson, R., Abraham, C., & Kokuryo, J. (2014). Sustaining life during the early stages of disaster relief with a frugal information system: Learning from the great east Japan earthquake. *Communications Magazine, IEEE*, *52*(1), 176–185. https://doi.org/10.1109/MCOM.2014.6710081

Shaw, R., Sakurai, A., & Oikawa, Y. (2021). New realization of disaster risk reduction education in the context of a global pandemic: Lessons from Japan. *International Journal of Disaster Risk Science*, *12*(4), 568–580. https://doi.org/10.1007/s13753-021-00337-7

Shek-Noble, L. (2023). Communicating vulnerability in disasters: Media coverage of people with disabilities in Hurricane Katrina and the Tōhoku earthquake and tsunami. In M. S. Jeffress, J. M. Cypher, J. Ferris, & J.-A. Scott-Pollock, Eds., *The Palgrave Handbook of Disability and Communication* (pp. 295–316). Springer International Publishing. https://doi.org/10.1007/978-3-031-14447-9_18

Shimoda, E. (2023). Construction of a support system for people requiring special care at evacuation shelters using Geographical Information System (GIS). *Japanese Journal of Disaster Medicine*, *28*(1), 12–18. https://doi.org/10.51028/jjdisatmed.28.1_12

Tanaka, Y. (2021). Social media technologies and disaster management. In M. Sakurai, & R. Shaw, Eds., *Emerging Technologies for Disaster Resilience: Practical Cases and Theories* (pp. 127–143). Springer Singapore. https://doi.org/10.1007/978-981-16-0360-0_8

Tokyo Metropolitan Government (2023). *Disaster prevention information*. https://www.bousai.metro.tokyo.lg.jp/bousai/1000026/1000316.html

United Nations Office for Disaster Risk Reduction (2017). *Terminology*. https://www.undrr.org/terminology

Usuda, Y. (2021). Decision support system and new technologies. In M. Sakurai, & R. Shaw, Eds., *Emerging Technologies for Disaster Resilience: Practical Cases and Theories* (pp. 241–260). Springer Singapore. https://doi.org/10.1007/978-981-16-0360-0_13

World Economic Forum (2023). *The global risks report 2023, 18th edition*. https://www3.weforum.org/docs/WEF_Global_Risks_Report_2023.pdf

WorldAtlas (2022). *The world's 10 most earthquake prone countries*. https://www.worldatlas.com/articles/the-world-s-10-most-earthquake-prone-countries.html

Author Bio

Mihoko Sakurai is an associate professor at the International University of Japan, Graduate School of International Management. She received Ph.D from Keio University, Japan. Prior to the current position, she worked for the department of Information Systems at the University of Agder (Norway). Her academic background is in management information systems and policy design. She has studied effective ways of using information communication technology in Japan's municipal governments. After the devastating Great East Japan Earthquake in 2011, she conducted field research and designed information systems to enhance the handling of future and unexpected disasters, especially for municipalities that have to deliver disaster relief to their residents. Her work related to the 2011 earthquake won the Best paper award at the International Telecommunication Union (ITU) Kaleidoscope conference (2013) and the Hawaii International Conference on System Sciences (HICSS) (2016). Her work including disaster risk communication research has been published in International Journal of Disaster Risk Reduction, International Journal of Information Systems for Crisis Response and Management, Progress in Disaster Science, Communications of the Association for Information Systems, Sustainable Cities and Society, IEEE communications magazine, European Journal of Information Systems, Sustainability and in the proceedings of the leading international conferences.

Crisis and Risk Communication Research in the Middle East

30

Crisis and Risk Communication Research in Israel

Eytan Gilboa, Clila Magen, and Ester Cohen-Rinski
School of Communication, Bar Ilan University, Ramat Gan, Israel

Introduction

In the past two decades, Israel has gone through a sequence of severe external and internal crises, requiring systematic utilization of crisis communication and risk communication (CRC) strategies and techniques. Israel is a highly developed industrial and technological state. It is a member of the Organisation for Economic Co-operation and Development (OECD) and one of the most "globalized" states in the world (Gilboa, 2008; Laor, 2018; Samuel-Azran et al., 2019). The economic prosperity turned Israel into a consumer society, much more opened and critical of political, economic, and social issues. Recently, Israel has gone through two major relatively long crises, both internal and external. A recent attempt by the Israeli government to control the judicial system led to the most severe domestic crisis in Israel's history. It was met with fierce opposition and mass protests (Meiri & Schrader, 2023). On October 7, 2023, the Palestinian terror organisation Hamas conducted the deadliest attack on Israel since the Holocaust. It killed 1,195 Israelis and foreign nationals, including 815 civilians, and took 251 hostages, including babies, children, women and the elderly. Hamas fighters raped women and burned people in their homes. Israel retaliated with a massive counterattack that lasted until the end of 2024 (Raine et al, 2023).

Successive and rapid transformations of the Israeli society have created increasing demands from both the public and private sectors for reliable information and accounting. The public has become more critical and less willing to take official information and media coverage at face value. To meet these new needs, many public relations (PR) agencies established departments specializing in CRC (Limor et al., 2014; Toledano & McKie, 2009). This study explores CRC research in Israel since 2016.[1] It covers the research output in terms of crises, publications, issues, and methodologies. It demonstrates not only progress but also lingering weaknesses and gaps between needs and knowledge, local and international research, and theory and practice. The survey begins with an analysis of the CRC research output including methodology and sources, a literature review, and findings from three major recent crises, both domestic and international. The study ends with a discussion of the findings and a few concluding remarks.

[1] Crisis and Risk Communication research in Israel before 2016 was presented and discussed in the contribution to the first edition of this handbook (Gilboa & Magen, 2016).

The Handbook of International Crisis and Risk Communication Research, Second Edition.
Edited by Andreas Schwarz, Matthew W. Seeger, and Sora Kim.

In this study, a crisis refers to severe disruption of routine conditions driven by stakeholders' perception of a critical challenge to their organization. Crises create ripple effects and damage various assets of states, organizations, and individuals. Leaders use CRC strategies to limit the scope and duration of these damages (Coombs et al., 2019, pp. 31–32). Essential elements of RC include "(1) an interactive communication processes that (2) seeks to increase awareness and response to a risk, (3) seeks to build tolerance for a risk, and (4) is premised on understanding and acknowledging perception of risk" (p. 32).

Research Output

We used several sources and keywords to identify scholarly and professional studies of Israeli CRC cases and practices published since 2016. The sources were "Google Scholar," the Electronic Data System (EDS) of Bar-Ilan University, which provides access to several databases, academic journals, think tanks, and papers presented at academic or professional conferences, in both Israel and abroad. The keywords were "Crisis Communication," "Risk Communication," and "Israel."

The journals' search included *Public Relations Review, Journal of Public Relations Research, The International Journal of Strategic Communication*, *The Journal of International Research in Crisis and Risk Communication,* and two communication journals in Hebrew: *Kesher* and *Media Frames.* All the datasets were coded according to issues and topics, methodological designs, dilemmas, and challenges.

To deepen the understanding of recent CRC research and practice in Israel, we analyzed CRC aspects in three major crises, all of which occurred in 2021. In the first edition of *The Handbook of International Crisis Communication Research,* we suggested a four-layer typology classified by the managing actor: international, national, organizational, and individual crises (Gilboa & Magen, 2016). The three cases in this review lie in between the first two. National crises mainly affect citizens of one country such as wide-scale natural disasters, military operations, and diplomatic entanglements. These crises are primarily managed by governmental agencies.

An international crisis involves several countries and potential global impacts such as global economic crises, epidemics, natural disasters, and acts of international terrorism. Although each country manages crises as an independent and sovereign body, in many instances, it has to pursue crisis management in cooperation with other states. The Meron crowd crush was a national crisis, the worst civilian disaster in Israel's history; the COVID-19 pandemic was a global crisis, which had its local unique aspects; and a military confrontation in Gaza in May 2021 was a national crisis, which lies between the national and international categories. The case studies explain and evaluate the CRC challenges, dilemmas, and techniques employed by the relevant Israeli policymakers.

The literature searches yielded a total of 116 publications: 89 from Google Scholar, 12 from EDS, 10 from journals, and 5 from think tanks. Mostly, 71 (82%) examined the management of CRC in Israel as one case within a comparative analysis of several states (Alasmari, 2018; Fermont et al., 2022; McGuire et al., 2020; Moran-Gilad et al. 2016; Tabak & Avraham, 2018). The rest dealt exclusively with CRC in Israel (Iftekhar et al., 2021). We also found that most studies addressed issues of RC rather than Crisis Communication (CC). In Google Scholar, out of the 89 items, 52 (46%) presented research on RC, while 37 (36%) explored CC. In the EDS search, all the articles were on RC. Of the 33 publications that focused exclusively on Israel, 21 dealt with RC and only 12 investigated CC.

Between 2016 and 2023, we found very few presentations of papers on Israeli CRC at the annual conferences of the academic Israel Communication Association (ISCA). The local professional Public Relations Association frequently publishes columns and blogs on CRC by both scholars and professionals, revealing high levels of interest in CRC among practitioners.

A search of papers presented at annual academic conferences of international associations such as the International Communication Association (ICA), the International Association for Media and Communication Research (IAMCR), or the National Communication Association (NCA) yielded similar very limited results of Israeli CRC research.

Findings

Issues

The identified CRC publications dealt with six main topics: COVID-19, medical risks other than COVID-19, earthquakes (Padan & Eskenazi, 2017), political and security crises (Tabak & Avraham, 2018; Toledano 2017), business and economic crises (Cottan-Nir & Lehman-Wilzig, 2022), and media challenges. For obvious reasons, since 2019, Israeli CRC coping with COVID-19 has been extensively researched. This will be discussed later in a separate section.

Studies of CRC either just on Israel or on Israel in a comparative setting with other states explored medical issues and disasters including campaigns against breast cancer (Hagoel, 2017); termination of pregnancy among Muslim Arab women (Gesser-Edelsburg & Shahbari, 2017); outburst of the wild poliovirus in culturally divided societies (Moran-Gilad et al., 2016); Parkinson (Sokol et al., 2017); a Salmonella outbreak (Savelli et al., 2021); outbreak of human leptospirosis in water bodies in Israel (Dadon et al., 2018); and genetic diseases among the Bedouin population in the Negev (Singer et al., 2020). Most studies dealt with the crisis or post-crisis periods. Very few dealt with the preparedness of CRC for crises.

Much of the research on CRC within the Israeli context was based on qualitative methods including questionnaires, interviews, and direct observations (Rosen et al., 2019; Shapira et al., 2020). Several studies offered general findings through reviews of the relevant literature (Roth-Cohen & Avidar, 2022). Other researchers collected information from various databases such as medical (Gesser-Edelsburg & Hijazi, 2020; Hagoel, 2017), official documents, and media reports and commentary (Tabak & Avraham, 2018). We didn't find a connection between a given topic and a specific methodological design.

Case Studies

For this study, we selected three diverse crises, which shed light on several aspects of Israeli CRC practices: the April 2021 Meron crowd crush – a national crisis, the worst civilian disaster in Israel's history; the COVID-19 pandemic – a domestic crisis connected to a global crisis; and a military confrontation in Gaza in May 2021– a national crisis with ripple effects on the international level. Each presented specific challenges, but since they all occurred almost simultaneously, the combined encounters were especially difficult to handle.

The Meron Crowd Crush

The Meron crowd crush happened on April 30, 2021, during an annual religious holiday, Rabbi Shimon Bar Yochai's pilgrimage at his tomb on Mount Meron. It was the deadliest civilian disaster in Israel's history. Forty-five ultra-Orthodox men and boys were killed, and more than 140 were injured (Heller & Richardson, 2021; Knell, 2021). In previous years, there were warnings about the undisciplined autonomous running of the place by Hassidic courts and insufficient safety measures, but no one attempted to reassert order and authority in the place.

The immediate CRC technique the relevant officials employed was the "blame game" as part of an image repair strategy. The religious officials responsible for the place and religious politicians, including ministers and parliament members, blamed the police (Shafir, 2021). The municipal authority blamed the religious officials and the Hassidic courts for defying its authority over the place. The regional police chief took some responsibility but was referring to pressure from politicians to allow more people to enter the narrow holy place, much beyond its capacity (Obel, 2022). He also said that a civilian safety expert approved the event.

One popular CRC technique in Israel is to establish a governmental Commission of Inquiry (COI) trusted to investigate disasters and policy failures. It operates under the leadership of a supreme court judge and has the authority and power to summon witnesses, assign blame, and demand punitive actions against those found guilty of negligence. Relatives of those killed and wounded called for the establishment of a COI to investigate the reasons for the crush and identify those responsible. But ultra-Orthodox spiritual leaders and politicians who were supposed to supervise the site resisted the call because they were enjoying much autonomy in running their communities, including the pilgrimage at Meron, and didn't want any governmental body to intervene in their affairs (Gur, 2021). They also feared the COI would accuse them of criminal negligence (Bhol Staff, 2021). A new government, however, decided in June 2021 to appoint a COI to investigate Meron (Sharon, 2021).

In March 2024, the COI issued a final report. It found much negligence, extraneous interests, loose supervision, and bad management. It held senior politicians and officials, including the then Prime Minister Binyamin Netanyahu, responsible for the disaster. Crowd crush disasters have been studied in Israel by governmental bodies (Still et al., 2020), and if lessons were systematically drawn from prior experiences and evidence-based research, the fiasco in Meron could have been prevented or its deadly results minored. The studies showed that social media could have helped to prevent the disaster by informing the public about the poor safety conditions at the location before and even during the event (Somerville, 2021). Others claimed that systematically studying the video footage of the disaster after the event could assist in revealing what exactly went wrong (Harrison & Earl, 2022).

These key recommendations missed a critical point; however, unique characteristics of ultra-Orthodox audiences required framing and dissemination of messages tailored specifically for their traditional closed communities. These communities have their own media outlets and unique internal jargon. Most avoid national outlets, new media, and social media, and they tend to treat information as reliable only when it comes from Rabbis – their spiritual leaders.

The Meron crowd crush disaster hasn't yet been sufficiently studied. We found only two relevant articles: The first analyzed the reactions and experiences in the ultra-Orthodox community (Gado & Fishof, 2023), while the second dealt with medical responses and issues (Daniel et al., 2022). Unfortunately, the critical aspect of understanding CRC needs of special audiences did not attract scholars. Other bodies, however, did investigate the disaster. The state comptroller released a critical report (2021), and the COI issued interim findings. The media published several detailed lengthy investigations of the events leading to the crash. Yet, all these sources haven't sufficiently addressed CRC's failures. Journalists and PR experts produced critical analysis and recommendations, much more than academic researchers. This also represents a failure of the academic community. In addition to available basic information on the crisis, CRC researchers could have used ethnographic methods, including interviews with relevant involved personalities to generate scholarly works. This research weakness will surface again in the next COVID-19 analysis.

The COVID-19 Pandemic

The COVID-19 outbreak was a global mass health crisis that resulted in considerable death especially among the elderly, hospitalization, mass vaccination, economic hardship, and social distress. Policymaking was complicated due to too many political considerations, emergency legislation, economic ramifications, health infrastructure, purchasing vaccines, communication and information campaigns, and enforcement (Amit et al., 2020; Fermont et al., 2022; Gesser-Edelsburg & Hijazi, 2020; Maor et al., 2020).

Combatting the pandemic also required close international cooperation and strict implementation of regional and international public health measures. CRC practices became especially critical for the handling of the pandemic during major outbursts of infections. The overwhelming magnitude of the crisis inspired much research and analysis of various medical, political, economic, and social aspects including CRC strategies (Fuller et al., 2022).

Studies of COVID-19 referred frequently to "health risk communication" (Berg et al., 2021). The CRC's main goal was to effectively reduce uncertainty, fake news, and conspiracy theories surrounding the pandemic (Sopory et al., 2019). Even before the crisis, Israel became a model for a country maintaining successful health communication practices (Betsch et al., 2016), mainly attributed to its reputation as a "startup nation" in healthcare, and effective utilization of digital technologies (Britnell, 2019, pp. 28–33). No wonder then, that many countries and researchers were observing and investigating the measures Israel took to cope with the crisis (Peleg et al., 2021). New Zealand (McGuire et al., 2020) and Zambia (Matenga et al., 2022) learned from the Israeli vaccination experience, Israel and the United Kingdom were presented as a model for countries that benefited from early vaccination campaigns (Iftekhar et al., 2021), and South Korea and Israel exchanged vaccines.

The main challenge CRC experts faced was public trust, essential to enforce compulsory severe restrictions and guidelines. One work that dealt with the effects of epidemic fatigue on vaccine hesitancy suggested that "risk communication employing fear tactics is losing its capacity to generate motivation for vaccination" (Bodas et al., 2023, p. 269). Studies of Israeli CRC practices confirmed one of the fundamental tenets of CRC management: Leaders must play crucial roles in building trust and confidence in their policies. Experts emphasized the need for transparency and accuracy to maintain trust in government decisions. The higher the public's trust in the governmental CRC management, the greater the public's compliance with guidelines (Berg et al., 2021; Gesser-Edelsburg et al., 2020; Mizrahi et al., 2021).

At the beginning of the pandemic, Israel swiftly mobilized its strong public health infrastructure to prevent or limit the spreading of massive infection. The Ministry of Health led the campaign, coordinated surveillance, and provided essential information via all available media outlets, both traditional and digital (McKee & Rajan, 2021; Waitzberg et al., 2020). The ministry appointed several outstanding public health physicians not only to run the operation but also to explain challenges, guidelines, and restrictions. It also provided relevant information to public health commentators, well-known senior and popular former directors of the Ministry of Health or hospitals, and the main television and radio stations employed in the daily news broadcasts.

Due to cultural and political barriers, two large minority groups, Israeli Arabs and ultra-Orthodox Jews, resisted government instructions, primarily quarantines (Waitzberg et al., 2020). As in the case of the Meron crowd crush, here too, understanding target audiences and addressing them properly were the main challenges. Both minority groups had very little trust in the government, and the challenge became even more acute during the respective family holidays of the two communities: the Jewish Passover and the Muslim Ramadan. Despite the clear differences between the two groups, there was one common characteristic: They consumed information differently than most Israelis. The State Comptroller Report (2021) pointed to the difficulty of transferring information and convincing the ultra-Orthodox and Arab populations to obey the government restrictions. He recommended to transfer powers to local authorities who know best how to reach their communities.

In the earlier phases of the pandemic, policymakers made many CRC mistakes in communicating with these two populations. To achieve maximum compliance, in later phases of the pandemic, the government opened direct communication channels with the leadership of the two communities (Saban et al., 2020; Waitzberg et al., 2020). The government imposed special measures during holidays including tough restrictions on mobility and public gatherings (Waitzberg et al., 2020). The building of public trust relied primarily on a strong health system, the reputation of high-level physicians who served in senior public health positions, and the formulation of suitable messages tailored to specific populations. Officials appeared daily on radio and television and reached diverse audiences via opinion leaders and a variety of mainstream and sectorial media channels (Levin-Zamir, 2020). They finally understood that not all Israeli citizens were on Facebook or Twitter.

Operation Guardians of the Walls

In May 2021, Hamas, the Palestinian Islamic ruler of Gaza, launched a barrage of missiles, rockets, and mortar shells on Israeli cities and towns. Israel retaliated with a limited military operation – "Guardian of the Walls." It lasted 11 days and was the most serious military confrontation between Hamas and Israel since 2014 (Moreno-Mercado & Calatrava-García, 2022). The operation also generated a series of violent attacks by Arabs on Jews living in mixed Israeli cities. The riots claimed human lives and caused much damage to Jewish houses, synagogues, public buildings, and vehicles (Lavie et al., 2021). During the operation, the government had to cope with both international and domestic information challenges (Vatikay, 2021). While defeated in the battleground, Hamas got the upper hand in the information battle (Tzoreff, 2021). It positioned itself as the defender of the Al-Aqsa Mosque in Jerusalem and attacked targets in Jerusalem and Tel Aviv.

Almost every military operation between Hamas and Israel created communication crises. There has always been a gap between external and internal perceptions of events in Gaza. Guardians of the Walls provided two glaring examples of this gap: the bombing of the Al Jalaa Tower in Gaza City and the underground tunnels Israel called "the metro" (Akram & Keath, 2021; Vatikay, 2021). In Israeli eyes, both targets were legitimate. The tower housed offices of Hamas's military intelligence as well as those of Al-Jazeera and Associated Press. Critics described the bombing of the tower as an attempt to curtail reporting and silence media criticism from Gaza (Moreno-Mercado and Calatrava-Garcia, 2022; Schweitzer et al., 2021). Israel argued that those who housed their media offices next to those of Hamas should have known that during the war, the tower could become a legitimate military target. In hindsight, several Israeli officials admitted that due to the international PR damage this action caused, it was a mistake to hit the building.

In another event, Israel claimed that Hamas used a system of tunnels to defend fighters and missiles and to penetrate the border and attack Israeli towns and villages. Calling this system "metro" (Gross, 2021) was a huge CRC blunder, because international audiences could have mistakenly understood the term as referring to a civilian underground train system essential for normal life (Vatikay, 2021). Consequently, the attack on the tunnels also triggered much criticism and negative reactions. Another more general mistake was to forbid foreign journalists from entering Gaza, thus abandoning the area to Hamas's media fixers. The Israel Defense Forces (IDF) used social media, especially Twitter, in several languages to disseminate credible information about the operation (Moreno-Mercado & Calatrava-García, 2022). But this effort failed because Israel's enemies had much more presence on social media and used it more effectively.

The CRC's failures yielded several lessons: routinely strengthen presence in the digital space, establish a national monitoring and information mechanism responsible for producing and coordinating messages to both domestic and international audiences, and allow entry of foreign correspondents into enemy territory (Schweitzer et al., 2021). As in previous Gaza military operations, Israel failed to effectively explain the reasons for the operation and specific military activities resulting in substantial damage to its reputation. The 2023-2024 Israel Hamas full scale war further demonstrated the CRC deficiencies described in the handling of the 2021 Guardians of the Wall operation. These events well demonstrated a common complexity in Israeli CRC in which operational dilemmas and challenges and reputational aspects frequently blend, complicating the already complex situation and stretching the crisis nexus between the national and international contexts.

Research about the Guardian of the Walls operation was conducted mainly by local research institutes specializing in strategic affairs. This was not the first operation in Gaza. Previously, there were several similar attacks and operations. After each of them, research and media commentary revealed a lack of preparedness and continuing failures in using CRC strategies. The military and other ministries and agencies produced CRC lessons, but they were only partially implemented due to political considerations and bureaucratic infighting. It seems that in this case, there was a more fundamental reason: too much reliance on hard power and insufficient attention to the importance of soft power, information battles, and reputational security.

Discussion

The literature review of Israeli CRC research combined with the case studies leads to three main insights – narrowing gaps between research and practice, better understanding of new media functions in CRC, and developing modern CRC contingency plans for future crises by both scholars and practitioners.

Narrowing Gaps Between Research and Practice

For many years, Israel has faced various crises, frequently, simultaneously. This intense cumulative experience created throughout the years CRC professionalism and best practices other countries have adopted. For instance, a group of researchers from six countries led by Shlomo Shpiro worked on a project specifically designed to provide effective CRC strategies for handling terrorist attacks, including a guide for public officials (Shpiro, 2011). University research centers and independent think tanks including the Institute for National Security Studies at Tel-Aviv University, the Jerusalem Institute for Strategy and Security, the Jerusalem Center for Public Affairs, and the BESA Center for Strategic Studies at Bar-Ilan University conducted research on terrorism and violence and occasionally addressed CRC issues.

This review also shows some "exporting" of Israeli CRC research and practical knowledge. The Israeli successful handling of the COVID-19 pandemic significantly contributed to the understanding of how CRC strategies can help to combat global pandemics. The Israeli practices were recognized as highly effective, and its vaccination campaign served as a model to other countries. Israel's success was attributed to a combination of factors including campaigns based on public trust through an integrated health system, familiar technology, transparency regarding vaccine safety information, culturally shaped messages in digital and offline media, acknowledging diverse health literacy needs, and active participation and role modeling by political religious opinion leaders. Israel's success in coping with another medical crisis, polio outbursts, was attributed to health communicators knowing their audience well, even before the outbreak of the crisis (Betsch, et al., 2016).

The survey reveals, however, that Israeli CRC research lacks cumulative practical experience. There is a clear gap between the increasing interest in CRC among Israeli practitioners and governmental actors and the relatively little attention Israeli CRC has received in academic platforms. For instance, studying Israel's ongoing coping with two independent, skeptical, resistant, and hard-to-convince two minority communities (ultra-Orthodox Jews and Arabs) could contribute very important, even critical insights to the universal body of CRC knowledge. In the Meron crowd crush, as well as in the first phases of COVID-19, Israel failed to use CRC strategies suitable for dealing with unique target audiences, but it gradually developed effective responses to these challenges. This CRC's crucial, unique experience didn't receive sufficient attention, and the Israeli academic community missed an opportunity to make a significant contribution to the field beyond Israel.

Several reasons explain the gap between research and practice. Despite the emergence of so many domestic and international crises in Israel, there are still very few PR academic scholars and CRC experts in the country and very few academic and research centers to house them. Consequently, the number of books, articles published in relevant journals, and papers presented at scholarly, local, and international conferences is meager.

All the departments and schools of communication in Israel offer courses in PR, and very few, however, deal exclusively or primarily with CRC. Only a few universities and colleges offer programs in PR, which include courses in CRC. A few schools of business have programs in marketing, but the bureaucratic artificial separation between PR and marketing is hindering teaching and research in CRC. PR firms do more and much better CRC work. There are still three major gaps between challenges and responses, local and international research, and theory and practice. The Council for Higher Education in Israel is responsible for the funding of public universities and the accreditation of degree programs in private institutions, and it should encourage research and teaching of CRC in Israel.

Understanding New Media

Social media has become a major PR instrument and is changing traditional CRC strategies (Cheng, 2018). Managing the COVID-19 crisis demonstrated the positive and negative effects of social media. On the one hand, it disseminated critical information about the pandemic, especially on restrictions, treatment, and vaccination. On the other hand, it also provided a platform for disinformation and conspiracy theories, primarily on vaccinations. This challenge became more serious when a noted physician, a former Director General of the Ministry of Health, called COVID-19 "a flu with PR," and a few of his colleagues disputed the value of vaccinations and the rationale of quarantines. Disinformation and conspiracy theories constitute a global crisis in several areas, not just in medicine. In health crises, however, believing fake news costs lives. States, international organizations, and nongovernmental organizations must cooperate, produce, and use creative CRC strategies to refute and limit dissemination and influence of disinformation.

Twitter enabled public health communicators to identify RC patterns and transmit effective messages to vulnerable populations (Sutton et al., 2020). Instagram performed a similar role (Pinto et al., 2020). Social networks allowed communication professionals to bypass gatekeepers in times of crisis, and many traditional journalists used them to strengthen relations with their audiences (Hedman, 2016). The Meron crowd crush and COVID-19 well demonstrated the need not only to effectively utilize social media in CRC but also to understand its limitations among traditional communities that consume information differently from most citizens.

Planning CRC Strategies

CRC is essential to effectively cope with different types of emergencies, whether caused by men, such as the Meron crowd crush, or nature, such as earthquakes. This requires extensive intergovernmental coordination and preparedness. As a product of lessons learned from the 2006 Second Lebanon War, in 2007, Israel established a National Emergency Authority (NEMA) tasked with coordinating and integrating all the organizations responsible for home-front defense during emergency scenarios. Yet, research and media reports found that NEMA didn't prepare well for the COVID-19 pandemic and for other potential emergencies such as earthquakes or crowd crushes of the type that happened in Meron.

It is well known that severe earthquakes occur in Israel approximately every century. The last happened in 1927; thus, if the historical pattern is still valid, then a major earthquake could happen in Israel in this decade. The government hasn't yet prepared a plan, including CRC strategies, to cope with earthquakes (Padan & Eskenazi, 2017). The literature review exposes a substantial lack of attention to CRC preparedness for crises. This critical aspect should and must be seriously addressed in future research.

Conclusion

This survey and the case studies revealed a mixed bag of successes and failures. Management of the COVID-19 pandemic was effective and successful but handling of the Meron crowd crush and Operation Guardians of the Walls was not. The success can be attributed to a better understanding of how CRC can help to manage risks and crises; highly motivated, talented, and experienced officials; the effective use of evaluation techniques; and the capability to identify and rapidly respond to changing circumstances. The failures resulted mainly from clear neglect of sufficient preparedness for crisis situations including CRC strategies.

This brief survey demonstrated much potential for scholarly and professional contributions to the field beyond Israel. CRC research and practice in Israel are growing and improving but still lack sufficient human and financial resources and programs, primarily in institutions of higher education and professional circles. In recent years, crises such as the COVID-19 pandemic inspired more research and analysis, but there is not enough CRC research, teaching, and training in universities and professional centers.

This work demonstrated the need to significantly expand Israeli CRC research and analysis. There are several encouraging indicators of potential progress in the next several years. First, there is more awareness about the significance of CRC in the public and private sectors as well as in professional and academic circles. Second, there are many more CRC cases and many efforts to deal with them by professional experts. Interesting and useful case studies are just waiting for academic research and analysis. Third, more young Israeli scholars are attracted to CRC; they conduct research for graduate degrees and participate in major domestic and international collaborative projects. The key is still a systematic expansion of teaching and research capabilities in Israeli universities and colleges and more effective collaboration between scholars and practitioners.

References

Akram, F., & Keath, L. (May 16, 2021). Israel strikes Gaza home of Hamas leader, destroys AP office. *AP News*. https://apnews.com/article/israel-west-bank-gaza-middle-east-israel-palestinian-conflict-7974cc0c03897b8b21e5fc2f8c7d8a79

Alasmari, A. O. A. (2018). A review of the challenges of the crisis management during the cyber-attacks. *Journal of Contemporary Scientific Research*, *7*(2), 1–9.

Amit, M. Kimhi, H., Bader, T., Chen, J., Glassberg, E., & Benov, A. (2020). Mass-surveillance technologies to fight coronavirus spread: The case of Israel. *Nature Medicine*, *26*(8), 1167–1169.

Berg, S. H., O'hara, J. K., Shortt, M. T., Thune, H., Brønnick, K. K., Lungu, D. A., Røislien, J., & Wiig, S. (2021). Health authorities' health risk communication with the public during pandemics: A rapid scoping review. *BMC Public Health*, *21*(1), 1–23.

Betsch, C., Böhm, R., Airhihenbuwa, C. O., Butler, R., Chapman, G. B., Haase, N., Herrman, B., & Uskul, A. K. (2016). Improving medical decision making and health promotion through culture-sensitive health communication: An agenda for science and practice. *Medical Decision Making*, *36*(7), 811–833.

Bhol Staff (May 25, 2021). Investigation of the Miron disaster: Who is trying to crack the ultra-Orthodox leadership. *Bhol*. https://www.bhol.co.il/news/1226063

Bodas, M., Kaim, A., Velan, B., Ziv, A., Jaffe, E., & Adini, B. (2023). Overcoming the effect of pandemic fatigue on vaccine hesitancy: Will belief in science triumph? *Journal of Nursing Scholarship*, *55*(1), 262–271.

Britnell, M. (2019). *Human: Solving the Global Workforce Crisis in Healthcare*. Oxford University Press.

Cheng, Y. (2018). How social media is changing crisis communication strategies: Evidence from the updated literature. *Journal of Contingencies & Crisis Management*, *26*(1), 58–68.

Coombs, W. T., Holladay, S. J., & Tachkova, E. (2019). Crisis communication, risk communication, and issues management. *Public Relations Theory: Application and Understanding*, 31–48. https://www.oreilly.com/library/view/public-relations-theory/9781119373155/c03.xhtml

Cottan-Nir, O., & Lehman-Wilzig, S. (2022). CEO brand equity: Implementation of a conceptual model, comparing CEO brand equity during successful and crisis periods. *International Journal of Strategic Communication*, *16*(1), 34–49.

Dadon, Y., Haas, E. J., Kaliner, E., Anis, E., Singer, S. R., Atiya-Nasagi, Y., Cohen-Dar, M., Abramovich, M., King, R., Sued, O., Goshen, T., Amit, S., Miskin, I., Gino, E., Yishai, R., Sheffer, R., Grotto, I., & Moran-Gilad, J. (2018). Outbreak of human leptospirosis linked to contaminated water bodies in Northern Israel, June to August 2018. *Eurosurveillance*, *23*(38), 1800486.

Daniel, D. T. G., Alpert, E. A., & Jaffe, E. (2022). The crowd crush at mount Meron: Emergency medical services response to a silent mass casualty incident. *Disaster Medicine and Public Health Preparedness*, *16*(6), 2691–2693.

Fermont, I. R., Livneh, A., & Benhamou, M. (2022). Risk communication on vaccines during the COVID19 pandemic: Is there room for small size or private initiatives? An Israeli experience. *Therapeutic Advances in Drug Safety*, *13*. http://doi.org/10.1177/20420986221112189

Fuller, R. P., Pyle, A., Riolli, L., & Mickel, A. (2022). Creating order out of chaos? Development of a measure of perceived effects of communication on the crisis organizing process. *International Journal of Business Communication*, *59*(2), 174–192.

Gado, T., & Fishof, D. (2023). Spectrum of response styles in a Religious-Orthodox Community to civilian disasters: The responses of the Haredi Community to the Meron Crowd Crush (2021) as a case study. *Religions*, *14*(3), 294.

Gesser-Edelsburg, A., & Hijazi, R. (2020). When politics meets pandemic: How Prime Minister Netanyahu and a small team communicated health and risk information to the Israeli public during the early stages of COVID-19. *Risk Management and Healthcare Policy*, *13*, 2985.

Gesser-Edelsburg, A., & Shahbari, N. A. E. (2017). Decision-making on terminating pregnancy for Muslim Arab women pregnant with fetuses with congenital anomalies: Maternal affect and doctor-patient communication. *Reproductive Health*, *14*(1), 1–12.

Gilboa, E. (2008). The evolution of the Israeli media. *Middle East Review of International Affairs*, *12*(3), 88–101.

Gilboa, E., & Magen, C. (2016). Crisis communication research in Israel: Growth and gaps. In A. Schwarz, M. W. Seeger, & C. Auer, Eds., *The Handbook of International Crisis Communication Research* (pp. 327–336). Wiley.

Gross, A. J. (May 14, 2021). IDF: Overnight bombardment targeted Hamas's tunnel network under Gaza City. *Times of Israel*. https://www.timesofisrael.com/idf-overnight-bombardment-targeted-hamass-tunnel-network-under-gaza-city/

Gur, R. H. (May 20, 2021). Forty-five people died at Meron. Why are Haredi parties blocking a probe? *Times of Israel*. https://www.timesofisrael.com/bid-to-block-meron-disaster-inquiry-sparks-first-glimmers-of-a-haredi-rebellion/

Hagoel, L. (2017). Existential suffering in the social context of cancer risk. In R. Anderson, Ed., *Alleviating World Suffering: The Challenge of Negative Quality of Life* (pp. 411–422). Springer.

Harrison, V., & Earl, C. (October 31, 2022). A visual guide to how the Seoul Halloween crowd crush unfolded. *The Guardian*. https://www.theguardian.com/world/2022/oct/31/how-did-the-seoul-itaewon-halloween-crowd-crush-happen-unfolded-a-visual-guide

Hedman, U. (2016). When journalists tweet: Disclosure, participatory, and personal transparency. *Social Media + Society*, *2*(1), 1–13. http://doi.org/10.1177/2056305115624528

Heller, J., & Richardson, A. (May 2, 2021). Israel observes day of mourning for religious festival dead. *Reuters*. https://www.reuters.com/article/us-israel-religion-crush-idCAKBN2CJ05J

Iftekhar, E. N., Priesemann, V., Balling, R., Bauer, S., Beutels, P., Valdez, A. C., Cuschierie, S., Czypionkaf, T., Dumpisg, U., Glaabb, E., Grillh, E., Hansoni, C., Hotulainenj, P., Klimekk, P., Kretzschmarl, M., Krügerm, T., Krutzinnan, J., Lowo, N., Machadop, H., Martinsq, C., McKeer, M., Bernd Mohra, S., Nassehih, A., Percs, M., Petelost, E., Pickersgillu, M., Prainsackv, B., Rocklövw, J., Schernhammerx, E., Stainesy, A., Szczurekz, E., Tsiodrasaa, S., Van Gucht, S., & Willeit, P. (2021). A look into the future of the COVID-19 pandemic in Europe: An expert consultation. *The Lancet Regional Health-Europe*, *8*, 100185.

Knell, Y. (April 30, 2021). Israel crush: Dozens killed at Lag B'Omer religious festival. *BBC News*. https://www.bbc.com/news/world-middle-east-56938657

Laor, T. (2018). Social pluralism on the air: Internet radio in Israel. *Israel Affairs, 24*(5), 830–847.
Lavie, E., Elran, M., Shahbari, I., Sawaed, K., & Essa, J. (May 31, 2021). *Jewish-Arab relations in Israel. INSS, 1474.* https://www.inss.org.il/wp-content/uploads/2021/05/no.-1474.pdf
Levin-Zamir, D. (2020). Communication, health literacy and a systems approach for mitigating the COVID-19 pandemic: The case for massive vaccine roll-out in Israel. *Journal of Health Communication, 25*(10), 816–818.
Limor, Y., Leshem, B., & Mandelzis, L. (2014). *Public Relations: Strategy and Tactics.* The Open University of Israel. [Hebrew]
Maor, M., Sulitzeanu-Kenan, R., & Chinitz, D. (2020). When COVID-19, constitutional crisis, and political deadlock meet: The Israeli case from a disproportionate policy perspective. *Policy and Society, 39*(3), 442–457.
Matenga, T. F. L., Zulu, J. M., Moonzwe Davis, L., & Chavula, M. P. (2022). Motivating factors for and barriers to the COVID-19 vaccine uptake: A review of social media data in Zambia. *Cogent Public Health, 9*(1), 2059201.
McGuire, D., Cunningham, J. E., Reynolds, K., & Matthews-Smith, G. (2020). Beating the virus: An examination of the crisis communication approach taken by New Zealand Prime Minister Jacinda Ardern during the Covid-19 pandemic. *Human Resource Development International, 23*(4), 361–379.
McKee, M., & Rajan, S. (2021). What can we learn from Israel's rapid roll out of COVID-19 vaccination? *Israel Journal of Health Policy Research, 10.* https://doi.org/10.1186/s13584-021-00441-5
Meiri, G., & Schrader, E. (March 9, 2023). Anti-judicial reform protesters up the ante with 'day of resistance' across Israel. *Ynet News.* https://www.ynetnews.com/article/s1fudwdyn
Mizrahi, S., Vigoda-Gadot, E., & Cohen, N. (2021). How well do they manage a crisis? The government's effectiveness during the Covid-19 pandemic. *Public Administration Review, 81*(6), 1120–1130.
Moran-Gilad, J., Kaliner, E., Gdalevich, M., & Grotto, I. (2016). Public health response to the silent reintroduction of wild poliovirus to Israel, 2013–2014. *Clinical Microbiology and Infection, 22,* S140–S145.
Moreno-Mercado, J. M., & Calatrava-García, A. (2022). Multilingual public diplomacy: Strategic communication of Israeli Defense Forces (IDF) in Twitter during operation guardian of the walls. *Media, War & Conflict.* https://doi.org/10.1177/17506352221082608
Obel, A. (August 30, 2022). Meron inquest finds Netanyahu, top cop Shabtai likely responsible for disaster. *Times of Israel.* https://www.timesofisrael.com/meron-inquest-finds-netanyahu-top-cop-shabtai-likely-responsible-for-disaster/
Padan, C., & Eskenazi, J. (July 20, 2017). Preparing for an earthquake: Responses by the public and the authorities. *INSS.* https://www.inss.org.il/publication/preparing-earthquake-responses-public-authorities/
Peleg, K., Bodas, M., Hertelendy, A. J., & Kirsch, T. D. (2021). The COVID-19 pandemic challenge to the all-hazards approach for disaster planning. *International Journal of Disaster Risk Reduction, 55,* 102103.
Pinto, P. A., Antunes, M. J. L., & Almeida, A. M. P. (June, 2020). Instagram as a communication tool in public health: A systematic review. *15th Iberian Conference on Information Systems and Technologies (CISTI).* https://doi.org/10.23919/CISTI49556.2020.9140809
Raine, A., Lau, C., Berlinger, J., Sangal, A., Poole, T., & Meyer, M. (November, 09, 2023). October 7, 2023: Israel says it is 'at war' after Hamas surprise attack. *CNN.* https://edition.cnn.com/middleeast/live-news/israel-hamas-gaza-attack-10-08-23/index.html October 8, 2023 Israel-Hamas war news | CNN
Rosen, L. J., Rier, D. A., Schwartz, R., Talitman, M., & Zwanziger, L. (2019). Knowledge and risk perceptions of Israelis towards combustible cigarettes: The need for immediate remedial action. *Israel Journal of Health Policy Research, 8,* 1–12. https://doi.org/10.1186/s13584-018-0276-2
Roth-Cohen, O., & Avidar, R. (2022). A decade of social media in public relations research: A systematic review of published articles in 2010–2020. *Public Relations Review, 48*(1). https://doi.org/10.1016/j.pubrev.2022.102154
Saban, M., Myers, V., & Wilf-Miron, R. (2020). Coping with the COVID-19 pandemic–the role of leadership in the Arab ethnic minority in Israel. *International Journal for Equity in Health, 19*(1). http://doi.org/10.1186/s12939-020-01257-6

Samuel-Azran, T., Laor, T., & Tal, D. (2019). Who listens to podcasts, and why? The Israeli case. *Online Information Review*, *43*(4), 482–495.

Savelli, C. J., Garcia Acevedo, R. F., Simpson, J., & Mateus, C. (2021). The utilization of tools to facilitate cross-border communication during international food safety events, 1995–2020: A realist synthesis. *Globalization and Health*, *17*(1), 1–21.

Schweitzer, Y., Siman Tov, D. & Michael, K. (May 25, 2021). The cognitive campaign in operation guardian of the walls: The battle over the narrative. *INSS*, 1467. https://www.inss.org.il/publication/guardian-of-the-walls/

Shafir, N. (May 2, 2021). Blame game begins after Meron disaster. *Globes*. https://en.globes.co.il/en/article-blame-game-begins-after-meron-lag-bomer-disaster-1001369411

Shapira, S., Aharonson-Daniel, L., Clarfield, A. M., & Feder-Bubis, P. (2020). Giving a voice to medically vulnerable populations: A mixed-methods investigation of their unique perceptions and needs in emergency situations. *Health & Social Care in the Community*, *28*(3), 811–822.

Sharon, J. (June 20, 2021). Gov't approves state committee of inquiry into Meron disaster. *Jerusalem Post*. https://www.jpost.com/israel-news/govt-approves-state-committee-of-inquiry-into-meron-disaster-671531

Shpiro, S. (2011). *Counter-terrorism crisis communications: Strategies for recovery and continuity*. https://cordis.europa.eu/project/id/218285/reporting

Singer, S., Davidovitch, N., Abu Fraiha, Y., & Abu Freha, N. (2020). Consanguinity and genetic diseases among the Bedouin population in the Negev. *Journal of Community Genetics*, *11*(1), 13–19. http://doi.org/10.1007/s12687-019-00433-8

Sokol, L. L., Young, M. J., & Jankovic, J. (2017). Counseling at-risk Parkinson's disease cohorts: Integrating emerging evidence. *Current Genetic Medicine Reports*, *5*, 100–107. https://doi.org/10.1007/s40142-017-0116-7

Somerville, P. (2021). Behavior and mechanics of crowd crush disasters. *Risk Frontiers*. https://riskfrontiers.com/insights/behaviour-and-mechanics-of-crowd-crush-disasters/

Sopory, P., Day, A. M., Novak, J. M., Eckert, K., Wilkins, L., Padgett, D. R., Noyes, J. P., Barakji, F. A., Liu, J., Fowler, B. N., Guzman-Barcenas, J. B., Nagayko, A., Nickell, J. J., Donahue, D., Daniels, K., Allen, T., Alexander, N., Vanderford, M. L., & Gamhewage, G. M. (2019). Communicating uncertainty during public health emergency events: A systematic review. *Review of Communication Research*, *7*, 67–108. http://doi.org/10.12840/ISSN.2255-4165.019

State Comptroller and Ombudsman (2021). *Publication of a special report: The Israeli government's handling of the Corona crisis* [Hebrew]. file:///C:/Users/ester/Downloads/2021-COVID-19-102-Mekomiyot.pdf

Still, K., Papalexi, M., Fan, Y., & Bamford, D. (2020). Place crowd safety, crowd science? Case studies and application. *Journal of Place Management and Development*, *13*(4), 385–407. https://doi.org/10.1108/JPMD-10-2019-0090

Sutton, J., Renshaw, S. L., & Butts, C. T. (2020). COVID-19: Retransmission of official communications in an emerging pandemic. *PLoS One*, *15*(9), e0238491.

Tabak, L., & Avraham, E. (2018). Country image repair strategies during an asymmetrical conflict: An analysis of the Gaza conflict in 2014. *International Journal of Strategic Communication*, *12*(3), 237–251. http://doi.org/10.1080/1553118X.2018.1464009

Toledano, M. (2016). Dialogue with the enemy: Lessons for public relations on dialogue facilitation drawn from the Israeli-Palestinian conflict. In *International public relations* (pp. 27–45). Routledge.

Toledano, M., & McKie, D. (2009). The Israeli PR experience: Nation building and professional values. In K. Sriramesh, & D. Verčič, Eds., *The Global Public Relations Handbook* (pp. 243–261). Routledge.

Tzoreff, Y. (May 30, 2021). The Palestinian arena after Operation Guardian of the Walls: What was is not what will be. *INSS*, 1475. https://www.inss.org.il/publication/pa-after-guardian-of-the-walls/

Vatikay, Y. (June 20, 2021). National strategic communications: Lessons from Operation Guardian of the Walls. *INSS*, Special publication. https://www.inss.org.il/publication/guardian-of-the-walls-strategic-communications/

Waitzberg, R., Davidovitch, N., Leibner, G., Penn, N., & Brammli-Greenberg, S. (2020). Israel's response to the COVID-19 pandemic: Tailoring measures for vulnerable cultural minority populations. *International Journal for Equity in Health*, *19*(1), 1–5. https://doi.org/10.1186/s12939-020-01191-7

Author's Bio

Eytan Gilboa has been a professor of International Communication and the founding head of both the School of Communication and the Center for International Communication at Bar-Ilan University in Israel. He also teaches public diplomacy at the University of Southern California. He received his MA and PhD degrees from Harvard University and has been a visiting professor at several leading American and European universities. He has published 15 books, most recently, A Research Agenda for Public Diplomacy (Elgar, 2023), and numerous articles on international communication. He has won several significant awards including most recently the ICOMM Distinguished Scholar Award from the International Studies Association. He has been an adviser to several ministries and nongovernmental organizations (NGOs) and a commentator on television and radio networks.

Clila Magen is a senior lecturer at the School of Communication and a research fellow at the Center for International Communication at Bar-Ilan University in Israel. Prior to joining academia, she served as a spokesperson for the Chair of the Committee of Defense and Foreign Affairs of the Knesset (Parliament). Her fields of research include strategic communication, crisis communication, nation branding, and interpersonal communications. She is the author of Behind the Seen: The Mossad, Shabak and the Israeli Media (2017) and has published articles in journals including *Journal of Public Relations Research, Public Relations Review, and The International Journal of Press/Politics.*

Ester Cohen-Rinski is a PhD candidate in communication at Bar-Ilan University, Israel, where she received her BA and MA degrees in Political Science and Communication. She has presented papers at various international scholarly conferences, including one selected in 2018 as an Outstanding Student Paper at the PR division of the International Communication Association. Her research deals with several aspects of crisis communication in Israel. She has served as an officer in the Israel Air Force and in the Israel Defense Forces Spokesperson's Unit for 20 years.

31

Risk and Crisis Communication Research

Contextual Characteristics and Perspectives from the GCC Countries[1]

Ilhem Allagui

Journalism and Strategic Communication Program, Northwestern University, Doha, Qatar

Introduction

The Arab states of the Arabian Gulf are home to more than 60 million people (Mati & Vacher, 2022). Situated in Western Asia, the region's largest area is the Kingdom of Saudi Arabia (KSA), with 36 million people, followed by the United Arab Emirates (UAE), which counts some 10 million people ("World Population Review," 2023). The other countries on the same arm of the Arabian Gulf are Bahrain, Kuwait, Oman, and Qatar. Except for Oman and Saudi Arabia, where the nationals (also called locals) outweigh the residents (see Table 31.1. Nationals vs. ex-pats in the GCC countries' population in appendix), in all of Bahrain, Kuwait, Qatar, and the UAE, the non-nationals represent most of the population ("World Population Review," 2023). They work in various services, including hospitality, education, business, and health, but the largest group is males from East and South Asia who migrated to work in construction.

The Arabian Gulf, also known as the Persian Gulf, extends to Iran and Iraq. In 1981, after the Iran–Iraq war, and initially for security reasons under Iranian threat, the Arab countries allied under the Gulf Cooperation Council (GCC), which aimed to develop shared goals and socio-political and economic agreements. The GCC countries (Bahrain, Kuwait, Oman, Qatar, Saudi Arabia, and the UAE) stretch over 2,672,700 km^2 and share Arabic as their official language and English as their Lingua Franca.

This chapter examines the research on risk and crisis communication in the GCC region from different perspectives. Given that the political and socio-cultural environments in the region significantly shape the research agenda, the chapter begins by introducing the regional context and elaborating on the unique characteristics of the political, economic, and socio-cultural environments. It then discusses the state of risk and crisis communication

1 This chapter honors the memory of Dr. Ibrahim Saleh and the knowledge he shared on risk and crisis communication in the first edition of this book. May God rest his soul.

The Handbook of International Crisis and Risk Communication Research, Second Edition.
Edited by Andreas Schwarz, Matthew W. Seeger, and Sora Kim.

Table 31.1 Nationals vs. expats in the GCC countries' population.

	Total population	*Nationals (%)*	*Non-nationals (%)*
Bahrain	1,485,509	47	53
Kuwait	4,310,108	30	70
Oman	4,644,384	54	46
Qatar	2,716,391	14	86
Saudi Arabia	36,947,025	63	37
United Arab Emirates	9,516,871	11	89
GCC countries	59,620,288	49	51

Source: Adapted from Hazem Shayah, 2019.

research in the area from an institutional, media, and audience perspective, supported by relevant examples and case studies. Additionally, this chapter highlights recent developments in corporate risk and crisis communication practices, including those handled by public relations (PR) consultants, which may affect future research in the area.

The Context of Risk and Crisis Communication Research in the GCC Countries

Historically, the GCC countries shared the same land. Arabian tribes moved from one place to another until they discovered oil and gas. Negotiations with the British rule since the nineteenth century "empowered and legitimized the ruling sheikhs (...) [and] insisted on a pure tribal lineage to qualify someone to negotiate, and their insistence on designating and prioritizing some tribes over others became crucial ultimately, not only to defining citizenship but also to assigning economic and political rights" (Cooke, 2014, pp. 33–34). Competition between tribes began, as some were gaining more stature over others.

Once relying on oil and gas resources, the rentier states realized their natural revenues would only last a while. They began modernizing their countries, embraced the globalization of flows, and ventured into diversifying their economies differently and competitively (Cooke, 2014) while choosing tourism, entertainment, or sports as alternatives to the energy sector.

Nevertheless, despite the religious, linguistic, cultural, economic, and political similarities among the six countries, and although they pledged mutual defense through their GCC alliance, the countries went through divides and crises, the most recent and critical of which is the blockade that Bahrain, the UAE, and Saudi Arabia imposed on Qatar in 2017, which will be discussed below.

The Politics of the GCC Countries

The GCC countries share the same ruling regime: They are monarchies, and the succession is hereditary. They apply unitary systems, except for the federal state of the UAE, and they all lack effective political participation (Al-Alkim, 1996; Al-Talei, 2021). The political participation index by the Gulf House for Studies and Publishing, a think tank based in London, United Kingdom, and run by Bahrainis, notes that in 2021, all GCC countries regressed regarding freedom of opinion and expression. All states failed to provide a safe political environment for citizens and practitioners that is favorable to the forming of political organizations (Al-Talei, 2021).

Although their coalition under the council postulates uniformity, the GCC countries' diplomacy diverges, especially regarding foreign policy and relationships with the United States, Russia, China, and Israel.

The Economy of the GCC Countries

The World Bank projected approximately US$2 trillion in 2022 for the economic output of the GCC countries (Nair, 2022). The KSA is the largest economy in the Middle East, followed by the UAE. The GCC countries enjoy the highest gross domestic product (GDP) levels in the Middle East region thanks to the energy sector; they account for at least 30% of the world's reserves. The International Monetary Fund (IMF) estimates the GDP per capita to be US$33,595.35 in 2022 (Mati & Vacher, 2022). Oil and gas remain the main growth drivers of the GCC states, as hydrocarbons top the good exports, followed by chemicals, plastic, and manufacturing materials (Mati & Vacher, 2022).

National economic developments of the Gulf countries have turned to diversification in non-energy sectors, the chief of which is the tourism sector. The global oil price drop in 2014–2016 extended to the GCC, making the region's economic crisis the most severe in its modern history (Al-Marri, 2017). The crisis led to austerity measures internally, including cuts in subsidies and military and security investments, while externally, they engaged in cuts in their foreign aid.

In Saudi Arabia, this economic crisis led to a socio-political crisis known as *the Saudi corruption crackdown*. In 2017, Mohammad Ben Salman, crown prince and prime minister of Saudi Arabia, arrested royals, military leaders, and wealthy business people, claiming no one was above the law (England, 2020). The arrests shocked the kingdom and won Ben Salman's public support. An anti-corruption committee was formed, and those billionaires arrested negotiated their freedom with a financial settlement that helped bring up Saudi's reserves (England, 2020).

Culture and Technology in the GCC Countries

The GCC countries enjoy the best technological infrastructure in the Middle East. Internet penetration rates among the population reached 98% in 2021 – compared to 63% worldwide – and 137% of the population are mobile subscribers, indicating that almost four out of ten people have more than one mobile subscription (Zawya, 2022).

Technology is shaping socio-cultural changes in the GCC region: While traditionally, social networks are articulated within a long heritage of Arab values based upon a collectivistic culture (Ayish & Breslow, 2014), technology enables the articulation of more individualistic culture, hindering some of the more collectivist features of Arab cultures (Allagui & Breslow, 2013). The Internet led to a shift in media consumption; as users migrated to digital, their media and news consumption turned fragmented: Users get updated with local news and events on group chats (i.e., WhatsApp) and social media, TikTok, Instagram, and Twitter (Dennis et al., 2019). However, Internet use has also led to tensions regarding security, the spread of rumors, and freedom of expression. The GCC countries adopted various cyberlaws to protect users from social and financial cybercrimes; however, they became perceived as justifications for regulating online usage and censoring political content (Al-Sumait et al., 2021).

Al-Talei (2021) argues that in times of crisis, the GCC states enforce control of freedom of expression through monitoring content, censorship, and intimidating techniques like penalties and arrests that induce fear and self-censorship that extends to journalists and academics alike. COVID-19 and the Qatar blockade are a few examples of when a control on freedom of expression was implemented and applied to nationals and expatriates, as discussed below. Moreover, Jones (2019) argues that Twitter bots were used to increase propaganda from the blockading countries against Qatar, Twitter trends were manipulated, and social media weaponized.

The State of Research in Risk and Crisis Communication in the GCC Countries

The crisis communication research in the Middle East and North Africa (MENA) region deals primarily with political issues, including the Israeli occupation of Palestine, struggles between authoritarianism and democracy, and the Arab uprising events (Saleh, 2016; Goby & Nickerson, 2015). This section focuses on the state of research in risk and crisis communication from institutional, audience, and media perspectives.

Institutional Perspective

Research in organizational crisis communication in the Arabian Gulf is lacking (Goby & Nickerson, 2015). Even in a field as vibrant as entrepreneurship, known for its high risk, start-ups in the MENA region are the least researched (Kiss et al., 2015). A review of the GCC countries' socio-cultural context can help understand why the institutional dimension of risk and crisis communication is little studied. A primary reason for this research gap is the limited access to corporate information and insights about risks or crises when they occur.

The economy of the Middle East is based on a family culture tradition; most businesses are family owned. A report by Ernest & Young (EY) in 2014 notes that 90% of companies in the Middle East are family-owned businesses (Ernst & Young, 2014). In the Arabian Gulf, foreign investment is limited and regulated; countries have set quotas for foreign capital participation or other legal measures to protect specific sectors and local businesses. This protectionist structure results in limited or no public records, as companies want to ensure the information is maintained within and no access is made available to the public or any third party (Watts, 2015). The information about the businesses becomes scarce, foreign investors interested in partnerships and acquisitions fail to conduct due diligence, and, most often, researchers face refusal to share records or conduct interviews. Only when turning public are companies legally required to share their books publicly; even then, they are reluctant to contribute to research unless connected through personal networks.

Further, to protect their books, businesses in the GCC countries care about protecting their reputation or *face* (Goby & Nickerson, 2015; Loewenberg, 2011). In collectivist cultures (Hofstede, 1994) such as those of the GCC, it is important not to expose mistakes or errors to keep face (Goby & Nickerson, 2015), leading to businesses keeping silent to contain their crises. Such was the case when a fatal accident occurred in Dubai Global Village in 2013 after a ferry cart fell on an Emirati man as he walked nearby. The CEO presented condolences, and the shopping center closed for the rest of the season, while the media attention lasted about a week (Afshan, 2013). Similarly, in 2012, a fatal fire broke out in Qatar's Villaggio shopping mall in a nursery operating without a legal license; it caused the death of 19 people, including 13 children and teachers (Sultan, 2013). The owners, Qatar's ambassador to the European Union, his wife, and managers of the mall were convicted to six years of prison, but no one has spent time in jail, according to a lawsuit filed by the parents of the victims (ITUC, 2014). The media coverage of the case was controlled and stopped by a court order (Sultan, 2013). The mall remained closed for a few months and reopened business as usual. At the time, the mall was a leader in its category, and no threat from the competition would shake the business. To our knowledge, no research on managing both crises with an institutional dimension has been conducted; however, research examining the Villaggio crisis from an audience perspective will be discussed below.

Government intervention to address local crises serves not only to control the media and their narratives; they step in beyond that, manifesting collective culture. For example, when Dubai Holding, a global personal investment holding company owned by Dubai ruler Sheikh Mohammed Bin Rashid, faced a crisis following the 2008 financial downturn that led to a decline in the Dubai real estate sector and a drop in investor confidence, Sheikh Khalifa Bin Zayed Al Nahyan, who was then the ruler of Abu Dhabi and president of the UAE, came to the rescue by injecting financial support into the emirate of Dubai. The tallest tower in the world, originally named Burj Dubai, was renamed Burj Khalifa in his honor as a tribute to his assistance. Therefore, culture plays a vital role in addressing business crises (Sawalha et al., 2017). Traditions and religious beliefs also influence individuals, including business people, and their responses to crises. Sawalha et al. (2017, p.25) write,

> It is also widely accepted in the Arab world that disasters and crises represent "God's will or expressions" of his wrath. Therefore, the normal response to these incidents is total submission and acceptance of the adverse impacts of these incidents with low levels of preparedness and pro-action. (…) As a result, CC [crisis communication] seems worthless under such conditions where people have already taken the decision to give up trying to respond effectively due to their religious views.

Although this may have been true half a century ago, business culture in the region has evolved. The impact of religion on institutions' handling of their crises is loosening with the arrival of a new generation of businessmen and women, educated and skilled, who are taking over family businesses and applying modern techniques in a market that is increasingly competitive and blended with local and foreign firms (Allagui, 2019). Local corporations or foreign companies increasingly use PR, hire PR consultants, and find high-value PR to address a PR crisis.

In Bahrain, AlSaqer (2018) argues that her research is the first to address strategic communication crisis planning in public and private organizations. Using an issue management theoretical framework, the study finds that crisis communication needs improvement to become proactive rather than reactive. Studying the COVID-19 crisis in the UAE, Abbas-Zaher et al. (2021) show that the UAE's crisis management included efficient governance, a public–private partnership, and expertise from a highly knowledgeable workforce.

In the academic literature, corporate scandals remain underexplored. For instance, the Villaggio Fire in Qatar and the Global Village accident in Dubai have, to our knowledge, not been studied by researchers. UAE Damas, a jewelry company majority-owned by the Abdullah family, experienced a scandal in 2010 involving allegations of fraud and mismanagement by its senior executives. The Abdullah brothers, who hold the majority of the company's shares, allegedly used company funds for personal reasons. Deeply in debt, the company underwent a restructuring before being acquired in 2012 by the Qatari corporation Al-Mannai Group. While this is a notable scandal in the UAE, significantly impacting the reputation of a longstanding family brand that has operated in the region for decades, we were unable to find any research addressing the crisis and reputation management of Damas.

Cybersecurity has been a significant threat in the region recently; research investigating cybersecurity crises deals with more than one country in the Gulf region since the countries enjoy a similar Internet infrastructure, and their laws about cybersecurity are fairly the same (Al-Shabib & Martins, 2022; Hassib & Shires, 2022). Most research studies deal with the information technology (IT) dimension and how to reduce threats and risks by favoring technical or managerial dimensions more than the reputation management dimension. However, some studies have examined the impact on countries and the survival of businesses. For instance, Shires (2019) studied the hack-and-leak operations in the Saudi–Yemen war, and Cherkaoui (2018) analyzed the cyber-attacks on government or public institutions that provoked crises in countries like KSA, UAE, and Qatar. The Saudi and UAE cyber-attacks on the Qatar news agency website in 2017 that caused the Qatar blockade have also been widely studied (Al-Rawi, 2021; Bianco & Stansfield, 2018; Ulrichsen, 2020).

Similarly, when the COVID-19 pandemic hit the Gulf countries, researchers tended to discuss and analyze the countries' risks and crises rather than a perspective about the institutions involved in the crisis and their reputation management. Similarly, with the Khashoggi murder on October 2, 2018, the KSA went through a damaging reputation crisis. For instance, Cherkaoui and Mohydin (2019) studied the narratives and counternarratives in the Khashoggi murder.

The 2017 Qatar blockade and the COVID-19 pandemic ushered in research that adopted a ***cross-national*** approach and discussed the GCC countries not as a block of homogeneous group members but as states in conflict or competition. Researchers focused on comparing governments' responses to the crisis and how they handled their risks separately despite the affinities among countries of the GCC alliance. For instance, studying the GCC countries' reactions to the COVID-19 pandemic crisis, Young (2020) writes that the countries held different economic, labor, and health positions and responses, respective of their national priorities and affordances, despite the economic and socio-cultural similarities the GCC countries share. Young (2020) notes that during the pandemic crisis, governments faced pressure to make trade-offs between various policies, including market liberalization, monetary and fiscal policies, work and immigration policies, and economic regulations that spoke to their national priorities and leadership visions, which became distinct rather than common to the other GCC countries.

In closing, from an institutional perspective, research in risk and crisis communication in the GCC countries has yet to develop. A deeply ingrained, protective corporate culture has prevailed, largely due to traditional practices and socio-cultural factors. However, there is reason to believe that the adoption of global business practices and the dissemination of knowledge have created a new framework that facilitates the sharing of business insights, cultural change, and the development of collaborative research programs.

Media Perspective

Initially, media outlets in the GCC countries have developed mainly as government-owned institutions funded and supported by the states. With the rise of satellite broadcasting, media reporting has evolved from merely covering officials' activities and news to a more diverse range of programming. However, their framing of events, problems, or crises remained positively biased toward their governments. While private media are independent in principle, in practice, they are often controlled by the state through laws and policies that regulate speech and freedom of the press. In times of a crisis, both public and private media must align with the state's framing to describe, explain, or interpret the crisis. Occasionally, when presenting opinions that do not align with the state's official position, local media would refer to foreign sources (Althaus et al., 1996; Guaaybess, 2019).

Researchers have extensively examined the media coverage of wars in the region, specifically Al-Jazeera's reporting on both Gulf Wars: 1991 (Iraq) and 2011 (Iraq and Afghanistan), as well as the uprisings in Syria and Bahrain post-2011. For example, Abdul-Nabi (2015) analyzed Al-Jazeera's reporting on Saudi intervention in Bahrain in 2011 and the chemical attack in Syria in 2013. He employed the peace journalism model to highlight the absence of peace journalism framing, which resulted in various biases favoring Qatar's foreign policy, as well as sectarianism and war propaganda. Gasim (2018) studied the Al-Jazeera coverage of the war in Yemen before and after the Qatari blockade led by Saudi Arabia and found that the news coverage increased after the start of the blockade, particularly the coverage dealing with the Saudi-led coalition in Yemen's war, suggesting the channel's alignment with Qatar. Along the lines of the media's impact on sparking or influencing crises, Sadig (2018) argues that Al-Jazeera partially gives voices to some but not all voiceless and that its programs and coverages have created and affected crises in the region, including the Arab Spring. Cherkaoui (2018) notes how AJA (AlJazeera Arabic) changed its tone of voice from being critical to countries of the region, including Qatar, in its early days to a state-funded broadcasting channel. "This media salvo may have been the prelude for a military invasion by Saudi/UAE forces," notes

Cherkaoui (2018, p. 137), arguing that AJA contributed to the crisis among GCC countries. Kirat (2014) suggests a *government press coalition theory*, as his study of three Gulf wars indicated that news organizations align with the country's position, often compromising journalism ethics, objectivity, and fairness.

Alternative media can play an equally important role in times of crisis; for instance, Ahmad and Hillman (2021) studied the information communicated to minority groups in Qatar at the time of the COVID-19 crisis. They concluded that the role of religious leaders and social media influencers was critical to raising awareness and communicating information to diverse minority language groups within Qatar. Jaziri and Miralam (2021) found that Saudi Arabia used a tri-dimensional framework to deal with the COVID-19 crisis in its disaster risk reduction system: strategic, operational, and tactic. This approach translates into being vigilant at the public level, flexible within a national management structure, and ensuring good governance at the local administrative level.

A new body of research has emerged that addresses the cyberwar involving trolls and misinformation, leading to various risks and crises. For instance, Jones (2019) found that the Twitter bots deployed during the 2017 Gulf crisis promoted fake news and aimed to amplify the crisis and increase the propaganda from the blockading countries toward Qatar. In examining the Saudi crisis and the Khashoggi killing, Al-Rawi (2021) discusses state-run misinformation campaigns as responses both before and after a crisis. He contends that Saudi Arabia deployed social media trolls to discredit Jamal Khashoggi and damage his reputation prior to the murder; afterward, these trolls circulated narratives claiming the killing was a staged event orchestrated by adversaries, specifically Qatar and Turkey. Abrahams and Leber (2021) analyzed media coverage of the Saudi crisis through Arabic hashtags, identifying 281 accounts among 2.4 million that generated 80% of the conversation from Saudi allies, showcasing a dominant narrative in support of Saudi Arabia's agenda and the government press coalition theory.

Research on risk and crisis communication from media perspectives has explored various approaches. While the government-affiliated media tends to frame crises in a certain way, the research delves into how different media outlets handle crises using a range of theoretical frameworks.

Audience Perspective

Research focusing on risk and crisis communication from the audience's perspective in the GCC region remains limited and sporadic. In comparison, studies on the Arab uprising crisis that delve into the perceptions of Arab citizens, particularly in Egypt and Tunisia, are abundant. This disparity can be attributed to the significant interest from global researchers, both local and international, who have mobilized to understand the massive protests against their regimes. Their efforts have yielded a wide range of publications about the crises in the Middle East, particularly regarding Tunisia, Libya, Syria, Egypt, and Yemen (for instance, Hudson et al., 2014; Masri, 2017; Ufheil-Somers & McMurray, 2013). In contrast, the GCC countries, apart from Bahrain, have not experienced a similar scale of events or research. It is important to be mindful of the nature of the GCC countries' regimes, which are non-democratic, during crises that lead to self-censorship. For example, during the Qatar blockade, the UAE banned any expression of sympathy toward Qatar by citizens who risk imprisonment between three and 15 years and more than $100,000 in fines. Under such conditions, audiences' participation in research becomes challenging, and researchers may feel unsafe conducting fieldwork, as pointed out in the opening of the 2018 Middle East Studies Association conference. Additionally, the International Journal of Communication's special section on the Qatar blockade crisis received no submission from the blockading countries Saudi Arabia, the UAE, Bahrain, and Egypt (Allagui & Akdenizli, 2019).

Nonetheless, not all research is inaccessible or controlled. Mitchell and Allagui (2019) used ethnographic interviews and visual analysis to discuss the impact of the Qatar blockade on the participation of nationals and expatriates in shared rituals of nationalism. They found evidence of a framing change of civic nationalism, to which both locals and expatriates henceforth belong.

Applying the social-mediated crisis communication model to the Villaggio fire crisis in Qatar, El-Gazzar (2015) studied the mediated role of social networks in crisis communication. The model clarifies "the two-way flows between key publics and information sources. Finally, the model adds five factors that affect how organizations respond to crises via the different forms of communication: crisis origin, crisis type, infrastructure, message content, and message form," says El-Gazzar (2015, p. 55). In addition to finding that social media was the primary source of information for audiences during this crisis, El Gazzar notes that audiences' behavior entails sharing news with their contacts. However, before sharing, they check the news on several sites to assess its trustworthiness and share it with selected groups of their contacts.

The field of risk and crisis communication research is both interesting and challenging from an audience perspective. Although people are eager to share their opinions on risks and crises in their environments, they may also have reservations about doing so. Additionally, the political climate can affect their willingness to participate in research initiatives and sway the agendas of risk and crisis communication research.

Handling of Crises: PR Consultants (Foreign vs. Local)

A Deloitte report (2011) notes, "Today, the Middle East lags behind the West in its understanding of public relations. However, numerous business executives are starting to realize the added value of PR, providing exposure at a minimal cost and being a highly-valuable tool in countering a crisis" (Nahas, 2011, p. 49). The business of PR has significantly developed over the last decade and is expected to double from US$1 billion in 2020 to US$2 billion in 2030 (Bridge, 2020). Thanks to the cutting-edge technological infrastructure in the GCC region, the establishment of global competing brands, and the vigorous event agenda in the UAE, Qatar, and Saudi Arabia, including the Dubai Expo 2020 and the FIFA World Cup in Qatar, risk and crisis management became a significant part of the PR business.

Providing an overview of the PR industry in Bahrain and Kuwait, Al-Saqer and Al-Hachemi (2019), as well as Almutairi and Dashti (2019), discuss how PR remains a new business in these countries, focusing more on tactical rather than strategic approaches, and relying on the will of senior management. Both studies note that the PR practice differs between the public and private sectors: Governments practice the publicity perspective of PR, as research and strategic planning are not within the scope of the PR function in public entities. In contrast, private companies, because of their exposure to foreign partnerships, have a better understanding of how research and strategy support and embrace PR functions. Along with Hall's (1976) high and low culture, both studies note the importance of local context to interpersonal and professional relationships and the impact of religious background on conducting business, including building image and persuading. Hall (1976) considers the Middle East a high culture where being direct and upfront does not work; PR relationships need to use a tone of indirectness and subtlety, and the conversations and relationships are very structured. Findings from interviews with PR practitioners in Bahrain (Al-Saqer & Al-Hashemi, 2019) show a tight relationship between religion and local traditions: "[T]he participants showed awareness of these Islamic ethics of public relations. For instance, interviewee V explained: 'Building good relationships with people from different cultures and religions is an important Islamic value that leads our practice in PR' (…) Islamic values affect our writing style in PR as we should use accepted words that respect our Islamic ethics," write AlSaqer and Al-Hashemi (2019, p. 18).

Almutairi and Dashti (2019) note how the invasion of Kuwait crisis in 1990 helped raise awareness about the function of PR and gain recognition of its usefulness and value. To manage the domestic crisis, Kuwait mandated PR and lobbying global firms, including US Hill & Knowlton, to shape American public opinion through PR efforts, including media relations, lobbying, public speaking, and video news releases. The authors add that these efforts have continued even after the Kuwait restoration "to maintain a positive image of its democratic political system to the world. Also, the exposure of the Kuwaiti people to the Western culture made them aware of public relations function in Western society" (Almutairi & Dashti, 2019, p. 43).

Bashir (2019) examined the PR business in Kuwait and concluded that there is a limited commitment to the principles of excellence in PR. She explains that PR professionals are little involved and empowered in the strategic management of PR due to little understanding of the business by the higher management and the lack of qualified practitioners.

In Saudi Arabia, Almahraj's (2019) research shows that PR consultants are valued and sought after during times of crisis, as the higher management would not handle their organizations' crises themselves but would hire PR practitioners to manage the crisis. This might not have been the case a decade ago, as earlier research (Al-Jaralh, 2011, cited by Almahraj, 2019) shows that in private companies, about 40% of PR departments chose to hire a consultant to handle the crisis, while in public companies, about 56% depended on their higher management to handle crises.

Crisis and Risk Management Research

In the GCC countries, the media is largely controlled by public structures and regulations that limit the creation of a public sphere. This environment restricts the sharing, acknowledgment, discussion, and research of corporate and organizational crises and scandals. Furthermore, the ruling regimes discourage opposing opinions and critiques, leaving scant opportunity for investigating crisis and risk management. Mellor (2021, p. 334) writes:

> If an editor crosses a line by publishing news critical of or unfavorable to certain royal family members, he will be relieved of his duties and forced to resign. (…) The late Saudi journalist Jamal Khashoggi (…) was relieved of his job as editor of an *al-Watan* newspaper in 2003. The reason given was he was critical of the religious authorities and their strict religious teachings. In his view, these led to the terrorist attacks in 2003, when two major bombings occurred in residential areas in Riyadh, killing 39 people; they were attributed to Islamic extremists who were said to be protesting the presence of US troops in the KSA.

This is one example of how Saudi Arabia addresses crises, as censorship, arrests, intimidation, and relief from duties are only a few examples of sanctions against freedom of expression, even if the crises are relevant to domestic public discussions. According to Mellor (2021), on the international stage, Saudi Arabia uses a reward system to buy loyalties (for instance, Hajj (pilgrim) rewards that include visa, airfare, and accommodation for Muslim editors that refrain from criticizing the kingdom) or neutralization and containment strategies also to prevent media crises:

> Neutralization and containment, in which the former strategy refers to buying out loyalties of international outlets so that they become neutralized or refrain from publishing negative news or criticism about the Arabian kingdom. The containment approach refers to buying out journalists' loyalty so that they praise the kingdom and are ready to attack critics of KSA. To facilitate this strategy, the KSA purchases hundreds or even thousands of subscriptions in selected publications in return for praise or refrain from attacking KSA (Mellor, 2021, p. 335).

Qatar used crisis management (Albasoos et al., 2021; Łukaszewicz & Grabowski, 2020) and a global network (Łukaszewicz & Grabowski, 2020) as the primary strategies to mitigate the sanctions imposed by Bahrain, Egypt, KSA, and the UAE during the Qatar blockade. Cherkaoui (2018) argues that Qatar turned to an international law framework and open dialogue to manage its blockade crisis and relied on its soft diplomacy, capitalizing on the relationships made through its billions of investments abroad and internally, it held the image of a country running its business as usual. Conversely, Harris (2018) and Hassan (2018) noted that the blockading quartet's communications suffered inconsistencies and imbalances.

Thus, risk and crisis management scholarship in the GCC countries captures conflicts and wars to a much greater extent than corporate and organizational crises. Growing competition among brands, exposure to PR practices, the rise of global PR firms in the region catering to their international clientele, and the prevalence of digital and social media all contribute to consolidating the business of PR in the region. Consequently, scholarship focusing on organizational risk and crisis communication might become a growing area of research.

Case Study: The Qatar Human Rights Allegations of Violations Followed by the Qatar Blockade

After Qatar had won the hosting of the 2022 FIFA World Cup and leading up to the World Cup, the country faced attacks on all fronts: First, it faced a crisis related to allegations of bribery and corruption; then, the crisis extended to accusations of human rights violations regarding the construction workers' conditions, leading to reputation crisis and inspiring researchers to study migration, race, labor, and economic and social conditions in the country. For instance, Babar's research on migration and working conditions includes the case of migrants in Qatar (Babar, 2015), female migrants in Qatar (Khattab et al., 2020), and power distribution in Qatar (Babar, 2015). Qatar involved public diplomacy and lobbying to control its narrative regarding improvements introduced to workers' conditions and its efforts and compliance with NGO recommendations. Qatar also enacted lobbying efforts to win the hearts of Western media and other stakeholders, a strategy used during the Qatar Blockade 2017.

The Qatar blockade crisis case spreads across all countries of the GCC; all countries are involved in how they engage with the crisis. Saudi Arabia, the UAE, Bahrain, and Egypt applied an economic and diplomatic embargo on Qatar, effective June 5, 2017. Kuwait opted for the mediator role, and Oman refused to take a position in the conflict. Qatar was found successful in its strategy of mobilizing foreign opinion in its favor. Al-Muftah (2019) describes the blockade as a war over narratives in which Qatar undermined the allegations against it and used public diplomacy to maximize its soft power and win the hearts of Western stakeholders. According to Cinzian & Gareth (2018), since the Qatar blockade, the region has become increasingly *fragmented*.

Conclusion and Areas of Future Research

This overview of the risk and crisis communication research shows that research published on conflicts and wars outweighs the research on organizational risk and crisis research.

This chapter discusses socio-cultural and political factors that impact the scholarship on risk and crisis communication emanating from within the region studied. Scholars must navigate challenging conditions, sometimes threatening to produce research on risk and crisis and most often opting to avoid researching sensitive topics. However, research on crises in the region involves not just the work of local scholars; academics from institutions worldwide have also contributed to the scholarship concerning the area. In the future, scholars should have the freedom to explore all subjects, including sensitive crises and case studies.

Research on risk and crisis communication in the future will explore various areas. In organizational communication, research will evolve due to the adoption of modern management practices by traditional and family-owned organizations, the competition between brands and organizations heightened with the new open economy of the region, the valorization of the PR profession that is increasingly valued for its role and support in times of crises, and the opportunities brought by digital and social media to expose scandals and crises subject to new areas of research.

Finally, with the expanding scope of risk and crisis communication research, and in light of modern business practices, we may encounter new strategies for addressing and managing risk and crisis communication that are informed by regional, political, socio-economic, cultural, and technological specifics. This locally-based approach can offer valuable insights and improve our understanding of risk and communication research on a global scale.

References

Abbas Zaher, W., Ahamed, F., Ganesan, S., Warren, K., & Koshy, A. (2021). COVID-19 crisis management: Lessons from the United Arab Emirates leaders. *Frontiers in Public Health, 9.* https://www.frontiersin.org/articles/10.3389/fpubh.2021.724494

Abdul-Nabi, Z. (2015). Based on the peace journalism model: Analysis of Al-Jazeera's coverage of Bahrain's uprising and Syria's chemical attack. *Global Media and Communication, 11*(3), 271–302. https://doi.org/10.1177/1742766515606300

Abrahams, A., & Leber, A. (2021). Framing a murder: Twitter influencers and the Jamal Khashoggi incident. *Mediterranean Politics, 26*(2), 247–259. http://doi.org/10.1080/13629395.2019.1697089

Afshan, A. (January 26, 2013). Three arrested over Global Village Ferris wheel death in Dubai. *The National UAE.* https://www.thenationalnews.com/uae/three-arrested-over-global-village-ferris-wheel-death-in-dubai-1.276740

Ahmad, R., & Hillman, S. (2021). Laboring to communicate: Use of migrant languages in COVID-19 awareness campaign in Qatar. *Multilingua, 40*(3), 303–337. https://doi.org/10.1515/multi-2020-0119

Al-Alkim, H. H. (1996). The prospect of democracy in the GCC countries. *Critique: Critical Middle Eastern Studies, 5*(9), 29–41. https://doi.org/10.1080/10669929608720090

Al-Jaralh, M. (2011). The efforts of public relations departments in facing the crises: A field study on private companies in Saudi Arabia [in Arabic]. *Saudi Association for Public Relations and Advertisement, 1*, 69–91.

Al-Marri, F. H. M. A. (2017). *The Impact of the Oil Crisis on Security and Foreign Policy in GCC Countries: Case Studies of Qatar.* KSA and UAE: Arab Center for Research & Policy Studies. http://www.jstor.org/stable/resrep12663

Al-Muftah, H. (2019). Qatar's response to the crisis: Public diplomacy as a means of crisis management: The Anatomy of a crisis. In A. Krieg, Ed., *Divided Gulf. Contemporary Gulf studies* (pp. 233–250). Palgrave Macmillan.

Al-Rawi, A. (2021). Disinformation under a networked authoritarian state: Saudi trolls' credibility attacks against Jamal Khashoggi. *Open Information Science, 5*(1), 140–162. https://doi.org/10.1515/opis-2020-011

Al-Shabib, H. N., & Martins, J. T. (2022). Cybersecurity: Perceived threats and policy responses in the Gulf Cooperation Council. *IEEE Transactions on Engineering Management, 69*(6), 3664–3675. http://doi.org/10.1109/TEM.2021.3083330

Al-Sumait, F., Dashti, A. A., & Kaposi, I. (2021). Chronicling Kuwait's media evolution. The politics of technology and regulation. In N. Miladi, & N. Nehor, Eds., *Routledge Handbook on Arab Media* (pp. 149–163). Routledge.

Al-Talei, R. (December 14, 2021). Why did GCC countries record disappointing results in the political participation index? *Carnegie Endowment for International Peace*. https://carnegieendowment.org/sada/85991

Albasoos, H., Hassan, G., & Zadjali, S. A. (2021). The Qatar crisis: Challenges and opportunities. *International Journal of Research in Business and Social Science, 10*(1), 2147–4478, Article 1. https://doi.org/10.20525/ijrbs.v10i1.1013

Allagui, I. (2019). *Advertising in MENA Goes Digital*. Routledge.

Allagui, I., & Akdenizli, B. (2019). The Gulf information war and the role of media and communication technologies. Editorial introduction. *International Journal of Communication, 13*, 1287–1300. https://ijoc.org/index.php/ijoc/article/view/8988/2599

Allagui, I., & Breslow, H. (2013). The disruption of online habitus: Flow, cyberculture, and the public sphere amongst diasporic groups in the UAE. In S. Baumann, Ed., *Cybercultures: Cultures in Cyberspace Communities* (pp. 167–182). Inter-Disciplinary Press.

Almahraj, Y. A. (2019). Public relations in Saudi Arabia. An Islamic perspective. In T. AlMutairi, & D. Drucker, Eds., *Public Relations in the Gulf Cooperation Council Countries. An Arab Perspective* (pp. 98–117). Routledge.

Almutairi, T. M., & Dashti, A. (2019). Public relations in Kuwait. A historical, practical, and theoretical perspective. In T. AlMutairi, & D. Drucker, Eds., *Public Relations in the Gulf Cooperation Council Countries. An Arab Perspective* (pp. 31–52). Routledge.

AlSaqer, L. (2018). The role of public relations in crisis communication planning in Bahraini organisations. *KnE Social Sciences, 3*(10), 76–87. https://doi.org/10.18502/kss.v3i10.3104

AlSaqer, L., & Al-Hashemi, S. (2019). The status and new directions of public relations practice in Bahrain. In T. AlMutairi, & D. Drucker, Eds., *Public Relations in the Gulf Cooperation Council Countries. An Arab Perspective* (pp. 5–30). Routledge.

Althaus, S. L., Edy, J. A., Entman, R. M., & Phalen, P. (1996). Revising the indexing hypothesis: Officials, media, and the Libya crisis. *Political Communication, 13*(4), 407–421.

Ayish, M., & Breslow, H. (2014). The need for interdisciplinary research of the Arab mass media. *Global Media Journal* Canadian edition, *7*(2), 57–73.

Babar, Z. (2015). Population, power, and distributional politics in Qatar. *Journal of Arabian Studies, 5*(2), 138–155. https://doi.org/10.1080/21534764.2015.1113680

Bashir, M. (2019). Toward excellence in public relations: identifying practices and barriers in Kuwaiti corporate, governmental and non-profit organizations. *Journal of Public Relations Research, 31*(3–4), 118–132. https://doi.org/10.1080/1062726X.2019.1679633

Bianco, C., & Stansfield, G. (2018, May). The intra-GCC crises: mapping GCC fragmentation after 2011. *International Affairs, 94*(3), 613–635. https://doi.org/10.1093/ia/iiy025

Bridge, S. (February 7, 2020). *Size of MENA's PR industry to double to $2bn by 2030, says Sunil John. Arabian Business*. https://www.arabianbusiness.com/world/439523-size-of-menas-pr-industry-to-double-to-2bn-by-2030-says-sunil-john

Cherkaoui, T. (2018). Qatar's public diplomacy, international broadcasting, and the Gulf Crisis. *Rising Powers Quarterly, 3*(3), 127–149.

Cherkaoui, T., & Mohydin, R. (2019). Murder in the consulate: The Khashoggi affair and the Turkish-Saudi war of narratives. *The Political Economy of Communication, 7*(2), 28–59. http://www.polecom.org/index.php/polecom/article/view/111/328

Cinzian, B., & Gareth, S. (2018). The intra-GCC crises: mapping GCC fragmentation after 2011. *International Affairs (London), 94*(3), 613–635.

Cooke, M. (2014). *Tribal Modern: Branding New Nations in the Arab Gulf* (1st ed.). University of California Press. https://www.jstor.org/stable/10.1525/j.ctt4cgfrq

Dennis, E. E., Martin, J. D., & Hassan, F. (2019). *Media Use in the Middle East, 2019: A Seven-Nation Survey*. Northwestern University in Qatar. www.mideastmedia.org/survey/2019

El-Gazzar, N. (2015). The use of social media among Qatari youth during crises – A survey. *The Scientific Journal of Public Relations & Advertising Research, 4*, 43–79. https://sjocs.journals.ekb.eg/article_88756_f8e779232d67ffe504690f53067c6df6.pdf

England, A. (March 16, 2020). Saudi Arabia arrests nearly 300 public servants in latest crackdown. *Financial Times*. https://www.ft.com/content/288fbb60-670b-11ea-800d-da70cff6e4d3

Ernst & Young (2014). *Family Businesses in the Middle East. Facts and Figures* (pp. 124–127). EY. Family Business Yearbook.

Gasim, G. (2018). The Qatari crisis and Al Jazeera's coverage of the war in Yemen. *Arab Media & Society, 25.* Winter/Spring. https://www.arabmediasociety.com/wp-content/uploads/2018/02/YemenWarQatarCrisis_Gasim.pdf

Goby, V. P., & Nickerson, C. (2015). The impact of culture on the construal of organizational crisis: Perceptions of crisis in Dubai. *Corporate Communications: An International Journal, 20*(3), 310–325. https://doi.org/10.1108/CCIJ-06-2014-0036

Guaaybess, T. (2019). *The Media in Arab Countries. From Development Theories to Cooperation Policies.* Wiley.

Hall, E. T. (1976). *Beyond Culture* (pp. 68–69). New York: Doubleday.

Hassib, B., & Shires, J. (2022). Cybersecurity in the GCC: From economic development to geopolitical controversy. *Middle East Policy, 29*, 90–103. https://onlinelibrary.wiley.com/doi/pdf/10.1111/mepo.12616

Harris, G. (February 9, 2018). In charm offensive, Qatar pushes for a comeback in Washington. *The New York Times.* https://www.nytimes.com/2018/02/09/us/politics/trump-qatar-lobbying-embargo.html

Hassan, H. (2018). *Qatar won the Saudi blockade, Foreign Policy.* https://foreignpolicy.com/2018/06/04/qatar-won-the-saudi-blockad

Hofstede, G. (1994). *Cultures and Organizations. Software of the Mind: Intercultural Cooperation and Its Importance for Survival.* London: Harper Collins.

Hudson, L., Iskander, A., & Kirk, M. (2014). *Media Evolution on the Eve of the Arab Spring.* Palgrave MacMillan.

ITUC International Trade Union Confederation (December 22, 2014). *Tensions rise as Villaggio fire appeal hearing drags on.* https://www.business-humanrights.org/en/latest-news/tensions-rise-as-villaggio-fire-appeal-hearing-drags-on/

Jaziri, R., & Miralam, M. S. (2021). The impact of crisis and disasters risk management in COVID-19 times: Insights and lessons learned from Saudi Arabia. *Ethics, Medicine and Public Health, 18*, 100705. https://doi.org/10.1016/j.jemep.2021.100705

Jones, M. O. (2019). Propaganda, fake news, and fake trends: The weaponization of Twitter bots in the Gulf Crisis. *International Journal of Communication, 13*, 1389–1415. https://ijoc.org/index.php/ijoc/article/view/8994/2604

Khattab, N., Babar, Z., Ewers, M., & Shaath, M. (2020). Gender and mobility: Qatar's highly skilled female migrants in context. *Migration and Development, 9*(3), 369–389. https://doi.org/10.1080/21632324.2020.1723216

Kirat, M. (2014). From news pools to embedded journalists: How media frame wars and conflicts? *Journalism and Mass Communication, 4*, 1–12.

Kiss, A. N., Danis, W. M., & Cavusgil, S. T. (2015). International entrepreneurship research in emerging economies: A critical review and research agenda. *Journal of Business Venturing, 27*(20), 266–290.

Loewenberg, P. (2011). Matteo ricci, psychoanalysis, and 'face' in Chinese culture and diplomacy. *The American Imago, 68*(4), 689–706.

Łukaszewicz, A., & Grabowski, W. (2020). Crisis management in the era of the global network. The case of Qatari responsive policy vs. the antiterror quartet sanctions. *European Journal of Transformation Studies, 8*(2), Article 2.

Mati, A. & Vacher, J. (November 29, 2022). Gulf countries should maintain reform momentum, despite oil boom. *IMF Country Focus.* https://www.imf.org/en/News/Articles/2022/11/28/cf-gulf-countries-should-maintain-reform-momentum-despite-oil-boom

Masri, M. S. (2017). *Tunisia.* An Arab Anomaly: Columbia University Press.

Mellor, N. (2021). The Saudi press – The combined power of wealth and religion. In N. Miladi, & N. Nehor, Eds., *The Routledge Handbook on Arab Media* (pp. 327–337). Routledge.

Mitchell, J. S., & Allagui, I. (2019). Car decals, civic rituals, and changing conceptions of nationalism. *The International Journal of Communication, 13*, 1368–1388. https://ijoc.org/index.php/ijoc/article/view/899

Nahas, A. (2011). *Is there a PR manager in the house? A Middle East point of view. Deloitte.* https://www2.deloitte.com/content/dam/Deloitte/xe/Documents/About-Deloitte/mepovdocuments/mepov4/dtme_mepov4_Is-there-a-PR-manager-in-the-house.pdf

Nair, D. (October 31, 2022). GCC economies projected to grow 6.9% in 2022, World Bank says. *The National Business.* https://www.thenationalnews.com/business/economy/2022/10/31/gcc-economies-projected-to-grow-69-in-2022-world-bank-says/
Sadig, H. B. (2018). In the heart of the storm: How Al Jazeera is contributing to changing the Gulf and the World. *International Journal of Crisis Communication, 2*, 21–31.
Saleh, I. (2016). Crisis communication research in the Middle East and North Africa (MENA). In A. Schwarz, M. W. Seeger, & C. Auer, Eds., *The Handbook of International Crisis and Communication Research* (pp. 313–326). John Wiley & Sons.
Sawalha, I. H., Shamieh, J. M., & Fendi, U. A. (2017). Insights on the influence of the attributes of the Arab culture on crisis communications. *International Journal of Crisis Communication, 1*, 21–28. http://dx.doi.org/10.31907/2617-121X.2017.01.01.04
Shires, J. (2019). Hack-and-leak operations: Intrusion and influence in the Gulf. *Journal of Cyber Policy, 4*(2), 235–256. https://doi.org/10.1080/23738871.2019.1636108
Sultan, Z. (2013). What went wrong with the media coverage of the Villaggio fire? *Business & Human Rights Resource Center.* https://www.business-humanrights.org/en/latest-news/what-went-wrong-with-the-media-coverage-of-the-villaggio-fire/
Ulrichsen, K. C. (2020). *Qatar and the Gulf Crisis.* Oxford University Press.
Ufheil-Somers, A., & McMurray, A. (2013). *The Arab Revolts. Dispatches on Militant Democracy in the Middle East.* Indiana University Press.
Watts, G. (2015). *Business conditions in the Arabian Gulf.* https://www.tamimi.com/law-update-articles/business-conditions-in-the-arabian-gulf/
World Population Review (2023). *GCC countries 2023.* Retrieved September 6, 2023 from https://worldpopulationreview.com/country-rankings/gcc-countries
Young, K. E. (2020). Twin crises deepen Gulf states' policy competition and independence. *Global Discourse, 10*(4), 481–487. https://doi.org/10.1332/204378920X16015780589771
Zawya (January 17, 2022). GCC's internet users soar over 98 percent, and mobile subscribers account for over 137 per cent of region's total population, says report. *Zawya.* https://www.zawya.com/en/press-release/gccs-internet-users-soar-over-98-per-cent-and-mobile-subscribers-account-for-over-137-per-cent-of-regions-u3jesjo7

Author Bio

Ilhem Allagui is a full professor at Northwestern University in Qatar. She received her Ph.D. in communication science at the University of Montreal, Canada (2006). Dr. Allagui authored *Advertising in MENA Goes Digital* (Routledge, 2019). Northwestern scholar, Dr. Allagui's research falls under two strands: strategic communication on the one hand and new media adoption and social transformations on the other hand. She published on corporate strategic communications, big data and the creative economy, digital media, and socio-political change in the Arab region. She is an editorial board member of the International Journal of Communication (ijoc.org) and Internet Histories (Taylor & Francis). Dr. Allagui was the president of the International Media Management Academic Association and chairwoman of its executive board. She remains a board member. Email: ilhem.allagui@northwestern.edu.

Crisis and Risk Communication Research in Europe

32

Crisis and Risk Communication Research in Germany

Andreas Schwarz
Institute of Media and Communication Science,
Technische Universität Ilmenau, Ilmenau, Germany

The Context of Crisis Communication Research in Germany

Since 1945, and especially after 1990, the reunified Germany has become a democratic country with more than 80 million inhabitants. The unified Germany is the biggest country in the European Union and the third largest economy in the world by gross domestic product in 2023 (World Bank, 2024). After the political experiences of the failed democracy of the Weimar Republic and the Nazi terror regime, the post-1949 German constitution defined principal human rights, federalism, and the separation of legislative, judical, and executive powers (Bentele & Wehmeier, 2003). The economy is organized as a social market economy that combines free trade with the idea of a social welfare state that, besides economic freedom, emphasizes social justice. Therefore, not only private companies but also trade unions, associations, and NGOs representing very diverse and often conflicting interests are important players that influence business, politics, and public opinion. The German constitution guarantees press freedom, allowing practically all persons to express and publish their opinion and even to call themselves journalists ("free profession") or public relations practitioners. The international NGO Reporters without Borders (2024) ranked Germany 10th on their World Press Freedom Index in 2024, ranking higher than countries like France (21st) or the United States (55th). However, as in other countries, the rise of right-wing extremist groups such as the Alternative for Germany (AfD) in the last decade, which consistently spreads disinformation about the work of free professional journalists, has contributed to an increase in open verbal and violent attacks on journalists as well as scientists. These political developments have been repeatedly linked to the efforts of the Russian government (Allweiss, 2024), especially since the invasion of Ukraine that began with the annexation of the Crimean Peninsula in 2014 and has intensified since Russia's attack on the entire country.

Hallin and Mancini (2004) assigned Germany to the North/Central Europe or democratic corporatist model of media systems together with countries like Austria, the Netherlands, and Sweden. This model is described by an early development of a mass-circulation press, including high levels of newspaper circulation. The media system is characterized by high levels of professionalization in journalism, where a majority of journalists perceive their role as

The Handbook of International Crisis and Risk Communication Research, Second Edition.
Edited by Andreas Schwarz, Matthew W. Seeger, and Sora Kim.

providing reliable information based on impartial observation, combating disinformation, shedding light on social issues, and empowering people to form opinions (Loosen et al., 2023). In terms of media outreach, the use of TV and radio (the most used media among Germans) has been rather constant in the last few years while the use of printed newspapers has been declining, especially among younger demographics. The most used social media platforms are YouTube (>40%), Facebook (35%), Instagram (31%), TikTok (14%), Snapchat (13%), and Twitter (10%) (Koch, 2022; Kupferschmitt & Müller, 2023).

Crises and the Emergence of Risk and Crisis Communication Research in Germany

Germany has a long history of severe economic and political crises, with the latter often culminating in devastating wars which not only caused tremendous damage and loss of human life in its own country but in many other countries in Europe, Africa, and even North America. After World War II, Germany was divided into two countries with a democratic and market-economy-based West Germany and a socialist East Germany that was ruled by a totalitarian one-party regime under Soviet Russian control. During this time the two countries experienced crises such as natural disasters (e.g., the storm tide of the North Sea in 1962), terrorist attacks (e.g., the assassinations and attacks of the Red Army Faction from 1970 to 1993), and industrial accidents or scandals (e.g., the Contergan scandal of Grünenthal Ltd. in 1961). In addition, the Cold War was experienced as a prolonged political crisis between the eastern and western blocs that threatened the lives and security of the German people. After massive protests in East Germany in 1989, the political and civil context of the time paved the way for a reunification of Germany.

The relatively quick fall of the Berlin Wall in November 1989 can anecdotally be attributed to, among other things, a fundamental "failure" of crisis communication during a press conference on November 9. During a press conference of the Eastern German government, the regime's spokesperson, Günter Schabowski, explained new relaxed travel regulations for East Germans based on handwritten notes. Apparently, he was unaware that the regulation included various conditions and was only to apply from the following day. In response to a question from an Italian and a Western German journalist, Schabowski erroneously replied, "As far as I know . . . this is immediate, without delay." Shortly thereafter, thousands of East Germans rushed to the border between East and West Berlin. The border police did not know how to handle the situation and finally opened the border at 23:29 as a result of a poorly prepared televised press conference (LEMO Lebendiges Museum Online, 2024).

After the reunification of the two Germanys, the country started to be actively involved in military conflicts again, this time as a member of international coalitions which intervened, for example, in the Kosovo War (1999) and the war in Afghanistan (2001). Germany has experienced several severe floods as a result of heavy precipitation. Floods are increasing in magnitude and cost and have been attributed to climate change. The flood in the Ahr Valley in 2021, for example, was a severe disaster in the recent past with 134 fatalities and an economic cost of 20 billion Euros, according to the German Research Centre for Geosciences (2024). Further consequences of weather events and climate change are an increase in droughts and wildfires. As with many other countries, Germany was significantly affected by the COVID-19 pandemic between March 2020 and 2023, with more than 180,000 deaths (German Federal Ministry of Health, 2024). Both the increase of extreme weather events and the pandemic triggered substantial research activities in risk and crisis communication in the country, as our literature review will show. In addition, economic crises have continued to affect Germany, such as the international financial crisis (since 2007), the European debt crisis (since 2009), or the economic recession, the increase of inflation after the COVID-19 pandemic, as well as

Russia's invasion of Ukraine in 2022. Large-scale corporate crises also keep occurring in Germany, including the Volkswagen diesel scandal in 2015, money laundering allegations against Deutsche Bank in 2017 and 2023, and the fraudulent financial reporting and bankruptcy of Wirecard in 2020.

Although Germany has experienced a wide variety of crises in all sectors of society, research on risk and crisis communication is still a fragmented field in the country. A survey of members of the German Communication Association (DGPuK) asking for their research activities between 2005 and 2009 showed that only 5% of the respondents were involved in projects on crisis or risk communication (Altmeppen et al., 2011). In its beginnings, mainly disaster and environmental sociologists such as Ortwin Renn (1984) and Wolf Dombrowsky (1987) contributed to the field with an initial focus on risk perception and risk communication concerning the civil use of nuclear power and other technological risks. This was inspired by the emergence of this new technology and the fears it generated in the German population, especially after the 1986 Chernobyl accident, which caused slight radioactive contamination effects in Germany. Relevant research institutions were, for example, the Research Center for Nuclear Power in Juelich and the Disaster Research Center at the University of Kiel. The Chernobyl disaster also inspired several media scholars who conducted content analyses of the media coverage and began to draw more attention to risk communication as a topic in German communication scholarship (e.g., Kepplinger, 1988; Ruhrmann, 1992; Teichert, 1987). However, the terms "crisis" or "crisis communication" were rarely used as theoretical concepts, as the focus was predominantly the perception and communication of social and environmental risks that resulted from the use of new technologies. The concept of crisis communication was emphasized more strongly in the early research on war reporting and the role of the media in framing, legitimizing, or delegitimizing armed conflicts with or without the involvement of the German military, especially by the German communication scholar Martin Löffelholz at Ilmenau University of Technology (Löffelholz, 1993).

Later in the 1990s, crisis communication became a more common term used for the study of different crisis types, including disaster, terrorism, war, political crises or scandals, as well as corporate crises. German communication scholars in the 1990s were strongly influenced by Niklas Luhmann's theory of autopoietic systems and cognitive constructivism. Kohring et al. (1996), for instance, argued that the observation of events as conflicts, wars, and disasters is the result of a complex process of social construction and that such events do not exist independently from the perception of their observers but depend on the observers' dispositions. The authors defined crises as observations of events that contradict or challenge usual expectancies of continuity and which are perceived as potential threats to existence and evaluated negatively (Kohring et al., 1996, p. 285). Crisis observations become socially manifest by communication. These observations and communications can substantially differ depending on the specific social system and its logic of observation. That may explain why not all wars, for example, are labeled as "crisis" by all observers or social systems. Löffelholz (1993, 2004) proposed a broader understanding of crisis and crisis communication that applies to all crises and all kinds of actors or systems that can be affected by crises. He defined crisis as assumed threats of crucial values of an observing system. They create high levels of uncertainty, involuntarily threaten dominant goals (e.g., of organizations), and are unpredictable in terms of consequences. The characteristics of crises are generated in cognitive and social processes; they do not "exist" in an ontological sense but stem from recursive observations which are coupled communicatively. War was described as a kind of ongoing crisis usually involving the use of violence (Löffelholz, 2004).

Hence, German communication scholars have considered war as crisis and the communication about war as crisis communication in the early phase of crisis communication research. Several publications appeared in the domain of journalism research and war reporting, most recently an edited volume on the war in Ukraine (Löffelholz et al., 2024). This emphasis on communication in the context of armed conflicts as crisis communication in Germany goes back to the history of the country, which before 1945 was heavily devastated by wars, usually caused by its own governments, who used propaganda and media censorship to legitimize these wars.

This has led to a rather broad understanding of crisis communication in German academia, comprising a broad range of crisis types (e.g., disaster, war, public health crises, industrial accidents, etc.) and crisis communicators (e.g., journalists, public relations professionals, politicians, NGOs, etc.). Based on this broad approach, Schwarz and Löffelholz (Schwarz, 2010; Schwarz & Löffelholz, 2014) characterized crisis communication as a social negotiation process in which observers intuitively or strategically attribute the status of a crisis to certain observed processes or events. From a process perspective, ***crisis communication*** refers to public and interpersonal communication processes in anticipation of crisis, during crisis, as well as in the aftermath of crisis. S***trategic*** crisis communication was conceptualized as the management of communication to proactively detect or prevent crises, to prepare for crises, to cope with ongoing crisis situations, and to deal with post-crisis concerns as well as to evaluate organizational crisis communication performance. The primary goal of strategic crisis communication is to protect crisis stakeholders from harm and to minimize the expected or observed loss of trust and reputation of organizations as perceived by relevant crisis stakeholders to maximize the scope of action of organizations to attain their strategic goals under crisis conditions. Depending on the type of organization (e.g., business organizations, disaster protection agencies, NGOs) and the type of crisis (e.g., disasters, public health crises, organizational crises), these goals refer to different values and standards, such as decreasing infection rates, assisting disaster victims, increasing donations in the third sector, or minimizing the loss of profits.

Another relevant context to understand crisis communication research in Germany is the institutionalization of the field in practice and academia. German practitioners increasingly recognize and emphasize the importance of the field. In public relations, for example, the data of an annual ranking of PR agencies showed that 48 out of 83 participating PR agencies reported to offer services in crisis communication (PR-Journal, 2024). In the German Public Relations Society (DPRG), one of the expert groups that meet on a regular basis is dedicated to crisis communication and issues management. The so-called "Crisisnavigator – Institute of Crisis Research," founded by the University of Kiel, organizes an annual conference on crisis communication for practitioners. Its main focus lies on commercial activities such as consulting and applied research without substantial publication output in academic books or journals. In addition, different government agencies, such as the German Federal Institute of Risk Assessment (BfR) or the Federal Office of Civil Protection and Disaster Assistance (BBK), offer seminars and training on different topics related to risk and crisis. Ilmenau University of Technology established a conference series on crisis communication with international attendance of scholars and practitioners. The conference started as a student congress for practitioners in 2006 and turned into a more academic international conference in 2009 entitled "Crisis Communication at the beginning of the 21st Century." Subsequently, the conference was continued as a biennial event of the European Communication Research and Education Association (ECREA) in several European countries such as Denmark, Germany, Portugal, Romania, Sweden, and the UK. The conference series has helped to raise awareness of risk and crisis communication as a field of study in Germany and has created strong links between the European and U.S. communities of scholars and practitioners. A further outcome of these activities was the foundation of the Risk and Crisis Communication Section within ECREA by the chapter's author, who chaired the section from 2011 to 2018. The section now counts more than 200 members and was chaired by the German professor Florian Meissner at the Macromedia University of Applied Sciences in Cologne until 2024. Both the start of the conference series in Ilmenau and the founding of the ECREA section have been described as important steps in the institutionalization of the field in Germany and Europe (Klingelhöfer, 2023).

Ilmenau University of Technology has been one of the more productive academic institutions in the field, also exemplified by Martin Löffelholz's foundation of the International Research Group on Crisis Communication in 2002. Other universities, which developed more than merely sporadic activities in risk and crisis communication research, have been the University of Mainz, the University of Siegen, the University of Münster, and the Free University of Berlin. The Research Institute for Sustainability at the Helmholtz Center Potsdam and the University of Stuttgart have been more productive in the fields of risk perception/communication and risk governance research.

The State of German Risk and Crisis Communication Research

Research on risk and crisis communication in its earlier stages, including non-peer-reviewed publications in German, was reviewed in the first edition of this handbook (Schwarz, 2016). Since the German academic system in the social sciences has increasingly shifted to the Anglo-American model with more emphasis on publishing in international and peer-reviewed journals, for this edition, the German contributions to risk and crisis communication were analyzed by using international literature databases such as Scopus and the Web of Science. This analysis will be presented in two steps. First, formal indicators will be assessed for a longer timespan (2010–2024) to get a broader overview of authorship, affiliations, important journals, etc. Second, the more recent publications (2020–2024) will be reviewed more thoroughly to understand recent developments in the field and the impact of societal trends. This review will be structured by the handbook's categories in section two (strategic institutional risk/crisis communicators), three (legacy/social media in risk and crisis communication), and four (audiences, citizens, and victims in risk and crisis contexts).

German Risk and Crisis Communication Scholarship from 2010 to 2024

To capture relevant publications, only journal articles in English or German listed in the database Scopus between 2010 and August 2024 were included. In addition, publications had to use the term "crisis communication" or "risk communication" either in titles or abstracts. The affiliation of at least one of the authors had to be in Germany. In addition, we limited the search to only those journals whose title indicated references to communication science (e.g., communication, media, public relations, journalism, health communication, etc.) or to risk, crisis, or specific types of risk and crisis (e.g., crisis, risk, hazard, disaster, climate change, war, etc.).

As a result, a total of 121 articles were found. On average, German risk and crisis communication scholarship in peer-reviewed journals grew substantially over time, with its peak in 2023 and 2024, which may be attributed to the impact of COVID-19 and more recent flood events in Germany, as later analysis will show (Figure 32.1). The most relevant journals were those in the fields of risk and disaster management or risk analysis such as *Risk Analysis* (12%), the *Journal of Risk Research* (11%), and the *International Journal of Disaster Risk Reduction* (9%) (Figure 32.2). The most relevant communication journals were mainly found in the field of PR and strategic communication such as *Public Relations Review* (6%) and the *Journal of Communication Management* (4%). The remaining papers were distributed across a wide array of journals related to health, crisis and disaster management, science communication, and environmental issues. In terms of disciplines, most of the research was classified by Scopus as social sciences (66%), business/management (36%), engineering (35%), medicine (27%), environmental science (20%), or earth and planetary sciences (16%). The involvement of co-authors from outside of Germany was mainly limited to Western scholars from the UK (19%), the US (10%), and Italy (8%). Only a few publications included co-authors from the Global South, with countries like Brazil, South Africa, or Vietnam with one or two publications each.

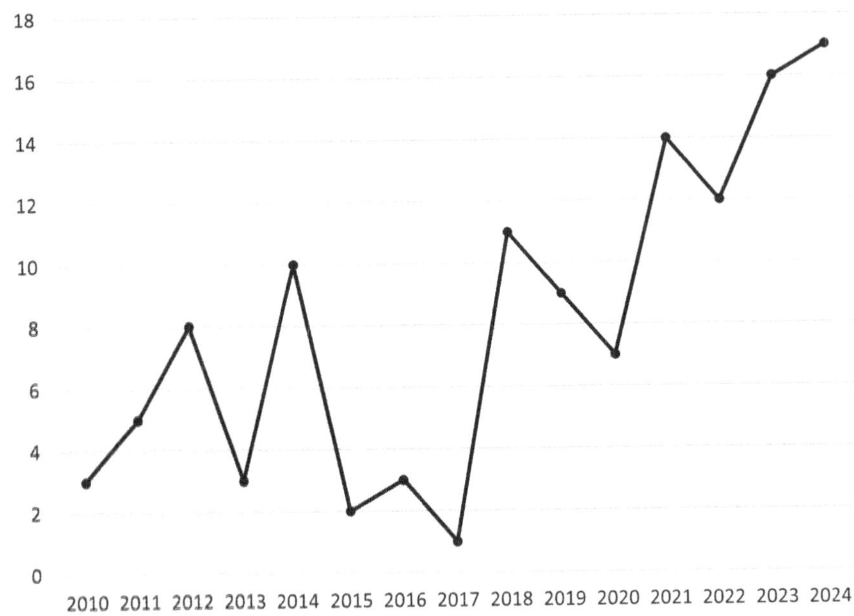

Figure 32.1 Number of peer-reviewed journal articles on risk and crisis communication with German affiliation from 2010 to 08/2024 (Scopus).

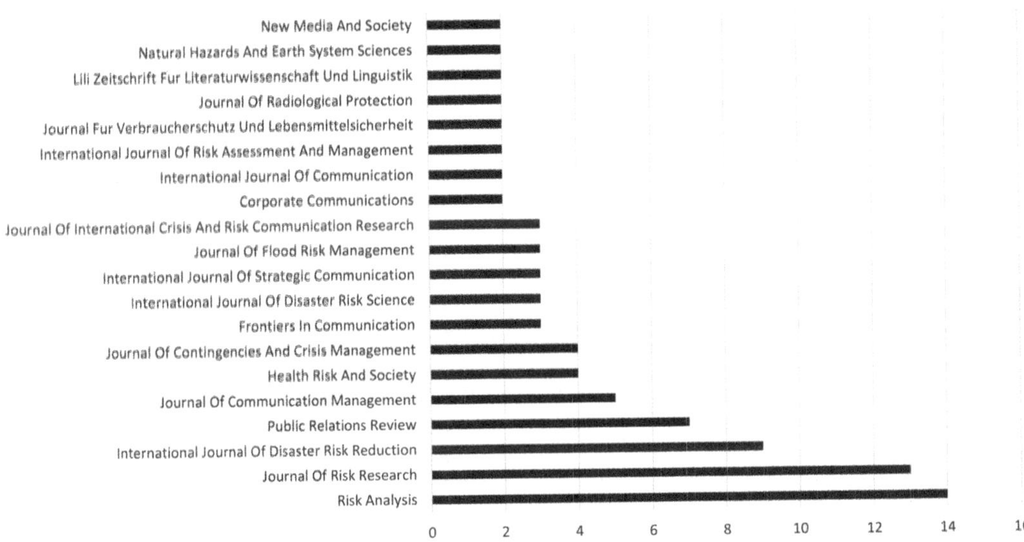

Figure 32.2 Number of peer-reviewed journal articles on risk and crisis communication with German affiliation by journal from 2010 to 08/2024 (Scopus).

From an institutional perspective, most of the research was published by German universities, with Ilmenau University of Technology (8%), Free University of Berlin (7%), the University of Potsdam (6%), and the University of Münster (6%) taking the lead (Figure 32.3). Also, a few government agencies contributed to that output, including the German Federal Institute for Risk Assessment (BfR) (4%) and the Federal Office for Radiation Protection (BfS) (3%). Prolific authors, besides the author of this chapter (7%) (e.g., Schwarz & Diers-Lawson, 2024), have been Annegret H. Thieken (4%), an environmental scientist from the

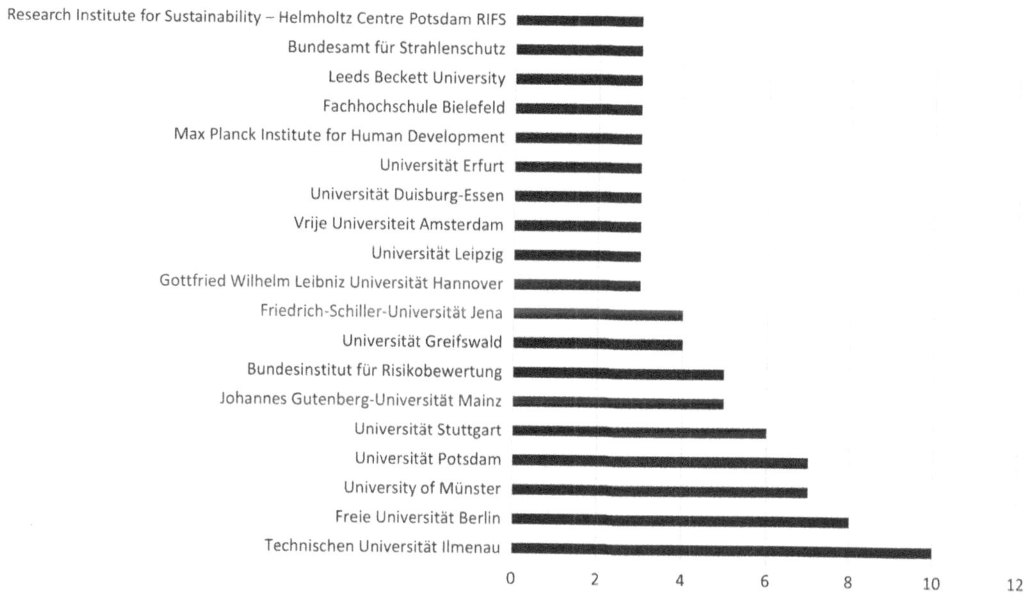

Figure 32.3 Number of peer-reviewed journal articles on risk and crisis communication by affiliation of authors from 2010 to 08/2024 (Scopus).

University of Potsdam with a strong emphasis on flood risk management and risk communication, who is also the president of the German Committee Disaster Risk Reduction (DKKV) (e.g., Thieken et al., 2022) (Figure 32.4). At the same institution and with a similar background is Philip Bubeck (3%) (e.g., Bubeck et al., 2024). Audra Diers-Lawson, a professor for risk and crisis communication at Kristiania University College in Norway, has been a frequent co-author of German scholars as well (3%) (Schwarz & Diers-Lawson, 2024). Ortwin Renn (3%), who played an important historical role in establishing risk perception and risk communication as a field of study in Germany, keeps being a productive contributor in the field of risk governance and communication (e.g., Bouder et al., 2021). Among other contributions, he was one of the co-authors who proposed the social amplification of risk framework (SARF), which to date is still an influential model in the field (Kasperson et al., 1988). Two authors from the German Federal Institute for Risk Assessment (BfR), Gaby Fleur Böl (3%) (e.g., Berger et al., 2023) and Severine Koch (3%) (e.g., Janzik et al., 2024), published on several aspects of risk perception and communication related to food safety and COVID-19, for example. Among German communication scholars, Juliana Raupp (3%) (e.g., Raupp, 2019) from the Free University of Berlin with a focus on public health threats as well as Thomas Koch (3%) (e.g., Koch et al., 2024) from the University of Mainz with a focus on corporate crises and CSR contributed notably to the body of literature according to Scopus and our search criteria. Most of the research related to German affiliations was funded by the research programs of the European Union (14%), followed by the German Federal Ministry of Education and Research (4%) and the German Research Foundation (DFG) (3%). Government agencies were scarcely listed for one or two publications each, including, for example, the German Federal Institute for Risk Assessment (BfR), the Federal Office for Civil Protection and Disaster Assistance (BBK), the Federal Office for Radiation Protection (BfS), and the German Aerospace Center (DLR), which is mainly funded by the German government and the EU.

This analysis shows that German research in the field is multidisciplinary, scattered across many disciplines and journals, with communication being a relatively minor contributor compared to other social sciences and other fields. Most of the published research in

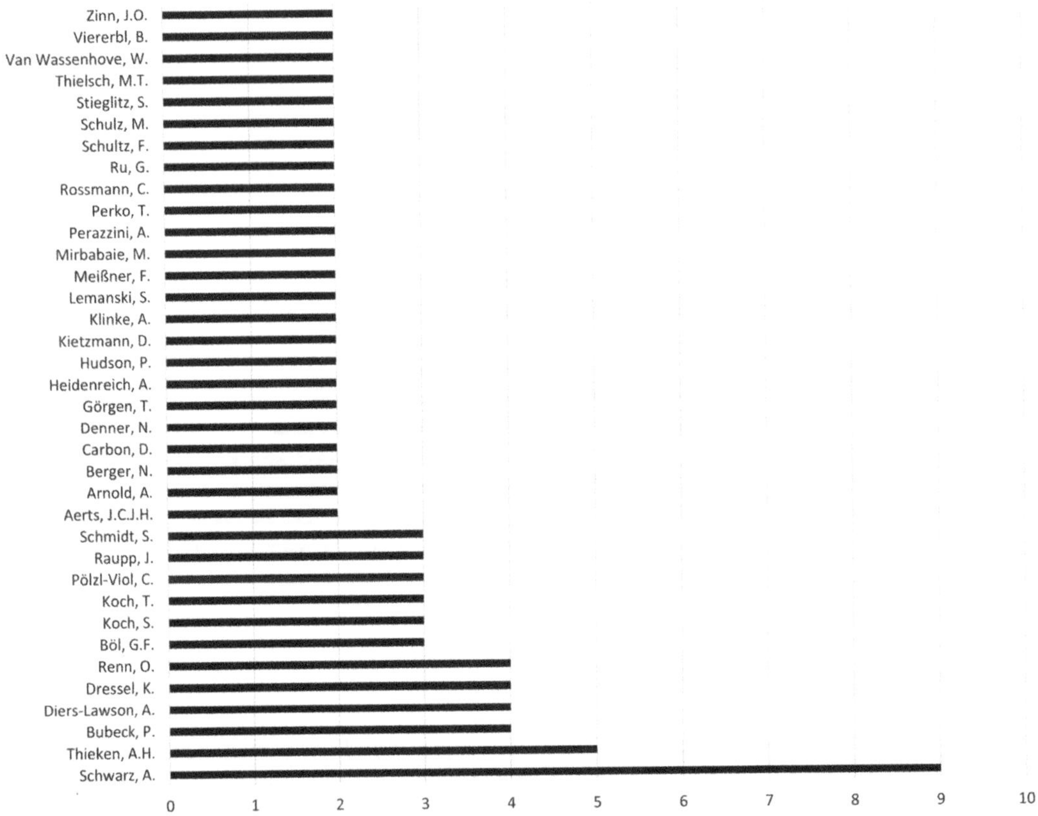

Figure 32.4 Number of peer-reviewed journal articles on risk and crisis communication with German affiliation by author from 2010 to 08/2024 (Scopus).

peer-reviewed outlets is concentrated on a few institutions based in Ilmenau, Berlin, Potsdam, and Münster. The results suggest that the perception, management, and communication of risk is the dominant perspective compared to crisis communication. In quantitative terms, the field seems to be growing significantly since 2018, with most of the funding coming from the European Union.

Recent Trends in German Risk and Crisis Communication Research (2020–2024)

To address recent developments in the field in Germany, we took a closer look at peer-reviewed journal publications from 2020 to August 2024. To capture as many relevant publications as possible, we combined searches in Scopus and the Web of Science with the same criteria as mentioned before, adapted to the available options in each database. A total of 67 papers were identified, most of them published after 2021, specifically in 2022 (30%), 2023 (24%), and the first seven months of 2024 (22%). Similar to our long-term analysis, most publications appeared in the *Journal of Risk Research* (16%), the *International of Disaster Risk Reduction* (13%), and *Risk Analysis* (12%). Relevant communication journals included Frontiers in Communication (4%), the *Journal of Communication Management* (4%), and the *Journal of International Crisis and Risk Communication Research* (JICRCR) (4%). We found two Germany-based communication journals with two articles each, including *Medien- und Kommunikationswissenschaft* and *Studies in Communication and Media*. Again, journals related to risk and disaster research largely dominated, while previously more important journals such as *Public Relations Review* were not among the publication titles at all. The latter seems to reflect a more recent editorial policy of that journal to divert risk and crisis communication studies to other journals such as *JICRCR* (4%) or the *Journal of Contingencies and Crisis Management* (6%). The most frequently listed affiliations were the University of Münster (9%), Ilmenau University of Technology (7%), and the University of Mainz (6%). The German Federal Institute for Risk Assessment (BfR) and the universities of Bergen (Norway), Bielefeld, Hamburg, and Potsdam, as well as Dortmund University of Technology, were represented with three papers each (4%). Most of the research was funded by the European Union and the German Federal Ministry of Education and Research. Most of the international collaborations of Germans were found for co-authors from the US (13%) and Norway (10%).

A systematic review of abstracts revealed that 75% of Germany-based publications actually dealt with risk/crisis *communication* as an explicit topic, while the remaining contributions were mainly addressing issues of perception, management, or governance of risks and crises. 79% of papers were empirical and 15% conceptual. At least 45% of the research actually collected data in Germany (in 19% of cases this was uncertain based on abstract descriptions). Only 16% of 67 studies collected data in more than one country. In terms of risk/crisis types, most publications dealt with pandemics (mostly COVID-19) (28%), followed by disasters (19%, mainly floods) and organizational crises (9%). Based on the terms the authors emphasized in their abstracts, titles, and keywords, most of the research used a risk communication perspective (45%) as opposed to a crisis communication perspective (24%).

A more in-depth review of publications was conducted for articles with an explicit reference to risk or crisis communication (abstract), excluding essays and fully conceptual papers, in total 36 articles. Out of these publications, we will summarize some of the most cited in consideration of the academic impact and the most recent articles in consideration of trends in German risk and crisis communication research.

Institutional Perspective

A lower share of Germany-based publications empirically analyzed institutional communicators and their risk and crisis communication strategies. With references to best practices in crisis communication and rhetorical arena theory (RAT), Drerup and Birkner (2022) computationally analyzed the 16 German state governments' responses to the COVID-19 pandemic on Facebook, Twitter, and in press releases in 2020. As a result, the authors found different emphases of topics between different state governments and communication channels. Many governments stressed topics related to solidarity in society as well as issues of education. Press releases were used for more complex topics such as future concerns or the economy, whereas social media were used more often for timely information such as infection numbers.

A study of crisis communication practices (interviews) and social media contents (automated content analysis) of the German state police showed that PR and social media managers mainly rely on Twitter to respond to crises, especially community-level crises such as mass shootings, while Facebook is seen more critically because of its algorithm's effect on crisis response (Jungblut et al., 2024). Social media content on Twitter and Facebook had a low share of crisis communication content. For organizational-level crises (e.g., allegations of police brutality), the authors found a higher share of dialogic communication than for community-level crises. Overall, the study shows that German police departments strongly rely on social media in their crisis response, predominantly on Twitter and for community-level crises.

Recent research with German participation also included cross-national studies. One example analyzed disaster management practices using social media in eight European countries, including German firefighters and emergency organizations (BBK), in response to a flood disaster and a shooting (Torpan et al., 2024). As a result, six predominant uses of social media were identified, including sharing educational guidelines, informing and warning the public, identifying citizens' concerns, identifying missing persons, sharing guidelines during disasters, and organizing volunteers. Another cross-national study analyzed practices of instructional internal risk communication at higher education institutions during the COVID-19 pandemic. The analysis was based on the IDEA model and semi-structured interviews with communication practitioners in 16 countries on five continents, including two practitioners in Germany (Schwarz et al., 2024). In general, messaging strategies emphasized behavioral recommendations (action) and channel selection (distribution) over communicating personal relevance (internalization) or explaining the pandemic in comprehensible language (explanation). Especially in Germany, practitioners did not see the need to translate messages to layperson terms and rarely used IDEA elements simultaneously in their risk messages.

Media Perspective

A common topic of German scholarship is environmental hazards as framed by the news media. A quantitative content analysis of media reports on plastics in selected German print and TV news media between 2015 and 2017 found that stories usually take an event-driven approach and focus on damages due to plastics that have already occurred as opposed to future potential threats (Welzenbach-Vogel et al., 2022).

A cross-national comparative study of 18 traditional news media outlets in six countries, including Germany, analyzed news frames of organizational crises related to nonprofit, nongovernmental, and intergovernmental organizations (IGOs) (Schwarz & Diers-Lawson, 2024). Based on an approach integrating framing, attribution theory, and situational crisis communication theory (SCCT), the authors identified three frames (critique, damage, victim) across countries with news media emphasizing different crisis types, quoting different sets of crisis response strategies, and moral evaluations that in part contradicted assumptions as formulated in SCCT. Overall, crisis reporting about nonprofits emphasized internal (e.g., sexual harassment scandals) over external crises (e.g., terrorism attacks). The most frequent crisis types were fraud and corruption, sexual violence/personal exploitation, and attacks on organizations. In comparison, German news media reported more positively about nonprofit and IGO crises, while they mainly focused on IGOs as organizations being victims of external attacks.

War is still a topic in German crisis communication research, as exemplified by a study on the framing of the Ukraine crisis by the German government, German newscasts, political talk shows, news satire shows, and the German version of the Russian broadcaster RT (in 2022 prohibited in Germany) in 2014 and 2015 after Russia's annexation of Crimea (Lichtenstein & Koerth, 2022). The authors used framing and the indexing hypothesis as a theoretical framework, according to which media coverage of violent conflicts largely reflects the dominant position of the political elites (see Chapter 4 in this volume by Schleicher). The results revealed a plurality of competing frames in the TV formats under study. The indexing hypothesis was confirmed in that German newscasts followed the German government's framing and RT the Russian government's position. Political talk shows and satire shows included much more criticism of governmental frames, partially even reflecting RT's frames, as in the case of one German satire show. Hence, the indexing hypothesis does only seem to apply to mainstream news media or propaganda channels such as RT.

Studies using a media perspective frequently analyze content on social media platforms. A framing study that integrates text and visual elements, for example, identified nine news frames of COVID-19 used by two German news media outlets on Twitter. The frames of politics and instructions, updated information, economic impact, and social impact had the highest thematic salience. Semiotic signs (indexical, symbolic and iconic) were used in news visuals to fulfill evidential, performative, and illustrative functions. The study is one of the few in the field using an approach of multimodal health crisis communication (Xu et al., 2024).

Using scandal theory and SCCT, Meier et al. (2023) analyzed the response to two scandals of the German Olympic team on Twitter/X (Tokyo 2020 Olympics), related to the racist slur by a German official during a cycling competition and a case of animal cruelty during a pentathlon event. The results show how scandals in niche sports can trigger substantial pressure for organizational reform due to a shift in public opinion. On the other hand, the adoption of reputation protection tactics by the affected organizations seemed to silence public criticism on social media.

Although media representations of the emerging technology of artificial intelligence (AI) have been frequently analyzed, authors rarely adopted an explicit risk communication perspective. Therefore, Schwarz and Unselt (2024) used an integrated framework of framing and the extended parallel processing model to identify risk frames of societal threat and efficacy of AI on YouTube. The authors identified four frames of AI, with videos using a low-threat perspective dominating over videos emphasizing risks of AI. Recommendations for measures of risk governance or societal risk mitigation were rarely addressed. Only one frame corresponded to standards of effective technological risk communication. This frame was found in a minority of videos and received the lowest share of attention on YouTube.

Audience Perspective

One of the most cited papers we identified dealt with the factors influencing COVID-19 vaccination conspiracy beliefs of the German population (Jensen et al., 2021). Based on a representative survey, the authors found that the lack of trust in government, science, or international institutions was related to higher levels of conspiracy beliefs. In addition, a migrant background along with the use of Twitter/X was correlated with conspiracy beliefs. Age, gender, or political orientation had only minor influence. Lower levels of conspiracy beliefs were related to a higher willingness to get vaccinated.

Another frequently cited paper studied the perceptions of internal crisis communication of employees in different German organizations – mostly business organizations – during the early stage of the COVID-19 pandemic (Ecklebe & Löffler, 2021). The survey revealed that mainly the dissemination of substantial information (informative, factual) as well as the frequency of communication influences the perception of high-quality internal crisis communication. Positive perceptions of internal crisis communication were related to higher levels of perceived trustworthiness, commitment, and employee satisfaction (i.e., employee-organization relationships).

Heidenreich et al. (2020) analyzed the effects of a number of workshops about private flood protection in towns and cities along the river Elbe in 2017. Based on protection motivation theory, the authors showed that such workshops can be employed as effective risk communication tools to increase people's knowledge about flood protection measures, perceived self-efficacy, and the motivation to engage in protective behavior.

Further studies focusing on audiences and message effects often used SCCT to analyze the effects of crisis response strategies during the COVID-19 pandemic (Hirschfeld & Thielsch, 2022) or in the context of terrorist attacks (Domschat et al., 2023). Others have experimentally tested the effects of CSR and CEO communication in contexts of corporate crises (Koch et al., 2022; Koch et al., 2024). In the context of climate change, the effects of heat warning messages were studied using the protective action decision model (PADM), showing that survey respondents felt better informed and willing to act when receiving warnings with action recommendations (Heidenreich & Thieken, 2024). Another study found no significant effects of targeting risk communication to specific stakeholder groups in the context of radon radiation risks in an online experiment (Dametto et al., 2023). A survey of German spontaneous volunteers during flood disasters showed that emergency response organizations should strengthen their coordination and cooperation with volunteers to motivate and engage them more effectively during disasters, especially via social media and online registration (Bier et al., 2023). Overall, we found German risk and crisis communication research addressing the audience perspective to be dominant compared to the media and institutional perspectives in recent years.

Conclusion and Outlook

This review of risk and crisis communication research in Germany from 2010 to 2024 has shown that authors cover a broad range of different risk/crisis types and perspectives in the communication process (professional communicators, media, audience/stakeholders). Most recent publications had a notable focus on the COVID-19 pandemic as well as flood disasters, reflecting the recent threat and crisis landscape of the country. Quantitatively, the literature review suggests a dominance of the risk communication perspective over a crisis communication perspective. Risk communication is primarily used as a concept in research on health, disaster, and technological threats, while crisis communication research is often focused on organizational crises or strategic communication concerns. It seems that only a few institutions and authors work consistently in the field of risk and crisis communication research. Many scholars only occasionally refer to risk/crisis as important concepts and are scattered across sub-disciplines such as health communication, environmental communication, science communication, media studies, and public relations. Previous literature reviews of research across sub-disciplines and countries related to media representations of COVID-19 or risks of AI technologies showed that studies often lack explicit conceptual references to the body of knowledge in risk and crisis communication, although the main object of study is risk and/or crisis (Schwarz et al., 2023; Schwarz & Faj, 2024). Hence, a great deal of published research may be somewhat relevant for the field but falls short in linking conceptual approaches and methodologies (measures) to the body of knowledge in risk and crisis communication research, both in Germany and globally.

In terms of international and cross-cultural comparative research, German scholars have looked at crises outside their own country since the early stages of risk and crisis communication research. However, a systematic, comparative, and theory-driven study of risk and crisis communication is still lacking. Global threats and crises, such as COVID-19 and climate change, have led to more international collaboration and research with German participation. Nevertheless, publications on cross-national aspects of risk and crisis communication as well as the involvement of countries in the Global South remain scarce.

In terms of limitations, our literature review may have missed some of the research and authors because of database features or the specified search criteria. Some research, for instance, was published in journals without obvious links to communication/media or risk/crisis types such as in the fields of medicine, public health, environmental studies, and computer science. Many publications empirically address issues of risk and/or crisis but do not refer explicitly to risk communication or crisis communication as concepts. In addition, many German scholars still publish their research as books or book chapters in German. A recent sociological analysis of crisis communication as a discipline by a German researcher showed, for example, that some of these authors publishing in German books are scarcely or not at all represented in international journals (Klingelhöfer, 2023). Some recent work in this regard includes an analysis of governmental crisis communication as perceived by German journalists (Drews, 2018) or the role of German journalists in crisis reporting (Dörner & Vogt, 2020). Several volumes have been published that address more applied aspects of crisis communication, mostly based on best practices, case studies, or literature reviews (e.g., Meißner & Schach, 2024; Ullrich & Brandstädter, 2016).

The increasing severity of global threats to Germany, including pandemics, climate change, the effects of migration, armed conflicts, and the impact of malicious actors' efforts to misinform and disinform the public, as well as the growing number of publications in international journals with German participation, suggest that risk and crisis communication research will gain importance in Germany. Whether this will lead to more institutionalization and sustainable research structures in terms of positions and funding beyond temporary, event-driven efforts remains uncertain. The engagement of German risk and crisis communication scholars in international associations, conferences, collaborative research, and international publication projects such as this handbook are promising indicators in this regard.

References

Allweiss, M. (2024). Pro-russische Propaganda quer durch Europa. Tagesschau. Retrieved December 8 from https://www.tagesschau.de/ausland/europa/tschechien-prorussische-propaganda-100.html

Altmeppen, K.-D., Weigel, J., & Gebhard, F. (2011). Forschungslandschaft Kommunikations- und Medienwissenschaft: Ergebnisse der ersten Befragung zu den Forschungsleistungen des Faches. *Publizistik*, *56*, 373–398. https://doi.org/10.1007/s11616-011-0132-7

Bentele, G., & Wehmeier, S. (2003). From literary bureaus to a modern profession: The development and current structure of public relations in Germany. In K. Sriramesh, & D. Verčič, Eds., *The Global Public Relations Handbook: Theory, Research, and Practice* (pp. 199–221). Lawrence Erlbaum.

Berger, N., Koch, S., Jungnickel, K., & Böl, G. F. (2023). Food safety in the aging population: Qualitative findings on what to communicate and how. *Risk Analysis*, *43*(9), 1843–1854. https://doi.org/10.1111/risa.14069

Bier, M., Fathi, R., Stephan, C., Kahl, A., Fiedrich, F., & Fekete, A. (2023). Spontaneous volunteers and the flood disaster 2021 in Germany: Development of social innovations in flood risk management [Article; Early Access]. *Journal of Flood Risk Management*, *20*. https://doi.org/10.1111/jfr3.12933

Bouder, F., Perko, T., Lofstedt, R., Renn, O., Rossmann, C., Hevey, D., Siegrist, M., Ringer, W., Pölzl-Viol, C., Dowdall, A., Fojtíková, I., Barazza, F., Hoffmann, B., Lutz, A., Hurst, S., & Reifenhäuser, C. (2021). The Potsdam radon communication manifesto. *Journal of Risk Research*, *24*(7), 909–912. https://doi.org/10.1080/13669877.2019.1691858

Bubeck, P., Pham, T. D. M., Nguyen, T. N. A., & Hudson, P. (2024). Disaster risk reduction on stage: An empirical evaluation of community-based theatre as risk communication tool for coastal risk mitigation and ecosystem-based adaptation. *Progress in Disaster Science*, *22*, 100323. https://doi.org/10.1016/j.pdisas.2024.100323

Dametto, D., Oertel, B., Pölzl-Viol, C., & Böhmert, C. (2023). Is targeting the solution? Evidence from an experiment on radon risk communication. *Journal of Risk Research*, *26*(4), 450–467. https://doi.org/10.1080/13669877.2023.2176913

Dombrowsky, W. R. (1987). *Das Tschernobyl-Syndrom: Katastrophen als verhaltensändernde Ereignisse.* Westdeutscher Verl.

Domschat, L., Stephens, M., & Saeed, H. (2023). Communication to protect brand image during a terrorism crisis: Application of situational crisis communication theory. *Journal of Contingencies & Crisis Management*, *31*(4), 913–927. https://doi.org/10.1111/1468-5973.12489

Dörner, A., & Vogt, L. (Eds.). (2020). *Mediale Störungen: Krisenkommunikation in Sondersendungen des Deutschen Fernsehens.* Springer VS. https://ebookcentral.proquest.com/lib/kxp/detail.action?docID=6179451

Drerup, F., & Birkner, T. (2022). Themes & timing crisis communication by German State Governments during the corona pandemic – A (semi-)automated content analysis of key communication channels. *Medien und Kommunikationswissenschaft*, *70*(3), 256–285. https://doi.org/10.5771/1615-634X-2022-3-256

Drews, J. (2018). *Risikokommunikation und Krisenkommunikation: Kommunikation von Behörden und die Erwartungen von Journalisten.* Springer VS. https://doi.org/10.1007/978-3-658-20015-2

Ecklebe, S., & Löffler, N. (2021). A question of quality: Perceptions of internal communication during the Covid-19 pandemic in Germany. *Journal of Communication Management*, *25*(3), 214–232. https://doi.org/10.1108/JCOM-09-2020-0101

German Federal Ministry of Health (2024). *Todesfälle im Zeitverlauf.* German Federal Ministry of Health. Retrieved December 8 from https://infektionsradar.gesund.bund.de/de/covid/todesfaelle

GFZ German Research Centre for Geosciences (2024). *On the flood situation in southern Germany.* Retrieved December 8 from https://www.gfz-potsdam.de/en/press/news/details/anlaesslich-der-hochwasserlage-in-sueddeutschland

Hallin, D. C., & Mancini, P. (2004). *Comparing Media Systems: Three Models of Media and Politics.* Cambridge University Press.

Heidenreich, A., Masson, T., & Bamberg, S. (2020). Let's talk about flood risk – Evaluating a series of workshops on private flood protection. *International Journal of Disaster Risk Reduction*, *50*, 10. Article 101880. https://doi.org/10.1016/j.ijdrr.2020.101880

Heidenreich, A., & Thieken, A. H. (2024). Individual heat adaptation: Analyzing risk communication, warnings, heat risk perception, and protective behavior in three German cities. *Risk Analysis*, *44*(8), 1788–1808. https://doi.org/10.1111/risa.14278

Hirschfeld, G., & Thielsch, M. T. (2022). Impact of crisis communication strategies on people's attitudes toward behavioral guidelines regarding COVID-19 and on their trust in local officials. *International Journal of Disaster Risk Science*, *13*(4), 495–506. https://doi.org/10.1007/s13753-022-00424-3

Janzik, R., Koch, S., Zamariola, G., Vrbos, D., White, M. P., Pahl, S., & Berger, N. (2024). Exploring public risk perceptions of microplastics: Findings from a cross-national qualitative interview study among German and Italian citizens. *Risk Analysis*, *44*(3), 521–535. https://doi.org/10.1111/risa.14184

Jensen, E. A., Pfleger, A., Herbig, L., Wagoner, B., Lorenz, L., & Watzlawik, M. (2021). What drives belief in vaccination conspiracy theories in Germany? *Frontiers in Communication*, *6*, 678335. https://doi.org/10.3389/fcomm.2021.678335

Jungblut, M., Kümpel, A. S., & Steer, R. (2024). Social media use of the police in crisis situations: A mixed-method study on communication practices of the German police. *New Media & Society*, *26*(8), 4647–4668. https://doi.org/10.1177/14614448221127899

Kasperson, R. E., Renn, O., Slovic, P., Brown, H. S., Emel, J., Goble, R., Kasperson, J. X., & Ratick, S. (1988). The social amplification of risk: A conceptual framework. *Risk Analysis*, *8*(2), 177–187. https://doi.org/10.1111/j.1539-6924.1988.tb01168.x

Kepplinger, H. M. (1988). Die Kernenergie in der Presse. Zum Einfluss subjektiver Faktoren auf die Konstruktion der Realität. *Kölner Zeitschrift für Soziologie und Sozialpsychologie*, *40*, 659–683.

Klingelhöfer, J. (2023). *The Power of Crisis Communication: A Qualitative Study of the Establishment of a Scientific Field*. Springer VS.

Koch, T., Denner, N., & Coutandin, F. (2022). A CEO but also a parent: How strategic communication of private information about the CEO affects perceptions of an organization during a crisis. *International Journal of Strategic Communication*, *16*(4), 620–632. https://doi.org/10.1080/1553118x.2022.2075749

Koch, T., Viererbl, B., Beckert, J., & Keilmann, J. (2024). CSR in times of crisis: Why CSR activities can be both a blessing and burden during an organizational crisis. *Journal of Communication Management*, *28*(3), 442–458. https://doi.org/10.1108/JCOM-09-2023-0095

Koch, W. (2022). Ergebnisse der ARD/ZDF-Onlinestudie 2022: Reichweiten von Social-Media-Plattformen und Messengern. *Media Perspektiven*, *10*, 471–478. https://www.ard-media.de/fileadmin/user_upload/media-perspektiven/ARD-ZDF-Onlinestudie/2022__Reichweiten_von_Social_Media_und_Messengern.pdf

Kohring, M., Görke, A., & Ruhrmann, G. (1996). Konflikte, Kriege, Katastrophen. Zur Funktion internationaler Krisenkommunikation. In M. Meckel, & M. Kriener, Eds., *Internationale Kommunikation. Eine Einführung* (pp. 283–298). Westdeutscher Verlag.

Kupferschmitt, T., & Müller, T. (2023). Aktuelle Ergebnisse der repräsentativen Langzeitstudie – ARD/ZDF-Massenkommunikation Trends 2023: Mediennutzung im Intermediavergleich. *Media Perspektiven*, *21*, 1–20. https://www.ard-media.de/fileadmin/user_upload/media-perspektiven/pdf/2023/MP_21_2023_MKT_Intermediavergeich_final.pdf

LEMO Lebendiges Museum Online (2024). *Dokument Original "Schabowski-Zettel"*. Retrieved December 8 from https://www.hdg.de/lemo/bestand/objekt/dokument-notizzettel-schabowski.html

Lichtenstein, D., & Koerth, K. (2022). Different shows, different stories: How German TV formats challenged the government's framing of the Ukraine crisis. *Media War and Conflict*, *15*(2), 125–145. Article 1750635220909977. https://doi.org/10.1177/1750635220909977

Löffelholz, M. (Ed.). (1993). *Krieg als Medienereignis: Grundlagen und Perpektiven der Krisenkommunikation*. Westdeutscher Verl.

Löffelholz, M. (Ed.). (2004). *Krieg als Medienereignis II. Krisenkommunikation im 21. Jahrhundert*. VS, Verl. für Sozialwiss.

Löffelholz, M., Schleicher, K., & Trippe, C. F. (Eds.). (2024). *Krieg der Narrative: Russland, die Ukraine und der Westen*. De Gruyter. https://doi.org/10.1515/9783111331508

Loosen, W., Garmissen, A. v., Bartelt, E., & Olphen, T. v. (2023). Journalismus in Deutschland 2023: Aktuelle Befunde zu Situation und Wandel. *Arbeitspapiere des Hans-Bredow-Instituts, 68*, 1–16.

Meier, H. E., Tickell, S., & Konjer, M. V. (2023). A tale of two scandals: Scale shift and the inefficacy of crisis communication management in Olympic scandals. *Frontiers. Communication, 8*, 1155747. https://doi.org/10.3389/fcomm.2023.1155747

Meißner, J., & Schach, A. (Eds.). (2024). *Professionelle Krisenkommunikation: Basiswissen, Impulse und Handlungsempfehlungen für die Praxis* (2nd ed.). Springer Fachmedien Wiesbaden. https://doi.org/10.1007/978-3-658-43639-1

PR-Journal (2024). Earned Media – Krisenkommunikation 2023. PR-Journal. Retrieved December 8 from https://datenbanken.pr-journal.de/pr-agenturrankings/pfeffers-pr-ranking.html?view=ranking&layout=detail&type=204

Raupp, J. (2019). Crisis communication in the rhetorical arena. *Public Relations Review, 45*(4), 101768. https://doi.org/10.1016/j.pubrev.2019.04.002

Renn, O. (1984). *Risikowahrnehmung der Kernenergie*. Campus-Verl.

Reporters Without Borders (2024). *2024 World Press Freedom Index – journalism under political pressure*. https://rsf.org/en/index

Ruhrmann, G. (1992). Risikokommunikation. *Publizistik, 37*(1), 5–24.

Schwarz, A. (2010). *Krisen-PR aus Sicht der Stakeholder: Der Einfluss von Ursachen- und Verantwortungszuschreibungen auf die Reputation von Organisationen*. VS Verl. für Sozialwissenschaften.

Schwarz, A. (2016). Crisis communication research in Germany. In A. Schwarz, M. Seeger, & C. Auer, Eds., *The Handbook of International Crisis Communication Research* (pp. 357–372). Wiley Blackwell. https://doi.org/10.1002/9781118516812.ch33

Schwarz, A., Alpers, F., Wagner-Olfermann, E., & Diers-Lawson, A. (2023). The global study of COVID news: Scope, findings, and implications of quantitative content analyses of the COVID-19 news coverage in the first two years of the pandemic. *Health Communication, 39*(8), 1568–1581. https://doi.org/10.1080/10410236.2023.2226932

Schwarz, A., & Diers-Lawson, A. (2024). Mediated crises and strategic crisis communication of third sector organizations: A content analysis of crisis reporting in six countries. *Corporate Communications, 29*(4), 567–591. https://doi.org/10.1108/ccij-08-2023-0117

Schwarz, A., & Faj, T. (2024). Communicating and perceiving risks of artificial intelligence as an emerging technology. In T. L. Sellnow, & D. D. Sellnow, Eds., *Communicating Risk and Safety* (pp. 503–526). De Gruyter Mouton. https://doi.org/10.1515/9783110752427-027

Schwarz, A., & Löffelholz, M. (2014). Krisenkommunikation: Vorbereitung, Umsetzung, Erfolgsfaktoren. In A. Zerfaß, & M. Piwinger, Eds., *Handbuch Unternehmenskommunikation: Strategie – Management – Wertschöpfung* (2nd ed., pp. 1303–1319). Springer Gabler. DOI:https://doi.org/10.1007/978-3-8349-4543-3_66

Schwarz, A., Sellnow, D. D., Sellnow, T. D., & Taylor, L. E. (2024). Instructional risk and crisis communication at higher education institutions during COVID-19: Insights from practitioners in the global south and north. *Journal of International Crisis and Risk Communication Research, 7*(1), 1–47. https://doi.org/10.56801/jicrcr.V7.i1.1

Schwarz, A., & Unselt, J. J. (2024). Rage against the machine? Framing societal threat and efficacy in YouTube videos about artificial intelligence. *Risk Analysis, 44*(10), 2377–2395. https://doi.org/10.1111/risa.14299

Teichert, W. (1987). Tschernobyl in den Medien: Ergebnisse und Hypothesen zur Tschernobyl-Berichterstattung. *Rundfunk und Fernsehen, 35*(2), 185–204.

Thieken, A. H., Samprogna Mohor, G., Kreibich, H., & Müller, M. (2022). Compound inland flood events: Different pathways, different impacts and different coping options. *Natural Hazards and Earth System Sciences, 22*(1), 165–185. https://doi.org/10.5194/nhess-22-165-2022

Torpan, S., Hansson, S., Orru, K., Jukarainen, P., Gabel, F., Savadori, L., Meyer, S. F., Schieffelers, A., Lovasz, G., & Rhinard, M. (2024). Mitigating vulnerabilities with social media: A cross-national study of European disaster managers' practices. *Risk, Hazards & Crisis in Public Policy, 15*(2), 162–179. https://doi.org/10.1002/rhc3.12286

Ullrich, T. W., & Brandstädter, M. (2016). *Krisenkommunikation: Grundlagen und Praxis: Eine Einführung mit ergänzender Fallstudie am Beispiel Krankenhaus*. Kohlhammer Verlag.

Welzenbach-Vogel, I. C., Werling, K., Barkela, B., & Milde, J. (2022). Plastics in mass media. A content analysis of german media coverage of plastic-associated risks and sustainable alternatives to plastics. *Environmental Communication*, *16*(2), 179–194. https://doi.org/10.1080/17524032.2021.1979618

World Bank (2024). *GDP (current US$)*. https://data.worldbank.org/indicator/NY.GDP.MKTP.CD?most_recent_value_desc=true

Xu, Y., Yu, J., & Löffelholz, M. (2024). Portraying the pandemic: Analysis of textual-visual frames in German News Coverage of COVID-19 on twitter. *Journalism Practice*, *18*(4), 858–878. https://doi.org/10.1080/17512786.2022.2058063

Author's Bio

Andreas Schwarz (PhD, TU Ilmenau, 2009) is a senior researcher in risk and crisis communication at Technische Universität Ilmenau in Germany where he serves as co-director of the International Research Group on Crisis Communication. He was the founding chair of the Crisis Communication Section of the European Communication Research and Education Association (ECREA), 2011–2018. His research interests include cross-cultural risk and crisis communication, crisis response of nongovernmental and higher education organizations, and the science and risk communication of emerging technologies such as artificial intelligence. Schwarz received research grants to study risk communication of COVID-19, crisis communication of child protective services and nonprofit organizations, and perceptions of artificial intelligence or automated mobility. His research has been published in journals like Health Communication, International Journal of Strategic Communication, Public Relations Review, Journal of Public Relations Research, Risk Analysis, Journal of Risk Research, and Science Communication. He has conducted trainings and consulted on risk and crisis communication for several government agencies, nonprofit organizations, and corporations.

33

Risk and Crisis Communication Research in the Nordic Countries

Finn Frandsen and Winni Johansen
Department of Management, Aarhus School of Business and Social Sciences, Aarhus University, Denmark

Introduction

In 2016, we introduced our contribution to *The Handbook of International Crisis Communication Research* (Schwartz et al., 2016) by claiming that the history of crisis communication research in Nordic countries such as Denmark, Finland, Iceland, Norway and Sweden was "short, but intense." The aim of our chapter was to provide an overview of this research. What are the characteristics of this type of research? How has it developed? And does it still make sense to operate with the idea of a so-called "Nordic model"? Now eight years later, we are asking the same questions. However, the crisis landscape has changed importantly since 2016. Risk and crisis management has seemingly become the new normal, and this has had and will continue to have a strong impact on the amount of research within risk and crisis communication in the future.

In this chapter we will first shortly take a look at the new crisis landscape and the interrelatedness between crisis management subfields that lead to a new understanding of risk and crisis communication. Next we will present a small section describing the context of risk and crisis communication in the Nordic countries (Denmark, Finland, Iceland, Norway, and Sweden), before we describe scholars, institutions, and research on risk and crisis from each country. Finally, we end by presenting selected findings and research related to COVID-19, concentrating on studies that have compared risk and crisis communication activities across the Nordic countries to identify differences and similarities between the countries in the Nordic region and discuss whether there is such a thing as a Nordic model of risk and crisis communication.

New Crisis Landscape and Interrelatedness Between Crisis Management Subfields

The new crisis landscape that has emerged since the 1st edition of this handbook includes crisis types such as: MeToo, DEI issues, and moral outrage (sticky crises); pandemics and health issues; war, conflicts, and geopolitics; climate and sustainability problems leading to emergency situations (e.g., floodings, fires); economic problems; and communication problems around fake news, misinformation, and polarization of beliefs and groups of people. This new crisis

The Handbook of International Crisis and Risk Communication Research, Second Edition.
Edited by Andreas Schwarz, Matthew W. Seeger, and Sora Kim.

landscape has caused changes in citizen and consumer habits, leading to changes among private and public sector organizations. With the rise of such new crisis types, we see private organizations acting as corporate citizens and as corporate politicians taking stances on socio-political issues and wars and conflicts, running the risks of getting criticized from polarized groups of people.

This development also plays out in the Nordic countries. With Covid-19, in particular, we have witnessed a rise in interest and research into risk and crisis communication. For the communication profession, COVID-19 can in fact be perceived as the golden age of communicators, as the work of communicators has been more appreciated than ever during the pandemic. The debate on *cold hands versus warms hands* (Frandsen & Johansen, 2022), and communicators perceived as less needed cold hands, in the Nordics has stopped – at least for this period of time.

Crisis management used to be divided into separate categories: public crisis management, political crisis management, and corporate crisis management. However, we have recently developed a new model describing the interrelatedness and intertwining of the three subfields that seems beneficial to almost any type of crisis (Frandsen & Johansen, 2020; Frandsen & Johansen, 2023b). In today's world this interrelatedness has become more true than ever. Natural disasters such as floods or forest fires are first and foremost dealt with by public emergency officers, but they quickly turn into crises for politicians responsible for climate-related decisions and for companies that are involved in the same local areas. Furthermore, a crisis to a company, such as a product harm or chemical spill, quickly gets the attention of politicians who may use such a crisis as an opportunity for criticizing public office holders (Boin et al., 2009; Frandsen & Johansen, 2020). With COVID-19, the strong intertwining between the three crisis management subfields stood out even more clearly.

Hence, by risk and crisis communication we understand the management and communication activities related to three intertwined and interrelated subfields within crisis management: public crisis management (natural disasters, health crises, and emergencies in society at large), political crisis management (political crises and scandals), and corporate crisis management (crises of private or public companies) (Frandsen & Johansen, 2020). Each subfield may be said to have a specific focus on risk and crisis communication and on specific risk and crisis stages: public risk and crisis management has a focus on the during the crisis stage and on communication for the safety of people (e.g., the CERC model); political crisis management has a focus on the post-crisis stage and the maintaining or gaining of political power; and corporate crisis management has a focus on the pre-crisis stage and the prevention of crisis and reputation management. See Frandsen & Johansen (2020) for theoretical elaboration and illustration on the case of the Great Belt Bridge train accident in Denmark in January 2019.

All three subfields are typically involved and overlapping when a crisis hits. This becomes even more evident if we take the new crisis landscape into account. As scholars we need to be familiar with theories and research from within all three fields. Now let's use this perspective for the following study of risk and crises and research in the Nordic countries.

The Context of Crisis Communication Research in the Nordic Countries

The Nordic countries form a geographical region in Northern Europe that consists of five relatively homogeneous societies: Denmark, Finland, Iceland, Norway, and Sweden, which for centuries have formed a social, economic, political, and linguistic community, as they all, except for Finland, speak the same language.

The Nordic countries are developed parliamentary democracies with a universal freedom of expression. They are among the richest countries in the world, and their approx. 28 million inhabitants are often described as the "happiest people" on earth (Booth, 2015; Bjørnskov, 2021). All five countries are ranked in the World Happiness Reports (UN) among the 10 best (out of 156 countries) for their happiness level. In 2022, Finland ranked No. 1, followed by Denmark No. 2, Iceland No. 3, Sweden No. 7 and Norway No. 8. What makes people so satisfied in the Nordic countries is seemingly the high level of institutional and interpersonal trust, tolerance (low level of polarization), and the personal and social freedom to choose the life they want (Bjørnskov, 2021).

The concept of the "Nordic model" refers to the political, economic, and organizational work-life systems in the region, which involve the combination of a free market economy with a welfare state, including free healthcare, childcare, and universities. This type of capitalism is only possible because of the high level of social trust and social freedom among the citizens (Bjørnskov, 2021). However, it is also important to stress that apart from Covid-19, the Nordic region has not faced a lot of severe political crises or natural disasters enabling distrust in the systems.

In the past decades, the media landscape in the Nordic countries has undergone important changes. In each of the five countries, there is a free news media sector, and public service radio and television still play an important role. The Nordic countries can be considered a "media welfare state" (Syvertsen et al., 2014), with a rather stable communication environment that still, to a high degree, relies on legacy media, and a high-choice media environment where citizens can use multiple sources to inform themselves, and social media and alternative media such as online and mobile communication have become important channels (Johansson et al., 2023).

Although the Nordic countries may not have experienced a lot of severe crises, some of the crises covered very intensively by national and international news media took place in this region. In the Nordic countries, apart from the Tsunami disaster in 2004 (see 1st edition of this handbook), the Cartoon Affair forms a *social icon* crisis, defined as "a past event which has become part of history in the present in specific ways" (Maier et al., 2019). It started in September 2005, when the Danish newspaper *Jyllands-Posten* published 12 editorial cartoons, many of them depicting the Islamic prophet Muhammad, creating a huge outrage in the Muslim world (Frandsen & Johansen, 2010). This crisis is constantly popping up again, e.g., in 2023, when a few right-wing persons conducted public burnings of the Quran in Sweden and Denmark, creating strong reactions again in the Muslim world against Nordic governments for accepting this kind of freedom of expression. It has led to a rise in the terror threat level in Sweden and Denmark. The mass shooting on the island of Utøya, where 69 people, mostly teenagers, were killed by the right-wing extremist Anders Behring Breivik on July 22, 2011, is yet another social icon crisis, which took place not far away from Oslo, the capital of Norway. However, today the most important and severe crisis in the Nordic region, leading to a huge increase in risk and crisis communication research, is without a doubt the worldwide pandemic COVID-19, that we will return to at the end of this chapter.

The Nordic region accounts for more than 110 universities, university colleges, and business schools, mostly public institutions offering free education. Among students, crisis management and crisis communication are very popular topics, but within research, this area is still mostly conducted at a minority of these higher educational institutions. However, as already mentioned, COVID-19 has created an increasing research interest in many institutions.

The Nordic research community has created a wide range of pan-Nordic forums for research collaboration, from funding of collaborative research projects to common academic associations, conferences, and publications, often initiated or supported by the Nordic Council of Ministers. Four examples of how research on crisis communication benefits from these forums: (1) The collaboration between the national emergency management agencies in Sweden, Norway, Finland, and Denmark, including a series of Pan-Nordic conferences on crisis communication where academics meet practitioners; (2) *NORDICOM*, a knowledge-sharing center for Nordic media research (media, journalism and mediated communication), located at the University in Gothenburg; and (3) *NORA*, the Nordic Alliance for Communication and Management, located at BI Norwegian Business School in Oslo, where communication executives meet communication and management scholars from Norway, Denmark, Finland, and Sweden to shape debate and develop research-based knowledge. Most recently, (4) *NordForsk* has supported the establishment of a research Centre for Societal Security at the Department of Strategy and War Studies in Copenhagen and a research project *RESECTOR* studying the public sector responsibility principles before, during, and after COVID-19 across Denmark, Norway, and Sweden to prepare for more complex crises in the future.

Before we start looking into risk and crisis communication research and activities in the five Nordic countries, it is important for us to emphasize that it has not been possible to do a complete overview of all the research conducted within the field. This means that the following descriptions are based on a selection of studies, conducted primarily since 2015, and scholars working regularly within risk and crisis communication.

Risk and Crisis Communication Research in Sweden

Sweden is the country, out of the five, which has contributed most substantially to the study of risk and crisis communication. This research is mainly going on in five Swedish research environments, and they have mostly adopted a societal perspective within the public sector and political crisis subfields.

The first and the largest of the five research environments that we have been able to identify for this study was created in 1997 under the Swedish National Defense College. It was named CRISMART (Crisis Management Research and Training). However, in January 2018, CRISMART was integrated into the Centre for Social Security (CTSS). The founding fathers were the Swedish scholars Bengt Sundelius and Eric Stern, who, together with two Dutch scholars, Arjen Boin and Paul 't Hart, have co-authored *The Politics of Crisis Communication: Public Leadership under Pressure* (Boin et al. 2005, 2017). For a more detailed introduction to political crisis management, see Frandsen & Johansen (2020).

The second research environment is located at Örebro University and consists mainly of media and communication scholars and rhetoricians. Among the members of the first generation of scholars, we find Stig Arne Nordstedt and Larsåke Larsson, two of the pioneers within this field. The former has coined the concept of the *threat* society, a complement to Ulrich Beck's (1992) theory of the *risk* society (Nohrstedt, 2011), and the latter has focused on organizational learning and a series of case studies (Larsson, 2010). Two scholars from the same university, Birgitte Mral and Orla Vigsø, created a new Centre for Crisis Communication (CCC) in 2012, which is now led by professor Mats Eriksson. The center has recently finished a research project on crisis communication in a digital age (Eriksson, 2015, 2018) and is now working on various projects, including pandemic rhetoric (Joel Rasmussen); internal dimensions of crisis communication in an ongoing crisis situation (Hogne Satoyen); and new motives for the citizen's home preparedness studying how citizens are preparing themselves at home for pandemics and the new security situation in Europe (Mats Eriksson).

The third research environment is Lund University, Campus Helsingborg (Department of Strategic Communication), where Jesper Falkheimer, Mats Heide, Charlotte Simonsson, Hui Zhao, Åsa Thelander, and others have conducted various research projects and published several articles, chapters, and books, including topics such as strategic improvisation, multicultural crisis communication, crisis communication of multinational corporations, visual crisis communication, internal crisis communication, to name a few (see for instance Falkheimer & Heide, 2023; Falkheimer & Zhao 2020; Falkheimer et al., 2022; Zhao, 2022; Zhao et al., 2017). Heide and Simonsson have also, in particular, contributed to the study of internal crisis communication. In 2019, they published a book entitled *Internal Crisis Communication: Crisis Awareness, Leadership, and Coworkership,* perceiving employees as co-workers that contribute actively to the crisis communication of organizations, and in 2021 they did a study on communicative coworkership during a pandemic, emphasizing a process approach to crisis communication (Heide & Simonsson, 2021).

The fourth research environment is located at Gothenburg University (Department of Journalism, Media and Communication). Among the group of scholars, we find professor Bengt Johansson, who is an expert on media and political communication. He studies risk and crisis communication and institutional trust from a power and democracy perspective (e.g., Johansson et al., 2023). One of his research projects, entitled KRISAMS (Crisis Communication and Social Trust in a Multi-public Society), is a study of how social trust affects crisis communication and back again. With professor Gabriella Sandstig, he also studies risk communication and self-protection (Johansson & Sandstig, 2024), and he is co-editor of the book: *Communicating a Pandemic: Crisis management and Covid-19 in the Nordic Countries* (2023); see the last section of this chapter. Among other scholars, we find Professor Orla Vigsø, who studies political communication and scandals as well as crisis communication from a rhetorical and organizational perspective (see for instance, Johansson & Vigsø, 2020; Mral & Vigsø, 2012; Strandberg & Vigsø, 2016); Professor Marina Ghersetti, whose primary research interest is the relationship between news journalism and news reporting of crises (e.g., Ghersetti et al., 2023); and Dr. Pavel Rodin, who has studied media and health communication from a multiplatform and multivocal perspective, applying rhetorical arena theory (e.g., Rodin, 2023).

Finally, the last research environment is The Risk and Crisis Research Center (RCR) at Mid Sweden University (Sundsval). The research at RCR focuses on risk and crisis from a societal perspective and is conducting projects such as: People, measures, and resilience: new ways to study risk communication, responsibility, and preparedness; resilience work in local governance; and simulation and experimental design in risk and crisis management. Many of the research projects are interdisciplinary and collaborative; see, for instance, (Petridou et al., 2023).

As it appears from above, scholars in Sweden have a main focus on public sector risk and crisis communication, media and political communication, and citizen behavior.

Risk and Crisis Communication Research in Denmark

In Denmark, crisis communication has also been a vibrant field of study for quite some time now. Unlike those in Sweden and Finland, Danish crisis communication researchers focus on organizational crises in the private sector, combining crisis communication with a managerial perspective. However, during Covid-19, a new team of researchers, around the HOPE project (hope-project.dk), led by professor Michael Bang Petersen at the Department of Political Science at Aarhus University, followed the development of citizen behavior, well-being, and risk and crisis reactions to COVID-19, as well as government decisions throughout the whole period of the COVID-19 crisis. The project was entitled: "How Democracies Cope with COVID-19 – a data driven approach," and included eight Western democracies: Denmark, Sweden, Germany, France, Italy, Hungary, the UK, and the US (see for instance Bor et al., 2023, on moralizing the Covid-10 pandemic, or Jørgensen et al., 2021).

As for the study of risk and crisis communication in the private sector, the crisis management research group at the Department of Management, at the School of Business and Social Sciences, Aarhus University, led by professor Finn Frandsen and professor Winni Johansen, is one of the important contributors in a Danish context. Frandsen and Johansen published their first article on Rhetorical Arena Theory in 2000 and further developed their multivocal, two-layered arena model in their book on *Krisekommunikation [Crisis Communication]* in 2007 (Johansen & Frandsen, 2007) and the study of the Cartoon Affair in 2010. Since then, they have continuously conducted research on the communicative complexity of a crisis to reveal patterns of interaction and communication among the multiple voices that enter the rhetorical arena when a crisis hits, having an important impact on the outcome of a crisis. The model works for any kind of crisis (corporate crises, public sector crises, political crises, health crises, emergencies, etc.). The idea behind the rhetorical arena is that every time a crisis breaks out, a multivocal arena opens up, where multiple *voices start communicating to, with, against, past and about one another* (see Frandsen & Johansen, 2010; Frandsen & Johansen 2020; Frandsen & Johansen 2023a). All voices do not necessarily want consensus. Dissensus and polarization also play out. Thus, RAT forms an agonistic and even antagonistic model. Among the voices, we find consumers, citizens, politicians, media, investors, NGOs, trade associations, etc., but also third parties using a crisis situation as an opportunity for promoting their own agenda, e.g., politicians, activists, trolls, hackers, and critics. The rhetorical arena, and the multivocal approach, has been applied to the analysis of complex crises such as the cartoon affair in 2005–2006 and Covid-19, as well as to the study of crises triggered on social media (e.g., Johansen et al., 2016, Frandsen & Johansen, 2017).

The crisis research group at Aarhus University has also conducted other studies. To examine the complexity of the rhetorical arena, Frandsen & Johansen have also studied the internal crisis management and crisis communication of Danish organizations (Frandsen & Johansen, 2011; Johansen et al., 2012) and made one of the first surveys on internal crisis communication among managers and employees (ICMCC 2011–2014), whistleblowing arrangements, trade associations as intermediaries (2018, 2023b), sub-arenas and polarization of voices (2023a), as well as crisis consulting (Johansen, 2020). Furthermore, they have studied the reframing of crisis management (2020), Covid-19 and corporate crisis management (2023b), and business crisis management during the Russian-Ukrainian war (Opatska et al., 2023). Associate professor Carmen D. Maier has a focus on visual (multimodal) crisis communication (Maier, 2020; Maier & Ravazzani, 2023; Maier et al., 2019), and on smoldering crises (Maier et al., 2022), and professor Heidi Salomonsen studies public sector crisis communication, investigating civil servants, reputation management, and political communication (Salomonsen and 't Hart, 2020).

However, crisis communication research in Denmark is not only conducted at Aarhus University. At Copenhagen University, scholars within interdisciplinary fields have established the Copenhagen Center for Disaster Research (COPE), which is a platform for research on disasters and climate issues. At Roskilde University, media scholars such as Mark Blach-Ørsten study political scandals (Pollack et al., 2018), as well as media, journalism, and COVID-19 in the Nordic countries (see last section of this chapter, and Blach-Ørsten et al., 2023). Finally, at Copenhagen University College, Nina Blom Andersen is head of a research unit named Societal Safety and Security that studies emergency risk management, climate challenges to small local communities in the Nordic countries, as well as spontaneous volunteering of citizens during crises.

Risk and Crisis Communication Research in Norway

In Norway, two professors of sociology, Tom Christensen, from the University of Oslo, and Per Lægreid, from the University of Bergen, have examined what makes a government's crisis management system. They claim that dealing with crises is a main responsibility of government authorities. They are first of all known for their work on New Public Management and the transformation of public reforms, but they also outline an organizational approach to crisis management by distinguishing between a *structural/instrumental* and a *cultural/institutional* perspective. See, for instance, their study on the Nordic way of crisis management of Covid-19 (Christensen & Lægreid, 2023).

Another important scholar within crisis management is Christer Pursiainen, who, since 2014, has been a Professor in Societal Safety and Environment at the Arctic University of Norway (UiT) in Tromsø. Pursiainen has published an important number of articles and books on societal security, crisis management, foreign policy, and international relations. In his book on *The Crisis Management Cycle* (2018), he applies a multidisciplinary approach to crisis management theory and practice by combining frameworks developed within safety and security studies, political studies, as well as business and behavior studies. We consider these management studies to be very inspirational to communication scholars who want to integrate crisis management and crisis communication.

Recently, the number of crisis communication publications has increased in Norway. However, scholars are still scattered over various institutions in Norway. Among these scholars, we find Professor Øyvind Ihlen, from the Department of Media and Communication at the University of Oslo, who published an article (Ihlen, 2002) on crisis response strategies during the Mercedes A-class crisis back in 1997. He is another co-editor of the book: *Communicating a Pandemic in the Nordic Countries* (2023), described in the specific section below. Two other scholars, both from the Inland Norway University of Applied Sciences have also written interesting books on crisis communication. Senior lecturer Tore Hafting edited an anthology in Norwegian entitled *Krisehaandtering: Planlegging og handling [Crisis management: Planning and action]* (2017), covering an impressive range of crisis handling topics including risk communication, resilience, internal crisis communication, and power and crisis management. His colleague, professor Martin Ndlela, has written several books on crisis communication, such as *Crisis communication: A stakeholder approach* in 2018. Most recently he published a book (2024) that studies the specific challenges to communicating messages during the coronavirus: *Risk and Crisis Communication During the Covid-19 Pandemic: Muddled Messages*, applying a multivocal approach, and including chapters on lockdown messages, uncertainty, trust, and misinformation. At BI Norwegian Business School, a group of communication scholars conducted a research project on how small and medium-sized companies (SMEs) in Norway dealt with COVID-19 (e.g., Frandsen & Johansen, 2023b). Finally, at Kristiania University College, Head of the Department of Communication, Ketil Raknes, conducts research on media, public diplomacy, and crisis communication. With Falkheimer, he studied the communication battle of Nordic neighbors in the pandemic crisis (Falkheimer and Raknes, 2022). Furthermore, Professor Audra Diers-Lawson conducts a new research project on "Risk communication and community engagement" aiming at strengthening the public's ability to conduct self- and community- protective behavior in future health and disaster crises.

Risk and Crisis Communication Research in Finland

In Finland, crisis communication research has primarily been conducted at three Finnish institutions. At the University of Jyväskylä, Professor Marita Vos took part in creating the crisis communication research group (CrisCom) and worked with a large research project aiming at developing a *Crisis Communication Scorecard*, as well as an EU-funded project on how to enable public empowerment for crisis management (the so-called PEP-project). In 2017, Vos published a book entitled: *Communication in Turbulent Times: Exploring Issue Arenas and Crisis Communication to Enhance Organisational Resilience*, aiming to increase the understanding of multistakeholder communication around an issue or a crisis and to discuss the contribution of communication to organizational resilience. Today, professors Vilma Luoma-aho and Chiara Valentini have both conducted several studies within media and crisis communication in the public sector, in particular during the COVID-19 pandemic, e.g, Luoma-aho has studied the public sector organizations' social media listening strategies during Covid-19 (Erkkilä & Luoma-aho, 2023), and Valentini, Badham, and Mykkänen conducted a comparative study of news media's roles and public perceptions in pandemic communications, including public trust in crisis narratives across six countries (including Finland and Sweden, Australia, Italy, South Korea, and USA) (Valentini et al., 2023).

At the University of Helsinki, we find professor Johanna Sumiala, who has studied media, terrorist events, and violence associated with religion for quite some time, including school shootings in Finland, Charlie Hebdo attacks, the Berlin truck attack, and more (e.g., Muschert & Sumiala, 2013; Sumiala & Haru, 2019; Sumiala & Räisä, 2020). Minttu Tikka, at Aalto University, who has collaborated with Sumiala, studies digital media, crisis sensemaking, trust, and resilience (see Tikka, 2019; Vaslaskivi et al., 2022). Finally, at Åbo Akademi, you find scholars such as university lecturer Jenny Lindholm, co-editor of the *Communicating a Pandemic* book (Johansson et al., 2023), conducting research on political communication and social media (Lindholm et al., 2023), and senior university lecturer Klas Backholm, who has studied authority communication during Covid-19 (Backholm & Nordberg, 2023) and studies psychological well-being among journalists having experienced terrorism, as well as trust in digital volunteers during crises (Ruohonen & Backholm, 2023).

Risk and Crisis Communication Research in Iceland

Iceland is a small island country with approximately 370,000 inhabitants. It has experienced severe crises such as the huge financial crisis in 2008 and natural disasters such as the volcanic eruption and ash cloud crisis in 2010 and the volcanic eruption of 2023. Although risk and crisis communication research is not forming a large research area, one important scholar at the University of Iceland (located in Reykjavik) is Deanne Bird, who is a research specialist at the Institute of Life and Environmental Sciences. Bird and colleagues are conducting research within the field of disaster risk management, including volcanos and floodings (e.g., Omarsdottir et al., 2022). In fact, a new cross-disciplinary approach seems to emerge within the field, combining the study of volcanos, risk communication, volcanic crisis communication, and tourism communication in Iceland. However, during COVID-19, cross-Nordic studies were conducted within media coverage, media reporting, and crisis communication, involving scholars such as Valgerdur Jóhanssdóttir at the University of Iceland and Birgir Gudmundsson at the University of Akureyri (Blach-Ørsten et al., 2023).

As it appears, we have witnessed an increasing amount of research during COVID-19 in each of the Nordic countries. Now, let's also take a look at important examples of cross-Nordic crisis research in the final section.

Case Study: Covid-19 and Cross-Nordic Risk and Crisis Communication Research

COVID-19 forms an interesting case study as Nordic scholars have studied the use of risk and crisis communication strategies across countries in the Nordic region. One example is the Nordicom book: *Communicating a Pandemic: Crisis Management and Covid-19 in the Nordic countries* edited by Johansson, Ihlen, Lindholm & Blach-Ørsten and published in 2023. The book includes 16 chapters and presents some of the many studies that compare communication strategies of governments, health authorities, lobbyists, interest organizations, and corporations, as well as media use, media coverage, and reactions by citizens between two or more Nordic countries during this long-term crisis.

The World Health Organization declared COVID-19 a pandemic on March 11, 2020. The Danish government decided to shut down the country the same day and to close the borders. Norway did the same type of lockdown the following day, and also Finland decided on a state of emergency in mid-March. Although Iceland did not do a full lockdown, various restrictions were made, and some businesses were closed. In contrast to the other Nordic countries, Sweden chose a different way. The Swedish government did not close the borders, and society remained open as they wanted to "meet the crisis with recommendations instead of regulations, trusting citizens' sense of responsibility," later referred to as the "Swedish experiment" (Johansson et al., 2023, p. 16). However, over time the Swedish strategy changed and became more similar to the other Nordic countries. According to Johansson et al. (2023), the Nordic countries remained more open, and the death tolls were lower compared to other European countries, even though Sweden had higher death tolls compared to the other Nordic countries, due to the chosen strategy in spring 2020. This means that "compared to the other Nordic countries, the Swedish Covid-19 strategy was less successful, but seen from a global perspective, Sweden did fairly well." (Johansson et al., 2023, p. 17). How can this be explained?

Public trust in government and health authorities was high; there were almost no political disputes between governments and the opposition. The distribution of roles and functions between government and health authorities worked well, and most citizens were happy with the COVID-19 crisis management of their country. Based and documented through the various comparative studies in the book, Johansson et al. (2023) also conclude that "the idea of a specific Nordic model and its importance for the handling of a global crisis is supported." High levels of trust in relation to public authorities and legacy news media, combined with a low level of polarization and a strong sense of cooperation between institutions, contribute to a society resilient to huge crises such as COVID-19.

As for *government and authorities*, it was important to communicate risks to make people change behaviors: staying home, keeping social distancing, wearing masks, becoming vaccinated, etc., and to communicate for sensemaking purposes and to emotional reactions by showing empathy and understanding (see Nord & Olsson Gardell, 2023, Rasmussen et al., 2023 for a comparison of communication by governments and health authorities in Denmark, Norway, and Sweden). In contrast to the other Nordic countries, where the governments were in charge of decision-making based on information from the health authorities, it was the Swedish health organization that was taking care of decisions and communications to the citizens. Communication channels such as press conferences, public campaigns, and social media were used as a way to get messages through to people. See, for instance, Kjeldsen, who did a study of the multimodal rhetoric of public health authorities and political leaders during press conferences in Denmark, Norway, and Sweden (Kjeldsen, 2023), and (Lindholm et al., 2023) for a study of the use of social media by all Nordic prime ministers and health authorities.

However, as COVID-19 turned out to be a long-term crisis, there was a need to change communication strategies over time to overcome crisis "fatigue." In this case, both Sweden and Denmark made use of humor in their public campaigns, for instance, to reach younger generations, whereas Norway mostly used rational informative strategies. For instance, Danish health authorities used videos on you tube applying humor as the main strategy (Almlund et al., 2023).

As for *corporations*, the study by Frandsen and Johansen (2023b) on Denmark, Norway, and Sweden shows that a lot of SMEs were struggling to make their businesses survive during COVID-19, and that they turned to their trade associations, who were quite successful in getting media attention (400–700% increase in media coverage during Covid) and obtaining support (in the form of compensation packages) from governments. Danish and Swedish trade associations also launched public campaigns, such as the "Safe to Visit" campaign, to make people remember that even if the borders were closed, they could still travel in their own country, supporting business.

As for *media*, Ghersetti et al. (2023) studied the news coverage in Iceland and Sweden, Blach-Ørsten et al. (2023) studied investigative reporting in Denmark, Iceland, and Sweden, and Kjeldsen (2023) did a study on the multiple press conferences in Denmark, Norway, and Sweden.

The Nordic countries have learned a lot from Covid-19. It has improved the crisis and health preparedness in all five Nordic countries, and it has led to new forms of research collaboration and multiple studies within risk and crisis communication during the pandemic as well as to new Nordic post-pandemic studies, such as studies on trust and self-protection among citizens and communities in future crises taking the new crisis landscape into account.

A Brief Look to the Future

Climate change and sustainability issues, the impact of continued global political and social turmoil, as well as continued issues in the private sector trying to embrace the new crisis landscape, are likely to create ongoing risks leading to crises within the Nordic region. While these risk factors are not necessarily distinct from other regions, their manifestation within the political, corporate, and media environments of the Nordic countries is distinct. In particular, taken together, the Nordic countries appear to have taken a proactive and aggressive stance toward the need for crisis communication research, in part supported by government funding. It is likely that this trend will gain traction, and the Nordic countries will continue to make substantial contributions to the risk and crisis communication scholarship.

References

Almlund, P., Kjeldsen, J. E., & Mølster, R. (2023). Expressions of governance, risk, and responsibility: Public campaigns in the crisis and risk management of Covid-19 in Denmark, Norway, and Sweden. In B. Johansson, Ø. Ihlen, J. Lindholm, & M. Blach-Ørsten, Eds., *Communicating a Pandemic: Crisis Management and Covid-19 in the Nordic Countries* (pp. 121–147). University of Gothenburg, Nordicom. https://doi.org/10.48335/9789188855688-6

Backholm, K., & Nordberg, C. (2023). Efficient authority communication in times of crisis: Examining how vulnerable language minorities experienced Covid-19 communication strategies in Finland, Norway, and Sweden. In B. Johansson, Ø. Ihlen, J. Lindholm, & M. Blach-Ørsten, Eds., *Communicating a Pandemic: Crisis Management and Covid-19 in the Nordic Countries* (pp. 325–346). University of Gothenburg, Nordicom. https://doi.org/10.48335/9789188855688-15

Beck, U. (1992). *Risk Society: Towards a New Modernity.* London: Sage.

Blach-Ørsten, M., Jönsson, A. M., Jóhannsdóttir, V., & Guðmundsson, B. (2023). The role of journalism in a time of national crisis: Examining criticism and consensus in Denmark, Iceland, and Sweden during the Covid-19 pandemic. In B. Johansson, Ø. Ihlen, J. Lindholm, & M. Blach-Ørsten, Eds., *Communicating a Pandemic: Crisis Management and Covid-19 in the Nordic Countries* (pp. 261–282). University of Gothenburg, Nordicom. https://doi.org/10.48335/9789188855688-1

Bjørnskov, C. (2021). *Happiness in the Nordic World.* Aarhus: Aarhus Universitetsforlag.

Boin, A., t'Hart, P., Stern, E., & Sundelius, B. (2005). *The Politics of Crisis Management: Public Leadership Under Pressure.* Cambridge, UK: Cambridge University Press.

Boin, A., McConnell, A., & t'Hart, P. (2009). Crisis exploitation: Political and policy impacts of framing contest. *Journal of European Public Policy, 16*(1), 81–106.

Boin, A., t'Hart, P., Stern, E., & Sundelius, B. (2017). *The Politics of Crisis Management: Public Leadership Under Pressure.* 2nd ed. Cambridge, UK: Cambridge University Press.

Booth, M. (2015). *The Almost Nearly Perfect People. Behind the Myth of the Scandinavian Utopia.* Vintage Publishing.

Bor, A., Jørgensen, F., Lindholt, M. F., & Petersen, M. B. (2023). Moralizing the COVID-19 pandemic: Self-interest predicts moral condemnation of other's compliance, distancing, and vaccination. *Political Psychology, 44*(2), 257–279. http://doi.org/10.1111/pops.12835

Christensen, T., & Lægreid, P. (2023). Crisis management of the COVID-19 pandemic: The Nordic Way and Swedish exceptionalism. In A. B. L. Cheung, & S. van Theil, Eds., *Crisis Leadership and Public Governance During the Covid-19 Pandemic: International Comparisons* (pp. 289–232). Singapore: World Scientific Publishing Company.

Eriksson, M. (2015). Crisis communication and improvisation in a digital age. In D. Holtzhausen, & A. Zerfass, Eds., *The Routledge Handbook of Strategic Communication* (pp. 508–519). New York: Routledge.

Eriksson, M. (2018). Lessons for crisis communication on social media: A systematic review of what research tells the practice. *International Journal of Strategic Communication, 12*(5), 526–551. http://doi.org/10.1080/1553118X.2018.1510405

Erkkilä, T., & Luoma-aho, V. (2023). Alert but somewhat unaligned: Public sector organisations' social media listening strategies during the COVID-19. *Journal of Communication Management, 27*(1), 120–135. http://doi.org/10.1108/JCOM-02-2022-0015

Falkheimer, J., Heide, M., Simonsson, C., & Anderson, R. (2022). Rally-around-the-organizational-flag. Internal communication in a professional organization during the Covid-19 pandemic crisis. *Corporate Communications: An International Journal, 27*(5), 23–38.

Falkheimer, J., & Heide, M. (2023). Strategic improvisation in crisis communication. In W. T. Coombs, & S. J. Holladay, Eds., *The Handbook of Crisis Communication* (2nd ed., pp. 405–420). Boston: Wiley-Blackwell.

Falkheimer, J., & Raknes, K. (2022). Nordic neighbors in pandemic crisis: The communication battle between Sweden and Norway. *Place Branding and Public Diplomacy, 18*, 26–29.

Falkheimer, J., & Zhao, H. (2020). Intercultural and multicultural approaches to crisis communication. In F. Frandsen, & W. Johansen, Eds., *Crisis Communication: Handbook of Communication Science* (pp. 523–539). Berlin: De Gruyter Mouton.

Frandsen, F., & Johansen, W. (2000). Retorik og krisekommunikation [Rhetoric and crisis communication]. *Rhetorica Scandinavica, 14*, 45–62.

Frandsen, F., & Johansen, W. (2010). Crisis communication, complexity, and the cartoon affair: A case study. In W. T. Coombs, & S. J. Holladay, Eds., *The Handbook of Crisis Communication* (pp. 425–448). Boston: Wiley-Blackwell.

Frandsen, F., & Johansen, W. (2011). The study of internal crisis communication: Towards an integrative framework. *Corporate Communications: An International Journal, 16*(4), 347–361. http://doi.org/10.1108/13563281111186977

Frandsen, F., & Johansen, W. (2017). *Organizational Crisis Communication – A Multivocal Approach.* London: Sage.

Frandsen, F., & Johansen, W. (2018). Voices in conflict? The crisis communication of meta-organizations. *Management Communication Quarterly, 32*(1), 90–120. https://doi.org/10.1177/0893318917705734

Frandsen, F., & Johansen, W. (2020). Reframing the field: Public crisis management, political crisis management, and corporate crisis management. In F. Frandsen, & W. Johansen, Eds., *Crisis Communication: Handbook of Communication Science* (pp. 59–102). Berlin: De Gruyter Mouton.

Frandsen, F., & Johansen, W. (2022). Strategic communication – A discipline in the making? In J. Falkheimer, & M. Heide, Eds., *Research Handbook on Strategic Communication* (pp. 14–32). Cheltenham: Edward Elgar Publishing.

Frandsen, F., & Johansen, W. (2023a). Rhetorial arena theory – Revisited and expanded. In W. T. Coombs, & S. J. Holladay, Eds., *The Handbook of Crisis Communication* (2nd ed., pp. 169–181). Boston: Wiley-Blackwell.

Frandsen, F., & Johansen, W. (2023b). Corporate crisis management. Managing Covid-19 in Denmark, Norway, Sweden. In B. Johansson, Ø. Ihlen, J. Lindholm, & M. Blach-Ørsten, Eds., *Communicating a Pandemic: Crisis Management and Covid-19 in the Nordic Countries* (pp. 173–194). University of Gothenburg, Nordicom.

Ghersetti, M., Ólafsson, J. G., & Ólafsdóttir, S. (2023). Watchdogs and government megaphones: The dual democratic roles of the news media during the Covid-19 pandemic in Iceland and Sweden. In B. Johansson, Ø. Ihlen, J. Lindholm, & M. Blach-Ørsten, Eds., *Communicating a Pandemic: Crisis Management and Covid-19 in the Nordic Countries* (pp. 217–240). University of Gothenburg, Nordicom. https://doi.org/10.48335/9789188855688-10

Hafting, T. (2017). *Krisehåndtering: Planlegging og handling [Crisis Management, Planning and Action].* Oslo: Fagbokforlaget.

Heide, M., & Simonsson, C. (2021). What was that all about? On internal communication and co-workership during a pandemic. *Journal of Communication Management, 25*(3), 256–275.

Ihlen, Ø. (2002). Defending the Mercedes A-Class: Combining and changing crisis response strategies. *Journal of Public Relations Research, 14*(3), 185–206. http://doi.org/10.1207/S1532754XJPRR1403_2

Johansen, B. F., Johansen, W., & Weckesser, N. M. (2016). Emotional stakeholders as "crisis communicators" in social media: The case of the Telenor customer complaints crisis. *Corporate Communications: An International Journal, 21*(3), 289–308. https://doi.org/10.1108/CCIJ-05-2015-0026

Johansen, W. (2020). Crisis management consulting: An emerging field of study. In F. Frandsen, & W. Johansen, Eds., *Crisis Communication: Handbook of Communication Science* (pp. 375–397). Berlin: De Gruyter Mouton.

Johansen, W., & Frandsen, F. (2007). *Krisekommunikation [Crisis Communication].* Frederiksberg: Samfundslitteratur.

Johansen, W., Aggerholm, H. K., & Frandsen, F. (2012). Entering new territory: The study of internal crisis management and crisis communication in organizations. *Public Relations Review, 38*(2), 270–279. http://doi.org/10.1016/j.pubrev.2011.11.008 (accessed November 25, 2015)

Johansson, B., Ihlen, Ø., Lindholm, J., & Blach-Ørsten, M. (2023). *Communicating a Pandemic: Crisis Management and Covid-19 in the Nordic Countries.* University of Gothenburg, Nordicom. https://www.nordicom.gu.se/en/publications/communicating-pandemic

Johansson, B., & Sandstig, G. (2024). In T. L. Sellnow, & D. D. Sellnow, Eds., *Communicating Risk and Safety* (pp. 321–338). Berlin: De Gruyter Mouton. https://doi.org/10.1515/9783110752427-019

Johansson, B., & Vigsø, O. (2020). Crisis communication and the political scandal. In F. Frandsen, & W. Johansen, Eds., *Crisis Communication: Handbook of Communication Science* (pp. 461–475). Berlin: De Gruyter Mouton.

Jørgensen, F., Bor, A., & Petersen, M. B. (2021). Compliance without fear: Individual level protective behaviour during the first wave of the COVID-19 pandemic. *British Journal of Health Psychology, 29*, 679–696.

Kjeldsen, J. E. (2023). Crafting a crisis: How the genre of the justifying press conference constituted the Covid-19 pandemic as an emergency and legitimized the power of authorities in Denmark, Norway, and Sweden. In B. Johansson, Ø. Ihlen, J. Lindholm, & M. Blach-Ørsten, Eds., *Communicating a Pandemic: Crisis Management and Covid-19 in the Nordic Countries* (pp. 97–120). University of Gothenburg, Nordicom.

Larsson, L. (2010). Crisis and learning. In W. T. Coombs, & S. J. Holladay, Eds., *The Handbook of Crisis Communication* (pp. 713–718). Boston: Wiley-Blackwell.

Lindholm, J., Carlson, T., Albrecht, F., & Hermansson, H. (2023). Communicating Covid-19 on social media: Analysing the use of Twitter and Instagram by Nordic health authorities and prime ministers. In B. Johansson, Ø. Ihlen, J. Lindholm, & M. Blach-Ørsten, Eds., *Communicating a Pandemic: Crisis Management and Covid-19 in the Nordic Countries* (pp. 149–172). University of Gothenburg, Nordicom. https://doi.org/10.48335/9789188855688-7

Maier, C. D. (2020). Visual crisis communication. In F. Frandsen, & W. Johansen, Eds., *Crisis Communication: Handbook of Communication Science* (pp. 213–233). Berlin: De Gruyter Mouton.

Maier, C. D., Frandsen, F., & Johansen, W. (2019). Visual crisis communication in the scandinavian press. Images of the MS Estonia disaster. *Nordicom, 40*(2), 91–109. http://doi.org/10.2478/nor-2019-0035

Maier, C. D., Frandsen, F., & Johansen, W. (2022). Understanding the arena of smoldering crises: A longitudinal study of discursive struggles after implementing a new IT health care platform. *Journal of Communication Management, 27*(3), 329–344.

Maier, C. D., & Ravazzani, S. (2023). Climate crisis communication in global news videos: A multimodal disourse approach to multifaceted knowledge and reaction Management. In W. T. Coombs, & S. J. Holladay, Eds., *The Handbook of Crisis Communication* (2nd ed., pp. 491–506). Boston: Wiley-Blackwell.

Mral, B., & Vigsø, O. (Eds.). (2012). *Krisretorik: Retoriske aspekter på krisekommunikation [The Rhetoric of Crisis: Rhetorical Aspects of Crisis Communication]*. Ödåkra: Retorikforlaget.

Muschert, G. W., & Sumiala, J. (Eds.). (2013). *School Shootings: Mediatized Violence in a Global Age*. London: Emerald.

Ndlela, M. N. (2018). *Crisis Communication: A Stakeholder Approach*. Cham: Palgrave Macmillan.

Ndlela, M. N. (2024). *Risk and Crisis Communication During the Covid-19 Pandemic: Muddled Messages*. New York: Routledge.

Nohrstedt, S. A. (Ed.). (2011). *Communicating Risk: Towards the Threat Society*. Gothenburg: Nordicom.

Nord, L., & Olsson Gardell, E.-K. (2023). Communicating the Covid-19 pandemic: A comparison of government communication in Denmark, Norway, and Sweden. In B. Johansson, Ø. Ihlen, J. Lindholm, & M. Blach-Ørsten, Eds., *Communicating a Pandemic: Crisis Management and Covid-19 in the Nordic Countries* (pp. 53–71). University of Gothenburg, Nordicom. https://doi.org/10.48335/9789188855688-3

Ómarsdóttir, I. L., Pétursdóttir, G., Bird, D. K., & Gísladóttir, G. (2022). Community resilience through the lens of support: Recovering from the 2010 Eyjafjallajökull eruption in Iceland. *International Journal of Disaster Risk Reduction, 81*. https://doi.org/10.1016/j.ijdrr.2022.103272

Opatska, S., Johansen, W., & Gordon, A. V. (2023). Business crisis management in wartime. Insights from Ukraine. *Journal of Contingencies & Crisis Management*. E-pub ahead of print. https://doi.org/10.1111/1468-5973.12513

Petridou, E., Sparf, J., Hemmingson, O., & Pihl, K. (2023). Immersive simulation and experimental desing in risk and crisis management: Implications for learning. *Journal of Contingencies & Crisis Management, 31*, 1009–1017.

Pollack, E., Allern, S., Kantola, A., & Ørsten, M. (2018). The new normal: Scandals as standard feature of political life in Nordic countries. *International Journal of Communication, 12*, 3087–3108.

Pursiainen, C. (2018). *The Crisis Management Cycle*. New York: Routledge.

Rasmussen, J., Ihlen, Ø., Kjeldsen, E., & J. (2023). Strategic Covid-19 management in communicational practice: At the crossroads to remain open or not in Denmark, Norway, and Sweden. In B. Johansson, Ø. Ihlen, J. Lindholm, & M. Blach-Ørsten, Eds., *Communicating a Pandemic: Crisis Management and Covid-19 in the Nordic Countries* (pp. 73–95). University of Gothenburg, Nordicom. https://doi.org/10.48335/9789188855688-4

Rodin, P. (2023). *Voices in the Arena: A Participation-Centred Study of Multivocal Risk and Crisis Communication on Social Media*. Doctoral thesis. Gothenburg: University of Gothenburg. ISBN: 78-91-8069-322-6 (PDF)

Ruohonen, H., & Backholm, K. (2023). Matter of trust: How to include digital volunteers in crisis management. *Journal of Contingencies & Crisis Management, 31*, 843–852. http://doi.org/10.1111/1468-5973.12484

Salomonsen, H. H., & 't Hart, P. (2020). Communicating and managing crises in the world of politics. In F. Frandsen, & W. Johansen, Eds., *Crisis Communication: Handbook of Communication Science* (pp. 436–460). Berlin: De Gruyter Mouton.

Schwartz, A., Seeger, M. W., & Auer, C. (Eds.). (2016). *The Handbook of International Crisis Communication Research*. Wiley Blackwell: Chichester.

Strandberg, J. M., & Vigsø, O. (2016). Internal crisis communication: An employee perspective on narrative, culture and sensemaking. *Corporate Communications: An International Journal, 21*(1), 89–102. https://doi.org/10.1108/CCIJ-11-2014-0083

Sumiala, J. M., & Harju, A. A. (2019). "No more apologies": Violence as a trigger for public controversy over Islam in the public sphere. *Journal of Religion, Media and Digital Culture, 8*(1), 132–152. https://doi.org/10.1163/21659214-00801007

Sumiala, J. M., & Räisä, T. (2020). 'No words are stronger': Re-inforcing boundaries through ritual work in a terrorist news event. *International Journal of Cultural Studies, 23*(3), 422–438. https://doi.org/10.1177/1367877919895992

Syvertsen, T., Enli, G., Mjøs, O. J., & Moe, H. (2014). *The Media Welfare State: Nordic Media in the Digital Era*. The University of Michigan Press. http://dx.doi.org/10.3998/nmw.12367206.0001.001

Tikka, M. (2019). Ritualisation of crisis communication: Crowd-enabled responses to the Stockholm terror attack on Twitter. *Nordicom Review*, *40*(1), 105–120. http://doi.org/10.2478/nor-2019-0006

Valentini, C., Badham, M., & Mykkänen, M. (2023). Covid-19 voices in finnish news media in the global context: A comparative study of news media's roles in pandemic communications and public perceptions across six countries. Jyväskylän yliopisto. *JYU Reports*, *27*. https://doi.org/10.17011/jyureports/2023/27

Valaskivi, K., Sumiala, J., & Tikka, M. (2022). Ambivalent rituals of belonging: (Re)theorising hybrid, vio-lent media events. *Nordic Journal of Media Studies*, *4*(1), 81–98. https://doi.org/10.2478/njms-2022-0005

Vos, M. (2017). *Communication in turbulent times: Exploring issue arenas and crisis communication to enhance organisational resilience*. Reports from the School of Business and Economics, Jyväskylä University, no. 40, Jyväskylä.

Zhao, H., Falkheimer, J., & Heide, M. (2017). Revisiting a social constructionist approach to crisis communication – Investigating contemporary crises in China. *International Journal of Strategic Communication*, *11*(5), 364–378. http://doi.org/10.1080/1553118X.2017.1363758

Zhao, H. (2022). When organizational crises meet nationalism: Crisis communication of multinational corporations in the Chinese context. *Public Relations Review*, *48*(3). https://doi.org/10.1016/j.pubrev.2022.102198

Author's Bio

Finn Frandsen is a Professor of Corporate Communication and Crisis Management in the Department of Management, Aarhus BSS, Aarhus University. His primary research interest is organizational crises, crisis management and crisis communication, including various aspects such as organizational legitimacy, internal crisis communication, visual crisis communication, crisis consulting, the crisis communication of trade associations and of public sector organizations. His research has been published in international journals and handbooks. He is the co-author of *Organizational Crisis Communication: A Multivocal Approach* (Sage, 2017) and the co-editor *Crisis Communication* (Mouton de Gruyter, 2020). In 2019, Finn Frandsen and Winni Johansen received the KOM' Prisen for their "outstanding work within institutionalization of corporate communication in Denmark," and in 2021 they received the Distinguished Public Relations Scholars Award of EUPRERA.

Winni Johansen, PhD, is a Professor of Corporate Communication and Crisis Management in the Department of Management, Aarhus BSS, Aarhus University. Her research interests include crisis management and crisis communication, strategic listening, social media, crisis consulting, internal crisis communication, environmental communication and strategic communication in private and public organizations. She is the co-author of *Organizational Crisis Communication: A Multivocal, Approach* (2017), and co-editor of *International Encyclopedia of Strategic Communication* (2018), and *Crisis Communication* (2020), and has published many scholarly articles or book chapters on crisis communication. Together with Finn Frandsen, she was awarded the KOM'Prisen 2019 by the Danish Union of Journalists and K-forum (Danish community for communication professionals) for their "outstanding work within the professionalization of corporate communication in Denmark, and for their internationally renowned crisis communication research."

34

Revisiting the Challenges of Crisis Management and Crisis Communication Research in Russia[1]

Sergei A. Samoilenko[1] and Greg Simons[2]
[1] Department of Communication, George Mason University, Fairfax, VA, USA
[2] Department of Journalism, Media & Communication, Daffodil International University in Dhaka, Bangladesh

Introduction

The Soviet Union and the countries that emerged from its collapse have experienced an immense number of crises of all types. While largely applauded in the West, the fall of the USSR in 1991 resulted in abrupt political, economic, and social transformations in each of the former Soviet republics. For instance, the economic crisis that swept through the former Soviet republics in the 1990s proved to be twice as severe as the Great Depression that plagued Western Europe and the United States in the 1930s (The World Bank, 2002). The decay of the Soviet system was marked by a succession of significant interethnic conflicts, emergencies, and disasters. These events left a lasting impact on Russia, which has been deeply traumatized by the numerous disasters and catastrophes that have struck the nation, many of which were exacerbated by state policies (see Samoilenko, 2016 for a list of the most notable crises). In Russian society, these moments are often remembered as pivotal instances when public officials displayed indifference and disregard for human life.

The field of crisis communication in the Russian context is more institutionalized within the domain of public relations (PR) than as an academic discipline. According to Gryzunova (2021), Russian PR specialists consider crisis communication primarily as a set of response strategies and tactics aimed at resolving an ongoing situation. Therefore, it is commonly referred to as "anti-crisis public relations" (*antikrizisny PR*). Crisis communication in the PR literature is usually associated with emergency public information, public awareness and national safety campaigns, corporate reputation management, and other related topics (Chumikov et al., 2016). Scholarship on crisis and risk communication in Russia is mainly conducted by researchers beyond communication studies. While crisis communication scholarship is

[1] This chapter is a considerably revised and updated version of the following chapter: Samoilenko, S. (2016). Crisis management and communication research in Russia. In A. Schwarz, M. W. Seeger, & C. Auer (Eds.), *The Handbook of International Crisis Communication Research* (pp. 397–410). Malden: John Wiley & Sons.

The Handbook of International Crisis and Risk Communication Research, Second Edition.
Edited by Andreas Schwarz, Matthew W. Seeger, and Sora Kim.

theoretically grounded in both conflict studies (Chumikov, 2021) and the sociology of management (Gryzunova, 2013), it is primarily the literature in the former field that prevails, frequently framing crises within the context of conflicting interests and competition in politics and business. Similarly, risk analysis and management in the Russian context are often associated with the *sociology of risk*, particularly through the works of Russian environmental sociologist Oleg Yanitsky (2000, 2012).

Moreover, it is worth noting that crisis management and crisis communication in Russia are not allied fields. Whereas crisis communication is overtly in the realm of academia, crisis management is primarily considered the domain of the Ministry of Extraordinary Situations (abbreviated as MChS, also known internationally as EMERCOM), the Ministry of International Affairs, and a few other federal departments. These "crisis" ministries largely rely on their own organizations for policy advice and research rather than turning to the academic community. Local academia often has limited access to primary documentation and data on hazards, accidents, and emergencies. Additionally, crisis management often refers to economic and organizational restructuring efforts in the banking or corporate sector when enterprises face financial issues or bankruptcy (Kruglova, 2010).

This chapter draws from a diverse range of original sources to illuminate how Russian cultural norms, social patterns, and new resolution tendencies are manifested in crisis communication practices. Throughout the text, crisis is principally understood as a situation that presents "a serious threat to basic values and norms with a great deal of uncertainty and considerable time constraints" (Shlykova, 2012, p. 178). Because power relations play a central role in Russian crises, a distinctive characteristic of most studies featured in this publication is that they are conducted through the power-aware prism of political communications. Porfiriev and Simons (2012, p. 3) employ the term *vlast'* (power) to define general authority within a hierarchical system that "guides and determines personal relations between various individuals in all spheres of Russian life," thereby contributing to substantial inequality and a lack of robust democratic institutions in society.

This chapter first describes the perceptions of risk and crisis and responses to them in Russian society. It then introduces three approaches to crisis communication research in Russia according to institutional, media, and public perspectives. Finally, it provides an outlook for crisis communication research in Russia and suggests areas for future development.

Perceptions and Responses to Risks and Crises

Crises are generally perceived as extraordinary situations (such as natural disasters) capable of exerting profound consequences for a political system and society as a whole (Porfiriev & Simons, 2012). A fundamental contradiction inherent in the concept of crisis is the tension "between a scarcity of information and the immediate demand of the public to know what is happening" (Asmolov, 2020, p. 235). The concept of *risk* is instrumental to our understanding of crises and emergencies. Risk is conceived and understood as a phenomenon that spans the various realms of human existence – the physical, the informational, and the cognitive. As Sandman (1987, p. 21) notes, risk "is the sum of hazard and outrage." In other words, a physical hazard can evolve into a source of public outrage that has long-term consequences, sometimes becoming imprinted in national memory for generations to come.

Crisis management is not only a matter of seeking to mitigate the problem at hand but also navigating the informational chaos that may emerge and influence public perception and response to a crisis event. Thus, as Minaeva and Nohrstedt (2002, p. 241) noted, "to successfully resolve a crisis situation very much depends upon how the problem is formulated and communicated to the social and political environment." If state leaders are unable to meet public expectations or respond to crises effectively, their incompetence will eventually undermine the public's perception of confidence and legitimacy in the state.

However, crises can also present political actors with potential opportunities to improve their standing and public image. Crucially, the ability to effectively respond to a crisis and construct an image of strength and integrity are of paramount importance for gaining public approval. For example, in the period of national crisis following the September 11th attacks, US President George W. Bush used extensive saber-rattling immediately after the tragedy and during the buildup to the invasions of Afghanistan and Iraq to cater to the media and help bolster public support (Wood, 2012). Consequently, his approval ratings skyrocketed to more than 85%, peaking at 92% after the attacks (Langer, 2011).

In authoritarian contexts, crisis communication entails the operationalization of two main elements (Asmolov, 2022a). The first involves controlling information about the crisis either through the use of concealment or by convincing the public that the situation is firmly under their control. The second revolves around managing mobilization and preventing any collective actions that could result in mass protests. Since autocracies lack free elections and other institutional mechanisms that allow the public to articulate their dissatisfaction with the authorities, mass protests remain one of the very few options for expressing frustrations and outrage in times of crisis.

Crisis Management Actors: State Versus the Rest

In times of crisis, the state is primarily represented by the President of the Russian Federation, the Ministry of Extraordinary Situations (EMERCOM), and the federal and regional authorities. State crisis management usually adheres to familiar top-down models within hierarchical and centralized systems of response ('t Hart et al., 1993). Numerous case studies (e.g., Porfiriev & Simons, 2012; Porfiriev & Svedin, 2002) have documented indifference, limited accountability, and a general lack of concern for the well-being of the populace demonstrated by both federal and local authorities during emergencies. These and other leadership characteristics were outlined by Malle (2009) in relation to Russia's Soviet legacy. In the Soviet Union, accidents at military sites and production facilities were largely kept secret. The submarine *Kursk* tragedy that occurred on August 12, 2000 (Minaeva & Nohrstedt, 2002) exemplified this Soviet *modus operandi* in action when "the values of military secrecy and human life came into conflict with one another" (Porfiriev & Simons, 2012, p. 276). In terms of attempting to manage risk and prevent or mitigate the effects of a disaster that could potentially develop into a crisis, Sidortsov et al. (2016) argued that the current Russian legal and regulatory regime often fails to provide an adequate basis for governing systemic risks.

Sometimes, indifference and negligence on the part of local and federal authorities can serve as the wellsprings for new crises. The crisis management during the 2012 flooding in the city of Krymsk is illustrative in this regard (Asmolov, 2013). Local authorities were aware of the approaching storm three hours in advance but failed to warn residents in a timely manner. Government officials also demonstrated a lack of foresight by failing to learn from their experiences with previous floods in the area, neglecting to improve water drainage, or install urgent alarm systems. Furthermore, the local government and EMERCOM officers were reluctant to share their monopoly for crisis management with volunteer groups and drove them out of the city on the spurious grounds that they disturbed local residents. Soon after the disaster, Russian senators proposed a new law seeking to regulate volunteers and charity drives and requiring legal contracts between volunteers and legally registered NGOs.

Other studies, however, have provided evidence that state institutions and authorities have come to understand the importance of crisis communication by engaging in open dialogue with the media and public (Gryzunova, 2021; Tran et al., 2021). Some government agencies have invested in a range of online services to improve emergency preparedness across different sectors. Since 2008, EMERCOM has been actively using its official website and social media accounts to stay connected with people in over 80 federal subjects across 11 time zones in Russia. Cell broadcast technologies are also now used in emergency situations, allowing simultaneous message delivery to mobile telephone users within a defined area.

Another illustrative example is the national program "Your Finances" (Vashi Financy)[2] launched by the Russian government and the International Bank for Reconstruction and Development to improve the financial literacy and retirement planning of Russian citizens following the negative impacts of the 2007–2008 financial crisis (Chumikov, 2021). The program was developed in response to a study that revealed Russian citizens' passive approach to managing their finances and their tendency to place responsibility for personal decisions and risks on the state. This national assistance program used a combination of online consulting services, games, and mobile applications to reduce citizens' financial risks.

As noted by Asmolov (2022a), authoritarian states have adapted to the new information environment by identifying novel ways to reduce independent citizen mobilization and civic engagement. These strategies go beyond traditional forms of censorship and scapegoating (such as shifting the blame from the federal government to local authorities for public criticism) by encouraging citizens to take responsibility for the actions of others and apply peer pressure and informal checks and balances to enforce compliance. For example, the government may choose to activate a wide range of control techniques to coerce citizens into monitoring their own behaviors through self-discipline, self-censorship, and intergroup policing.

An effective mechanism of this type of *governmentality* is outsourced moralization, whereby pro-government activists are often rewarded by the state for their efforts to identify and condemn divergent behavior, thus helping sustain institutional norms (Samoilenko, 2021). The distinction between legality and morality is often subtle in traditionalist societies; for example, accusations of blasphemy may invoke both legal sanctions and outrage from the conservative majority (Weiss, 2016). In Russia, moral sanctioning is often delegated to various groups, including patriotic youth, veterans, retirees, conservative activists, and nationalist organizations (Laruelle, 2025). These ideological entrepreneurs often seek ways to put pressure on dissenting voices both online and offline by accusing them of divergent or unpatriotic political convictions. However, it would be mistaken to interpret conservative attitudes among the Russian population as stimulated by state-sponsored ideological narratives alone. Laruelle (2023) argues that research focused solely on Russia's top-down conservatism has overlooked the more grassroots-based origins of the phenomenon, which are premised on different grounds and inspired by other ideological sources (e.g., Orthodoxy).

Despite the increasing authoritarian climate, Russian society continues to be influenced by grassroots activism, evidenced by various self-help, volunteer, and charitable organizations that frequently intervene to tackle social issues during crises when local authorities are slow to act. For example, in December 2024, thousands of environmental activists and volunteers engaged in cleanup activities after a storm had damaged two oil tankers, resulting in the spillage of thousands of tons of heavy fuel along the southern coast of Russia's Black Sea (Moscow Times Reporter, 2024; Novokreshennova, 2024).

The Role of the Media as a Crisis Actor

The public perception of a crisis has become increasingly shaped by the media, which often turns a crisis situation into a political issue (Simons & Strovsky, 2006). Extensive and transparent media coverage is typically associated with greater public expectations when it comes to the abilities of authorities to manage crises. Thus, higher media coverage coupled with increased

[2] https://vashifinancy.ru/.

politicization of a crisis is often considered a threat to the legitimacy of the government. In the early 2000s, the Russian media strongly criticized the government's crisis response and management capabilities, including its handling of the sinking of the submarine *Kursk* in August 2000 and the 2002 Nord-Ost siege crisis. Both events are remembered for their extensive and uncensored media coverage that resulted in the subsequent introduction of a broad array of anti-terrorism legislation. The state gradually diminished the role of the media to addressing minor societal issues and maintaining public calm during emergencies.

In 2000, Russian President Vladimir Putin introduced the Information Security Doctrine, which outlined the state's intention to increase its information security. The 2000 Information Security Doctrine was legitimized as necessary for protecting the country's national interests in the information sphere across individual, societal, and state levels. The document called for a "single information space" to counter external threats to Russian information security, among these: international competition for information technology, terrorism, and world powers' growing technological edge over Russia. The 2016 Information Security Doctrine superseded its predecessor by addressing "internal and external information threats" and explicitly mentioning foreign countries that are building up their information technology capacities to influence the information infrastructures in Russia" (President of Russia, 2016). The doctrine stated the importance of improving the competitiveness of Russian technology companies and eliminating dependence on foreign technology.

In the early 2000s, the Russian media strongly criticized the government's crisis response and management capabilities, including its handling of the sinking of the submarine *Kursk* in August 2000 and the 2002 Nord-Ost siege crisis. Both events are remembered for their extensive and uncensored media coverage that resulted in the subsequent introduction of a broad array of anti-terrorism legislation. The state gradually diminished the role of the media to reporting on minor socioeconomic matters and maintaining public calm during emergencies.

As noted by Simons and Strovsky (2006), the threat of terrorism in Russia has provided authorities with both a problem and an opportunity to censor media coverage during emergencies under the pretext of maintaining law and order. According to Simons (2010, p. 190), terrorism can be considered a form of propaganda in the sense of being an "act of causing a public spectacle in order to attract mass media attention." By attempting to conceal damaging information following an act of terrorism, the Russian government undermines its credibility as a reputable source of information and potentially hands the initiative to its opponents. In the information vacuum that proceeds from an act of terrorism, public fear and uncertainty can grow to a fever pitch.

Currently, traditional media, such as television, are the principal means of communicating state interests and policies to the public. The reliance on these forms of media has fostered a kind of symbiosis between political and media agendas that is strictly controlled by the bureaucratic hierarchy created by media managers. This symbiosis has resulted in the censorship of certain topics. For example, in line with the Russian president's promotion of conservative and traditional values, discussions surrounding issues of gay rights have disappeared from the media agenda (Reporters Without Borders, 2023).

Social networking sites have become particularly crucial in crisis communication, as they help solve everyday problems and compensate for the shortcomings of more formal institutions, including the traditional media (Asmolov, 2013). Between 2008 and 2012, the Russian Internet (Runet) became an alternative news source to state-controlled media, spurred by the rise of participatory online culture. For urban users, Runet significantly undermined the monopoly traditionally held by television over agenda-setting and news consumption. During this time, Runet served as a system of checks and balances against discriminatory practices and misdeeds of political and business elites. Some examples include calling out government officials or corporate executives for avoiding criminal charges, denouncing the Ministry of

Transport's decision to build a high-speed road through the Khimki Forest near Moscow, and bringing to light multiple cases of high-level corruption, among other issues. In a short while, Runet turned into a public space for networking, fundraising for political and humanitarian purposes, and social mobilization (Alexanyan, 2013).

Furthermore, digital self-help communities have emerged that engage in various forms of participatory activity, such as crowdsourcing, gathering data to develop an operational understanding of a crisis, and offering help and advice (Asmolov, 2020). For example, when the traditional media and Russian authorities downplayed the scale of the wildfires that broke out near Moscow in the summer of 2010, the Russian blogosphere quickly responded by launching a LiveJournal community to coordinate volunteer firefighters and provide assistance to victims via the crowdsourcing platform Help Map (Asmolov, 2013; Yanitsky, 2012).

The power of the well-developed network society that emerged in Russia in the late 2000s demonstrated that interpersonal relations can prevail over the low trust in social institutions. During the 2012 Krymsk floods, online communities became social hubs for improving the surveillance of the disaster and fact-checking the information provided by the mass media. Similar to the way Help Map was used during the 2010 wildfires, a crowdsourced database map was established to help people locate humanitarian aid stations, provide assistance to victims via virtual "situation rooms," and coordinate relief efforts. The Krymsk disaster motivated thousands of volunteers to collect humanitarian aid, organize transportation and cargo logistics, and control the public panic. Bloggers set up a system for verifying rumors about the disaster through a variety of credible sources, such as eyewitnesses, local residents, and journalists (Rodchanina, 2017). A follow-up survey of Krymsk residents showed that the highest levels of trust were placed in relatives, neighbors, friends, and volunteers who came to their rescue during and after the flood, while the "least helpful" were commercial organizations, regional administration, and the police (Higher School of Economics, 2012).

The lessons of the 2010 Moscow wildfires and the 2012 Krymsk floods prompted the Russian government to become more proactive in minimizing the political risks associated with the country's growing volunteer movement. Their solution was an advanced system of vertical crowdsourcing that put state institutions in charge of volunteer mobilization while also allowing them to control the forms and scope of mobilization in crisis situations (Asmolov, 2015). The development of state-sponsored volunteering resources was channeled into specific causes through the allocation of grants, training programs, awards, and other forms of financial aid and symbolic recognition. For example, the website Dobro.ru[3] is a state-sponsored unified volunteer engagement network system with the goal of facilitating participation in state-supported non-governmental initiatives. In 2020–2021, the platform mobilized hundreds of thousands of volunteers to help medical workers, the elderly, and people with limited mobility during the coronavirus pandemic.[4]

Crowdsourcing work has also been integrated into a new collaborative vision of the Moscow government that offers a range of online platforms for addressing urban issues, thus allowing Moscow residents to contribute to local initiatives (Chumikov, 2021). For example, "Crowdsourcing projects" [5] allow residents to suggest, comment, and discuss ideas on a given topic. The platform "Moscow is Our City"[6] welcomes comments and complaints from residents, which help the executive authorities to address problems with the city's infrastructure, including roadway development, transport hubs, lighting, cleaning, and landscaping.

[3] https://dobro.ru/.
[4] https://xn--b1agazb5ah1e.xn--p1ai/covid19.
[5] https://crowd.mos.ru/.
[6] http://gorod.mos.ru.

Finally, the "Active Citizen" platform[7] which engages a substantial audience of more than 2 million users, allows residents to vote for various city development projects, giving bonuses that can be used as payment for public services to those who vote. However, voters can only select projects that have already been approved by the Mayor's Office. For example, in 2017, the Mayor's Office made a unilateral decision regarding the reconstruction of historical buildings that caused strong public outrage from some local politicians concerned with protecting Russian historical heritage. This issue demonstrates the need for independent city media that could monitor the situation in Moscow and report on the oversight of the municipal authorities and their public information apparatuses (Pichugina, 2022).

The Russian government has been creative in resolving a dilemma concerning the degree of control over the digital environment, which provides timely and reliable information that is essential to crisis response while also potentially undermining political stability and the regime's legitimacy (Asmolov, 2022a). For instance, Asmolov observed how, during COVID-19, state officials used digital platforms to control the spread of information and manage the public's reaction to the crisis. In addition, the authorities invested in efforts to confront independent volunteer projects by encouraging critics who questioned their legitimacy and authenticity as digital activists. Vigilantes began identifying online content that provided alternative interpretations of the pandemic's management and statistical data and labeled it as "fake." These accusations of fake news allowed state agencies to confront information that challenged their efforts to address the crisis. Furthermore, state-sponsored media launched local city forums, various tracking systems, and online maps for resident surveillance and encouraged people to report on their neighbors and relatives. These actions aimed at diverting public attention away from the activities of the state to the moral conduct of quarantine violators.

Following the election falsification protests in 2012, Runet went through major structural changes due to state centralization and increased censorship. These changes included the adoption of laws introducing administrative and criminal penalties for posting and sharing content identified by the state as "extremist," "unlawful," or "violating regulations" (Human Rights Watch, 2020). Many anti-terrorism regulations, such as the 2014 "blogger law," were implemented to further strengthen internet censorship. Moreover, professional "troll factories" aimed to counter anti-government sentiment by disseminating pro-government narratives (Gaufman, 2021).

The state's increased control over digital domains has served to limit the scope of digital innovation in crisis situations, restrict independent crisis-related activities, and channel digital activists into state-sponsored resources. As Asmolov (2022b, p. 253) pointed out, "Although this type of regulation mitigates crisis-related political risks for the authorities, it also limits the social resilience of a society in the face of a crisis." The implementation of laws intended to control digital spaces has brought a new level of surveillance and information control, culminating in the creation of an internet "kill switch" that would allow the state to disconnect Runet from the global network in an emergency situation (Muravyeva & Gurkov, 2021).

Audience Perceptions of Risks and Safety

Low personal safety is a significant issue in Russia. This absence of a safety culture can be characterized as a general lack of an "atmosphere in which safety is understood to be, and is accepted as, the number one priority" (Cullen, 1990, p. 300). Multiple case studies have demonstrated the disregard for personal safety at hazardous facilities, such as those in Dzerzhinsk (Jones, 2001) and Karabash (Mozgovaia, 2002). It is quite typical for workers

---

[7] https://ag.mos.ru/.

at environmentally hazardous facilities to be more interested in keeping their jobs than, say, in seeking treatment when they first notice adverse health issues. Researchers have also addressed how residents of the areas contaminated by the Chernobyl accident were largely uneducated about the hazards of radiation (Marchenko et al., 2014).

Some research has attempted to understand how and why the past influences perceptions of risk and safety in contemporary contexts. For example, Shok and Beliakova (2020) argued that the response of Russia's public health system to the COVID-19 pandemic can be attributed to the legacy of Soviet crisis management. They observed how a paternalistic approach to state governance of public health, intertwined with certain "neo-Soviet" trends, such as a culture of silence, doublethink, and non-disclosure, substantially influenced the response to the pandemic.

Other studies contend that strict state regulatory and managerial control has hindered critical cultural processes of modernization, including the development of independent and pragmatic individual skills (Tarasova, 2009; Yakovenko, 2006). These studies suggest that underlying cultural traits and collective attitudes have contributed to man-made risks and disasters. These factors include: (1) the influence of traditional Russian values, such as collectivism and paternalism; (2) the influence of state industrial policies that encourage the abuse of natural and human resources and environmentally dangerous practices; and (3) low compliance with technological instructions.

Over the course of Russian history, civil society cells and networks have been remarkably resilient and viable regardless of critical transformations (Yanitsky, 2020). Many Russian citizens have become immune to emergencies and tend to embrace risk-laden environments as typical after being continually exposed to threats and dangers. The memories of significant cultural traumas, such as World War II, often make local crises and misfortunes appear insignificant by comparison, thereby compelling many Russians to "face increasing hardships with stoicism rather than outrage and dissatisfaction" (Shevchenko, 2001, p. 86). The monitoring conducted by the Institute of Sociology of the Russian Academy of Sciences shows during the observation period from 2011 to 2024, the proportion of Russians seeing the national situation as a crisis consistently remained above 50% (Barash, 2024). This perception of reality somewhat explains the indifference shown by the majority of Russians regarding Western sanctions since 2022, with + a steady decline in public concern in March 2023:34% of respondents state that they are not worried about sanctions at all and another 30% that they are not worried that much (Levada Center, 2023). Also, in 2023, the percentage of those who considered the situation terrible declined from 16% to 8% (Barash, 2024).

After the fall of the Soviet Union, a crucial expression of "weapons of the weak" (see Scott, 1985 for more information) displayed by ordinary Russians was the use of *consumption narratives*. These consumption narratives involved a range of discursive practices, such as discussing price differences and purchasing strategies with relatives and friends, that helped individuals make sense of growing inflation, cope with stressful situations, and adapt to the political and economic chaos of the 1990s (Shevchenko, 2009). Another technique involves nostalgic practices, which serve as a coping mechanism to help individuals recognize the necessary break from the Soviet past. Research has also mentioned the use of humor by ordinary Russians as a coping mechanism for stressful events, such as natural disasters and financial problems (Artemyeva, 2013).

The Russian public's predisposition for adaptation strategies in times of crisis was demonstrated in a 1998 national poll by the polling agency VTsIOM (Dubin, 2004). The survey showed several key adaptation strategies displayed by Russian citizens, including viability, patience, long-term aptitude to put up with hardships and deprivations, and the ability to find contentment in times of scarcity. These findings undergird Gudkov's (2011, 2021) description of Russian society as one defined by the *inertia of passive* (or reductive) *adaptation*. This society adapts to the measures taken by a repressive and kleptocratic state by focusing on survival strategies within current circumstances and reducing demands for the government

(Strzelecki, 2017). This overall adaptation is reinforced by "a self-fulfilling prophecy," whereby "having no faith in the institutions' capacity to resolve their grievances, individuals may opt not even to bother trying" (Shevchenko, 2002, p. 859). This readiness for internal mobilization could be viewed as a sign of nonviolent opposition "between us and them." This division between the people and the state is typical of the Russian rhetorical tradition (Shlapentokh, 1986), illustrated by the popular Russian saying, "If you're in trouble, you're on your own."

Historically in Russia, one often feels more protected when they belong to an established social network of others, also known as a "*svoi*." A study conducted by Levinson (2009) revealed that social capital is considered by many Russians as the most valuable resource in times of crisis. Research has also found that ordinary Russians are motivated to act and respond to daily risks and threats not only when they reach a certain level of dissatisfaction with their quality of life but also when they feel solidarity with other groups and have a shared desire to improve the situation (Aleinikov et al., 2020). Importantly, major crises and disasters may expand the possibility of creating social networks, reduce sentiments of alienation among citizens, and help establish more meaningful relationships between people (Yanitsky, 2004). According to Yanitsky, the community of *risk-consumers* begins mobilizing social networks and other grassroots resources to ensure its own survival and, thus, challenge the hazards caused by major *risk-producers*.

There is also evidence that crises and emergencies have created new opportunities for ordinary Russians. For example, the 1998 financial crisis sparked the rise of e-commerce, which became a catalyst for the entrepreneurial activities of many Russians (Gurova & Morozova, 2021). The economic recession in the wake of the international sanctions imposed on Russia in 2014 had a significant effect on the development of various rental services, such as Airbnb, in many Russian cities.

Studies have also shown that there are critical differences in crisis resilience displayed by Russian men and women. While Russian women explored new opportunities and faced the challenges of the new capitalist society of the 1990s, Russian men appeared to be more deeply impacted by the radical social shifts and the economic and political turmoil that plagued the post-Soviet era (Andreevskikh & Muravyeva, 2021). In particular, Russian men faced a crisis of masculinity by being deprived of their professional dignity, achievements, and their role as the primary breadwinner of the family. Fueled by the state-sponsored ideology that espoused traditional values, one of the responses to the post-Soviet crisis of masculinity has been a rise in paramilitary, masculinist, and even anti-feminist movements (Turovskiy, 2015).

Although these attitudes may differ for members of Generation Z, who live in a different, post-Soviet reality, many young people still demonstrate tolerance of cronyism, nepotism, and other informal practices much like the older generations of Russians. Furthermore, many young Russians do not identify with what is commonly perceived as "Western" culture and are distrustful not only towards their own state institutions but also towards international and European institutions (Gudkov et al., 2020).

Future Research and Conclusions

This chapter reveals that many of the specific characteristics of crisis management and communication in Russia are deeply rooted in cultural and political experiences, highlighting three overarching themes:

1. The Soviet legacy of political leadership is still entrenched in approaches to crisis communication and management in Russia. The state has historically acted as both the primary crisis manager and risk producer. Inadequate state responses to crises often aggravate already disastrous scenarios and carry the risk of instigating subsequent crises.

2. The lessons of the 2010 Moscow wildfires and the 2012 Krymsk floods have prompted the Russian government to seek more proactive communication strategies to minimize the political risks associated with volunteer movements in the country. Furthermore, as demonstrated during the COVID-19 pandemic, state agencies have exerted control over digital spaces by rerouting volunteers to government-run channels and delegitimizing alternative narratives.
3. In an environment characterized by low trust in state institutions, interpersonal networks become vital mechanisms for coping with crises. The increase in volunteer activities can be considered a form of solidarity and communal empathy among citizens who have low trust in the authorities and live in an unstable political and economic environment. Overall, Russian citizens show remarkable resilience in crisis situations by developing their own unique communication strategies and pragmatic approaches to survive and maintain control over their social environment. Furthermore, crises and economic sanctions have ironically become drivers for new opportunities and improvements.

As mentioned in the previous edition of this chapter, changes toward a developed civil society in Russia are rather seasonal and linked to external influences. After 2012, the Russian state has significantly reduced opportunities for independent volunteers and alternative media to become capable crisis actors in emergency situations. These measures included the adoption of repressive laws introducing administrative and criminal penalties for posting and sharing content identified by the state as extremist or fake. Since the beginning of the Russia-Ukraine War in February 2022, nearly all independent media outlets have been banned, blocked, or declared "foreign agents" or "undesirable organizations," while other media outlets have been subject to military censorship (Reporters Without Borders, 2023).

This publication has identified a deficit of culturally relevant scholarship regarding crisis management and communication in Russia. In part, this is explained by rather rudimentary partnerships between the Russian research community and the aforementioned "crisis" ministries, which prevent academics from accessing primary documentation and data on crises, accidents, and emergencies. The lack of systematic industry research means that scholars have little empirical evidence with which to advance theory. In addition, Russian universities do not offer graduate programs in communication studies, which negatively impacts the state and quality of academic research on the topic, resulting in a very small number of scholarly publications on risk and crisis communication.

While Soviet legacy has been identified among the key influencers of crisis response in the Russian context, this assumption needs testing and assessment in the current sociopolitical context. It may be that young Russians live in a different, post-socialist reality and have little or no memory of the Soviet Union. Future research should focus on generational differences in attitudes towards extraordinary political and economic crises and public reactions to state crisis management policies.

References

Aleinikov, A. V., Artemov, G. P., & Pinkevich, A. G. (2020). Risk reflections as a factor for choosing forms of political participation (Results of the all-Russian survey). *RUDN Journal of Sociology, 20*(4), 847–863. https://journals.rudn.ru/sociology/article/view/25215

Alexanyan, K. (2013). *The Map and the Territory: Russian Social Media Networks and Society [Doctoral Dissertation]*. Columbia University. http://hdl.handle.net/10022/AC:P:19097

Andreevskikh, O., & Muravyeva, M. (2021). Doing gender online: Digital spaces for identity politics. In D. Gritsenko, M. Wijermars, & M. Kopotev, Eds., *The Palgrave Handbook of Digital Russia Studies* (pp. 205–220). Palgrave.

Artemyeva, T. V. (2013). Humor as a form of coping behavior among Russian students. *Middle-East Journal of Scientific Research, 16*(3), 348–351.

Asmolov, G. (2013). Natural disasters and alternative modes of governance: The role of social networks and crowdsourcing platforms in Russia. In S. Livingston, & G. Walter-Drop, Eds., *Bits and Atoms: Information and Communication Technology in Areas of Limited Statehood* (pp. 98–114). Oxford University Press.

Asmolov, G. (2015). Vertical crowdsourcing in Russia: Balancing governance of crowds and state–citizen partnership in emergency situations. *Policy & Internet, 7*(3), 292–318.

Asmolov, G. (2020). Runet in crisis situations. In S. Davydov, Ed., *Internet in Russia: A Study of the Runet and Its Impact on Social Life* (pp. 231–250). Springer.

Asmolov, G. (2022a). Crisis Communication in authoritarian systems and digital innovation: How do autocracies resolve the dictator's dilemma in crisis situations? In W. Timothy Coombs, & S. J. Holladay, Eds., *The Handbook of Crisis Communication* (pp. 209–227). Wiley.

Asmolov, G. (2022b). Internet regulation and crisis-related resilience: From Covid-19 to existential risks. *The Communication Review, 25*(3–4), 235–257.

Barash, R. E. (2024). Predstavlenija rossijan o kljuchevyh sostavljajushhih kachestva zhizni i social'noj spravedlivosti: srez obshhestvennogo mnenija v 2024 g. [Russians' perceptions of key components of the quality of life and social justice: a cross-sec tion of public opinion in 2024]. *Vestnik Instituta Sotziologii, 15*(4), 82–109. https://doi.org/10.19181/ vis.2024.15.4.7

Chumikov, A. N. (2021). *Antikrizisnie kommunikatsii [Crisis Communications]*. Prospekt.

Chumikov, A. N., Bocharov, M. S., & Samoilenko, S. A. (2016). *Reklama i svyazi s obshestvennostyu. Professionalnye kompetentsii [Advertising and Public Relations. Professional Competencies]*. Delo.

Cullen, W. D. (1990). *The Public Inquiry Into the Piper Alpha Disaster*. HMSO.

Dubin, B. V. (2004). *Intellektualnye gruppy i simvolicheskie formy: Ocherki sociologii sovremennoi kultury [Intellectual Groups and Symbolic Forms: Essays on the Sociology of Contemporary Culture]*. Novoe Izdatelstvo.

Gaufman, E. (2021). Cybercrime and punishment: Security, information war, and the future of Runet. In D. Gritsenko, M. Wijermars, & M. Kopotev, Eds., *The Palgrave Handbook of Digital Russia Studies* (pp. 115–134). Palgrave MacMillan. https://doi.org/10.1007/978-3-030-42855-6_7

Gryzunova, E. (2013). Models of governmental crisis communications and information management. *Disaster, Conflict and Social Crisis Research Network Newsletter, 51*(14), 19–22.

Gryzunova, E. (2021). Hybridity of crisis communication professional discourse in Russia. In K. Tsetsura, & D. Kruckeberg, Eds., *Strategic Communications in Russia: Public Relations and Advertising* (pp. 193–205). Routledge.

Gudkov, L. (2011). Inertsiya passivnoi adaptatsii [Inertia of passiv adaptation]. *Pro et Contra, 15*(1–2), 20–42. https://bit.ly/3ELh2eZJanuary–April.

Gudkov, L. (2021). *Kak my dumaem [How We Think]*. Levada Center. http://bit.ly/3rtbLpn

Gudkov, L., Zorkaya, N., Kochergina, E., Pipiya, K., & Ryseva, A. (2020). *Russia's 'generation Z': Attitudes and values 2019/2020*. Friedrich-Ebert-Stiftung. https://library.fes.de/pdf-files/bueros/moskau/16134.pdf

Gurova, O., & Morozova, D. (2021). Digitalization of consumption in Russia: Online platforms, regulations and consumer behavior. In D. Gritsenko, M. Wijermars, & M. Kopotev, Eds., *The Palgrave Handbook of Digital Russia Studies* (pp. 221–240). Palgrave MacMillan. https://doi.org/10.1007/978-3-030-42855-6_7

Higher School of Economics (August 20, 2012). *Bedstvie v Krymske [Disaster in Krymsk]*. https://spb.hse.ru/news/67792938.html

Human Rights Watch (June 18, 2020). *Russia: Growing internet isolation, control, censorship*. https://bit.ly/3PFl5ir

Jones, M. (December 16, 2001). Disregard for health is killing Russians. *Los Angeles Times*. https://www.latimes.com/archives/la-xpm-2001-dec-16-mn-15468-story.html

Kruglova, N. (2010). *Antikrizisnoe upravlenie [Crisis Management]*. Knorus.

Langer, G. (October 1, 2011). Poll: Bush approval rating 92 percent. *ABC News*. https://abcnews.go.com/Politics/story?id=120971&page=1

Laruelle, M. (2023). A grassroots conservatism? Taking a fine-grained view of conservative attitudes among Russians. *East European Politics, 39*(2), 173–193. https://doi.org/10.1080/21599165.2022.2045962

Laruelle, M. (2025). *Ideology and Meaning-Making Under the Putin Regime*. Stanford University Press.

Levada Center (April 6, 2023). *Public perceptions of Western sanctions: March 2023*. https://bit.ly/3Lv7Xux

Levinson, A. (February 24, 2009). Nashe "my: Taynoe obshestvo [Our "we": Secret society]. *Vedomosti*, https://bit.ly/3PMP0X5

Malle, S. (2009). Soviet legacies in Post-Soviet Russia: Insights from crisis management. *Post-Soviet Economies*, *24*(3), 249–282.

Marchenko, T. A., Melnitskaya, T. B., Belykh, T. V., Krikunova, L. V., & Khavylo, A. V. (2014). *Resultaty ocenki urovnya sformirovannostu kultury bezopasnosti zhiznedeyatelnosti naseleniya Rossii, prozhivayushego na radioaktovno zagryaznennyh territoriyah* [The assessment results of safety culture among Russian residents living in radioactive contaminated areas]. *Psikhologicheskie Nauki*, *6*, 1057–1066. https://bit.ly/3RxoYYX

Minaeva, L., & Nohrstedt, D. (2002). The Kursk submarine accident: Coping with value complexity and a credibility crisis. In B. Porfiriev, & L. Svedin, Eds., *Crisis Management in Russia: Overcoming Institutional Rigidity and Resource Constraints* (pp. 223–260). Swedish National Defence College.

Moscow Times Reporter (December 23, 2024). 'Left to fend for themselves': Volunteers step up as Russian government falters in Black Sea oil spill response. *The Moscow Times*. https://www.themoscowtimes.com/2024/12/23/left-to-fend-for-themselves-volunteers-step-up-as-russian-government-falters-in-black-sea-oil-spill-response-a87429

Mozgovaia, A. (2002). Crisis management of the ecological disaster in the town of Karabash. In B. Porfiriev, & L. Svedin, Eds., *Crisis Management in Russia: Overcoming Institutional Rigidity and Resource Constraints* (pp. 205–222). Swedish National Defence College.

Muravyeva, M., & Gurkov, A. (2021). Law and digitization in Russia. In D. Gritsenko, M. Wijermars, & M. Kopotev, Eds., *The Palgrave Handbook of Digital Russia Studies* (pp. 77–93). Palgrave.

Novokreshennova, V. (December 19, 2024). Bolee 1,5 tysjachi volonterov i voennyh uchastvujut v ochistke pljazhej Anapy ot mazuta [More than 1.5 thousand volunteers and military personnel are participating in cleaning the beaches of Anapa from fuel oil]. *Telekanal Krasnodar*. https://tvkrasnodar.ru/obshchestvo/2024/12/19/bolee-1-5-tysyachi-volonterov-i-voennykh-uchastvuyut-v-ochistke-plyazhey-anapy-ot-mazuta/

Pichugina, O. (2022). Urban communication and media in Russia. In M. Minielli, M. Lukacovic, S. A. Samoilenko, M. Finch, & D. Uecker, Eds., *Communication Theory and Application in Post-Socialist Contexts* (pp. 45–58). Lexington Books.

Porfiriev, B., & Simons, G. (2012). *Crises in Russia: Contemporary Management Policy and Practice from a Historical Perspective*. Ashgate.

Porfiriev, B., & Svedin, L. (2002). *Crisis Management in Russia: Overcoming Institutional Rigidity and Resource Constraints*. Stockholm: Swedish National Defence College.

President of Russia (2016). Ukaz Prezidenta Rossijskoj Federacii ot 05.12.2016 No. 646. "Ob utverzhdenii Doktriny informacionnoj bezopasnosti Rossijskoj Federacii" [Decree of the President of the Russian Federation dated December 5, 2016 No. 646 "On approval of the Information Security Doctrine of the Russian Federation"]. http://publication.pravo.gov.ru/Document/View/0001201612060002

Reporters Without Borders (2023). *Russia*. https://rsf.org/en/country/russia

Rodchanina, L. (July 7, 2017). "Yedinstvennoye, chto imeyet smysl, — eto pomoshch' lyudyam". Volontery o tragedii v Krymske spustya 5 let ["The only thing that makes sense is helping people." Volunteers about the tragedy in Krymsk 5 years later]. *Yuga*. https://www.yuga.ru/articles/society/8089.html

Samoilenko, S. A. (2016). Crisis management and communication research in Russia. In A. Schwarz, M. Seeger, & C. Auer, Eds., *The Handbook of International Crisis Communication Research* (pp. 399–409). Wiley-Blackwell.

Samoilenko, S. A. (2021). Character assassination: The sociocultural perspective. *Journal of Applied Social Theory*, *1*(3), 186–205.

Sandman, P. M. (1987). Risk communication: Facing public outrage. *EPA Journal*, *13*, 21–22.

Scott, J. C. (1985). *Weapons of the Weak: Everyday Forms of Peasant Resistance*. Yale University Press.

Shevchenko, O. (2001). Bread and circuses: Shifting frames and changing references in the ordinary Muscovites' political talk. *Communist and Post-Communist Studies*, *34*(1), 77–90.

Shevchenko, O. (2002). Between the holes: Emerging identities and hybrid patterns of consumption in post-socialist Russia. *Europe-Asia Studies, 54*(6), 841–866.
Shevchenko, O. (2009). *Crisis and the Everyday in Postsocialist Moscow*. Indiana University Press.
Shlapentokh, V. (1986). *Soviet public opinion and ideology: Mythology and pragmatism in interaction*. Praeger.
Shlykova, E. (2012). Social security policy for the Chernobyl clean-up and rescue workers: Crisis chronology and lessons. In B. Porfiriev, & G. Simons, Eds., *Crises in Russia: Contemporary Management Policy and Practice from a Historical Perspective* (pp. 177–204). Ashgate.
Shok, N., & Beliakova, N. (2020, September). How Soviet legacies shape Russia's response to the pandemic: Ethical consequences of a culture of non-disclosure. *Kennedy Institute of Ethics Journal, 30*(3-4), 379–400.
Sidortsov, R., Ivanova, A., & Stammler, F. (2016). Localizing governance of systemic risks: A case study of the Power of Siberia pipeline in Russia. *Energy Research & Social Science, 16*, 54–68.
Simons, G. (2010). *Mass Media and Modern Warfare: Reporting on the Russian War on Terrorism*. Ashgate.
Simons, G., & Strovsky, D. (2006). Censorship in contemporary Russian journalism in the age of the war against terrorism: A historical perspective. *European Journal of Communication, 21*, 189–211.
Strzelecki, J. (2017). *Painful Adaptation: The Social Consequences of the Crisis in Russia*. (Publication No. 60). OSW Centre for Eastern Studies. https://bit.ly/3t24v4r
t'Hart, P., Rosenthal, U., & Kouzmin, A. (1993). Crisis decision making: The centralization thesis revisited. *Administration and Society, 15*(1), 12–15.
Tarasova, V. V. (2009). *Spetsifika svyazei s obshestvennostyu MChS Rossii v usloviyakh riskogennosti sociokulturnoi sredy*. The specifics of EMERCOM public relations in a risk-producing sociocultural environment. Doctoral dissertation. https://core.ac.uk/download/pdf/197388374.pdf
The World Bank (2002). *A New World Bank Report: Transition – The First Ten Years: Analysis and Lessons for Eastern Europe and the Former Soviet Union*. The World Bank. http://siteresources.worldbank.org/ECAEXT/Resources/complete.pdf
Tran, V. D., Pak, T. V., Gribkova, E. I., Galkina, G. A., Loskutova, E. E., Dorofeeva, V. V., Dewey, R. S., Nguyen, K. T., & Pham, D. T. (2021). Determinants of COVID-19 vaccine acceptance in a high infection-rate country: a cross-sectional study in Russia. *Pharmacy Practice (Granada), 19*(1), 2276. https://dx.doi.org/10.18549/pharmpract.2021.1.2276
Turovskiy (September 22, 2015). *Stroiteli oflayn-gosudarstva [Offline state builders]. Meduza*. https://bit.ly/3MQHYwV
Weiss, D. (2016). The new Russian Legislation on blasphemy and swearing: the parliamentary debates. *Zeitschrift für Slavische Philologie, 72*(2), 289–321.
Wood, B. D. (2012). *Presidential Saber Rattling: Causes and Consequences*. Cambridge University Press.
Yakovenko, I. G. (2006). *Riski socialnoi tranformatsii rossiyskogo obshestva: Kultorologicheskiy aspekt [The Social Risks of Transforming Russian Society: Culturological Aspect]*. Progress-Traditsiya.
Yanitsky, O. N. (2000). Sustainability and risk: The case of Russia. *Innovation: The European Journal of Social Science Research, 13*(3), 265–277.
Yanitsky, O. N. (2004). Rossiya kak obshestvo riska: Metodologiya analiza i kontury kontseptsii [Russia as a risk society: Research methodology and conceptual outlines. Social sciences and modernity]. *Obshestvennye Nauki i Sovremennost, 2*, 5–15. http://ecsocman.hse.ru/text/18235966/
Yanitsky, O. N. (2012). The 2010 wildfires in Russia. *An Ecosociological Analysis Sociological Research, 51*(2), 57–75.
Yanitsky, O. N. (2020). On the volunteers and volunteering: The case of Russia. *Creative Education, 11*(03), 307–320. https://www.scirp.org/html/11-6304857_98913.htm

Author's Bio

Sergei A. Samoilenko is an assistant professor and co-founder of the Research Lab for Character Assassination and Reputation Politics (CARP) in the Department of Communication at George Mason University. He authored and co-authored numerous books and publications on character assassination and reputation management, political and crisis communication, and post-socialist issues. His latest book project includes two anthologies – *Media and Public Relations Research in Post-Socialist Societies* and *Communication Theory and Application in Post-Socialist Contexts* – published by Lexington Books. https://orcid.org/0000-0002-8607-3053.

Greg Simons (PhD, University of Canterbury, New Zealand) is currently a professor at the Department of Journalism, Media and Communication at Daffodil International University in Dhaka, Bangladesh. His research interests include changing political dynamics and relationships, mass media, public diplomacy, political marketing, crisis management communications, media and armed conflict, and communication aspects of the Russian Orthodox Church. He also researches the relationships and connections between information, politics, and armed conflict more broadly, such as the Global War on Terrorism (GWOT) and Arab Spring, as well as the interpretation and representation of the evolving global geopolitical order.

ORCHID 0000-0002-6111-5325.

35

Risk and Crisis Communication Research in Romania

Corina Buzoianu[1], Monica Bîră[1], and Alina Bârgăoanu[2]
[1,2] National Univeristy of Political Studies and Public Administration (SNSPA), Bucharest, Romania

Societal Context of Risk and Crisis Communication in Romania

The chapter addresses the history and current state of crisis communication in Romania, exploring the development of research and practices in crisis communication after the fall of communism. Influenced by the transition period that followed the 1989 events, the fields of communication and, consequently, the crisis in communication have been subject to imports from US and Western European theories, means, and practices. The first post-graduate program in communication and public relations was established in 1991. It was followed four years later by the set-up of Romania's first professional public relations association. In 1998, in Bucharest, a newly established state university devoted to political studies and public administration, SNSPA, opened the first program dedicated to BA studies in communication and public relations. One year later, in 1999, the PR specialist job title was officially recognized in the national occupations directory. The arrival of multinational corporations in the local market and the resulting economic changes spurred the growth of Romania's communication and public relations field to meet an emerging need. However, crisis communication was perceived as a niche topic and did not benefit from the same attention in its early beginning (Balaban, 2013; Buzoianu et al., 2019; Coman, 2008b; Dobrescu, 2008).

Studies looking at the complex and challenging transition process in Eastern Europe, especially regarding the field of communication, are still scarce. For the purpose of this chapter, we have to keep in mind that the transition from a totalitarian regime to a democracy and from a state-controlled, centrally planned economy to a market economy puts individuals and societies through a long and struggling process. This required people to form new communication relationships as they became stakeholders of multinational companies, brands, organizations, state institutions, political parties, and other entities. Transitioning from one role to another encompassed several changes, discussed below.

First, prior to 1989 and especially during the last decade of the regime, a large part of the population struggled to obtain essential goods and foods with power outages, heating and

The Handbook of International Crisis and Risk Communication Research, Second Edition.
Edited by Andreas Schwarz, Matthew W. Seeger, and Sora Kim.

warm water shortages being frequent. As the economy shifted towards a market-oriented system, consumers were enabled to choose and voice expectations. During the 1990s, American brands such as Coca-Cola, Pepsi, and McDonald's were extremely popular among the public as aspirational brands. Their name relates to events that entered the collective memory, such as Michael Jackson's first concert in Eastern Europe (September 1992), sponsored by Pepsi. The opening of the first McDonald's restaurant in Bucharest in 1995 was attended by more than 16.000 and needed the support of the police to maintain order (Voinea & Delcea, 2015a; Voinea & Delcea, 2015b). In addition, American brands entering the Romanian market directly impacted the development of the communication and advertising industry, as they brought in know-how and large budgets in advertising (Barbu, 2014). Although few sources are available to document the beginning of crisis communication in Romania, we can trace its initial stage in the early 1990s. The first press release we could identify so far was written in the new framework of the market economy. During the fall of 1991, there was media scrutiny in Romania over the quality of soft drinks distributed nationwide by TEC, a Romanian-American company selling carbonated beverage dispensers supplied by Cornelius, which is still a player in this specific market relevant today. In response, the TEC Company issued a press release announcing the launch of an initiative aimed at "restoring consumer confidence" (Voinea, 2013).

Second, a comrade-citizen in a totalitarian regime, where the lines between party and state were confounded, became a citizen of a state where several political parties could compete for power in free elections. Political communication emerged alongside electoral marketing, following a similar pathway as advertising and public relations (Bardan, 2001; Teodorescu et al., 2005), with university courses being taught towards the end of the 1990s and introductory books and syntheses being published during the decade 2000–2010 (Pripp, 2002; Stoiciu, 2000). Crisis communication in broader political and social contexts also entered its first stages of action towards the end of the 90s, when large-scale social movements took place, such as the miners' march towards Bucharest (in February 1999) and other unions' protests (e.g., teachers' unions). Among these, the miners' movement triggered a major governmental crisis response and the set-up of one of the first crisis management teams. The event was widely covered by the media, both television and print, and was punctuated by frequent press statements, government meetings, and meetings of national and local authorities. The threat of miners marching to Bucharest to press for their demands created polarization in society and exacerbated preexisting social tensions. When crafting and delivering their messages, national authorities considered public opinion, carefully navigating the tensions of various stakeholders (Gavril, 2007).

Third, a consumer of state-controlled and censored media, with only a few hours per day of television, turned gradually into a member of the audience exposed to a state-owned "free television" and printed outlets presenting multiple points of view. Since 1992 onwards, several privately owned TV channels started to broadcast, and some western TV channels (e.g., CNN, TV5) were available to the public, thus enlarging the Romanian media landscape. Translated TV commercials and locally produced ads were broadcast on radio and TV, gradually forging a relationship between Western brands and local producers on the one hand, and consumers on the other hand. Oral testimonies documenting the beginnings of advertising (Barbu, 2014; Voinea & Delcea, 2015c) highlight the essential role that US brands and NGOs played in this development (Berend, 2009).

Last but not least, the political establishment was interested in encouraging Western investors and specifically American brands to develop business operations in Romania because of the widely held belief in society that, at an international level, a country improves its reputation in the eyes of prospective investors and presents enough guarantees for economic and social stability when significant businesses and brands are operating there. The idea is emphasized by the ones involved in developing post-1990 media structures and market communication/advertising companies (Barbu, 2014; Voinea & Delcea, 2015c).

Academic Context of Risk and Crisis Communication in Romania

Risk and crisis communication in Romania follows the development of the field of communication in the country and, from its early beginning, was based on imports from both French and Anglo-Saxon epistemologies and practices. After the fall of communism, Romania and other countries in the region reopened academic programs outlawed before 1989 and launched new ones like communication studies. From the early beginning of importing the field of communication, Romanian scholars faced some significant challenges that impacted the domain's development (Buzoianu et al., 2019; Coman, 2008a; Dobrescu, 2008) and related topics like crisis communication.

Among these challenges, it is worth mentioning that in the early 1990s, only very few Romanian scholars were able to read in English because this language was not widespread in teaching curricula, and dedicated infrastructure was poor (Tribuna Şcolii, 1971; Tribuna Şcolii, 1981). During a short timeframe, between 1968 to the mid-1970s, Romania's openness to international business prompted an increase in modern foreign languages being taught in middle and high school (Giurescu, 2001) and in universities (Muzeul Universităţii Bucureşti, 2022) including French, English, Spanish and Italian. However, although the Russian language was mandatory in Romanian schools only for two decades, due to available resources such as teaching personnel and educational materials and Romania's affiliation with the Council for Mutual Economic Assistance, it continued to be widely taught (Giurescu, 2001; Institutul de Ştiinţe ale Educaţiei, 2004; Verzea, 2003). Thus, with the main foreign languages being French and Russian, most of the literature on communication and crisis communication was initially used by Romanian scholars in French. The import of knowledge and concepts in crisis communication started with Libaert (2008, 2009), Mucchielli (2008), Barus-Michel et al. (1998), and d'Humières (1993). Only some years later, academic literature in English was used, in most cases, with the English language being sometimes self-taught or improved, building on very thin bases established in secondary schools and high school. In the years that followed, as the English language became more widely used, Anglo-Saxon literature began to penetrate the field and crisis communication topics began to expand.

When discussing the development of a field and its topics, the role of translating fundamental works should not be ignored. Translations are not only about providing access to a particular literature but also (at least for a while) orienting in a particular direction or trend. Ideas, concepts, and theoretical frames are introduced in academia and amongst prospective practitioners, shaping their understanding of the domain. Translations also showcase the existing degree of awareness, access to information (that influences decisions about what authors and books to translate), networks, contacts, and the capacity to allocate resources. At the end of the 1990s and the beginning of the 2000s, several publishing houses built a name for themselves by printing translations of fundamental works and handbooks focused on social sciences. Tracking back to the 1990s, all the published works focused on communication; however, since the early 2000s, a mix of translations from French and English can be documented, with most of the titles referring to the general practice of public relations, and only a few focused on crisis communication.

Furthermore, in the initial phases of crisis communication in Romania, the first communication scholars often came from diverse academic backgrounds, such as philosophy, philology, sociology, psychology and, in certain instances, history (Anghelache et al., 2018). Consequently, the first courses in crisis communication were taught by scholars and teaching staff with no previous academic training in communication or crisis communication. The initial class materials in crisis communication heavily relied on concepts, theories, and methods from their major studies and from disciplines, authors and approaches that they were familiar with from their previous university training, such as psychology and sociology. At that time, theoretical elements like social representation and public opinion adopted from French literature grounded the first conceptualizations of crisis communication in Romania (Neculau, 1995; Zamfir & Vlăsceanu, 1993; Zlate, 1998). Following the borrowings from French literature in public relations (e.g., Barus Michel et al., 1998; Kapferer, 1993) and crisis communication (Lagadec, 1991; Lagadec, 1993; Lagadec, 1995; Libaert, 2008; Libaert, 2009), studies in English, either in original or translations (Coombs, 1999; Fearn-Banks, 1996; Pauchant, 1992; Regester & Larkin, 2003) acquired a prominent place within Romanian scholars' works.

Moreover, in the early 1990s, once multinational companies opened offices in Romania and local companies were established, for the first job positions in communication, people without previous experience or background in communication, public relations (Coman, 2008b), or advertising were hired (Barbu, 2014). Although this situation is less discussed today, there is evidence that a degree in communication, public relations, and advertising is not mandatory to work in the field even now. This idea is supported by previous studies (Buzoianu et al., 2019) and can easily be observed when looking at most of the job requirements listed on online recruiting platforms in Romania. This follows a broader trend in communication, in which a university degree in communication is still not required to become a communication professional. The reports issued by the European Communication Monitor, the largest transnational study on strategic communication, emphasize the prevalence of this practice (Zerfaß et al., 2022).

In addition, multinationals introduced jobs and roles in communication and crisis communication. Therefore, the entire workflow, framework and crisis response were structured from corporate headquarters outside Romania. In this respect, the Danone crisis of 2007 highlights several important issues related to crisis management, decision-making, and communication during an EU-wide outbreak of suspected food poisoning. The crisis was triggered in the context of a suspected food poisoning when a contaminated food additive manufactured in India reached dairy products in Europe by accident. The European Commission used the Rapid Alert System for Food and Feed to draw attention to the potential danger to all EU countries. The Romanian media exacerbated the issue, while panic and suspicion spread amongst consumers. Despite working with the authorities to identify and withdraw the suspected batches, Danone failed to address the public's concerns properly. During a more than 10-day crisis, the company issued two statements and organized a press conference (Chiciudean & David, 2011). On the one hand, the public was not accustomed to the widespread practice of product recall, and, on the other, local authorities responsible for food safety were ill-prepared to communicate publicly and to be seen cooperating with FMCG producers. In addition, Danone's local management had to wait for the response from the Paris headquarters, resulting in a significant delay in addressing the situation. When the negative results of lab tests on suspected batches were shared, the president of Danone was present at the press conference, and an image repair campaign was launched during the subsequent months. Instead of organizing an FMCG product recall, Danone's crisis response generated considerable media coverage and was transformed into a series of vivid controversies and tensions among authorities, consumers, and journalists, with a significant drop in sales during two months.

Perspectives of Risk and Crisis Communication Research in Romania

Although there is a significant number of crises going on in different sectors in Romania, dedicated academic courses, in-house and open training offered by consultants and agencies, and teams and experts working in the field, risk and crisis communication is still not a well-established discipline. Reviewing the existing studies and research in Romania (Balaban, 2013; Barbu & Cmeciu, 2019; Chiciudean & Tones, 2010; Coman, 2009a; Corbu et al., 2012; David & Chiciudean, 2016), and the current practices of risk and crisis communication (Bîră et al., 2021), shows that despite a vivid and noticeable growth of the field during the last years,

(Bârgăoanu et al., 2022; Buzoianu & Bîră, 2021; Buzoianu et al., 2022; Cmeciu et al., 2022; Corbu et al., 2021; Palade & Balaban, 2020), there is still much work to be done. While universities have offered academic courses in crisis communication for more than 20 years, and agencies have had their own crisis management departments for more than 13 years now, crisis communication is still in its infancy in Romania.

Institutional Perspective

The examination of crisis communication in Romania from an *institutional perspective* needs to consider the following four areas: (1) the set-up of the first academic programs in communication in the country after the fall of the communist regime; (2) research and publications on risk and crisis communication by the Romanian academia; (3) the development of the communication and public relations industry; (4) national framework and regulations for academic programs in communication.

Academic Programs

When talking about the origins of crisis communication studies and programs in Romania, we must consider the establishment of university programs on communication and public relations in the early 1990s (see Dobrescu, 2008; Nastasia, 2011), and the emergence of the first communication and public relations agencies. In addition, the appointment of media relations officers in multinational companies (Coman, 2008b) that began to operate in Romania following the downfall of the communist regime is key to the development of communication and crisis communication. As mentioned previously, due to constraints related to infrastructure and human resources, in the early beginning, the field of communication and crisis communication in Romania was based on imports from Western European and US epistemologies and methodologies, and practices.

In the first decade of crisis communication, the development was subject to borrowings and a multi-disciplinary approach (Coman, 2008b; Dobrescu, 2008). Although the first academic courses dedicated to risk and crisis communication were established in 1998 (Chiciudean & Tones, 2002), the first manuals and handbooks on this topic were published later. Starting in 2000, along with several other changes and developments in academic programs in communication, an increase in the number of university courses dedicated to crisis communication became noticeable. Risk and crisis management and crisis communication are constantly present in the academic curricula of communication programs for both BA and MA, but also in business management, international relations, and other fields.

Research and Academic Publications

Exploring the academic literature and research infrastructure dedicated to risk and crisis communication in Romania reveals that there is still much to be done to reach a solid development of this topic in the country. As in the case of other countries in the region (Schwarz et al., 2016), until now, Romanian scholars did not managed to produce a research tradition on crisis communication. Looking at the timeline of crisis communication research, the first books on this topic by Romanian scholars were published between 2000 and 2010 (Abrudan, 2010; Chiciudean & Țones, 2002/2010; Chifu & Ramberg, 2007; Coman, 2009a; Coman, 2009b) following the initial issues of The Romanian Journal of Communication and Public Relations, the main Romanian journal in communication. Since its launch in 1998, the journal has published several articles dedicated to the crisis, most of them tackling crises from broader perspectives, not necessarily communication and public relations.

The initial books and articles were followed by a broader set of research and publications (Chiciudean, 2012; Corbu et al., 2012; Palade & Balaban, 2020; Pop-Flanja, 2020). In most cases, the literature relies on the dominant theories of crisis communication and image repair (e.g., Coombs and Benoit) but also tackle conflicts and social crises, like protests, economic crises and political scandals (Balaban et al., 2014; Radu & Ştefăniţă, 2012; Stoica, 2012; Vincze et al., 2021). Most of the Romanian academic research only partially addresses crisis communication, with numerous studies focused on sociological analyses of crises and protests, thus creating awareness for research dedicated to conflicts rather than contributing to the development of crisis communication studies. The interdisciplinary nature of communication may not fully explain this situation. Instead, the scarce number of Ph.D. supervisors in communication and crisis communication and the limited funding opportunities and grants for research on this topic may be considered significant obstacles. In addition, the scarcity of research articles on topics related to crisis and risk communication in academic journals in Romania may be easily confirmed by a swift perusal of journal archives. For example, The Journal of Media Research (published at the Babes Bolyai University in Cluj) features only a few articles addressing crisis communication during its 15 years of existence. In addition, it also publishes a slightly higher number of papers addressing crises and conflicts from other fields, like sociology, media studies, political communication and health communication. Furthermore, according to its available online archive between 2010 and 2018, an academic journal that includes "communication sciences" in its title (The Scientific Annals of "Alexandru Ioan Cuza" University of Iasi. Communication Sciences) did not publish papers on crisis communication, risk, emergency or conflict. Instead, this journal published articles bordering philosophy and communication (Fârte 2008; Stoica, 2011).

In recent years, Romanian scholars have increasingly focused on crisis communication and its current conceptualizations (Buzoianu & Bîră, 2021; Cmeciu & Coman, 2018; Pop-Flanja, 2020), with a majority of these studies examining the impact of social media platforms in crisis escalation (Barbu & Cmeciu, 2019). However, these investigations primarily rely on crisis conceptualizations in the context of social media, such as *paracrisis* (Coombs & Holladay, 2012) or the social-mediated crisis communication model (Austin et al., 2012). Considering the evident reflexive efforts in discussing theoretical models of crisis communication, these studies could be considered a step further in the advancement of crisis communication. Moreover, an emerging topic related to crisis communication in Romania is dedicated to social media listening and its role in spotting risks and anticipating crisis and crisis response (Bîră et al., 2021; Buzoianu & Bîră, 2021).

Topics relevant to *risk and safety* are examined by Romanian scholars from disciplines outside the field of communications, such as geography and civil engineering. Some of these studies are related to discussions about plans concerning the seismic risk in Bucharest. Although local authorities and NGOs are constantly communicating on topics related to preparedness (ISUBIF, n.d.) and the collective memory has retained the 1977 earthquake in Bucharest as a traumatic event for the nation, research published on this topic is produced in domains such as civil engineering and geography, being focused on monitoring, model simulation, estimation of damage, losses, and casualties and vulnerability assessment of various areas including protected areas (Armaş & Rădulian, 2014; Florescu et al., 2014; Georgescu et al., 2014; Pavel & Văcăreanu, 2016; Ţigănescu et al., 2022). Some studies are addressing the general population's perceptions related to earthquake risks in Bucharest and factors that could influence it, (Armaş, 2006; Armaş et al., 2017) meanwhile others are concerned with low knowledge transfer and dissemination of information available to seismology and earthquake engineers towards various other stakeholders (Craifaleanu et al., 2016). However, there remains a necessity for further efforts to bridge the existing body of knowledge with authorities' preparedness, particularly in the context of risk and safety communication and/or disaster relief communication.

In Romania, crisis communication is accompanied by a low level of debate on theories and methodologies and on terminology and taxonomy. This situation follows the challenges outlined previously and is expected to last for a period of time, keeping in mind that crisis communication is currently an emerging field that will also have to accommodate the significant changes brought by digital communication and social media. In Romania, most of the conceptualizations of crisis communication refer to the crisis as a PR disaster and reputation crisis and, consequently, discuss crisis communication as a means of image repair (Chiciudean & David, 2011; Chiciudean & Tones, 2010; Coman, 2008a). The titles of the courses and crisis communication training show that, in most cases, crises are referred to as image problems or situations affecting the image of an organization. Some of the research carried out in crisis communication comes from political communication (Beciu, 2002; Corbu et al., 2017), media studies (See *The Journal of Media Research* (2008–2024) collection), and international relations (Herta & Flanja, 2021; Miculescu 2001; Pop-Flanja, 2020) and addresses crisis-related topics in the case of major events (e.g., Colectiv, COVID-19). To these, we add studies emerging from the communication field addressing social media's role in crisis escalation (Cmeciu & Coman, 2018).

Development of the Communication and Public Relations Industry

The currently limited academic and industry events dedicated to risk and crisis communication, and scarce interest in bridging academia with practitioners in crisis communication, contribute to the existing boundaries of crisis communication in Romania. Upon reviewing the programs and keynotes of events in communication and public relations, it becomes evident that crisis communication is rarely addressed and that there is low interest in tackling this topic. This is also reflected by the fact that although the Romanian PR Award, the main competition dedicated to communication and public relations in Romania, has been annually organized since 2003, it was not until 2017 that introduced a category dedicated to crisis communication and issues management. In addition, the professionalization of the field is still emerging. As previously stated, most job ads (for entry-level positions) demonstrate that a communication and public relations degree is not mandatory for related positions, with many job adverts emphasizing higher education without specifying the specialization and, for advanced roles and positions, experience is required. Despite the existence of several professional associations, their role in the development of communication and crisis communication in Romania is limited. Amongst them, IAA Romania, established in 1993 as a branch of the International Advertising Association (IQads, n.d.), is the most active and engaged in events dedicated to communication professionals, students, and scholars, with two noticeable initiatives: the *IAA School* and a CSR project, *AcademIAA*. The first initiative, the *IAA School*, comprises a series of workshops and modules dedicated to PR and advertising and targeting young professionals, students and recent graduates that aim to gain further access to the industry and expand their practical skills and their professional network. Examining the list of available modules and courses, one can notice that their main efforts go towards PR and advertising, while crisis communication has been only recently added and is framed as a digital marketing topic (Şcoala IAA, n.d.). On the other hand, AcademIAA started as a transversal partnership bridging academia and the marcom industry and has been functioning at a small pace (Academiaa, n.d.). Other organizations, with relevant activity during the 1990s and early 2000, such as the *Romanian Association of Public Relations* (ARRP) and the *PR Companies Club* (CCRP) (Coman, 2008b) have drastically reduced their involvement in growing the sector or animating meaningful events or initiatives aiming to further establish the domain during the last decade.

National Framework and Regulations for Academic Programs

In relation to the national framework and regulations for academic programs in communication, crisis communication is not included yet as a mandatory course in the curricula for communication and public relations degrees at the BA or MA level in Romania, according to the national regulatory agency for higher education institutions. There are, however, several other disciplines where themes related to crisis communication could fit in. To our knowledge, the Romanian Agency for Quality Assurance in Higher Education listed a crisis communication course only in the case of a new (since 2019) BA study program in communication and emerging media, taught in English. The course is included on a 17-discipline list that can be used by universities to choose from in accordance with their resources and educational aims. In addition, crisis communication as a distinct discipline is found under the name of crisis management in BA degrees in defense and military.

Media Perspective

Drawing on the existing literature, we notice that research on the *media perspective* on crisis communication in Romania is scarce. Although there are a few studies investigating crises from a media studies perspective (see Vincze, 2014; Vincze & Balaban, 2022), we need more analysis of the way journalists and media professionals refer to crises and crisis communication. Existing research on media and journalism in Romania (Avădani, 2017; Milewski et al., 2014) does not explore how crises are perceived and instrumentalized and the means and practices of reporting about different types of crises. The current situation can be attributed to the emerging professionalization of crisis communication in Romania and the limited resources and efforts in bridging different perspectives, such as communication and PR agencies and in-house communication departments who have experience in dealing with a crisis, a company's management protective attitude when sharing information about crisis and academia. However, it is also worth noting that crisis communication is not a compulsory subject in either undergraduate or graduate journalism programs, which could also account for the lack of attention given to this topic.

Framing theory (Corbu et al., 2017; Radu & Ştefăniţă, 2012; Vincze, 2013; Vincze, 2014), agenda setting (Buturoiu & Voloc, 2021), and thematic analysis (Vincze & Balaban, 2022) are the predominant approaches used in crisis-related research from a media perspective in Romania. These studies investigate from different standpoints and methodologies how mass media refer to crises, attribute guilt, and construct meaning in different contexts. As Vincze (2014) points out, in Romanian media, the term crisis has been used as a catchphrase, with a broad understanding and range of events and meanings. In a study exploring the salience of crisis in Romanian media in 2008–2009, Vincze (2013) showed that media created a "generalized sense of crisis," with reference to social, economic and political areas. The analysis of online media coverage of recent crises and conflicts (Balaban et al., 2022; Corbu et al., 2017; Vincze & Balaban, 2022; Vincze et al., 2021), along with studies looking to understand how crises are referred to on social media platforms (Barbu & Cmeciu, 2019; Bârgăoanu & Durach, 2020; Buzoianu & Bîră, 2021; Corbu et al., 2022), show the prevalence of several meta-narratives related to crises, like anti-establishment (both political and economic) or the lack of trust in state institutions, experts and corporations (Eurocomunicare, 2020).

Audience Perspective

Given the current lack of research explicitly investigating the perspective of the Romanian *audience* with regard to crisis and crisis communication, we examine extant studies that explore audience-related viewpoints by analyzing representations during crises (Eurocomunicare, 2020; Eurocomunicare, 2022; Stanciu et al., 2020), predictors of trust and media consumption (Bârgăoanu et al., 2022; Mureşan et al., 2021). The results emerging from current research are in line with the above-mentioned meta-narratives. They point to consistent anti-establishment attitudes and expressed opinions as outcomes of low levels of trust in public institutions (both national and European), experts and media among the Romanian public. Two surveys (Eurocomunicare, 2020) conducted during the COVID-19 pandemic (March 2020 and October 2020) show a decrease in trust levels in the crisis context. This should be linked to the emergence of conspiracy myths, disinformation and information pollution. It has been reported (Bârgăoanu & Durach, 2020) that throughout the COVID-19 pandemic in Romania, disinformation narratives included anti-establishment rhetoric that depicted political leaders as malevolent figures scheming for personal gain. One of the earliest conspiracy theories to emerge claimed that the virus had been intentionally engineered to establish a new global order, either under US or Chinese leadership, or to benefit the Deep State. Other disinformation narratives implicated the political elite (both at the European and national levels) or the economic sector (particularly Big Pharma) in schemes involving mandatory vaccination, surveillance and control measures such as enforced lockdowns and implanted microchips, and even population control intended to eliminate the elderly, impoverished, or vulnerable members of society (Eurocomunicare, 2022). Furthermore, upon examining stakeholders' reactions during April and May of 2020, when two important private hospitals faced resentment and criticism, we observed a similar trend and narratives (Buzoianu & Bîră, 2021).

Concerning media consumption and information seeking and vetting, data emerging from a survey conducted in 2021 (*Eurocomunicare,* 2022) in the context of the COVID-19 pandemic report that there is an increased risk of dilettantism among the Romanian public as they tend to seek information from family and friends instead of experts. Relying on personal experience, seeking information from personal contacts, and checking opinion leaders' standpoints on some issues describe Romanians' most frequent information-seeking and vetting behavior in crises. The survey points out that although Romanians have relatively low trust in information obtained through social media, they continue to access Facebook as their primary source of information. Earlier studies (Eurocomunicare, 2020) conducted at the onset of the COVID-19 pandemic indicated comparable media consumption trends, with social media serving as the most frequently accessed source of information on a daily basis, followed by traditional media platforms such as television, radio, and print.

Conclusion

Following the gradual institutionalization and professionalization of public relations and communication in Romania, crisis communication has been introduced as a niche specialization within the broader domain of communication, PR, and advertising. Academic courses and various specialized workshops and modules delivered by professionals within the industry on risk and crisis communication topics are an established part of PR foundational teaching and training. Nevertheless, their position is heavily influenced by crisis communication being an emerging field, despite significant advances during the last decade. With opportunities for development being few and context-based, risk and crisis communication research continues to demand a significant amount of work to broaden its reach. This includes efforts to answer challenges from the digital transition and social media landscape, to further incorporate debates on crisis conceptualization, and to become an integrated part of risk and crisis communication domain.

References

Abrudan, M. (2010). *Criza şi media. Criza economică şi reflectarea ei în mass-media. [The Economic Crisis and How it is Reflected by the Media].* Tritonic.

Academiaa (n.d.). *Despre Academiaa* [About us]. Retrieved March 25, 2023 from https://academiaa.ro/

Anghelache, C., Petrescu, I., Anghel, M. G., & Gogu, E. (2018). *Evoluția centenară a învățământului în România. [100 years of education in Romania]*. Economică.

Armaş, I. (2006). Earthquake risk perception in Bucharest, Romania. *Risk Analysis, 26*(5), 1223–1234.

Armaş, I., & Rădulian, M. (2014). Spatial multi-criteria risk assessment of earthquakes from Bucharest, Romania. In M. Bostenaru Dan, I. Armaş, & A. Goretti, Eds., *Earthquake Hazard Impact and Urban Planning* (pp. 127–149). Springer. https://doi.org/10.1007/978-94-007-7981-5_7

Armaş, I., Cretu, R. Z., & Ionescu, R. (2017). Self-efficacy, stress, and locus of control: The psychology of earthquake risk perception in Bucharest, Romania. *International Journal of Disaster Risk Reduction, 22*, 71–76.

Austin, L., Fisher Liu, B., & Jin, Y. (2012). How audiences seek out crisis information: Exploring the social-mediated crisis communication model. *Journal of Applied Communication Research, 40*(2), 188–207.

Avădani, I. (2017). Of journalists and money: The employment of journalists in Romania and its influence on media freedom and quality. *International Journal of Communication, 11*(19328036), 23.

Balaban, D. C., Iancu, I., & Mucundorfeanu, M. (2014). Framing Obama's re-election. A comparative analysis of German, French and Romanian media coverage. *Romanian Journal of Communication & Public Relations, 16*(2), 75.

Balaban, D. C., Mucundorfeanu, M., & Naderer, B. (2022). The role of trustworthiness in social media influencer advertising: Investigating users' appreciation of advertising transparency and its effects. *Communications, 47*(3), 395–421.

Balaban, D. C. (2013). Development of communication science in Romania. Challenges and perspectives. *Professional Communication and Translation Studies, 6*, 1–2.

Barbu, P. (2014). *Primul an de publicitate. [The First Year of Advertising]*. Bucureşti: Tandem Media.

Barbu, R., & Cmeciu, C. (2019). Crisis communication in Romania and social media influencers and followers. Case study: Patient's death at the Sanador hospital. *Journal of Media Research, 12*(3), 5–17.

Bardan, A. (2001). *Marketing politic în România înainte şi după 1989 [Political Marketing in Romania Before and After 1989]*. Bucureşti: Tritonic.

Bârgăoanu, A., & Durach, F. (2020). The COVID-19 infodemic–an accelerated version of the new digital ecosystem. *Romanian Journal of Communication and Public Relations, 22*(2), 125–129.

Bârgăoanu, A., Corbu, N., Buturoiu, R., & Durach, F. (2022). Managing the COVID-19 pandemic: Predictors of trust in institutions in Romania. *Kybernetes, 51*(7), 2398–2415.

Barus-Michel, J., Giust-Desprairies, F., & Ridel, L. (1998). *Crize: abordare psihosocială clinică [original title in French: Crises: approche psychosociale clinique]*. Iaşi: Polirom.

Beciu, C. (2002). *Comunicare politică [Political Communication]*. Bucureşti: Comunicare.ro.

Berend, I. T. (2009). *From the Soviet bloc to the European Union: The Economic and Social Transformation of Central and Eastern Europe since 1973*. Cambridge University Press.

Bîră, M., Stroe, L., Buzoianu, C., & Răducu, R. (2021). Hearing out your audiences: Models, means, and practices for social media listening. In C. Brătianu, A. Zbuchea, F. Anghel, & B. Hrib, Eds., *Strategica International Academic Conference. Shaping the Future of Business and Economy* (pp. 328–336). Tritonic. https://strategica-conference.ro/wp-content/uploads/2022/04/25-2.pdf

Buturoiu, D. R., & Voloc, A. (2021). Media coverage in times of crisis. Intermedia agenda-setting of COVID-19–related topics. *Romanian Journal of Communication and Public Relations, 23*(2), 7–22.

Buzoianu, C., Bîră, M., & Duduciuc, A. (2019). Building a discipline. The setup of communication as an academic discipline in Romania. *Studies and Scientific Researches. Economics Edition, 30*, 14–22.

Buzoianu, C., & Bîră, M. (2021). Using social media listening in crisis communication and management: New methods and practices for looking into crises. *Sustainability, 13*(23), 13015.

Buzoianu, C., Bîră, M., Rădudu, R., & Stroe, L. (2022). *Branduri în conversații. Instrumente de monitorizare şi analiză pentru relațiile publice online [Brands in Conversations. Monitoring and Analysis Tools for Online Public Relations]*. Bucureşti: Comunicare.ro.

Craifaleanu, I. G., Georgescu, E. S., & Dragomir, C. S. (2016). Lessons from M 7.2 seismic event and how to preserve awareness forty years later: The case of the Vrancea, Romania, March 4, 1977 Earthquake. *IOP Conference Series: Earth and Environmental Science* (Vol. 44, No. 4, p. 042043). IOP Publishing.

Chiciudean, I., & Ţoneş, V. (2002). *Gestionarea crizelor de imagine. [Image Crisis Management].* Comunicare.ro.

Chiciudean, I., & Ţoneş, V. (2010). *Gestionarea crizelor de imagine. [Image Crisis Management].* Comunicare.ro.

Chiciudean, I. (2012). Development of crisis communication content. In N. In Corbu, L. Becker, R. Pricopie, & T. Vlad, Eds., *Crisis Communication. Professional and Academic Perspectives.* Comunicare.ro.

Chiciudean, I., & David, G. (2011). *Managementul comunicării în situaţii de criză [Crisis Communication].* Comunicare.ro.

Chifu, J., & Ramberg, B. (Eds.). (2007). *Crisis Management in Transitional Societies: The Romanian Experience.* Crisis Management Europe Research Program, Volume 33. Sweedish National Defence College: CRISMART.

Cmeciu, C., & Coman, I. (2018). Twitter as a means of emotional coping and collective (re) framing of crises. Case study: The Collective crisis in Romania. *Social Communication, 4*(2), 6–15.

Cmeciu, C., Anton, A., & Nicola, A. (2022). Information-seeking behaviour and governmental communication assessment during the COVID-19 pandemic in Romania. In R. Tench, J. Meng, & Á. Moreno, Eds., *Strategic Communication in a Global Crisis* (pp. 282–302). Routledge.

Coman, C. (2008a). Comunicarea de criză şi strategiile de restaurare a imaginii [Crisis communication and image restoration strategies]. *Revista Română de Jurnalism şi Comunicare, [Romanian Journal of Journalism and Communication], 3*(4), 30.

Coman, C. (2008b). Instituţionalizare şi profesionalizare în relaţiile publice din România. [Institutionalisation and profesionalisation of public relations in Romania]. *Revista Română de Comunicare şi Relaţii Publice. [Romanian Journal of Communication and Public Relations], 12*, 83–98.

Coman, C. (2009a). *Comunicarea de criză: tehnici şi strategii [Crisis Communication: Techniques and Strategies].* Iaşi: Polirom.

Coman, C. (2009b). *Relaţiile publice: modele teoretice şi studii de caz [Public Relations: Theoretical Models and Case Studies].* Bucureşti: Editura Universităţii din Bucureşti.

Coombs, W. T., & Holladay, J. S. (2012). The paracrisis: The challenges created by publicly managing crisis prevention. *Public Relations Review, 38*(3), 408–415.

Coombs, W. T. (1999). *Ongoing Crisis Communications.* Thousand Oaks, California: Sage Publications Inc.

Corbu, N., Becker, L., Pricopie, R., & Vlad, T. (2012). *Crisis Communication. Professional and Academic Perspectives.* Comunicare.ro.

Corbu, N., Buturoiu, R., & Durach, F. (2017). Framing the refugee crisis in online media: A Romanian perspective. *Romanian Journal of Communication and Public Relations, 19*(2), 5–18.

Corbu, N., Negrea-Busuioc, E., Udrea, G., & Radu, L. (2021). Romanians' willingness to comply with restrictive measures during the COVID-19 pandemic: Evidence from an online survey. *Journal of Applied Communication Research, 49*(4), 369–386.

Corbu, N., Bârgăoanu, A., Durach, F., & Ştefăniţă, O. (2022). Predictors of engagement on social media and instant messaging platforms during the COVID-19 pandemic: Evidence from Romania. *Romanian Journal of Communication and Public Relations, 24*(3), 7–23.

d'Humières, P. (1993). *Management de la communication d'entreprise.* Paris: Editions Eyrolles.

David, G., & Chiciudean, I. (2016). Golden reputation wanted for a gold producer. The case of the Rosia Montana gold corporation. *Romanian Journal of Communication and Public Relations, 16*(3), 89–104.

Dobrescu, P. (2008). 18 ani de comunicare [18 years of communication]. *Revista Română de Comunicare şi Relaţii Publice [Romanian Journal of Communication and Public Relations], 14*, 9–18.

Eurocomunicare (2020). Public perception about covid-19 vaccination in Romania. *Public opinion survey (2022, October).* Retrieved March 25, 2023, from https://www.eurocomunicare.ro/wp-content/uploads/2020/11/EN_Research-study-vaccination_final.pdf

Eurocomunicare (2022). *Disinformation societal resilience and Covid-19 (2022; May).* Retrieved March 25, 2023, from https://www.eurocomunicare.ro/wp-content/uploads/2022/05/DISINFORMATION-SOCIETAL-RESILIENCE-AND-COVID19_Report-FINAL-1.pdf. Publication supported by NATO Public Diplomacy Division

Fârte, G. I. (2008). How can we evaluate public relations activities? *The Scientific Annals of "Alexandru Ioan Cuza" University of Iasi. Communication Sciences, 1*(1), 37–48.

Fearn-Banks, K. (1996). *Crisis Communication: A Casebook Approach.* New Jersey: Lawrence Erlbaum.

Florescu, T., Moscu, C. I., Gociman, C. O., Georgescu, M. S., Dragomir, C. S., Craifaleanu, C. S., & Georgescu, E. S. (2014). Urban heritage and multi-hazard threats. Case study of seismic vulnerability assessment and mapping in a protected area of Bucharest, Romania. *Proceedings the 1st Huixian International Forum on Earthquake Engineering for Young Researchers.*

Gavril, C. (2007). 1998–1999 Miners' Crisis. In J. Chifu, & B. Ramberg, Eds., *Crisis Management in Transitional Societies: The Romanian Experience.* Crisis Management Europe Research Program, Volume 33. Sweedish National Defence College: CRISMART.

Georgescu, E. S., Craifaleanu, I. G., Gociman, C. O., Florescu, T., Moscu, C., & Georgescu, M. S. (2014). Tools for assessment, mapping and risk mitigation in urban fabrics in the aftermath of March 4, 1977 Vrancea earthquake. *Proceedings of the Fifth National Conference on Earthquake Engineering and First National Conference on Earthquake Engineering and Seismology–5CNIS & 1CNISS, Bucharest, Romania* (pp. 403–409).

Giurescu, D. C. (2001). *Învăţământul din România între 1948 şi 1989. [The education and training in Romania between 1948 and 1989].* Retrieved March 2023 from: https://www.ucv.ro/pdf/international/informatii_generale/doctor_honoris/68.pdf

Herta, L. M., & Pop-Flanja, D. (2021). Public Perception on the Western Balkan States' accession to the EU. Social-constructivist interpretations. *Studia Universitatis Babes-Bolyai. Studia Europaea, 66*(2), 135–161.

Institutul de Ştiinţe ale Educaţiei [Institute of Education Sciences] (2004). *Antologia legilor învăţământului din România. [The Anthology of Laws on Education in Romania].* Bucureşti: Institutul de Ştiinţe ale Educaţiei [Institute of Education Sciences].

IQads (n.d.). *IAA Romania.* Retrieved March 25, 2023, from https://www.iqads.ro/catalog/13305/iaa-romania

ISUBIF (n.d.). *Campanie naţională de informare şi pregătire a populaţiei. Inspectoratul pentru situaţii de urgenţă Bucureşti* – Ilfov. [Information and preparedness national campaign]. https://isubif.ro/local/campania-nu-tremur-la-cutremur/ (accessed March 25, 2023).

Kapferer, J. N. (1993). *Zvonurile: cel mai vechi mijloc de comunicare din lume.* Humanitas.

Lagadec, P. (1991). *La gestion des crises. Outils de réflexion à l'usage des décideurs.* Paris: McGraw-Hill.

Lagadec, P. (1993). *Apprendre à gérer les crises.* Paris: Editions d'organisation.

Lagadec, P. (1995). *Cellules de crise.* Paris: Editions d'organisation.

Libaert, T. (2008). *Comunicarea de criză.* C. H. Beck.

Libaert, T. (2009). *Planul de comunicare: cum să-ţi defineşti şi să-ţi organizezi strategia de comunicare [original title in French: Le plan de communication: définir et organiser votre stratégie de communication].* Polirom.

Mureşan, R., Sălcudean, M., & Pintea, A. (2021). Information and news consumption. Perception on the communication of authorities and journalists during the covid-19 pandemic. *Postmodern Openings, 12*(4), 104–123.

Miculescu, S.-M. (2001). *Relaţii publice internaţionale în contextul globalizării. [International Public Relations in a Global Context].* Comunicare.ro.

Milewski, N., Barczyszyn, P., & Lauk, E. (2014). Three countries, one profession: The journalism cultures in Poland, Romania and Moldova. *Journalism that Matters. Views from Central and Eastern Europe. Frankfurt am Main–Bern–Bruxelles–New York–Oxford–Warsawa–Wien: Peter Lang, 2,* 97–114.

Pauchant, T. (1992). *Transforming the Crisis-Prone Organizations; Preventing Individual, Organizational and Environmental Tragedies.* San Francisco, California: Jossey-Bass.

Mucchielli, A. (2008). *Comunicarea in institutii si organizatii [Communication in Institutions and Organisations].* Polirom.

Museum Universităţii Bucureşti (2022). Învăţământul superior de limbi străine [Higher education in foreign languages. Digital exhibition. Ideas and sources for a history of higher education in Romania]. *Laboratorul de surse şi idei pentru istoria universitară,* Expoziţia digitală.

Nastasia, S. (2011). A cross-country comparison of public relations practices employing critical theories and mixed methods. *Revista Română de Comunicare şi Relaţii Publice [Romanian Journal of Communication and Public Relations], 13*(3), 7–20.

Neculau, A. (Ed.). (1995). *Psihologia câmpului social: Reprezentările sociale [Social Psichology: Social Representations]*. Bucureşti: Editura Societate Ştiinţă şi Tehnică S.A.

Palade, I., & Balaban, D. C. (2020). An analysis of COVID-19-related fake news from Romania. A pilot qualitative study. *Journal of Media Research, 13*(2), 27–43.

Pavel, F., & Vacareanu, R. (2016). Scenario-based earthquake risk assessment for Bucharest, Romania. *International Journal of Disaster Risk Reduction, 20*, 138–144.

Pop-Flanja, D. (2020). Cross-cultural differences in risk perception and risk communication. A case study on the COVID-19 outbreak. *Redefining Community in Intercultural Context, 9*(1), 68–74.

Pripp, C. (2002). *Marketingul politic [Political Marketing]*. Nemira.

Radu, L., & Ştefăniţă, O. (2012). Framing the economic crisis in the Romanian online media. *Romanian Journal of Communication & Public Relations, 14*(2), 29–48.

Regester, M., & Larkin, J. (2003). *Managementul crizelor şi al situaţiilor de risc*. Comunicare.ro.

Schwarz, A., Seeger, M. W., & Auer, C. (Eds.). (2016). *The Handbook of International Crisis Communication Research*. John Wiley & Sons.

Şcoala IAA (n.d.). *Scoala IAA*. Retrieved from: https://www.scoalaiaa.ro/v1/cursuri/modulul-digital/#ceinveti (accessed March 15, 2023).

Stanciu, S., Radu, R. I., Sapira, V., Bratoveanu, B. D., & Florea, A. M. (2020). Consumer behavior in crisis situations. Research on the effects of COVID-19 in Romania. *Annals of the University Dunărea de Jos of Galati: Fascicle: I, Economics & Applied Informatics, 26*(1), p. 5–13.

Stoica, C. A. (2012). Faţetele multiple ale nemulţumirii populare: o schiţă sociologică a protestelor din Piaţa Universităţii din ianuarie 2012. [Multiple facets of social discontent: A sociological approach of January 2012 protests in Piaţa Universităţii protests]. *Romanian Sociology [Sociologie Româneasca], 10*(1), 6–13.

Stoica, D. (2011). Despre dificultatea construirii unui model global al comunicării [On the difficulty of building a global model of communication]. *The Scientific Annals of "Alexandru Ioan Cuza" University of Iasi. Communication Sciences, 4*(1), 7–28.

Stoiciu, A. (2000). *Comunicarea politică. Cum se vând idei şi oameni. [Political Communication. How to Sell Ideas and People*. Libra.

Teodorescu, B., Guţu, D., & Enache, R. (2005). *Cea mai bună dintre lumile posibile. Marketingul politic în România – 1990-2005 [The Best Possible World. Political Marketing in Romania – 1990-2005]*. Comunicare.ro.

Tiganescu, A., Craifaleanu, I. G., Aldea, A., Grecu, B., Vacareanu, R., Toma-Danila, D., & Dragomir, C. S. (2022). Evolution, recent progress and perspectives of the seismic monitoring of building structures in Romania. *Frontiers in Earth Science, 10*, 819153.

Tribuna Şcolii [The School Magazine] (1971). Ministerul Educaţiei şi Învăţământului & Uniunea Sindicatelor din Învăţământ şi Cultură. Tribuna Şcolii, 1971 [The Ministry of Education & The Unions in Education and Culture. *The School Magazine]*. 1971.

Tribuna Şcolii [The School Magazine] (1981). Ministerul Educaţiei şi Învăţământului & Uniunea Sindicatelor din Învăţământ Şi Cultură. Tribuna Şcolii, 1981 [The Ministry of Education & The Unions in Education and Culture. *The School Magazine]*. 1871.

Verzea, M. (2003). Desovietizarea culturii româneşti la începutul deceniului şapte [Desovietisation of Romanian culture during the 1970's]. *Arhivele totalitarismului, [The Archives of Totalitarianism], 11*(40–41), 3–4.

Vincze, H. O., & Balaban, D. C. (2022). Between conflict and solidarity: Pandemic media coverage of Romanian intra-EU labour migrants. *Media and Communication, 10*(2), 265–275.

Vincze, H. O., Meza, R., & Balaban, D. C. (2021). Frame variation in the news coverage of the refugee crisis: The Romanian perspective. *East European Politics and Societies, 35*(1), 113–135.

Vincze, H. O. (2014). 'The Crisis' as a journalistic frame in Romanian news media. *European Journal of Communication, 29*(5), 567–582.

Vincze, H. O. (2013). The salience of crisis in Romanian news media. *Studia Universitatis Babes-Bolyai-Ephemerides, 58*(1), 145–154.

Voinea, M., & Delcea, C. (August 8, 2015a). *Interviu: Povestea venirii McDonald's în România: "16.000 de oameni au spart geamurile la deschidere", Adevărul, [Interview: The story of McDonald's coming to Romania – 16.000 people, broken windows at the opening. The Truth]*. https://adevarul.ro/stiri-interne/societate/interviu-povestea-venirii-mcdonalds-in-romania-1647888.html (accessed March 15, 2023).

Voinea, M., & Delcea, C. (August 26, 2015b). *Povestea omului care a transformat Cico în Coca-Cola. "M-am consultat cu nevasta şi le-am scris americanilor o scrisoare". Adevărul. [The story of the man who transformed Cico in Coca Cola: I talked to my wife and we wrote a letter to the Americans". The Truth].* https://adevarul.ro/stiri-interne/societate/povestea-omului-care-a-transformat-cico-in-1646834.html (accessed March 15, 2023).

Voinea, M. (June 6, 2013). Anii '90 şi apogeul sucurilor la dozator. Firma TEC susţinea că „E-urile "fac bine: Consumul regulat reduce riscul de boli cardio-vasculare". *Adevărul. [The 90's and the highlight of soda dispenser. TEC claimed that E-s are beneficial to one's health: "Regularly intake reduces the risk of cardio-vascular diseases". The Truth].* https://adevarul.ro/stiri-interne/societate/anii-90-si-apogeul-sucurilor-la-dozator-firma-1451075.html (accessed March 15, 2023).

Voinea, M., & Delcea, C. (April 25, 2015c), ANII '90. Cum a schimbat America faţa României. Milioane de dolari pentru ONG-uri, televiziuni, sindicate şi mişcări politice. *Adevărul. [*The 90's. How America changed the look of Romania. Milions of dollars for NGOs, televisions, unions and political movements. *The Truth].* https://adevarul.ro/stiri-interne/societate/anii-90-cum-a-schimbat-america-fata-romaniei-1617643.html (accessed March 15, 2023).

Zamfir, C., & Vlăsceanu, L. (1993). *Dicţionar de sociologie [Disctionary of sociology].* Babel.

Zerfaß, A., Tench, R., Verčič, D., Moreno, A., & Buhmann, A. (2022). European communication monitor. In *Exploring Diversity and Empathic Leadership, CommTech and Consulting in Communications. Results of a Survey in 43 Countries.* Brussels: EUPRERA/EACD. https://www.communicationmonitor.eu/2022/07/07/ecm-european-communication-monitor-2022/ (accessed March 15, 2023)

Zlate, M. (1998). *Psihologia mecanismelor cognitive [Psichology of Cognitive Mechanisms].* Polirom.

Author's Bio

Corina Buzoianu, PhD, is currently an associate professor at SNSPA, Romania, teaching crisis communication in social media. For the past 11 years, Corina Buzoianu has engaged in qualitative research within the realm of communication and crisis communication, collaborating with teams at both national and international levels. Currently, she focuses on crisis communication in online platforms and social media listening. Before joining academia, Corina Buzoianu was a PR consultant and in-house communication specialist.

Monica Bîră, PhD, is currently an associate professor at SNSPA, Romania, teaching social media listening methods and techniques and PR measurement. In the last eight years, Monica has engaged in projects on monitoring online environments and analyzing data emerging from different media platforms. She is currently working closely with agencies and companies, developing media monitoring and social media listening tools and techniques in an approach that aims to bridge academic research and practices in the field of social media listening.

Alina Bargaoanu, PhD, is a Romanian communication scholar with a strong interest in disinformation, media and information literacy, government communications, and the impact of technology on democracy; member of the Advisory Board of European Digital Media Observatory (EDMO) and of EDMO's taskforce on the war in Ukraine; Marcin Król Fellow at Visegrad Insight; visiting fellow at Minda de Gunzburg Center for European Studies at Harvard University; member of the High-Level Expert Group on Fake News and Online Disinformation (EC); she has published extensively on the topics of disinformation, cognitive warfare, visualization mechanisms on social media, trust in institutions.

36

Crisis and Risk Communication Research in Eastern Europe

Katerina Tsetsura[1], Marta N. Lukacovic[2], and Iuliia Dolmatova[1]

[1] Gaylord College of Journalism and Mass Communication, University of Oklahoma, Norman, OK, USA

[2] Department of Communication and Mass Media, Angelo State University, San Angelo, TX, USA

Main Regional Trends in Crisis and Risk Communication

This chapter presents an overview of the crisis communication research in the region broadly identified as Eastern Europe. In this chapter, we focus on describing the trends and issues in research centered around crisis communication to demonstrate the breadth and depth of research completed in a number of countries in this region over the past decade. Much of the crisis communication research in the region is driven largely by two factors: (1) the Western/U.S. influence on crisis communication research theory and practice and (2) unique ways that highlight a multidisciplinary nature of approaches to studying crisis communication in Eastern Europe.

Much of the U.S.-driven crisis communication research was adopted over the years by multiple scholars from the region who studied at Western and/or U.S. universities and/or collaborated with researchers who had Western training. Additionally, many crisis communication researchers from this region started their scholarly journeys outside the field of communication per se, and thus the influence of interdisciplinary approaches and a comprehensive understanding of the importance of applied research to solve challenges prevails among scholars to this day.

In what follows, we present a review of the literature published on crisis communication, broadly defined, over the past decade. Due to the limitations of the authors of this chapter to read the research published only in five languages, Czech, English, Russian, Slovak, and Ukrainian, we do not claim to present a comprehensive review of the crisis communication literature of the region. Because of the linguistic limitations (after all, the region we are attempting to cover here has people who speak more than 40 languages), we might have well missed identifying a thriving crisis communication literature in a particular country, written in one specific language not accessible to the authors. Simply put, we do not know what we do

The Handbook of International Crisis and Risk Communication Research, Second Edition.
Edited by Andreas Schwarz, Matthew W. Seeger, and Sora Kim.

not know. However, because English is a dominant language for international and global academic research, with the vast majority of leading communication and similar academic journals published in English, and major international communication conferences (such as ICA) using English as the working language, we feel confident that we can capture some, if not all, major trends in crisis communication research in Eastern Europe.

So rather than thinking about this chapter as a catch-all database of crisis communication research, we see it as a gateway to familiarize readers with the research on the topic in this region. We also share observations of how crisis communication scholars from the region influenced one another and what commonalities and trends arise from scholars' interests, based on the geographical areas and clusters.

The chapter is structured in the following way: first, we will provide some context to better understand contemporary crisis communication studies in the region. Next, we present crisis communication literature by several geographical clusters within the region. We offer the literature review that is organized into two main clusters: (1) Ukraine and the Baltic countries of Latvia, Lithuania, and Estonia, and (2) the V4 countries: Czech Republic (or Czechia), Hungary, Poland, and Slovakia. Finally, we share our reflections on trends and issues relevant to crisis communication in the region and propose ideas for future studies on the topic.

Context of Crisis Communication Studies

The literature originating in various countries of Eastern Europe comprises identifiable general trends in terms of *context*, which allowed us to organize our findings into corresponding contextual categories: (1) Crisis communication theory and discourse; (2) Historical and cultural perspective; (3) Media perspectives; (4) Institutional perspectives; (5) Professional/applied strategic communication perspectives; and (6) Audience perspectives. Within these categories, a wider array of separate *topics* surfaces, which we further discuss in dedicated sections and break down into several tables for each major geographic cluster that we cover. The main areas that are covered include societal, political, and business/commercial risk and crisis communication.

Eastern European crisis communication research is strongly driven by distinct large crises specific to the region or the particular country. Overall, a region-specific theory development is rare, with the exception of Russia. We also notice a more pronounced emphasis on illuminating particular instances elsewhere: for instance, a large portion of the contemporary V4 countries' studies explores the migration/refugee crisis in Europe. It also is apparent that an atypical and massive crisis event like the COVID-19 pandemic stimulated an exponential growth of the crisis communication literature, particularly in the V4 countries, but also in the reviewed Balkan countries. Even though crisis communication is rarely identified as a coherent sub-field in Eastern Europe – and it is not institutionalized in the region as of today – our review illustrates that some general observations, conclusions, implications, and predictions about future tendencies can be extracted.

Ukraine and the Baltic Countries

This subsection summarizes the recent studies on crisis communication and management in Ukraine and the countries in the Baltic region (Estonia, Latvia, Lithuania). It is meaningful to look at these countries due to the historical legacy and cultural peculiarities they share (Jaakkola, 2020; Poissonnier, 2017). The studies are organized thematically and by the country or the region. The examination of the crisis communication literature in the selected countries helped identify major research themes, including crisis communication theory and discourse, cultural/historical perspective, the role of mass media, the influence of the state government, and the audience perspective.

The research published by major researchers of the topic in local universities and by U.S.- based researchers is examined. One thing to note is that scholars studying crisis communication in selected countries heavily adopt and build upon Western frameworks and theories on crisis communication. The crisis communication literature in the discussed countries also has a clear focus on the governmental role in handling various crises, be it direct management of the situations or the state influence on media framing or the actions of the crowd (Akimovich, 2018; Asmolov, 2020; Bilokonenko, 2021; Kumar & Baglay, 2021; Samoilenko, 2016; Struberga & Ozoliņa, 2022; etc.). Additionally, in recent years, there was more emphasis on communication during the COVID-19 pandemic (Bilokonenko, 2021; Kumar & Baglay, 2021; Patel et al. 2020; Rožukalne et al., 2022; Struberga & Ozoliņa, 2022).

Ukraine

Kushnir and Izhutova (2020) discussed crisis communication policies implemented by the Ministry of Defense of Ukraine in response to Russian information aggression against Ukraine between 2016 and 2018. The researchers noted that the specialists at the Ukrainian Ministry of Defense are skilled in crisis management due to years of experience in managing Russian aggression. They further analyzed existing documents on crisis communication response. The documents, such as the Draft of Strategic Communications Doctrine of the Armed Forces of Ukraine and the Instruction on the Organization of Crisis Communications, provided sequential steps that need to be taken following the crisis emergence. For example, according to the Instruction on the Organization of Crisis Communications, the first comment on the crisis should be provided an hour after the crisis announcement and report to the Ministry. The authors also offered a set of recommendations for enhancing the official crisis response system in the country (Kushnir & Izhutova, 2020). Bilokonenko (2021) conducted a sociolinguistic analysis of the statements on the COVID-19 pandemic given by Ukraine's President Volodymyr Zelenskyi. Overall, in his speeches, the President demonstrated confidence and compassion, and appeals to national values and symbols that communicate the hope for victory over the pandemic.

Patel et al. (2020) examined disinformation surrounding the health communication crisis in Ukraine during the COVID-19 pandemic. They found evidence of disinformation campaigns, primarily conducted by Russia or Russian-backed parties, that undermined trust in the accuracy of official COVID-19 messaging and misleading about the availability of COVID-related resources. Based on the evidence, recommendations for tackling the disinformation issue were provided. See Table 36.1 for the tendencies in the Ukraine-focused literature.

Table 36.1 Crisis communication perspectives in Ukraine.

Context	*Topic*	*Key takeaways*
Institutional perspective	The Ministry of Defense of Ukraine Crisis Communications in Response to Russian Aggression	• The current crisis communication of the Armed Forces of Ukraine in response to the Russian information aggression against Ukraine in 2016–2018 and further recommendations on countering the aggression (Kushnir & Izhutova, 2020)
	Crisis Communication of the President of Ukraine during COVID-19	• Sociolinguistic features of V. Zelenskyy's statements on counteracting COVID-19 (Bilokonenko, 2021).
	Healthcare Disinformation during COVID-19 Crisis	• Disinformation landscape on health crisis Communication During the global pandemic (Patel et al., 2020).

The latest active phase of the war in Ukraine that Russia started on February 24, 2022, has accelerated tremendously the demand for crisis communication practices in Ukraine. However, due to the ongoing war as we wrote this chapter, much of the academic research in Ukraine, including the crisis communication research, is on hold. Ukrainian communication researchers are actively pursuing applied research that can help to bring the country closer to victory. Special attention is currently given to studies of countering mis- and disinformation in times of war and the psychological effects of war (as an extreme type of crisis) on the population. Additionally, many non-Ukrainian scholars from the region and beyond are currently investigating various aspects of crisis communication practices of Ukraine and Ukrainians, with a few studies starting to appear in academic journals (Boatwright & Pyle, 2023; Tasente, 2023) or as presentations at the international research conferences (e.g., research panel presentations and roundtable discussions at PRSA, NCA, and ICA conferences in 2022–2023). As time progresses, crisis communication research will continue to expand its presence within the field of communications studies in Ukraine.

Baltic Countries

Historical and Cultural Perspective

As defined by Harro-Loit et al. (2012), cultural experience of crisis (CEC) is "the synthesis of mediated crisis experiences, media and fictional narratives, collective memories of societal disasters, conversations, and immediate crisis experiences of witnesses and victims" (p. 26). Based on qualitative analysis of interviews and focus groups conducted in Estonia, the authors propose a CEC model with four dimensions of cultural experience of crisis: proximity versus distance and knowledge vs. emotions. This model is elaborated based on the Estonian study about the perceptions of the nuclear-pollution crisis messaging. The study highlights the differences in the reception of crisis messages depending on the cultural context and different experience spheres.

Overall, the interest in historical and cultural perspectives on crisis and risk communication in Baltic countries has been closely related to these countries' common history and legacy (Jaakkola, 2020). As countries have been under the Soviet regime for a big part of the twentieth century, the current communication research addresses various aspects of how the post-Soviet structures affect crisis and risk communications in these countries today.

Institutional Perspective

Struberga and Ozoliņa (2022) examined whether Latvian officials' messaging in response to COVID-19 was effective in reaching all social groups, including a Russian-speaking community. Focus groups were conducted to assess the public perception of the Latvian governmental communication. Overall, communication with the Latvian officials was less effective in reaching Russian-language speakers, which led to vaccination resistance, deeper distrust in the government, and the feeling of isolation. This research demonstrated the importance of inclusion in governmental crisis communication, especially for a multicultural society such as Latvia.

Alas et al. (2010) investigated crisis management implementation and strategies in two countries that were under the communist regime – Estonia and China. Estonian organizations had the biggest share of human resource (HR) crises while the majority of Chinese crises were related to reputation and economics. The most important stakeholders in both countries were employees. Chinese organizations were less prepared for managing crises beforehand and used a more authoritarian approach. However, most companies in both Estonia and China use reactive strategies to address crises. Lastly, a triangular model for crisis management is proposed and further recommendations to Chinese and Estonian companies are provided.

The case-based study by Šontaitė-Petkevičienė (2014) analyzed the crisis response of the retail chain "Maxima" operating in Lithuania, Latvia, Estonia, and Bulgaria. The chain dealt with a human-error accident, in which the roof of the store in the western part of Riga collapsed killing 54 people and injuring dozens of others. The authors analyzed the crisis from the corporate reputation perspective, building their analysis on Coombs' SCCT. The researchers found that although the retail chain made several mistakes in its communication responses in the aftermath of the collapse (e.g., inconsistent messaging), overall, it managed the crisis properly. Most importantly, it engaged in rebuilding crisis response strategies, offering apologies and compensation for victims and creating a plan to address previous mistakes in the future. The authors concluded that no significant reputational damage should be expected.

Audience Perspective

Acknowledging a so-called rally "round the flag" effect in times of crisis, Rožukalne et al. (2022) investigated relationships between trust in various information sources about COVID-19 and perceived disease risk. They find positive relationships with almost all information sources, except friends, relatives, and colleagues, and confirm that the perception of risk is dependent on socio-demographic characteristics, except gender. The authors further concluded that with heightened risk perception and trust in government and media institutions, the government can better manage the COVID-19 crisis. For an overview of the Baltic region's studies, see Table 36.2.

The war in Ukraine also changed the trajectory of research interests toward crisis communication among scholars in Baltic countries. Many European research entities, including organizations such as the Estonian Research Council (www.etag.ee/en) now offer funding to support research by Ukrainian scholars in various fields, including communication. More and more scholars are now combining their efforts to study crisis communication practices in the region in times of war. It seems that it will be only a matter of time before we will see an array of published research on various aspects of war-related crisis communication.

Table 36.2 Crisis communication perspectives in the Baltic countries.

Context	*Topic*	*Key takeaways*
Historical and cultural perspective	Cultural Experience in Crisis Communication Planning	• The model of cultural experiences of crises highlighting the differences in the perception of crisis messages based on the cultural context and different experience spheres (Harro-Loit et al., 2012).
Institutional perspective	Latvian Government Crisis Communication in Response to the COVID-19	• Crisis communication of the Latvian government and how effective it is in reaching Latvian and Russian-speaking communities in the country (Struberga & Ozoliņa, 2022).
	Organizational strategies of crisis management	• The implementation of crisis management in Estonian and Chinese organizations through the content analysis of interview data (Alas et al., 2010).
	Crisis Management and Corporate Reputation	• Crisis management analysis of a Baltic retail chain (Šontaitė-Petkevičienė, 2014).
Audience perspective	Trust in Various Information Sources about COVID-19 and Perceived Disease Risk	• Positive correlations between the level of trust in information sources (all except personal connections) and COVID-19 risk perception (Rožukalne et al., 2022).

The V4-Cluster: Czech Republic, Hungary, Poland, and Slovakia

As a subgroup of states, it is meaningful to look at the developments of crisis communication in the so-called V4 countries, also referred to as the Visegrád Group or the Visegrád Four, which includes the Czech Republic, Hungary, Poland, and Slovakia. The V4 partnerships have been actively happening since the turn towards the post-socialist transition more than three decades ago. Besides the political, cultural, and other meaningful relationships, many collaborations between scholars, academic institutions, and other scholarly endeavors across the V4 countries are common. Similar trends across the Visegrád states are apparent in the field of communication in general, and when looking at crisis communication in particular. For example, many studies consider two or more V4 countries for illustrative cases or comparison (e.g., Kovář, 2023; Kreutler et al., 2022; Lukacovic & Sellnow-Richmond, 2023; Mihelj et al. 2022).

In terms of the local trends in V4 crisis communication, several tendencies are evident. The authors cite local V4 scholars and Western scholars. Scholarship from non-Western or non-V4 authors is very rarely used, which is symptomatic of a broader limitation of communication research in this region (Demeter et al., 2023). Interestingly, the Western literature on the crisis and risk communication subfield is rather rarely cited. Instead, V4 authors support their analyses from a variety of communication and interdisciplinary perspectives, including journalism and media studies, business communication, political communication, critical-cultural studies, etc. Paradigmatically, the approaches range from social scientific to political economy outlooks, and from theoretical studies to applied research. However, empirical approaches are dominant.

The crisis communication literature in V4 has been characterized by the focus on the migration/refugee crisis that has been unfolding in Europe within the last decade (Demeter, 2018; Kotišová, 2017; Kovář, 2023; Kreutler et al., 2022; Ostrowska, 2019; Rosenfeldová & Vochocová, 2022; Tkaczyk, 2017; Urbániková & Tkaczyk, 2020; Vallo et al., 2020; Zvada, 2018). The vast majority of these studies were conducted with a focus on journalism, media, and new/digital media. The heavy emphasis on media is symptomatic of the general tendencies of communication research in V4. Furthermore, the media in V4 countries have covered the migration issues extensively, unlike, for instance, the Russian media, which have not presented migration issues as particularly salient (Kreutler et al., 2022).

In the more recent years, the focus of the V4 crisis communication research has shifted toward the COVID-19 pandemic (Biernacka-Ligieza, 2021; Darázs & Šalgovičová, 2021; Gálik & Gáliková Tolnaiová, 2022; Lukacovic, 2022; Lukacovic & Sellnow-Richmond, 2023; Mihelj et al., 2022; Přikrylová & Pátík, 2022; Szabó & Szabó, 2022; Tworzydlo et al., 2022; Ušák & Bednárik, 2022). A significantly more diverse spectrum of perspectives is utilized in the analyses of the pandemic crisis, including institutional, government, media, audience, and theory-development-oriented perspectives.

The next subsection of this chapter discusses the key takeaways from the crisis communication-related research in the Czech Republic, Hungary, Poland, and Slovakia. We begin with the most heavily represented perspectives; starting with (1) media, (2) institutional, and (3) audience perspectives, and then feature the subsection with (4) crisis communication theory and discourse-centered takeaways.

Media Perspective

The migration/refugee-focused literature has pointed out the pervasive problems with crisis journalism (e.g., Tkaczyk, 2017) and the problems with the user-generated public sphere such as the online discussion comments in the V4 region (Rosenfeldová & Vochocová, 2022). The COVID-19 pandemic reflects the same concerns. Furthermore, the pandemic research in the

V4 offers recommendations for improved crisis journalism (Gálik & Gáliková Tolnaiová, 2022), improved local government approaches to digital media crisis communication (Biernacka-Ligieza, 2021), and improved international communication policies to address the contemporary threats to digital media such as the malicious use of AI (Lukacovic & Sellnow-Richmond, 2023). The findings on the role of traditional media, new media, film, and lastly government and media relationship are detailed further on. A particular attention was given to the studies of media nontransparency practices in traditional and online media, in the Eastern European region between 2005 and 2015, with particular attention on Poland (Tsetsura, 2005), Romania (Klyueva & Tsetsura, 2010), Russia (Tsetsura & Luoma-aho, 2010), and Ukraine (Tsetsura & Grynko, 2009), among others. Media nontransparency studies violations of stakeholder expectations of professional and ethical obligations of the media and PR professionals. As part of media nontransparency, news media publish favorable news articles (or sometimes unfavorable information about competitors) in exchange for payments or free services from the company. Tsetsura (2011) and Tsetsura and Kruckeberg (2017) extensively examined this phenomenon and its regional implications for crisis communication, ethical decision-making, and for media trust.

Traditional Media

Tkaczyk (2017) employed quantitative content analysis to explore the performance of the Czech media in coverage of the European migration/refugee crisis. The author found evidence the Czech government set the agenda of politicization and securitization that was dominantly echoed via the reporting of influential online media platforms. Other perspectives, such as the humanitarian dimension of the crisis, were sidelined in the media coverage. The content analysis of the most popular Czech dailies by Urbániková and Tkaczyk (2020) revealed that the most dominant frame depicts the migrants and refugees in Europe as "a burden on host society" (p. 580). Very similar trends were detected by Kovář's (2023) content analysis of the main Czech and Slovak TV broadcasters. Kotišová (2017) explored the "emotional culture" of the Czech TV crisis journalists. Specifically in the context of the refugee crisis and terrorism, Kotišová detected high levels of cynicism among the Czech journalists. Furthermore, the author explored how the cynical approach pairs with the expectations and demands of the profession. Finally, Kreutler et al. (2022) demonstrated different tendencies in coverage of the migration crisis in journalism across different countries, including several European countries, Russia, and the US. In terms of the tendency and comparison to other countries, the media from the Czech Republic, Hungary, and Poland used negative framing in depictions of the crisis. However, the authors specify that various media outlets in these countries demonstrate different tendencies, which seems to suggest a degree of pluralism in the media.

In the case of the migration/refugee crisis, the findings in the V4 echo the same tendencies of politicization and securitization of the migration issue, while sidelining the actual perspective and lived experiences of the migrants and refugees themselves. It appears that journalists were rather reflecting the elite framing than setting a specifically different frame in the depictions of the immigration issues. Thus, crisis journalism in the region suffers from some serious limitations. Other crises serve as cases to further document issues in the journalistic performance.

Hejlová et al. (2021) conceptualized "discursive responsibility" to capture the media culpability in the situation when the risk messages are not fully and accurately conveyed through the media coverage of the issue. They argued that discursive responsibility could potentially grow into a crisis if not properly addressed, and dangers could be documented. Using the context of the Red Sludge Disaster in Hungary, Sarlos and Szondi (2014) analyzed the content of legacy media coverage across political divides in the country. Their findings suggested that media are important stakeholders who construct several different realities in depictions of the crisis, which reflect the political and economic motivations of particular media organizations.

Slovak researchers Gálik and Gáliková Tolnaiová (2022) scrutinized what they characterize as an actual *crisis* of the crisis journalism that has been exposed by the COVID-19 pandemic. They proposed that social responsibility should be upheld by all influential crisis communicators, including journalists. Authors further envisioned some ways to mitigate the problems of crisis journalism by pointing out areas such as the personal-professional responsibility of journalists in upholding ethical standards and noetic (critical-thinking) skills, but also the necessity of appropriate media education.

New Media

While many studies explore the traditional media's framing of the migration/refugee crisis in Central Eastern Europe (CEE), Rosenfeldová and Vochocová's study (2022) filled the gap in the research of the internet user-generated discussions about this crisis. The authors find that while the Czech online comment contributors' frames tend to reflect the main framing of the given online medium, some stories tend to produce a higher frequency of counterreaction. For instance, human-rights-type stories were frequently met with rejections in the user comments. Vallo et al. (2020) investigated the Czech political Twitter framing of the migration crisis. The authors detected politicization, securitization, and Islamophobic positions. The authors wrote that the Czech political communication on Twitter that bases Islamophobic positions on securitization is doing so in the name of proverbial "freedom" and "democracy" instead of "nation, people, or state" (p. 170). Hence, Czech populism resembled tendencies in the Western European countries.

Biernacka-Ligieza (2021) studied crisis management and strategic communication via digital media during the COVID-19 outbreaks in Poland in comparison to Italy and the UK. The results showed that, for instance, disinformation played a detrimental role in all examined cases as it contributed to diminishing public trust in the institutions and deteriorating dialogue between the organizations and stakeholders.

Lukacovic and Sellnow-Richmond (2023) explored various cases including the Czech Republic, Poland, and Slovakia to draw lessons about the role of malicious artificial intelligence (AI) on digital media platforms such as social media during the acute stages of the COVID-19 crisis. The authors argued that the theoretical prisms of mega-crisis and securitization are specifically useful in scholarly analysis of the cases and in the crafting of policy-related and communication-related recommendations that are appropriate for the cumbersome demands of the current digital era.

Film

Ostrowska (2019) used the example of a human rights-focused film festival in the Czech Republic as an example of how social change can be approached via this medium. The author pointed out the realities of anti-immigration positions, which are very common in the Central-Eastern European region. Ostrowska then elucidated how the combination of film and emphasis on the local heritage of the dissident movement with the central figure Václav Havel, can serve as a counterbalance to short-term political gains that tend to fuel the negative orientations toward the refugees.

The Relationship between the State and the Media

Demeter (2018) demonstrated how the Hungarian government of Viktor Orbán instrumentalized state media and favorable private media in launching a campaign with propagandistic characteristics during the migration crisis in Europe. Demeter argued that the real target of the entity to be portrayed negatively through the smear campaign were not the migrants, but the European Union (EU). Furthermore, Demeter stressed that the crisis is two-dimensional, with the actual migrant influx crisis as the backdrop for the created political crisis that stems from Hungary, which is one of the "member states striking at the EU itself" (p. 177).

Szabó and Szabó's (2022) analysis illuminated how the Hungarian PM, Viktor Orbán used the COVID-19 crisis to discursively legitimize and delegitimize certain international partners. In particular, the authors discuss how the V4 partner states were legitimized and the Western European states and supranational EU institutions were delegitimized through the PM's metaphorical discourse. Furthermore, Szabó and Szabó contemplated to what degree their findings may be particular to Hungary or represent a rather theoretically generalizable trend of political discourse that exploits a crisis to advance political persuasive goals. Similarly, as Demeter (2018) noted, Orbán used the migration crisis to fuel another political crisis. Szabó and Szabó (2022) also pointed out that Orbán used the pandemic to polarize and thus contribute to political risk and crisis.

Institutional Perspective

Přikrylová and Pátík (2022) analyzed data related to companies and stakeholders in the Czech Republic to determine preferable branding strategies during serious crises such as the COVID-19 pandemic and the war in Ukraine. The authors recommended that branding should include a holistic focus on all important stakeholders. Furthermore, the stakeholders should be treated with a high degree of empathy, sincerity, and consistency.

Ušák and Bednárik (2022) surveyed consumers of mid-sized Slovak companies to inquire about purchasing behaviors specifically during the COVID-19 pandemic. Their findings suggested that consumers are paying attention to companies' commitments to corporate social responsibility (CSR) and their purchasing decisions are impacted by whether they perceive the company as socially responsible. Hence, CSR is a wise business strategy and should be voiced via corporate communication. These findings echo the growing attention to CSR in the region (e.g., Molnár, 2017).

Darázs and Šalgovičová (2021) assessed online marketing strategies of Slovak organizations and content creators in the field of tourism during the COVID-19 pandemic. They detected a shift in focus on local audiences instead of long-distance or foreign audiences. Darázs and Šalgovičová also suggested that the experience with the COVID-19 crisis should motivate initiatives to create materials that can serve organizations and content creators in specific industries in coping with and adapting to possible future crises.

The survey of Polish public relations (PR) practitioners by Tworzydlo et al. (2022) shed light on the trends that are anticipated by these professionals in the field in the aftermath of the COVID-19 pandemic. The practitioners expect a particular growth in crisis management PR and digital PR.

Audience Perspective

The perceptions and experiences of audiences during crises are rarely examined in the V4 region. An important exception is the study by Mihelj et al. (2022) who conducted semi-structured interviews with participants in the Czech Republic, Hungary, and Poland, and Serbia, to shed more light on the audience's trust in experts during crises. As the authors point out, Central-Eastern Europe is the region with one of the highest levels of vaccine hesitancy in the world, while also having low levels of general trust in political institutions and science, but high affinity towards populism and illiberalism. Mihelj and colleagues' research revealed additional factors to enrich the theories on trust in experts; (1) experts' independence from political elites; and (2) personal contact with experts. For an overview of the V4 region studies, see Table 36.3.

Table 36.3 Crisis communication perspectives in the V4 countries.

Context	*Topic*	*Key takeaways*
Crisis communication theory/discourse	CSR (Corporate Social Responsibility)	• Theorization of stakeholder relations, ethics in organizational communication, and environmental and social dimensions of corporate responsibility (Molnár, 2017).
	Normative Strategic Communication in Crises	• Normative recommendations for strategic crisis communication in the instances of security threat that is to be mitigated by problematic countermeasures (Lukacovic, 2022).
Media perspective	The Role of Traditional Media	• The role of tendencies and pluralism in crisis reporting (Kreutler et al., 2022). • The role of agenda setting; presenting a crisis through a politicized and/or securitized frame (Kovář, 2023; Sarlos & Szondi, 2014; Tkaczyk, 2017; Urbániková & Tkaczyk, 2020). • Problems with the "emotional culture" of crisis journalism (Kotišová, 2017). • Conceptualization of "discursive responsibility" in risk & and crisis journalism (Hejlová et al., 2021). • Mitigation of the problems of crisis journalism by, for example, the personal-professional responsibility of journalists in upholding ethical standards as well as noetic skills (Gálik & Gáliková Tolnaiová, 2022).
	The Role of New Media	• The role of user-generated discussions on digital media platforms in framing crises (Rosenfeldová & Vochocová, 2022). • The role of political communication on digital media platforms in framing crises (Vallo et al., 2020). • Detriments of disinformation on digital media platforms during crises (Biernacka-Ligieza, 2021). • Detriments of malicious AI (artificial intelligence) on digital media platforms during crises (Lukacovic & Sellnow-Richmond, 2023).
	Film	• Film and film festivals as ways to impact communication tendencies during crises (Ostrowska, 2019).
Relationship between the state and the media	Political Communication	• Instrumentalization of media and of the crisis itself to execute a persuasive campaign (Demeter, 2018). • Problematization of the use of propagandistic devices in the government's crisis communication (Demeter, 2018).
Institutional perspective	Strategic Communication During Crisis	• Adaptation of industries/fields and their communication to crises (Darázs & Šalgovičová, 2021). • Crisis branding to include a holistic focus on all stakeholders, empathy, sincerity, and consistency (Přikrylová and Pátík, 2022).
	CSR in Institutional Strategic Communication	• Normative dimensions of CSR in organizational communication (Molnar, 2017). • Competitive value of CSR for business communication in crises (Ušák & Bednárik, 2022).

Table 36.3 (Continued)

Context	*Topic*	*Key takeaways*
	Political Communication	• Problematization of the populist tendencies in crisis political communication (Demeter, 2018; Szabó & Szabó, 2022). • Identification of civilizations securitization and prejudicial trends in political communication during crises (Zvada, 2018).
Professional/ Applied strategic communication perspective	Anticipated Impacts of a Crisis	• Expected growth of crisis management PR and digital PR (Tworzydlo et al., 2022).
Audience perspective	Trust in Scientists/Experts	• Newly determined factors that impact the audience's trust in experts: (1) experts' independence from the political elites; and (2) the audience's contact with the experts (Mihelj et al., 2022).

Crisis Communication Theory and Discourse in the V4 Countries

Interestingly, the most commonly employed theoretical outlook across the V4 crisis communication literature is securitization theory according to the Copenhagen School on security and international relations (Buzan et al., 1998), including the studies by Kovář (2023), Lukacovic (2022), Lukacovic and Sellnow-Richmond (2023), Tkaczyk (2017), Urbániková and Tkaczyk (2020), Vallo et al. (2020), and Zvada (2018). This lens is uncommon in the North American crisis communication literature. Lukacovic (2022) outlined some possibilities of interconnecting the literature of the U.S. strategic communication and the European securitization by examining how the COVID-19 pandemic was securitized in Slovakia. What it means is that the crisis was not just labeled a security threat, but also the countermeasures against the pandemic were extraordinary. By extraordinary they meant that under normal circumstances such measures would have been frowned upon in a democratic society. The author proposed several normative recommendations for strategic crisis communication in such securitized circumstances, in which something that is presented as a threat indeed is seen as such by particular audiences.

Another important theoretical direction in the V4 countries involves the concept of CSR (corporate social responsibility). Molnár (2017) examined Hungarian corporate communication to assess and advance the theories surrounding CSR (corporate social responsibility), stakeholder relations, and ethics in organizational communication. The study by Molnár in particular relates to crisis and risk communication with its focus on environmental and social dimensions of CSR. Furthermore, Ušák and Bednárik (2022) pointed out how the COVID-19 pandemic relates to a paradigm shift in consumer demand for products and services that originate from CSR-committed organizations, which adds a new dimension to the theorization of and advocacy for CSR that goes beyond the normative level to the business competition level.

Later, the attention shifts toward multi-level crises, such as the pandemic and also seems to enhance the prospects of crisis communication that evolve into its specific and unique iterations in the V4 region with the findings that offer meaningful insights. For instance, Demeter (2018) described the hijacking of the migration crisis by the populist leadership in Hungary to fuel a political crisis, while Szabó and Szabó (2022) described the role of communication in hijacking the pandemic to further fuel this political crisis. As Szabó and Szabó contemplated, the detected phenomenon may not be idiosyncratic to Hungary, especially with the growth of the global inclinations towards political populism and simultaneously the high likelihood of various crises occurring in the future.

In summary of the crisis communication developments in the V4 countries, the interest in this subfield of communication is increasing. The scholars from the V4 can productively use their interconnections with each other, the regional interconnections for comparative studies, and bring in different ideas from the local and Western literature. However, the V4 scholarship would benefit from a less Western-centric and a more global orientation (Demeter et al., 2023). Likewise, the other global hubs of crisis and risk communication research, especially the U.S., would benefit from drawing not just on the examples and cases from the Visegrád countries, but on the stimulating ideas and theoretical proposals originating from the Czech, Hungarian, Polish, and Slovak authors.

Trends and Issues in Crisis Communication Research in the Region

As evident from the review of the literature in all two geographical clusters, there are several trends and issues on which crisis communication scholars in this region. First, a definite media perspective on crisis communication prevails in much of the research in the region. Second, much of the contemporary research in the region has an institutional perspective on crisis communication. This approach is driven by how institutions understand and respond to crises and how they think about the time before, during, and after crises. We have seen the institutional perspective present in the literature, in particular. Third, the crisis communication theory discourse that serves as a foundation for many empirical studies is predominantly Western and/or utilizes Western literature (e.g., the works by Coombs on SCCT, by Benoit on image restoration theory).

Next, many scholars offer their takes on the crisis, heavily based on context rather than on theoretical underpinnings. That might be a result of the limited original knowledge production and accumulation of crisis communication theory in the region as practice-focused descriptions case studies to this day, for the most part, dominate academic literature. For example, many studies simply describe responses of organizations and companies, through the case study approach, during and shortly thereafter crises, without critiquing or interrogating the organization-centric approach.

Finally, in our literature analysis, we have not come across studies that are focused on the post-crisis recovery of organizations from the public-centered perspective (Slovenia was an exception). How do organizations in the region learn from crises? In V4 countries post-crisis recovery is rarely mentioned (and if so, then it was mentioned only marginally). Future research on crisis communication in the region would benefit from learning from the contemporary studies of organizational learning in post-crises and a more systematic, comprehensive investigation of structural changes organizations make to respond to crises. Given the global nature of the public relations practice, we believe such examples exist in the region (e.g., a mass exodus of Western companies from the Russian market following the start of the Russian war against Ukraine in 2022). However, regional scholars have yet to publish English-language literature based on such examinations. In another example, the crisis communication research that originates in the successor countries of former Yugoslavia has not been especially abundant. However, a few published works demonstrate a wide range of diversity of approaches from Western-oriented, empirical, and corporate-communication perspectives (e.g., Jugo, 2017) to locally-rooted, critical, and political-economy perspectives (e.g., Vobič et al., 2014). As in many other Eastern European nations, COVID-19 has stimulated a growing body of research in this region (e.g., Grbeša, 2020). Hence, possibly the pandemic focus can further aid the creation of a more defined and independent crisis communication field in the region.

In conclusion, this review can serve to gain insight into trends and idiosyncrasies of risk and crisis communication in Eastern Europe. While we do not claim to offer an all-inclusive and comprehensive assessment of the field, we believe our findings are representative of some of the especially noteworthy developments that Eastern European crisis communication research conveys. Eastern European perspectives should be represented in the truly inclusive global collections about communication, along with other severely underrepresented cultural groups and geographical regions from around the world.

References

Akimovich, E. V. (2018). Obobshchennaya model' krizisnykh kommunikatsii organov gosudarstvennoi vlasti v situatsiyakh sotsial'noi napryazhennosti [Synthesis model of crisis communication of government authorities in situations of social tension]. *Teorii i problemy politicheskikh issledovanii [Theories and Problems of Political Studies]*, *7*(5A), 128–136. (in Russian)

Alas, R., Gao, J., & Vanhala, S. (2010). The crisis management in Chinese and Estonian organizations. *Chinese Management Studies*, *4*(1), 18–36. https://doi.org/10.1108/17506141011032981

Asmolov, G. (2020). Runet in crisis situations. In S. Davydov, Ed., Internet in Russia: An integral study of the Runet and its Impact on Social Life *Societies and Political Orders in Transition* (pp. 231–250). Cham, Switzerland: Springer.

Biernacka-Ligieza, I. (2021). The significance of digital media in local public space crisis management: The case of Poland, the United Kingdom and Italy. *Journal of Arab & Muslim Media Research*, *14*(1), 47–70. https://doi.org/10.1386/jammr_00024_1

Bilokonenko, L. (2021). Crisis communication of president of Ukraine Volodymyr Zelenskyi on counteracting COVID-19: Sociolinguistic features. In *International Conference on New Trends in Languages, Literature and Social Communications (ICNTLLSC 2021)*: Conference Proceedings. (pp. 262–270). Kyiv, Ukraine: Atlantis Press. (in Ukrainian). https://doi.org/10.2991/assehr.k.210525.031May

Boatwright, B. C., & Pyle, A. S. (2023). "Don't Mess with Ukrainian Farmers": An examinationof Ukraine and Kyiv's official Twitter accounts as crisis communication, public diplomacy, and nation building during Russian invasion. *Public Relations Review*, *49*. https://doi.org/10.1016/j.pubrev.2023.102338

Buzan, B., Waever, O., & de Wilde, J. (1998). *Security: A New Framework for Analysis*. Boulder, CO: Lynne Rienner Pub.

Darázs, T., & Šalgovičová, J. (2021). Impact of the corona crisis on marketing communication focused on tourism. *Communication Today*, *12*(1), 148–160. https://communicationtoday.sk/wp-content/uploads/10_DARAZS_SALGOVICOVA_CT-1-2021.pdf

Demeter, M. (2018). Propaganda against the West in the Heart of Europe. A masked official state campaign in Hungary. *Central European Journal of Communication*, *11*(2), 177–197. https://doi.org/10.19195/1899-5101.11.2(21).5

Demeter, M., Vozab, D., & Segado Boj, F. J. (2023). From Westernization to internalization: Research collaboration networks of communication scholars from Central and Eastern Europe. *International Journal of Communication*, *17*, 1211–1231. https://ijoc.org/index.php/ijoc/article/view/20176

Gálik, S., & Gáliková Tolnaiová, S. (2022). Media coverage and its determinants in the context of the COVIC-19 pandemic. *Communication Today*, *13*(1), 46–58. ProQuest Central|ID: covidwho-1863912

Grbeša, M. (2020). Communicating COVID-19 pandemic: Media coverage of the Headquarters and the use of persuasion strategies in Croatia. *Anali Hrvatskog politološkog društva: časopis za politologiju*, *17*(1), 57–78. https://doi.org/10.20901/an.17.03

Harro-Loit, H., Vihalemm, T., & Ugur, K. (2012). Cultural experience as a (critical) factor in crisis communication planning. *Journal of Contingencies & Crisis Management*, *20*(1), 26–38. https://doi.org/10.1111/j.1468-5973.2011.00657.x

Hejlová, D., Schneiderová, S., Klabíková Rábová, T., & Kulhánek, A. (2021). Užívání necigaret není bez rizika" aneb Diskurz o zahřívaných tabákových produktech v médiích ["The use of non-cigarettes is not without risk": The discourse on heated tobacco products in the media]. *Naše řeč [Our Speech]*, *104*(3), 167–183. https://www.researchgate.net/publication/362344572_Uzivani_necigaret_neni_bez_rizika_aneb_Diskurz_o_zahrivanych_tabakovych_produktech_v_mediich

Jaakkola, M. (2020). Editor's introduction Media and information literacy research in countries around the Baltic Sea. *Central European Journal of Communication, 13*, 146–161. https://doi.org/10.19195/1899-5101.13.2(26).1

Jugo, D. (2017). Reactive crisis strategies application of the corporate sector in Croatia. *Journal of Communication Management, 21*(2), 201–214. https://doi.org/10.1108/JCOM-11-2016-0088

Klyueva, A., & Tsetsura, K. (2010). Media non-transparency research: A case of Romania. *Public Relations Journal, 4*(4), 24. http://www.prsa.org/Intelligence/PRJournal/Documents/2010Fall KlyuevaTsetsura.pdf

Kotišová, J. (2017). Cynicism ex machina: The emotionality of reporting the 'refugee crisis' and Paris terrorist attacks in Czech television. *European Journal of Communication, 32*(3), 242–256. https://doi.org/10.1177/0267323117695737

Kovář, J. (2023). Media framing of immigrants in central Europe in the period surrounding the refugee crisis: Security, negativity, and political sources. *Communications: The European Journal of Communication Research, 48*(1), 5–27. https://doi.org/10.1515/commun-2020-0087

Kreutler, M., Fengler, S., Asadi, N., Bodrunova, S., Budivska, H., Diop, L., Ertz, G., Gigola, D., Katus, E., Kovacs, D., Kuś, M., Láb, F., Litvinenko, A., Mack, J., Maier, S., Pinto Martinho, A., Matei, A., Miller, K. C. et al. (2022). Migration coverage in Europe, Russia, and the United States: A comparative analysis of coverage in 17 countries (2015-2018). *Central European Journal of Communication, 15*(2), 202–226. https://doi.org/10.51480/1899-5101.15.2(31).2

Kumar, Y., & Baglay, B. (2021). Government crisis communications during the COVID-19 pandemic: The case of Kazakhstan and Russia. *BULLETIN of L.N. Gumilyov Eurasian National University. Pedagogy. Psychology. Sociology Series, 1*(134), 226–233. https://repository.apa.kz/xmlui/handle/123456789/568

Kushnir, V., & Izhutova, I. (2020). Analysis of Ministry of Defence of Ukraine crisis communications within the Russian Federation information aggression against Ukraine in 2016–2018. *Reality of Politics, 12*, 59–68. https://doi.org/10.32523/2616-6895-2021-134-1-226-233

Lukacovic, M. N. (2022). The normative dimension of securitization as a strategic communication theory; Lessons from the COVID-19 pandemic in Central & Eastern Europe. *Social Communications: Theory and Practice, 14*(1), 192–204. https://doi.org/10.51423/2524-0471-2022-14-1-8

Lukacovic, M. N., & Sellnow-Richmond, D. D. (2023). COVID-19 pandemic and the rise of MUAI threats to national and international psychological security. In E. Pashentsev, Ed., *The Palgrave Handbook of Malicious Use of AI and Psychological Security* (pp. 175–201). Palgrave Macmillan.

Mihelj, S., Kondor, K., & Štětka, V. (2022). Establishing trust in experts during a crisis: Expert trustworthiness and media use during the COVID-19 pandemic. *Science Communication, 44*(3), 292–319. https://doi.org/10.1177/10755470221100558

Molnár, B. (2017). Organization, discourse ethics and the interpretation of "political CSR". *KOME – An International Journal of Pure Communication Inquiry, 5*(1), 1–23. https://doi.org/10.17646/KOME.2017.11

Ostrowska, D. (2019). "The migrant gaze" and "the migrant festive chronotype" – programming the refugee crisis at the European human rights and documentary film festivals. The case of the One World International Human Rights Documentary Film Festival (2016). *Studies in European Cinema, 16*(3), 266–281. https://doi.org/10.1080/17411548.2019.1631532

Patel, S. S., Moncayo, O. E., Conroy, K. M., Jordan, D., & Erickson, T. B. (2020). The landscape of disinformation on health crisis communication during the COVID-19 pandemic in Ukraine: Hybrid warfare tactics, fake media news and review of evidence. *JCOM, Journal of Science Communication, 19*(5). https://doi.org/10.22323/2.19050202

Poissonnier, A. (2017). The Baltics: Three countries, one economy? European economy – economic briefs 024, directorate general economic and financial affairs (DG ECFIN), *European Commission*. https://ideas.repec.org/p/euf/ecobri/024.html

Přikrylová, J., & Pátík, L. (2022). The position of the brand and its marketing communication in the crisis period. *Communication Today, 13*(2), 178–195. http://cejsh.icm.edu.pl/cejsh/element/bwmeta1.element.cejsh-ecb8ba24-3d7b-4ea7-837e-267a6935dead

Rosenfeldová, J., & Vochocová, L. (2022). "Untouched by your do-gooder propaganda": How online user comments challenge the journalistic framing of the immigration crisis. *Central European Journal of Communication, 15*(2), 227–245. https://doi.org/10.51480/1899-5101.15.2(31).3

Rožukalne, A., Kleinberga, V., Tīfentāle, A., & Strode, I. (2022). What is the flag we rally around? Trust in information sources at the outset of the COVID-19 pandemic in Latvia. *Social Sciences*, *11*(3), 123. https://doi.org/10.3390/socsci11030123

Samoilenko, S. A. (2016). Crisis management and communication research in Russia. In A. Schwarz, M. W. Seeger, & C. Auer, Eds., *The Handbook of International Crisis Communication Research* (pp. 397–410). Wiley. https://doi.org/10.1002/spiepr LINEBREAK9781118516812.ch36

Sarlos, G., & Szondi, G. (2014). Crisis communication during the red sludge spill disaster in Hungary – a media consent analysis-based investigation. *Journal of Public Affairs*, *15*(3), 277–286. https://doi.org/10.1002/pa.1526

Šontaitė-Petkevičienė, M. (2014). Crisis management to avoid damage for corporate reputation: The case of retail chain crisis in the Baltic countries. *Procedia-Social and Behavioral Sciences*, *156*, 452–457. https://doi.org/10.1016/j.sbspro.2014.11.220

Struberga, S., & Ozoliņa, Ž. (2022). Crisis communication and resilience: Are Russian and Latvian speakers in the same boat? *Social Sciences*, *11*(5), 216. https://doi.org/10.3390/socsci11050216

Szabó, L. P., & Szabó, G. (2022). Attack of the critics; Metaphorical delegitimization in Viktor Orbán's discourse during the Covid-19 pandemic. *Journal of Language and Politics*, *21*(2), 255–276. https://doi.org/10.1075/jlp.21068.sza

Tasente, T. (2023). Online communication in European public institutions and NATO during the crisis in Ukraine (February 24, 2022 – December 24, 2022). *Technium Social Sciences Journal*, *39*, 195–206. https://doi.org/10.47577/tssj.v39i1.8187

Tkaczyk, M. (2017). Between politicization and securitization: Coverage of the European migration crisis in Czech online news media. *Communication Today*, *8*(2), 90–110. https://www.communicationtoday.sk/download/22017/07.-TKACZYK-E28093-CT-2-2017.pdf

Tsetsura, K. (2005). *Bribery for news coverage: Research in Poland. Institute for Public Relations Online: International Research*. http://www.instituteforpr.org/bribery-poland-2005/.

Tsetsura, K. (2011). Cultural and historical aspects of media transparency in Russia. In A. G. Nikolaev, Ed., *Ethics Issues in International Communication* (pp. 172–182). New York: Palgrave Macmillan.

Tsetsura, K., & Grynko, A. (2009). An exploratory study of the media transparency in Ukraine. *Public Relations Journal*, *3*(2), 1. http://www.prsa.org/SearchResults/download/6D-030205/0/An_Exploratory_Study_of_the_Media_Transparency_in

Tsetsura, K., & Kruckeberg, D. (2017). *Transparency, public relations and the mass media: Combating the hidden influences in news coverage worldwide*. New York: Taylor and Francis/Routledge.

Tsetsura, K., & Luoma-aho, V. (2010). Innovative thinking or distortion of journalistic values? How the lack of trust creates non-transparency in the Russian media. *Ethical Space: The International Journal of Communication Ethics*, *7*(4), 30–38.

Tworzydlo, D., Gawronski, S., Lach, M., & Bajorek, K. (2022). Changes in crisis management PR and digital PR caused by the COVID-19 pandemic. *Central European Journal of Communication*, *15*(3), 396–415. https://doi.org/10.51480/1899-5101.15.3(32).4

Urbániková, M., & Tkaczyk, M. (2020). Strangers ante portas: The framing of refugees and migrants in the Czech quality press. *European Journal of Communication*, *35*(6), 580–596. https://doi.org/10.1177/0267323120928224

Ušák, P., & Bednárik, J. (2022). Changes in purchasing behavior after the onset of the COVID-19 pandemic related to the application of corporate social responsibility. *Communication Today*, *13*(1), 180–189. http://cejsh.icm.edu.pl/cejsh/element/bwmeta1.element.cejsh-f8368370-fb8f-4b93-aca6-a5f78db5ab35

Vallo, Z., Jaworek, R., & Matlach, V. (2020). Islamophobic discourse of Czech politicians and political parties on Twitter during the 2015 migration crisis. *Journal of Nationalism, Memory & Language Politics*, *14*(2), 152–176. https://doi.org/10.2478/jnmlp-2020-0009

Vobič, I., Slaček Brlek, A. S., Mace, B., & Prodnik, J. A. (2014). Changing faces of Slovenia; Political, socio-economic and news media aspects of the crisis. *Javnost – The Public*, *21*(4), 77–97. https://doi.org/10.1080/13183222.2014.11077104

Zvada, Ľ. (2018). Securitization of the migration crisis and Islamophobic rhetoric: The 2016 Slovak parliamentary elections as a case study. *Journal of Nationalism, Memory & Language Politics*, *12*(2), 216–235. https://doi.org/10.2478/jnmlp-2018-0010

Authors' Bio

Katerina Tsetsura, Ph.D. (Purdue University), is a Gaylord Family Full Professor of Public Relations and Strategic Communication at the Gaylord College of Journalism and Mass Communication at the University of Oklahoma in the USA. Dr. Tsetsura is internationally known for her work in global public relations and media transparency. She is a co-author of "*Transparency, public relations, and the mass media: Combating hidden influences in news coverage worldwide*" (2017, Taylor & Francis) and co-editor of "*Strategic Communications in Russia: Public Relations and Advertising*" (2021, Taylor & Francis) and has over 100 academic publications.

Currently, Dr. Tsetsura serves as a co-PI on the multi-disciplinary NSF-funded research project to enable the t**RAN**sition to **G**reen **E**nergy in gas-producing regions (RANGE) using a unique proposition: To engage local communities in the co-development of research goals related to the hydrogen energy transition. Dr. Tsetsura leads the team in developing and testing a transparent, socially just, community-focused framework for fundamental knowledge creation in carbon-free hydrogen production and storage (https://www.oucheps.org/).

In 2021–2023, Dr. Tsetsura served as a PI on a multidisciplinary research project to study community resilience to information pollution in times of crisis.

In 2018, Dr. Tsetsura received the Outstanding Educator of the Year award, the highest national award in public relations teaching from the Public Relations Society of America. Dr. Tsetsura is a member of the Arthur W. Page Society.

Marta N. Lukacovic, Ph.D., received her doctorate from Wayne State University, Detroit-Michigan, USA. She is an Assistant Professor of Communication and Mass Media at Angelo State University (Texas Tech University System), USA. Her research is focused on the intersection of communication through digital media platforms and the matters of security. Particularly she analyzes the contexts of global mega-crises such as pandemics, political violence, disinformation, and malicious use of artificial intelligence (MUAI). She co-edited a two-volume book project with Lexington Books of the publishing house Rowman & Littlefield on public relations, media, and communication in post-socialist nations of Eastern Europe and Central Asia. Her work was supported through the South Carolina Humanities Award-CARES NEH grant, Summer Research Fellowship at Furman University, SC, and T.C. Rumble Fellowship at Wayne State University, MI. She presented at numerous scholarly conferences across the USA and at international conferences in Canada, the Czech Republic, France, the Netherlands, and Russia. Her research appeared in prominent publications such as *Journal of Applied Communication Research*, *International Journal of Communication*, and *Journal of International Crisis and Risk Communication Research*. She is a member of the Board of Directors of La Esperanza Clinic, which is a non-profit organization that prioritizes providing high-quality primary and preventive healthcare to underserved communities in West Texas. She serves as the president of CAER (Communication Association of Eurasian Researchers) and as a co-chair of the Education and Professional Development Working Group of the ICRCA (International Crisis and Risk Communication Association).

Iuliia Dolmatova received her Master of Arts in Strategic Communication from the University of Oklahoma, USA and her Bachelor's degree in Advertising and Public Relations from Saint Petersburg State University in Russia. Iuliia's master's research investigates strategic communication in art institutions. As part of her thesis, she developed an integrated marketing communication campaign for the University of Oklahoma's art museum. During her graduate studies, Iuliia also contributed to multiple research projects on media disinformation, misinformation and disinformation online, and crisis communication. Currently, Dolmatova is an Associate Director at an international strategic fundraising consulting firm, CCS Fundraising, where she supports business development and strategic marketing efforts across multiple geographic regions.

Crisis and Risk Communication Research in the Americas

37

Risk and Crisis Communication Research in North America

Shari R. Veil
College of Journalism and Mass Communications, University of Nebraska-Lincoln, Lincoln, NE, USA

Risk and crisis communication research involves multidisciplinary approaches and requires coordinated efforts to address the challenges posed by unexpected and fast-moving harmful events. Although emergency response and disaster management as organized activity has existed in the United States since at least the early 1900s, the development of risk and crisis communication research programs largely developed in the 1970s and 80s (Quarantelli, 2000). This work was driven by specific disaster events and a recognition that communication initially in the form of alerts and warnings was essential. The Great Galveston Hurricane of 1900, for example, demonstrated the need for a robust national weather service to issue predictions and warnings of impending natural disasters.

Risk communication research emerged in the fields of environmental and health risk, while crisis communication research emerged out of organizational rhetoric and public relations (Palenchar, 2020; Reynolds & Seeger, 2005). Both areas of research were born out of an organization-centric approach, oftentimes prioritizing the needs and reputations of organizations and government agencies over the health and well-being of risk bearers.

As risk and crisis communication research matured, scholars better understood the cyclical nature of a risk that becomes a crisis that exposes additional risk (Veil et al., 2008). Catastrophic events including terrorist attacks, natural disasters and global pandemics, along with the government agencies funding interdisciplinary research to understand and manage these events, pushed scholars out of their academic silos and elevated research and best practices that demonstrate a more holistic approach to issues and events that can cause significant harm. This chapter describes the evolution of risk and crisis communication research in North America, including major themes, theories and models.

Risk Communication

In 1980, the Love Canal environmental disaster in Niagara Falls, New York, prompted the U.S. Congress to enact the Comprehensive Environmental Response, Compensation and Liability Act (CERCLA). This act was designed to confront the threats of unchecked hazardous waste, establishing a program for emergency responses, data collection and analysis, and

The Handbook of International Crisis and Risk Communication Research, Second Edition.
Edited by Andreas Schwarz, Matthew W. Seeger, and Sora Kim.

site remediation. CERCLA also instituted the Hazardous Substance Response Trust Fund (commonly known as Superfund), aimed at funding emergency interventions and cleanup. As part of this initiative, the U.S. Environmental Protection Agency leveraged risk communication to foster open, informed, and value-laden discussions about risks linked to hazardous activities and toxic substances (Palenchar & Heath, 2007).

The National Research Council (NRC) initiated the study of risk communication in "recognition that technological issues, in addition to being critically important, are complex, difficult, and laden with political controversy" (NRC, 1989, p. ix). Leiss (1996) identified three phases in the evolution of risk communication. Phase I (1975–1985) emphasized our capacity to manage risks at an exacting level of detail. Public perceptions were considered irrelevant to the risk faced and therefore ignored. Phase II (1985–1994) focused on creating a shared understanding through persuasive one-way messages. Lindell and Perry (2004) suggested that this shift can be traced back to a risk communication conference held in Washington D.C. in 1986 that brought together more than 500 scholars, government officials and industry representatives to advance the field. Phase III (1995+) recognized the social context and sought to build consensus and trust. Town hall meetings became common practice to engage in "open" discussions between risk managers and risk bearers.

Sutton and Veil (2017) proposed that Phase III ended around 2004 when Facebook was invented, smartphones increased accessibility, and activist organizations went online to launch competing risk narratives. Phase IV (2005–2014) saw the rise of Digital Humanitarians who used social media to crowd-source information to share with risk mitigators, and Phase V (2015+) includes the use of "Big Data" and artificial intelligence to search for, vet, verify, and catalog usable risk information.

According to the National Research Council (1989), risk communication "involves multiple messages about the nature of risk or expressing concerns, opinions or reactions to risk messages" (p. 322). In short, risk communication helps to define a problem and solicit involvement and action to reduce risk. Reynolds and Seeger (2005) describe risk communication as a process of informing people about risks and persuading them to modify their behavior to reduce risks. Risk perception influences an individual's willingness to comply with risk messages. Therefore, much of the early risk communication research sought to identify factors that affect risk perception. The following themes and theories highlight the advances in risk communication research over time.

Risk Perception Models

The Social Amplification of Risk Framework explains how risk events interplay with psychological, social, institutional, and cultural factors. This interaction can either heighten or lessen risk perceptions and influence how individuals behave towards those risks (Kasperson, et al., 1988). Covello et al. (2001) pinpointed 15 factors that can shift the public's degree of concern about risks, either intensifying or diminishing their emotional reactions to risks. These factors span from characteristics of the risk itself, like its controllability or how familiar it is, to broader societal considerations such as its ethical/moral implications or whether it's of human or natural origin. Determining the impact of these factors is crucial for influencing risk perception, changing behaviors, and adjusting attitudes in response to communicated risk messages (Ferrante, 2010).

Slovic (1987) emphasized the intricacies of risk perception. He posited that individuals don't necessarily evaluate risks solely based on facts or statistics. Instead, personal feelings, cultural values, and inherent biases play pivotal roles in shaping risk perception. His research underscores that purely factual communication strategies may fall short if they fail to address these subjective elements of risk.

Sandman (2003) wrote extensively about risk communication. His conceptualization of Risk = Hazard + Outrage is widely quoted. In this context, "Hazard" represents the real event at the heart of the communication, whether it's a looming potential event or one currently unfolding. These hazardous situations can range from barely noticeable to utterly catastrophic. A crucial aspect of effective communication is ensuring the audience, typically the public or a specific stakeholder group, grasps the severity of the event. Their comprehension significantly influences the effectiveness of the message and the subsequent actions they take. "Outrage," on the other hand, pertains to the emotional reactions and actions of the audience based on their assessment of the presented hazard. Just as with hazards, outrage can vary from intense to mild. The emotional triggers and factors highlighted by Covello and Slovic can heighten this outrage, thus amplifying the perception of risk, even when the actual threat is limited.

Mental Noise and Sensemaking

The Mental Noise Model provides a means for understanding how the public processes information in periods of high stress and anxiety (Covello et al., 2001). As the perceived threat rises, an individual's ability to process information decreases. The creation of this "mental noise" effectively blocks the individual's ability to hear the message and affects their willingness and ability to process the message. Risks associated with a lack of control, which are perceived to be low in benefits or are thought to be unfair, create the highest levels of mental noise (Ferrante, 2010). An individual's ability to engage in rational discourse has substantial implications for professionals attempting to deliver a message dedicated to changing attitudes and behaviors.

Weick (1993) refers to mental noise as a "cosmology episode" (p. 633). He suggests that individuals instinctively try to comprehend a threatening situation by relating it to past events. When current experiences don't align with our established frames of reference, we experience a sudden loss of meaning in which we do not have control over our understanding of the world. Weick (1988) defines sensemaking as an individual's capacity to rationalize their situation based on prior experiences and personal interpretations. Following a cosmology episode, sensemaking unfolds in three phases: enactment, in which a person responds through speech, action, or actively attuning to information; selection, where the action's outcome is interpreted; and retention, wherein this interpretation guides the categorization of future information. Weick et al. (2005) describe this process as a dance between "action and interpretation" (p. 409). By taking action to address a threat, we gain a clearer perspective on the risk confronting us. This clarity enables us to assimilate information about similar risks in the future, restoring our grasp on reality.

Risk Information Seeking and Messaging

The Risk Information Seeking and Processing (RISP) Model suggests that an individual's drive to seek and process risk information mainly hinges on their personal evaluation of the difference between their current knowledge about a risk and the amount of information they believe they need to adequately respond to the risk (Griffin et al., 1999; Griffin et al., 2004; Griffin et al., 2012). This assessment of the information gap is influenced by numerous factors, such as personal attributes like socioeconomic status and ideological leanings, perceptions of the risk's dangers, anxiety levels regarding the risk, and societal expectations to be informed about the risk. While RISP acknowledges emotional aspects of risk, unlike risk perception models, its foundation is primarily cognitive. Studies on RISP over various risks and timeframes show that people are more inclined to thoroughly seek and analyze risk information if they feel societal pressures to be informed or believe they lack sufficient data for decision-making. Based on RISP, individuals who feel social pressure to be informed about a risk will be more open and receptive to risk messaging.

Research by Mileti and colleagues (Mileti & Fitzpatrick, 1991; Mileti & Sorensen, 1990) focused on how to craft a risk message that will invoke desired action. The recipients of the information must (1) receive the information, (2) understand that information, (3) understand that the message relates to them directly, (4) understand the risks they face if they do not follow the protective action provided, (5) decide that they should act on the information, (6) understand the actions they need to take, and (7) actually be able to take action. Effective risk communication must ensure that recipients comprehend the information, its relevance, the associated risks, and the proposed protective measures, as presented by a trusted entity (Windahl et al., 1992). According to Palenchar and Heath (2007), the chief aim of risk communication is not mere understanding but cultivating a supportive social relationship, which becomes a vehicle for communicating values and identities as much as addressing the risk itself.

Heath (2006) describes crisis as risk manifested. While closely related, there are theoretical distinctions between the terms risk communication and crisis communication. Risk communication is more preventative in nature and is employed to convey the probability of a potential threat and how to mitigate that threat. Crises, however, pose actual or perceived threats, necessitate fast responses, and cause heightened uncertainty (Ulmer et al., 2007); thus, crisis communication is often more strategic and time-sensitive.

Crisis Communication

Crisis creates rhetorical problems that demand that the organization experiencing the crisis understand and respond to both the crisis event and perceptions about decisions the organization made (or did not make) that contributed to the onset of the crisis. When an organization's action or inaction is viewed as contrary to expected social norms, an expectation gap occurs. Negative stakeholder perceptions, created by the expectation gap, can threaten the organization's reputation and even its long-term legitimacy. Perceptions of the crisis communication efforts also are critical to maintaining confidence in the organization's ability to manage the crisis.

Heath and Millar (2004) explain that the "exigencies created by a crisis center on the organization's actions and statements to regain control of the circumstances" (p. 10). As such, the response must provide an explanation to stakeholders about what happened, and ultimately, provide a solution or a process for identifying a solution for the problem. Communication responses to the crisis include instructional information for physical protection, adjusting information to help stakeholders cope psychologically with the crisis, and reputation management responses to protect the reputation of the organization both during and following the crisis (Sturges, 1994).

While crisis communication scholars agree the ethical imperative is to focus first on instructional messages that seek to explain risks and what the public can do to protect themselves in a crisis, failure to bolster the reputation of the organization can negatively impact stakeholder perceptions. Thus, theories grounded in apologia and attribution of responsibility, including image repair theory, situation crisis communication theory, and crisis renewal theory have dominated the literature.

Apologia and Image Repair

Ware and Linkugel (1973) were one of the first to examine crisis response strategies as communication used to defend one's reputation from public attack. Their concept of apologia did not necessarily involve an apology but rather a form of argumentative self-defense. They suggested that individuals make strategic rhetorical choices based on the nature of the accusation and their relationship with the audience. These choices are aimed at maintaining credibility and are considered in the broader context of situational demands and constraints. Their work laid the groundwork for future studies on crisis communication and reputation management, influencing theories like Image Repair Theory.

Image Repair Theory builds on theories of apologia and accounts to address how individuals and organizations manage and restore their image in the face of reputational threat. The theory aims to guide the response to accusations or events that might damage the public image, suggesting various tactics to mitigate negative effects, restore credibility, and maintain positive relationships with stakeholders.

According to Benoit (1997), a crisis response is required for image repair if an organization is seen as responsible for an action (or inaction) and if that action (or inaction) is viewed as offensive by stakeholders and creates a reputation threat. Image repair theory identified five broad categories of crisis response strategies used to bolster reputation including (1) denial, (2) evasion of responsibility, (3) reducing offensiveness, (4) corrective action, and (5) mortification. Hearit (2006) suggested that mortification, which includes an apology, should adhere to the following criteria: admitting wrongdoing, taking responsibility, expressing regret, identifying with affected stakeholders, seeking forgiveness, striving for stakeholder reconciliation, full disclosure, providing a proper explanation, offering corrective action and proposing suitable compensation. Research on image repair most often utilizes interpretive case study methods and textual analysis, to distill meaning from individual and organizational statements.

Situational Crisis Communication Theory

Situational Crisis Communication Theory (SCCT) is grounded in attribution theory, which suggests that people seek to understand the causes of events, particularly negative ones, and attribute responsibility or blame to others (Coombs, 2004). Attribution of responsibility is based on (1) isolated stability, if the organization or related industry is frequently involved in similar events; (2) external control, if outside sources or agents other than the organization involved had some responsibility for the event; and (3) locus of control, if the organization could have done something to prevent the event (Weiner, 1995).

According to SCCT, prior stakeholder relationships also impact the attribution of crisis responsibility. Organizations with positive prior stakeholder relationships may experience a halo effect whereby stakeholders are hesitant to believe the organization would act outside stakeholder expectations. Alternatively, a Velcro effect can occur when organizations do not have a strong organizational reputation with their stakeholders before a crisis. A history of crisis and continued stakeholder disappointment can have a Velcro-like effect by snagging additional reputational damage (Coombs & Holladay, 2006).

The theory outlines three crisis types (victim, accidental, intentional) and corresponding crisis response strategies (denial, diminish, rebuild). The response strategies are aligned with the crisis types from least accommodating to most accommodating based on the level of responsibility attributed. Coombs (2007) suggested that the level of accommodation in the crisis response strategy should match the level of reputational damage generated by the crisis. If crisis communication strategies are selected according to stakeholder perceptions of responsibility, the aligned response has the potential to positively impact the organization's reputation and improve the crisis. Accordingly, organizations that select strategies that do not align with stakeholder assessments of control and responsibility will not benefit from the protective powers that would be offered by an aligned response strategy. Bolstering strategies can be used to supplement the primary response strategies.

Crisis Renewal Theory

Ulmer and Sellnow (2002) proposed renewal discourse as a crisis response strategy to provide a more optimistic perspective of rebuilding and renewal than the traditional blame and apology at the heart of image repair and SCCT. Crisis Renewal Theory posits that crisis, while inherently challenging and potentially damaging, also presents organizations with opportunities for renewal and positive change. This perspective shifts the focus from crisis management, which is primarily about minimizing harm and restoring the status quo, to leveraging the lessons learned from the crisis to improve the organization.

Ulmer et al. (2007) suggested renewal discourse is most successful when (1) crises are natural disasters rather than human-caused, (2) responding organizations have strong pre-crisis relationships with stakeholders, (3) responding organizations can demonstrate a commitment to making changes and building a better organization and response system, and (4) the discourse allows the organization's publics and stakeholders to change the rhetorical frame of the crisis into a prospective vision for the future.

The theory is founded on the belief that how an organization responds to a crisis can lead to improved processes, stronger relationships with stakeholders, and enhanced organizational learning. The central tenets of renewal discourse include (1) learning, (2) ethical communication, (3) positive organizational rhetoric, and (4) prospective vision (Ulmer et al., 2007). The theory encourages organizations to go beyond mere survival and to use the crisis as a catalyst for introspection, innovation, and transformation. By embracing change and being open to learning from the crisis, organizations can emerge stronger, more resilient, and with a better strategic position than before the crisis occurred.

Stage Models and Best Practices

Although crisis communication strategies like image repair and SCCT address reputation threats, and renewal theory provides for adjusting information to help stakeholders psychologically cope with the crisis, these strategies do not address the public risk in a crisis. Crisis stage models demonstrate the cyclical nature of a risk that becomes a crisis and produces additional risk. Describing elements of a crisis through the stage models helps researchers and practitioners identify what communication strategies are needed during particular phases of the crisis cycle. The U.S. Centers for Disease Control and Prevention and Health Canada developed their own evidence-based models to better inform communication processes. The collective wisdom distilled from these models is crucial for guiding organizations through the intricate dance of crisis management, from preemption to learning and back to preparedness, now enriched with insights from past experiences. The best practices were derived from this grounded theory approach and provide guidelines for practitioners throughout the crisis cycle (Veil et al., 2008).

Crisis Stage Models

Fink (1986) was one of the first to develop a crisis stage model. While his research was primarily on for-profit corporations, Fink described crisis through the metaphor of a medical illness with four stages: (1) *prodromal*, when warning signals of a potential crisis emerge; (2) *acute*, when the trigger event and ensuing damage of the crisis occur; (3) *chronic*, when lasting effects of the crisis continue and clean up begins; and (4) *resolution*, when the crisis is no longer a concern to stakeholders. Fink describes a crisis with a starting and ending point, yet he notes that warning signals emerge before the onset of a crisis.

Mitroff (1994) suggested there are opportunities to interrupt the crisis lifecycle. Also specific to organizational crises, his approach focused on strategic actions for crisis prevention through (1) *signal detection*, when warning signs can be identified and acted upon to prevent a crisis; (2) *probing and prevention*, when organization members should be searching for known crisis risk factors and working to reduce potential harm; (3) *damage containment*, the onset of crisis during which organization members try to limit the damage; (4) *recovery*, working to return to normal business operation as soon as possible; and (5) *learning*, which involves reviewing and critiquing the crisis management process. Gonzalez-Herrero and Pratt (1995) extended Mitroff's work to include learning as a continuation of the recovery phase that will improve signal detection for organizations at the start of the cycle.

Drawing from emergency management and the work of Fink and Mitroff, Coombs (2012) described the crisis lifecycle through four interrelated factors: (1) *prevention*, detecting warning signals and taking action to mitigate the crisis; (2) *preparation*, diagnosing vulnerabilities and developing the crisis plan; (3) *response*, applying the preparation components and attempting to return to normal operations; and (4) *revision*, evaluating the crisis response to determine what was done right or wrong during the crisis management performance.

The three-stage approach is most commonly used to separate the events surrounding a crisis for further analysis (Seeger et al., 2003): (1) *pre-crisis* includes crisis preparation and planning; (2) *crisis* includes the trigger event and ensuing damage; and (3) *post-crisis* includes learning and resolution, which then informs the pre-crisis stage. This macro approach to crisis furthers the notion of a crisis cycle. If an organization survives the stages of pre-crisis, crisis, and post-crisis, it will once again find itself in the stage of pre-crisis, only better equipped to prepare for another crisis. While the cycle returns to pre-crisis, lessons learned from the crisis should inspire a different mindset in preparing for the next crisis (Veil, 2011).

Crisis and Emergency Risk Communication

Leading up to and following the 9/11 terrorist attacks and subsequent anthrax attacks in the U.S. in 2001, communication professionals at the U.S. CDC developed an integrated model titled Crisis and Emergency Risk Communication (CERC) as a tool to educate and equip public health professionals for the expanding communication responsibilities of public health in emergency situations (Reynolds, 2002). The model organizes a crisis into five stages: (1) pre-crisis, (2) initial event, (3) maintenance, (4) resolution, and (5) evaluation and lists specific communication objectives for each phase of the crisis lifecycle. Training for public health officials on the CERC framework and the accompanying handbook was launched in 2002.

According to Veil et al. (2008), the communication objectives of the CERC framework address the nuanced nature of risks and crises, emphasizing the unique information demands they produce. Continuous, interactive communication is crucial for public understanding and decision-making in the face of such ambiguous threats, as communication dynamics will inevitably shift, introducing new challenges at each stage. How risk is communicated prior to a crisis can shape future perceptions and actions, which then feed back into ongoing risk communication efforts. A hallmark of the CERC model is that effective communication empowers people to take protective actions, but the diverse characteristics and needs of the affected populations influence their communication requirements and abilities during a crisis. The critical components of crisis communication outlined by the CERC Model are summarized as (1) Be First, (2) Be Right, (3) Be Credible, (4) Express Empathy, (5) Promote Action, and (6) Show Respect.

Dialogue-based Strategic Risk Communications Process

While the CERC Model was being developed in the U.S., Health Canada was developing their own Decision-making Framework for Identifying, Assessing and Managing Health Risks (DMF) to help guide risk management efforts. The DMF outlined five Guiding Principles of Strategic Risk Communication: (1) strategic risk communication is integral to integrated risk management; (2) stakeholders are the focal point, specifically, "those who face the greatest risk deserve the most attention, as do those most concerned with managing particular risks" (Minister of Health Canada, 2006, pp. 2–5); (3) decisions are evidence-based, tapping both social and natural sciences; (4) risk management and risk communication processes are transparent; and (5) the Strategic Risk Communications Process requires continuous improvement through evaluation.

In 2004, a steering team of representatives across Health Canada, chaired by the Communications Directorate, was formed to help guide mental models research to identify important elements in the thinking and behavior of professionals with respect to risk management practices and risk communications. The resulting Dialogue-based Strategic Risk Communications Process and accompanying handbook were published in 2006. The process requires seven steps: (1) define the opportunity; (2) characterize the situation; (3) assess stakeholder perceptions of the risks, benefits and tradeoffs; (4) assess how stakeholders perceive the options; (5) develop and pre-test strategies, risk communications plans and messages; (6) implement risk communications plans; and (7) evaluate risk communications effectiveness. The framework also outlined specific roles and responsibilities related to the implementation of risk communications.

Best Practices in Risk and Crisis Communication

The U.S. Department of Homeland Security National Centers of Excellence, established in the wake of 9/11, at the University of Southern California (Risk and Economic Analysis of Threats and Emergencies), University of Minnesota (Food Protection and Defense) and University of Maryland (Consortium for the Study of Terrorism and Responses to Terrorism) included risk and crisis communication as critical components of the centers' programmatic research. Based on an extensive synthesis of literature and in-depth discussions of organizational crisis planning and response by an expert panel convened by these Centers of Excellence, a theoretical framework of Best Practices in Risk and Crisis Communication was developed and summarized by Seeger (2006) in a special issue of the *Journal of Applied Communication Research*. Prominent risk and crisis communication scholars (Heath, 2006; Reynolds, 2006; Ropeik, 2006; Sandman, 2006; Venette, 2006) provided critiques of the summary.

Additional research has since applied, analyzed, validated, and expanded the best practices in a variety of crisis contexts. In 2020, Veil and colleagues published 15 Essential Guidelines for Ongoing Risk and Crisis Communication in the *Handbook of Applied Communication Research* including (1) plan ahead for a prompt response; (2) establish a crisis communication network with credible sources; (3) prioritize the safety and wellbeing of the public; (4) accept uncertainty and avoid public speculation; (5) listen to the public's concerns; (6) provide instruction for self-protection; (7) tailor messages to affected audiences; (8) communicate with honesty, candor, and openness; (9) communicate with compassion, concern, and empathy; (10) acknowledge and account for vulnerable populations; (11) acknowledge and account for cultural differences; (12) form partnerships with the public; (13) meet the needs of the media and remain accessible; (14) complete and communicate recovery efforts; and (15) continuously evaluate and update crisis plans (Veil et al., 2020).

While the best practices provide a holistic approach to risk and crisis communication throughout the crisis life cycle, they are not a panacea. Research continues to develop and improve recommendations for each of the practices. For example, Sellnow and Sellnow (2010) have been developing the IDEA (internalization, distribution, explanation, action) Model as a situationally generalizable framework for designing effective instructional messages for self-protection (Sellnow & Sellnow, 2010; Sellnow et al., 2017), while Jin and Austin (2022) have focused extensively on the role of social media in crisis communication to both listen to the public's concerns and communicate with honesty, candor, and openness.

Conclusion

The goal of this chapter was to provide an overview of risk and crisis communication research in North America. As much of the discipline originated in the U.S., this overview needed to be limited in scope and only cover major trends and theories. Leading risk and crisis communication scholars in the field are already engaging and publishing with scholars from around the world. For example, the newly established International Crisis and Risk Communication Association (ICRCA) grew out of an annual conference hosted by the Nicholson School of

Communication and Media at the University of Central Florida. Members of ICRCA collaborate extensively with the European Communication Research and Education Association's (ECREA) Risk and Crisis Communication Section, which hosts the ECREA Crisis Communication conference every other year. Similarly, the Crisis Communication Think Tank in the Grady College of Journalism and Mass Communication at the University of Georgia has now launched an international hub in Europe. While risk and crisis communication scholarship continues to have Western bias, as the field evolves, being able to differentiate the research and scholarship in one country compared to another will become increasingly difficult.

References

Benoit, W. L. (1997). Image restoration discourse and crisis communication. *Public Relations Review, 23*, 177–186.

Reynolds, B. (2002). *Crisis and Emergency Risk Communication.* Atlanta, GA: Centers for Disease Control and Prevention.

Coombs, W. T. (2004). Impact of past crises on current crisis communication. *Journal of Business Communication, 41*(3), 265–289.

Coombs, W. T. (2007). Protecting organization reputations during a crisis: The development and application of situational crisis communication theory. *Corporate Reputation Review, 10*, 163–176.

Coombs, W. T. (2012). *Ongoing Crisis Communication: Planning, Managing, and Responding* (3rd ed.). Thousand Oaks, CA: SAGE Publications, Inc.

Coombs, W. T., & Holladay, S. J. (2006). Unpacking the halo effect: Reputation and crisis management. *Journal of Communication Management, 10*(2), 123–137.

Covello, V., Peters, R., Wojtecki, J., & Hyde, R. C. (2001). Risk communication, the West Nile Virus epidemic and bioterrorism: Responding to the communication challenges posed by the intentional or unintentional release of a pathogen in an urban setting. *Journal of Urban Health: Bulletin of the New York Academy of Medicine, 78*(2), 382–391.

Ferrante, P. (2010). Risk and crisis communication: Essential skills for today's SH&E professionals. *Professional Safety, 55*(6), 38–45.

Fink, S. (1986). *Crisis Management: Planning for the Inevitable.* New York: AMACOM.

Gonzalez-Herrero, A., & Pratt, C. B. (1995). How to manage a crisis before – or whenever – it hits. *Public Relations Quarterly, 40*(1), 25–29.

Griffin, R. J., Dunwoody, S., & Neuwirth, K. (1999). Proposed model of the relationship of risk information seeking and processing to the development of preventive behaviors. *Environmental Research, 80*(2), S230–S245.

Griffin, R. J., Dunwoody, S., & Yang, Z. J. (2012). Testing the robustness of a risk information processing model. *Communication Yearbook, 36*, 323–362.

Griffin, R. J., Neuwirth, K., Dunwoody, S., & Giese, J. (2004). Information sufficiency and risk communication. *Media Psychology, 6*, 23–61.

Hearit, K. M. (2006). *Crisis management by apology: Corporate response to allegations of wrongdoing.* Mahwah, New Jersey: Lawrence Erlbaum.

Heath, R. L. (2006). Best practices in crisis communication: Evolution of practice through research. *Journal of Applied Communication Research, 34*(3), 245–248.

Heath, R. L., & Millar, D. P. (2004). A rhetorical approach to crisis communication: Management, communication processes, and strategic responses. In R. L. Heath, & D. P. Millar, Eds., *Responding to Crisis: A Rhetorical Approach to Crisis Communication* (pp. 1–18). Mahwah, NJ: Lawrence Erlbaum.

Jin, Y., & Austin, L. L. (2022). *Social Media and Crisis Communication* (2nd ed.). New York: Routledge.

Kasperson, R. E., Renn, O., Slovic, P., Brown, H. S., Emel, J., Goble, R. et al. (1988). The social amplification of risk: A conceptual framework. *Risk Analysis, 8*(2), 177–187.

Leiss, W. (1996). Three phases in the evolution of risk communication practice. *The Annals of the American Academy of Political and Social Science, 545*, 85–94.

Lindell, M. K., & Perry, R. W. (2004). *Communicating Environmental Risk in Multiethnic Communities.* Thousand Oaks, CA: Sage.

Mileti, D. S., & Fitzpatrick, C. (1991). Communication of public risk: Its theory and its application. *Sociological Practice Review, 2*(1), 20–18.
Mileti, D. S., & Sorensen, J. H. (1990). *Communication of Emergency Public Warnings: A Social Science Perspective and state-of-the-art Assessment (ORNL-6609)*. Oak Ridge, TN: Oak Ridge National Laboratory.
Minister of Health Canada (2006). *Strategic risk communications framework and handbook for Health Canada and the Public Health Agency of Canada, 1*(1), http://www.riskcommunications.gc.ca (accessed November 1, 2023).
Mitroff, I. I. (1994). Crisis management and environmentalism: A natural fit. *California Management Review, 36*(2), 101–113.
National Research Council (1989). *Improving Risk Communication*. Washington, DC: National Academy Press.
Palenchar, M. J. (2020). Historical trends of risk and crisis communication. In R. L. Heath, & H. D. O'Hair, Eds., *Handbook of Risk and Crisis Communication* (pp. 31–52). Routledge.
Palenchar, M., & Heath, R. (2007). Strategic risk communication: Adding value to society. *Public Relations Review, 33*(2), 120–129.
Quarantelli, E. L. (2000). Disaster planning, emergency management and civil protection: The historical development of organized efforts to plan for and to respond to disasters.
Reynolds, B. (2006). Response to best practices. *Journal of Applied Communication Research, 34*(3), 249–252.
Reynolds, B., & Seeger, M. W. (2005). Crisis and emergency risk communication as an integrative model. *Journal of Health Communication, 10*(1), 43–55.
Ropeik, D. (2006). Best practices response. *Journal of Applied Communication Research, 34*(3), 253–256.
Sandman, P. M. (2006). Crisis communication and best practices: Some quibbles and additions. *Journal of Applied Communication Research, 34*, 257–262.
Sandman, P. M. (2003). Four kinds of risk communication. *The Synergist, 8*, 26–27. https://www.petersandman.com/col/4kind-1.htmApril
Seeger, M. W. (2006). Best practices in crisis communication: An expert panel process. *Journal of Applied Communication Research, 34*(3), 232–244.
Seeger, M. W., Sellnow, T. L., & Ulmer, R. R. (2003). *Communication and Organizational Crisis*. Westport, CT: Praeger.
Sellnow, D. D., Lane, D. R., Sellnow, T. L., & Littlefield, R. S. (2017). The IDEA Model as a best practice for effective instructional risk anbd crisis communication. *Communication Studies, 68*(5), 552–567.
Sellnow, T. L., & Sellnow, D. D. (2010). The instructional dynamic of risk and crisis communication: Distinguishing instructional messages from dialogue. *The Review of Communication, 10*(2), 112–126.
Slovic, P. (1987). Perceptions of risk. *Science, 236*(4799), 280–285.
Sturges, D. L. (1994). Communicating through crisis: A strategy for organizational survival. *Management Communication Quarterly, 7*(3), 297–316.
Sutton, J., & Veil, S. R. (2017). Risk communication and the social media. In R. Kasperson, Ed., *Risk Conundrums: Solving Unsolvable Problems* (pp. 96–111). New York: Earthscan Routledge.
Ulmer, R. R., & Sellnow, T. L. (2002). Crisis management and the discourse of renewal: Understanding the potential for positive outcomes of crisis. *Public Relations Review, 28*(4), 361–365.
Ulmer, R. R., Sellnow, T. L., & Seeger, M. W. (2007). *Effective Crisis Communication: Moving from Crisis to Opportunity*. Thousand Oaks, CA: Sage.
Veil, S. R. (2011). Mindful learning in crisis management. *Journal of Business Communication, 48*(2), 116–147.
Veil, S. R., Anthony, K., Sellnow, T. L., Staricek, N., Young, L., & Cupp, P. (2020). Revisiting the best practices in risk and crisis communication: A multi-case analysis. In H. D. O'Hair, & M. J. O'Hair, Eds., *Handbook of Applied Communication Research* (pp. 377–396). New York: Wiley.
Veil, S. R., Reynolds, B., Sellnow, T. L., & Seeger, M. W. (2008). Crisis & emergency risk communication as a theoretical framework for research and practice. *Health Promotion Practice, 9*(4), 26S–34S.
Venette, S. J. (2006). Special section introduction: Best practices in risk and crisis communication. *Journal of Applied Communication Research, 34*(3), 229–231.

Ware, B. L., & Linkugel, W. A. (1973). They spoke in defense of themselves: On the generic criticism of apologia. *The Quarterly Journal of Speech*, *59*, 273–283.

Weick, K. E. (1988). Enacted sensemaking in a crisis situation. *Journal of Management Studies*, *25*, 305–317.

Weick, K. E. (1993). The collapse of sensemaking in organizations: The Mann Gulch disaster. *Administrative Science Quarterly*, *38*, 628–652.

Weick, K. E., Sutcliffe, K. M., & Obstfeld, D. (2005). Organizing and the process of sensemaking. *Organization Science*, *16*(4), 409.

Weiner, B. (1995). *Judgments of Responsibility: A Foundation for a Theory of Social Conduct*. New York: Guilford.

Windahl, S., Signitzer, B., & Olson, J. T. (1992). *Using Communication Theory: An Introduction to Planned Communication*. Newbury Park, CA: Sage.

Author Bio

Shari R. Veil, MBA, Ph.D., is a professor and dean of the College of Journalism and Mass Communications at the University of Nebraska-Lincoln. She oversees the strategic, programmatic, financial, fundraising, and management operations that support the mission and vision of the college and its role within the university and state. Veil also serves as a research fellow with the National Strategic Research Institute, a Department of Defense-designated University Affiliated Research Center focused on developing solutions for complex problems across the spectrum of chemical, biological, radiological, nuclear, and explosive threats. Her research has been funded by the National Science Foundation, Department of Agriculture, Environmental Protection Agency, and the Department of Homeland Security's National Center for Food Protection and Defense and National Center for Risk and Economic Analysis of Terrorism Events. She's served on expert working groups for the Centers for Disease Control and Prevention and the Food and Drug Administration. Veil earned a Bachelor of Science in communication and a Master of Business Administration from the University of Mary in North Dakota. Her doctorate in communication, with a research focus on risk and crisis communication, is from North Dakota State University.

38

Risk and Crisis Communication in Latin America

Jesús Arroyave[1] and Ana María Erazo-Coronado[2]

[1] Departamento de Comunicación Social, Universidad del Norte, Barranquilla, Colombia
[2] Dirección Especialización Endodoncia, Universidad Metropolitana, Barranquilla, Colombia

The Context of Risk and Crisis Communication in Latin America

Although Latin America stands out internationally for its exuberant nature, great raw material resources, and beautiful landscapes, it also faces significant challenges in crises of various kinds and a wide range of risks. In fact, Latin America and the Caribbean region pertain to the second most disaster-prone regions in the world (UN OCHA, 2020). In the first two decades of this century, nearly 1,205 disasters have affected 152 million people in the region. In addition, several political, social, and economic crises, including the assassination and imprisonment of presidents, massive internal migration within the continent, and the loss of 25 million jobs as a result of the COVID-19 pandemic, have had a dramatic impact on the region and led to the breakdown of institutionalism in some countries.

In terms of the different types of risk to which the region has been exposed, floods have been the most common type of disaster in the first two decades of this century. From 2000 to 2019, there have been 548 floods that cost more than $26 billion, affecting 41 million people in the region. While Brazil has been the most flood-prone country and has been impacted by 70 floods since the beginning of this century, Guyana has been proportionally the most impacted country, mainly due to its lack of preparedness and limited response capacity. As stated by UN OCHA (2020), floods are considered to be one of the costliest natural disasters because of "the wide array and extent of damages caused by flood events, from direct damages and losses to physical and environmental assets, including human belongings and shelter, ecological systems and production across economic sectors, to health-related issues and the loss of human life" (p. 16).

However, this was not the sole catastrophe wreaking havoc upon the region. From 2000 to 2019, around 330 storms, including several hurricanes, made landfall in the Caribbean and coastal nations. The hurricane season of 2017 marked the third most devastating on record, regarding the count of disasters and impacted countries and the scale of destruction incurred. Earthquakes also cast their shadow often, with 75 quakes recorded in Latin America and the Caribbean, 20 of which registered a magnitude of 7.0 or higher. In addition, droughts hold a recurring place in the region's disasterscape, affecting an enormous swath of individuals. A staggering 74 droughts struck the area, impacting 54 million people and causing over US$1.3 trillion in losses. Particularly hard-hit were the Central American countries. Furthermore,

The Handbook of International Crisis and Risk Communication Research, Second Edition.
Edited by Andreas Schwarz, Matthew W. Seeger, and Sora Kim.

other events with substantial ramifications have unfolded, including landslides (66), extreme temperature events (50), volcanic eruptions (38), and forest fires. Many of these disasters exhibit cyclical patterns intricately connected to stationary natural processes.

Parallel to this, different social, political, and economic crises have affected the region at different times during the present century. On the one hand, organized crime is one of the problems that most afflict the region. While only 9% of the world's population lives in Latin America and the Caribbean (LAC), the region accounts for 30% of the world's homicides. Countries such as Venezuela and Honduras register the highest number of homicides in the region and are among the deadliest on the planet (Sahd et al., 2023). The weakness of the state in responding to organized crime, the corruption of the judicial system, and the expansion of criminal groups such as the Jalisco Cartel – New Generation, the Sinaloa Cartel, and the Aragua Train throughout the region have led to various crises that have affected the institutional framework and plunged the inhabitants into a sense of insecurity and powerlessness. As summarized by Sahd et al. (2023), "The region suffers from the weakening of the rule of law, the increase in organized crime and other manifestations of violence, generating a growing sense of insecurity, increased corruption and frustration in the face of impunity for criminal acts" (p. 11).

There is also a political crisis alongside the public order crisis. On the one hand, there are countries such as Nicaragua and Venezuela, where left-wing governments have become entrenched in power, preventing any form of criticism, restricting the freedom of the press, and weakening attempts at change in favor of democratic processes. For its part, Peru has experienced a series of institutional crises in this century. Since 2000, the country has had 11 presidents, five of them in the last four years. Congress has dismissed some, and several have been imprisoned. In Haiti, the country's institutional foundations were destabilized by the assassination of President Jovenel Moïse in 2021. In El Salvador, the right-wing government of Nayib Bukele has been firm in its control of the various criminal gangs that have plagued the country and turned it into a failed state under gang rule. However, the Latin American Political Risk Report led by Sahd et al. (2023) considers that "it stopped being a democracy to become a hybrid regime" (p.13), making dictatorial decisions without respecting public powers.

The humanitarian crisis caused by the migration crisis is another phenomenon that has exploded in the region. Although it is not the only country in the continent, the most dramatic case corresponds to Venezuela, where more than 7 million Venezuelans have migrated or sought refuge in the world. Eighty-five percent have settled in various Latin American countries, including Colombia (1.8 million), Peru (1.2 million), Ecuador (500,000), Chile (448,000), and Brazil (345,000). The crisis manifests itself in issues such as access to health care, housing, education, and employment opportunities, as several Latin American countries have been unprepared to absorb the large flow of migrants. As a result, sexual exploitation, cheap labor that makes working in different countries precarious, and involvement in organized crime have become common, exacerbating xenophobia. Some forms of aggression, such as "the burning of migrants' homes in northern Brazil, aggressions against Venezuelan migrants on public transport in Colombia, or the burning of migrants' belongings during anti-immigration demonstrations in Chile" (Sahd et al., 2023, p. 23) are taking place in the region. This crisis is even more evident in light of the region's loss of 25 million jobs due to the COVID-19 pandemic (IMF).

This concise overview only scratches the surface of the numerous regional risks and crises. These challenges have been further exacerbated by the ongoing pandemic's devastating impact, the escalating political polarization in various nations, and the persistent governance crises that plague the area. Despite the region grappling with a disproportionately higher count of crisis-related predicaments compared to other continents, scholarly exploration and reflection of these matters have remained sparse, particularly within esteemed journals registered in high-impact databases like WoS and Scopus.

Given this landscape, our attention was focused on conducting a methodological examination of the body of research disseminated in crisis and risk communication. Our choice of the WoS and Scopus databases stems from their international prominence and alignment with the pursuit of robust empirical investigations that adhere to rigorous methodological benchmarks. The next section details the procedures followed to compile a comprehensive cross-section of risk and crisis communication research in Latin America.

Methodology

A descriptive, longitudinal, systematic review type research was conducted based on the PRISMA Statement (Page et al., 2021). The research question was constructed using the PICO methodology (P- Problem, I- Intervention, C- Comparison, and O- Outcomes), considering the acronyms P I O because there was no comparison. The research question was: What is the institutional, media, and audience perspective in risk and crisis communication research in Latin America?

The Web of Science (WoS) and Scopus databases were chosen due to their significant impact on scientific research, spanning the study period from 1982 to 2022. When searching for Risk Communication, the keywords employed were as follows: "Comunicación de riesgo," "América Latina," "Investigación," "Temas y abordajes" (in Spanish), and "Risk Communication," "Latin America," "Research," "Issues and Approaches" (in English), linked by the Boolean operator "AND." While it is acknowledged that the term "Latin America" might not explicitly encompass the individual names of Latin American countries, this broader terminology aligns with our comprehensive research objectives. These terms were combined in the search queries, yielding no results for the Spanish combinations. In contrast, the English combinations identified 25 articles in WoS and 78 articles in Scopus, resulting in a cumulative total of 103 articles.

For the search in Crisis Communication, the keywords used were *Comunicación de crisis, América Latina, Investigación, Temas y Enfoques* (Spanish); and in *English: Crisis Communication, Latin America, Research, Issues, and Approaches,* using the Boolean operator "AND."The combination of words in the search boxes yielded no results for the words in Spanish, while for the words in English, 22 articles were initially obtained in WoS and 14 in Scopus, for a total of 36 articles.

Inclusion criteria were original articles and risk and crisis communication topics, while exclusion criteria were review articles, books, book chapters, editor's notes, and health communication topics. The filters were applied manually, eliminating duplicate articles, followed by a filter by title, as they were not related to the subject studied, then by abstract, as they were not available in full text. Finally, the exclusion criteria were applied, resulting in 15 articles on Risk Communication and five on Crisis Communication. Figure 38.1 illustrates the search process according to the PRISMA model for both topics.

Subsequently, a table was prepared according to the general and specific objectives, questions derived from them, and response categories to systematize the information extracted from the articles and proceed to their analysis in Excel (Table 38.1).

Results

For risk communication, 103 articles were identified from the WoS (N = 25) and Scopus (N = 78) databases, resulting in 15 articles for the final analysis, as evidenced in the flow chart. Even though the search period covered the last 40 years (1982–2022), the final articles obtained were published between 2003 and 2022, with a higher scientific production on the subject studied in the last 2 years: 2022 (4 articles) and 2021 (7 articles). In the period

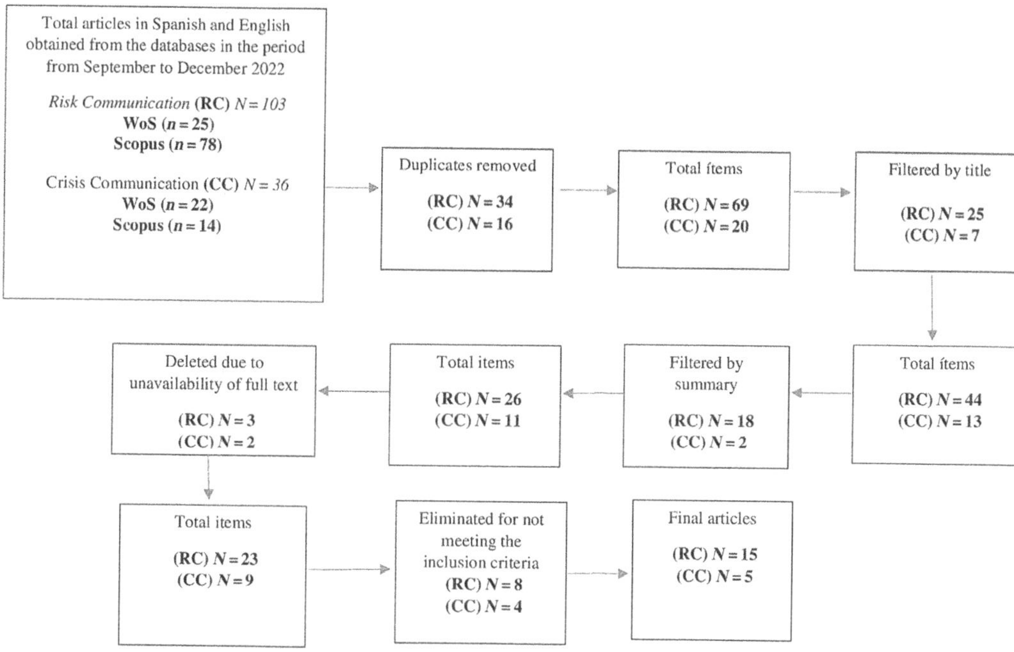

Figure 38.1 Risk and crisis communication flowchart.

between 2020 and 2003, the production was lower, corresponding to one article in 2020, two articles in 2015, and one article in 2003.

In general, all the categorized regions – Southern Cone, Andean countries, Island-Caribbean region, Central America, and Hispanic North America – were the subject of study in the 15 selected articles, highlighting that five studies focused their attention on Latin America as a whole (Azócar et al., 2020; Bancroft et al., 2022; Henríquez-Coronel et al., 2021; Lee et al., 2015; Moyano & Lay Mendivil, 2021).

Regarding the authors' affiliations, 66.6% of the publications were made by authors coming exclusively from university institutions (Azócar et al., 2020; Cárdenas & Pineda, 2021; Coates, 2021; Henríquez-Coronel et al., 2021; Holston et al., 2021; Jensen et al., 2021; Lee et al., 2015; Marcillo-Delgado et al., 2022; Perez & Dabis, 2003). The 33.3% corresponds to collaborations between university academics and research institutes.

For crisis communication, 36 articles were identified from the WoS (N = 22) and Scopus (N = 14) databases, resulting in 5 articles for the final analysis, as evidenced in the flow chart. Although the search period covered the last 40 years (1982–2022), the final articles obtained were published between 2020 and 2022, showing a scientific production on the subject studied during this period as follows: 2022 with 1 article (Marcillo-Delgado et al., 2022), 2021 with two articles (Contreras-Pacheco et al., 2021; Rodelo, 2021) and 2020 with two articles (Cazzamata, 2020; Mira et al., 2020).

In general terms, all the categorized regions – Southern Cone, Andean Countries, Insular Caribbean, Central America, and Hispanic North America – were studied in the five selected articles, noting that only one study focused on Latin America as a whole (Cazzamata, 2020).

Eighty percent of the publications were written by authors from university institutions only (Cazzamata, 2020; Contreras-Pacheco et al., 2021; Marcillo-Delgado et al., 2022; Rodelo, 2021), while 20% corresponded to collaborations between university academics and research institutes (Mira et al., 2020).

Table 38.1 Relationship between objectives, questions, and response categories.

Objectives – research questions – response categories			
General objective	*Specific objectives*	*Questions*	*Categories*
Determine the institutional aspects, media, and audiences of risk and crisis communication research in Latin America.	Establish the year, geographic region where the research was conducted, and type of affiliation of the authors.	During what period of time were the publications made?	Year of publication
		What were the geographic regions studied?	Southern Cone, Andean Countries, Insular-Caribbean Region, Central America, Hispanic North America.
		What is the origin of the authors' affiliations from an institutional point of view?	Academics, Governmental Agencies, United Nations
	Analyze the institutional aspects, media, and audiences addressed in research on risk and crisis communication in Latin America.	How has risk and crisis communication research been approached from an institutional perspective?	Institutional communication, government agencies, NGOs, international organizations
		How have the media addressed risk and crisis communication research?	Traditional mass media, digital media, and alternative media.
		How has risk and crisis communication research been approached from the audience's perspective?	Types of audience, strategies to reach the audience, prevailing approaches (vertical – horizontal, etc.), types of messages.

Institutional Perspective of Risk and Crisis Communication Research in Latin America

A recurring theme from an institutional perspective relates to the difficulties/obstacles/limitations that exist at the level of government agencies or official institutions to respond to the multiple disaster risk or crises that exist in the region (Dookie & Spence-Hemmings, 2022; Marcillo-Delgado et al., 2022; Sell et al., 2020). On the one hand, some studies highlight resource limitations (Sell et al., 2020), the ability to generate or access timely knowledge for decision-making, or even the capacity to respond to environmental challenges affecting certain countries or regions, some of them cyclical (Dookie & Spence-Hemmings, 2022).

In the systematic review conducted by Dookie and Spence-Hemmings (2022), researchers found that the average response time to learn of storms or hurricanes that could potentially affect Caribbean countries was 24 hours. While the analysis shows that there has been a gradual decrease in the time taken by the agencies in charge in the Caribbean, the ability to do so has changed from weekdays to weekends. As the researchers note, "Since there is likely to be a 'weekend effect', i.e., the capacity of agencies to assimilate and disseminate risk information may be less on a weekend than on a weekday, such short awareness periods indicate a challenge to effective preparedness" (p. 123). The researchers concluded that this circumstance poses a challenge that affects decision-making to deal with sometimes dramatic events such as hurricanes and effective preparedness activities to prevent significant impacts. This issue is of great concern given that storms are the second most crucial factor affecting the region, with 330 storms and an average of 17 hurricanes per year in the period 200–2019 (UN OACH, 2020).

Marcillo-Delgado et al. (2022) conducted a systematic review of 29 documents related to strategic communication planning for risk and disaster management (RDM) systems in seven Spanish-speaking South American countries (ssSAc). The researchers identified five components of communication planning to achieve a permanent communication strategy during the pre-disaster, disaster, and post-disaster phases. These elements are (1) early communication planning, (2) information and communication system management planning, (3) quality management planning of communication and communicators, (4) awareness-raising for RDM, and (5) consolidation of stakeholders.

A notable finding emphasized by the researchers is that most countries accorded higher significance to raising awareness for Risk and Disaster Management (RDM). This prioritization established it as the most prominent communication strategy within the ssSAc. Conversely, early communication planning and stakeholder consolidation could have been more relevant. The study's comparative analysis employing these categories concluded that Chile, Ecuador, and Paraguay exhibited stronger associations with preparatory communication ahead of disasters. At the same time, Bolivia and Colombia were aligned with communication strategies during disasters. Argentina and Peru, on the other hand, demonstrated a closer alignment with the communication recommendations outlined by PAHO (Pan American Health Organization).

Nonetheless, the study underscores two significant conclusions drawn from the review of planning documents across the region. Firstly, the absence of post-disaster planning in South American nations positions them as reactive rather than proactive in disaster management. Secondly, aspects like early communication planning and establishing communication networks remained unexplored during the prevention phase in South American countries, underscoring the need for more solidified communication planning.

The institutional perspective in the research also highlights the politicization of disaster preparedness and management, which poses a significant issue in the region. Policies related to preparedness often change with shifts in government, leading to disruptions and discontinuity of programs. Official agencies become political arenas, with new governments undoing or altering their predecessors' initiatives. Conflicting political viewpoints further hinder disaster education and risk planning efforts, undermining community well-being. Coates (2021) presents a Brazilian case study demonstrating how politicized disaster education confuses rather than provides clear guidance. Politics negatively impact community preparedness and training strategies, ultimately weakening community agency and management due to the competing influences of social, institutional, and political-economic factors.

Contreras-Romero et al. (2021) investigated how four extractive companies managed crisis communication when faced with adverse or offensive situations. The researchers identified various strategies employed by these companies in response to the crises. One company projected an image of controlling the situation, despite the contrary reality (PDVSA). Another chose to conceal all or part of the incident (Drummond), while a different company resorted to lying about the causes of the crisis (Grupo México). The fourth company initially downplayed the magnitude of the crisis but eventually acknowledged its severity over time. These strategies were problematic and had detrimental effects on the organization's image.

Apart from the identified strategies, the researchers discovered additional secondary tactics. These included maintaining deception by altering specific facts, delaying the official report of the incident, searching for a scapegoat to divert attention, and obstructing third-party inquiries into the crisis events. However, the companies' responses were unsatisfactory when questioned about their actions during the crises. The researchers also noted that it seemed almost obligatory for these companies to counterattack either the government (or environmental regulators) or media representatives who raised questions about their crisis management actions.

The study of the institutional dimension underscores the importance of thoroughly examining the roles played by government agencies, private companies, and NGOs in crisis and risk situations. This expands the landscape of comprehensive research that contributes to addressing various regional challenges. Building on the work of Dookie and Spence-Hemmings (2022), Marcillo-Delgado et al. (2022), and Contreras-Romero et al. (2021), there is a clear need to explore strategies for improving risk communication and crisis management in both the public and private sectors.

Media Perspective of Risk and Crisis Communication Research in Latin America

The global shift toward digitization, known as the digital turn, has significantly impacted crisis management and risk communication in Latin America, as noted in regional studies that focus on different forms of media, including traditional and social media. Traditional communication channels, with their infrastructure requirements and limited accessibility, have been replaced by easily accessible social media platforms, which allow for widespread content creation and distribution through devices such as phones, computers, and tablets. The COVID-19 pandemic has further accelerated the adoption of social media for communication and knowledge sharing. Government agencies increasingly use social media to share critical crisis prevention and management information. Recent academic contributions in the region examine government strategies for disseminating information and assess the quality and effectiveness of information provided through these official online platforms.

For example, in their study, Cárdenas and Pineda (2021) examined the use of social networks in risk communication management in 12 Latin American countries concerning the COVID-19 pandemic, specifically Facebook. The researchers found that recommendations for self-care and collective care and biosafety protocols for socioeconomic activities, which were expected to be central themes in each country, were not the most important in the region. In Brazil, for example, these issues were not central on Facebook, with some messages showing denial and apathy. Mexico also had none of these priority issues on Facebook. The authors concluded that "only five of the twelve countries surveyed included self-care recommendations as their first agenda item" (p. 89).

Similarly, Moyano and Lay Mendivil (2021) found significant gaps in the thematic and cross-cutting treatment of the diversity of communication products "with little adaptation to different languages – in a context where most Latin American (LAC) countries have indigenous populations" (p. 7). In fact, after analyzing 3,253 information products published on the official websites of the Ministries of Health in 47 LAC countries and territories, the researchers expressed concern about the lack of gender focus, which demonstrated the failure to adapt interventions and messages to the different groups in the pieces used. Worsting was that "messages were found to contain information that was not supported by scientific data and was largely based on hearsay" (p. 7). Based on what the researchers found, it is clear that some of these portals needed more help in dealing with a crisis as significant as COVID-19 in the region.

Cárdenas and Pineda (2021) present interesting findings highlighting a distinction between traditional and digital media. The authors point to a significant contrast in the communication strategies employed in digital and non-digital contexts. In the digital realm, there appears to be a strong tendency to focus risk communication on educational issues with a public health orientation. In contrast, in traditional media, many presidents are often portrayed as engaging with issue experts on online platforms, fostering a more politically oriented discourse, and using the pandemic to advance their governmental agendas and future electoral interests. Nevertheless, the researchers observed increased followers for presidential and Ministry of Health accounts. In cases such as Colombia, this surge represented a remarkable 1,162% increase, underscoring the central role of this tool in everyday life.

Holston et al. (2021) conducted a successful pilot study in Managua, Nicaragua, using the social media platform DengueChat to control the Aedes aegypti mosquito and reduce dengue virus transmission. This approach combined digital communication with face-to-face interactions, increasing community engagement and vector control effectiveness. In contrast, Henríquez-Coronel et al. (2021) found shortcomings in digital tools for official disaster response in 20 Latin American countries. Limited mechanisms for immediate response to natural hazards and a lack of updates were identified, highlighting risk and disaster prevention challenges.

Sell et al. (2020) engaged policymakers and practitioners in discussions about Zika information practices during the outbreak in Brazil. Constrained resources and insufficient collaborations hindered public health communication capabilities. The study highlighted the importance of alliances between the public sector and local communities to overcome communication barriers, but sustaining these partnerships demands significant investments. Furthermore, Rodelo's (2021) content analysis of COVID-19 portrayal in Mexico's media identified prevalent frames like responsibility attribution, human interest, and political action, while the scientific information frame was notably underutilized in both newspapers and television news broadcasts. This raises questions about the necessity of rigorous evaluations for the effectiveness of interventions in the region.

In summary, our findings highlight the potential significance of media during times of crisis or risk situations, although the conclusions drawn from studies are varied. On the one hand, proponents of digital risk prevention and communication strategies often present positive and impactful outcomes. However, empirical evaluations of such experiences often yield unfavorable results with minimal influence. Consequently, further research is imperative to comprehend the media's potential within risk management and crisis communication processes, especially concerning emerging digital platforms.

Audience Perspective of Risk and Crisis Communication Research in Latin America

Studies focusing on audience perceptions of crisis and risk messages in Latin America are relatively limited but highlight key message comprehension challenges. For instance, Jensen et al. (2021) interviewed recycling workers in Colombia, revealing disparities between perceived and actual mercury exposure risks due to limited environmental health literacy and reliance on informal sources. This underscores the need for better public health communication regarding workplace hazards. The need for more Spanish-language resources and the challenges of accessing online information also hinder awareness.

The focus on the human role in disasters has gained prominence in Latin America, spurred by influential figures like Mercer (2010), who have revolutionized the comprehension of natural disasters. Nonetheless, disregarding the human element poses a challenge, as disasters frequently stem from human activities. This is exemplified by recurring floods devastating areas along riverbanks or slopes susceptible to landslides. Acknowledging human accountability is pivotal in reshaping risk scenarios through comprehensive developmental models, both rural and urban planning, and initiatives for secure housing. The findings of the climate change study align with this perspective. Through their analysis of survey data encompassing 119 countries, Lee et al. (2015) discovered that comprehending the anthropogenic origins of climate change is the most potent predictor of climate change risk perceptions. This holds especially true for Latin America and Europe.

The research focused on climate change and risk perceptions in Latin America underscores the importance of considering the perspectives of audiences and stakeholders. De Mel et al. (2021) identified barriers to stakeholders' use of climate risk information, including lack of access to such information, resource constraints, and institutional challenges. Bancroft et al. (2022) examined outbreaks of mosquito-borne diseases in Brazil and identified challenges in ensuring compliance with repellent use and the disproportionate responsibility placed on women for control measures, leading to their exhaustion. The lack of cooperation between communities and local governments has affected the response to this disease. In Colombia, a school-based HIV prevention program (Pérez & Dabis, 2003) successfully increased knowledge and awareness through peer education and classroom sessions, demonstrating the effectiveness of such interventions in promoting sexual health. The strategy of comprehensive education, combining school-based initiatives with events and supported by effective interpersonal communication, such as peer education, classroom teaching, and community involvement, is emerging as an effective primary prevention approach to the sexual transmission of HIV.

Case Study: Risk and Crisis Communication During the COVID-19 Pandemic in Latin America and Colombia

During the recent COVID-19 pandemic, six Latin American countries, including Brazil, Peru, Mexico, Colombia, Chile, and Argentina, were among the 12 most severely affected nations. Amid this crisis, Brazil faced allegations of corruption related to procuring virus detection tests and misallocating funds. In Chile, authorities faced criticism for changing methodologies in tracking death counts, leading to public dissatisfaction. Crisis communication from an institutional perspective, as Riorda (2008) advocates, involves consistent updates on public policies and direct communication with the public, employing digital strategies, and maintaining the presence of the current leader.

However, some leaders exhibited detrimental denialism in handling the crisis. For instance, Brazil's President Jair Bolsonaro downplayed the virus, likening it to the flu, thus undermining preventive measures and fostering misinformation. Consequently, the WHO identified Brazil, along with the United Kingdom and India, as having mishandled the pandemic (Lilleker et al., 2021). In Colombia, President Iván Duque, who started with low public approval ratings, navigated the crisis differently. Early risk communication efforts involved announcing diagnostic tests and preventive measures through various platforms. Utilizing a panel of experts and focused communication strategies, including the CoronApp and the television program "Prevention and Action," the government aimed to provide information, reduce uncertainty, establish credibility, and demonstrate crisis management results. However, as the pandemic transitioned to economic concerns, the communication focus shifted toward economic reactivation (Ramirez, 2021).

Conclusion

Crisis and risk communication research in Latin America and the Caribbean encompasses different crises and risks, often linked to disasters and natural phenomena. Despite this, the region needs more systematic research leading to concrete interventions, even though many recurrent disasters stem from cyclical and fixed phenomena. Effectively addressing these challenges requires a comprehensive approach to planning, risk reduction, and crisis prevention across the region.

In addition, Latin America and the Caribbean have experienced political and economic crises that have led to various problems, including political instability and numerous upheavals with potentially fatal consequences. In order to comprehensively address these issues and explore effective solutions, developing new theoretical frameworks and applied research is imperative. By fostering a deeper understanding of the issues at hand and paving the way for innovative alternatives, such research efforts have the potential to bring about significant positive change.

References

Azócar, G., Billi, M., Calvo, R., Huneeus, N., Lagos, M., Sapiains, R., & Urquiza, A. (2020). Climate change perception, vulnerability, and readiness: Inter-country variability and emerging patterns in Latin America. *Journal of Environmental Studies and Sciences*, 1–15. https://doi.org/10.1007/s13412-020-00639-0

Bancroft, D., Power, G. M., Jones, R. T., Massad, E., Bernstein Iriart, J., Preet, R., Kinsman, J., & Logan, J. G. (2022). Vector control strategies in Brazil: A qualitative investigation into community knowledge, attitudes and perceptions following the 2015-2016 Zika virus epidemic. *BMJ Open*, *12*, e050991. https://doi.org/10.1136/ bmjopen-2021-050991

Cárdenas Ruiz, J. D., & Pineda Rodríguez, N. C. (2021). Managing risk communication through Facebook: Exploratory analysis of the initial strategies of 12 Latin American governments in the face of the COVID-19 pandemic. *Revista de Comunicación*, *20*(2), 73–91. https://doi.org/10.26441/RC20.2-2021-A4

Cazzamata, R. (2020). Crises as catalysts of foreign reporting on Latin America: An evaluation of the German press over 15 years. *Media, War & Conflict*, *15*(3), 315–333. https://doi.org/10.1177/1750635220945737

Coates, R. (2021). Educational hazards? The politics of disaster risk education in Rio de Janeiro. *Disasters*, *45*(1), 86–106. https://doi.org/10.1111/disa.12399

Contreras-Pacheco, O. E., Claasen, C., & Garrigós-Simón, F. J. (2021). Engaging with untruthful company crisis communication: The understanding of decoupling in the face of crisis. *Intangible Capital*, *17*(1), 33–51. https://doi.org/10.3926/ic.1775

De Mel, M., Solecki, W., Horton, R., Bartlett, R., Hehmeyer, A., Martin, S., & Rosenzweig, C. (2021). Perceptions of climate risk and use of climate risk information by natural resource conservation stakeholders participating in ADVANCE projects in Asia and Latin America. *Weather, Climate, and Society*, *13*, 423–436. https://doi.org/10.1175/WCAS-D-20-0010.1

Dookie, D. S., & Spence-Hemmings, J. (2022). The timing of storm awareness in the Caribbean: The utility of climate information for improved disaster preparedness. *Disasters*, *46*(S1), S101–S127. https://doi.org/10.1111/disa.12540

Henríquez-Coronel, P., Zambrano-Yepez, C., Herrera-Tapia, J., & Barreiro-Moreno, M. (June 23–26, 2021). Risk communication in the portals of public organizations in latin america. *Towards an initial assessment.* 16th Iberian Conference on Information Systems and Technologies (CISTI). Spain.

Holston, J., Suazo-Laguna, H., Harris, E., & Coloma, J. (2021). Dengue chat: A social and software platform for community-based arbovirus vector control. *The American Journal Tropical Medicine and Hygiene*, *105*(6), 1521–1535. https://doi.org/10.4269/ajtmh.20-0808

Jensen, M., Combariza Bayona, D. A., & Sripada, K. (2021). Mercury exposure among E-waste recycling workers in Colombia: Perceptions of safety, risk, and access to health information. *International Journal of Environmental Research and Public Health*, *18*(17), 9295. https://doi.org/10.3390/ijerph18179295

Lee, T. M., Markowitz, E. M., Howe, P. D., Ko, C. Y., & Leiserowitz, A. A. (2015). Predictors of public climate change awareness and risk perception around the world. *Nature Climate Change*, *5*, 1014–1020. https://doi.org/10.1038/nclimate2728

Lilleker, D., Coman, I. A., Gregor, M., & Novelli (Eds.). (2021). *Political communication and COVID-19. Governance and Rhetoric in Times of Crisis.* Routledge.

Marcillo-Delgado, J. C., Alvarez- García, A., & García- Carrillo, A. (2022). Communication strategies on risk and disaster management in South American countries. *International Journal of Disaster Risk Reduction*, *76*, 102982. https://doi.org/10.1016/j.ijdrr.2022.102982

Mercer, J. (2010). Disaster risk reduction or climate change adaptation: Are we reinventing the wheel? *Journal of International Development, 22*(2), 247–264. https://doi.org/10.1002/jid.1677

Mira, J. J., Carrillo, I., García-Elorrio, E., Andrade-Lourenção, D. C. D. E., Pavan-Baptista, P. C., Franco-Herrera, A. L., Campos-Castolo, E. M., Poblete, R., Limo, J., Siu, H., & Sousa, P. (2020). What Ibero-American hospitals do when things go wrong? A cross-sectional international study. *International Journal for Quality in Health Care, 32*(5), 313–318. https://doi.org/10.1093/intqhc/mzaa031

Moyano, D., & Lay Mendivil, L. (2021). Communication products for COVID-19 prevention promoted by Latin American and Caribbean governments. *Revista Panamericana de Salud Pública, 45*(e111), 1–10. https://doi.org/10.26633/RPSP.2021.111

Page, M. J., Mckenzie, J. E., Bossuyt, P. M., Boutron, I., Hoffmann, T. C., Mulrow, C. D., Shamseer, L., Tetzlaff, J. M., Akl, E. A., Brennan, S. E., Chou, R., Glanville, J., Grimshaw, J. M., Hróbjartsson, A., Lalu, M. M., Li, T., Loder, E. W., Mayo-Wilson, E., McDonald, S. et al. (2021). The PRISMA 2020 statement: An updated guideline for reporting systematic reviews. *Systematic Reviews, 10*(89), 10–10. https://doi.org/10.1186/s13643-021-01626-4

Perez, F., & Dabis, F. (2003). HIV prevention in Latin America: Reaching youth in Colombia. *AIDS Care: Psychological and Socio-medical Aspects of AIDS/HIV, 15*(1), 77–87. https://doi.org/10.1080/0954012021000039789

Ramírez Salcedo, J. S. (2021). *Coronavirus Crisis: Governmental Communication in Iván Duque's Presidency.* Degree thesis, Pontificia Universidad Javeriana. https://repository.javeriana.edu.co/bitstream/handle/10554/57806/Trabajo%20de%20Grado%20final.pdf?sequence=3 (accessed January 29 2024).

Riorda, M. (2008). Gobierno bien pero comunico mal: análisis de las Rutinas de la Comunicación Gubernamental. *Revista del CLAD Reforma y Democracia, 40*, 25–52. Available at https://www.redalyc.org/pdf/3575/357533671002.pdf

Rodelo, F. V. (2021). Framing of the Covid-19 pandemic and its organizational predictors. *Cuadernos Info, 50*, 91–112. https://doi.org/10.7764/cdi.50.37525

Sahd, J., Zovatto, D., & Rojas, D. (2023). *Riesgo político en América Latina.* Centro UC, Estudios Internacionales CEIUC.

Sell, T. K., Ravi, S. J., Watson, C., Meyer, D., Pechta, L. E., Rose, D. A., Lubell, K. M., Podgornik, M. N., & Schoch-Spana, M. (2020). A public health systems view of risk communication about Zika. *Public Health Reports, 135*(3), 343–353. https://doi.org/10.1177/0033354920912215

UN- OCHA (March -2020). Natural disasters in Latin America and the Caribbean 2000-2019. Report-UN-OCHA: Ancon: Panama.

Author's Bio

Jesús Arroyave is a full professor in the Department of Communication and Journalism at the Universidad del Norte. His professional interests focus on journalism and media studies, health and risk communication, and communication for development and social change. His research has been published in journals such as *Journalism, Journalism Studies, International Journal of Communication, Feminist Media Studies, Cuadernos.info, Palabra Clave, and Signo y Pensamiento.* He has extensive experience as a consultant to various United Nations agencies in health communication and communication for development and social change. He has been a visiting scholar/scientist in Spain, Germany, the United Kingdom, and the United States.

Ana María Erazo-Coronado is a Dentist (Universidad de Cartagena, Colombia), Endodontist (Universidade Estadual de Campinas, UNICAMP, Brasil) and has a PhD in Communication (Universidad del Norte, Colombia). She is a full professor at the School of Dentistry of Universidad Metropolitana, Barranquilla, Colombia. She has extensive knowledge and experience in dentistry, risk and crisis communication, and the design, implementation, and evaluation of health communication strategies. She participated in health communication projects of national and international organizations to provide tools that generate the capacities of vulnerable populations to deal with health problems.

39

Risk and Crisis Communication Research in Brazil

Rodrigo Soares[1], Rozália Del Gáudio Soares[2], and Paulo Henrique Soares[3]

[1] University of Vermont, Department of Agriculture, Landscape & Environment, Burlington, VT, USA

[2] Inspiria 3 Consulting, São Paulo, SP, Brazil

[3] Brazilian Mining Institute, Belo Horizonte, MG, Brazil

The advancement of social science research in Brazil, including communication research, coincides with the period when the federal government began to invest in science and technology, starting in 1930 and intensifying after 1970. Initially, the government invested in the expansion of public higher education institutions and in the establishment of a national education and research system. The approach aimed at funding the creation of graduate programs and providing resources to graduate school faculty to foster scientific research within the University system (Romancini, 2007).

Regarding Communication research, specifically, Peruzzo (2018) conducted a systematic review of the literature and recognized the diversity of themes covered by communication research in Brazil. Although diverse, the main focus has been on themes related to journalism and, more recently, subjects related to the internet and cyberculture. The review criticizes the lack of methodological rigor on part of the communication research in Brazil. González (2017) mentions the pressure of the current science and technology policies, which makes researchers focus more on quantity rather than on scientific quality. Therefore, there are some challenges when it comes to the exigence and robustness of communication research in Brazil.

Our goal with this chapter is to provide an assessment of the state of the risk and crisis communication research in Brazil. We found that the field is not as prominent as it is in North America, some European countries, and other parts of the world. This was first proved by the difficulty we faced when defining our search strategy. There are no specific conference thematic divisions or journals dedicated to risk and crisis communication, unlike in other countries, such as the United States, where there are journals dedicated to the field (e.g., Journal of Contingencies and Crisis Management – JCCM). To conduct our search, we relied on the Scielo platform, the Brazilian Scientific Electronic Online Library, and found one thematic publication under the communication search criterion: *Intercom – Revista Brasileira de Comunicação* (Brazilian Journal of Communication). It was listed under the broader field of applied social sciences. We also searched the Brazilian Digital Library of Theses and Dissertations

The Handbook of International Crisis and Risk Communication Research, Second Edition.
Edited by Andreas Schwarz, Matthew W. Seeger, and Sora Kim.

(BDTD) and found that less than 1% of the communication theses and dissertations listed were related to risk and/or crisis communication.

Lastly, for a more targeted assessment, we searched a database of scientific research in risk and crisis communication in Brazil created by the *Universidade Federal de Santa Maria* (Santa Maria Federal University). Although it also lacks a more rigorous methodology for selecting what is included, the list contains book chapters, journal articles, reports, and other publications related to the field. This part of our investigation showed a strong focus on organizational crises and qualitative methods, mainly case studies, interviews, and thematic analyses. Most studies are also practical and non-theoretical in essence.

Our chapter will begin with an analysis of the state of the scientific research on risk and crisis communication in Brazil. The following section will describe and analyze three recent crises that happened in the country and the lessons learned. Lastly, we will discuss some opportunities and recommendations to expand the field of risk and crisis communication research in the country.

The State of Risk and Crisis Communication Research in Brazil

As described in the previous section, the first challenge we faced while writing this chapter was the definition of a research strategy. We had difficulties in finding available data about risk and crisis communication research in Brazil for one simple reason: the field is underexplored from a scientific perspective. Peruzzo (2018) described the lingering focus on discussing the epistemology of what is communication, its object, and whether or not it should be considered a science or a field of study. The review also emphasizes the diversity of themes and methodologies. Regarding the latter, there is criticism about the superficiality of the methodological description in communication studies. Furthermore, there is no association or institute dedicated to the field of risk and crisis communication. The Brazilian Association of Business Communication (ABERJE) offers short-term practical training in crisis communication, but the association has a broader business communication focus. Scientific research in communication, in its broader sense, is still in a developmental phase as compared to other countries (Marchiori & Oliveira, 2009). The sub-field of risk and crisis communication is, therefore, in its early stage in Brazil.

During our search, we identified three main sources that provided an overview of the state of risk and crisis communication research in Brazil. The first one was identified through the Scielo platform, the Intercom – *Revista Brasileira de Comunicação* (Brazilian Journal of Communication). We conducted an analysis of all issues over the past five years (2019–2023). During this period, the journal published a total of 150 articles covering a variety of communication topics (journalism, social media, broadcast television etc.). Among these 150 articles, only 3 (2% of the total) were related to risk and crisis communication research. These few articles covered risk and crisis communication directly or indirectly while focusing on different research objectives.

Silva and Baldissera (2021) assessed strategies taken by organizations with the goal of reducing their visibility on social media in various situations, including crisis responses. The study also analyzed such strategies from the publics' perspective, considering their ethical and legal implications. In line with Peruzzo's (2018) findings, the study did not include a specific methods section, although it describes the use of interviews and content analysis.

A study conducted by Cajazeira et al. (2022) looked at the news coverage during the COVID-19 pandemic. The study identified three political crises triggered by the federal government that worsened the already serious crisis created by the pandemic. Besides using exploratory and bibliographical research, the study employed content analysis as its main methodology, which was clearly described in a specific section.

Gramacho (2022) took a different route and assessed the media effects of TV commercials that "glorify risks and long-term associations, such as the use of violent videogames, on the attitudes of young people towards driving experiences" (p. 1). The study used a between-subjects experiment to understand people's perceptions of risk based on different treatments (TV commercials) shown to the participants during commercial breaks in popular TV shows. After being exposed to the treatments, participants responded to a questionnaire to address their risk attitudes.

These studies show the diversity of topics and methods used by Brazilian researchers. But as previously mentioned, they represent only 2% of the articles published on Intercom.

The second source used in our investigation was the Brazilian Digital Library of Theses and Dissertations (BDTD). We conducted an analysis to identify how risk and crisis communication have been influencing the production of scientific knowledge by early career researchers. We considered the same timeframe used for the analysis of Intercom (2019–2023). Using the keyword *communication* as the main search criterion for theses and dissertations written in Portuguese, we found 3,833 research projects. When we narrowed the criterion to include not only *communication* but also *crisis*, we found only 18 studies. Adopting the same approach but using *risk* and *communication* as the keywords, we found 25 studies. In order to test a different search criterion, we used the (Title) field, rather than the (Subject) one. With this approach, we were able to find 27 studies with the word *crisis* in the title and 20 studies with *risk* as part of the title (see Table 39.1).

This specific source supported our assessment that research in risk and crisis communication is still in its early stages in Brazil. Just less than 1% of the communication theses and dissertations completed in the country over the past five years had risk and/or crisis communication as its main research topic.

These crisis communication studies also showed a thematic diversity, although the majority of them focused on journalism and the perspective of the media during different crisis stages. Moreover, some studies considered organizational communication as their main object of analysis of how crises unfolded and how these organizations responded.

Motta (2020) analyzed the communication strategies used by the Brazilian Department of Health to address the vaccination crisis, more specifically, the Polio and Measles 2018 vaccination campaign. The study used a triangulation of methods (codification cycles, historical descriptive analysis, and descriptive analysis). Results showed that the campaign lacked a dialogical focus, prioritizing information over communication.

Ceni (2021) assessed the crisis communication approach taken by the Brazilian mining company Vale after the collapse of one of its dams, a tragedy that resulted in the loss of 270 lives. They also analyzed the perspective of an NGO that was created to monitor this crisis response process. The study discussed the post-crisis sensemaking-sensegiving process through the collection and analysis of secondary data from the internet and social media.

When it comes to risk communication, the thematic diversity was even more salient. Public communication campaigns, journalism, and organizational communication were some of the perspectives considered as researchers analyzed how risks were managed and communicated.

Table 39.1 Brazilian digital library of theses and dissertations (BDTD, 2019–2023).

Search criterion	*N*	*%*
Subject: Communication	3833	
Subject: Communication + Crisis	18	0.47
Subject: Communication + Risk	25	0.65
Subject: Communication/Title: Crisis	27	0.70
Subject: Communication/Title: Risk	20	0.52

Table 39.2 Publications on risk and crisis communication listed in the Observatório de Comunicação de Crise (UFSM, 2019–2023).

Topics	*N*	%
Organizational Communication	20	41.7
Journalism	7	14.6
Internet/Social Media	6	12.5
Public Communication/Political Communication	5	10.4
Others	10	20.8

Souza (2023) studied how journalism deals with the risks of disasters in a highly vulnerable scenario. The study approached risk communication in the news as a social construction of reality. Risks related to the mining sector were the main focus of a content analysis of news coverage of recent mining disasters. The author found that there is a more intense discussion in the news about risks during the post-crisis stage and that risk communication tends to fade over time.

Leitao (2020) assessed risk communication convergence and its impact on the credibility of Anvisa, the Brazilian Health Regulatory Agency. The study used a 2 × 2 experiment to test how actionable the risk messages were in the communication of a fictitious drug. Among other results, the study found a positive relationship between consistency in risk communication messages and Anvisa's credibility; when risk communication messages were consistent, Anvisa's credibility was perceived as higher.

The last source we explored was the database *Observatório de Comunicação de Crise* (Crisis Communication Observatory) created by the *Universidade Federal de Santa Maria* (Santa Maria Federal University). The list is the only exclusive thematic collection of studies in the field that we could identify. They used some of the same sources we used in our analyses, such as the Brazilian Digital Library of Theses and Dissertations, but they also include conference proceedings and other scientific sources. There are no categories, filters, or order, which makes the database difficult to use. It shows, though, that there is a large focus on organizational crises and descriptive case studies as the main methodology applied by researchers.

Although the database includes studies since 2010, our search considered the list of published articles and conference proceedings, written in Portuguese, and published between 2019 and 2023 ($N = 48$). Table 39.2 shows the diversity of topics covered by these studies. More than 40% of the articles analyzed crises faced by organizations, with a clear focus on descriptive case studies. Almost 15% of the studies explored crises and their impacts from a journalistic perspective. Internet and social media aspects of crises were the object of 12.5% of the research projects, while around 10% of the studies investigated the political implications of crises. The remaining 20.8% of the studies covered a variety of topics out of these categories.

The analyses above support our assessment that the risk and crisis communication research in Brazil is in an early stage. However, these examples also show great opportunities for researchers in the country to expand the field and explore its research gaps.

The next section will shift from research into practice and describe how recent crises in Brazil have been managed and how the crisis communication process has influenced public and media perceptions.

Risk and Crisis Communication in Brazil – Relevant cases from the past 10 years

The recent major crises in Brazil have shown a precarious assessment of operational and business risks while also exposing Brazil's hierarchical cultural traits. As observed by De Barros and Prates (1996), Brazilian culture generally shows characteristics of concentration of power based on hierarchy, subordination, personalism, paternalism, more passive attitudes among non-leaders, and a sense of impunity. Brazilians tend to protect relationships and avoid conflicts. Consequently, issues signaling latent crises either take longer to be addressed or are not brought up by teams, contributing to an environment with greater tolerance for risk and failures. Recently, NGOs, governmental organizations, and high-profile retail and industrial organizations have experienced situations of great negative exposure in both traditional and social media, extensive lawsuits, and, in many cases, financial liability.

Some of these crises resulted from inefficient risk assessment and communication processes. As a consequence, there has been a structured movement from various regulatory agencies and civil society – worth highlighting the role of the Brazilian Central Bank – in strengthening regulations by offering credit to entities engaged in the assessment of social and environmental risks.

For example, with regard to environmental risks, the Central Bank issued Resolution 4327, created in 2014 and expanded in 2021. The resolution focused on establishing important socio-environmental requirements to be met by financial institutions. This piece of legislation aimed to emphasize these organizations' duty of diligence regarding their credit policies, aiming at improving their risk management processes and, consequently, minimizing the risk of crises (Youssif et al., 2022).

Despite this important advancement in the regulatory framework regarding risk assessment and communications, some recent crises show that there are opportunities to improve the management, governance, control systems, and communication processes related to risk and crises in Brazil.

In this section of our chapter, we will summarize three recent relevant crises in Brazil by describing how the entities responded and what lessons can be learned from these events. We used secondary data from news websites and portals to structure the narrative around what each crisis situation encompassed, how the response processes unfolded from a communicational standpoint, and which lessons we could learn from them.

Leadership Insensitivity During the COVID-19 Pandemic and the Impact on People

In January 2021, during one of the peaks of the COVID-19 pandemic in Brazil, hospitals in the city of Manaus, capital of the state of Amazonas, faced a critical shortage of medical oxygen, which is essential for the treatment of seriously ill patients. Demand exceeded supply capacity, resulting in a highly impactful emergency scenario with patients dying and others demanding emergency transfers to other states. A succession of missteps led to the oxygen crisis in Manaus ("A sucessão," 2021).

Under normal circumstances, the daily demand of medical oxygen would be fully met by the only gas manufacturer in the state, White Martins. However, due to the volume of infected people, the state government warned that production would not be sufficient. Even after the warnings, important public health measures to contain the spread of the disease, such as the closing of businesses, were suspended. This exposed the population to new strains of the virus, leading to an explosion of cases and exacerbating the oxygen shortage.

With the demand critically increasing, an exchange of accusations began between state and federal governments about responsibilities. Brazil's President at that time, Jair Bolsonaro, asked the minister of health, Eduardo Pazuello, to intervene in the state. However, rather than prioritizing the support to the state government with supply of oxygen, the federal government took the opportunity to engage in a rhetorical effort to promote medications – such as Hydroxychloroquine – that had not been scientifically proven to be effective in treating the disease. By January 14th, oxygen ran out in all Manaus hospitals, leading to an unconfirmed number of 41 deaths (Schimidt, 2021).

There was intense mobilization of civil society, private companies, NGOs, and other stakeholder groups to help normalize the supply. These entities took on the role of what Millner et al. (2011) called proxy communicators and filled the void left by the Brazilian Federal Government.

President Jair Bolsonaro was criticized for making a controversial statement while the critical situation in Manaus was unfolding. During a visit to the state of Maranhão, Bolsonaro made a joke imitating a person choking and sarcastically suggesting that the situation in Manaus was under control, minimizing the seriousness of the disease. A few months later, and with the pandemic still raging in the country, the President kept imitating patients with shortness of breath in his live broadcasts, as this rhetoric resonated with his political base ("Em transmissão," 2021).

Within a context where Brazilians, particularly those residing in Manaus, had been profoundly affected by the pandemic, the President´s actions, coupled with the lack of organization and a swift government response, resulted in intense and negative media coverage, thereby worsening the crisis. This underscored the need for more effective and empathetic leadership to navigate the challenges posed by the ongoing public health emergency. As the nation faces the consequences of the pandemic, a critical reflection on the President´s approach becomes imperative for informed and responsible decision-making in the future.

Lessons learned:

- Empathy, especially from top leadership, is an essential component of an effective crisis response (König et al., 2020; Schoofs et al., 2019). The lack of empathy on the part of the federal government turned what was at the time a critical, but mainly logistical situation, into an unnecessary rhetorical crisis during a mega-crisis that the country and the world were already facing.
- People forget, but the internet does not. Leaders should be careful about controversial statements and rhetorical mockery of human pain. During the 2022 presidential campaign, then-president and re-election candidate Jair Bolsonaro denied that he had made impressions of COVID-19 patients suffering during the pandemic. However, traditional media and other presidential candidates widely disseminated the videos, contributing to eroding the President's image during the campaign. He ended up defeated and not being re-elected, but the real victims of the lack of sensitivity were those who suffered from a life-threatening disease and who could not have access to basic treatment due to political disputes between different levels of government.

The Water Crisis in São Paulo

Between 2014 and 2015, the state of São Paulo, the most economically developed state in Brazil, faced a significant water supply crisis. The crisis was caused by a combination of adverse climate factors, inadequate management of water resources, and population growth. During these two years, there was below-average rainfall, which lowered the water levels in the reservoirs. It was also a period marked by a decline in infrastructure investments due to the slowdown in the domestic and global economies. This combination resulted in a widespread water shortage in the region, impacting the provision of basic services to the population (Custódio, 2015).

The state government then implemented a rigorous water rationing plan that restricted access to water for the population and local businesses. As a result, industrial production processes had to be reviewed or placed on a contingency mode, which affected basic services.

The economic impact was significant, especially in sectors such as agriculture, industry, and tourism. For example, during the peak of the crisis, restaurants in São Paulo had to close their doors due to water shortages. A survey conducted by FIESP – São Paulo Industries' Federation showed that almost 70% of the industries were worried about the possibility of water rationing, and 65% understood that a water interruption would severely impact their finances (Martín, 2014).

Private organizations, local governments, and non-governmental organizations joined forces and developed campaigns to encourage water savings. On an emergency basis, new infrastructure investments were made, including the construction and expansion of reservoirs and the improvement of water capture, treatment, and reuse systems. This adverse scenario, associated with the recognition of climate change as a critical issue, led to the review of integrated water resources management plans and public policies related to water distribution and consumption (Rossi, 2014).

Communication during the crisis focused not only on providing the population with instructions on how to reduce consumption and save water but also on sharing daily reports on the water levels in the state's main supply system. This system reached zero capacity in May 2014. The government then decided to expand the use of another water system, including the capture of what is called "dead volume" – water that had never been used. The measure required an intense communication effort as the population and the federal government questioned the quality of the water, among other potential issues.

It is important to highlight that the water and sewage services in São Paulo are carried out by public and private companies, consortiums, or PPPs (public-private partnerships). This can make the crisis response process even more complex, limiting the capacity of consensus among various stakeholders and possibly creating failed sensemaking (Nowling & Seeger, 2020).

Martirani and Peres (2016) evaluated this crisis communication response and found that while there was extensive media coverage that contributed to public awareness of the state's water supply problems, there was also silence regarding the structural causes of the problem and the public policies that may have contributed to the issue. The crisis response and the positions taken by the stakeholders provided clarity on what was being done and how the population could help; on the other hand, there was a lack of discussions about broader and long-term implications.

Lessons learned:

- Importance of translating technical information into clear instructional messages. Crisis response messages must be clear, relevant, and actionable (Frisby et al., 2014; Soares et al., 2022). Since the outbreak of the crisis and the beginning of the rationing measures, people from São Paulo have become accustomed to consuming information from both traditional and social media about rainfall forecasts and the volume of water in the reservoirs. This happened as a consequence of effective crisis communication, which included instructional messages about individual actions to be taken with a collective emergency approach.
- Transparency throughout the crisis response process helped to engage the population, as their participation was necessary and a key success factor in the crisis response. Sharing the responsibility with the public or ensuring a collective understanding that a collaborative effort between the government and the population can bring faster and more meaningful results than individual actions (Soares, 2018).

Failure to Learn: The Case of Vale and the Collapse of Two Mining Dams

In January 2019, a tailings dam owned by the global mining company Vale collapsed in the municipality of Brumadinho, in the state of Minas Gerais. The tragedy resulted in 665 victims, of which 270 were fatalities. Thousands of people were left homeless. The disaster also had environmental impacts, as the mining waste reached the Parauapebas River.

The dam was built in 1976 and suddenly shut down in 2016, a few months after another dam, partially owned by the same company, collapsed in the town of Mariana. This disaster, which occurred four years before the Brumadinho tragedy, also had serious environmental and social impacts, including the loss of human lives.

During his inauguration speech, a statement by Vale's CEO, Fábio Schvartsman, became a motto among employees: "Mariana, never more." He committed to taking all necessary measures to avoid failures in dam management, such as the ones that happened in Mariana. Unfortunately, this commitment did not hold up, and the Brumadinho dam collapsed in January 2019.

In addition to exposure on traditional and social media, Vale faced severe questions from investors, local communities, government authorities, and environmental organizations. There was a significant drop in the company's market value, and several legal actions were taken against the company, including in the United States, where the SEC – Securities and Exchange Commission – decided to sue the company in 2022, arguing that the mining company had violated securities laws by failing to disclose information adequately before the disaster. The company chose to reach agreements to end the process in 2023, paying a fine of almost U$ 56 million ("Regulador dos EUA", 2022). This was not the only agreement that was settled, though.

Vale was also summoned by a Parliamentary Commission of Inquiry, both at state and federal levels, and forced to pay compensation and fines, totaling around R$ 27 billion (Brazilian Reais) to repair and decommission all dams built using the same method as the one that collapsed ("Brumadinho: Vale," 2022).

This crisis also led to broader discussions about corporate social responsibility and the need for more rigorous environmental risk management practices. Additionally, as described in the executive summary of an independent investigation report commissioned by Vale's Board of Directors, improvements were recommended in aspects such as internal controls, governance, composition of the board itself, and the company's culture (CIAEA, 2020).

Immediately following the dam collapse, the company initiated a crisis management protocol that included support for the media, victims and their families, and government and regulatory agencies. Social media was extensively utilized to communicate with the public. The company's website became an information hub for the media and the victims. In addition, there were advertising spots during commercial breaks of major Brazilian news shows. The company established a humanitarian aid committee to assist the families of the victims. ("Vale e Governo," 2019). Nonetheless, given the dimension of the tragedy and the fact that it was a second disaster with the involvement of the same organization in a period of four years in the same state, the repercussions escalated very quickly, not just in the country but internationally.

The company's narrative about its prior knowledge of the dam's problems, the possible causes of the rupture, and the effectiveness of its geotechnical process was confronted by the disclosure of internal documents based on official investigations, which amplified the damage to the company.

Lessons learned

- When responding to a crisis, especially the ones that involve human tragedies, organizations should avoid overpromising.
- Spokespersons should communicate truthfully and accurately about what is known and now known and not neglect facts that will ultimately be contradicted by the company's own documentation.
- An internal culture of openness, transparency, and discussion of issues and risks can help organizations minimize the impact of a crisis while also reducing the risk of repeated or similar crises.

- Organizations should face crises as opportunities to learn. This case shows that after the first disaster, the organization either failed to learn, to communicate, or to implement lessons learned. As Soares (2022) found:
  Learning must be collective and systemic in nature if it is to result in meaningful change within an organization. Through this collective process, post-crisis lessons must offer a clear vision of how the organization will change to address the problems and, equally important, engage organizational members at all levels in enacting those changes. Without such a commitment to learning, organizations risk repeating the same failures and experiencing a similar crisis (p. 104).

Conclusion

This chapter aims to provide an assessment of the state of risk and crisis communication research in Brazil. The field is still in its infancy in terms of volume, methodological rigor, and theoretical grounding. The country is facing serious issues that require research-based risk and crisis communication. From disease outbreaks such as Dengue and the Zika virus to environmental disasters and social issues, organizations and government institutions would benefit from partnerships that can bridge the gap between research and practice. Scholars can follow the example of *Universidade Federal de Santa Maria* and create initiatives to foster research in risk and crisis communication, establishing a knowledge base that can not only move the field forward in the country but, more importantly, benefit society and communities.

References

Cajazeira, P. E. S. L., Souza, J. J. G. D., Antoniutti, C. L., Vasconcelos, W. G. I., Sales, L. S. G., & Silva, T. S. S. D. (2022). Análise comparativa entre os meses iniciais de 2020 e 2021 no processo de monotematização da cobertura jornalística durante a pandemia da COVID-19 no Jornal Nacional. *Intercom: Revista Brasileira de Ciências da Comunicação, 45*, e2022105. https://doi.org/10.1590/1809-58442022105pt

Ceni, J. C. (2021). *Performatividade narrativa e ficção: a comunicação da Vale S.A. e da ONG Gabinete de Crise Pós-rompimento em Brumadinho.* Doctoral dissertation, Universidade.

CIAEA. (February 20, 2020). *Extraordinary independent consulting committee for investigation.* December 27, 2023. https://vale.com/documents/44618/1683677/20.02.20_ciaea_report_i.pdf/79d3ab94-7fed-712c-1c15-647d8bc9e72e?version=1.0&t=1668174428036&download=false (accessed December 27 2023).

CNN Brasil (April 28, 2022). *Regulador dos EUA processa Vale por fraude a investidores em caso Brumadinho.* https://www.cnnbrasil.com.br/economia/regulador-dos-eua-processa-vale-por-fraude-a-investidores-em-caso-brumadinho/ (accessed December 27 2023).

Custódio, V. A. (2015). A Crise Hídrica na Região Metropolitana de São Paulo (2014-2015). *GEOUSP Espaço e Tempo, 19*(3), 445–463. https://doi.org/10.11606/issn.2179-0892.geousp.2015.102136

De Barros, B. T., & Prates, M. A. S. (1996). *O estilo brasileiro de administrar.* Editora Atlas.

Frisby, B. N., Veil, S. R., & Sellnow, T. L. (2014). Instructional messages during health-related crises: Essential content for self-protection. *Health Communication, 4*, 347–354. https://doi.org/10.1080/10410236.2012.755604

González, J. A. (2017). Entrevista. *Tríade – Comunicação. Cultura e Mídia, 5*(9), 246–253.

Gramacho, W. (2022). É perigoso: a glorificação do risco na mídia e as atitudes dos jovens em relação à direção no trânsito. *Intercom: Revista Brasileira de Ciências da Comunicação, 45.* https://doi.org/10.1590/1809-58442022114pt

König, A., Graf-Vlachy, L., Bundy, J., & Little, L. M. (2020). A blessing and a curse: How CEOs' trait empathy affects their management of organizational crises. *Academy of Management Review, 45*(1), 130–153. https://doi.org/10.5465/amr.2017.0387

Leitao, L. O. (2020). *Transparência e ação: os efeitos da (in)consistência da comunicação de riscos de medicamentos nas atitudes e comportamentos de proteção de profissionais da saúde.* Master's thesis, Fundação Getulio Vargas - FGV]. Biblioteca Digital Brasileira de Teses e Dissertações – BDTD.

Marchiori, M., & de Lourdes Oliveira, I. (2009). Perspectives, challenges, and future directions for organizational communication research in Brazil. *Management Communication Quarterly*, *22*(4), 671–676. https://doi.org/10.1177/0893318909332070

Martín, M. (August 1, 2014). Indústria faz alerta sobre impacto econômico da crise hídrica em SP. *El País.* https://brasil.elpais.com/brasil/2014/08/01/politica/1406847379_070354.html (accessed December 27 2023).

Martirani, L. A., & Peres, I. K. (2016). Crise hídrica em São Paulo: cobertura jornalística, percepção pública e o direito à informação. *Revista Ambiente e Sociedade.*, *19*(1), 01–20.

Meio & Mensagem. (January 29, 2019). *Vale e Governo Federal vão à TV para gerenciar crise.* https://www.meioemensagem.com.br/marketing/vale-e-governo-federal-vao-a-tv-para-gerenciar-crise (accessed December 27 2023).

Millner, A. G., Veil, S. R., & Sellnow, T. L. (2011). Proxy communication in crisis response. *Public Relations Review*, *37*(1), 74–76. https://doi.org/10.1016/j.pubrev.2010.10.005

Motta, J. R. (2020). *Comunicação pública e campanhas nacionais de vacinação em contexto de midiatização: as estratégias comunicacionais do Ministério da Saúde na crise da cobertura vacinal de 2018. 2020.* Master's thesis, Universidade Federal de Goiás. Biblioteca Digital Brasileira de Teses e Dissertações – BDTD.

Nowling, W. D., & Seeger, M. W. (2020). Sensemaking and crisis revisited: The failure of sensemaking during the Flint water crisis. *Journal of Applied Communication Research*, *48*(2), 270–289. https://doi.org/10.1080/00909882.2020.1734224

Dia, O. (July 5, 2021). *Em transmissão ao vivo, Bolsonaro volta a imitar paciente com falta de ar.* https://odia.ig.com.br/brasil/2021/05/6140611-em-transmissao-ao-vivo-bolsonaro-volta-a-imitar-paciente-com-falta-de-ar.html (accessed December 27 2023).

Peruzzo, C. M. K. (2018). Apontamentos para epistemologia e métodos na pesquisa em Comunicação no Brasil. *Comunicação e sociedade*, *33*, 25–40. https://doi.org/10.17231/comsoc.33(2018).2905

Poder 360 (January 19, 2021). *A sucessao de erros que levou à crise de oxigenio em Manaus.* https://www.poder360.com.br/brasil/a-sucessao-erros-manaus-dw/ (accessed December 27 2023).

Romancini, R. (2007). *O campo científico da comunicação no Brasil: institucionalização e capital científico. São Paulo: ECA/USP, 2007.* Doctoral dissertation, Universidade de Sao Paulo. https://doi.org/10.11606/t.27.2006.tde-07052009-150949

Rossi, M. (September 26, 2014). Crise hídrica no Estado de São Paulo: "Resta água para apenas 38 dias". *El País.* https://brasil.elpais.com/brasil/2014/09/26/politica/1411739708_069324.html (accessed December 27 2023).

Shimidt, S. (January 14, 2021). Morrer sem oxigênio em Manaus, a tragédia que escancara a negligência política na pandemia. *El País.* https://brasil.elpais.com/brasil/2021-01-15/morrer-sem-oxigenio-em-uma-maca-em-manaus-a-tragedia-que-escancara-a-negligencia-politica-na-pandemia.html (accessed December 27 2023).

Schoofs, L., Claeys, A. S., De Waele, A., & Cauberghe, V. (2019). The role of empathy in crisis communication: Providing a deeper understanding of how organizational crises and crisis communication affect reputation. *Public Relations Review*, *45*(5), 101851. https://doi.org/10.1016/j.pubrev.2019.101851

Silva, D. W. D., & Baldissera, R. (2021). Comunicação organizacional e interesse público: estratégias de (in) visibilidade nas mídias sociais. *Intercom: Revista Brasileira de Ciências da Comunicação*, *44*, 157–174. https://doi.org/10.1590/1809-5844202128

Soares, R. (2018). The evolution of shared responsibility and instructional risk communication in Brazil's campaign against the Zika virus.

Soares, R., Dumitrescu, S., Sims, T., Sellnow, T. L., Sellnow, D. D., & Seeger, M. W. (2022). Opportunities for instructional crisis communication through social media: Communicating self-protective actions for food safety during the COVID-19 pandemic. In *Social Media and Crisis Communication* (pp. 273–284). Routledge. https://doi.org/10.4324/9781003043409-32

Soares, R. A. (2022). Post-crisis organizational learning thresholds, pitfalls and the risk of repeated crises: clarifying the discourse of renewal theory.

Souza, E. A. (2023). *Risco é notícia? A relevância jornalística dos riscos nos grandes desastres da mineração brasileira*. Doctoral dissertation, Universidade Federal de Santa Maria. Biblioteca Digital Brasileira de Teses e Dissertações – BDTD.

Youssif, B., Piffer, G., Grilo, L., & Dias, G. (2022). *Apertos de parafuso" na regulação Social, Ambiental e, agora, também Climática pelo Banco Central do Brasil. Visão prudencial, eventos de risco, fundamentos para gestão, perdas e oportunidades como mitigantes*. Resultante.

Authors' Bio

Rodrigo Soares is a Postdoctoral Associate at the University of Vermont. He bridges more than 15 years of experience as a leading practitioner in the corporate communication field with more than 8 years of applied research in risk and crisis communication. His research provides both theoretical advancements and applications for strategic communication practitioners. His investigations analyzed diseases outbreaks, such as the Zika virus in Brazil and the COVID 19 pandemic through a message design perspective. He also tested the adequacy of crisis communication theories in explaining the failures of institutions facing repeated crises, expanding the understanding of post-crisis learning. He holds a PhD in Strategic Communication and a master's degree in mass communication, both from the University of Central Florida, and a bachelor's degree in communication from Universidade Estacio de Sa, in Brazil.

Rozália Del Gáudio is a Corporate Communication and Sustainability expert, with over 25 years of experience in strategic reputation management for large companies operating in Brazil, such as Vale S.A., C&A and McDonalds. Currently, she holds the position of Professor in MBA programs offered by ABERJE (Brazilian Association for Business Communication) in partnership with Fundação Getúlio Vargas and in a Graduate program in Strategic Communication and Public Relations Management from the Universidade de São Paulo – USP. Additionally, she serves as a Board Member at the Ronald McDonald House of Charities in Brazil. She holds a PhD in Social Sciences, from the University of Paris 1 – Panthéon-Sorbonne, a master´s degree in Business Administration and a Journalism degree from Universidade Federal de Minas Gerais. Rozália was named the Communication Professionals of the Year twice in Brazil by ABERJE, in 2015 and 2021.

Paulo Henrique Soares: Prior to his current role as director of the Brazilian Mining Institute (IBRAM), Mr. Paulo Henrique Soares was the Corporate Communication and External Relations Director for the Brazilian mining organization Vale S.A. The company is Brazil's largest logistics operator and one of the largest mining companies in the world. Mr. Paulo Henrique worked with Vale for more than 20 years, in several roles within the Communication department. He was especially effective in roles that heavily demanded the understanding of social concerns, given Vale's impact on local communities in Brazil and abroad. Along with his professional roles, Mr. Paulo Henrique served as Director of The Brazilian Association of Business Communication (Aberje) in Rio de Janeiro, and as Executive Board Member of the International Association of Business Communicators (IABC), institution who conferred him the ABC title (Accredited in Business Communication). He holds a bachelor's and master's degrees in Communication from Pontificia Universidade Catolica (PUC-MG) in Brazil, and a doctoral degree in Business at the same Institution. He was named the Communication Professionals of the Year twice in Brazil by Aberje, and he has been on the list of the "100 Most Influential Communicators in the World" according The PRovoke Media for six consecutive years (2015–2020).

40

Crisis, Risk, and Media Cases in Argentina

Damián Fernández Pedemonte
Universidad Austral, Graduate School of Communication, Buenos Aires, Argentina

Introduction

The systematic, although not abundant, publication of academic studies on crisis and risk communication in Argentina began in 2001. That year, the country witnessed the largest economic and political crisis in the history of the democracy. As a field, communication already had an important history since the early seventies, when its founders stood out in areas such as semiotics, cultural studies, and critical studies on communication media (Rivera, 1987). Since 2001, the creation of university graduate programs, the consolidation of specialized academic journals, and the recognition of the discipline on the part of the National Scientific and Technical Research Council (CONICET, acronym in Spanish), Argentina's main agency for scientific promotion (Zarowski & Justo von Lurzer, 2018)[1], increased the impact of communications researchers on society. They played, for example, a leading role during the debate on the new Media Law that was passed in Argentina in 2009.

According to Silvio Waisbord, the "de-Westernization" (Curran & Park, 2000) of communication studies should contribute to theoretical development from peripheral areas. In Latin America, research tends to produce results that are mainly of interest to local specialists rather than being in tune with important theoretical debates (Waisbord, 2013). This applies to the case of Argentine academic production on crisis and risk communication.

Originally, this research study was associated with the public relations paradigm, foreign to the founding academic tradition. In Argentina, initial practical professional training in certain multinational company subsidiaries (Carbone & Montaner, 2014; Ferrari & França, 2011) dates back to the 50s, and in 1964, the first public relations undergraduate degree was created in the *Universidad Argentina de la Empresa* (UADE) (Gutiérrez-García & Sadi, 2020).

Subsequently, another area that fostered the systematic research of crises was political communication. Several activities related to public opinion and politics were led by experts who provided professional services to political parties, candidates, and the State (Adrogué, 1998). Among its pioneers is Manuel Mora y Araujo (Bulcourf & Jolías, 2016), who produced a public opinion theory (Mora y Araujo, 2005) but did not address public crises. As of 2001,

[1] For this chapter, we compiled articles from journals belonging to the CONICET Basic Core of Publications, the CONICET's digital repository and books with a wide circulation.

The Handbook of International Crisis and Risk Communication Research, Second Edition.
Edited by Andreas Schwarz, Matthew W. Seeger, and Sora Kim.

certain researchers centered on government crisis management (Elizalde, 2004; Fernández Pedemonte, 2010; Riorda & Cabas, 2005) or on risk communication management (Fontana & Maurizi, 2014).

These contributions already distinguish communication crisis from communication risk. The former is strictly reactive (Noguera, 2005): The government is forced to respond to a situation that is posed by the context. In turn, the latter is proactive. It involves a planned public policy, laid out strategically and penetrating across all levels of society (Amadeo, 2016).

Empirical research findings on corporate or government crises, based on up-to-date and comprehensive theoretical frameworks, were published as early as the beginning of the new millennium. This chapter summarizes these studies' major contributions, with an emphasis on those authors who are in tune with major current theoretical debates, as requested by Waisbord. They will be presented in three sections according to a presentation criterion which is roughly chronological and thematic. The three sections include the following: (1) before 2001: corporate crises; (2) since 2001: media cases; and (3) during the pandemic: risk management. Each section will present major research findings in crisis and corporate communications, media communications, and political communication, respectively, with case studies serving as illustrations. The conclusion outlines the most relevant concepts within each sub-area of study while showing their points of convergence and respective contribution to a comprehensive vision of public crises (Auer et al., 2016) in Argentina.

Before 2001: Corporate Crisis

In Argentina, during the nineties, a privatization process of State-owned companies such as public services took place: gas network, electricity, telecommunication, water, and sewage systems. These companies were the first to create institutional management departments. In parallel, the first master's programs in corporate communication management were created at private universities.

The professionalization of the Director of Communications (DirCom) role gained more importance following a few public crises that affected the reputation of private companies and jeopardized their profitability. The disruptive nature of this situation initially stood out perhaps due to its novelty in the Argentine market. *The End of Zero Risk*, translated in 2002 in Argentina, understands crisis as a sudden change in the normal performance of an organization which affects its image and natural equilibrium. It is a complex, unexpected, and atypical situation which combines urgency and destabilization: an event that explodes and quickly resonates in the environment (Lagadec & Guilhou, 2002).

The practices that are taught in new academic programs, drawn from multinational companies or American corporate communication manuals, include protocols for the design of communication plans and for crisis contingencies. This perspective, the evolution of public relations, puts emphasis on issues management through planned messages. Federico Rey Lennon draws on the work of Edwards Bernays (Rey Lennon, 2006) to propose communication processes that are appropriate for the new business environment. The 2001 crisis allowed the field of communication to develop greater theoretical elaboration of the concept of crisis and its connection to conflict and social change (Fraga, 2015).

According to Rey Lennon, the objectives of issues management include the following: (1) anticipating changes in the environment; (2) changing the negative impact on the organization or on its products and services, if the crisis does occur; and (3) establishing a platform for the organization's future (Rey Lennon & Bartoli, 2020).

Under this perspective, risk is the step prior to a crisis: It should be evaluated and prevented through tools that allow analyzing the context as compared with historical crises, classifying risks according to severity and probability of occurrence, and knowing the company's resources and vulnerabilities. The expected result would be to have an inventory of strengths and weaknesses and the establishment of vulnerability indices.

In contrast to some of these corporate communications' manuals that reduce the complexity of public crises to a recipe, Luciano Elizalde applies a broad concept of strategy that stems from game theory (Schelling, 1980), which consists of rebuilding implicit rationality in the actions of the protagonists of crises.

"A crisis is a complex social and psychic process that someone experiences, which originates in a dissent between agents with a certain degree of power over who will suffer the crisis" (Elizalde, 2004, p. 15). The reason for conceptually demarcate the crisis is because the response will depend on what the agent understands by it.

In addition to game theory, this strategy for crisis management is indebted to Norbert Elias's (1998) concept of power: interdependence and capacity to generate consensus between agents. Indeed, a crisis is an experience that affects the relative power of those parties that are implicated. Conflicts, in turn, are tense social relationships that do not compromise the balance of power. The position of power is, thus, the payment of the crisis (Elizalde, 2010).

According to Elizalde (2004), those who suffer crises often experience them as a disruptive, sudden, and chaotic event, but these crises are pre-structured within the relationships that organizations systematically maintain with their environments. If a crisis is experienced subjectively as a process of personal and organizational disruption, this is due to a combination of the loss of power, behaviors that are out of control, a lack of responsiveness, and emotional shock.

Communication comes into play because there are two sides to every crisis: an administrative aspect and a social one, proceeding from the dissent among agents. Elizalde refers to a big power outage that took place in 1999 in the city of Buenos Aires that was caused by a technical failure at the Edesur electricity utility company. There were several days without supply in the neighborhoods, which generated much discomfort among the population. During the first days of the crisis, the number of individuals affected decreased, but public criticism of the company increased. Electrical power was restored yet the problem was resolved only several weeks later when the company reached an agreement with the parties affected. The core of the crisis was not the outage itself but the dissent that it caused.

The early analysis of the power structure is fundamental to this model. During the prevention stage, the crisis committee becomes operational. The committee must direct its communications to those agents serving as Backups, that is, responsible for providing certainty (e.g., a strategic partner with a good reputation), and as Guarantors, that is, responsible for maintaining rules of engagement (such as the State). Elizalde adds two examples of Argentine crises. In 2001, McDonalds faced a report of spoiled food. McDonalds was defended because its products underwent a safety and hygiene analysis provided by a prestigious laboratory, which defended the company and thus its own work. The Guarantor was the State, which had to determine whether it would proceed to close down company stores, and informing the public of the reasons. Following the LAPA airplane crash in 1998, the company's president, in a press conference, declared that its airplanes and pilots were certified by the required aviation bodies. There was a negative response from victims and the public. The communication of Backups and Guarantors was inadequate.

Elizalde's *crisis management* model later evolved toward *dissent management.* If the *crisis management* model centered on the need to prepare a spokesperson, the leader needs to be prepared for the crisis. In the past, one had to simply work with a crisis manual, now a team that specializes in complex problems is required. In *crisis management,* key messages had to be formulated, while *dissent management* proposes knowing the interpretative background of players so as to succeed with the most comprehensive and acceptable language. Crisis management focused on communicating with the press, whereas managing dissent requires developing a direct or mediated conversation between all players: The digital media system has incorporated many actors to the public discussion (Elizalde, 2017).

Hence, it is necessary to count on a leader with decision-making and communication skills and a team that serves as a communication channel to the leader which carries out the action protocol. These stakeholders should think of the communication strategy as a series of social situations prepared for talking with the involved parties.

Dissent is a medium used to force a decision. It is the result of a disparity in positions over change in the organization. Positive change is only possible when dissent is a mechanism operated from management or is creatively controlled.

Change in the media environment has brought about new crisis contingencies. Nowadays, they often emerge in social media, which company employees share with external publics, activists, and influencers. This interconnected scenario compels dialogue between new stakeholders (Ennova Lead, 2021). Social media can be used by stakeholders and the general public to stay informed. The worst thing in a crisis is not to know what is happening (Rey Lennon & Bartoli, 2020). This perspective is in line with the findings of an international research study. Sng et al. (2021) signal influencers as potential originators of a type of crisis developing in new social media.

Since 2001: Media Cases

In 1987, Eliseo Verón, while living in France, studied the news coverage there on the crisis of the Three Mile Island nuclear plant. He did so with the understanding that the media are producers of current events: a reality in the making of which social actors have a collective experience. The media construct the only crisis accessible to indirect witnesses (Verón, 1987).

For the generation of communication researchers that succeeded the founding generation, the notion of mediatization became mainstream. This approach concerns the relationship that the media system has with other social systems in every stage of its history. The various cultural practices such as politics, culture, and education, change in the face of the media (Verón, 1994; Verón, 2001), due to the fact that there are media in the middle. Nowadays, the concept of mediatization attempts to capture the nature of this relationship between the historical changes in the media and other social transformation processes (Hepp, 2012). In 2011, Sandra Valdettaro (2016) created the Center for Research in Mediatizations (CIM) at the National University of Rosario (Zarowski & Justo von Lurzer, 2018).

Although media semiotics in Argentina has not directly dealt with public crises, its theoretical developments are essential to understanding the role of the media in the social construction of the problem, an issue that is sometimes treated naïvely and externally by corporate communications. One of the factors of the propagation of public crises is the tendency of the Argentine media to treat certain outstanding news as cases. "Case" refers to the interruption of a successive chain of events, of a foreseeable sequence. A break from "normality" associated with chance or misfortune. Aníbal Ford (2001) postulated that in Argentina, these types of journalistic cases have created more political debate over social issues than their promotion by official instances of public deliberation such as the National Congress. Thus, for example, the dynasty that governed a province collapsed because of its involvement in the crime of young María Soledad, in1990, an event that was widely covered by the media. Compulsory military service was abolished due to public pressure following the journalistic investigations into the chain of cover-ups within the Army over the responsibility for the death of Private Carrasco, in 1994 (Fernández Pedemonte, 2010). Following a line of research in crime, Gabriel Kessler delves into the capacity that news about individual crimes have to produce political change (Gayol & Kessler, 2019).

Fernández Pedemonte (2010) defines commotional media cases as follows: "A case is established when the representation of certain events in the media makes a latent structural conflict surface in the discourse, which has been covered up by a dominant public discourse of politicians or the media themselves, which insists on a manifest conjunctural conflict of the opposite sign."

A generalization among several analyzed cases allows us to describe their structure, which consists of the following components: (1) The media themselves present the cases as cases, by means of headlines and specific headings. (2) The case stages the contrast between two conflicts: a conjunctural one and a structural one: a new agenda erupts. (3) The social representation of the institution and social group involved in the case may change during media coverage. There is a leveling out of the knowledge about them among expert and non-expert audiences. (4) The media put into play two types of hypotheses. In the first news, diverse hypotheses come into play. Among these conjectures, one of them points to the central conflict that appears in the case. (5) The media seem to capture a public opinion atmosphere that places pressure on the institution to drastically rectify the pernicious effects of the crisis. (6) The media – public actors, though invisible – act not only as witnesses in cases but also as protagonists, visible actors. (7) Finally, the choice of a narrative format to cover the incidents is related to placing concrete individuals at the center of the stage (Fernández Pedemonte, 2010).

The media case influences social memory (Olick & Robbins, 1998) to the extent that its representation remains active (Fernández Pedemonte, 2012), which from a media communications perspective requires its connection to the current media agenda (Raiter et al., 2002). Elvira Navajas de Arnoux (2019) studies the call to remembrance of 2001 in a debate of Argentine legislators about a social protest that occurred in front of Congress on the occasion of a liberal labor reform law. The event becomes fixed through its naming (Dosse, 2010), and this turns the 2001 crisis into a word-event (Moirand, 2007), which conveys representations and emotions, linked to knowledge, facts, and know-how. One of the concepts that is rekindled by these recollections is that of crisis.

Media cases eventually evolved into post-media cases. At this stage, in Argentina, conventional media coexist with digital native media in a hybrid media system (Chadwick, 2017), resulting from the interaction of old and new media and their associated technologies, genres, standards, behaviors, and organizations. Argentine semiotician Carlos Scolari resorts to an ecological metaphor to distinguish media evolution on the diachronic axis from the media ecosystem on the synchronic axis (Scolari, 2010).

National Prosecutor Alberto Nisman was found dead in his apartment in the posh Buenos Aires neighborhood of Puerto Madero on the night of Sunday, January 18, 2015. He was supposed to appear before the Senate the next day to explain the contents of his criminal complaint of an alleged secret agreement between the Cristina Kirchner's government and the Iranian authorities to exonerate former Iranian officials who were accused in the case of the bombing of the AMIA Jewish Mutual Association headquarters (July 18, 1998) where 85 people died.

Those typical elements found in the cases analyzed in the era of mass media are repeated in the Nisman case. There are other characteristics that differentiate the case of the Prosecutor's death from preceding ones and allow it to be described as a post-media case – specifically the fact that information about the case does not exclusively circulate through the mass media nor does it originate from them. The first announcement of the Prosecutor's death was made by a journalist from his personal Twitter account. Many other contributions are made in social networks where non-media expert opinions discuss with those of the public. When referring to Nisman's death, President Cristina Kirchner published two texts in Facebook during the first week with a journalistic rather than governmental tone (Fernández Pedemonte, 2021a).

The case had a strong impact on Twitter, with 4.500.000 tweets with the #Nisman hashtag were published in the first 40 days from over 700 thousand accounts. About 50% of all tweets in that period were sent by 1% of tweeters. The accounts that published the most were those of institutional users. The so-called rift between the center-left-wing populist Kirchnerist government and the self-proclaimed republican and liberal opposition is reflected on Twitter through the polarization of the event's interpretative frameworks in two frames: murder versus suicide. During the case, the distance is maximal between the communities aligned with one frame or the other on Twitter (Calvo, 2015). The media are no longer the only or the main place where information about major public crisis is enunciated.

During the Pandemic: Managing Risk

From a government communications perspective, early and open reporting have been seen as central to crisis communication strategy, even when the news that need to be delivered is bad news. "Crisis management means providing certainty" (Riorda, 2012). This idea, however, still responds to a linear and controlled model where information circulates from institutions to interested publics through the media, which are seen as powerful and centralized: a vision that no longer corresponds to the evolution of the media system.

Today, crises require a leader's ability not only to inform but to generate legitimacy and trust in his plan, symbolic and political power (Thompson, 2013) to guide actions in the direction set by his strategy. *Anyone has a plan until they get hit in the face*, a book co-authored by Silvia Bentolilla and Mario Riorda (Riorda & Bentolilla, 2020), addresses the personal consequences of crises on their protagonists. In one of the book's epigraphs, Argentine writer Samanta Schweblin asks: "Is any apocalypse not personal?" It is just that a crisis for those who experience it is a loss of references, a rupture of psychological balance, a general mental and emotional disturbance, stress due to excessive demands, and the lack of resources to cope with them.

The book focuses on political leaders who manage the crises of "crises-prone" governments, their loss of power and legitimacy, their functional and dysfunctional ego management, but also on crisis victims, particularly those of violent episodes. It describes a dialectic between the strategic consideration from the subjective point of view of leaders and the ethics of care from the perspective of the resilience of victims. Crisis management and care ethics involve two opposing communication models in tension, as experienced by so many organizations during the COVID-19 crisis. Crises are a time for bringing certainties, for building trust and cooperation, for modifying behavior and intensifying the perception of risk. But they are also vital ruptures that require restoration, attention to bodies, self-care, and empathetic companionship.

In a previous article, Riorda (2020) discusses the difference between crisis communication and risk communication management. In crises, leaders are expected to reduce uncertainty and provide an authoritative narrative about what is happening, why it is happening and what needs to be done. The prevailing maxim in political crises is that they must end as soon as possible. Risk communication, in turn, does not aim to close processes or to generate positive appreciations, but basically, to prevent, raise awareness and modify habits. The success of change depends on whether the idea turns into a specific behavior or not (Heath & Heath, 2011).

The International Strategy for Disaster Reduction (ISDR) of United Nations defines risk as the potential detrimental consequences or expected losses as a result of the conjunction of natural or anthropogenic threats and conditions of vulnerability. In T*he Politics of Risk*, Riorda et al. (2022) summarize this in the following equation: Risk = Threat × Vulnerability. Therefore, the population's perception of risk comes into play.

For Mary Douglas, risk arises from probability theory: "expectations that an individual rational agent forms about the probable actions of other individual rational agents as well as the probability that said expectations turn into permanent conventions with agreed forms of signaling" (Douglas, 1996, p. 42). Risk perception is a way that diverse sectors of society are aware of the level of risk and how they perceive themselves within the problem. In general, it is characterized by a lack of information and the omission of background information that would allow recognizing the risk and taking notice of one's own vulnerability.

The material side of risk is disaster, which occurs when a situation exceeds the responsiveness of the population. Disasters are not only natural; they are the result of the process of building vulnerability situations that are man-made and triggered by inadequate development policies.

Fontana and Maurizi maintain that "disaster risk management is a paradigm that has gained strength since the 90's, especially when major international organizations called the reduction of disaster risks to the attention of world Heads of State" (Fontana & Maurizi, 2014, p. 9).

The issue of environmental risk has evolved from the promotion of good practices for journalism that must cover disasters (Camps, 2017) to a complete challenge to the "neo-extractive" production model and its tragic externalities: climate change, loss of biodiversity, alteration of life cycles, in accordance with the anthropocene paradigm, according to which humans are the cause of unprecedented planetary risks (Svampa, 1919). Flavia Costa (2021) refers to the technocene, adding the environmental impact of highly complex and risky technologies to this era.

As in the case of a crisis, risk management involves two dimensions: disaster management and communication. For the former, Riorda (Riorda et al., 2022) advocates governance understood as a collaborative style of governing between government agencies and private and social organizations. Risk communication, on the other hand, occurs in two different moments: in normal situations, when risks are treated as hypothetical, and in crises, when risk manifestations already exist. Various political and social actors are also involved in the discursive framework. Risk communication aims at changing the perception and behavior of the population, based on existing gaps in risk perception between the non-specialized public and the expert public, both for which a specific rhetoric must be constructed.

The limits of technical rationality are narrow and reductionist, while the limits of cultural rationality are broad and include the use of analogies and historical precedents. In the first perspective, risks are depersonalized and there is an emphasis on probability, while, in the other, risks are personalized and there is an emphasis on impacts on the family and the community. Risk estimation oscillates between objectivist extremes – in the context of Big Data – that aim at the precise calculation of the occurrence probability of the adverse event and constructivist extremes that understand risk only on the basis of culturally and socially shaped subjective perspectives. Instead, communication should include a persuasive component on the prudence in preparing for the most likely scenarios and precautions against the most negative ones.

Zero risk is impossible. Therefore, the need to coexist with uncertainty must be accepted. It is necessary to raise the risk thresholds of groups that do not perceive risk, given that people only respond to risks they perceive, and at the same time, combat exaggerated emotionally conditioned perceptions. It is about building audience capabilities and motivating behavioral change.

One bias that can be particularly important for policymakers during a crisis is the "hindsight bias." People generally believe that an outcome was always more likely once they know it happened. This can lead to the perception that the authorities "should have known" where events were headed, when in fact the uncertainty was too great. The general rule of risk communication is that it is preferable to opt for excessive warning criteria rather than to underestimate damage, for reasons of credibility concerning the communicating authority. However, appealing to panic reduces the chances of obtaining the best response. Empirical evidence indicates that cooperation and orderly rule-governed behavior prevail in disaster situations. Relaxation is more common than panic in situations that are protracted.

According to Fernández Pedemonte (2021b), the discursive strategy of Argentine President Alberto Fernández to manage the COVID-19 crisis initially consisted of a monologic discourse by a personalistic enunciator who argued with data and provided explanations based on a leadership that sought to rely on two legitimacies – that of the State, whose high authority is responsible for managing the crisis and which allows him to initiate a political project in which the State plays a central role, and that of the scientific community, represented by the group of experts who advise him. With this strategy, he presents himself as a leader who has taken the fight against the virus as something personal, out of pure responsibility toward the health of the population and appealing to the national unity that the magnitude of the crisis demands.

The crisis management strategy was based on restriction of movement through a strict and extensive quarantine and other social distancing measures that lasted for a year and a half. The aim was to communicate the drastic measures with authority, appealing to fear of the disease or of the penalties due to non-compliance. From the discourse, this was supported by a framing of the pandemic as a war against an invisible enemy in solidarity with the activation of social alarm, although not so much with the ethics of care, in the sense that it could have contributed to the stigmatization of the infected individuals.

Although the health strategy remained constant, the communication model implicit in the discourse that supported it changed after six months. If at the beginning it was a risk and crisis communication which seeks to influence the behavior of citizens and promote the coordination of social actors, then the discourse became contaminated with political aspects to the detriment of professional ones.

The polemical dimension appeared increasingly, by citing to disqualify the words of critics to the health strategy or, more generally, government policy. In 2021, the polemical nature of the discourse was also at the service of electoral competition.

Conclusion

The scientific production on crisis and risk is recent and lateral with respect to the great tradition of communication studies in Argentina. It is growing on par with reflection on public crises in both business and government spheres, which have increased since the institutional crisis of 2001, cases which are referred to in the preceding pages.

However, important developments by communication researchers in the field of mediatization and political communication nourish the theoretical framework with the most relevant contributions in crisis and risk communication outlined here.

These authors face two challenges. On the one hand, being able to articulate the furthering and updating of theoretical study with the applicability of case studies to the management of communications in organizations playing a central role in crises. There is the risk of falling into inadequate simplistic recipes for an increasingly complex reality or remaining in a terrain that is too abstract or too detailed to be translated into an action plan.

Crises are increasingly a public phenomenon where the rationale of the media, organizations, and politics should be taken into account simultaneously. The place where these perspectives, which have been separated in this occasion, integrate is that of strategic communication. Communication, in addition to being managed, is something by which to manage.

Theory is essential because management first requires appropriate conceptualization. Based on what is understood by crisis or risk, of whether we are in the presence of one phenomenon or the other, a plan will be followed. In this sense, a more fluent dialogue between experts in corporate, media, and political communication could contribute to reduce the relationship between crisis and risk and contribute to the naming and social construction of situations. Getting the communication model right in the proposed discourse is fundamental for the success of the management. In addition to knowledge management, today, we need management with knowledge.

Another challenge that the authors reviewed here find is monitoring the evolution of addressees, who nowadays are also enunciators in the digital environment. The new stakeholders of companies, media audiences, and political parties are involved both in the genesis of crises and in their management. A shift in the focus placed by researchers from leaders to audiences is crucial to the understanding of post-pandemic crises.

References

Adrogué, G. (1998). Estudiar la opinión pública. Teoría y datos sobre la opinión pública argentina [Studying public opinion. Theory and data on Argentine public opinion]. *Desarrollo Económico*, 387–407. https://doi.org/10.2307/3467385

Amadeo, B. (2016). El estudio de la comunicación gubernamental [The study of government communication: Lines of inquiry and future challenges]. *Austral comunicación*, *5*(2), 155–181. https://doi.org/10.26422/aucom.2017.0502.ama

Auer, C., Schwarz, A., & Seeger, M. W. (2016). Communication. Conclusions for an integrative approach to international crisis communication research. In A. Schwarz, M. W. Seeger, & C. Aurer, Eds., *The Handbook of International Crisis Communication Research* (pp. 66–72). Wiley-Blackwell. https://doi.org/10.1002/9781118516812.ch7

Bulcourf, P., & Jolias, L. (2016). El desarrollo de la ciencia política en la Argentina: agendas temáticas y nuevos desafíos [The development of political science in Argentina: Thematic agendas and new challenges]. *Revista Andina de Estudios Políticos*, *6*(1), 18–51. https://doi.org/10.5354/0716-1077.2012.22649

Calvo, E. (2015). *Anatomía política de Twitter en Argentina: tuiteando #Nisman [Political Anatomy of Twitter in Argentina: Tweeting #Nisman]*. Ciudad Autónoma de Buenos Aires, Argentina: Capital Intelectual.

Camps, S. (2017). *Periodismo sobre desastres: cómo cubrir desastres, emergencias y siniestros en medios de transporte [Disaster Journalism: How to Cover Disasters, Emergencies and Transport Claims]*. Eudeba.

Carbone, C., & Montaner, M. (2014). Argentina. In T. En Watson, Ed., (Coord.) *Latin American and Caribbean Perspectives on the Development of Public Relations: Other Voices* (pp. 5–16). Palgrave Pilot. https://doi.org/10.1057/9781137404329

Chadwick, A. (2017). *The Hybrid Media System: Politics and Power*. Oxford University Press.

Costa, F. (2021). *Tecnoceno: algoritmos, biohackers y nuevas formas de vida [Technocene: Algorithms, Biohackers and New Forms of Life]*. Buenos Aires: Taurus.

Curran, J., & Park, M. J. (Eds.). (2000). *De-Westernizing Media Studies*. Londres: Arnold.

Dosse, F. (2010). Reinhart Koselleck entre semántica historica y hermenéutica crítica [Reinhart Koselleck between historical semantics and critical hermeneutics]. In C. Delacroix, F. Dosse, & P. García, Eds., *Historicidades*. Buenos Aires: Waldhuter Editores.

Douglas, M. (1996). *La aceptabilidad del riesgo según las ciencias sociales [Risk Acceptability According to Social Science]*. Barcelona: Paidós.

Elias, N. (1998). *On Civilization, Power, and Knowledge: Selected Writings*. University of Chicago Press.

Elizalde, L. H. (2004). *Estrategias en las crisis públicas: la función de la comunicación [Strategies in Public Crises: The Role of Communication]*. La Crujía.

Elizalde, L. H. (2010). Conflictividad y conflictos en el escenario público argentino. Estado, empresas, organizaciones y vecinos" al borde de un ataque de nervios" [Conflictivity and conflicts in the Argentine public scenario. State, companies, organizations and neighbors" on the verge of a nervous breakdown"]. *Conexiones: revista iberoamericana de comunicación*, *2*(1), 79–98.

Elizalde, L. (2017). *Manejando el disenso: estrategias, tácticas y modelos de gestión [Managing Dissent: Strategies, Tactics and Management Models]*. Buenos Aires: La Crujía.

Ennova Lead (2021). El liderazgo stakeholder en la práctica. Aprendizaje de la red Ennova Lead 2021. [Stakeholder Leadership in practice. Learning from the Ennova Leads Network].

Fernández Pedemonte, D. (2010). *Conmoción pública: los casos mediáticos y sus públicos [Public Commotion: Media Cases and their Publics]*. Buenos Aires: La Crujía.

Fernandez Pedemonte, D. (2012). Media cases and social memory in Argentina post 2001. *Journal for Communication Studies*, *5*(10), 61.

Fernández Pedemonte, D. (2021a). El Caso Posmediático.: Circulación de la información sobre la muerte del fiscal Nisman [The post-media case. Circulation of information about the death of prosecutor Nisman]. *Question/Cuestión*, *3*(70). https://doi.org/10.24215/16696581e629

Fernández Pedemonte, D. (2021b). Modelos de comunicación en el discurso del presidente argentino Alberto Fernández durante la crisis de la pandemia [Communication models in the doscourse of Argentine President Alberto Fernandez during the pandemic crisis]. *Más poder local, 46*, 74–95.

Ferrari, M., & França, F. (2011). *Relaciones públicas. Naturaleza, función y gestión en las organizaciones contemporáneas [Public Relations. Nature, Role and Management in Contemporary Organizations]*. Buenos Aires: La Crujía.

Fontana, S., & Maurizi, V. (2014). *Comunicando el riesgo. Estrategias comunicativas frente al riesgo de desastres [Communicating Risk. Communication Strategies in the Face of Disaster Risk]*. Buenos Aires: La Crujía.

Ford, A. (2001). *La marca de la bestia: identificación, desigualdades e infoentretenimiento en la sociedad contemporánea [The Mark of the Beast: Identification, Inequalities and Infotainment in Contemporary Society]*. Grupo Editorial Norma.

Fraga, E. (2015). *La pregunta por el cambio social y su conceptualización en términos de contradicción, conflicto y crisis [The Question of Social Change and Its Conceptualization in Terms of Contradiction, Conflict and Crisis]*. Question/Cuestión.

Gayol, S., & Kessler, G. (2019). *Muertes que importan: Una mirada sociohistórica sobre los casos que marcaron la Argentina reciente [Deaths that Matter: A Sociohistorical Look at the Cases that Marked Recent Argentina]*. Siglo XXI editores.

Gutiérrez-García, E., & Sadi, G. (2020). Capacidades profesionales para el mañana de la comunicación estratégica: contribuciones desde España y Argentina [Professional capabilities for the future of strategic communication: Contributions from Spain and Argentina]. *Revista de Comunicación, 19*(1), 125–148. https://doi.org/10.26441/RC19.1-2020-A8

Heath, C., & Heath, D. (2011). *Switch*. Vintage Español.

Hepp, A. (2012). *Cultures of Mediatization*. London: Politic Press.

Lagadec, P., & Guilhou, X. (2002). *El fin del riesgo cero [The End of Zero Risk]*. Buenos Aires: El Ateneo.

Moirand, S. (2007). Discours, mémoires et contextes: à propos du foncitionnement de l'allusion dans la presse. *Corela, HS-6*. http://journals.openedition.org/corela/1567

Mora y Araujo, M. (2005). *El poder de la conversación: elementos para una teoría de la opinión pública [The Power of Conversation: Elements for a Theory of Public Opinion]*. La Crujía.

Narvaja de Arnoux, E. (2019). *Crisis política en la Argentina. Memoria discursiva y componente emocional en el debate sobre la Reforma Previsional [Political Crisis in Argentina. Discursive Memory and Emotional Component in the Debate on the Pension Reform.]*. Bielefeld University Press.

Noguera, F. (2005). La campaña permanente [Permanent campaign]. In R. Izurieta, C. Arterton, & R. Perina, Eds., *Estrategias de comunicación para gobiernos* (pp. 77–101). La Crujía: Buenos Aires.

Olick, J. K., & Robbins, J. (1998). Social memory studies: From" collective memory" to the historical sociology of mnemonic practices. *Annual Review of Sociology, 24*, 105–140.

Raiter, A., Sánchez, K., & Zullo, J. (2002). *Representaciones sociales [Social Representations]*. Buenos Aires: Eudeba.

Rey Lennon, F. (2006). *Edward Bernays: el inventor de las relaciones públicas [Edward Bernays: Inventor of Publoc Relations]*. Buenos Aires: Educa.

Rey Lennon, F., & Bartoli, J. (2020). *Manual de comunicación en las organizaciones [Handbook of Organizational Communication]*. Buenos Aires: Rey Lennon Ediciones.

Riorda, M. (2012). Quiero salir. . . sólo y si se puede, bien [I want to go out. . . just and if it's possible, fine]. *Más poder local, 10*, 38–40.

Riorda, M. (2020). Antes de comunicar el riesgo o la crisis: hay que diferenciarlos [Before communicating the risk or the crisis: It is necessary to differentiate between them]. *Más poder local, 41*, 20–23.

Riorda, M., & Bentolilla, S. (2020). *Cualquiera tiene un plan hasta que le pegan en la cara [Anyone has a Plan Until they get Hit in the Face]*. Buenos Aires: Paidós.

Riorda, M., & Cabas, P. (2005). Si los rojos no fueran rojos: la gestión de la comunicación de crisis del gobierno de la Alianza [If the reds were not red: The crisis communication management of the Alliance government]. *Revista SAAP: Sociedad Argentina de Análisis Político, 2*(2), 257–283.

Riorda, M., Fontana, S., & Conrero, S. (2022). *La política del riesgo. Construcción social, liderazgo y comunicación [The Politics of Risk. Social Construction, Leadership and Communication]*. Buenos Aires: La Crujía.

Rivera, J. (1987). *La investigación en comunicación social en la Argentina [Social Communication Research in Argentina]*. Buenos Aires: Punto sur editores.

Schelling, T. C. (1980). *The Strategy of Conflict: With a new Preface by the Author.* Harvard University Press.
Scolari, C. (2010). Ecología de los medios. Mapa de un nicho teórico [Media ecology. Map of a theoretical niche]. *Cuaderns del CAC, 34*(1), 17–25.
Sng, K., Au, T. Y., & Pang, A. (2021). Social media influencers as a crisis risk in strategic communication: Impact of indiscretions on professional endorsements. In *Social Media Influencers in Strategic Communication* (pp. 68–87). London: Routledge.
Svampa, M. (1919). *Antropoceno. Lecturas globales desde el sur [Anthropocene. Global Readings from the South].* Córdoba: La Sofía cartonera.
Thompson, J. B. (2013). *Political Scandal: Power and Visability in the Media Age.* London: John Wiley & Sons.
Valdettaro, S. (2016). Mediatizaciones: hacia la consolidación de un campo de estudios [Mediatizations: Towards the consolidation of a field of Studies]. *Inmediaciones de la Comunicación, 11*, 21–29. https://doi.org/10.18861/ic.2016.11.2614
Verón, E. (1987). *Construir el acontecimiento [Constructing the Event].* Barcelona: Gedisa.
Verón, E. (1994). Mediatización, comunicación política y mutaciones de la democracia [Mediatization, political communication and mutations of democracy]. *Semiosfera, 2*, 5–36.
Verón, E. (2001). *El cuerpo de las imágenes [The Body of Images].* Buenos Aires: Grupo Editorial Norma.
Waisbord, S. (2013). Cambios y continuidades: La agenda de investigación de la comunicación política en América Latina [Changes and continuities: The investigative agenda of political communication in Latin America]. *Austral Comunicación, 2*(1), 105–131. https://doi.org/10.26422/aucom.2013.0201.wai
Zarowsky, M., & Justo von Lurzer, C. (2018). Communication research in Argentina (2001–2015): Between expansion and intellectual intervention. *Communication Theory, 28*(2), 202–223. https://doi.org/10.1093/ct/qtx012

Author Bio

Damián Fernández Pedemonte has a PhD in Language from the Universidad Nacional de La Plata, Argentina, with post-doctorate programs in Ohio University (USA) and Universitá Cattolica Di Milano (Italy). He is a professor of discourse analysis for media and organizations at the Universidad Austral, visiting scholar and professor in communications graduate programs of Europe and Latin America. He also works as a researcher at CONICET the National Council for Scientific and Technical Research and is the director of the Graduate School of Communication at the Universidad Austral. Fernández Pedemonte is the author of ten academic books and about fifty papers and academic articles, among them, *Grieta entre el relato y la conversación. Comunicación política argentina, del 2001 a la pandemia* (The crack between the story and the conversation. Argentine political communication, from 2001 to the pandemic) (2023) and *Comunicación aplicada: Teoría y método* (Applied communication: Theory and method) (2014). His research project focuses on the relationship between political and corporate systems and media systems during different crises. He also conducted applied research projects such as Key Communication Indicators (KCI), instrument that measures all the corporate communication functions developed with American Chamber of Commerce in Argentina (AMCHAM).

Crisis and Risk Communication Research in Australia and Oceania

41

Risk and Crisis Communication in Australia and New Zealand

Christopher Galloway and Theodore E. Zorn
Massey Business School, Massey University, Auckland, New Zealand

Introduction

This chapter addresses the Australian and New Zealand contexts of risk and crisis communication research and key areas in which it is conducted. We explore not only organization-specific risks and crises but also "public" crises, that is, community- and societal-level crises, which have received relatively more attention in Australia and New Zealand. Thus, the main institutional actors in the context of our discussion will include not only business organizations but also government agencies and NGOs.

The chapter updates aspects of what we outlined in the previous edition of the *Handbook* and touches on major developments in the intervening years. After this introduction, we move to discussing the social, political, and media context of crisis and risk communication in Australia and New Zealand, before tackling the traditional terrain of research into organization-specific crisis communication. We then review communication surrounding public crises before examining trends, offering some conclusions, and proposing angles of approach for future scholarship, including a call for a return to organizational crisis communication studies better informed by theory than the typical cases and enhanced by the inclusion of indigenous perspectives.

In the first edition of the *Handbook*, Galloway (2016) reviewed crisis communication research in Australia, proposing that while much crisis communication research is undertaken in the northern hemisphere, Australian scholars were making original and, in some cases, influential contributions to the international body of crisis management and communication scholarship. In their chapter in the previous edition, Zorn et al. (2016) found that academic research into crisis communication in New Zealand was very limited and much published work took the form of practitioner case studies. Zorn and his colleagues also called for the involvement of indigenous Māori as vital partners in research endeavor. Echoing this appeal, researchers in both countries now place much more emphasis on eliciting indigenous contributions. The relative lack of them so far is itself a crisis of sorts.

Over the last 10 years or so, crisis communication research centered on Australia and New Zealand has largely focused on analyses of communication about catastrophes such as the COVID-19 pandemic, a destructive – of both lives and landscape – volcanic eruption in New

The Handbook of International Crisis and Risk Communication Research, Second Edition.
Edited by Andreas Schwarz, Matthew W. Seeger, and Sora Kim.

Zealand and devastating flooding, particularly in food-producing regions of New Zealand. However, there has been little fresh theorizing, a paucity of innovative explorations of organizational crisis scenarios and their possible paths.

Context

Australia and New Zealand are connected by their relative proximity geographically, a shared history of (mainly British) colonization and membership in the Commonwealth of Nations, and a long history of cooperation, trade, and friendly rivalry. That said, there are also important differences between the two countries.

New Zealand

In New Zealand, with its population of only around five million, some of the larger corporates[1] are Crown (i.e., government-owned) Research Institutes (CRIs). Others are known as state-owned enterprises, such as Transpower New Zealand, which operates the country's electricity grid, and KiwiRail, which runs New Zealand's rail system. Cooperatives are also found: The largest example is Fonterra, owned by around 9,000 farmers and their families. The company is responsible for around 30% of the world's dairy exports. Another large co-operative is Foodstuffs New Zealand, one of the major players in New Zealand's supermarket duopoly. While these organizations may have a social good purpose, all are mandated to deliver a surplus.

Like Australia, New Zealand operates a Western type of parliamentary democracy. It is distinguished from that in Australia by its foundation on a treaty, signed in 1840, between the British Crown and representatives of the indigenous Māori people. The treaty is even today a contested document whose interpretation is debated, sometimes intensely, but whose outcomes have – after years of breached commitments – resulted in government forms of redress such as land transfers, money, and other assets.

English-language broadcasters operate alongside Māori Television, a nationwide channel whose programming is predominantly in Māori, and a range of other ethnically focused publications, radio stations, and websites (over 20 in Chinese in Auckland alone, a city in which more than 45% of the residents identify with an ethnic minority). The government operates both television and radio stations which compete with private enterprises.

Several of New Zealand's eight universities have started or expanded communication programs in the last decade, and the majority now offer courses in risk and/or crisis communication. However, few scholars based in New Zealand have contributed to the literature on crisis and risk communication within the past decade.

Australia

Across the Tasman Sea, Australia is a mature, developed, bicameral, Western-style parliamentary democracy with the twelfth largest economy in the world even though its 26.3 million people account for only around 0.3% of the globe's population. Political institutions are robust and regulatory regimes strong, even though a reform agenda focused on competition, regulation, and human capital was agreed by federal, state, and territory governments (OECD, 2010, p. 6). In Australia, the media sector is lively but ownership is heavily concentrated, with private control complemented by government-funded broadcasters the Australian Broadcasting Corporation (ABC) and the Special Broadcasting Service (SBS). Culturally diverse, Australia

[1] "Corporate" is often used as a noun in New Zealand and Australia as a synonym for corporation or large private company.

not only has an aboriginal population of ancient origin but also integrates immigrants from many countries into its society. Immigrants account for 30% of the population, the highest proportion among major Western countries. The higher education sector includes 39 universities, many of which attract international students.

Crisis communication is taught by such leading universities as the University of Sydney, the Queensland University of Technology, and the University of Canberra. At the University of Adelaide, crisis communication is presented together with risk communication, while both the University of Queensland and Melbourne-based Monash University combine issues and crisis management. Several Australia-based scholars contribute to the crisis literature and we include their work in the review that follows.

Organization-Specific Crises and Risks

While attention given to corporate or organization-specific crises has been less than public crises, a few noteworthy studies on organization-specific crisis communication have been done in the Australia-New Zealand context. An interesting example is examination of 17 large Australian organizations' use of social media for crisis communication, analyzing thousands of Facebook and Twitter messages. The authors suggested that familiar theories on crisis communication might not adequately represent the social media context. They noted that relevant literature fell short of providing what is needed to help organizational crisis managers choose an appropriate crisis response strategy; when large Australian organizations responded to crises, they were not fully aware of social media's potential for crisis communication.

Australian studies by Grebe illustrate how crisis response can go wrong when the corporate reaction is disingenuous and an apology is not only seen as inauthentic but also worsens the crisis in question. Grebe's study (2012) examined the process for drafting an apology within a scandalized organization suffering reputational damage; an organization that sought to suppress significant documents and the testimony of key personnel. The crisis centered on the Australian Wheat Board (AWB) paying bribes and kickbacks to the Iraqi Government between 1999 and 2003 in exchange for the right to sell wheat to Iraq under the terms of the United Nations Oil-for-Food program – an arrangement which was plagued by corruption and mismanagement. AWB initially tried to manage the impact of the scandal, rather than address its causes, which could have helped it to rebuild trust and reputation. In a follow-up study (2013), Grebe discussed how "Things can get worse: How mismanagement of a crisis response strategy can cause a secondary or double crisis: the example of the AWB corporate scandal." His article showed that the company's original defensive apologia crisis response strategy fell short, as it was seen as inappropriate, resulting in further embarrassment to the AWB.

Not surprisingly given the prominence of the sport of rugby in New Zealand culture, a scandal involving the All Blacks, the country's national rugby team – typically dominates front page news. Jackson and Thaker's (2021) study "Letting the team down? Examining sport fans' reactions to Aaron Smith's 'toilet tryst' on social media" focused on a romantic liaison with the All Black rugby player in a disability toilet in the airport at Christchurch, New Zealand. Smith was sent home from a tour of South Africa and was given an official warning after New Zealand Rugby found him guilty of serious misconduct. Jackson and Thaker's (2021) study comparatively analyzes the crisis communication messages voiced by Smith and All Blacks management, reviewed associated elite opinion in media coverage, and undertook comparative analysis of communication strategies used by fans across a range of social media networks. While Smith and the All Blacks employed traditional strategies of apology, the authors found that fans on social media often defended Smith and the All Blacks using newer strategies of expression of disappointment and humor to diminish and curtail reputational impact. However, while there was a little variation in crisis response strategies between the social media networks, there was more in the sub-rhetorical spaces within a social media platform. Jackson and Thaker suggested that their work helped extend Coombs' Situational Crisis Communication Theory (SCCT) in the context of athlete reputational crises.

A very different sort of analysis (Brunton & Jeffrey, 2019) used the critical incidents technique to explore the practice of communication management in a sample of practitioners in New Zealand and Finland – two geographically distant countries. Critical incidents technique is a set of procedures for systematically identifying behaviors that contribute to success or failure of individuals or organizations in specific situations. The critical incidents reviewed mostly related to managing crisis communication across both countries. To manage the incidents, communication practitioners predominantly used two competencies: stakeholder relationship management and external interface management. In addition, the personal attribute of adaptability was most commonly employed in both countries. Despite the similarity of incidents and the competencies and attributes required to manage them, variability in practitioners' strategic and personal responses was also evident in the authors' findings.

Other contributions to crisis communication scholarship focused on effective leadership. Melbourne-based crisis scholar and public relations practitioner Tony Jaques set out his analysis of crisis lmanagement in "Crisis leadership: A view from the executive suite" (2012). The heavily regulated chemical industry is seen as something of a bellwether for crisis management, and the study details the perspective from leaders themselves, namely top executives in the chemical and petrochemical industry in Australia, representing some of the world's largest multinational corporations. The study explores the reasons perceived at the executive level for why top executives often fail to provide the necessary openness, leadership, and prioritization to prevent and prepare for organizational crises. Crisis leadership has become a strong element of crisis management scholarship, yet much of the published research is primarily observational, based on the performance of leaders in crises or prescriptions for preferred behavior. By contrast, the study builds on in-depth interviews with CEOs and top executives who provide a rare and remarkably frank view from the executive suite about the current state of crisis management and in particular about the role of corporate leaders in crisis prevention and preparedness.

Jaques also explored crisis leadership in an analysis titled "The leadership role in crisis prevention" (2013a). Jaques, a prolific author, also produced a second study titled "Ensnared in a gay health controversy: A comparative study in responding to issue activism" (2013b). This latter case study describes competing activist campaigns triggered by a provocative poster promoting safe gay sex, which became one of the most complained-about outdoor advertisements in Australia. Drawing on issue management theory and personal interviews, Jaques analyses the contrasting strategies followed by two outdoor advertising companies caught up in the controversy, where family value advocates failed to consistently present their objections, whereas supporters of the same-sex equality effectively mobilized traditional and social media to frame the case as advertising free speech. Jaques argued that leadership in response to a crisis is reasonably well understood – albeit not always well executed. In contrast, leadership in terms of crisis preparedness and crisis prevention is less well understood and still developing as a management discipline. In his view, one of the conundrums of modern crisis management is that most top executives recognize nothing damages an organization faster or deeper than a crisis or issue mismanaged. Yet many of these same executives fail to take proper steps to prevent a crisis happening in the first place.

Public Crises and Risks

In this section, we consider risk and crisis communication studies focused on the public crises that authorities in Australia and New Zealand dealt with and in some cases, such as the impacts of severe flooding, are continuing to do so. Public crises include COVID-19 and its associated health and public order issues, natural disasters such as devastating wildfires and floods, a deadly terror attack, and "smoldering" crises (Maier et al., 2022). Such events, though often termed disasters, can properly be considered also as crises. Al-Dahash et al. (2016, p. 1191) note that "Despite the fact that there is a difference between the terms disaster, crisis and emergency, they are closely interconnected, interdependent and overlap significantly."

COVID-19 and Public Health Crises

Sydney-based scholars Bromfield and McConnell (2021) described the COVID-19 global pandemic in 2020 as "a crisis personified." As they explained,

> "It exhibits classic crisis ingredients of high and cascading threats, deep levels of uncertainty about their impact, and exceptional time pressures for action (Weible et al., 2020). It is also an exemplar of transboundary crises, the 'ultimate nightmare' of crisis managers (Boin, 2019, p. 95), where volatile and interlinked threats cascade across national borders."

As with many other countries, New Zealand was forced to confront the spread of COVID-19 and its initial "go early, go hard" elimination strategy won plaudits globally, prompting analyses such as McGuire et al. (2020) study of the crisis communication approach taken by the then Prime Minister, Jacinda Ardern. Their study found that the Prime Minister's "positive and consistent messaging inspire[d] confidence and social solidarity." Similarly, New Zealand scholars Beattie and Priestly (2021) studied Ardern's daily press briefings during the crisis using reflexive thematic analysis to identify three key themes: (1) open, honest and straightforward communication; (2) distinctive and motivational language; and (3) expressions of care.

The Australian Prime Minister's crisis communication was also studied, with Bernard et al. (2021) basing their analysis on the Crisis and Emergency Risk Communication (CERC) principles as recommended by the WHO and the US Centers for Disease Control and Prevention. Their study led to the suggestion of new frames and themes for the current CERC framework which the authors proposed could be transferable to other crises in Australia and elsewhere.

Macnamara (2021), a distinguished Sydney professor, contributed to crisis communication theory in his writing about the pandemic and its "flow-on crises." He noted the effects of "crisis contagion" for a range of organizations including international airlines, tourism operators, and local businesses and commented that his analysis

> "provides a relatively rare "inside" (*emic*) perspective through ethnography and autoethnography conducted by a senior decision-maker in the organization studied, which expands traditional outside (*etic*) perspectives and offers new insights into crisis communication."

Macnamara also suggested that

> "an expansion of SCCT [Situational Crisis Communication Theory] is needed to include at least one additional crisis type that recognizes failure of an organization to meet stakeholder and/or societal expectations even when it is not at fault through intention, or by accident, or involved as a victim (2021, p. 256)."

He proposed that this added crisis type "could be called 'ineffectual' and applied to organizations that are a 'downstream [from the crisis] participant'."

Gluckman and Bardsley (2020) reviewed the post-pandemic crisis landscape in New Zealand in a study about "Resetting the way a nation is run, post-pandemic, to cope with potentially permanent changes to how we do business, learn, etc." Their focus was the future direction for the country – a recognition that the post-crisis period can be even more demanding than crisis response for crisis managers.

In the only non-COVID health-related crisis communication study in this period, through a case study analysis, Galloway et al. (2019) examined how scientific testing was involved in both the triggering and the resolution of the largest food safety scare ever to hit New Zealand. The study examines the practical applications for communicators dealing with food-safety-based risks and discusses how, when dealing with crises, they need to consider lay publics' biases toward assurances of zero risk. This should be part of determining audiences' information needs and of calibrating the provision of scientific information, including information about necessary testing, in ways that meet these needs. Doing so will help build trust, including about the scientific method and the organizations applying it to determine not only the nature of a given risk but also to assess how best it might be mitigated. While distrust might surface in a risk-based crisis, communicators should focus on messaging that addresses uncertainty through providing consistent and credible information.

Crises Resulting from Natural Disasters

Both Australia and New Zealand have experienced traumatic natural catastrophes in the last few years, including floods, wildfires, and a volcanic eruption. A disastrous volcanic eruption occurred on Whakaari/White Island, New Zealand, in 2019 in which 22 people died and 25 were injured, and devastating flooding occurred in three food-producing regions of the country in 2023 as a result of a ferocious Cyclone Gabrielle. Similarly, Australia faced multiple natural disasters – a prolonged drought, bushfires, and Cyclone Debbie, a 2017 weather event ranked as one of the most severe to hit the coast of Queensland in decades. Communication scholars have not been particularly active in this domain, but there has been relevant work done on risk and crisis communication from other disciplines, particularly science.

New Zealand straddles the Pacific and Australian tectonic plates, the so-called Pacific Rim of Fire, the region where most of earth's volcanoes and earthquakes occur. Thus, a vigorous sector of inquiry studies not only quakes but also volcanic activity. Earthquakes of small to moderate size are frequent, leading to the sobriquet "The Shaky Isles" – but major tremors struck the southern city of Christchurch in 2010 and 2011. More than 180 people died in the 2011 earthquake; hundreds of buildings in the central business district and some 10,000 dwellings were assessed as being unlivable.

The White Island volcanic eruption was the focus of Kotlarsky et al.'s (2022) study of the use of Twitter in a crisis. The New Zealand-based investigators found that while media agencies tweeted and retweeted more messages, private individuals and emergency response agencies achieved the most significant reach and impact per tweet posted.

The city of Auckland alone sits on over 50 identifiable volcanoes. The consensus among scientists is that the existing volcanoes are not likely to become active again, but the Auckland volcanic field itself is still active, meaning further eruptions are possible. Not surprisingly then, volcanic crisis communication has become a major focus of inquiry in New Zealand, with a recent edited book devoted to the subject (Fearnley et al., 2018), with two of the editors based in Australia and New Zealand. Most scholars doing research in volcanic crisis communication are more aligned with science (particularly geology and environmental science) than communication programs, but the work clearly has overlap with the interests of communication scholars. A major focus is on preparing communities and relevant government agencies to communicate effectively in the event of an eruption (e.g., Dohaney et al., 2015).

Kotlarsky et al.'s (2022) study of tweets referring to the 2019 eruption of New Zealand's most active volcano (Whakaari/White Island) in which 22 people died and 25 people were injured. The New Zealand-based investigators found that while media agencies tweeted and retweeted more messages, private individuals and emergency response agencies achieved the most significant reach and impact per tweet posted.

In New Zealand, the National Institute of Water and Atmospheric Research (NIWA) investigates ways to predict flooding so that planners are better able to judge areas at risk and more able to predict water depths and velocities should flooding occur. Such studies are vital because the country has suffered severe flooding, especially in early 2023. Significant floods and landslides resulting from Cyclone Gabrielle hit the largest city, Auckland, and two important food-producing regions, Hawkes Bay and Gisborne. The northland province was also severely affected. Deaths totaled 15 and swathes of productive land were inundated with water and heavy deposits of silt. The cyclone, "the most significant weather event New Zealand has seen this century," according to the Prime Minister Chris Hipkins (McClure, 2023., February 14) "exposed a shocking litany of failed leadership, faulty communication, and inadequate crisis preparedness in New Zealand's largest city" (Jaques, 2023). In response, the government allocated more than NZD1 billion for cyclone and flood recovery in its 2023 budget. As New Zealand authorities' subpar responses in this case demonstrated, core practices of research-supported crisis management can be more honored in the breach than the observance: an independent review of their work saw it as "damning," evidencing "system failure" (Sowman-Lund, 2023, April 12).

Risk is also a concern in Dharmasena et al. (2020) "The role of public relations in building community resilience to natural disasters: Perspectives from Sri Lanka and New Zealand." The study identifies a role for public relations in disaster management by analyzing disaster and communication managers' understanding of community resilience and their use of communication in the context of two different cultural environments. The authors acknowledged that because nations are complex multicultural realities, the findings cannot be generalized to make claims about how natural disasters are managed in different national contexts. They contend that by supporting efforts to build community resilience to disasters, public relations practitioners can contribute to social well-being in times of catastrophic natural disasters.

In a study of risk communication devoted to potential dam failure, Australia-based Mehta et al. (2020) argued not only that this communication is prudent and relevant to downstream communities but also that because dam failures "are typically scarce, simply asking questions to understand assumptions is insufficient to guide communication planning." Rather, they suggested, planning should involve testing of messages in focus groups "to identify how content triggers responses from downstream community members" (2020, p. 2). The authors found that both public and expert participants in their research generally agreed on key concepts to do with dam failure. There was also "general community recognition for the impacts of dam failure, challenging historical research findings that identify this knowledge as located more strongly in expert groups" (2020, p. 2). Mehta et al. (2020) also, however, identified "problematic" divergences in how expert and public participants viewed dam failure. They advocated for five proposals for dam failure risk communication, including the need to personalize risk impact (2020, p. 10).

In 2022, a different group (except for Mehta's participation) examined how citizens could be encouraged to evacuate their properties in the face of bushfire warnings (Mehta et al., 2022). They noted that "Warnings that do not include clear behavioral guidance can challenge clarity and behavioral uptake." Their research findings showed that including behavioral inputs into social media warnings can intentions to take protective action (2022, p. 1).

Another collection of Australian researchers (Howes et al., 2015) noted that climate change is likely to exacerbate the serious stress placed on scarce public resources when major disasters such as bushfires or floods occur. They advocated an integrated approach to disaster risk management and climate change adaptation, arguing for a strategy to improve interagency communication and collaboration, pointing to the context of "rapidly growing public expectations at a time when the public sector is already stretched to its limits" (2015, p. 1). Boon (2016) predicts that Australia will "face more intense and frequent disasters in the 21st century as a result of climate change" (2016, p. 1). She found a concerning "eroding of public trust in scientific communications about the environment, whether arising from the media or from government" (2016, p. 13).

University-level studies of such developments can be found at institutions such as Brisbane-based Griffith University, which brings together crisis and disaster in its curriculum offering, "Communication in Crises and Disasters." While Australia can, and does, experience devastating wildfires, more citizens are killed by floods than bushfires (FitzGerald et al., 2010). In 2021, the Australian Government funded Natural Hazards Research Australia for 10 years to address the major challenges arising from natural hazards, including bushfires, floods, cyclones, heatwaves, storms, and other hazards. The aim is to deliver usable research and knowledge that creates safer and more resilient communities.

Crises Resulting from Terrorism

According to Australian scholar Sky Marsen (2020), studies of terrorism are part of a broadening of scope in some areas of crisis communication research, an extension she views as a challenge to existing definitions of crisis "by bringing into play governmental responses to multifaceted events that involve a wide range of stakeholders as well as the reputation building activities of individuals" (2020, p. 166).

New Zealand and Australia have mostly been free from such crises, with the glaring exception of the 2019 Christchurch Mosque terrorist attack which cost the lives of 51 people, and had international as well as local ramifications. Fakhrurroja et al. (2019) examined the use of Twitter after the tragedy, concluding that an individual might have more information-spreading power than authority or government institutions, while Prastya and Dewi (2020) conducted a framing analysis of government crisis communication in terrorist attacks, using the Christchurch case and another based in Sri Lanka.

Smoldering Crises

At the risk of stretching the definitions of risk and crisis communication too far, we wish to briefly address situations that can be seen as "smoldering" crises (Maier et al., 2022) lurking in the two nations' social fabric. Doyle et al. (2015) refer similarly to "creeping disasters," which they describe as "failing to recognize the accumulation of many small changes which can amount to a major crisis; normalization bias; and personnel fatigue and performance issues for long duration events" (Doyle et al., 2015, p. 86).

In short, there is a crisis of perceived inequities and institutional racism affecting indigenous peoples: Aboriginal and Torres Strait Islander people in Australia and Māori and Pasifika people in New Zealand. For example, MacGillivray and Baldry (2013, abstract) note that

> "the over-representation of Aboriginal and Torres Strait Islander people with mental and cognitive impairment in the Australian criminal justice systems ('CJS'), particularly in prisons, is of grave concern. Social justice, human rights and anti-discrimination challenges emerge from the systematic enmeshment of this group in criminal justice systems in all Australian jurisdictions."

In New Zealand, researcher Heather Came (2012) asserted that health policy was a "monocultural domain" which was (and arguably remains)

"dominated by western bio-medical discourses that preclude and under-value Māori, the indigenous peoples of this land, in the conceptualisation, structure, content, and processes of health policies" notwithstanding historic promises to "protect Māori interests."

Elers et al. (2021) pick up the cultural issue of social inequities, viewed in the context of a COVID-19 lockdown, in an article titled "Hegemonic health communication literature ignores inequities in NZ health experience." Recognizing that New Zealand's public health crisis communication approach was effective in mobilizing the nation into a strict lockdown; nevertheless, they sought to investigate the question, "How did communities situated amongst the 'margins of the margins' … navigate through the existing structural barriers to health during the pandemic"?

Future Research and Conclusions

Australasian organizations are no less afflicted by crises than counterparts in other countries – yet antipodean scholars seem to have been drawn more to public crises than to the dilemmas of corporations and other organizations, perhaps due in part to the tremendous impact of natural disasters and public health crises on social well-being. Furthermore, as noted above, while there is some theorizing, there is room for more to complement the cases studies which have long been the staple fare of crisis communication research. Equally, as natural disasters – some linked to climate change – multiply, there is a need for more crisis scholars to expand their investigations into how crises are framed and crisis managers handled their communication responsibilities.

While crisis retains its attraction as a component of university courses and a focus for some researchers, a new school of analysts is needed to grapple with the challenges of social media and artificial intelligence (AI) – facilitated crises. Social media is well-known as a vehicle through which crisis communication can be turbo-charged; it may be too early to assess the potential impacts of powerful AI communication (and disinformation) engines. These emergent dilemmas also call for critical thinking about ethics in handling new crisis types: AI implementations can produce ethical dilemmas, such as algorithmic bias, disinformation on an accelerated trajectory, and much more. Yet this is in itself nothing new: It has long been asserted that crisis response and the communication that is essential to it must be based on ethical, transparent decision-making. Future research might usefully explore how crisis communicators can best recruit AI and the new tools it powers to the task of better crisis identification, strategy formulation, and quick, appropriate communication.

References

Al-Dahash, H. F., Thayaparan, M., & Kulatunga, U. (2016). Understanding the terminologies: Disaster, Crisis and Emergency. In P.W. DChan & Nielson (eds.). *Proceedings of the 32nd Annual ARCOM Conference,* 5–7 September, Manchester, UK. Association of Researchers in Construction Management, *2*, pp. 1191–1200.

Beattie, A., & Priestley, R. (2021). Fighting COVID-19 with the team of 5 million: Aotearoa New Zealand government communication during the 2020 lockdown. *Social Sciences & Humanities Open*, *4*(1), 100209.

Bernard, N. R., Basit, A., Sofija, E., Phung, H., Lee, J., Rutherford, S., Sebar, B., Harris, N., Phung, D., & Wiseman, N. (2021). Analysis of crisis communication by the Prime Minister of Australia during the COVID-19 pandemic. *International Journal of Disaster Risk Reduction*, *62*, August 2021, 102375. https://doi.org/10.1016/j.ijdrr.2021.102375

Boin, A. (2019). The transboundary crisis: Why we are unprepared and the road ahead. *Journal of Contingencies & Crisis Management*, *27*(1), 94–99. https://doi.org/10.1111/1468-5973.12241

Boon, H. J. (2016). Perceptions of climate change in four disaster-impacted rural Australian towns. *Regional Environmental Change*, *16*(1), 137–149. http://dx.doi.org/10.1007/s10113-014-3

Bromfield, N., & McConnell, A. (2021). Two routes to precarious success: Australia, New Zealand, COVID-19 and the politics of crisis governance. *International Review of Administrative Sciences*, *87*(3), 518–535. https://doi.org/10.1177/0020852320972465

Brunton, M. A., & Jeffrey, L. M. (2019). Margaret Ann Brunton & Lynn Maud Jeffrey (2010) Using the critical incident technique for triangulation and elaboration of communication management competencies. *Journal of Vocational Education and Training*, *62*(3), 239–255. https://doi.org/10.1080/13636820.2010.499475

Came, H. (2012). *Institutional racism and the dynamics of privilege in public health.* Doctoral dissertation, University of Waikato.

Dharmasena, M. K. G. I., Toledano, M., & Weaver, C. K. (2020). The role of public relations in building community resilience to natural disasters: Perspectives from Sri Lanka and New Zealand. *Journal of Communication Management*, *24*(4), 301–317. https://doi.org/10.1108/JCOM-11-2019-0144

Dohaney, J., Brogt, E., Kennedy, B., Wilson, T. M., & Lindsay, J. M. (2015). Training in crisis communication and volcanic eruption forecasting: Design and evaluation of an authentic role-play simulation. *Journal of Applied Volcanology*, *4*, 1–26.

Doyle, E. E. H., Paton, D., & Johnston, D. M. (2015). Enhancing scientific response in a crisis: Evidence-based approaches from emergency management in New Zealand. *Journal of Applied Volcanology: Society and Volcanoes*, *4*(1), 1–26. https://doi.org/10.1186/s13617-014-0020-8

Elers, C., Jayan, P., Elers, P., & Dutta, M. J. (2021). Negotiating health Amidst COVID-19 lockdown in low-income communities in Aotearoa New Zealand. *Health Communication*, *36*(1), 109–115. https://doi.org/10.1080/10410236.2020.1848082

Fakhrurroja, H., Atmaja, M. N., Panjaitan, J. N. C. G., Alamsyah, A., & Munandar, A. (2019). Crisis communication on twitter: A social network analysis of Christchurch terrorist attack in 2019, *2019 International Conference on ICT for Smart Society (ICISS)*, Bandung, Indonesia, pp. 1–6, https://doi.org/10.1109/ICISS48059.2019.8969839.

Fearnley, C. J., Bird, D. K., Haynes, K., McGuire, W. J., & Jolly, G. (Eds.). (2018). *Observing the Volcano World: Volcano Crisis Communication.* Cham: Springer International Publishing.

FitzGerald, G., Du, W., Jamal, A., Clark, M., & Hou, X.-Y. (2010). Flood fatalities in contemporary Australia. *Emergency Medicine Australia (1997-2008)*, *22*(2), 180–186. https://doi.org/10.1111/j.1742-6723.2010.01284.xApril,

Galloway, C. (2016). Crisis communication research in Australia. In A. Schwartz, M. W. Seeger, & C. Auer, Eds., *The Handbook of International Crisis Communication Research* (pp. 337–346). Wiley. https://doi.org/10.1002/9781118516812.ch31

Galloway, C., Ashwell, D., Croucher, S., & Diers-Lawson, A. R. (2019). Testing times: Communicating the role and uncertainty of analytical procedures in a food safety crisis. *Asian Journal of Communication*, *20*(2), 42–58. ISSN 0129-2986

Gluckman, P., & Bardsley, A. (2020). *The Future is Now: Exploring the Post-pandemic Direction for Aotearoa New Zealand.* Koi Tu: The Centre for Informed Futures. https://apo.org.au/organisation/305163

Grebe, S. K. (2012). Getting it right from the start: How the initial crisis response by scandalized organizations is critical to repairing reputational damage. *Asia Pacific Public Relations Journal*, *13*(2). https://www.pria.com.au/public/38/files/Asia%20Pacific%20PR%20Journal/Volume%2013%20(2)/AWB_rebuilding_reputation_manuscript_print_version.pdf

Grebe, S. K. (2013). Things can get worse: How mismanagement of a crisis management strategy can cause a secondary or double crisis: The example of the AWB corporate scandal. *Corporate Communications: An International Journal*, *18*(1), 70–86. https://doi.org/10.1108/13563281311294137

Howes, M., Tangney, P., Reis, K., Grant-Smith, D., Heazle, M., Bosomworth, K., & Burton, P. (2015). Towards networked governance: Improving interagency communication and collaboration for disaster risk management and climate change adaptation in Australia. *Journal of Environmental Planning and Management*, *58*(5), 757–776. https://doi.org/10.1080/09640568.2014.891974

Jackson, J., & Thaker, J. (2021). Letting the team down? Examining sport fans reactions to Aaron Smith's 'Toilet Tryst' on social media. *Communication Research and Practice*, *7*(2), 148–172. https://doi.org/10.1080/22041451.2021.1905942

Jaques, T. (2012). Crisis leadership: A view from the executive suite. *Journal of Public Affairs*, *12*(4), 366–372. https://doi.org/10.1002/pa.1422

Jaques, T. (2013a). The leadership role in crisis prevention. In A. J. Du Brin, Ed., *Handbook of Research on Crisis Leadership in Organizations* (pp. 270–289). Elgaronline. https://doi.org/10.4337/9781781006405.00023

Jaques, T. (2013b). Ensnared in a gay health controversy: A comparative study in responding to issue activism. *Journal of Public Affairs, 13*(1), 53–60. https://doi.org/10.1002/pa.1442

Jaques, T. (May 1, 2023). Lessons in leadership and communication from a city flood crisis. *Managing Outcomes, 14*(9) [e-newsletter]. https://us1.campaign-archive.com/?u=12234fd351f8df7c1f4324 8ea&id=d442cb5ce1

Kotlarsky, J., Kishore, S., Branicki, L., & Sullivan-Taylor, B. (2022). How the world understood the white Island Eruption: The tales that different social media actors tell us. *The University of Auckland Business School Research Paper Series, European Conference of Information Systems (ECIS)*, 2022 Research-in-Progress Papers, p. 1342.

MacGillivray, P., & Baldry, E. (2013). Indigenous Australians, mental and cognitive impairment and the criminal justice system: A complex web. *Indigenous Law Bulletin, 8*(9), 22–26.

Macnamara, J. (2021). New insights into crisis communication from an "inside" emic perspective during COVID-19. *Public Relations Inquiry, 10*(2), 237–262. https://doi.org/10.1177/2046147X21999972

Maier, C. D., Frandsen, F., & Johansen, W. (2022). Understanding the arena of smoldering crises: A longitudinal study of discursive struggles after implementing a new IT health care platform. *Journal of Communication Management*, Vol. ahead-of-print No. ahead-of-print. https://doi.org/10.1108/JCOM-12-2021-0136

Marsen, S. (2020). Navigating crisis: The role of communication in organizational crisis. *International Journal of Business Communication, 57*(2), 163–276.

McClure, T. (February 14, 2023). Cyclone Gabrielle worst storm to hit New Zealand this century, says PM. TheGuardian.com. https://www.theguardian.com/world/2023/feb/13/cyclone-gabrielle-new-zealand-declares-national-state-of-emergency (accessed November 8, 2023).

McGuire, D., Cunningham, J. E. A., Reynolds, K., & Matthews-Smith, G. (2020). Beating the virus: An examination of the crisis communication approach taken by New Zealand Prime Minister Jacinda Ardern during the Covid-19 pandemic. *Human Resource Development International, 23*(4), 361–379. https://doi.org/10.1080/13678868.2020.1779543

Mehta, A. M., Weeks, C. S., & Tyquin, E. (2020). Towards preparedness for dam failure: An evidence base for risk communication for downstream communities. *International Journal of Disaster Risk Reduction, 50*, 101820.

Mehta, A. M., Murray, S., McAndrew, R., Jackson, M., & Tippett, V. (2022). Encouraging evacuation: The role of behavioural message inputs in bushfire warnings. *International Journal of Disaster Risk Reduction, 67*, 102673.

OECD (2010). *OECD Reviews of Regulatory Reform: Australia 2010: Towards a Seamless National Economy*, OECD Reviews of Regulatory Reform, OECD Publishing, Paris, https://doi.org/10.1787/9789264067189-en

Prastya, N. M., & Dewi, M. (2020). Framing analysis of government crisis communication in terrorist attacks (Case in New Zealand and Sri Lanka). *Informasi, 50.* https://doi.org/10.21831/informasi.v50i2.31444December,

Rajan, R. P. (2022). 'Go Hard, Go Early': New Zealand's COVID-19 elimination strategy. In S. Pachauri, & A. Pachauri, Eds., *Health Dimensions of COVID-19 in India and Beyond* (pp. 319–333). Springer. https://doi.org/10.1007/978-981-16-7385-6_18

Sowman-Lund, S. (April 12, 2023). Damning review into Auckland flood response finds 'system failure'. *The Spinoff.* https://thespinoff.co.nz/politics/12-04-2023/damning-review-into-auckland-flood-response-finds-system-failure (accessed November 2023).

Weible, C. M., Nohrstedt, D., Cairney, P., Carter, D. P., Crow, D. A., Durnová, A. P., Heikkila, T., Ingold, K., McConnell, A., & Stone, D. (2020). COVID-19 and the policy sciences: Initial reactions and perspectives. *Policy Sciences, 53*(2), 225–241. https://doi.org/10.1007/s11077-020-09381-4. Epub 2020 18 April. PMID: 32313308; PMCID: PMC7165254.

Zorn, T., Comrie, M., & Fountaine, S. (2016). Crisis communication research in Aotearoa/New Zealand. In A. Schwartz, M. W. Seeger, & C. Auer, Eds., *The Handbook of International Crisis Communication Research* (pp. 347–356). Wiley.

Author's Bio

Dr Christopher Galloway is an honorary research associate of Massey University, Auckland, New Zealand. He is an internationally recognized crisis and communication scholar whose most recent research and publications focus on Artificial Intelligence. He combines academic research with experience as a senior corporate manager in national New Zealand organizations.

Theodore E. Zorn (PhD, University of Kentucky) is a professor of Organizational Communication at Massey University in New Zealand. He is the former Dean of Massey Business School and former Deputy Vice-Chancellor at Massey University and has held other leadership roles at Massey and other universities. His teaching and research specialties are organizational communication, organizational change processes, and enhancing workplace well-being. He has published widely in communication and management journals and has consulted with a wide range of companies, government organizations, and not-for-profit organizations. He is the Past Editor of the journal *Management Communication Quarterly*, and a past recipient of the International Communication Association's Frederic Jablin Award for Outstanding Contribution to Organizational Communication. Ted's current research focuses on changing leaders' meanings and unspoken rationales for their work as well as on political polarization in the workplace.

Part VI

Emerging Topics, Challenges, Theory, and Methods

Conceptual and Theoretical Developments and Challenges in Crisis and Risk Communication

42

International Crises as Wicked Problems and Mega-crises: Opportunities for Building Crisis Communication Theory on an International Level

Rodrigo Soares[1] and Timothy L. Sellnow[2]
[1] Department of Agriculture, Landscape & Environment, University of Vermont, Burlington, VT, USA
[2] Department of Communication, Clemson University, Clemson, SC, USA

Introduction

Simple observation reveals the international attributes of crises and the need for an international response. Wildfires degrading air quality across borders, refugees fleeing oppression and creating controversy at international borders, and most obviously pandemics such as COVID-19 are only a few examples of the expansive reach crises manifest. In response to the span and intensity of crises, scholars are called to embrace an international focus in their research. Spence and Lachlan (2016), for example, admonish crisis communication scholars to bear in mind crises do not recognize or adhere to human-made borders separating countries. Coombs (2008) laments a distorted emphasis on crises occurring within the United States and calls for more international research. Beck (1992) offers compelling evidence that the risks humans endure are not only local but simultaneously global in stature. Sellnow and Veil (2016) observed both the need for and lack of research focusing on international crisis communication in their chapter published in the first edition of this handbook. More than half a decade later, the question persists: Are crisis communication scholars addressing the international dimensions of crises?

In answering this question, our chapter begins with a discussion of the evolving nature of crises in the forms of wicked problems and mega-crises and the increasing need for international crisis communication research and theory building. We then provide a brief assessment of international crisis communication scholarship in the seven years since the first edition of this handbook was published. We next highlight growing opportunities for international crisis communication research. We conclude by delineating opportunities for building theory that encompasses crisis communication on an international level.

The Handbook of International Crisis and Risk Communication Research, Second Edition.
Edited by Andreas Schwarz, Matthew W. Seeger, and Sora Kim.

The Increasing Complexity of Crises and Crisis Communication

Two concepts generating increased attention from crisis communication scholars, wicked problems and mega-crises, reveal the need for international research and response. In this section, we characterize wicked problems and mega-crises, providing further exemplification of the need for international collaboration in resolving an increasingly complex array of global crises.

Wicked Problems

Increasingly, some risks and crises are, by their nature, progressing to the level of wicked problems (Mitroff & Silvers, 2010). The term "wicked" as a characterization of a problem has been used since the late 1960s, when C. West Churchman, a philosopher and systems scientist, classified as wicked the problems that are confusing or not well formulated. The solutions to these problems can, at times, make the situation even worse. These solutions "are not true-or-false, but good or bad" (Willis, 2016, p. 307). Think, for example, how software solutions intending to make global financial transactions faster and easier have opened the door to cyberextortion and ransomware attacks.

Wicked problems foster an intensity that makes them too complex for individuals, organizations, agencies, or communities to resolve independently (Mitroff & Silvers, 2010; Willis et al., 2018). Unfortunately, wicked problems often linger without resolution or manifest suddenly with little anticipation. Because they are complex, addressing wicked problems effectively requires strategic engagement among a "diverse set of stakeholders," often in the form of an international alliance (Mitroff & Silvers, 2010, p. 37). Willis et al. (2018) recommend deliberative and collaborative engagement as a means for addressing the complex nature of wicked problems. They define deliberative engagement as a form of collaboration intended to assure the views of multiple stakeholders are considered. Without such collaboration, they argue wicked problems cannot be resolved.

Engaging multiples stakeholders, including international collaboration, creates an opportunity for shared learning. This form of post-crisis learning is widely advocated in the best practices crisis communication literature (Sellnow et al., 2017). Learning from crises collaboratively can stimulate "better understanding of the view of others" that, in turn, creates "a heightened sense of agency, social intelligence, self-fulfillment, and a sense of belonging to a shared undertaking" (Willis et al., 2018, p. 385). To achieve this end, resolving wicked problems relies often on an international dialogue devoted to mitigating complex crises.

From a crisis communication perspective, dialogue is the means through which collaborative relationships produce shared knowledge and lessons learned (Sellnow & Seeger, 2021). For example, during the early months of the COVID-19 pandemic, the International Food and Information Council (IFIC) used Twitter to dialogically engage scientists, journalists, healthcare professionals, and the public (Soares et al., 2022). Dialogue on this level, however, is far more than awareness and conversation. To achieve an international collaboration, dialogue requires relationships where statements are received and addressed with a "positive, respectful, and inclusive" attitude (Lane & Kent, 2018, p. 62). Further, dialogue requires the acceptance of risk associated with change, a mutual respect among all parties, a sense of propinquity or closeness in an ongoing relationship, empathy among all parties, and a commitment to maintaining the conversation (Kent & Taylor, 1998; Kent & Taylor, 2002; Lane & Kent, 2018). In short, for engaged dialogue to address wicked problems, "the question of who initiates the communication is irrelevant: the repeated pattern of responsiveness means the focus is on the progress of communication toward a mutually acceptable conclusion" (Lane & Kent, 2018, p. 62). Overall, wicked problems create complex situations that require learning through a collaborative commitment to dedicating the time and resources needed to overcome the international intersections of risk and crisis.

Mega-Crisis

Like wicked problems, mega-crises pour over human-made borders, demanding a shared response. Mega-crises, however, are more than a single exceptionally large event. Rather, mega-crises are a series of simultaneous crises transcending borders and individual governments (Lukacovic & Sellnow-Richmond, 2023). Thus, mega-crises are inherently international or often global in nature. As with wicked problems, mega-crises appear with greater frequency or clarity now than in the past. Disasters, many initiated by climate change, regularly traverse borders. The shifting landscape of digital technology, in general, and social media, specifically, gives rise to cybercrime and voice to dissident threats. Along with globalization comes the increasing threat of pandemics – complex, transboundary, and creeping in nature (Christensen & Lægreid, 2020). These, among many other impending risks, make the study of crisis communication on an international level increasingly imperative.

The study of mega-crises began with a focus on cataclysmic events such as massive earthquakes, exceptionally powerful hurricanes, and massive floods creating expansive devastation to broad regions (Helsloot et al., 2012). Such disasters challenge traditional thinking about crisis response, demanding "a paradigm shift in terms of decision-making capabilities and public policy commitments" (Helsoot et al., 2012, p. 7). Such disasters also defy traditional views of crises where, within a foreseeable span of time, the crisis moves from the acute stage to resolution, and a return to pre-crisis boundary spanning (Sellnow & Seeger, 2021). The duration of mega-crises greatly exceeds the confines of smaller, more typical crisis events. This added time invites speculation by often outraged publics who turn to new media to vent and to access advice from opinion leaders – some of whom have limited knowledge about the scientific reality of the event. These multiple views, not necessarily based on facts, create lack of convergence, which negatively impact people's perceptions of risk (Soares et al., 2023). Moreover, the expanse of mega-crises also frequently requires a multinational response through a variety of communication channels.

The complexity, magnitude, and duration of wicked problems and mega-crises defy attempts to establish or reinforce existing forms of resilience. Rather, they demand novel solutions and coping mechanisms that cannot emerge from individual communities, agencies, or nations (Sellnow & Sellnow, 2023). With wicked problems and mega-crises advancing in our awareness, the expectation is that more crisis communication research would address them and, in so doing, reflect an international focus. The remainder of this chapter is dedicated to assessing the extent of international crisis communication research since the first publication of the Handbook of International Crisis Communication Research in 2016. To do so, we begin by identifying the frequency and form of international crisis communication research in the two most relevant journals: *Journal of Contingencies and Crisis Management (JCCM)* and the *Journal of International Crisis and Risk Communication Research (JICRCR)*.

Frequency and Form of Recent International Risk and Crisis Communication Research

To assess the frequency and form of recent international risk and crisis communication research, we conducted a simple content analysis of publications in the JCCM and the JICRCR from 2017 to 2022. We chose these two journals because they are, by design,

Table 42.1 Topics of international risk and crisis communication research.

Topic	*Total articles*
International disasters	18
Social media/digital communication	17
Epidemics/pandemics	8
Cultural comparison	2
War	1
Total	**42**

intended to publish international scholarship on crisis communication. They are also the only two journals dedicated exclusively to crisis communication. Articles were identified as having an international focus if more than one country was included in the analysis and dataset. The two authors served as coders. The simplicity of the criteria afforded few discrepancies between the coders, with any disagreement being resolved through conversation.

Despite the call for more international crisis communication research, fewer than one in five articles published in the JCCM and in the *JICRCR* involve crisis research focused on more than one country. We reviewed 239 articles in the above-mentioned refereed journals: $N = 181$ (JCCM) and $N = 58$ (JICRCR). The analyses showed that 42 (17.6%) established an international research focus (covering more than one country). Divided by journal, of the 58 articles published in JICRCR, 8 (13.8%) established an international research focus, while 34 (18.8%) of 181 articles published in the JCCM did so. Regardless of the lower than anticipated frequency, the quality of research and insight produced by the international research is notable. The majority of international crisis communication studies focused on international disasters and the use of social media as a means to establish post-crisis dialogue. Pandemics also garnered a notable number of studies (see Table 42.1). Next, we provide a general overview of the international research content by topic, providing representative examples for clarity.

International Research on Disasters

The international research on disasters provides generalizations extending beyond individual countries. In the JCCM, for example, Dalgas (2018) investigated the opportunities and constraints migrants experience when attempting to channel needed resources to assist residents in their home countries who are enduring disasters. Dalgas observed both constraints for migrants to contribute their resources and calls for a reconsideration of how remittances flow in disaster relief, particularly for migrants. Lai and Hsu (2019) compared the communication networks employed in the response to four disasters affecting multiple countries. In addition to observing differences among crisis type, Lai and Hsu also noted variability in the resilience and success of existing networks based on prior experience and network redundancy. Turcanu et al. (2021) assessed perceived compliance by residents of three European countries with recommendations provided by authorities during a nuclear emergency. They found many respondents were likely to comply with recommendations, excluding those recommendations to leave their children at school and to minimize phone use. Inclusive of all three countries, they conclude that comprehending and responding to society concerns enhances societal resilience in the aftermath of a nuclear accident. Fu and Lai (2021) observed a lack of research informing humanitarian organizations of how to best engage in disaster risk relief. In response, they studied 104 such agencies. Their study revealed the importance of external communication capacity through interorganizational collaboration across the broad sample of agencies in providing effective disaster risk reduction.

Similarly, generalizability across countries was noted in the international disaster research published in JICRCR. For instance, Novak et al. (2019) conducted a systematic review of literature focused on engaging communities. They found public benefits from emergency risk communication across countries during all crisis stages, pre-crisis, during, and post-crisis. The authors also cautioned, however, that the observed importance of grounding the communication in local contexts also limited generalizability of some strategies. Similarly, Miller et al. (2021) conducted a systematic review of studies applying the Center for Disease Control and Prevention's (CDC's) Crisis Emergency Risk Communication (CERC) model. The principles of the model were applied internationally with favorable results reported in cases studies. Empirical support for the model's central propositions was less clear.

International Research on Digital Crisis Communication

Multiple international studies in both journals also focused on international aspects of digital and social media use during crises. As illustration, in the *JCCM,* Bentley et al. (2018) analyzed organizational responses to data breaches experienced by many international companies. They observed a willingness by organizations to accept responsibility when they were to blame and a tendency to emphasize self-protection for customers when the organizations were victimized by sophisticated cyber criminals. Backman (2021) conceptualized cybercrime as a transboundary crisis and compared responses from organizations in two countries. Results indicated organizations benefit from alacrity and flexibility, while acknowledging a greater need for multi-organizational collaboration than in other crisis types. Several studies also provided international assessments of social media use during crises. Reuter and Kaufhold (2018) provide a retrospective look at applications of social media in crisis contexts over the past 15 years. They observed a maturation of both social media technology and its application over the selected period, thereby increasing the demands on practitioners to provide timely messages over diverse message channels. Cheng (2018) observed a similar evolution of crisis response opportunities and expectations in a global crisis context. Cheng noted similar shifts due to social media condensing the time expectations for a public response to crisis by organizations and government agencies. A deficiency of dialogic interaction with publics was also observed.

Observations of scholarship on digital communication in the JICRCR offer similar findings. Miller and Kendall (2018) documented a blurring of the distinction between personal and organizational identity in crises involving political protest and unrest. Kang et al. (2019) compared posts on Twitter among Australia, South Korea, and the USA focusing on the Samsung Galaxy Note 7 explosion crisis. They identified a consistently negative sentiment in posts across the sample, suggesting the potential for global audiences to influence an organization's crisis response.

International Research on Pandemics

Pandemics were another crisis type inspiring international scholarship. In the *JCCM* for example, Willems et al. (2022) studied the resource pressures international nonprofits experienced in responding to COVID-19. Pressures were experienced involving a variety of stakeholders on an international level. Petridou and Zahariadis (2021) conducted a comparative analysis of effectiveness and efficiency in the leadership decisions and actions in Greece and Sweden during COVID-19. They recognized leaders are not bound to a single "correct" strategy in crisis response, but instead have many viable options for how they respond.

Similar examples were found in the JICRCR in three separate crisis environments. For instance, Sellnow-Richmond et al. (2018) noted the presence of mega-crisis attributes in the 2014 Ebola outbreak in Western Africa. In doing so, they observed the necessity for international collaboration and consistency in the instructional risk and crisis communication process. Brunson et al. (2020) identified a series of generalizable communication lessons for all pandemic stages through an intricately designed simulation, the SPARS pandemic. Littlefield (2020) applied the theory of Dialectical Tensions to the Zika epidemic, noting the evolution of decision-making tensions throughout lifecycle of crises.

International Research on "Other" Topics

Other topical areas appearing with less frequency focused on international alliances, cultural comparisons, and war. For instance, Luoma-aho et al. (2017) provided a cultural comparison of Finland and Spain regarding crisis communication. Petridou et al. (2019) observed how various European Union states communicate about the risk of war with their citizens.

Conclusions and Implications

In the 2016 *Handbook of International Crisis Communication Research*, Sellnow and Veil (2016) described the challenges created by potentially competing voices in international crisis communication. They further identified potential arguments over responsibility and blame as additional detractors to international collaboration in crisis response activities. These concerns, however, are subsumed by the greater challenges of wicked problems and mega-crises – both of which inherently demand an international response. Simply put, the tragic consequences of communication failures in such expansive events are far greater than the reputational matters of responsibility and blame. Despite the urgency for developing international crisis communication strategies and theories to address wicked problems and mega-crises, fewer than one in five articles published between the previous handbook's publication and now have taken an international focus.

Although somewhat disappointing in frequency, the existing international research is fitting with the expectations and demands of wicked problems and mega-crises. Disasters, digital media, and pandemics comprised the most common areas of international study. All three of these topic areas are identified as key concerns in the literature on wicked problems and mega-crises. Thus, the existing literature on international risk and crisis communication is aligned with the shifting nature and intensification of crises. Those authors committed to collecting international datasets are modeling a way forward accounting for the changing nature of crises. The impacts of major crises are rarely confined within a single country. Thus, international datasets reflect the public informational needs during crises. Likewise, those scholars who recognize the internationality of social media networks are in step with the shifting form of crisis communication. Relatedly, the threat to cybersecurity is a matter no nation can sufficiently address alone. In short, the existing international crisis communication literature, though limited in volume, is well aligned with the evolving crisis environment.

An unforeseen dimension of the literature identified for this study is the inconsistency in application of theory. Nearly half, 20 of 42, of the articles taking an international focus did not clearly identify a theory guiding their research. Those articles applying a theory used a wide range of approaches such as imager repair, SCCT, resilience, sensemaking, framing, and organizational learning/instructional communication. The lack of theory may be due to the descriptive or comparative nature of the research. Another likely reason is the lack of a clearly dedicated line of theory building dedicated to international risk and crisis communication research. This situation is less a problem and more an opportunity. Scholars have the opportunity to isolate crises that span borders as a recurring system state in need of description, interpretation, evaluation, and, ultimately, prediction and control. The time is right for scholars to step forward and engage in theorizing about the nuances of communication in crises that span borders, persist beyond the typical time-frame assumed in many theories, and require collaborative messaging and solutions.

Finally, opportunities for scholars from different countries to unite in research teams continue to expand. Organizations such as the European Communication Research and Education Association and the International Association for Media and Communication Research sponsor interest areas specific to crisis communication where scholars from various countries can share their research and discuss opportunities for collaboration. Additionally, the newly formed International Crisis and Risk Communication Association hosts an annual conference dedicated to risk and crisis communication scholarship that attracts scholars from North America, South America, Europe, Africa, and Australia. Alliances formed from interaction at such conferences better positioned scholars for conducting international research.

Crises, though always challenging, are steadily increasing in their global frequency and intensity (Beck, 2016). Crisis responses and related communication are increasingly dependent on the actions of others – frequently transcending international boundaries. Though crisis communication scholars recognize the need for an international focus in their research, the frequency of such studies lags far behind single-nation or single-organization studies. The existing international research conducted over the past seven years, however, is well aligned with the needs of wicked problems and mega-crises. Thus, a solid foundation for continued and expanded research and theorizing exists. For this reason, we remain optimistic.

References

Backman, S. (2021). Conceptualizing cyber crises. *Journal of Contingencies & Crisis Management, 29*(4), 429–438. https://doi.org/10.1111/1468-5973.12347

Beck, U. (1992). *Risk Society: Towards a New Modernity (M. Ritter, Trans.)*. SAGE.

Beck, U. (2016). *The Metamorphosis of the World*. Polity.

Bentley, J. M., Oostman, K. R., & Shah, S. F. A. (2018). We're sorry but it's not our fault: Organizational apologies in ambiguous crisis situations. *Journal of Contingencies & Crisis Management, 26*(1), 138–149. https://doi.org/10.1111/1468-5973.12169

Brunson, E. K., Chandler, H., Gronvall, G. K., Ravi, S., Sell, T. K., Shearer, M. P., & Schoch-Spana, M. (2020). The SPARS pandemic 2025-2028: A futuristic scenario to facilitate medical countermeasure communication. *Journal of International Crisis and Risk Communication Research, 3*(1), 71–102. https://doi.org/10.30658/jicrcr.3.1.4

Cheng, Y. (2018). How social media is changing crisis communication strategies: Evidence from the updated literature. *Journal of Contingencies & Crisis Management, 26*(1), 58–68. https://doi.org/10.1111/1468-5973.12130

Christensen, T., & Lægreid, P. (2020). The coronavirus crisis – crisis communication, meaning-making, and reputation management. *International Public Management Journal, 23*(5), 713–729. https://doi.org/10.1080/10967494.2020.1812455

Coombs, T. W. (2008). The future of crisis communication from an international perspective. *Krisenmanagement in der Mediengesellschaft: Potenziale und Perspektiven der Krisenkommunikation*, 275–287. https://doi.org/10.1007/978-3-531-91191-5_19

Dalgas, K. (2018). Translocal disaster interventions: The role of individual relief channels in Philippine disasters. *Journal of Contingencies & Crisis Management, 26*(3), 377–384. https://doi.org/10.1111/1468-5973.12204

Fu, J. S., & Lai, C. H. (2021). Determinants of organizational performance in disaster risk reduction: A preliminary study of global humanitarian NGOs. *Journal of Contingencies & Crisis Management, 29*(3), 232–247. https://doi.org/10.1111/1468-5973.12346

Helsloot, I., Boin, A., Jacobs, B., & Comfort, L. K. (2012). The new challenges of mega-crises. In I. Helsloot, A. Boin, B. Jacobs, & L. K. Comfort, Eds., *Mega-crises: Understanding the Prospects, Nature, Characteristics and the Effects of Cataclysmic Events* (pp. 5–11). Charles C. Thomas, Publisher, LTD.

Littlefield, R. S. (2020). The tensions of strategic communication decision-making: An exploratory examination of theory and practice. *Journal of International Crisis and Risk Communication Research, 3*(2), 211–242. https://doi.org/10.30658/jicrcr.3.2.4

Kang, S., Shim, K., & Kim, J. (2019). Social media posts on the Samsung Galaxy Note 7 explosion: A comparative analysis of crisis framing and sentiment in three nations. *Journal of International Crisis and Risk Communication Research, 2*(2), 259–289. https://doi.org/10.30658/jicrcr.2.2.5

Kent, M. L., & Taylor, M. (1998). Building dialogic relationships through the World Wide Web. *Public Relations Review, 24*(3), 321–334.

Kent, M. L., & Taylor, M. (2002). Toward a dialogic theory of public relations. *Public relations review, 28*(1), 21–37. https://doi.org/10.1016/S0363-8111(02)00108-X

Lai, C. H., & Hsu, Y. C. (2019). Understanding activated network resilience: A comparative analysis of co-located and co-cluster disaster response networks. *Journal of Contingencies & Crisis Management, 27*(1), 14–27. https://doi.org/10.1111/1468-5973.12224

Lane, A., & Kent, M. L. (2018). Dialogicengagement. The handbook of communication engagement, 61–72.

Lukovic, M. N., & Sellnow-Richmond. (2023). The COVID-19 pandemic and the rise of malicious use of AI threats to national and international psychological security. In E. Pashentsev, Ed., *The Palgrave Handbook of Malicious Use of AI and Psychological Security* (pp. 175–202). Palgrave MacMillan. https://doi.org/10.1007/978-3-031-22552-9_7

Luoma-aho, V., Moreno, Á., & Verhoeven, P. (2017). Crisis response strategies in Finland and Spain. *Journal of Contingencies & Crisis Management, 25*(4), 223–231. https://doi.org/10.1111/1468-5973.12163

Miller, A. N., Collins, C., Neuberger, L., Todd, A., Sellnow, T. L., & Boutemen, L. (2021). Being first, being right, and being credible since 2002: A systematic review of Crisis and Emergency Risk Communication (CERC) research. *Journal of International Crisis and Risk Communication Research, 4*(1), 1–27. https://doi.org/10.30658/jicrcr.4.1.1

Miller, K. E., & Kendall, M. C. (2018). Blurred (identity) lines: A content analysis of the #deleteuber crisis on Twitter. *Journal of International Crisis and Risk Communication Research, 1*(2), 253–277. https://doi.org/10.30658/jicrcr.1.2.4

Mitroff, I. I., & Silvers, A. (2010). *Dirty Rotten Strategies: How We Trick Ourselves and Others into Solving the Wrong Problems Precisely*. Stanford University Books.

Novak, J. M., Day, A. M., Sopory, P., Wilkins, L., Padgett, D., Eckert, S. et al. (2019). Engaging communities in emergency risk and crisis communication: A systematic review and evidence synthesis. *Journal of International Crisis and Risk Communication Research, 2*(1), 61–96. https://doi.org/10.30658/jicrcr.2.1.4

Petridou, E., Danielsson, E., Olofsson, A., Lundgren, M., & Große, C. (2019). If crisis or war comes: A study of risk communication of eight European Union member states. *Journal of International Crisis and Risk Communication Research, 2*(2), 207–232. https://doi.org/10.30658/jicrcr.2.2.3

Petridou, E., & Zahariadis, N. (2021). Staying at home or going out? Leadership response to the COVID-19 crisis in Greece and Sweden. *Journal of Contingencies & Crisis Management, 29*(3), 293–302. https://doi.org/10.1111/1468-5973.12344

Reuter, C., & Kaufhold, M. A. (2018). Fifteen years of social media in emergencies: A retrospective review and future directions for crisis informatics. *Journal of Contingencies & Crisis Management, 26*(1), 41–57. https://doi.org/10.1111/1468-5973.12196

Sellnow, D. D., Lane, D. R., Sellnow, T. L., & Littlefield, R. S. (2017). The IDEA model as a best practice for effective instructional risk and crisis communication. *Communication Studies, 68*(5), 552–567. https://doi.org/10.1080/10510974.2017.1375535

Sellnow-Richmond, D., George, A., & Sellnow, D. (2018). An IDEA model analysis of instructional risk communication messages in the time of Ebola. *Journal of International Crisis and Risk Communication Research, 1*, 135–166. https://doi.org/10.30658/jicrcr.1.1.7

Sellnow, T. L., & Sellnow, D. D. (2023). *Before Crisis: The Practice of Effective Risk Communication*. Cognella.

Sellnow, T. L., & Seeger, M. W. (2021). *Theorizing Crisis Communication* (2nd ed.). John Wiley & Sons.

Sellnow, T. L., & Veil, S. R. (2016). Preparing for international and cross-cultural crises: The role of competing voices, inclusivity, and the interplay of responsibility in global organizations. In A.

Schwarz, M. W. Seeger, & C. Auer, Eds., *The Handbook of International Crisis Communication Research* (pp. 489–497). Wiley Blackwell. https://doi.org/10.1002/9781118516812.ch44

Spence, P. R., & Lachlan, K. A. (2016). Reoccurring challenges and emerging threats: Crises and the new millennium. In A. Schwarz, M. Seeger, & C. Auer, Eds., *Handbook of International Crisis Communication* (pp. 212–223). Wiley-Blackwell. https://doi.org/10.1002/9781118516812.ch20

Soares, R., Dumitrescu, S., Sims, T., Sellnow, T. L., Sellnow, D. D., & Seeger, M. W. (2022). Opportunities for instructional crisis communication through social media: Communicating self-protective actions for food safety during the COVID-19 pandemic. In Y. Jin, & L. Austin, Eds., *Social Media and Crisis Communication* (2nd ed., pp. 273–284). Routledge. https://doi.org/10.4324/9781003043409-32

Soares, R., Jin, X., Spence, P. R., & Sellnow, T. L. (2023). Interacting arguments in crisis communication: The influence of message convergence on risk and crisis messages. *Journal of Contingencies & Crisis Management*. https://doi.org/10.1111/1468-5973.12456

Turcanu, C., Sala, R., Perko, T., Abelshausen, B., Oltra, C., Tomkiv, Y. et al. (2021). How would citizens react to official advice in a nuclear emergency? Insights from research in three European countries. *Journal of Contingencies & Crisis Management*, *29*(2), 143–169. https://doi.org/10.1111/1468-5973.12327

Willems, E. L., Van Puyvelde, S., Jegers, M., & Raeymaeckers, P. (2022). Responding to COVID-19: International nonprofits' stakeholder channels, resource pressures and governance responses. *Journal of Contingencies & Crisis Management*, *30*(3), 270–280. https://doi.org/10.1111/1468-5973.12421

Willis, P. (2016). From humble inquiry to humble intelligence: Confronting wicked problems and augmenting public relations. *Public Relations Review*, *42*(2), 306–313. https://doi.org/10.1016/j.pubrev.2015.05.007

Willis, P., Tench, R., & Devins, D. (2018). Deliberative engagement and wicked problems: From good intentions to practical action. In K. A. Johnston, & M. Taylor, Eds., *The Handbook of Communication Engagement* (pp. 383–396). Wiley Blackwell. https://doi.org/10.1002/9781119167600.ch26

Authors' Bio

Rodrigo Soares is a Postdoctoral Associate at the University of Vermont. He bridges more than 15 years of experience as a leading practitioner in the corporate communication field with more than 7 years of applied research in risk and crisis communication. His research provides both theoretical advancements and applications for strategic communication practitioners. His investigations analyzed diseases outbreaks, such as the Zika virus in Brazil and the COVID-19 pandemic through a message design perspective. He also tested the adequacy of crisis communication theories in explaining the failures of institutions facing repeated crises, expanding the understanding of post-crisis learning.

Timothy L. Sellnow is a professor of strategic communication, and Pegasus Professor, at the University of Central Florida (UCF). His research focuses on risk and crisis communication. He has conducted funded research for the Department of Homeland Security, the United States Department of Agriculture, the Centers for Disease Control and Prevention, the Environmental Protection Agency, the United States Geological Survey, and the World Health Organization. He has also served in an advisory role for the National Academy of Sciences, the Federal Emergency Management Agency, and the Food and Drug Administration. He is past winner of the National Communication Association's Gerald Phillips Award for Distinguished Applied Communication Scholarship and UCF's Luminary Scholar award for research. He has co-authored seven books on risk and crisis communication and has published many journal articles in such publications as *Journal of Applied Communication Research, Critical Studies in Media Communication, Communication Education, Health Communication, and Journal of Health communication.* His most recent book, co-authored with Dr. Deanna Sellnow, is *Before Crisis: Strategies for Effective Risk Communication.*

43

Instructional Communication Theories, Models, and Constructs in Risk/Mega-Risk and Crisis/Mega-Crisis

Deanna D. Sellnow
Department of Communication, Clemson University, Clemson, SC, USA

Decades have come and gone since Ulrich Beck (1986) described our global risk society as wrought with a multiplicity of omnipresent and interacting ecological, financial, military, terrorist, biochemical, and informational risks. Anthony Giddons (1990) claimed it emerged from a preoccupation with the future and safety. More than two decades later, Helsloot et al. (2012) extended the debate by introducing mega-crises as interconnected global threats manifested in ways that impact diverse populations in multiple ways. More recently, Sellnow and Sellnow (2024) proposed the notion of mega-risk as inextricably interconnected risks and crises that, "when left unchecked, can manifest into existential risk," which may exacerbate mega-crises and cause global, terminal, and permanent damage (p. 152). Whereas mega-crises are "risks already manifested into crises," mega-risks both "precede and supersede mega-crises by focusing on the interaction of [interconnected and seemingly distinct] risks not yet manifested" (p. 154).

These projections made over the years appear to have come to fruition as local and global communities struggle to navigate the complex risks embedded in mega-crises such as climate change, pandemics, war, data capitalism, cybersecurity, political conflict/polarization, and bioterrorism, among others. Thus, scholars dedicated to risk and crisis communication are at a crossroads where existing theories and models are no longer adequate for navigating the complex challenges that pervade the global risk society we find ourselves living and working in today (e.g., Avery et al., 2010; Sellnow & Sellnow, 2024).

I begin this chapter by articulating some of the driving forces that challenge existing notions of risk and crisis and, by extension, risk and crisis communication. From there, I propose instructional communication research as a resource for expanding risk and crisis communication theories and models to better address some of the complexities embedded in our global risk society. I close with a summary of how these tenets, theories, and constructs ground the IDEA model as one effective instructional risk and crisis communication theoretical model that has demonstrated utility when focusing on a variety of risk situations and crisis events occurring around the world.

The Handbook of International Crisis and Risk Communication Research, Second Edition.
Edited by Andreas Schwarz, Matthew W. Seeger, and Sora Kim.

Driving Forces for Theory Expansion

Several factors serve as driving forces that complicate existing definitions, rules, and best practices of both risk and crisis communication. These factors are related directly to theoretical limitations based on time, space, uncertainty, and communication.

One factor is rooted in how we conceptualize time. For example, the time parameters imposed by many existing theories of crisis are inadequate in describing prolonged mega-crises such as the coronavirus pandemic that began in 2020. One question we find ourselves grappling with is as follows: How do we define crisis stages in prolonged crises and mega-crises that may last for several months, years, and even decades? Consider, for example, existing models for identifying crisis stages and pandemic phases (e.g., Sellnow & Seeger, 2021; World Health Organization, 2009). Neither the pre-established crisis stages nor the WHO phases in their current forms necessarily matched the coronavirus pandemic shifts as they occurred in different countries and regions over time. At any given point during the "three years, three months and five days" of the global pandemic (Lenharo, 2023), one region was overwhelmed by hospitalizations and deaths (acute crisis response), while others were anticipating a peak in infections (pre-crisis). Still others were experiencing declining numbers of cases, hospitalizations, and deaths (post-crisis). Existing definitions of crisis stages and pandemic phases do not readily account for these realities related to time.

Another time-related reality yet to be addressed adequately can be described as a vigilance/fatigue dialectic. Fatigue clearly plays a role in how people attend to potential threats and perceived risks, as well as the degree to which they comply with recommendations for self-protection. In the case of the COVID-19 pandemic, people became less inclined to follow risk mitigation protocols (e.g., wearing a mask, maintaining physical distance, avoiding crowds) as weeks turned into months and then months turned into years (e.g., Harvey, 2020; Petherick et al., 2021). What will motivate people to remain vigilant when imminent high impact threats shift into risk management issues as threat impact probabilities fluctuate and even decrease over time?

Still another time-related reality we must now grapple with can be described as an interest/apathy dialectic. When the long-term effects of potential threats – even high impact ones – are barely perceptible and seemingly inconsequential in the short term, overcoming indifference may become a significant barrier to motivating short-term behavioral change, as well as sustaining that change over time (e.g., Anderson & Hobolt, 2022; Steen & Brandsen, 2020). For example, scientists have been documenting climate change as a potential threat to people and society(ies) for decades. Recommendations for mitigating harms based on a wealth of empirical data-driven research often falls on deaf ears due to apathy. What will motivate people to engage in recommended risk management actions when the consequences of inaction are not readily apparent in the short term? The aforementioned factors are a few time-related realities to be accounted for in new and expanded risk and crisis communication theories and models.

In addition to these time-related realities is the complicating factor of space. Most existing crisis theories frame them (and the potential threats and perceived risks embedded in them) as events bounded by geographic location (Schwarz et al., 2016). However, globalization (ongoing interaction among people and organizations worldwide) has rendered that distinction virtually obsolete. For example, when the coronavirus first surfaced in Wuhan, China, it was described as a crisis occurring within the borders of China. The consequences of this inadequate description of what we now understand as a prolonged mega-crisis quickly became apparent as the outbreak in China transcended geographic boundaries and traveled across countries and continents. Another example is evidenced in the 2023 wildfires in Canada: the smoke from which impacted air quality for large portions of the entire North American continent. Certainly, as Quarantelli (1998) explains, all disasters are local; however, the impacts of the wildfires clearly extended beyond those local region(s) to other communities and countries.

Moreover, as crises cross borders both within and beyond countries, their characteristics may change as they interact with new publics and environments. The coronavirus, for example, mutated multiple times as it crossed borders. Scientists identified dozens of variants over the course of the pandemic and continue to identify them via comprehensive and ongoing surveillance. One consequence of globalization is the fact that when a risk situation crosses border, as was the case with the coronavirus, "it has new opportunities to change and may become more difficult to stop" (CDC, n.d.).

As crises cross borders and impact diverse people and groups, both the actual risks and risk perceptions associated with them may differ, as well (Dutta, 2008). Cultural norms and values, financial and economic constraints, and political ideologies may influence risk perception, recommendations, and compliance. When the U.S. Centers for Disease Control and Prevention (CDC) recommended wearing masks and maintaining physical distance during COVID-19, it was difficult and sometimes impossible for some people and communities to comply because masks were not accessible to them; they lived in multi-family/multi-generational homes and were considered essential workers (Sellnow et al., 2023a). Certainly, political polarization played a similar role in the degree to which people chose to comply with U.S. CDC recommendations (Bekalu et al., 2021).

A third complicating factor has to do with the role of uncertainty and how we address it. Uncertainty has long been acknowledged as a characteristic of both risk and crisis. Many existing theories acknowledge the need to share what is known, what is not yet known, and what is being done to find out during all stages of a crisis (Sellnow & Seeger, 2021). Most theories describe uncertainty during crises as related to surprise. Inherent in this description, however, is an assumption that once answers have been discovered about what came as a surprise, the uncertainty will be resolved. However, the nature of uncertainty inherent in risks and mega-risks in prolonged and mega-crises is ongoing and ever-changing. In this case, uncertainty is a constant to manage rather than an unexpected problem to be understood. This perpetual uncertainty/certainty dialectic must be acknowledged in both risk and crisis communication theories and strategies (Sellnow & Sellnow, 2024).

To illustrate, as the COVID-19 virus traveled and mutated, what was known and unknown about it did so, as well. The ever-changing uncertainty/certainty dialectic poses a threat to attaining and maintaining both trust and credibility. This became painfully clear throughout the COVID-19 pandemic as public perceptions of (dis)trust toward government officials, public health officials, and the scientific community, as well as of media journalists reporting on their behalf, grew exponentially. Theories and models focused on communicating uncertainty must go beyond seeking answers to initial questions about risks and crises to managing ever-changing realities about what is known and unknown continues to evolve (Sellnow & Sellnow, 2024).

A fourth complicating factor that serves as a driving force for expanding our theoretical understanding of effective risk and crisis communication is rooted in information digitization (the process of converting information into a digital format) (Malecki et al., 2021). In fact, infodemic, a term coined by Rothkopf (2003) to describe the breadth of risk information that spreads quickly over the Internet, quickly became part of the popular culture vernacular in myriad countries during the COVID-19 pandemic (World Health Organization, n.d.). Having 24/7 access to information via the Internet and other technological affordances increases opportunities for misunderstandings rooted in issues of translation across languages, disparate literacy levels, and misinformation, disinformation, and malinformation. All these concerns point to the need to better equip people with tools to evaluate information and sources through educational training and campaigns (Liu et al., 2020). Consequences of information digitization in terms of risk and crisis were realized throughout the COVID-19 pandemic as information-seekers turned to the Internet and social media to learn about and make decisions regarding the crisis and various risks associated with it. Regarding information digitization, what is (and is not) the responsibility of risk and crisis communicators in terms of teaching stakeholders how to discern fact from fiction?

These are some of the driving forces for extending risk and crisis communication theory and practice. This chapter focuses specifically on the role of instructional communication theories, tenets, and constructs as they may effectively enhance the study of risk/mega-risk and crisis/mega-crisis communication. Although they originated in traditional classroom contexts, they may be relevant to any communication context where learning is the goal and teaching is the means for achieving it. In other words, instructional communication focuses on the role of communication in instruction regardless of setting – including risk and crisis contexts.

Instructional Communication

To ascertain the role of instructional communication theory, tenets, and constructs in informing effective risk and crisis communication, two key misconceptions about what constitutes instructional communication require clarification. First, although the *sharing of information* does occur while engaging in instructional communication, information-sharing alone does not constitute instructional communication (Mottet & Beebe, 2006). Second, although *giving directions* also occurs while engaging in instructional communication, simply telling people what to do also does not constitute instructional communication (Gayle et al., 2006). In other words, merely providing information or simply telling people what to do are insufficient to achieve learning, which is the goal of instructional communication. Effective instructional communication in any context must achieve three fundamental learning outcomes: affective, cognitive, and behavioral.

Affective learning is achieved when learners realize the relevance and value of a given topic (Lane et al., 2022). Affective learning is often measured by the degree to which learners are motivated to engage with a topic. Do learners realize the significance of the topic or issue for themselves (personal) and for others (societal)? Cognitive learning is achieved when learners accurately understand the topic at hand. Cognitive learning is measured via knowledge comprehension (Hosek et al., 2022). Do learners accurately understand the meaning of a given topic or issue for themselves and others? Behavioral learning is achieved when learners adequately perform desired actions (Afifi et al., 2022). Behavioral learning is measured via the assessment of skills performed. To what degree do learners enact certain skills, tasks, or other desired behaviors? Perceived efficacy (self and/or collective) is central to achieving behavioral learning (Bandura, 1997). In other words, simply realizing the relevance of a topic (affective learning) and understanding its meaning (cognitive learning) will not lead to appropriate performance (behavioral learning) unless learners believe they can properly execute the recommended actions (efficacy). Using the COVID-19 pandemic as an example, people may realize the potential impact of the virus on them and their loved ones (affective learning) and how the virus spreads through the air via droplets (cognitive learning). Even if they also want to comply with recommendations to wear a mask in public settings, however, behavioral learning outcomes (i.e., mask-wearing) will not be realized if they cannot get access to such masks (efficacy). With these characteristics clarified, the next section highlights several tenets and constructs of instructional communication as they may inform effective communication in various risk situations and crisis events.

Theoretical Tenets and Constructs of Instructional Communication

Extant research identifies several theoretical tenets and constructs of communication that predict student learning. To illustrate how they operate in effective risk and crisis communication, the following paragraphs focus on effective instructional communication as both learner-centered and learning outcome-driven.

Effective Instructional Communication is Learner-Centered

To be effective, instructional communication is learner (rather than teacher)-centered. It follows that in contexts of risk and crisis, instructional communication must be receiver (rather than sender)-oriented (e.g., Littlefield et al., 2014; Sellnow et al., 2015). To be learner-centered, communication must first and foremost engage and empower learners based on the knowledge and experiences they bring to the occasion (e.g., Brookfield, et al., 2024; Dewey, 1938; Rogers, 1983).

In *Pedagogy of the Oppressed*, now considered a classic among education scholars, Paulo Freire (1968/1972) debunked what he called the "banking" concept of instructional communication – a.k.a. teacher-centered pedagogy – as a "a form of oppression" that can only be overcome through dialogue among teacher(s) and students(s). Teacher-centered communication is ineffective because it fails to honor the fact that students come to the occasion with legitimate knowledge based on their unique lived experiences. bell hooks (1994/2020) extended Freire's theories by proposing "engaged pedagogy" as it transforms traditional notions of teacher(s) and student(s) by conceiving of classrooms as "sites of resistance" that emphasize "mutual participation between teacher and student" (p. 204).

Risk and crisis communication theories ought to similarly embrace learner-centered communication that honors the knowledge risk bearers bring to the occasion. Doing so is more likely to motivate receivers to attend to the topic at hand and participate actively in the process, which leads to better learning outcome achievement (Sellnow et al., 2015). This is particularly critical when communicating cross-culturally both within countries and across them (Dutta, 2018). In their analysis of failed instructional communication between government leaders and farmers living on Mount Elgon in eastern Uganda, for example, Napakol and colleagues (2023) highlight the fact that residents did not believe their needs and concerns were adequately considered in the relocation proposals offered by the government officials. In this sense, government officials were not learner-centered. Similarly, Salazar (2021) illustrated how and why the Spanish versions of U.S. CDC COVID-19 recommendations failed to achieve compliance among Hispanic populations based in large part on the fact that they were not receiver-oriented (a.k.a. learner-centered).

Risk and crisis communication scholars and practitioners also continually grapple with how to manage public perceptions regarding (dis)trust as it influences willingness to believe spokespersons (a.k.a. credibility), as well as to comply with recommended actions for risk mitigation and self-protection (e.g., Cologna & Siegrist, 2020; Jennings et al., 2021; Niu et al., 2022; Suiter & Fletcher, 2020; Wang et al., 2021). A substantial body of research explores the challenges in building credibility and fostering trust among diverse publics before, during, and after crises; as well as in restoring trust once it is lost (e.g., Frandsen & Johansen, 2015; Seeger & Sellnow, 2019; Ulmer et al., 2023). Some of these inherent challenges in building and rebuilding trust among disparate publics were made abundantly clear throughout the COVID-19 pandemic. Research suggests that strategies for (re)establishing trust must be grounded in a clear understanding of the rhetorical situation (e.g., topic, audience, and occasion).

Risk and crisis spokespersons can again draw from the wealth of instructional communication research focused on teacher strategies for building credibility and maintaining trust with diverse learners, which is attained via a comprehensive awareness of the rhetorical situation.

As hooks (1994/2020) explains, this means going beyond a tendency to hear, acknowledge, and nurture only the voices and experiences of "particular individuals," to instead seek opportunities to intentionally "embrace everyone" in discussions and decision-making (p. 198).

For risk and crisis communication, this means inviting those living and working at the margins (as well as the margins of the margins) of society into the conversation (Dutta, 2008). All risk bearers must be invited to share their unique stories and experiences – especially because those stories are likely to shed light on perspectives of a situation that might be overlooked and even disregarded or ignored. Inherent in this pedagogical strategy is to listen with empathy and to acknowledge diverse experiences as valid and valuable to informing the topic and occasion. The literature describes this as student-to-teacher and student-to-student engagement (in addition to or even in place of teacher-to-student engagement) (e.g., Svinicki & McKeachie, 2014). This same learner focus has demonstrated utility in some risk and crisis communication contexts, particularly in terms of narrative storytelling (Seeger & Sellnow, 2016). People in any context – not just students in classrooms – want to be heard, valued, and validated before they are necessarily willing to hear from spokesperson "expert(s)" (Sellnow & Sellnow, 2024). To build and maintain trust, spokespersons must be receiver-oriented and "show that [they] care" by listening with empathy, encouraging storytelling, and cultivating dialogue as a means to co-construct meaning before risk-bearers will be willing to trust what they have to say (Sellnow & Sellnow, 2024, pp. 65–71).

Effective Instructional Communication is Learning Outcome-Driven

When engaged in strategic risk or crisis communication, primary goals are typically to arouse interest, raise awareness, increase understanding, gain compliance, and elicit certain behaviors. The following paragraphs illustrate how each of them can be measured via instructional communication theories and metrics.

Effective instructional communication is learning outcome-driven. In other words, effective teaching is measured by the degree to which students (i.e., learners) achieve affective learning, cognitive learning, and behavioral learning. In the contexts of risk and crisis, effective instructional communication may also be measured by the degree to which people and publics learn. Affective learning is achieved when learners are interested in, aware of, and motivated to pay attention to the risk or crisis topic as relevant to them. Cognitive learning is achieved when they accurately understand the risk issue or crisis event (e.g., what it is, what is causing it, why it is happening, potential causes/effects, what is being done about it) and what they can do about it. Finally, behavioral learning is achieved when risk bearers actually comply with recommended actions in the short term and over time, as well as across contexts and in different situations and locations.

Affective Learning

Two theories that have been particularly useful in achieving affective learning outcomes in traditional classroom settings and seem potentially fruitful for doing so in risk and crisis communication are immediacy and narrative. As previously mentioned, learner-centered pedagogy confirms that students must perceive the teacher as trustworthy and credible before they will be motivated to listen to and learn from them (Witt et al., 2004). Effective teachers build trust and cultivate credibility among learners by employing communication strategies that foster immediacy (e.g., Frymier & Houser, 2000; Gorham, 1988).

Albert Mehrabian (1966) conceptualized immediacy theory, which suggests that employing certain verbal and nonverbal behaviors will reduce the psychological distance between communicators. In other words, "people are drawn toward persons and things they like, evaluate highly, and prefer" and "avoid or move away from things they dislike, evaluate negatively, or do not prefer" (Mehrabian, 1971, p. 1). Instructional communication scholars adapted

Mehrabian's theory to identify teacher behaviors that reduce psychological distance with students and, consequently, increase student perceptions of teacher trustworthiness. When students trust the teacher, they become motivated to engage with and learn from them (Witt et al., 2004). In fact, perceived teacher immediacy tends to be the most powerful predictor of students' willingness to comply with teacher requests (Kearney et al., 1988).

Sellnow and Sellnow (2024) extend immediacy theory further as it informs affective learning in effective risk and crisis communication. Risk and crisis spokespersons, like teachers, must "be perceived as trustworthy by the at-risk people and groups with whom we are communicating" by saying and doing things intentionally and transparently to "foster that perception" (p. 67). Spokespersons can do so by listening with empathy, encouraging storytelling, and co-constructing meaning through dialogue. As Slovic (1996) clarifies, even the most well-intentioned altruistic efforts are likely to fail unless risk bearers trust the spokespersons. Employing communication that fosters immediacy is a means by which to do so.

Cognitive Learning

Just as perceived trust is fundamental to achieving affective learning outcomes, perceived teacher credibility is essential to achieving cognitive learning outcomes. In fact, teacher credibility is one of the most prominent constructs examined in the instructional communication literature (Finn et al., 2009). Teachers in any context are perceived as credible when they appear competent (intelligent, trained, informed), trustworthy (honest, honorable, ethical), and caring (understanding, empathetic, responsive) (McCroskey & Teven, 1999; Sellnow & Sellnow, 2024). Perceived teacher credibility is merely a foundation, however, for achieving cognitive learning outcomes. Two lines of instructional communication research that can inform cognitive learning about risks and crises are teacher clarity and engaged dialogue for meaning co-construction.

Cruickshank and Kennedy (1986) define teacher clarity as "a cluster of teacher behaviors [verbal and nonverbal] that result in learners gaining knowledge or understanding of a topic" (p. 43). A plethora of studies have been published that confirm the significant relationship between teacher clarity and both affective and cognitive learning (e.g., Titsworth et al., 2015). In addition to being accurate, precise, coherent, and organized, clarity is also achieved when teachers (1) acknowledge transparently what they know and do not know and (2) articulate learner relevance through personal examples and stories shared by both teacher and students (Mazer, 2022). Thus, clarity is ascertained when teacher and students engage in dialogue as a "co-operative enterprise, not a dictation" (Dewey, 1938, p. 72). Because managing uncertainty is critical in effective risk and crisis communication, these same constructs can inform necessary goals of "information accuracy, transparency, and intelligibility" (Sellnow & Sellnow, 2024, p. 101).

Behavioral Learning

Behavioral learning focuses on behavior change or reinforcement brought about as a result of a teaching and learning experience. Behavioral learning outcomes are measured via psychomotor skill performance (Dave, 1967; Krathwohl, 2002). Perhaps most critical to effective instructional risk and crisis communication are social learning theory and experiential learning theory.

Social learning theory, also sometimes described as social cognitive theory, focuses on behavioral learning as the goal and cognitive learning as key to achieving it (Bandura, 1986). The theory presumes that learning occurs in a social environment wherein people observe and imitate actions of those they perceive as models. Models are those people that learners observe engaging in certain behaviors and enjoying positive consequences as a result. Learners also benefit by observing anti-models as they endure negative consequences as a result of certain (in)actions. Embedded in this theory is the notion of efficacy. That is, learners also need to believe they can perform the recommended behaviors, and they must believe that doing so will make a meaningful difference for themselves and/or others (Bandura, 1997). To do so, communicators must provide precise directions with sufficient details using multiple modes (e.g., visual, aural, written). They must also appropriately tailor the recommendations to the target population in ways that make doing so both achievable and desirable. Effective instructional risk and crisis communication can employ modeling via, for example, live and in-person demonstrations, infographics and audiovisual training modules, and VR and AI games and simulations (Merrill et al., 2019; Sellnow & Sellnow, 2024).

Experiential learning theory as conceptualized in a variety of related models (e.g., Dewey, 1938; Lave & Wenger, 1991; Sellnow & Sellnow, 2019; Tan, 2021) is also grounded in the assumption that effective learning is situated in real-life contexts. What makes experiential learning theory so relevant to instructional risk and crisis communication is that what is learned in one context can be translated and applied effectively across contexts. The transferable skill is embedded in the process of engaging with the material via the dynamic and ongoing interaction among knowing (actual lived experiences), thinking (cognitive knowledge), doing (active experimentation), and reflecting (perceived relevance). Experiential learning theory can inform instructional communication in contexts of risk and crisis by (1) acknowledging the past and present lived experiences of diverse publics, (2) engaging in dialogue to co-construct accurate knowledge about the risk or crisis, (3) working together to identify and employ achievable actions for risk management and protection of self and others, and (4) identifying future directions for renewal among individuals, local communities, and global society. Research suggests that appealing to diverse learning styles can effectively restore order during the chaos of the acute phase of a crisis event by impacting risk-bearer receptivity to messages (Sellnow et al., 2012).

IDEA Model

One theoretical framework that draws from this extant body of work is the IDEA model for effective instructional risk and crisis communication (e.g., Sellnow & Sellnow, 2019; Sellnow & Sellnow, 2024; Sellnow et al., 2023b). Although the IDEA model has demonstrated utility across a variety of risk and crisis types, as well as among disparate people and groups, it is not intended to be the only such model, particularly as the nature of risks/mega-risks and crises/mega-crises continue to grow in complexity across time and space. However, it could serve as a prototype on which to build new models and theories going forward.

IDEA is essentially an acronym for the key elements to be addressed in effective instructional risk and crisis communication. "I" stands for internalization and encompasses the constructs required to achieve affective learning. "D" stands for distribution and points to the need to communicate via multiple modes and channels, as well as in ways that engage ongoing dialogue with diverse stakeholders. "E" stands for explanation and represents the communication strategies required to achieve cognitive learning. Finally, "A" stands for action and embodies the processes for achieving desired behavioral learning outcomes. The IDEA model is an easy-to-use framework for designing and assessing risk and crisis communication grounded firmly in rigorous and empirically tested theories. To date, eleven primary propositions of this "comprehensive and relationship-centered framework" have been tested via both qualitative and quantitative methods (Sellnow et al., 2023a, pp. 228, 237–238). However, its success will ultimately be measured not just as it is used to inform effective risk and crisis communication but also as it evolves to account for new complexities that spur the development of additional models grounded in instructional communication theory and research.

A growing body of research confirms the utility of instructional communication to inform best practices in risk situations and crisis events. These publications appear in a variety of national and international outlets and focus on topics ranging from natural disasters (e.g., Herovic et al., 2019; Johannson et al., 2021; Napakol et al., 2023; Sellnow et al., 2019; Sellnow et al., 2021) and foodborne illnesses (e.g., Frisby et al., 2014; Littlefield et al., 2014; Sellnow et al., 2015; Sellnow et al., 2017;; Sellnow et al., 2019; Soares et al., 2022) to disease outbreaks (e.g., Sellnow-Richmond et al., 2019; Sheppard et al., 2020) and biosecurity (e.g., Edwards et al., 2020; Edwards et al., 2023; Merrill et al., 2019; Sellnow et al., 2017; Sellnow et al., 2019). They also focus on engaged communication between and among diverse cultural groups within countries (e.g., Cook et al., 2021; Napakol et al., 2023; Sellnow & Salazar, 2021; Sellnow et al., 2023a; Sellnow-Richmond et al., 2023) and across national and international borders (e.g., David et al., 2023; Johansson et al., 2021; Sellnow et al., 2021).

For example, Napakol and colleagues used instructional communication theory to examine failed efforts made by the Ugandan government to relocate farmers and families living on and around the mudslide-prone Mount Elgon. Soares et al. (2022) used instructional communication theory to explore how social media might be employed to communicate self-protective actions for food safety among diverse populations during the COVID-19 pandemic. David et al. (2023) compared COVID-19 media messages and compliance among populations living in the United States and Canada, and others have examined instructional communication targeting children (Cook et al., 2021), as well as other indigenous and underrepresented people and groups (e.g., Littlefield et al., 2014; Napakol et al., 2023; Sellnow et al., 2023a). This array of research suggests that instructional communication theory can extend our understanding of effective risk and crisis communication that occurs across both time and space and is embedded in larger mega-risk and mega-crisis phenomena.

Conclusion

We live in a global risk society where mega-crises wrought with complex, interconnected risks and uncertainties transcending both time and space are quickly becoming the norm for risk and crisis communication. Accurately ascertaining and communicating effectively about the nature of these far-reaching and rapidly spreading issues and events has been exacerbated by globalization, digitization, and informatization. Consequently, many of the existing theories and models are inadequate for predicting and explaining the complexities of risks and crises today. Thus, this chapter explored the utility of several instructional communication theories and constructs not as replacements to but, rather, as a means for expanding existing theories and models of risk and crisis communication to account for ever-evolving challenges of risk and crisis in a global risk society. In adopting a learner-centered and learning outcome-driven approach, we may more effectively address some of our most perplexing challenges rooted in (dis)trust, credibility, (mis)interpretation, and compliance and – in so doing – increase our impact in achieving our utmost goals of reducing harms and saving lives.

References

Afifi, T. D., Denes, A., & Salehuddin, A. (2022). Contemporary approaches to studying biological and physiological markers in a changing instructional context. In M. L. Houser, & A. M. Hosek, Eds., *Handbook of Instructional Communication: Principles and Practices of Teaching Rhetorical and Relational Perspectives* (3rd ed., pp. 385–406). Kendall Hunt.

Anderson, C. J., & Hobolt, S. B. (2022). Creating compliance in crisis: Messages, messengers, and masking up in Britain. *West European Politics*, *46*(2), 300–323. https://doi.org/10.1080/01402382.2022.2091863

Avery, E. J., Lariscy, R. W., Kim, S., & Hocke, T. (2010). A quantitative review of crisis communication research in public relations from 1991 to 2009. *Public Relations Review*, *36*(2), 190–192. https://doi.org/10.1016/j.pubrrev.2010.01.001

Bandura, A. (1986). *Social Foundations of Thought and Action: A Social Cognitive Theory.* Prentice-Hall.

Bandura, A. (1997). *Self-efficacy: The Exercise of Control.* W. H. Freeman.

Beck, U. (1986). *Risk Society: Towards a New Modernity.* Sage.

Bekalu, M. A., Dhawan, D., McCloud, R., Pinnamaneni, R., & Viswanath, K. (2021). Adherence to COVID 19 mitigation measures among American adults: The need for consistent and unified messaging. *Health Education Research*, *36*(2), 178–191. https://doi.org/10.1093/her/cyab002

Brookfield, S. D., Rudolph, J., & Tan, S. (2024). *Teaching Well: Understanding Key Dynamics of Learning-centered Classrooms.* Routledge.

Centers for Disease Control and Prevention (n.d.). *COVID data tracker.* https://covid.cdc.gov/covid-data-tracker/#variant-summary (accessed August 1, 2024).

Cologna, V., & Siegrist, M. (2020). The role of trust for climate change mitigation and adaptation behaviour: A meta-analysis. *Journal of Environmental Psychology*, *69*, 101428.

Cook, J., Sellnow, T. L., Sellnow, D. D., Parrish, A., & Soares, R. (2021). Communicating science in COVID-19: *Meet the helpers.* In H. D. O'Hair, & M. J. O'Hair, Eds., *Communicating Science in Times of Crisis* (pp. 172–188). Wiley-Blackwell.

Cruickshenk, D. R., & Kennedy, J. J. (1986). Teacher clarity. *Teaching and Teacher Education*, *2*, 43–67. https://doi.org/10.1016/0742-051X(86)90004-1

Dave, R. (1967). *Psychomotor Domain.* Berlin: International Conference of Educational Testing.

David, M., Lane, D., Champagne-Poirer, O., Sellnow, D. D., Carignan, M., Sellnow, T. L., & Boutemen, L. (2023. Predicting compliance during the coronavirus global pandemic: The IDEA model for effective instructional health risk communication in Canada and the USA. *National Communication Association Conference*, 16–19 November, 2023, National Harbor, MD.

Dewey, J. (1938). *Experience and Education.* Simon & Schuster.

Dutta, M. J. (2008). *Communicating Health: A Culture-centered Approach.* Polity.

Dutta, M. J. (2018). Culture-centered approach in addressing health disparities: Communication infrastructures for subaltern voices. *Communication Methods and Measures*, *12*(4), 239–259. https:/doi.org/10.1080/19312458.2018.1453057

Edwards, A. L., Sellnow, T. L., Sellnow, D. D., Iverson, J., Parrish, A., & Dritz, S. (2020). Communities of practice as purveyors of instructional communication during crises. *Communication Education*, *70*(1), 49–70. https://doi.org/10.1080/03634523.2020.1802053

Edwards, A. L., Freihaut, R., Sellnow, T. L., Sellnow, D. D., Getchell, M. C., & Parrish, A. (2023). Engaged learning: Lessons learned by subject-matter experts from COVID-19 in the U.S. swine industry. *Journal of Applied Communication Research*, advanced online publication. https://doi.org/10.1080/00909882.2023.2178853

Finn, A. N., Schrodt, P., Witt, P. L., Elledge, N., Jernberg, K. A., & Larson, L. M. (2009). A meta-analytical review of teacher credibility and its associations with teacher behaviors and student outcomes. *Communication Education*, *58*(4), 516–537. https://doi.org/10.1080/03634520903131154

Frandsen, F., & Johansen, W. (2015). Organizations, stakeholders, and intermediaries: Towards a general theory. *International Journal of Strategic Communication*, *9*(4), 253–271.

Freire, P. (1968/1972). *Pedagogy of the Oppressed.* Herder and Herder.

Frisby, B. N., Veil, S. R., & Sellnow, T. L. (2014). Instructional messages during health-related crises: Essential content for self-protection. *Health Communication*, *4*, 347–354. https://doi.org/10.1080/10410236.2012.755604

Frymier, A. B., & Houser, M. L. (2000). The teacher-student relationship as an interpersonal relationship. *Communication Education*, *11*(1), 207–219. https://doi.org/10.1080/03634520009379209

Gayle, B. M., Preiss, R. W., Burrell, N., & Allen, M. (Eds.). (2006). *Classroom Communication and Instructional Processes: Advances Through Meta-analysis.* Lawrence Erlbaum.

Giddens, A. (1990). *Consequences of Modernity.* Polity Press.

Gorham, J. (1988). The relationship between verbal teacher immediacy behaviors and student learning. *Communication Education*, *37*(1), 40–53. https://doi.org/10.1080/03634528809378702

Harvey, N. (2020). Behavioral fatigue: Real phenomenon, naïve construct, or policy contrivance? *Frontiers in Psychology*, *2960*. https://doi.org/10.3389/fpsyg.2020.589892

Helsloot, I., Boin, A., Jacobs, B., & Comfort, L. K. (2012). *Mega-crises: Understanding the Prospects, Nature, Characteristics, and the Effects of Cataclysmic Events.* Charles C. Thomas.

Herovic, E., Sellnow, T. L., & Sellnow, D. D. (2019). Challenges and opportunities for pre-crisis emergency risk communication: Lessons learned from the earthquake community. *Journal of Risk Research*, 1–16. https://doi.org/10.1080/13669877.2019.1569097

Hosek, A. M., Hannah, M., & n., & Densmore, C. (2022). Cognitive approaches in the instructional context. In M. L. Houser, & A. M. Hosek, Eds., *Handbook of Instructional Communication: Principles and Practices of Teaching Rhetorical and Relational Perspectives* (3rd ed., pp. 337–360). Kendall Hunt.

Jennings, W., Stoker, G., Valgarðsson, V., Devine, D., & Gaskell, J. (2021). How trust, mistrust and distrust shape the governance of the COVID-19 crisis. *Journal of European Public Policy, 28*(8), 1174–1196. https://doi.org/10.1080/13501763.2021.1942151

Johansson, B., Lane, D. R., Sellnow, D. D., & Sellnow, T. L. (2021). No heat, no electricity, no water, oh no!: An IDEA model experiment in instructional risk communication. *Journal of Risk Research.* https://doi.org/10.1080/13669877.2021.1894468

Kearney, P., Plax, T. G., Smith, V. R., & Sorensen, G. (1988). Effects of teacher immediacy and strategy type on college student resistance to on-task demands. *Communication Education, 37*(1), 54–67. https://doi.org/10.1080/03634528809378703

Kolb, D. (1984). *Experiential Learning: Experience as the Source of Learning and Development.* Prentice-Hall.

Krathwohl, D. R. (2002). A revision of Bloom's taxonomy: An overview. *Theory Into Practice, 41*(4), 212–218. https://doi.org/10.1207/s15430421tip4104_2

Lane, D. R., Frey, K., & Tatum, N. T. (2022). Affective approaches in the instructional context. In M. L. Houser, & A. M. Hosek, Eds., *Handbook of Instructional Communication: Principles and Practices of Teaching Rhetorical and Relational Perspectives* (3rd ed., pp. 361–384). Kendall Hunt.

Lave, J., & Wenger, E. (1991). *Situated Learning: Legitimate Peripheral Participation.* Cambridge University Press.

Lenharo, M. (May 23, 2023,). WHO declares end to COVID-19's emergency phase. *Nature.* Retrieved from: https://www.nature.com/articles/d41586-023-01559-z (accessed August 10, 2024).

Littlefield, R. S., Beauchamp, K., Lane, D., & Sellnow, D. D. (2014). Instructional crisis communication: Connecting ethnicity and sex in the assessment of receiver-oriented message effectiveness. *Journal of Management and Strategy, 5*(3). http://dx.doi.org/10.5430/jms.v5n3p16

Liu, B. F., Jin, Y., Austin, L., Kuligowski, E., & Young, C. E. (2020). The social-mediated crisis communication (SMCC) model: Identifying the next frontier. In Y. Jin, B. H. Reber, & G. J. Nowak, Eds., *Advancing Crisis Communication Effectiveness* (pp. 214–230). Routledge.

Malecki, K. M., Keating, J. A., & Safdar, N. (2021). Crisis communication and public perception of COVID-19 risk in the era of social media. *Clinical Infectious Diseases, 72*(4), 697–702. https://doi.org/10.1093/cid/ciaa758

Mazer, J. P. (2022). Instructor message variables. In M. L. Houser, & A. M. Hosek, Eds., *Handbook of Instructional Communication: Principles and Practices of Teaching Rhetorical and Relational Perspectives* (3rd ed., pp. 29–54). Kendall Hunt.

McCroskey, J. C., & Teven, J. J. (1999). Goodwill: A reexamination of the construct and its measurement. *Communication Monographs, 66*(1), 90–103. https://doi.org/03637759909376464

Mehrabian, A. (1966). Immediacy: An indicator of attitudes in linguistic communication. *Journal of Personality, 34*(1), 26–34. https://doi.org/10.1111/j.1467-6494.1966.tb01696.x

Mehrabian, A. (1971). *Silent Messages.* Wadsworth.

Merrill, S. C., Moegenburg, S., Koliba, C. J., Zia, A., Trinity, L., Clark, E., Bucini, G., Wiltshire, S., Sellnow, T., Sellnow, D., & Smith, J. M. (2019). Willingness to comply with biosecurity in livestock facilities: Evidence from experimental simulations. *Frontiers in Veterinary Science, 6*, 156. https://doi.org/10.3389/fvets.2019.00156

Mottet, T. P., & Beebe, S. A. (2006). Foundations of instructional communication. In T. P. Mottet, V. P. Richmond, & J. C. McCroskey, Eds., *Handbook of Instructional Communication: Rhetorical and Relational Perspectives* (pp. 3–32). Pearson.

Napakol, A., Miller, A. N., Sellnow, T. L., Sellnow, D. D., Mugunga, A., & Khaukha, J. (2023). Risk and crisis communication: Considering catastrophic mudslides in Uganda's bududa district. In H. D. O'Hair, & M. J. O'Hair, Eds., *Communication and Catastrophic Events: Strategic Risk and Crisis Management* (pp. 191–205). Wiley. https://doi.org/10.1093/cid/ciaa758

Niu, C., Jiang, Z., Liu, H., Yang, K., Song, X., & Li, Z. (2022). The influence of media consumption on public risk perception: A meta-analysis. *Journal of Risk Research, 25*(1), 21–47. https://doi.org/10.1080/13669877.2020.1819385

Offerdal, T. S., Just, S. N., & Ihlen, O. (2021). Public ethos in the pandemic rhetorical situation strategies for building trust in authorities' risk communication. *Journal of International Crisis and Risk Communication Research, 4*(2), 247–270. https://doi.org/10.30658/jicrcr.4.2.3

Petherick, A., Goldszmidt, R., Andrade, E. B., Furst, R., Hale, T., Pott, A., & Wood, A. (2021). A worldwide assessment of changes in adherence to COVID-19 protective behaviours and hypothesized pandemic fatigue. *Nature Human Behavior, 5*, 1145–1160. https://doi.org/10.1038/s41562-021-01181-x

Quarantelli, E. L. (1998). *What is a Disaster?: Perspectives on the Question*. Routledge.

Rogers, C. R. (1983). *Freedom to Learn for the 80's*. Charles E. Merrill Publishing Company.

Rothkopf, D. J. (, May 11, 2003). "When the buzz bites back." *The Washington Post*. https://www.washingtonpost.com/archive/opinions/2003/05/11/when-the-buzz-bites-back/bc8cd84f-cab6-4648-bf58-0277261af6cd/ (accessed August 11, 2024).

Salazar, E. S. (2021). The IDEA Model as an effective instructional crisis and risk communication framework to analyze the CDC's messages aimed at Hispanics in the COVID-19 era. *Proceedings of the International Crisis and Risk Communication Conference*, Vol. 4 (pp. 45–48). Orlando Fl: Nicholson School of Communication and Media. https://doi.org/10.30658/icrcc.2021.11

Schwarz, A., Seeger, M. W., & Auer, C. (2016). *The Handbook of International Crisis Communication Research*. Wiley.

Seeger, M. W., & Sellnow, T. L. (2016). *Narratives of Crisis: Telling Stories of Ruin and Renewal*. Stanford University Press.

Seeger, M. W., & Sellnow, T. L. (2019). *Communication in Times of Trouble*. Wiley.

Sellnow, T. L., & Seeger, M. W. (2021). *Theorizing Crisis Communication*. John Wiley & Sons.

Sellnow, D. D., & Sellnow, T. L. (2019). The IDEA model for effective instructional risk and crisis communication by emergency managers and other key spokespersons. *Journal of Emergency Management* (Weston, Mass.), *17*(1), 67–78. https://doi.org/10.5055/jem.2019.0399

Sellnow, T. L., & Sellnow, D. D. (2024). *Before Crisis: The Practice of Effective Risk Communication*. Cognella.

Sellnow, T. L., Sellnow, D. D., Lane, D. R., & Littlefield, R. S. (2012). The value of instructional communication in crisis situations: Restoring order to chaos. *Risk Analysis: An International Journal, 32*(4), 633–643. https://doi.org/10.1111/j.1539-6924.2011.01634.x

Sellnow, D. D., Lane, D., Littlefield, R. S., Sellnow, T. L., Wilson, B., Beauchamp, K., & Venette, S. (2015). A receiver-based approach to effective instructional crisis communication. *Journal of Contingencies & Crisis Management, 23*(3), 149–158. https://doi.org/10.1111/1468-5973.12066

Sellnow, D. D., Lane, D. R., Sellnow, T. L., & Littlefield, R. (2017). The IDEA model as a best practice for effective instructional risk and crisis communication. *Communication Studies, 68*, 552–567. https://doi.org/10.1080/10510974.2017.1375535

Sellnow, D. D., Jones, L. M., Sellnow, T. L., Spence, P., Lane, D. R., & Haarstad, N. (2019). The IDEA model as a conceptual framework for designing earthquake early warning (EEW) messages distributed via mobile apps. In J. Santos-Reyes, Ed., *Earthquakes: Impact, Community Vulnerability and Resilience* (pp. 11–20). InTechOpen.

Sellnow, T. L., Sellnow, D. D., & Reis, C. D. (2021). Calming giants in the earth: The internalization, distribution, explanation, and action (IDEA) model as strategic communication in with competing narratives. In Y. Jin, B. H. Reber, & G. J., Eds., *Advancing Crisis Communication Effectiveness: Integrating Public Relations Scholarship with Practice* (pp. 198–213). Routledge.

Sellnow, D. D., Carballo, S. E. S., & Sellnow, T. L. (2023a). Applied communication and pandemics: Expanding the IDEA model of instructional risk and crisis communication. In S. M. Croucher, & A. Diers-Lawson, Eds., *Pandemic Communication* (pp. 141–155). Routledge.

Sellnow, T. L., Sellnow, D. D., Johansson, B., Lane, D. R., & Seeger, M. W. (2023b). The IDEA model theoretical framework: An explication of risk communication as engaged public relations. In C. H. Botan, & E. J. Sommerfeldt, Eds., *Public Relations Theory III* (pp. 228–246). Routledge.

Sellnow-Richmond, D., Strawser, M. G., & Sellnow, D. D. (2019). Student perceptions teaching effectiveness and learning achievement: A comparative examination of online and hybrid delivery format. *Communication Teacher, 1-16*. https://doi.org/10.1080/17404622.2019.1673456

Sellnow-Richmond, D. D., George, A., Lukacovic, M. N., Salazar, S., & Sellnow, D. D. (2023). A comparative analysis of state government communication and resident compliance to CDC COVID-19 guidelines. *Journal of Applied Communication Research, 53*(4), 380–403. https://doi.org/10.1080/00909882.2023.2165885

Sheppard, R. J., Sellnow, T. L., Sellnow, D. D., Parrish, A. J., & Brand, J. D. (2020). Instructional crisis communication for an industry: Model and anti-model biosecurity standards for the prevention and control of Highly Pathogenic Avian Influenza. *Journal of Applied Communications, 104*(3). https://doi.org/10.4148/1051-0834.2330

Slovic, P. (1996). Risk perception and trust. In V. Molak, Ed., *Fundamentals of Risk Analysis and Risk Management* (pp. 233–245). CRC Press.

Soares, R., Dumitrescu, S., Sims, T., Sellnow, T. L., Sellnow, D. D., & Seeger, M. W. (2022). Opportunities for instructional crisis communication through social media: Communicating self-protective actions for food safety during the COVID-19 pandemic. In Y. Jin, & L. Austin, Eds., *Social Media and Crisis Communication* (2nd ed., pp. 273–284). Routledge.

Steen, T., & Brandsen, T. (2020). Coproduction during and after the COVID-19 pandemic: Will it last? *Public Administration Review, 80*(5), 851–855.

Suiter, J., & Fletcher, R. (2020). Polarization and partisanship: Key drivers of distrust in media old and new? *European Journal of Communication, 35*(5), 484–501.

Svinicki, M. D., & McKeachie, W. J. (2014). *McKeachie's Teaching Tips: Strategies, Research, and Theory for College and University Teachers* (14th ed.). Wadsworth Cengage.

Tan, O. S. (2021). *Problem-based Learning Innovation: Using Problems to Power Learning in the 21st Century*. Gale Cengage Learning.

Titsworth, S., Mazer, J. P., Goodboy, A. K., Bolkan, S., & Myers, S. (2015). Two meta-analyses exploring the relationship between teacher clarity and student learning. *Communication Education, 64*(4), 385–418. https://doi.org/10.1080/03634523.2015.1041998

Ulmer, R. R., Sellnow, T. L., & Seeger, M. W. (2023). *Effective Crisis Communication: Moving from Crisis to Opportunity*. Sage.

Wang, X., Shi, J., & Kong, H. (2021). Online health information seeking: A review and meta-analysis. *Health Communication, 36*(10), 1163–1175. https://doi.org/10.1080/10410236.2020.1748829

Witt, P. L., Wheeless, L. R., & Allen, M. (2004). A meta-analytical review of the relationship between teacher immediacy and student learning. *Communication Monographs, 71*(2), 184–207. https://doi.org/10.1080/036452042000228054

World Health Organization (2009). *Pandemic Influenza Preparedness and Response: A WHO Guidance Document*. World Health Organization.

World Health Organization (n.d.). *Infodemic*. World Health Organization. https:www.who.int/health-topics/infodemic#tab=tab_1

Author Bio

Deanna D. Sellnow is professor and Chair of the Department of Communication at Clemson University, Clemson, SC, USA. Her primary area of research focuses on strategic instructional risk and crisis communication in a variety of contexts (e.g., natural disasters, health epidemics/pandemics, biosecurity, terrorism, and agricultural biotechnology). She has conducted funded research for such agencies as the United States Geological Survey (USGS), the United States Department of Agriculture (USDA), the Department of Homeland Security (DHS), the National Oceanic and Atmospheric Administration (NOAA), and the U.S. CDC. She has presented her research in many countries around the world, including Canada, China, Czech Republic, Denmark, Egypt, England, Germany, Hong Kong, India, Indonesia, Ireland, Italy, Japan, Senegal, Singapore, Spain, Sweden, Turkey, United States, and Vietnam. She served as President of the Central States Communication Association where she was inducted into the Hall of Fame in 2018. She has authored or co-authored numerous books, book chapters, and refereed national and international journal articles. Her most recent book, co-authored with Timothy Sellnow, is *Before Crisis: The Practice of Effective Risk Communication.*

44

Risk-based Approaches to Crisis Management and Communication

Frederic Bouder

Faculty of Science and Technology, Department of Safety, Economic and Planning, University of Stavanger, Stavange, Norway

Introduction

Back in the 1990s, sociologists drew attention to deep societal transformations that were happening within Western societies. Late modernity was moving toward a reality where new risks strain the secure basis of emotional security – the human need for "ontological security" – and therefore the personality and identity of people (Giddens, 1990). The rise of the *risk society* characterized by "a systematic way of dealing with hazards and insecurities induced and introduced by modernization itself" (Beck, 1992, p. 21). We should not underestimate the triggering role that *crises* played in this development. In the last part of the twentieth century, the West was plagued with a series of acute failures that shook and transformed the social order: first in the United States with high profile events such as the Love Canal and Three Mile Island controversies and later in Europe with the Thalidomide disaster, the Bovine spongiform encephalopathy (BSE) scandal the Chernobyl meltdown, the HIV Tainted Blood contamination of hemophiliacs, to mention only a few. It should also be noted that other parts of the world also experienced similar events, sometime worse in terms of the number of fatalities. One such event with both local and global repercussions was the Bhopal disaster in 1984. Bhopal had long-lasting repercussions including in the northern hemisphere, which is the focus of this chapter.

Where are we, 30 years after the groundbreaking work of Giddens and Beck? On the one hand, the way of dealing with hazard and insecurities has become ever more systematic. For instance, many organizations both in the public and private sectors now mandate exhaustive risk assessments, and many agencies are moving toward "risk-based regulation" (Rothstein et al., 2006). Enormous progress has also been achieved in the area of risk communication (Balog-Way et al., 2020). The notion that risk should be sensibly handled and governed has stimulated the formulation of holistic frameworks (IRGC, 2005; Renn, 2008). It may even be argued that "risk science" is becoming a distinctive scientific field with its own "fundamental concepts, principles, approaches, methods and models for how to understand, assess, communicate, manage and govern risks" (Aven & Thekdi, 2021). Yet, the twentieth century does not seem to have progressed toward uneventful normality. Risk events are often – maybe more than ever – conceptualized as crises. From high profile product recalls to

The Handbook of International Crisis and Risk Communication Research, Second Edition.
Edited by Andreas Schwarz, Matthew W. Seeger, and Sora Kim.

environmental disasters, the number of risk events leading to a sense of crisis seems to be on the increase. Thus, crises seem to have become an ordinary feature of modern life. Moreover, even events that lack a sense of paroxysmic acuity may be publicly labeled as crisis. We hear about the ongoing "climate crisis," the "COVID crisis," and even the "disinformation crisis."

Arguably, one of the objectives of sound risk management is precisely to prevent escalation into full-blown crisis. What has happened then? Have we failed to connect the dots? Should we better equip crisis managers with risk management skills? This chapter explores the features of an approach to crisis management and communication that is grounded in several decades of risk studies. After revisiting the definitions of crisis and risk, the chapter offers a plea for a better integration of the two concepts. Then, it provides concrete suggestions such as the formulation of "dos" and "don'ts" as well as principles of "survival."

Definitions: Crisis and Risk

The word crisis comes from medical Latin, derived from the Greek κρίσις /krisis. It means "decision" or "judgment," from krinein, "to decide." The term has been used at least since the seventeenth century to describe "the turning point for better or worse in an acute disease or fever." Nowadays, a crisis often addresses "a difficult or dangerous situation that needs serious attention" (Merriam-Webster dictionary, 2023 edition).

If one examines the origin of the word "risk" in an etymological dictionary, we are led via the French "risque" and the Italian "risco" and in some dictionaries ultimately to an original Greek derivation, which came to English through the Latin [resignum], with the meaning of sailing "dangerously close to the rocks" connected with a term which means cliff or rock (Wolff, 2000). Risk first became widely used as a way of describing a danger of pecuniary loss in merchant trade and insurance (Covello et al., 1988). According to Bernstein's closer account of the concept, the development of the notion risk is the result of a "Promethean" emancipation from a fatalistic worldview. At an early stage, risk may have been seen largely as unavoidable danger that results from uncontrollable events. Yet, the Italian verb "risicare" – which means to dare and from which "risco" (risk) derives – suggests an already more complex linguistic pattern, whereby risk is a choice rather than a fate (Bernstein, 1998, p. 8). In 2018, the Society for Risk Analysis (SRA) gave mandate to an expert group to develop a risk analysis glossary. Among other things, the authors of this document stock of the scientific and normative (ISO) definitions of risk. They concluded that, for a given activity, risk may be defined as "a relation to the consequences (effects, implications) of this activity with respect to something that humans value. The consequences are often seen in relation to some reference values (planned values, objectives, etc.), and the focus is often on negative, undesirable consequences. There is always at least one outcome that is considered as negative or undesirable" (Aven et al., 2018, p. 4).

Why does Risk Science Matter?

These etymological considerations shed an interesting light on the relationship between the two concepts of crisis and risk. Both are grounded in decision and judgment, one (risk) emphasizing the need and opportunity of decision-making, while the other (crisis) pointing to the urgency and irreversibility of the choices to be made. Poor risk choices are a missed opportunity that increase the chance of "unfortunate events" (Slovic, 1987b) likely to trigger indirect costs for exceeding the initial event. The likelihood of crises is also heightened in the context of complex systemic risks (Renn & Klinke, 2004). Finally, the urgency of a looming crisis adds pressure to act swiftly, which may lead to methodological errors, such as the following:

- Crucial evidence to support the decisions may be assembled too quickly;
- Important knowledge may be overlooked;
- Studies developed to inform the response may be rushed;
- Scientific advice may draw on narrow and limited disciplinary inputs;
- Extreme scenarios are likely to be given more weight than they should (Aven & Bouder, 2020).

These problems underline the need to develop crisis responses that are grounded in science and go beyond empirically validated "best practices."

Another critical aspect relates to the relationship between trust and crisis communication. In Europe, the major crises that took place in the 1990s played a significant role in shaping negative attitudes toward the governance system and regulators (Löfstedt, 2005). In particular, the BSE scandal in the United Kingdom (Powell & Leiss, 1997; Ratzan, 1999) and beyond (Sinaceur et al., 2005), the dioxin-in-chicken scandal in Belgium (Lok & Powell, 2000), and the tainted-blood scandal in France (Bouder, 2006) resulted in acute political crisis, in addition to the substantial economic losses. As a result, public trust in policymakers, industry officials, and opinion-shapers declined significantly – a trend highlighted by opinion polls, surveys, and research (House of Lords, 2000; Löfstedt, 2005; Newton & Norris, 2000; Pharr & Putnam, 2000). The consequences of these inadequacies often triggered some level of insecurity within management especially so when not anticipated yet socially amplified (Kasperson et al., 1988; Pidgeon et al., 2003). One senior regulator involved in the management of the vaccine Measles, Mums, and Rubella (MMR) crisis (Horton, 2004) once confessed:

> "The MMR crisis was a surprise; it was unpredictable. We had no idea that the public could be so sensitive about such a trivial issue. What should have been the right move? I do not know" (Bouder, 2008, p. 208).

The combination of poor management and declining public trust typically has the effect of framing the response to future events in a restrictive way (Löfstedt, 2011). Regulators become extremely sensitive to public expressions of distrust, especially when key opinion leaders are suggesting that the regulator is failing the public (Löfstedt et al., 2011). As a result, they tend to become less science-based and more precautionary (Löfstedt, 2005; Löfstedt, 2011). In the food area, for instance, the BSE crisis exposed the incompetence of the consensual regulation practices of the time. The precautionary principle has been the main response of the regulator to regain trust (Löfstedt, 2005).

To sum up, crises involving risks to health and the environment, when poorly "risk-managed" tend to result in (1) a failure that creates a sense of betrayal (2) which leads to a collapse of the trust vested in the regulator (3) that is conducive to tougher regulations. The general outcome of research undertaken in other areas can be summarized as follows (Bouder, 2008):

- Safety-related scares, especially those having to do with sensitive human health issues, have a decisive impact on regulatory practices;
- Scares are amplified when low levels of trust in the regulatory process or its proponents (scientific experts, government, and industry) existed prior to the outbreak. When not properly addressed, scares tend to generate further public distrust in regulatory processes and their key proponents.

This destructive path may lead to a vicious circle of risk aversion (Bouder, 2008, p. 46). Figure 44.1 offers a visual representation of this phenomenon.

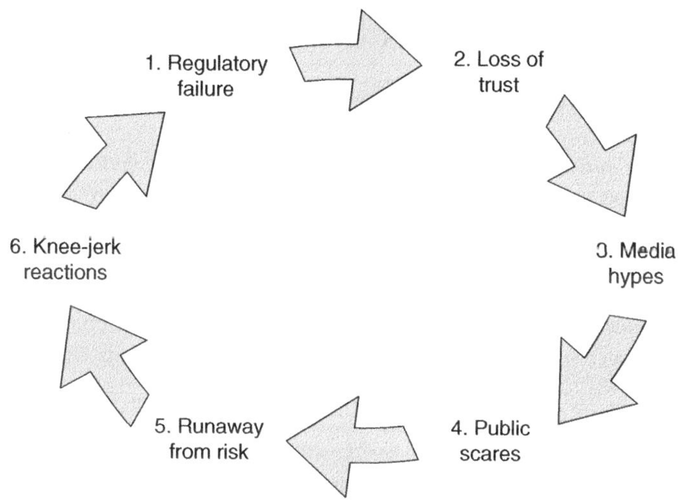

Figure 44.1 Post-trust vicious cycle of risk aversion.

A better understanding of trust factors, coupled with a mapping of actual levels of trust vested in key stakeholders, will be essential to develop more effective crisis communication. Before defining their communication strategy, regulators could have benefited from acknowledging the collapse of trust as well as changing public attitudes to policymaking.

In addition to the procedural principles of public risk communication, key lessons have been developed at the crossroads of routine and urgent situations, namely:

a. A two-way proactive communication style is likely to be more effective than a top-down one-way messaging style (Eriksson, 2018; Fischhoff, 1995; Fischhoff, 2005; Fischhoff, 2009; Johansson & Bäck, 2017; Leiss 1996; McComas, 2006) unless reliable studies have established that trust in the policymakers and the process is high (Löfstedt, 2005).
b. Communication needs to be conducted honestly, candidly, and receptively. Crisis communicators need to represent the truth accurately, which also implies a duty to inform the public about uncertainty and knowledge gaps (Fischhoff & Scheufele, 2019; Seeger, 2006).
c. Leadership matters enormously for positive outcomes (Nyenswah et al., 2016; Wardman, 2020). This involves not only a commitment to playing a leading role but also to integrate knowledge between communities (Hyvärinenand & Vos, 2015; Reynolds & Seeger, 2005). Tightening control and shutting down dialogue including on social media (Austin & Jim, 2017) are the opposite of leadership.

As already discussed, a crucial variable that cuts through most crises is the challenge that it poses to trust. This was identified early in the history of risk communication as a field of research (Siegrist, 2021; Slovic, 1993). Following in the steps of earlier efforts, especially the illuminating book on Risk Management in Post-Trust Society by Löfstedt (2005), the author of this chapter co-developed studies to test trust dynamics in concrete situations and offer concrete advice (European Medicines Agency [EMA], 2010; Health and Safety Executive [HSE], 2010). A summary of "dos" and "don'ts" is presented in Box 44.1.

A Survivor's Guide for Crisis Management and Communication

Since the mid-1990s, repeated efforts have been made to offer and receive guidance on how crises could be best managed and communicated. Examples of international documents and standards that offer direct advice to decision-makers and crisis managers include, among

Box 44.1 Dos and don'ts of Risk Communication in Crises

1. **Maintain frequent communication with key stakeholders (government, industry, journalists, etc.)**
   It is not because you don't like what they stand for that you should ignore them. In the context of a crisis, this also implies to engage with those who are skeptics and hesitant about specific measures designed to manage or contain the risk.
2. **Avoid unnecessary confrontation**
   It is not because you don't agree with them that you should get into a fight. In a crisis, it is particularly important to maintain a positive and constructive debate. For instance, it is essential to show empathy when discussing the pros and cons of specific measures/ actions.
3. **Rely on neutral third parties**
   You may think you are best placed to speak, yet it is not necessarily the case. Someone with no vested interest or stake is likely to be more trusted than you. In a crisis, when trust in government is challenged, scientists with high credentials and who do not have major conflicts of interest can play a key role for building trust in the science. This may prove critical to generate consensus on practical science-informed measures.
4. **Avoid the lawyers as long as possible**
   Think twice before you bring your lawyers in, as their role is to protect your legal interest, which often involves advice to shut communication channels. In a crisis, many conflicts are likely to arise. Legal actions (e.g., between NGOs and a risk producer, or between a company and a government agency) can be very destructive and should not be considered lightly.
5. **Local decision-makers matter**
   Bypassing local decision-makers may seem like a shortcut, but remember that they are likely to be trusted and not involving them can be counter-productive as you need them on your side. Most crises "start somewhere" and have local ramifications and impacts. Subsidiarity is particularly important in contexts where local authorities play a critical role in the problem identification and resolution.
6. **NGOs are increasingly shaping outcomes**
   Don't ignore pressure groups like NGOs as they may not ignore you. Civil society organizations and especially at-risk groups should be part of the discussion as they play a role in the response as they are often influential in shaping opinions. This does not mean that their views or positions should be uncritically translated into crisis management measures, but that a discussion with clear procedural steps needs to take place.
7. **Always take responsibility**
   It may be tempting to blame others for one's mistake or not do your bit. The problem is you cannot fool people. It will backfire eventually. In a crisis context, it has become apparent that strong leadership and not evading one's responsibilities is a key factor of success.

Source: Adapted from HSE (2010) and Bouder and Löfstedt for EPO (2016).

several others, the United Nations Crisis Communication Toolkit, the OECD Strategic Crisis Management report, the CDC Crisis Emergency Risk Communication Checklists, or the ISO 22361 standard for crisis management. Many similar documents also exist at national and subnational levels as well as in private and nonprofit organizations. These documents have often been developed by the end users themselves with the help of consultants, yet with limited input from science. The cheer number and the repetitive nature of the exercise suggest that practitioners are still struggling. While crisis management experts have contributed to inject more science into the discussion (Heath, 2006; Seeger, 2006; Veil et al., 2008), risk scientists have also observed that the same practitioners are making too little use of the scientific approach to risk communication (Árvai & Rivers, 2013; Kasperson, 2014; Wardman, 2008; Wardman, 2014; Wardman, 2020). One of the reasons is the persistence of the so-called deficit model (Gregory & Lock, 2008; Renn, 2014) whereby "experts" develop top-down communication toward lay "publics" with the expectation that this would change lay behavior (Balog-Way et al., 2020). Expert-led communication often fails to properly address:

- Lay perceptions (Fischhoff et al., 1978; Slovic, 1987a), biases (Kahneman & Tversky, 1979), and feelings (Slovic et al., 2004), with experts often relying on their preconceptions of what the general public may think and how it will behave
- Trust factors (Löfstedt, 2005; Renn & Levine, 1991; Slovic, 1993), with experts often overestimating the trust vested in them
- Barriers to expected behavioral change (Evensen et al., 2023; Way et al., 2017), with experts often overestimating their ability to ensure compliance

In 2009, the author worked with the UK Risk and Regulation Advisory Council, the UK Government Office for Science, and the UK Department for Business, Innovation and Skills (BIS) to develop guidance that would translate the latest consensus in risk science into practical advice to support the needs of policy makers (Bouder, 2009). The goal was to move away from the deficit model and start from risk science. Principles should be defined on the basis of scientifically tested evidence instead of empirically observed "best practices." While the intent was not aiming at crises, it became quite clear that the managers' "needs" were primarily crisis-focused. A crucial question was how policymakers could be helped to anticipate public risks, how they may best survive risk events and ensure damage control, and finally how they could best learn their lessons after the event. These preoccupations mirror the traditional conceptual distinction between pre-crisis (prodromal phase), crisis (acute phase), response (chronic phase), and post-crisis (resolution or recovery phase).

The document contains five procedural principles – the so-called five As of public risk communication – drawing on decades of research on risk communication combined with direct input from leading researchers and senior practitioners from the United Kingdom, the United States, and Europe. Each principle was supplemented with key questions to guide implementation. The document, despite being almost 15 years old, is still in demand. For instance, the five principles have been adapted to specific field requirements, including vaccine risk communication and COVID-19 (Bouder, 2015; Bouder, 2022). This section will consider how the principles (presented in Box 44.2) may be helpful to crisis managers.

Assembling the Evidence

This first principle draws attention to the importance of the scientific basis of the decisions, in terms of both generating science and risk assessment and ensuring that the latest knowledge is communicated to the decision-makers. Translated into the context of crisis management, this implies to pay special attention to the robustness and broadness of the scientific input. First, we need to define *what is the risk*? For instance, is the crisis about a defined risk to health or the environment, and what is this risk? Are there other factors to consider? If one looks back at the Horse Meat Scandal that shocked the United Kingdom in 2013, the issue was less about an actual risk to health than misleading information/outright lies regarding the content of certain foods (e.g., horse meat in "beef" lasagna). A proper characterization of the risk or problem at the root of the crisis is therefore essential not only in terms of controlling possible adverse events but also in terms of public perception and communication. The second question is *have we used the best available information*? Too often, decisions are made without the

Box 44.2 Principles of Public Risk Communication

1. **Assembling the evidence**
   Concretely, this means that risk communicators need to demonstrate that they understand the risk and therefore have a credible basis for their decisions. Questions that may guide communicators include the following:
   - What is the risk?
   - Have you used the best available information to define the problem at stake?
   - Are you aware of the chance that the hazard may occur?
   - Are you aware of the size of the hazard?
   - Who will benefit and who will suffer if the hazard occurs? Will everyone be equally affected?
   - Have you considered complexity, ambiguity, and uncertainty?
2. **Acknowledgement of public perspectives**
   Acknowledging public perspectives should include a commitment to generate and draw on robust studies as to better understand the nature of public perception as well as showing an ongoing commitment to test for trust. Questions to bear in mind:
   - Do you understand how members of the public perceive the risk?
   - Do you understand how influential risk actors view the risk?
   - Have you identified the risk entrepreneurs that are likely to fear the risk the most?
   - Have you identified those groups that are likely to want to amplify or diminish the risk, or others' perceptions of the risk, for their own benefit?
   - Have you considered those groups that are negatively affected by the risk, especially where those groups are seen as particularly vulnerable?
3. **Analysis of options**
   The quality of risk communications will benefit from openly discussing the broad range of options and the associated trade-offs that drive a specific policy or response. Crucially, this implies for institutional actors to devise a clear communication of the expected impacts, costs, and benefits of action as well as inaction. Questions include the following:
   - Can you demonstrate that you have weighed the costs and benefits of the risk and the options for managing it?
   - Do you have good arguments for assigning the necessary trade-offs between conflicting objectives and goals?
   - Are you clear about the impact of doing too much, too little or nothing?
   - When time permits, do you look for a range of options and select the one that promises the best balance of "upsides" and "downsides"?
   - When you have the opportunity, do you reduce those risks that are easy and inexpensive to reduce?
4. **Authority in charge**
   Risk communicators need to define the nature of their involvement with the risk. It is important to face up to one's responsibilities, yet it is equally important to avoid overstepping one's competences as well as leaving space to other stakeholders, and trusted parties viewed as independent and neutral. Questions to consider include the following:
   - What are the reasons for your organization to step in?
   - Have you identified conflicting views within your organization?
   - Have you made sufficient efforts to ensure that your organization speaks with one voice?
   - Do you periodically check how well trusted you are?

- Should any other public body be speaking out on this issue?
- Have you identified independent third parties that are more trusted than you and may facilitate the public debate?

5. **Interacting with the audience**
   Effective communication requires interacting with the right audience using a factual approach that refrains from triggering emotions, as well as the right methods depending on the context (e.g., face-to-face versus Internet). Supportive questions include the following:
   - Have you clarified who the audience of your message is likely to be?
   - Have you clarified how you will interact with other groups (through information, consultation, and deliberation)?
   - Are you clear whether messages are intended to inform your organization, organized groups, or the general public?
   - Have you used communication methods that have worked in similar circumstances?
   - Do you select and train effective communicators and learn from examples of similar situations where messages have proven successful?

Source: Adapted from Bouder (2009) and Bouder (2022).

backing of a strong risk assessment – this was for instance the issue in the initial phase of the BSE crisis. Of course, the novelty of the issue and, consequently, the lack of evidence may be partly responsible: Yet more often than not, the main problem is about which relevant scientific information is shared and communicated. For instance, effective communication channels between risk assessors and risk managers need to be in place. This can be particularly challenging when the decision requires to draw on a large number of scientific sources. One issue that was identified during the COVID-19 crisis, for instance, was the fact that some disciplines were overrepresented (e.g., epidemiological modeling) (Aven & Bouder, 2020). The next three questions – ***are you aware of the chance that the hazard may occur, of the size of the hazard*** and of ***who will benefit and will suffer?*** – suggest more directly to use the approaches and techniques that are well established in risk science (Aven & Thedkdi, 2021), namely probabilistic estimates as well as risk-benefit and cost-benefit analyses. Generating this knowledge at the prodromal phase will be much beneficial as such will be difficult to assemble at the acute phase of the crisis. Monitoring programs in sensitive areas should be encouraged, from seismic activity to pandemic surveillance. One possible danger of monitoring would be to reduce information to simple calculus translated into risk "fact sheets." Modern crises typically involve unknowns, multiple relationships, and ripple effects. Sophisticated systems also suffer from vulnerabilities. Therefore, specific attention should be paid to ***complexity, ambiguity, and uncertainties*** (Renn, 2008).

Acknowledgement of Public Perspectives

The second principle offers concrete suggestions to get away from the deficit model and move toward a multi-way communication approach (Balog-Way et al., 2020). The first question – ***do you understand how members of the public perceives the risks?*** – may be answered by commissioning perception studies that will look into peoples' concerns as well as preferences. This may take the different forms (provided they are scientifically robust), that is, opinion surveys or qualitative interviews. A well-established fact, for instance, is the fear of nuclear risks – or "dread" factor (Slovic, 1987a). Any crisis involving a nuclear risk dimension will likely require special attention and proactive communication to lessen anxiety. Perceptions of other risks may attenuate the sense of urgency and seriousness. This is typically the case of recurring natural disasters such as flooding. The next two questions – *do you understand how influential risk actors view the risk? Have you identified the risk entrepreneurs (. . .)?* – underline the importance of mapping out the views of the key stakeholders that are likely to voice their concerns and shape opinions. Opinions leaders may be as diverse as patient representatives (EMA, 2010) or local politicians (HSE, 2010). As part of this mapping exercise, specific attention ought to be paid to the people and factors that may *amplify or attenuate* the event (Kasperson et al., 1988; Pidgeon et al., 2003). Finally, ethical considerations include to pay specific attention to those individuals and groups who are *particularly vulnerable* and may be *negatively affected* by the risk at play and/or the crisis response measures. Worries that this may not be the case were clearly expressed during the COVID-19 crisis (Evensen et al., 2023).

Analysis of Option

The next principle is particularly important at the acute and chronic phases of the crisis. The second, third, and fourth questions focus on effectiveness that helps crisis managers to increase the chances that the measures will bear the expected results. First, they will need to reassure citizens that they have *good arguments to assign the necessary trade-offs between conflicting objectives and goals.* This implies working toward an honest exchange of information between experts and lay audiences (Clarke & Freudenburg, 1993). Decision-makers will need to demonstrate clarity about the impact of *doing too much or too little* as well as presenting the *upsides and downsides* of the key options (Aven & Thedkdi, 2021). The first and fifth questions aim at ensuring efficiency, that is, minimizing the waste of time, effort, and money. Can decision-makers demonstrate that they have *weighed the costs and benefits of the options*? Can they show that they have first and foremost *reduced those risks that are easy and inexpensive to reduce*? Well-established techniques such as cost-benefit analysis (CBA) are obvious candidates to guide decisions about efficiency. They already do so in the legislative process. In the United States, for example, a requirement was introduced in 1995 to conduct a quantitative analysis of the expected costs and benefits for all regulatory actions with an annual cost of more than $100 million (Hattis & Minkowitz, 1997). While this commitment to efficiency is crucial, it is not an easy task during a crisis as decision-makers may be tempted to promise to do "whatever it costs" to protect the population from a specific risk. This was the strategy explicitly adopted by the French government during the COVID-19 crisis. This, however, generated much criticism in the end and was rather interpreted by large sections of the public as a lack of discernment and leadership. A well-established risk communication rule is that perceived efficiency is positively correlated to trust (Löfstedt, 2005)

Authority in Charge

The next set of questions is more directly concerned with the allocation of crucial decision-making responsibilities across the four stages of crisis management. First, organizations need to *provide justification for stepping in.* Confusion about who is supposed to do what is likely to damage trust in the response process since recognized competence is a key component contributing to trust, along with fairness and efficiency (Löfstedt, 2005). The ability to *overcome conflicting views* within an organization and *speaking with one voice* are crucial factors that strengthen perceived competence and trust. Regularly *testing for trust* is also important as a specific organization may lack the necessary public support to make a positive impact. When trust is low, an organization may have to rely on *other public bodies* and *independent third parties* – such as scientists or well-respected leaders (Bouder & Löfstedt, 2016; HSE, 2010; Löfstedt, 2005). This raises the fundamental issue of leadership that is so crucial to crisis management (Wardman, 2020) yet so difficult to attain (Boin & Hart, 2003). Effective leadership of the authority in charge requires crucially to

- Enact and integrate knowledge (Hyvärinen & Vos, 2015)
- Bridge gaps between key knowledge communities (Reynolds & Seeger, 2005)
- Offer direction and contextualize information (Seeger, 2006)
- Maintain open dialogue channels on crucial platforms (Austin & Jin, 2017)
- Ensure that dialogue is two-way (Jacques, 2012; Löfstedt, 2005)

Interacting with the Audience

The final set of questions relates to interactions with the audience broadly defined as those involved in the crisis whether as risk producers, risk assessors, and managers, as well as those directly affected by the risk. Advice primarily applies to the chronic and resolution phases of the crisis. However, the need to interact with various publics may be felt at earlier stages, for instance, when an issue is generating polarized discussions in society – which was for instance the case in the early 2000s when food derived from genetically modified organisms (GMOs), and later, nanotechnology became controversial topics of discussion. The first question – *have you clarified who the audience of your message is likely to be?* – suggests to keep track of the various audiences. Background work on acknowledging and understanding public perceptions (principle 2) can play an important role in characterizing their expectations. The second and third questions are also about clarity, regarding *how* the interaction should best take place as well as the clarity of the *messages* and the nature of the interlocutors (*organizations, organized groups, or the general public*). The last two questions are about learning from experience and knowledge transfer. Learning from *communication methods that have worked in the past* and learning from *similar situations*. Far too often decision-makers may take a crisis as a one-off event – after all there was "one" BSE crisis, one COVID-19 crisis, etc. – and while doing so failing to recognize the value of looking for similarities and patterns as well as looking for lessons from past events. There is, however, increasing evidence of positive lessons coming from the systematic analysis of crises. Some final points from the author's research will be discussed below in the concluding section.

Conclusion

Toward the end of the twentieth century, regulatory crises changed the risk communication environment durably and gave rise to a "post-trust" environment (Lofstedt, 2005). By the early to mid-2000s, the general features of the new model became apparent throughout Europe (Löfstedt, 2011; Löfstedt et al., 2011), with important effects:

- The first trend was to allocate benefits and risks in a more inclusive fashion, to encourage greater public and stakeholder participation in the policy process;
- Regulators were also urged to make their strategies more transparent to meet demands for more accountable decisions;
- Finally, the status and role of science were increasingly challenged, as scientists are seen by society as just one of many voices.

With time, this new "paradigm" has become ever more salient. In a context marked by repetitive crisis events, citizens and the media have become more critical about governments and scientists. While we may not yet have reached the point of a "post-truth" society where scientific facts bear little credibility (Roozenbeek & van der Linden, 2019; Roozenbeek et al., 2020; Saladino et al., 2020; van der Linden & Löfstedt, 2019), we may not be too far off. If anything, the recent COVID-19 crisis has exacerbated the trust deficit (Balog-Way & McComas, 2020; Bouder, 2022) and led to renewed calls for transparency (Mercuri, 2020; Rajan et al., 2020). Boyd (2019) expresses well the paradox of modern government when it comes to risk:

> "Democratic governments are generally very risk averse because the political consequences of even quite small risks materialising as real and adverse outcomes can magnify non-linearity. (…) But it would probably be misguided of governments to imagine that the control of this kind of risk comes about through strong risk aversion and, therefore, by setting a low level of risk tolerance. (…) Ironically and perhaps counter-intuitively, those governments which have a strong aversion to risk resulting in a culture of control are likely to be less trusted, will bring upon themselves greater costs, and are therefore more likely to suffer (…)" (Boyd, 2019, p. 71).

Against the backdrop, the fact that crises tend to act as catalysts of precautionary and restrictive action suggests that urgent action should be taken to prevent a worrying downward spiral. To stop the vicious circle of crisis-risk aversion, it is becoming urgent and vital to better connect the fields of crisis and risk sciences. This chapter is only a small step in that direction. We believe that crisis management and communication, which is an emerging field of research, can benefit from risk science methodological advancements. In particular, risk decision models can supplement crisis management at every stage, that is, scanning, preparing, managing, recovering, and reflective learning. Finally, a focus on crisis management may also be beneficial to risk science as a way to provide concrete opportunity to test concepts in different national and cultural setting, therefore reinforcing its international/multicultural dimension.

References

Árvai, J., & Rivers, L., III (Eds.). (2013). *Effective Risk Communication* (pp. 23–39). Oxon, UK: Routledge.

Austin, L. L., & Jin, Y. (Eds.). (2017). *Social Media and Crisis Communication*. New York: Taylor & Francis.

Aven, T., & Bouder, F. (2020). The COVID-19 pandemic: How can risk science help? *Journal of Risk Research*. https://doi.org/10.1080/13669877.2020.1756383

Aven, T., & Thekdi, S. (2021). *Risk Science: An Introduction*. Milton Park, Abingdon: Routledge. ISBN 9780367742683

Aven, T., Ben-Haim, Y., Boje Andersen, H., Cox, T., López Droguett, E., Greenberg, M., Guikema, S., Kröger, W., Renn, O., Thompson, K.M., & Zio, E. (2018). *Society for risk analysis glossary*. Retrieved January 14, 2025 from https://www.sra.org/wp-content/uploads/2020/04/SRA-Glossary-FINAL.pdf

Balog-Way, D., & McComas, K. (2020). COVID-19: Reflections on trust, tradeoffs, and preparedness. *Journal of Risk Research*. https://doi.org/10.1080/13669877.2020.1758192

Balog-Way, D., McComas, K., & Besley, J. (2020). The evolving field of risk communication. *Risk Analysis*, *40*(S1), 2240–2262.

Beck, U. (1992). *Risk Society: Towards a New Modernity*. London: Sage. (Original work published 1985)

Bernstein, P. L. (1998). *Against the Gods: The Remarkable Story of Risk*. New York: John Wiley & Sons.

Boin, A., & Hart, P. T. (2003). Public leadership in times of crisis: Mission Impossible? *Public Administration Review*, *63*(5), 544–553. https://doi.org/10.1111/1540-6210.00318

Bouder, F. (2006). A contribution to transnational risk analysis: Comparative analysis of risk perception related to human health issues. In I. K. Richter, S. Berking, & R. Müller-Schmid, Eds., *Risk Society and the Culture of Precaution* (pp. 1967–1983). Basingstoke: Palgrave Macmillan.

Bouder, F. (2008). *Defining a Tolerability of Risk framework for pharmaceutical products in a context of scientific uncertainty*. PhD thesis, London.

Bouder, F. (2009). *A Practical Guide to Public Risk Communication: The Five Essentials of Good Practice. Pamphlet for the Risk and Regulation Advisory Council, Department for Business, Innovation and Skills*. London: BIS.

Bouder, F. (2015). Communicating vaccine safety to the media and general public. *Special issue Vaccine Safety Communication, Current Drug Safety, 10*, 9–15.

Bouder, F. (2022). *Principles and Challenges of Risk Communication/Crisis Communication, Specifically Addressing Issues Relating to Pandemic*. Underlagsrapport till SOU 2022:10 Sverige Under Pandemin. ISBN 978-91-525-0334-8

Bouder, F. and Löfstedt, R. (2016). *Bringing policy relevance to EPO's Occupational and Safety Risk Assessment 2016*. Report. European Patent Office.

Boyd, I. (2019, 2019). Risk and uncertainty in the context of government decision-making. In S. van der Linden, & R. E. Löfstedt, Eds., *Risk and Uncertainty in a Post-Truth Society* (1st ed., pp. 54–73). London: Routledge. https://doi.org/10.4324/9780429280290

Clarke, L., & Freudenburg, W. R. (1993). Rhetoric, reform, and risk. *Society, 30*, 78–81.

Covello, V. T., Sandman, P., & Slovic, P. (1988). *Risk Communication, Risk Statistics, and Risk Comparison: A Manual for Plant Managers*. Washington, DC: Chemical Manufacturers Association.

Eriksson, M. (2018). Lessons for crisis communication on social media: A systematic review of what research tells the practice. *International Journal of Strategic Communication, 12*(5), 686–693.

European Medicines Agency (EMA) (2010). *Benefit/Risk Communication by the European Medicines Agency: A Study of Influential Stakeholders' Expectations and Attitudes*. EMA Publisher.

Evensen, D., Warren, G., & Bouder, F. (2023). Satisfaction with governmental risk communication both increases and decreases COVID-19 mitigation behaviors. *International Journal of Public Health, 68*, 1604966.

Fischhoff, B. (1995). Risk perception and communication unplugged: Twenty years of process. *Risk Analysis, 15*(2), 137–145.

Fischhoff, B. (2005). Scientifically sound pandemic risk communication. *Prepared for House Science Committee Briefing Gaps in the National Flu Preparedness Plan: Social Science Planning and Response*. Retrieved January 14, 2025 from https://www.researchgate.net/profile/Baruch_Fischhoff/publication/228632978_Scientifically_sound_pandemic_risk_communication/links/57442b7808ae298602f0ff71/Scientifically-sound-pandemic-risk-communication.pdf

Fischhoff, B. (2009). Risk perception and communication. In R. Detels, R. Beaglehole, M. A. Lansang, & M. Gulliford, Eds., *Oxford Textbook of Public Health* (5th ed., pp. 940–952). Oxford: Oxford University Press.

Fischhoff, B., & Scheufele, D. (2019). The science of science communication III. *PNAS, 116*(16), 7632–7633. In N. K. Chater (Ed.), Judgement and Decision Making. London: SageGiddens, A. (1990) The Consequences of Modernity, Cambridge: Polity Press

Fischhoff, B., Slovic, P., & Lichtenstein, S. (1978). How safe is safe enough? A psychometric study of attitudes towards technological risks and benefits. *Policy Sciences, 9*, 127–152.

Giddens, A. (1990). *The Consequences of Modernity*. Cambridge: Polity Press.

Gregory, J., & Lock, S. J. (2008). The evolution of "public understanding of science": Public engagement as a tool of science policy in the UK. *Sociology Compass, 2*(4), 1252–1265.

Hattis, D., & Minkowitz, W. S. (1997). Risk evaluation: Legal requirements, conceptual foundations, and practical experiences in the United States. In G. Pfister, & O. Renn, Eds., *Reports on risk regulation procedures in several countries (Introduction to Discussion Paper No. 91)* (pp. 1–109). Stuttgart: Akademie für Technikfolgenabschätzung in Baden-Württemberg.

Health and Safety Executive (HSE) (2010). Improving health and safety: An analysis of HSE's risk communication in the 21st century [Report]. *HSE*. Retrieved January 14, 2025 from https://www.hse.gov.uk/research/rrpdf/rr785.pdf

Heath, R. L. (2006). Best practices in crisis communication: Evolution of practice through research. *Journal of Applied Communication Research, 34*(3), 245–248. https://doi.org/10.1080/00909880600771577

Horton, R. (2004). *MMR: Science and Fiction*. London: Granta Books.

House of Lords (2000). *Select Committee on Science and Technology, Science and Society*. London: The Stationary Office.

Hyvärinen, J., & Vos, M. (2015). Developing a conceptual framework for investigating communication supporting community resilience. *Societies, 5*(3), 583–597. https://doi.org/10.3390/soc5030583

International Risk Governance Council (IRGC) (2005). *Risk governance: Towards an integrative approach*. Retrieved January 14, 2025 from https://irgc.org/wp-content/uploads/2018/09/IRGC_WP_No1_Risk_Governance_reprinted_version_3.pdf
Jaques, T. (2012). Crisis leadership: A view from the executive suite. *Journal of Public Affairs, 12*(4), 366–372. https://doi.org/10.1002/pa.1422
Johansson, C., & Bäck, E. (2017). Strategic leadership communication for crisis network coordination. *International Journal of Strategic Communication, 11*(4), 324–343.
Kahneman, D., & Tversky, A. (1979). Prospect theory: An analysis of decision under risk. *Econometrica, 47*, 263–291.
Kasperson, R. (2014). Four questions for risk communication. *Journal of Risk Research, 17*(10), 1233–1239.
Kasperson, R. E., Renn, O., Slovic, P., Brown, H. S., Emel, J., Goble, R., & Ratick, S. (1988). The social amplification of risk: A conceptual framework. *Risk Analysis, 8*(2), 177–187.
Leiss, W. (1996). Three phases in the evolution of risk communication practice. In H. Kunreuther, & P. Slovic, Eds., *Challenges in Risk Assessment and Risk Management* (Vol. 545, pp. 84–95). Special Issue of the Annals of the American Academy of Political and Social Science.
Löfstedt, R. E. (2005). *Risk Management in Post-trust Societies*. Basingstoke: Palgrave.
Löfstedt, R. E. (2011). Risk versus hazard – how to regulate in the 21st century. *European Journal of Risk Regulation, 2*(2), 149–168.
Löfstedt, R., Bouder, F., Wardman, J., & Chakraborty, S. (2011). The changing nature of communication and regulation of risk in Europe. *Journal of Risk Research, 14*(4), 409–429. https://doi.org/10.1080/13669877.2011.557479
Lok, C., & Powell, D. (2000). *The Belgian Dioxin Crisis of the Summer of 1999: A Case Study in Crisis Communication and Management*. Guelph, Ont.: Department of Food Science, University of Guelph.
McComas, K. A. (2006). Defining moments in risk communication research: 1996–2005. *Journal of Health Communication, 11*(1), 75–91.
Mercuri, M. (2020). Just follow the science: A government response to a pandemic [Editorial]. *Journal of Evaluation in Clinical Practice*. https://doi.org/10.1111/jep.13491
Newton, K., & Norris, P. (2000). Confidence in public institutions. In S. J. Pharr, & R. D. Putnam, Eds., *Disaffected Democracies: What's Troubling the Trilateral Countries* (pp. xx–xx). Princeton, NJ: Princeton University Press.
Nyenswah, T., Engineer, C. Y., & Peters, D. H. (2016). Leadership in times of crisis: The example of Ebola virus disease in Liberia. *Health Systems and Reform, 2*(3), 194–207. https://doi.org/10.1080/23288604.2016.1222793
Pharr, S., & Putnam, R. (Eds.). (2000). *Disaffected Democracies*. Cambridge, MA: Harvard University Press.
Pidgeon, N., Kasperson, R., & Slovic, P. (2003). *The Social Amplification of Risk*. New York, NY: Cambridge University Press.
Powell, D., & Leiss, W. (1997). *Mad Cows and Mother's Milk: The Peril of Poor Risk Communication*. Montreal, Canada: McGill-Queen's University Press.
Rajan, D., Koch, K., Rohrer, K., Bajnockzi, C., Socha, A., Voss, M., Nicod, M., Ridde, V., & Koonin, J. (2020). Governance of the COVID-19 response: A call for more inclusive and transparent decision-making. *BMJ Global Health, 5*, e002655.
Ratzan, S. (Ed.). (1999). *The Mad Cow Crisis: Health and the Public Good*. London, UK: University College London Press.
Renn, O. (2008). *Risk Governance: Coping with Uncertainty in a Complex World*. London, UK: Earthscan.
Renn, O. (2014). Four questions for risk communication: A response to Roger Kasperson. *Journal of Risk Research, 17*(10), 1277–1281.
Renn, O., & Klinke, A. (2004). Systemic risks: A new challenge for risk management. *EMBO Reports, 5*(Spec. No. S41-6). https://doi.org/10.1038/sj.embor.7400227
Renn, O., & Levine, D. (1991). Credibility and trust in risk communication. In R. E. Kasperson, & P. J. Stallen, Eds., *Communicating Risk to the Public: International Perspectives* (pp. xx–xx). Amsterdam, Netherlands: Kluwer.

Reynolds, B., & Seeger, M. (2005). Crisis and emergency risk communication as an integrative model. *Journal of Health Communication, 10*(1), 43–55. https://doi.org/10.1080/10810730590904571
Roozenbeek, J., & van der Linden, S. (2019). The fake news game: Actively inoculating against the risk of misinformation. *Journal of Risk Research, 22*(5), 570–580.
Roozenbeek, J., Schneider, C. R., Dryhurst, S., Kerr, J., Freeman, A. L. J., Recchia, G., van der Bles, A. M., & van der Linden, S. (2020). Susceptibility to misinformation about COVID-19 around the world. Royal Society Open. *Science, 7*(201199). https://doi.org/10.1098/rsos.201199
Rothstein, H., Huber, M., & Gaskell, G. (2006). A theory of risk colonisation: The spiralling regulatory logics of societal and institutional risks. *Economy and Society, 35*(1), 91–112.
Saladino, V., Algeri, D., & Auriemma, V. (2020). The psychological and social impact of Covid-19: New perspectives of well-being. *Frontiers in Psychology, 11*, 577684. https://doi.org/10.3389/fpsyg.2020.577684
Seeger, M. W. (2006). Best practices in crisis communication: An expert panel process. *Journal of Applied Communication Research, 34*(3), 232–244.
Siegrist, M. (2021). Trust and risk perception: A critical review of the literature. *Risk Analysis*. https://doi.org/10.1111/risa.13325
Sinaceur, M., Heath, C., & Cole, S. (2005). Emotional and deliberative reactions to a public crisis – Mad Cow disease in France. *Psychological Science, 16*(3), 247–254.
Slovic, P. (1987a). Perception of risk. *Science, 236*, 280–285.
Slovic, P.Ripples in a pond: Forecasting industrial crises., Ed. (1987b). *Industrial Crisis Quarterly*. https://doi.org/10.1177/108602668700100403
Slovic, P. (1993). Perceived risk, trust and democracy. *Risk Analysis, 13*, 675–682.
Slovic, P., Finucane, M. L., Peters, E., & MacGregor, D. G. (2004). Risk as analysis and risk as feelings: Some thoughts about affect, reason, risk, and rationality. *Risk Analysis, 24*(2), 311–322.
Van der Linden, S., & Löfstedt, R. E. (2019). *Risk and Uncertainty in a Post-truth Society*. London; New York: Routledge, Taylor & Francis Group.
Veil, S., Reynolds, B., Sellnow, T., & Seeger, M. (2008). Crisis and emergency risk communication (CERC) as a theoretical framework for research and practice. *Health Promotion Practice, 9*(4 Suppl), 26–34. https://doi.org/10.1177/1524839908322113
Wardman, J. K. (2008). The constitution of risk communication in advanced liberal societies. *Risk Analysis, 28*(6), 1619–1637.
Wardman, J. K. (2014). Sociocultural vectors of effective risk communication. *Journal of Risk Research, 17*(10), 1251–1257.
Wardman, J. K. (2020). Recalibrating pandemic risk leadership: Thirteen crisis ready strategies for COVID-19. *Journal of Risk Research*. https://doi.org/10.1080/13669877.2020.1842989
Way, D., Blazsin, H., Löfstedt, R., & Bouder, F. (2017). Pharmaceutical benefit–risk communication tools: A review of the literature. *Drug Safety, 40*(1), 15–36.
Wolff, H. (2000). Introductory Remarks, Science, Risk and the Regulation of New Technologies, Merton College, Oxford, 24 March – 1 April.

Author Bio

Frederic Bouder is Professor in Risk Management at the University of Stavanger, Norway. He is a recognized expert in risk policy analysis and has deployed this expertise to develop and maintains strategic international policy networks. In particular, he has integrated cognitive insights from decision science into making risk policy more science-informed. Frederic Bouder has directed several research programs focusing primarily on health and energy risks. He has made tangible impacts on policy; in particular, several of his recommendations have been endorsed and implemented by European and national regulators and policymakers. In 2009, Frederic Bouder was appointed National Expert to the European Medicines Agency where he carried an evaluation of specific safety cases. In 2012, he was appointed Scientific Advisor to the network of pharmaceutical National Competent Authorities across Europe as part of the EU project on Strengthening Collaboration for Operating Pharmacovigilance in Europe (SCOPE) Joint Action. Frederic Bouder has advised a range of regulators including the European Food Safety Authority (EFSA), the UK Sustainable development Commission, the UK Department for BIS, the UK HSE, the Dutch Ministry of Infrastructure and the Environment (IenM), the Dutch Ministry of Economic Affairs (MInezek), and the European Patent Office (EPO). In addition, many medical and non-medical regulators across Europe and in North America have invited him to provide policy advice and state-of-the-art training on risk analysis.

Methodological Developments and Challenges in Crisis and Risk Communication Research

45

Aligning the Field: Embracing the Interdisciplinary, Conceptually Divergent, and Methodological Diverse Reality of Good Research in Risk and Crisis Communication

Audra Diers-Lawson
Institute for Communication, Kristiania University of Applied Sciences, Oslo, Norway

Though the first volume of this book was only published in 2016, the world and our understanding of risk and crisis communication are evolving. COVID-19 was a significant disruption in our lives, prompting change because it is a societal-level crisis Diers-Lawson & Omondi (2024). Reeves et al. (2020) argue that because societal-level crises disrupt all aspects of our lives, they can fundamentally reshape our beliefs and behaviors across domains. But of course, COVID-19 is not the only disruption in people's lives. We have seen a proliferation of political crises around the world, whether it is the Russian invasion of Ukraine, the January 6, 2021, insurrection in the United States, the January 8, 2023, insurrection in Brazil, or countless other political crises. Moreover, wicked problems like climate change, refugee crises, and human trafficking are emerging as crises affecting lives – often in understudied populations and parts of the world. Global supply chain shortages, labor difficulties, and network security are becoming increasingly difficult problems for many organizations to manage, from small businesses to governments and global corporations. All of this is played out in cross-platform communication from local to global legacy media organizations as well as social media platforms. Across the domains of organizational strategy, public health, governance, and citizen engagement, there is emerging a common need to mitigate the effects of crises. This requires us to think in terms of crisis prevention, resilience, and engagement, as well as cross-sector roles that can be played (Dahal et al., 2020; Hunt & Eburn, 2018; Hyvärinen & Vos, 2015; Kim, 2020; Mochizuki et al., 2018; Rela et al., 2020; Willems, 2016; Žilinskas & Sakalauskas, 2021). Therefore, it is right that the field of "crisis communication" redefines itself as "risk and crisis communication" because the crisis communication process does not begin when a crisis is triggered; instead, it should be thought of as an ongoing process of risk and crisis communication (see Figure 45.1).

This change of nomenclature requires us to reconsider the assumptions and positioning of risk and crisis communication research. Crisis communication is often operationalized as a tool of business to protect, repair, and promote its image or reputation. For example, two major reviews of the field of crisis communication (Ha & Boynton, 2014) and a review of the field

The Handbook of International Crisis and Risk Communication Research, Second Edition.
Edited by Andreas Schwarz, Matthew W. Seeger, and Sora Kim.

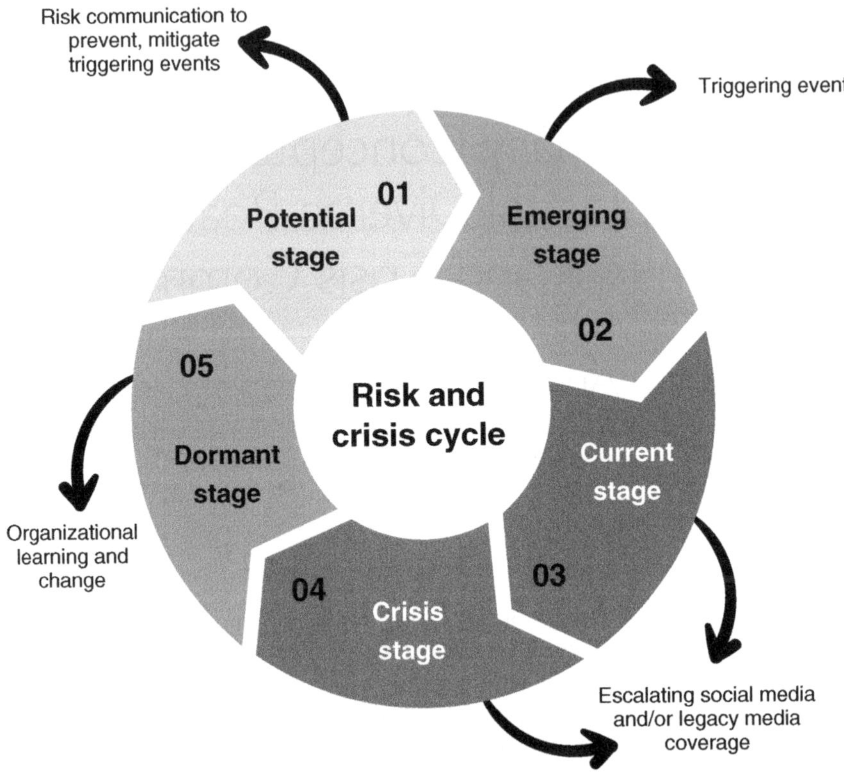

Figure 45.1 Risk and crisis cycle. *Source*: See Diers-Lawson (2020)/Taylor and Francis.

of public relations (Kim et al., 2014) both place crisis communication squarely within the field of public relations and identify image repair theory (Benoit, 1997) and situational crisis communication theory (Coombs, 2006) as the dominant theories in the field. Yet, in a more comprehensive review of literature on crisis communication from 1953 to 2015, I found that while these theories are certainly foundational in the evolution of the field as a distinctive subfield in communication, they only represent about 11% of the published research (Diers-Lawson, 2020), which suggests that when research is theory-driven, risk and crisis communication has always been more theoretically diverse than it is often described. In fact, in my review of the field I identified more than 100 different theories in three broad categories that had been used (see Figure 45.2). Moreover, the field has further diversified since the review was completed; therefore, it is reasonable to assume that the theories used and developed have also diversified. Yet, anecdotally, researchers in risk and crisis communication often find it difficult to publish in some "traditional" public relations and strategic communication journals simply because they have not used "traditional" or "dominant" perspective.

The conceptual diversity that has always been present in the field has a direct tie to research design in risk and crisis communication. Meißner and Diers-Lawson (2022) argued that the interdisciplinary needs in risk and crisis communication are reflected in the methodological innovations in the field. In the previous volume of this book, Coombs (2016) rightly argued that challenges of culture, nations, frameworks, and focus represented important methodological challenges in crisis communication. Coombs (2016) did not provide a comprehensive review of the state of the art of research in the field; however, since this volume focuses on setting an interdisciplinary research agenda for risk and crisis communication, I will do so. More specifically, my objectives for this chapter are to: (1) discuss the two dominant

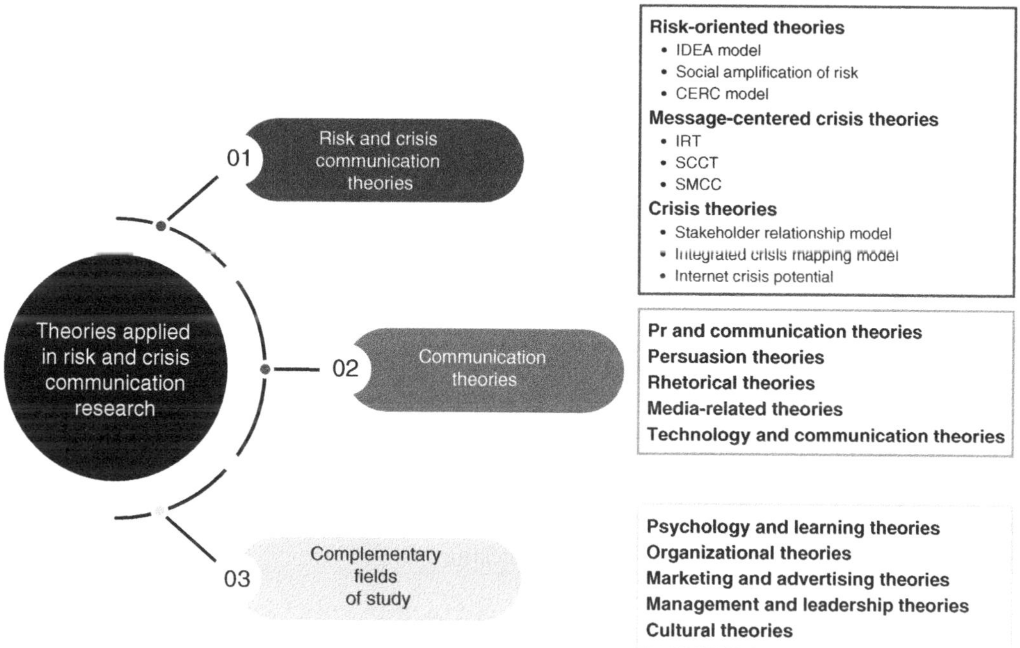

Figure 45.2 Theories applied in risk and crisis communication research. *Source*: Adapted Meißner and Diers-Lawson (2022), Diers-Lawson (2020).

epistemologies in risk and crisis communication; (2) provide a data-based summary of the methodological and interdisciplinary diversity in risk and crisis communication; and (3) explore the current needs for research design in risk and crisis communication to suggest a methods-based research agenda in our field.

Two Paths Diverging in the Woods: Risk and Crisis Communication Epistemology

In September 2022, at the annual European Public Relations Education Research Association (EUPRERA) convention, there was a broad discussion about the nature of public relations and strategic communication tied to publishing outlets. What emerged from that conversation was a clear articulation of the two paths to take: one path suggests that strategic communication research should be organization-centric (i.e., focused on safeguarding the organization's reputation), and the other is that to develop and meet strategic communication objectives, strategic communication research should be stakeholder-centered. In exploring this argument within the context of pandemic communication, I compared the evolution of the field of organizational communication versus public relations and concluded that the stakeholder perspective was more aligned with the traditions of organizational communication, whereas the organization-centric perspective was more aligned with the traditions of public relations (Diers-Lawson, 2023). This is not to suggest there is a "good" or "bad" path to take; rather, there are two distinctive ideologically and historically grounded epistemologies underlying the field of risk and crisis communication.

If we define epistemology as the study of how we acquire knowledge connecting how our minds relate to reality and how we filter information from the world around us (Croucher &

Cronn-Mills, 2018), then it is not surprising that it influences our approach to research in risk and crisis communication. Epistemology asks basic questions like:

- What do we know?
- What does it mean to say we know something?
- How do we know what we know?

Therefore, if we think in terms of traditional schools of thought in epistemology, we may view knowledge attainment through perceptual observation (i.e., empiricism), reasoning from observations (i.e., rationalism), decide that we learn through action and experience (i.e., pragmatism), or we may decide that knowledge produced by systems where oppression was rife is fundamentally corrupted and needs to be rebuilt (i.e., decolonial epistemology). As fields institutionalize, epistemological perspectives also develop to define "legitimate" questions that fields ask to differentiate themselves from other related fields. For example, though communication broadly borrows from sociology, social psychology, political science, and several other fields, what makes the field of communication distinctive is that we focus on communication within these contexts; therefore, our epistemological stance suggests that legitimate questions to ask must center on some aspect of communication.

PR Epistemology in Risk and Crisis Communication

In a risk and crisis communication context, a *PR-based epistemology* puts the organization at the center of knowledge creation about risk and crisis communication needs. It is well-aligned with business models of knowledge that often argue that the only purpose of business is to be profitable (Volk, 2016). Of course, this does not suggest that other social objectives cannot be pursued or might not be important, but it does explain why those might be secondary or rationalized in terms of what they do to support an organization's reputation (and thus its profitability/survivability). As such, risk and crisis communication research aligned with PR epistemology would focus broadly on questions about how organizations can protect, rebuild, or develop their reputation before or after crises. There are literally hundreds of journal articles, book chapters, and books in crisis communication that focus on these questions. For example, Benoit's use of case studies analyzing companies like Sears (1995) or US Air (1997) or public figures like Queen Elizabeth (1999) or President Bush (2009). Other authors used this focus to emphasize the importance of limiting rumors (DiFonzo et al., 1994), discussing the impact of news coverage on reputation (Einwiller et al., 2010), considering the use of emotion as a tool for crisis communication (Claeys et al., 2013), connecting crisis response and advertising (Kim & Atkinson, 2014), or more recently focusing on the impact of pre-crisis corporate associations with post-crisis response strategy (Tao & Song, 2020). Certainly, in this context, Coombs and Holladay's development and application of situational crisis communication theory (SCCT) has been instrumental beginning with their adaptation of attribution theory (Coombs & Holladay, 1996) and use of it throughout the last 25 or so years (Coombs, 2015; Coombs & Holladay, 2009).

Organizational Communication Epistemology in Risk and Crisis Communication

In risk and crisis communication, an *organizational communication epistemology*, however, is more concerned with questions of the stakeholder voice (Pearson & Clair, 1998), experience (Granville et al., 2016; Sellnow & Seeger, 2001), and serving the broader societal good (Hunt &

Eburn, 2018; Xu & Li, 2013). The roots of the organizational communication epistemology in risk and crisis communication can be connected with research like racial and moral crises (Campbell & Pettigrew, 1959), public dissent to policy making (Chesler & Schmuck, 1964), exploring tensions between victims and shareholders in corporate decision-making (Marcus & Goodman, 1991), and stronger post-crisis commitment to stakeholders (Seeger & Ulmer, 2002). As the organizational communication epistemology grew in risk and crisis communication research, we began to see a more diverse focus in research in terms of context like health (Menon & Goh, 2005), politics or government (Førde et al., 2019; Wukich & Mergel, 2015), non-governmental organizations (Schwarz & Pforr, 2011), sports (Jin et al., 2010; Sellnow & Brand, 2001), or cross-industry engagement (Bacchi, 2014) as well as broader topics of consideration like employee experience (Mazzei et al., 2012; Ravazzani, 2016), emotion (Hajibaba et al., 2015; Jin & Pang, 2010; Rhee & Yang, 2014), culture (Falkheimer & Heide, 2006; Shim et al., 2018), terrorism and war (Falkheimer, 2014; Petridou et al., 2019), ethnicity (Spence et al., 2013), gender (Goby & Nickerson, 2015; Rowsell et al., 2000), and encouraging self-protective behaviors (Sellnow-Richmond et al., 2018). The organizational communication epistemological position is, therefore, interested in a broader and more diverse set of questions related to risk and crisis contexts.

Methodological and Disciplinary Diversity in Risk and Crisis Communication Research

When we can position the epistemological views of risk and crisis communication research, it frames the discussion of the methodological and disciplinary diversity in risk and communication research. For example, in an analysis of the first four volumes (2018-2021) of the *Journal of International Crisis and Risk Communication Research* (*JICRCR*), Diers-Lawson and Meißner (2022) found that while there is a greater need for methodological diversity – specifically, qualitative research, big data, and experimental research are underdeveloped methods – the journal reflects a broad spectrum of research methodologies. The question is how do these findings reflect the field's development over time? This section will summarize both the methodological and disciplinary diversity evident in the field's development from 1953 to 2015 (for a full summary of the research methodology see Diers-Lawson, 2017). This review provides context for the richness of this field as well as the differences in the field based on epistemological views.

Methodological Diversity in Risk and Crisis Communication Research

Generally, the findings from the first four volumes of *JICRCR* are consistent with the field's evolution (see Figure 45.3). Across both the field's history and in the last four years, about 30% of articles published have been non-data-based; they are conceptual, theoretical, or focused on articulating "best practices" in risk and crisis communication. There is also a sizeable proportion of the research in the field's development that is rhetorical – including research using thematic analysis or critical perspectives. Third, there is also a sizeable amount of research that is quantitative – either questionnaire or content analysis-based. However, the methodologies that are comparatively underdeveloped in risk and crisis communication research are qualitative methods – including ethnographic or interview-based methods – and "big-data" based approaches. This is part of the reason why Meißner and Diers-Lawson (2022) called for more innovation in research methods in risk and crisis communication research.

Diversity in both research methods and sample has long been identified as a priority within the European risk and crisis research community. For example, as the Chair of ECREA's Crisis Communication division, Andreas Schwarz polled the division's members to identify the most

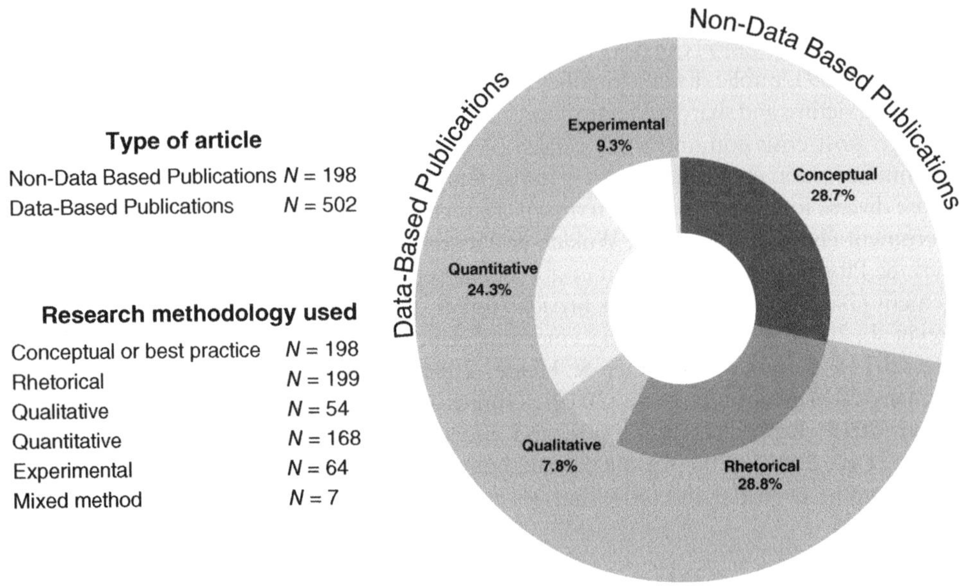

Figure 45.3 Summary of research methods in risk and crisis communication 1953–2015.

important research needs in 2015. Methods and cross-cultural research were rated as one of the most important research trends. Seven years later, these issues remain on scholars' research agendas. This suggests a need to further develop research methodologies in risk and crisis communication to improve theory development, testing, and application – often better aligning them with fields of practice. For example, whereas global public health is presently emphasizing a community engagement approach to understanding risk and crisis communication strategy (WHO, 2022), with public health officials in places like the Western Balkans or Central Asia talking about the importance of going into the communities during crises to listen to community concerns, there are only a handful of studies published in risk and crisis communication research that meet these engagement needs. One example of this approach was interviews conducted door-to-door in housing estates in Sweden reaching out to hard-to-reach populations (Arroyo et al., 2021). Similarly, in the Scottish context of the simultaneous crises of Brexit and COVID-19, one of the ways that I was able to better understand the complex interaction between pro-independence advocacy, "British history," and the role of crisis was to conduct in-depth interviews with Scots (Diers-Lawson, 2022). Likewise, there is a distinct need for developing theoretically rich "big data" analyses of risk and crisis communication because they can be used to address disasters and conduct ongoing "social listening" for many reasons (Allan & Peters, 2015; Dahal et al., 2020; Liu et al., 2015; Vogler & Meissner, 2020).

Disciplinary Diversity in Risk and Crisis Communication Research

Instead of building an argument for the primacy of quantitative questionnaire-based research because international marketing research experts argue for more experimental and survey-based research design (Coombs, 2016), risk and crisis communication research should more readily broaden its focus to better represent the interdisciplinary nature of the research. Moreover, because both the epistemological approaches I have outlined have rich traditions and histories within the field's development, it simply makes no sense to proscribe a limited view for research design in risk and crisis communication. In fact, if we focus on a data-based argument about what fields constitute risk and crisis communication, advocacy for a business-centered PR approach to research design simply does not reflect the reality of the risk and crisis communication's evolution because there are meaningful differences in how different disciplines approach the topics. In my analysis of risk and crisis communication research, 690 journal articles were analyzed. Field assessments were judged based on the journal the research was published in and SCIMAGO's categorization of the discipline(s) represented by the journals. Figure 45.4 summarizes the comparative findings. Peer-reviewed risk and crisis communication was primarily represented in five disciplines: science, engineering, and technology; management; communication; social sciences and humanities; and medicine and health. Then for each of the disciplines, the articles were analyzed for methodology differences (ANOVA), regional differences (correlations), and conceptual differences (correlations). Therefore, Figure 45.4 provides a summary of the significant findings. For example, in journals categorized within the management field, there were only significant differences in which regions were represented in crisis communication research and which concepts were addressed. By comparison, within journals categorized in the broader social sciences and humanities, crisis communication articles varied based on regions studied, concepts addressed, and methodologies used. It is noteworthy however, that only communication and social science journals demonstrated significant differences in the methodologies used in published crisis communication research.

In social science and humanities journals, we are significantly more likely ($F(5, 553) = 2.59$, $p = 0.03$; $\eta^2_p = 0.02$) to see articles using rhetorical methods ($M = 1.81$) compared to qualitative ($M = 1.48$) or conceptual[1] approaches ($M = 1.51$) and also experimental methods ($M = 1.75$) compared to conceptual ($M = 1.51$) approaches (see Table 45.1).

In communication journals, there was also significant two-way interaction (see Figure 45.5) between article type and research method. Qualitative research methods were meaningfully incorporated into both theory-building pieces as well as cross-section research design; however, they were seldom used in applied or case-study designs. Quantitative and experimental research methods were incorporated relatively evenly across theoretical, applied, and case study, and cross-sectional designs. Rhetorical research methods were seldom used in theory-building but were used often in both applied or case study designs as well as cross-sectional research. Finally, mixed methods were only meaningfully incorporated into applied or case study designs and not into cross-sectional research.

Because there were no method differences for article types appearing in medicine and health; science, engineering, and technology; or management journals, this would seem to reflect a methodological bias – whether conscious or not – in communication ($F (8, 671) = 2.69$, $p = 0.01$; $\eta^2_p = 0.03$) as well as general social sciences and humanities journals. In communication journals, while rhetorical methods ($M = 1.69$), quantitative ($M = 1.60$), and quantitative experimental ($M = 1.73$) are preferred compared to mixed methods ($M = 1.29$), conceptual ($M = 1.36$), and qualitative articles ($M = 1.45$) Scheffe post hoc tests found two homogeneous subsets, with the most preferred methods separated from the least preferred. Given these methodological biases do not emerge in the other three fields analyzed, it suggests that traditionally scholars trying to publish in our fields were either less likely to conduct qualitative, mixed-method, or conceptually grounded research *or* they found it more difficult to be published in the field's journals. This is a meaningful limitation in the types of journals where risk and crisis communication research is often published, particularly compared to other disciplines. This is also a meaningful limitation in the development of risk and crisis-specific theory and practice. Therefore, if communication scholars find it difficult to publish qualitative or mixed-methods research in our journals ***and*** we have preeminent scholars in the discipline arguing that the discipline should favor quantitative and experimental methods simply because

[1] In this case, "conceptual" papers refer to any non-data driven work published. This can include theory or best practices peer-reviewed articles.

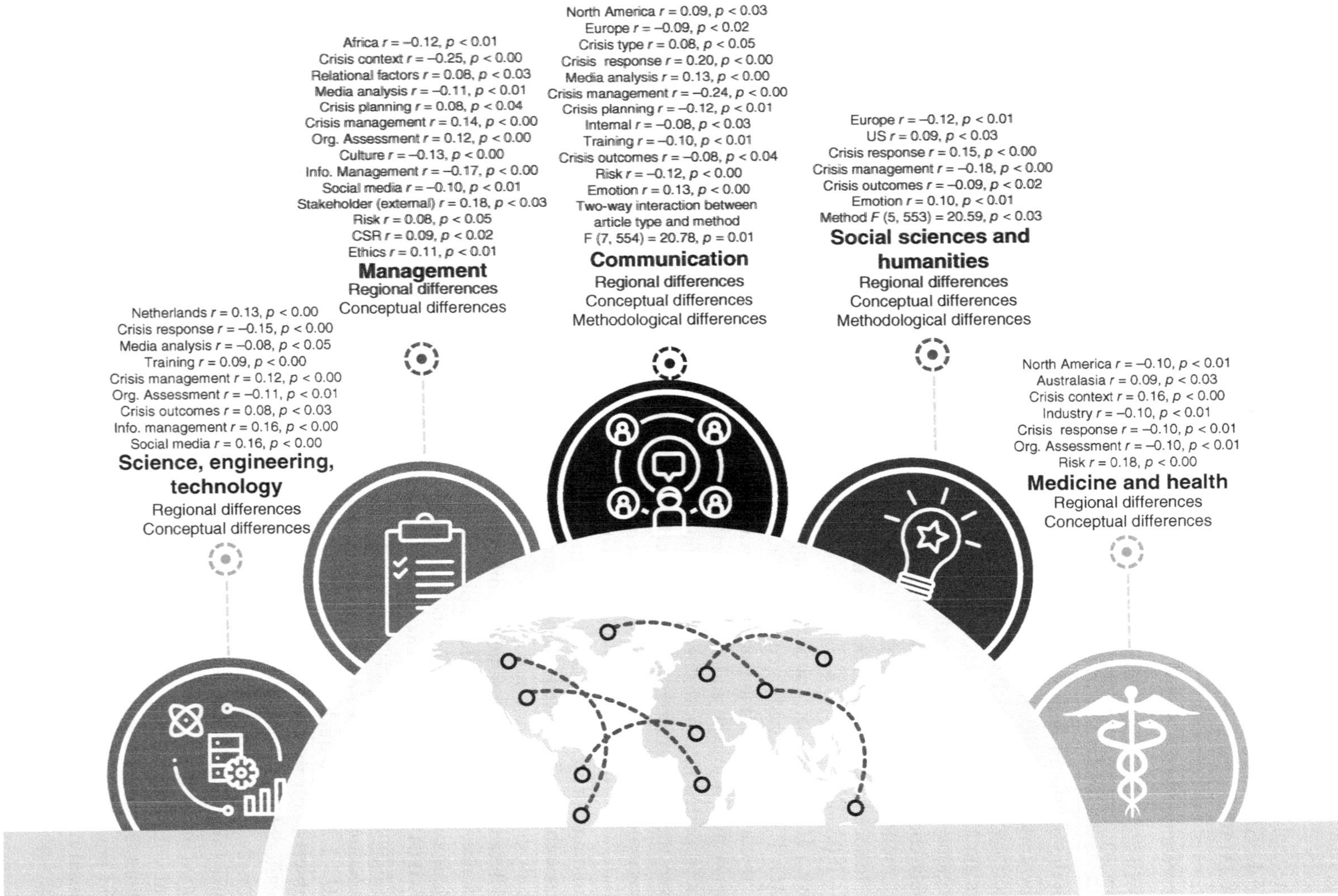

Figure 45.4 Cross-disciplinary risk and crisis communication research 1953–2015.

Table 45.1 Significant post hoc results for differences in research method for crisis articles published in social sciences and humanities journals.

Post hoc I	*Post hoc J*	*I-J*	*Sig.*
Rhetorical	Qualitative	0.33	0.00
	Conceptual/best practices	0.30	0.00
Experimental (quantitative)	Conceptual/best practices	0.24	0.00

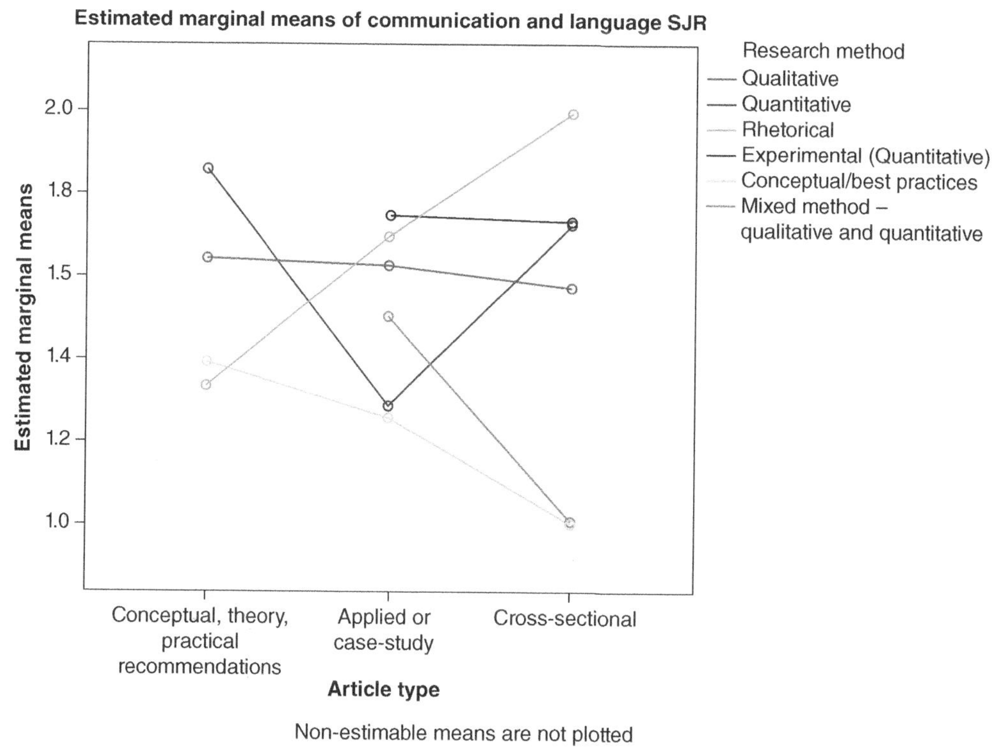

Figure 45.5 Significant two-way interaction between article type and method.

they believe that business-related disciplines do so, then it would seem that traditional communication journals are failing to support adequate theoretical and conceptual development in risk and crisis communication.

Current Needs for Improving Research Design in Risk and Crisis Communication

From both epistemological and evidence-based research design perspectives, while risk and crisis communication demonstrates a rich history and trajectory for theoretical, conceptual, and methodological development as an interdisciplinary subject, there is yet work to do to improve the quality and variety of research in the field. There are two areas for development that reflect both the field's development and current methodological concerns in risk and crisis communication: (1) ensuring diverse voices and perspectives are represented and (2) aligning theory and research design to avoid tendencies to be too descriptive and not analytical or predictive enough.

Supporting Diverse Voices in Risk and Crisis Communication Research

There have been consistent arguments and research demonstrating that risk and crisis communication research should represent more diverse voices during crises because it is often too Western or US-centric, business-centric, and/or simply lacks diverse perspectives (Diers-Lawson, 2017; Goby & Nickerson, 2015; Lachlan et al., 2014a; Schwarz & Fritsch, 2014; Sellnow-Richmond et al., 2018; Zhao, 2021, Zhao, 2014). There are some methodological and research design considerations to address some of these issues, and there are several ways to improve the diversity of voices represented.

First, ***develop teams of researchers reflecting different disciplines, nationalities, and perspectives.*** There are many examples of this that include large funded projects like the DECIPHER grant developed by a team of researchers at Technische Universität Ilmenau that includes scholars from across Germany, Italy, the Netherlands, Spain, Sweden, the UK, and the US with the aim of better understanding the communication strategies, structures, and outcomes of governmental risk and crisis communication (Technische Universität Ilmenau, 2022). However, there are also non-funded or small-grant-funded collaborative projects like the one that Professor Stephen Croucher put together exploring issues connected to COVID-19 and blame. Using a standardized questionnaire, colleagues from 22 countries collected data that are producing important cross-cultural comparisons between countries (Croucher et al., 2023a; Croucher et al., 2023b).

Second, ***develop research in diverse national contexts.*** For the most part, we tend to produce research from national contexts with which we are familiar, which makes intuitive sense. While the methodological problems of equivalence and bias have been widely addressed in the literature over time (Hanitzsch & Esser, 2012) and the field of risk and crisis communication has improved in its efforts to internationalize, it remains a valid critique of the field (Diers-Lawson & Meissner, 2021). Given the number of risk and crisis communication scholars from the US and Northern Europe, there still remains a US and Northern Europe (or more broadly a "Western") bias in risk and crisis communication research (Diers-Lawson, 2017; Zhao, 2014). Of course, one way to address this is to diversify our research teams – both in terms of seeking more international collaborations and being more conscious of inclusiveness in terms of communities represented on our research teams. Another way is to consider part of the development of methodological skills to include the development of cultural knowledge so that researchers have the efficacy to research outside their own national contexts. A third option is to seek out opportunities for collaborations with nongovernmental or intergovernmental organizations. For example, in the last couple of years, I have attended regional WHO workshops in the Western Balkans and Central Asia and worked on developing collaborative relationships with people from other national and cultural perspectives to support internationalizing my own research agenda. These connections have all emerged from attending international conferences. If we are to produce research that is diverse and we happen to come from "dominant" perspectives, then we must consider how we can address those limitations through collaboration and research development.

Third, ***within our own countries and communities, researchers should be seeking out unheard voices.*** In recent years, a clear narrative has emerged that in most any country, people from different backgrounds have had profoundly different crisis experiences (Ali & Ocha, 2018; Berg, 2022; Falkheimer & Heide, 2006; Willis et al., 2021) and have different views of government recommendations for self-protective behaviors (El-Far Cardo et al., 2021; Wagner et al., 2021; Wollebæk et al., 2022). For example, Black and Asian minorities in countries like the US and UK were slower to be vaccinated for COVID-19 because of problems of epistemic mistrust (Lindholt et al., 2021). Similarly, one of the challenges that has emerged in

Scandinavian countries is a de facto societal segregation for immigrants, which has resulted in demonstrably worse health outcomes for those immigrant populations (Mangrio & Strange, 2022). This is not a new lesson learned; we have known that minority communities are often the most susceptible to the worst effects of crises and disasters for decades (Cheng, 2013; Duhamel, 2013); however, research has also demonstrated that methodologies that explore age, sex, ethnicity, religion, and language can provide insights to improving risk and crisis communication (de Fatima Oliveira, 2013; Lachlan et al., 2014b). This has implications both in terms of research design and research partners. From a research design perspective, this is also likely to require more qualitative, rhetorical, and/or big data-based research projects to explore these unheard voices across platforms and crisis contexts. However, from a research partner perspective, there are several ways to improve diversity. For example, when possible, diversifying our research teams is a meaningful way to improve the representation of different community perspectives. However, that may not always be realistic. Therefore, risk and crisis communication scholars ought to be building relationships with members of different communities – as members of research consortia, as partners for projects – and generally embracing a public health perspective of "community engagement." The logical implication is that researchers build relationships with community actors over time, and in building those relationships, they gain access to diverse communities. This has emerged as a best practice for evidence-led decision-making in public health (WHO, 2022) and is certainly something that can be translated into scholarly research as well.

These recommendations for embracing diverse voices, projects, and approaches to risk and crisis communication also mean that antiquated assumptions about theoretical, epistemological, ontological, and methodological "value" within risk and crisis communication need to be left behind. Instead of aligning research to a particular set of assumptions about our preferred theories, research approaches, and methodologies, we should be aligning research to the problems that need to be tackled. From the data about the interdisciplinary development of risk and crisis communication, it is the communication journals that most need to broaden the methodological perspectives to be aligned with the other fields publishing research on risk and crisis communication.

Aligning Theory and Research Design

The analysis of the development of risk and crisis communication also demonstrates that approximately one-third of the research in the field is non-data driven. While this can be a challenge to ensure that published research is more than glorified "best practices" pieces, many of these non-data-driven pieces focus on theory development and the coordination of scholarship and practice in risk and crisis communication. However, what has emerged in the last few years with COVID-19 and the rapid publication of research on the topic is a trend in the opposite direction – too much data reported without theoretical grounding. There is an ongoing debate about the advantages and disadvantages of rapid publication of research related to the pandemic and especially media and big data studies devoid of theoretical grounding (King, 2020; Steinberg, 2020); therefore, critical evaluations of existing research are periodically needed. Yet, rapid increases in the rate of publication about risk and crisis communication are not new – we have experienced periods of significant growth before (Diers-Lawson, 2020). Therefore, there is already precedent in the field for evaluating the quality of the field's development (An & Cheng, 2010; Diers-Lawson, 2017; Ha & Boynton, 2014).

For example, there are many risk and crisis communication theories or models that provide insights regarding how people judge risk and/or adopt self-protective behaviors in public health contexts (e.g., Cho & Witte, 2005; Sellnow-Richmond et al., 2018). However, many studies published in the first year of the COVID-19 pandemic did not include sufficient conceptual grounding. This is a core weakness in research design emerging as a publication "norm" in risk and crisis communication. Instead, in publications, we should aim for a minimum standard of theory-based studies, meaning (1) reference to a main theory or conceptual grounding; (2) a demonstrable connection between the theory and research design; (3) reference to the extant body of related risk and crisis communication research; and (4) identification of implications for theory and/or practice. Yet, in the case of "big data" media studies, there are very few studies that meet these criteria (e.g., Hossain et al., 2022; Morissan et al., 2020; Ophir et al., 2021; Tejedor et al., 2020).

If research on risk and crisis communication fails to align theory and research design, while researchers might identify valuable "problems" or contexts of study, the research is unlikely to articulate clear contributions to theory or even transferrable knowledge, despite the clear connections in the findings to the extant body of risk and crisis research. The risks and crises that the world is confronting are complex because the modern global environment is seemingly more crisis prone than ever; they are fissures created by COVID-19, there are problems of cross-border political crises, and a challenging global business environment. Unfortunately, what seems to be emerging is a lot of descriptive research but little predictive research. While it is good for the field to have such a growth in interest from all sectors, we must also consider the field's development to ensure that epistemological questions, inclusion challenges, and their implications for aligned research design are also considered. This chapter has laid out a data-based argument for who we are as a field, what the methodological needs and challenges are, and ultimately has provided recommendations for ensuring the theoretical and conceptual growth of risk and crisis communication as an interdisciplinary field of research.

One of the exciting aspects of doing risk and crisis communication research is that we can contribute to protecting people and organizations. We can put a human face on the crises and disasters that our communities, regions, countries, and global community face. We also can influence practice, policy, and action. However, that is only possible if the research that we conduct addresses the diverse needs related to risk and crisis communication in action. This chapter has offered a formal analysis of the two emergent epistemological perspectives in risk and crisis communication and provided a data-based perspective on the valuable methodological diversity in the field so that it could identify arguments for a methodological research agenda for the field in the coming years to meet the field's needs.

References

Ali, J. A., & Ocha, W. (2018). East Africa refugee crisis: Causes of tensions and conflicts between the local community and refugees in Kakuma refugee camp, Kenya. *Journal of Social Science Studies*, *5*(1), 298–315.

Allan, S., & Peters, C. (2015). Visual truths of citizen reportage: Four research problematics. *Information, Communication & Society*, *18*(11), 1348–1361. https://doi.org/10.1080/1369118X.2015.1061576

An, S.-K., & Cheng, I.-H. (2010). Crisis communication research in public relations journals: Tracking research trends over thirty years. In W. T. Coombs, & S. J. Holladay, Eds., *The Handbook of Crisis Communication* (pp. 65–90). Wiley-Blackwell.

Arroyo, I., Montesino, N., Johansson, E., & Yahia, M. W. (2021). Social integration through social connection in everyday life. Residents' experiences during the COVID-19 pandemic in SällBo collaborative housing, Sweden. *Archnet-IJAR: International Journal of Architectural Research*, *15*(1), 79–97. https://doi.org/10.1108/ARCH-10-2020-0236

Bacchi, U. (2014). Ebola: French government orders air France to cancel flights to Sierra Leone. *International Business Times*. Retrieved April 14, 2015, from http://www.ibtimes.co.uk/ebola-french-government-orders-air-france-cancel-flights-sierra-leone-1462855

Benoit, W. L. (1995). Sears' repair of its auto service image: Image restoration discourse in the corporate sector. *Communication Studies*, *46*(1–2), 89–105.
Benoit, W. L. (1997). Image repair discourse and crisis communication. *Public Relations Review*, *23*(2), 177–187.
Benoit, W. L., & Brinson, S. L. (1999). Queen Elizabeth's image repair discourse: Insensitive royal or compassionate queen? *Public Relations Review*, *25*(2), 145–156.
Benoit, W. L., & Czerwinski, A. (1997). A critical analysis of USAir's image repair discourse. *Business Communication Quarterly*, *60*(3), 38–57.
Benoit, W. L., & Henson, J. R. (2009). President Bush's image repair discourse on Hurricane Katrina. *Public Relations Review*, *35*, 40–46.
Berg, M. (2022). Information-precarity for refugee women in Hamburg, Germany, during the COVID-19 pandemic. *Information, Communication & Society*, 1–17. https://doi.org/10.1080/1369118X.2022.2129271
Campbell, E. Q., & Pettigrew, T. F. (1959). Racial and moral crisis: The role of little rock ministers. *American Journal of Sociology*, 509–516.
Cheng, S. S. (2013). Crisis communication failure: A case study of typhoon Morakot. *Asian Social Science*, *9*(3), 18. https://doi.org/10.5539/ass.v9n3p18
Chesler, M., & Schmuck, R. (1964). Student reactions to the Cuban crisis and public dissent. *Public Opinion Quarterly*, 467–482.
Cho, H., & Witte, K. (2005). Managing fear in public health campaigns: A theory-based formative evaluation process. *Health Promotion Practice*, *6*(4), 482–490. https://doi.org/10.1177/1524839904263912
Claeys, A.-S., Cauberghe, V., & Leysen, J. (2013). Implications of stealing thunder for the impact of expressing emotions in organizational crisis communication. *Journal of Applied Communication Research*, *41*(3), 293–308.
Coombs, W. T. (2006). The protective powers of crisis response strategies: Managing reputational assets during a crisis. *Journal of Promotion Management*, *12*(3/4), 241–260. https://doi.org/10.1300/J057v12n03•13
Coombs, W. T. (2015). The value of communication during a crisis: Insights from strategic communication research. *Business Horizons*, *58*(2), 141–148. https://doi.org/10.1016/j.bushor.2014.10.003
Coombs, W. T. (2016). Methodological challenges of international crisis communication research. In A. Schwarz, M. W. Seeger, & C. Auer, Eds., *The Handbook of International Crisis Communication Research* (pp. 456–464). Wiley Blackwell.
Coombs, W. T., & Holladay, S. J. (1996). Communication and attributions in a crisis: An experimental study in crisis communication. *Journal of Public Relations Research*, *8*(4), 279–295.
Coombs, W. T., & Holladay, S. J. (2009). Further explorations of post-crisis communication: Effects of media and response strategies on perceptions and intentions. *Public Relations Review*, *35*(1), 1–6. https://doi.org/10.1016/j.pubrev.2008.09.011
Croucher, S. M., & Cronn-Mills, D. (2018). *Understanding Communication Research Methods: A Theoretical and Practical Approach*. Routledge.
Croucher, S. M., Cullinane, J., Murray, N., Rocker, K. T., & Nguyen, T. (2023a). Health communication and behaviors during the COVID-19 pandemic: A 22-nation exploration of mask wearing. In S. M. Croucher, & A. Diers-Lawson, Eds., *Pandemic Communication* (pp. 12–43). Routledge.
Croucher, S. M., Nguyen, T., Ding, G. G., Diers-Lawson, A., Spencer, A., Eskiçorapçı, N., Girardelli, D., Permyakova, T. M., Dutta, M. J., Turdubaeva, E., Ashwell, D., Bustamante, S., & Gomez, O. (2023b). Intergroup communication during the COVID-19 pandemic: A 20-nation analysis of prejudice. In S. M. Croucher, & A. Diers-Lawson, Eds., *Pandemic Communication* (pp. 174–197). Routledge.
Dahal, L., Idris, M. S., & Bravo, V. (2020). "It helped us, and it hurt us" The role of social media in shaping agency and action among youth in post-disaster Nepal. *Journal of Contingencies & Crisis Management*, *28*(4). online. https://doi.org/10.1111/1468-5973.12329
Diers-Lawson, A. (2017). A state of emergency in crisis communication an intercultural crisis communication research agenda. *Journal of Intercultural Communication Research*, *46*(1), 1–54.
Diers-Lawson, A. (2020). *Crisis Communication: Managing Stakeholder Relationships*. Routledge.
Diers-Lawson, A. (2022). iScotland: Crises, the integrated model of activism and Twitter. In L. Austin, & Y. Jin, Eds., *Social Media and Crisis Communication* (Vol. 2, p. pp. 13).). Routledge.

Diers-Lawson, A. (2023). The new normal: Pandemic communication and sustainable organizations. In S. M. Croucher, & A. Diers-Lawson, Eds., *Pandemic Communication* (pp. 96–116). Routledge.

Diers-Lawson, A., & Meissner, F. (2021). Editor's essay: Moving beyond western corporate perspectives: On the need to increase the diversity of risk and crisis communication research. *Journal of International Crisis and Risk Communication Research*, *4*(1), 165–176. https://doi.org/10.30658/jicrcr.4.1.6

Diers-Lawson, A., & Meißner, F. (2022). Editorial essay: A reflection on methodological diversity in the journal of international crisis and risk communication research. *Journal of International Crisis and Risk Communication Research*, *5*(1), 1–8. https://doi.org/10.30658/jicrcr.5.1.0

Diers-Lawson, A., & Omondi, G. (2024). Ripples, waves, and riptides: Reconceptualizing wicked, novel, and ongoing crises as prolonged crises. In B. Liu, & A. Mehta, Eds., *Handbook for Risk, Crisis, and Disaster Communication* (pp. 179–196). Routledge. https://doi.org/https://doi.org/10.4324/9781003363330

DiFonzo, N., Bordia, P., & Rosnow, R. L. (1994). Reining in rumors. *Organizational Dynamics*, *23*(1), 47–62.

Duhamel, C. (2013). Using lessons from SARS in tackling swine flu: Looking inward to develop a crisis communication model. *Journal of Communication in Healthcare*, 395–410. https://doi.org/10.1179/cih.2009.2.4.395

Einwiller, S. A., Carroll, C. E., & Korn, K. (2010). Under what conditions do the news influence corporate reputation? The roles of media dependency and need for orientation. *Corporate Reputation Review*, *12*(4), 299–315.

El-Far Cardo, A., Kraus, T., & Kaifie, A. (2021). Factors that shape people's attitudes towards the COVID-19 pandemic in Germany – the influence of MEDIA, politics and personal characteristics. *International Journal of Environmental Research and Public Health*, *18*(15), 7772. https://doi.org/10.3390/ijerph18157772

Falkheimer, J. (2014). Crisis communication and terrorism: The Norway attacks on 22 July 2011. *Corporate Communications: An International Journal*, *19*(1), 52–63. https://doi.org/10.1108/CCIJ-08-2012-0053

Falkheimer, J., & Heide, M. (2006). Multicultural crisis communication: Toward a social constructionist perspective. *Journal of Contingencies & Crisis Management*, *14*(4), 180–189.

de Fatima Oliveira, M. (2013). Multicultural environments and their challenges to crisis communication. *Journal of Business Communication*, 0021943613487070. https://doi.org/10.1177/0021943613487070

Førde, J. S., Lægreid, P., Rubecksen, K., & Rykkja, L. H. (2019). Organizing for societal security and crisis management in Germany, the Netherlands, Norway, Sweden and the UK. In P. Laegreid, & L. H. Rykkja, Eds., *Societal Security and Crisis Management* (pp. 27–51). Springer.

Goby, V. P., & Nickerson, C. (2015). The impact of culture on the construal of organizational crisis: Perceptions of crisis in Dubai. *Corporate Communications: An International Journal*, *20*(3), 310–325.

Granville, F., Mehta, A., & Pike, S. (2016). Destinations, disasters and public relations: Stakeholder engagement in multi-phase disaster management. *Journal of Hospitality and Tourism Management*, *28*, 73–79. https://doi.org/10.1016/j.jhtm.2016.02.001

Ha, J. H., & Boynton, L. (2014). Has crisis communication been studied using an interdisciplinary approach? A 20-year content analysis of communication journals. *International Journal of Strategic Communication*, *8*(1), 29–44. https://doi.org/10.1080/1553118X.2013.850694

Hajibaba, H., Gretzel, U., Leisch, F., & Dolnicar, S. (2015). Crisis-resistant tourists. *Annals of Tourism Research*, *53*, 46–60. https://doi.org/10.1016/j.annals.2015.04.001

Hanitzsch, T., & Esser, F. (2012). Challenges and perspectives of comparative communication inquiry. In F. Esser, & T. Hanitzsch, Eds., *The Handbook of Comparative Communication Research* (pp. 501–516). Routledge.

Hossain, A., Wahab, J. A., & Khan, M. S. R. (2022). A computer-based text analysis of Al Jazeera, BBC, and CNN news shares on Facebook: Framing analysis on Covid-19 issues. *SAGE Open*, *12*(1), 215824402110684. https://doi.org/10.1177/21582440211068497

Hunt, S., & Eburn, M. (2018). How can business share responsibility for disaster resilience? *Australian Journal of Public Administration*, *77*(3), 482–491. https://doi.org/10.1111/1467-8500.12320

Hyvärinen, J., & Vos, M. (2015). Developing a conceptual framework for investigating communication supporting community resilience. *Societies, 5*(3), 583–597. https://doi.org/10.3390/soc5030583

Jin, Y., & Pang, A. (2010). Future directions of crisis communication research: Emotions in crisis–The next frontier. In W. T. Coombs, & S. J. Holladay, Eds., *Handbook of Crisis Communication* (pp. 677–682). Wiley.

Jin, Y., Park, S.-A., & Len-Ríos, M. E. (2010). Strategic communication of hope and anger: A case of Duke University's conflict management with multiple publics. *Public Relations Review, 36*(1), 63–65.

Kim, Y. (2020). Organizational resilience and employee work-role performance after a crisis situation: Exploring the effects of organizational resilience on internal crisis communication. *Journal of Public Relations Research, 32*(1–2), 47–75. https://doi.org/10.1080/1062726X.2020.1765368

Kim, S., & Atkinson, L. J. (2014). Responses toward corporate crisis and corporate advertising. *Journal of Promotion Management, 20*(5), 647–665. https://doi.org/10.1080/10496491.2014.946201

Kim, S.-Y., Choi, M.-I., Reber, B. H., & Kim, D. (2014). Tracking public relations scholarship trends: Using semantic network analysis on PR Journals from 1975 to 2011. *Public Relations Review, 40*(1), 116–118. https://doi.org/10.1016/j.pubrev.2013.11.017

King, A. (2020). Fast news or fake news? The advantages and the pitfalls of rapid publication through pre-print servers during a pandemic. *EMBO Reports, 21*(6), e50817. https://doi.org/10.15252/embr.202050817

Lachlan, K. A., Spence, P. R., & Eith, C. A. (2014a). Risk, crisis, and emergency communication in developing countries: Identifying the needs of urban populations. In C. C. Okigbo, Ed., *Strategic Urban Health Communication* (pp. 65–76). Springer.

Lachlan, K. A., Spence, P. R., & Lin, X. (2014b). Expressions of risk awareness and concern through Twitter: On the utility of using the medium as an indication of audience needs. *Computers in Human Behavior, 35*, 554–559. https://doi.org/10.1016/j.chb.2014.02.029

Lindholt, M. F., Jørgensen, F., Bor, A., & Petersen, M. B. (2021). Public acceptance of COVID-19 vaccines: Cross-national evidence on levels and individual-level predictors using observational data. *BMJ Open, 11*(6), e048172. https://doi.org/10.1136/bmjopen-2020-048172

Liu, B. F., Fraustino, J. D., & Jin, Y. (2015). Social media use during disasters: How information form and source influence intended behavioral responses. *Communication Research, 43*(5), 626–646. https://doi.org/10.1177/0093650214565917

Mangrio, E., & Strange, M. (2022). Segregation within welfare societies–communication barriers to migrants' healthcare in Scandinavia. In D. K. D. Kim, & G. L. Kreps, Eds., *Global Health Communication for Immigrants and Refugees* (pp. 112–125). Routledge. https://doi.org/10.4324/9781003230243

Marcus, A. A., & Goodman, R. S. (1991). Victims and shareholders: The dilemmas of presenting corporate policy during a crisis. *Academy of Management Journal, 34*(2), 281–305.

Mazzei, A., Kim, J.-N., & Dell'Oro, C. (2012). Strategic value of employee relationships and communicative actions: Overcoming corporate crisis with quality internal communication. *International Journal of Strategic Communication, 6*(1), 31–44. https://doi.org/10.1080/1553118X.2011.634869

Meißner, F., & Diers-Lawson, A. (2022). Editorial essay: Innovation in risk and crisis communication: Towards new topics, theories, and methods. *Journal of International Crisis and Risk Communication Research, 5*(2), 1–10. https://doi.org/10.30658/jicrc.5.2.1

Menon, K., & Goh, K. T. (2005). Transparency and trust: Risk communications and the Singapore experience in managing SARS. *Journal of Communication Management.* https://doi.org/10.1108/13632540510621614

Mochizuki, J., Keating, A., Liu, W., Hochrainer-Stigler, S., & Mechler, R. (2018). An overdue alignment of risk and resilience? A conceptual contribution to community resilience. *Disasters, 42*(2), 361–391. https://doi.org/10.1111/disa.12239

Morissan, W. J. A., Siang, T. G., & Cahyowati, T. D. (2020). Media Framing on Covid-19 Pandemic in Malaysian and Indonesian Newspapers. *International Journal of Academic Research in Business and Social Sciences, 10*(10). https://doi.org/10.6007/IJARBSS/v10-i10/8016

Ophir, Y., Walter, D., Arnon, D., Lokmanoglu, A., Tizzoni, M., Carota, J., D'Antiga, L., Nicastro, E., & DAntiga, L. (2021). The framing of COVID-19 in Italian media and its relationship with community mobility: A mixed-method approach. *Journal of Health Communication, 26*(3), 1–13. https://doi.org/10.1080/10810730.2021.1899344

Pearson, C. M., & Clair, J. A. (1998). Reframing crisis management. *Academy of Management Review*, *23*(1), 58–76.

Petridou, E., Danielsson, E., Olofsson, A., Lundgren, M., & Große, C. (2019). If crisis or war comes: A study of risk communication of eight European union member states. *Journal of International Crisis and Risk Communication Research*, *2*(2), 3. https://doi.org/10.30658/jicrcr.2.2.3

Ravazzani, S. (2016). Exploring internal crisis communication in multicultural environments. *Corporate Communications: An International Journal*, *21*(1), 73–88. https://doi.org/10.1108/CCIJ-02-2015-0011

Reeves, M., Carlsson-Szlezak, P., Whitaker, K., & Abraham, M. (2020). Sensing and shaping the post-COVID era. *T. B. H. Institute*. https://web-assets.bcg.com/img-src/BCG-Sensing-and-Shaping-the-Post-COVID-Era-Apr-2020-rev_tcm9-244426.pdf (accessed September 17, 2020).

Rela, I. Z., Awang, A. H., Ramli, Z., Sum, S. M., & Meisanti, M. (2020). Effects of environmental corporate social responsibility on environmental well-being perception and the mediation role of community resilience. *Journal of Contingencies & Crisis Management*, *28*(2). https://doi.org/10.1002/csr.1956

Rhee, H. T., & Yang, S.-B. (2014). Consumers' emotional reactions to negative publicity and crisis management in the health care industry a multiple case study of lipitor and oxyelite pro. *Social Science Computer Review*, *32*(5), 678–693. https://doi.org/10.1177/0894439314525901

Rowsell, B., Norris, P., Ryan, K., & Weenink, M. (2000). Assessing and managing risk and uncertainty: Women living with breast implants. *Health, Risk & Society*, *2*(2), 205–218.

Schwarz, A., & Fritsch, A. (2014). Communicating on Behalf of Global Civil Society: Management and Coordination of Public Relations in International Nongovernmental Organizations. *Journal of Public Relations Research*, *26*(2), 161–183. https://doi.org/http://dx.doi.org/10.1080/1062726X.2013.864242

Schwarz, A., & Pforr, F. (2011). The crisis communication preparedness of nonprofit organizations: The case of German interest groups. *Public Relations Review*, *37*(1), 68–70. https://doi.org/10.1016/j.pubrev.2010.10.002

Seeger, M., & Ulmer, R. R. (2002). A post-crisis discourse of renewal: The cases of Malden Mills and Cole Hardwoods. *Journal of Applied Communication Research*, *30*(2), 126–142.

Sellnow, T. L., & Brand, J. D. (2001). Establishing the structure of reality for an industry: Model and anti-model arguments as advocacy in Nike's crisis communication. *Journal of Applied Communication Research*, *29*(3), 278–296.

Sellnow, T. L., & Seeger, M. (2001). Exploring the boundaries of crisis communication: The case of the 1997 Red River Valley flood. *Communication Studies*, *52*(2), 153–168.

Sellnow-Richmond, D., George, A., & Sellnow, D. (2018). An IDEA model analysis of instructional risk communication in the time of Ebola. *Journal of International Crisis and Risk Communication Research*, *1*(1), 135–166. https://doi.org/10.30658/jicrcr.1.1.7

Shim, K., Cho, H., Kim, S., & Yeo, S. L. (2018). Impact of moral ethics on consumers' boycott intentions: A cross-cultural study of crisis perceptions and responses in the United States, South Korea, and Singapore. *Communication Research*, 1–25. https://doi.org/10.1177/0093650218793565

Spence, P. R., Lachlan, K. A., Westerman, D., & Spates, S. A. (2013). Where the gates matter less: Ethnicity and perceived source credibility in social media health messages. *Howard Journal of Communications*, *24*(1), 1–16.

Steinberg, I. (2020). Coronavirus research done too fast is testing publishing safeguards, bad science is getting through. *The Conversation*, *9*, 2020. Available at: https://www.researchgate.net/profile/Irving-Steinberg/publication/341089534_Coronavirus_research_done_too_fast_is_testing_publishing_safeguards_bad_science_is_getting_through/links/5eac631092851cb2676cdc31/Coronavirus-research-done-too-fast-is-testing-publishing-safeguards-bad-science-is-getting-through.pdf

Tao, W., & Song, B. (2020). The interplay between post-crisis response strategy and pre-crisis corporate associations in the context of CSR crises. *Public Relations Review*, *46*(2), 101883. https://doi.org/10.1016/j.pubrev.2020.101883

Technische Universität Ilmenau (2022). *DECIPHER at a Glance*. Ilmenau Technical University. Retrieved 11 January, 2023 from https://www.tu-ilmenau.de/en/universitaet/fakultaeten/

fakultaet-wirtschaftswissenschaften-und-medien/profil/institute-und-fachgebiete/institut-fuer-medien-und-kommunikationswissenschaft/forschung/decipher/at-a-glance

Tejedor, S., Cervi, L., Tusa, F., Portales, M., & Zabotina, M. (2020). Information on the COVID-19 pandemic in daily newspapers' front pages: Case study of Spain and Italy. *International Journal of Environmental Research and Public Health*, *17*(17). https://doi.org/10.3390/ijerph17176330

Vogler, D., & Meissner, F. (2020). How users tweet about a cyber attack: An explorative study using machine learning and social network analysis. *Journal of Digital Media & Policy*, *11*(2), 195–214. https://doi.org/10.1386/jdmp_00016_1

Volk, S. C. (2016). A systematic review of 40 years of public relations evaluation and measurement research: Looking into the past, the present, and future. *Public Relations Review*, *42*(5), 962–977. https://doi.org/10.1016/j.pubrev.2016.07.003

Wagner, A. L., Shotwell, A. R., Boulton, M. L., Carlson, B. F., & Mathew, J. L. (2021). Demographics of vaccine hesitancy in Chandigarh, India. *Frontiers in Medicine*, *1062*. https://doi.org/10.3389/fmed.2020.585579

WHO (2022). *Risk communication and community engagement*. https://www.who.int/europe/publications/i/item/WHO-EURO-2022-6186-45951-66353 (accessed January 9, 2023).

Willems, J. (2016). Organizational crisis resistance: Examining leadership mental models of necessary practices to resist crises and the role of organizational context. *VOLUNTAS: International Journal of Voluntary and Nonprofit Organizations*, *27*(6), 2807–2832. https://doi.org/10.1007/s11266-016-9753-9

Willis, D. E., Andersen, J. A., Bryant-Moore, K., Selig, J. P., Long, C. R., Felix, H. C., Curran, G. M., & McElfish, P. A. (2021). COVID-19 vaccine hesitancy: Race/ethnicity, trust, and fear. *Clinical and Translational Science*, *14*(6), 2200–2207. https://doi.org/10.1111/cts.13077

Wollebæk, D., Fladmoe, A., Steen-Johnsen, K., & Ihlen, Ø. (2022). Right-wing ideological constraint and vaccine refusal: The case of the COVID-19 vaccine in Norway. *Scandinavian Political Studies*, 1–26. https://doi.org/10.1111/1467-9477.12224

Wukich, C., & Mergel, I. (2015). Closing the Citizen-Government communication gap: Content, audience, and network analysis of government tweets. *Journal of Homeland Security and Emergency Management*, *12*(3), 707–735.

Xu, K., & Li, W. (2013). An ethical stakeholder approach to crisis communication: A case study of Foxconn's 2010 employee suicide crisis. *Journal of Business Ethics*, *117*(2), 371–386. https://doi.org/10.1007/s10551-012-1522-0

Zhao, Y. (2014). Communication, crisis, & global power shifts: An introduction. *International Journal of Communication*, *8*, 26.

Zhao, H. (2021). Beyond culture: Advancing the understanding of political and technological contexts in crisis communication. *International Communication Gazette*, *83*(5), 517–537. https://doi.org/10.1177/1748048521 1029066

Žilinskas, R., & Sakalauskas, L. (2021). Exploring crisis governance: Quest for functional resilience during COVID-19 in Lithuania. *Scientific Journal of the Military University of Land Forces*, *53*(4), 763–798.

Author Bio

Audra Diers-Lawson (PhD, 2006 University of Texas-Austin) is a Professor of Risk and Crisis Communication and Head of the PhD in Communication and Leadership at Kristiania University of Applied Sciences in Oslo, Norway. With more than 35 scientific publications in the last five to six years alone, serving on editorial boards or as a reviewer for more than 20 journals, and serving as a section Vice-Chair and Chair for the Crisis Communication Division of the ECREA and serving as an inaugural Executive Committee member and Secretary/Treasurer from the International Crisis and Risk Communication Association, Diers-Lawson is a leader in the field of risk and crisis communication. Her research focuses on the connections between risk, crisis, stakeholders, and organizations. Diers-Lawson's monograph, *Crisis Communication: Managing Stakeholder Relationships* (2020) brought together more than 50 years of research on risk and crisis communication to identify important common themes, evaluate theory and practice, and articulate a comprehensive argument for adopting a stakeholder perspective in risk and crisis communication. Finally, she translates her research for practice with collaborations and applied research projects with organizations like the EU, World Health Organization, and Asia-Europe Foundation. Diers-Lawson also serves as the Head of the WHO-Europe Collaboration Centre for Risk Communication, Community Engagement, and Infodemic Management at Kristiania University of Applied Sciences.

46

Opportunities and Pitfalls of Computational Communication Science for International Risk and Crisis Communication Research

Daniel Vogler
Research Center for the Public Sphere and Society (fög), University of Zurich, Zurich, Switzerland

Crisis communication scholars increasingly highlight the international dimension of risk and crises (Schwarz et al., 2016; Ulmer & Pyle, 2016). In the digital media environment, risks and crises are, by default, international in scope. Communication on digital channels like social media platforms enables crises to quickly spread internationally (Valentini & Kruckeberg, 2016). Thus, many risks and crises are potentially global and can only be understood in a comprehensive manner when including their international dimension (Diers-Lawson & Meissner, 2021; Schwarz et al., 2016).

However, the study of risk and crises often remains restricted to regional or national contexts. Research in risk and crisis communication has only slowly started "reflecting the global environment and diverse crisis and risk contexts" (Diers-Lawson & Meissner, 2021, p. 165) and taking into account "emerging issues that are global in their manifestation and treatment, including environmental threats (e.g., global warming), the globalization of human rights and social justice, as well as global security, as it is linked to international arms trade, war, and terrorism" (Schwarz et al., 2016, p. 1). Even though advances in the direction of more diverse scholarship have been made in recent years (Schwarz et al., 2023), the focus of scholarship remains on Western countries. In contrast, studies of countries from the Global South or other regions, including but not limited to Latin America, Africa, Southeast Asia, and Eastern Europe, remain scarce. These shortcomings have already been articulated by communication scholars in general (e.g., Cruz & Sodeke, 2021) as well as by risk and crisis communication scholars in particular (Diers-Lawson & Meissner, 2021; Schwarz et al., 2016).

Computational communication science (CCS) is a relatively new discipline within communication science and offers the possibility to overcome these limitations and biases. At the same time, it is also susceptible to reproducing them. Even though the COVID-19 pandemic has undoubtedly boosted the quantity of CCS studies on risk and crisis communication, the field has not yet fully embraced these new methods. Thus, many recent studies on crisis communication that use computational methods do not apply theories and concepts from risk and crisis communication and mainly stem from other subdisciplines of communication, for instance,

The Handbook of International Crisis and Risk Communication Research, Second Edition.
Edited by Andreas Schwarz, Matthew W. Seeger, and Sora Kim.

journalism, health communication, and political communication. However, not considering (international) risk and crisis communication often leads to missing analytical depth or insufficient theoretical foundation. Thus, if we want to implement CCS into international risk and crisis communication research beneficially, we need to be more aware of the opportunities, challenges, and pitfalls of its methods and procedures.

In this chapter, I will provide central definitions, give an overview of the state of research of CCS in the field of risk and crisis communication, and discuss the opportunities, challenges, and pitfalls of computational methods. Even though the chapter focuses on international risk and crisis communication research, it also touches on the general implications of computational methods for communication research that are necessary for a thorough understanding of the matter. The chapter concludes with suggestions on how to address the limitations and leverage the opportunities of CCS in international risk and crisis communication research.

Definition of Terms and Scope

CCS, as a subfield of computational social sciences, is used as an umbrella term for computer-assisted methods to collect, analyze, and present data for studying communication processes in a broad sense (Lazer et al., 2020; van Atteveldt & Peng, 2018). Theocharis and Jungherr (2021, p. 4) define CCS "as an interdisciplinary scientific field in which contributions develop and test theories or provide systematic descriptions of human, organizational, and institutional behavior through the use of computational methods and practices." CCS relies on the application of so-called computational methods (Domahidi et al., 2019; van der Meer & Kroon, 2022), a term that is frequently used as a synonym for CCS in the field of communication.

Looking at CCS, one of the most evident trends is the increasing use of natural language processing (NLP) approaches for automated content analysis (Boumans & Trilling, 2016; Schäfer & Hase, 2023). NLP consists of techniques "aimed at automatically analyzing and comprehending human language" (Kang et al., 2020, p. 139). Thus, the term NLP is not limited to a specific method but includes different computational approaches to analyzing and making sense of human language, usually in the form of written text like newspaper articles or social media posts (Boumans & Trilling, 2016). Typical methods in the realm of NLP are sentiment analysis (Öztürk & Ayvaz, 2018), different variations of topic models like LDA or structural topic models (Jacobi et al., 2016), automated analysis of geospatial data with geo-parsing, detection of entities with named entity recognition (NER), and text classification algorithms (Boumans & Trilling, 2016). These techniques rely on different computational approaches, like supervised and unsupervised machine learning, or so-called dictionaries (for an overview of the field of crisis communication, see van der Meer & Kroon, 2022; Vogler & Meissner, 2022).

Communication researchers have also increasingly started to integrate methodological concepts from the natural sciences. A frequently used method is (social) network analysis (van Atteveldt & Peng, 2018) for analyzing relations between individuals or organizations (e.g., Rauchfleisch et al., 2021) and semantic network structures within or between documents (e.g., van der Meer et al., 2014). With the emergence of social media, large numbers of social interactions are recorded and available to researchers, boosting the application of social network analysis in the field of communication. Another method with roots in the natural sciences that has been used in communication research is agent-based modeling (for an overview, see Waldherr et al., 2021). Agent-based modeling is based on a computer model for simulating the behavior of a population of agents, for instance, individuals or organizations, which may be exposed to different conditions in a given environment (Waldherr & Wettstein, 2019).

Following the rise of generative artificial intelligence (AI), so-called large language models (LLMs) are starting to be used for research. LLMs have significant potential for communication research, as they can be used for machine translation of text for subsequent analysis with NLP techniques and for data collection, especially for coding or annotation of data. Initial explorative studies with LLMs to analyze communication processes have already been conducted (e.g., Gilardi et al., 2023). However, the risks of applying LLMs to the research process, including the lack of transparency, low validity, or even generation of false data, are a frequent topic of discussion (Reiss, 2023).

The Present: Primary Issues, Topics, and Areas of Work

Even though CCS, or at least its broad application, was introduced to communication research mainly throughout the last decade (Lazer et al., 2020), computational approaches have previously been widely used. This is also the case for risk and crisis communication research. Widespread computer-based applications include basic techniques, like surveys via websites instead of pen and paper or telephone, digital databases and archives, and software to annotate text (for an overview, see Mahrt & Scharkow, 2013), which we take for granted as researchers nowadays. Basic data collection, analysis, and presentation have been digitalized since the advent of personal computers in the late 1970s, with tools like R Studio, SPSS, Stata, and not least Microsoft Excel becoming a standard in most research labs. Also, more sophisticated approaches, like computer-assisted cluster analysis with survey data (e.g., Coombs & Holladay, 2005), belong to the basic methodological toolkit of most communication researchers. In addition to the continuous digitalization of research, more elaborate computational methods were also adopted early on by crisis communication researchers. For instance, the seminal study on the concept of stealing thunder by Arpan and Pompper (2003) applied semantic network analysis to measure frames in news media articles.

CCS, as defined by Theocharis and Jungherr (2021), includes the study of risk and crisis communication and related behavior through computational methods and practices. At the moment, the focus in the CCS literature lies on crisis rather than risk communication. Crises indeed are events that produce large amounts of data, which are well suited to analysis by computational methods.

Even though computational approaches are used to simulate and model risks (Burger et al., 2019; Zechman, 2011) and disaster responses (Lewis et al., 2013) using methods like agent-based modeling to detect risks (for instance, wildfires) based on extensive data (Larsen et al., 2021), there is almost no work that is actually related to risk *communication*. A noteworthy exception is the study by Reinhold et al. (2023), which used NLP techniques in combination with qualitative approaches for risk message testing. In addition, there is a growing body of literature on news coverage of risk and technology that focuses on technologies like AI (Sun et al., 2020) and nanotechnology (Dudo et al., 2011), which uses computational approaches, such as topic models or dictionaries for topic identification.

Most CCS studies in crisis communication investigate public debates about crises for which data is actually available – typically news media articles or social media posts and, to a lesser degree, communicator data like press releases. Recent societal crises, such as the COVID-19 pandemic, the refugee crisis, and the climate crisis, have stimulated extensive research on crisis communication. These global crises have led to a plethora of studies in a diverse range of countries (Schwarz et al., 2023), some international comparative studies (Mellado et al., 2021; Vu & Lynn, 2020), and investigations in multilingual countries like Switzerland (Rauchfleisch et al., 2021). However, the research often stems from fields like journalism or political communication and rarely works with theories and concepts of risk and crisis communication (Schwarz et al., 2023) and is grounded in more general concepts like framing or (news) diversity (e.g., Mellado et al., 2021; Pakvis & Hendrickx, 2023; Vu & Lynn, 2020).

CCS in Crisis Communication Research

CCS methods are used at all stages of the empirical research process in crisis communication, but especially for the retrieval, collection, and analysis of large datasets. CCS methods used for data retrieval include web scraping (e.g., Rauchfleisch et al., 2023), queries to established data providers like Factiva or LexisNexis (e.g., Gerken & van der Meer, 2019), and digital trace data collection from social media platforms or mobile phones (e.g., Crawford & Finn, 2015). Data from social media platforms is usually accessed through application programming interfaces (API). Similar to communication research in general, studies in crisis communication mostly use Twitter data (e.g., Jin, 2020; Vogler & Meissner, 2020). While the emphasis on Twitter may be a general limitation, its free API (until 2023) has enabled scholars from the Global South to do research with big data, often focused on the area and language of their region. There is a notable stream of research on crisis communication in countries like Iran (Mohammad Ali Kermani et al., 2022), Turkey (Öztürk & Ayvaz, 2018), and India (Kaur et al., 2021) using Twitter data gathered through its API. However, access to data from most larger social media platforms (e.g., Facebook, Instagram, Twitter, TikTok, YouTube) and messenger apps (e.g., WhatsApp or Telegram) is increasingly being restricted or completely denied by the platforms, so that it is unavailable, only partially available, or exclusively provided to selected teams of researchers (Walker et al., 2019). The availability of reliable and diverse data is, thus, seen as a major challenge for leveraging the potential of CSS in the future (Lazer et al., 2020).

For data analysis, most CCS studies on crisis communication rely on methods from the field of NLP, meaning automated content analysis in various forms and to different kinds of data (Vogler & Meissner, 2022). A typical case is the analysis of media coverage of crises like the COVID-19 pandemic (Mellado et al., 2021; Ort et al., 2023), the refugee crisis (Öztürk & Ayvaz, 2018; Vu & Lynn, 2020), the climate crisis (Chen et al., 2023; Rauchfleisch et al., 2023), and organizational crises (van der Meer et al., 2014; Vogler & Meissner, 2020). The methods are applied most frequently to news media and social media data, but they are also applied to texts such as press releases (Gerken & van der Meer, 2019). The studies use established NLP methods like topic models (Ort et al., 2023), framing analysis (Gerken & van der Meer, 2019; Pakvis & Hendrickx, 2023), and sentiment analysis (Kaur et al., 2021; Yantseva, 2020). However, they mostly focus on a single case (e.g., in organizational crises), a single country, or a single language, with a few notable exceptions, for instance, a study of sentiments in Turkish and English on the Syrian refugee crisis (Öztürk & Ayvaz, 2018).

Another common case in crisis communication research is studies that conduct social network analysis with social media data. In most cases, network analysis is used to investigate the relationship between the users of social media platforms. It typically analyzes disasters (Getchell & Sellnow, 2016; Hagen et al., 2018; Jin, 2020; Liu et al., 2018), terrorist attacks (Mirbabaie & Marx, 2020), public health crises, and pandemics (Kaur et al., 2021; Rauchfleisch et al., 2021; Wang et al., 2021), as well as organizational crises (Biddix et al., 2023; Vogler & Meissner, 2020). Again, these analyses are mostly based on Twitter data. Studies on other platforms like Facebook (Gerken et al., 2016; Kim & Hastak, 2018) are comparably rare, as data accessibility has become restricted over the last few years (Walker et al., 2019).

Furthermore, network analysis is also applied to texts to identify semantic networks (Gerken et al., 2016; Schultz et al., 2012). For instance, Gerken et al. (2016) used posts and comments on Air Asia's Facebook page to investigate if the framing of the company's online crisis communication following the crash of flight QZ8501 had been aligned with the public framing.

The Future: Opportunities, Challenges, Pitfalls

CCS offers a variety of tools for crisis communication research, in which researchers are often confronted with large datasets (van der Meer & Kroon, 2022; Vogler & Meissner, 2022). Automated procedures can help scale analyses and deliver results comparably quickly, which can be relevant for practitioners who need to react to crises quickly. Once properly validated, computational methods enable rapid and cost-effective scaling of research efforts (Trilling & Jonkman, 2018). Therefore, CCS is regarded as an opportunity to prevent, mitigate, and manage crises, for instance, by using big data (Larsen et al., 2021). Conducting swift analyses of news media and social media data can provide significant practical advantages for authorities and organizations in their efforts to implement immediate and effective crisis mitigation measures.

However, since the rollout of CCS methods, there has been a critical debate about their limitations and weaknesses. These discussions point out shortcomings such as missing analytical depth and related issues of validity (Muddiman et al., 2019; van Atteveldt & Peng, 2018), weak or missing theoretical foundations (Mahrt & Scharkow, 2013), a focus on isolated single-country cases (Theocharis & Jungherr, 2021), and insufficient ethical guidelines and considerations (Lazer et al., 2020; Shahin, 2016). Computational approaches can also reproduce existing biases and blind spots in research (Schäfer & Hase, 2023; van Atteveldt & Peng, 2018). The introduction of generative AI and LLMs might enforce biases in research as they are trained with data from the past; thus, results might mirror and reproduce existing biased structures in society (Grossmann et al., 2023).

Methodological challenges have been identified for data collection and analysis (Vogler & Meissner, 2022). From an international (comparative) stance, multilingual datasets pose a particularly challenging case. Conducting truly international risk and crisis communication research with CCS methods often means conducting analyses in more than one language when doing comparative studies or adapting existing procedures that were initially developed for English or Western languages like German or Spanish into other languages.

However, many computational methods are language-sensitive. They do not necessarily deliver valid results in a different language than the one they were initially developed for. For instance, Botometer, a widely used tool for detecting bots on Twitter, has been shown to deliver poor results when applied to non-English languages (Rauchfleisch & Kaiser, 2020). Therefore, the validation of computational approaches remains crucial, especially when using so-called off-the-shelf tools (Muddiman et al., 2019). The problem of adaptation is often circumvented by machine translations into English with services like Google Translate and DeepL, where the analysis is subsequently conducted in English. Such procedures have delivered valid results (Maier et al., 2022; Reber, 2019). The recent improvements in machine translation following the introduction of LLMs present even more promising avenues for researchers, as established procedures can now be readily applied to data from basically any language. However, concerns about the validity of such procedures have been raised by some researchers, as the nuances and structures of a language might get lost during the process of translation (Maier et al., 2022). Furthermore, applying a computational procedure in English instead of the original language might solve the validity issues. However, researchers will still need expertise in data interpretation and contextual knowledge. Understanding the background and peculiarities of analyzed cases or countries is a neglected and often underestimated aspect of CCS.

Recently, multilingual research methods have gained attention (Lind et al., 2019; Maier et al., 2022). This might be an especially promising path for international crisis communication research. Instead of translating all texts into one language, usually English, the procedures are designed to deliver valid and comparable results in several languages. An established procedure is the construction of multilingual dictionaries (Lind et al., 2019), which "operationalize categories of interest through a comprehensive list of indicative expressions in multiple languages" (Maier et al., 2022, p. 23). However, until now, few examples of multilingual studies based on computational methods exist in crisis communication. Even though multilingual analyses can be seen as a promising future path for risk and crisis communication research, challenges persist in various dimensions of the research process, for instance, the problem of data availability for specific platforms or regions, access to tools and training, and the need to develop and adapt procedures for specific non-Western languages.

Conclusion

This chapter gives an overview of the concepts, methods, and state of CCS research in the field of international risk and crisis communication. It shows that CCS offers new opportunities for the field but also comes with challenges and pitfalls. Thus, I conclude by outlining five areas that need to be addressed in the future for further advancing CCS in risk and crisis communication research: (1) an integrative and reflexive view on CCS; (2) the combination of CCS with theories from risk and crisis communication; (3) method triangulations of CCS with established quantitative and qualitative research methods of communication research; (4) accessibility to data, tools, and training; and (5) the development of multilingual CCS methods. These suggestions are not all specifically related to international risk and crisis communication but apply to communication research in general. However, some areas are especially relevant with regard to their international dimension.

First, given the strengths and weaknesses of computational methods, scholars should take an integrative and reflexive stance on CCS (cf. Schäfer & Hase, 2023), which includes a critical discussion about strengths, weaknesses, and limitations, as well as the suitability of computational methods for the research objectives. Judging how to integrate (or not integrate) such methods does not require everyone to be able to apply computational methods. However, cultivating an understanding of the strengths and limitations of CCS methods in the field of international crisis and risk communication will be crucial in the future. Strengthening such a mindset is not, however, easy to do. Lazer et al. (2020) noted the slow process of "integrating computational training directly into social science (e.g., teaching social scientists how to code) and social science into computational disciplines (e.g., teaching computer scientists research design)" (Lazer et al., 2020, p. 1060). Therefore, we need more interdisciplinary collaborations between communications researchers and computer scientists (Lazer et al., 2020), as well as the implementation of basic computational training in the curricula of communication science departments, including ethical guidance for researchers (Shahin, 2016).

Second, many computational studies show a lack of theoretical foundation (Schäfer & Hase, 2023; Theocharis & Jungherr, 2021). Even though the COVID-19 pandemic has boosted the research on crisis communication, most research stems from other disciplines and is often not related to the literature and theories of risk and crisis communication (Schwarz et al., 2023). Combining CCS with theories from risk and crisis communication seems a fruitful path worth pursuing in the future. It will allow crisis communication scholars to bring their expertise to the table.

Third, computational studies often suffer from a lack of analytical depth and insufficient validity. Method triangulations with established and newly developed quantitative and qualitative methods are a way to address these limitations (Shahin, 2016). Such approaches would allow researchers to gain additional insights into the research object and to better systematically validate the results of the automated procedures. This aspect becomes especially important for international risk and crisis communication when applying multilingual approaches, adapting procedures from one language to another, and using LLMs for data annotation or machine translation.

Fourth, as "the implementation of computational models necessitates a high level of computational resources and skills" (Guo et al., 2023, p. 281), the advancement of CCS can potentially amplify existing biases in research. Therefore, ensuring broad accessibility to data, tools, and training is especially relevant for the international risk and crisis communication research community. There is an ongoing discussion as to whether computational methods empower scholars to conduct research, thereby lowering entry barriers, or whether these methods create new gaps and exacerbate existing ones, given that the specific skills and training they demand are typically provided by leading universities in Western countries (Guo et al., 2023). On the one hand, we see reduced costs of computational power and widespread access to data science toolkits (Theocharis & Jungherr, 2021). On the other hand, obtaining and utilizing relevant data, from, for instance, social media platforms, still requires specific skills and resources.

Fifth, international risk and crisis communication scholars should emphasize the development of procedures for multilingual analysis and the adaptation of tools for multiple languages. This means embracing new multilingual methods that are yet to be implemented in the realm of international crisis communication (e.g., Lind et al., 2021; Maier et al., 2022). Notably, these advanced methods are becoming more accessible through open access and are designed to be user-friendly for researchers with limited or no programming experience (Guo et al., 2023). Strengthening multilingual CCS would empower researchers with limited resources to conduct substantial analyses. This represents a crucial stride in narrowing the existing gaps in international risk and crisis communication research.

References

Arpan, L. M., & Pompper, D. (2003). Stormy weather: Testing "stealing thunder" as a crisis communication strategy to improve communication flow between organizations and journalists. *Public Relations Review*, *29*(3), 291–308. https://doi.org/10.1016/S0363-8111(03)00043-2

Biddix, J. P., Park, H., Collom, G. D., Bailey, M. R., & Park, H. W. (2023). Discourse about higher education on Twitter in early phases of COVID-19: A crisis management social network analysis. *Education and Information Technologies*, *28*, 9957–9983. https://doi.org/10.1007/s10639-023-11590-2

Boumans, J. W., & Trilling, D. (2016). Taking stock of the toolkit. *Digital Journalism*, *4*(1), 8–23. https://doi.org/10.1080/21670811.2015.1096598

Burger, A., Oz, T., Kennedy, W. G., & Crooks, A. T. (2019). Computational social science of disasters: Opportunities and challenges. *Future Internet*, *11*(5), 1–31. https://doi.org/10.3390/fi11050103

Chen, K., Molder, A. L., Duan, Z., Boulianne, S., Eckart, C., Mallari, P., & Yang, D. (2023). How climate movement actors and news media frame climate change and strike: Evidence from analyzing Twitter and news media discourse from 2018 to 2021. *The International Journal of Press/Politics*, *28*(2), 384–413. https://doi.org/10.1177/19401612221106405

Coombs, T., & Holladay, S. J. (2005). An exploratory study of stakeholder emotions: Affect and crises. In N. M. Ashkanasy, W. J. Zerbe, & C. E. J. Härtel, Eds., *The Effect of Affect in Organizational Settings* (pp. 263–280). Emerald. https://doi.org/10.1016/S1746-9791(05)01111-9

Crawford, K., & Finn, M. (2015). The limits of crisis data: Analytical and ethical challenges of using social and mobile data to understand disasters. *GeoJournal*, *80*(4), 491–502. https://doi.org/10.1007/s10708-014-9597-z

Cruz, J. M., & Sodeke, C. U. (2021). Debunking eurocentrism in organizational communication theory: Marginality and liquidities in postcolonial contexts. *Communication Theory*, *31*(3), 528–548. https://doi.org/10.1093/ct/qtz038

Diers-Lawson, A., & Meissner, F. (2021). Moving beyond western corporate perspectives – on the need to increase the diversity of risk and crisis communication research. *Journal of International Crisis and Risk Communication Research*, *4*(1), 165–176. https://doi.org/10.3316/INFORMIT.101581291736024

Domahidi, E., Yang, J., Niemann-Lenz, J., & Reinecke, L. (2019). Computational communication science. Outlining the way ahead in computational communication science. *International Journal of Communication*, *13*, 3876–3884. https://ijoc.org/index.php/ijoc/article/view/10533

Dudo, A., Dunwoody, S., & Scheufele, D. A. (2011). The emergence of nano news: Tracking thematic trends and changes in U.S. newspaper coverage of nanotechnology. *Journalism and Mass Communication Quarterly*, *88*(1), 55–75. https://doi.org/10.1177/107769901108800104

Gerken, F., Van der Land, S. F., & van der Meer, T. G. L. A. (2016). Crisis in the air: An investigation of AirAsia's crisis-response effectiveness based on frame alignment. *Public Relations Review*, *42*(5), 879–892. https://doi.org/10.1016/j.pubrev.2016.09.002

Gerken, F., & van der Meer, T. (2019). Crises frame dynamics: Frame diversity in news media and the role of governmental actors. *Journal of International Crisis and Risk Communication Research*, *2*(2), 149–180. https://doi.org/10.30658/jicrcr.2.2.1

Getchell, M. C., & Sellnow, T. L. (2016). A network analysis of official Twitter accounts during the West Virginia water crisis. *Computers in Human Behavior*, *54*, 597–606. https://doi.org/10.1016/j.chb.2015.06.044

Gilardi, F., Alizadeh, M., & Kubli, M. (2023). ChatGPT outperforms crowd workers for text-annotation tasks. *Proceedings of the National Academy of Sciences*, *120*(30), e2305016120. https://doi.org/10.1073/pnas.2305016120

Grossmann, I., Feinberg, M., Parker, D. C., Christakis, N. A., Tetlock, P. E., & Cunningham, W. A. (2023). AI and the transformation of social science research. *Science*, *380*(6650), 1108–1109. https://doi.org/10.1126/science.adi1778

Guo, L., Su, C., Paik, S., Bhatia, V., Akavoor, V. P., Gao, G., Betke, M., & Wijaya, D. (2023). Proposing an open-sourced tool for computational framing analysis of multilingual data. *Digital Journalism*, *11*(2), 276–297. https://doi.org/10.1080/21670811.2022.2031241

Hagen, L., Keller, T., Neely, S., DePaula, N., & Robert-Cooperman, C. (2018). Crisis communications in the age of social media: A network analysis of Zika-related tweets. *Social Science Computer Review*, *36*(5), 523–541. https://doi.org/10.1177/0894439317721985

Jacobi, C., van Atteveldt, W., & Welbers, K. (2016). Quantitative analysis of large amounts of journalistic texts using topic modelling. *Digital Journalism*, *4*(1), 89–106. https://doi.org/10.1080/21670811.2015.1093271

Jin, X. (2020). Exploring crisis communication and information dissemination on social media: Social network analysis of hurricane Irma tweets. *Journal of International Crisis and Risk Communication Research*, *3*(2), 179–210. https://doi.org/10.30658/jicrcr.3.2.3

Kang, Y., Cai, Z., Tan, C.-W., Huang, Q., & Liu, H. (2020). Natural language processing (NLP) in management research: A literature review. *Journal of Management Analytics*, *7*(2), 139–172. https://doi.org/10.1080/23270012.2020.1756939

Kaur, M., Verma, R., & Otoo, F. N. K. (2021). Emotions in leader's crisis communication: Twitter sentiment analysis during COVID-19 outbreak. *Journal of Human Behavior in the Social Environment*, *31*(1–4), 362–372. https://doi.org/10.1080/10911359.2020.1829239

Kim, J., & Hastak, M. (2018). Social network analysis: Characteristics of online social networks after a disaster. *International Journal of Information Management*, *38*(1), 86–96. https://doi.org/10.1016/j.ijinfomgt.2017.08.003

Larsen, A., Hanigan, I., Reich, B. J., Qin, Y., Cope, M., Morgan, G., & Rappold, A. G. (2021). A deep learning approach to identify smoke plumes in satellite imagery in near-real time for health risk communication. *Journal of Exposure Science & Environmental Epidemiology*, *31*(1), 170–176. https://doi.org/10.1038/s41370-020-0246-y

Lazer, D., Pentland, A., Watts, D. J., Aral, S., Athey, S., Contractor, N., Freelon, D., Gonzalez-Bailon, S., King, G., Margetts, H., Nelson, A., Salganik, M. J., Strohmaier, M., Vespignani, A., & Wagner, C. (2020). Computational social science: Obstacles and opportunities. *Science*, *369*(6507), 1060–1062. https://doi.org/10.1126/science.aaz8170

Lewis, B., Swarup, S., Bisset, K., Eubank, S., Marathe, M., & Barrett, C. (2013). A simulation environment for the dynamic evaluation of disaster preparedness policies and interventions. *Journal of Public Health Management and Practice*, *19*, 42–48. https://doi.org/10.1097/PHH.0b013e31829398eb

Lind, F., Eberl, J.-M., Heidenreich, T., & Boomgaarden, H. G. (2019). Computational communication science. When the journey is as important as the goal: A roadmap to multilingual dictionary construction. *International Journal of Communication, 13*, 4000–4020. https://ijoc.org/index.php/ijoc/article/view/10578

Lind, F., Heidenreich, T., Kralj, C., & Boomgaarden, H. G. (2021). Greasing the wheels for comparative communication research: Supervised text classification for multilingual corpora. *Computational Communication Research, 3*(3), 1–30. https://doi.org/10.5117/CCR2021.3.001.LIND

Liu, W., Lai, C., & Xu, W. (2018). Tweeting about emergency: A semantic network analysis of government organizations' social media messaging during Hurricane Harvey. *Public Relations Review, 44*(5), 807–819. https://doi.org/10.1016/j.pubrev.2018.10.009

Mahrt, M., & Scharkow, M. (2013). The value of Big Data in digital media research. *Journal of Broadcasting & Electronic Media, 57*(1), 20–33. https://doi.org/10.1080/08838151.2012.761700

Maier, D., Baden, C., Stoltenberg, D., De Vries-Kedem, M., & Waldherr, A. (2022). Machine translation vs. multilingual dictionaries assessing two strategies for the topic modeling of multilingual text collections. *Communication Methods and Measures, 16*(1), 19–38. https://doi.org/10.1080/19312458.2021.1955845

Mellado, C., Hallin, D., Cárcamo, L., Alfaro, R., Jackson, D., Humanes, M. L., Márquez-Ramírez, M., Mick, J., Mothes, C., I-Hsuan Lin, C., Lee, M., Alfaro, A., Isbej, J., & Ramos, A. (2021). Sourcing pandemic news: A cross-national computational analysis of mainstream media coverage of COVID-19 on Facebook, Twitter, and Instagram. *Digital Journalism, 9*(9), 1261–1285. https://doi.org/10.1080/21670811.2021.1942114

Mirbabaie, M., & Marx, J. (2020). 'Breaking' news: Uncovering sense-breaking patterns in social media crisis communication during the 2017 Manchester bombing. *Behaviour & Information Technology, 39*(3), 252–266. https://doi.org/10.1080/0144929X.2019.1611924

Kermani, M. A., Maghsoudi, M., Hamedani, M. S., & Bozorgipour, A. (2022). Analyzing the interorganizational collaborations in crisis management in coping with COVID-19 using social network analysis: Case of Iran. *Journal of Emergency Management, 20*(3), 249–266. https://doi.org/10.5055/jem.0623

Muddiman, A., McGregor, S. C., & Stroud, N. J. (2019). (Re)claiming our expertise: Parsing large text corpora with manually validated and organic dictionaries. *Political Communication, 36*(2), 214–226. https://doi.org/10.1080/10584609.2018.1517843

Ort, A., Rohrbach, T., Diviani, N., & Rubinelli, S. (2023). Covering the crisis: Evolution of key topics and actors in COVID-19 news coverage in Switzerland. *International Journal of Public Health*, Advance Online Publication. https://doi.org/10.3389/ijph.2022.1605240

Öztürk, N., & Ayvaz, S. (2018). Sentiment analysis on Twitter: A text mining approach to the Syrian refugee crisis. *Telematics and Informatics, 35*(1), 136–147. https://doi.org/10.1016/j.tele.2017.10.006

Pakvis, M., & Hendrickx, J. (2023). Media consolidation and news content diversity: A deductive framing analysis of Belgian refugee news coverage. *Journalism Practice*, Advance Online Publication. https://doi.org/10.1080/17512786.2023.2263414

Rauchfleisch, A., & Kaiser, J. (2020). The false positive problem of automatic bot detection in social science research. *PLoS One, 15*(10), e0241045. https://doi.org/10.1371/journal.pone.0241045

Rauchfleisch, A., Siegen, D., & Vogler, D. (2023). How COVID-19 displaced climate change: Mediated climate change activism and issue attention in the Swiss media and online sphere. *Environmental Communication, 17*(3), 313–321. https://doi.org/10.1080/17524032.2021.1990978

Rauchfleisch, A., Vogler, D., & Eisenegger, M. (2021). Public sphere in crisis mode: How the COVID-19 Pandemic influenced public discourse and user behaviour in the Swiss Twitter-sphere. *Javnost – The Public, 28*(2), 129–148. https://doi.org/10.1080/13183222.2021.1923622

Reber, U. (2019). Overcoming language barriers: Assessing the potential of machine translation and topic modeling for the comparative analysis of multilingual text corpora. *Communication Methods and Measures, 13*(2), 102–125. https://doi.org/10.1080/19312458.2018.1555798

Reinhold, A. M., Raile, E. D., Izurieta, C., McEvoy, J., King, H. W., Poole, G. C., Ready, R. C., Bergmann, N. T., & Shanahan, E. A. (2023). Persuasion with precision: Using natural language processing to improve instrument fidelity for risk communication experimental treatments. *Journal of Mixed Methods Research, 17*(4), 373–395. https://doi.org/10.1177/15586898221096934

Reiss, M. V. (2023). Testing the reliability of ChatGPT for text annotation and classification: A cautionary remark. *arXiv*. https://doi.org/10.48550/arXiv.2304.11085

Schäfer, M. S., & Hase, V. (2023). Computational methods for the analysis of climate change communication: Towards an integrative and reflexive approach. *WIREs Climate Change, 14*(2), e806. https://doi.org/10.1002/wcc.806

Schultz, F., Kleinnijenhuis, J., Oegema, D., Utz, S., & van Atteveldt, W. (2012). Strategic framing in the BP crisis: A semantic network analysis of associative frames. *Public Relations Review, 38*(1), 97–107. https://doi.org/10.1016/j.pubrev.2011.08.003

Schwarz, A., Alpers, F., Wagner-Olfermann, E., & Diers-Lawson, A. (2023). The global study of COVID news: Scope, findings, and implications of quantitative content analyses of the COVID-19 news coverage in the first two years of the pandemic. *Health Communication*, Advance Online Publication. https://doi.org/10.1080/10410236.2023.2226932

Schwarz, A., Seeger, M. W., & Auer, C. (2016). Significance and structure of international risk and crisis communication research. In A. Schwarz, M. W. Seeger, & C. Auer, Eds., *The Handbook of International Crisis Communication Research* (pp. 1–10). John Wiley & Sons, Ltd. https://doi.org/10.1002/9781118516812.ch1

Shahin, S. (2016). When scale meets depth: Integrating natural language processing and textual analysis for studying digital corpora. *Communication Methods and Measures, 10*(1), 28–50. https://doi.org/10.1080/19312458.2015.1118447

Sun, S., Zhai, Y., Shen, B., & Chen, Y. (2020). Newspaper coverage of artificial intelligence: A perspective of emerging technologies. *Telematics and Informatics, 53*, 101433. https://doi.org/10.1016/j.tele.2020.101433

Theocharis, Y., & Jungherr, A. (2021). Computational social science and the study of political communication. *Political Communication, 38*(1–2), 1–22. https://doi.org/10.1080/10584609.2020.1833121

Trilling, D., & Jonkman, J. G. F. (2018). Scaling up content analysis. *Communication Methods and Measures, 12*(2–3), 158–174. https://doi.org/10.1080/19312458.2018.1447655

Ulmer, R. R., & Pyle, A. S. (2016). International organizational crisis communication. In A. Schwarz, M. W. Seeger, & C. Auer, Eds., *The Handbook of International Crisis Communication Research* (pp. 108–118). John Wiley & Sons, Ltd. https://doi.org/10.1002/9781118516812.ch11

Valentini, C., & Kruckeberg, D. (2016). The future role of social media in international crisis communication. In A. Schwarz, M. W. Seeger, & C. Auer, Eds., *The Handbook of International Crisis Communication Research* (pp. 478–488). John Wiley & Sons, Ltd. https://doi.org/10.1002/9781118516812.ch43

van Atteveldt, W., & Peng, T.-Q. (2018). When communication meets computation: Opportunities, challenges, and pitfalls in computational communication science. *Communication Methods and Measures, 12*(2–3), 81–92. https://doi.org/10.1080/19312458.2018.1458084

van der Meer, T. G. L. A., & Kroon, A. (2022). Crisis communication and computational methods. In W. T. Coombs, & S. J. Holladay, Eds., *The Handbook of Crisis Communication* (pp. 1–16). John Wiley & Sons, Ltd. https://doi.org/10.1002/9781119678953.ch1

van der Meer, T. G. L. A., Verhoeven, P., Beentjes, H., & Vliegenthart, R. (2014). When frames align: The interplay between PR, news media, and the public in times of crisis. *Public Relations Review, 40*(5), 751–761. https://doi.org/10.1016/j.pubrev.2014.07.008

Vogler, D., & Meissner, F. (2020). How users tweet about a cyber attack: An explorative study using machine learning and social network analysis. *Journal of Digital Media & Policy, 11*(2), 195–214. https://doi.org/10.1386/jdmp_00016_1

Vogler, D., & Meissner, F. (2022). Tackling the information overload. In W. T. Coombs, & S. J. Holladay, Eds., *The Handbook of Crisis Communication* (pp. 53–65). John Wiley & Sons, Ltd. https://doi.org/10.1002/9781119678953.ch4

Vu, H. T., & Lynn, N. (2020). When the news takes sides: Automated framing analysis of news coverage of the Rohingya crisis by the elite press from three countries. *Journalism Studies, 21*(9), 1284–1304. https://doi.org/10.1080/1461670X.2020.1745665

Waldherr, A., Hilbert, M., & González-Bailón, S. (2021). Worlds of agents: Prospects of agent-based modeling for communication research. *Communication Methods and Measures, 15*(4), 243–254. https://doi.org/10.1080/19312458.2021.1986478

Waldherr, A., & Wettstein, M. (2019). Computational communication science. Bridging the gaps: Using agent-based modeling to reconcile data and theory in computational communication science.

International Journal of Communication, 13, 3976–3999. https://ijoc.org/index.php/ijoc/article/view/10588
Walker, S., Mercea, D., & Bastos, M. (2019). The disinformation landscape and the lockdown of social platforms. *Information, Communication & Society, 22*(11), 1531–1543. https://doi.org/10.1080/1369118X.2019.1648536
Wang, Y., Hao, H., & Platt, L. S. (2021). Examining risk and crisis communications of government agencies and stakeholders during early-stages of COVID-19 on Twitter. *Computers in Human Behavior, 114*, 106568. https://doi.org/10.1016/j.chb.2020.106568
Yantseva, V. (2020). Migration discourse in Sweden: Frames and sentiments in mainstream and social media. *Social Media+ Society, 6*(4), 1–16. https://doi.org/10.1177/2056305120981059
Zechman, E. M. (2011). Agent-based modeling to simulate contamination events and evaluate threat management strategies in water distribution systems. *Risk Analysis, 31*(5), 758–772. https://doi.org/10.1111/j.1539-6924.2010.01564.x

Author Bio

Daniel Vogler (PhD) is the research director of the Research Center for the Public Sphere and Society (fög) at the University of Zurich and a research associate at the Department of Communication and Media Research at the University of Zurich (IKMZ). His research focuses on crisis communication, public relations, journalism, online communication, and computational communication science.

47

Methodological Challenges of International Crisis Communication Research[1]

W. Timothy Coombs

Centre for Crisis and Risk Communicaitons, Calgary, Canada

Introduction

Marion Pinsdorff (1991) was among the first to call for an international view of crisis communication with her article in *Public Relations Review*. She felt so strongly about the international aspect of crisis communication that her 2004 book was titled *All Crises Are Global* (Pinsdorff, 2004). Lee (2005) is another who has called for a more international view of crisis communication. I amplified these clarion calls in 2008 (Coombs, 2008). These calls are not just an academic exercise but are driven by reality – more and more crises are international in scope. Thankfully, more international crisis communication literature is emerging, representing authors from around the world. Perfect illustrations of the point are the 2012 book *Case Studies in Crisis Communication: International Perspectives on Hits and Misses* (George & Pratt, 2012) and the development of the rhetorical arena theory for crisis communication emerging from Denmark (e.g., Frandsen & Johansen, 2010a; Frandsen & Johansen, 2010b). These works demonstrate an international interest in crisis communication and an analysis of crisis cases that are international in scope.

The point of this chapter is not to be a comprehensive review of all the research published on international crisis communication. Instead, the focus of this chapter is the difficulties facing researchers seeking to pursue specific types of international crisis communication research. The first section of the chapter provides a short overview of the different types of international crisis communication research. That includes the distinction between nation and culture and the dominant analytic national culture frameworks available to researchers seeking to examine the international aspect of crisis communication. The next section provides a more detailed examination of the key challenges crisis communication research faces when attempting to execute international crisis communication research. The chapter ends with an identification of the central concerns for future international crisis communication research.

[1] This chapter is a reprint of Chapter 41 in the first edition of the Handbook of International Crisis Communication Research (2016).

The Handbook of International Crisis and Risk Communication Research, Second Edition.
Edited by Andreas Schwarz, Matthew W. Seeger, and Sora Kim.

Basic Research Concerns: Culture, Nations, Analytic Frameworks, and Focus

This first section provides a review of key concerns and analytic tools that are relevant to any international research. Given the relatively recent emergence of international crisis communication research, it is instructive to examine how more established areas, such as international marketing, have identified and addressed basic concerns for international research.

Nations and Cultures

The idea of international research in any field involves a mixing of nations and cultures. A nation has geographic boundaries, whereas culture can be defined as "people who are domestic speakers of a common distinct language and who belong to either the same state or the same contact group" (Malhotra et al., 1996, p. 25). There can be overlap between the two concepts captured in the term national culture. "A culture can be validly conceptualized at the national level if there exists some meaningful degree of within-country commonality and between-country differences in culture" (Steenkamp, 2001, p. 36). We can even use the term national values to capture the overlap. National values are "collectively held values at a general level" (Soyez, 2012, p. 625). While related, nation and culture are not necessarily isomorphic. Nation and culture seem to have increasing differences as nations become more heterogeneous (Steenkamp, 2001).

Still, most international research will compare data in two or more countries while using culture as an explanatory tool. The international research reflects intercultural research concerns of discovering if culture makes a difference and the importance of a specific cultural influence. It is fair to say that the international research often has a component of intercultural research. The rationale for using culture is its explanatory power. "Cultural norms and beliefs are powerful forces shaping people's perceptions, dispositions, and behaviors" (Steenkamp, 2001, p. 30). However, I am using the phrase "international research" to capture both elements because using "international/intercultural" or "international and intercultural" is too cumbersome. The situation becomes even more complex when we consider the existence of meta and micro culture. Meta cultures are groupings of similar cultures into clusters. An example would be the ten societal clusters found in the GLOBE research, such as Latin Europe, the Middle East, and Southern Asia (House et al., 2004). Micro cultures are subcultures that exist within a nation, such as the Flemish and Walloons in Belgium (Steenkamp, 2001). We will return to the issues of meta and micro cultures in the next section. The point is that national boundaries are used to demarcate segments; the cultural factors are used to understand any differences and similarities between the cultural segments.

Analytic Frameworks for National Culture

When comparing samples from different nations, there needs to be some theoretically driven framework for understanding national culture. The most commonly used analytic frameworks for national culture are Hofstede (1980), House et al. (2004), Schwartz (1997), and Trompenaars and Hampden-Turner (1997). These frameworks each conceptualize culture as multidimensional. We must quickly return to the issue of culture and nation for clarification of terminology. Hofstede's (1980) work illustrates how the data is divided by nations and conclusions drawn about the dimensions of a nation's culture. The mixing of nation and culture works when the level of analysis is the nation. However, we cannot apply these national cultures to the individual level because "the national culture dimensions can be used to explain other national-level phenomena" (Brewer & Venaik, 2012, p. 679). This section provides a short overview of these four analytic frameworks for national culture. The analytic frameworks are critical to international comparisons because they provide a theoretical explanation for differences and similarities, a point I will expand upon in the next section.

Hofstede's (1980) work might be the best known of the national culture analytic frameworks. It is also the oldest, which raises questions about its current applicability. Hofstede's (1980) research originally identified four dimensions of national culture that were later extended to six: power distance, individualism versus collectivism, uncertainty avoidance, masculinity versus femininity, long-term versus short-term orientation, and indulgence versus restraint. House et al. (2004) call their national culture analytic framework GLOBE. GLOBE has nine cultural dimensions: performance orientation, institutional collectivism, gender egalitarianism, uncertainty avoidance, in-group collectivism, future orientation, humane orientation, assertiveness, and power distance. Schwartz (1994) has three dimensions: conservatism versus autonomy, hierarchy versus egalitarianism, and mastery versus harmony.

Trompenaars and Hampden-Turner (1997) have seven dimensions: universalism versus pluralism, individualism versus communitarianism, specific versus diffuse, affectivity versus neutrality, inner-directed versus outer-directed, achieved status versus ascribed status, and sequential time versus synchronic time. Table 47.1 lists and defines the various dimensions of national culture.

General Research Approach

International crisis communication research can be pursued utilizing a variety of general research approaches that are qualitative or quantitative. In fact, most of the extant international crisis communication research is composed of qualitative studies that employ a case study method (e.g., Denis-Remis et al., 2013). There is also a growing set of international crisis communication studies that use content analysis of legacy and digital media messages during a crisis (e.g., Haruta & Hallahan, 2003). The focus of this chapter is on quantitative international crisis communication research. The rationale is derived from international marketing research. International marketing research has a longer history and body of work than international crisis communication researchers. Experts there argue the need for more experimental and survey studies. Cases provide some speculation about relationships while survey data can verify those relationships. Moreover, the experimental studies verify if there are causal relationships between cultural factors and marketing factors (e.g., Taylor et al., 2011). The consideration of research issues in the following section will emphasize quantitative research, but there are some applications to qualitative as well.

Key Challenges for International Crisis Communication Researchers

The challenges facing international research can fill and have filled books. This section draws out two sets of key challenges for seeking to conduct quantitative international crisis communication research. The two sets of challenges are informed by the international marketing research because of the similarities between the two fields. The first set of challenges reflects the different concerns that arise during the various steps in the research process and is informed by the work of Malhotra et al. (1996). The second set of challenges is based upon the criteria Taylor et al. (2011) utilized to evaluate the quality of international research in marketing.

Challenges in the Research Process

During each step in the research process, there are concerns/challenges for international researchers. Table 47.2 presents a list of the key challenges identified for international crisis communication researchers. The list focuses on only four steps in the research process: problem definition, research design, data analysis, and report preparation.

Table 47.1 Analytic frameworks for national culture.

Hofstede:
1. Power distance: degree of power differential people are willing to accept
2. Individualism versus collectivism: how tight or loose-knit a society is
3. Uncertainty avoidance: degree to which people feel uncomfortable with ambiguity
4. Masculinity versus femininity: degree to which a society favors competition or cooperation
5. Long-term versus short term orientation: degree to which society favors thrift and long-term results or savings and quick returns
6. Indulgence versus restraint: degree to which gratifications are suppressed

Globe:
1. Performance orientation: degree to which innovation and performance improvement are rewarded by society
2. Institutional collectivism: degree to which society rewards and encourages collective action and distribution of rewards
3. Gender egalitarianism: degree to which society minimizes gender inequality
4. Uncertainty avoidance: degree to which norms and rules used by society to reduce unpredictability of the future
5. In-group collectivism: degree to which people express loyalty and cohesion in families and organizations
6. Future orientation: degree to which society rewards future-oriented behaviors
7. Humane orientation: degree to which society rewards being caring and kind to others
8. Assertiveness: degree to which people are assertive and aggressive toward others
9. Power distance: degree to which society accepts power differences and status privileges

Schwartz:
1. Conservatism versus autonomy: people are part of a collective or free to express themselves
2. Hierarchy versus egalitarianism: society has fixed rules and resource distribution or works together to solve problems
3. Mastery versus harmony: people control world and mold it to their desires or act and preserve world instead of exploiting it

Trompenaars & Hampden-Turner:
1. Universalism versus pluralism: degree of emphasis on rules or relationships
2. Individualism versus communitarianism: degree to which people view selves as part of collective or as individuals
3. Specific versus diffuse: degree to which responsibility is diffused or assigned
4. Affectivity versus neutrality: degree to which people display or conceal emotions
5. Inner directed versus outer directed: degree to which people feel they are controlled by the environment or that they control the environment
6. Achieved status versus ascribed status: degree to which people are given status or must prove they have earned it
7. Sequential time versus synchronic time: degree to which people accomplish one task at a time or multiple tasks at one time

Table 47.2 Challenges in the research process.

Problem definition
Research design
  Measurement
  Sampling
Data analysis
  Standardization
  Level of analysis
Report preparation

For problem definition, the dominant challenge is functional equivalence. The phenomenon being examined must be related to the same functional problem in every culture being studied. Another way to phrase it is that each culture must have the same problem. As a result, international research demands an extremely clear articulation of the problem being studied (Malhotra et al., 1996; Young & Javalgi, 2007). One implication is that any problem related to crisis communication must be found in all of the cultures being utilized in a particular study. A specific concern for international crisis communication researchers is specifying what is meant by crisis. More specifically, researchers must take care in identifying the crisis type or types being studied. We have disasters, public health crises, and an array of organizational crises that all have significant differences from one another (Coombs, 2010). Research must be specific about the crisis type and evaluate its functional equivalence. For instance, Huang (2006) examined crises experienced by politicians. It is difficult to then compare those results with findings using organizational or corporate crises. There is no functional equivalence between political and organizational crises. Similarly, comparing utilizing health crises to organizational crises violates functional equivalence.

The key challenges with research design involve measurement and sampling. The measurement challenges revolve around equivalence. Construct equivalence is concerned that the construct has the same meaning in each culture. One concern might be a particular type of crisis generating different meanings between cultures. If there is too much variance in the construct due to culture, that skews the results of the research. Functional equivalence relates to the concept of serving the same function in each culture. An issue in crisis communication is that crisis communication serves the same functions in each culture. Finally, there are some basic challenges related to language. Each scale demands translation. First, a scale is translated from language A to language B. Then a different person translates the scale from language B to A. The final translated version of the scale is then compared with the original to see if they remain consistent. Researchers also need to be careful about the "anchors" used for Likert and semantic differential scales. The selected anchors must be appropriate for each culture (Malhotra et al., 1996; Taylor et al., 2011).

One implication for crisis communication research is a need to utilize a consistent set of scales to measure central concepts in the research rather than continually developing new scales to assess the same or very similar concepts. A common set of scales would allow for further checks on the validity of their use in international crisis communication research. For example, there are multiple scales used to measure organizational reputations in the crisis communication research (e.g., Coombs & Holladay, 2002; Dean, 2004). The reputation measure is an important concern because organizational reputation frequently is a central variable in the research. Therefore, research is necessary to determine how similar the various organizational reputation measures are to see if comparisons between the studies are acceptable.

Sampling can be an issue if the international researchers need to draw participants from a particular population. International marketing research frequently draws from consumers. There are times when crisis researchers identify specific stakeholder groups, such as community members or consumers, for study. Researchers should realize the sampling frame is much more complicated for international research and should review other studies to determine the appropriate sampling strategies (Malhotra et al., 1996). If crisis researchers are using, for example, a consumer sample, they should review the specific strategies used in international marketing. However, if the crisis researchers are examining general psychological human reactions, a general sample can be used. For instance, Laufer et al. (2005) use a more general sample when they examined cultural differences in attributions of blame in a crisis. There was not a need to specify a specific subset of respondents in that study.

The key challenges for data analysis are whether or not to standardize the data and the level of analysis. International researchers are divided on whether or not to standardize their data. Arguments have been made for both sides (Malhotra et al., 1996). International crisis researchers should review the arguments and decide which argument is most salient to their research project. The other concern is the level of analysis. International research tends to use the individual, within the national culture, and across the national cultures (Malhotra et al., 1996). The level of analysis should be driven by the needs of the study. International crisis communication researchers must remember that the national culture analytic frameworks were not designed for the individual level even though they are often misapplied to that level. If crisis researchers are using cultural dimensions, the study should include an assessment of those dimensions. For example, if the research compares reactions to crisis response strategies in Argentina and Germany because of supposed differences in ambiguity tolerance, the researchers should assess the ambiguity tolerance of the participants to determine if the anticipated differences on the variable really did occur in the sample.

The challenge for report preparation is avoiding ethnocentrism. The results and data analysis require interpretation. Of particular concern is trying to understand the potential effect of a national culture dimension. To avoid ethnocentrism, the research team should be multicultural. A researcher or researchers from a particular culture should analyze and report on the results relevant to their culture (Malhotra et al., 1996; Yaprak, 2008). If a US researcher collected data on perceptions of events as crises in the United States and China, it is problematic if the US researcher is the only one to interpret the results of the data analysis. A researcher from China, sensitive to cultural concerns, should provide their interpretations as well.

As noted earlier, the focus of this section is on quantitative research. However, qualitative research has been used for comparative purposes employing case studies. When comparing cases, there is a need to give careful consideration to equivalence. Researchers must match the crisis cases along all relevant factors. Researchers will need to determine the "relevant factors" for their studies. One example is the comparison of airline crashes. The researchers took care in matching the nature of the crises (Haruta & Hallahan, 2003). Qualitative researchers must determine how issues of equivalence and ethnocentrism in interpreting results could impact their studies.

Evaluative Criteria for International Research

Taylor et al. (2011) developed a set of criteria they used to evaluate six years of international marketing research. There was some overlap between the Taylor, Bowen, and Bang criteria and those used for the research process. Table 47.3 presents the unique criteria from Taylor et al. (2011) that hold relevance for international crisis communication researchers.

The variety of cultures recommends that nations from diverse cultural contexts are used in the study. Ideally, nations from different cultural clusters are utilized – meta culture becomes a factor in selection. A recognized problem is that the nations are often a convenience sample rather than purposefully selected for their cultural variation. Moreover, there is a call to include Brazil, Russia, India, and China due to their increasing international

Table 47.3 Evaluative criteria for international research.

Utilize a variety of cultures
Provide strong rationale for each nation
Employ a cross-national research team
Collect a variety of data
Establish a clear link between culture and other variables
Use advanced analytic techniques
Check for equivalence after data collection
Verify if the cultural differences exist

importance (Taylor et al., 2011). International crisis communication researchers should make cultural variation one of their selection criteria when developing international research teams.

The rationale for selecting nations is a function of the conceptual or theoretical ideas that support the research project. If a particular dimension of national culture is anticipated to be relevant, the nations must differ on that concept (Taylor et al., 2011). Again, international crisis communication researchers must have a rationale for why each nation fits with the research project. For instance, if uncertainty avoidance is believed to affect the decision to treat a situation as a crisis, the nations used in the study must represent varying degrees of uncertainty avoidance.

The cross-national research team returns to the value of having a multicultural interpretation of the results. The argument is extended by Taylor et al. (2011) to include the ability to capture emic (culture bound) and etic (across cultures) perspectives.

The types of data collected refer to the overreliance in international marketing research on content analysis. There is a strong element of content analysis research in international crisis communication research as well. Taylor et al. (2011) call for more research using surveys and experiments to explore relationships and to develop causal claims. International crisis communication research would benefit from experiments that validate relationships and build causal claims. We are far from a point in international crisis communication research where we can simply utilize normative studies. We know very little about the dynamics of international crisis communication to be able to make prescriptive claims devoid of data. Such "speculation" can do more damage than good for researchers and practitioners.

The clear link between culture and other field-specific variables places an emphasis on research being driven by theory. The theories driving international research are a combination of the national culture frameworks and theories from the researchers' own fields (Taylor et al., 2011). International crisis communication researchers should provide strong links for the projects between theory and practices in crisis communication and some national culture framework to articulate how the study will explain the effect of some national culture concept on some aspect of crisis communication such as the selection of crisis response strategies.

The advanced analytic techniques criterion is an extension of the request for more research using surveys and experiments. The idea is that such data permits the utilization of more advanced analytic techniques such as regression analysis and structural equation models (SEM) (Taylor et al., 2011). Once more we have an argument for international crisis communication researchers to develop studies that employ surveys and experimental methods.

The equivalence of data after it is collected adds to the equivalency discussions from the previous section. Confirmatory factor analysis can be used to determine if the constructs and their measures were equivalent across cultures (Steenkamp & Baumgartner, 1998; Taylor et al., 2011). International crisis communication researchers should include confirmatory factor analysis in their quantitative studies to check for the equivalence of measures.

Verification of cultural differences is a warning not to assume that simply because a sample is from a particular nation, it will manifest the traditional scores for the national culture dimensions. Increasing heterogeneity is a risk for researchers, and verifying the cultural differences is a way to check for that problem (Taylor et al., 2011). Here the issue is the potential for microcultures influencing the research results. International crisis communication researchers should include a measure for any national cultural dimension that is relevant to their study. The researchers would have specified the relevant national cultural dimensions to satisfy the clear link between culture and variables. By including the measure of the national cultural dimension or dimensions, researchers can test to determine if their samples actually varied the way the national cultural dimension frameworks specified that they would or if some microculture was actually sampled. Researchers can consider this as a type of manipulation check because the national culture is often an independent variable in international research.

Summary

There are a myriad of challenges facing researchers when seeking to examine international crisis communication. This section has reviewed the key challenges. The challenges were divided into two sets: the research process and evaluative criteria for international research. The research process challenges identified the common problems faced in international research. The evaluative criteria reflect what researchers feel are recommended practices for international research. Combined, the two lists of challenges can help to shape future international crisis communication research. One emerging recommendation would be the formation of cross-national teams composed of researchers from different cultural clusters that utilize survey or experimental studies. Such teams can utilize the research process challenge list to guide their research projects.

Conclusion

The percentage of crisis communication research that is truly international is rather small. Taylor (2000) was among the first to use national cultural dimensions to explain crisis communication. Within this scant body of literature, most of the research is case studies set in a particular culture (e.g., Schwarz, 2012) or efforts to understand crisis communication by applying US theories in other cultures to see if the theories still have merit (e.g., Claeys & Cauberghe, 2010; Huang et al., 2005; Verhoeven et al., 2012). Haruta and Hallahan (2003) is one of the truly international studies because it involved a cultural comparison. Like early international marketing research, the method is content analysis rather than surveys or experiments. However, the area of international crisis communication is still young, and these case studies and single-nation studies are useful in building a base of knowledge.

The greatest challenge facing international crisis communication researchers is to aspire to comparative studies that are empirically based. We must begin to form multinational teams to conduct comparative international crisis communication research. Moreover, we must find concepts that can be studied across a variety of national cultures and develop measures that are valid across national cultures. As this chapter indicates, there are many issues an international crisis communication research team will face. However, if we do not rise to meet the challenge, we are doomed to know precious little about the effects of national culture on central concepts in crisis communication. This lack of knowledge impoverishes the field for both researchers and practitioners.

References

Brewer, P., & Venaik, S. (2012). On the misuse of national culture dimensions. *International Marketing Review, 29*(6), 673–683. https://doi.org/10.1108/02651331211277991

Claeys, A. S., & Cauberghe, V. (2010). Crisis response and crisis timing strategies: Two sides of the same coin. *Public Relations Review, 38*(1), 83–88.

Coombs, W. T. (2008). The future of crisis communication from an international perspective. In T. Nolting, & A. Thießen, Eds., *Krisenmanagement in der Mediengesellschaft. Potenziale und Perspektiven der Krisenkommunikation [Crisis Management in Media Society. Potentials and Perspectives of Crisis Communication]* (pp. 275–287). Wiesbaden: VS Verlag für Sozialwissenschaften.

Coombs, W. T. (2010). Parameters for crisis communication. In W. T. Coombs, & S. J. Holladay, Eds., *Handbook of Crisis Communication* (pp. 17–53). Malden, MA: Blackwell.

Coombs, W. T., & Holladay, S. J. (2002). Helping crisis managers protect reputational assets initial tests of the situational crisis communication theory. *Management Communication Quarterly, 16*(2), 165–186.

Dean, D. H. (2004). Consumer reaction to negative publicity effects of corporate reputation, response, and responsibility for a crisis event. *Journal of Business Communication, 41*(2), 192–211.

Denis-Remis, C., Lebraty, J. F., & Philippe, H. (2013). The 2008 anti-French demonstrations in China: Learning from a social media crisis. *Journal of Contingencies & Crisis Management, 21*(1), 45–55. https://doi.org/10.1111/1468-5973.12010

Frandsen, F., & Johansen, W. (2010a). Apologizing in a globalizing world: Crisis communication and apologetic ethics. *Corporate Communications: An International Journal, 15*(4), 350–364.

Frandsen, F., & Johansen, W. (2010b). Crisis communication, complexity, and the cartoon affair: A case study. In W. T. Coombs, & S. J. Holladay, Eds., *The Handbook of Crisis Communication* (pp. 425–448). Boston, MA: Wiley-Blackwell.

George, A. M., & Pratt, C. B. (Eds.). (2012). *Case Studies in Crisis Communication: International Perspectives on Hits and Misses.* New York: Routledge.

Haruta, A., & Hallahan, K. (2003). Cultural issues in airline crisis communication: A Japan-US comparative study. *Asian Journal of Communication, 13*(2), 122–150.

Hofstede, G. (1980). *Culture's Consequences: Comparing Values, Behaviours, Institutions and Organizations.* Beverly Hills, CA: Sage.

House, R. J., Hanges, P. J., Javidan, M., Dorfman, P. W., & Vipiin, G. (2004). *Culture, Leadership, and Organizations: The GLOBE Study of 62 Societies.* Thousand Oaks, CA: Sage.

Huang, Y. H. (2006). Crisis situations, communication strategies, and media coverage: A multicase study revisiting the communicative response model. *Communication Research, 33*(3), 180–205.

Huang, Y. H., Lin, Y. H., & Su, S. H. (2005). Crisis communicative strategies in Taiwan: Category, continuum, and cultural implication. *Public Relations Review, 31*, 229–238.

Laufer, D., Gillespie, K., McBride, B., & Gonzalez, S. (2005). The role of severity in consumer attributions of blame: Defensive attributions in product-harm crises in Mexico. *Journal of International Consumer Marketing, 17*(2–3), 33–50.

Lee, B. K. (2005). Crisis, culture, and communication. In P. J. Kalbfleisch, Ed., *Communication Yearbook 29* (pp. 275–308). Mahwah, NJ: Lawrence Erlbaum.

Malhotra, N. K., Agarwal, J., & Peterson, M. (1996). Methodological issues in cross-cultural marketing research. *International Marketing Review, 13*(5), 7–43. https://doi.org/10.1108/02651339610131379

Pinsdorff, M. K. (1991). Flying different skies: How cultures respond to airline disaster. *Public Relations Review, 17*(1), 37–56.

Pinsdorff, M. K. (2004). *All Crises are Global: Managing to Escape Chaos.* New York: Fordham University Press.

Schwartz, S. H. (1994). Are there universal aspects in the structure and contents of human values? *Journal of Social Issues, 50*(4), 19–45.

Schwartz, S. H. (1997). Values and culture. In D. Munro, S. Carr, & J. Schumaker, Eds., *Motivation and Culture* (pp. 69–84). New York: Routledge.

Schwarz, A. (2012). How public use social media to respond to blame games in crisis communication: The Love Parade tragedy in Duisburg 2010. *Public Relations Review, 38*, 430–437.

Soyez, K. (2012). How national cultural values affect pro-environmental consumer behavior. *International Marketing Review, 29*(6), 623–646. https://doi.org/10.1108/02651331211277973

Steenkamp, J. B. E. M. (2001). The role of national culture in international marketing research. *International Marketing Review, 18*(1), 30–44. https://doi.org/10.1108/02651330110381970

Steenkamp, J. B. E. M., & Baumgartner, H. (1998). Assessing measurement equivalence in cross-national consumer research. *Journal of Advertising Research, 25*(2), 78–90.

Taylor, C. R., Bowen, C. L., & Bang, H. K. (2011). The state of methodological practice in international marketing research. In M. Sarstedt, M. Schwaiger, & C. R. Taylor, Eds., *Measurement and Research Methods in International Marketing* (pp. 143–168). Bingley, UK: Emerald.

Taylor, M. (2000). Cultural variance as a challenge to global public relations: A case study of the Coca-cola scare in Europe. *Public Relations Review, 26*, 277–293.

Trompenaars, F., & Hampden-Turner, C. (1997). *Riding the Waves of Culture: Understanding Cultural Diversity in Business* (2nd ed.). London: Nicholas Brealey.

Verhoeven, J. W. M., Van Hoof, J., Jeurs, H. T., & Van Vuuren, M. (2012). Effects of apologies and crisis responsibility on corporate and spokesperson reputation. *Public Relations Review, 38*, 501–504.

Yaprak, A. (2008). Culture study in international marketing: A critical review and suggestions for future research. *International Marketing Review*, *25*(2), 215–229. https://doi.org/10.1108/02651330810866290

Young, R. B., & Javalgi, R. G. (2007). International marketing research: A global project management perspective. *Business Horizons*, *50*, 113–122. https://doi.org/10.1016/j.bushoz.2006.08.003

Author Bio

W. Timothy Coombs (PhD, Purdue University) is a former university professor and currently is on the Advisory Board for the Centre for Crisis and Risk Communications and is the Editor-in-Chief of the *Journal of Contingencies and Crisis Management*. Dr. Coombs has been researching crisis communication for the past 30 years and developed the situational crisis communication theory. His crisis communication research has won multiple awards from professional organizations including the Jackson, Jackson & Wagner Behavioral Science Prize from the Public Relations Society of America and the Pathfinder Award from the Institute of Public Relations in recognition of his research contributions to the field and the practice. His books include the award-winning book *Ongoing Crisis Communication*, coediting the *Handbook of Crisis Communication* (first and second editions), and co-writing *Communicating in Extreme Crises: Lessons from the Edge*. Dr. Coombs also is an ICA Fellow and an Academic Core member of the University of Georgia Crisis Communication Think Tank.

Technologies and Practices in International Crisis and Risk Communication

48

Technologies in Crisis Communication: Tools, Systems, and Infrastructures

Rob Grace
University of Cincinnati, School of Information Technology, Cincinnati, OH, USA

Technologies are integral to ***risk and crisis communication***, processes of sending and receiving messages between senders and receivers for the purpose of managing potential and imminent threats to public safety (Frandsen & Johansen, 2020; Seeger & Sellnow, 2019; Sellnow & Seeger, 2021). In this context, technologies allow public safety authorities and citizens to share and manage information that supports interdependent activities of mitigation, preparation, response, and recovery required to manage small-scale emergencies and large-scale disasters (Sakurai & Murayama, 2019). Consequently, studies examine the use of technologies in contexts of risk and crisis communication to define requirements and develop sociotechnical systems that improve authorities and citizens' abilities to access, manage, and communicate information that, in turn, can improve their abilities to manage risks and crises.

The study of technologies in risk and crisis communication is highly multidisciplinary. Outside of disciplines such as communications and organizational studies, research in emergency management, information science, and human-computer interaction, including the multidisciplinary field of crisis informatics (Palen & Anderson, 2016), focuses on the role that technologies play in the management of risks and crises. In particular, research published in the Proceedings of the Information Systems for Crisis Response and Management (ISCRAM) Conference (iscram.org) and recent edited collections concerning crisis information management systems (Scholl et al., 2023) and emergency management information systems (Van de Walle et al., 2014) focus on the design, use, and evaluation of technologies in crisis management, to include processes of risk and crisis communication that support activities of crisis mitigation, preparation, response, and recovery (Reynolds & Seeger, 2005).

Scope

In the next section, we begin by defining three approaches to the study of technology in risk and crisis communication that understand technology as tools, systems, and infrastructures. The following section shows how these approaches guide research on technologies that can support communications between public safety authorities and citizens. Lastly, using these three approaches as starting points, we explore future directions for research on human-AI and human-autonomy teaming that will be required to understand how semi- and fully autonomous agents can support emerging and future contexts of risk and crisis communication.

The Handbook of International Crisis and Risk Communication Research, Second Edition.
Edited by Andreas Schwarz, Matthew W. Seeger, and Sora Kim.

Technology as Tool, System, and Infrastructure

To understand the role of technologies in risk and crisis communication, we begin by reviewing how researchers have understood technologies as tools, systems, and infrastructures. Each of these perspectives foregrounds aspects of people's interactions with technology that help us understand how public safety authorities and citizens access, share, and use risk- and crisis-related information and to what extent these interactions contribute to risk and crisis management outcomes.

Technology as Tool

Approached as tools or *information and communications technologies (ICT)*, studies examine technologies as integrations of hardware, software, and network components which perform information processing tasks (input, processing, storage, output) that allow end users to access, share, and use information to manage risks and crises. Examples of ICT commonly used by citizens include radio, television, personal computers, smartphones, websites, social media, applications such as personal safety/public warning apps and Generative AI chatbots, and networked devices such as building intrusion detection systems and smartwatches, as well as ICT often used by teams and organizations, including analytics software, decision-support systems, and common operation picture (COP) platforms (Schwarz et al., 2016).

Studies that understand technologies as tools examine how public safety authorities and citizens use ICT to cope with risks and crises and assess the outcomes of these user behaviors and experiences against utility, usability, and user experience criteria defined by users themselves, e.g., user satisfaction (Nielsen, 2009), or task-related criteria defined by other stakeholders, e.g., task efficiency (Norman, 2005). For example, studies of risk and crisis communication examine how local citizens' used Facebook and Twitter to access and share information during the 2014 Oso Mudslide and assess ICT utility and usability by, for example, examining the outcomes of public safety authorities' use of software designed to monitor multiple social media streams during an emergency (Grace et al., 2024; Hughes & Shah, 2016).

By understanding the processes and outcomes of people's use of technologies as tools, researchers inform the design of ICT that helps authorities and citizens' access risk- and crisis-related information they need to cope with these threats. Generally, studies in risk and crisis communication contribute to the human-centered design of ICT by (1) understanding how authorities and citizens access, share, and use information to manage risks and crises, (2) assessing users' information needs to define functional and non-functional design requirements, and (3) designing and evaluating prototypes against these requirements to design ICT that can improve authorities and citizens' abilities to access, share, and use risk- and crisis-related information (Gjøsæter et al., 2021; Palen & Liu, 2007).

Technology as System

Approached as *sociotechnical systems* or *information systems*, studies examine technologies as integrations of ICT, people, and information, typically at team, organizational, or work system levels (Winter et al., 2014), which perform information processing tasks that allow end users to access, share, and use information to manage risks and crises. Examples of sociotechnical systems include the integrations of ICT and personnel in law enforcement agencies that process reports of child abduction and communicate AMBER Alerts to citizens in U.S. communities. These systems consist of multiple ICT tools, such as web-based forms and Wireless Emergency Alert (WEA) technology, and "social" components such as law enforcement agency personnel, standard operating procedures (SOP), organizational structure, and legal authority (Uzzell, 2012).

Studies that understand technologies as systems examine the performance and effectiveness of information processing tasks performed by integrations in which "human participants and/or machines perform work (processes and activities) using information, technology, and other resources to produce specific products/services for specific internal and/or external customers" (Alter, 2013). Thus, studies might examine the performance of law enforcement agencies that process reports of child abduction (i.e., inputs) and communicate AMBER alerts (i.e., outputs) to citizens living in U.S. jurisdictions (i.e., users).

Other studies examine the performance and effectiveness of sociotechnical systems to improve work processes based on criteria defined by end users and stakeholders. For example, law enforcement agencies and victims' families may assess the effectiveness of AMBER Alerts based on the number and quality of citizen tips that lead to the safe return of abducted children (Uzzell, 2012). However, studies suggest that AMBER Alerts do not typically result in these outcomes (Griffin et al., 2016; Griffin et al., 2022), as citizens who receive these and similar alerts can experience alert fatigue and may not effectively monitor and report persons and vehicles of interest (Gier et al., 2017; Miller et al., 2009). Consequently, research explores opportunities to integrate additional sensors into the systems that process AMBER alerts, including traffic cameras that identify and track vehicles (Zhang et al., 2018), so that these systems may more effectively locate abducted children and other missing persons.

Like research that approaches technologies as tools, studies of sociotechnical or information systems for risk and crisis communication contribute design-oriented knowledge. However, these studies define requirements for the sociotechnical integration of ICT within organizations and work systems (Challenger & Clegg, 2011). This involves understanding how the design of "social" components that include SOPs, policies, regulations, worker training, and organizational structure and culture affect the performance and effectiveness of sociotechnical work processes (Clark-Ginsberg & Slayton, 2019; Murata, 2021; Wolbers, 2021).

Technology as Infrastructure

When approached as *infrastructure*, studies also address technologies as integrations of ICT, people, and information, but focus on systems that support information processing by other systems and massively distributed end users (Star & Ruhleder, 1996). Typically examined at inter-organizational and macro-social levels of analysis, studies of technology as infrastructure examine relationships between distributed uses of ICT, e.g., citizens using NextDoor to coordinate recovery work with neighbors following Hurricane Havey (Page-Tan, 2021), and the design and maintenance of the "pervasive enabling resources in network form" that support distributed ICT use (Bowker et al., 2010), e.g., the cloud-based services, software engineers, algorithms, and data that allow NextDoor users across the world to communicate information on the platform during periods of stability and crisis.

Following what Bowker termed "infrastructural inversion," studies of technology-as-infrastructure examine the otherwise-invisible work processes that design and maintain the networked resources or "infrastructure" supporting visible uses of ICT for risk and crisis communication (Soden & Palen, 2016; Star & Bowker, 2002). In the case of AMBER Alerts, infrastructure including telecommunications and Emergency Services IP networks and Next-Generation 911 Core Services allow emergency communications centers to receive and process 9-1-1 calls, including those reporting child abductions. These networked resources and systems provide, in turn, the infrastructure for law enforcement agencies to receive and process these reports for the communication of AMBER Alerts to citizens. By doing so, law enforcement agencies provide, in turn, additional infrastructure that supports the "response system" of citizens tasked with identifying and reporting the child, suspect, and/or vehicle described in the alert to 9-1-1 (Mileti & Sorensen, 1990). Studies that approach technology as infrastructure, therefore, examine the interdependencies between sociotechnical or information systems that support distributed information processing by other systems and individuals using ICT for risk and crisis communication in inter-organizational or macro-social contexts.

From an infrastructure perspective, studies of performance and effectiveness become challenging if the networked resources that support risk and crisis communication remain opaque. For social platforms like NextDoor, the processes of sociotechnical interaction between users and algorithms that organize the functionality of the platform remain invisible or difficult to explain. As a consequence, research can struggle to define the functionality of platforms that "not only help us find information, [but] provide a means to know what there is to know and how to know it" (Gillespie, 2013). Moreover, as these sociotechnical processes both enable and are shaped by the actions of numerous, massively distributed end users, their outcomes can vary across contexts and local practices of risk and crisis communication. Crucially, therefore, research that illuminates these processes and outcomes allows us to evaluate the performance and effectiveness of infrastructure underpinning risk and crisis communication. For example, studies that examine the distributed work processes of volunteers contributing spatial data to OpenStreetMap (Palen et al., 2015), and evaluate maps created by volunteers against the needs of disaster responders (Anderson et al., 2018; Eckle & de Albuquerque, 2015), contribute design knowledge that can improve the performance and effectiveness of infrastructures supporting disaster response activities, especially crisis communications, that depend on accurate and timely maps of disaster-affected areas.

Research on Technologies in Crisis Communication

Research on risk and crisis communication examines information sharing among public safety authorities and citizens supported by technologies that function as tools, systems, and infrastructures. Figure 48.1 presents a matrix of information flows outlined by Quarantelli (1988), Reuter (2015), Reuter and Kaufhold (2018) which we use to identify exemplar technologies that support communications from authorities to citizens (A2C), citizens to citizens (C2C), citizens to authorities (C2A), and authorities to authorities (A2A). For each exemplar, we summarize state-of-the-art research that frames and examines the technology as a tool, system, and infrastructure.

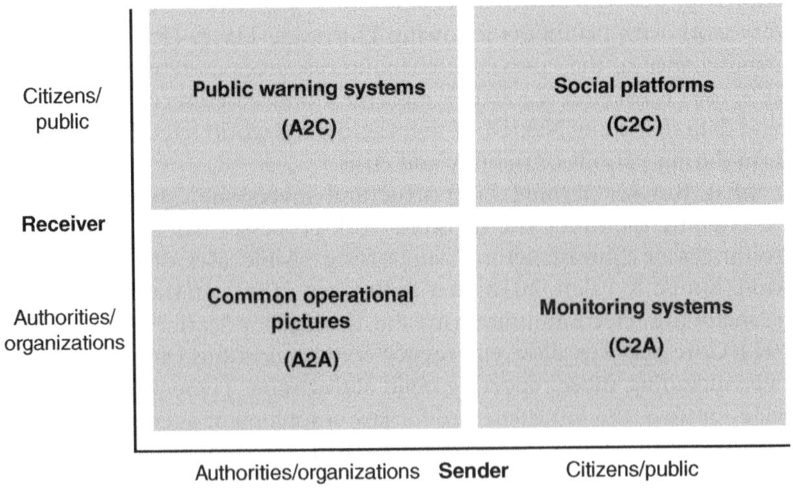

Figure 48.1 Information flows between public safety authorities and citizens. *Source*: Adapted from Reuter (2015).

Importantly, Figure 48.1 offers a framework for organizing research on technologies supporting risk and crisis communication, but does not describe the complexity of information flows characterizing contexts of risk and crisis communication. A single crisis involves multiple crisis management activities that each involve information flows among professional responders and citizens. For example, during the 2022 McKinney Fire that burned over 60,000 acres in Northern California (InciWeb, 2022), the Yreka Fire Department communicated evacuation orders to residents of Siskiyou County (i.e., A2C). In response, residents communicated with family and friends about the evacuation order (i.e., C2C) and called 9-1-1 and 3-1-1 to report incidents and request information from authorities, respectively (i.e., C2A). Meanwhile, officials in the Yreka Fire Department communicated with emergency managers and other public safety organizations to coordinate inter-agency efforts to facilitate the evacuation, respond to 9-1-1 requests for assistance, and contain the fire (i.e., A2A).

A2C: Public Warning Systems

Studies often focus on ***public warning systems*** that authorities use to communicate warnings and other information to citizens in imminent danger from hazards such as heatwaves, hurricanes, and tornados (Lindell, 2018; Lowe et al., 2011). According to Mileti and Sorenson (1990), a public warning system is composed of integrated subsystems for crisis detection, management, and response. Traditionally, detection involves authorities such as meteorologists who use ICT (embedded in systems and infrastructures) to collect and process data to assess the likelihood, severity, and, if imminent, timing of a crisis. These assessments are communicated to authorities such as emergency managers who, as part of the management subsystem, communicate warning messages to the public across multiple channels. Public warning systems like ShakeAlert in the Northwest USA, for example, make use of various channels that include WEA, push notifications to purpose-built mobile and social media apps, as well as broadcast media such as print, radio, television, and web-based news sources (McBride et al., 2020). The response subsystem then focuses on citizens who receive warning messages and take responsive actions, which include communicating informal warnings to family and friends (Mileti & Sorensen, 1990). While studies have examined these subsystems in isolation (Sorensen, 2000), state-of-the-art research examines opportunities for their integration through the design of tools, systems, and infrastructures that support interdependent, data-driven processes of detection, management, and response.

As tools, studies examine public warning systems as ICT which authorities and citizens use to send and receive warnings, respectively. Regarding the latter, studies have long recognized that citizens receive warning messages from multiple sources via multiple channels and then proceed to share warnings with family, friends, and other citizens in online and offline social networks (Kasperson et al., 1988; Lindell & Perry, 2012). However, state-of-the-art research on public warning systems examines the use of multiple channels, including disaster apps and social media platforms, among citizens and organizations sharing official and unofficial messages. In these contexts, crisis communication must be coordinated across decentralized networks and disinformation becomes a major challenge to timely and effective warning and response. In contrast to traditional channels such as warning sirens, studies of general-purpose apps such as Twitter or Sina Weibo and purpose-built mobile apps such as Red Cross New Zealand's Hazard App (Tan et al., 2017) address unique issues of adoption and user experience that shape "people's routine channel access and preferences" in the periods leading up to a crisis warning event (Lindell, 2018). These studies include surveys of targeted users, such as surveys of citizens' perceptions of the utility and acceptability of a proposed earthquake early warning system (Becker et al., 2020). As the European Emergency Number Association (2019) concludes, one of the major challenges for the deployment of public warning apps "is to get an adequate number of people to install the app" (p. 16).

As systems, studies examine the sociotechnical work processes that perform the detection, management, and response functions of public warning subsystems (McBride et al., 2020). Focusing on the management subsystem, for example, studies develop and evaluate prototype dashboards that public information officers (PIOs) can use alongside commercial tools like Hootsuite to manage multi-channel, many-to-many communications with citizens using traditional channels, official public warning apps, and social platforms like Facebook and Twitter (Hughes & Shah, 2016; Wukich & Mergel, 2015). As Hughes and Palen (2012) explain, communicating across multiple channels requires PIOs to analyze public information-as-data and communicate public information-as-warnings inside and outside emergency management agencies, respectively. Other research focuses on collective behavior that shapes the (re-)distribution of official messages. Sutton et al. (2014, 2015), for example, examine factors that influence the redistribution, i.e., retweeting, of official warnings among citizens using Twitter.

Lastly, studies address the infrastructure supporting detection, management, and response in integrated public warning systems. Describing the networked resources supporting crisis communication in rural Oso, Washington, where a 2014 landslide killed 43 people, Daily and Starbird (2017) summarize these resources:

> "The phone lines in the newsroom are VOIP. Google productivity tools are the back-end of reporting. Print production and website production both happen through web-based services. Excluding the bodies of the journalists and the printing presses, almost everything else of the "most local" newspaper is mediated by software-based networked services ... reliance on so many tools that function from a distance raises questions about how a local news organization might perform their role as local communication infrastructure in the absence of these tools—for example—if networked ICTs were disrupted in a large scale natural disaster."

This centralization and interdependence of networked resources supporting public warning systems create vulnerabilities in critical infrastructure that can contribute to escalating and cascading failures during a disaster (Scholz et al., 2022). Studies therefore address opportunities to improve the resilience of critical infrastructure supporting risk and crisis communications such as power grids (Comes & Van de Walle, 2014), as well as issues, including smartphone state-of-charge (Lukau et al., 2023), that can determine the effectiveness of public warning systems during power outages (Reuter, 2013).

C2C: Social Media

Focusing on citizen-to-citizen communication, studies investigate how people use *social media* to cope with risks and crises (Reuter et al., 2018). Here we refer to social media broadly, to include apps like Facebook, Sina Weibo, and Twitter/X, and messaging apps such as WhatsApp. Research on social media also approaches these technologies as tools, systems, and infrastructures that support risk and crisis communication.

As tools, studies examine how citizens use social media apps to share and access information about risk and crises. During disasters, for example, citizens typically use social media to share expressions of sympathy, opportunities for volunteering and donation, warnings and advice, and situation-specific details, e.g., hazard information, response updates, etc. during a crisis (Olteanu et al., 2015; Reuter et al., 2018; Vieweg et al., 2010). Significantly, compared to information posted by media organizations and remote citizens, relatively little information is posted by eyewitnesses or local citizens, especially regarding critical infrastructure damage or requests for assistance (Grace, 2020; Olteanu et al., 2015). Studies also show that citizens use social media to access information about risks and crises and often expect public safety authorities to monitor information posted on social platforms (Petersen et al., 2020; Reuter & Spielhofer, 2017; Reuter et al., 2015; Reuter et al., 2017). This information also serves as a backchannel to information broadcast by news media and government agencies (Sutton et al., 2008). For example, during floods impacting Chennai, India, in 2015, citizens preferred Facebook and WhatsApp over traditional broadcast media for real-time updates (Bhuvana & Arul Aram, 2019).

As systems, social platforms consist of networks of app users who collaboratively share, filter, annotate, and (re)distribute information resources for citizens coping with risks and crises. Starbird et al. (2010) describe three collective information behaviors observed on social media platforms during a crisis: Generative behaviors occur when citizens post eyewitness observations about crisis events; synthetic behaviors involve "digesting, filtering, relaying, and adapting" information generated by local eyewitnesses or official sources; and derivative behaviors occur when citizens redistribute (e.g., retweet) generative and synthetic information across networks of social platform users (Starbird et al., 2010). These information behaviors can contribute to collective sensemaking during a crisis by providing citizens with timely and accurate information about developing events (Fischer-Preßler et al., 2019; Stieglitz et al., 2018). However, studies also show that crowd-based processes contribute to misinformation (Starbird et al., 2019), such as rumors that spread across social platforms about the perpetrators of the Boston Marathon bombing (Fischer-Preßler et al., 2019; Krafft et al., 2017).

Lastly, the collective behaviors of citizens using social media, together with these platforms' algorithms, "not only help us find information, they provide a means to know what there is to know and how to know it" during a crisis (Gillespie, 2013). As such, social media provides infrastructure that public safety authorities and citizens rely on to share and access risk- and crisis-related information. As explained above, public warning systems rely on multiple channels, including social media, to distribute timely warnings to the public. Furthermore, as sources of real-time data, social media platforms, especially those with open APIs (Anderson & Schram, 2011), provide the infrastructure for monitoring systems that public safety authorities use to gather risk- and crisis-related information generated by citizens (Castillo, 2016). As we explain below, monitoring systems support information flows from citizens to public safety authorities who use this information to detect and characterize events ranging from traffic jams to disease outbreaks (Yousefinaghani et al., 2019).

C2A: Monitoring Systems

Research examines risk and crisis communication from citizens to public safety authorities through channels that include emergency and non-emergency telephone numbers (Grace et al., 2023; Morand et al., 2023; Pamukcu et al., 2021) and social media platforms (Hughes, & Palen, 2012; Wukich & Mergel, 2015). However, research on monitoring, sensing, and surveillance systems looks to these channels as sources of real-time data to detect and characterize events, processes, and system statuses in a geographic area (Fertier et al., 2020). These *monitoring systems* consist of tools, systems, and infrastructures that support the continuous and systematic collection, analysis, and interpretation of data related to public health and safety (WHO, 2022).

As tools, monitoring systems consist of ICT that public safety authorities use to collect and analyze data from heterogeneous sensors. These sensors include physical sensors such as water level sensors and citizens who serve as "social sensors" by producing data about real-time events (Jiang & McGill, 2010). In a participatory sensing model, citizens voluntarily produce data by responding to purpose-built app requests or posting information on social platforms like Twitter/X and Sina Weibo that are subsequently gathered by monitoring systems (Bauman et al., 2017; Tien et al., 2016). In contrast, opportunistic sensing enlists citizens as "custodians" of smartphones or other networked devices installed with applications that share data without citizens' direct involvement (Lane et al., 2008). An example of participatory sensing, LastQuake is an earthquake monitoring system that integrates traditional seismic data with crowdsourced reports from people who respond to tremors by sharing information on the

LastQuake app (Bossu et al., 2018). Together with data gathered from in-situ and remote sensors, including satellite, airborne, and ground-based sensors, monitoring systems provide opportunities to detect, characterize, and predict events occurring in built and natural environments that can support crisis mitigation, preparation, response, and recovery applications.

As systems, monitoring systems involve work performed by public safety authorities using ICT to effectively detect and characterize events in a geographic jurisdiction. For example, studies examine changes in emergency call taking and dispatch that result from the integration of multiple, heterogeneous sensors, including 9-1-1 callers, vehicle and smart home alarms, and traffic cameras into emergency communications centers (Grace, 2021; Grace & Potts, 2022). Similarly, other studies examine the sociotechnical work processes of virtual operations support teams (VOST), volunteers who use off-the-shelf and purpose-built ICT to gather, filter, and summarize posts made by citizens across multiple social platforms during crises (Fathi & Fiedrich, 2022). VOSTs provide information resources to emergency management agencies that have also adapted to monitor real-time streams of multisource information (Purohit et al., 2018).

As infrastructures, monitoring systems gather and analyze data from heterogeneous sensors to detect and characterize events, thereby supporting authority-to-citizen communication through public warning systems (see preceding section) and authority-to-authority communication through systems such as common operational pictures (see next section). Furthermore, historical datasets created by monitoring systems create resources for machine learning and simulation applications that, for example, help emergency communications centers make data-driven staffing decisions (Petitdemange et al., 2020) or pre-position ambulances based on observed emergency call patterns (Landsberg et al., 2020). Conversely, as monitoring systems incorporate social sensors, the adoption and usage behaviors of purpose-built and social media app users provide the infrastructure for participatory and opportunistic sensing that supports effective and timely event detection and characterization.

A2A: Common Operational Pictures

A *common operational picture* (COP) is a real-time information display that provides collocated or distributed actors with a shared view of the status of crisis management contexts and assets, typically displayed as map layers as part of geographic-information systems (GIS) (Hwang & Yoon, 2020; Steen-Tveit & Erik Munkvold, 2021). COPs integrate data from various monitoring systems to display information on crisis contexts and crisis management processes. As such, COPs support situational awareness and communication among public safety authorities, which can improve the coordination and performance of risk and crisis management operations.

As tools, studies examine COPs to understand how public safety authorities use shared information displays to manage crises such as simulated terrorist attacks (Steen-Tveit & Radianti, 2019). These studies often examine COP effectiveness based on measures of authorities' situational awareness (SA), which, according to Endsley (1995), involves the perception, comprehension, and projection of elements in an environment. These studies show that while a COP might represent real-time information on map-based displays, authorities' SA depends on how they interpret this information based on tacit knowledge gained through experience in professional roles, formally represented by standard operating procedures and organizational structures, while engaged in situated activities of crisis mitigation, preparation, and response (Danielsson et al., 2014; Klein, 2008).

As systems, however, studies examine COPs as integrations of shared information displays (i.e., the "technical") within work practices of authorities working in and across organizations such as emergency management agencies (i.e., the "social"). Focusing on how COP designs can support shared SA among public safety authorities (Steen-Tveit & Erik Munkvold, 2021), these studies also show that information displays alone are insufficient for shared understanding and coordination in crisis situations (Treurniet & Wolbers, 2021). Wolbers and Boersma (2013), for example, show that authorities interpret COP displays differently based on their tacit knowledge and work practices, and, as a result, must negotiate the meaning of shared information displays to coordinate intra- and inter-organization operations. Consequently, along with a COP, authorities use various ICT and information resources to negotiate the meaning of shared information displays during a crisis (Borglund, 2017).

Lastly, studies examine the infrastructures supporting authorities' use of COP tools, including wireless and satellite networks that provide access to shared information displays during crises such as Hurricane Harvey (Danaher et al., 2022). However, few studies assess COPs as a key component of sociotechnical systems that infrastructure risk and crisis communication among distributed public safety authorities and citizens. For example, 9-1-1 call takers and dispatchers use computer-aided dispatch systems to communicate situational awareness information to first responders using radio and mobile data terminals (Grace et al., 2023). Assessing the effectiveness of this work requires understanding how the design of a COP like CAD can support team processes of call taking and dispatch (i.e., performance) to provide information resources that first responders – often using other COP tools – require for emergency response (i.e., effectiveness).

Future Research Directions

Future research on technologies in crisis communication must address the roles of AI-based technologies that involve human supervision and, increasingly, those that do not. While humans interact with non-human agents that operate at different levels of automation/autonomy, research broadly distinguishes between human-automation and human-autonomy teaming (Parasuraman et al., 2000). In the former, non-human agents, such as generative AI chatbots, automate specific work tasks under the direction and supervision of humans. In contrast, human–autonomy teaming refers to one or more humans and one or more autonomous, non-human agents working interdependently toward a common goal or outcome (O'Neill et al., 2022). In human-autonomy teams, the autonomous agent, such as a robot that can independently search a collapsed building for survivors (Chitikena et al., 2023), functions at a high level of autonomy characterized by independent decision-making and task execution that does not require human prompting or direction (McNeese et al., 2018; O'Neill et al., 2022).

To address the role of non-human, automated and autonomous agents in crisis communication, future research will involve continuities and discontinuities with past research. Below we briefly consider how emerging research on human-automation and human-autonomy teaming develops from and breaks with past research that has approached technologies as tools, systems, and infrastructures.

From Tools to Teammates

First, studies of future crisis communication will need to consider non-human agents as teammates rather than tools (National Academies, 2022). In contrast to ICT, automated agents such as generative AI chatbots will perform human tasks and exhibit human behaviors developed from human-generated training data. Addressing these technologies as teammates is important, as studies show that humans exhibit different levels of trust in automated and autonomous agents, and the extent to which humans trust their non-human teammates affects the performance and effectiveness of human-automation/autonomy teams (McNeese et al., 2018).

For research on public warning systems, for example, trust and social cues are important factors in risk perception and protective action decision-making (Lindell, 2018). How does this change when citizens interact with AI agents to access personalized warnings and other information during a crisis? Studies will need to investigate citizens' use of chatbots and other generative AI systems that may be indistinguishable from human sources. Beyond traditional concerns with usability, this research can look to studies of (human) teamwork to guide analyses of the performance and effectiveness of human-automation/autonomy teams involved in accessing, sharing, and using risk- and crisis-related information (O'Neill et al., 2022). However, continuities with past research will be found in studies of user experience that consider, for example, perceptions of trust as important criteria for the acceptability, adoption, and use of disaster warning apps (Tan et al., 2020a; Tan et al., 2020b).

Delegation and Monitoring in Human-Automation/Autonomy Systems

Second, future research will need to examine how risk and crisis communication tasks and roles can be delegated to autonomous agents, and how public safety authorities and citizens can effectively monitor and coordinate with autonomous agents during crises. Although the sociotechnical perspective has often been questioned as a framework for examining interdependencies between the "social" and "technical" components of work systems (Griffith & Dougherty, 2002), new human/non-human interdependencies emerge when non-human teammates begin performing tasks and roles formerly performed by public safety authorities and citizens within systems constituted by teams of human-automation/autonomy teams. At team and system levels, research will need to examine how public safety authorities and citizens delegate crisis communication work to non-human teammates and then monitor the performance and effectiveness of automated/autonomous agents performing this work (Lyytinen et al., 2021). Furthermore, issues of explainability arise when humans do not understand the logic or factors that determined an AI/autonomous system's actions and resulting outcomes (Endsley, 2023).

Studies of COPs, for example, now explore designs that support monitoring of autonomous agents, like unmanned aerial vehicles, to which public safety authorities have delegated tasks such as wildfire detection and monitoring (Akhloufi et al., 2021). Future research will need to examine how shared information displays support effective crisis communication among authorities working to coordinate the activities of human-automation/autonomy teams and systems. These studies might explore how these technologies support communication by understanding requirements for coordination work in sociotechnical systems (Schmidt, 2008) or approaches to explainability that can inform the design of communications between human and non-human teammates engaged in crisis management and response (Hoffman et al., 2019).

Infrastructures and AI Biases

Lastly, future research must examine hidden biases in the infrastructures that shape the design of AI-based technologies that support crisis communication among distributed public safety authorities and citizens. Following work in critical data studies that challenges the neutrality of data generated by people using, for example, social media during crises (Mulder et al., 2016; Shelton et al., 2014), research will need to examine biases that result from human, institutional, and computational infrastructures used to design and maintain AI systems for crisis communication (Schwartz et al., 2022). However, because the operations of AI systems are often opaque, these biases will likely be hidden from and variously perceived by authorities and citizens interacting with AI systems. While risk and crisis communication research has always attempted to understand the factors that shape the content and distribution of information about hazards (Kasperson et al., 1988), future studies will be required to explore factors that include the datasets, testing, evaluation, and supervision of AI systems to understand how these technologies shape information access and sharing during emergencies and disasters.

Conclusion

Crisis communication research has understood technologies as tools, systems, and infrastructures. These approaches have guided studies of technologies that support crisis communication among public safety authorities and citizens. Examples of these technologies include public warning systems, social media platforms, monitoring systems, and common operational pictures. However, to address the role of non-human, automated, and autonomous agents in crisis communication, future research must navigate both continuities and discontinuities with past approaches.

References

Akhloufi, M. A., Couturier, A., & Castro, N. A. (2021). Unmanned aerial vehicles for wildland fires: Sensing, perception, cooperation and assistance. *Drones*, *5*(1), 15. https://doi.org/10.3390/drones5010015

Alter, S. (2013). Work system theory: Overview of core concepts, extensions, and challenges for the future. *Journal of the Association for Information Systems*, *14*(2), 72–121. https://doi.org/10.17705/1jais.00323

Anderson, K. M., & Schram, A. (2011). Design and implementation of a data analytics infrastructure in support of crisis informatics research. *Proceeding of the 33rd International Conference on Software Engineering – ICSE '11*, 844. https://doi.org/10.1145/1985793.1985920

Anderson, J., Soden, R., Keegan, B., Palen, L., & Anderson, K. M. (2018). The crowd is the territory: Assessing quality in peer-produced spatial data during disasters. *International Journal of Human Computer Interaction*, *34*(4), 295–310. https://doi.org/10.1080/10447318.2018.1427828

Bauman, K., Tuzhilin, A., & Zaczynski, R. (2017). Using social sensors for detecting emergency events. *ACM Transactions on Management Information Systems*, *8*(2–3), 1–20. https://doi.org/10.1145/3052931

Becker, J. S., Potter, S. H., Vinnell, L. J., Nakayachi, K., McBride, S. K., & Johnston, D. M. (2020). Earthquake early warning in Aotearoa New Zealand: A survey of public perspectives to guide warning system development. *Humanities and Social Sciences Communications*, *7*(1), 138. https://doi.org/10.1057/s41599-020-00613-9

Bhuvana, N., & Arul Aram, I. (2019). Facebook and Whatsapp as disaster management tools during the Chennai (India) floods of 2015. *International Journal of Disaster Risk Reduction*, *39*, 101135. https://doi.org/10.1016/j.ijdrr.2019.101135

Borglund, E. A. M. (2017). The role of artefacts in creating a common operational picture during large crises. *Proceedings of the 14th ISCRAM Conference*, 191–203.

Bossu, R., Roussel, F., Fallou, L., Landès, M., Steed, R., Mazet-Roux, G., Dupont, A., Frobert, L., & Petersen, L. (2018). LastQuake: From rapid information to global seismic risk reduction. *International Journal of Disaster Risk Reduction*, *28*, 32–42. https://doi.org/10.1016/j.ijdrr.2018.02.024

Bowker, G. C., Baker, K., Millerand, F., & Ribes, D. (2010). Toward information infrastructure studies: Ways of knowing in a networked environment. In J. Hunsinger, L. Klastrup, & M. Allen, Eds., *International Handbook of Internet Research* (pp. 97–117). Netherlands: Springer. https://doi.org/10.1007/978-1-4020-9789-8_5

Castillo, C. (2016). *Big Crisis Data: Social Media in Disasters and Time-Critical Situations*. Cambridge University Press.

Challenger, R., & Clegg, C. W. (2011). Crowd disasters: A socio-technical systems perspective. *Contemporary Social Science*, *6*(3), 343–360. https://doi.org/10.1080/21582041.2011.619862

Chitikena, H., Sanfilippo, F., & Ma, S. (2023). Robotics in search and rescue (SAR) operations: An ethical and design perspective framework for response phase. *Applied Sciences*, *13*(3), 1800. https://doi.org/10.3390/app13031800

Clark-Ginsberg, A., & Slayton, R. (2019). Regulating risks within complex sociotechnical systems: Evidence from critical infrastructure cybersecurity standards. *Science and Public Policy*, *46*(3), 339–346. https://doi.org/10.1093/scipol/scy061

Comes, T., & Van de Walle, B. (2014). Measuring disaster resilience: The impact of hurricane sandy on critical infrastructure systems. *Proceedings of the 11th International ISCRAM Conference*, 190–199.

Dailey, D., & Starbird, K. (2017). Social media seamsters: Stitching platforms & audiences into local crisis infrastructure. *Computer Supported Cooperative Work (CSCW)*. https://doi.org/10.1145/2998181.2998290

Danaher, L. T., Wood, E., & Frazier, T. (2022). Rescue coordination common operating picture: Enhancement through satellite technology. *Journal of Emergency Management*, *20*(8), 73–90. https://doi.org/10.5055/jem.0682

Danielsson, E., Alvinius, A., & Larsson, G. (2014). From common operating picture to situational awareness. *International Journal of Emergency Management*, *10*(1), 28. https://doi.org/10.1504/IJEM.2014.061659

Eckle, M., & de Albuquerque, J. P. (2015). Quality assessment of remote mapping in openstreetmap for disaster management purposes. *Proceedings of the ISCRAM 2015 Conference.*

EENA (2019). *Public warning systems: Update.* European Emergency Number Association (EENA) August 3, 2024. https://eena.org/wp-content/uploads/2019_09_25_PWS_Document_FINAL_Compressed.pdf

Endsley, M. R. (1995). Toward a theory of situation awareness in dynamic systems. *Human Factors: The Journal of the Human Factors and Ergonomics Society*, *37*(1), 32–64. https://doi.org/10.1518/001872095779049543

Endsley, M. R. (2023). Supporting human-AI teams: Transparency, explainability, and situation awareness. *Computers in Human Behavior*, *140*, 107574. https://doi.org/10.1016/j.chb.2022.107574

Fathi, R., & Fiedrich, F. (2022). Social media analytics by virtual operations support teams in disaster management: Situational awareness and actionable information for decision-makers. *Frontiers in Earth Science*, *10*. https://doi.org/10.3389/feart.2022.941803

Fertier, A., Montarnal, A., Barthe-Delanoë, A.-M., Truptil, S., & Bénaben, F. (2020). Real-time data exploitation supported by model- and event-driven architecture to enhance situation awareness, application to crisis management. *Enterprise Information Systems*, *14*(6), 769–796. https://doi.org/10.1080/17517575.2019.1691268

Fischer-Preßler, D., Schwemmer, C., & Fischbach, K. (2019). Collective sense-making in times of crisis: Connecting terror management theory with Twitter user reactions to the Berlin terrorist attack. *Computers in Human Behavior*, *100*, 138–151. https://doi.org/10.1016/j.chb.2019.05.012

Frandsen, F., & Johansen, W. (2020). . In F. Frandsen, & W. Johansen, Eds., *Crisis Communication*. De Gruyter. https://doi.org/10.1515/9783110554236

Gier, V. S., Kreiner, D. S., & Lampinen, J. M. (2017). Factors affecting recognition of senior citizens in a silver alert. *Journal of Police and Criminal Psychology*, *32*(3), 185–196. https://doi.org/10.1007/s11896-016-9210-0

Gillespie, T. (2013). The relevance of algorithms. In T. Gillespie, P. Boczkowski, & K. Foot, Eds., *Media Technologies: Essays on Communication, Materiality, and Society* (pp. 167–193). MIT Press.

Gjøsæter, T., Radianti, J., & Chen, W. (2021). Universal design of ICT for emergency management from stakeholders' perspective: a systematic literature review. *Information Systems Frontiers*, *23*(5), 1213–1225. https://doi.org/10.1007/s10796-020-10084-7

Grace, R. (2020). Toponym usage in social media in emergencies. *International Journal of Disaster Risk Reduction*, *52*, 101923. https://doi.org/10.1016/j.ijdrr.2020.101923

Grace, R. (2021). Overcoming barriers to social media use through multisensor integration in emergency management systems. *International Journal of Disaster Risk Reduction*, *66*, 102636. https://doi.org/10.1016/J.IJDRR.2021.102636

Grace, R., & Potts, M. (2022). Opportunities for multisensor integration in public-safety answering points. *Proceedings of the 19th ISCRAM Conference*, 895–904.

Grace, R., Montarnal, A., Petitdemange, E., Rutter, J., Rodriguez, G. R., & Potts, M. (2023). Collaborative information seeking during a 911 call surge: A case study. *Proceedings of the 20th ISCRAM Conference, 649-662.* http://dx.doi.org/10.59297/ZFAY5505

Grace, R., Pang, F., & Kropczynski, J. (2024). Cues facilitating collective sensemaking during emergencies: Gaps, inconsistencies, and indicators. *International Journal of Disaster Risk Reduction*, *114*, 104897. https://doi.org/10.1016/j.ijdrr.2024.104897

Griffin, T., Williams, J. H., Wooldredge, J., & Miller, D. (2016). Does AMBER Alert 'save lives'? An empirical analysis and critical implications. *Journal of Crime and Justice*, *39*(4), 490–511. https://doi.org/10.1080/0735648X.2014.1003577

Griffin, T., Williams, J. H., & Kadleck, C. (2022). AMBER alert effectiveness reexamined. *Criminal Justice Policy Review*, *33*(1), 23–44. https://doi.org/10.1177/08874034211026366

Griffith, T. L., & Dougherty, D. J. (2002). Beyond socio-technical systems: Introduction to the special issue. *Journal of Engineering and Technology Management*, *19*(2), 205–216. https://doi.org/10.1016/S0923-4748(02)00018-8

Hoffman, R. R., Mueller, S. T., Klein, G., & Litman, J. (2019). Metrics for explainable AI: Challenges and prospects. *ArXiv Preprint ArXiv*, *1812*(04608), 1–50.

Hughes, A., & Palen, L. (2012). The evolving role of the public information officer: An examination of social media in emergency management. *Journal of Homeland Security and Emergency Management*, *9*(1). https://doi.org/10.1515/1547-7355.1976

Hughes, A., & Shah, R. (2016). Designing an application for social media needs in emergency public information work. *Proceedings of the 19th International Conference on Supporting Group Work – GROUP '16*, 399–408. https://doi.org/10.1145/2957276.2957307

Hwang, G. H., & Yoon, W. C. (2020). A new approach to requirement development for a common operational picture to support distributed situation awareness. *Safety Science*, *125*, 104569. https://doi.org/10.1016/j.ssci.2019.104569

InciWeb (November 7, 2022,). *McKinney Fire*. Incident Information System. https://inciweb.nwcg.gov/incident-information/caknf-mckinney-fire

Jiang, M., & McGill, W. L. (2010). Human-centered sensing for crisis response and management analysis campaigns. *Proceedings of the 7th International ISCRAM Conference*.

Kasperson, R. E., Renn, O., Slovic, P., Brown, H. S., Emel, J., Goble, R., Kasperson, J. X., & Ratick, S. (1988). The social amplification of risk: A conceptual framework. *Risk Analysis*, *8*(2), 177–187. https://doi.org/10.1111/j.1539-6924.1988.tb01168.x

Klein, G. (2008). Naturalistic decision making. *Human Factors: The Journal of the Human Factors and Ergonomics Society*, *50*(3), 456–460. https://doi.org/10.1518/001872008X288385

Krafft, P., Zhou, K., Edwards, I., Starbird, K., & Spiro, E. S. (2017). Centralized, parallel, and distributed information processing during collective sensemaking. *Proceedings of the 2017 CHI Conference on Human Factors in Computing Systems – CHI '17*, 2976–2987. https://doi.org/10.1145/3025453.3026012

Landsberg, L., Ganske, D., Munschauer, C., & Mudimu, O. A. (2020). Using existing data to support operational emergency response in Germany: Current use cases, opportunities and challenges. *Proceedings of the 17th ISCRAM Conference*, 406–415.

Lane, N. D., Eisenman, S. B., Musolesi, M., Miluzzo, E., & Campbell, A. T. (2008). Urban sensing systems. *Proceedings of the 9th Workshop on Mobile Computing Systems and Applications – HotMobile '08*, 11. https://doi.org/10.1145/1411759.1411763

Lindell, M. K. (2018). Communicating imminent risk. In H. Rodríguez, W. Donner, & J. E. Trainor, Eds., *Handbook of Disaster Research* (pp. 449–477). Cham: Springer. https://doi.org/10.1007/978-3-319-63254-4_22

Lindell, M. K., & Perry, R. W. (2012). The protective action decision model: Theoretical modifications and additional evidence. *Risk Analysis*, *32*(4), 616–632. https://doi.org/10.1111/j.1539-6924.2011.01647.x

Lowe, D., Ebi, K. L., & Forsberg, B. (2011). Heatwave early warning systems and adaptation advice to reduce human health consequences of heatwaves. *International Journal of Environmental Research and Public Health*, *8*(12), 4623–4648. https://doi.org/10.3390/ijerph8124623

Lukau, E., Schiller, J., & Meissen, U. (2023). Towards efficient post-blackout emergency communication based on citizens' smartphone state of charge. *Proceedings of the 20th ISCRAM Conference*.

Lyytinen, K., Nickerson, J. V., & King, J. L. (2021). Metahuman systems = humans + machines that learn. *Journal of Information Technology*, *36*(4), 427–445. https://doi.org/10.1177/0268396220915917

McBride, S. K., Bostrom, A., Sutton, J., de Groot, R. M., Baltay, A. S., Terbush, B., Bodin, P., Dixon, M., Holland, E., Arba, R., Laustsen, P., Liu, S., & Vinci, M. (2020). Developing post-alert messaging for ShakeAlert, the earthquake early warning system for the West Coast of the United States of America. *International Journal of Disaster Risk Reduction*, *50*, 101713. https://doi.org/10.1016/j.ijdrr.2020.101713

McNeese, N. J., Demir, M., Cooke, N. J., & Myers, C. (2018). Teaming with a synthetic teammate: Insights into human-autonomy teaming. *Human Factors: The Journal of the Human Factors and Ergonomics Society*, *60*(2), 262–273. https://doi.org/10.1177/0018720817743223

Mileti, D. S., & Sorensen, J. H. (1990). Communication of emergency public warnings: A social science perspective and state-of-the-art assessment. https://doi.org/10.2172/6137387

Miller, M. K., Griffin, T., Clinkinbeard, S. S., & Thomas, R. M. (2009). The psychology of AMBER Alert: Unresolved issues and implications. *The Social Science Journal, 46*(1), 111–123. https://doi.org/10.1016/j.soscij.2008.12.004

Morand, O., Larribau, R., Safin, S., Pages, R., Soichet, H., & Rizza, C. (2023). The integration of live video tools to help bystanders during an emergency call: Protocol for a mixed methods simulation study. *JMIR Research Protocols, 12*, e40699. https://doi.org/10.2196/40699

Mulder, F., Ferguson, J., Groenewegen, P., Boersma, K., & Wolbers, J. (2016). Questioning big data: Crowdsourcing crisis data towards an inclusive humanitarian response. *Big Data & Society, 3*(2), 205395171666205. https://doi.org/10.1177/2053951716662054

Murata, A. (2021). Cultural aspects as a root cause of organizational failure in risk and crisis management in the Fukushima Daiichi disaster. *Safety Science, 135*, 105091. https://doi.org/10.1016/j.ssci.2020.105091

National Academies (2022). *Human-AI Teaming: State-of-the-art and Research Needs*. National Academies Press. https://doi.org/10.17226/26355

Nielsen, J. (2009). What is usability? In C. Wilson, Ed., *User Experience Re-mastered: Your Guide to Getting the Right Design* (pp. 3–22). Elsevier Science.

Norman, D. (2005). Human-centered design considered harmful. *Interactions, 12*(4), 14–19. https://interactions.acm.org/archive/view/july-august-2005/human-centered-design-considered-harmful1

O'Neill, T., McNeese, N., Barron, A., & Schelble, B. (2022). Human–autonomy teaming: A review and analysis of the empirical literature. *Human Factors: The Journal of the Human Factors and Ergonomics Society, 64*(5), 904–938. https://doi.org/10.1177/0018720820960865

Olteanu, A., Vieweg, S., & Castillo, C. (2015). What to expect when the unexpected happens. *Proceedings of the 18th ACM Conference on Computer Supported Cooperative Work & Social Computing – CSCW '15*, 994–1009. https://doi.org/10.1145/2675133.2675242

Page-Tan, C. (2021). An analysis of social media use and neighbor-assisted debris removal in Houston following Hurricane Harvey. *International Journal of Disaster Risk Reduction, 63*, 102450. https://doi.org/10.1016/j.ijdrr.2021.102450

Palen, L., & Anderson, K. M. (2016). Crisis informatics: New data for extraordinary times. *Science, 353*(6296), 224–225. https://doi.org/10.1126/science.aag2579

Palen, L., & Liu, S. B. (2007). Citizen communications in crisis: Anticipating a future of ICT-supported public participation. *Proceedings of the SIGCHI Conference on Human Factors in Computing Systems – CHI '07*, 727. https://doi.org/10.1145/1240624.1240736

Palen, L., Soden, R., Anderson, T. J., & Barrenechea, M. (2015). Success & scale in a data-producing organization: The socio-technical evolution of openstreetmap in response to humanitarian events. *Proceedings of the 33rd Annual ACM Conference on Human Factors in Computing Systems*, 4113–4122. https://doi.org/10.1145/2702123.2702294

Pamukcu, D., Zobel, C., & Gu, Y. (2021). Analysis of Orange County 311 system service requests during the COVID-19 pandemic. *Proceedings of the 18th ISCRAM Conference*, 208–217.

Parasuraman, R., Sheridan, T. B., & Wickens, C. D. (2000). A model for types and levels of human interaction with automation. *IEEE Transactions on Systems, Man, and Cybernetics – Part A: Systems and Humans, 30*(3), 286–297. https://doi.org/10.1109/3468.844354

Petersen, L., Fallou, L., Reilly, P., & Serafinelli, E. (2020). Public expectations of critical infrastructure operators in times of crisis. *Sustainable and Resilient Infrastructure, 5*(1–2), 62–77. https://doi.org/10.1080/23789689.2018.1469358

Petitdemange, E., Lamine, E., Fontanili, F., & Lauras, M. (2020). Enhancing emergency call centers' performance through a data-driven simulation approach. *Proceedings of the 17th ISCRAM Conference*, 218–227.

Purohit, H., Castillo, C., Imran, M., & Pandey, R. (2018). Social-EOC: Serviceability model to rank social media requests for emergency operation centers. *2018 IEEE/ACM International Conference on Advances in Social Networks Analysis and Mining (ASONAM)*, 119–126. https://doi.org/10.1109/ASONAM.2018.8508709

Quarantelli, E. L. (1988). Disaster crisis management: A summary of research findings. *Journal of Management Studies, 25*(4), 373–385. https://doi.org/10.1111/j.1467-6486.1988.tb00043.x

Reuter, C. (2013). Power outage communications: Survey of needs, infrastructures and concepts. *Proceedings of the 10th ISCRAM Conference*, 884–889.

Reuter, C. (2015). *Crisis 2.0: Towards a Systematization of Social Software Use (IJISCRAM). In Emergent Collaboration Infrastructures* (pp. 35–48). Springer Fachmedien Wiesbaden. https://doi.org/10.1007/978-3-658-08586-5_4

Reuter, C., & Kaufhold, M.-A. (2018). Fifteen years of social media in emergencies: A retrospective review and future directions for crisis Informatics. *Journal of Contingencies & Crisis Management*, *26*(1), 41–57. https://doi.org/10.1111/1468-5973.12196

Reuter, C., & Spielhofer, T. (2017). Towards social resilience: A quantitative and qualitative survey on citizens' perception of social media in emergencies in Europe. *Technological Forecasting and Social Change*, *121*, 168–180. https://doi.org/10.1016/J.TECHFORE.2016.07.038

Reuter, C., Ludwig, T., Friberg, T., & Pratzler-Wanczura, S. (2015). Social media and emergency services? Interview study on current and potential use in 7 European countries. *International Journal of Information Systems for Crisis Response and Management*, *7*(2), 36–58. https://doi.org/10.4018/IJISCRAM.2015040103

Reuter, C., Kaufhold, M. A., Spielhofer, T., & Hahne, A. S. (2017). Social media in emergencies: A representative study on citizens' perception in Germany. *Proceedings of the ACM on Human-Computer Interaction*, *1*(CSCW), 1–19. https://doi.org/10.1145/3134725

Reuter, C., Hughes, A. L., & Kaufhold, M. A. (2018). Social media in crisis management: An evaluation and analysis of crisis informatics research. *International Journal of Human-Computer Interaction*, *34*(4), 280–294. https://doi.org/10.1080/10447318.2018.1427832

Reynolds, B., & Seeger, M. W. (2005). Crisis and emergency risk communication as an integrative model. *Journal of Health Communication*, *10*(1), 43–55. https://doi.org/10.1080/10810730590904571

Sakurai, M., & Murayama, Y. (2019). Information technologies and disaster management – benefits and issues. *Progress in Disaster Science*, *2*, 100012. https://doi.org/10.1016/j.pdisas.2019.100012

Schmidt, K. (2008). *Cooperative Work and Coordinative Practices* (pp. 3–27). London: Springer. https://doi.org/10.1007/978-1-84800-068-1_1

Scholl, H. J., Holdemon, E. E., & Boersma, K. F. (2023). . In H. J. Scholl, E. E. Holdeman, & F. K. Boersma, Eds., *Disaster Management and Information Technology* (Vol. 40). Springer International Publishing. https://doi.org/10.1007/978-3-031-20939-0

Scholz, C., Schauer, S., & Latzenhofer, M. (2022). The emergence of new critical infrastructures. Is the COVID-19 pandemic shifting our perspective on what critical infrastructures are? *International Journal of Disaster Risk Reduction*, *83*, 103419. https://doi.org/10.1016/j.ijdrr.2022.103419

Schwartz, R., Vassilev, A., Greene, K., Perine, L., Burt, A., & Hall, P. (2022). *Towards a Standard for Identifying and Managing Bias in Artificial Intelligence*. NIST. https://doi.org/10.6028/NIST.SP.1270

Schwarz, A., Binetti, J., Broll, W., & Mitschele-Thiel, A. (2016). New technologies and applications in international crisis communication and disaster management. In A. Schwarz, M. W. Seeger, & C. Auer, Eds., *The Handbook of International Crisis Communication Research* (pp. 465–477). Wiley. https://doi.org/10.1002/9781118516812.ch42

Seeger, M. W., & Sellnow, T. L. (2019). *Communication in Times of Trouble*. Wiley.

Sellnow, T. L., & Seeger, M. W. (2021). *Theorizing Crisis Communication*. Wiley.

Shelton, T., Poorthuis, A., Graham, M., & Zook, M. (2014). Mapping the data shadows of hurricane sandy: Uncovering the sociospatial dimensions of 'big data.'. *Geoforum*, *52*, 167–179. https://doi.org/10.1016/J.GEOFORUM.2014.01.006

Soden, R., & Palen, L. (2016). Infrastructure in the wild: What mapping in post-earthquake Nepal reveals about infrastructural emergence. *Proceedings of the 2016 CHI Conference on Human Factors in Computing Systems – CHI '16*, 2796–2807. https://doi.org/10.1145/2858036.2858545

Sorensen, J. H. (2000). Hazard warning systems: Review of 20 years of progress. *Natural Hazards Review*, *1*(2), 119–125. https://doi.org/10.1061/(ASCE)1527-6988(2000)1:2(119)

Star, S. L., & Bowker, G. (2002). How to infrastructure. In L. Lievrouw, & S. Livingstone, Eds., *Handbook of New Media: Social Shaping and Consequences of ICTs* (pp. 230–245). Sage. https://doi.org/https://doi.org/10.4135/9781848608245

Star, S. L., & Ruhleder, K. (1996). Steps toward an ecology of infrastructure: Design and access for large information spaces. *Information Systems Research*, *7*(1), 111–134. https://doi.org/10.1287/isre.7.1.111

Starbird, K., Palen, L., Hughes, A. L., & Vieweg, S. (2010). Chatter on the red what hazards threat reveals about the social life of microblogged information. *Proceedings of the 2010 ACM Conference on Computer Supported Cooperative Work – CSCW '10*, 241. https://doi.org/10.1145/1718918.1718965

Starbird, K., Arif, A., & Wilson, T. (2019). Disinformation as collaborative work. *Proceedings of the ACM on Human-Computer Interaction*, *3*(CSCW), 1–26. https://doi.org/10.1145/3359229

Steen-Tveit, K., & Erik Munkvold, B. (2021). From common operational picture to common situational understanding: An analysis based on practitioner perspectives. *Safety Science*, *142*, 105381. https://doi.org/10.1016/j.ssci.2021.105381

Steen-Tveit, K., & Radianti, J. (2019). Analysis of common operational picture and situational awareness during multiple emergency response scenarios. *Proceedings of the 16th ISCRAM Conference*, 199–208.

Stieglitz, S., Mirbabaie, M., & Milde, M. (2018). Social positions and collective sense-making in crisis communication. *International Journal of Human Computer Interaction*, *34*(4), 328–355. 10.1080/10447318.2018.1427830

Sutton, J., Palen, L., & Shklovski, I. (2008). Emergent uses of social media in the California wildfires backchannels on the front lines: Emergent uses of social media in the 2007 southern California wildfires. *Proceedings of the 5th International ISCRAM Conference*, 624–632. http://www.iscram.org/legacy/dmdocuments/ISCRAM2008/papers/ISCRAM2008_Sutton_etal.pdf

Sutton, J., Spiro, E. S., Johnson, B., Fitzhugh, S., Gibson, B., & Butts, C. T. (2014). Warning tweets: Serial transmission of messages during the warning phase of a disaster event. *Information, Communication & Society*, *17*(6), 765–787. https://doi.org/10.1080/1369118X.2013.862561

Sutton, J., Gibson, C. B., Phillips, N. E., Spiro, E. S., League, C., Johnson, B., Fitzhugh, S. M., & Butts, C. T. (2015). A cross-hazard analysis of terse message retransmission on Twitter. *Proceedings of the National Academy of Sciences of the United States of America*, *112*(48), 14793–14798. https://doi.org/10.1073/pnas.1508916112

Tan, M. L., Prasanna, R., Stock, K., Hudson-Doyle, E., Leonard, G., & Johnston, D. (2017). Mobile applications in crisis informatics literature: A systematic review. *International Journal of Disaster Risk Reduction*, *24*, 297–311. https://doi.org/10.1016/j.ijdrr.2017.06.009

Tan, M. L., Prasanna, R., Stock, K., Doyle, E. E. H., Leonard, G., & Johnston, D. (2020a). Understanding end-users' perspectives: Towards developing usability guidelines for disaster apps. *Progress in Disaster Science*, *7*, 100118. https://doi.org/10.1016/j.pdisas.2020.100118

Tan, M. L., Prasanna, R., Stock, K., Doyle, E. E. H., Leonard, G., & Johnston, D. (2020b). Usability factors influencing the continuance intention of disaster apps: A mixed-methods study. *International Journal of Disaster Risk Reduction*, *50*, 101874. https://doi.org/10.1016/j.ijdrr.2020.101874

Tien, I., Aibek, M., Benas, D., & C. Pu. (2016). Detection of damage and failure events of critical public infrastructure using social sensor big data. *Proceedings of International Conference on Internet of Things and Big Data.*

Treurniet, W., & Wolbers, J. (2021). Codifying a crisis: Progressing from information sharing to distributed decision-making. *Journal of Contingencies & Crisis Management*, *29*(1), 23–35. https://doi.org/10.1111/1468-5973.12323

Uzzell, D. (2012). *AMBER Alert Best Practices (NCJ 232271).*

Van de Walle, B., Turoff, M., & Hiltz, S. R. (2014). *Information Systems for Emergency Management.* Routledge.

Vieweg, S., Hughes, A. L., Starbird, K., & Palen, L. (2010). Microblogging during two natural hazards events: What twitter may contribute to situational awareness. *Proceedings of the 28th International Conference on Human Factors in Computing Systems – CHI '10*, 1079. https://doi.org/10.1145/1753326.1753486

WHO (2022). *Surveillance in Emergencies.* World Health Organization.

Winter, S., Berente, N., Howison, J., & Butler, B. (2014). Beyond the organizational 'container': Conceptualizing 21st century sociotechnical work. *Information and Organization*, *24*(4), 250–269. https://doi.org/10.1016/j.infoandorg.2014.10.003

Wolbers, J. (2021). Understanding distributed sensemaking in crisis management: The case of the Utrecht terrorist attack. *Journal of Contingencies & Crisis Management.* https://doi.org/10.1111/1468-5973.12382

Wolbers, J., & Boersma, K. (2013). The common operational picture as collective sensemaking. *Journal of Contingencies & Crisis Management, 21*(4), 186–199. https://doi.org/10.1111/1468-5973.12027

Wukich, C., & Mergel, I. (2015). Closing the citizen-government communication gap: Content, audience, and network analysis of government tweets. *Journal of Homeland Security and Emergency Management, 12*(3), 707–735. https://doi.org/10.1515/jhsem-2014-0074

Yousefinaghani, S., Dara, R., Poljak, Z., Bernardo, T. M., & Sharif, S. (2019). The assessment of twitter's potential for outbreak detection: Avian influenza case study. *Scientific Reports, 9*(1), 18147. https://doi.org/10.1038/s41598-019-54388-4

Zhang, Q., Zhang, Q., Shi, W., & Zhong, H. (2018). Distributed collaborative execution on the edges and its application to AMBER alerts. *IEEE Internet of Things Journal, 5*(5), 3580–3593. https://doi.org/10.1109/JIOT.2018.2845898

Author Bio

Rob Grace is an Assistant Professor at the University of Cincinnati where he specializes in the areas of crisis communication and emergency management. His research focuses on the socio-technical design of technologies and work organizations adopted in emergency communications systems that support situational awareness, collaboration, and decision-making among citizens and first responders during emergencies. Rob received a PhD in Informatics from The Pennsylvania State University. He is the current President of the Information Systems for Crisis Response and Management (ISCRAM) Association.

49

Preparing for International and Cross-Cultural Crises: The Challenges of Research in Action, Competing Voices, Inclusivity, and the Interplay of Responsibility in Global Organizations

Ben Duncan[1] and Audra Diers-Lawson[2]
[1] Self-employed crisis and risk communication consultant, Consultant to WHO Health Emergencies Programme, Brussels, Belgium
[2] Institute for Communication, Kristiania University of Applied Sciences, Oslo, Norway

The COVID-19 pandemic is an example of a societal-level health crisis because it disrupted all aspects of people's lives and reshaped beliefs and behaviors across multiple domains and has threatened most countries' societal security (Bajrami et al., 2021; Reeves et al., 2020). Governmental COVID-19 containment policies also changed the way we work, consume, and interact – at least in the short term – and potentially paved the way to new behaviors, policy, and procedures emerging across domains of social and work activities (Reeves et al., 2020). While effective communication is important during all crises, during societal-level crises, it is essential that governments and public health successfully disseminate fact-based and relevant information to ensure compliance with recommendations and rules (Diers-Lawson et al., 2022). They must also avoid reinforcing false health beliefs because once these false beliefs take hold in a population, they are difficult to undo (Lewandowsky et al., 2013). Credible information and instructive guidance from governments, health officials, and other organizations are essential for saving lives by reducing risk, reinforcing desirable attitudes, and building institutional trust (Diers-Lawson et al., 2022). Islam et al. (2020) also argue effective communication is crucial for stopping the spread of conspiracy theories, misinformation, and disinformation, all of which decrease trust in governments and international health agencies.

Because of the truly global nature of the COVID-19 pandemic, practitioners and researchers are developing a rich set of insights into international and cross-cultural crises. Unsurprisingly, there has been an unprecedented amount of scientific and professional research published about it from around the world with well over 125,000 scientific articles and reports published

The Handbook of International Crisis and Risk Communication Research, Second Edition.
Edited by Andreas Schwarz, Matthew W. Seeger, and Sora Kim.

(Fraser et al., 2021) with national and cross-national comparisons of COVID-19 experiences and policies from Asia (Dai et al., 2020; Nguyen et al., 2020), to Europe (Breakwell & Jaspal, 2020; Meier et al., 2020), or the Americas (Bruine de Bruin & Bennett, 2020; Glenn et al., 2020). This affords us the opportunity to reflect on previous frameworks for international and cross-cultural crises. For example, in the first edition of this handbook, Sellnow and Veil (2016) expressed optimism that social media would create an opportunity for inclusive dialogue between various national and international organizations managing multi-country crises and the different communities affected by it. Using the severe acute respiratory syndrome (SARS) pandemic as the key case, they provided a framework for exploring the complexities of international and cross-cultural crises arguing that organizations are best served when they work collaboratively and inclusively to respond to international crises. In this chapter, we will (1) explore the foundations and functions of international response to cross-border crises; (2) consider the challenges of coordinating research and emergency response, competing voices, and inclusivity; and (3) reflect on the interplay of responsibilities in global organizations using the COVID-19 pandemic as an example.

Foundations and Functions of International Response to Cross-Border Crises

The COVID-19 pandemic revealed three communication challenges with which governments, public health, corporations, and cross-national organizations have had to contend. First, the infodemic is associated with rampant problems of misinformation, disinformation, and so-called "fake news" all of which limit the adoption of self-protective behaviors (Balarabe & Kumar, 2020; Cheng & Luo, 2020). Second, there have been challenges in developing effective international and national responses and communication because of the high levels of politicization associated with the COVID-19 initial emergence, transmission, and emergent pandemic (Bruine de Bruin et al., 2020; Salvi et al., 2021). Third, in many national contexts, it was necessary to develop new communication strategies to improve the public's willingness to adopt self-protective behaviors (Papageorge et al., 2021; Sun et al., 2020).

The context for international and cross-cultural crises is inherently complex, colored by competing institutional and political agendas, and even where the response is governed by a relatively detailed framework of rules (e.g., health emergencies), it can still become messy during a crisis. For example, during the first few months of the pandemic, citizens, governments, and public health organizations were working to make sense of the evolving nature of COVID-19. In particular, leaders of governments and health authorities were engaging in a challenging process of sensemaking, making meaning, and making decisions all at the same time (Glenn et al., 2020; Mikac, 2020). The questions being asked by governments were as follows: "What should we do?" "What if there has been someone with COVID at a hotel, on a plane, or in a meeting?" "How should we disinfect rooms to keep people COVID-safe?" During those early days, governments wanted answers from health authorities at the national and international level and there was not a lot of demand for participative decision-making. As it became clear that COVID-19 was going to be around for an extended period, cross-governmental discussions and political debates began to emerge regarding lockdowns and school closures, and while substantial feedback and guidance for citizen self-protective behaviors were provided by the WHO and national health authorities, different governments took different actions.

Actions became more complex as controversial policy considerations emerged for risk reduction such as implementing travel restrictions. In this case, the WHO sat resolutely on the fence about travel restrictions throughout 2020 because providing guidance posed both a political and legal challenge related to its mandate to coordinate the international response to health emergencies and maintain good institutional relations with member states. Therefore, the recommendation throughout 2020 was that countries should do their own risk assessments.

In this chapter, we work to unpack many of the complexities surrounding international crises, and while we focus on the COVID-19 pandemic, it is important to note that the same types of complexities, competing agendas, international legal frameworks, and exchange between local, regional, national, and international bodies will apply across different international crises – it is only that some of the actors and legal regulations change. We should also note these complexities do not account for differences in cultural factors within and between countries that substantially influence the relative success of the public health response (De Vries et al., 2021).

Foundations: Legal Framework for International Health Emergency Response

Responses to the COVID-19 pandemic were grounded by work from the public health sector at the national and international levels to improve pandemic preparedness since at least 2003 because the SARS epidemic – the key case in the last edition of this text – was widely seen as a "near miss" as a global pandemic requiring improved pandemic response capacity (Sellnow & Veil, 2016). Therefore, the 2005 International Health Regulations (IHRs) introduced an ambitious new legal framework by the WHO and its member states on how they should manage multi-country health emergencies (WHO, 2005b). Unlike earlier frameworks that focused on just three diseases (i.e., yellow fever, plague, and cholera), the IHRs (2005) took an all-hazards approach because it applies to any disease or health threat with potential cross-border impact. The IHR was also noteworthy because it placed a strong emphasis on preparedness and prevention compared with just response.

The IHR underscored the importance of intergovernmental organizations (IGOs) and nongovernmental organizations (NGOs) to effective crisis response (Kaltenbrunner & Reichel, 2018; Mason & Fiocco, 2017; Schwarz & Fritsch, 2014). For example, within the context of international and cross-cultural health crises, the WHO is a vital part of the global coordination and response effort (Kluge & Ammon, 2022; Sellnow-Richmond et al., 2018). Additionally, the IHR framework is grounded in effective communication and cross-agency cooperation by including the following key principles:

- Member states have an obligation to alert the WHO and each other about health threats that could spread internationally.
- Once alerted to a situation, the WHO director general has power to declare it a Public Health Emergency of International Concern (PHEIC).
- WHO's role is to coordinate response actions of the United Nations (UN) system and member states to avoid unnecessary impediments to travel and trade.
- All member states are obliged to build and maintain a core capacity to detect, assess, and respond to health threats.

Functions: WHO Doctrine for International Risk and Crisis Communication

The IHR and the system built around it are certainly not an international risk or crisis communication framework; however, it laid the groundwork for a multi-cultural and multi-national cooperative approach to crisis response. For instance, the IHR's principles demonstrate the critical role of information sharing, sensemaking, and communication. This has been an inherent part of WHO policy and action for two decades and is therefore an established doctrine in risk and crisis communication. While the most detailed "standards" are established in the IHR Joint External Evaluation Tool (WHO, 2022c), WHO doctrine is drawn from multiple sources and curated by a tight-knit community of expert practitioners in and around the WHO. For example, the most authoritative written texts on WHO risk and crisis communication doctrine were established in WHO guidelines that supported its implementation of IHR (2005) (WHO, 2005b), WHO's strategic communication framework (WHO, 2017), and its risk communication and community engagement guidance issued during the COVID-19 response (WHO, 2022d). The doctrine has also emerged from post-crisis "lessons learned" reports from the 2009–2010 H_1N_1 influenza pandemic, the 2014–2015 Ebola epidemic in West Africa, the 2018 Zika virus epidemic, and many other outbreaks (WHO, 2018). WHO doctrine in responding to health crises is built around the organization's dual role as one of the key voices in international discourse about emerging health hazards and providing technical support to countries around the world to enable them to conduct their national risk communication in line with "best practice" guidelines.

During the COVID-19 crisis, the WHO provided substantial technical support to different countries. The technical and operational support WHO and its UN partners gave to national public health authorities during the pandemic amounted to tens of millions of US dollars worldwide (WHO, 2022a). Additionally, the WHO provided critical international guidance documents on risk communication and numerous national-level capacity-building initiatives between 2005 and 2019 (WHO, 2020b). Conducting a comprehensive evaluation of all this work would be a valuable project, but it is not one we undertake in this chapter; we just observe that the literature, including professional reports published by the WHO, is beginning to be published that highlights the positive impact this work has had on the quality of risk communication about COVID-19 (WHO, 2020a; WHO, 2021a; WHO, 2021b). This support includes supporting national health authorities' engagement with at-risk and vulnerable communities and implementing a range of two-way communication social listening activities (WHO, 2021a). However, by identifying WHO's five emergent functions in responding to cross-border crises, we can establish a template for considering the role of IGOs and NGOs in international crisis contexts.

Function 1: Naming and Framing International Crises

One of the positive contributions WHO made to the COVID-19 pandemic response was naming and framing the pandemic. There is a long history of medical sociology research that has found that "disease" is typically co-constructed with cultural meaning. It is socially constructed at the experiential level and the way in which the language (i.e., naming and framing) of a disease affects its prevalence, treatment, health outcomes, and policymaking around it (Brown, 1995; Conrad & Barker, 2010).

However, the framing of the disease was not the only necessary function to help support and guide policy; the WHO also named the disease COVID-19 to avoid (or reduce) the stigmatization of any country or community. Research on disease and stigma has long established the negative health outcomes associated with stigmatizing populations (Bragazzi et al., 2022; Rimal et al., 1996), but in the case of COVID-19 the question of blame attribution has been challenging with different populations being blamed depending on social and political ideology (Chang et al., 2020; Croucher et al., 2023). WHO's approach to naming helped to establish and change the language used about the disease stood in direct competition with bad-will actors like US President Donald Trump calling it "the Chinese Virus" during his previous term, which was connected to a rise in anti-Asian racism and discrimination in the United States (Reja, 2021). Therefore, an important function of IGOs in responding to international and cross-cultural crisis is naming and framing the crisis to ensure that the language used does not harm the response and community engagement about the crisis.

Function 2: Consensus Building

One of the core challenges with international and cross-cultural crises is a tendency for conflict to become the dominant approach rather than consensus building among different national and international interest groups. In the COVID-19 context, within countries where there were elevated levels of conflict about the disease, there were measurably worse health outcomes (Bíró-Nagy & Szászi, 2022; Bruine de Bruin et al., 2020; Szabó & Szabó, 2022). However, one of the critical functions that IGOs, like WHO, can serve is as consensus-building institutions. We will discuss the challenges in consensus building later, but there is evidence that the WHO contributed to creating consensus around the importance of COVID-19 and the development of vaccination programs. For example, countries consistently adopted COVID-19 vaccination programs suggesting a relatively consistent global consensus in government sensemaking and major action recommendations about the pandemic.

Function 3: Advocacy for Less Powerful Countries (and/or Vulnerable Populations)

Of course, each country's government is directly responsible to and for its own citizens. This truism creates the potential for conflict and exploitation in international and cross-cultural crises. A core risk is that the wealthy and by extension wealthier countries will consume a disproportionate share of the financial, material, technical, and medical resources needed to fight a pandemic, while lower- and middle-income citizens and countries will be left with shortages. Therefore, one of the key functions and obligations that NGOs and IGOs serve is to advocate for vulnerable or poorer people and countries. The WHO's work with the European Union (EU)'s joint vaccine procurement program, which gave its poorer member states equal access to vaccines, was one such example. As vaccines became available, the WHO became a powerful advocate for vaccine equity by coordinating programs like the COVID-19 Vaccine Delivery Partnership with UNICEF and Gavi. The WHO also coordinated with international partners and governments to improve COVID-19 vaccination in 34 low-coverage countries (WHO, 2023). This approach is one that can and must be replicated across different types of international disasters and crises to address the real needs of the most vulnerable populations.

Function 4: Long-Term Preparation

Long-term planning is central to the success of any major international health emergency. This is apparent in WHO's doctrine for international crisis response and necessary for the first three functions we discuss to succeed. There are many examples from around the world where lessons from previous pandemics informed the response to COVID-19. For example, in Asia, health authorities, the Asia-Europe Foundation, and the WHO have had significant experience with outbreaks like Avian flu, SARS, and Middle East respiratory syndrome (MERS). Their experience and long-term approach to preparation not only shaped their approach and recommendations to COVID-19 but also people's willingness to take self-protective behaviors (Diers-Lawson et al., 2021).

Many millions of dollars of national and international funding have gone into building and strengthening IHR core capacities in the years since it was established (WHO, 2022b). Yet, while the upscaling of work to build capacity for global health emergencies must have helped in the COVID-19 response, the pandemic also showed the relationship between technical preparedness and effective crisis response is not straightforward. For example, Fran Baum et al. (2021) charted countries' COVID-19 deaths up to October 2020 against their preparedness score calculated by the Global Health Security Index (GHSI) and found little correlation. The United States and the United Kingdom, for instance, "should" have been best prepared according to the GHSI, yet they performed comparatively badly. They diagnose three problems: a rich country bias in the GHSI, an undervaluing of the role of civil society, and a failure to account for the role of political leadership.

Another part of the long-term preparation process for international and cross-cultural crises involves IGOs and NGOs collaborating with countries at multiple levels to improve crisis response. For example, WHO country offices generally work with and through national health authorities while WHO headquarters (HQ) and regional offices communicate independently of national authorities about cross-border issues. This multi-level coordination allows WHO to develop long-term relationships and provide long-term capacity building for countries. As the acute stage of the COVID-19 pandemic waned in 2022, the emphasis on "crisis response" shifted to longer-term risk communication and community engagement capacity building to prepare for the next pandemic or health-related crisis.

This approach to learning and organizational change after crises is consistent with a large body of literature arguing that one of the critical post-crisis functions for all organizations is identifying critical lessons learned and implementing plans to mitigate risk or respond better in the future (Antonacopoulou & Sheaffer, 2014; Keen et al., 2020). However, despite this clearly established need, many organizations do not critically reflect and implement change because (1) as crisis wanes, so too does the urgency to act and (2) organizational reflection is often connected with blame taking, which is often viewed as undesirable at individual, departmental, and institutional levels (Antonacopoulou & Sheaffer, 2014; Roux-Dufort, 2000). Therefore, IGOs and NGOs must be able to navigate the political and face-saving challenges when engaging with governments and other organizations to facilitate improved long-term crisis planning and preparation.

Function 5: Collecting and Disseminating Best Practices

In the case of the WHO, collecting and disseminating best practices is a central post-crisis strategy. For example, WHOEurope coordinated workshops in the Western Balkans, Southeastern Europe, and Central Asia to collect and disseminate best practices among different communities of practice (and regions) – focusing on those that are often ignored in public health practice and academic research. Embracing this post-crisis learning strategy, the WHO has multiple approaches for collecting and disseminating best practices in risk and crisis communication. In addition to workshops, one approach for collecting best practices is through the institution's use of Technical Advisory Groups (TAGs) that bring together academic experts and expert practitioners to reflect on recent, current, and emerging risks for cross-disciplinary feedback. These function as one way to put research and experience into action. Another example of how the WHO collects and disseminates best practices is through critical case studies. For example, in Duncan's reflection on the importance of putting risk and crisis communication alongside medical interventions for improving health crisis outcomes, he explains how WHO learned from early errors in the communicative response to Ebola in West Africa in subsequent interventions (see Diers-Lawson, 2020). Using case studies is a point of critical reflection to develop and disseminate best practice and provide real-world contexts for reflecting on best practices.

As a result of this process of critical institutional reflection, providing platforms for diverse voices to contribute to lessons learned, and providing opportunities for cross-sector collaboration, the outcome has been the development of a WHO risk communication "doctrine" with the following key elements:

- Announce early: Communicate in an open and transparent way, being clear about what is known and unknown. Avoid false reassurance. This standard of timely and transparent communication emerged from lessons identified during SARS in 2003 (WHO, 2005a; WHO, 2005c).

- There should be ***cross-government and, if possible whole-of-society, coordination of risk communication*** during an emergency. The principle of multi-level, multi-sectoral coordination of all aspects of health emergency response is written into the evaluation framework for IHR core capacities (WHO, 2022b).
- Risk communication should include the ***real-time exchange*** of information, advice, and opinions between experts/officials and people who face health threats. Its aim is that ***people at risk are empowered to take informed decisions to protect their health*** and the health of their loved ones (Sellnow & Veil, 2016; WHO, 2018).
- ***Risk communication needs to be integrated into health emergency response systems.*** This advice has been given since 2008 and was codified in the 2018 Guideline (WHO, 2018).
- ***Communities at risk need to be engaged with when developing the health emergency response.*** This was a key lesson identified in the evaluation of WHO's response to the 2014–2015 Ebola epidemic (WHO, 2022c). It is also written in the 2018 Guideline (WHO, 2018).

In the context of international crises and cross-national response, the type of process reflected in the WHO example for developing and disseminating best practices over time reflects one of the critical functions that IGOs and NGOs serve in coordinating intelligence development and improving risk and crisis communication (Gilstrap et al., 2016; Kaltenbrunner & Reichel, 2018; Schwarz & Fritsch, 2014). In fact, in a reflection on the deadly MERS epidemic in South Korea, research found that better applying disaster response tools and best practices from public health institutions like the WHO, the US Center for Disease Control, or Public Health England could have improved disaster response leading to fewer deaths (Choi et al., 2015).

Challenges in International Risk and Crisis Communication

Using the COVID-19 pandemic as a critical case for learning about the foundation and functions of international risk and crisis communication response and WHO's doctrine of response as a benchmark, we have established several important principles for responding to these complex crises and established a clear and vital role for IGOs and NGOs in such crises. However, these crises are also inherently tangled. Therefore, we identify four challenges in meeting the conditions of inclusivity and collaboration that Sellnow and Veil (2016) articulated as optimal for organizations addressing international and cross-cultural crises.

Coordinating Research and Emergency Response Practice

One of the challenges in developing and evaluating "best practice" in international and cross-cultural crisis response is the limited interaction between scholarly research, theory development, and real-world application. In fact, this is a subject being tackled in workshops, conferences, and professional discussions in organizations like the European Communication Research and Education Association (ECREA), International Association of Risk and Crisis Communication (IARCC), Chartered Institute of Public Relations (CIPR), and the International Crisis and Risk Communication Conference (ICRCC). The fact of the matter is that scholars and practitioners seemingly do not always make easy bedfellows because each has different needs, priorities, and often different paces of work.

Risk and Crisis Communication in Practice

Risk and crisis communication in the health sector is one of the core capacities mandated by the WHO under the IHR. Though approaches vary considerably among national health authorities, there has been growing consensus (particularly since 2020) on the core tasks and output of the risk communication and community engagement function during health emergencies with WHO largely responsible for setting standards and defining good practice. This has specific implications for the type of information that practitioners consult. As a result, WHO's reports and policy documents (i.e., "grey literature") are much more likely to be used compared to peer-reviewed or scholarly research. In part, this is also attributable to the accessibility of the scholarly literature – both because most scholarly research is hidden behind paywalls and because most practitioners in WHO and national health authorities are unlikely to have the time to stay current in the scholarly research. This is a common theme in what often seems like a chasm between academic scholarship and practice.

Further, both practitioners and many scholars often assume that "theory" is a rigid construct, and if a theory is not perfectly applied, then the scholarship is not being used properly. As a result, practitioners across the field often reject theory as being useless "in the real world" and scholars often reject practitioners as "anti-intellectual." Neither conclusion is particularly useful. If we consider that, for example, WHO's standards or doctrine of good practice for risk communication have evolved over time and with experience across health crises as a way for establishing what is replicable across space and time, these standards are an example of theory in practice. Likewise, if we consider that most risk and crisis communication theories, over time, have established a common set of factors influencing citizen attitudes and behaviors, then we can say that academic scholarship has identified a set of predictable contingencies that should help guide risk and crisis communication practice (Diers-Lawson, et al., 2021). As such, we need not worry about rigidly applying theory but rather using established standards of theory in practice. The point is that when both approaches are reviewed, the conclusions are nearly identical in their recommendations (Seeger, 2006). The challenge, therefore, is not that scholarship and practice are fundamentally different, but the challenge is that the two simply fail to engage one another meaningfully, which limits knowledge exchange and improves applied risk and crisis communication strategy.

Bridging the Academic and Practitioner Chasm to Improve Crisis Preparation

One of the central premises in global public health risk and crisis communication is that risk reduction, crisis preparation, emergency interventions, and institutional learning are evidence led (WHO, 2018; WHO, 2022d). As such, bridging the academic and practitioner chasm is a matter of preparing for international and cross-cultural crises because the convergence of experience and research from both are needed. Yet, open collaboration remains a challenge. Even if we assume goodwill between academics and practitioners, the challenge of engagement is also affected by workflows and work patterns. For example, of course in emergency situations, responders need to make decisions quickly and often based on incomplete information. Dr. Mike Ryan, Executive Director of WHO's Health Emergencies Programme, often says, "If you wait until you are certain, it will be too late." Applied in WHO's guidance on communicating during health emergencies, the recommendation is to "announce early," control the message, and gather data from a variety of sources making the best decisions based on the available data. Unsurprisingly, this confirms most academic research on crisis response (Petridou et al., 2019; Sellnow et al., 2019; Spence et al., 2014).

So, why is it difficult to get practitioners and scholars together? Simply stated – the pacing and prioritization of academic work are nearly incompatible with being an emergency responder. Most work around their teaching obligations, institutional demands for "service" work, and lengthy research revision processes that often last from roughly three months to two years to get a single piece of research out – and that is after the research is conducted, data analyzed, and the results written. For young and mid-career scholars, there is a growing pressure on academic publication and producing (large) funded research projects. In many cases, practice-oriented research may not be publishable in peer-reviewed publications because, for example, of the nature of the data (small sample size, "quick and dirty" study design). From a professional development perspective, this means that if an academic commits to practice-oriented projects and cannot get at least one peer-reviewed publication from projects, it can damage prospects for promotion.

For more senior scholars, however, many of these issues are less problematic because as "full professors" these scholars typically have more flexibility and freedom. Moreover, the career progression and development priorities can be somewhat different with a greater expectation on the "impact" of research. In an academic context, impact may be about the number of citations that a scholar has across their career, but it is increasingly being defined in applied fields like communication as the degree to which scholarly research influences practice in the real world. This means that as scholars advance in their careers, they are often interested in opportunities for their research to be used "in the real world," which might be the difference between being promoted to "professor" and not being promoted. It can also make the difference in establishing the case for their research to be funded by large funding bodies or not. Therefore, being mindful of the challenges in practice needs and academic ability to deliver is one way to build constructive opportunities for more meaningful engagement between practitioners and academic researchers.

Inclusivity

Beyond pragmatic questions about research-informed communication strategy, one of the challenges is identifying whose voices matter within international and cross-cultural crises. For example, research on COVID-19 across Europe highlighted the importance of producing culturally relevant messaging both between countries and within countries to acknowledge the different pandemic experiences by minority communities (de Vries et al., 2022; Kamburova & Georgieva, 2021; Varghese et al., 2021). In context, "community engagement" is a vitally important part of risk and crisis communication; yet, giving minority communities voice is one of the challenges in producing materials that effectively target and address the intersection of historic, cultural, political, social, and health concerns of these populations because they often look and think very differently to the majority populations within those countries. In part, one of the core challenges with engaging these communities is the history of oppression and inherent mistrust of institutions within the minority communities – particularly with issues of health (Khan et al., 2021; Mehmood et al., 2021; Sullivan et al., 2023).

In national contexts where there is low trust – either overall or within the context of disenfranchised portions of the population, as we see with the Roma in Bulgaria, Indigenous peoples in places like Canada or India, or places like the United Kingdom where the legacy of colonial history and systemic racism leave minority communities with low trust in government initiatives, accessing these communities is challenging, let alone persuading these communities to adopt recommendations for self-protective behaviors (Bielicki, 2021; Lee & Li, 2021; Mesch & Schwirian, 2015). These are just a few examples, but we see this challenge – especially across the Global South as well. This means that countries have to manage these low-trust environments differently. For example, in a country like Uzbekistan, one of the most successful strategies for community engagement involved public health officials reaching out directly to influencers within communities across the country. This meant building personal relationships with community leaders and religious leaders and spending time (re)building trust within those communities. In other countries in Central Asia, there were extensive community outreach programs that involved health officials going directly into the communities and knocking on doors. These kinds of time-intensive inclusivity strategies are likely necessary during crises to ensure that vulnerable and disenfranchised communities are reached. However, these strategies during crises can also create avenues for long-term community engagement as well that can improve the planning for future crises.

There is, however, a challenge in the concept of inclusivity – are we communicating to empower individuals to make decisions that are in their best interest or are we integrating their interests into the response and engaging communities in the response? The principle of risk communication and community engagement inherent in inclusivity would suggest that risk and crisis communication *ought* to be about building relationships, creating value for both sides, and co-creating the response to crises like the COVID-19 pandemic. However, though health officials may talk about co-creation, there is a greater (unconscious?) tendency to view community engagement within the context of persuasion and traditional campaigns that assume that the "right" answer is known and simply needs to be effectively disseminated in a way that is appealing to different populations. This is not an easy answer, but if institutions look beyond the immediate crisis to creating more resilient communities and lasting opportunities for engagement, then an approach that co-creates value should be preferred. In fact, among ethnically diverse communities and low-resource availability communities, research is consistently suggesting that co-creation not only is a more cost-effective approach to improve inclusivity and health outcomes but also leads to longer-term health benefits (Halvorsrud et al., 2021; Lazo-Porras et al., 2020).

Competing Voices

If we look at the big picture, what stands out most about the global conversation around COVID-19 is the decision of many actors to pursue narrative competition and conflict, rather than to build authentic consensus. Given the scale of the damage caused by the pandemic, it was inevitable that the response would be politicized at some point (Bruine de Bruin et al., 2020; Salvi et al., 2021). In some countries, political leaders came together and built a consensus in support of the public health response to COVID-19. Unfortunately, in some countries, the appearance of "consensus" was more important, and so dissenting voices were silenced. Finally, in other countries – most notably Brazil and the United States – political leaders from different parties took dramatically different views on the risk posed by COVID-19 and the measures that should be taken to protect people. In these countries, whether someone wore a mask or practiced social distancing became seen as a test of their political allegiance rather than a health decision (Bruine de Bruin et al., 2020; Croucher et al., 2022; Sun et al., 2020).

From an international perspective, what was most notable – and most depressing – about the discussion was the degree of narrative competition and acrimony exhibited between countries. This was exhibited between the EU and the United Kingdom for a while on the issue of who should have access to the first vaccines against COVID-19 (Copeland & Maccaferri, 2022). Misinformation and disinformation about COVID-19 were weaponized by Russia to pursue "information warfare" against its neighbors and global competitors (Sukhankin, 2020). However, the most high-profile conflict was between the United States and China during 2020 and 2021 about the origins of COVID-19 – and whether China suppressed information about the start of the outbreak (Croucher et al., 2021; Hart et al., 2020). The WHO was caught in the middle of this controversy, with the United States at one point giving notice of its intention to leave the organization (later withdrawn, post-President Trump).

That said, many countries and regions worked to manage or mitigate the competing voices and narratives of conflict (Wolff & Ladi, 2020). However, state-level controversies helped to fuel existing institutional mistrust that already existed in many countries and also created conditions for the agitated and negative emotional states that facilitated increased belief in misinformation and disinformation allowing "fake news" to spread like wildfire in some communities (Martel et al., 2020; Pierre, 2019; Sun et al., 2020). Jacob et al.'s (2023) comprehensive summary of pan-European research on COVID-19 drew a direct connection between countries where increased narratives of conflict were well-documented and increased COVID-19 deaths compared to countries embracing a more collaborative approach to pandemic response. These problems were certainly amplified by the news media and social media. Globally, research suggests that both traditional and social media contributed to the spread of misinformation largely because of the use of conflict as a critical tool in gaining attention for stories and posts (Apuke & Omar, 2021; Martel, et al., 2020; Soares & Recuero, 2021). Therefore, it is fair to suggest that one of the critical challenges in international and cross-cultural crises is overcoming competitive narratives and conflict because it risks citizen lives and well-being both in terms of more disease-related deaths (e.g., Jacob et al., 2023) and in terms of well-documented increases in prejudice and violence against minority groups (Croucher et al., 2023).

Interplay of Responsibilities

Conflicting responsibilities – or at least the perception of conflicts in responsibilities – is the final challenge to achieving Sellnow and Veil's (2016) objective of inclusivity and collaboration that we can document based on the COVID-19 experience and WHO context. COVID-19 revealed significant fragility in international agreements and opportunities for collaboration because governments, IGOs, and NGOs all serve multiple stakeholders who often have competing interests. For example, under former President Trump, the conflict of interest between his administration's objectives and global health objectives was so severe that it led the United States to withdraw from the WHO until changes in government changed the conflict perception.

Stakeholder-related approaches to crisis response clearly suggest balancing competing stakeholder interests can damage collaboration because different stakeholders' interests are often in competition with one another (Diers-Lawson, 2020; Heath & Palenchar, 2009). Therefore, COVID-19 challenged core and long-standing legal frameworks and partnerships because different perceptions of responsibilities by governments and organizations increasingly politicized the pandemic at both national and international levels. Certainly, the conflicts between the United Kingdom and the EU, the United States and China, and within different countries like Bulgaria, Hungary, Brazil, and Tanzania provide illustrations of this point. These conflicts exposed the fragility of international legal frameworks, like the IHR, on which much of WHO's "authority" during health emergencies is based. For example, despite the IHR legal obligations, China did not communicate in a timely and transparent manner about the emergence of a novel human disease with pandemic potential. Rather, the authorities delayed and downplayed their communication about the outbreak during December 2019 and most of January 2020. China then limited its cooperation with the WHO's investigation into the source of the outbreak. This undermined the IHR's objective because it was explicitly negotiated to highlight the importance of notifying WHO and other member states about emerging health threats in a timely and transparent way (WHO, 2022c). Unironically, this is also something that China failed to do in 2002–2003 as SARS emerged in Southern China.

There are pragmatic health concerns when countries fail to share information but also this poses a significant threat to the operational legitimacy of institutions like the WHO and their ability to execute the five functions identified in this chapter. From the operating assumption that international cooperation is essential to reducing the damage and death posed by international and cross-cultural crises (Sellnow & Veil, 2016), then risks to the legitimacy of the NGO and IGO actors that facilitate collaboration represent a very credible threat in the global community's ability to meaningfully respond to these crises. In the case of the failure of the IHR to ensure early and transparent communication about the emergence of COVID-19, the WHO has already launched negotiations with member states on a new pandemic treaty (WHO, 2022b). However, whether the outcome of the negotiations is successful will only be tested with the next epidemic or pandemic and still relies on the goodwill of governments and other international actors. Therefore, fostering trust and transparency between governments remains an ongoing (and unending) challenge in managing international and cross-cultural crises.

Conclusions

In this chapter, our objective was to build on Sellnow and Veil's (2016) lessons learned about international and cross-national crises from reflecting on the SARS pandemic with a critical reflection on COVID-19 and the global response to it. We highlighted the foundations and functions of international responses to transnational crises and identified unresolved challenges in international crisis response. Our analysis also suggests that the dynamics and interest in cross-national collaboration will change depending on the phase of risk and crisis management that we are looking at. In a crisis lifecycle, the long-term preparation – encompassing both post-crisis learning and risk mitigation activities before crises – along with the acute phase of a crisis, represents the opportunities for the most cohesive collaboration: between countries, sectors, and for building research-based partnerships with academics because the timing, competing voices, and interplay of responsibilities are less problematic. However, the buildup to a crisis, early emergence, and long tail of the crisis response produces the conditions least suited for transparency and collaboration and most suited for competition and blame-shifting. Yet, there will be challenges in identifying voices, translating science, building collaborative relationships, and defining the priority on community persuasion or community engagement throughout. This suggests there is a need for a pragmatic approach to integrating research into action, community engagement, public diplomacy, and long-term stakeholder relationship management. NGOs and IGOs like the WHO play an integral part in this approach because they should be able to serve as a conduit for information, best practice, and support. Beyond the challenges of international relations and organizational collaboration, what communication scholars and practitioners can affect is communication strategy. It is vital to remember that one of the central lessons learned from the COVID-19 pandemic is that the failure to consider diversity, incorporate diverse communicative needs into the crisis response, and directly target vulnerable groups cost lives (Jacob et al., 2023).

References

Antonacopoulou, E. P., & Sheaffer, Z. (2014). Learning in crisis rethinking the relationship between organizational learning and crisis management. *Journal of Management Inquiry*, *23*(1), 5–21. https://doi.org/10.1177/1056492612472730

Apuke, O. D., & Omar, B. (2021). Fake news and COVID-19: Modelling the predictors of fake news sharing among social media users. *Telematics and Informatics*, *56*, 101475. https://doi.org/10.1016/j.tele.2020.101475

Bajrami, D. D., Terzić, A., Petrović, M. D., Radovanović, M., Tretiakova, T. N., & Hadoud, A. (2021). Will we have the same employees in hospitality after all? The impact of COVID-19 on employees' work attitudes and turnover intentions. *International Journal of Hospitality Management*, *94*, 102754. https://doi.org/10.1016/j.ijhm.2020.102754

Balarabe, U. B., & Kumar, R. (2020). Perspectives and impacts of social media, fake news and misinformation narratives about coronavirus. *Journal of Humanities and Social Science*, *25*(7), 62–66. https://doi.org/10.9790/0837-2507086266

Baum, F., Freeman, T., Musolino, C., Abramovitz, M., De Ceukelaire, W., Flavel, J., Friel, S., Giugliani, C., Howden-Chapman, P., & Huong, N. T. (2021). Explaining covid-19 performance: what factors might predict national responses? *BMJ*, *372*, 1–4. https://doi.org/https://www.bmj.com/content/372/bmj.n91.full

Bielicki, A. (2021). Societal trust and nation-thinking in the midst of a pandemic–Central Europe and Scandinavia. *Köz-gazdaság*, *16*(2), 61–77. https://doi.org/10.14267/RETP2021.02.05

Bíró-Nagy, A., & Szászi, Á. J. (2022). The roots of COVID-19 vaccine hesitancy: Evidence from Hungary. *Journal of Behavioral Medicine*, 1–16. https://doi.org/10.1007/s10865-022-00314-5

Bragazzi, N. L., Khamisy-Farah, R., Tsigalou, C., Mahroum, N., & Converti, M. (2022). Attaching a stigma to the LGBTQI+ community should be avoided during the monkeypox epidemic. *Journal of Medical Virology*. https://doi.org/10.1002/jmv.27913

Breakwell, G. M., & Jaspal, R. (2020). Identity change, uncertainty and mistrust in relation to fear and risk of COVID-19. *Journal of Risk Research*, *24*(3/4), 1–17. https://doi.org/10.1080/13669877.2020.1864011

Brown, P. (1995). Naming and framing: The social construction of diagnosis and illness. *Journal of Health and Social Behavior*, 34–52. https://doi.org/10.2307/2626956

Bruine de Bruin, W., & Bennett, D. (2020). Relationships between initial COVID-19 risk perceptions and protective health behaviors: A national survey. *American Journal of Preventative Medicine*, *59*(2), 157–167. https://doi.org/10.1016/j.amepre.2020.05.001

Bruine de Bruin, W., Saw, H. W., & Goldman, D. P. (2020). Political polarization in US residents' COVID-19 risk perceptions, policy preferences, and protective behaviors. *Journal of Risk and Uncertainty*, *61*, 177–194. https://doi.org/10.1007/s11166-020-09336-3

Chang, A., Schulz, P. J., Tu, S., & Liu, M. T. (2020). Communicative blame in online communication of the COVID-19 pandemic: Computational approach of stigmatizing cues and negative sentiment gauged with automated analytic techniques. *Journal of Medical Internet Research*, *22*(11), e21504. https://doi.org/10.2196/21504

Cheng, Y., & Luo, Y. (2020). The presumed influence of digital misinformation: Examining US public's support for governmental restrictions versus corrective action in the COVID-19 pandemic. *Online Information Review*. https://doi.org/10.1108/OIR-08-2020-0386

Choi, J. W., Kim, K. H., Moon, J. M., & Kim, M. S. (2015). Public health crisis response and establishmentof a crisis communication system in South Korea: Lessons learned from the MERS outbreak. *Journal of the Korean Medical Association*, *58*(7), 624–634. https://doi.org/10.5124/jkma.2015.58.7.624

Conrad, P., & Barker, K. K. (2010). The social construction of illness: Key insights and policy implications. *Journal of Health and Social Behavior*, *51*(1_suppl), S67–S79. https://doi.org/10.1177/0022146510383495

Copeland, P., & Maccaferri, M. (2022). The UK, the EU, and COVID-19: Media reporting, the recontextualisation of Eurosceptic discourse, and the fait accompli of Brexit. *Politics*, 02633957221122322. https://doi.org/10.1177/02633957221122322

Croucher, S. M., Nguyen, T., Pearson, E., Murray, N., Feekery, A., Spencer, A., Gomez, O., Girardelli, D., & Kelly, S. (2021). A comparative analysis of Covid-19-related prejudice: the United States, Spain, Italy, and New Zealand. *Communication Research Reports*, *38*(2), 79–89. https://doi.org/10.1080/08824096.2021.1885371

Croucher, S., Nguyen, T., Ashwell, D., Spencer, A., Permyakova, T., & Gomez, O. (2022). COVID-19 prejudice towards Afro-Brazilians. *Journal of Intercultural Communication Research*, *51*(4), 383–399. https://doi.org/10.1080/17475759.2021.1957702

Croucher, S. M., Nguyen, T., Ding, G. G., Diers-Lawson, A., Spencer, A., Eskiçorapçı, N., Girardelli, D., Permyakova, T. M., Dutta, M. J., Turdubaeva, E., Ashwell, D., Bustamante, S., & Gomez, O. (2023). Intergroup communication during the COVID-19 pandemic: A 20-nation analysis of prejudice. In S. M. Croucher, & A. Diers-Lawson, Eds., *Pandemic Communication* (pp. 174–197). Routledge.

Dai, B., Fu, D., Meng, G., Liu, B., Li, Q., & Liu, X. (2020). The effects of governmental and individual predictors on COVID-19 protective behaviors in China: a path analysis model. *Public Administrative Review*. https://doi.org/10.1111/puar.13236

Diers-Lawson, A. (2020). *Crisis Communication: Managing Stakeholder Relationships*. Routledge.

Diers-Lawson, A., Johnson, S., Clayton, T., Kimoto, R., Tran, B. X., Nguyen, L. H., & Park, K. (2021). Pandemic communication: Information seeking, evaluation, and self-protective behaviors in viet-

nam and the republic of korea. *Frontiers in Communication*, *6*(731979), 160. https://doi.org/10.3389/fcomm.2021.731979
Diers-Lawson, A., Omondi, G., & Hillier, S. (2022). Shooting from the Hip or Taking Careful Aim? Developing the VISTA analytic framework comparing the English and Scottish visual campaigns for self-protective behavior throughout the COVID-19 pandemic. *Journal of Visual Political Communication*, *9*, 59–97. https://doi.org/https://doi.org/10.1386/jvpc_00017_1
Fraser, N., Brierley, L., Dey, G., Polka, J. K., Pálfy, M., Nanni, F., & Coates, J. A. (2021). The evolving role of preprints in the dissemination of COVID-19 research and their impact on the science communication landscape. *PLoS Biology*, *19*(4), e3000959. https://doi.org/10.1371/journal.pbio.3000959
Gilstrap, C. A., Gilstrap, C. M., Holderby, K. N., & Valera, K. M. (2016). Sensegiving, leadership, and nonprofit crises: How nonprofit leaders make and give sense to organizational crisis. *VOLUNTAS: International Journal of Voluntary and Nonprofit Organizations*, *27*(6), 2787–2806. https://doi.org/10.1007/s11266-015-9648-1
Glenn, J., Chaumont, C., & Dintrans, P. V. (2020). Public health leadership in the times of COVID-19: a comparative case study of three countries. *International Journal of Public Leadership*, *17*(1), 81–94. https://doi.org/10.1108/IJPL-08-2020-0082
Halvorsrud, K., Kucharska, J., Adlington, K., Rüdell, K., Brown Hajdukova, E., Nazroo, J., Haarmans, M., Rhodes, J., & Bhui, K. (2021). Identifying evidence of effectiveness in the co-creation of research: A systematic review and meta-analysis of the international healthcare literature. *Journal of Public Health*, *43*(1), 197–208. https://doi.org/10.1093/pubmed/fdz126
Hart, P. S., Chinn, S., & Soroka, S. (2020). Politicization and polarization in COVID-19 news coverage. *Science Communication*, *42*(5), 679–697. https://doi.org/10.1177/1075547020950735
Heath, R. L., & Palenchar, M. J. (2009). *Strategic Issues Management* (2nd ed.). Sage.
Islam, M. S., Sarkar, T., Khan, S. H., Kamal, A.-H. M., Hasan, S. M., Kabir, A., Yeasmin, D., Islam, M. A., Chowdhury, K. I. A., & Anwar, K. S. (2020). COVID-19–related infodemic and its impact on public health: A global social media analysis. *The American Journal of Tropical Medicine and Hygiene*, *103*(4), 1621.
Jacob, C., Hausemer, P., Zagoni-Bogsch, A., & Diers-Lawson, A. (2023). *The Effect of Communication and Disinformation During the Covid-19 Pandemic (Special Committee on the COVID-19 Pandemic: Lessons Learned and Recommendations for the Future, Issue*. E. Parliament. http://www.europarl.europa.eu/supporting-analyses
Kaltenbrunner, K., & Reichel, A. (2018). Crisis response via dynamic capabilities: A necessity in NPOs' capability building. *VOLUNTAS: International Journal of Voluntary and Nonprofit Organizations*, *29*(5), 994–1007. https://doi.org/10.1007/s11266-017-9940-3
Kamburova, M., & Georgieva, S. (2021). The impact of the COVID-19 epidemic and anti-epidemic measures in the Roma neighborhood in Bulgaria. *European Journal of Public Health*, *31*(Supplement_3), ckab164. 244. https://dx.doi.org/10.1093%2Feurpub%2Fckab164.244
Keen, P. K., Gilkey, R., & Baker, E. L. (2020). Crisis leadership – from the haiti earthquake to the COVID pandemic. *Journal of Public Health Management and Practice*, *26*(5), 503–505. https://doi.org/10.1097/PHH.0000000000001207
Khan, M. S., Ali, S. A. M., Adelaine, A., & Karan, A. (2021). Rethinking vaccine hesitancy among minority groups. *The Lancet*, *397*(10288), 1863–1865. https://doi.org/10.1016/S0140-6736(21)00938-7
Kluge, H., & Ammon, A. (2022). Monkeypox in Europe and beyond–tackling a neglected disease together. *Eurosurveillance*, *27*(24), 2200482. https://doi.org/10.2807/1560-7917.ES.2022.27.24.2200482
Lazo-Porras, M., Perez-Leon, S., Cardenas, M. K., Pesantes, M. A., Miranda, J. J., Suggs, L. S., Chappuis, F., Perel, P., & Beran, D. (2020). Lessons learned about co-creation: Developing a complex intervention in rural Peru. *Global Health Action*, *13*(1), 1754016. https://doi.org/10.1080/16549716.2020.1754016
Lee, Y., & Li, J. Y. Q. (2021). The role of communication transparency and organizational trust in publics' perceptions, attitudes and social distancing behaviour: A case study of the COVID-19 outbreak. *Journal of Contingencies & Crisis Management*, *29*(4), 368–384. https://doi.org/10.1111/1468-5973.12354

Lewandowsky, S., Gignac, G. E., & Oberauer, K. (2013). The role of conspiracist ideation and worldviews in predicting rejection of science. *PLoS One*, *8*(10), e75637. https://doi.org/10.1371/journal.pone.0075637

Martel, C., Pennycook, G., & Rand, D. G. (2020). Reliance on emotion promotes belief in fake news. *Cognitive Research: Principles and Implications*, *5*(47). https://doi.org/10.1186/s41235-020-00252-3

Mason, D. P., & Fiocco, E. (2017). Crisis on the border: Specialized capacity building in nonprofit immigration organizations. *VOLUNTAS: International Journal of Voluntary and Nonprofit Organizations*, *28*(3), 916–934. https://doi.org/10.1007/s11266-016-9754-8

Mehmood, Q., Tebha, S. S., & Aborode, A. T. (2021). COVID-19 vaccine hesitancy among Indigenous people in India: An incipient crisis. *Ethics, Medicine, and Public Health*, *19*, 100727. https://doi.org/10.1016%2Fj.jemep.2021.100727

Meier, K., Glatz, T., Guijt, M. C., Piccininni, M., van der Meulen, M., Atmar, K., Jolink, A. C., Kurth, T., Rohmann, J. L., Zamanipoor Najafabadi, A. H., & Group, C.-S. S. (2020). Public perspectives on protective measures during the COVID-19 pandemic in the Netherlands, Germany and Italy: A survey study. *PLoS One*, *15*(8), e0236917. https://doi.org/10.1371/journal.pone.0236917

Mesch, G. S., & Schwirian, K. P. (2015). Social and political determinants of vaccine hesitancy: Lessons learned from the H1N1 pandemic of 2009-2010. *American Journal of Infection Control*, *43*(11), 1161–1165. https://doi.org/10.1016/j.ajic.2015.06.031

Mikac, R. (2020). Covid-19 pandemic and crisis management in the Republic of Croatia. *Anali Hrvatskog politološkog društva: časopis za politologiju*, *17*(1), 31–55. https://doi.org/10.20901/an.17.02

Nguyen, N. P. T., Hoang, T. D., Tran, V. T., Vu, C. T., Siewe Fodjo, J. N., Colebunders, R., Dunne, M. P., & Vo, T. V. (2020). Preventive behavior of Vietnamese people in response to the COVID-19 pandemic. *PLoS One*, *15*(9), e0238830. https://doi.org/10.1371/journal.pone.0238830

Papageorge, N. W., Zahn, M. V., Belot, M., van den Broek-Altenburg, E., Choi, S., Jamison, J. C., & Tripodi, E. (2021). Socio-demographic factors associated with self-protecting behavior during the Covid-19 pandemic. *Journal of Population Economics*, *34*, 691–738. https://doi.org/10.1007/s00148-020-00818-x

Petridou, E., Danielsson, E., Olofsson, A., Lundgren, M., & Große, C. (2019). If crisis or war comes: A study of risk communication of eight european union member states. *Journal of International Crisis and Risk Communication Research*, *2*(2), 3. https://doi.org/10.30658/jicrcr.2.2.3

Pierre, J. M. (2019). Mistrust and misinformation: A two-component, socio-epistemic model of belief in conspiracy theories. *Journal of Social and Political Psychology*, *8*(2), 617–641. https://doi.org/10.5964/jspp.v8i2.1362

Reeves, M., Carlsson-Szlezak, P., Whitaker, K., & Abraham, M. (2020). *Sensing and Shaping the Post-COVID Era*. T. B. H. Institute. https://web-assets.bcg.com/img-src/BCG-Sensing-and-Shaping-the-Post-COVID-Era-Apr-2020-rev_tcm9-244426.pdf

Reja, M. (2021). Trump's 'Chinese Virus' tweet helped lead to rise in racist anti-Asian Twitter content: Study shows. *ABC News*. Retrieved January 18, 2023, from https://abcnews.go.com/Health/trumps-chinese-virus-tweet-helped-lead-rise-racist/story?id=76530148

Rimal, N. R., Fogg, B., & Flora, J. A. (1996). Moving ntoward a framework for the study of risk communication: Theoretical and ethical issues. *Communication Yearbook*, *18*, 320–342.

Roux-Dufort, C. (2000). Why organizations don't learn from crises: The perverse power of normalization. *Review of Business*, *21*, 25–30.

Salvi, C., Iannello, P., Cancer, A., McClay, M., Rago, S., Dunsmoor, J. E., & Antonietti, A. (2021). Going viral: How fear, socio-cognitive polarization and problem-solving influence fake news detection and proliferation during COVID-19 pandemic. *Frontiers in Communication*, *5*, https://doi.org/10.3389/fcomm.2020, 562588.

Schwarz, A., & Fritsch, A. (2014). Communicating on behalf of global civil society: Management and coordination of public relations in international nongovernmental organizations. *Journal of Public Relations Research*, *26*(2), 161–183. https://doi.org/10.1080/1062726X.2013.864242

Seeger, M. W. (2006). Best practices in crisis communication: An expert panel process. *Journal of Applied Communication Research*, *34*(3), 232–244.

Sellnow, T. L., & Veil, S. R. (2016). Preparing for international and cross-cultural crises: The role of competing voices, inclusivity, and the interplay of responsibility in global organizations. In A. Schwarz, M. W. Seeger, & C. Auer, Eds., *The Handbook of International Crisis Communication Research* (pp. 489–498). Wiley and Blackwell. https://doi.org/10.1002/9781118516812.ch44

Sellnow, D. D., Johansson, B., Sellnow, T. L., & Lane, D. R. (2019). Toward a global understanding of the effects of the IDEA model for designing instructional risk and crisis messages: A food contamination experiment in Sweden. *Journal of Contingencies & Crisis Management*, *27*(2), 102–115. https://doi.org/10.1111/1468-5973.12234

Sellnow-Richmond, D., George, A., & Sellnow, D. (2018). An IDEA model analysis of instructional risk communication in the time of ebola. *Journal of International Crisis and Risk Communication Research*, *1*(1), 135–166. https://doi.org/10.30658/jicrcr.1.1.7

Soares, F. B., & Recuero, R. (2021). How the mainstream media help to spread disinformation about COVID-19. *M/C Journal*, *24*(1), 1–17. https://doi.org/10.5204/mcj.2735

Spence, P. R., Lachlan, K. A., Omilion-Hodges, L. M., & Goddard, A. K. (2014). Being first means being credible? Examining the impact of message source on organizational reputation. *Communication Research Reports*, *31*(1), 124–130. https://doi.org/10.1080/08824096.2013.846259

Sukhankin, S. (2020). COVID-19 as a tool of information confrontation: Russia's approach. *The School of Public Policy Publications*, *13*(3), 1–10. https://doi.org/https://ssrn.com/abstract=3566689

Sullivan, P., Starr, V., Dubois, E., Starr, A., Acharibasam, J. B., & McIlduff, C. (2023). Where past meets present: Indigenous vaccine hesitancy in Saskatchewan. *Medical Humanities*. https://doi.org/10.1136/medhum-2022-012501

Sun, Y., Chia, S. C., Lu, F., & Oktavianus, J. (2020). The battle is on: Factors that motivate people to combat anti-vaccine misinformation. *Health Communication*. https://doi.org/10.1080/10410236.2020.1838108

Szabó, L. P., & Szabó, G. (2022). Attack of the critics: Metaphorical delegitimisation in Viktor Orbán's discourse during the Covid-19 pandemic. *Journal of Language and Politics*, *21*(2), 255–276. https://doi.org/10.1075/jlp.21068.sza

Varghese, N. E., Sabat, I., Neumann-Böhme, S., Schreyögg, J., Stargardt, T., Torbica, A., van Exel, J., Barros, P. P., & Brouwer, W. (2021). Risk communication during COVID-19: A descriptive study on familiarity with, adherence to and trust in the WHO preventive measures. *PLoS One*, *16*(4), e0250872. https://doi.org/10.1371/journal.pone.0250872

de Vries, M., Claassen, L., Te Wierik, M. J., van den Hof, S., Brabers, A. E., de Jong, J. D., Timmermans, D. R., & Timen, A. (2021). Dynamic public perceptions of the coronavirus disease crisis, the Netherlands, 2020. *Emerging Infectious Diseases*, *27*(4), 1098. https://doi.org/10.3201%2Feid2704.203328

de Vries, H., Verputten, W., Preissner, C., & Kok, G. (2022). COVID-19 vaccine hesitancy: The role of information sources and beliefs in dutch adults. *International Journal of Environmental Research and Public Health*, *19*(6), 3205. https://doi.org/10.3390/ijerph19063205

WHO (2005a). *Outbreak Communication: Best Practices for Communicating with the Public During an Outbreak* Communicable Disease Surveillance and Response, Issue. W. H. Organization. https://apps.who.int/iris/handle/10665/69138

WHO (2005b). *WHO Global Influenza Preparedness Plan: The Role of WHO and Recommendations for National Measures Before and During Pandemics*. Geneva: WHO. (Epidemic Alert and Response, Issue. https://apps.who.int/iris/handle/10665/68998

WHO (2005c). *WHO Outbreak Communication Guidelines*(Emergency Preparedness, Issue. W. H. Organization. https://www.who.int/publications/i/item/who-outbreak-communication-guidelines

WHO (2017). *WHO Strategic Communications Framework for Effective Communication*. WHO. https://www.who.int/mediacentre/communication-framework.pdf

WHO (2018). *Communicating Risk in Public Health Emergencies: A WHO Guidelines for Emergency Risk Communication (ERC) Policy and Practice*. Geneva: WHO. (Emergencies Preparedness, Guidelines Review Committee, Issue

WHO (2020a). *Coronavirus Disease (COVID-19) Advice for the Public*. World Health Organization. Retrieved July 30, 2021 from https://www.who.int/emergencies/diseases/novel-coronavirus-2019/advice-for-public

WHO (2020b). *WHO Outbreak Communication Guidelines*. Geneva: WHO. https://www.who.int/publications/i/item/who-outbreak-communication-guidelines

WHO (2021a). *COVID-19 Global Risk Communication and Community Engagement Strategy*. World Health Organization. Retrieved June 27, 2020 from https://www.who.int/publications/i/item/covid-19-global-risk-communication-and-community-engagement-strategy

WHO (2021b). *Fighting Misinformation in the Time of COVID-19, one Click at a Time*. World Health Organization. Retrieved June 27, 2020 from https://www.who.int/news-room/feature-stories/detail/fighting-misinformation-in-the-time-of-covid-19-one-click-at-a-time

WHO (2022a, December 21, 2022). *Coronavirus Disease (COVID-19) Donors & Partners: WHO Says Thank You!* WHO. Retrieved 3 January from https://www.who.int/emergencies/diseases/novel-coronavirus-2019/donors-and-partners/funding

WHO (2022b). *Intergovernmental Negotiating Body*. World Health Organization. Retrieved 24 January from https://inb.who.int/

WHO (2022c). *International Health Regulations: Joint External Evaluation Tool* (Country Capacity for IHR, Issue. W. H. Organizaiton.

WHO (2022d). *Risk Communication and Community Engagement: a compendium of case studies in times of COVID-19*. Copenhagen: WHO. https://www.who.int/europe/publications/i/item/WHO-EURO-2022-6186-45951-66353

WHO (2023). *Vaccine equity*. Retrieved January 18 from https://www.who.int/campaigns/vaccine-equity

Wolff, S., & Ladi, S. (2020). European Union responses to the COVID-19 pandemic: Adaptability in times of permanent emergency. *Journal of European Integration*, *42*(8), 1025–1040. https://doi.org/10.1080/07036337.2020.1853120

Author's Bio

Ben Duncan (LL.M, 1989, University of Edinburgh) is a senior risk communication and community engagement (RCCE) practitioner who worked on pandemic communication preparedness for nearly 18 years before COVID-19 struck. His career has included 13 years of working for the European Union, during which time he was part of the start-up team for the European Centre for Disease Prevention and Control (ECDC), as well as assignments for the WHO across Europe, Asia, Africa, and the Americas. In 2020, he worked on the frontline of the COVID-19 response at the WHO headquarters and then the WHO Country Office in Lao PDR. Between 2021 and 2024, he was one of the senior RCCE consultants working for WHO's Regional Office for Europe. He was the lead researcher and author of a compendium of case studies on good practices and lessons learned from across Europe and Central Asia published by the WHO in October 2022. He has also helped design and facilitate sub-regional lessons learned meetings on COVID-19 RCCE for WHO/Europe in the Balkans, the Caucuses, and Central Asia in 2022, as well as being one of the faculty for its RCCE School to train practitioners.

Audra Diers-Lawson (PhD, 2006, University of Texas-Austin) is a professor of risk and crisis communication and head of the PhD in Communication and Leadership at Kristiania University of Applied Technology in Oslo, Norway. With more than 35 scientific publications in the last five to six years alone, serving on editorial boards or as a reviewer for more than 20 journals, serving as a section vice-chair and chair for the Crisis Communication Division of the ECREA, and serving as an inaugural Board member and Secretary Treasurer for the International Crisis and Risk Communication Association, she is a leader in the field of risk and crisis communication. Her research focuses on the connections between risk, crisis, stakeholders, and organizations. Her monograph, *Crisis Communication: Managing Stakeholder Relationships* (2020), brought together more than 50 years of research on risk and crisis communication to identify important common themes, evaluate theory and practice, and articulate a comprehensive argument for adopting a stakeholder perspective in risk and crisis communication. Finally, she translates her research for practice with collaborations and applied research projects with organizations like the EU, the World Health Organization, and the Asia-Europe Foundation. Diers-Lawson is also the head of the WHO-Europe Collaboration Centre for Risk Communication, Community Engagement, and Infodemic Management at Kristiania.

Summing Up & Looking Ahead: The Future of International Risk & Crisis Communication Research

50

The Expanding and Dynamic Field of Crisis and Emergency Risk Communication: Summary, Implications, and Outlook

Andreas Schwarz[1], Matthew W. Seeger[2], and Sora Kim[3]

[1] Institute of Media and Communication Science, Technische Universität Ilmenau, Ilmenau, Germany

[2] Center for Emerging and Infectious Disease, Wayne State University, Detroit, MI, USA

[3] School of Journalism and Communication, Chinese University of Hong Kong, Shatin, Hong Kong

Introduction

The second edition of the *International Handbook of Crisis and Risk Communication Research* builds upon the goals of the first edition, including representing research from diverse regions not always included in academic journals, growing the global research community, and bolstering efforts to understand risk and crisis communication as simultaneously a local and global challenge. Crises and disasters are always grounded in a specific location at a specific time, yet often transcend international borders both physically and symbolically (Schwarz et al., 2016). In addition, the second edition illustrates that the larger communication ecosystem has become both more complex and more interconnected. More and more diverse state, NGO, and corporate actors actively communicate about crises and risks using more diverse channels, enabled by new technologies, including an array of social media platforms and artificial intelligence tools. In addition, the cultural lens is increasingly important in understanding risk and crises as global phenomena, and multidisciplinary perspectives are necessary to understand the complexity of these events.

Although the second edition confirms that this area of work is still dominated by European and North American approaches and perspectives, programs of research are proliferating, including in the global south. This may be in part a consequence of the COVID-19 pandemic and its global impact. Moreover, the pandemic was a powerful illustration of the level of disruption and harm that can come from a crisis, that crises do not respect boundaries, and that communication is an essential process for any response. COVID-19, as many of the chapters in this edition illustrate, drove a considerable amount of research throughout the world.

The Handbook of International Crisis and Risk Communication Research, Second Edition.
Edited by Andreas Schwarz, Matthew W. Seeger, and Sora Kim.

In this general summary, we review major themes of Part I (History and Trends), Part II (Institutional and Strategic Perspectives), Part III (Legacy Media and Social Media Perspectives) Part IV (Audience, Citizen, and Victim Perspectives), Part V (The State of Risk and Crisis Communication Research Around the Globe), and Part VI (Emerging Topics, Challenges, Theory, and Methods). We conclude by offering our thoughts about future directions and the opportunities and challenges of the continued growth and globalization of this field.

An Expanding, International Field, Driven by Events (Part I)

As illustrated in the introductory chapters, hazards and risks are proliferating and crises appear to be more frequent and impact more people. They are also more complex, interconnected, and international (Chapter 1, Schwarz). The rapid growth of new technologies of communication, social media, and AI has created both opportunities and significant challenges for research and practice. This was vividly demonstrated by COVID-19 and other crises, such as the war in Ukraine and climate-driven disasters, floods, droughts, and extreme heat events. Moreover, despite a growth in risk and crisis research over the last 15 years, the research has not adequately embraced a diverse set of global perspectives. The field continues to be dominated by North American and European researchers, with significant contributions from researchers in Asia. The field is also interdisciplinary and, as noted by others, cross-national or cross-cultural crisis and risk communication research is limited.

The introduction chapters in Part I show how the practice and study of crisis and risk communication is closely associated with the development of societies and their effort to collectively manage hazards and respond to risks. The formalized, academic study of crisis and risk communication began in the 1940s and 1950s, centered in North America and Europe. Research was facilitated by the development of strong university systems and the realization of the devastation that arose from global conflicts and the threat of nuclear war. The history of crisis and risk communication also demonstrates that risk communication research and practice, in particular, was driven by state-based actors and agencies, and to a lesser degree, corporate actors addressing product and production-related risks. Crisis communication, in contrast, was driven by natural disasters, such as hurricanes, floods, wildfires, and tornadoes, and emphasized warnings and alerts and preparedness and response messages, such as evacuation measures, shelter in place, etc. As the discussion of history demonstrates, both areas of research and practice have expanded significantly with new and re-emerging hazards, higher expectations that communities will be safe, the ubiquity of communication systems and messages, and a general recognition of audience diversity.

The introductory chapters also explore the complexities of crisis and risk communication as an intercultural and trans-border phenomenon. Culture is a complex and multidimensional construct that is linked to different levels of culture, including the macro-level (national culture) the meso-level (industry culture) and the micro-level (organizational culture). Culture interacts with the scope and nature of the crisis/risk. Culture also impacts crisis management strategies, public perceptions, and behavioral reactions (Chapter 3, Kim). This underscores the imperative for culturally tailored approaches to crisis and risk communication. COVID-19 clearly demonstrated what crisis scholars have argued for some time; that is, crises transcend physical, national, and cultural boundaries, and that the study and practice of crisis and risk communication necessitate understanding culture. Moreover, culture plays an essential role in the ways risks are understood and managed, how risk messages are interpreted, and "crisis is a deeply culture-sensitive social construct" (Chapter 3, Kim, p. 28). Although the construct of culture has been the focus of considerable communication scholarship, limited research, especially theory-driven research, has focused on culture, crisis, and risk communication.

The concept of culture, however, can help move the study of crisis and risk away from North American and European perspectives. More researchers are taking non-Western perspectives and exploring risk and crisis communication issues outside of Western regions. This includes investigating national-level (macro) cultural differences and how these differences influence crises and risks and the identification of cross-cultural disparities. In addition, some cross-cultural comparisons have bolstered the understanding of both differences and disparities and also how institutions working across global contexts can enhance preparedness and response.

The Emergence of more, and more Diverse Organizational and Institutional Actors (Part II)

Much of crisis and risk communication research has been driven by organizational, institutional, and strategic perspectives. This has helped further the view that crisis and risk communication is a strategic institutional and management function designed to create specific outcomes. It has also furthered the critique that crisis and risk communication serve primarily to protect institutions and maintain or exert power. Institutional actors may be divided roughly as state actors, agencies, political institutions, the military, and NGOs, private corporations, media organizations, aid agencies, etc.

Organizational crises, those associated with NGOs, private companies, and public corporations, and those cases where crises disrupt corporate activity, are increasingly common and increasingly multinational. Crises associated with multinational organizations can have global consequences in part because of the power and control over resources these organizations exert. These institutional crises are often managed strategically to minimize disruption to organizations, their reputations, profitability, and stakeholders. Significant research has been directed toward understanding the role of strategic communication in limiting harm to organizations (Chapter 8, Pyle, Fuller, & Ulmer). A much smaller body of work emphasizes the ways open, honest, and equitable communication can create shared understanding of risk, emphasize and clarify common values, and help reconstitute order and help renew systems.

Among the most salient crises that engage institutional actors is war. Although not always included as a form of crisis, war, as the armed conflict between groups, has been recognized by researchers as a form of crisis in terms of the direct harm inflicted and by secondary impacts such as population displacement, disease, and economic disruption. War, along with terrorism, is somewhat distinct in that it involves the creation of intentional harm. In addition, war is by definition mediatized and influenced by communication processes (Chapter 4, Schleicher). Institutional actors, therefore, seek to manage the communication processes, including media coverage, public access to information, and the associated public opinion. Media coverage, including the traditional watchdog function of journalism, can change the behavior of actors during armed conflict. In addition, as with many cases of crises involving institutions, new voices are enabled by new technologies of social and digital media. Institutions have also embraced digital media as another channel for the dissemination of strategic messages.

Many of the same processes are evident with crisis events characterized as terrorism. Although there is no universal agreement about the term, terrorism is generally viewed as an ideologically driven attack or series of attacks designed to create chaos, disruption, fear, and revulsion. Terrorism often has the strategic goal of generating public attention through dramatic and destructive acts, and the management of terrorism involves strategic use of communication in preparedness, response, and recovery phases. As with war, investigators are increasingly using the lens of crisis and risk communication to examine terrorism (Chapter 5, Ruggiero & Tikka).

An additional form of crisis that intersects with and activates institutional actors is the political crisis. As with war and terrorism, political crises are intertwined with other crisis forms

(Chapter 9, Johansson & Vigsø). These may include the management of crises of various types and severity at various levels, including various types of political scandals. The success of crisis management is assessed by outcomes such as the level of harm, speed of recovery, and overall responsiveness of the political actors. Scandals typically require some level of public accountability. Political crises are also associated with a variety of institutional actors who often rely on strategic communication to achieve their goals. The metaphor of an arena has been used to describe the context of multiple actors within democratic systems participating in discursive activity associated with an issue such as a risk or crisis.

The political arena is influenced by the quality of information available to institutional actors. The quality of risk and crisis information is "currently being bombarded by a post-truth communication environment of fake news and intentionally misleading information" (Chapter 6, Palenchar & Heath, p. 71). The phenomenon of misinformation and disinformation threatens to overwhelm basic understanding of crises and risks, including established theory and research paradigms. Post-truth views, fake news, individual and organized group disinformation and misinformation, and the sheer volume of messages along with the resulting information overload threaten the effectiveness of risk and crisis communicators' efforts and campaigns. The ubiquity of social media and its global reach and various AI-enabled tools for creating misleading and distorting messages, in combination with the motivation to use mis- and disinformation strategically, has created a paradigm shift in both the study and practice of risk and crisis communication. The fundamental processes for making sense of and responding to risks and their manifestation in crises have been disrupted. Current models of risk and crisis communication are simply inadequate, and risk communicators and crisis managers struggle to find appropriate and effective ways to respond.

Institutional actors, both state and NGO, are the primary voices in crisis and risk communication. The research programs examining institutional actors are still dominated by European and North American approaches. The need for global perspectives is driven by the fact that neither disasters nor messages respect international boundaries. Moreover, the quality and volume of information produced by actors vary considerably, complicating the larger communication ecosystem.

The Rise of Mis/Disinformation, the Impact of AI, and the Lack of Global South Perspectives: The Role of News Media and Social Media in Global Risk and Crisis Communication (Part III)

The review of crisis communication research and the role of journalism/news media has shown that armed conflicts and war need to be considered an important subject in the field (Chapter 10, Sarısakaloğlu & Gidget Estella). Many researchers consider war as a manifestation of crisis that either results from other crises (e.g., political conflicts over resources or territory), amplifies existing crises, and/or leads to further crises (killing civilians, famine, diseases, etc.). Research on war reporting has been conducted from different epistemological and normative perspectives with concepts such as "war journalism" or "peace journalism." While the field is still highly fragmented and scattered across journalism studies, international relations research, or political science, commonly used approaches such as framing, agenda setting, news values theory, or the indexing hypothesis. The research output has substantially increased over the last decades. Mainstream news media have been criticized for either one-sidedly emphasizing conflicts with the involvement of elite nations (usually Western) or with high geographic proximity (usually to Western countries), while many severe conflicts in the Global South stay unnoticed. Whenever they are noticed, news media tend to perpetuate stereotypes related to developing countries as marginalized, poor, and violent. As in many other chapters of this handbook (e.g., Chapter 15, Larsen & Ihlen), Russia's aggression and invasion of Ukraine plays a notable role. They refer to research showing how Russian actors managed to shape the news coverage in Europe about Ukraine more than European actors themselves. In addition, case studies described the use of disinformation campaigns on social media used by Russia and Ukraine as analyzed by Larsen and Ihlen (Chapter 15). Given the increasing impact of emerging technologies such as artificial intelligence (AI) and drones, Sarısakaloğlu and Gidget Estella call for more research efforts: "As information warfare becomes an integral part of modern conflict, and as new technologies allow both massive deception and audience empowerment, scholarship has to keep pace with innovative and more critical approaches" (Chapter 10, p. 129). This also means that future research should take into account the transnational nature of both the conflicts themselves and the mediated communication about these conflicts in the news media and on social media.

A dominance of Western normative perspectives was diagnosed by Rothenberger and Verhovnik-Heinze (Chapter 11) in their analysis of media research on terrorism and shooting incidents. More research analyzing media content on terrorist attacks or shootings cross-nationally, but also social media strategies by terrorist organizations or lone-wolf shooters in different contexts, is needed. A cross-national perspective is also crucial, as many terrorist groups are organized and operate transnationally, related to both attacks and communication (disinformation, recruiting, etc.). Some case studies showed how perpetrators use social media in preparation of attacks as well as during their attacks by either receiving instructions until the very last moment or by transmitting their deeds live on platforms like Facebook (e.g., the Christchurch attack in 2019). While governmental or societal pressure on social media companies such as Meta has helped to decrease the presence of terrorists on their platforms, they continue to thrive on other less regulated platforms (e.g., Telegram).

The crucial role of social media was also emphasized for disasters and the field of environmental risk communication (Chapter 12, Palenchar & White). While social media help to inform and engage crucial stakeholders related to issues like climate change, they also suffer from substantial trust and credibility limitations. This weakness is accentuated by the observation that science communication research and practice often favor one-way communication, which can increase public distrust in science. Further risks originate in the increasing use of misinformation/disinformation on social media, partly created, targeted, and/or amplified by new technologies such as AI to amplify distrust in climate science. This has been related to right-wing and/or conservative groups and media and their efforts to create an anti-science intellectual climate. This tendency is not confined to the US but can be observed in many countries and, hence, warrants a more global approach by risk and crisis communication researchers.

The media are evidently influential during public health crises such as the COVID-19 pandemic, which has claimed more than seven million lives worldwide as of August 2024 (World Health Organization, 2024). In the US, inaccurate and contradictory statements by the government led to a media narrative of public confusion and poor governmental communicators (Chapter 13, Liu & Baur). One of the reasons may have been the lack of inclusion of risk and crisis communication experts in advising the government on COVID-19 response issues. In addition, the full potential of monitoring social media regarding the effectiveness of messages has not always been used during different outbreaks. In general, as for other risk and crisis types as well, social media were both important channels for timely risk communication and sources of misinformation. Misinformation spread by trolls, bots, and malicious actors was often counteracted too late by different governments during COVID-19, while in some cases the government itself was the source of misinformation (e.g., the US, Brazil). The media, on the other hand, contributed to reinforcing stereotypes and stigmata about elder and obese people or national prejudices (e.g., the "Chinese virus"). Liu and Baur therefore caution against marginalizing messages addressing specific audiences, such as ethnic minorities or other vulnerable groups, which points to the government, but also the media, as responsible communicators.

Understanding the media environment is therefore essential for all types of risks and crises, including organizational crises (Chapter 14, Jin & van de Mer). According to mediatization theory, organizations have become more visible and under more scrutiny by the media, especially in crisis situations. This has led to an increasing politicization of corporate communication, which, especially for larger and transnational organizations, is a complex situation considering their international stakeholder networks. In this context, social media have gained a significant role in shaping and amplifying risks and crises from an organizational perspective, as described by the social-mediated crisis communication (SMCC) model. Triggering or amplifying novel risks in crisis management in organizations has become a greater challenge with the emergence of AI and its application to create and disseminate disinformation. Jin and van de Mer therefore recommend new forms of disinformation readiness, which organizations have to incorporate in their crisis prevention and preparation approaches across media types and national/cultural backgrounds.

The Interconnectedness of Audiences, Citizens, and Victims in Crisis Dynamics (Part IV)

Part IV delves into the profound impact that audiences, citizens, and victims have on international crises, highlighting their roles across various contexts – including war (Chapter 16, Haigh), terrorism (Chapter 17, DeFoster), pandemics (Chapter 19, Wiedicke & Rossmann), organizational crisis (Chapter 20, Claeys & Schwarz), and political crisis (Chapter 21, Samoilenko & Simons). This section demonstrates how these groups have transitioned from passive recipients of information to active participants whose perceptions and reactions can significantly shape the dynamics and outcomes of crises.

Historically, audiences, citizens, and victims were often seen as passive observers of crises, receiving information from traditional media sources and responding to events in relatively subdued ways. However, the advent and proliferation of social media and new technologies have drastically transformed this dynamic. Today, these groups are not merely absorbing information but are actively engaging with it, influencing public discourse, and shaping crisis outcomes (Chapter 18, Spence & Lachlan).

Wars, for example, were historically reported through newspapers and radio broadcasts, with audiences having limited means to interact with or influence the narrative. However, the rise of social media has changed this landscape. Platforms like X (formerly Twitter), Facebook, and Instagram allow for real-time reporting and immediate public feedback. This shift has empowered audiences to rapidly disseminate information and disinformation, challenge official narratives, share alternative viewpoints, and mobilize support or opposition based on their perspectives (Chapter 16, Haigh).

Similarly, terrorism acts, often framed as dramatic spectacles, leverage media coverage to amplify their impact (Chapter 17, DeFoster). In the past, terrorism might have been reported as isolated incidents with limited public engagement. Today, however, the extensive coverage and sensationalism often associated with terrorist attacks can lead to heightened public fear and increased support for stringent security measures. Responses of audiences and victims to media portrayals of terrorist acts can escalate fear and influence policy shifts, such as increased support for security measures or heightened prejudice against certain groups. Victims of terrorism also play a crucial role in shaping public perceptions and policy responses. Their stories, when highlighted by media, can evoke strong emotional reactions and drive humanitarian responses. The portrayal of victims as innocent and vulnerable can galvanize public support for intervention and reform while also influencing political agendas and policy decisions (Chapter 17, DeFoster).

In the realm of natural disasters and pandemics, individuals' active information-seeking behavior and citizen activism to regain a sense of control and reduce uncertainty have been emphasized in the complex interactions among crisis, media, and audiences or citizens (Chapter 18, Spence & Lachlan; Chapter 19, Wiedicke & Rossmann). During health crises such as the COVID-19 pandemic, for example, social media platforms became essential tools for disseminating information, sharing personal experiences, and mobilizing public health efforts. Citizens used these platforms to advocate for public health measures, share updates, and support each other. Grassroots movements and advocacy groups often drive public pressure, pushing governments and organizations to take more decisive actions. Victim narratives and personal testimonies can humanize abstract public health issues, making them more relatable and urgent to the general public. This active engagement demonstrates that citizens and victims are instrumental in shaping how crises are managed and addressed (Chapter 19, Wiedicke & Rossmann).

The role of audiences in the context of political scandals and crises is also significant. With the increasing complexity of managing reputational risks in the digital era, where information spreads rapidly and public scrutiny is intense, political actors must carefully navigate media coverage, public perception, and social media feedback to protect their reputations and mitigate damage. Political figures and institutions must be adept at managing their public image, responding to criticisms, and engaging with their audience to rebuild trust and maintain support (Chapter 21, Samoilenko & Simons).

In the information-seeking and consumption process of crisis, Spence and Lachlan (Chapter 18) also highlight the varying responses among different demographic groups, noting that marginalized communities may have less access to information and may respond differently to crisis communication. They discuss the psychological impact of vivid and emotionally charged media portrayals on secondary audiences (those not directly affected by a disaster but still influenced by media coverage). Such can lead to overestimations of risk, causing undue fear and anxiety among these audiences. This reveals how diverse demographic groups respond differently to crisis communication, emphasizing the importance of addressing varied needs and the necessity for culturally sensitive communication strategies in global crises.

From the publics' perspective in crisis, cultural aspects should also be considered. Audiences, citizens, and victims interpret and respond to crisis communication in varied ways. In this process, cultural differences play an important role. For example, Western audiences might prefer direct and transparent communication, while other cultures like Asia may value more indirect or nuanced approaches (Chapter 3, Kim). Understanding these cultural differences is essential for crafting effective crisis communication strategies. Organizations must navigate this complex landscape, balancing the need for clear messaging with cultural sensitivities to maintain their reputations and address diverse audience concerns. In this regard, Claeys and Schwarz (Chapter 20) underscore the need for cross-cultural research to better understand how diverse audiences interpret and respond to crises.

Part IV illustrates the interconnectedness of audiences, citizens, and victims in shaping the dynamics of international crises. Whether through media consumption, public opinion, activism, or direct participation, these groups influence the discourse, outcomes, and management of crises in profound ways. The section highlights the importance of understanding these roles not just in isolation but as part of a broader, interactive system where media, communication strategies, and public perceptions continuously influence each other.

In today's globalized world, where information spreads rapidly across borders and cultural contexts, the role of audiences, citizens, and victims in crisis dynamics has never been more critical. Understanding and addressing the diverse needs and perspectives of these groups is essential for effective crisis management, whether in the context of war, terrorism, public health emergencies, or political scandals. As Part IV demonstrates, the ability to navigate these complex interactions is key to managing and resolving international crises in a way that is both effective and humane.

Risk and Crisis Communication Research in Different World Regions: Global Threats, Local Challenges, and Emerging Global South Perspectives (Part V)

The second edition of this handbook includes additional and updated overviews on risk and crisis communication research in specific countries and regions of the world. The goal was to offer insights and contextualization to international scholars and practitioners, which improves understanding of distinct national/cultural environments and potentially facilitates collaboration across boundaries.

Risk and crisis communication research in the US and Europe still dominates international publication outlets and has been growing significantly after the COVID-19 pandemic. In addition, the increasingly visible manifestations of climate change (e.g., disasters, extreme temperature events) and the detrimental effects of misinformation/disinformation before and during crises are of growing concern in these countries and the scientific community. Although ethnocentric approaches still dominate, risk and crisis communication research in the US has become more international because of more international conferences and research collaboration across countries (Chapter 37, Veil). Within Europe, the UK, Germany (Chapter 32, Schwarz), and the Scandinavian countries (Chapter 33, Frandsen & Johansen) continue to be the most productive, especially with more transnational funding opportunities from the European Union related to COVID-19, disaster and climate change research, and security concerns (Ukraine). While the research output from Eastern Europe is less prevalent, in many countries such as Romania (Chapter 35, Buzoianu et al.), the Baltic countries, the Czech Republic, Hungary, Poland, and Slovakia (Chapter 36, Tsetsura et al.), COVID-19 has led to a surge of publications. Since the fall of the Iron Curtain in 1989, these countries have been going through a significant transformation to democracy and a free (social) market economy, which has also led to a broad adoption of Western theories and research practices. In many cases, a predominance of case studies of organizational crises (PR perspective) and media research was observed. In Ukraine, risk and crisis communication research has co-developed with the continuing and increasing aggression of Russia against the country, focusing in particular on Russia's disinformation campaigns related to COVID-19, Russia's invasion of the country, and the Ukrainian government in general. As of 2024, risk and crisis communication research in Ukraine is on hold because of the ongoing war, with researchers trying to produce knowledge that helps the country more directly deal with the Russian threat (Chapter 36, Tsetsura et al.). Risk and crisis communication in Russia (Chapter 34, Samoilenko & Simons) was diagnosed to be deeply rooted in the country's cultural and political experiences, where the state has historically acted as both the primary crisis manager (e.g., disasters), crisis aggravator (COVID-19), and risk producer (e.g., the invasion of Ukraine). Disasters or the COVID-19 pandemic triggered government responses that, rather than supporting people, aimed to control or suppress volunteers and maintain government communication channels as the dominant source of information. The authors concluded that the Russian population tends to have higher levels of risk tolerance and crisis resilience, often taking pragmatic approaches to deal with difficult situations. The low academic output in risk and crisis communication research is explained by the lack of academic communication programs and restricted access of scholars to official data on different types of risks or crises.

A strong and growing community of risk and crisis communication scholars is based in East Asia. Research from this region has had an important influence on the international literature, especially in countries like Japan (Chapter 29, Sakurai), South Korea (Chapter 25, Kim & Kim), Singapore (Chapter 26, Pang et al.), and China (Chapter 27, Ji & Wan). Many of these countries have long-term experience with disaster threats, in particular Japan, as well as infectious diseases. COVID-19 has affected the region and stimulated extensive research. However, although some of these countries were rather successful in containing the SARS-CoV-2 virus (e.g., South Korea, Singapore), the governments' performance did not necessarily translate to higher levels of institutional trust (e.g., Chapter 25, Kim & Kim). In China, the political context has significant influence on risk and crisis communication (Ji & Wan, Chapter 27). The tightly regulated media, for example, were found to frame crises and risks very positively, emphasizing the government's successful risk and crisis management efforts. Besides a substantial growth in publications, the authors observe an increasing intersection between risks, crises, and social issues in China's literature. There is strong consensus among our Asian contributors, including Sriramesh and Dhanesh from India (Chapter 28), that Western theories such as situational crisis communication theory (SCCT), image restoration theory (IRT), the extended parallel process model (EPPM), or the risk information seeing and processing model (RISP) strongly dominate in the region. Pang et al. (Chapter 26), therefore, point to the need for concepts and models that are more indigenized to the Asian political, historical, and socio-cultural context.

Risk and crisis communication research in the Middle East is strongly shaped by the conflicts (e.g., Israeli-Palestinian conflict) and political issues in the region (Chapter 31, Allagui; Chapter 30, Gilboa et al.). For the GCC countries (Bahrain, Kuwait, Oman, Qatar, Saudi Arabia, UAE), Allagui points to a lack of research on organizational crises, where organizations often stress reputation (face saving) over victim support. While governments exert a strong control of the media, traditions and religious beliefs have some influence as well. In the past, disasters and crises were often regarded as god's will, which was related to low motivations to prepare for crises. However, this has changed since new generations of business people have introduced modern management approaches. The field of risk and crisis communication research is still emerging in the GCC countries, also because many scholars decide to avoid sensitive issues that might cause problems for them personally. Prevailing topics in the Israeli literature were COVID-19, medical risks, earthquakes, political and security crises, business/economic crises, and media challenges (Chapter 30, Gilboa et al.). Risk communication research was found more frequently than crisis communication publications.

Another not well-represented region in the international research literature is Sub-Saharan Africa. The region has experienced a multitude of, in part, long-lasting crises, including disasters, terrorism, political unrest, or infectious diseases such as Ebola, HIV/AIDS, and COVID-19. In East African countries such as Uganda, Kenya, and Tanzania (Chapter 22, Napakol et al.) police brutality and violence against journalists have led to low levels of trust in the authorities and their crisis management. This was also observed in countries like Nigeria (Chapter 24, George & Adamolekun) and Ethiopia (Chapter 23, Abas & Beyene). The population in these regions often turns to traditional leaders rather than elected officials. Therefore, these leaders need to be included in risk and crisis response practices to reach larger parts of the often multilingual and multicultural population and to provide trusted information. The governments of Nigeria, for example, often poorly managed crisis situations such as the Boko Haram insurgency (terrorism), the #EndSARS protests, and the flooding of 2022, with responses including denial of crises, minimizing impact, or broken promises (Chapter 24, George & Adamolekun). While most governments struggle to deploy effective crisis communication, in part because of political instability in many regions, some progress was reported for East Africa, such as the establishment of disaster management agencies in Tanzania and Kenya. Overall, our African contributors stated a lack of research within and from the region. Some of the common topics in the literature include accountability and transparency, misinformation, culture and crisis communication, mobile communication, the role of social media, health communication, and tourism (Chapter 22, Napakol et al.). While massive disinformation operations of actors such as Russia and its mercenaries are considered a severe threat to the already fragile democracies in many African countries, the topic has not received the necessary scholarly attention (Akinola & Ogunnubi, 2021).

One of the least represented regions in English-language research publications is Latin America (Chapter 1, Schwarz), despite being the second most disaster-prone region in the world (Chapter 38, Arroyave & Erazo-Coronado). Floods, storms, droughts, landslides, extreme temperatures, volcanic eruptions, and wildfires pertain to the common types of disasters. Latin America suffers from multinational organized crime (e.g., drug cartels), high levels of violence, and humanitarian crises (e.g., Venezuela). The resulting migration flows often amplify political conflicts and xenophobia in the unprepared countries receiving refugees. In many South American countries, governments lack measures of disaster planning. This is partly due to the politicization of disaster preparedness and management, with policies often changing as new administrations take office. This leads to disruptions and discontinuities in programs since new governments reverse or modify the initiatives of their predecessors. Case studies of corporate crises often revealed strategies of downplaying, lying, concealing information, falsely claiming control, etc. In terms of government responses to public health crises (e.g., COVID-19, Zika, Dengue), our Latin American contributors diagnose a lack of emphasis on instructional (emergency) risk communication to provide recommendations for self-protective behavior. Authorities often fail to address the multicultural and multilingual diversity in many countries, where indigenous communities in some nations altogether represent almost half the population (e.g., Bolivia, Guatemala) – sometimes still labeled as ethnic "minorities" – and speak different languages other than Spanish (e.g., Quechua, Q'eqchi', or Nahuatl). The neglect of this diversity, partly rooted in Spanish colonialism and racism, has had tragic consequences, as in the case of the eruption of the Volcán de Fuego in Guatemala in 2018, where many of the local Mayan population died because they were not warned in time and not in their language. The need for more consideration of indigenous voices, especially in disaster contexts, has also been stressed by scholars in Australia and New Zealand (Chapter 41, Galloway & Zorn).

In addition, COVID-19 has stimulated reflection and research in Latin America. A Brazilian case study of the city of Manus (Amazonas state) showed how a succession of missteps led to a severe lack of medical oxygen (Chapter 39, Soares et al.). The situation was aggravated by the mismanagement and misinformation spread by the then President Jair Bolsonaro, who, similar to Donald Trump in the US, downplayed the pandemic's severity. The authors explain how an intense mobilization of civil society and private companies helped to normalize the oxygen supply and compensate for the failures of the federal government. Although risk and crisis communication research in Latin America is still emerging, the field is described as a growing sub-discipline of communication studies (Chapter 40, Fernández Pedemonte). However, despite the disproportionately high level of threats and crises in these countries, scholarly exploration and peer-reviewed publications in risk and crisis communication remain scarce (Chapter 39, Soares et al.).

Summary

Altogether, these reviews of issues, concepts, research, and practice revealed several global trends as they stimulated and situated risk and crisis communication research across countries. In the last part of this volume (Part VI), the authors build on these trends and discuss recent developments and their implications for the theory, methodology, practice, and technology of risk and crisis communication. Overall, we can summarize as follows:

1. As with other outbreaks of infectious diseases, the COVID-19 pandemic led to a significant increase in research and reflection in almost all regions of the world. This is consistent with other work that suggests that the field is driven by crisis events.

2. Climate change and its consequences (e.g., disasters, migration) are observable across regions and lead to more publications and likely enhanced research funding in some countries. The hazards associated with climate change will continue to drive research and will be a focal point as countries seek to manage and mitigate the harm.
3. Misinformation and disinformation, partly disseminated by malicious state actors to either destabilize countries (Russia's global disinformation campaigns) and/or maintain power by manipulating public opinion (Donald Trump in the US or Jair Bolsonaro in Brazil), have increased threats and cost lives in several countries and regions. The post-truth communication ecosystem will continue to pose significant challenges to practice and will be an essential focus of research.
4. The emergence of AI has not only contributed to the advancement of the risk and crisis communication practices but also increased concerns about the abuse of the technology for disinformation campaigns (deepfakes) and cybersecurity threats posed by both state and non-state actors. The role of AI in crisis and risk communication is evolving and expanding, and the implications of this technology for research and practice are not clear.
5. Many scholars, especially in the Global South, point to the general lack of attention, if not disregard, of vulnerable groups and minorities in risk and crisis communication practices, which is often related to the lack of acknowledging idiosyncrasies in culture, languages, resources, or leadership in different regions and/or communities. This was especially evident during COVID-19, where underlying disparities among minority communities resulted in a disproportional impact.
6. The comparison of the Global North and South suggests a sharp regional contrast in terms of resources for risk and crisis communication practice at the governmental level, as well as for academic research. Available resources appear to be negatively correlated with the severity of threats and crises in these regions, with richer and safer countries having more resources and generally experiencing fewer crises than less developed and more crisis-prone countries.
7. Scholars in Asia, Africa, and Latin America see a need to further indigenize concepts, models, and theories to their specific historical, political, and socio-cultural contexts, where a few Western approaches still dominate (e.g., SCCT, IRT, EPPM, etc.). The representation of culture in crisis and risk communication research is growing and providing important insights.
8. Audiences, victims, and citizens have transitioned from passive recipients of information to active participants whose perceptions and reactions can significantly shape the dynamics and outcomes of crises. The crisis and risk arena is increasingly characterized by multiple voices with diverse experiences, values, and perspectives.
9. Citizen activism can significantly influence crisis responses. Grassroots movements and advocacy groups often drive public pressure, pushing governments and organizations to take more decisive actions in crisis and in response to risks.
10. The media environment, including new and legacy media, has altered risk and crisis communication in fundamental ways and seems to accelerate the creation of more segmented audiences, enhance the speed of dissemination, and allow for the inclusion of more and more diverse actors. This evolving media landscape creates additional challenges for practice.

Conclusions

This compilation of global crisis and risk communication research demonstrates that crisis and risk communication is a dynamic, expansive, multinational, multidisciplinary field of study. The trends of research addressing a diverse set of hazards using multiple methods across contexts create many opportunities and challenges.

The expanding field creates opportunities to apply risk and crisis communication broadly and to address a wider range of hazards, senders, and receivers than have traditionally been examined. Moving beyond corporate crises and image repair strategies is an important trend in expanding the field. Public health hazards, climate change, and wars, for example, have emerged as important research topics. Examining crisis and risk in non-Western contexts provides the basis for a broader understanding of how these forms of communication interact with different cultures, communities, media systems, and governmental forms. This trend has also promoted comparative analyses of crisis communication.

The authors represented here also make compelling arguments about the essential role of communication in managing and mitigating risks and crises. As several of the chapters demonstrate, communication is the process through which management occurs. Researchers should take advantage of the opportunities afforded by crises such as COVID-19 and risks such as climate change that illustrate the central role of communication. These and other cases may help investigators in pursuing funding and support and facilitate positioning communication as an essential strategic management function.

The expansion of crisis and risk communication research also creates opportunities to demonstrate the relevance of this work to other fields and to the practice of crisis and risk management. As demonstrated throughout the *Handbook*, crises and risks are multi-disciplinary phenomena. They cannot be adequately understood without the methods and theories from a variety of fields of study. This multidisciplinary perspective is especially relevant with crises and risks that are transnational in scope.

In addition to opportunities, the *Handbook* also reveals important challenges. Many of the crises and risks examined are expansive in terms of scope, impact, and duration. Sometimes described as mega-crises, they defy simple characterization and clear parameters. Examining risks and crises such as climate change and pandemics stretches both research methods and resources. These investigations require longer time frames, multiple methods, larger research budgets, and more diverse teams. Researchers are often incentivized to focus on smaller, more manageable cases and issues and avoid the larger, more consequential risks and crises. Although the scope of many of the current risks and crises can be overwhelming, it is essential that researchers engage these larger cases and risks.

Finally, the *Handbook* reveals the rich diversity of the field, and it also demonstrates a growing lack of conceptual and theoretical coherence. The loss of a conceptual center complicates the development of a broader understanding of these events. It is increasingly difficult to access, organize, and apply this diverse, dynamic, and growing body of scholarship. Projects such as this *Handbook*, the development of dedicated research journals, research centers and institutes, and multinational research teams and consortia are essential to connecting research and maintaining the coherence of this increasingly important field of practice and research.

References

Akinola, A. E., & Ogunnubi, O. (2021). Russo-African Relations and electoral democracy: Assessing the implications of Russia's renewed interest for Africa. *African Security Review*, *30*(3), 386–402. https://doi.org/10.1080/10246029.2021.1956982

Schwarz, A., Seeger, M. W., & Auer, C. (2016). Significance and structure of international risk and crisis communication research: Toward an integrative approach. In A. Schwarz, M. W. Seeger, & C. Auer, Eds., *The Handbook of International Crisis Communication Research* (pp. 1–10). Wiley Blackwell. https://doi.org/10.1002/9781118516812.ch1

World Health Organization (2024). *Number of COVID-19 deaths reported to WHO*. Retrieved August 15 from https://data.who.int/dashboards/covid19/deaths

Author's Bio

Andreas Schwarz (PhD, TU Ilmenau, 2009) is a senior researcher in risk and crisis communication at Technische Universität Ilmenau in Germany where he serves as co-director of the International Research Group on Crisis Communication. He was the founding chair of the Crisis Communication Section of the European Communication Research and Education Association (ECREA), from 2011 to 2018. His research interests include cross-cultural risk and crisis communication, crisis response of nongovernmental and higher education organizations, and the science and risk communication of emerging technologies and space exploration. Schwarz received research grants to study risk communication of COVID-19, crisis communication of child protective services and nonprofit organizations, and perceptions of artificial intelligence or automated mobility. His research has been published in journals like *Health Communication*, *International Journal of Strategic Communication*, *Public Relations Review*, *Journal of Public Relations Research*, *Journal of Risk Research*, *Risk Analysis*, and *Science Communication*. He has conducted trainings and consulted on risk and crisis communication for several government agencies, nonprofit organizations, and corporations.

Matthew W. Seeger (PhD) is a Distinguished University Professor of Communication, Dean Emeritus, and Fellow of the International Communication Association. His work has appeared in over 200 peer-reviewed journal articles, book chapters, and conference proceedings and 13 books. He is the co-author of the Centers for Disease Control and Prevention handbook for *Crisis and Emergency Risk Communication* (Second Edition, 2015). His other books include *Communication and Organizational Crisis* (2003), *Crisis Communication and the Public Health* (2008), *Effective Crisis Communication*, 5th Edition (2007), *Effective Risk Communication* (2009), *Theorizing Crisis Communication*, 2nd Edition (2021), *Narratives of Crisis: Stories of Ruin and Renewal* (2016), and the *International Handbook of Crisis Communication* (2016). He has been quoted in the *Washington Post*, *New York Times*, *The Atlanta Journal-Constitution*, and *Rolling Stone*, and he has appeared on CNN.

Sora Kim is a professor in the School of Journalism and Communication and the director of the M.S.Sc. in Corporate Communication program at the Chinese University of Hong Kong. Her research focuses on crisis and corporate social responsibility (CSR) communication. She has published more than 130 publications including refereed international journal articles, conference papers, book chapters, and other publications. Her work has been published in top international journals across communication, business, management, and ethics. She has presented at leading international conferences, received six prestigious top research awards, and secured significant research funding from organizations such as the General Research Fund (GRF)/Research Grants Council (RGC), Toyota Foundation Research Grants, and the Arthur W. Page Center. Sora Kim has been recognized on the Top 2% Scientists list by Stanford University in the subfield of communication and media studies for five consecutive years, from 2020 to 2024.

Index

The Handbook of International Crisis and Risk Communication Research, Second Edition.
Edited by Andreas Schwarz, Matthew W. Seeger, and Sora Kim.

Printed and bound by CPI Group (UK) Ltd, Croydon, CR0 4YY
17/09/2026
14964250-0006